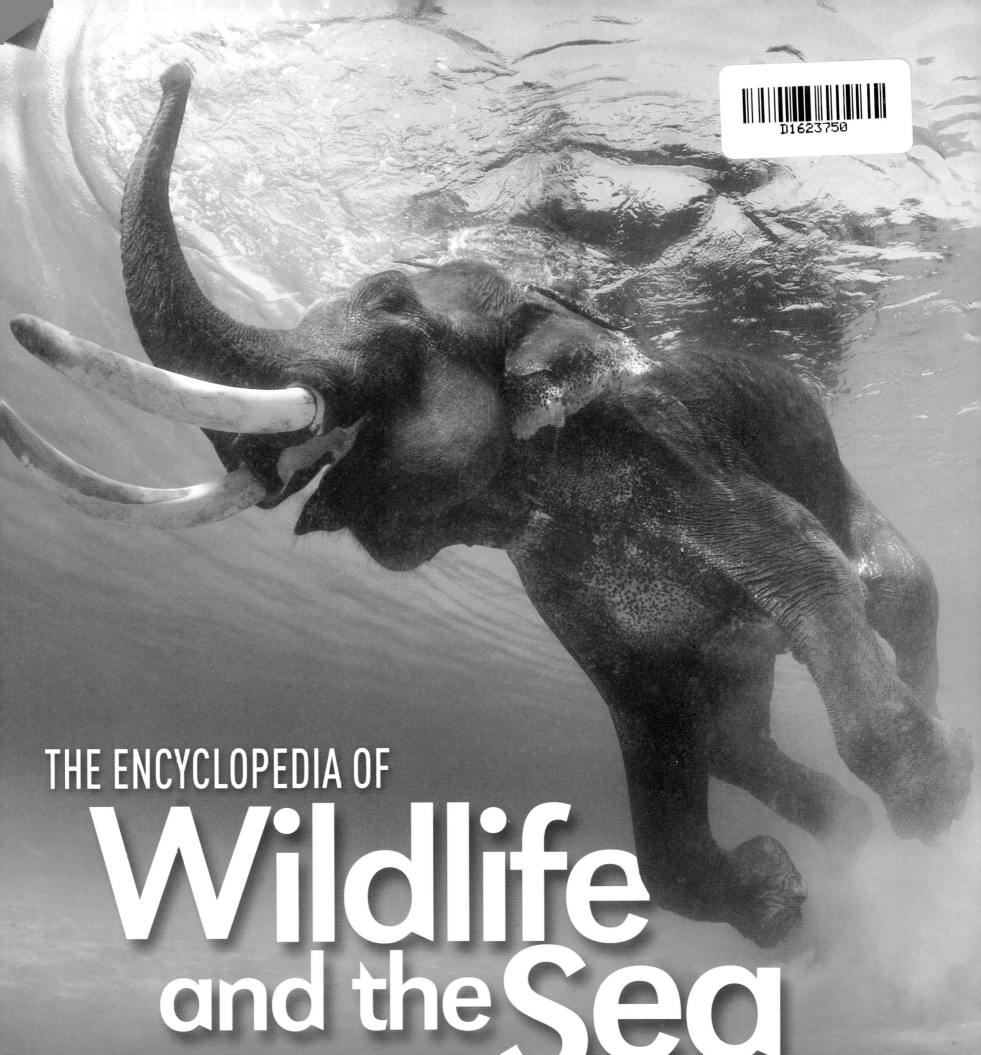

THE ENCYCLOPEDIA OF
Wildlife
and the Sea

WELDON OWEN

Conceived and produced by Weldon Owen Pty Ltd
59–61 Victoria Street, McMahons Point
Sydney NSW 2060 Australia
www.weldonowen.com

Chief Executive Officer Sheena Coupe
Creative Director Sue Burk
Art Manager Trucie Henderson
Senior Vice President, International Sales Stuart Laurence
Sales Manager: United States Ellen Towell
Vice President Sales: Asia and Latin America Dawn Low
Administration Manager, International Sales Kristine Ravn
Production Manager Todd Rechner
Production Coordinators Lisa Conway, Mike Crowton
Production Assistant Nathan Grice

The Encyclopedia of Wildlife

Managing Editor Jennifer Taylor
Project Editors Jenni Bruce, Averil Moffat
Copy Editor Amanda Burdon
Picture Researcher Jo Collard
Designers Michelle Cutler, Gabrielle Green
Cover Designer John Bull, The Book Design Company
Cartographers Will Pringle/Mapgraphx, Laurie Whiddon/Map
Information Graphics Andrew Davies/Creative Communication
Index Jo Rudd

The Encyclopedia of the Sea

Managing Editor Jennifer Taylor
Project Editors Averil Moffat, Jasmine Parker
Picture Researcher Jo Collard
Designers John Bull, The Book Design Company, Gabrielle Green
Cartographers Will Pringle/Mapgraphx, Laurie Whiddon/Map
Information Graphics Andrew Davies/Creative Communication
Index Jo Rudd

ISBN 978-1-74252-091-9

Color reproduction by Chroma Graphics (Overseas) Pte Ltd
Printed by Craft Press
Manufactured in Singapore

A WELDON OWEN PRODUCTION

Grizzly bear
A grizzly bear (*Ursus arctos horribilis*) brings a
freshly caught salmon to her cubs. These bears
roam large areas of open wilderness in north
America and in northern Europe. They generally
feed on berries, grasses, shoots, and small
animals. As winter approaches they must eat
as much as possible before hibernating.

Authors and Consultants

The Encyclopedia of Wildlife

Dr. Channa Bambaradeniya
Coordinator of the Asia Regional Species
   and Biodiversity Program
International Union for Conservation of Nature
Sri Lanka

Cinthya Flores
International Communications Consultant and Journalist
Former Communications Officer of WWF Central America
Costa Rica

Dr. Joshua Ginsberg
Vice President for Global Programs
Wildlife Conservation Society
Washington DC, USA

Dwight Holing
Natural History and Environmental Author
Orinda CA, USA

Dr. Susan Lumpkin
Research Associate
Smithsonian Institution's National Zoological Park
Washington DC, USA

George McKay
Consultant in Conservation Biology
Chair, NSW National Parks and Wildlife Advisory Council
Sydney NSW, Australia

Dr. John Musick
Marshall Acuff Professor Emeritus in Marine Science
Virginia Institute of Marine Science
College of William and Mary
Virginia, USA

Dr. Patrick Quilty
Honorary Research Professor
School of Earth Sciences
University of Tasmania, Australia

Dr. Bernard Stonehouse
Emeritus Associate
Scott Polar Research Institute
University of Cambridge, UK

Dr. Eric J Woehler
Honorary Research Associate
School of Zoology
University of Tasmania, Australia

Dr. David Woodruff
Professor of Biological Sciences
Ecology, Behavior and Evolution Section
Division of Biological Sciences
University of California, San Diego, USA

The Encyclopedia of the Sea

Dr Stephen Hutchinson
Senior Research Fellow
National Oceanography Centre
Southampton, UK

Professor Johann R. E. Lutjeharms
Department of Oceanography
University of Cape Town, South Africa

Beverly McMillan
Science writer and author
Virginia, USA

Dr John Musick
Marshall Acuff Professor Emeritus in Marine Science
Virginia Institute of Marine Science
College of William and Mary
Virginia, USA

Dr Bernard Stonehouse
Emeritus Associate
Scott Polar Research Institute
University of Cambridge, UK
Honorary Research Fellow
Maritime Historical Studies Centre
University of Hull, UK

Dr Matthias Tomczak
Emeritus Professor of Oceanography
Flinders University
South Australia

THE ENCYCLOPEDIA OF
Wildlife

CONTENTS

Humphead wrasse (below left)
The distinctive humphead wrasse is a common inhabitant of coral reefs but is also found in cooler waters. Easily recognized by the prominent bulge on its head, it is among the largest reef fish.

Red-spotted purple butterfly (below)
The red-spotted purple butterfly is common in the eastern United States on aspen and poplar trees. It avoids predation by birds by mimicking the pipevine swallowtail, which is poisonous.

Burchell's sandgrouse (above)
A Burchell's sandgrouse takes flight from a waterhole after drinking and soaking its belly feathers. This desert-dwelling bird flies long distances, returning with water held in its feathers for its chicks to "drink."

Ring-tailed lemur (left)
Ring-tailed lemurs, natives of Madagascar, spend much of their time on the ground, but early in the day they are likely to be found in the treetops, warming themselves in the sun.

Bobcat (far left)
The secretive, solitary bobcat, an inhabitant of eastern forests in the United States, is an efficient hunter. It remains out of sight by day but seeks its prey—cottontail rabbits and small rodents—at night.

FOREWORD

What always surprises me is not the richness of the world's biological heritage, but just how little we know about it. In recent years we have sequenced the human genome, rapidly advanced our understanding of atomic structure, and continued to explore and advance our understanding of the universe. In contrast, our best estimates suggest that there are 10 to 50 million species on Earth. Whatever the error in this number, we have only described 1.5 million species, at best 10 percent of the world's diversity. Our understanding of ecological communities is, at best, rudimentary.

Study of biodiversity is, increasingly, a time limited endeavor. Humans are growing in number and in their individual demands for resources. Habitats such as the Amazon, Borneo, and the Congo forests, once thought to be vast, wild, and infinitely resilient, are either highly fragmented and degraded, or under increasing threat from conversion. Some ecosystems, such as the North American sagebrush and grasslands, are represented by a small percentage of their original extent. Europe, dominated by humans for thousands of years, still harbors a remarkable diversity of wildlife, but many species are confined to small islands of their former range, a pattern likely soon to be seen globally. Australia and Oceania have some of the most unusual and unique biological diversity on Earth, but the islands and reefs of the Pacific, initially threatened by habitat conversion, pollution, and a phalanx of introduced species, now face the new threats of climate change, warming oceans, and rising seas. It is not surprising that island species show the highest rate of extinction across all taxa.

However, conservation efforts, while always an uphill battle, show that we can reverse some of the threats to the world's biological heritage, and mitigate others. While recent data suggest that perhaps 50 percent of the world's primates are threatened with extinction, a recent discovery of 125,000 western lowland gorillas by staff and colleagues of the Wildlife Conservation Society expanded the options for conservation of this species. The discovery may lead to new protected areas in northern Congo that will aid the conservation of not just gorillas, but dozens of primates, and thousands of species. In the last two decades, the proportion of Earth's surface under formal protection has continued to expand, and efforts now focus on extending protection of coastal and high seas. And because protected areas, while necessary, are not sufficient, new conservation initiatives work with industry, local and indigenous communities, and private landowners to expand conservation beyond park boundaries, to ensure connectivity and freedom for animals to roam.

The Illustrated Atlas of Wildlife helps us better understand both the diversity of life, and the threats that face wildlife and wildlands around the world. In a day and age where seemingly limitless information is on the web, why buy a book? For many of us, the physical act of holding a book, especially one this beautiful and well designed, will never be replaced by a web page and laptop. More importantly, this book is written by experts in their fields and the quality and accuracy of information is remarkable, drawing not just on information widely available, but on some of the most recent scientific research and unpublished studies that are not yet "popular" and hence not yet online. Finally, this book allows you to learn about the ecoregional structure of the entire world, and of the wildlife that inhabits these diverse environments. Hold it in your hands, and enjoy your global tour.

Joshua Ginsberg
Vice President, Global Conservation, Wildlife Conservation Society

How to Use this Atlas

This atlas is arranged in three main sections. The first, "Living Earth," provides an overview of how and where natural life occurs on Earth, including pages devoted to different kinds of habitats, the relationship between animals and their environment, and the impact of one animal species on another. The second section, which is the core of the book, is a chapter-by-chapter survey of the world's main continents and oceans, and the animal life they support. The third, reference, section consists of a detailed factfile on the animals presented in the book, a glossary, and an index.

Wildlife regions of the world
Each continent is divided into key wildlife regions. A double page is dedicated to a survey of the habitats and resident animal life found in each region, accompanied by an introductory overview and a locator and regional map.

Regional map
Regional maps are shaded to show the area within the continent that is being described for its animal life.

Conservation watch
At-risk animals are described under this heading. Symbols flag species that are either critically endangered or endangered.

Lavish photographs
Taken by leading wildlife photographers, these portray the habits and habitats of different species.

Feature box
Special-interest subjects are shown in a feature box, with their own introduction and selected photographs or illustrations.

Locator
These small maps locate the region within its continent.

Climate chart
Accompanying each map is a climate chart, showing average temperature and rainfall in the region.

Stunning illustrations
Individual species are beautifully illustrated. Habitat scenes show animals in context with each other and their surrounds.

Introduction
Each chapter opens with an overview of the featured continent and its natural life.

Regional overview
Each region covered in the chapter is identified with a map and a captioned wildlife photograph.

Main map
Geographical and political maps of the continent show borders, topography, and key physical features.

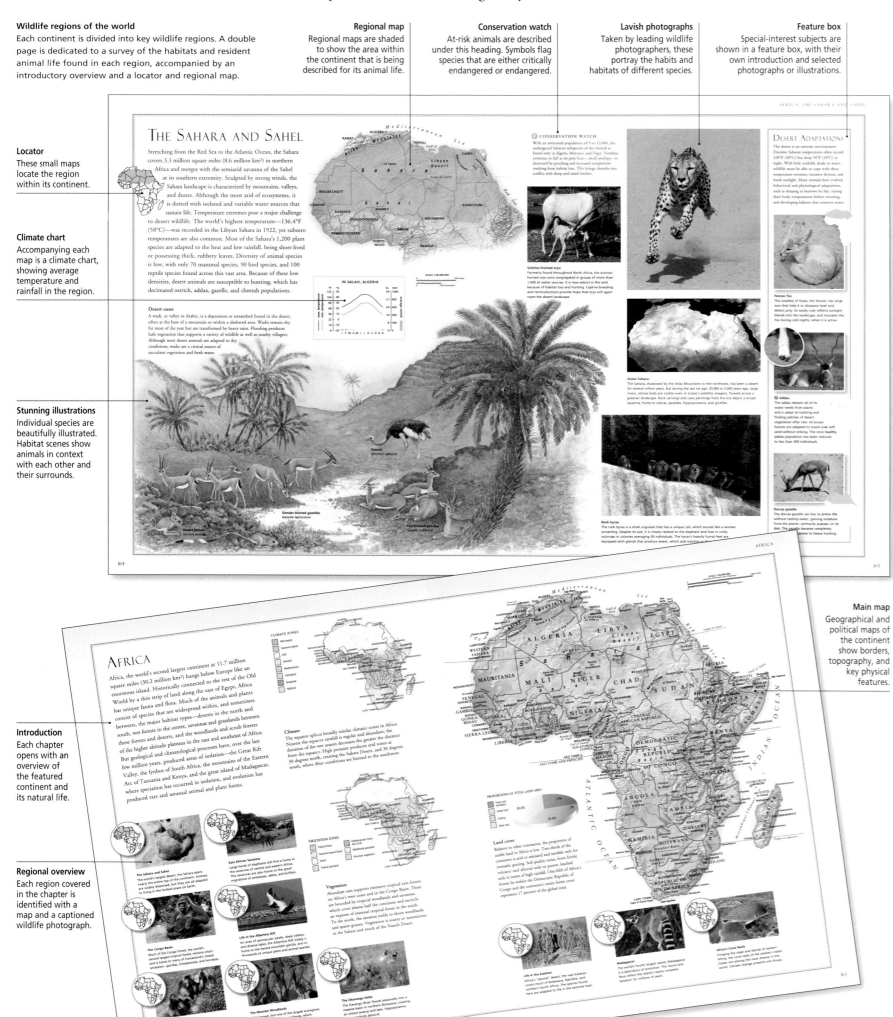

Living Earth

Introductory pages provide an overview of a range of wildlife subjects, including the origins and ecology of animals, the variety of Earth's habitats—from polar to desert and forest to sea—the threats facing many wildlife species, ecological balance, and conservation measures for endangered animals.

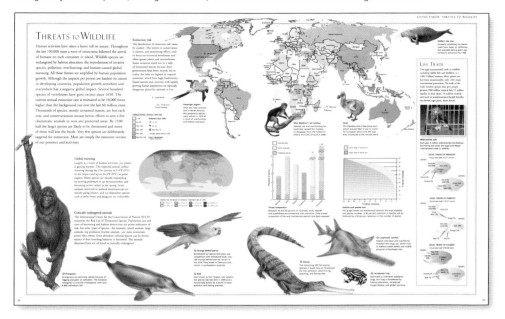

Special Subject

Throughout the chapters special-interest pages take a closer look at a particular animal, or group of animals. In the example below the cockatoos and parrots of Australia are displayed to show their variety and color, as well as the differences between them in nesting and feeding.

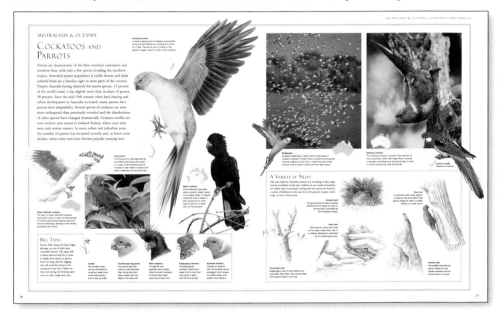

Animal Factfile

This detailed factfile profiles the common and scientific name, distribution, habitat, size, weight, diet, and conservation status of each captioned species in the atlas. The factfile is arranged by class and includes maps that show each order's global range. Refer to the index for a quick link to entries in the factfile.

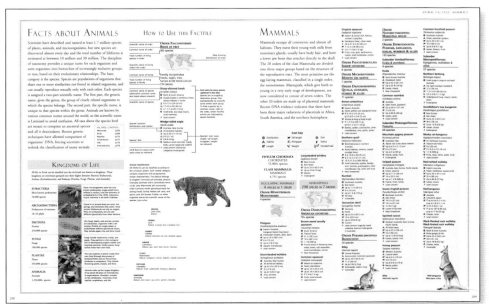

VISUAL KEYS

Map legend

The maps in this atlas contain a variety of labels, symbols, and other graphic devices to provide detailed information such as altitude and ocean floor topography, and the location of mountains, rivers, cities, and country borders.

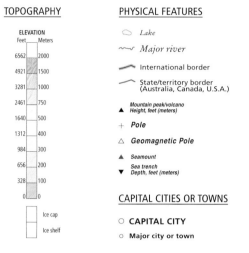

TOPOGRAPHY

Feet	Meters
ELEVATION	
6562	2000
4921	1500
3281	1000
2461	750
1640	500
1312	400
984	300
656	200
328	100
0	0

Ice cap

Ice shelf

PHYSICAL FEATURES

- Lake
- ~ Major river
- International border
- State/territory border (Australia, Canada, U.S.A.)
- ▲ Mountain peak/volcano Height, feet (meters)
- + Pole
- △ Geomagnetic Pole
- ▲ Seamount
- ▼ Sea trench Depth, feet (meters)

CAPITAL CITIES OR TOWNS

- ○ CAPITAL CITY
- ○ Major city or town

Conservation icons

The conservation status of endangered and critically endangered animals, as determined by the IUCN Red List of Threated Species, is indicated by a red or yellow icon.

- 🔴 Critically endangered
- 🟡 Endangered

Charts, tables, and graphs

Additional details about regions, or the animal life found there, is provided in the form of tables, charts, or graphs. This at-a-glance information adds to captions and photographs.

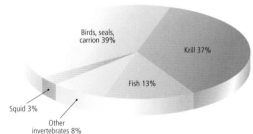

LEOPARD SEAL DIET

Birds, seals, carrion 39%
Krill 37%
Fish 13%
Squid 3%
Other invertebrates 8%

THE FACTS

Area	More than 1.3 million sq miles (+3.4 million km²)
Number of countries	6
Length of Congo River	2,900 miles (4,700 km)
Habitat	Rain forest, woodland, swamp, savanna, freshwater
Estimate of mammal species	More than 400
Estimate of fish species	More than 700
Estimate of bird species	More than 1,000

Range maps

Individual range maps accompanying some captions show the current (and former) range of selected species.

Each year at the end of the rainy season, millions of zebra, gazelles, and wildebeest migrate to Kenya from the grassy plains of the Serengeti National Park, Tanzania. In one of Earth's most impressive migrations, masses of wildebeest cross the Mara River into the Masai-Mara Reserve, Kenya—many drown in the crush to cross.

LIVING EARTH

LIVING EARTH

Life as we know it occurs only on Earth, where it assumes a fascinating diversity of forms. Of the millions of animal species, humans are the only one to appreciate the role of living organisms in creating a habitable planet. Without life, without plants and microorganisms releasing oxygen into the atmosphere, our planet would be a very different and inhospitable place. The world's wildlife depends on plants and phytoplankton and the billions of little things—bacteria, single-celled protists, and decomposing fungi—that make the biosphere work. Animal species are broadly distributed into eight biogeographic realms. Although many species are shared between realms, a good naturalist, blindfolded and put down anywhere on Earth, could quickly work out the location by observing the local assemblage of animals.

The effect of life

The Gaia hypothesis proposes that all life, working together as a superorganism, maintains the planet's atmosphere and temperature.

CONDITION	WITHOUT LIFE	WITH LIFE
Carbon dioxide	98%	0.03%
Nitrogen	1.9%	78%
Oxygen	Trace	21%
Temperature	419°F (215°C)	59°F (15°C)

SPECIES TALLY

Individual organisms are grouped into populations of interbreeding or genetically similar individuals called species. The total number of living species is estimated to be between 10 million and 30 million, with most of these being microscopic lifeforms. Vertebrates amount to only 5 percent of all known animal species. There are at least twice as many species of fungi and six times as many species of plants.

Estimated number of animal species
10 million

Known animal species
1.3 million (13%)

Invertebrates 95%

Vertebrates 5%

Fish 48%

Amphibians 9%

Mammals 9%

Reptiles 15%

Birds 19%

Animal groups

At least 30 animal groups and about 1.3 million living animal species are known. The vast majority are invertebrates and include marine sponges, flatworms, corals, segmented worms, mollusks, sea stars, and arthropods such as crustaceans, spiders, and insects. The vertebrates are a minority group that share 400 million years of evolutionary history. These conspicuous consumers of plants and microorganisms dominate most habitats.

Mammals

The giraffe is one of about 4,800 living mammal species, all of which have milk glands. Mammals comprise a few egg-laying monotremes, 298 pouched marsupials, and diverse placentals, including 291 species of primates.

Biogeographic realms

Recognizable clusters of species characterize the eight biogeographic realms and tell us much about the geological history of continents and islands and the evolutionary history of different groups of animals. Life in the oceans is less clearly partitioned because of the homogenizing effects of global currents and the ancient connections of the ocean basins, but there are clear regional differences in the nutrient-based richness of coastal faunas.

Nearctic Realm
The species of the Nearctic and Palearctic are so alike that they form a super-realm, the Holarctic. Bald eagles typify North America but related eagles occur in the Palearctic.

Reptiles

Like most of the other 8,000 reptile species, the spotted harlequin snake lays eggs with protective membranes. Turtles, crocodiles, and most lizards possess two pairs of limbs, but snakes have lost these ancestral features.

Birds

The toco toucan and 10,000 other species of living birds share ancestry with the dinosaurs. Defined by their feathered forelimbs (wings), most are superbly adapted for flight.

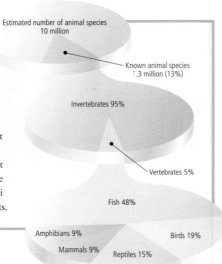

Palearctic Realm

The Palearctic includes Eurasia and northern Africa. Now hunted to near extinction, wild goats such as the alpine ibex once ranged from Spain to the Himalayas.

Neotropic Realm

Encompassing Central and South America, the Neotropic Realm includes more tropical rain forest than any other realm. The rich fauna includes the vivid blue poison-dart frog.

Afrotropic Realm

The Afrotropic covers all of sub-Saharan Africa and is almost entirely tropical. Its distinctive wildlife includes lions, elephants, giraffes, and baboons and other primates.

Indomalay Realm

Extending across most of South and Southeast Asia, the Indomalay contains forests that still harbor a few hundred tigers. Habitat loss and hunting have devastated tiger numbers.

Australasian Realm

This realm comprises Australia, New Zealand, New Guinea, and part of Indonesia. On isolated Australia marsupials such as kangaroos filled niches occupied by placental mammals elsewhere.

Oceanic Realm

Islands colonized by species that could swim, float, or fly make up the Oceanic Realm. In the absence of competitors, colonists evolved into unique species such as the Fiji banded iguana.

Antarctic Realm

Comprising Antarctica and some southern islands, this realm presents great challenges to wildlife. The emperor penguin is one of the few species that survives on the ice cap.

ARCTIC OCEAN

Arctic Circle

Siberia

Palearctic Realm

EUROPE

ASIA

Gobi Desert

NORTH PACIFIC OCEAN

Mediterranean Sea

Himalaya

Tropic of Cancer

Sahara

India

Mekong

Oceanic Realm

Sahel

AFRICA

Ethiopian Highlands

Philippines

Indomalay Realm

Equator

Congo Basin

Ruwenzori

Great Rift Valley

Sunda Shelf

Wallace Line

New Guinea

Afrotropic Realm

Madagascar

INDIAN OCEAN

Cape York

Great Barrier Reef

Fiji

Kalahari Desert

Australasian Realm

Tropic of Capricorn

SOUTH ATLANTIC OCEAN

AUSTRALIA

New Zealand

Antarctic Realm

SOUTHERN OCEAN

Antarctic Circle

ANTARCTICA

SCALE 1:108,000,000
Robinson Projection

Ray-finned fish

Yellowtail scad are among the 25,000 species of ray-finned fish. Found in both freshwater and marine habitats, ray-finned fish share their ancestry and bony skeletons with lobe-finned fish such as lungfish.

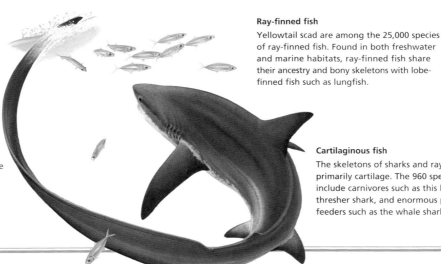

Amphibians

The 5,500 living amphibian species include frogs, legless burrowing caecilians, and salamanders such as this European fire salamander. Most depend on water for the embryonic and larval phases of life.

Cartilaginous fish

The skeletons of sharks and rays are primarily cartilage. The 960 species include carnivores such as this long-tailed thresher shark, and enormous plankton feeders such as the whale shark.

Invertebrates

Beetles, such as this seven-spotted ladybug, comprise more than 370,000 of the 1 million known species of insects and are the most species-rich animal group.

EVOLUTION

Evolution is life's little secret: a suite of processes that enable populations to change over time. Without the ability to evolve, no species could survive Earth's constant environmental changes. The fundamental process, natural selection, ensures that the individuals best adapted to their environment survive and pass on their genes to the next generation. Other processes, such as mutations and sexual reproduction, ensure the creation of the new genetic variation upon which evolution works. Animal evolution over the past 600 million years is a story of adaptation leading to solutions to life's challenges, played out in an ever-changing ecological theater. Occasional catastrophic change can eliminate even the most apparently successful species. Today's animal species, including our own, are here as much by sheer luck as by adaptive success. Time, process, and chance are responsible for the incredible diversity of species alive today and all their amazing fossil ancestors.

Continental drift

The slow movement of Earth's surface plates has reconfigured its continents and islands over time, a process known as continental drift. About 200 million years ago, the supercontinent Pangaea started splitting into the northern Laurasia and southern Gondwana landmasses. By 90 million years ago, these, in turn, had begun separating into today's continents. The continents continue to slowly change their positions.

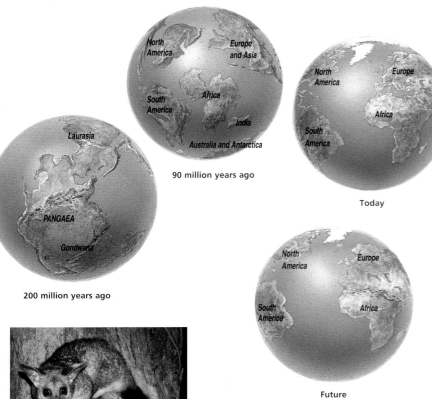

90 million years ago

Today

200 million years ago

Future

African vulture
The lappet-faced and other African vultures share looks and behavior with American vultures, but they are unrelated. African vultures are related to eagles.

American vulture
The turkey vulture is an American scavenger related to storks. Although unrelated to African vultures, it developed similar adaptations, a process called convergent evolution.

Parallel evolution
The brushtail possum of Australia (above left) and the common opossum of South America (left) are both marsupials. Once globally distributed, marsupials were replaced by placental mammals in most places. They survived only on the two southern landmasses of Australia and South America, where they became isolated by continental drift and evolved separately for more than 65 million years.

Rate of extinction

Extinctions are not distributed evenly through time. In the past 450 million years, there were at least five mass extinction events, when more than 50 percent of animal species and a high proportion of genera died out. Each event had different causes. The ongoing biodiversity crisis may soon qualify as the sixth mass extinction.

KEY
mya Million years ago
● Mass extinction

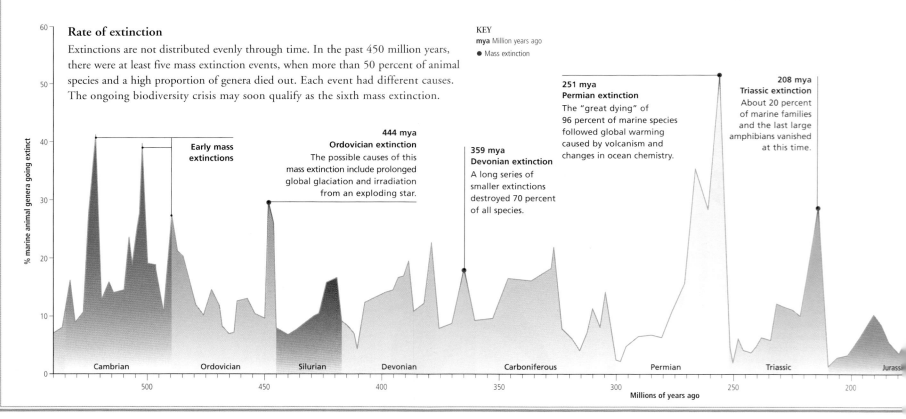

Early mass extinctions

444 mya
Ordovician extinction
The possible causes of this mass extinction include prolonged global glaciation and irradiation from an exploding star.

359 mya
Devonian extinction
A long series of smaller extinctions destroyed 70 percent of all species.

251 mya
Permian extinction
The "great dying" of 96 percent of marine species followed global warming caused by volcanism and changes in ocean chemistry.

208 mya
Triassic extinction
About 20 percent of marine families and the last large amphibians vanished at this time.

% marine animal genera going extinct

Cambrian | Ordovician | Silurian | Devonian | Carboniferous | Permian | Triassic | Jurassic

500 | 450 | 400 | 350 | 300 | 250 | 200

Millions of years ago

KEY

mya Million years ago

bya Billion years ago

● Mass extinction

Cambrian

Ordovician

Silurian

Devonian

Carboniferous

Permian

Triassic

Jurassic

Cretaceous

Tertiary

Quaternary

PALEOZOIC ERA

MESOZOIC ERA

CENOZOIC ERA

A B C D E F G H I J K L M

NATURAL SELECTION

A single African species of vanga colonized the island of Madagascar, where it evolved into 14 different species. Through the process of natural selection, the birds developed different bill shapes, for feeding on different insects, and various feather colors. Such adaptive radiations are often found on islands where colonizing species have few competitors. Hawaiian honeycreepers and Galápagos finches have evolved from insect-eating birds to also become seed eaters, nectar feeders, and even vampires.

Blue vanga

Pollen's vanga

Helmet vanga

Sickle-billed vanga

History of living Earth

The vast expanse of time since Earth's formation is represented here by a 12-hour clockface. In this scheme, the first bacteria-like organisms appeared about 9½ hours ago. The first photosynthetic bacteria, which released oxygen into the oceans and atmosphere, appeared roughly seven hours ago. Animals and fungi are latecomers, turning up in the past 90 minutes. Our own species evolved merely a few seconds ago.

EVENTS OF THE PAST 535 MILLION YEARS

A. 535–488 mya: Extraordinary diversity of shallow marine invertebrate fossils known as "the Cambrian explosion."

B. 488–444 mya: Trilobites and first fishlike vertebrates. Plants and fungi start slow colonization of land.

C. 444–416 mya: First jawed fish, first land plants, first small land animals.

D. 416–359 mya: Fish diversify, first insects and amphibians, first seed plants and trees.

E. 359–299 mya: First reptiles, first winged insects, first conifers.

F. 299–251 mya: Mammal-like reptiles.

G. 251–208 mya: First dinosaurs.

H. 208–144 mya: Dinosaurs diversify, first true mammals, first birds.

I. 144–65 mya: First flowering plants, first placental mammals and marsupials.

J. 65–59 mya: First large mammals, first primates.

K. 59–34 mya: Early horses, camels, rodents, elephants, monkeys, bats, whales.

L. 10 mya: Mammals, birds, and insects diversify rapidly.

M. 1.8 mya to present: Spread of *Homo erectus* and *Homo sapiens* around the world, and disappearance of much of the megafauna.

65 mya
Cretaceous extinction

An asteroid impact and massive volcanism plunged the world into years of "impact winter," finished off the non-avian dinosaurs, and eliminated half of all marine species.

0 to future
Sixth mass extinction?

A dramatic increase in species extinctions began with the disappearance of Pleistocene megafauna and continues today. Cause: humans.

Cretaceous | Tertiary | Quaternary

150 | 100 | 50 | 0

Earth forms

4.6 bya Newly formed solar system includes planet Earth.

Atmosphere forms

4.3 bya Comet impacts and volcanic eruptions release chemicals that form atmosphere.

Ediacaran biota
565–535 mya The earliest global community of diverse complex larger organisms.

Snowball Earth
750–580 mya Period of repeated global glacial activity.

Multicellular organisms

1.2 bya First fossils of multicellular algae-like organisms.

Prokaryotes

3.6 bya The earliest fossils belong to prokaryotes, single-celled organisms without a nucleus.

ARCHEAN ERA

PROTEROZOIC ERA

Eukaryotes

2.1 bya Eukaryotes, the first single-celled organisms with a nucleus, evolve from symbiotic interactions among several bacteria.

Oxygenated atmosphere

2.7 bya Oceans release excess oxygen (produced by photosynthetic bacteria) into the atmosphere.

WHERE ANIMALS LIVE

Biogeographers study where animals live today and how climate, vegetation, and competition affect their distribution. Species numbers tend to be highest in tropical rain forests and coral reefs, and lowest in hot deserts and polar regions. Some places, such as Madagascar, have a high number of endemics—species found nowhere else—and are of special interest to conservationists. Each species has a preferred habitat, its surroundings, and niche, what it does there, which determine the extent of its range. Although most animals are found in only one area, a few, such as rats and house sparrows, have worldwide distributions. Humans move such invasive species accidentally or intentionally, and they often become major pests in areas where they have no natural enemies. The ranges of species change over time. During the last glacial period, much of northern Europe was covered in ice, forcing animals to move south. Once the ice caps melted 18,000 years ago, the animals moved back north. Many species are now shifting their ranges because of global warming.

Feral rabbits
In 1859 European rabbits were introduced into Australia. Their populations exploded in the absence of native predators and competitors. They spread rapidly across the continent, destroying vegetation, soils, and grazing lands. Controlling introduced species that become pests is an expensive challenge.

Endemic lemur
Isolated on the island of Madagascar, lemurs radiated into 40 or so endemic species, including the ring-tailed lemur (right), and ranging from mouse-size lemurs to recently extinct species larger than gorillas. These unique primates are found nowhere else.

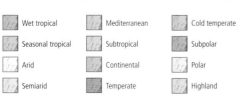

Vanished mammoth
Ice age woolly mammoths ranged across the northern continents. By 10,000 years ago, they had all but disappeared as a result of climate and vegetation changes and overhunting.

Biodiversity around the world

Biodiversity varies dramatically across the continents and islands. This map shows the number of vascular plant and vertebrate species—species richness—in each country, as well as which countries have high numbers of endemic vertebrates. Two-thirds of all animal species live in tropical forests, so conservationists are especially active in such biodiversity hotspots.

BIODIVERSITY LEVELS

Highest	**Countries with more than 100 endemic species**
Medium high	Mammals
Medium	Birds
Medium low	Reptiles
Lowest	Amphibians

SCALE 1:92,000,000
Robinson Projection

Today's climate zones

Animals are sensitive to both local day-to-day weather and regional year-round climate. Climates vary by latitude, altitude, and distance from the sea, and are characterized by temperature, rainfall, and seasonality. Human activities, such as the burning of fossil fuels and the clearing of forests, are changing weather and climate on a global scale.

Wet tropical	Mediterranean	Cold temperate
Seasonal tropical	Subtropical	Subpolar
Arid	Continental	Polar
Semiarid	Temperate	Highland

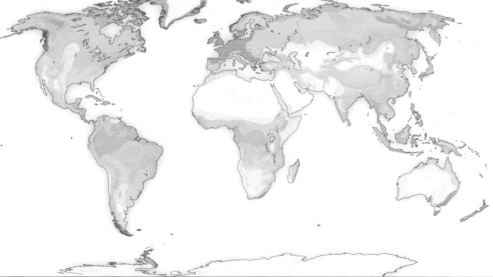

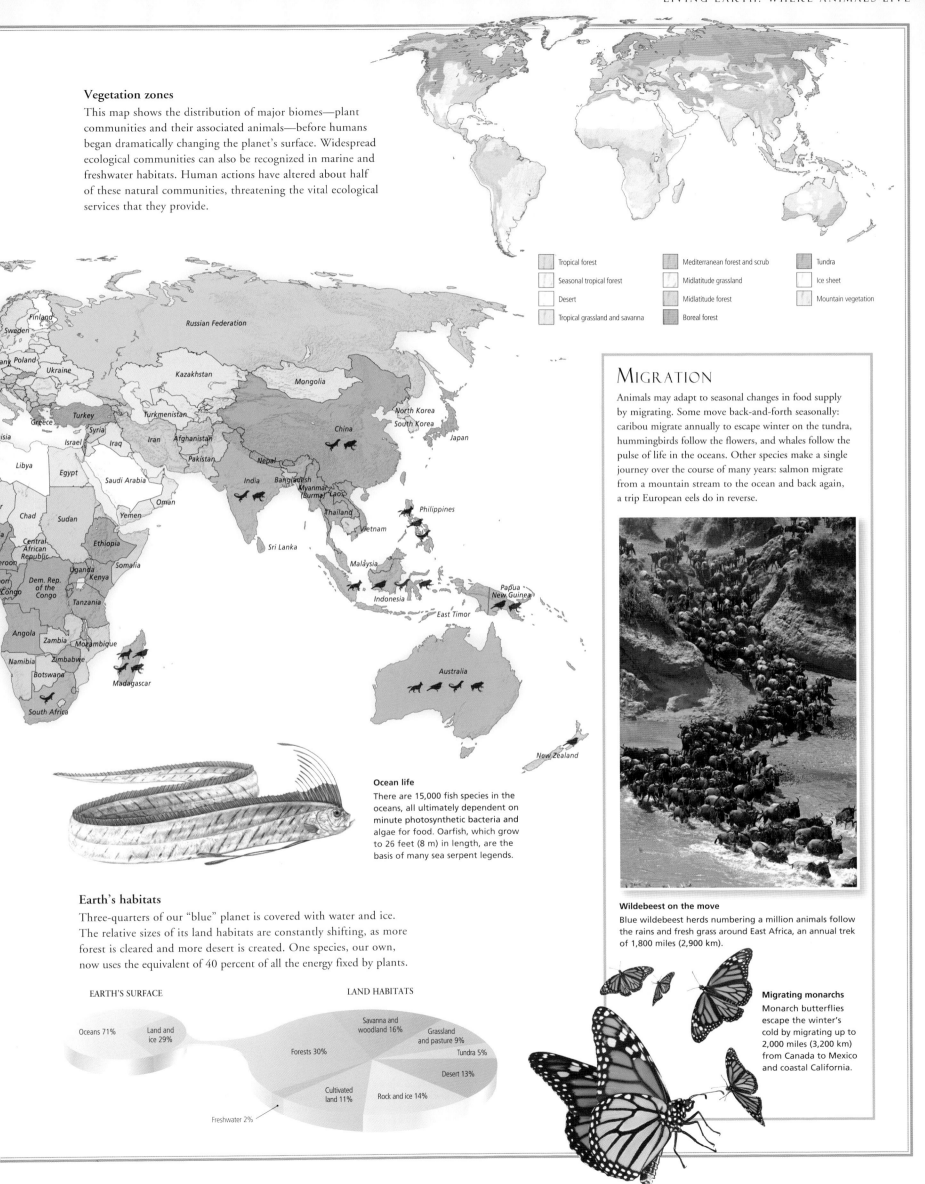

Vegetation zones

This map shows the distribution of major biomes—plant communities and their associated animals—before humans began dramatically changing the planet's surface. Widespread ecological communities can also be recognized in marine and freshwater habitats. Human actions have altered about half of these natural communities, threatening the vital ecological services that they provide.

Tropical forest

Seasonal tropical forest

Desert

Tropical grassland and savanna

Mediterranean forest and scrub

Midlatitude grassland

Midlatitude forest

Boreal forest

Tundra

Ice sheet

Mountain vegetation

MIGRATION

Animals may adapt to seasonal changes in food supply by migrating. Some move back-and-forth seasonally: caribou migrate annually to escape winter on the tundra, hummingbirds follow the flowers, and whales follow the pulse of life in the oceans. Other species make a single journey over the course of many years: salmon migrate from a mountain stream to the ocean and back again, a trip European eels do in reverse.

Ocean life
There are 15,000 fish species in the oceans, all ultimately dependent on minute photosynthetic bacteria and algae for food. Oarfish, which grow to 26 feet (8 m) in length, are the basis of many sea serpent legends.

Wildebeest on the move
Blue wildebeest herds numbering a million animals follow the rains and fresh grass around East Africa, an annual trek of 1,800 miles (2,900 km).

Earth's habitats

Three-quarters of our "blue" planet is covered with water and ice. The relative sizes of its land habitats are constantly shifting, as more forest is cleared and more desert is created. One species, our own, now uses the equivalent of 40 percent of all the energy fixed by plants.

EARTH'S SURFACE

Oceans 71%

Land and ice 29%

Freshwater 2%

LAND HABITATS

Savanna and woodland 16%

Grassland and pasture 9%

Forests 30%

Tundra 5%

Desert 13%

Cultivated land 11%

Rock and ice 14%

Migrating monarchs
Monarch butterflies escape the winter's cold by migrating up to 2,000 miles (3,200 km) from Canada to Mexico and coastal California.

19

BALANCING ACT

Nature is very good at providing us with food, water, and oxygen, the essentials of life. Energy is captured from sunlight, and shared with community members. Minerals are converted into useful nutrients and body tissues, then carefully recycled. At first glance nature seems perfectly organized, with plants to feed the herbivorous animals, predators to hunt the herbivores, and fungi to clean up after them, but this image of nature is too simple. Competition and cooperation are actually more important than the "tooth and claw" of a few fierce animals. Many species are totally dependent on others; most trees, for example, must live symbiotically with microscopic fungi in order to grow and defend themselves. Although natural communities may appear balanced and harmonious, they are in fact constantly changing in membership, as individual species come and go and as the environment changes. Ecology is the study of all these interactions: the study of our home.

Competition between species
Lions may stalk and kill their prey but must compete with other species, such as hyenas and vultures, for the food. Competition for space and resources is a hallmark of community ecology.

Harvester ant

Competition within species
These male stag beetles are fighting over a female. Competition between individuals over resources underpins much animal behavior. In social species, such as ants and humans, related individuals may cooperate to enhance their competitiveness.

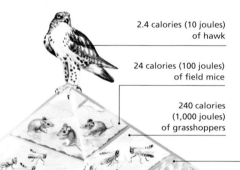

2.4 calories (10 joules) of hawk

24 calories (100 joules) of field mice

240 calories (1,000 joules) of grasshoppers

2,400 calories (10,000 joules) of prairie grasses

A pyramid of energy
In a Michigan field, sunlight is transformed into plant tissue that feeds grasshoppers and, in turn, field mice and hawks. As energy transfer between levels of the food chain is imperfect, fewer animals are supported at higher levels and the community has a pyramid-shaped structure.

FOOD WEB ROLES

Producers
Decomposers and scavengers
Herbivores
Carnivores
Top carnivores

Acacia tree

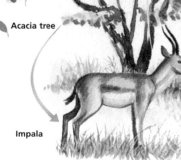

Impala

Organization of nature
Ecologists recognize five levels of complexity ranging from the individual animal to the entire biosphere. It is clear that no animal can survive without lots of others; it is less clear how many species can be lost and how many communities can be destroyed before the biosphere fails to provide the ecological services we take for granted.

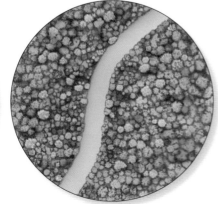

Organism
This level involves the individual, such as the lar, or white-handed, gibbon of Asia's rain forests, as well as its interactions with other members of its own species, other species, and the environment.

Population
A population comprises the members of a species living in one place. Lar gibbons live in monogamous family groups. Adult pairs defend a territory and sing to advertise their presence.

Community
All the populations of many interdependent species living in one place and all their ecological interactions make up a community. The lar gibbon is part of the rain-forest canopy community.

Biome
A biome is an association of similar communities distributed over large areas. The major biomes, such as tropical rain forest, are usually named after the dominant vegetation type.

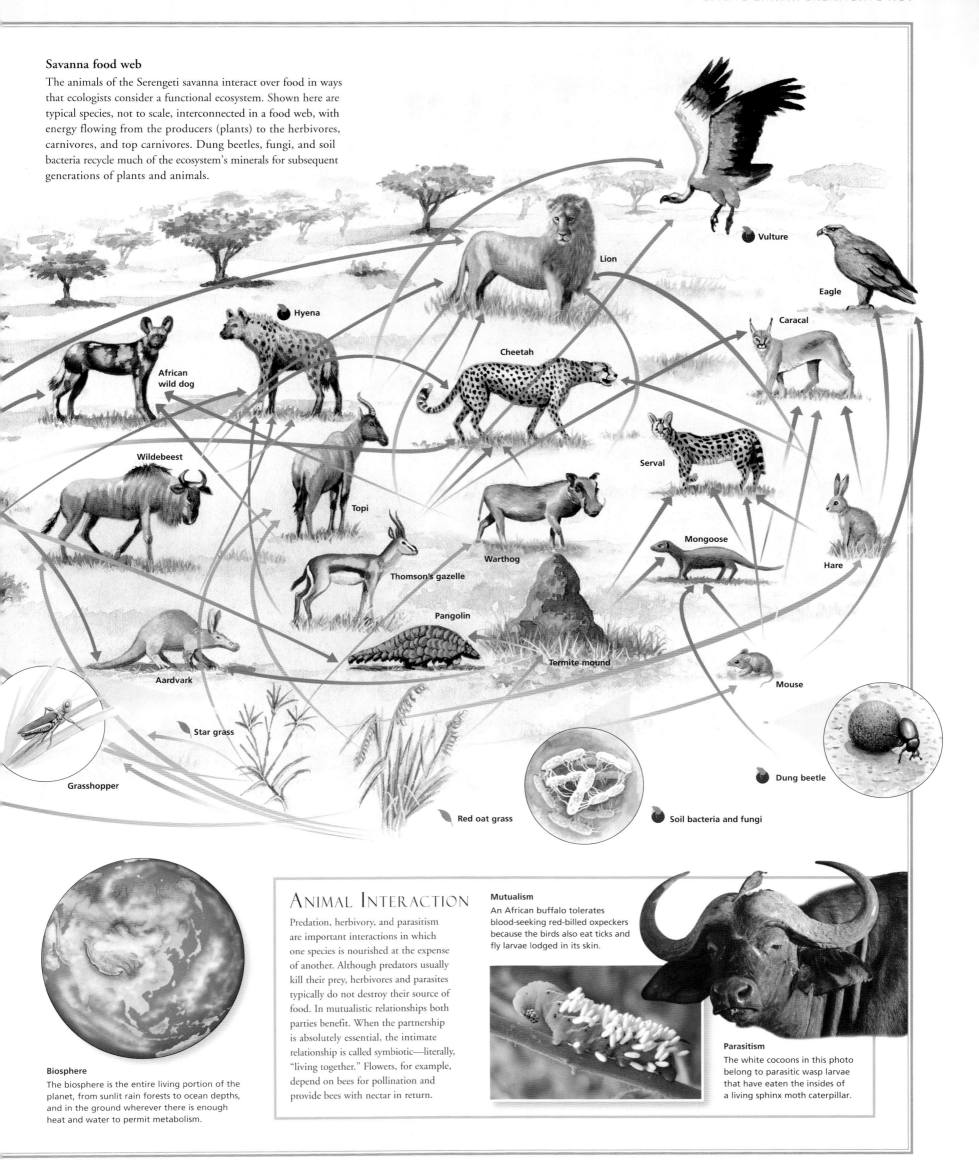

Savanna food web

The animals of the Serengeti savanna interact over food in ways that ecologists consider a functional ecosystem. Shown here are typical species, not to scale, interconnected in a food web, with energy flowing from the producers (plants) to the herbivores, carnivores, and top carnivores. Dung beetles, fungi, and soil bacteria recycle much of the ecosystem's minerals for subsequent generations of plants and animals.

Vulture

Eagle

Lion

Caracal

Hyena

Cheetah

African wild dog

Serval

Wildebeest

Topi

Warthog

Mongoose

Hare

Thomson's gazelle

Pangolin

Aardvark

Termite mound

Mouse

Star grass

Grasshopper

Dung beetle

Red oat grass

Soil bacteria and fungi

Biosphere

The biosphere is the entire living portion of the planet, from sunlit rain forests to ocean depths, and in the ground wherever there is enough heat and water to permit metabolism.

ANIMAL INTERACTION

Predation, herbivory, and parasitism are important interactions in which one species is nourished at the expense of another. Although predators usually kill their prey, herbivores and parasites typically do not destroy their source of food. In mutualistic relationships both parties benefit. When the partnership is absolutely essential, the intimate relationship is called symbiotic—literally, "living together." Flowers, for example, depend on bees for pollination and provide bees with nectar in return.

Mutualism

An African buffalo tolerates blood-seeking red-billed oxpeckers because the birds also eat ticks and fly larvae lodged in its skin.

Parasitism

The white cocoons in this photo belong to parasitic wasp larvae that have eaten the insides of a living sphinx moth caterpillar.

FOREST HABITATS

At least one trillion trees cover 30 percent of the land's surface, and two-thirds of all animals are forest dwellers. From the lush vegetation of the tropics to the snow-covered conifers of the north, forests grow in a wide range of climates. Their three-dimensional structure provides different microhabitats that feed and shelter an extraordinary diversity of wildlife. Some species spend their entire lives in the canopy, climbing, swinging, gliding, or flying from branch to branch. Forests play a vital role in the health of our planet. Through exchanges of energy, water, and carbon dioxide, they influence climates on a regional and global scale. Much of the world's original forest has been cleared for cropland or pasture. Reforestation efforts are under way but natural regrowth supports not even half the original biodiversity, and plantation forests support even less. Forest management, especially in the tropics, will help to determine both how much wildlife is lost and how much warmer the planet will become.

The world's forests

Determined largely by climate and soil, the major forest types occur across Earth in roughly horizontal bands that merge into one another. Year-round warmth and high rainfall near the equator result in lush evergreen rain forests. Further north and south, trees cope with seasonal temperature and rainfall variation by dropping leaves or becoming dormant. The most northern forest is boreal, where hardy conifers endure bitter winters.

Boreal forest
The boreal forest, or taiga, is Earth's largest biome. It is dominated by evergreen conifer (needle-leaf) trees such as firs, spruce, and pines. The moose is a year-round resident.

Forest wildlife

A million species of forest animals show exquisite adaptations to the trees in which they feed, shelter, and reproduce. Just moving around without falling out of the trees can be challenging. Although all forest wildlife is directly or indirectly dependent on trees, few species actually eat the woody trunks and branches; those that appear to, such as termites, rely on bacteria and fungi to break down the wood's indigestible cellulose.

Northern flicker
This North American woodpecker spends more time on the forest floor catching ants than it does drumming on tree trunks for insect larvae.

Northern flying squirrel
This nocturnal rodent can glide from tree to tree using a pair of furry membranes that extend between its front and rear legs.

Red-eyed tree frog
Climbing easily with sucker-padded toes, this amphibian spends most of its life in the trees of the always-humid tropical rain forest.

Carpet python
Arboreal snakes such as the Australian carpet python wait for days to feed on birds and mammals. At night they can detect prey by body temperature.

Map labels: North American boreal forest · Pacific Northwest temperate rain forest · NORTH AMERICA · California coniferous forest · Eastern deciduous forest · Central American rain forests · Monteverde cloud forest · Amazon rain forest · Brazilian shield seasonal tropical forest · SOUTH AMERICA · Southern temperate rain forest

Disappearing forests

The largest cause of species extinction is the loss of 27,000 square miles (70,000 km²) of forest to logging and agriculture each year. Nearly half the forests that were present 2,000 years ago are gone. Frontier forests are undisturbed areas that are large enough to maintain their biodiversity. Efforts to set aside remaining forests are often frustrated; protected areas act like "honeypots" and attract poor settlers to their edges.

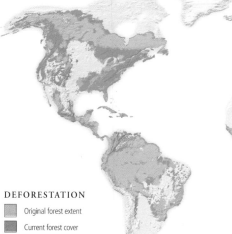

DEFORESTATION
- Original forest extent
- Current forest cover
- Remaining frontier forest

Temperate deciduous forest
A blaze of colors precedes leaf-fall as the forest prepares for winter dormancy. Spring begins with a wildflower show on the forest floor until new leaves provide shade again.

Temperate rain forest
High rainfall, coastal fog, and mild winters characterize these cool wet forests. In North America's Pacific Northwest, tall conifers are festooned with mosses, lichens, and ferns.

Seasonal tropical forest
In seasonal tropical areas, such as Indonesia's Komodo Island, the forest trees lose their leaves during the hot dry season. Komodo dragons stalk prey on the open forest floor.

Tropical rain forest
Ever-wet rain forests are home to more species of animals than any other biome. Scarlet macaws live high in the forest canopy, which is closed 100 feet (30 m) above the ground.

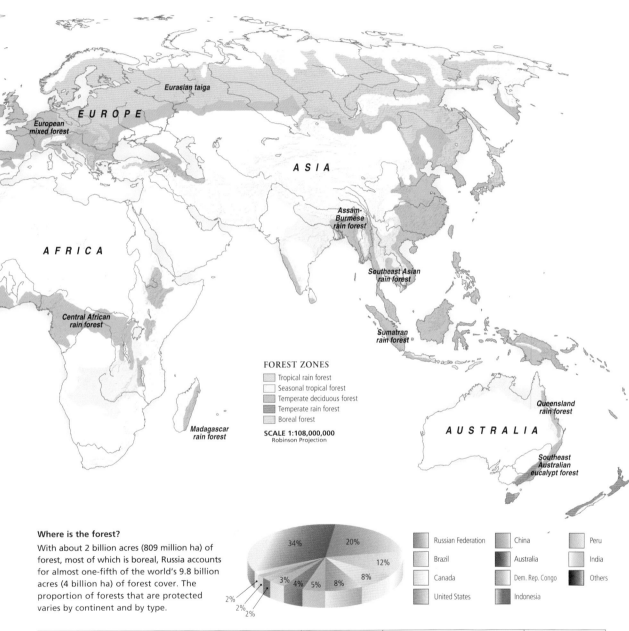

EUROPE

European mixed forest

Eurasian taiga

ASIA

AFRICA

Assam-Burmese rain forest

Southeast Asian rain forest

Central African rain forest

Sumatran rain forest

Madagascar rain forest

Queensland rain forest

AUSTRALIA

Southeast Australian eucalypt forest

FOREST ZONES
- Tropical rain forest
- Seasonal tropical forest
- Temperate deciduous forest
- Temperate rain forest
- Boreal forest

SCALE 1:108,000,000
Robinson Projection

CARBON STORAGE

Of the 8.8 billion tons (8 billion t) of carbon dioxide released into the atmosphere by humans each year, about one-fifth comes from deforestation, and the rest comes from fossil fuel use. Through photosynthesis, forests absorb 37.5 percent of this carbon dioxide. The oceans absorb the same amount, but the remaining 25 percent stays in the atmosphere and is the major cause of global warming. By storing carbon, the world's forests provide a vital ecological service.

Vanishing rain forest
Forest loss reduces both carbon storage and biodiversity. In this satellite image, pale green and tan deforested tracts break up the darker green Amazon rain forest.

DEFORESTATION OF NATURAL FORESTS

Millions of acres/year | Millions of hectares/year

Brazil, Indonesia, Russian Federation, Mexico, Papua New Guinea, Peru, United States, Bolivia, Sudan, Nigeria

The big emitters
Although the United States emits 25 percent of the world's carbon emissions, mostly from fossil fuel use, Brazil and Indonesia are the largest contributors based on deforestation.

Where is the forest?
With about 2 billion acres (809 million ha) of forest, most of which is boreal, Russia accounts for almost one-fifth of the world's 9.8 billion acres (4 billion ha) of forest cover. The proportion of forests that are protected varies by continent and by type.

20%, 12%, 8%, 8%, 5%, 4%, 3%, 2%, 2%, 2%, 34%

- Russian Federation
- Brazil
- Canada
- United States
- China
- Australia
- Dem. Rep. Congo
- Indonesia
- Peru
- India
- Others

Region	Tropical Forest	Protected	Non-tropical Forest	Protected
Europe (incl. Russia)	Nil	n/a	3,828,000 sq. miles (9,914,000 km²)	3%
North America	1,700 sq. miles (4,400 km²)	7%	2,649,000 sq. miles (6,837,000 km²)	9%
Central & South America	2,669,000 sq. miles (6,914,000 km²)	12%	233,000 sq. miles (605,000 km²)	11%
Asia	814,000 sq. miles (2,108,000 km²)	16%	510,000 sq. miles (1,321,000 km²)	5%
Africa & Middle East	1,731,000 sq. miles (4,482,000 km²)	9%	70,000 sq. miles (180,000 km²)	3%
Australasia & Oceania	207,000 sq. miles (536,000 km²)	9%	105,000 sq. miles (271,000 km²)	19%

Grassland Habitats

Earth's great grasslands still cover about 10 percent of the land. Most of a grassland community's biomass lies below the ground in a rich, nutrient-storing root-mat, or sod. This enables grasses and herbs to survive and quickly recover from frequent drought and fire. Seasonality dominates the ecology. Animals usually feed and reproduce during the rainy season, and switch to survival mode (or migrate) during the hot dry season or cold season. Historically, grasslands were home to vast herds of grazing and browsing mammals, but today these populations can be found only in Africa. The grasses themselves depend on grazing, and without large numbers of herbivores, the vegetation changes to scrub or thorny woodland. Taking advantage of the fertile soil, humans have converted half the grassland biome for crops, grazing, and urban development. The remaining grasslands and their wildlife are also threatened by growing human populations and the increasing numbers of domestic sheep, goats, and cattle.

The Lost Prairies

The great interior plains of the United States were once a sea of grass extending thousands of miles, home to about 60 million bison. Between 1830 and 2000, the prairies' extent shrank by two-thirds, and the bison were hunted down to about 100 animals. European settlers converted almost all the eastern tallgrass prairie to cornfields, while further west they farmed wheat, cattle, and sheep. Non-native plants invaded and now account for up to 90 percent of vegetation.

ORIGINAL PRAIRIE COVER

CURRENT PRAIRIE COVER

- ▮ Tallgrass prairie
- ▯ Midgrass prairie
- ▮ Shortgrass prairie

The world's grasslands

Known as savannas, or llanos in South America, the grasslands bordering the tropics often include scattered trees. They are warm year-round but have a pronounced dry season. The temperate grasslands are treeless plains with hot dry summers and cold winters. They are called prairies in North America, pampas in South America, veldt in South Africa, and steppe in Eurasia. The large herbivores associated with grasslands include North American bison, South American guanacos, African gazelles, Asian wild horses, and Australian kangaroos.

NORTH AMERICA

Urban 19% — Remaining grasslands 10%

Croplands 71%

SOUTH AMERICA

Urban 6% — Remaining grasslands 22%

Croplands 72%

Fire on the steppe

Wildfire is an essential component of grassland ecology, helping to break down dead matter, recycle nutrients, and prevent shrubs from taking over. In many grassland regions, farmers also deliberately light fires to clear land for agriculture or to regenerate pasture for grazing animals. In this false-color satellite image of Central Asia's Kazakhstan steppe, vegetation appears green, burned areas are deep reddish brown, and the red dots represent burning fires.

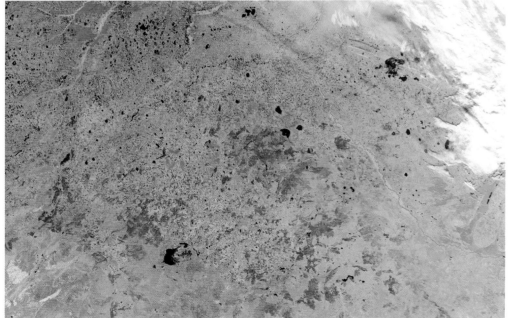

Region	Grassland & Savanna Area	Name
Europe (incl. Russia)	541,000 sq. miles (1,401,000 km²)	Steppe
North America	675,000 sq. miles (1,749,000 km²)	Prairie
Central & South America	1,911,000 sq. miles (4,950,000 km²)	Pampas
Asia	10,253,000 sq. miles (26,555,000 km²)	Steppe
Africa & Middle East	3,958,000 sq. miles (10,251,000 km²)	Savanna
Australasia & Oceania	1,186,000 sq. miles (3,072,000 km²)	Grassland

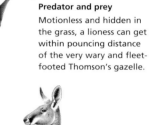

Foot patrol
Grassland residents include the tall flightless running birds—ostrich, emu, and rhea—as well as the long-legged African secretary bird, a reptile-eating eagle that patrols the savanna on foot.

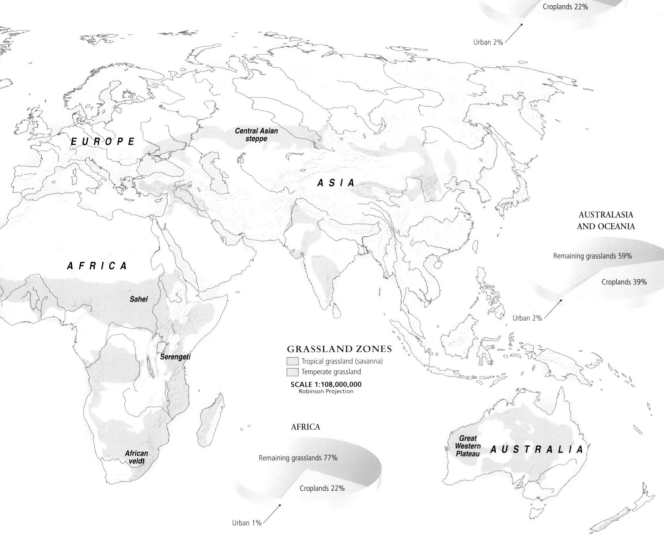

EUROPE AND ASIA
Remaining grasslands 76%
Croplands 22%
Urban 2%

AUSTRALASIA AND OCEANIA
Remaining grasslands 59%
Croplands 39%
Urban 2%

GRASSLAND ZONES
Tropical grassland (savanna)
Temperate grassland
SCALE 1:108,000,000
Robinson Projection

AFRICA
Remaining grasslands 77%
Croplands 22%
Urban 1%

EUROPE
ASIA
Central Asian steppe
AFRICA
Sahel
Serengeti
African veldt
AUSTRALIA
Great Western Plateau

Predator and prey
Motionless and hidden in the grass, a lioness can get within pouncing distance of the very wary and fleet-footed Thomson's gazelle.

Outback grazer
Adapted to Australia's driest grasslands, the red kangaroo times its activities to the daily temperature regime, and its reproduction to the sporadic rainfall.

Grassland wildlife

Hot dry summers and cold winters with little food present grassland animals with challenges. With no trees to hide in, many predators and prey have adopted the burrowing habit and the ability to run fast. The huge standing crop of vegetation is regrown annually and supports large populations of vertebrate and invertebrate herbivores. Grasshoppers and their alter-egos, plague locusts, are notorious residents.

Burrower
Many grassland mammals and birds, such as America's burrowing owl (left), live underground, where they can hide from predators and escape the heat of summer and the cold of winter.

Termite eater
Termites are responsible for 90 percent of the decomposition of dead grass. The South American giant anteater visits termite mounds to feed on these abundant insects.

Grazing herds
Large grazing herds once characterized most grasslands but they survive only in parts of Africa, where zebras, wildebeest, and gazelles feed sequentially to reduce competition.

Dry Habitats

Life as we know it depends on water, so animals face special challenges when they inhabit areas of little rain and extreme temperatures. In hot deserts, daytime temperatures regularly exceed 100°F (38°C) and the ground surface may reach 170°F (77°C). In cold deserts, water may be frozen and unavailable. Under such conditions, there is little vegetation and limited animal life. Few animals are about during the day. Most shelter beneath the sand or in whatever shade is available. Desert animals often have coats and scales that resist desiccation, and many use evaporative heat-loss mechanisms such as panting and sweating to keep the body and brain cool. A few animals become dormant and estivate for months or even years. At night the desert comes alive as its animals emerge and feed. Rain, when it comes, brings about a sudden transformation as desert plants bloom briefly and animals quickly reproduce. Then most animals go back into hiding and patiently await the next life-sustaining storm.

Western scrub jay
In summer in its chaparral or semidesert habitat, this bird gets all its water from its food, seeks shade at midday, and sheds heat from its unfeathered feet.

Hyperarid to humid
Much of the global land surface is already arid or semiarid. These areas have little topsoil and are susceptible to wind-erosion. Global warming and poor land-use practices are likely to increase the proportion of drylands, with significant negative consequences for both people and wild animals.

WORLD ARIDITY

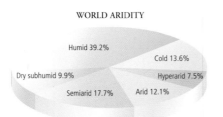

Humid 39.2%
Cold 13.6%
Dry subhumid 9.9%
Hyperarid 7.5%
Semiarid 17.7%
Arid 12.1%

DRY ZONES
- Desert
- Semidesert
- Coastal scrub
- ❋ Hot desert
- ☼ Cold desert

SCALE 1:108,000,000
Robinson Projection

The world's dry zones
Drylands circle the globe in two bands 20 to 30 degrees north and south of the equator. Deserts cover about 13 percent of Earth's land, but up to one-third of the land can be called arid or semiarid. Desert and semidesert biomes merge into grasslands, thornwoods, and coastal scrub (Mediterranean-type vegetation such as maquis, chaparral, fynbos, and mallee).

NORTH AMERICA
Great Basin ☼
Mojave Desert ❋
Californian chaparral
Sonoran Desert ❋   Chihuahuan Desert

SOUTH AMERICA
Peruvian Desert ☼
Atacama Desert ☼
Chilean mattoral
☼ Patagonian Desert

Desertification

A decline in land productivity called desertification is occurring at the edges of many drylands. The major causes are climate change, overgrazing, poor soil management in croplands, and local human population growth. Currently, about 30 million acres (12 million ha) of agricultural land become useless each year. As the 1930s "dust bowl" in North America's Great Plains and the 1980s Sahelian drought show, desertification can destroy human societies and wildlife habitats.

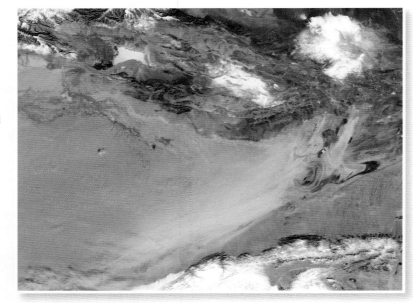

Dust storm
Poor management of drylands is increasing dust storms, such as this one over the sand dunes of China's Taklimakan Desert. By removing soil and organic matter, dust storms reduce agricultural productivity at desert margins.

DESERTIFICATION RISK
- Low
- Moderate
- High
- Very high
- Desert
- Not vulnerable

A drier world
Significant areas of grassland are at risk of desertification as a result of global warming and local land-use practices.

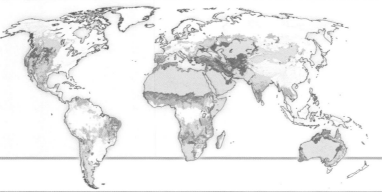

Southern grasshopper mouse
This nocturnal burrower obtains its water from its meals of other mice, scorpions, and beetles. The male stands and sings loudly to advertise his territory.

Greater roadrunner
Roadrunners sun themselves in the morning to warm up without burning food calories. Later they stand in the shade, spread their wings, and pant to stay cool.

Desert	Region	Type	Area
Sahara	Northern Africa	Hot	3,500,000 sq. miles (9,100,000 km²)
Arabian	Arabian Peninsula	Hot	1,000,000 sq. miles (2,600,000 km²)
Gobi	China, Mongolia	Cold	500,000 sq. miles (1,300,000 km²)
Patagonian	Argentina	Cold	260,000 sq. miles (670,000 km²)
Great Victoria	Australia	Hot	250,000 sq. miles (650,000 km²)

EUROPE

ASIA

☼ Gobi Desert

Karakum Desert ☼

☼ Taklimakan Desert

Mediterranean maquis

☼ Iranian Desert

☀ Lut Desert

☀ Sahara Desert

☀ Thar Desert

Arabian Desert

AFRICA

Namib Desert ☼

Kalahari Desert ☀

South African fynbos

Bactrian camel
Gobi desert camels have broad feet, long eyelashes, and closeable nostrils to deal with sand. Two fatty humps provide metabolic water.

Central bearded dragon
This lizard's display scares away predators. The color of its scales can slightly lighten or darken to optimize its temperature regulation.

☀ Great Sandy Desert

AUSTRALIA
☀ Simpson Desert

☀ Great Victoria Desert

Southern Australian mallee

Fog-basking beetle
This Namibian beetle emerges from the sand at night and climbs a dune to bask head-down in the passing fog, gathering water that then trickles to its mouth.

Burchell's sandgrouse
This desert bird has the habit of "belly wetting" when it drinks at a pool just after sunrise; it then carries the water to its chicks.

Indian wild asses
These wild asses can survive in the barren desert of northwest India as long as they live within a couple of miles of a waterhole.

Deserts and semideserts

Semidesert regions (such as the Galápagos Islands, right, with giant tortoise) receive less than 10 inches (250 mm) of rain annually and feature well-spaced cacti and thorn scrub. True deserts (such as the Namib Desert, far right) receive less than 2 inches (50 mm) of rain annually and support few plants, and years or decades may pass between rains. The Namib's sidewinding adder hides during the day with only its eyes and nostrils above the sand.

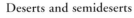

FROZEN HABITATS

The last ice age ended only 18,000 years ago, and many cold-adapted species from that time survive around the polar ice caps and on polar and alpine tundra. The treeless polar tundra is underlain by frozen soil known as permafrost, and characterized by a short cool summer and a long frigid winter when the sun never rises. Animals require special adaptations to survive in frozen habitats year-round. Many species are migratory and walk, swim, or fly toward the equator to escape the bitter winter cold. Some that stay, such as polar bears, shelter in snow caves and live off their body fat; others, such as lemmings, burrow beneath the snow, where they nibble on what is left of the vegetation. Insulation, physiological adaptations, and social behavior enable penguins to overwinter on Antarctica's ice. Within days of the sun's return to polar regions, life is in full swing as newborns and hatchlings must be rushed though their development during the two- to four-month-long summer day.

Ice and tundra habitats

The three major ice caps cover all the Antarctic continent and Greenland with ice up to 16,000 feet (5,000 m) thick. The Arctic tundra remains extensive but is changing rapidly as the planet becomes warmer. In the southern hemisphere, tundra occurs on subantarctic islands. Alpine tundra is found in restricted mountainous areas of all continents and is associated with glaciers in a few places.

FROZEN ZONES

- Arctic tundra
- Alpine tundra
- Polar ice

SCALE 1:96,000,000
Robinson Projection

WARMER POLES

The polar regions are warming at three times the rate of the tropics. The 50-year decline in Antarctic winter sea ice (below) and the projected loss of Arctic permafrost and ice cover (right) are illustrative. Sea levels are projected to rise 3 to 6 feet (1–2 m) this century, but if all the world's 7.2 million cubic miles (30 million km³) of ice caps and glaciers melt, global sea levels could rise by as much as 256 feet (78 m).

Loss of Arctic permafrost
This map shows the projected impact of global warming on Arctic permafrost and ice cover. Animals such as caribou and walrus, which depend on tundra and sea ice, will face new stresses.

ARCTIC WARMING

- Current permafrost area
- Projected permafrost area 2100
- Current sea ice
- Projected sea ice 2070–90

Antarctic sea ice decline
Life around Antarctica depends on winter sea ice, which is shrinking every year. The algae that shelter beneath the ice provide for the growth of populations of shrimplike krill, which in turn sustain penguins, seals, and whales.

Legend:
- MSA* ice core record
- MSA long-term trend
- Sea ice extent satellite data

*MSA (methanesulphonic acid) is produced by phytoplankton and associated with sea ice extent.

Summer in Siberia

Still-frozen lakes dot the tundra east of the Lena River delta in Siberia, and cracked sea ice connects the New Siberia Islands to the mainland. The platform of sea ice enables polar bears to hunt seals, and as it melts with global warming, the bears and their cubs will starve. The lakes and permafrost are also melting and releasing methane, a potent greenhouse gas, and further contributing to climate change.

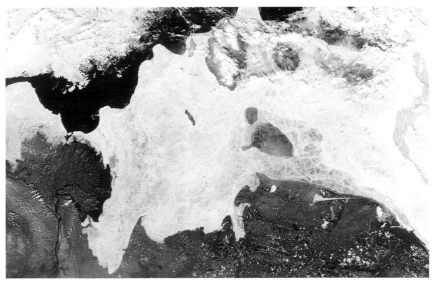

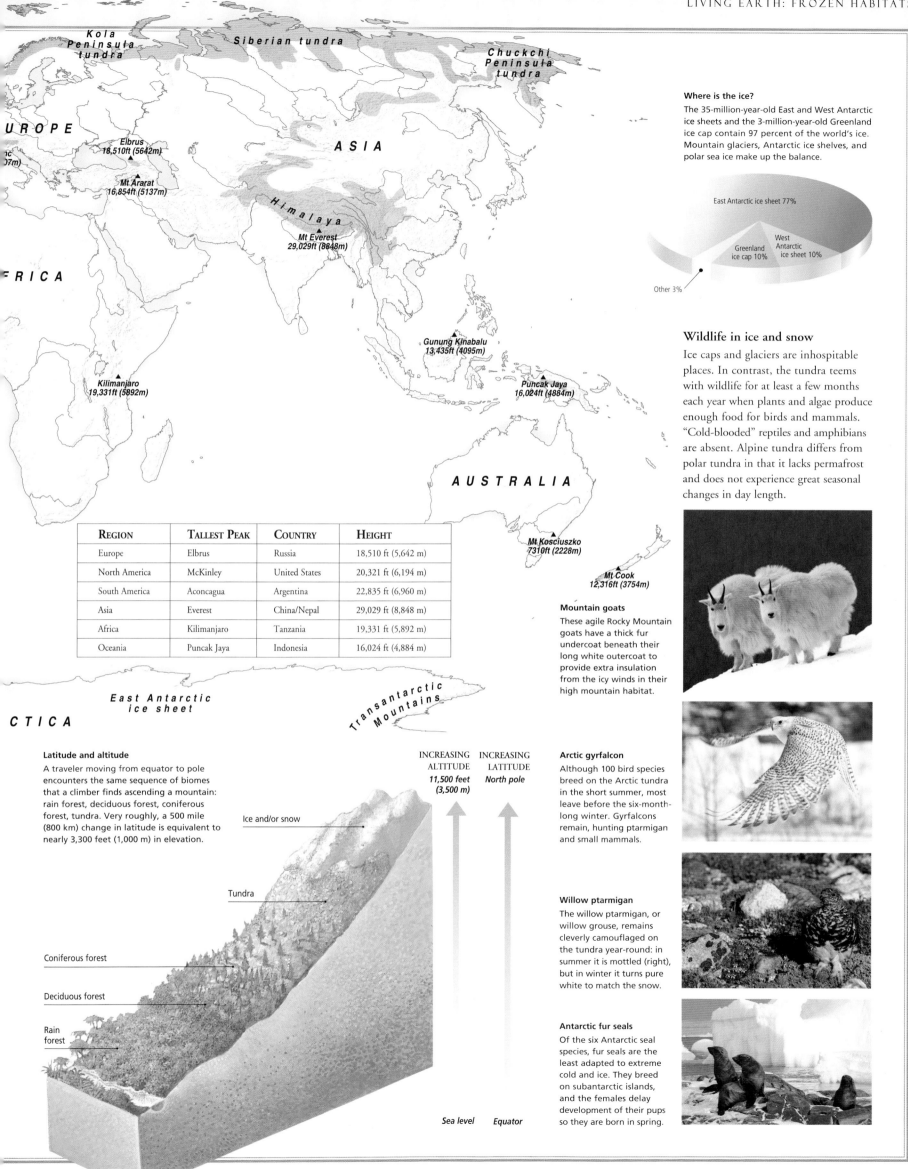

Kola
Peninsula
tundra

Siberian tundra

Chuckchi
Peninsula
tundra

EUROPE

ASIA

Elbrus
18,510ft (5642m)

Mt Ararat
16,854ft (5137m)

Himalaya

Mt Everest
29,029ft (8848m)

AFRICA

Gunung Kinabalu
13,435ft (4095m)

Kilimanjaro
19,331ft (5892m)

Puncak Jaya
16,024ft (4884m)

AUSTRALIA

Mt Kosciuszko
7310ft (2228m)

Mt Cook
12,316ft (3754m)

Where is the ice?

The 35-million-year-old East and West Antarctic ice sheets and the 3-million-year-old Greenland ice cap contain 97 percent of the world's ice. Mountain glaciers, Antarctic ice shelves, and polar sea ice make up the balance.

East Antarctic ice sheet 77%

Greenland
ice cap 10%

West
Antarctic
ice sheet 10%

Other 3%

Wildlife in ice and snow

Ice caps and glaciers are inhospitable places. In contrast, the tundra teems with wildlife for at least a few months each year when plants and algae produce enough food for birds and mammals. "Cold-blooded" reptiles and amphibians are absent. Alpine tundra differs from polar tundra in that it lacks permafrost and does not experience great seasonal changes in day length.

REGION	TALLEST PEAK	COUNTRY	HEIGHT
Europe	Elbrus	Russia	18,510 ft (5,642 m)
North America	McKinley	United States	20,321 ft (6,194 m)
South America	Aconcagua	Argentina	22,835 ft (6,960 m)
Asia	Everest	China/Nepal	29,029 ft (8,848 m)
Africa	Kilimanjaro	Tanzania	19,331 ft (5,892 m)
Oceania	Puncak Jaya	Indonesia	16,024 ft (4,884 m)

East Antarctic
ice sheet

Transantarctic
Mountains

ANTARCTICA

Mountain goats
These agile Rocky Mountain goats have a thick fur undercoat beneath their long white outercoat to provide extra insulation from the icy winds in their high mountain habitat.

Latitude and altitude

A traveler moving from equator to pole encounters the same sequence of biomes that a climber finds ascending a mountain: rain forest, deciduous forest, coniferous forest, tundra. Very roughly, a 500 mile (800 km) change in latitude is equivalent to nearly 3,300 feet (1,000 m) in elevation.

Ice and/or snow

Tundra

Coniferous forest

Deciduous forest

Rain
forest

INCREASING
ALTITUDE
11,500 feet
(3,500 m)

INCREASING
LATITUDE
North pole

Sea level   Equator

Arctic gyrfalcon
Although 100 bird species breed on the Arctic tundra in the short summer, most leave before the six-month-long winter. Gyrfalcons remain, hunting ptarmigan and small mammals.

Willow ptarmigan
The willow ptarmigan, or willow grouse, remains cleverly camouflaged on the tundra year-round: in summer it is mottled (right), but in winter it turns pure white to match the snow.

Antarctic fur seals
Of the six Antarctic seal species, fur seals are the least adapted to extreme cold and ice. They breed on subantarctic islands, and the females delay development of their pups so they are born in spring.

AQUATIC HABITATS

Aquatic habitats span a greater range of physical conditions than are found on land, so life in water is even more diverse. Coral reefs rival rain forests in terms of complexity, and salt marshes are among the most productive ecosystems on the planet. Compared to our intensive study of terrestrial life, however, aquatic habitats are relatively unexplored and they continue to surprise us. Tiny planktonic algae in sunlit ocean water, and not land plants, are responsible for producing most of the oxygen that land animals depend on. Life thrives in total darkness on the deep ocean floor where 660°F (350°C) water and hydrogen sulfide are released from underwater volcanic vents. One-fifth of the world's much-loved coral reefs are already gone, and half are doomed by present trends. Wetlands store 20 percent of the world's carbon and, if they continue to be destroyed, could release their carbon dioxide as a planet-warming "carbon bomb." Clearly, it is time to pay more attention to aquatic habitats.

Freshwater and marine habitats

Animals in aquatic habitats may be either permanent residents or visitors with adaptations to both land and water. Many more types of animals are found in salt water than in fresh, as oceans are the ancestral habitat of all lifeforms and are easier to live in metabolically. Nevertheless, freshwater ponds, lakes, rivers, and wetlands are the permanent home of diverse invertebrates, fish, waterfowl, and other vertebrates.

Ponds and lakes
Living between worlds, painted turtles must warm up in the sun before feeding in cool water. But when the water freezes in winter, turtles hibernate in the pond's muddy bottom.

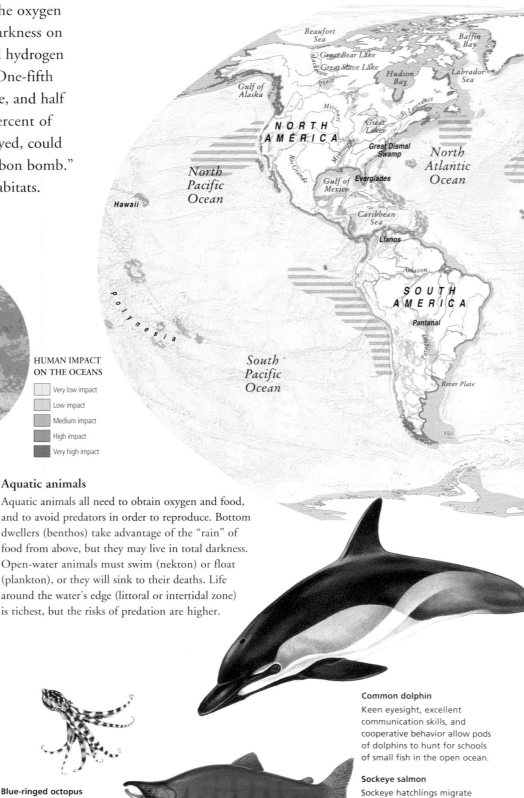

HUMAN IMPACT ON THE OCEANS

- Very low impact
- Low impact
- Medium impact
- High impact
- Very high impact

The cost of human activities

Humans have destroyed much freshwater and coastal habitat, sacrificing clean water, flood control, and biodiversity in the process. Most oceanic communities have been damaged by overfishing, habitat destruction, pollution, and global warming. Chemicals discharged by polluted rivers are linked to large dead zones in coastal seas, where there is not enough oxygen to support life, and to the increased frequency of the noxious plankton blooms known as red tides.

Aquatic animals

Aquatic animals all need to obtain oxygen and food, and to avoid predators in order to reproduce. Bottom dwellers (benthos) take advantage of the "rain" of food from above, but they may live in total darkness. Open-water animals must swim (nekton) or float (plankton), or they will sink to their deaths. Life around the water's edge (littoral or intertidal zone) is richest, but the risks of predation are higher.

Wetland protection
Adopted in 1971, the Ramsar Convention on Wetlands of International Importance supports conservation efforts at 1,759 freshwater, estuarine, and coastal marine sites in 158 countries. Wetlands that shelter migratory waterfowl are given particular attention.

1,759 RAMSAR SITES PROTECT 398 MILLION ACRES (161 MILLION HA) OF WETLANDS

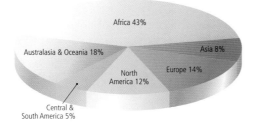

- Africa 43%
- Australasia & Oceania 18%
- Asia 8%
- Europe 14%
- North America 12%
- Central & South America 5%

Blue-ringed octopus
This small tide-pool octopus is usually well-camouflaged, but quickly flashes its bright colors when disturbed, a warning that its venomous bite is deadly.

Common dolphin
Keen eyesight, excellent communication skills, and cooperative behavior allow pods of dolphins to hunt for schools of small fish in the open ocean.

Sockeye salmon
Sockeye hatchlings migrate from their mountain-stream birthplace to the ocean, where they feed for years before returning to the same stream to reproduce and die.

Wetlands
Wetlands and the rivers that feed them are highly productive habitats that support many invertebrates, fish, and birds. Roseate spoonbills hunt crustaceans and fish in shallow water.

Mangroves
Mangroves receive nutrients from both land and sea and support great numbers of algae, plants, invertebrates, and fish, as well as birds such as this yellow-crowned night heron.

Coral reefs
Corals grow in warm, clear, nutrient-poor seas, but a symbiosis between the coral animals and algae fuels their great productivity. A reef's structure provides niches for many animals.

Oceans
Oceanic fish tend to specialize as bottom-, surface-, or mid-water feeders. The head of the scalloped hammerhead shark has sensory organs that guide it to buried stingrays.

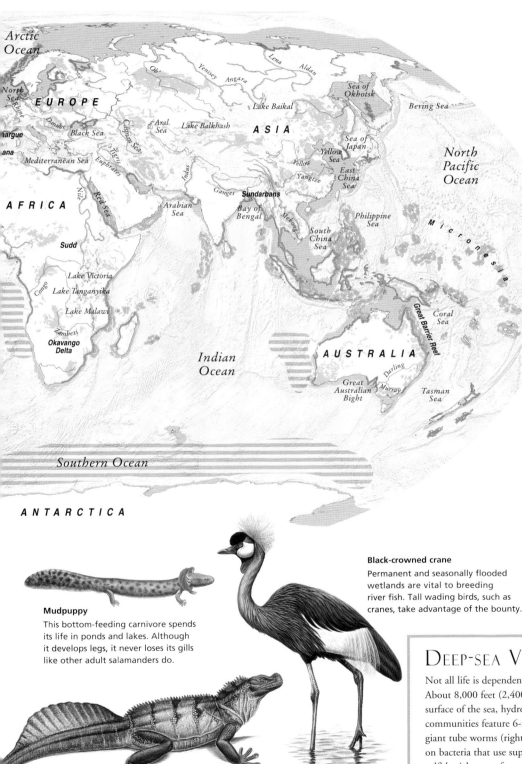

The world's waters

The great rivers, lakes, and wetlands are treasure troves of freshwater life that harbor thousands of fish species, amphibians, and aquatic turtles, snakes, birds, and mammals. Salt marshes and mangroves anchor the coastlines, serve as fish nurseries, and sustain millions of birds. Ocean habitats themselves are partitioned according to water temperature, light, depth, and nutrients (concentrated in upwelling zones). Coral reefs are the fragile crown jewels of the aquatic world.

AQUATIC HABITATS

- Major river
- Lake
- Wetland
- Salt marsh
- Mangrove
- Coral reef
- Deep-sea coral
- Continental shelf
- Upwelling zone
- Open ocean

SCALE 1:104,000,000
Robinson Projection

ALL WATER ON EARTH

Oceans 97.5%
Fresh water 2.5%

Ice caps and glaciers 79%
Groundwater 20%
Accessible surface fresh water 1%

Water in lakes 52%
Water in soil 38%
Water vapor in atmosphere 8%
Water in rivers 1%
Water in living organisims 1%

Where is the water?
The vast majority of water on our blue planet is salty. Less than 3 percent is fresh water, and most of this is locked up as either ice or groundwater. Less than 0.3 percent sustains life in lakes, rivers, and wetlands.

Mudpuppy
This bottom-feeding carnivore spends its life in ponds and lakes. Although it develops legs, it never loses its gills like other adult salamanders do.

Black-crowned crane
Permanent and seasonally flooded wetlands are vital to breeding river fish. Tall wading birds, such as cranes, take advantage of the bounty.

Sail-tailed water lizard
When threatened by a predator, this Central American lizard can make a quick escape. Fringed toes give its feet enough area to run across the surface of streams.

Deep-sea Vents

Not all life is dependent on sunlight. About 8,000 feet (2,400 m) below the surface of the sea, hydrothermal vent communities feature 6-foot (2-m) giant tube worms (right) and depend on bacteria that use superheated sulfide-rich water for energy. Scientists have recently found similar microbial life living in very hot groundwater in rock cracks up to 6 miles (10 km) below the surface of land, ice, and sea around the world.

Human Habitats

Our complicated relationship with wild animals plays out in human-dominated rural and urban environments. On the one hand, our agricultural practices have disturbed ecosystems and replaced natural vegetation with monocultures, opening the door for invasive species and allowing some animals to become pests. On the other hand, a growing number of people want to reconnect with nature and are feeding birds and mammals in gardens and parks. Changing attitudes, coupled with the movement of people from rural areas to cities, reduces pressure on remaining wildlife habitats. Humans have already co-opted nearly half of Earth's surface, so the ultimate fate of wildlife is tied to our use of land. If urbanization continues throughout the 21st century and we manage rural areas in more sustainable ways, wildlife will have a future. Until that time, most people will only encounter nature around their urban homes. Although urban areas seem to be unnatural habitats for animals, they play an important role both in educating the public about wildlife and in maintaining the world's ecological balance.

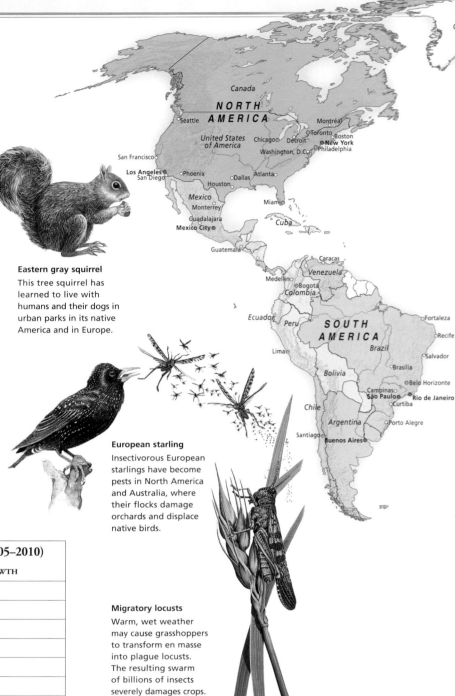

Eastern gray squirrel
This tree squirrel has learned to live with humans and their dogs in urban parks in its native America and in Europe.

European starling
Insectivorous European starlings have become pests in North America and Australia, where their flocks damage orchards and displace native birds.

Migratory locusts
Warm, wet weather may cause grasshoppers to transform en masse into plague locusts. The resulting swarm of billions of insects severely damages crops.

Largest Populations (2010)		Fastest-growing Countries* (2005–2010)	
Country	Population	Country	Annual Growth
China	1,347,563,498	Liberia	4.5%
India	1,184,090,490	Burundi	3.9%
United States	309,162,581	Afghanistan	3.85%
Indonesia	242,968,342	Western Sahara	3.72%
Brazil	201,103,330	Timor-Leste	3.5%
Pakistan	179,659,223	Niger	3.49%
Bangladesh	159,765,367	Eritrea	3.24%
Nigeria	152,217,341	Uganda	3.24%
Russia	139,390,205	Democratic Republic of the Congo	3.22%
Japan	126,804,433	Occupied Palestinian Territory	3.18%

* Countries with more than 100,000 inhabitants

Other 37%
Arable and permanent cropland 12%
Permanent pasture 27%
Forest 24%

Global land use
Humans have converted 35 percent of land to agriculture, and 40 percent of its biological productivity for their own use. Much of this use is unsustainable, and agriculture will need to use less land more intensively in future.

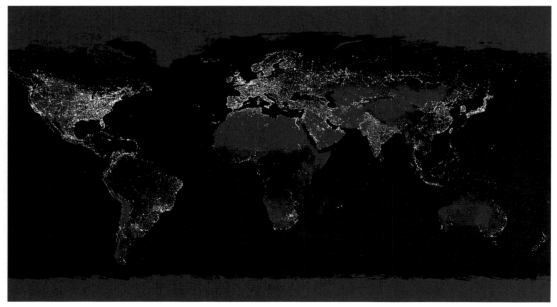

Earth at night

Our planet glows in the darkness of space. This composite satellite image of Earth at night illustrates the extent of urbanization. The United States, Europe, and Japan are brightly lit by their cities, while the interiors of Africa, Asia, Australia, and South America remain, for now, dark and lightly populated. Of the world's 18 megacities (cities with more than 10 million people), 14 are located in developing countries. Half the global human population lives in cities and towns.

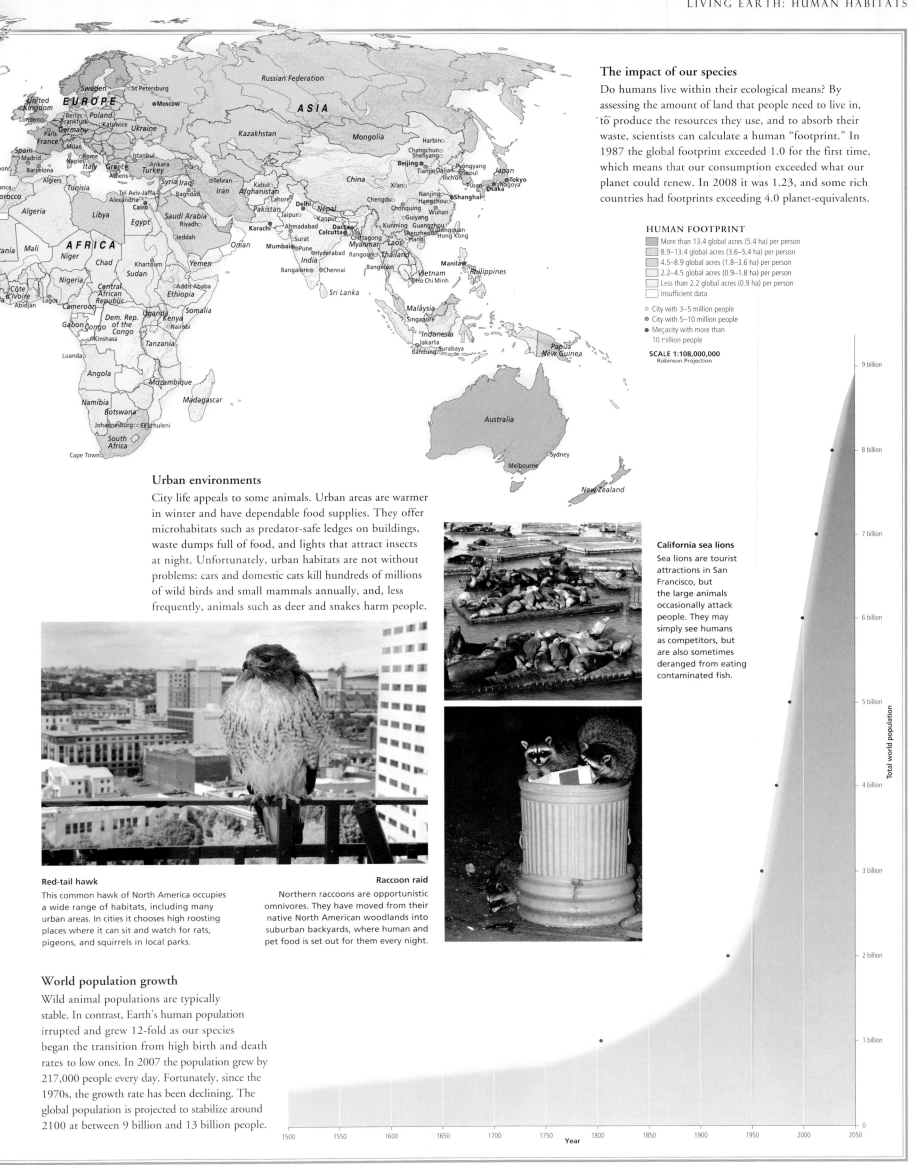

The impact of our species

Do humans live within their ecological means? By assessing the amount of land that people need to live in, to produce the resources they use, and to absorb their waste, scientists can calculate a human "footprint." In 1987 the global footprint exceeded 1.0 for the first time, which means that our consumption exceeded what our planet could renew. In 2008 it was 1.23, and some rich countries had footprints exceeding 4.0 planet-equivalents.

HUMAN FOOTPRINT

More than 13.4 global acres (5.4 ha) per person
8.9–13.4 global acres (3.6–5.4 ha) per person
4.5–8.9 global acres (1.8–3.6 ha) per person
2.2–4.5 global acres (0.9–1.8 ha) per person
Less than 2.2 global acres (0.9 ha) per person
Insufficient data

○ City with 3–5 million people
◉ City with 5–10 million people
● Megacity with more than 10 million people

SCALE 1:108,000,000
Robinson Projection

Urban environments

City life appeals to some animals. Urban areas are warmer in winter and have dependable food supplies. They offer microhabitats such as predator-safe ledges on buildings, waste dumps full of food, and lights that attract insects at night. Unfortunately, urban habitats are not without problems: cars and domestic cats kill hundreds of millions of wild birds and small mammals annually, and, less frequently, animals such as deer and snakes harm people.

California sea lions
Sea lions are tourist attractions in San Francisco, but the large animals occasionally attack people. They may simply see humans as competitors, but are also sometimes deranged from eating contaminated fish.

Red-tail hawk
This common hawk of North America occupies a wide range of habitats, including many urban areas. In cities it chooses high roosting places where it can sit and watch for rats, pigeons, and squirrels in local parks.

Raccoon raid
Northern raccoons are opportunistic omnivores. They have moved from their native North American woodlands into suburban backyards, where human and pet food is set out for them every night.

World population growth

Wild animal populations are typically stable. In contrast, Earth's human population irrupted and grew 12-fold as our species began the transition from high birth and death rates to low ones. In 2007 the population grew by 217,000 people every day. Fortunately, since the 1970s, the growth rate has been declining. The global population is projected to stabilize around 2100 at between 9 billion and 13 billion people.

THREATS TO WILDLIFE

Human activities have taken a heavy toll on nature. Throughout the last 100,000 years a wave of extinctions followed the arrival of humans on each continent or island. Wildlife species are endangered by habitat alteration, the introduction of invasive species, pollution, overhunting, and human-caused global warming. All these threats are amplified by human population growth. Although the impacts per person are hardest on nature in developing countries, population growth anywhere and everywhere has a negative global impact. Several hundred species of vertebrates have gone extinct since 1650. The current annual extinction rate is estimated to be 10,000 times higher than the background rate over the last 60 million years. Thousands of species, mostly unnamed insects, are lost each year, and conservationists mount heroic efforts to save a few charismatic animals in zoos and protected areas. By 2100 half the larger species are likely to be threatened and many of them will lose the battle. Very few species are deliberately targeted for extinction. Most are simply the innocent victims of our presence and activities.

Extinction risk

The distribution of extinction risk varies by country. The interest in conservation is uneven, and monitoring efforts tend to focus on terrestrial vertebrates and often ignore plants and invertebrates. Some countries stand out in a tally of threatened species because their governments keep better records, but in reality the risks are highest in tropical countries, which have high biodiversity. Island nations and countries with rapidly growing human populations are especially dangerous places for animals to live.

🌾 - Cook Islands

🌼 79 extinctions
French Polynesia

THREATENED ANIMAL SPECIES

☐ 0–49	**Extinctions since 1600***
☐ 50–99	🌾 10–29
☐ 100–199	🌿 30–50
☐ 200–299	🌼 More than 50
☐ 300–399	* including species extinct in wild
■ More than 400	**SCALE 1:98,000,000** Robinson Projection

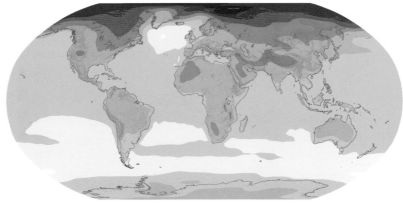

Passenger pigeon
Once the most common bird in North America, this gregarious species went extinct in 1914 as a result of overhunting and habitat alteration.

Global warming

Largely as a result of human activities, our planet is getting warmer. The expected annual surface warming during the 21st century is 5.4°F (3°C) in the tropics and up to 14.4°F (8°C) in polar regions. Many species are already responding by moving poleward or up mountainsides, and becoming active earlier in the spring. Some animals restricted to isolated mountaintops are already going extinct, and ice-dependent species such as polar bears and penguins are vulnerable.

PROJECTED INCREASE IN SURFACE TEMPERATURE BY 2099

☐ 0–1.8°F (0–1°C)	☐ 3.6–5.4°F (2–3°C)	☐ 7.2–9°F (4–5°C)	■ 10.8–12.6°F (6–7°C)
☐ 1.8–3.6°F (1–2°C)	☐ 5.4–7.2°F (3–4°C)	☐ 9–10.8°F (5–6°C)	■ 12.6–14.4°F (7–8°C)

Critically endangered animals

The International Union for the Conservation of Nature (IUCN) maintains the Red List of Threatened Species. Population size and rates of harvesting and habitat destruction are prime indicators of risk, but some types of species—for example, island animals, large animals, top predators, fearless animals—are more extinction-prone than others. Even abundant colonial species can be driven extinct if their breeding behavior is disturbed. The animals illustrated here are all listed as critically endangered.

🔴 Orange-bellied parrot
Devastated by habitat alteration and competition with introduced birds, only 180 orange-bellied parrots remain in the wild. They breed in Tasmania and winter in southeastern Australia.

🔴 Orangutan
Orangutans are declining rapidly because of logging and palm oil cultivation. The Sumatran orangutan is critically endangered, with only 6,600 individuals left.

🔴 Baiji
Also known as the Yangtze river dolphin, this species was last seen in 2004 and is functionally extinct as a result of water pollution and fishing practices.

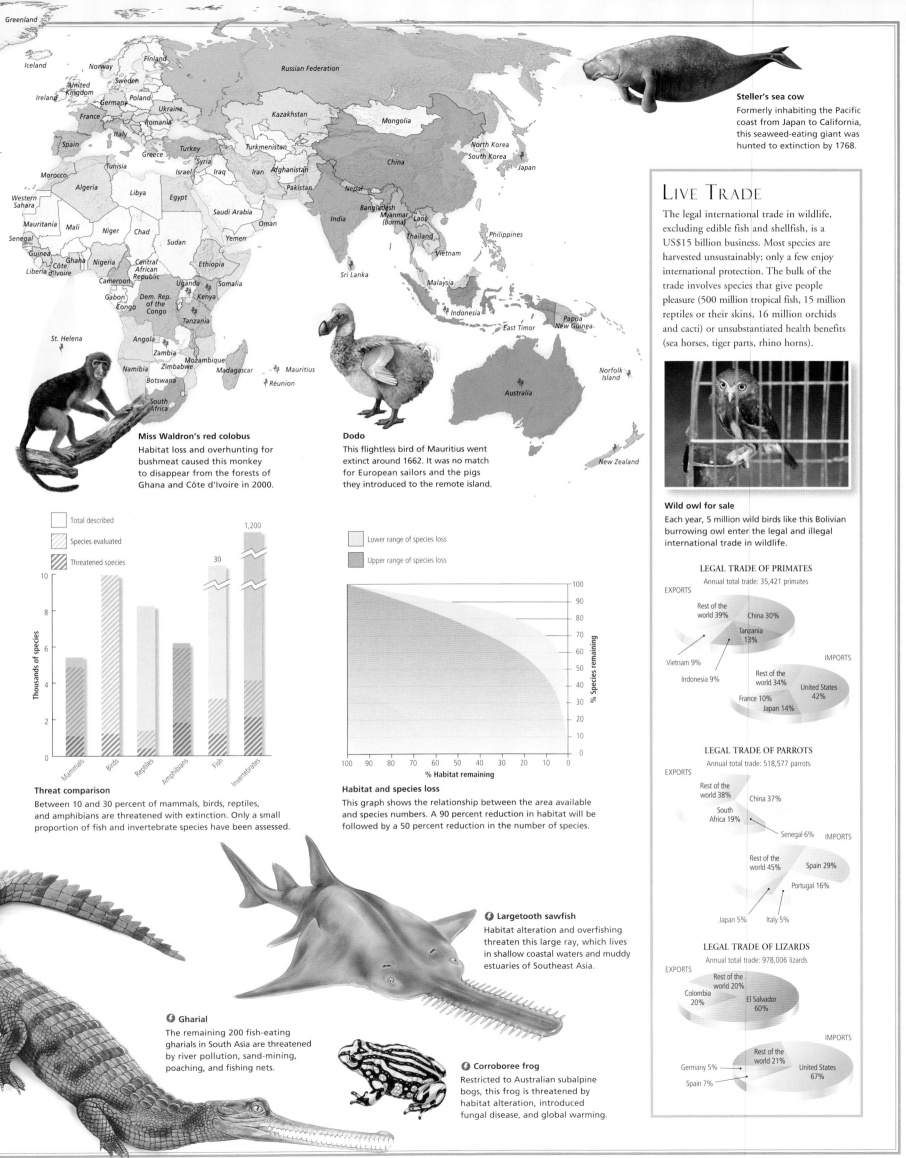

Steller's sea cow
Formerly inhabiting the Pacific coast from Japan to California, this seaweed-eating giant was hunted to extinction by 1768.

LIVE TRADE

The legal international trade in wildlife, excluding edible fish and shellfish, is a US$15 billion business. Most species are harvested unsustainably; only a few enjoy international protection. The bulk of the trade involves species that give people pleasure (500 million tropical fish, 15 million reptiles or their skins, 16 million orchids and cacti) or unsubstantiated health benefits (sea horses, tiger parts, rhino horns).

Wild owl for sale
Each year, 5 million wild birds like this Bolivian burrowing owl enter the legal and illegal international trade in wildlife.

LEGAL TRADE OF PRIMATES
Annual total trade: 35,421 primates

EXPORTS
Rest of the world 39%
China 30%
Tanzania 13%
Vietnam 9%
Indonesia 9%

IMPORTS
Rest of the world 34%
United States 42%
France 10%
Japan 14%

LEGAL TRADE OF PARROTS
Annual total trade: 518,577 parrots

EXPORTS
Rest of the world 38%
China 37%
South Africa 19%
Senegal 6%

IMPORTS
Rest of the world 45%
Spain 29%
Portugal 16%
Japan 5%
Italy 5%

LEGAL TRADE OF LIZARDS
Annual total trade: 978,006 lizards

EXPORTS
Rest of the world 20%
Colombia 20%
El Salvador 60%

IMPORTS
Rest of the world 21%
United States 67%
Germany 5%
Spain 7%

Miss Waldron's red colobus
Habitat loss and overhunting for bushmeat caused this monkey to disappear from the forests of Ghana and Côte d'Ivoire in 2000.

Dodo
This flightless bird of Mauritius went extinct around 1662. It was no match for European sailors and the pigs they introduced to the remote island.

Threat comparison
Between 10 and 30 percent of mammals, birds, reptiles, and amphibians are threatened with extinction. Only a small proportion of fish and invertebrate species have been assessed.

Total described
Species evaluated
Threatened species

Thousands of species
Mammals
Birds
Reptiles
Amphibians
Fish
Invertebrates
30
1,200

Habitat and species loss
This graph shows the relationship between the area available and species numbers. A 90 percent reduction in habitat will be followed by a 50 percent reduction in the number of species.

Lower range of species loss
Upper range of species loss
% Species remaining
% Habitat remaining

Largetooth sawfish
Habitat alteration and overfishing threaten this large ray, which lives in shallow coastal waters and muddy estuaries of Southeast Asia.

Gharial
The remaining 200 fish-eating gharials in South Asia are threatened by river pollution, sand-mining, poaching, and fishing nets.

Corroboree frog
Restricted to Australian subalpine bogs, this frog is threatened by habitat alteration, introduced fungal disease, and global warming.

CONSERVATION

The most effective response to the biodiversity crisis is to create the largest possible protected areas. About 10 percent of ice-free lands are now reserved for wildlife. National parks alone are not enough, however, as animals do not recognize reserve boundaries and they are affected by what humans do around each reserve. The attitudes of local people to wildlife are vitally important, so projects that benefit them are an essential part of conservation. Environmental NGOs (non-government organizations), with their armies of supporters, have successfully integrated human development into conservation efforts, especially when governments lack the will or funds to act. Protected areas provide us with all sorts of ecological services, including oxygen, clean air and water, medicines, and recreation. As the value of nature's services exceeds US$33 trillion per year—twice the value of all other human activities—wildlife conservation directly affects our well-being.

Wildlife tourism
The tourism industry is worth US$600 billion per year, and about 20 percent of this is wildlife-focused or ecotourism. Although tourists can harm wildlife habitat, well-planned activities benefit both local people and wildlife.

Biodiversity hotspots

More than half the planet's species occur in only 2.3 percent of its land area. Conservation International's 34 global hotspots, indicated on the map, contain an extremely large proportion of the world's biodiversity. Protecting these areas would help conserve many species found nowhere else, including 50 percent of endemic vascular plants and 42 percent of endemic vertebrates. When more widely distributed species are also considered, these small areas contain 77 percent of all terrestrial vertebrate species.

▢ Biodiversity hotspots

% Percentage of original vegetation remaining

SCALE 1:90,000,000
Robinson Projection

Resplendent quetzal
Restricted to montane cloud forests and declining in numbers, males still make "joy flights" in Costa Rican national parks.

NORTH AMERICA

California Floristic Province 25%

Madrean Pine-Oak Woodlands 20%

Caribbean Islands 10%

Mesoamerica 20%

Tumbes-Chocó-Magdalena 24%

SOUTH AMERICA

Tropical Andes 25%

Cerrado 22%

Atlantic Forest 8%

Chilean Winter Rainfall-Valdivian Forests 30%

Guinean Forests of West Africa 15%

🐾 **Iberian lynx**
Habitat conversion, declining wild rabbit populations, and fatal traffic accidents threaten the last hundred of these cats in Spain, even in Doñana National Park.

Spectacled bear
The only neotropical bear survives in generally unprotected Andean forests. It is killed for its valuable gall bladder and because it raids crops.

🦛 **Pygmy hippopotamus**
Perhaps 2,000 of these hippos survive in Liberia and nearby countries, but their riverine forest habitat is fast disappearing.

PROTECTED AREAS
- Less than 1%
- 1–5%
- 5–10%
- 10–20%
- More than 20%
- Insufficient data

Parks and reserves

Countries vary in how much land they have reserved for wildlife, and national parks are no guarantee of protection—nearly half are affected by the activities of indigenous people who have long lived inside the park boundaries, poor settlers, poachers, loggers, and developers. Creating buffer zones around parks and habitat corridors between reserves will help to address the needs of wildlife.

Wasteful harvest
The great white shark is legally protected in many areas, but it is still among the 250,000 sharks killed daily for sport, for their fins (for Chinese soup), and as accidental bycatch of other fisheries.

Ivory trade
Poaching reduced African elephant populations from about 20 million to 500,000. The 1989 CITES (Convention on International Trade in Endangered Species) ban on ivory trade reversed the trend, but elephant conservation remains challenging.

HOTSPOT FACTS

First outlined by British ecologist Norman Myers in 1988, the biodiversity hotspot concept has been refined by Conservation International, which identifies the following 34 hotspots (also shown on map). All these hotspots are home to high numbers of endemic species and face serious threats.

Endemic threatened birds
Endemic threatened mammals
Endemic threatened amphibians

Atlantic Forest: Tropical rain forest
55 21 14

California Floristic Province:
Chaparral to sequoia forest
4 5 8

Cape Floristic Region: Evergreen shrublands
0 1 7

Caribbean Islands: Montane forests to cactus shrublands
48 18 143

Caucasus: Arid vegetation
0 2 2

Cerrado: Woodland-savanna
10 4 2

Chilean Winter Rainfall-Valdivian Forests: Coastal to alpine forests
6 5 15

Coastal Forests of Eastern Africa:
Moist and dry forests
2 6 4

East Melanesian Islands: Volcanic islands, diverse vegetation
33 20 5

Eastern Afromontane:
Mountains and lakes
35 48 30

Guinean Forests of West Africa:
Lowland forests
31 35 49

Himalaya: High mountains
8 4 4

Horn of Africa: Arid bushland and grassland
9 8 1

Indo-Burma: Tropical forests and rivers
18 25 35

Irano-Anatolian:
Mountains and basins
0 3 2

Japan: Subtropical to northern temperate island habitats
10 21 19

Madagascar and Indian Ocean Islands: Isolated island habitats
57 51 61

Madrean Pine-Oak Woodlands:
Rugged mountains and canyons
7 2 36

Maputaland-Pondoland-Albany:
Warm temperate forests
0 2 6

Mediterranean Basin:
Maquis shrublands
9 11 14

Mesoamerica: Dry and moist forests
31 29 232

Mountains of Central Asia:
Glaciers to desert
0 3 1

Mountains of Southwest China:
Temperate to alpine mountains
2 3 3

New Caledonia: Pacific islands
7 3 0

New Zealand: Mountainous islands
63 3 4

Philippines: Rain-forest fragments
56 47 48

Polynesia-Micronesia:
Diverse island habitats
90 8 1

Southwest Australia: Forest to heath
3 6 3

Succulent Karoo: Arid succulent flora
0 1 1

Sundaland: Tropical rain forests
43 60 59

Tropical Andes: Montane cloud forests
110 14 363

Tumbes-Chocó-Magdalena:
Coastal habitats
21 7 8

Wallacea: Tropical rain forests
49 44 7

Western Ghats and Sri Lanka:
Tropical forests to grasslands
10 14 87

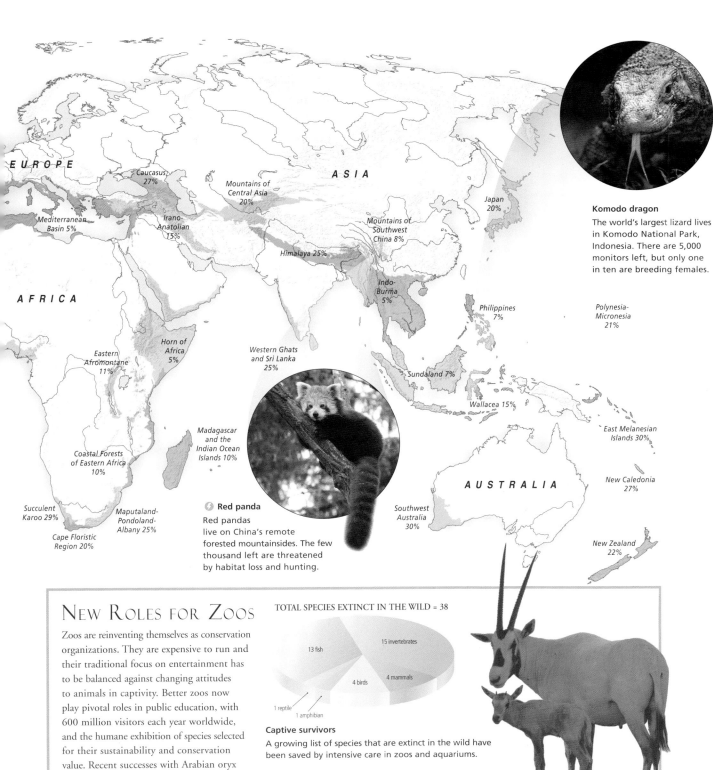

EUROPE

Caucasus 27%

Mountains of Central Asia 20%

ASIA

Mountains of Southwest China 8%

Japan 20%

Mediterranean Basin 5%

Irano-Anatolian 15%

Himalaya 25%

Indo-Burma 5%

Philippines 7%

Polynesia-Micronesia 21%

AFRICA

Horn of Africa 5%

Western Ghats and Sri Lanka 25%

Sundaland 7%

Wallacea 15%

Eastern Afromontane 11%

Madagascar and the Indian Ocean Islands 10%

East Melanesian Islands 30%

Coastal Forests of Eastern Africa 10%

New Caledonia 27%

AUSTRALIA

Succulent Karoo 29%

Maputaland-Pondoland-Albany 25%

Southwest Australia 30%

Cape Floristic Region 20%

New Zealand 22%

Komodo dragon
The world's largest lizard lives in Komodo National Park, Indonesia. There are 5,000 monitors left, but only one in ten are breeding females.

Red panda
Red pandas live on China's remote forested mountainsides. The few thousand left are threatened by habitat loss and hunting.

NEW ROLES FOR ZOOS

Zoos are reinventing themselves as conservation organizations. They are expensive to run and their traditional focus on entertainment has to be balanced against changing attitudes to animals in captivity. Better zoos now play pivotal roles in public education, with 600 million visitors each year worldwide, and the humane exhibition of species selected for their sustainability and conservation value. Recent successes with Arabian oryx and Californian condors show that zoos can serve as "arks" by providing animals for reintroduction into the wild.

TOTAL SPECIES EXTINCT IN THE WILD = 38

13 fish
15 invertebrates
4 birds
4 mammals
1 reptile
1 amphibian

Captive survivors
A growing list of species that are extinct in the wild have been saved by intensive care in zoos and aquariums.

Return to the wild
The Arabian oryx was hunted to extinction in the wild, but captive breeding in North American zoos allowed its reintroduction to the Arabian Peninsula.

Deep in the deciduous forests of Germany, a red deer stag stands
guard among females. Stags such as this one collect a harem,
which they rigorously defend against other males throughout
the mating season. Red deer are browsers, feeding on grasses,
leaves, shoots, and buds. They range across Western Europe.

EUROPE

EUROPE

With an area of 3.9 million square miles (10.2 million km²), Europe makes up less than 7 percent of Earth's land. Topography can vary greatly in relatively small areas. Mountains dominate the south, descending into hills before flattening into broad plains in the north. Uplands and mountains curve along the western edge of Britain and Ireland and eastward into Norway. Mixed forest once covered much of Europe, but more than half has been lost because of the long-time presence of humans. This has led to widespread disruption of native wildlife—some species have become extinct, others are confined to habitat pockets. The large predatory mammals such as bear, wolf, and lynx have experienced the greatest impact from the spread of urban areas but herbivores, including red deer, moose, chamois, and ibex are well-represented. Europe has a diversity of bird species, from large raptors, to migratory waterfowl, to tiny passerines. Many different species of marine mammals and fish inhabit the Mediterranean Sea and coastal waters.

CLIMATE ZONES
- Semiarid
- Mediterranean
- Subtropical
- Temperate
- Continental
- Cold temperate
- Subpolar
- Highland

Climate

Polar winds are largely responsible for the cold winters experienced by northern Europe, which also records shorter, cooler summers than southern climates. More temperate conditions in western Europe are largely because of the Gulf Stream, which carries warm water to Europe's coastline and heats the prevailing westerly winds. More dramatic weather extremes—from bitingly cold winters to scorching summers—are common across the eastern interior. Southern Europe generally enjoys warm, dry summers and mild, wet winters.

VEGETATION ZONES
- Midlatitude forest
- Boreal forest
- Mountain vegetation
- Midlatitude grassland
- Tundra
- Mediterranean forest and scrub
- Ice sheet

Vegetation

Broadleaf deciduous forests of oak, ash, elm, beech, and birch once covered most of western and central Europe. Large areas of Scandinavia, northwestern Russia, and alpine mountain regions continue to support boreal forests of fir, spruce, and pine. On the tundra of the far north, mosses, small shrubs, and summer wildflowers grow on the permanently frozen soils. Dry areas of eastern Europe are swathed in grasslands.

Deciduous Woodlands
Five vegetation zones layer the broad swath of deciduous woodlands that sweep across Europe, providing many types of habitat for wildlife, such as badgers, to choose from.

The Mediterranean
A monkey, devil ray, viper, and bone-eating vulture are some of the more unusual animal species found in and around the Mediterranean Sea.

River Valleys
Dozens of major rivers drain the continent and support the entire spectrum of animal life, from tiny invertebrates to fish, birds, and mammals, such as this river otter.

Coniferous Forests of Northern Europe
Only wildlife species that are well adapted to the conditions can survive on the limited vegetation, and withstand the severe climate, of the far north coniferous forests.

Mountain Ranges
Born from continental collision, Europe boasts some of the steepest and most rugged mountain ranges on the planet where living relics from the Ice Age still dwell.

Life Along the Shore
The seashore varies dramatically along Europe's relatively long coastline, ranging from rocky tidepools to sandy dunes, and animals take advantage of the selection.

Marshes and Wetlands
Every country in Europe boasts a wetland or marsh, and no habitat is more productive in terms of supporting every link in the wildlife food chain.

SCALE 1:17,000,000

0   400 miles

0   400 kilometers

PROPORTIONS OF TOTAL LAND AREA

Forest and woodland

Arable land

Grazing

Other land

21.8%

33.6%

16.4%

28.2%

Land cover

Urban and industrial areas, roads, and railways cover much of Europe. The surviving forests and woodlands are found mostly in European Russia and Scandinavia and the highest proportions of arable land and pasture are in Western Europe.

DECIDUOUS WOODLANDS

Europe's deciduous woodlands extend from as far north as Scotland, south to France, and east to the Urals. The term deciduous describes trees such as the oak, elm, birch, lime, and alder, which lose their leaves in autumn. Much of the broad swath of deciduous woodlands that once covered the continent was cleared long ago for agriculture and pastures, towns, and cities. What remains are pockets of woodland protected within preserves and parks. Woodlands have an average temperature of 50°F (10°C) and annual rainfall of 30–60 inches (762–1,524 mm). The relatively mild weather, with warm to cool summers and moderately cold winters, is because of the moderating effects of the Atlantic Ocean. The five vegetation strata of the woodlands—trees, small trees and saplings, shrubs, herbs, and the ground zone—provide habitats for a variety of wildlife. Woodland animals range from deer to small mammals and birds. When flowers are in bloom numerous delicate butterflies appear.

SCALE 1:32,000,000

Butterflies

Deciduous trees and flowering plants in open glades and meadows provide a plentiful food source for caterpillars and butterflies. Many of Europe's 576 butterfly species are found here.

White letter hairstreak
Satyrium album

Map butterfly
Araschnia levana

Lesser purple emperor
Apatura ilia

Silver-washed fritillary
Argynnis paphia

Camberwell beauty
Nymphalis antiopa

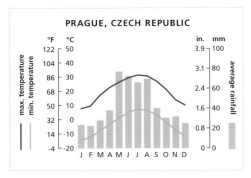

PRAGUE, CZECH REPUBLIC

Raccoon dog
Though the raccoon dog resembles a raccoon, it is a member of the dog family, Canidae. Small rodents are its preferred food but it is an omnivore, so can seek food widely. It hibernates in winter.

Fallow deer
Fallow deer are notable for their flattened antlers and long tails. They live in two separate herds, one comprising females and fawns, the other bucks living alone or in bachelor groups.

Red fox
The red fox has keen senses of sight, smell and hearing, earning it a reputation for intelligence. A skilled hunter, it is capable of feeding on a wide variety of prey.

Red squirrel
Sciurus vulgaris

Black woodpecker
Dryocopus martius

Little owl
Athene noctua

Badger
Meles meles

European mole
Talpa europaea

Clouded yellow butterfly
Colias croceus

The deciduous forest

A single tree can support myriad species of wildlife. Red squirrel and black woodpecker nest in cavities in mature trees that also provide an abundant source of seeds and insects. The little owl perches on the high limbs while looking for prey. The soft soil beneath a tree makes digging easier for the badger and European mole.

CONSERVATION WATCH

The long tail of the red squirrel helps it balance when jumping from tree to tree and provides winter warmth. Although the red squirrel is common in many parts of Europe, the introduction of the North American gray squirrel has driven the red species from much of its range in Britain. Conservation efforts are underway.

SPRING

Life in the woodlands is dominated by the changing of the seasons. Plants and animals must be able to survive the winter, then take full advantage of the spring, when the days lengthen and the temperature rises, to propagate and perpetuate their species. First come the wildflowers that bloom before the canopy of leaves shades them from sunlight. The flowers provide food for insects, which, in turn, attract migrating birds that arrive from their wintering grounds to breed and raise their young.

Bluebells
Bell-shaped and slightly fragrant, the bluebell blooms in woodlands all along the Atlantic seaboard, from Scotland to Spain. Some of its ingredients are being tested for their medicinal properties.

THE EUROPEAN BADGER

The badger is an Old World member of the weasel family that also includes the otter and pine marten, and dates back 2.4 million years. There are nine species of badger globally, but only *Meles meles* occurs in the wild in Europe. It is found throughout the British Isles and on the continent, though not in northern Scandinavia or the Mediterranean islands. The badger prefers to live in woodlands and grassy fields. While it resides in complex burrow systems, often in locations that experience cold winters and deep snowfalls, it does not hibernate. Animals enter into a state of torpor that can last for several weeks, living off fat reserves accumulated during the rest of the year. Much of the badger's survival success is because of its highly opportunistic and omnivorous feeding habits, which often bring it into conflict with farmers. The badger requires large territories of up to 405 acres (164 ha) in which to forage.

BADGER'S DIET

A forager rather than hunter, the nocturnal badger spends half its time looking for food, relying on its keen sense of smell and hearing. Though it has carnivorous incisors, its molars are flattened for grinding, making it a true omnivore. Its diet ranges from acorns, fruits, seeds, and mushrooms to earthworms, insects, reptiles, birds, and small mammals. It even eats carrion.

COMPOSITION OF DIET

Insects 24%
Earthworms 35%
Cereals 18%
Birds 6%
Mammals 8%
Fruits 9%

Worms
Earthworms make up much of the badger's diet, especially in grassy fields on damp nights when a badger can suck up to 200 wigglers in one sitting.

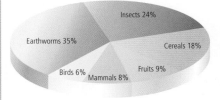

Fruit
Badgers feast seasonally, eating tree fruit that falls to the ground, including apples and pears, as well as stripping berries from bushes.

Baby hedgehogs
A hedgehog's spiny fur and its ability to roll into a tight ball are no defense against a hungry badger, which relies on its powerful front claws to pry open its prickly prey.

Sett
The communal burrow, or sett, has numerous entrances, passages, and chambers. It is typically constructed on sloping ground in woodland or on the periphery of a field. Spoil piles of dirt mark its entrances. Setts are often used for decades and continually grow in size and complexity.

Fresh bedding
Badgers line their beds with insulating grass or leaves, which they drag backward into the den. The vegetation is changed regularly and occasionally spread out at the sett's entrance in the morning to air in the sunlight for an hour or two.

Taking to water
While the badger can swim, it prefers walking around ponds and lakes or crossing over streams and canals using fallen trees as bridges. When forced to swim it paddles with its front paws much like a dog.

A proficient digger

The badger's digging ability is legendary. Stories of the animal outpacing humans with shovels abound. Scientists estimate badgers had moved almost 27.5 tons (25 t) of soil at one 1,000-foot-long (305-m) tunnel network. Long claws break up earth; webbed front feet scoop it out. Badgers remove the soil by pushing it out with their back legs, and are capable of carrying large rocks.

Family group
Highly communal badgers live in clans, generally containing up to 12 individuals. Cubs are weaned by six months and will forage with sows, often initiating play with other cubs and adults. Non-breeding sows sometimes serve as babysitters. Badgers use scent and vocalization to recognize clan members.

Predator
Full-grown badgers don't have any natural predators, though bears and wolves sometimes kill them to reduce competition for food. Cubs, however, are prey to the bears and wolves, as well as lynx and wolverines. The eagle owl (right) and golden eagle also eat young badgers.

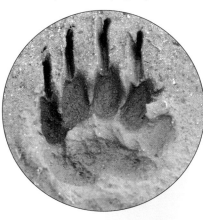

Claws
The badger has five toes on each foot, with broad plantar pads and bare soles. The front claws can be as long as 2 inches (5 cm). A badger often places its back foot exactly where its front foot has stepped.

RIVER VALLEYS

The islands of Ireland and Britain and the European continent are etched with major rivers that form fertile valleys, including the Guadalquivir, Ebro, Loire, Danube, Vistula, Biebrza, Volga, and Lemmenjoki. River valleys are biologically important, creating a wide spectrum of ecosystems, from brackish lagoons at the mouth to freshwater springs at the source. The sheer variety of habitats supports a vast array of wildlife. The mix of water and lush vegetation are both a home and a source of food for insects, amphibians, reptiles, birds, and mammals. River valleys also serve as wildlife corridors, providing anadromous fish such as Atlantic salmon access to freshwater spawning grounds, and migrating waterfowl a road map as well as a resting spot in fall and spring. Both predator and prey are drawn by water. While rich in species, river valleys are also among the landscapes most impacted by human activity. Farming, industrialization, and the construction of dams have all taken their toll.

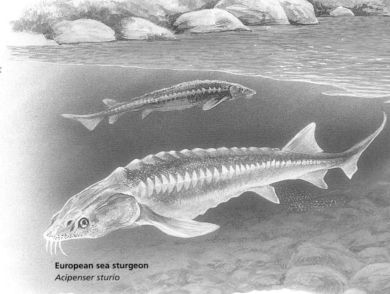

SCALE 1:30,000,000

0   400 miles

0   400 kilometers

Ebro River

Spain's longest river, the Ebro, springs from the Cantabrian Mountains in the north and flows 565 miles (910 km) southeast to the Mediterranean coast. Fed by more than 200 tributaries, the Ebro discharges more water than any other Spanish river.

Layers of life

A cross-section of a river valley reveals layers of life, each reliant on the other. Water supports nutrients and vegetation in the river and along its banks. This first link in the food chain leads to insects, invertebrates, fish, birds, and mammals. No two river valleys are the same, so speciation occurs. Climate, topography, and humans help determine which species are found where.

Wild boar
The wild boar is a highly aggressive omnivore. Adult males sport large tusks that are sharpened by grinding and used as weapons. Females guard their numerous young. The stiff bristles of the boar's fur are used to make hairbrushes.

European sea sturgeon
Acipenser sturio

FLAMINGOS

The greater flamingo lives in colonies numbering in the hundreds. The birds flock to shallow river mouths along the Mediterranean Sea because the mix of fresh and salt water makes for a rich stew of nutrients. These nutrients, in turn, generate large amounts of algae, insect life, and crustaceans, which are the bird's favorite foods.

Flamingo
The greater flamingo is the tallest of six flamingo species and dates back 30 million years.

Vistula River

Poland's longest river drains an enormous area measuring 75,000 square miles (194,250 km²), or nearly half the country's landmass. Industrialization and farming have brought changes but the Vistula still retains a semi-natural character for much of its length. The river valley supports more than 1,000 plant species. Bordering forests and meadows provide homes for the Eurasian lynx and other mammals.

European beaver
Once hunted to near extinction for its fur and scent glands, which are thought to have medicinal properties, this largest of European rodents is semi-aquatic. It dams streams with sticks and mud and creates lodges where it can find protection from predators. The dams also help to create ponds for easier access to food.

European kingfisher
The common, or European, kingfisher hunts for fish from an overhanging perch or while hovering above water. Small fish are swallowed immediately, head-first, while bigger fish are carried to a tree limb and beaten against it. A pair may have to catch 100 fish a day to feed their hungry nestlings.

Muskrat
Ondatra zibethica

Common rabbit
Oryctolagus cuniculus

Black stork
Ciconia nigra

Souslik
Citillus citillus

WARSAW, POLAND

RIVER VALLEY	COUNTRY	WILDLIFE SPECIES
Ebro	Spain	Auduoin's gull, catfish
Loire	France	Little bittern, wild cat
Danube	Germany-Ukraine	White pelican, sturgeon
Vistula	Poland	Beaver, pine marten
Volga	Russia	Great white egret, Volga lamprey
Lemmenjoki	Finland	Reindeer, Siberian jay

European hedgehog
Erinaceus europaeus

Danube River

The Danube drains the Black Forest in Germany and flows 1,770 miles (2,850 km) across 10 countries to the Black Sea. The river basin supports a diverse range of habitats and is home to many species of flora and fauna, including 100 types of fish. Five species of sturgeon swim its waters.

Black stork
A wading bird, the black stork feeds in the shallow waters of rivers, marshes, and ponds. This broad-winged bird flies with its long neck outstretched and migrates to Africa for the winter.

Eurasian otter
The Eurasian otter is well-adapted to aquatic life, with its slim body, webbed toes, and rudder-like tail. The otter can close its ears and nostrils while underwater and uses its sensitive whiskers to detect the movement of its prey.

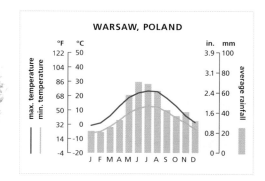

RIVER VALLEYS

THE DELTA OF COTA DONANA

The Guadalquivir is the second longest river in Spain and drains an area of 22,400 square miles (58,000 km²). It begins in the Cazorla Mountains and empties into the Gulf of Cádiz. Its delta is a complex system of marshes, dunes, and coastal lagoons. Much of the delta is protected as Doñana National Park, a UNESCO World Heritage site. One of the largest and best-known wetlands in Europe, Doñana is a land of contrasts, lying at the crossroads of two continents and influenced by both the Atlantic Ocean and the Mediterranean Sea. The array of habitats translates into a rich concentration of wildlife. Some 750 plant species live here, along with 20 species of fish, 10 amphibians, 19 reptiles, and 30 mammals, including the rare Iberian lynx, small-spotted genet, and wildcat. More than half of Europe's birds occur here, many of them in huge numbers, including flocks of up to 70,000 greylag geese and 200,000 teal.

Waters teem with life
Birds flock to the delta's shallow, brackish waters because they are nutrient-rich and full of food, including shrimp, crabs, insects, and larvae. Wading birds, such as egrets and herons, have an advantage over smaller, short-legged shorebirds, such as plovers and sandpipers.

Greater flamingo
Greater flamingos are social birds, forming colonies numbering up to 300 individuals. They can travel 373 miles (600 km) in a single night when migrating, preferably in cloudless skies and with favorable tailwinds.

Polecat
The polecat is related to the weasel, mink, otter, and stout. Mostly nocturnal, it feeds on rodents, amphibians, and birds, and makes its den in stream banks or under tree roots.

Horseshoe bat
Mediterranean horseshoe bats live in colonies called clouds, roosting in caves and tunnels where the average temperature is 50°F (10°C). They use echolocation to find their prey.

Spiny-footed lizard
The spiny-footed lizard owes its name to the comblike spines along its back legs, which allow it to run on sand. This species is found widely in the Mediterranean.

BIRD BEAKS

Birds have evolved to occupy certain niches, even in the same ecosystem, such as a delta. The most important function of a bird's bill is feeding, and it is shaped according to what the bird eats. For waterbirds, long, pointed bills suit probing and spearing; flat bills are adapted for straining and scooping.

Common spoonbill
The convex upper bill acts like an airfoil, creating swirling currents that suspend crustaceans and fish when swept from side to side in the water.

Common spoonbill
The common, or black-billed, spoonbill occurs in the intertidal flats and shallows of fresh and saltwater wetlands. It sweeps its bill from side to side in its quest to trap tiny fish.

Glossy ibis
The ibis uses its long, down-curved beak to probe in the mud for frogs, fish, insects, and snails. Nostrils at the base of the beak allow the bird to breathe.

Glossy ibis
The glossy ibis breeds in the warmer regions of Europe, where it nests colonially in trees. A strong flier and gregarious feeder, this widespread species migrates to Africa for the winter.

Purple heron
The 5-inch-long (13-cm) spiky beak of the purple heron is used to seize or harpoon prey. Food is swallowed whole.

Lataste's viper
Lataste's viper is one of five venomous snakes found in Spain. Stout with a triangular head, it is recognizable by the wavy or zigzag stripe that runs along its back.

Eurasian curlew
Females have longer decurved beaks than males, measuring up to 6 inches (15 cm). They feed by probing sand and mud for insects.

European weasel
It may be small, but the European weasel is known as a ferocious species. Medieval legend recognizes the weasel for killing the mythical basilisk.

Greater flamingo
The flamingo's keel-shaped bill is lined with rows of keratinous plates covered with tiny hairs. This enables the bird to filter invertebrates in a similar fashion to baleen whales.

Mountain Ranges

Like folds in skin, the European continent is creased with mountain ranges. They were created by the collision of jigsaw puzzle-shaped tectonic plates that form Earth's crust. Between five and 30 million years ago the northward-moving African plate slammed into the more stable European plate, pushing up sediments that once lay beneath a separating ocean made extinct by the collision. Collectively, the Alps, Scandes, Pyrenees, Carpathians, Rhodopes, Urals, Caucasia, and Dinaric landforms constitute what is known as the alpine biogeographic region. While the mountainous areas share common features, their varying gradients, climate, and soil types have influenced the distribution and diversity of species. The result is an amazing array of wildlife that includes 129 mammal species, 359 birds, 40 amphibians, and 65 reptiles. Plant life is also rich on the continent. The 5,000 species of vascular plants comprise half of all plant types native to Europe.

SCALE 1:25,000,000

Apollo butterfly
The beautiful Apollo butterfly, with distinctive "eye" marks on its wings, can be found in flowery alpine meadows as high as 6,400 feet (1,950 m). Life in a rugged mountain habitat has led to the development of many subspecies, some restricted to a single alpine valley. Medium-sized and tail-less, the Apollo has three pairs of walking legs.

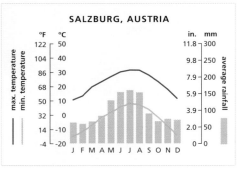

SALZBURG, AUSTRIA

Eagle wing
Eagle wings are a miracle in lightweight design. Bones are hollow and primary feathers spread like fingers to reduce drag. Most of the power for flying comes from the downward stroke.

Wildcat
Once found throughout Europe, the wildcat dates back to the Early Pleistocene. Hunting and habitat loss have reduced its range and numbers. It is generally solitary and is one-third larger, and has a thicker coat, than its direct descendant, the domestic cat.

European brown bear
Brown bears once occurred throughout Europe, but were driven almost to extinction. Protecting habitat and raising cubs in captivity has helped. Today, about 55,000 bears survive, most in Eastern Europe and Russia.

Golden eagle

Everything about an eagle is perfectly designed for hunting, from its keen eyesight, powerful wings, and aerodynamic feathers, to its sharp beak and talons. Eagles use several methods for capturing prey, but soaring and swooping are the most common. Snatching the animal by the head with one foot, the eagle drives the talons of its other foot into the prey's lungs as it carries it away.

RELICS OF THE GLACIERS

Plant and animal species that survived the Ice Age are known as glacial relics. A mountainous region of Poland, now protected as Karkonoski National Park, has a high proportion of glacial relics, including the arctic whorl snail, Sudetic wolf spider, and the bird known as the ring ouzel.

Rivers of ice
Glaciers are rivers of ice, always moving and churning up rocky debris. When they melt or retreat, they leave this debris behind in moraines.

Dotterel
A small wader, a member of the plover family, the migrating dotterel winters in the semiarid deserts of North Africa and the Middle East and breeds in the Alps and northern Europe, nesting in a bare ground scrape. The males are responsible for incubation.

Red kite

An extremely agile flier, the red kite has a small body relative to its wing size. If a predator approaches its nest the mother will signal her young to "play dead."

Tengmalm's owl
A small, ancient bird, Tengmalm's owl is found in boreal forests. It builds its nest in a tree cavity drilled by woodpeckers and successive generations occupy the same site. The male sings to attract a mate.

Dormouse
The dormouse's feet are adapted for grasping trees; the soles have cushioned pads and the toes have curved claws. Its hind feet can be turned backward, which allows it to dangle from a branch.

The Mountaineers

Animals that live in the mountains have developed special physical characteristics that help them cope in a challenging environment marked by severe cold, rugged topography and reduced oxygen. With the exception of some insects, most of the animals living at altitude are warm-blooded. These animals adapt to the cold by hibernating in winter, such as the marmot; migrating to lower, warmer areas; or huddling together in burrows, such as the snow vole. Mountain animals tend to have shorter appendages in order to reduce heat loss, such as the alpine hare, which has smaller ears than its lowland counterpart. Animals such as the ibex have larger lungs and more blood cells because of the increased pressure and lack of oxygen at higher altitudes. Other physical adaptations include special hooves such as those of the chamois, to aid in climbing, or the footpads of the lynx, which are broad and well-furred compared to other felines as an adaptation for walking on snow.

Alpine hare
The hare's brown coat turns white before winter, providing camouflage from predators and greater warmth. Shorter daylight hours trigger hormones that inhibit the production of brown pigment in the new coat. The hollow white hairs improve insulation and allow more sunlight to be absorbed.

Marmot den
As sociable animals, marmots live in large burrows with several generations of their family. They excavate the burrow using their forepaws and hind feet and remove stones with their teeth. Entrances are sited between large rocks to avoid detection and flooding, and living areas are lined with dried grass. Burrows are enlarged to accommodate new generations; the newborn remain in the burrow for their first 40 days.

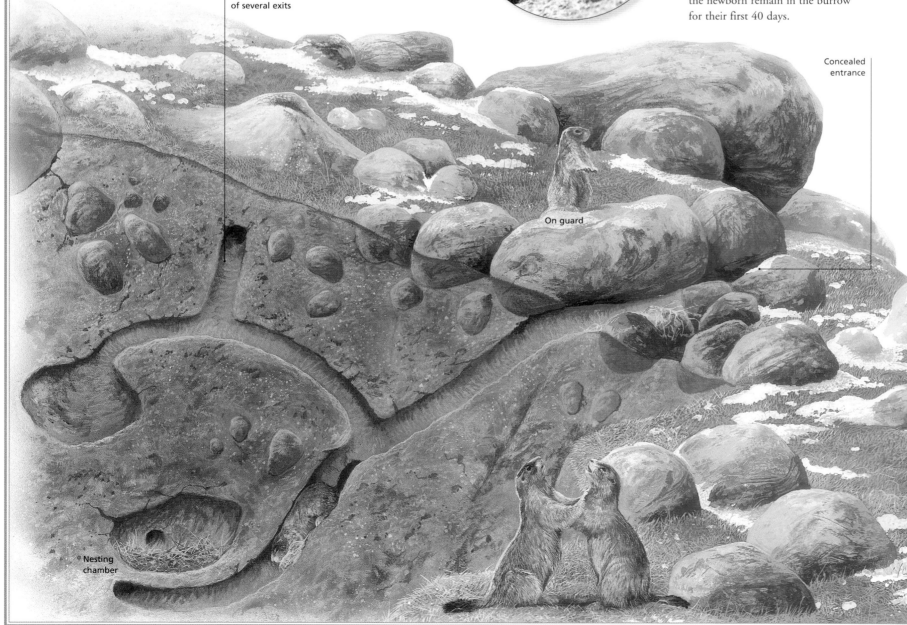

Tunnel to one of several exits

Concealed entrance

On guard

Nesting chamber

CHAMOIS AND IBEX

Split hooves that can spread enable chamois and ibex to climb near-vertical cliffs and smooth, slick rock faces. The hooves have a hard, thin rim surrounding a soft and sponge-like interior, and these cushioned pads can grip slippery surfaces. Well-developed leg muscles and a low center of gravity aid in climbing and jumping. A chamois can leap as high as 6.5 feet (2 m) and as long as 20 feet (6 m).

Chamois
In summer, herds of chamois graze in alpine meadows above 6,000 feet (1,800 m). As winter approaches, they descend to shelter in forests near steep cliffs. Chamois were once hunted for their hides.

Ibex
Horn size distinguishes male and female ibex. The defensive horns start growing at sexual maturity and never stop, reaching lengths up to 3 feet (1 m) in the male.

Snow vole
Relatively large compared to other species, the snow vole is generally found above the timberline in high rocky mountainsides above 5,000 feet (1,500 m). Though voles burrow under rocks, they do not hibernate in winter.

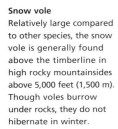

Eurasian lynx
Mainly nocturnal and solitary, the Eurasian lynx is seldom seen or heard. A highly efficient hunter, it preys on rabbits, rodents, and deer in a hunting territory of some 20 square miles (50 km²). It can live up to 17 years in the wild.

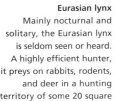

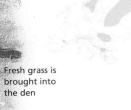

Fresh grass is brought into the den

THE MEDITERRANEAN

An enclosed sea, the Mediterranean covers nearly 1 million square miles (2.6 million km²), with a coastline that extends 28,500 miles (46,000 km) and runs through 22 countries. The Mediterranean Sea represents only one percent of the planet's ocean surface, yet it contains approximately six percent of its marine species. Its rocky reefs, seagrass meadows, and upwelling areas support enormous biological diversity. Marine mammals include the fin whale, harbor porpoise, and striped dolphin, and shark species occurring in the Mediterranean include the great white and blue sharks. Coastal and inland areas are also important habitats for wildlife, with wading and shorebirds dependent upon shallow estuaries, and mammals ranging in size from tiny mice to 200-pound (90-kg) deer found in the oak, pine, and wild olive forests. Wildlife, however, is under extreme pressure from human activities, including coastal development, overfishing, agricultural and industrial runoff, and wildfire.

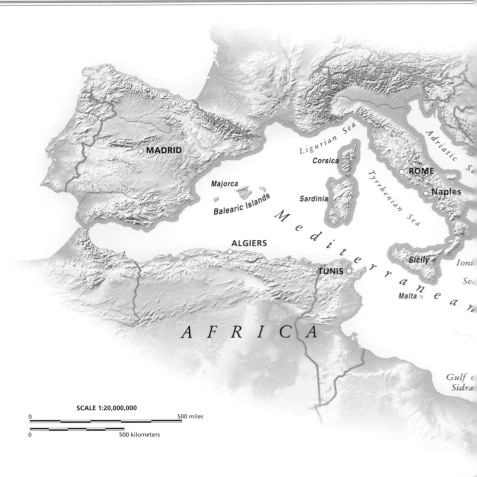

SCALE 1:20,000,000

WILDFIRES

Wildfires are commonplace throughout the Mediterranean. On average, 50,000 fires sweep through as many as 2.47 million acres (1 million ha) of forest and woodland every year. Up to 95 percent are caused by people. Hot, dry summers and a buildup of fuel compound the problem. Natural wildfires keep forests healthy and ensure plant diversity, but too much burning can impoverish habitat and contribute to climate change.

Forest fire
Wildfires have devastating effects on animals, from those with limited mobility, such as snails, snakes, and tortoises, to small and large mammals. Though birds can escape the flames, they lose their food supply of seeds, insects, and rodents.

Italian wall lizard
The Italian wall lizard, typical of the small reptiles at risk from wildfires, is found throughout the Mediterranean and as far away as Japan and the United States. It has been successful at adapting to new environments.

⚡ CONSERVATION WATCH

The Mediterranean monk seal is one of the most endangered marine mammals in the world, with fewer than 600 individuals in existence. They were once hunted for their pelts and blubber, which was turned into oil, and commercial fishermen considered them pests. The establishment of protected marine zones now holds the key to their continued survival.

Sharks

The Mediterranean Sea has one of the greatest diversities of sharks on the planet, but a high proportion are endangered. Of the 71 species of sharks and rays found here, 30 are deemed threatened with extinction, including the great white, shortfin mako, and porbeagle sharks.

Mako shark
Isurus oxyrinchus

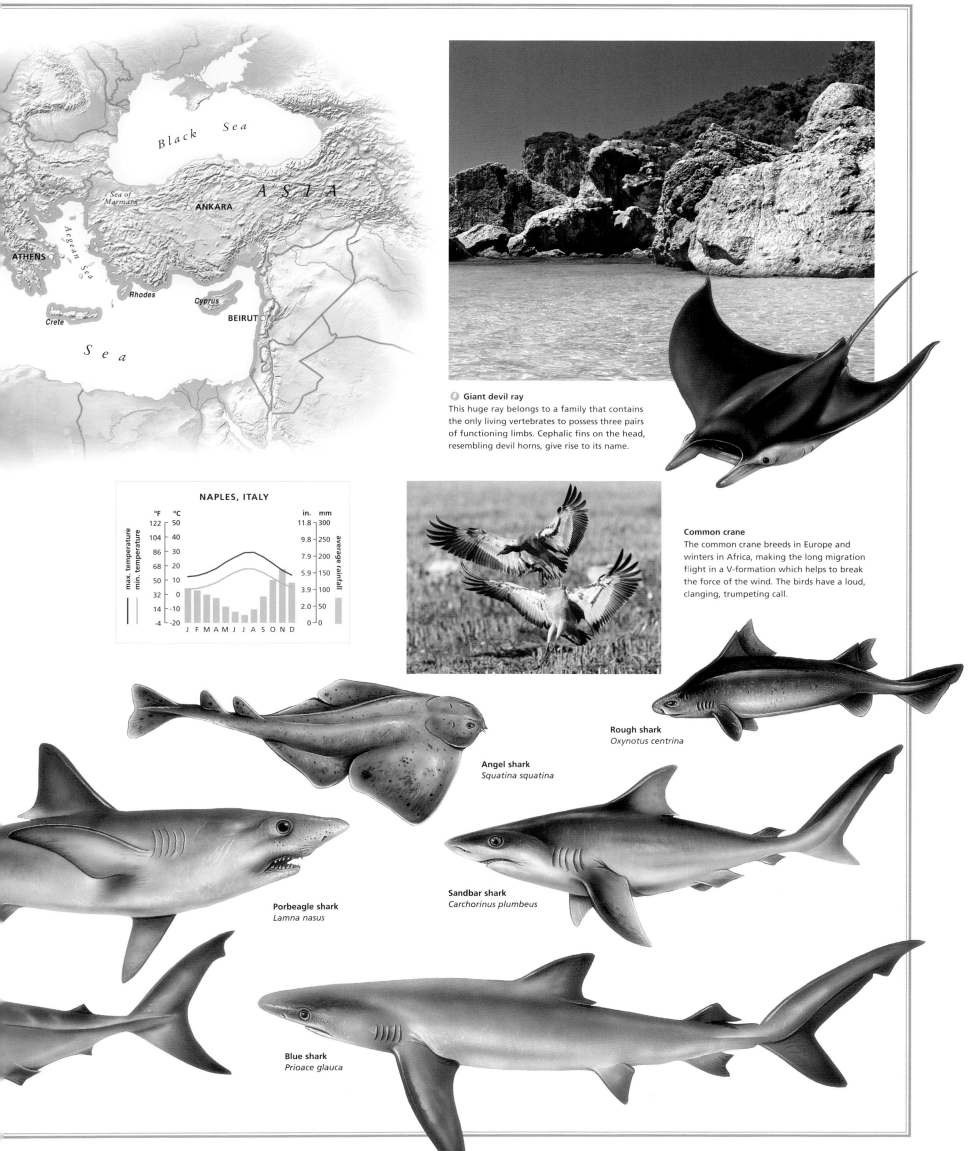

Giant devil ray
This huge ray belongs to a family that contains the only living vertebrates to possess three pairs of functioning limbs. Cephalic fins on the head, resembling devil horns, give rise to its name.

NAPLES, ITALY

Common crane
The common crane breeds in Europe and winters in Africa, making the long migration flight in a V-formation which helps to break the force of the wind. The birds have a loud, clanging, trumpeting call.

Rough shark
Oxynotus centrina

Angel shark
Squatina squatina

Porbeagle shark
Lamna nasus

Sandbar shark
Carchorinus plumbeus

Blue shark
Prioace glauca

55

MEDITERRANEAN ISLANDS

Five thousand islands, ranging from tiny islets to enormous Sicily, pepper the Mediterranean, making it one of the largest island groups in the world. Variations in size as well as altitude, geology, and isolation produce a wide range of habitats that support a diverse array of species. The limited or non-existent exchange of genetic material between island and mainland species has resulted in an exceptionally high rate of endemism. Isolation has also helped some ancient island plant species survive the last glacial period, when their mainland relatives perished. More than 125 plant species, 10 bird species, and the Cyprus mouflon, a wild sheep, are found on Cyprus and nowhere else. The islands also serve as resting and refueling stops for birds migrating between Europe and Africa. More than 100 different species, including the red-footed falcon and golden oriole, visit Corsica.

Eleonora's falcon
The medium-sized Eleonora's falcon lives in colonies of 100 pairs or more on rocky cliffs in Greece. It winters in Madagascar and is named for the 14th-century Sardinian princess who introduced laws to protect it. In the Middle Ages, falcons were trained and used for hunting.

Bearded vulture
Also known as the Lammergeier, this vulture inhabits high mountains. It feeds almost exclusively on bones, swallowing small ones whole and allowing gastric fluids to digest them. It smashes larger bones on rocks.

Sardinian wild deer
About 1,500 endemic Sardinian red deer live in mountainous areas of Sardinia. Once close to extinction, the deer is now protected and numbers are growing. Males compete for harems, first by bellowing and trying to chase competitors away, then by battling with their antlers.

BARBARY MACAQUE

The vulnerable Barbary macaque, commonly, but mistakenly called an ape, is the only wild primate found in Europe. It is restricted to Gibraltar, and though there is fossil evidence of the species in other parts of Europe, the 100 surviving macaques actually descended from North African populations that were introduced by the British from the 18th century. The British Army has assumed responsibility for the macaque's care.

ISLAND	AREA IN SQ MILES (KM²)	POPULATION
Sicily	9,926 (25,708)	5,017,509
Sardinia	9,301 (24,090)	1,655,677
Cyprus	3,572 (9,252)	788,457
Corsica	3,351 (8,680)	281,000
Crete	3,219 (8,336)	623,666

Common dolphin
Common dolphins are distinguished from other dolphins by their unique crisscross color pattern: dark on the back, light grey on the flank, with a pale yellow thoracic patch and white abdomen. They live in large schools and jump and splash together.

Blue tit
On Corsica, blue tits line their nests with aromatic plants, such as mint, lavender, and citronella, to help protect their chicks from blowflies, mosquitoes, and other blood-sucking parasites. The herbal potpourri, which parents constantly replenish, is also thought to repel fungi and bacteria.

CONSERVATION WATCH

Hunting and competition from livestock left the population of Cyprus's largest wild land mammal, the mouflon, down to just a few dozen by the beginning of the 20th century. The population has increased, in part, because of the establishment of special watering holes that protect the mouflon from diseases carried by domestic cattle, sheep, and goats.

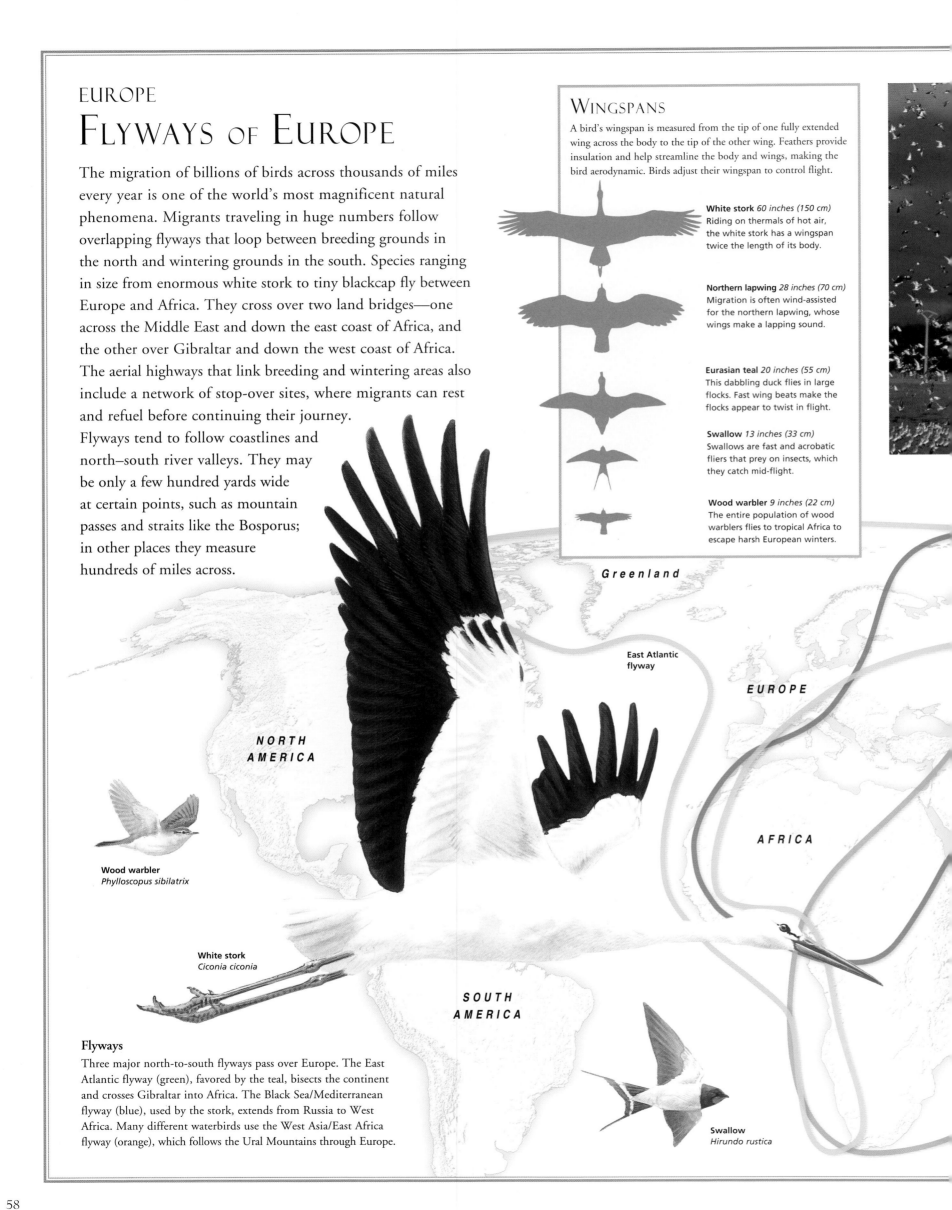

EUROPE
FLYWAYS OF EUROPE

The migration of billions of birds across thousands of miles every year is one of the world's most magnificent natural phenomena. Migrants traveling in huge numbers follow overlapping flyways that loop between breeding grounds in the north and wintering grounds in the south. Species ranging in size from enormous white stork to tiny blackcap fly between Europe and Africa. They cross over two land bridges—one across the Middle East and down the east coast of Africa, and the other over Gibraltar and down the west coast of Africa. The aerial highways that link breeding and wintering areas also include a network of stop-over sites, where migrants can rest and refuel before continuing their journey. Flyways tend to follow coastlines and north–south river valleys. They may be only a few hundred yards wide at certain points, such as mountain passes and straits like the Bosporus; in other places they measure hundreds of miles across.

WINGSPANS

A bird's wingspan is measured from the tip of one fully extended wing across the body to the tip of the other wing. Feathers provide insulation and help streamline the body and wings, making the bird aerodynamic. Birds adjust their wingspan to control flight.

White stork *60 inches (150 cm)*
Riding on thermals of hot air, the white stork has a wingspan twice the length of its body.

Northern lapwing *28 inches (70 cm)*
Migration is often wind-assisted for the northern lapwing, whose wings make a lapping sound.

Eurasian teal *20 inches (55 cm)*
This dabbling duck flies in large flocks. Fast wing beats make the flocks appear to twist in flight.

Swallow *13 inches (33 cm)*
Swallows are fast and acrobatic fliers that prey on insects, which they catch mid-flight.

Wood warbler *9 inches (22 cm)*
The entire population of wood warblers flies to tropical Africa to escape harsh European winters.

Greenland

East Atlantic flyway

EUROPE

NORTH AMERICA

AFRICA

Wood warbler
Phylloscopus sibilatrix

White stork
Ciconia ciconia

SOUTH AMERICA

Flyways

Three major north-to-south flyways pass over Europe. The East Atlantic flyway (green), favored by the teal, bisects the continent and crosses Gibraltar into Africa. The Black Sea/Mediterranean flyway (blue), used by the stork, extends from Russia to West Africa. Many different waterbirds use the West Asia/East Africa flyway (orange), which follows the Ural Mountains through Europe.

Swallow
Hirundo rustica

Blackcap
Sylvia atricapilla

Flock of plovers
Birds flock for defense, to locate food, and to navigate during migration. The coordinated movements of flocks such as these plovers result from the second-to-second decisions of individual birds reacting to their neighbors.

Eurasian teal
Anas crecca

A S I A

**Black sea/
Mediterranean flyway**

**West Asia/
East Africa flyway**

*Indian
Ocean*

Northern lapwing
Vanellus vanellus

SPECIES	WINTERING AREA	MIGRATION DISTANCE
Swallow	South Africa	5,600 miles (9,000 km)
Wood warbler	Central Africa	4,660 miles (7,500 km)
Eurasian teal	East Africa	3,400 miles (5,500 km)
White stork	East Africa	3,400 miles (5,500 km)
Blackcap	East Africa	3,400 miles (5,500 km)
Northern lapwing	North Africa	1,900 miles (3,000 km)

BIRDS OF PREY

Bird-eating raptors and owls prey on migrating species. The peregrine falcon nests near wetlands that attract large flocks of shorebirds and waterfowl to ensure an abundance of food for its young. Golden eagles time their own migration with that of prey species, such as warblers and songbirds. Another bird-eater is the European eagle owl. It nests on cliffs that overlook forests and open fields so that it can capture passing birds.

Osprey
The osprey snatches fish from shallow depths. Before hitting the water, it thrusts its talons forward, pushes out its breast, and holds its wings back, ready to clutch its catch headfirst.

Peregrine falcon
The peregrine falcon can reach speeds of up to 200 miles per hour (320 km/h) as it dive-bombs its prey, usually medium-sized birds, such as pigeons, ducks, and shorebirds. As strong as it is speedy, a peregrine can carry off prey half its own body weight.

Lanner falcon
Lanner falcon, also called Feldegg's falcon, resides in southeast Europe and breeds in Africa. It hunts by horizontal pursuit rather than diving from above, and is one of the few raptors that attack its prey head on, often resorting to ambush. Bats are favorite targets.

CONIFEROUS FORESTS OF NORTHERN EUROPE

The coniferous forest, or taiga, stretches across the upper part of Europe in a green band bordered by tundra to the north and deciduous trees to the south. It gets its name from the dominant vegetation: cone-bearing trees, including pine and spruce, that possess needles instead of leaves. The advantage of needles is that they contain little sap and do not freeze during the long, cold winters, when average temperatures drop below freezing for half the year. Needles are also dark and can better absorb what little sunlight there is present. Since they are not deciduous, the trees do not need to expend energy regenerating during the short growing season. The lack of plant diversity compared to other European biomes translates into fewer animal species, too. Resident mammals that have adapted to the harsh conditions include hearty specialists, such as moose, bears, lynx, and pine marten.

Barents Sea

REYKJAVÍK

Norwegian Sea

Ostersund

HELSINKI

OSLO STOCKHOLM TALLINN

North Sea RĪGA MOSCOW

COPENHAGEN

VILNIUS

LONDON AMSTERDAM BERLIN WARSAW

BRUSSELS KIEV

PARIS PRAGUE

BERN VIENNA BUDAPEST

BELGRADE BUCHAREST

MADRID

ROME

SCALE 1:30,000,000

0 — 400 miles

0 — 400 kilometers

Great gray owl
The scientific name for one of the world's largest owls, the great gray, is *Strix nebulosa*, derived from the Latin word meaning misty or foggy. It pants when hot and cools off by exposing its skin.

FOREST	COUNTRY	WILDLIFE SPECIES
Bohemian	Czech Republic, Austria, Germany	Wolf, hazel grouse
Bavarian	Germany	Bison, lynx
Trillemarka	Norway	Siberian jay, golden eagle
Pokka-Pulju	Finland	White-backed woodpecker, flying squirrel

European wolf
Wolves still survive in many European countries despite centuries of hunting and habitat loss. This highly social animal forms packs comprising the extended family of a dominant male.

Red deer
Only male red deer have antlers. Made of bone, the antlers grow about one inch (2.5 cm) a day from spring until they are shed in winter. Red deer graze in the early morning and late evening. They do not migrate.

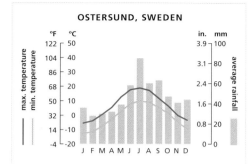

OSTERSUND, SWEDEN

Pine marten
Semi-retractable claws allow the pine marten to climb trees. A bushy tail helps it balance when scurrying from limb to limb, and fur on the soles of its paws aids insulation and creates built-in snowshoes for winter.

Black grouse
Black grouse, also known as blackgame, engage in an elaborate courtship ritual. Cocks fan their lyre-shaped tails and make a bubbling, spitting call while competing for hens.

Whooper swan
Whooper swans mate for life, jointly building a nest beside a shallow lake or slow-moving river. The male stands guard while the female incubates the eggs. The cygnets live with their parents for their first year, all migrating to warmer lands for winter.

Alpine newt
Though an amphibian, the alpine newt lacks webbed toes and spends much of its time on land, usually in undergrowth. It moves to the cool water of forest pools during the spawning season.

MOOSE

The largest of the deer family, moose are one of Europe's oldest species. Stone Age hunters depicted them in cave paintings. They are ideally suited to survival in northern forests from Norway to Russia—long legs ease travel through bogs and deep snow, especially when chased by wolves and bears. Moose defend themselves by flailing and kicking, their large size acting as a deterrent to would-be predators.

Adult male
Bulls grow antlers in summer. During the rut, August–October, they splash urine-soaked mud on hairy skin flaps under their jaws to attract females. They battle other males to win a mate.

Female and calf
Cows reach sexual maturity at 1.5 years. The gestation period varies, lasting anywhere between 215 and 243 days. Twins are common and mothers fiercely defend their calves.

LIFE ALONG THE SHORE

At 202,500 miles (325,900 km), Europe's shoreline is relatively long in relation to its land area compared to other continents. With a wide continental shelf, the seashore varies dramatically, ranging from rocky coastlines to sandy beaches to muddy tidal flats. Saltmarshes, coastal dunes, estuaries, and bays are some of the habitats that support an enormous variety of plants and animals. Tidal pools form along the rocky coastline and provide oases for limpets, mussels, crabs, and fish. Bivalve mollusks burrow under the surface on sandy beaches. Deposits of mud and silt in the sheltered waters of estuaries and bays are high in nutrients and provide homes for worms and other invertebrates. These, in turn, satisfy waders and shorebirds, such as the heron, stilt, oystercatcher, and stork. The coastline is also delicate. Development and changing land use threatens wildlife habitat, and erosion is a problem. Europe's coastlines are retreating, on average, by 1.6 to 6 feet (0.5–1.8 m) each year.

Little gull
The aptly named little gull is the smallest gull in the world. Often mistaken for a tern because of its size, coloring, and behavior, it snatches insects from the air and plucks food off the water. Highly migratory, the little gull nests in floating vegetation among reeds.

Sea urchin
The purple sea urchin's spines offer it protection from predatory fish as it feeds on kelp and other marine plants. Strong rasping teeth also allow the sea urchin to break off coral polyps and it can cause considerable damage. Sea urchins, like starfish, belong to the echinoderm group of invertebrates.

BREST, FRANCE

Starfish
Starfish are spiny-skinned animals called echinoderms with five or more "arms" that radiate from a disk. The common starfish is the most familiar. It is typically 4 to 12 inches (10–30 cm) in diameter and orange, pale brown, or violet in color. Others include the spiny sun star, sand starfish, and cushion star.

Sea slug
Sea slugs are essentially snails that have lost their shells or are in the process of losing them. There are hundreds of species, ranging from spectacular multicolored fanlike nudibranchs to primitive bubble shells. A muscular foot that produces sticky mucus aids their crawling movement.

Life in a tidal pool

Inside a tidal pool the environment is always changing with the movement of the sun, wind, and tide. Survival means avoiding being washed away or drying out. The hardiest animals, namely barnacles and whelks, live in the splash zone. Starfish and sea urchins cling to the middle zone and tiny fish stick to deeper pools. Hermit crabs and sea anemones dwell on the bottom.

Starfish underside
Tubelike feet aid starfish locomotion and feeding. The central mouth leads to two stomachs, one of which can be everted so the starfish can digest food outside its body.

Anemone
A sea anemone's body is a column with a single opening, used to ingest food and expel wastes. When touched, surrounding tentacles inject a poison and hold the prey for digestion.

Herring gull
A common gull found throughout the North Atlantic, the herring gull can drink either freshwater or sea water. It excretes the salt through special glands located above its eyes. A scavenger, the gull's call is a loud, clear bugle.

European harbor seal
Common harbor seals can be found from Ireland to the east coast of Sweden and north from Holland to the Arctic. They have two sets of flippers. The pectorals have five webbed digits with claws used for grooming and defense. The hind flippers are kicked for forward propulsion.

Eurasian oystercatcher
The tip of the oystercatcher's bill changes shape. Most of the year it is broad so that the coastal bird can pry open mollusks and hammer through shells. By the time the oystercatchers move inland to breed the tip has worn down to a point perfectly shaped for digging up worms.

| SHORELINE CREATURES AND THEIR HABITAT ||
CREATURES	HABITAT
Common moon jellyfish	Bay
Gray sea slug	Rocky shore
Chiton	Rocky shore
Little egret	Estuary
Harbor porpoise	Bay

MARSHES AND WETLANDS

Wetlands are either continuously submerged or intermittently inundated by seasonal flooding or daily tides. Enormously diverse in size and shape according to their origins and geographical location, they include marshes, fens, bogs, peatlands, ponds, and coastal estuaries. Wetlands occur in every country in Europe. One-eighth of the United Kingdom's entire landmass is covered in wetlands. Among the most biologically diverse habitats on Earth, nearly 900 European wetlands have been declared of international importance. Dynamic, complex, and renowned for their high levels of endemic species, they are a sanctuary for a wide variety of plants, invertebrates, fish, amphibians, reptiles, and mammals, as well as a high concentration of birds, including millions of migratory and sedentary waterfowl. Wetlands play an important role in maintaining an ecological balance, serving as the planet's natural kidneys by filtering runoff as well as controlling erosion and floods. They also act as buffers from storms.

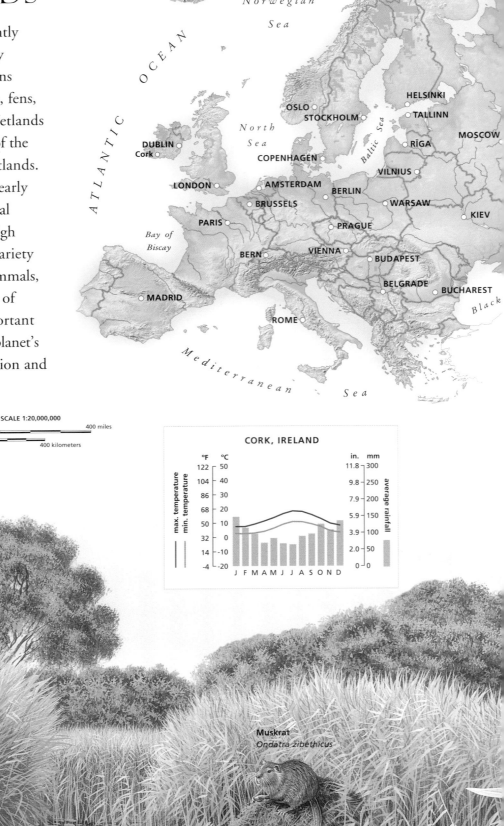

SCALE 1:20,000,000

0 — 400 miles

0 — 400 kilometers

Life in a marshland

The entire food chain is represented in a marsh, from plant to prey to predator. The sediment-rich water promotes algal and plant growth, which nourishes invertebrates, insects, and fish. These serve as food for purple heron and semi-aquatic rodents, such as the water shrew and muskrat, which, in turn, provide sustenance for birds of prey, such as the marsh harrier.

CORK, IRELAND

Purple heron
Ardea purpurea

Muskrat
Ondatra zibethicus

Water shrew
Noemys fodiens

European perch
Perca fluviatilis

Marsh harrier
Circus aeruginosus

Azure damselfly
Coenagrion puella

Country	Territory Area in acres (ha)	Wetland Area in acres (ha)
France	134,828,000 (54,563,000)	3,953,700 (1,600,000)
Sweden	101,542,500 (41,092,800)	26,440,300 (10,700,000)
United Kingdom	59,698,200 (24,159,000)	7,355,300 (2,976,585)
Estonia	10,674,500 (4,320,000)	3,325,800 (1,345,900)
Slovenia	5,005,400 (2,025,600)	296,500 (120,000)

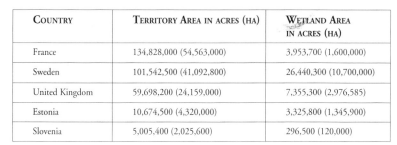

Dalmatian pelican
The largest of seven pelican species, the Dalmatian can be distinguished from the more common white pelican by its size, curly nape feathers, and light ash plumage. It catches fish in its huge bill pouch. Habitat loss has made it vulnerable to extinction.

Horned lark
Known as the shore lark in the United Kingdom, this small bird winters on seashore flats, then heads inland to breed. Its nest, on the open ground, is lined with grass and one side often has a flat doorstep of pebbles.

Wigeon
The wigeon is a dabbling duck, so named because it grazes by upending on the water surface rather than diving. When spooked, wigeons can spring straight up to take flight. During the breeding season males sport colorful plumage, with pink breasts and a yellow crown stripe.

Dragonfly

Dragonflies spend most of their lives as larvae underwater. They metamorphose by crawling onto plants. Exposed to air, their skin splits and the adult dragonflies emerge. Dragonflies have two pairs of wings and can fly at a speed of 100 body-lengths per second.

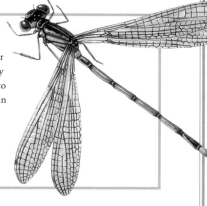

Water shrew
The water shrew lives in shallow burrow systems, often with underwater entrances. A fast swimmer, it uses hairs on the underside of its tail as a rudder. Venomous saliva helps immobilize prey, ranging from aquatic larvae and insects to small fish, frogs, slugs, and snails.

The bald eagle is found throughout North America and as far south as Mexico. This swooping bald eagle spreads its wings to slow its descent as it prepares to land on the Kenai Peninsula, Alaska. These eagles feed mainly on fish that they pluck from the water, but are also known to steal food from other birds.

NORTH AMERICA

NORTH AMERICA

Mysterious evergreen woods, parched deserts, temperate rain forests, vast grassy plains, snow-capped mountain peaks, oak forests bursting with life, swamps, and sandy beaches; all are found in North America. From northern Mexico through the United States and Canada, the continent is extraordinarily varied climatically and topographically, and this is reflected in its diverse flora and fauna. North America shares some of its wildlife wealth with other continents; awesome brown bears and moose haunt Eurasia, and pumas prey on white-tailed deer in South America. Many of its most beautiful songbirds migrate to and from North America every year. But many animals are unique, from pronghorns and bison to spotted salamanders and Gila monsters. However, humans have taken a huge toll on this land. Some species, such as passenger pigeons, have disappeared entirely and some habitats, including sagebrush and grasslands, are mere shadows of their former glory.

CLIMATE ZONES

- Wet tropical
- Seasonal tropical
- Arid
- Semiarid
- Mediterranean
- Subtropical
- Continental
- Temperate
- Cold temperate
- Subpolar
- Highland
- Polar

Climate

North America's remarkably varied climates encompass most extremes of weather. In the far north, low temperatures and polar winds keep sea and land frozen for much of the year. To the south, the cold temperate zone experiences heavy winter snowfalls and short summers. Winter snow is also abundant in the northeastern USA, where summers are hot and humid. The greatest aridity occurs in the southwestern USA and northwestern Mexico.

The Boreal Forest
Vast, cold, and remote, the boreal coniferous forest shrouds northern North America from sea to sea below the Arctic and supports a small but splendid wildlife assemblage.

The Great Plains
The vast expanse of grasses that flowed through the center of North America has nearly vanished, but traces of its glory remain in remnant bison herds and prairie dog towns.

Pacific Northwest Coniferous Forest
Boasting the tallest trees on Earth, the Pacific Northwest coniferous forest teems with wildlife, from fish in its coursing rivers to insects living in the treetops.

The Great Basin
The forbidding extremes of the Great Basin, a cold desert dominated by sagebrush and species that depend on it, are succumbing to human and plant invaders.

VEGETATION ZONES

- Tropical forest
- Seasonal tropical forest
- Desert
- Tropical grassland
- Mediterranean forest and scrub
- Midlatitude grassland
- Midlatitude forest
- Boreal forest
- Tundra
- Mountain vegetation
- Ice sheet

Natural Vegetation

A permanent cover of ice swathes most of Greenland. South of the arctic tundra—a barren region of bogs, mosses, and scattered conifers—a huge belt of boreal forest blankets most of Canada and reaches southward along the western ranges. Grasslands flank the Rocky Mountains, stretching across the interior to the broadleaved forests of the east, merging with Mediterranean scrub near the west coast. Deserts extend from the southwestern USA across much of northern Mexico.

The Rocky Mountains
The Rocky Mountains' tall peaks and low basins are the home of some of the continent's most spectacular wildlife including bison, bears, bobcats, and wolves.

Deserts of the Southwest
In the hot, dry expanses of the deserts of the southwest, diverse plants and animals have evolved ingenious strategies for conserving water and keeping cool.

Eastern Deciduous Forest
Rolling mountains and majestic trees that burst into brilliant fall colors define the eastern deciduous forest, where songbirds, salamanders, and flowering shrubs abound.

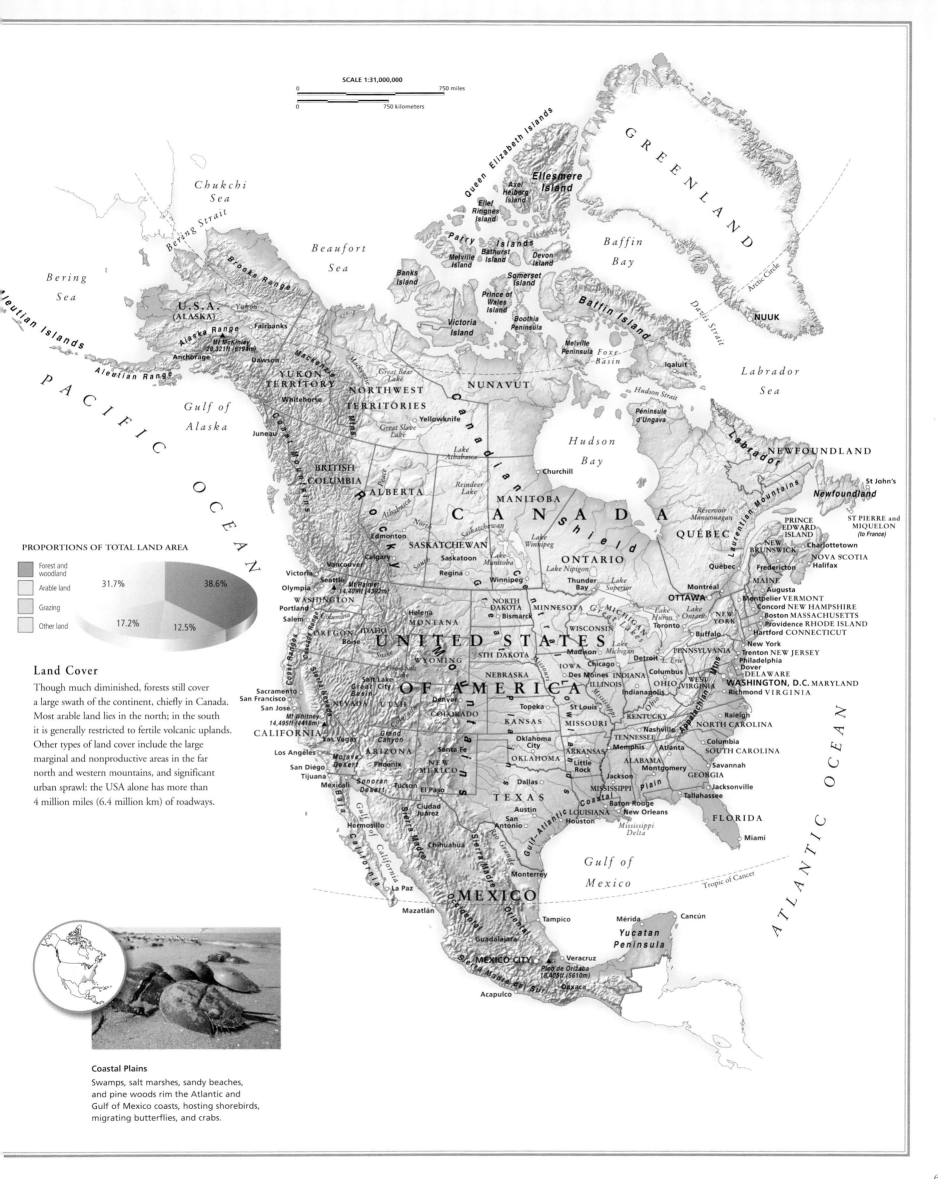

SCALE 1:31,000,000

0   750 miles

0   750 kilometers

PROPORTIONS OF TOTAL LAND AREA

Forest and woodland

Arable land

Grazing

Other land

38.6%

31.7%

17.2%

12.5%

Land Cover

Though much diminished, forests still cover
a large swath of the continent, chiefly in Canada.
Most arable land lies in the north; in the south
it is generally restricted to fertile volcanic uplands.
Other types of land cover include the large
marginal and nonproductive areas in the far
north and western mountains, and significant
urban sprawl: the USA alone has more than
4 million miles (6.4 million km) of roadways.

Coastal Plains

Swamps, salt marshes, sandy beaches,
and pine woods rim the Atlantic and
Gulf of Mexico coasts, hosting shorebirds,
migrating butterflies, and crabs.

69

THE BOREAL FOREST

Covering about one-quarter of North America, the boreal forest stretches from the interior of Alaska to the fringes of Newfoundland. Named for the Greek god of the North Wind, Boreas, this forest is also called taiga, a Russian word meaning "land of little sticks." Long, cold, snowy winters and infertile soils prevent the spruce, fir, and other coniferous trees that dominate this landscape from growing taller than about 50 feet (15 m). Along with these evergreens, birch, aspen, and a few other hardy deciduous trees thrive, all adapted to the natural fires that regularly ravage the forest. The harsh climate limits wildlife diversity, but about 85 mammal species make their homes here, and the boreal forest in summer abounds in breeding migratory birds, when some 3 billion birds of about 300 species feast on its abundant insects. Few people live in the boreal forest, but it is threatened by resource extraction, pollution, and global warming, which could create warmer and drier conditions, insect outbreaks, and more frequent fires.

SCALE 1:35,000,000

0 — 500 miles

0 — 500 kilometers

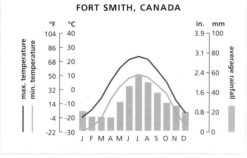

FORT SMITH, CANADA

Common loon
The haunting, wailing calls of breeding common loons emanate from boreal forest lakes and rivers across Canada and Alaska, the northernmost lower 48 US states, and into Yellowstone National Park. These fish-eating water birds rarely go ashore except to mate or to lay and incubate eggs.

Wetlands

Countless lakes, ponds, bogs, and other wetlands dot the boreal forest. More than 13 million migratory ducks breed, feed, and rest in these wetland habitats, as do millions of other waterbirds, including loons, grebes, cranes, and kingfishers. Wetlands and the boreal forest's many rivers are also home to about 130 species of fish and aquatic mammals, such as beavers, whose dams actually create wetlands.

Eared grebe
Eared grebes breed in large, raucous colonies in shallow wetlands in the western boreal forest and other parts of western North America. In summer, they hunt for aquatic insects and spiders on the water's surface and also dive underwater for them.

Whooping crane
Nearly the entire world population of endangered whooping cranes, about 70 breeding pairs, summers in the boreal forest wetlands of Canada's Wood Buffalo National Park and its surrounds. Living 20 to 30 years, whooping cranes raise only one chick a year.

Moose
The boreal forest is the primary habitat of the moose, the largest of all deer. In a sense, moose manage the boreal forest. They graze extensively on the forest's aspens and other deciduous trees, preferring them to conifers. As a result, moose grazing makes room for spruces and other conifers to grow.

CONSERVATION WATCH

The boreal forest is a stronghold of the solitary wolverine, which ranges widely. It was never abundant but is declining in most of its North American range, and may be extinct elsewhere. Trapping for their fur and poisoning, largely by ranchers, has taken a toll on wolverines, which are easily disturbed and prefer to live and breed in remote wildernesses.

Least weasel
Least weasels prefer to live and hunt in grassy meadows intermixed with forest. Their long, slender bodies enable them to follow mice and voles into their burrows and, in winter, through tunnels in the snow. This weasel needs to eat one or two prey a day, equal to about half its body weight.

Hungry hunters

Seven of North America's 11 species of mustelids live in various boreal forest habitats. These luxuriously-furred carnivores range from tiny least weasels, which weigh just one or two ounces (28–56 g), to husky wolverines that weigh up to 500 times more. Predators with voracious appetites, mustelids eat almost any animal they can catch as well as feeding on carrion.

Mink
Neovison vison

American marten
Martes americana

Least weasel
Mustela vison

Fisher
Martes pennanti

Wolverine
Gulo gulo

Porcupine
A North American porcupine is studded with about 30,000 barb-tipped quills for protection. If a predator attacks, the porcupine drives its quills into the assailant, injuring and sometimes killing the victim.

Northern river otter
Excellent swimmers and divers, semi-aquatic northern river otters ply the rivers and lakes of the boreal forest. They hunt, usually alone and at night, for fish, frogs, turtles, birds, eggs, and sometimes muskrats. A layer of oil underlying their thick fur insulates their bodies in cold water.

CARIBOU ON THE MOVE

Caribou, known as reindeer outside of North America, are superbly adapted to life in the cold boreal forest as well as the high Arctic tundra. Two subspecies occupy parts of the North American boreal forest. The woodland caribou lives here year-round in small groups, while barrenland caribou live further north. Barrenland caribou migrate in huge herds as far as 3,100 miles (5,000 km) a year between summer tundra calving grounds and winter boreal forest habitats. Woodland caribou may migrate too, but over much shorter distances of 9 to 50 miles (15–80 km) within the forest. Their numbers have steadily declined over the past century, disappearing entirely from most of the more southerly sections of their former range. Logging, mining, oil exploration, roads, and other human impacts on the boreal forest are the major reasons for this decline. Barrenland caribou are more secure, but climate change threatens the security of both this subspecies and its woodland counterpart.

CONSERVATION WATCH

Summer brings swarms of mosquitoes and black, bot, and warble flies that disturb caribou foraging and force them into patches of snow, where there are fewer insects. Higher summer temperatures because of global warming will boost insect numbers, which may compromise caribou health and reproduction.

Swimmers
Always on the move, whether migrating or just grazing, caribou are not deterred by lakes or rivers. They are strong swimmers, reaching speeds of up to six miles per hour (10 km/h) and air trapped between their double layer of fur aids buoyancy. A dip also brings some relief from pesky biting insects.

Grazing
A caribou's summer fare consists of a variety of grasses, flowering plants, leaves of willows and birches, and even mushrooms. Caribou shed their antlers every alternate year and, unique among deer, females bear them, too.

Adapted to Life in the Snow

Traveling through the deep snow that blankets the boreal forest for most of the year is hard work that requires a lot of energy. Some mammals, including Canada lynx, snowshoe hares, and caribou, have evolved "snowshoes." Specific adaptations make their feet extra large and this keeps them from sinking far into the snow. The willow ptarmigan, a forest bird, has evolved a different strategy: its feet are densely feathered.

Canada lynx
Medium-sized cats with tufted ears and keen eyesight, Canada lynx specialize in hunting snowshoe hares, which make up about 80 percent of their diet. Predator and prey are so closely linked that fluctuations in hare populations are mirrored in lynx numbers.

Lynx paw
The Canada lynx's paws are huge for the cat's size. They are furred above and below, serving to improve insulation, much like a pair of mittens.

On the move

The caribou that make up the Porcupine Herd spend most of the year on the move. They travel north on fairly fixed routes from their boreal forest wintering habitat, to calve in the northern foothills of the Brooks Range and on the Alaskan Coastal Plains. In the fall they return along more diffuse routes.

Snowshoe hare paw
Very large hind feet covered in dense fur and stiff hairs, and long toes that spread widely, allow a snowshoe hare to race over deep snow.

The hunted
Even snowshoes and fur that turns from brown to white to blend into the winter snow do not keep snowshoe hares from the jaws of Canada lynx. The hares dine on willow and aspen, which defend themselves with nasty chemicals when the hares over-browse.

Porcupine Herd Migration route

Shoveling for food
Green food is scarce in the boreal forest winter and the lichen that makes up much of the caribou's winter diet is buried beneath snow. Caribou use their sharp-edged hooves to shovel off the snow. This requires a lot of energy, so caribou try to steal the patches others have cleared.

Mackenzie

ORTHWEST RRITORIES

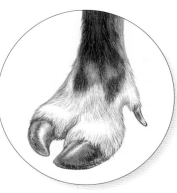

Caribou paw
Two large, half-moon-shaped front toes and two smaller back toes spread to make a caribou's hooves wide and long. This enables it to tiptoe through snow without getting bogged.

PACIFIC NORTHWEST CONIFEROUS FOREST

Stretching 1,300 miles (2,090 km) along the coast from Alaska to northern California, and just 40 to 75 miles (65–120 km) wide, the Pacific Northwest coniferous forest of North America is one of the richest forests on Earth. Mild temperatures and abundant rainfall of 30 to 115 inches (760–2,900 mm) per year combine to produce dense stands of towering, long-lived evergreen trees, such as Douglas fir, western hemlock, western red cedar, sitka spruce, and coast redwood. These coastal old-growth forests, through which many rivers course, are home to a diverse array of wildlife. Some species, such as the northern spotted owl and the Pacific giant salamander, are found nowhere else, and scientists are regularly discovering new species of insects and spiders in the forest canopy. Brown bears grow fat on the abundant salmon and trout that ply the rivers, while orcas lurk offshore seeking prey. Logging, dams built for hydroelectric power, and other human activities pose the major threats to this habitat.

Bald eagle
The majestic bald eagle uses its strong legs and powerful toes, tipped with sharp talons, to snatch salmon and trout, its favorite prey. This large raptor depends on old-growth coniferous or deciduous forest near large bodies of water. It roosts, perches, and builds its immense nest, which can weigh a ton (1,000 kg), in forest trees.

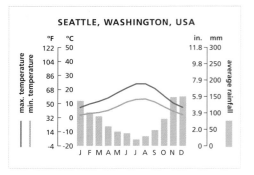

SEATTLE, WASHINGTON, USA

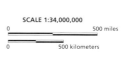

SCALE 1:34,000,000

Pacific banana slug
The second-largest land-living slug does, indeed, reach the size of a banana. The Pacific banana slug inhabits the Pacific Coast's coniferous rain forests, where it eats fungus, dead leaves, and animal droppings on the moist forest floor.

Marbled murrelet
Shy and secretive, marbled murrelets nest in coastal forest trees, usually selecting the largest trees available. They hunt small fish offshore, sometimes traveling 12 miles (19 km) or more from their nest to forage. In pursuit of a meal, murrelets often work synchronously in pairs at shallow depths, "flying" through the water by using their muscular wings like flippers and their webbed feet to steer.

Brown bear
Pacific coastal brown bears enjoy a food bonanza in summer, feasting on the abundant salmon swimming upriver to spawn. With food so plentiful, the usually solitary bears gather in numbers at prime fishing spots, often where waterfalls and other obstructions slow the fish down.

Salmon in stages

A female sockeye salmon lays eggs in the same river in which it hatched years before. Eggs hatch as alevin with the yolk sac still attached. Days later, an alevin becomes a free-swimming fry and, later, a parr that lives in freshwater for several years. A silver-colored smolt is ready to enter the sea, where it will grow into a large adult. Adults returning to rivers to spawn have red bodies and green heads.

Fish diet
The high-protein, high-fat salmon diet on the Pacific coast produces the largest brown bears in the world. Adult males reach a massive 1,300 pounds (600 kg) or more, and may stand 9 feet (2.8 m) tall. When hunting is good, these bears can eat 10 large salmon a day.

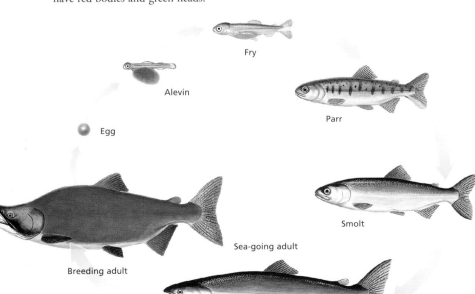

Fry

Alevin

Parr

Egg

Smolt

Sea-going adult

Breeding adult

Sockeye salmon
At four or so years old, male and female sockeye salmon leave the ocean and enter rivers to breed, returning to the same systems in which they hatched. By then, both sexes have turned bright red on their back and sides, a signature of their adult breeding status.

THE ROCKY MOUNTAINS

The Rocky Mountains divide North America in half. Stretching from Alberta, in Canada, to New Mexico in the United States, and varying from 60 to 350 miles (95–563 km) wide, the Rockies include 100 different ranges. The highest peaks reach 14,400 feet (4,390 m) but among them are large, low basins and troughs. Habitat diversity is enormous, ranging from snow-capped peaks to alpine meadows to boreal and deciduous forest and arid steppes, but coniferous forest dominates in the generally cool, dry climate. Wildlife diversity is limited in the Rockies. Relatively few insects, amphibians, and reptiles live here, and many of the fish species in the region's plentiful lakes and rivers have been introduced. However, at the heart of the Rockies, in Yellowstone National Park, exists the most impressive array of large mammals in North America. Bison, moose, elk, bighorn sheep, mountain goats, mule and white-tailed deer, pronghorn, grizzly and black bears, gray wolves, coyotes, pumas, wolverines, Canada lynx, bobcats, and more come together in this region.

SCALE 1:35,000,000

0 _____ 500 miles

0 _____ 500 kilometers

Common raven
The common raven is one of the Rockies' most conspicuous birds. Sociable and seemingly fearless, it is often seen scavenging gray wolf kills and will even swoop or chase these carnivores to steal a bite for its hungry nestlings.

Western rattlesnake
Although armed with deadly venom, western rattlesnakes are not aggressive and are seldom seen. In hot weather they hunt at night and spend cold winters hibernating in caves and other animals' burrows. Females give birth to up to 20 young in the fall.

Rattle structure
Each segment of the rattle is composed of tough skin that is not shed. The loosely interlocking rattles bounce against each other when the snake vibrates its tail.

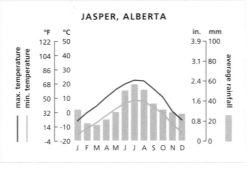

JASPER, ALBERTA

Numerous trout species

The lakes and streams of Yellowstone National Park, many of which were once fishless, are now home to about a dozen native fish species, including cutthroat trout and Arctic grayling. Four species of trout—rainbow, brown, brook, and lake—were also introduced for sport fishing from the late 19th century to the mid-20th century. The non-natives are now outcompeting the natives, some of which have sharply declined.

Cutthroat trout
Native cutthroat swim the same streams as non-native rainbows, which have robbed them of food and habitat. Consequently, the cutthroat is now highly vulnerable.

Mountain goat

Spending most of their time on severely steep, rocky slopes in alpine areas of the northern Rockies, where they are safe from predators, mountain goats nibble small plants that grow among the rocks. Powerful front legs help them to climb and descend the steep slopes, and rough pads on the undersides of their split hooves provide traction. The hooves are capable of pinching around a rock edge or spreading out for braking.

Mule deer
Mule deer prefer drier habitats than the white-tailed deer that also inhabit the Rocky Mountains. During most of the year, mule deer live in small groups of two or three, feeding on a wide range of plant species. When food is scarce in winter, larger groups gather at food sources.

American beaver
Energetic American beavers build lodges of tree branches and trunks they fell using their chisel-shaped front teeth. Their lips close behind their front teeth so they can carry branches underwater without fluid entering their lungs. Beavers have dense fur and webbed hind feet.

COYOTE

Adaptable and opportunistic, coyotes thrive almost everywhere in North America, from the high Rockies to large cities such as Washington DC. They took advantage of the extermination of gray wolves to expand well beyond their original, mostly western, range. However, where wolves reign, as they do once again in Yellowstone National Park, coyote numbers have decreased.

Facial expressions
Among other signals, such as vocalizations and postures, social coyotes use a variety of facial expressions to communicate. They may live alone, in breeding pairs, or packs of several individuals.

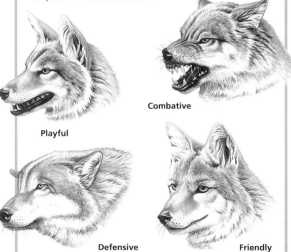

Playful

Combative

Defensive

Friendly

THE GRAY WOLF

Gray wolves once prowled throughout North America, coast to coast from the Arctic to central Mexico. They are still relatively abundant in Alaska and Canada but extermination programs and habitat loss over several hundred years combined to nearly eliminate these predators from the lower 48 US states. By the 1930s only a small number remained in a few northern strongholds. However, in 1995 and 1996, amid great controversy, 66 wolves were reintroduced to Yellowstone National Park and central Idaho, where they had not bred since 1926. By 2007, these wolf populations had increased to about 1,500 animals. Conservation programs and natural re-colonization from Canada have led to growing wolf numbers in Minnesota, Wisconsin, and Michigan. Efforts to reintroduce the Mexican gray wolf subspecies in the southwest, however, have thus far met with little success. The ecology of Yellowstone, where the wolves' impact has been best studied, has changed dramatically as wolves have flourished on meals of abundant elk.

Former range

Current range

CONSERVATION WATCH

Success can have a price. In 2008, the US government removed the thriving Rocky Mountains wolf population from its Endangered Species List. The population in Minnesota, Wisconsin, and Michigan, numbering about 4,000, was "de-listed" in 2007. Conservationists fear that state wildlife agencies may be less careful stewards of a species once persecuted as vermin.

Wolf cubs
A breeding wolf pair produces a litter of five to six cubs in spring or summer after mating about two months earlier. Born helpless, the cubs remain in a den for two months before joining the pack's hunting forays a few weeks later. Cubs do not hunt themselves until aged eight months.

Leaders of the pack

Wolves prey mostly on elk, mule deer, and white-tailed deer. They generally hunt in packs of five to 10 or more members, led by a dominant breeding pair, most often accompanied by members of their own recent litters. But a pair or even a single wolf can bring down elk and deer alone, so the benefit of pack hunting may lie in the pair sharing the surplus of their kills with their young.

Howling

The haunting sound of wolves howling can be heard up to 10 miles (15 km) away, and sometimes wolves howl to reunite stray members of the pack. Wolf packs also howl together at dusk, before heading out to hunt, which may reinforce the bonds between family members.

CASCADING EFFECTS OF WOLF REINTRODUCTION

Elk form about 90 percent of the prey of Yellowstone's wolves. As a result, their numbers are about half what they were before wolves returned. With fewer elk browsing, streamside vegetation including willows, aspens, and cottonwoods, is flourishing where once it was disappearing. Wolves have also reduced coyote numbers, which has led to greater survival rates among pronghorn calves, the coyotes' favorite prey. Other species have similarly been advantaged or disadvantaged by the return of the wolves.

Top scavenger
The presence of wolves helps grizzly bears, which are able to usurp wolf kills. Stolen carcasses are especially important to grizzlies when they emerge, starving, from winter hibernation. Scavenging ravens and eagles are increasing, too.

Birds abound
The recovery of willows and other streamside vegetation that was once overbrowsed by elk has improved the prospects for songbirds that nest in this habitat. Species such as the yellow warbler are increasing in number.

Hunting party
Although bison are harder to kill, wolves increasingly hunt them as elk numbers diminish. Large packs such as this one may be the key to wolves' success in bringing down these huge beasts.

More moose
Willow regrowth has provided new habitat for American beavers, which prefer to eat small willow trees. New beaver dams, in turn, have created more habitat for water-loving moose.

Return of the aspen
Aspen stands were once abundant along streams, but stopped growing about the same time as wolves disappeared from Yellowstone. With the wolves' return, aspen are again thriving.

Rodents on the rise
Semi-aquatic muskrats have found new homes in ponds created by beaver dams, as have river otters. More rodents taking up residence means more prey for foxes and birds of prey.

THE GREAT PLAINS

The Great Plains cover an immense swath of the continent's center, stretching about 1,000 miles (1,600 km) east from the foothills of the Rocky Mountains. Once a vast, largely treeless dry sea of perennial grasses, most of the Great Plains now form some of the world's best agricultural land, covered in fields of wheat and corn, and cattle. Though the plains may seem monotonous, closer inspection reveals a landscape of great diversity. The climate is dry, with rainfall of 24 inches (610 mm) at most recorded each year, but rainfall increases from west to east, dividing the region into western short-grass prairie, eastern tall-grass prairie, and mixed grass in between. Topography ranges from pancake flat to rolling hills. Amid the grassy expanses, trees and shrubs flourish along streams. Bison, whose enormous herds once thundered across the plains and supported the region's wolves and grizzly bears, typify this near-vanished ecosystem.

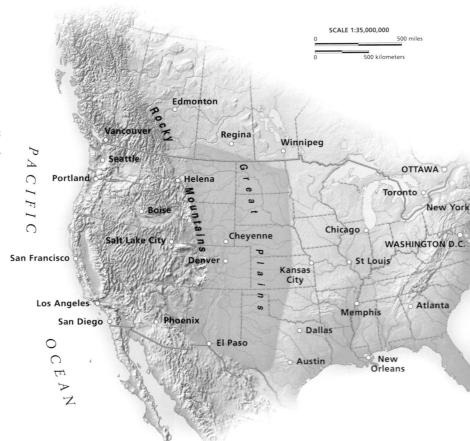

SCALE 1:35,000,000

American bison
The largest male bison reach the size of a small car, and can run at speeds of up to 40 miles per hour (64 km/h). The beasts are front-loaded: their head and shoulders are massive while their rear ends are relatively slender. In combat over females, two males may charge each other, butting heads with such force that one may be flipped head over heels.

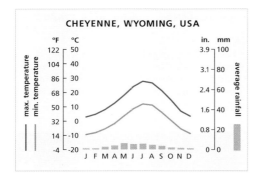

CHEYENNE, WYOMING, USA

Bobcat
Shy and secretive, bobcats thrive in agricultural areas with some natural vegetation or rocky outcrops that provide shelter. Cottontail rabbits, pocket gophers, wood rats, and ground hogs are among their favorite prey, but these cats will also take deer fawns or birds.

Greater short-horned lizard
These lizards defend themselves from coyotes and other predators by squirting blood from their eyes. The blood contains formic acid, obtained from the bodies of their primary food—ants.

Bison's head and neck
A bison's massive head is supported by a short yet wide neck and a large muscular hump between its shoulder blades, connected by a heavy ligament. A bison swings its strong head back and forth to sweep feeding areas clear of snow as deep as two to three feet (60–90 cm).

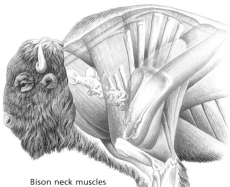

Bison neck muscles

CONSERVATION WATCH

The long, paddle-shaped snouts that give the American paddlefish its name are densely spotted with electrical sensors. These enable a paddlefish to locate its zooplankton prey in murky water by sensing its electric field. This exquisite sensory system, however, has not protected the paddlefish from overfishing, dams that block access to spawning grounds, and water pollution. The species is considered vulnerable to extinction.

Temperature extremes

Winters on the windswept Great Plains are brutally cold; summers are scorching hot. A bison's winter coat, with 10 times as many hairs as a cow's, helps keep it from freezing to death when temperatures plummet. The deep black fur, which absorbs the heat of the sun, is shed in summer but bison still have to pant to lose heat. If they failed to do so, they would not survive.

Bird life

The Great Plains host about 300 species of breeding migratory birds in summer, such as lark buntings, as well as permanent residents, such as greater sage grouse. Here the birds find, or once did, abundant grasshoppers and other insects, seeds, and herbs to feed their nestlings. However, with so much of the prairie gone, most of these species are in decline.

Western meadowlark
Sturnela neglecta

Grasshopper sparrow
Ammodramus savannarum

Lark bunting
Calamospiza melanocorys

Greater sage grouse
Centrocercus urophasianus

Snakeweed grasshopper
Hesperotettix viridis

81

THE GREAT PLAINS
PRAIRIE DOGS

More than 5 billion black-tailed prairie dogs once colonized the Great Plains, living in aggregations large enough to be called towns. The largest recorded single town numbered some 400 million of these burrowing rodents, spread over 25,000 square miles (65,000 km²). Four other less-widespread prairie dog species also inhabit the United States and Mexico. Vegetation shorn by the herbivorous animals and the pockmarks of their mounded burrow entrances make even the small towns that remain today conspicuous in the landscape. The animals themselves, which are active during the day, are conspicuous too. Scientists call prairie dogs keystone species because so many other species are affected by their presence. Many predators, such as coyotes and golden eagles, eat them. Burrowing owls, rabbits, snakes, insects, and others occupy their burrows, and prairie dog burrowing churns up the soil so it can better support plants. In turn, the plants attract grazers, such as pronghorn and bison, many rodents, and rabbits.

Model mounds
The mounds around entrances to prairie dog burrows are carefully constructed. Besides offering access, they are elevated so as to allow the animals to scan for predators. The mounds also help prevent flooding during rain storms and improve ventilation in the underground tunnels and chambers.

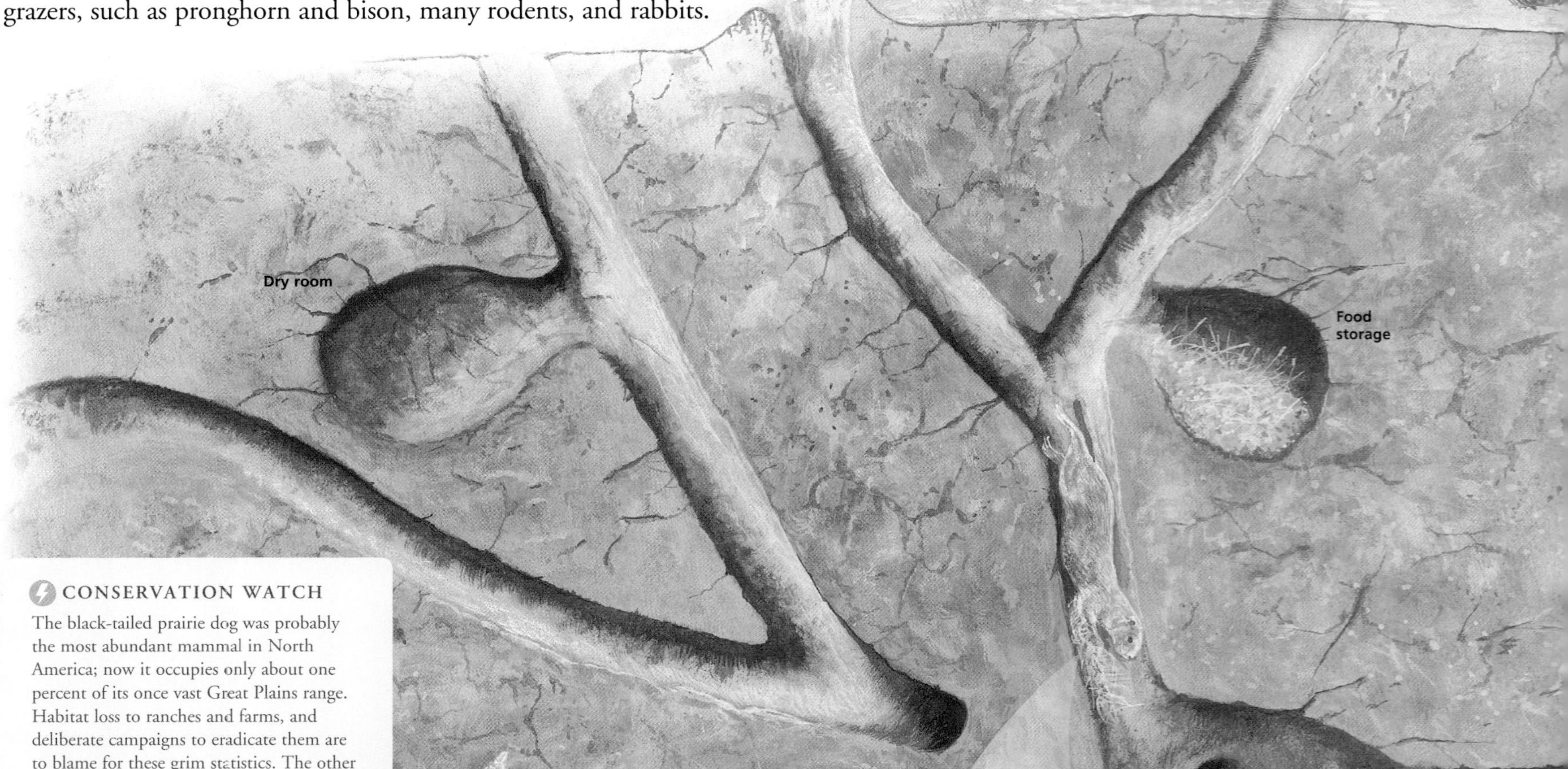

Emergency exit

Dry room

Food storage

⚡ **CONSERVATION WATCH**

The black-tailed prairie dog was probably the most abundant mammal in North America; now it occupies only about one percent of its once vast Great Plains range. Habitat loss to ranches and farms, and deliberate campaigns to eradicate them are to blame for these grim statistics. The other prairie dog species are in similar straits.

Nesting chamber
Throughout her 33-day pregnancy a female prairie dog collects dry grass to line her nesting chamber. Although other parts of the burrow system are shared by all family members, a female aggressively defends her nesting chamber from others that may wish to kill her babies.

Sleeping chamber

Home underground

A prairie dog town is divided into coteries—social groups of an adult male, two or three adult females, and one or two youngsters. Coteries defend territories that include their underground burrow system, which the rodents use to escape predators and bad weather, raise young, and spend the night. Multiple entrances give way to tunnels as long as 110 feet (33 m) and as deep as 16 feet (5 m).

Alarmed

With so many prairie dogs active at the same time, a few are always on the lookout for predators. On sighting a threat, a prairie dog instantly sounds the alarm, calling to alert others before diving into the burrow for its own protection.

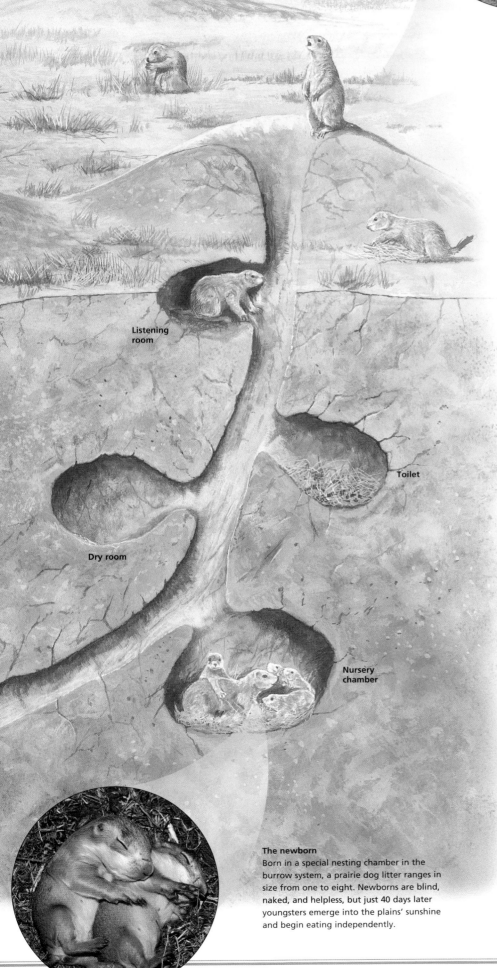

Listening room

Dry room

Toilet

Nursery chamber

The newborn

Born in a special nesting chamber in the burrow system, a prairie dog litter ranges in size from one to eight. Newborns are blind, naked, and helpless, but just 40 days later youngsters emerge into the plains' sunshine and begin eating independently.

PRAIRIE DOG PREDATORS

Only about half of the prairie dogs that emerge from their natal burrows live more than a year, although males can reach five years of age and females eight years. Disease, such as flea-borne bubonic plague, and many predators, from carnivores to birds of prey to snakes, take their toll on prairie dogs of all ages. Juveniles and subadults are particularly vulnerable to predation.

Aerial attack

Prowling slowly over the plains, the medium-sized northern harrier is just one of 10 or so day-hunting birds that feasts on prairie dogs.

Tunnel invaders

Black-footed ferrets live in prairie dog burrows and eat their hosts. They have lithe bodies that easily slink through tunnels to find a meal. The decline of prairie dogs, coupled with disease, almost rendered the ferrets extinct. The species was saved only by a zoo breeding program.

Night visitors

American badgers use their strong claws to dig their own complex burrow systems, but also visit prairie dog towns in search of food. Hunting at night, a badger may dig into a prairie dog burrow to catch one of its sleeping occupants unawares.

THE GREAT BASIN

North America's only cold desert south of the Arctic, the Great Basin, covers most of Nevada and parts of California, Idaho, Utah, Wyoming, and Oregon. At altitudes of 3,900–5,250 feet (1,200–1,600 m) in the rain shadow of western mountains, this is a land of extremes. The precipitation range is 4–12 inches (100–305 mm), mostly in the form of snow, but years of severe drought may be followed by wet years. Winter temperatures rarely climb above freezing and summer nights can be frosty, but summer days may be as hot as 90°F (32°C) with frequent violent thunderstorms. Dominated by sagebrush, the Great Basin appears desolate but 800 plant species eke out a living here and animal life is surprisingly abundant. A curious feature of the Great Basin is that its rivers and streams do not drain to the sea. Water is lost only to evaporation, so most of the fish species known here are found nowhere else. Human population growth, wildfires, and invasive species are threats to this habitat.

SCALE 1:35,000,000

0   500 miles

0   500 kilometers

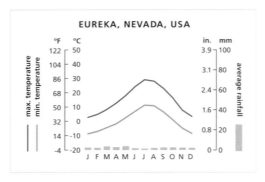

EUREKA, NEVADA, USA

Animal	Top Speed in mph (km/h)
Pronghorn	62 (100)
Black-tail jackrabbit	40 (65)
Coyote	40 (65)
Gray wolf	40 (65)
Mule deer	38 (61)
Puma	35 (56)
Brown bear	30 (48)
Bighorn sheep	30 (48)

Black-tailed jackrabbit
The black-tailed jackrabbit thrives in the Great Basin desert thanks, in part, to its amazing thermoregulation abilities. By increasing or decreasing blood flow to its enormous ears, the jackrabbit can either store or lose heat, thereby enabling it to regulate its body temperature. The jackrabbit is also most active after dusk.

Wild horses
They seem a timeless emblem of the Great Basin but wild horses did not exist here until about 1680. Domestic horses that arrived with the Spanish were soon adopted by Native Americans. Today, the Great Basin hosts the largest number of wild horses, 50,000–75,000, which are descended from released and escaped animals. At one time, herds in the west may have been several million strong.

THE PRONGHORN

Speedy hoofed mammals, able to race across the range at up to 62 miles per hour (100 km/h), pronghorns are a uniquely North American enigma. Scientists are unsure as to their closest relatives, but cows, deer, or giraffes are all possibilities. Adapted to arid and semiarid habitats, pronghorns range widely and migrate seasonally in search of nutritious food and to escape deep snow or drought.

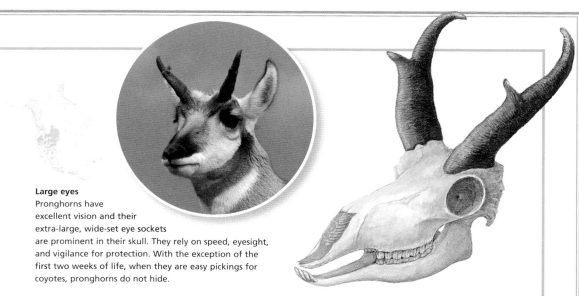

Exceptional speed

It remains a puzzle why pronghorns run so fast, clocking up speeds way beyond those required to escape any living predator they might encounter. One intriguing theory is that they evolved alongside speedier hunters, such as the American cheetah, which are now extinct.

Large eyes

Pronghorns have excellent vision and their extra-large, wide-set eye sockets are prominent in their skull. They rely on speed, eyesight, and vigilance for protection. With the exception of the first two weeks of life, when they are easy pickings for coyotes, pronghorns do not hide.

CONSERVATION WATCH

Hunting, habitat loss, and competition with wild horses and domestic livestock, especially sheep that transmit diseases, all conspired to reduce bighorn sheep numbers by 90 percent by the early 1900s. Some populations were completely eliminated. Protection and translocation programs have helped them recover, but several bighorn populations remain endangered.

Puma

Though not as fast as a pronghorn, a puma can catch one in broken, bushy terrain. It is harder for pronghorns to reach top speeds in these environments and they offer cover for a puma to stealthily approach its quarry.

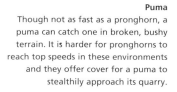

THE GREAT BASIN
SAGEBRUSH COUNTRY

The country dominated by big sagebrush once blanketed more than 23,000 square miles (60,000 km²) of western North America. This arid, high-elevation habitat is a mosaic of sagebrush species, grasses, shrubs, small green plants, and wildflowers, interspersed with woodlands, streams, and wetlands. Some animals evolved in sagebrush habitats and many, such as the sage grouse and sage vole, can live nowhere else. They get sustenance from sagebrush's soft, evergreen leaves, seek shelter under its branches, or both. But the sagebrush country and its 350 associated plants and animals are imperiled. People have eliminated about half the sagebrush habitat and what remains is influenced to varying degrees by human activities. Much sagebrush was simply destroyed, to be replaced by farms and forage more palatable to the cattle that arrived in the late 1800s. Invasive exotic cheatgrass and other weeds have edged out still more, and a host of other impacts have degraded or denuded the unique sagebrush country.

Cheatgrass
A native of Asia, cheatgrass has successfully invaded sagebrush country. This annual plant produces vast numbers of seeds that can survive five years of drought. Seeds also germinate and grow roots faster than perennial natives, quickly taking up vital water. Cheatgrass provides little or no nutrition except for a brief period in the spring so it is useless as food for mule deer and other grazers.

SAGEBRUSH IN THE GREAT BASIN

Current sagebrush habitat

Agriculture/ industry/ urban

Other habitats

Big sagebrush
Big sagebrush is found only in the dryland of western North America. Growing up to 10 feet (3 m) tall, but usually shorter, it can live as long as 100 years, however wildfires usually cut short its life. The silvery-gray shrub has brilliant yellow flowers in late summer, and year-round bears soft green leaves with fine hairs that may help keep the plant cool and conserve water.

Sagebrush community

Many animals rely on sagebrush habitats for survival in all or part of their range. Among the mammals and birds, pronghorns, pygmy rabbits, and white-tailed prairie dogs feed on sagebrush, as do Gunnison sage grouse and sage sparrows. In turn, ferruginous hawks hunt the rabbits, jackrabbits, and prairie dogs.

SAGEBRUSH COUNTRY ANIMALS

Mammals 20%

Reptiles 13%

Birds 21%

Invertebrates 46%

Spiders 36%

Aphids 26%

Beetles 11%

Ants 11%

Gall midges 16%

Sagebrush checkerspot
Female butterflies lay their eggs under the leaves of host plants in the sagebrush community. Caterpillars feed in groups on leaves and flowers.

Brewer's sparrow
Brewer's sparrows are abundant in summer in remaining Great Basin sagebrush habitats, but their numbers are declining.

Brown-headed cowbird
Recent additions to the sagebrush community, brown-headed cowbirds arrived only after farms and ranches appeared and created suitable feeding habitat for them.

Desert spiny lizard
The shy desert spiny lizard often shelters in desert woodrat nests and hunts by day for insects.

Desert woodrat
Desert woodrats are common in sagebrush habitats, where they eat leaves and other vegetation.

CONSERVATION WATCH

With greater sage grouse almost entirely dependent on sagebrush, it is not surprising that as sagebrush habitat has declined, so too have the grouse. The population of these large, showy birds has fallen by about one-third in the past 40 or so years and they have completely disappeared from five states and one province they once called home.

Greater sage grouse
Greater sage grouse eat sagebrush all year and in winter it comprises their entire diet. Females nest under a sagebrush canopy, insects attracted to sagebrush are fed to chicks, and the canopy conceals them from predators.

Mule deer
Named for their large ears, mule deer rely on sagebrush in many parts of their western range to get them through the harsh winter, when other plants are scarce. However, their diet is diverse, including hundreds of plants and shrubs, berries, and acorns.

DESERTS OF THE SOUTHWEST

The Mojave, Sonoran, and Chihuahuan deserts comprise the hot deserts of southwestern United States and northern Mexico. At fairly high elevations, the Mojave is a transition from the Great Basin and is the smallest of the deserts. From 1.5 to almost 11 inches (38–279 mm) of precipitation falls here and summer temperatures average 86–104°F (30–40°C). Its low elevation makes the Sonoran the hottest of these deserts. Summer temperatures soar to more than 105°F (40°C) and rainfall ranges from none to two inches (50 mm) a year in the driest western part of this desert. The Chihuahuan is the largest desert and fairly temperate because of its high elevation, annual rainfall of 6–16 inches (152–406 mm), and average annual temperatures of 65°F (18°C). Despite harsh conditions, many desert-adapted plants and animals populate these arid expanses. Some, such as the saguaro cactus and desert tortoises, live nowhere else.

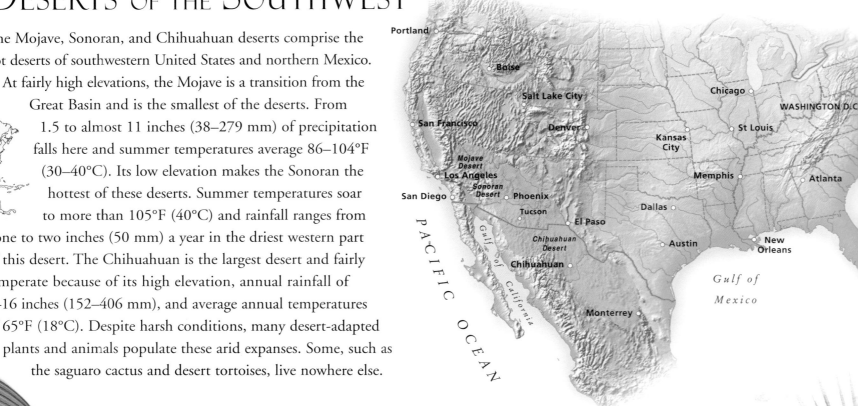

TUCSON, ARIZONA, USA

SCALE 1:30,000,000

0 — 500 miles

0 — 500 kilometers

Hummingbirds
More hummingbird species live in the southwest deserts than anywhere else in the United States and Canada. Southwestern Arizona boasts 15 species of these birds, which occur only in the New World. Costa's hummingbird breeds and winters here, sipping nectar from flowers.

Curved-billed thrasher
Common in the Sonoran and Chihuahuan deserts, the curved-billed thrasher builds a deep, grass-lined cup nest in cholla cacti. Breeding pairs share nest construction, incubation, and chick feeding responsibilities.

Burrowing owls
Burrowing owls may be year-long residents or winter migrants from more northerly extremes. These small owls nest and store food in other animals' burrows, such as those of desert tortoises. The owls hunt for insects, scorpions, rodents, frogs and toads, reptiles, and birds.

Ringtails
Although cat-like in appearance, ringtails are closely related to raccoons. Agile climbers, they scamper up and down canyon sides and trees. Their ankles rotate 180 degrees so they can easily descend a tree headfirst.

Desert dominants

Major vegetation types distinguish the three southwest deserts. Cacti are rare in the Mojave, where creosote bush and bur sage dominate. Joshua trees are prominent here and most plants are perennial shrubs, many found nowhere else in the world. In the Sonoran, creosote bush and bur sage occur at low elevations, but higher elevations host blue palo verde, ironweed, agave, and many cacti species. Prickly pear, yucca, and acacias characterize the Chihuahuan.

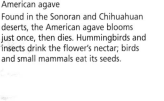

American agave
Found in the Sonoran and Chihuahuan deserts, the American agave blooms just once, then dies. Hummingbirds and insects drink the flower's nectar; birds and small mammals eat its seeds.

Chuckwallah
A large, robust lizard, the chuckwallah spends its mornings basking and its afternoons foraging. If it is cool, hot, or threatened, the lizard retreats to a rock crevice. If a predator approaches, it puffs up its body so that it cannot be dislodged.

CONSERVATION WATCH

Gila monsters and closely related beaded lizards are the only venomous lizards but their toxic bite has not stopped them declining in the face of threats posed by urban sprawl, pets, and cars. Fearful of the beasts, people often move them away from their neighborhoods and few, if any, of these lizards survive.

Desert tortoise

The only land turtle in its southwestern desert range, the football-sized desert tortoise spends most of its time in a burrow. It may go two years without a meal, even though its diet of green plants and wildflowers is its only source of water. Males often fight when they meet, using a horn on their shell to try to flip over their opponent. Fires, disease, urban sprawl, vehicle traffic, and skyrocketing numbers of ravens that eat hatchlings all threaten desert tortoises. Females do not breed until 15–20 years old.

DESERTS OF THE SOUTHWEST
SAGUARO CACTUS COMMUNITY

Found only in the Sonoran Desert, the saguaro cactus is a central component of this ecosystem and used by a variety of desert dwellers, including people. Birds such as gilded flickers dig nest holes in its flesh and Harris's hawks build stick nests in its arms. Abandoned nest holes are inhabited by other birds, such as finches and sparrows, and hawk nests are often reused by ravens and great horned owls. Bats, birds, and insects, especially bees, sip nectar from the cacti's large flowers and provide vital pollination services in return. Coyotes, jackrabbits, cactus wrens, and others eat its nutritious, water-rich fruit and seeds, then play their part in dispersing the seeds. Native Americans also eat the fruit, and once used the saguaro's strong ribs to construct houses. The cactus owes its success to amazing adaptations for storing and utilizing the region's scant water supplies.

Sonoran Desert
The satellite image of the Sonoran Desert shows the Salton Sea (bottom left) and the Gulf of California (right).

Saguaro cactus
With its tall, thick, trunk-bearing arms upturned toward the sky, the saguaro cactus dominates the Sonoran Desert landscape. These stately cacti grow as high as 50 feet (15 m) but attain that height slowly, after more than 125 years of growth. They do not begin to sprout arms until they are 65 to 75 years old and do not flower until about 35 years of age.

Southern long-nosed bat
Southern long-nosed bats specialize in eating the nectar and pollen of desert plants, such as agave and saguaro cactus. Flitting between flowers, the bats pollinate the plants. Some species, such as the organ pipe cactus, could not reproduce without them.

Nest hole
A Gila woodpecker pair digs a nest hole in a saguaro but will not make use of it for several months, until the inner pulp has dried into a solid casing around the hole.

Vantage point
Peering out of its secure nest cavity, a Gila woodpecker can survey the landscape for potential predators, such as bobcats, coyotes, foxes, hawks, and snakes.

Insect hunting
Gila woodpeckers leave the shelter of their holes to hunt for insects on the saguaro. Males probe the trunk and main branches; females focus on the edges.

Gila woodpecker
Permanent desert residents, Gila woodpeckers depend on saguaro cacti for nesting sites and for the insects that live on their trunks and branches. These birds help the cacti by cutting away flesh infected by disease-causing insect larvae.

Cactus wrens
These small birds, which get all the water they need from juicy insects and fruit, build their nests in cacti. The spines keep predators at bay, protecting eggs, nestlings, and adults. Cactus wrens are often seen singing from a perch atop a tall agave.

Greater earless lizard
These lizards are fast-moving, heat-loving reptiles that are active by day. They tunnel under the sand to seek shelter from heat and to nest. Scientists speculate that they lack external ear openings to keep sand out of their ears.

Kangaroo rat
Merriam's kangaroo rats hop across the sandy desert at night, gathering seeds of plants, such as mesquite and creosote bush. They store the seeds in their fat cheek pouches and, once full, cache the seeds in small sandy holes within their home range.

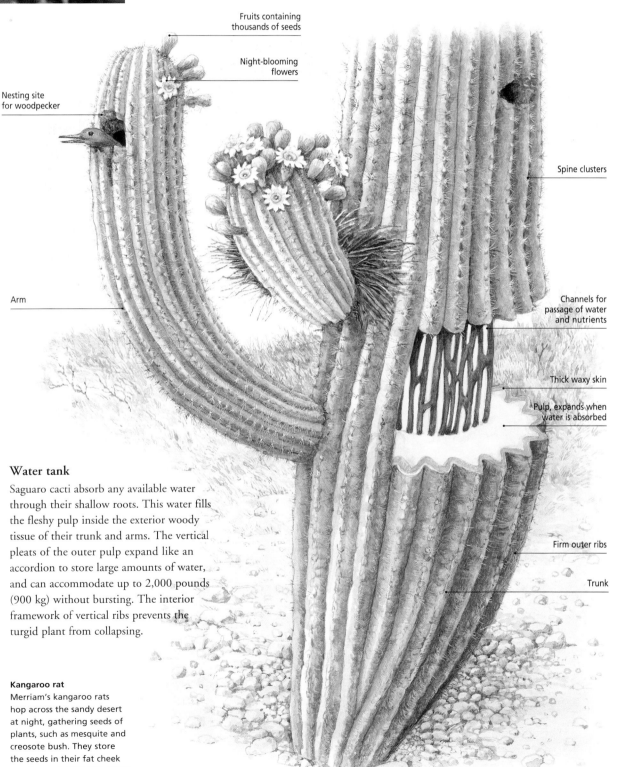

Fruits containing thousands of seeds

Night-blooming flowers

Nesting site for woodpecker

Arm

Spine clusters

Channels for passage of water and nutrients

Thick waxy skin

Pulp, expands when water is absorbed

Firm outer ribs

Trunk

Water tank

Saguaro cacti absorb any available water through their shallow roots. This water fills the fleshy pulp inside the exterior woody tissue of their trunk and arms. The vertical pleats of the outer pulp expand like an accordion to store large amounts of water, and can accommodate up to 2,000 pounds (900 kg) without bursting. The interior framework of vertical ribs prevents the turgid plant from collapsing.

EASTERN DECIDUOUS FOREST AND THE APPALACHIANS

The great eastern deciduous forest was once unbroken from central Florida to northern New England and southeastern Canada, and west to the Mississippi River. Dominated by tall trees that drop their leaves in the fall, such as oaks, maples, beech, chestnuts, and hickory, this forest boasts a rich understory of smaller trees, bushes, shrubs, ferns, fungi, and green plants. Winters are cold, but fall and spring are mild, and summers are long and warm. Water is abundant, with high levels of precipitation year-round. The Appalachian Mountains, which extend from Labrador, in Canada, to Alabama, in the United States, bisect and define this region. The diversity of wildlife in eastern deciduous forests is outstanding, with especially rich bird and amphibian faunas. Much of the forest was logged and farmed between the 1600s and the late 1800s. As the economy changed and many farmers moved west, farms were abandoned. Large fragments of forest have returned, but major urban and suburban centers dominate this region.

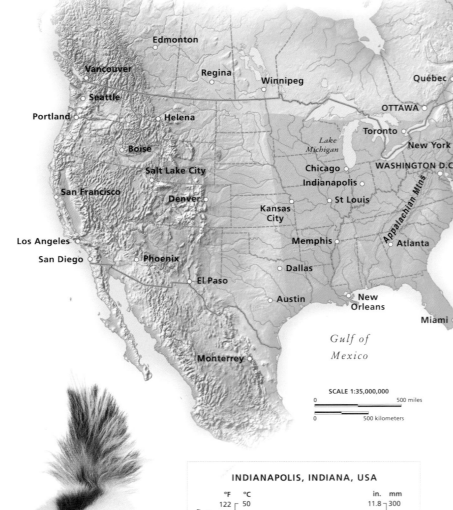

INDIANAPOLIS, INDIANA, USA

Striped skunk
Striped skunks emit a foul-smelling spray from their anal glands when threatened but that does not deter great horned owls from preying on them. Many skunks in eastern North America are also killed by vehicles and disease, such as rabies.

American black bear
The only bear in eastern North America is the American black bear, which overlaps with brown bears elsewhere. The black bear occupies diverse habitats, from deciduous forests and rain forests to swamps, tundra, and even suburbia.

Wild turkey
Habitat loss and hunting eliminated the wild turkey from the forests of the eastern United States by the early 1900s, but it has rebounded, thanks to protection and reintroductions. Traveling in noisy flocks, these birds forage on the ground for nuts.

Eastern chipmunk
Chattering eastern chipmunks are conspicuous members of the eastern forest community during summer. To endure cold winters, they hibernate in burrows, waking every few days to consume some of the nuts and seeds they cached in the fall.

Forest flier

Widely distributed in northern North America, the northern flying squirrel is found in isolated populations in the southern Appalachians, where it overlaps with the smaller southern flying squirrel. Mushrooms and other fungi are their favorite foods and the squirrels help disperse fungal spores throughout their forested habitats. Active only at night, they forage on the ground and in the treetops, where they are hunted by predators, such as owls and hawks.

Parachuting
Flying squirrels do not fly, but glide 65–295 feet (20–90 m) from tree to tree. The gliding membrane that stretches between their limbs, called a patagium, acts like a parachute. It keeps the squirrel aloft after it launches itself from on high.

Bobcat
While bobcats are fairly common in eastern forests they are seldom seen. Spending the day sheltering in rocky outcrops, brush piles, and dense bushes, they prowl the forest at night in search of a meal. Cottontail rabbits are favorites, but bobcats also prey on mice and white-tailed deer.

THE RACCOON

Northern raccoons are North America's ultimate generalist carnivores. With catholic tastes, they find food almost anywhere, from fields and forests to urban backyards, and shelter under porches as well as in tree holes and dens. Bobcats and foxes are among their predators in eastern forests, while the raccoons, themselves, prey on small mammals, birds, crustaceans, fish, mollusks, and insects, as well as eating fruit, seeds, and carrion.

Handy paws
The skeleton of a raccoon's forepaw bears a striking resemblance to that of a human hand, giving it great manual dexterity. It moves its forepaws through streams and ponds, plucking out crayfish and other aquatic creatures with its "fingers."

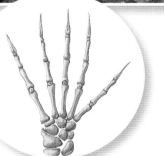

Raccoon paw   Human hand

Deciduous forest landscape

Autumn leaves in the eastern deciduous forest clothe the landscape in brilliant yellows, rich golds, and reds as vibrant as the feathers of a northern cardinal. However, this spectacle presages the tough winter, when food becomes scarce for many animals.

Northern cardinal
Cardinalis cardinalis

EASTERN DECIDUOUS FOREST AND THE APPALACHIANS
OAK FORESTS

The eastern United States is dominated by hardwood forests, of which oak forests are the main type. About 30 oak species live here in various associations with maples, beech, hickory, northern conifers, pines, and southern evergreens. Oaks flourish in areas disturbed by both natural and man-made fires, which were frequent in this part of North America until wildfire suppression programs were introduced. Fires removed other tall trees, whose shade prevented oak seedlings from thriving. Today, without fires, oaks have a hard time replacing themselves. Gypsy moth larvae, introduced insect pests that defoliate oaks and other eastern hardwoods, add to the stress on these forest ecosystems. Oaks produce huge crops of hard, nutritious seeds called acorns, although the size of the crop varies from year to year. Acorns, or mast, are a critical food source for about 50 species of mammals and birds. In addition, oak trees offer leafy forage for plant-eaters and provide shelter for many species.

Oak–Pine
Oak–Chestnut
Oak–Hickory

American robin
American robins nest in small trees under the canopy of oak forests as well as in urban backyards. They forage for earthworms between trees and also eat berries. One of the first birds to breed in the spring, the robin produces up to three clutches of three or four chicks per year.

Acorn harvest
White-tailed deer, black bears, squirrels, mice, turkeys, grackles, blue jays, and woodpeckers are among the many species that depend on acorns for fall and winter survival. Animals that store acorns in larders to tide them over the winter are important in dispersing the acorns throughout the forest.

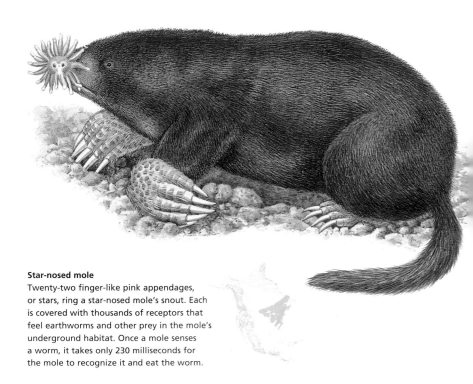

Star-nosed mole
Twenty-two finger-like pink appendages, or stars, ring a star-nosed mole's snout. Each is covered with thousands of receptors that feel earthworms and other prey in the mole's underground habitat. Once a mole senses a worm, it takes only 230 milliseconds for the mole to recognize it and eat the worm.

Blue jay
Raucous, boldly colored blue jays are year-round residents of the eastern deciduous forest. To survive winter, they collect and cache thousands of acorns, beechnuts, and pecans in the fall, storing the nuts in the ground. These birds also eat insects, green vegetation, and birds' eggs.

Virginia opossum
The only marsupial in North America north of Mexico, the Virginia opossum is best known for its habit of "playing possum" (acting dead) in response to danger. Although it lives just a year or two, the opossum has high rates of reproduction. A litter averages seven to nine young.

ECOLOGICAL INTERACTION

Oak trees produce bumper crops of acorns every two to six years, and few in between. Acorn eaters, such as white-tailed deer, white-footed mice, and chipmunks, flourish in the good acorn years, as do their ticks. This raises the risk of humans catching Lyme disease from a tick's bite. On the positive side, chipmunks prey on gypsy moths, an invasive species that defoliates oak trees.

White-tailed deer
Odocoileus virginianus

White-footed mouse
Peromyscus leucopus

Chipmunk
Tamius minimus

Acorn
Quercus velutina

Gypsy moth
Lymantria dispar

Black-legged tick
Ixodes scapularis

White-tailed deer
The only hoofed mammal in the eastern deciduous forest today, the white-tailed deer has recovered from habitat loss and overhunting. With forest returning, hunting now carefully managed, and the absence of their one-time wolf predator, the deer are considered "over abundant."

FOREST SALAMANDERS

At least 55 species of salamander, more than are found anywhere else on Earth, live in the forests of the southern Appalachian Mountains. About 20 are exclusive to the mountains. What is more, the group of lungless salamanders, which breathe through their skin, evolved here and, numbering 34 species, dominate the salamander fauna. The once-towering peaks of the ancient Appalachian range have eroded into gentle ridges and valleys. This process isolated salamanders, which rarely venture far from where they hatch, in different watersheds and on mountaintops, where they evolved into new species. For the same reason, this well-watered region is also rich in freshwater fish, turtles, mussels, crayfish, and insects. Because they live in and along streams and in other moist places under rocks, logs, and on the forest floor, salamanders are threatened by water pollution and habitat degradation. Even small changes due to global warming loom large for salamander species with restricted ranges.

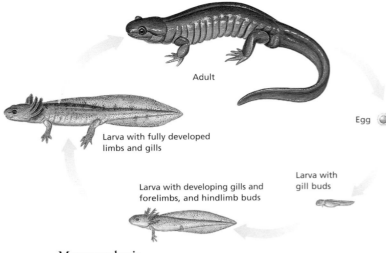

Adult

Egg

Larva with fully developed limbs and gills

Larva with developing gills and forelimbs, and hindlimb buds

Larva with gill buds

Metamorphosis

Many salamanders lay their eggs in water. The eggs hatch into larvae, which have gills and swim in search of prey, such as aquatic insects and their larvae. When salamander larvae reach a certain size they begin the process of metamorphosis, to change their body to better suit life on land. They grow tails and sprout legs and, except in the lungless species, develop lungs. In some salamander species, this transformation takes place within the egg.

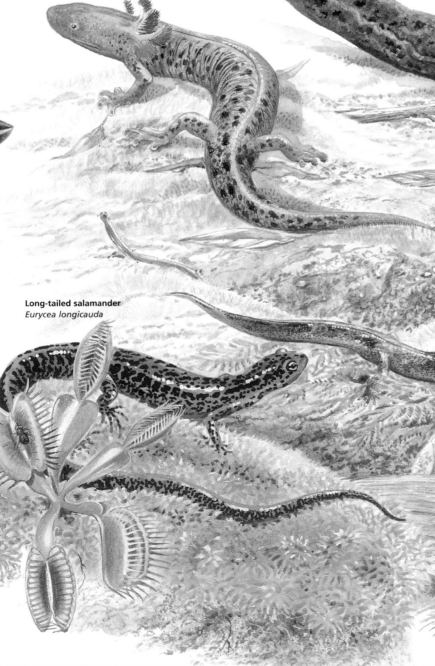

Mudpuppy
Necturus maculosus

Long-tailed salamander
Eurycea longicauda

Insect haven

Insects abound in the eastern deciduous forest, from the lofty heights of the canopy to the forest floor. Although mostly small, their combined weight probably exceeds that of the remaining animal life combined. Moths, butterflies, and their caterpillars are important food for many forest birds. Fierce yellowjacket wasps also prey on caterpillars, flies, and bees. Salamanders eat beetles and a host of other insects and their larvae.

Striped hawk moth
Hyles livornica

Lunar moth
Actius luna

Common yellowjacket
Paravespula vulgaris

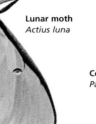

Stag beetle
Lucanus sp.

Venus flytrap
The Venus flytrap, a carnivorous plant, lures insects to its two-part leaves ringed with spiny teeth, with bright color and sweet secretions.

Red salamander
The red salamander eats small insects, worms, and other invertebrates, as well as smaller salamanders. It takes just 11 milliseconds to snatch prey using its long tongue, which is supported by a skeleton and tipped with a sticky pad.

Spotted salamander
Found only in deciduous forest, the spotted salamander spends much of its time hiding under logs or within the burrows of other animals. However, on a few warm, wet spring evenings these salamanders emerge in large numbers and migrate to small ponds to breed.

Salamanders

The salamanders of eastern North America range from the diminutive pigmy salamander, which is not as long as a small finger, to the arm's-length eastern hellbender. Whatever their size and secretive habits, salamanders are key players in their ecosystems. They are predators, prey, and nutrient recyclers. Many eat tiny insects, linking these creatures in the food chain to larger vertebrates, such as the birds and mammals that eat salamanders.

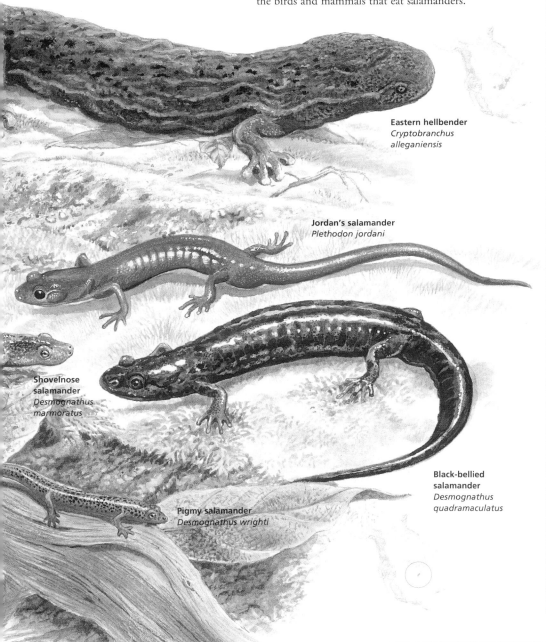

Eastern hellbender
*Cryptobranchus
alleganiensis*

Jordan's salamander
Plethodon jordani

**Shovelnose
salamander**
*Desmognathus
marmoratus*

**Black-bellied
salamander**
*Desmognathus
quadramaculatus*

Pigmy salamander
Desmognathus wrighti

FRUITFUL FUNGI

More than 2,000 species of mushroom, or fungi, are found in the damp forests of the Smoky Mountains National Park. Some live on organic material, such as leaf litter and animal dung, hastening its breakdown. Others enjoy a symbiotic relationship with trees. Called mycorrhizzae, these fungi extract carbohydrates from the tree and, in return, provide it with nutrients that it could not extract from the soil.

Witches' butter
Witches' butter is a kind of jelly fungi, a species whose fruiting bodies are gelatinous and often irregularly shaped. Found on oaks, beech, alder, and other deciduous tree wood, witches' butter is actually a parasite on other fungi that live on decaying wood.

Collared earthstars
Collared earthstars grow in the leaf litter of the deciduous forest, usually in groups. Visible in the foreground are newly sprouted fruiting bodies (mushrooms), with pointed tips, and an older earthstar, with the rounded top and collar that gives the species its name.

Shelf fungi
Shelf, or bracket, fungi, like the sulfur shelf, grows on dead oak wood as well as on living trunks, where it is a pathogen known as brown rot. The sulfur shelf is also known as the chicken of the woods. When cooked, its taste and texture are reminiscent of chicken.

THE COASTAL PLAINS

The Atlantic and Gulf of Mexico coastal plains encompass pine woodlands, moist deciduous forest, cypress swamps, salt and brackish marshes, and sandy beaches. Running along the coast from New York, around Florida, and west to east Texas, the plains are characterized by frequent fires, sandy soils, and wetlands. Chesapeake Bay, the largest estuary in the United States, is a prominent feature of the Atlantic coastal plains. Its 64,000-square-mile (165,760-km²) watershed includes parts of six states and the District of Columbia. However, little of the diverse natural plains habitats remains intact. They are now densely populated and, apart from major urbanization, have been logged and converted to agriculture, and beachside areas have been developed for recreation. Still, the coastal plains are rich in wildlife, especially migratory birds that frequent them during stopovers on their lengthy journeys between winter homes in South America and breeding sites as far north as the Arctic.

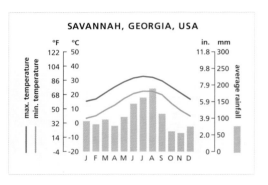

SAVANNAH, GEORGIA, USA

CONSERVATION WATCH

An isolated subspecies of the puma, the Florida panther lives in the swamps of south Florida. Pumas once ranged throughout eastern North America but hunting and habitat loss eliminated them from all but this retreat. Less than 100 of the critically endangered cats remain and they risk collisions with speeding vehicles.

Least bittern
The tiny least bittern has the uncanny ability to disappear among the reeds in which it forages. An alarmed least bittern will stand very tall, with its bill pointed skyward, to imitate a reed. It even sways in the wind, much like the reeds do.

Ancient species

Horseshoe crabs are an ancient species, some 540 million years old. They existed even before flowering plants and dinosaurs, and have changed little since. The North American species spawns on Atlantic beaches in spring. The massive clutches of eggs feed as many as a million shorebirds during their northward migration. Nesting sea turtles and fish also partake of the feast.

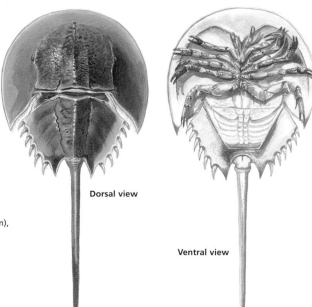

Dorsal view

Ventral view

Horseshoe crab
Female horseshoe crabs, with an average width of 9.5 inches (24 cm), are about 60 percent larger than their male counterparts. The first of six paired appendages on its underside is used to place food into the crab's central mouth.

Great blue heron
The largest heron in North America, the great blue heron, stands more than 4 feet (1.2 m) tall. Males and females perform elaborate courtship rituals to secure their bond before nesting begins. They raise their crests, puff their feathers, and joust with their bills.

Black skimmer
The black skimmer's large red and black bill is unusual in that the lower mandible is distinctly longer than the upper. Flying low over the surface of the water, these seabirds skim the water with their lower mandible to catch small fish. They often hunt at night.

Yellow-crested night heron
Rather large, hulking birds, yellow-crested night herons often nest in colonies, where they build stick nests overhanging water. These birds were nearly eliminated from the coastal plains of the United States in the late 1800s and early 1900s. Hunters killed and sold them as meat and their beautiful plumes decorated women's hats.

Nine-banded armadillo
Its body covered in shell-like plates, the nine-banded armadillo has expanded its range in the southeastern United States. First seen north of the Rio Grande, Texas, in about 1850, it has since ventured as far north as Kansas and Nebraska, and east to Florida.

Canebrakes for cover

Thickets of North American bamboos, called canes, once stood 20 feet (6 m) tall and stretched for miles along the coastal plains. Cut down to make way for farming, these thickets now survive only in scattered stands. They make a great wildlife habitat, providing cover, food, or both, for birds and mammals, and food for the caterpillars of moths and butterflies.

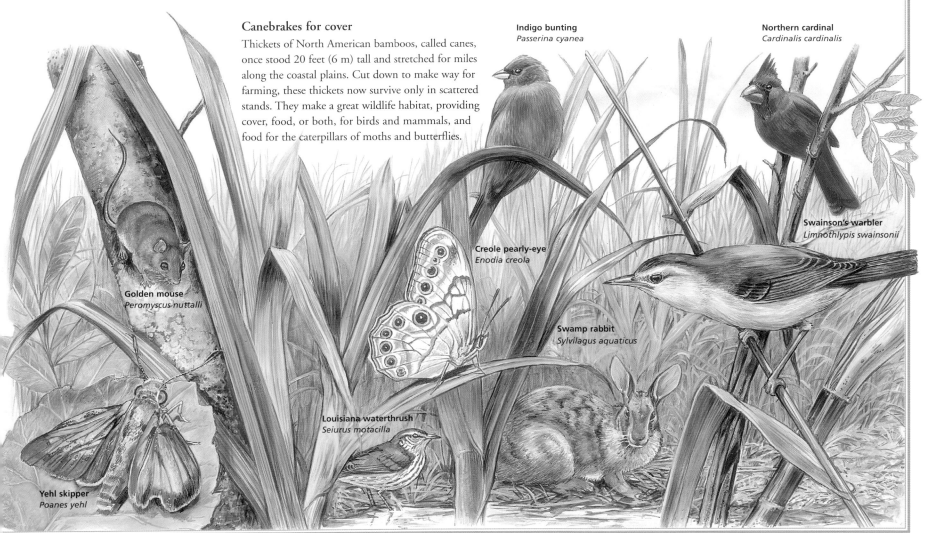

Indigo bunting
Passerina cyanea

Northern cardinal
Cardinalis cardinalis

Swainson's warbler
Limnothlypis swainsonii

Creole pearly-eye
Enodia creola

Golden mouse
Peromyscus nuttalli

Swamp rabbit
Sylvilagus aquaticus

Louisiana waterthrush
Seiurus motacilla

Yehl skipper
Poanes yehl

THE COASTAL PLAINS
BIRD MIGRATION

Birds have migrated across the Americas for millions of years. Some 200 species breed in summer in North America as far north as the Arctic Circle, when insect and plant food is abundant. They wing their way south as far as Tierra del Fuego, at the southern tip of South America, to avoid the meager fare available to them in winter, then retrace their flight the next spring. It is a spectacular phenomenon involving billions of birds in spring and fall, with huge numbers of these winged wanderers converging on a few choice stopover spots, such as Cape May, New Jersey. A million migratory shorebirds break their journey here in spring to feast on horseshoe crab eggs. But the fall is even more amazing. Funneled by geography, tens of thousands of migrating seabirds, raptors, and songbirds pour into this small peninsula on a single autumn day. However, many of the warblers and other migrants that pass through are in trouble, beset by habitat loss and fragmentation.

Red-winged blackbirds
Found throughout North and Central America south of the Arctic, red-winged blackbirds are the continent's most abundant birds. Some populations do not migrate but others, namely those that breed in Canada and northern United States, migrate to the south. Huge feeding flocks of several million birds may form during winter.

Sharp-shinned hawk
Migrating south from Canada in the fall, sharp-shinned hawks concentrate in large numbers at a few stopover sites on the Atlantic coast. Observers once counted 11,000 of these small, bird-eating hawks at Cape May on a single day in October.

Least bittern
Wetland habitats in both the least bittern's breeding and wintering range in North and South America are some of the world's most threatened.

Laughing gull
Laughing gulls that breed in the marshes and beaches of the northeast Atlantic coast migrate to Florida in winter.

American kestrel
Most kestrels that breed up north migrate south in the fall, perhaps tracking migrating green darner dragonflies, which kestrels prey on.

Piping plover
Diminutive piping plovers nest on Atlantic beaches and migrate in winter to similar habitats further south, from North Carolina to Mexico and the Caribbean. These ground-nesting birds are endangered due to habitat loss and human disturbance.

Black-throated blue warbler
Climate change threatens birds such as the black-throated blue warbler because it may influence food availability at breeding, stopover, and wintering sites.

Rose-breasted grosbeak
Rose-breasted grosbeaks that breed in the eastern parts of their range follow the Atlantic flyway through Central America and northwest South America to winter in southern Mexico. Those breeding in the north and west follow the Mississippi flyway.

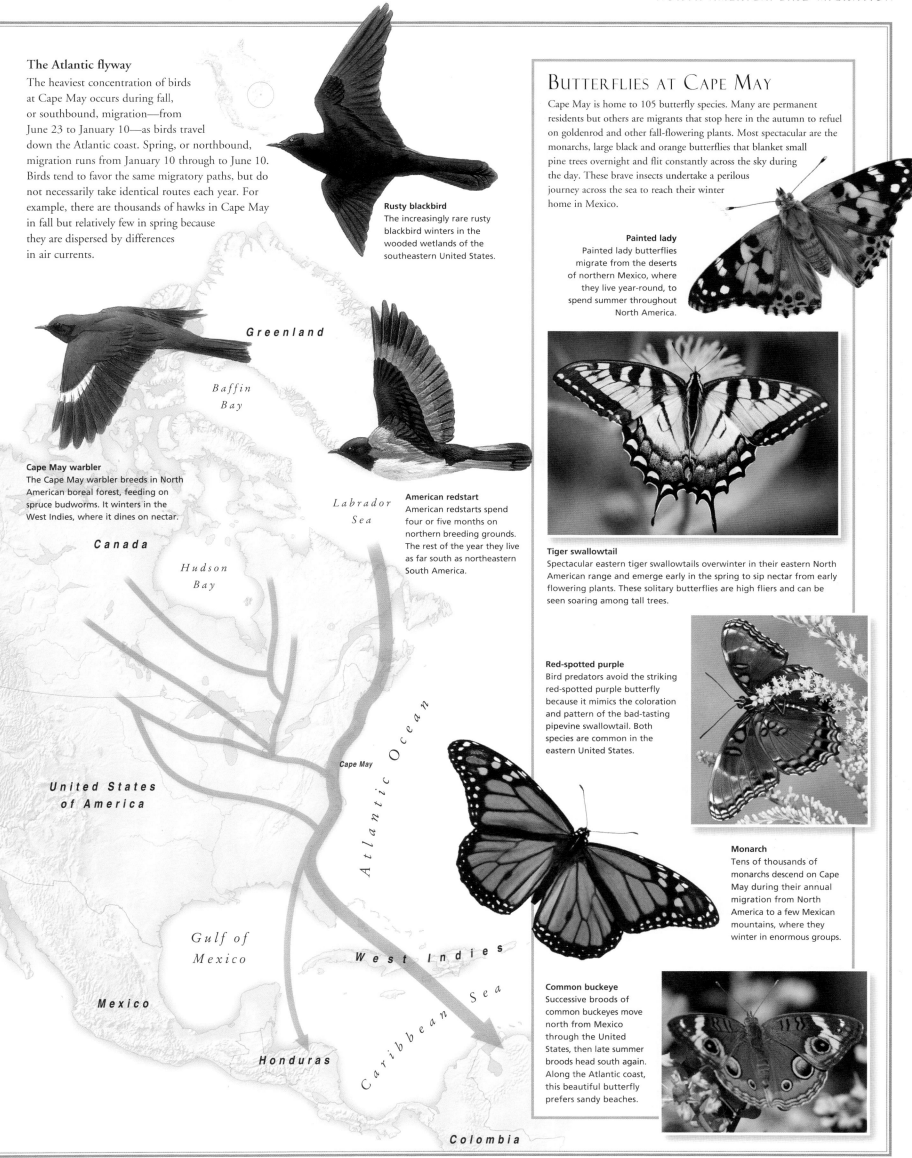

The Atlantic flyway

The heaviest concentration of birds at Cape May occurs during fall, or southbound, migration—from June 23 to January 10—as birds travel down the Atlantic coast. Spring, or northbound, migration runs from January 10 through to June 10. Birds tend to favor the same migratory paths, but do not necessarily take identical routes each year. For example, there are thousands of hawks in Cape May in fall but relatively few in spring because they are dispersed by differences in air currents.

Rusty blackbird
The increasingly rare rusty blackbird winters in the wooded wetlands of the southeastern United States.

Cape May warbler
The Cape May warbler breeds in North American boreal forest, feeding on spruce budworms. It winters in the West Indies, where it dines on nectar.

American redstart
American redstarts spend four or five months on northern breeding grounds. The rest of the year they live as far south as northeastern South America.

Greenland

Baffin Bay

Labrador Sea

Canada

Hudson Bay

United States of America

Atlantic Ocean

Cape May

Gulf of Mexico

West Indies

Caribbean Sea

Mexico

Honduras

Colombia

BUTTERFLIES AT CAPE MAY

Cape May is home to 105 butterfly species. Many are permanent residents but others are migrants that stop here in the autumn to refuel on goldenrod and other fall-flowering plants. Most spectacular are the monarchs, large black and orange butterflies that blanket small pine trees overnight and flit constantly across the sky during the day. These brave insects undertake a perilous journey across the sea to reach their winter home in Mexico.

Painted lady
Painted lady butterflies migrate from the deserts of northern Mexico, where they live year-round, to spend summer throughout North America.

Tiger swallowtail
Spectacular eastern tiger swallowtails overwinter in their eastern North American range and emerge early in the spring to sip nectar from early flowering plants. These solitary butterflies are high fliers and can be seen soaring among tall trees.

Red-spotted purple
Bird predators avoid the striking red-spotted purple butterfly because it mimics the coloration and pattern of the bad-tasting pipevine swallowtail. Both species are common in the eastern United States.

Monarch
Tens of thousands of monarchs descend on Cape May during their annual migration from North America to a few Mexican mountains, where they winter in enormous groups.

Common buckeye
Successive broods of common buckeyes move north from Mexico through the United States, then late summer broods head south again. Along the Atlantic coast, this beautiful butterfly prefers sandy beaches.

This remarkably colored red-eyed tree frog clasps a heliconia in a Costa Rican rain forest. Most tree frogs have adhesive pads on their fingers and toes that help them stick to leaves and branches. Some even have an opposable first finger, like a thumb, that allows them to grasp twigs and stems.

CENTRAL &
SOUTH AMERICA

CENTRAL & SOUTH AMERICA

Highly distinctive species from every class in the animal kingdom are found in Central and South America. Biodiversity is particularly remarkable in Central America, which supports around 7 percent of Earth's species on less than one-half a percent of its land. The spectacular landscapes in which these animals live, dramatically exemplified by the continent's physical geography, are every bit as varied. The region is dominated by large river systems and wetlands, but also renowned for its imposing mountain chains and volcanoes, deserts, lakes, vast grasslands, and tropical forests. Coastal and marine life is abundant amid the tropical coral reefs, mangroves, and seagrass beds. At its southernmost tip South America also supports sea ice.

Central America
Located at the junction of two continental masses and the world's largest oceans, this region is rich in biodiversity.

The Gran Chaco
Climatic extremes and wooded grasslands that become swamps in the rainy season are typical of this region.

Amazon Rain Forest
The largest rain forest in the world, which crosses nine international borders, features wildlife and ecosystems barely seen elsewhere.

Patagonia
Dramatic mountainous landscape at America's southern extreme adjoins the rugged coast, where Antarctic animals are regular visitors.

The Andes Wilderness
Low valleys grazed by camelids and snowy peaks patrolled by the spectacular condor typify the wild beauty of these mountains.

Life in the Caribbean
Shallow warm waters harbor magnificent coral reefs and their resident turtles, fish, and crustaceans in the stunning Caribbean.

The Galápagos Islands
The fascinating species found here are supremely adapted to the harsh life on one of Earth's major tropical archipelagos.

CLIMATE ZONES
- Wet tropical
- Seasonal tropical
- Arid
- Semiarid
- Mediterranean
- Subtropical
- Continental
- Temperate
- Cold temperate

Climate

The northwest coast, parts of the northeast and east coasts, and much of the Amazon Basin experience hot, wet weather year-round. Moist onshore winds are the main drivers of the subtropical conditions that extend down the east coast. Cold ocean currents off the west coast dry the air, producing an arid coastal strip. Conditions vary across the Andes; generally it is hot and wet in the north, hot and dry in the center, and cold and wet in the far south. Patagonia, east of the Andes, has low rainfall.

VEGETATION ZONES
- Tropical forest
- Seasonal tropical forest
- Desert
- Tropical grassland
- Mediterranean forest and scrub
- Midlatitude grassland
- Midlatitude forest
- Boreal forest

Vegetation

Amazon rain forests extend over much of the great river basin, giving way to cloud forest in the Andes and tropical deciduous woodlands in the north and east. The savanna grasslands that characterize the Gran Chaco and the Brazilian Highlands merge to the southeast with more temperate grasses on the Pampas. Thick stands of temperate rain forest occur on the southern Andes but the Central Andes and Patagonia are sparsely vegetated. The Atacama Desert is virtually devoid of plant life.

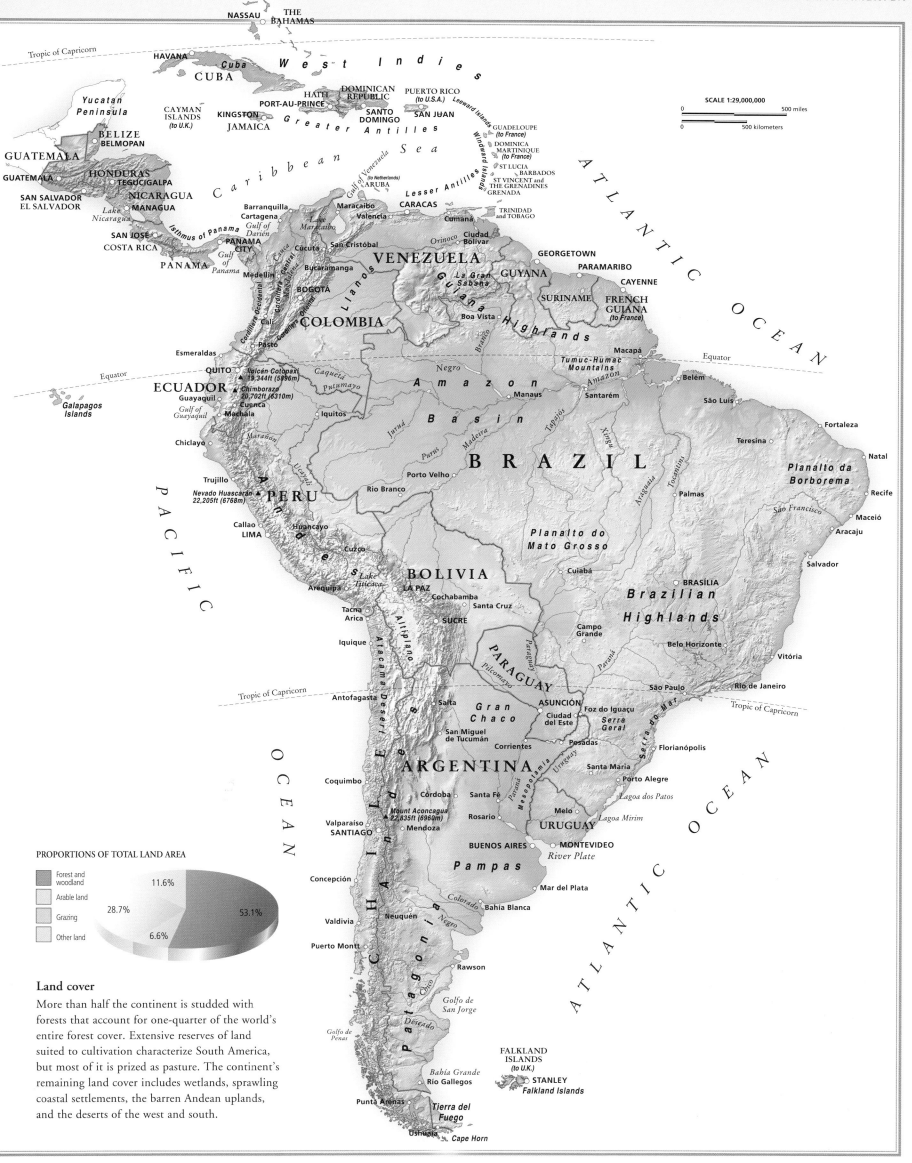

Land cover

More than half the continent is studded with forests that account for one-quarter of the world's entire forest cover. Extensive reserves of land suited to cultivation characterize South America, but most of it is prized as pasture. The continent's remaining land cover includes wetlands, sprawling coastal settlements, the barren Andean uplands, and the deserts of the west and south.

PROPORTIONS OF TOTAL LAND AREA
- Forest and woodland — 53.1%
- Arable land — 11.6%
- Grazing — 28.7%
- Other land — 6.6%

CENTRAL AMERICA

The near-equatorial isthmus of Central America connects the South and North of the American continent and serves as a terrestrial bridge between the Pacific and Atlantic oceans. This narrow strip of land, measuring 202,000 square miles (523,000 km²), formed 3 million years ago and is today the territory of seven countries: Guatemala, Honduras, El Salvador, Belize, Nicaragua, Costa Rica, and Panama. It holds a greater concentration of plant and animal life than anywhere else in the world. Central America is characterized by contrasting landscapes, ranging from dry, sea-level forests to those shrouded in mist, and from lofty peaks and coastal marshes to fertile valleys that continue to be shaped by volcanic activity. The abundant natural bounty here includes rivers and lakes, islands, thermal springs, lagoons, estuaries, beaches, and reefs. Distinct climates meet and merge in Central America as a result of topography rather than seasonal change. Average annual temperatures fall within the narrow range of 65–86°F (18–30°C).

SCALE 1:13,000,000

0   300 miles

0   300 kilometers

SAN SALVADOR, EL SALVADOR

Capybara
The largest of all the 1,729 rodent species, the semi-aquatic capybara is extremely agile in the water, using its partly webbed toes like tiny paddles. Troops, containing up to 20 animals, live along riverbanks where young capybaras are sometimes preyed on by caimans. However, this adult has little to fear—it is too large a meal for the surrounding caimans, which are more likely to hunt for fish or frogs.

 Scarlet macaws
Scarlet macaws are large, colorful parrots that are often seen perched on cliffs. Here they consume clay, which helps them digest poisonous chemicals found in the unripe fruit they feed on. Macaws fly in pairs or small groups and can reach speeds of 35 miles per hour (56 km/h).

Boa constrictor
The boa constrictor is a large, solitary snake with powerful muscles that allow it to squeeze its prey until it suffocates. The snake can open its jaws wide and swallows its prey whole, head-first. Strong acids in its stomach help the constrictor digest its meal.

White-faced capuchin
The white-faced capuchin is easy to spot in the wild. Small and inquisitive, it usually travels in groups from tree to tree with the aid of its prehensile tail. These monkeys forage for fruit and insects at all forest levels and communicate using chatters and shrieks.

Mantled howler monkey
The mantled howler monkey is often heard before it is seen. Even in dense rain forest its roars and piglike grunts travel for more than half a mile (0.8 km). A particularly large hyoid bone in the monkey's throat allows it to make such a resonant noise.

Tayra
The tayra is a mustelid related to the otter, but it lives in trees. It hunts small vertebrates, such as rabbits and lizards, and also feeds on carrion and fruits. Similar to a weasel, this skilled climber is able to jump from tree to tree when threatened.

TENT-MAKING BATS

Honduran white bats are among the few bat species that construct their own roosts. They bite the veins of large heliconia leaves until they collapse downward, forming a partially enclosed, tent-like space beneath which the bats hang upside down. These "tents" provide protection from jungle rains, sunlight, and predators such as snakes. One male and five or six females usually roost together.

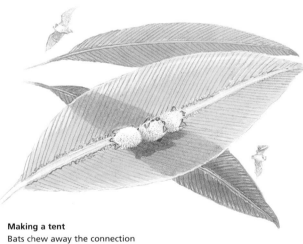

Making a tent
Bats chew away the connection between the midrib and edge of the leaf until it droops.

Protected roost
The little Honduran white bats roost in the tent they have created.

CENTRAL AMERICA
RAIN FORESTS

Central American rain forests are found in the tropical zone between the Tropic of Cancer and Tropic of Capricorn, where the weather is hot and humid year-round. Days and nights are of almost equal length and there is little seasonal variation, with an average temperature throughout the year of 80.6°F (27°C) and ample sunlight. Abundant rainfall, no less than four inches (100 mm) per month, is a result of cooling moisture produced by wind and ocean currents. Viewed from above, the tree canopy is an evergreen cover of towering trees that reach heights of 60 to 150 feet (20–50 m). These giants are laced with vines and lianas, and their trunks coated with epiphytes, bromeliads, and orchids. The forest's lower layers are densely planted with smaller trees and shrubs, and the deeply shaded forest floor is covered with decaying plant material. Birds of every size and color are found here, as are bats, monkeys, reptiles, ants, and many other insects that share a symbiotic relationship with plants as seed dispersers.

DEFORESTATION
- 1800
- 1960
- Present

Blue morpho butterfly
The blue morpho butterfly owes its coloring to tiny ridges on its wings that reflect light, giving it dazzling visibility. By contrast, the wing undersides are brown. Generally the butterfly rests with its wings closed to make it less visible to enemies.

FROGS AND TOADS

The frogs and toads of Central American rain forests include climbers that inhabit the canopy and ground-dwelling species that shelter in caves, burrows, or rock crevices. Most, however, live in ponds and streams. Their bulging eyes enable them to see in any direction, and their sticky tongues are adept at capturing insect prey. Rain forests echo with loud frog and toad calls during the mating season.

Harlequin frog
(Atelopus varius)

Poison dart frog
While some frogs rely on camouflage to remain unobtrusive, the brilliant red skin and blue legs of the poison dart frog serve as a warning to predators. The toxic excretions of this 2.3-inch (6-cm) frog were used by native people on the tips of their arrows.

Most tadpoles must stay in water, but the rain forest air is so moist that the poison dart frog can carry its young on its back.

Red-eyed tree frog
(Agalychnis callidryas)

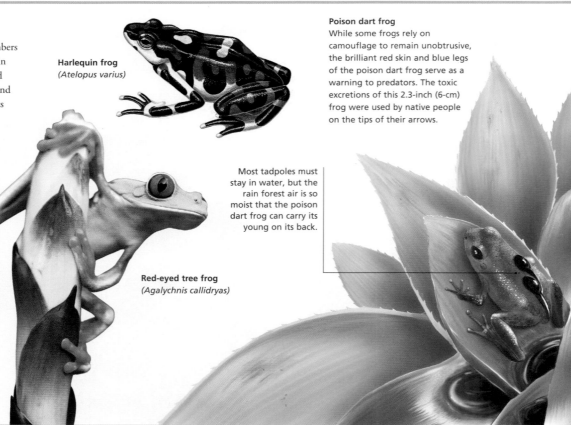

Golden toad
The golden toad, an endemic species of Costa Rica, is thought to be extinct in the wild. During the rainy season, hundreds of black females and yellow males used to gather in small ponds to mate. Females produced 200 to 400 eggs and, after hatching, the larvae remained in water for about five weeks as they progressed toward adulthood.

Three-toed sloth
Although sometimes taken for a primate, the brown-throated three-toed sloth is more closely related to the armadillo. Its movements and metabolism are slow; the sloth takes almost a month to digest a single meal and moves at an average speed of 1.2 miles per hour (2 km/h). Sloths are strictly arboreal and descend to the ground only to defecate.

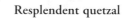

Kinkajou
The kinkajou is also known as the sugar bear because of its habit of eating honey, nectar, and sweet fruits. It licks nectar from flowers with its flexible tongue. Pollen that sticks to its fur is carried from flower to flower, making it an important pollinator.

Resplendent quetzal

The quetzal is often found in wild avocado trees, the fruits of which it swallows whole. This bird constructs its nest in the cavity of a dead tree, choosing a soft trunk that is in an advanced state of decomposition. The two feathers that form its tail, which can be 23 inches (59 cm) long, protrude from the nest to protect them from damage.

Spectacled owl
White "glasses" in the region of its yellow eyes give the spectacled owl its name. Juveniles, such as the bird on the left, have the markings in reverse; it takes years to reach the full adult plumage of the bird on the right.

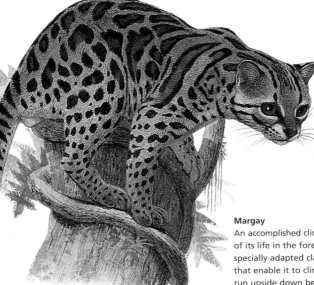

Margay
An accomplished climber, the margay spends most of its life in the forest canopy. This agile cat has specially adapted claws and rotating ankle joints that enable it to climb down trees headfirst and run upside down beneath branches.

Keel-billed toucan
Although it appears weighty, the keel-billed toucan's bill is light and hollow, and supported by thin rods of bone. The toucan employs its bill skillfully; using its feather-like tongue to catch insects and flick fruits down its throat.

CENTRAL AMERICA
THE JAGUAR

The jaguar is a top terrestrial predator in Central and South America, and plays an important role in stabilizing ecosystems and regulating the populations of its prey species. Its survival depends on more than one habitat and its presence is also critical for other animals. The jaguar's range has severely contracted to Mexico and Central America, mainly in Costa Rica, northern Guatemala, and Belize. Some populations are also found in Mato Grosso, Brazil, and in the Pantanal, an ecoregion bordering Brazil, Bolivia, and Paraguay. Factors that influence the jaguar's future prospects include its persecution by humans, because it is seen as a threat to people and livestock; hunting for fur and sport; a shortage of prey; loss of habitat, including the conversion of land for cattle ranching; and inadequate protection measures. Its survival depends on an intimate understanding of its habitat, gathering population data for both the jaguar and its prey, monitoring disease, education to mitigate conflicts with cattle ranchers, and developing protection measures.

Climbing
Jaguars depend on forest for their survival; it is their original and preferred habitat for hunting. They climb trees to lie in wait for wild prey below. But because of forest loss as a result of new settlements and clearing for pasture, some jaguars now also kill domestic animals and livestock in areas close to human populations.

Present
Former

CONSERVATION WATCH

Historically, the jaguar's range stretched from the southwestern United States to southern Argentina, but today it is extinct in the United States and numbers have drastically declined in Mexico and Argentina. Recovery programs have included on-the-ground monitoring, predator controls, minimizing livestock conflicts, and creating jaguar reserves.

Swimming
The jaguar is an excellent swimmer and thrives near rivers, lakes, and streams. When hunting fish it stalks, under cover, on its target's blind spot, before leaping into the water to catch its prey. The jaguar is also capable of carrying a large kill while swimming.

Fish prey
Like other big cats, jaguars routinely catch fish for the proteins and essential fatty acids they contain. Apart from fish, cats rarely prey on small animals because of their relatively low nutritional value. However, rabbits are an exception, and are highly sought after by leopards.

Coat
The jaguar can be distinguished by the presence of small dots within the larger rosette markings on its magnificent coat. Each marking has a unique pattern that is like a fingerprint.

Leopard-like ancestors

Jaguars are thought to have evolved from leopard-like ancestors in Eurasia, and to have arrived on the American continent 1.8 million to 10,000 years ago via the Bering land bridge. The modern jaguar is smaller and has shorter legs than its cousin the leopard, although both these members of the genus *Panthera* have muscular bodies, roar, climb trees, and enjoy swimming. Female jaguars reach sexual maturity at the age of three and males at four years.

Offspring
Female jaguars bear a litter of one to four cubs after a gestation period of 91 to 111 days, with births peaking during the rainy season when prey is most abundant. The cubs are born blind but gain their sight at two weeks. Females mother the cubs for two years, after which time they are ready to find their own territory.

Teeth
Four canine teeth, up to 2 inches (5 cm) long, are used for killing, while the sharp, scissor-like carnassial teeth enable the jaguar to crush bones, or to hold meat and cut it at the same time.

Eyes
The pupils of the night-hunting jaguar can contract to mere slits and its night vision is up to seven times better than that of a human. It also has excellent binocular vision for judging distances.

PREY

Jaguars are known to eat more than 85 species of prey, taking advantage of the diversity of animals that are found in rain forests. They prefer to hunt at night, but may capture prey during the day if it is available. Jaguar prey ranges from domestic livestock to tapirs, deer, sloths, peccaries, capybaras, agoutis, crocodiles, snakes, monkeys, and fish. They can consume up to 55 pounds (25 kg) of meat in one sitting, followed by periods of famine.

Capybara
Because capybaras live in groups, a jaguar has a good chance of taking at least one while it feeds underwater, or catching one on land, where capybaras are less agile.

Sloth
Like many other predators, jaguars prey on sloths. A green coating of algae on the sloth's fur aids its camouflage in the rain forest canopy.

Baird's Tapir
Baird's tapir becomes active at dusk, foraging along riverbanks. It is easily detected by a stalking jaguar employing its highly effective night vision.

Amazon Rain Forest

The Amazon rain forest is the oldest and largest tropical forest in the world. It extends across the Amazon River basin, a region of 2.6 million square miles (6.7 million km²) drained by the Amazon River. Sixty-two percent of the basin is in Brazil but it also covers parts of Peru, Bolivia, French Guyana, Suriname, Guyana, Venezuela, Colombia, and Ecuador. This huge expanse of rain forest contains an amazing collection of wildlife, including amphibians, birds, insects, mammals, and reptiles. Tarantulas, caterpillars, scorpions, anacondas, caimans, jaguars, sloths, tamarins, toucans, and vampire bats all occur in this region. Although some soils in the Amazon rain forest have declined in fertility, the area is a web of diverse landscapes and ecosystems. Dense, jungle-like forests filled with towering trees merge with open forests shaded by palms and tangled with lianas. High humidity, abundant rainfall, and an average temperature of 75°F (24°C) are common characteristics across the basin.

SCALE 1:37,500,000

0 .... 500 miles

0 .... 500 kilometers

Big River Creatures

Amazon River waters have a high diversity of fish, estimated at more than 3,000 species. During each rainy season extensive forested areas adjacent to the river are flooded and many fish, reptiles, and mammals move into the newly flooded areas to feed, mainly on fallen fruits from the trees. They also reproduce here, returning to the main channels when the floodwaters recede.

Pink river dolphin
The pink river dolphin is the largest and most common of the world's five freshwater dolphins. It uses echolocation to find prey in the muddy rivers of flooded jungles. Age, water clarity, temperature, and location determine its body colors, which can vary from pink to gray or white.

Black caiman
The black caiman is the largest member of the Alligatorinae family. This predator lives along slow-moving rivers and lakes, and in the seasonally flooded savannas of the Amazon basin. Its prey includes capybaras, fish, turtles, and deer.

Amazon River
The Amazon River is the world's second longest river. Its 3,976-mile (6,400-km) course, which includes 15,000 tributaries, meanders from the Andes to the Atlantic Ocean. The Amazon is the source of almost 20 percent of all river water that flows into the oceans.

Giant river otter
Only a few thousand giant river otters are thought to survive in the wild because of hunting by humans. With a body length of 80 inches (2 m), this is the world's longest river otter. It propels itself through water using its powerful paddle-shaped tail.

Pirarucu
The carnivorous, air-breathing pirarucu, the world's largest freshwater fish, is thought to be 200 million years old. It can grow to up to 120 inches (3 m) in length and weigh up to 400 pounds (180 kg).

Rain forest

The Amazon rain forest can be divided vertically into four layers, each representing a unique ecosystem. At the emergent level, eagles and parrots inhabit the tallest trees. The broad crowns of these giants form the canopy, which is home to snakes, toucans, tree frogs, monkeys, parakeets, orchids, and bromeliads. In the understory, shrubs and ferns grow larger leaves to capture sunlight, but only a thin layer of decaying organic matter is found on the forest floor.

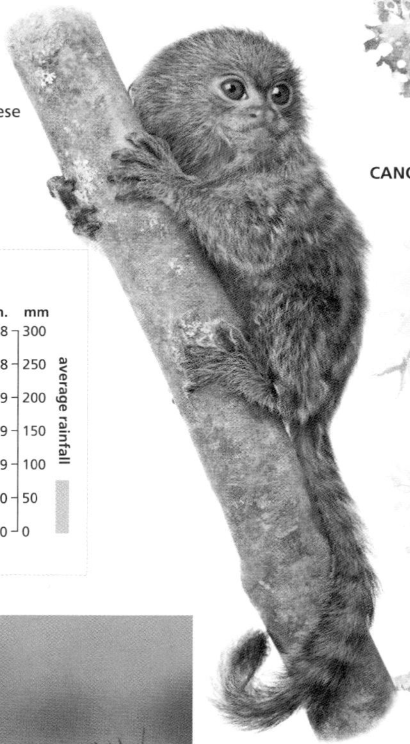

Pygmy marmoset
Inhabitants of rain forests canopies, pygmy marmosets are the smallest monkeys. Habitat destruction does not seem to have affected these primates, but some populations have declined because of the pet trade. Public education is aimed at reducing human disturbances and helping to monitor the trade.

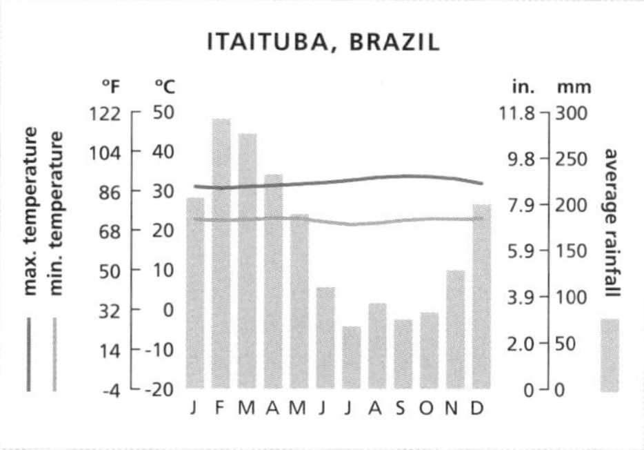

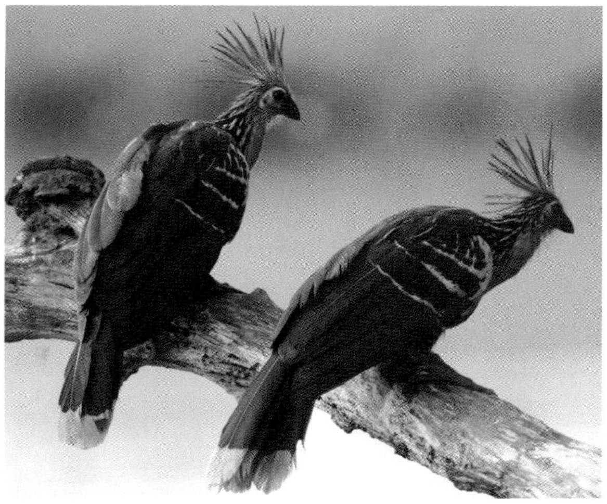

ITAITUBA, BRAZIL
°F °C
122 50
104 40
86 30
68 20
50 10
32 0
14 -10
-4 -20
in. mm
11.8 300
9.8 250
7.9 200
5.9 150
3.9 100
2.0 50
0 0
max. temperature
min. temperature
average rainfall
J F M A M J J A S O N D

Hoatzin
The hoatzin, which belongs to a primitive bird family, lives in flocks of 50 or more. These birds perch on low or middle branches that overhang water, and eat green leaves and buds. They have a large food-storage pouch and esophagus for converting plant carbohydrates into sugars they can digest.

CONSERVATION WATCH

Since 1970, more than 232,000 square miles (600,000 km²) of Amazon rain forest has been destroyed, occupied, or altered by human activity. It continues to be threatened by hunting, unsustainable logging, illegal gold mining, agriculture and cattle ranching, dam construction, fire, and gas and oil mining operations. At the current rate of loss, 55 percent of the rain forest could be gone by 2030.

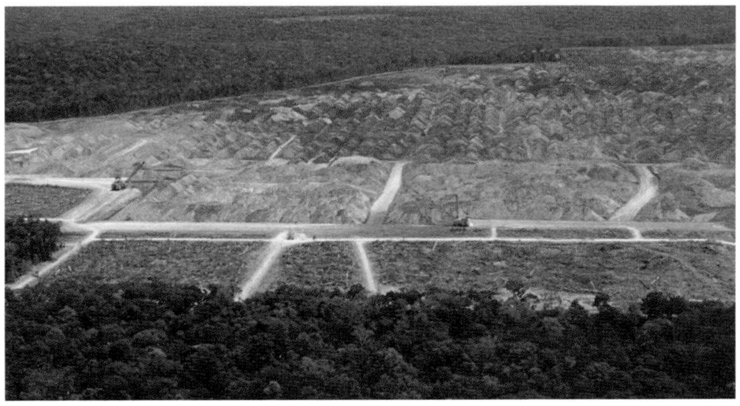

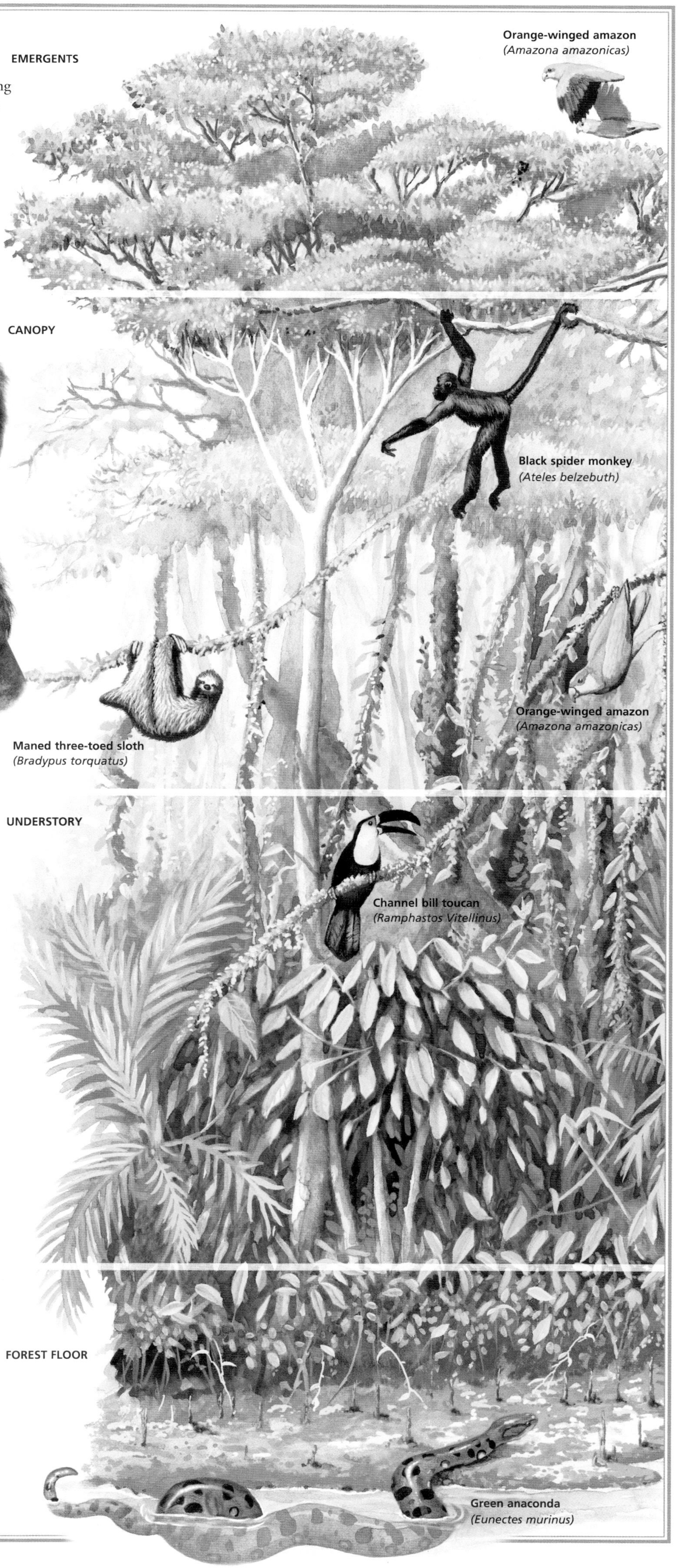

EMERGENTS
Orange-winged amazon
(Amazona amazonicas)
CANOPY
Black spider monkey
(Ateles belzebuth)
Orange-winged amazon
(Amazona amazonicas)
Maned three-toed sloth
(Bradypus torquatus)
UNDERSTORY
Channel bill toucan
(Ramphastos Vitellinus)
FOREST FLOOR
Green anaconda
(Eunectes murinus)

AMAZON RAIN FOREST
LIFE IN THE TREETOPS

Most of the species diversity within tropical rain forests is concentrated in the canopy, just below the top, emergent, layer. This dense ceiling of closely spaced trees, which rarely interlock, stretches for vast distances. Canopy dwellers are well-adapted to deal with the forest openings by climbing, jumping, or flying. It is estimated that biodiversity within the canopy includes 40 percent of all plant and animal species globally. Some of the world's loudest birds and primates, which rely on sound signals to communicate because the dense leaf cover precludes visual territorial displays, are found here. Other important species are bats and small mammals that coexist with a high number of insects and their allies. These, in turn, have evolved camouflage coloration to protect themselves from birds of prey, lizards, and frogs. All creatures of the canopy are adapted to take advantage of treetop resources, such as nesting sites, transit routes, hiding places, and a diet of insects, fruits, seeds, flowers, and leaves.

Toucan barbet
The colorful toucan barbet hops from branch to branch, feeding on a diet of insects and fruit, from the ground right up to the forest canopy. Its distinctive call is a repetition of short, foghorn-like notes. Breeding pairs nest in hollows in dead trees.

Storing carbon, releasing oxygen
Forest canopies absorb carbon dioxide from the atmosphere and convert it into oxygen. The canopy thereby plays an important part in global climate regulation because it enables the exchange of heat, water vapor, and atmospheric gases.

Common fruit bat
Fruit bats digest food quickly, without microbial fermentation in the stomach, so they must constantly forage for meals. As a consequence, these bats are a key species in the pollination of tropical fruits, and many plants rely on fruit bats for the dispersal of seeds.

Julia butterfly
A yellow-orange tropical butterfly with long forewings, the Julia butterfly is a fast-flying, long-lived species. It is active during the day, feeding on the nectar of flowers, such as lantana and shepherd's needle.

Hairy protection
Julia butterfly females lay their eggs on new passionflowers, the leaves of which nourish their larvae. Caterpillars rely on their short antennae to locate food, and defend themselves with fine, irritating bristles that lodge in the skin of their predators.

Emperor tamarin
The emperor tamarin lives in groups and communicates using strident squeaks. The male is an attentive father, assisting at the birth of its offspring and taking responsibility for their grooming and transportation. This tiny monkey is territorial and fiercely defends its area.

Red howler monkey
The red howler monkey travels through the forest by clambering along tree branches and lianas, but also descends to the ground, where it walks and runs. It is most active in the morning and evening. Its calls carry more than 1.5 miles (3 km) through the forest.

Versicolored barbet
The versicolored barbet, which is distinguished by the bristles that border its heavy bill, is a member of the Ramphastidae family and is closely related to toucans. Like all fruit-eating species, this arboreal bird plays an important role in seed dispersal, regurgitating seed pits throughout the forest.

⚡CONSERVATION WATCH
The pied tamarin, which has one of the smallest ranges of any primate, is dying out in the forests of the Amazon. Its habitat has been reduced, and is now fragmented and isolated because of urban expansion and agriculture. This small monkey, which weighs just 0.9 pounds (400 g), lives in groups of two to 10, and has a lifespan of just nine years.

Brown-eared woolly opossum
The woolly opossum's large, protruding eyes face forward, giving it a monkey-like appearance. Its hands and feet are adapted for climbing and gripping, and its flexible prehensile tail provides extra support. It is usually solitary, but opossums gather where fruit is plentiful.

Orange-winged parrot
The sociable orange-winged parrot moves through the crowns of tall trees searching for ripe fruits and nuts. True to its name, this parrot has a brilliant orange patch on its wings, visible as it flies over the forest at dawn.

Harpy eagle
The largest and most powerful raptor of the tropical rain forest is the harpy eagle, which preys upon tree-dwelling mammals. Like other birds of prey, it brings green twigs to its nest to protect its young from insects and parasites, and to ensure a cooler home environment.

THE ANDES WILDERNESS

The Andes is the world's longest mountain range. It stretches for 5,000 miles (8,000 km) and mountain peaks reach higher than 12,000 feet (3,600 m) along half its length. The mountain system forms the western border of South America and extends through Colombia, Venezuela, Ecuador, Peru, Bolivia, Chile, and Argentina. Glaciers, snow-capped volcanoes, desert plateaus, cloud forests, deep gorges incised by rivers, and peaceful valleys characterize the landscape. Conifers and ferns abound and wildlife is richly varied: 50 percent of the plant and animal species found here are unique to the area. The movement of sedimentary rocks and tectonic forces that helped form the Andes some 199 million years ago continue to cause earthquakes and volcanic eruptions even today. The weather varies significantly, depending on the location, elevation, and proximity to the sea. It ranges from wet and warm conditions averaging 64°F (18°C) to freezing temperatures above the snow line.

SCALE 1:37,500,000

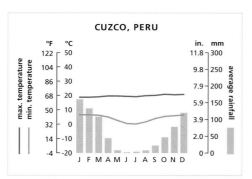

CUZCO, PERU

Treetop platform

The spectacled bear's diet consists of fruits and bromeliads, which grow on high tree branches that cannot support the animal's weight. To reach the fruit and flowers, the bear bends the branches toward itself. Smaller branches that snap off are used by the bear to build a rough nest that serves as a strong feeding and sleeping platform for several days.

Spectacled bear

The spectacled or Andean bear lives mainly in cloud forests. It is the only representative of the family Ursidae in South America and the only surviving member of the genus *Tremarctos,* thanks largely to its ability to climb even the tallest trees. It has good eyesight and is named for the markings around its eyes.

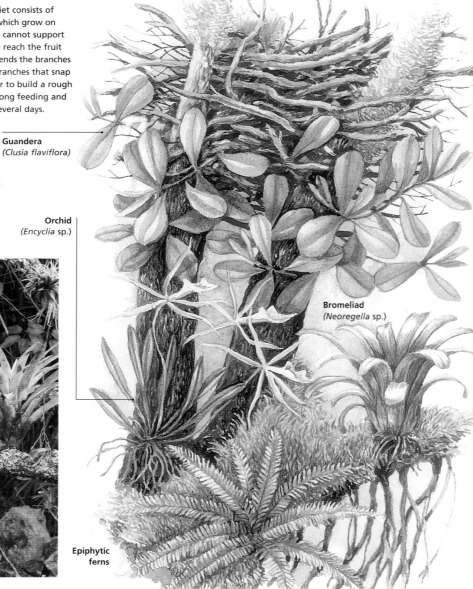

Bear's nest

Guandera
(*Clusia flaviflora*)

Orchid
(*Encyclia* sp.)

Bromeliad
(*Neoregella* sp.)

Epiphytic
ferns

Rugged beauty
Spectacular granite pillars and black sedimentary peaks dominate the rugged Andean landscape in locations such as Torres del Paine National Park, in Chile. Aconcagua, the highest point in the Americas and the tallest peak in the world outside Asia, is another iconic Andean view.

Taruca
Throughout the day, taruca of both sexes and all ages gather in tight-knit herds, led by an adult female. During the summer months the herds move up to higher slopes, but in winter these animals, also known as huemul, shelter in the lower valleys of the Andes.

Andean cock-of-the-rock
The female cock-of-the-rock builds a shallow nest of mud and vegetation on rock walls, hence the bird's name. The polygamous males compete in a mating ritual that includes dances, gymnastics, plumage displays, and vocal challenges.

CONSERVATION WATCH

The Brazilian tapir, a large animal with a distinctive fleshy snout, prefers water to land. Its peaceful nature and meaty physique make it a favorite hunting target. However, the tapir is now vulnerable because of such illegal hunting, combined with the destruction of its tropical forest habitat. After a gestation of 400 days, females produce just one offspring.

Andean red fox
A long-lived solitary hunter, the Andean red fox is one the greatest predators of this region. It hunts mostly small mammals but also takes poultry and livestock, bringing it into conflict with farmers. The fox is under pressure from hunters, who prize its fur.

Giant anteater
As its name suggests, the giant anteater feeds voraciously on ants and termites, consuming up to 30,000 in a day. It claws open termite mounds and uses its tubular snout and long sticky tongue to gather up insects. Though generally docile, it can defend itself against pumas and jaguars.

THE ANDES WILDERNESS
THE CONDOR

Considered to be the largest flying bird, the Andean condor is in danger of extinction across a significant portion of its range. Its decline has been most marked since 1973, in part caused by aggressive hunting, loss of habitat and therefore food, air pollution, water contamination, and collisions with structures such as power lines. The condor's vulnerability to threats is undoubtedly increased by its slow rate of reproduction and years spent reaching breeding maturity. Population decline has been most dramatic in Ecuador, Venezuela, and Peru. Biologists estimate that a few thousand birds remain in the wild, concentrated mostly along the southern section of the Andes mountains. This bird of prey and its close cousin, the California condor, are part of the New World vultures, a family more closely related to storks than to the vultures of Africa. Standing nearly 3 feet (90 cm) tall, the condor feeds on the carrion of animals such as deer, elk, cows, and llamas.

PREY ON NEWBORNS

Condors prefer open areas to search for carrion, newborns, and dying animals, which are their main food sources. If a meal has been particularly large, they may have to spend hours on the ground or perched on a low branch before they are able to take off again. Condors can travel 200 miles (320 km) a day soaring at great heights while foraging for food. They are able to survive without a meal for at least two weeks.

● Puma
The puma is one of the main carnivorous predators in the Andes, but even this successful hunter must protect its cubs from condors that circle overhead.

● Northern pudu
The world's smallest deer, the 12-inch (30-cm) tall pudu is one of the condor's favorite meals. It also feeds on the remains of sheep, llama, vicuña, cattle, seals, and the eggs of seabirds.

Carrion diet

Condors are not hunters. They locate carrion by sight or by following smaller birds. This helps other scavengers because the condor is capable of tearing through the tough hides of some carcasses. The only member of the genus *Vultur*, the condor can live for up to 50 years and mates for life. It communicates by grunting and hissing.

Dining
The average weight of a condor is 30 pounds (15 kg) and it can eat up to 4.5 pounds (2 kg) in one sitting. Older condors eat before the younger birds.

The largest bird of prey

Condors are well-adapted carcass feeders. Since they are not outfitted to stalk, their feet have rounded claws instead of the sharp talons of raptors. Bare skin on a condor's head and neck keeps it safe from bacteria when it sticks its heads into carcasses, and its beak is tailored for tearing fleshy tissue.

Naked head
A naked head and neck enables the condor to feed off carcasses without soiling its feathers. Blood vessels concentrated over the head help to radiate heat and keep the bird cool.

Feet
The condor has strong legs but relatively weak, blunt nails that are more like toenails than talons. The feet are thus better adapted to walking than grasping.

Inflatable neck
Condors do not possess vocal cords, so they inflate air sacs in their neck when agitated or excited. This gives them the appearance of being larger than they really are.

In flight
Condors flap their wings to lift off the ground, but rarely do so when flying. Instead, they rely on thermal air currents to stay aloft. A condor's wingspan can exceed 10 feet (3 m), which enables it to fly in a way that expends as little energy as possible.

CONSERVATION WATCH

Efforts are being made to breed condors in captivity for return to the wild as part of the American Zoo and Aquarium Association's Species Survival Plan program. Thirty-nine condors reared in North America and Colombia have been reintroduced to Peru, Colombia, and Venezuela. Colombian biologists satellite-tracking the birds found that they survived and are now breeding—a major milestone.

GALAPAGOS ISLANDS

Nineteen islands and more than 40 islets comprise the Galápagos archipelago, located in the Pacific Ocean some 620 miles (1,000 km) off the coast of Ecuador. It has changed little in millions of years. Ongoing seismic and volcanic activity reflects the processes that formed the islands, which, together with their isolation, led to the development of some of the most unusual species on Earth. All the Galápagos reptiles, half the birds, 32 percent of the plants and 25 percent of the fish, as well as many invertebrates, are found nowhere else. Ocean currents, the merging of cold and warmer waters, warm air temperatures, high rainfall, and a lack of predators have all contributed to the evolution of this unique suite of species. Endemic mockingbirds, seabirds, finches, and marine life inspired Charles Darwin's theory of evolution following his visit in 1835. The islands are now a World Heritage site and protected within the Galápagos National Park.

Galápagos hawk
A permanent resident found only in the Galápagos, the Galápagos hawk often uses tortoises as observation posts from which to sight prey, such as giant centipedes, locusts, small lava lizards, snakes, and rodents. It also takes small marine and land iguanas, hatchling tortoises, and sea turtles.

Giant tortoises
Eleven of the 13 subspecies of giant tortoise that evolved from a single species survive today. Five live on Isabela Island, separated by wide lava fields; five are found on Santa Cruz, San Salvador, San Cristobal, Pinzon, and Española islands, respectively; and the Pinta tortoise can be seen at the Charles Darwin Research Station, Santa Cruz. Each species has a different shell, or carapace, and has evolved adaptations to suit the environment in which it lives.

SANTA CRUZ, GALAPAGOS

Variety of shells
Tabletop shells are distinct from the dome shells of tortoises from wetter islands. The shell of the smaller saddle-backed tortoise allows it to extend its head high to feed. Tabletop shells afford more protection than saddle-backs, but domed shells provide the most protection.

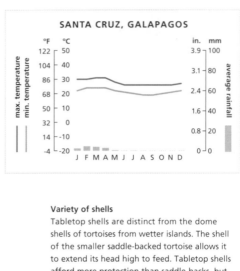

**Saddle-backed shell
ventral view**

Domed shell ventral view

Saddle-backed shell

Tabletop shell

Domed shell

Galápagos land iguana
Galápagos land iguanas are vegetarians, subsisting mostly on the fruit and pads of *Opuntia* cactus. They use their front feet to scrape away larger cactus thorns, then gulp down cactus fruit in a few swallows. These iguanas live in dry areas and in the mornings they bask in the hot equatorial sun.

Blue-footed booby
Male blue-footed boobies pick up their distinctive blue feet and perform an exaggerated step-walk during their courtship dance. The world's 40,000 breeding pairs, half of which inhabit the Galápagos Islands, breed opportunistically.

Marine iguana
The only seagoing lizard, the marine iguana develops its colors with age. Young iguanas are black, while adults can be shades of green, red, gray, or black, depending on their island home. Males favor sunny, rocky shores during the day, where sea breezes keep them cool.

Sea lion
Graceful and inquisitive, sea lions always seem to be playing with something, whether it is with each other, marine iguanas, penguins, or red crabs. They often splash brown pelicans, which share a similar diet that includes mussels, clams, anchovies, and sardines.

Animal Types	No. of Species
Giant tortoises	13
Lava lizards	7
Iguanas	3
Land reptiles	23
Insects	1,600

FINCHES

Thirteen species of finch, belonging to four genera, live on the Galápagos Islands. All evolved from a single pair of birds similar to the blue-black grassquit finch commonly found along the Pacific Coast of South America. Finches have bills of varying size and shape, suited to their particular diet and lifestyle. According to Darwin's theory of evolution, beaks changed as the birds developed different tastes for fruits, seeds, or insects.

Ancestral ground finch
Probably ate seeds

Sharp-billed finch
Pecks seabirds to drink blood

Tree finch
Feeds on insects

Warbler finch
Extracts insects from twigs

Woodpecker finch
Raps rotten wood for insects

Tree finch
Feeds on plant material

Large ground finch
Cracks and eats large seeds

Large cactus ground finch
Feeds on cactus flowers and seeds

THE GRAN CHACO

One of the major wooded grasslands of South America, the Gran Chaco comprises savannas and thorn forests so impenetrable that until relatively recently they had barely been explored. The region covers a total of 250 square miles (650 km²), extending northward from the foothill plains of Argentina into western Paraguay, eastern Bolivia, and a small area of southwestern Brazil. The Chaco is divided into the Boreal, Central, and Austral regions by its two main rivers, the Pilcomayo and Bermejo. As this region is a low, flat, alluvial plain, the climate is hot and dry in summer, but river flooding during the rainy season converts large areas into swamps. The resident wildlife continues to amaze scientists, with animals such as the Chacoan peccary, rediscovered in 1975, and at least 18 species of armadillo. However, the Chaco is threatened by unrestricted forest clearing, overgrazing, cattle ranching, oil and gas exploration, and road construction.

SCALE 1:45,000,000

0 — 750 miles
0 — 750 kilometers

LAS LOMITAS, ARGENTINA

Nine-banded armadillo
Solitary and nocturnal, but more diurnal during winter, the nine-banded armadillo can have between seven and nine bands. It can jump up to 4 feet (1.2 m) straight into the air to escape predators. The armadillo's armored skin is composed of hard, bony plates. Since it cannot store large reserves of body fat to keep warm, it forages actively and often grunts as it searches for food.

To defend itself from predators the three-banded armadillo rolls into a tight ball using its thick bony plating like armor.

Three-banded armadillo
Contrary to popular belief, the nine-banded armadillo is incapable of rolling completely into a ball; it has too many bony dermal plates. Only the three-banded armadillo is capable of this.

Guira cuckoo
The Guira cuckoo is a large ground-feeding bird that gives off a sharp, penetrating smell. It inhabits scrubby and open areas, and bands of six to 18 individuals perch, feed, and roost together.

Maned wolf
The maned wolf looks like a cross between a wolf and a fox. It has evolved long legs for roaming long distances in tall grass. This wolf takes one partner for life, but only interacts with its mate during the breeding season. Just 1,500 maned wolves remain in the wild, and numbers continue to decline because of threats such as habitat loss, agriculture, and hunting.

Paradox frog
The tadpoles of the paradox frog may be four times the length of the adult. The frog lives amid vegetation at the bottom of lakes, ponds, and lagoons, where it feeds on larvae and insects at night. Its skin secretions are being used to treat diabetes.

Blue-fronted parrot
In parrot society, the blue-fronted parrot is regarded as one of the best talkers and singers. It uses a repertoire of whistles, shrieks, and yapping notes. Active, intelligent, and graceful, this bird is commonly kept as a pet.

Burrowing owl
The burrowing owl may be spotted standing near its burrow, which can consist of a labyrinth of tunnels. In this undergound refuge the owl breeds, nests, and sleeps during the day. The tunnel also serves as protection and can be used to trap prey.

Chacoan peccary
The Chacoan peccary emits a strong odor from a scent gland on its back when frightened or to mark its territory. It is the largest of the four peccary species that live in South America, and is distinguished by its long bristles and shaggy appearance. The Chacoan peccary was thought to be extinct until 1975, when it was rediscovered.

PATAGONIA

At the southern end of the American continent, stretching from the Atlantic to the Pacific Ocean through the Andes, is geographically diverse and dramatic Patagonia. It is a region of immense beauty, and includes habitats as varied as treeless plains, forests, snow-capped mountains, large deserts, fertile valleys, wide seashores, impressive lakes, and gigantic glaciers. Its climate is equally variable, from long cold winters averaging 36°F (2°C) to scorching summers, when temperatures reach 105°F (40°C). The Andes in Patagonia receive 80 inches (2,000 mm) of rain annually, but the land becomes drier near the Atlantic zone, with only 8 inches (200 mm) recorded. Some parts of Patagonia preserve untouched vegetation, others are sparsely populated, while the human influences of ranching and mining prevail elsewhere. Vastly different environments across the region result in an abundance of rare vertebrates, from wild grazing mammals to the puma, Andean cat, river otter, and gray fox. Patagonia is also noted for its coastal and marine animals, freshwater fish, and birds.

Antarctic accent

Patagonia is renowned for its rugged coastlines, which are rich in animals that depend on the sea, such as great colonies of Magellanic penguins, seals, and sea lions. The climate is mostly temperate, but it becomes colder to the south. The meeting of cool air from the Antarctic with moist Pacific air masses, combined with low sea-surface temperatures, accounts for the region's high rainfall.

SCALE 1:35,000,000

0 — 500 miles

0 — 500 kilometers

NEUQUEN, ARGENTINA

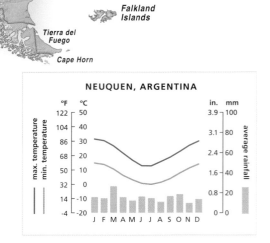

Southern elephant seal

The southern elephant seal is so named for its enormous size and the bull's habit of inflating its trunk to impress rivals. The female comes ashore to give birth and does not leave the beach until her pup is weaned, losing weight as her offspring thrives.

Magellanic penguins

Magellanic penguins enact a courtship ritual with the same partner every six months, when they return to breed at the rookery where they were born. Parents share the task of incubating the eggs for 42 days, then raise the chicks together for the next 29 days.

SPECIES	ONSHORE SIGHTING
Killer whale or orca	February to April and October to November
Southern elephant seal	August to March
Black-browed albatross	September
Magellanic penguin	September to April
Southern right whale	June to December
Dark dolphin	December to March
South American sea lion	April to November
Commerson's dolphin	April to December

Geoffroy's cat
A small, solitary wild cat, Geoffroy's cat has razor-sharp claws that help it climb trees. These claws are also used to stab and secure prey, such as small lizards, rodents, insects, frogs, and fish. Humans are the cat's only predators.

Patagonian mara
The mara is a large rodent, the fourth largest in the world, yet belongs to the guinea-pig family. Its hind legs are slightly larger than its front legs, giving it the ability to make agile jumps. The mara is also able to run fast and is capable of reaching speeds of 28 miles per hour (45 km/h).

Southern viscacha
Populations of the southern viscacha, a medium-sized rodent, have greatly declined because of illegal hunting for its woolly coat and for its meat. It is extremely agile, often running with no difficulty on rocky territories, where it lives in burrows.

Patagonian gray fox
The survival of the Patagonian gray fox has depended on its ability to eat everything from meat and fruit to eggs and carrion. When eating cooperatively, foxes without litters bring food to families with pups. This fox evolved from the wolf family 6 to 7 million years ago.

BIRDS OF THE PAMPAS

The Pampas is one of the richest grazing lowland areas in the world, but also one of the most endangered habitats on Earth. Found primarily in Argentina and Uruguay, it covers an area of 300,000 square miles (800,000 km²) from the Andes mountains to the Atlantic Ocean. With a humid and moist climate, the northern region has an average temperature of 64°F (18°C) and well distributed rainfall throughout the year produces fertile soils suitable for agriculture. To the south, the semiarid Pampas is known for its marshes and wetlands. Grasshoppers are one of the most abundant herbivores throughout the Pampas, but it is also home to rodents, deer, viscachas, and marsupials such as opossums. Migration has enabled birds to adapt to life in these windy grasslands. Marine and coastal birds make a stopover in the region to feed and rest, and more than 300 bird species have been recorded here, including 18 species of stork, ibis, heron, gull, and spoonbill. Land birds are not as common, but among the most notable are the tinamou and rhea.

⚡ **CONSERVATION WATCH**

There are only a few hundred white-winged nightjars left in Brazil and about 50 in Paraguay. Populations have declined as a result of the destruction of tropical savanna and open grasslands, the spread of invasive grasses, fire, the expansion of eucalyptus plantations, and the impacts of agriculture.

Greater rhea
The greater rhea is the largest South American bird. Although flightless, it can run at speeds of 37 miles per hour (60 km/h). Males mate with multiple females, who each lay eggs in the nest he has prepared. It is then his task to incubate the 30 to 60 eggs and to take care of the striped chicks that hatch.

Great pampas finch
The great pampas finch feeds on seeds and grain. It lives near marshes and in association with tall grasses and shrubs, and is usually seen in a bush calling, or on top of a tree or branch singing. It belongs to one of the most diverse terrestrial vertebrate orders, the Passeriformes, which encompass more than half of all bird species.

Baby toucan
Toco toucans nest high in tree cavities or holes made by woodpeckers. Three to four young fledge some 50 days after hatching and receive care for about eight weeks.

OCEANS OF GRASS

This treeless region comprises a continuous terrain made up of different grasses. Its distinctive vegetation is the tall, coarse-leaved pampas grass, with feathery spikes extending some 8 feet (2.5 m). Only trefoils, flowers, and other herbs grow between its tussocks. Grasses are categorized into hard pastures, which include the large, tussock-forming species, and soft pasture species with more tender undergrowth of greater nutritional value to grazers. Vertebrates are the main seed-eaters because the tall grass grants them refuge from carnivorous predators.

Uruguayan pampas grass
(Cortaderia selloana)

Tussock paspalum
(Paspalum quadrifarium)

Wild cane
(Gynerium sagittatum)

Puna grass
(Achnatherum caudatum)

Buff-necked ibis
The buff-necked ibis, also known as the white-throated ibis, uses its curved bill to feed on insects, reptiles, frogs, and small mammals and is easy to spot on the pampas.

Chalk-browed mockingbird
The chalk-browed mockingbird is skilled at imitating the melodies of other birds. During the breeding season the male performs a nuptial dance that involves flying from branch to branch and landing slowly with its tail splayed.

Toco toucan
The toco toucan is the largest of nearly 40 species in the toucan family. It feeds on fruit, but when nesting it also consumes a variety of insects as a source of protein. The toucan resides in the jungle canopy and actively flies in noisy flocks of six birds.

CENTRAL & SOUTH AMERICA
LLAMAS AND RELATIVES

The South American or New World camelids originated in North America 45 to 40 million years ago. They belong to the Camelidae family composed of llamas, alpacas, guanacos, and vicuñas, although the term llama is commonly used to refer to all four races. Their habitat includes near-waterless environments located in cool, dry mountain valleys and the Altiplano—the high Andean plateau distinguished by its steep, rocky mountain ledges that extends through Bolivia, Peru, Argentina, and Chile. Camelids are adapted to life at high altitude: thick wool coats protect them from the cold temperatures, and their extra-large lungs and hearts supply their bodies with sufficient oxygen to cope with the thin air. Throughout history, these mammals have played important roles in the culture and economies of indigenous communities. While the guanaco and vicuña live in the wild, the llama and alpaca were domesticated between 4000 and 3500/¥ and used for transportation, milk, meat, and fiber.

Grass grazing
These llamas are grazing along a line of snow-capped volcanoes in the Paranicota Volcano Shadows, located in the Chilean Altiplano on the border with Bolivia. This remote, harsh, and cold region is also home to condors, pumas, and flamingos.

Curious camelids
Camelids are herbivores that use their protruding lower incisor teeth and cleft upper lip to snip grass and tear off leaves. They have long legs, necks, and eyelashes, and slender heads. Camelids lack functional hooves and, instead, have feet made up of just two toes covered by a nail. These social herd animals require little water and can rest on their stomachs by bending their hind limbs when seated. They move their front and back legs on the same side in unison when walking.

Guanaco
Considered as ancestors of llamas and alpacas, guanacos can survive for long periods without drinking. While grass constitutes the bulk of their diet, they also graze on trees and range from sea level to elevations of 13,000 feet (4,000 m).

Vicuña
Mountain-grazing vicuñas range from elevations of 10,000 to 16,000 feet (3,000–5,000 m). They use one territory for day foraging and a higher, and therefore safer, territory for sleeping. Their fleece once clothed Inca royalty.

Habitat under threat
The ice fields of southern Patagonia are the natural home of guanacos, as well as foxes, rheas, maras, armadillos, wild cats, and bats. Since the early 1980s, this ecosystem has been severely threatened by overgrazing from introduced sheep and livestock.

PREDATOR

Pumas are the main predators of llamas. A puma stalks a llama before ambushing it. Leaping from the ground, the puma typically pounces on the llama's back and breaks its neck. Until the puma has finished its meal, it covers the carcass with leaves and twigs to hide it from hungry competitors.

ANIMAL	FINENESS OF WOOL (IN MICRONS)
Vicuña	6–10
Alpaca	10–27.7
Merino	12–20
Angora rabbit	13
Cashmere	15–19
Yak	15–19
Camel	16–25
Guanaco	16–18
Llama	20–40
Chinchilla	21
Mohair	25–45

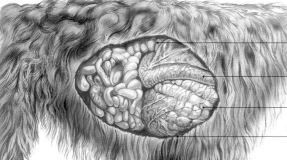

Small intestine

Third stomach chamber

First stomach chamber

Second stomach chamber behind first

Digestion
Llamas have a three-chambered stomach and chew their cud, a mouthful of swallowed food that is regurgitated from the first stomach. Once swallowed, the cud moves to the next two chambers to be fully digested, thereby extracting as much energy as possible from the food. Llamas spit their mouth contents or a foul-smelling fluid from their first stomach chamber to defend themselves.

Wool
A llama's coat consists of a double layer of fibers. About 20 percent is the protective outer coat of long and coarse guard hairs, while the inner layer comprises short, wavy fibers that are fine and soft.

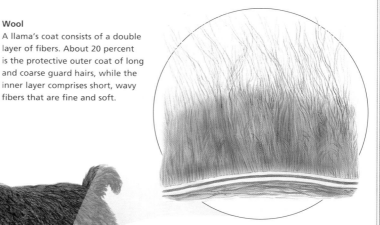

Alpaca
The most numerous camelid, the alpaca, is reared in the Andean mountains for its fiber, which is finer than cashmere. Most concentrated in the southern highlands of Puno, the alpaca can be distinguished by its fringe.

Llama
The llama was one of the first animals to be domesticated, some 4000 years ago. As pack animals, they can carry loads of 50 to 75 pounds (25–35 kg) and cover up to 20 miles (30 km) in a day.

THE CARIBBEAN SEA

The warm, tropical waters of the Caribbean Sea cover an area of about 1,050,000 square miles (2,700,000 km²). This sea is renowned for its coral reefs and clear waters. The Atlantic meets the Caribbean in the Anegada Passage that lies between the Lesser Antilles and Virgin Islands, and the Windward Passage between Cuba and Haiti. A nursery ground for an array of marine animals, the Caribbean Sea is home to saltwater crocodiles, dozens of species of stony corals, sea snails, spiny lobsters, and more than 500 species of fish. Red mangroves are one of the key habitats of the region, providing food and shelter, above and below the water, for creatures such as manatees, kingfishers, crabs, egrets, common black hawks, and boa constrictors. Mangroves, fringing the shores, also protect against land erosion and storm damage, and filter pollutants.

SAN JUAN, PUERTO RICO

SCALE 1:20,000,000

Whale shark
Fishermen once feared the whale shark, the biggest fish in the world. However, it was eventually discovered that the species is not a man-eater but feeds on plankton by sucking in huge quantities of plankton-rich water, then expelling the water through its gills.

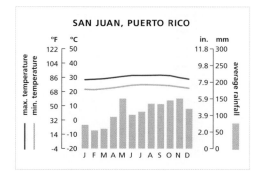

Cuban tody
The Cuban tody is endemic to Cuba and the oldest survivor of five tody species confined to the Greater Antilles. The bird often appears inactive as it feeds on flies from a perch. However, its bright red throat bristles when issuing its "tot-tot-tot" call.

Mesoamerican Reef

The world's second largest reef system, the Mesoamerican Reef covers the northern end of the Yucatan Peninsula in Mexico, the coasts of Belize and Guatemala, and stretches to the Bay Islands in northern Honduras. This tropical region hosts productive ecosystems, such as barrier and fringing reefs, atolls, patch reefs, and seagrass beds. It is at risk from rising water temperatures and increasing tourism.

West Indian manatee
Ancient mariners mistook manatees for sirens or mermaids, perhaps because of their long tails. This gentle mammal can swim vertically or upside down, and dense bones enable it to stay suspended at, or below, the water's surface.

Reef octopus
The Caribbean reef octopus is able to squeeze its body through tiny cracks in the reef. It can maneuver its head, beak, and each of its eight arms through a space the size of a keyhole.

Parrotfish
The parrotfish grazes on algae that grows on rocks or coral, pulverizing the algae with its grinding teeth to aid digestion. It later excretes the undigested coral, which then forms much of the sand in the fish's range.

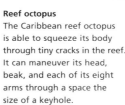

Barracuda
Barracudas live around the margins of coral reefs. They are formidable predators. The barracuda's projecting lower jaw is spiked with knifelike teeth and its silvery coloration reduces its visibility to prey, enabling it to herd fish schools into shallow water.

SOLENODON

The solenodon is one of the world's few poisonous mammals. It lives in burrows and is nocturnal. Although it resembles a rat, it can be distinguished by its elongated, flexible snout. Endemic to Cuba, the solenodon inflicts its venomous bite when fighting, provoked, or agitated by one of its own kind.

Grooved tooth
Venomous saliva is secreted by the submaxillary gland that flows through the grooved second lower incisor, which delivers the poisonous bite.

OCEAN
Leeward Islands
SAN JUAN
Windward Islands
Lesser Antilles
RACAS

This Bengal tiger, charging through the water at the mouth of the Ganges River, India, is a skilled swimmer. It can swim rivers more than 3 miles (5 km) wide and is a formidable predator. Its large canines, long, sharp, retractable claws, and massive forelimbs and shoulders allow it to single-handedly overpower prey much bigger than itself.

ASIA

Asia

Asia is the world's largest continent, covering 8.6 percent of Earth's surface area. It is bounded on the east by the Pacific Ocean, on the south by the Indian Ocean, and on the north by the Arctic Ocean. Asia stretches from north of the Arctic Circle to south of the equator—from east to west, Asia stretches nearly halfway around the world. This vast area has many different kinds of climate, with some of the coldest and some of the hottest, some of the wettest and some of the driest places on Earth. The subregions of Asia include West Asia, Central Asia, South Asia, Southeast Asia, Eastern Asia, and Russia. The high, cold deserts of Central Asia are known for their vast areas of barren landscape. Several biogeographic areas are considered biodiversity hot spots, harboring unique plants and animals. Among the many rivers that traverse the Asian continent, 32 rivers exceed 1,000 miles (1,600 km) in length. The Yangtze River in China is the longest at 3,915 miles (6,300 km).

CLIMATE ZONES

- Wet tropical
- Seasonal tropica
- Arid
- Semiarid
- Mediterranean
- Subtropical
- Continental
- Cold temperate
- Subpolar
- Highland

Climate

The Malay Archipelago and Malay Peninsula climate is dominated by heat and humidity. Southern Asia and the Indochina Peninsula experience more seasonal rains, often associated with monsoonal winds. The arid interior owes its temperature extremes largely to the Himalaya, which block moisture-bearing winds. A band of almost constant high pressure creates hot, arid conditions in the southwest. Cold polar air prevails in the north.

The Steppes of Central Asia
The steppes are Asia's unique grassland ecosystem that harbors grazing herbivores and burrowing rodents. The flat-bottomed lakes here attract numerous waterbirds.

The Himalayas
This is the world's longest and highest mountain range. About one-third of the mountain animals in the world occur here, and are well adapted for the environment.

VEGETATION ZONES

- Tropical forest
- Seasonal tropical forest
- Desert
- Tropical grassland
- Mediterranean forest and scrub
- Midlatitude grassland
- Midlatitude forest
- Boreal forest
- Tundra
- Mountain vegetation

The Siberian Wilderness
The Siberian wilderness is the world's largest remaining wilderness, dominated by taiga forests. The wildlife here includes carnivores such as the brown bear and the Siberian tiger.

The Indian Subcontinent
The junction between the east and the west, this region has a great diversity of natural forest and wetland ecosystems that harbor a rich wildlife.

Vegetation

The Arctic Ocean is flanked by a strip of tundra. To its south, stretching from the Urals to northern Japan, is a broad belt of coniferous forest that yields to deciduous and mixed forests that extend down the east coast, steppe grasslands, and scrub. Either sparse, arid-adapted plants or none at all typify large areas of the interior and southwest. In Southeast Asia, high rainfall supports some of the most extensive tropical forests in the world.

Hot and Cold Deserts
These are semiarid areas with extremely harsh climates. Many of the wildlife species here burrow underground for insulation against the extreme heat and aridity.

The Mountains of Southwest China
This region is known to be the most botanically rich temperate region in the world. Many species of rare and threatened wildlife, including the giant panda, live here.

East Asia
Located at the intersection of three of Earth's tectonic plates, this region contains numerous volcanoes, hot springs, and mountains, and is prone to earthquakes.

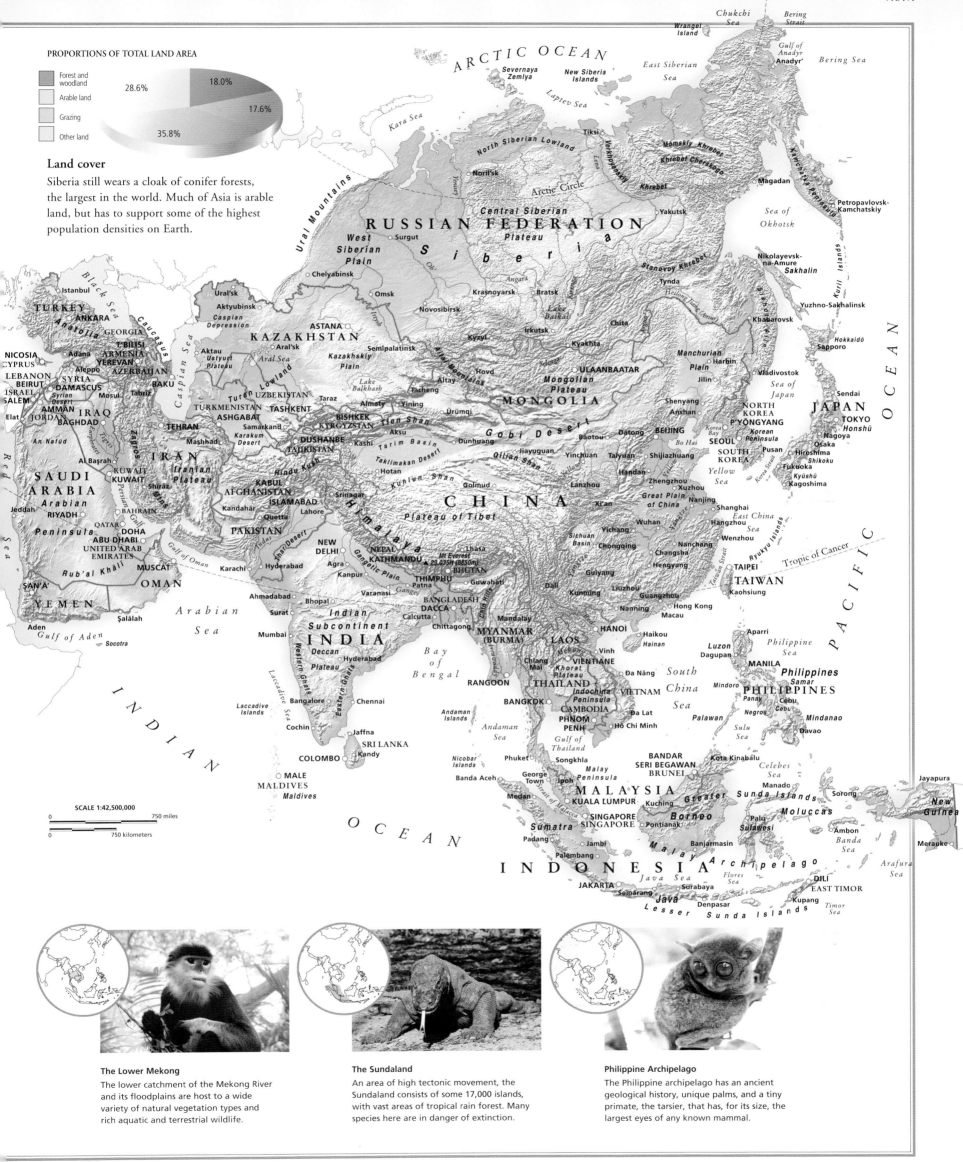

PROPORTIONS OF TOTAL LAND AREA

Forest and woodland
Arable land
Grazing
Other land

28.6%
18.0%
17.6%
35.8%

Land cover

Siberia still wears a cloak of conifer forests, the largest in the world. Much of Asia is arable land, but has to support some of the highest population densities on Earth.

SCALE 1:42,500,000

0   750 miles

0   750 kilometers

The Lower Mekong

The lower catchment of the Mekong River and its floodplains are host to a wide variety of natural vegetation types and rich aquatic and terrestrial wildlife.

The Sundaland

An area of high tectonic movement, the Sundaland consists of some 17,000 islands, with vast areas of tropical rain forest. Many species here are in danger of extinction.

Philippine Archipelago

The Philippine archipelago has an ancient geological history, unique palms, and a tiny primate, the tarsier, that has, for its size, the largest eyes of any known mammal.

THE STEPPES OF CENTRAL ASIA

The steppes are a unique grassland ecosystem that occurs in the lower slopes, foothills, and basins of Central Asia's mountain ranges. These areas may be semidesert, or covered with grasses and shrubs, depending on the season and the latitude. The climate is continental and temperate, with hot, windy summers, periodic droughts, and cold winters. The topography in some parts of this region can be either completely flat, low plain or a gently hilly plain–plateau. Several large rivers, such as the Ural and the Irtysh, and their tributaries, cross the region and there is an abundance of wetlands that include many flat-bottomed lakes. Compact turf or cushion-like vegetation is common here and several endemic species of tulips grow in the meadow zones. The wildlife is dominated by grazing species, such as antelope, sheep, and wild horses, and small burrowing rodents such as hamsters, voles, and lemmings. Several species of water birds also inhabit the wetlands or are seasonal visitors.

SCALE 1:47,000,000

TASHKENT, UZBEKISTAN

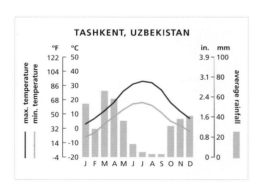

Great bustard
A large, ground-dwelling bird, the great bustard has an omnivorous diet, feeding on seeds, insects, worms, and frogs. The males develop a gular pouch and long white whiskers during the breeding season and carry out a flamboyant display to attract females.

GROUND DWELLERS

The small ground-dwelling animals of the steppe include a variety of rodents such as ground squirrels, hamsters, voles, jerboas, and marmots, and lagomorphs such as pikas and hares. They contribute to the natural disturbance regime in the steppes because their burrowing habits cause the recycling of nutrients, which sustains the ecosystem.

Steppe lemming
Lemmings eat shoots, leaves, and seeds and are most active at night. Solitary by nature they live in burrows on the steppes but do not hibernate. Litters range from four to 10 pups. Populations undergo phases of rapid growth and subsequent crashes.

Black-bellied hamster
This, the largest species of hamster, lives solitarily in burrows. Stores of cereal grains, seeds, and peas are kept in its winter burrow, which can reach more than six feet (2 m) below the surface.

Saiga antelope

The saiga is recognizable by its over-sized, flexible nose, which is thought to warm the air as it breathes in winter and to filter out the dust in summer. Saigas occur in large herds that move across the semidesert steppes grazing on several species of plants, including some that are poisonous to other animals. Males compete for females, fighting with their horns and head-butting.

High-altitude steppes
The high steppes of Central Asia can be a challenging environment for both animals and plants. Cold winters cause the surface water to freeze and the flat, open terrain exposes all living things to strong winds. Vegetation is low-growing and hardy.

Wild horses of the steppe
Przewalski's horse is the last surviving subspecies of wild horse. Compared with the domestic horse this animal is stockily built, with a large head, shorter legs, and a muscular body. In the wild it lives in a social group comprising a dominant stallion, a dominant lead mare, other mares, and their offspring.

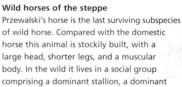

⚡ CONSERVATION WATCH

Przewalski's horse once roamed freely on the steppe along the Mongolia–China border. The wild population declined in the 20th century because of hunting, harsh climate, and habitat loss. It was dying out in Mongolia in the 1960s and was designated "extinct in the wild." These horses have since been bred in captivity and have recently been reintroduced in Mongolia.

THE SIBERIAN WILDERNESS

The Siberian wilderness is the world's largest remaining wilderness and provides a safe home for many species of plants and animals. The climate is continental, with hot summers, above 104°F (40°C), and extremely cold winters, below -76°F (-60°C). The average annual temperature is below freezing, but the snow cover is relatively thin. Annual precipitation ranges from 16 to 24 inches (400–600 mm) in the west, decreasing to eight inches (200 mm) in the east. The area is dominated by taiga forests, characterized by coniferous trees such as spruce and pines. In taiga forests the trees are widely spaced, and carpets of mosses and lichens cover the ground. The wildlife here includes large herbivores such as moose and caribou (reindeer), and carnivores such as the red fox, lynx and wolves. Brown bears are also found here. Among the high upland ridges mountain goats and alpine sheep graze on rocky slopes, and small burrowing mammals such as lemmings and voles search for insects and fresh shoots.

SCALE 1:50,000,000

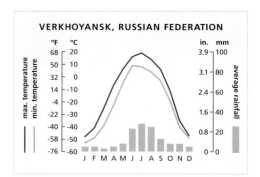

VERKHOYANSK, RUSSIAN FEDERATION

Siberian jay
The small-bodied Siberian jay is a widely distributed species in the wild coniferous forests of the north. It is commonly found in unspoilt forests with small natural clearings, marshy hollows, and ancient spruce trees. The birds have various alarm calls to warn others if predators are near.

Remote forests
Taiga forests dominate this landscape and the vast forests across Siberia act as a valuable carbon sink. Much of the region falls within the watershed of the Lena river system. The eastern Siberian taiga also has an extensive network of rivers.

Hazel grouse
The hazel grouse can fly but does so only infrequently. It nests on the ground, laying a clutch of three to six eggs in a nest concealed by grasses. It feeds mostly on plants, but also eats insects in the breeding season. During the non-breeding season, males and females associate as loosely bound pairs.

Ural owl
The Ural owl, a medium- to large-sized bird, has a wide distribution in the taiga forests where it feeds at night on rodents and other medium-sized birds. It is an aggressive owl and will chase birds of prey from its territory. It nests in hollow tree trunks.

Reindeer
Reindeer are large herbivores that live in herds and travel long distances annually. They feed on the leaves of willows and birches, as well as grazing on sedges and grasses. During winter, when snow covers much of their range, their main food source is lichens.

Siberian brown bear
This is a subspecies of the brown bear (*Ursus arctos*), and has a larger skull and luxuriant fur. It is generally a solitary animal and, when it meets other animals in its range, is usually aggressive. It has an omnivorous diet, feeding on plants, fish, insects, and small mammals.

Sable
A member of the Mustelidae family, this small carnivore was once hunted for its coat of thick fur, which was highly prized by fur traders. A careful, secretive predator with acute senses of smell and hearing, it feeds on birds, small mammals, and fish.

⚡ CONSERVATION WATCH

The Siberian tiger is a rare subspecies that is confined to the Amur region in the Russian Far East where it preys primarily on wild boar and red deer. It is considered to be the largest wild cat in the world but is endangered, with only about 480 to 520 individuals occurring in the wild.

Hot and Cold Deserts

The hot and cold deserts of Central Asia are semiarid regions with extremely harsh climates. Wide temperature variations are experienced on a daily basis, with fiercely hot temperatures during the day and below freezing temperatures at night. The landscape in these areas consists of sand dunes, barren mountains, and pebble grounds that cover vast plains. The weather typically includes dry air, strong winds, extremely hot summer temperatures, and swirling dust storms. These deserts generally receive less than 10 inches (254 mm) of rainfall per year. The plant cover is sparse and is limited to species that are able to tolerate drought. Animals that live in desert regions have developed adaptations that allow them to cope with the lack of water, the extreme temperatures, and the shortage of food. Desert dwellers such as rodents and reptiles burrow underground, where they are insulated from the heat and aridity. They emerge at night to feed.

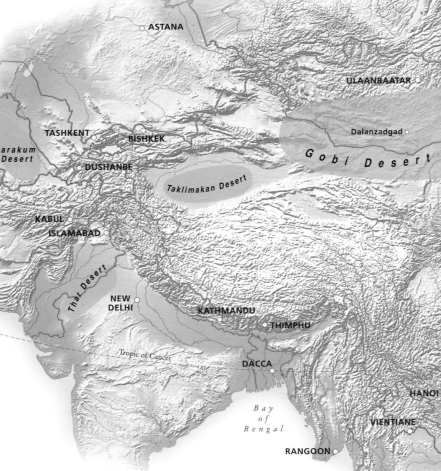

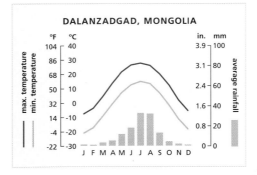

DALANZADGAD, MONGOLIA

Bactrian camel
The critically endangered Bactrian camel occurs in north-western China and Mongolia. It is identifiable by the two humps on its back, where it stores fat that can be converted into water and energy. These camels develop a thick, shaggy coat in winter.

Cold desert
A cold desert is one that has snow in winter, such as the Gobi Desert in China, with temperatures as low as -40°F (-40°C). The small animals that live here burrow underground to keep warm. These deserts are also home to animals such as gazelles, jerboas, Bactrian camels, and sand grouse.

Sand grouse
This ground-dwelling bird lives in semiarid grass-covered plains and sandy desert habitats, often with a cover of scrub, where it feeds on legume seeds. It nests in a ground scrape, where two or three greenish eggs with cryptic markings are laid. It is found in large flocks during the non-breeding season.

Gray monitor
The gray monitor is a burrowing lizard, widely distributed in deserts. It is active during the early hours of the day and feeds on vertebrates such as rodents, lizards, snakes, birds, frogs, and toads. It also eats eggs. These monitors become relatively inactive during the winter period.

SCALE 1:35,000,000

0   500 miles

0   500 kilometers

Lebetine viper
A large, venomous snake, the Lebetine viper has a wide distribution in dry and semiarid areas. It has a broad triangular head and a blunt, rounded snout. Primarily nocturnal or crepuscular, it hunts rodents and birds.

Hot desert
Hot deserts, such as the Thar Desert in India and Pakistan, are warm throughout the fall and spring seasons and extremely hot during the summer, when temperatures can rise to 129°F (54°C). These areas receive little rainfall during winter. The animals in hot deserts burrow to keep cool during the day.

LONG-EARED JERBOA

Jerboas are small jumping rodents in the Dipodidae family. The several species all have long hind legs, a long tail, and nocturnal feeding habits. The long-eared jerboa is recognizable by its exceptionally large ears. Classified as endangered, it is at home in the Gobi Desert in China.

Jerboa
The long-eared jerboa has the general appearance of a mouse but with long hind legs and feet. It has a tuft at the end of its tail.

Skeleton
The illustration of a jerboa skeleton reveals how long its hind legs are in relation to the rest of the body. It is these legs that give the jerboa its agile, jumping gait.

Jerboa burrow
The jerboa burrows in sand, where it digs with the aid of its fore feet, and throws the sand out with its long hind feet.

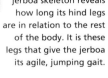

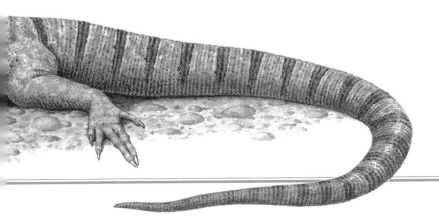

THE HIMALAYAS

The Himalayas, a massive mountain range in Asia, separates the Indian subcontinent from the Tibetan Plateau. The Himalayan system is the longest—1,490 miles (2,400 km) west to east—as well as the highest mountain range in the world. The climate here ranges from tropical at the base of the mountains to permanent ice and snow at the highest elevations. The distribution of plants and animals of the Himalayas varies with climate, rainfall, altitude, and soils. The vegetation varies from the unexplored tropical rain forests of the Eastern Himalayas, to the dense subtropical and alpine forests of the Central and Western Himalayas, to the sparse desert vegetation of the cold desert areas of the Transhimalaya. The wildlife is characterized by species adapted to life in cold and mountainous regions and about one-third of the mountain animal species in the world are found here. Many species of goat antelope, including the mountain goat, Himalayan tahr, chiru, and takin make this region their home.

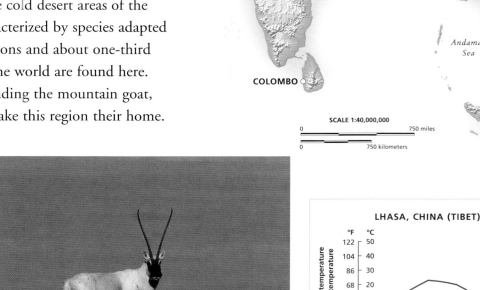

Chiru antelope
Chiru antelopes usually congregate in herds of more than 100 individuals and they live in the high mountain grassland and semidesert areas of the Tibetan plateau. The species has been over-exploited for its skin and is now endangered.

Indian wild ass
This is the largest among wild asses and is native to the high, cold habitat of the Tibetan Plateau. These animals live in cohesive herds of up to 400 individuals, led by an old female. Mature males are solitary, although they form, and defend, harems during the breeding season.

LHASA, CHINA (TIBET)

Himalayan tahr
This is a wild goat species that inhabits the rugged wooded hills and mountain slopes in the Himalayas. The tahr spends the summers grazing in high pastures, then descends to lower elevations to form mixed-sex herds in the winter.

Markhor
The markhor is an Asian mountain goat found in the western Himalayas, at elevations as high as 11,800 feet (3,600 m), in scrub forests of oaks, pines, and junipers. Males are solitary; females and their young live in small herds.

BIRDS OF THE MOUNTAINS

The diversity of habitats in the Himalayan region is reflected in the richness of its bird fauna, which includes many endemic species. Among the larger birds found here are kites, eagles, vultures, and pheasants. Many birds move to higher altitudes during the summer and return to the shelter of valleys during winter.

Monal pheasant
This large-sized pheasant is the national bird of Nepal. The males have a long, metallic green crest and brightly colored plumage. They occur in pairs during the breeding season and form large groups that roost communally during the winter.

Western tragopan
A medium-sized brightly plumaged pheasant found along the Himalayas, the western tragopan is considered the rarest of all living pheasants. It is mostly arboreal but also feeds on the ground.

Yak
Wild yaks live in treeless mountains and plateaus feeding on grasses, lichens, and other plants. Vegetation in their habitat is scarce, so they must travel great distances to find sufficient food. They live at altitudes between 10,500 and 17,500 feet (3,200–5,400 m) but are insulated by a thick coat of shaggy hair.

Big Cats

The Asian big cats are the large mammalian top predators in Asia. They include the Asiatic lion, tiger, leopard, and the snow leopard. The Asiatic lion is restricted to the Gir Forest in the state of Gujarat in India's west. The tiger, with six subspecies, is more widely distributed across Asia. The Bengal tiger is found in the Indian subcontinent and Burma, the Siberian tiger occurs in eastern Siberia, the Indochinese tiger in the Mekong region, the Sumatran tiger in Sumatra (Indonesia), and the South China tiger—critically endangered—occurs in South China. There are seven subspecies of leopard distributed throughout Asia. The snow leopard is native to the rugged mountain ranges of Central Asia. The tiger, the largest and most powerful wild cat in the world, is a highly adaptable predator. As it is a territorial animal that needs large contiguous areas of habitat that support its prey, it often faces conflicts with humans. All the big cats in Asia are threatened with extinction today, because of loss of habitats, poaching, and increasing human–wildlife conflict.

Sri Lankan leopard
The Sri Lankan leopard is a subspecies of leopard endemic to Sri Lanka. A solitary hunter, it is the island's top mammalian predator and occurs widely in a variety of habitats, including dry monsoon forests, montane forests, thorn scrub, and lowland tropical rain forests.

Bengal tigers fighting
The Bengal tiger is a solitary and extremely territorial animal. Adult tigers guard their territories fiercely. Males in particular will not tolerate any incursions by other males into their territory, often leading to fights that can end in the death of one of them, or cause severe wounds to both.

Big Cat	Group Size	Litter Size	Life Expectancy in the Wild
Bengal tiger	Solitary	2–4	15–20 years
Sri Lankan leopard	Solitary	2–3	10–15 years
Asiatic lion	2–5	1–4	12–16 years
Snow leopard	Solitary	1–4	15–18 years

Former range
Current range

Asiatic lion
The Asiatic lion is a subspecies of lion restricted to the Gir Forest National Park of western India. They are highly social animals that live in prides led, usually, by two adult females. The males are less social, and associate with the pride mostly for mating and during the hunting of large prey.

Prey

In the wild, tigers feed mostly on large and medium-sized prey, such as deer, sambar, and buffalo. However, if large prey is scarce they will often capture smaller prey, such as small mammals, ground-dwelling birds, and reptiles in order to feed themselves and their offspring. Depending on the habitat, tigers may also eat peafowl, monkeys, fish, porcupines, frogs, crabs, and large monitor lizards.

Careful capture
After a careful stalk, tigers make a short rush toward prey, such as this Indian muntjac, usually approaching from the side or back to avoid hooves and antlers.

Protecting the kill
If a kill is made in the open, a tiger usually drags the carcass, in this case that of an axis deer, into dense cover before beginning to feed.

Bengal tiger cubs
A tiger litter is made up of three or four cubs, which are raised by the mother. They remain in their birth den until they are about eight weeks old, then emerge to watch their mother hunt. They do not become independent of her for about 18 months.

⚡ CONSERVATION WATCH

The total wild population of the snow leopard is estimated to be 4–7,500 individuals. It lives in the rugged mountainous regions—up to 17,000 feet (5,180 m)—of Central Asia. Snow leopards are illegally hunted because of the high demand for their thick pelt. They also run into conflict with humans when they attack livestock, which happens when other prey is scarce.

THE INDIAN SUBCONTINENT

The Indian subcontinent is a large section of Asia consisting of countries lying mainly on the Indian tectonic plate. These include countries on the continental crust (India, Pakistan, Bangladesh, Nepal, and Bhutan), an island country on the continental shelf (Sri Lanka), and an island archipelago (the Maldives). The subcontinent has a tropical monsoon climate, with a wet and a dry season. Mainland India harbors a diversity of natural ecosystems, including forests, and an array of wetlands influenced by large rivers such as the Brahmaputra, Ganges, and Indus. A long mountain range, the Western Ghats, runs north to south along the western edge of the subcontinent. Many species of animals, including several endemic amphibians and reptiles live here. The ranges also serve as a wildlife corridor, allowing the seasonal migration of the endangered Asian elephant. The continental island of Sri Lanka is separated from southern India by the narrow Palk Strait. Although the plants and animals in Sri Lanka show affinities with those of peninsular India, many species on the island have evolved in isolation.

SCALE 1:35,000,000

Nilgai
The nilgai, closely related to wild cattle, is a large herbivore that generally lives in small herds of up to 20 individuals. Mature males have a gray–blue coat and are sometimes known as "blue bulls." The nilgai is able to live in dry conditions, sometimes surviving without water for several days, by deriving water only from the vegetation it feeds on.

Gaur
A species of wild cattle, the gaur is recognizable by its humped back and large body supported by slim white legs. It is the heaviest and most powerful of all wild cattle and lives in herds of up to 40 individuals, led by an old female. Adult males may be solitary.

AGRA, INDIA

⚡ CONSERVATION WATCH

The Asian elephant is the largest terrestrial mammal in Asia. There are two subspecies in the region, occurring in peninsular India and Sri Lanka respectively. A small percentage of the adult males bear tusks. These elephants have a semi-prehensile "finger" at the tip of their trunk, which enables them to gather plant matter for feeding. They live in herds, led by an old female; mature males live a solitary life.

Animal Common Name	Population in India (% of world)
Tiger	60%
Asian elephant	50%
Asiatic lion	100%
One-horned rhinoceros	80%

Indian rhinoceros

Indian rhinoceros are generally solitary although their home ranges may overlap and they sometimes gather in small, short-term groups. These large herbivores have one horn, a good sense of smell, but poor eyesight. They can run at speeds of up to 25 miles per hour (40 km/h).

Peacock dance

The male peafowl, the "peacock" bears a group of colorful display feathers on its tail coverts. During the breeding season the peacock expands these feathers and performs a dance in front of peahens to entice them for mating. These feathers are shed annually during the non-breeding season.

Common langur

The common langur is a sub-arboreal species of monkey that spends much of its time on the ground. It lives in medium to large groups of 10 to 64 individuals led by a dominant male. The group is likely to have a home range of 495 to 2,965 acres (200–1,200 ha).

KING COBRA

The largest poisonous snake in the world, the king cobra feeds almost exclusively on other snakes. It hunts its prey during the day, and is able to swallow snakes that are much bigger than its own head. King cobras are capable of killing a human with a single bite.

Cobra–mongoose battles

The mongoose is a natural predator of cobras, including king cobras. When a cobra encounters a mongoose, it flattens its upper body by spreading its ribs, forming the distinctive hood on its neck. It emits a high-pitched hiss and strikes at the predator. The mongoose expands its fur and jumps around the cobra to avoid being bitten, waiting for the ideal moment to jump on the snake's neck to give it a lethal bite.

THE MOUNTAINS OF SOUTHWEST CHINA

This region stretches across 100,400 square miles (260,000 km²) of temperate to alpine mountains, characterized by extremely complex topography, ranging from less than 6,500 feet (2,000 m) above sea level in some valley floors to 24,800 feet (7,558 m) at the summit of Gongga Shan. Mountain ridges are oriented in a generally north–south direction. The area has a wide range of climatic conditions and temperatures. Tributaries of several temperate and tropical rivers originate from these mountains. There is also a wide variety of vegetation types, including broad-leaved and coniferous forests, bamboo groves, scrub communities, savanna, meadow, prairie, freshwater wetlands, and alpine scrub. The region is the most botanically rich temperate region in the world. The wild animals that make their home here include more than 200 mammals and 600 bird species, including many that are rare and globally threatened. The world's best-known flagship species for conservation, the giant panda, is restricted to the shrinking forests of this region.

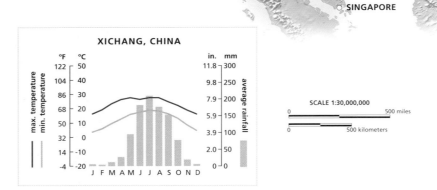

XICHANG, CHINA

SCALE 1:30,000,000

0   500 miles

0   500 kilometers

Golden monkey
Golden monkeys are an arboreal species that inhabit temperate montane forests. These monkeys feed mainly on lichens and other plant matter, supplemented with insects. Found in groups of 20 to 30, they have a large home range of up to 15 square miles (40 km²).

Red goral
The red goral, the smallest of the currently recognized goral species, lives at high elevations of 6,500 to 13,000 feet (2,000–4,000 m). It feeds primarily on lichens, supplemented with tender stems, leaves, and twigs from shrubs. It is agile, moving easily and with speed over rough terrain.

Takin
The takin, a goat–antlope, is found in bamboo forests at altitudes of 6,500 to 14,500 feet (2–4,500 m). It feeds during the day on grasses, buds, and leaves. Takin gather in small herds in winter and herds of up to a hundred individuals in summer.

GIANT PANDA

Giant pandas live in dense bamboo and coniferous forests at altitudes of 5–10,000 feet (1,500–3,000 m). Their diet consists mainly of bamboo leaves, stalks, and roots, which they crush with their powerful jaws and teeth. A single adult panda must eat 20 to 40 pounds (9–18 kg) of food a day to survive, and spends up to 15 hours a day feeding. Although principally terrestrial, pandas can climb trees.

Baby panda
Female pandas give birth to one or two cubs weighing four to eight ounces (100–200 g) each, in a sheltered den. A female in general raises only one cub, if more than one is born.

Bamboo
Bamboo groves are one of the main vegetation types in the mountains of southwest China but they are subject to periodic die-off after mass flowering. The giant panda depends on bamboo species such as the umbrella bamboo.

Former range

Current range

Giant panda
The panda's thick, woolly coat keeps it warm in cool forests. Each adult has a defined territory and females are not tolerant of other females in their range. Giant pandas communicate through vocalization and scent marking of trees.

⚡ CONSERVATION WATCH

Red pandas, which are arboreal and generally solitary, occur in both deciduous and coniferous forests. They rest during the day in the branches of trees and in tree hollows. Their primary food is bamboo, but they also feed on berries, blossoms and leaves of other plants. They are threatened by deforestation and other human activities, and are classified as endangered.

THE SUNDALAND

The Sundaland covers the western half of the Indo-Malayan archipelago, and consists of some 17,000 equatorial islands. They are dominated by two of the largest islands in the world: Borneo 279,925 square miles (725,000 km²) and Sumatra 164,980 square miles (427,300 km²). Earthquakes and volcanic eruptions are a common natural hazard here; there are more than 20 active volcanoes on the island of Java. The landscape is dominated by lowland rain forests, which have several strata of vegetation. Sandy and rocky coastlines support scrubland, muddy shores are lined with mangrove forests, and large peat-swamp forests occur further inland. Montane forests, where plants such as mosses, lichens, and orchids are plentiful, occur at higher elevations. Higher still, scrubby subalpine forests are dominated by rhododendrons. Sundaland fauna is diverse, with nearly 3,000 species of vertebrates, one-third of them endemic. The Sundaland also has the highest number of species threatened with extinction in the Asian region.

INDONESIAN MARINE LIFE

The waters around the Indonesian archipelago are relatively shallow and warm and the rich nutrients support a diversity of marine life. These waters also serve as an important migratory area for more than 30 species of marine mammals. More than one-third of all known whale and dolphin species can be found in the Indonesian seas, including the rare and endangered blue whale—the largest mammal in the world.

SCALE 1:40,000,000

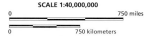

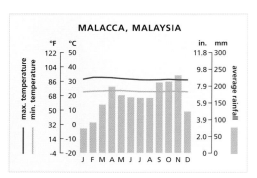

MALACCA, MALAYSIA

Marine turtles
Six of the world's seven marine turtle species are found in Indonesia. There are important nesting and foraging grounds on the many islands, and migration routes converge at the crossroads of the Pacific and Indian oceans.

Nudibranch
These are a group of marine slugs—mollusks without an external shell. A variety of colorful nudibranchs are found in the coral reefs around Indonesia. They store toxic chemicals in their body for their defense.

Tail
The dragon's muscular tail is as long as its body. It is used for balance and when capturing prey, and in fights with other males, especially when standing on its hind legs.

Red Helen butterfly
This large swallowtail butterfly is common in evergreen forests. It has a white patch on the upper hindwing, which is characteristic of the species. The larvae feed on plants of the Rutaceae family, which includes citrus plants.

⚡ Sumatran rhinoceros
The Sumatran rhinoceros is the smallest of the living rhino species. A solitary browser, it eats up to 110 pounds (50 kg) of leaves, saplings, twigs, and shoots a day. Individual bulls have territories as large as 20 square miles (50 km²).

Former range
Current range

Crested langur
The crested langur lives in groups of up to 50 individuals, which include a single adult male, several adult females, and immature individuals. It feeds mainly on leaves, supplemented with fruits, nuts, young shoots, and flowers. The young are born orange-colored and become gray as they grow.

Sun bear
This, the smallest member of the bear family, is a solitary, nocturnal omnivore. It feeds on termites, birds' eggs, vertebrates, fruits, insects, berries, and shoots. The sun bear spends much of its time in trees. It has a long, slender tongue that may be up to 10 inches (25 cm) long, which it uses to extract honey from beehives.

Komodo dragon

The world's largest lizard, the venomous Komodo dragon is restricted to Komodo and a few neighboring islands. Although these lizards usually feed on carrion, they have been known to kill large animals such as goats, deer, and cattle by ambushing them on paths through thick undergrowth. Previous belief that damaging bites were due to bacterial infection are now better understood as resulting from tissue-destroying venom.

Claws
Strong claws help the Komodo dragon dig burrows for resting. They are also used as weapons and to disembowel prey.

Skin
The scales in the dragon's skin, some of which are reinforced with bone, have sensory plaques connected to nerves that facilitate its sense of touch.

Tongue
The Komodo's sense of smell functions through its tongue, which samples the air then "smells" by touching the roof of its mouth.

TROPICAL RAIN FORESTS OF SOUTHEAST ASIA

Lowland tropical rain forests are forests that receive high rainfall, more than 80 inches (2,000 mm) annually, with a mean annual temperature of 75°F (24°C), and an average relative humidity of 85 percent. These forests occur in a belt around the equator, between the Tropic of Cancer and the Tropic of Capricorn, at elevations of less than 3,300 feet (1,000 m). Among the continents that harbor tropical rain forests, Asia is the second largest region, with Indonesia, Malaysia, and the Philippines all in the tropical zone. Tropical rain forests are characterized by a closed canopy formed by tall broadleaf evergreen trees, several layers of vegetation—the emergent overstory, canopy, sub-canopy, understory—a relatively open and shaded forest floor with a thick layer of litter, and many thousands of species of plants and animals. The diverse wildlife in tropical rain forests in southeast Asia is well adapted to live in the trees, and includes birds, arboreal amphibians, reptiles, and mammals.

Dipterocarp trees
The tropical lowland rain forests in Borneo are dominated by towering trees of the Dipterocarpaceae family, which often exceed 145 feet (45 m) in height. A majority of these dipterocarp species undergo a mass flowering event, occurring roughly every four years and coinciding with the onset of dry weather. At these times the forest canopy bursts into color.

THE ORANGUTAN

Among the great apes of the world, orangutans are the most arboreal, spending most of their time in trees. They are generally solitary, with large territories. A major portion of their diet consists of fruits, supplemented with young leaves, shoots, seeds, bark, flowers, insects, and small vertebrates. They are remarkably intelligent great apes and are known to use tools for feeding. In the evening they construct a "nest" in a tree, using leaves and branches, and rest there for the night.

⊘ Orangutan
Orangutans usually move by swinging from one branch to another. Their powerful arms, twice as long as their legs, enable them to easily bear their body weight, which is 100 to 200 pounds (45–90 kg).

Baby orangutan
Females give birth to a single offspring, and care for it for some six to seven years. Newborn infants weigh around three pounds (1.5 kg). They begin to take soft food from their mother's lips at about four months.

Hornbill nest

Hornbills nest in cavities in living trees. The male locates a possible site and invites the female to inspect it. Once she is satisfied with the choice of nest, the birds mate and the female then seals herself inside the nest chamber using rotten wood, clay, regurgitated food, and other materials supplied by the male. The sealing process usually takes three to seven days. The female lays her eggs, incubates them, then rears the chick inside the nesting cavity.

Epiphytic orchid
Phalenopsis sp.

Fern
Drymoglossum piloselloides

Delivering food
The male delivers food to its mate, and later to the chicks. In most large forest species, the female remains in the nest until the chick is fledged, a total period of incarceration of up to five months.

Flying frog
A large tree frog with brilliant colors, Wallace's flying frog is well adapted to life in the treetops. Its fingers and toes are webbed and a membrane of skin stretches between the limbs.

Flying lizard
This is an arboreal lizard that can spread out folds of skin attached to its movable ribs to form "wings" that it uses to glide from tree to tree over distances of more than 26 feet (8 m).

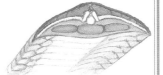

Regular body shape   Flattened for flying

Flying snake
These arboreal snakes are able to glide between trees, by flattening their bodies to up to twice their usual width from the back of the head to the vent.

White-handed gibbon
The white-handed gibbon is a small, tailless ape with dense, shaggy fur that varies from black to pale gray. It has long, slender arms and the upper side of its hands and feet are white. Its opposable thumb is used for climbing or grooming.

Rain forest life

An estimated 70 to 90 percent of life in the rain forest exists in the trees above the shaded forest floor. A variety of epiphytes, such as colorful orchids and mosses, occur in the trees. Arboreal animals such as flying squirrels, tree frogs, and flying lizards feed, nest, and rest among the foliage.

Gliding lemur
Galeopterus variegates

Orchid
Vanda sp.

Red-eyed tree frog
Agalychnis callidryas

Pygmy tree shrew
Tupaia minor

Proboscis monkey
The male of this primate species has a distinct, enlarged, protruding nose, which can be up to seven inches (17 cm) long. It also has an enlarged belly. It is found in small groups of 10 to 32, living on a diet of seeds, leaves, shoots, and fruit.

Slow loris
The slow loris, a nocturnal, arboreal primate, is known for its slow, deliberate movements and powerful grasp. It can be difficult to remove the slow loris from a branch. These animals live alone or in small family groups. As opportunistic carnivores, they typically eat insects, birds' eggs, and small vertebrates.

Orchid
Coelogyne sp.

Orchid
Dendrobium sp.

Flying lizard
Draco volans

EAST ASIA

This region includes the Japanese archipelago, which consists of more than 3,000 islands, Korea, and southeast Russia. The archipelago sits at the intersection of three tectonic plates—resulting in numerous volcanoes, hot springs, mountains, and earthquakes. The area stretches from humid subtropics in the south to a temperate zone in the north. Vegetation on the islands of the Japanese archipelago ranges from boreal mixed forests of fir, spruce, and pine, to subtropical broadleaf evergreen forests and mangrove swamps. Higher elevations support alpine vegetation; subalpine vegetation and beech shrublands occur throughout the region. About half the mammal, reptile, and amphibian species in Japan are endemic. The long, north–south stretch of the Korean Peninsula and its complex topography have resulted in wide climatic variations. Wildlife here includes the roe deer, Amur goral, sable, brown bear, tiger, lynx, northern pika, water shrew, and Manchurian ring-necked pheasants. Species such as the black bear, mandarin vole, river deer, fairy pitta, and ring-necked pheasant are found in the lowlands.

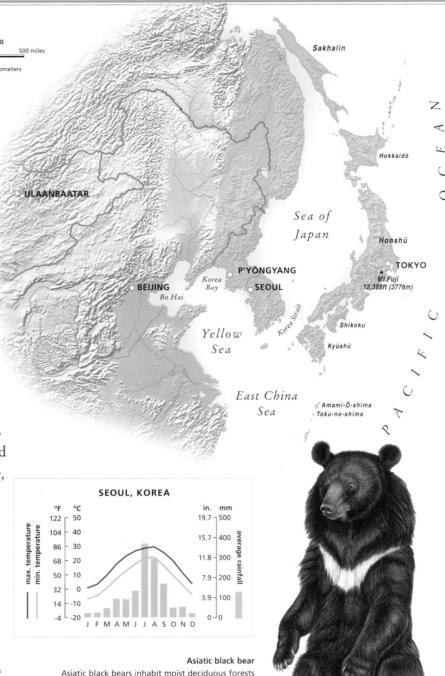

SEOUL, KOREA

Mandarin duck
The male mandarin duck has a red bill, whiskers on its face, and stunning color patterns on its body feathers. This duck breeds in wooded areas near shallow lakes, marshes, or ponds. It nests in cavities in trees close to water and feeds mainly on plants and seeds.

Asiatic black bear
Asiatic black bears inhabit moist deciduous forests and brushy areas. They migrate into the mountains during summer, returning to valleys for winter. They are excellent tree climbers and strong swimmers. They are sometimes known as "moon bears" because of the white patch on the chest.

Azure-winged magpie
A member of the crow family, the azure-winged magpie inhabits various types of coniferous and broadleaf forest, including parks and gardens. It feeds in family groups of up to 30 individuals and its diet includes seeds, nuts, invertebrates, and fruits. It nests in loose, open colonies with a single nest in each tree.

Oriental fire-bellied toad
This is a mostly aquatic frog, which spends much of its time in shallow pools. It has a brightly colored body, with bright green and black coloration on its back, and brilliant orange and black on its underside—warning predators of its toxicity. When disturbed, it secretes a milky toxin from its abdominal skin.

Amami rabbit
An endemic rabbit that is restricted to two islands in Japan, Amami-O-shima and Toku-no-shima, the amami rabbit is found mainly in dense old-growth forests. It has primitive morphological traits that resemble those found in fossils from the Miocene Epoch. It digs burrows for resting and breeding.

CONSERVATION WATCH

Red-crowned cranes are among the rarest cranes in the world and, weighing from 15 to 20 pounds (7–10 kg), are the heaviest. They breed in Siberia and parts of Mongolia and migrate to east Asia in the fall. Adults reinforce their pair bond in a synchronized courtship dance. They inhabit wetlands and have a broad diet that includes insects, frogs, and grasses.

Staying warm
These macaques have a thick coat of fur, which helps them withstand cold winter temperatures. Mothers protect their young from the cold by huddling closely together.

Japanese macaques

The Japanese macaque is an omnivorous, semi-terrestrial primate that lives in groups of 10 to 160. Its home range depends on the availability of food and is around one-and-a-half square miles (3.5 km²). It is an excellent swimmer, able to swim distances of 500 yards (0.5 km). In Shiga Heights, in central Japan, macaques remain near hot springs in winter, which helps to maintain their body temperature.

Mount Fuji
Among the many mountains in Japan, Mount Fuji is the highest, its summit reaching 12,400 feet (3,776 m). It is an active volcano, which last erupted about 300 years ago. Its symmetrical cone is covered with snow for several months of the year.

Japanese giant salamander
This, the second largest salamander in the world, grows up to five feet (1.5 m) in length. It is an aquatic species restricted to mountain streams that have clear, cool water. It has poor eyesight but feeds at night on insects, crabs, frogs, and fish.

THE LOWER MEKONG

The Lower Mekong region includes Laos, Cambodia, Vietnam, and southern parts of Thailand and Myanmar. It contains the lower catchment of the Mekong river and its floodplains. A wide variety of vegetation types is found in this region, including mixed wet evergreen, dry evergreen, deciduous, and montane forests. There are also patches of shrublands and woodlands on karst limestone outcrops and, in some coastal areas, scattered heath forests. Other distinctive, localized, vegetation formations include floodplain swamps, mangroves, and seasonally inundated grasslands. The area supports amazing bird diversity, some 1,300 species, and the largest waterbird populations in Southeast Asia. Four species of ungulates new to science have been discovered in this region over the past two decades. They include the Annamite muntjac, the large-antlered muntjac, the leaf deer, and the saola. The region also supports the highest diversity of freshwater turtles in the world.

SCALE 1:30,000,000

0 — 500 miles

0 — 500 kilometers

Big-headed turtle
This freshwater turtle is distinguished by its large head and long tail. It is found in rivers and streams and is also known to climb trees, using its beak. It cannot withdraw its head into its shell, but the top of the head is covered with a large bony scute for protection. It feeds on fish and snails.

White-throated kingfisher
Halcyon smyrnensis

PHNOM PENH, CAMBODIA

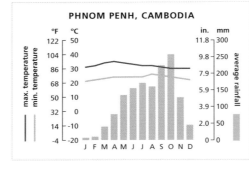

Burmese python
Burmese pythons are among the largest snakes on Earth. They may reach 23 feet (7 m) or more in length and can weigh up to 200 pounds (90 kg). They are nocturnal carnivores, killing by constriction, and survive primarily on small mammals and birds. They are also excellent swimmers.

The Mekong River
The Mekong is the longest river in Southeast Asia, with an estimated length of 2,703 miles (4,350 km), draining an area of 306,950 square miles (795,000 km²). The river links numerous habitats that attract a variety of animals. Islands in the river enhance habitat diversity, with sandy shores, shallow ponds, sediment flats, and reed beds.

Capped gibbon
Capped gibbons live together as monogamous pairs, spending most of their time in the trees. They eat mainly fruits, leaves, and small animals. The males are black; females are black on the belly and head but pale gray elsewhere.

Red-shanked douc monkey

This colorful arboreal monkey lives in primary and secondary evergreen forests and moist deciduous forests. It forms groups of 4 to 15 individuals, which socialize by grooming each other, led by dominant males. The monkeys communicate through facial expressions and vocalization. They feed on flowers, leaves, fruits, seeds, and buds.

Clouded leopard

This medium-sized wild cat has a tawny coat, bearing cloud-shaped patterns, and a stocky build. It is known to have the longest canine teeth, two inches (5 cm), of any living feline. It is tree-dwelling, solitary, and secretive.

⚡ CONSERVATION WATCH

The freshwater Siamese crocodile occurs in swamps, oxbow lakes, and slow-moving sections of streams and rivers. It feeds predominantly on fish, but also amphibians, reptiles, and possibly small mammals. Females construct a mound nest during the annual wet season and lay 20 to 50 eggs. The species is critically endangered in the wild because of habitat destruction, over-exploitation for farming, accidental entanglement and drowning in fishing nets, and hunting.

Eld's deer

The rare, medium-sized Eld's deer is found in dry dipterocarp forests. It lives in small groups of four to seven animals, but also gathers in herds of up to 50 individuals. Adult stags are solitary, joining herds during the rut. Eld's deer are active at dusk and rest at forest edges during the day.

Life in the river

Riverine wetlands along the Lower Mekong consist of a mosaic of habitat types, influenced by the movement of water over the riverbed. Sandbars, mudflats, perennial river channels, rock outcrops, waterfalls, deep pools, and rapids are all found here. The wildlife is richly varied. Crocodiles bask on the muddy banks, turtles and frogs hunt for insects, long-legged waders fish by the shore, and giant carp cruise the waters.

Black-necked crane
Grus nigricollis

Giant ibis
Pseudibis gigantean

Siamese crocodile
Crocodylus siamensis

Irrawaddy dolphin
Orcaella brevirostris

Smooth-coated otter
Lutrogale perspicillata

Siamese giant carp
Catlocarpio siamensis

Mekong wagtail
Motacilla samveasnae

Fishing cat
Prionailurus viverrinus

Giant Asian pond turtle
Heosemys grandis

Spiny-breasted giant frog
Paa fasciculispina

THE PHILIPPINE ARCHIPELAGO

The Philippine archipelago includes more than 7,100 islands covering 114,741 square miles (297,179 km²) in the Pacific Ocean. The isolated fragments of the archipelago have an ancient geological history—some date back 30 to 50 million years—and include 17 active volcanoes. The Philippines has a tropical climate with three pronounced seasons: wet (June–October); cool and dry (November–February); and hot and dry (March–May). The archipelago is within a typhoon belt and is affected by a number of cyclonic storms every year. Once covered with thick tropical lowland rainforests, the islands have been cleared extensively and only isolated patches of forest remain today. There is still a rich diversity of vascular plants, about one-third of which is endemic, dominated by orchids, palms, begonias, and dipterocarps. Among the many terrestrial vertebrate species in the Philippines more than 50 percent are endemic. Birds are the largest vertebrate group, with more than 600 species found in the region.

SCALE 1:12,000,000

Tarsier

Just the size of a human fist, this small arboreal mammal is a forest-dweller. Its eyes cannot turn in their sockets but a special adaptation in its neck has enabled the tarsier to rotate its head through 180 degrees. Its eyes are considered to be, for its size, the largest of any known mammal. The tarsier is a solitary animal, with a specific home range, travelling up to a mile (1.5 km) across the forest. It is primarily an insectivore, but also feeds on lizards and birds.

Cloud rat

A nocturnal, arboreal rodent, the cloud rat has large hind feet and long claws that facilitate its excellent tree-climbing ability. A herbivore, it feeds on leaves and flowers and is endemic to the island of Luzon in the Philippines, where it is found in the northern highlands.

MANILA, PHILIPPINES

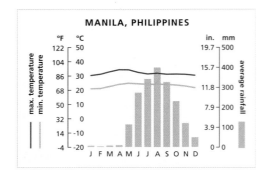

Tarsier hands and feet

The tarsier's second and third toes have sharp claws specially adapted for grooming. Its long digits are tipped with rounded pads that allow it to cling easily to trees.

Sleeping tarsier

The tarsier sleeps during the day, usually in dark hollows close to the ground, near the trunks of trees and shrubs deep in thick bushes and forests. These animals sleep in groups, or as solitary individuals, becoming active at night.

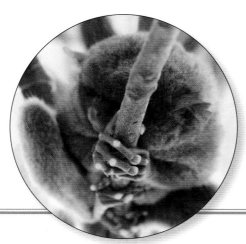

Philippine eagle

One of the largest and most powerful birds of prey, the Philippine eagle builds a large nest in emergent dipterocarp trees, about 98 feet (30 m) from the ground. The female lays only one egg and the parents care for the hatchling for about 20 months. Each breeding pair requires a home range of 9 to 19 square miles (25–50 km²).

CONSERVATION WATCH

The tamaraw, also known as the Mindoro dwarf buffalo, is a small hoofed mammal endemic to the island of Mindoro in the Philippines. It is the largest terrestrial mammal in the country, with an average height of three feet (1 m). It is a diurnal grazer that feeds on grass and bamboo shoots. Adults live a solitary, reclusive life.

Philippine crocodile

A relatively small freshwater crocodile endemic to the Philippines, the Philippine crocodile has a broad snout and heavy dorsal armor. It feeds on aquatic invertebrates, fish, and small vertebrates. The female constructs a small nest mound, where 7 to 20 eggs are laid.

Luzon mangrove snake

This is one of the biggest cat snake species, between six and eight feet (1.8–2.5 m) long, with vividly marked bold yellow bands on a black body. It is a nocturnal feeder and its prey includes small mammals, lizards, frogs, other snakes, and fish.

GOLDEN-CAPPED FRUIT BAT

One of the largest fruit bats in the world, this species bears a patch of golden-tipped hairs on the top of its head. It roosts in colonies during the day and flies long distances, up to 19 miles (30 km) during the night in search of fruits, mainly the fruits of fig trees. It uses its excellent eyesight to locate food, rather than the echolocation used by other bat species.

Heavyweight bat

The golden-capped fruit bat is probably the heaviest bat in the world, weighing up to two-and-a-half pounds (1.2 kg).

Visayan spotted deer

Endemic to the Philippines, this small, short-legged deer is found in steep dipterocarp forests that are relatively inaccessible to humans. It feeds at night, grazing on cogon grass and young low-growing leaves and buds within the forest.

Wide wingspan

This bat's wingspan is more than five feet (1.5 m). It may travel more than 25 miles (40 km) each night in search of food.

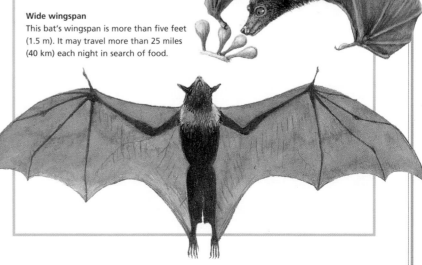

African elephants are the largest land animals on Earth. This herd of African elephants moves through the Etosha National Park, Namibia. Three-quarters of an elephant's life is devoted to feeding or moving toward food or water. Female elephants, or cows, live in family groups with their young, but adult bulls roam on their own.

AFRICA

AFRICA

Africa, the world's second largest continent at 11.7 million square miles (30.2 million km²) hangs below Europe like an enormous island. Historically connected to the rest of the Old World by a thin strip of land along the east of Egypt, Africa has unique fauna and flora. Much of the animals and plants consist of species that are widespread within, and sometimes between, the major habitat types—deserts in the north and south, wet forests in the center, savannas and grasslands between these forests and deserts, and the woodlands and scrub forests of the higher altitude plateaus in the east and southeast of Africa. But geological and climatological processes have, over the last few million years, produced areas of isolation—the Great Rift Valley, the fynbos of South Africa, the mountains of the Eastern Arc of Tanzania and Kenya, and the great island of Madagascar, where speciation has occurred in isolation, and evolution has produced rare and unusual animal and plant forms.

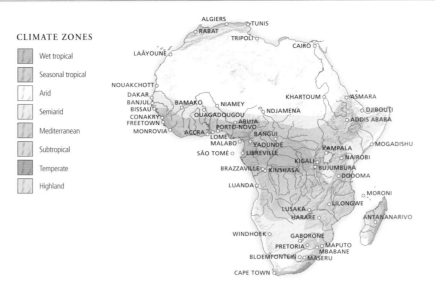

CLIMATE ZONES

- Wet tropical
- Seasonal tropical
- Arid
- Semiarid
- Mediterranean
- Subtropical
- Temperate
- Highland

Climate

The equator splices broadly similar climatic zones in Africa. Nearest the equator rainfall is regular and abundant; the duration of the wet season decreases the greater the distance from the equator. High pressure produces arid zones at 30 degrees north, creating the Sahara Desert, and 30 degrees south, where drier conditions are limited to the southwest.

The Sahara and Sahel
The world's largest desert, the Sahara spans nearly the entire top of the continent. Animals are widely dispersed, but they are all adapted to living in the hottest place on Earth.

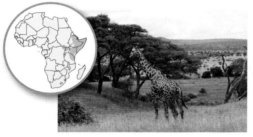

East African Savanna
Large groups of giraffes still find a home in the savannas of central and eastern Africa. The savannas are also home to the great migrations of antelopes, zebra, and buffalo.

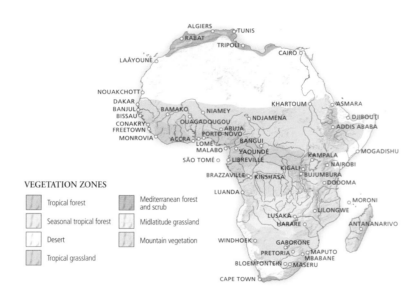

VEGETATION ZONES

- Tropical forest
- Seasonal tropical forest
- Desert
- Tropical grassland
- Mediterranean forest and scrub
- Midlatitude grassland
- Mountain vegetation

Vegetation

Abundant rain supports extensive tropical rain forests on Africa's west coast and in the Congo Basin. These are bounded by tropical woodlands and savannas, which cover almost half the continent and encircle an expanse of seasonal tropical forest in the south. To the north, the savanna yields to thorn woodlands and sparse grasses. Vegetation is scanty or nonexistent in the Sahara and much of the Namib Desert.

The Congo Basin
Much of the Congo forest, the world's second largest tropical forest, remains intact and is home to many of humankind's closest ancestors—gorillas, chimpanzees, and bonobos.

Life in the Albertine Rift
An area of spectacular peaks, deep valleys, and diverse lakes, the Albertine Rift Valley is home to the famed mountain gorilla, and to thousands of unique plant and animal species.

The Ethiopian Highlands
The Ethiopian Highlands are high islands cut off from the rest of Africa by their altitude. The Simien and Bale mountains are home to many unique animals species.

The Miombo Woodlands
Little known, but one of the largest ecoregions in Africa, the Miombo woodlands, which provide a habitat for Africa's largest elephant herds, span much of south-central Africa.

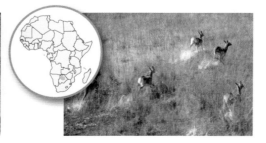

The Okavango Delta
The Kavango River floods seasonally into a massive basin in northern Botswana, creating an inland swamp and lake. Hippopotamus and waterbirds abound.

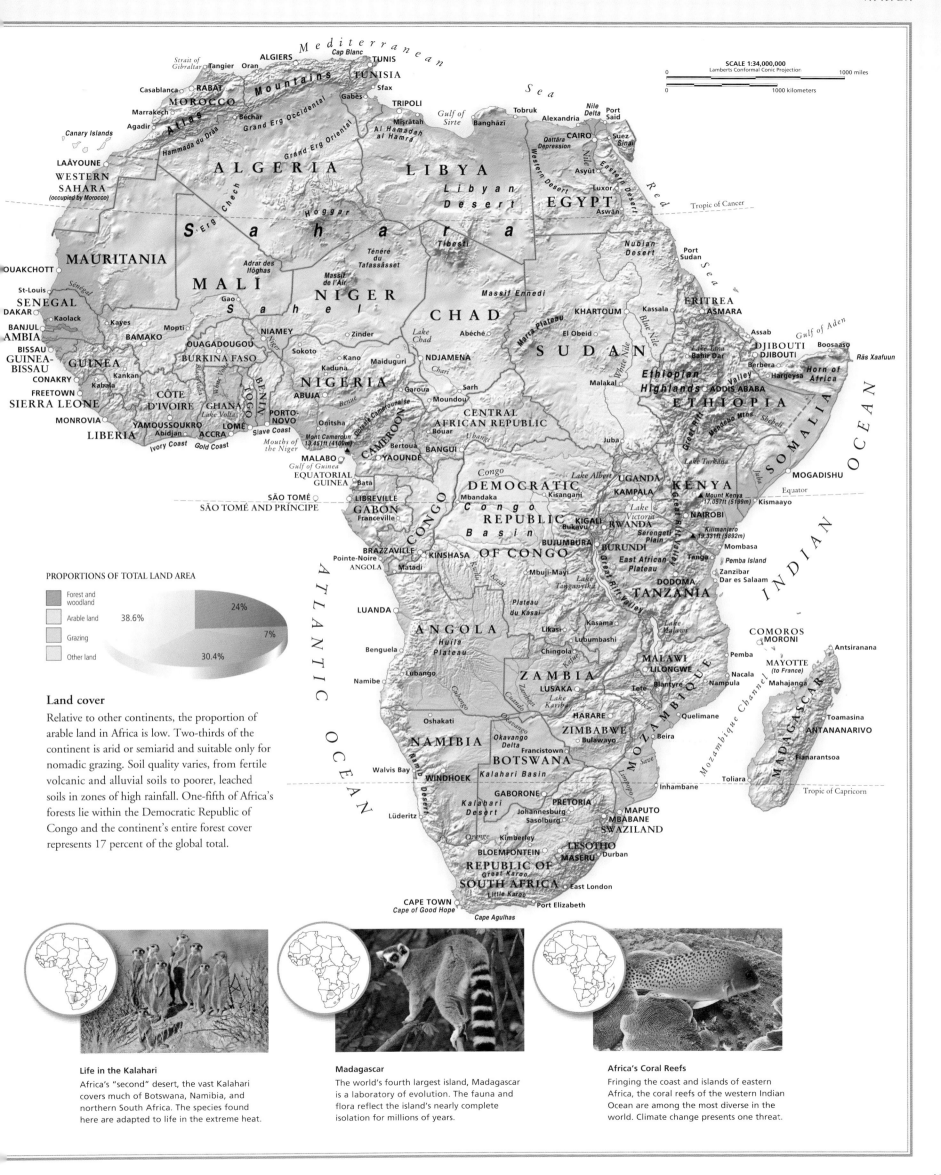

SCALE 1:34,000,000
Lamberts Conformal Conic Projection

PROPORTIONS OF TOTAL LAND AREA

- Forest and woodland
- Arable land 38.6%
- Grazing
- Other land

24%
7%
30.4%

Land cover

Relative to other continents, the proportion of arable land in Africa is low. Two-thirds of the continent is arid or semiarid and suitable only for nomadic grazing. Soil quality varies, from fertile volcanic and alluvial soils to poorer, leached soils in zones of high rainfall. One-fifth of Africa's forests lie within the Democratic Republic of Congo and the continent's entire forest cover represents 17 percent of the global total.

Life in the Kalahari
Africa's "second" desert, the vast Kalahari covers much of Botswana, Namibia, and northern South Africa. The species found here are adapted to life in the extreme heat.

Madagascar
The world's fourth largest island, Madagascar is a laboratory of evolution. The fauna and flora reflect the island's nearly complete isolation for millions of years.

Africa's Coral Reefs
Fringing the coast and islands of eastern Africa, the coral reefs of the western Indian Ocean are among the most diverse in the world. Climate change presents one threat.

THE SAHARA AND SAHEL

Stretching from the Red Sea to the Atlantic Ocean, the Sahara covers 3.3 million square miles (8.6 million km²) in northern Africa and merges with the semiarid savanna of the Sahel at its southern extremity. Sculpted by strong winds, the Sahara landscape is characterized by mountains, valleys, and dunes. Although the most arid of ecosystems, it is dotted with isolated and variable water sources that sustain life. Temperature extremes pose a major challenge to desert wildlife. The world's highest temperature—136.4°F (58°C)—was recorded in the Libyan Sahara in 1922, yet subzero temperatures are also common. Most of the Sahara's 1,200 plant species are adapted to the heat and low rainfall, being short-lived or possessing thick, rubbery leaves. Diversity of animal species is low, with only 70 mammal species, 90 bird species, and 100 reptile species found across this vast area. Because of these low densities, desert animals are susceptible to hunting, which has decimated ostrich, addax, gazelle, and cheetah populations.

Desert oases

A wadi, or valley in Arabic, is a depression or streambed found in the desert, often at the base of a mountain or within a sheltered area. Wadis remain dry for most of the year but are transformed by heavy rains. Flooding produces lush vegetation that supports a variety of wildlife as well as nearby villagers. Although most desert animals are adapted to dry conditions, wadis are a critical source of succulent vegetation and fresh water.

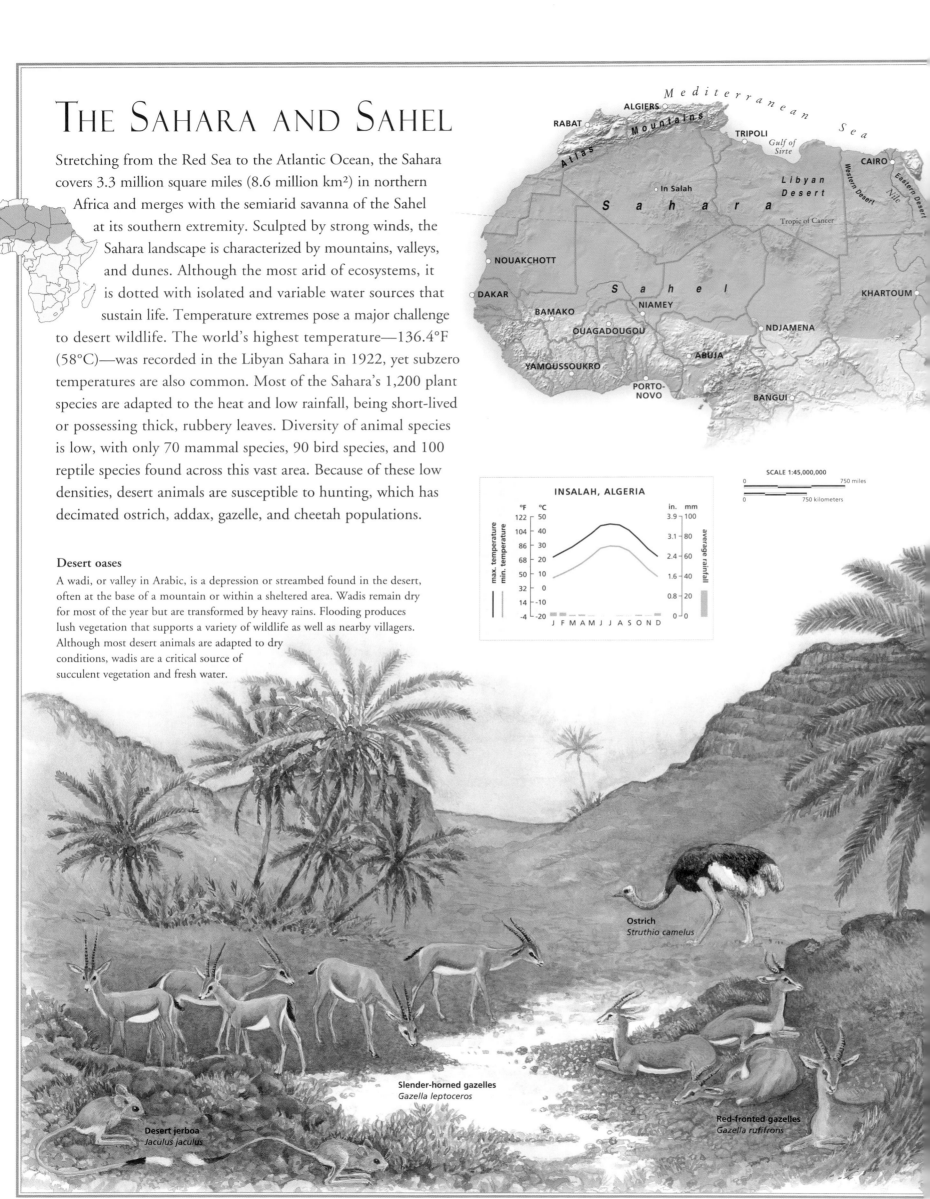

INSALAH, ALGERIA

max. temperature
min. temperature
average rainfall

SCALE 1:45,000,000
750 miles
750 kilometers

Ostrich
Struthio camelus

Slender-horned gazelles
Gazella leptoceros

Red-fronted gazelles
Gazella rufifrons

Desert jerboa
Jaculus jaculus

⚡ CONSERVATION WATCH

With an estimated population of 9 to 12,000, the endangered Saharan subspecies of the cheetah is found only in Algeria, Morocco, and Niger. Numbers continue to fall as its prey base—small antelope—is destroyed by poaching and increased competition resulting from habitat loss. This brings cheetahs into conflict with sheep and camel herders.

Scimitar-horned oryx
Formerly found throughout North Africa, the scimitar-horned oryx once congregated in groups of more than 1,000 at water sources. It is now extinct in the wild because of habitat loss and hunting. Captive breeding and reintroductions provide hope that oryx will again roam the desert landscape.

Green Sahara
The Sahara, shadowed by the Atlas Mountains to the northwest, has been a desert for several million years. But during the last ice age, 20,000 to 5,000 years ago, large rivers, whose beds are visible even in today's satellite imagery, flowed across a greener landscape. Rock carvings and cave paintings from this era depict a broad savanna, home to zebras, gazelles, hippopotamus, and giraffes.

Rock hyrax
The rock hyrax is a small ungulate that has a unique call, which sounds like a woman screaming. Despite its size, it is closely related to the elephant and lives in rocky outcrops in colonies averaging 50 individuals. The hyrax's heavily furred feet are equipped with glands that produce sweat, which aids traction in its rocky habitat.

DESERT ADAPTATIONS

The desert is an extreme environment. Daytime Saharan temperatures often exceed 100°F (38°C) but drop 50°F (10°C) at night. With little available shade or water, wildlife must be able to cope with these temperature extremes, excessive dryness, and harsh sunlight. Many animals have evolved behavioral and physiological adaptations, such as sleeping in burrows by day, raising their body temperatures before sweating, and developing kidneys that conserve water.

Fennec fox
The smallest of foxes, the fennec, has large ears that help it to dissipate heat and detect prey. Its sandy coat reflects sunlight, blends into the landscape, and insulates the fox during cold nights, when it is active.

⚡ Addax
The addax obtains all of its water needs from plants and is adept at tracking and finding patches of desert vegetation after rain. Its broad hooves are adapted to travel over soft sand without sinking. The once healthy addax population has been reduced to less than 300 individuals.

Dorcas gazelle
The dorcas gazelle can live its entire life without tasting water, gaining moisture from the plants—primarily acacias—in its diet. The gazelle became completely nocturnal in response to heavy hunting.

THE CONGO BASIN

The Congo Basin forest spans six countries across about two-thirds of the African continent, from the Gulf of Guinea in the west, to the East African Rift in the east. The Congo is second only to the Amazon in size, covering more than 700,000 square miles (1.8 million km²), which includes 25 percent of the world's remaining tropical forest. Unlike much of the Amazon, the Congo is largely undeveloped, but increased road-building, agricultural expansion, mining, and forestry activity destroy up to 2 million acres (810,000 ha) a year and threaten the future of these forests. The Congo is not a single ecosystem but a patchwork of ecosystems that includes rivers, swamps, and flooded forests. The size of the forest basin is rivalled only by its diversity. More than 10,000 species of plants, 1,000 bird species, and 400 species of mammals, including forest elephants, four species of great ape, and a wide variety of forest antelopes and monkeys make their home here.

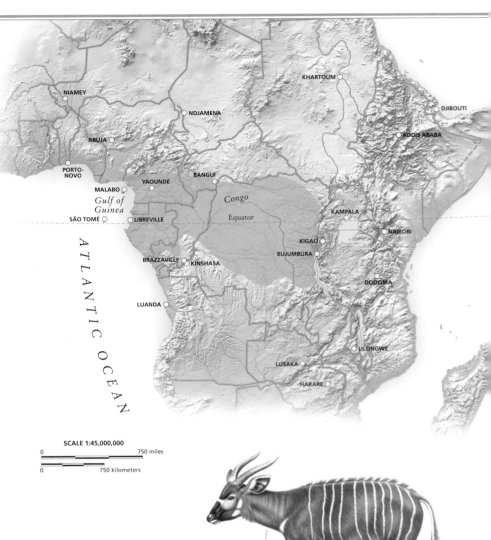

SCALE 1:45,000,000

0 ————— 750 miles

0 ————— 750 kilometers

Red river hog
Traveling in large groups, or sounders, of up to several dozen animals, red river hogs use their strong snouts to dig for tubers and roots in the forest floor. Adept swimmers, they are often found in swamps. While adults are characterized by a red coat and contrasting black and white stripe down their back, piglets are darker.

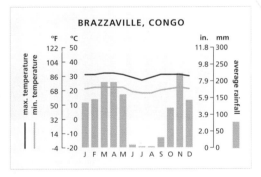

BRAZZAVILLE, CONGO

Congo bongo
Easily recognized by its striped coat and the spiral horns sported by both sexes, the bongo is one of Africa's largest antelopes. Like other African herbivores, it prefers to graze on nutrient-rich grasses found in small forest clearings. Females are social; males solitary.

CONSERVATION WATCH

The okapi resembles a zebra but is in fact the only living relative of the giraffe. Not described by science until 1901, the okapi is found only in the north and east of the Democratic Republic of Congo, formerly Zaire. In the late 1980s, the government established the Okapi Wildlife Reserve to protect the species from hunting and habitat destruction. The initiative has been largely successful, despite near-constant civil war.

Lady Ross's turaco
A social bird that lives in flocks of up to 30 individuals, the Lady Ross's turaco emits a noisy call. Turacos mate while traveling in groups, and the male and female share responsibility for incubating the eggs. The bird's characteristic red crest can rise up to 2 inches (5 cm) when it is excited.

Giant swallowtail
The largest of hundreds of African butterfly species, the giant swallowtail has long, narrow wings. Females tend to remain in the canopy, where they lay their eggs, while males are more frequently encountered near streams on the forest floor, where they engage in territorial disputes.

African gray parrot
With striking red tail feathers, the African gray parrot is endemic to the forests of central and western Africa and renowned for its mimicking ability. Studies suggest that up to 21 percent of these parrots are taken annually for the pet trade. As well, the trees they nest in are frequently harvested for their timber.

Complete ecosystem
The Congo Basin's dense vegetation, rivers, and swamps, constitute a self-contained ecosystem. This structure, when combined with the hot and humid conditions, regulates water flow and creates a stable climate that has enabled the forest's biological diversity to evolve and endure.

Congo River
The Congo is the second-largest river in the world. It contains more than 4,000 islands and water may take six months to traverse the African continent. With more than 500 endemic fish species, the Congo's productive fisheries support millions of people.

THE FACTS	
Area	More than 1.3 million sq miles (+3.4 million km²)
Number of countries	6
Length of Congo River	2,900 miles (4,700 km)
Habitat	Rain forest, woodland, swamp, savanna, freshwater
Estimate of mammal species	More than 400
Estimate of fish species	More than 700
Estimate of bird species	More than 1,000

BUSH MEAT

The number of Congo animals killed and sold as bush meat is growing, with estimates of more than 2 billion pounds (1 billion kg) being traded each year. This trade is facilitated by a growing network of logging roads that penetrate the forest, and many wildlife managers are calling for stricter legislation and improved management to curb unsustainable hunting.

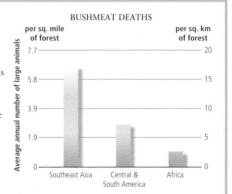

BUSHMEAT DEATHS

per sq. mile of forest / per sq. km of forest

Average annual number of large animals

7.7 — 20
5.8 — 15
3.9 — 10
1.9 — 5
0 — 0

Southeast Asia | Central & South America | Africa

Blue duiker
One of the smallest species of antelope living in central Africa, blue duikers are commonly found in bush-meat markets. Hunting threatens not only the duiker but also its predators, which rely heavily on the duiker as a food source.

THE CONGO BASIN
PRIMATES OF THE CONGO

The forests of the Congo Basin are some of the most diverse and extensive tropical forests remaining in the world. Home to 33 of the 79 African primate species, these forests are also critical to primate evolution and conservation. However, it is not the number of species but their evolutionary and ecological significance that makes the primates of the Congo Basin so important. All of Africa's great apes, humankind's closest relatives, are found in the Congo—bonobos, gorillas, and chimpanzees. The smaller monkeys—colobus monkeys, drills, and guenons—are keystone species, eating fruits and spreading or dispersing their seeds, which helps regenerate the forest. The habitat is under increasing pressure from the timber and mining industries, but the single greatest threat to primates is the direct hunting by humans for food, with thousands of animals entering the bush-meat trade annually.

The Congo Basin
A mosaic of forests, swamps, woodlands, and flooded forests, this vast region stretches across central Africa. The Congo Basin's tropical forests are critical to storing carbon and preventing global warming. Rates of deforestation have been lower here than in other tropical forest areas of Asia and the Amazon, but threats and access to the area are increasing.

Skeleton
The ape skeleton reveals adaptations for both terrestrial walking and arboreal climbing, including a flat chest, short legs, long arms, no tail, and the ability to walk with weight bearing down on the knuckles.

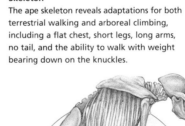

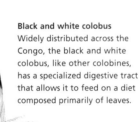

Black and white colobus
Widely distributed across the Congo, the black and white colobus, like other colobines, has a specialized digestive tract that allows it to feed on a diet composed primarily of leaves.

⏺ Bonobo
Bonobos are the gentlest of the great apes, living in large, cohesive groups. Peaceful relations are reinforced by sexual interactions rather than aggression.

⏺ Chimpanzee
Chimpanzees are humans' closest relative and share 98 percent of our DNA. Highly intelligent, they are often observed using tools.

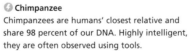

⏺ Drill
With a restricted range in west Africa, the drill is one of the most endangered primates. Drills live in social units of up to 20 individuals, but groups may merge to form troops of up to 200 individuals. Males may be twice the size of females, some weighing 55 pounds (25 kg).

Mandrill
One of the largest and most striking of the terrestrial monkeys, mandrills are distinguished by the vibrant coloration of the snout and hindquarters of males. While males are higher ranking, the enduring bonds in these highly social animals, which form groups of up to 1,350 individuals, are among females.

Playful

Frightened

Hungry

Submissive

Aggressive

Attentive

Making faces
Wild chimpanzees communicate with a greater range of facial expressions than any of the other large primates, except for humans.

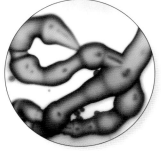

Ebola virus
First identified in humans in 1976 in Africa, the ebola virus kills 50 to 90 percent of its human victims and it is equally dangerous for gorillas and chimpanzees. Recent outbreaks in the Congo Basin have decimated great ape populations and caused outbreaks in humans who have killed apes or scavenged the bush meat from carcasses. Scientists are testing vaccines that would protect people and apes alike.

⚡ CONSERVATION WATCH

In the late 1970s, hopes for the conservation of mountain gorillas were few. Populations were in decline and habitat shrinking. Since then, focused conservation action and a vibrant gorilla tourism program in Rwanda have led to stable or increasing populations and declining threats from poaching and habitat loss, despite years of military conflict and instability in many parts of the species' range.

🔵 Mountain gorilla
Mountain gorillas live in small groups of about nine individuals, led by a large silverback male. Although the largest of the primates, mountain gorillas are rarely aggressive and spend most of the day eating leaves and stems.

🔵 Western gorilla
The western gorilla has the widest distribution of any gorilla subspecies and is often found in swampy habitats or forest clearings feeding on fruits and herbs. A recent discovery has more than doubled population estimates that now stand at more than 200,000 gorillas.

THE ETHIOPIAN HIGHLANDS

The Ethiopian Highlands, sometimes referred to as "the roof of Africa," encompass a vast expanse of high-altitude habitat. They are mainly contained within modern-day Ethiopia—just 5 percent of their 200,000 square-mile area (518,000 km²) is in Eritrea and Somalia—and are divided by the Great Rift Valley into northwest and southeast sections. The base of the highlands is a plateau that formed 70 million years ago and begins at 5,000 feet (1,500 m), but rises to up to 15,000 feet (4,570 m), completely isolating the region's flora and fauna. National parks have been designated in the two best known areas—the Simien Mountains in the northwest and the Bale Mountains in the southeast. The region's unique flora and fauna bears its own name—Afromontane. Eleven percent of the highlands's 5,200 vascular plant species are endemic, including several species of wild coffee. The highlands are also home to 193 mammal species, 33 percent of them endemic; 59 species of amphibians, 39 percent of which are found nowhere else; 80 species of reptiles; and 680 bird species.

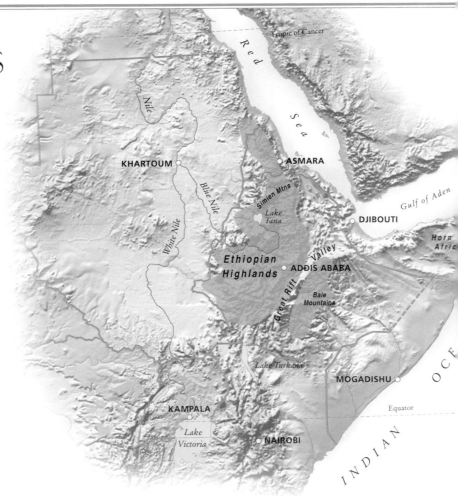

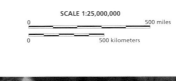

SCALE 1:25,000,000

ADDIS ABABA, ETHIOPIA

Abyssinian blue-winged goose
This goose is primarily terrestrial, feeding on grasses and other plants. During the courtship ritual, the male struts around the female whistling and displaying its blue wings, its head arched over its back and its bill pointed skyward. The species is protected by local religious beliefs.

Rouget's rail
Typically found at high elevations, this bird is commonly associated with water, where it searches for aquatic insects, crustaceans, and snails. It is primarily threatened by the loss of its habitat to domestic livestock grazing and the collection, for building construction, of thatch, which degrades the rail's habitat.

Giant mole rat
The giant mole rat spends most of its day underground, only surfacing to gather plants. It may reach densities of up to 10 rats per acre (22 per ha) and forms a vital part of the diet of the Ethiopian wolf. Higher wolf densities correspond with large rat populations.

⚡ CONSERVATION WATCH

The Ethiopian wolf, an ancient lineage, is more closely related to the gray wolf than any African canid. The wolf is found in six isolated populations, with the largest single population of several hundred individuals surviving in the Bale Mountains. Habitat conversion is the primary cause of its decline, but domestic dogs also bring a multitude of threats to small wolf populations: disease, competition for prey, and hybridization.

Gelada baboon

Found only in the high plateaus of Ethiopia, the gelada travels in small harems dominated by a large male. Dozens of these harems often gather to escape predators, with herds of up to 600 individuals sometimes sleeping on cliffs. Gelada are adapted to feeding on grasses in these open areas and tend to forage in an upright sitting position, shuffling along the ground. The chest skin is a dramatic red color, replacing the sexual signaling usually visible on the hindquarters of other baboons.

Walia ibex

The walia ibex, a mountain goat, is another rare endemic species of the Ethiopian Highlands. Closely related to the Nubian ibex, it has large horns, most prominent in the males. Once avidly hunted, it survives in the Simien Mountains, within a 400-strong remnant population.

🌐 Mountain nyala

The mountain nyala, only the males of which have spiraled horns, was the last African antelope to become known to science, in 1910. Its endangered status can, in part, be attributed to hunting for meat and medicinal use.

THE FACTS	
Area	200,000 sq. miles (520,000 km²)
Altitude	5,000–15,000 ft (1,500–4,600 m)
Habitat	Montane grassland, shrubland
Endemic mammals species	63
Endemic bird species	27
Endemic amphibian species	23

AFRICA
ENDEMIC BIRDS

More than 2,300 bird species, or 23 percent of the current list of 9,917 living birds worldwide, are found across the 58 countries that comprise Africa, Madagascar, and the African island nations. Sixty percent of these, or more than 1,400 bird species, are found nowhere else in the world. Like other continents, Africa has many species that are threatened with extinction—about 10 percent, or 234 of its birds, slightly less than the international average. But threats are increasing because of a growing population of 800 million people; advancing climate change; increased desertification in the Sahara; and competition for land, water, and wetlands. More than 5 billion birds migrate annually between Africa and Eurasia. Of 36 species that migrate between Africa and Britain, 60 have declined sharply since 1967 and two—the red-backed shrike and wryneck—have become extinct in Britain. Further evidence of problems can be found among the 522 migratory waterbirds on the African–Eurasian flyways, 41 percent of which are in decline.

Martial eagle
The largest of the African birds of prey, the martial eagle feeds on a variety of mammals and birds, ranging from hyraxes to antelope. Its slow reproduction rate—one egg every two years—makes the eagle vulnerable to population declines in areas where it comes into conflict with humans.

SECRETARY BIRD

The sole member of the family Sagittariidae, the secretary bird is endemic to sub-Saharan Africa. It can fly but spends more time hunting on the ground than other birds of prey—often covering 20 miles (30 km) on foot each day. It stomps on clumps of grass to flush out grasshoppers and lizards before chasing them down and, shielded by its large wings, will repeatedly strike a snake until it is stunned.

Impressive nest
Secretary birds forage separately but may roost together at night. Nests are enormous structures of interwoven sticks that often span 98 inches (2.5 m) across and 20 inches (0.5 m) deep. They may use the same nest for years.

Lesser kestrel
The migratory lesser kestrel spends the winter in the grasslands of sub-Saharan Africa. As a small falcon, it relies on its keen eyesight and gliding abilities to seek out prey, such as small rodents. Rather than build its own nest, the kestrel resumes the nests of other birds.

Distinctive crest
The secretary bird is easily recognized by the black, quill-like feathers that form a crest on the back of its head. It has the body of an eagle but stands on storklike legs.

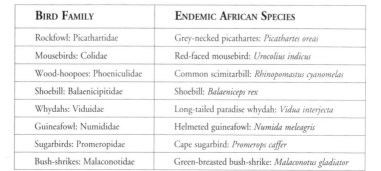

BIRD FAMILY	ENDEMIC AFRICAN SPECIES
Rockfowl: Picathartidae	Grey-necked picathartes: *Picathartes oreas*
Mousebirds: Colidae	Red-faced mousebird: *Urocolius indicus*
Wood-hoopoes: Phoeniculidae	Common scimitarbill: *Rhinopomastus cyanomelas*
Shoebill: Balaenicipitidae	Shoebill: *Balaeniceps rex*
Whydahs: Viduidae	Long-tailed paradise whydah: *Vidua interjecta*
Guineafowl: Numididae	Helmeted guineafowl: *Numida meleagris*
Sugarbirds: Promeropidae	Cape sugarbird: *Promerops caffer*
Bush-shrikes: Malaconotidae	Green-breasted bush-shrike: *Malaconotus gladiator*

Ostrich

Flightless birds such as the ostrich exist in many avian families around the world. As well as being the globe's largest bird, the ostrich is the only bird species with two-toed feet. Its long, strong legs make it one of the fastest animals on land, capable of reaching speeds of up to 45 miles per hour (72 km/h). Once widespread, its range is now restricted to western, eastern, and southwestern Africa.

Cape sparrows
Cape sparrows live in many habitats in southern Africa. They typically forage for insects on the ground and can be found in small groups or large flocks. They are monogamous and nest in loose colonies of up to 100 pairs with up to 15 nests in one tree.

Female ostrich
Unlike the black and white male, the female ostrich is a brownish-gray, which aids camouflage. Females will lay 12–14 eggs in a clutch, and up to four clutches a year. Males, because of their color, incubate at night. After 40 days, the young hatch, and clutches of several females often join together in large creches.

Yellow-billed hornbill
Like all hornbills, the yellow-billed species is characterized by a large, curved, colorful beak. Only males have a casque, or bony, air-filled cavity atop the bill, which serves to attract mates and broadcast their loud call. Southern yellow-billed hornbills forage on the ground for insects and build nests in the cavities of woodland trees.

Ground-hornbill
The southern ground-hornbill is a large, terrestrial, turkey-like bird with a booming call. It has bright red skin on its throat, accentuated by a blue patch on the female. Ground-hornbills often breed cooperatively and all family members may assist a female to rear her single chick.

EAST AFRICAN SAVANNA

Though considered the cradle of humankind, the savannas of East Africa are best known for their animals—elephants, giraffes, rhinoceros, wildebeest, impala, gazelles, lions, hyenas, and jackals, to name a few. Savanna across Central Africa is sandwiched between the Sahara Desert and Sahel to the north, and the Congo forest to the south, arcing down through South Sudan into Ethiopia, Kenya, and Somalia, before ending in northern Tanzania. Savanna vegetation ranges from dry forest and scrub to the spectacular grasslands of Tanzania's Serengeti and the Masai Mara of Kenya. With seasonal rainfall varying from 12 to 47 inches (300–1,200 mm) annually, animals often migrate, following the rains and subsequent grass growth. This open vegetation has been maintained for tens of thousands of years by virtue of the interaction between the rains, grazing by the abundant wildlife, and fires, both natural and lit by humans, that suppress the growth of dense, woody vegetation.

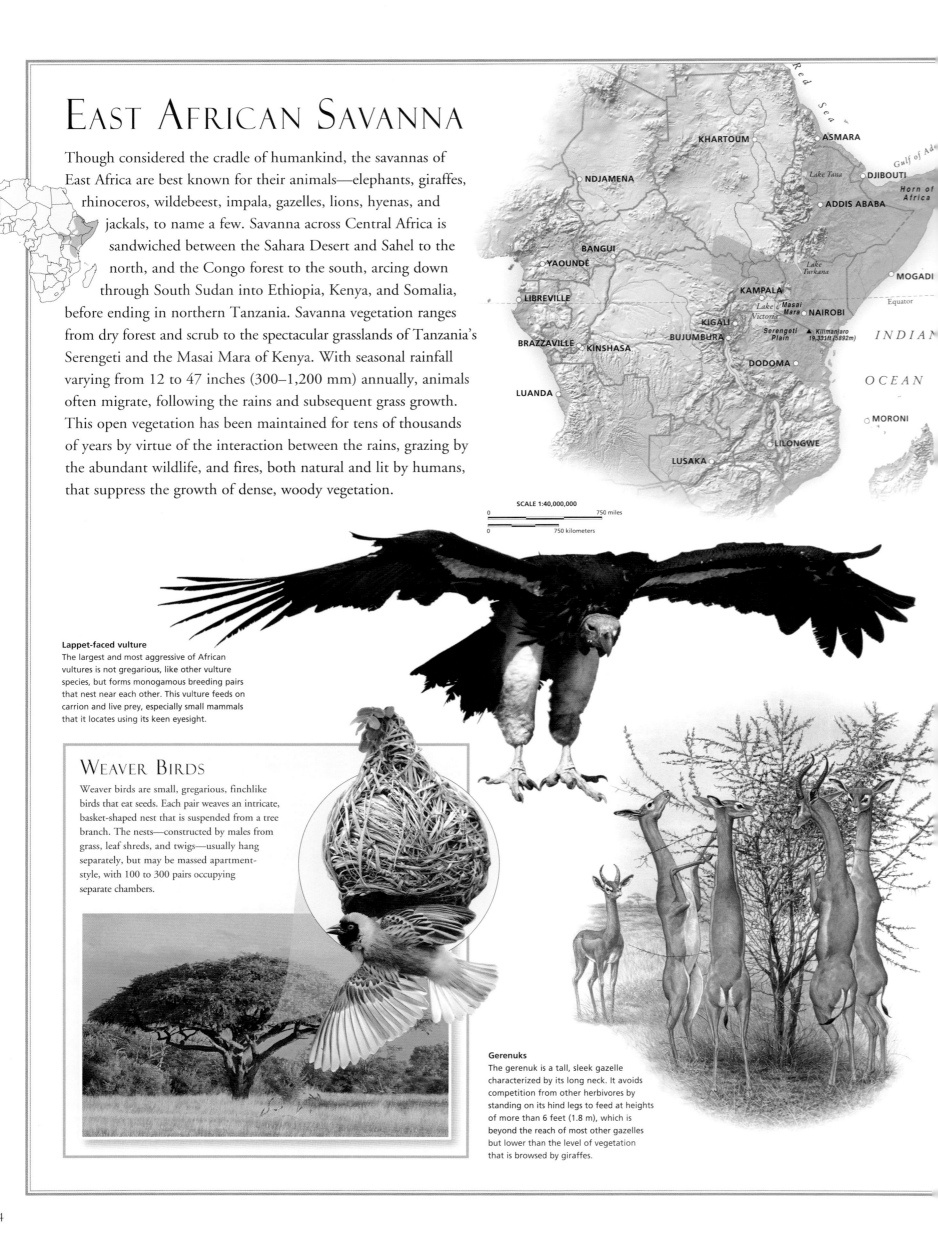

SCALE 1:40,000,000

Lappet-faced vulture
The largest and most aggressive of African vultures is not gregarious, like other vulture species, but forms monogamous breeding pairs that nest near each other. This vulture feeds on carrion and live prey, especially small mammals that it locates using its keen eyesight.

WEAVER BIRDS

Weaver birds are small, gregarious, finchlike birds that eat seeds. Each pair weaves an intricate, basket-shaped nest that is suspended from a tree branch. The nests—constructed by males from grass, leaf shreds, and twigs—usually hang separately, but may be massed apartment-style, with 100 to 300 pairs occupying separate chambers.

Gerenuks
The gerenuk is a tall, sleek gazelle characterized by its long neck. It avoids competition from other herbivores by standing on its hind legs to feed at heights of more than 6 feet (1.8 m), which is beyond the reach of most other gazelles but lower than the level of vegetation that is browsed by giraffes.

Savanna engineers

Elephants are often called ecosystem engineers because of their direct impacts, but termites may play a greater role in savanna structure and function. Termites, which are incredibly abundant, increase soil porosity, allowing water to infiltrate the soil. They also bring nutrients to the surface in tall mounds that may rise 6 to 9 feet (2–3 m) high. These nutrients influence larger scale patterns of vegetation, and hence animal distribution.

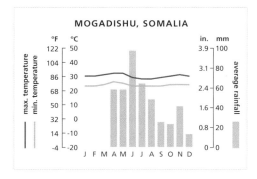

Safari ants
Safari or army ants may live in colonies of 20 million individuals. When food is scarce, columns containing up to 50 million ants from several colonies may form to find resources.

MOGADISHU, SOMALIA

Giraffe
At 18 feet (5.5 m) tall, the giraffe is the tallest land mammal. Recent genetic evidence suggests that there may be as many as six species of giraffe, with variations in color and pattern. Males swing their long necks in combat and when competing for partners.

Striped hyena
A skilled scavenger, the striped hyena has strong teeth and jaw muscles that allow it to crush and digest bones. It is primarily solitary but may rest in pairs. At kill sites, striped hyenas are outcompeted by lions and other carnivores.

African elephants
Males are primarily solitary so elephant societies are dominated by female groups, led by an old matriarch. Elephants rely on their good memory to recall widely dispersed water holes. They also communicate across distances using rumbling infrasound, which can carry for three miles (4.8 km).

EAST AFRICAN SAVANNA
GRASSLAND GRAZERS

From South Africa to just south of the Sahara, grassland ecosystems are dominated by hoofed animals, or ungulates, that come in a wide variety of shapes and sizes. Some of these animals browse or eat woody vegetation, but the greatest densities are among those species that live off seasonally abundant and nutritious grasses—the grazers. The largest grazer is the white rhinoceros, weighing in at 5,000 pounds (2,200 kg), while smaller grazing gazelles, such as the oribi, may weigh as little as 20 pounds (9 kg). In the Serengeti and other large grasslands, zebra eat the taller, rougher grasses, allowing wildebeest to follow in their wake and clip off the shorter, more nourishing grasses. This grazing pattern spurs new growth, and small gazelles such as the Grant's or Thomson's are among the first to dine on the lush, short swards of new grass. This succession of grazers enhances grassland productivity and may explain the abundance of wildlife in the savannas of Africa.

African buffalo
The African buffalo is one of Africa's most abundant of large herbivores. It usually lives in herds of up to a few hundred but buffalo sometimes congregate in their thousands. Although their sight and hearing is poor, a well developed sense of smell allows them to detect predators on the open plains.

Grazing succession
Grazing animals move gradually from raised slopes to lower, damper pockets in their search for good herbage. Larger animals such as zebra are followed by wildebeest, then the smaller gazelles.

 Zebra
 Wildebeest
Thomson's Gazelle

White-eared kob
Africa's best-kept secret was recently revealed when conservationists announced that more than 1.2 million white-eared kob, tiang antelope, and Mongalla gazelle continued to migrate in South Sudan, despite 30 years of civil war. The kob migration had not only survived, but thrived, with numbers rivaling those of the Serengeti.

CONSERVATION WATCH

The two subspecies of white rhino have different histories. Nearly extinct in the early 1900s, the southern white rhino has staged a remarkable recovery, with more than 10,000 now living in South Africa. However, the northern white is now virtually extinct, with only eight to 10 surviving in the wild. The declines are because of demand for rhino horn.

MIGRATION MILES

Each year 2 million animals follow a migration path around the vast plains of the Serengeti. More than one million wildebeest, half a million zebras, and tens of thousands of African buffalo and Thomson's gazelles make the annual move, covering more than 1,000 miles (1,600 km). Not all paths traverse national parks; migrating animals still spend up to 10 percent of their journey in unprotected areas.

River crossings
Lurking crocodiles and raging rapids pose the greatest hazards during river crossings. As many as 200,000 wildebeest die during each migration from being caught in stampedes, falling victim to predators, or drowning.

Grassland communities

Grasslands, dominated by large grazing ungulates above ground and termites below ground, host a diversity of other wildlife. Rodents can occur at densities equaling the grazers. Dozens of carnivore species—from small serval cats to hyenas, leopards, cheetahs, and lions—take advantage of the variety of prey, which ranges from elephants to mice. Birds are abundant, from small larks and nightjars to the world's largest bird, the ostrich.

Thomson's gazelle
The Thomson's gazelle is known for its graceful leaps, which often reach more than 8 feet (2.5 m) in height. When stalked by predators, it will bounce or "stot" to signal that it is escaping. During migration, males establish territories that they rigorously defend in the hope of herding passing females.

Zebra
The plains zebra (above), found across eastern and southern Africa, is one of three zebra species. Grevy's zebra, found only in northern Kenya and southern Ethiopia, has fine stripes and a white belly. The mountain zebra of South Africa and Namibia has wide stripes over its hindquarters. Studies suggest that a zebra's stripes may play a role in thermoregulation—the maintenance of a stable body temperature.

MIGRATION MAP

→ Migration routes

Kenya

Mara R

4

3

5

Serengeti
National Park

2

1

Tanzania

Lining up
A winding column of blue wildebeest crosses the Serengeti–Masai Mara Nature Reserve, tracing a route used annually as they migrate across the grasslands.

Birth on the run
Approximately 400,000 wildebeest are born in the rainy season preceding migration, but births also occur along the way, placing calves at great risk. However, youngsters can stand and run within an hour of birth.

LIFE IN THE ALBERTINE RIFT

Thirty-five million years ago, the African continent almost divided in two. This event created a 6,000-mile (9,600-km) long split, or fissure, known as the East African or Great Rift Valley. An area of spectacular peaks, deep valleys, and diverse lakes, the northern section of the rift, named the Albertine Rift for England's Prince Albert, stretches from the northern tip of Lake Albert to the southern tip of Lake Tanganyika and straddles five countries—the Democratic Republic of Congo, Uganda, Rwanda, Burundi, and Tanzania. Its geographic variety has produced spectacular biological diversity. The region is home to a vast array of vertebrate species: 39 percent of Africa's mammal species, 50 percent of its birds, 19 percent of its amphibians, 14 percent of its reptiles, and a high number of freshwater fish. Representatives of these five groups, alone, total more than 7,500 species. Many are found nowhere else on Earth and a high proportion are critically endangered due to habitat loss or change.

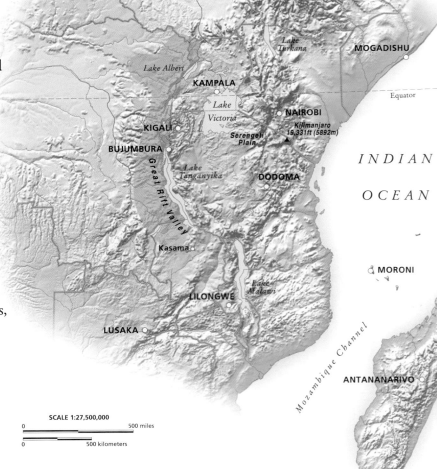

SCALE 1:27,500,000

0   500 miles

0   500 kilometers

Owl-faced monkey
Little is known about this endangered monkey. Limited to the forests of the Democratic Republic of Congo and Rwanda, it uses its elongated fingers to cling to bamboo. Infants are born with a yellowish-brown coat that darkens in colour as they mature.

CONSERVATION WATCH

The golden monkey is so closely related to the blue monkey that they were mistakenly classed as a single species. With a soot-black coat, highlighted by a gold-orange mantle across its back and head, this endangered species is found only in the Virunga Volcanoes—home of the more famous mountain gorilla—and Nyungwe National Park, in Rwanda.

Blue monkey
The paucity of hair on the faces of these silvery-gray furred monkeys gives them a blue appearance. They often feed and travel in groups with other primates, such as red-tailed monkeys, red colobus, and mangabeys. Such multiple species groups enhance efforts to discover new food sources and afford greater protection from predators.

High-altitude variety

The Albertine Rift is home to some of the world's most spectacular plants and animals. At altitudes above 10,000 feet (3,050 m), the giant lobelia provides nectar for many species of sunbirds. Mountain gorillas are visitors to areas dominated by heath at elevations of 9,000 to 12,000 feet (2,800–3,600 m).

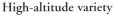

KASAMA, ZAMBIA

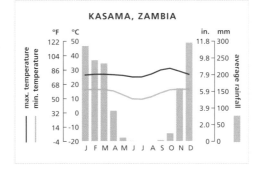

Mountain gorilla
Gorilla beringei beringei

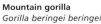

Erica
Erica cruenta

Yellow-eyed black flycatchers
Melaenornis ardesiacus

**Rwenzori
double-collared sunbirds**
Cinnyris stuhlmanni

Giant lobelia
*Lobelia
rhynchopetalum*

Purple breasted sunbird
Nectarinia purpureiventris

Flamingos
Alkaline soda lakes have developed across this region
as a result of the deposition of fine volcanic ash.
The lakes are home to both the lesser and greater
flamingos. Flamingos are filter feeders—they use
their bills, which are lined with fine hairs, to strain
water and capture small shrimplike animals. The
prey contains a red pigment that gives flamingos
their pink color.

Regal sunbird
Cinnyris regia

Bushbaby
The bushbaby is more closely related
to the Madagascan lemurs than the
monkeys of continental Africa. It uses
its large, round eyes and ears to hunt
insects and other prey at night. During
the day it sleeps in tree-hollow nests.

CHAMELEONS

This family of lizards is best known for the ability
to change color. While commonly considered a
camouflage strategy, the color variation actually
results from physiological changes and may be a
means of communication. The upper and lower
lids on a chameleon's eyes are fused, leaving it only
a pinhole to see through. It grips prey—usually
large insects—using suction cups on its tongue.

Johnston's chameleon
Endemic to the Albertine Rift,
the male Johnston's chameleon
resembles a mini triceratops. It uses
its horns when fighting for a mate.

Strange-horned chameleon
A popular pet, famed for the bump
on its nose, this over-collected
chameleon is now endangered and
lives only in the Rwenzori Mountains.

THE MIOMBO WOODLANDS

This vast habitat spans much of south-central Africa, from southern Tanzania through Malawi, Zambia, Zimbabwe, and west to Angola through the southern part of the Democratic Republic of Congo. The Miombo woodlands covers more than 1.1 million square miles (3 million km²), which is 10 percent of the African continent, and takes its name from the Bantu word for the dominant tree genus, *Brachystegia*. The Miombo is characterized by a single, long wet season, when 30 to 39 inches (760–1000 mm) of rain falls, in contrast to the two rainy seasons of the savanna. Plant diversity is high, with more than 8,500 species, and the Miombo's suite of animals includes less common but specialized ungulates, such as Lichtenstein's hartebeest, eland, sable antelope, and black rhino. The region supports a high number of primates, including red colobus, and yellow and chacma baboons, but is perhaps best known as the home of the Gombe Stream Game Reserve, where Jane Goodall conducted her chimpanzee study.

SCALE 1:35,000,000

HORNED CREATURES

The ungulates of the Miombo woodlands are adorned with some of the most spectacular horns of any of the African hoofed animals. Horns, which unlike antlers are not shed, serve a dual function—to protect the animals from predators and as weapons in combat between males for access to females. As a result males usually have larger, more elaborated horns than females.

Greater kudu
The corkscrew horns of the greater kudu indicate rank among males. Males interlock their horns when fighting, in an attempt to push each other off balance.

Sable antelope
Male sable antelope drop to their knees when in battle and fight with their horns, which can reach up to 40 inches (1 m) in length. They have been known to successfully defend themselves against lions.

Oryx
Supremely adapted to dry conditions, oryx occur in large herds and can survive for long periods without water. Their straight horns are extremely sharp, and can fend off lions.

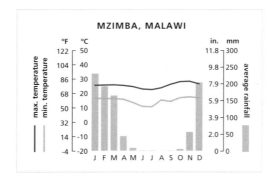

MZIMBA, MALAWI

⚡ CONSERVATION WATCH

The black rhinoceros is critically endangered—only around 4,000 remain in the wild. These rhinoceros have been heavily hunted, particularly for their horns, which are used in traditional medicine. Long, prehensile lips assist the black rhinoceros as it browses for leaves and twigs.

Animals of the woodlands

The animals of the Miombo woodlands must deal with a long, dry season each year. During the long rainy season, when water is plentiful, wildlife densities are low, and animals spread out across the landscape. When water dries up, animals congregate at high densities around the few permanent waterholes. Elephants, the dominant animal by weight, are also critical to excavating waterholes, allowing other animals access to water.

Dung beetle
The dung beetle serves an important function by improving soil composition and nutrient cycling. It locates dung using its keen sense of smell, rolls it into a ball, and buries it. Females lay their eggs inside the balls, which nourish the developing larvae.

Northern carmine bee-eater
The striking carmine bee-eater catches bees on the wing and hits them against hard surfaces to remove their stings. It nests in or near riverbanks in large colonies, where the multiple nesting tunnels resemble high-rise apartments.

Puff adder
Short and wide, the puff adder produces an extremely toxic venom and is one of the deadliest snakes in Africa. It lies in wait to ambush prey, such as small mammals and birds. When disturbed, the adder inflates its head and makes a loud hiss.

Ground pangolin
Pangolins are covered with large plate-like scales. When threatened, they curl up into a ball and the scales form a protective armor. Pangolins do not have teeth; instead, they rely on their specialized tongues to feed on ants.

Woodland home
The Miombo woodlands are home to some of Africa's most iconic predators, including leopards, wild dogs, cheetahs, hyenas, and lions. Recent studies have shown a sharp decline in the number of lions, once common across Africa, because of loss of habitat and direct persecution.

Nile crocodile
An aggressive and feared predator, the Nile crocodile consumes a variety of mammals, ranging from the sitatunga to the wildebeest. Unlike most reptiles, it buries its eggs. Both parents diligently guard them and the mother continues to care for the hatchlings. Nile crocodiles have been known to live for up to 100 years.

Rhinoceros defense
Rhinoceros have two forms of defense—their great bulk and long horn. Males use their horn when competing for females, and females use their horn to defend their young from predators. This critical function was demonstrated when rhinoceros were dehorned in Namibia to deter poachers. Juvenile mortality rose as a result.

THE OKAVANGO DELTA

The Okavango Delta, in the heart of southern Africa, is one of the largest water systems in the world that does not flow to an ocean. With its headwaters in the Cubango River, in Angola, the Okavango River runs through Namibia and terminates in a vast floodplain in northern Botswana. About 10,000 years ago, the waters fed the vast inland Lake Makgadikgadi, but earthquakes and faulting have since destroyed the lake. The delta experiences an annual cycle of flooding and retreat. Rains in Angola, beginning in October, swell the Okavango River and flood the delta. By April, dry conditions have returned, and the delta, which may then cover 6,200 square miles (16,000 km²), shrinks to nearly half that area. The lack of industry or agriculture along the river has kept its waters exceptionally pure, but proposed dams, increased human settlement, and agricultural irrigation threaten its quality and flow. The delta supports a wealth of wildlife—300 species of plants, 450 bird species, and 20 ungulate species.

SCALE 1:30,000,000

THE HIPPOPOTAMUS

Hippopotamuses generally live in small groups, or pods, usually containing one male, several females, and their young. Sensitive to sunlight, they spend much of the day in water, venturing on to land at dusk to feed on grasses. Hippopotamus are hunted for their meat and ivory teeth. When threatened, they express their aggression by opening their mouths wide.

Community group
Hippopotamus pods are led by a bull, which strongly defends its territory and harem from other males. Congregations of up to 100 individuals have been observed; in some rivers hippopotamus densities are high.

Skin protection
The skin of the hippopotamus is sensitive to the harsh African sun. It secretes a red-tinted fluid that protects it against ultraviolet rays and may also have antibiotic properties.

Swamp society

The hippopotamus, widespread across Africa, commonly grazes on dry land at night. But in delta swamps it plays a critical role in maintaining pathways through thick vegetation—water lilies, papyrus, and water cabbage. These hippopotamus channels often connect lakes in the permanent swamps where waterbirds, such as the hammerkop and wattled crane, and the Cape clawless otter make their living.

Hammerhead stork
Scopus umbretta

Hippopotamus
Hippopotamus amphibius

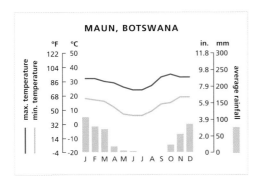

MAUN, BOTSWANA

Waters of the delta
The floodplains of the Okavango Delta expand and retreat seasonally, but there are areas of permanent swamp.

Seasonal floodplains
Permanent swamp
Channels

Red lechwe
The red lechwe, a medium-sized antelope, is an important food source for lions in the delta but is skilled at evading capture. Its hind quarters are longer than its forelimbs, giving it superior leaping abilities. When threatened, members of a lechwe herd disperse in different directions, effectively confusing potential predators.

Sitatunga
Sitatunga are well adapted to swamp life. Strong swimmers with water-resistant coats, they can submerge all but their nostrils and use their splayed hooves to negotiate boggy marshes. However, sitatunga are hunted for their meat and fall victim to snares set on swampy trails.

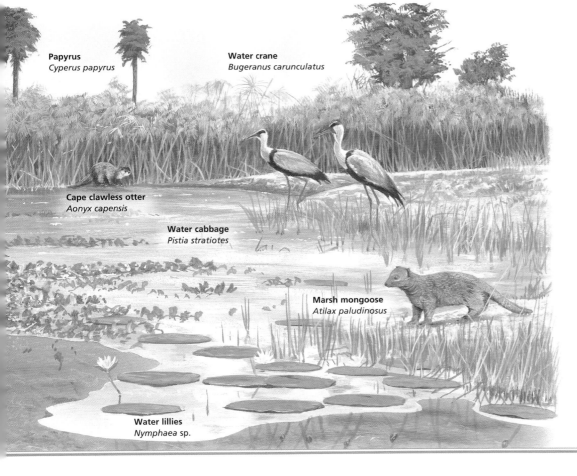

Papyrus
Cyperus papyrus

Water crane
Bugeranus carunculatus

Cape clawless otter
Aonyx capensis

Water cabbage
Pistia stratiotes

Marsh mongoose
Atilax paludinosus

Water lillies
Nymphaea sp.

AFRICA
BIG CARNIVORES

The plains and forests of Africa still support a spectacular group of large carnivores that survive by eating animals much larger than themselves. Carnivorous cats and rarer canids, similar to those still found in Africa, once prowled North America, Asia, and Europe, but were mostly exterminated 10,000 years ago. Lions, hyenas, cheetahs, leopards, and wild dogs are among the widest-ranging species found in Africa, however their pattern of vast movement puts them in direct conflict with an ever-growing human population. As available habitat is reduced, these animals begin competing with one another for food and a defined hierarchy operates, governed by those species that can successfully steal a kill from the others. The lion remains the undisputed king of beasts; hyenas trump wild dogs and cheetah; almost all species are capable of stealing from leopards, which drag their prey into trees in an effort to avoid such theft; and cheetahs employ their unsurpassed speed and cunning to outpace the competition.

AFRICAN CARNIVORE	TOP SPEED IN MILES PER HOUR (KM/H)	GROUP SIZE	LITTER SIZE
Cheetah	70 (112)	1–4	3–5
Lion	50 (80)	5–15	3–5
African wild dog	45 (72)	3–25	5–17
Hyena	40 (60)	2–90	1–2
Leopard	40 (60)	1	2–3

Spotted hyena
Spotted hyenas are among the most effective hunters on the African plains. They kill most of their own food and hunt in packs, chasing down weak or young animals. They efficiently crush bones using their massive teeth and strong jaw muscles, ingesting and digesting body parts that many other predators leave behind. Females are the dominant sex and possess sexual organs that are masculine in appearance. An alpha or dominant female leads each complex hyena clan, which may number up to 80 individuals.

Leopard
The leopard is an opportunistic, solitary hunter that prefers mid-sized antelope. Graceful and elegant, it silently stalks its prey. Like the cheetah and wild dog, the leopard hunts in areas and at times not favored by lions and hyenas, caching fresh kills in trees. Males have large ranges that encompass several female home ranges, but leopards are almost never seen in groups.

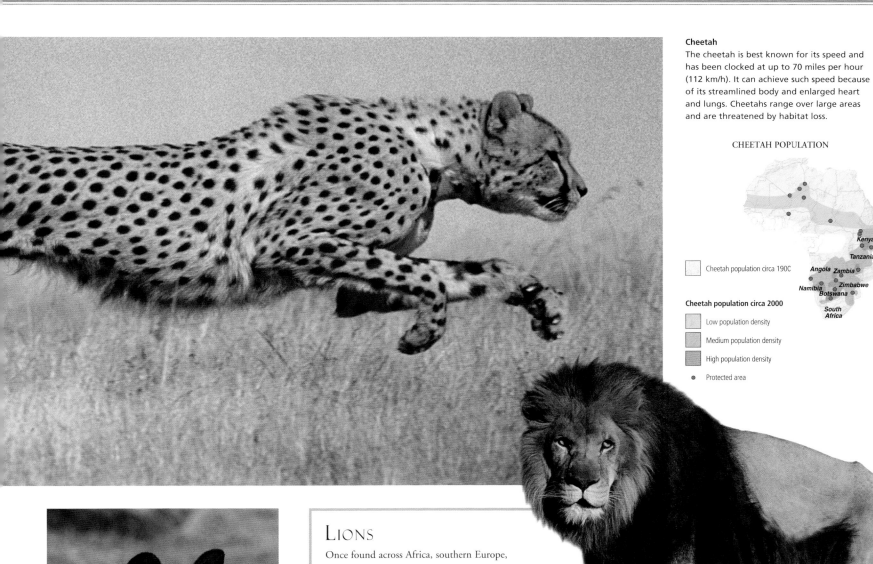

Cheetah
The cheetah is best known for its speed and has been clocked at up to 70 miles per hour (112 km/h). It can achieve such speed because of its streamlined body and enlarged heart and lungs. Cheetahs range over large areas and are threatened by habitat loss.

CHEETAH POPULATION

Kenya
Somalia
Tanzania
Angola
Zambia
Zimbabwe
Namibia
Botswana
South Africa

Cheetah population circa 1900

Cheetah population circa 2000

Low population density

Medium population density

High population density

• Protected area

LIONS

Once found across Africa, southern Europe, and western Asia, lions are now restricted to the savannas and grasslands of eastern and southern Africa. The largest of the African carnivores, they live in prides consisting of five to 10 related females and a coalition of two to three males. Loss of habitat forces them into conflict with humans and livestock, and populations have recently plummeted.

Mane
Only male lions have manes. The mane size and color indicates male quality, but not without a cost. The dark manes preferred by females raise a male's body temperature, demanding more energy use, and make the male more conspicuous.

⚡ CONSERVATION WATCH

Once found across Africa in every habitat except true rain forest, the African wild dog has been exterminated from 32 African countries and fewer than 5,000 remain. Disease contracted from domestic dogs, habitat fragmentation, roads, snaring, and direct persecution have all contributed to the wild dog's decline. However, recent conservation efforts appear to be helping the species recover. Wild dogs hunt in packs of up to 20 adults and communally rear a single litter of puppies born to the dominant female.

Cubs
A lioness gives birth to a litter of up to four cubs, which are introduced to the pride at six weeks. Females may synchronize the timing of births and often nurse each others' offspring.

Hunting
Females are the hunters of the pride, chasing down prey as a unit. They kill by strangulation or delivering a bite to the neck or head. Males may feed first, despite contributing little to the kill.

Life in the Kalahari

The Kalahari describes a vast plateau in southern Africa. It includes both a large desert of about 200,000 square miles (518,000 km²) that covers part of Botswana, South Africa, and Namibia; and a much larger basin measuring some 400,000 square miles (1.03 million km²) that extends north into Angola and Zambia. This basin skirts the western edge of Zimbabwe and includes the whole Okavango River and delta system. At an altitude of approximately 3,000 feet (915 m), the Kalahari is not a true desert but a semi-desert, where stationary sand dunes are covered by grasslands, acacia woodlands, and acacia scrub. The flush of grass that follows annual rain supports some of the most significant wildlife populations in the region, including species once common across Africa, such as the giraffe, elephant, rhinoceros, and lion. Parks in the region include the Central Kalahari Game Reserve, the world's second largest protected area, and the Kgalagadi Transfrontier Park. San Bushmen have long wandered this landscape, living nomadically in the Kalahari for the past 20,000 years.

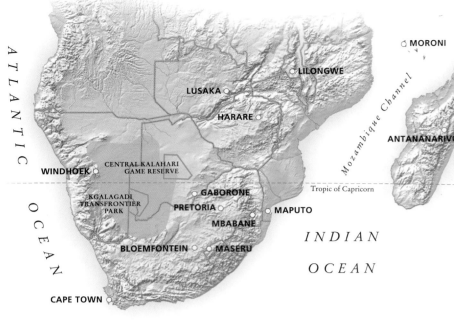

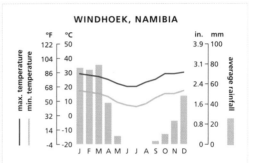

WINDHOEK, NAMIBIA

Desert Adaptations

Wildlife in the Kalahari have adapted to the harsh environment primarily by living at low densities, being active at night, and traveling vast distances. Water, not food, is the key limiting resource. During the wet season, animals fan out across the Kalahari; they survive the drier periods by retreating to the seasonal riverbeds. Elephants—which excavate water holes in the rivers—are critical to the survival of many other species.

Elephant memory
The desert-dwelling elephants of Namibia are smaller than other elephants and can endure many days without water. Like others of their kind, they have a fine memory and may travel more than 45 miles (70 km) to reach water holes and feeding grounds they recall previously visiting.

Lion economies
The lions of the desert have lighter fur and black manes as an adaptation to the extreme daytime temperatures. They travel in smaller groups, over larger ranges, and hunt smaller mammals than lions living elsewhere.

Cape fox
The Cape fox is nocturnal and avoids the heat of the day by resting in burrows underground. It enjoys a varied diet of small mammals, insects, and reptiles, and may cache, or hide, its food.

Aardwolf
Despite being a member of the hyena family, the nocturnal aardwolf subsists on a diet of ants, consuming as many as 200,000 a night. It extracts them from mounds using its sticky tongue and is capable of detoxifying soldier ants. The aardwolf defends itself by secreting a substance similar to that of a skunk.

Springbok
The springbok is named for its tendency to "pronk," or repeatedly leap up to 13 feet (4 m), when escaping predators. During the pronk, a fold of skin with a crest of white fur is exposed on the rump. The springbok can survive for extended periods without water and tends to feed before dawn, when vegetation is most succulent, and at night, when dew has settled on plants.

Gemsbok
The gemsbok, or oryx, relies mainly on water contained within grass for moisture. It has a distinctive black pattern on its white face, with black stripes extending down its back and belly. Oryx have graceful horns that can reach 30 inches (76 cm), with the female growing taller and thinner horns than those of her male counterpart.

Aardvark
Powerful legs, special claws, a long snout and sticky tongue enable the aardvark to dig through termite mounds and ant nests (right), its thick skin wards off bites from prey. Aardvarks regularly dig themselves new burrows (above), which allows other mammals to use their abandoned shelters.

Meerkats

Meerkats, an iconic Kalahari species, live in clans of up to 50 individuals, dominated by a single breeding pair. Family members excavate burrows, help raise pups, and watch out for predators. Meerkats mostly eat insects, excavated using their non-retractable claws. While foraging, at least one clan member serves as sentry, scanning for predators. Meerkats often stand in the morning sun to warm their belly skin.

MADAGASCAR

More than 100 million years ago, Madagascar broke off from the African continent and for much of its history has been completely isolated. It is the world's fourth largest island, with an area of 226,000 square miles (587,000 km²). Its isolation, as well as the variety of habitats on the island, has contributed to the unusual diversity of wildlife that is found in Madagascar and nowhere else on Earth. The western and southern regions of the island are dominated by dry forests and thorny deserts and they harbor animals adapted to dry conditions. Along the eastern side of the island habitats are wetter and some of the most diverse tropical forests are found here. Overall, Madagascar is home to an astonishing 5 percent of the world's species, and 80 percent of them are endemic. Best known are the lemurs—a group of approximately 70 primate species. Despite the island being densely populated by humans and poor by global standards, the Madagascan government is making huge efforts to save the island's natural heritage.

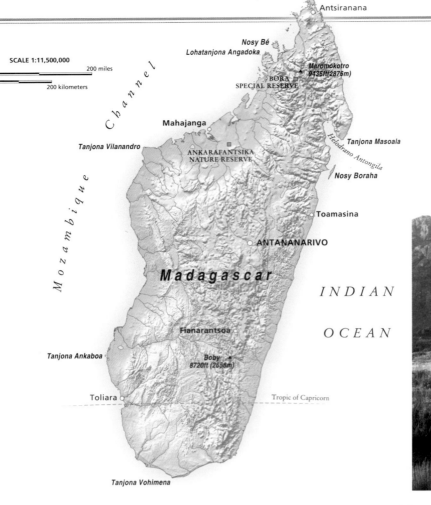

SCALE 1:11,500,000

SMALL FOREST CREATURES

With more than 400 species of reptiles and 300 species of frogs, Madagascar hosts a wide diversity of reptiles and amphibians. Half of the world's chameleon species exist only in Madagascar. Some evolutionary affinities are unexpected: pythons do not occur here but an endemic boa constrictor has its closest relatives in South America.

Giant leaf-tailed gecko
A master of camouflage, the giant leaf-tailed gecko spends much of its day resting while hanging upside down by its tail. If disturbed, it will stand with head and tail erect and emit a loud hiss.

Panther chameleon
Found throughout Madagascar's tropical forest, the male panther chameleon is nearly twice the size of the female, and more vibrantly colored. Chameleons' coloration and patterns are social signals.

Spider tortoise
Named for the weblike pattern of yellow lines on its shell, the spider tortoise has adapted to life in dry habitats by burrowing underground during the driest times of the year and remaining buried until the rainy season begins.

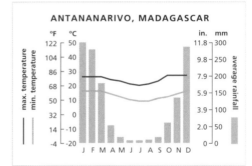

ANTANANARIVO, MADAGASCAR

Tomato frog
Despite its bright red color, the tomato frog sits quietly as it waits to ambush its insect prey. Its coloration acts as a warning to predators; if attacked it puffs up its body and gives off a toxic sticky substance.

Fossa
The fossa is the dominant and largest predator on Madagascar. More than 50 percent of its diet is made up of lemurs. Closely related to the mongoose, it is agile both on the ground and in trees. Widely distributed, it is always found at low densities, which makes it vulnerable to extinction.

Lemur diversity

The sifakas, wooly lemurs, and the indri, all in the Indriidae family, are the largest lemurs: indris may weigh up to 22 pounds (10 kg). The world's smallest primate, the gray mouse lemur, weighs one to two ounces (40–60 grams). Mid-sized lemurs, such as the red-bellied lemur, weigh about 3 pounds (1.4 kg). The ruffed lemurs are the only primates to produce young in litters.

Gray mouse lemur
Microcebus murinus

Indri
Indri indri

⚡ **Red-ruffed lemur**
Varecia variegata rubra

Red-bellied lemur
Eulemur rubriventer

Island landscape
The weathering of rocky outcrops in the south of Madagascar has created some spectacular landforms. Also found here is a unique habitat, characterized by tall, spiny vegetation. Baobabs, aloes, and cactus-like euphorbia are common, but the most distinctive plants are the endemic Dideraceae trees, inlcuding the octopus tree.

Ring-tailed lemur
The ring-tailed lemur is the most terrestrial of the lemurs and is often found "sunbathing" in an upright stance. Like most lemurs, females are dominant. Aggressive interactions often include "stink fights," which involve flicking tails coated with a scent from glands in the wrist.

Malagasy civet
Found throughout Madagascar, the Malagasy civet, which looks like a small fox, typically lives in pairs that share a territory. Its diet is made up of small animals—rodents, birds, reptiles, and frogs. To cope with times of food shortage the fat stored in its tail may comprise up to 25 percent of its body weight.

AYE-AYE

Perhaps the most distinctive of the Malagasy primates, the nocturnal aye-aye was originally mistaken for a rodent. In part this is because of its strange appearance as well as its rodent-like incisors that continue to grow throughout its life. It is the largest nocturnal primate, with big eyes and large, sensitive ears. Some local traditions identify aye-ayes with bad luck, often leading to their persecution.

Claws
Pointed claws allow aye-ayes to hang from branches. The distinctive elongated middle finger is used to tap tree branches to find and extract insect grubs inside.

Mother and young
Aye-ayes live a primarily solitary life with the only long-term bond being the one between a mother and her young.

AFRICA'S CORAL REEFS

While corals fringe the African continent, true reefs are mostly found off the east coast, from the Red Sea south to Mozambique and across to Madagascar. West and Central Africa, on the Atlantic coast, also possess some diverse corals, particularly on the islands of Cape Verde, but a combination of high rainfall and strong Atlantic currents, with cold oceanic upwellings, largely inhibits reef formation. Coral reefs are biologically diverse, highly productive, and critical to local fisheries and subsistence fishermen. This is particularly true for the densely populated coasts of Kenya, Tanzania, Mozambique, and Madagascar. Industrial run-off and pollutants, untreated sewage, and increasing sediment flows in rivers all threaten these coastal ecosystems. But most serious of all are the threats posed by global climate change. Sea surface temperature increases—the result of climate change and a particularly severe El Niño in 1997–98—hit the Western Indian Ocean particularly hard, killing 90 percent of corals across a large expanse.

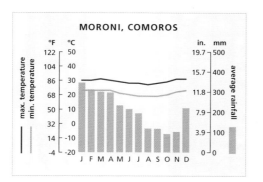

MORONI, COMOROS

ORNAMENTAL SHELLS

Mollusk shells are multilayered. The mother-of-pearl layer is made up primarily of calcium carbonate and gives the shell its luster and distinctive pattern. Shells are a protective fortress for the soft-bodied mollusks living within, their color and patterns providing camouflage from a multitude of predators. Algae may live along the lips of clam shells, where they trap sunlight and deliver the clam an energy-rich supply of food.

Cowrie
Cowries live under rocks and feed on algae at night. Their smooth, porcelain-like shells are wrapped in a mantle that is often brilliantly colored. In Africa, the shells were once used as currency and for decorating cloth and baskets.

Maxima clam
Clams are bivalves, having two shells to protect their soft bodies. The maxima clam lives in shallow waters near the top of the reef, where it attaches itself to the coral rubble or limestone surface and filters water to trap plankton.

Mantis shrimp
The stalked, compound eyes of the mantis shrimp are among the most complex of the animal kingdom. These active hunters use their robust claws to repeatedly smash prey, employing forces so strong that they have been known to crack glass.

Starfish
Starfish lack a centralized brain, but have two stomachs to digest their prey, and at least five arms, which they can regenerate if severed. A covering of spines prevents organisms from colonizing the skin of starfish, all of which can reproduce sexually and asexually.

Sweetlips
As its name suggests, the black-spotted sweetlip that lives in the Indian Ocean can be recognized by its lips and spots. Juveniles have six lines down their back, which later develop into spots. Sweetlips feed at night on invertebrates and can grow up to 18 inches (45 cm) in length.

Humphead wrasse
One of the largest fish inhabiting the coral reef, the humphead wrasse is distinguished by a large bulge on its head. Highly sedentary, it is active by day and rests in reef caves at night. A long lifespan—about 32 years—and slow breeding rate make the humphead wrasse vulnerable to over-fishing.

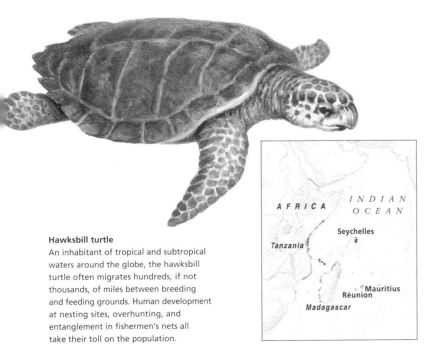

Hawksbill turtle
An inhabitant of tropical and subtropical waters around the globe, the hawksbill turtle often migrates hundreds, if not thousands, of miles between breeding and feeding grounds. Human development at nesting sites, overhunting, and entanglement in fishermen's nets all take their toll on the population.

AFRICA

INDIAN OCEAN

Seychelles

Tanzania

Mauritius

Réunion

Madagascar

ESTIMATED THREAT TO CORAL REEF

Low
Medium
High

Potato grouper
Found in the Red Sea and Indo-West Pacific, the potato grouper is a large fish that feeds on other reef fish and crustaceans. It is highly territorial and known for its aggression, but its size makes the grouper susceptible to spear-fishing.

Frilled lizards are found in New Guinea and the tropical north and east coast of Australia. The capelike frill that lies over the lizard's shoulders flares up when it is frightened or angry, making it appear twice its actual size. The lizard opens its mouth wide, hisses loudly, and pushes up on its front legs to ward off predators.

AUSTRALASIA
& OCEANIA

AUSTRALASIA & OCEANIA

The biogeographic region of Australasia extends from the easternmost islands of the Indonesian archipelago to New Guinea and Australia. The region known as Oceania incorporates all the island groups in the southern Pacific Ocean, including New Zealand. Most of the land in these two regions consists of three remnants of what was once the ancient continent Gondwana; Australia and New Guinea being the largest, and New Zealand and New Caledonia the smaller fragments. The remaining island groups are mainly volcanic in origin or formed as coral atolls perched atop submerged volcanic remnants. The flora and fauna of Australasia and Oceania is rich in old endemic species that had ancestors in the forests of Gondwana. Foremost among the floral relicts are the Araucaria pines and southern beeches. Among the fauna, the large flightless ratite birds, monotremes, and marsupial mammals are also reminders of previous Gondwanan wildlife.

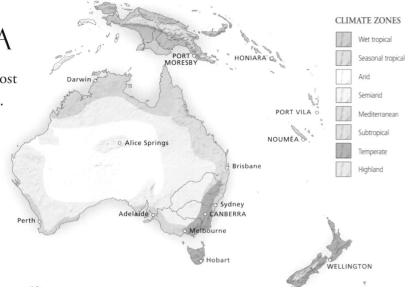

CLIMATE ZONES
- Wet tropical
- Seasonal tropical
- Arid
- Semiarid
- Mediterranean
- Subtropical
- Temperate
- Highland

Climate

Close proximity to the equator produces warm, humid conditions across much of Oceania. Hurricanes, known locally as cyclones, occur above 5 degrees south during the summer and extend to the northern latitudes of Australia. The middle latitudes are cooler, and moist onshore winds ensure regular rainfall in New Zealand and on Australia's east coast. However, the Australian interior is arid; less than 12 inches (300 mm) of rainfall is recorded each year across about half the continent.

New Guinea Highlands
The rain forests of the New Guinea highlands are home to many unique species of mammals and birds, including the tree kangaroos and birds-of-paradise.

The Tropical North
The "Top End" of Australia, with its iconic magnetic termite mounds, is home to many unique species adapted to the extremes of heavy summer rains and dry winters..

New Zealand
The kiwi is synonymous with New Zealand. It is one of the few survivors of an ancient line of flightless birds that once inhabited the great southern continent of Gondwana.

The Great Barrier Reef
Australia's Great Barrier Reef is the largest fringing coral reef in the world and its abundant coral and fish species make it an important global biodiversity hot spot.

The Australian Outback
The deserts of central Australia are home to arid-adapted species such as the bearded dragon, but oases in the form of artesian springs and ephemeral lakes occur here too.

Islands of the Southeast Pacific
Lord Howe Island is home to a host of seabirds that nest on its predator-free shores. Other islands are a sanctuary for endemic species including flightless birds.

Wildlife of Cape York
Cape York is both the bridge and the barrier between Australia and New Guinea, and its flora and fauna contain a fascinating mix of species from both major landmasses.

Temperate Southern Forests and Heathlands
Like the eucalyptus trees on which it feeds, Australia's iconic animal, the koala, is one of the most readily identified inhabitants of the temperate southern forests.

PROPORTIONS OF TOTAL LAND AREA

- Forest and woodland — 23.6%
- Arable land — 6.6%
- Grazing — 49.4%
- Other land — 20.4%

Land cover

Most of the Australian continent, as well as New Zealand, is suited to grazing, but in Australia livestock must roam widely to find sufficient food. Overall, one-quarter of Oceania is covered with forests. Arable land is scarce on many Pacific Islands, except where good rainfall and volcanic soils ensure agricultural productivity.

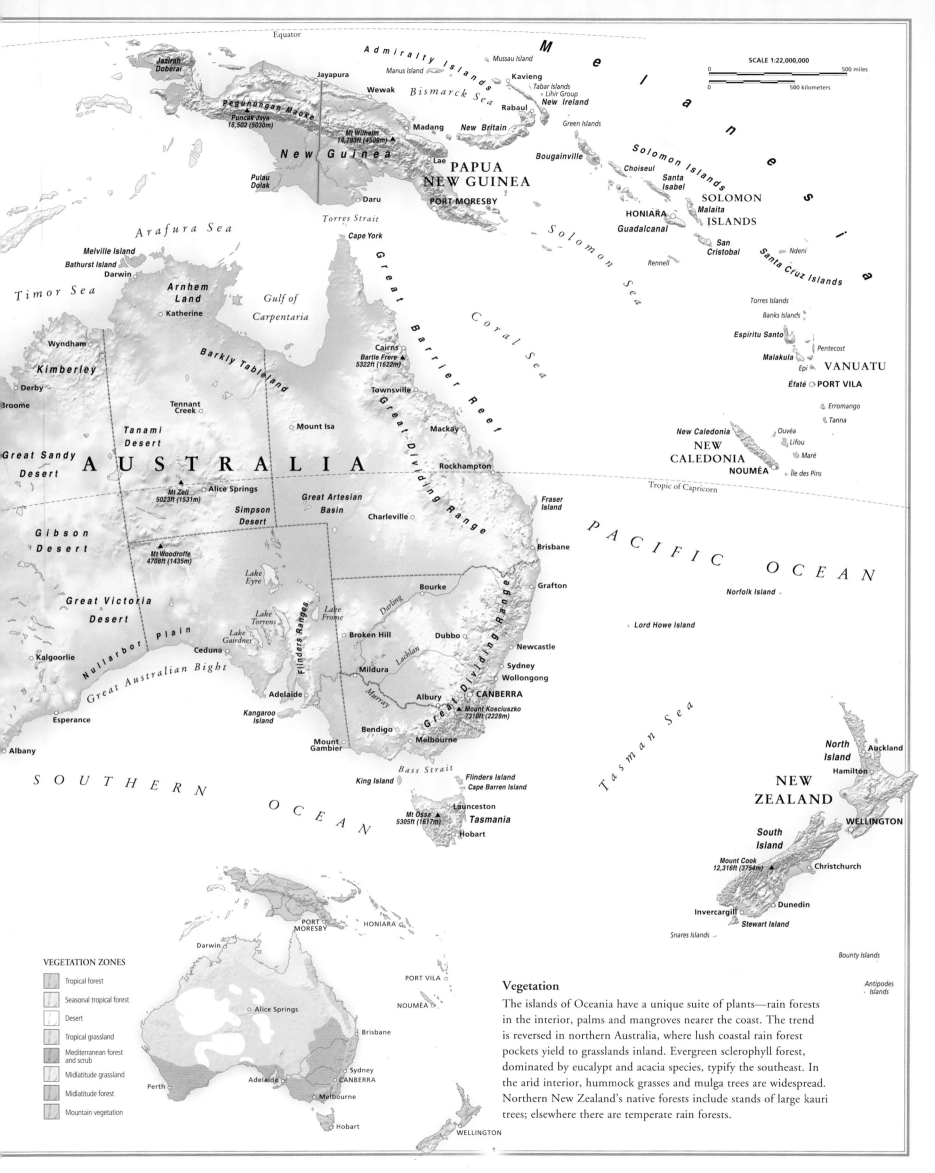

Equator

Melanesia

SCALE 1:22,000,000
0   500 miles
0   500 kilometers

Jazirah
Doberai

Admiralty Islands
Mussau Island
Manus Island
Jayapura   Kavieng
Wewak   Tabar Islands
Bismarck Sea   Lihir Group
New Ireland
Pegunungan Maoke   Rabaul
Puncak Jaya   Madang   New Britain
16,502 (5030m)   Green Islands
Mt Wilhelm
14,793ft (4509m) ▲   Madang
New Guinea   Lae   Bougainville   Choiseul
Pulau   **PAPUA**   Santa
Dolak   **NEW GUINEA**   Isabel   SOLOMON
Daru   **PORT MORESBY**   ISLANDS
Torres Strait   HONIARA   Malaita
Guadalcanal   ISLANDS
Solomon Sea   San
Arafura Sea   Cristobal   Santa Cruz Islands
Cape York   Rennell   Ndeni

Melville Island   Coral Sea   Torres Islands
Bathurst Island   Banks Islands
Darwin   Espíritu Santo
Timor Sea   Arnhem   Gulf of   Pentecost
Land   Carpentaria   Malakula
Katherine   Epi   **VANUATU**
Wyndham   Cairns   Éfaté ○ **PORT VILA**
Bartle Frere
Kimberley   Barkly Tableland   5322ft (1622m) ▲   Erromango
Derby   Townsville   Tanna
Broome   Tennant   Great Barrier Reef
Creek   Mount Isa   New Caledonia   Ouvéa
Tanami   Mackay   **NEW**   Lifou
Great Sandy   Desert   **CALEDONIA**
Desert   Great Dividing Range   Maré
A U S T R A L I A   Rockhampton   **NOUMÉA**   Île des Pins
Tropic of Capricorn
Mt Zeil   Alice Springs   Fraser
5023ft (1531m) ▲   Simpson   Great Artesian   Island   **P A C I F I C   O C E A N**
Gibson   Desert   Basin
Desert   Mt Woodroffe   Charleville   Brisbane
4708ft (1435m) ▲   Lake   Norfolk Island
Eyre
Bourke   Grafton
Great Victoria   Lake   Darling   Lord Howe Island
Desert   Torrens   Lake
Frome   Broken Hill   Dubbo
Lake   Newcastle
Kalgoorlie   Nullarbor   Gairdner   Lachlan   Sydney
Plain   Ceduna   Mildura   Wollongong
Esperance   Great Australian Bight   Murray   Albury   **CANBERRA**
Adelaide   ▲ Mount Kosciuszko
Albany   Kangaroo   7310ft (2228m)   Tasman Sea
Island   Bendigo
Flinders Ranges   Melbourne   North
Mount   King Island   Bass Strait   Flinders Island   Island   Auckland
Gambier   Cape Barren Island   Hamilton
S O U T H E R N   Launceston   **NEW**
Mt Ossa ▲   **Tasmania**   **ZEALAND**
5305ft (1617m)
O C E A N   Hobart   South   **WELLINGTON**
Island
Mount Cook
12,316ft (3754m) ▲   Christchurch
Invercargill   Dunedin
Stewart Island
Snares Islands

Bounty Islands

Antipodes
Islands

Vegetation

The islands of Oceania have a unique suite of plants—rain forests
in the interior, palms and mangroves nearer the coast. The trend
is reversed in northern Australia, where lush coastal rain forest
pockets yield to grasslands inland. Evergreen sclerophyll forest,
dominated by eucalypt and acacia species, typify the southeast. In
the arid interior, hummock grasses and mulga trees are widespread.
Northern New Zealand's native forests include stands of large kauri
trees; elsewhere there are temperate rain forests.

VEGETATION ZONES

Tropical forest
Seasonal tropical forest
Desert
Tropical grassland
Mediterranean forest and scrub
Midlatitude grassland
Midlatitude forest
Mountain vegetation

PORT MORESBY   HONIARA
Darwin
PORT VILA
Alice Springs   NOUMÉA
Brisbane
Sydney
Perth   CANBERRA
Adelaide
Melbourne
Hobart   WELLINGTON

MONOTREMES AND OTHER UNIQUE ANIMALS

Australia has unique remnants of the fauna that existed on the southern supercontinent, Gondwana, 200 million years ago. These include lungfish, ratites (large flightless birds), endemic turtles and frogs, and monotremes. Monotremes, or egg-laying mammals, are the only survivors of the early mammals that arose while dinosaurs dominated Earth. Fossil monotremes are found in South America and Australia, but the living species occur only in Australia and New Guinea. The surviving platypus species is found only in eastern Australia and the two echidna species, with short and long beaks, occur in Australia and New Guinea respectively. Until the Pleistocene period, 50,000 years ago, the long-beaked echidna's relatives also occurred in Australia. Monotremes have advanced mammalian characteristics, such as hair, mammary glands, although not teats, and a large cerebral cortex, but they retain some primitive reptilian features.

Short-beaked echidna
The short-beaked echidna is a spiky, rotund creature widely distributed throughout Australia and lowland New Guinea, where its preferred prey are plentiful. The echidna's diet consists of ants and termites, which it consumes in enormous quantities. It is frequently seen foraging by day, except during the hottest months of the year. When threatened, it can dig vertically into the soil, leaving only a few spines visible.

Claws and tongue
Echidnas use their powerful claws to excavate the nests and feeding tunnels of ants and termites. They then insert their long, sticky tongues into the galleries to lap up the insects.

Monotremes

Monotremes lay eggs, which hatch after a short incubation period in either a nest or the mother's pouch. The young lap milk from the mother's mammary glands. In echidnas, the mammary glands lie within a pouch on the mother's belly. The highly specialized diet of the platypus includes freshwater crustaceans and insect larvae; the long-beaked echidna eats worms. All monotremes have a daily period of torpor (a deep sleep when the body temperature is lowered) and, in southern latitudes, the short-beaked echidna may hibernate in winter.

Platypus
Platypus swim with their webbed front feet, using their hind feet to steer. When diving, they close their eyes and ears and search for food using electroreceptors within their beak, which detect the movement of prey. They are found in streams, rivers, and lakes in eastern Australia.

CURIOUS CREATURES

In addition to monotremes, Australia is home to many other unique animals. Among the most recognizable are the emu and cassowary, large flightless birds related to the ostrich of Africa and rheas of South America. Rarely seen inhabitants of inland waters, the lobe-finned lungfish and soft-shelled turtle also have relatives in Africa and South America. Ground frogs and toadlets, once considered part of an American family, are now recognized as uniquely Australian.

Pig-nosed turtle
Found only in Australia's far north, pig-nosed turtles are notable for their soft shells, which lack bony dermal plates. They live and breed in freshwater, flood-prone rivers, where the rising waters stimulate their eggs to hatch.

Australian lungfish
These air-breathing fish are restricted to two rivers in Queensland. Their lungs allow them to breathe air when caught in shallow pools but, unlike their African and American cousins, they cannot survive in mud alone.

Platypus young

The mother platypus incubates her eggs for two weeks in a nest near the end of a long burrow. She then suckles her young until they are old enough to forage, leaving them briefly to feed herself.

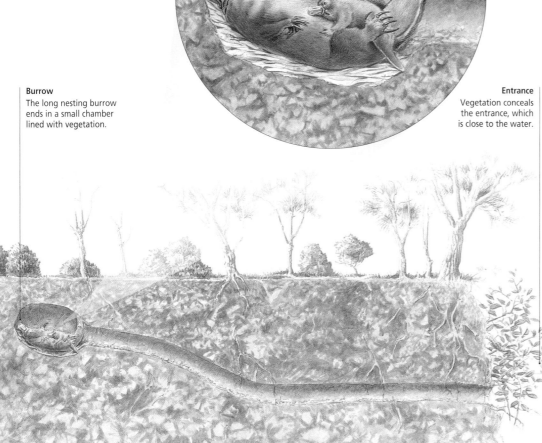

Burrow
The long nesting burrow ends in a small chamber lined with vegetation.

Entrance
Vegetation conceals the entrance, which is close to the water.

● Corroboree frog
This colorful frog is restricted to sphagnum bogs above 3,500 feet (1,000 m) in the Australian Alps. It has a short breeding season and lays its large eggs in deep burrows.

Emu
Widespread over most of Australia, emus eat the leaves and flowers of a variety of native plants, as well as insects. The male incubates the eggs and cares for the young for at least six months. At maturity, emus can reach 8 feet (2.5 m) in height.

AUSTRALIA'S MARSUPIALS

Marsupials evolved on the great southern continent of Gondwana around the time it was breaking up, and formed a major part of the early mammal fauna of both South America and Australia. In Australia they became the dominant mammals for much of the early Tertiary period, 65 million years ago. Marsupials have a more primitive brain and skeletal features, particularly the skull, than placental mammals. They deliver live young, but the young are born at an embryonic stage of development and newborns attach themselves to a teat, generally enclosed in a pouch on the mother's belly, where they are fed until they are fully furred and able to move around. Australia's living marsupials range in size from the tiny, three-inch (8 cm) planigale, which lives in grasslands, to the red kangaroo, which stands at 5 feet (1.5 m). However, the fossil record reveals more impressive marsupials of times gone by, such as giant wombats that reached the size of a modern-day rhinoceros.

Koala
The koala looks sleepy because it lives on a diet of highly toxic eucalypt leaves. It has the ability to detoxify the poisons but the effort required leaves little energy to spare. Koalas do not make nests but simply sleep in the fork of a tree.

Common wombat
The stout frame and limbs of the common wombat make it a formidable landscape architect, capable of excavating extensive burrow systems with nesting chambers and multiple entrances. A grazer, the wombat forages for food at night. Its large colon enables it to live, like a horse, on dry grasses.

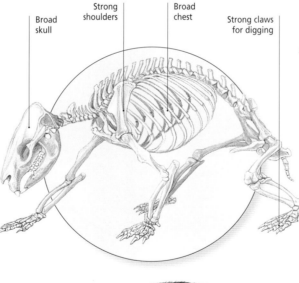

Broad skull · Strong shoulders · Broad chest · Strong claws for digging

Southern brown bandicoot
Isoodon obesulus

Diverse habitats

Marsupials live in a variety of habitats. Trees provide shelter and food for possums, gliders, and the koala; rocky slopes are home to rock wallabies and wallaroos; and grassy nests hide the brown bandicoot. The elusive marsupial mole ploughs through soft sand without making a permanent burrow.

⚡ CONSERVATION WATCH

The Tasmanian devil, a carnivorous marsupial, is under severe threat from a virus that causes debilitating facial tumors. This contagious, fatal disease seems to be transferred between animals through biting. Efforts are continuing to establish a vaccine and an isolated, disease-free population. It is feared that the wild population could become extinct. Of Australia's 170 marsupial species, 10 are extinct, a further 34 are listed by the International Union for Conservation of Nature (IUCN) as threatened, and 26 are on the verge of threatened status.

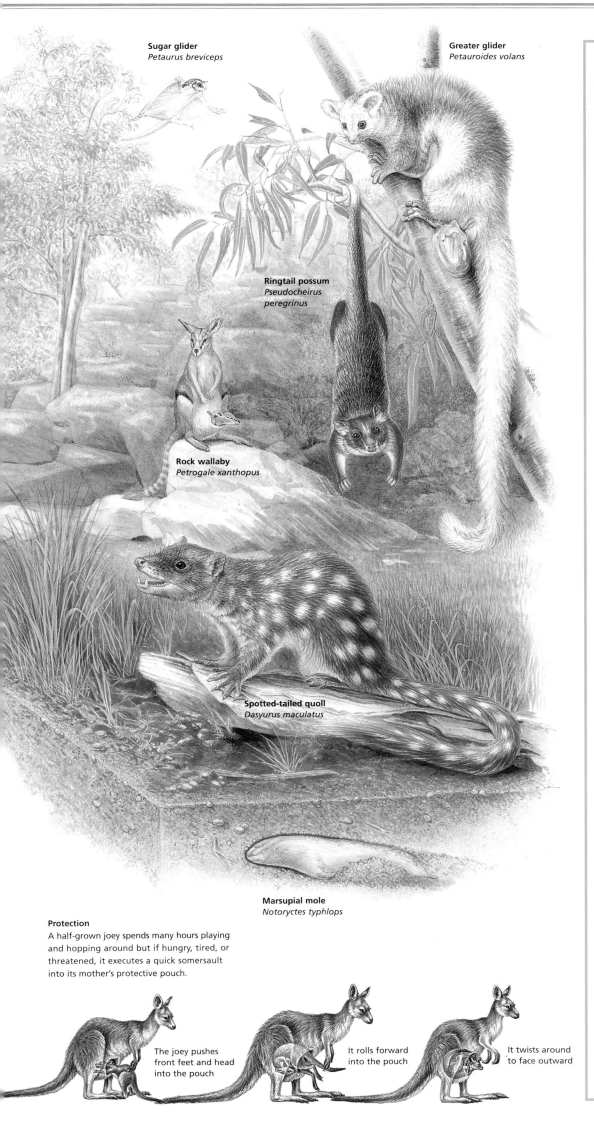

Sugar glider
Petaurus breviceps

Greater glider
Petauroides volans

Ringtail possum
Pseudocheirus peregrinus

Rock wallaby
Petrogale xanthopus

Spotted-tailed quoll
Dasyurus maculatus

Marsupial mole
Notoryctes typhlops

Protection
A half-grown joey spends many hours playing and hopping around but if hungry, tired, or threatened, it executes a quick somersault into its mother's protective pouch.

The joey pushes front feet and head into the pouch

It rolls forward into the pouch

It twists around to face outward

MARSUPIALS LARGE AND SMALL

Marsupials in Australia occur in all terrestrial habitats but are most numerous in wetter forested areas with more dense and diverse vegetation. Despite this, the majority of marsupials occupy select feeding niches. More than half are carnivores or insectivores/omnivores and most of the remainder are herbivores. The koala and greater glider can eat highly toxic eucalypt leaves. Termites, pollen and nectar, gums, resins, and fungi comprise other specialized marsupial diets.

Honey possum
Mouselike honey possums feast on pollen and nectar, reaching their brush-tipped tongues into the flowers of banksias and other heathland plants.

Brown antechinus
The brown antechinus, a small carnivorous marsupial, nests in hollow logs or in rock crevices, emerging at night to feed on beetles and spiders.

Red kangaroo
Widespread across Australia's inland, the red kangaroo browses on grasses and shrubs. It rests under trees by day, feeding mostly at dawn and dusk.

New Guinea Highlands

The highlands of New Guinea are generally considered to include land over 3,000 feet (914 m). They consist of a central cordillera running east-west along the island, two large outliers on the Vogelkop and Huon peninsulas, and several smaller isolated mountain ranges. These highland areas amount to nearly 30 percent of New Guinea's total land area. The vegetation found here ranges from palm forests and rain forest in the wettest areas to tree-fern savannas and grasslands on the drier slopes. The extensive open grasslands characteristic of many highland valleys, known as kunai grasslands, may not be the result of human clearing but a natural vegetation type in areas of lower rainfall and soil fertility. Among the native mammal and bird species there is considerable variability in different regions. Subspecies or local variants might occur along the central range while related but distinct species are found on the peninsulas.

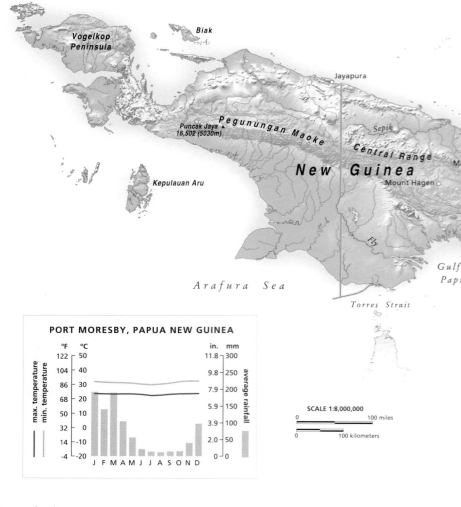

PORT MORESBY, PAPUA NEW GUINEA

SCALE 1:8,000,000

0 — 100 miles
0 — 100 kilometers

CONSERVATION WATCH

The long-beaked echidna was once a common resident of the rain forests above 2,000 feet (600 m) throughout New Guinea. It was, however, a delicacy for the Papuan peoples. Hunting, combined with a drastic loss of habitat, has resulted in it becoming endangered.

Remote landscapes

The rugged terrain of the New Guinea highlands and the small population, found mostly in scattered villages, has resulted in much of the densely forested country remaining undisturbed. The animal life found here—the cuscus, tree kangaroo, colorful Birds-of-Paradise, and the long-beaked echidna —are adapted to forest living. But, increasingly, human activities are causing habitat loss.

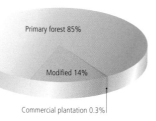

Primary forest 85%

Modified 14%

Commercial plantation 0.3%

Forests

The forests of New Guinea's highlands vary in nature according to altitude. On the lower slopes rain forests support flowering, fruit-bearing trees, which attract fruit bats, numerous birds, and some of the world's largest birdwing butterflies. On higher slopes the forest thins, gradually giving way to small subalpine trees and grasses.

Birdwing butterfly

The male Poseidon birdwing butterfly is often seen as a brilliant flash of iridescent green and yellow as it flits through the dappled light of the forest understory. Larvae of the birdwing feed on rain forest vines of the genus *Aristolochia*.

Goodfellow's tree kangaroo
Living in the rain forests of the Central Highlands, Goodfellow's tree kangaroo has suffered habitat loss because of forest-clearing for agriculture. However, it remains the most widespread species within the ornate tree kangaroo group.

Spotted cuscus
One of the most widespread mammals of New Guinea, the spotted cuscus occurs in all habitat types. It has long been a favorite food of the Papuan people, and has been transported to many of New Guinea's neighboring islands.

BIRDS-OF-PARADISE

Birds-of-paradise are synonymous with the island of New Guinea and the bright plumes the birds employ in their spectacular displays have been adopted by the local peoples in their equally colorful headdresses. The birds' range extends to Indonesia and subtropical Australia, but the center of diversity is in the New Guinea highlands. The bright, gaudy males perform elaborate acrobatic displays.

Raggiana bird-of-paradise
The Raggiana bird-of-paradise is the most common species in this family. Males gather in groups known as leks to perform their spectacular dance routines, which are accompanied by high-pitched calls.

King of Saxony
The male King of Saxony is unique, with its two long head plumes, but the female is easily mistaken for a drab honeyeater. Solitary males display from a dead limb high in the canopy.

Superb bird-of-paradise
The male superb bird-of-paradise is unmistakable, with electric-blue false wings on its chest and lustrous black erectile back feathers.

Huon astrapia
Huon astrapias are, like other astrapias, quiet birds of the middle to upper canopy. They fly in a characteristic flap-and-glide pattern, with their enormous tails trailing behind.

Blue bird-of-paradise
The male blue bird-of-paradise is solitary, unlike its close relative the Raggiana bird-of-paradise. It is also secretive, displaying in the treetops high on a hillside.

Great Barrier Reef

The Great Barrier Reef, a magnificent strand of coral reefs and islands set in clear, warm tropical waters, was one of Australia's first World Heritage nominations and was inscribed on the World Heritage List in 1981. Running parallel to the far northeast coast and spanning nearly 14 degrees of latitude the reef is the largest World Heritage Area. It covers some 134,286 square miles (347,800 km^2) and The Great Barrier Reef Marine Park, which was declared in 1975 and which affords protection to the reef and its wildlife, contains most of the designated WHA. Despite its name, the reef is not one long barrier, but a series of 760 separate fringing reefs and more than 2,000 other reefs and cays inside the barrier, which range in size from less than 2.5 acres (1 ha) to more than 250,000 acres (100,000 ha). The shallow tropical water, with surface temperatures in the range of 75–86°F (24–30ºC), is an ideal environment for a wide variety of marine animals.

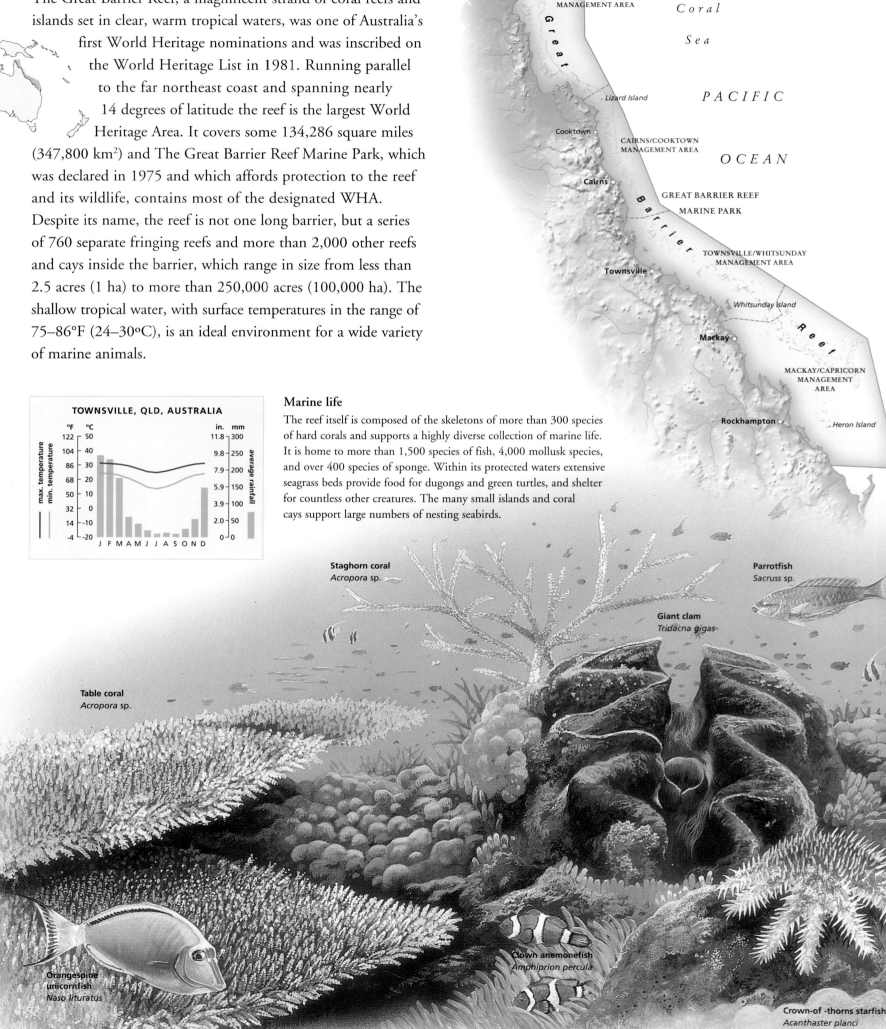

SCALE 1:11,000,000

0   200 miles
0   200 kilometers

Cape York

Coral Sea

FAR NORTHERN MANAGEMENT AREA

PACIFIC

Lizard Island

Cooktown

CAIRNS/COOKTOWN MANAGEMENT AREA

OCEAN

Cairns

GREAT BARRIER REEF MARINE PARK

TOWNSVILLE/WHITSUNDAY MANAGEMENT AREA

Townsville

Whitsunday Island

Mackay

MACKAY/CAPRICORN MANAGEMENT AREA

Rockhampton

Heron Island

TOWNSVILLE, QLD, AUSTRALIA

°F	°C		in.	mm
122	50		11.8	300
104	40		9.8	250
86	30		7.9	200
68	20		5.9	150
50	10		3.9	100
32	0		2.0	50
14	-10		0.0	0
-4	-20			

max. temperature / min. temperature

average rainfall

J F M A M J J A S O N D

Marine life

The reef itself is composed of the skeletons of more than 300 species of hard corals and supports a highly diverse collection of marine life. It is home to more than 1,500 species of fish, 4,000 mollusk species, and over 400 species of sponge. Within its protected waters extensive seagrass beds provide food for dugongs and green turtles, and shelter for countless other creatures. The many small islands and coral cays support large numbers of nesting seabirds.

Staghorn coral
Acropora sp.

Parrotfish
Sacruss sp.

Giant clam
Tridacna gigas

Table coral
Acropora sp.

Clown anemonefish
Amphiprion percula

Orangespine unicornfish
Naso lituratus

Crown-of-thorns starfish
Acanthaster planci

Minke whale
What was once referred to as the minke whale is now recognized as two species of small rorqual, one of which migrates to warmer waters during the southern winter. It is a frequent visitor to the coastal waters of the Great Barrier Reef, where it often swims close to divers, and the Western Australian coast.

Dugong
The dugong once inhabited extensive shallow waters around the Indian Ocean but now occurs only as small, remnant populations including the waters of northern Australia. Here seagrass beds provide food and shelter from predators.

Loggerhead turtle
The loggerhead turtle is one of several species of marine turtles that coexist in shallow tropical waters. Although sharing the same range they may have different diets. The loggerhead mainly eats mollusks and its powerful jaws are capable of crushing even large shells.

CONSERVATION WATCH

The greatest current threats to the Great Barrier Reef are from agricultural chemical runoff, coral predation by the crown-of-thorns starfish, and physical damage caused by the anchors of tourist vessels. Potential threats include oil spillage from large ships and the introduction of exotic marine organisms in their ballast, but rising sea levels is by far the greatest looming danger. Four plans of management contain strategies for dealing with these threats.

Sooty tern
Many small, inaccessible islands within the Great Barrier Reef provide a safe haven, free from the threat of terrestrial predators, for roosting and nesting seabirds. On such islands sooty tern colonies can nest safely on the sand.

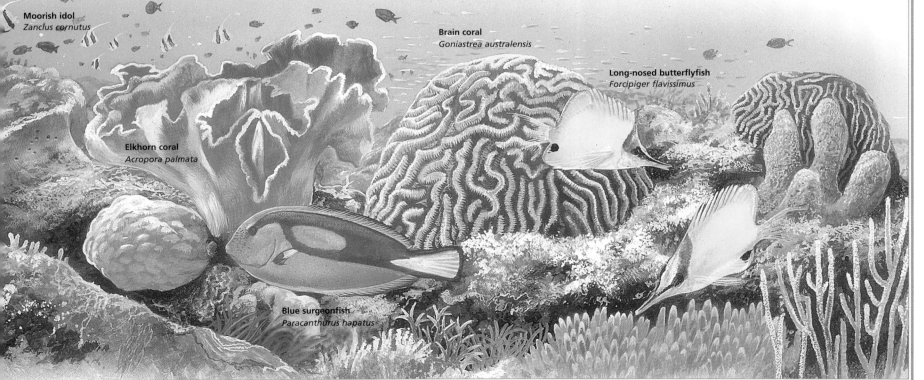

Moorish idol
Zanclus cornutus

Brain coral
Goniastrea australensis

Long-nosed butterflyfish
Forcipiger flavissimus

Elkhorn coral
Acropora palmata

Blue surgeonfish
Paracanthurus hapatus

WILDLIFE OF CAPE YORK

Cape York Peninsula is literally the northern finger of Australia pointing to the rest of the world. Torres Strait was not always water, and the flora, fauna, and peoples of this region bear witness to the close relationship between Australia and its nearest neighbor, the island of New Guinea. Cape York is significant because it demonstrates how recently the island of New Guinea became isolated from Australia. Many plants and animals have distributions that span the strait, such as the short-beaked echidna, striped possum, spotted cuscus, palm cockatoo, and birdwing butterfly. Many other groups have closely related, yet distinct species on either side of the strait, such as the tree kangaroos, pademelons, and dasyurids. Ancient rain forests once covered the entire area. As the continent of Australia entered a prolonged dry period its rain forests shrank. This coincided with the separation of Australia from New Guinea, which retained more of the ancient rain forest.

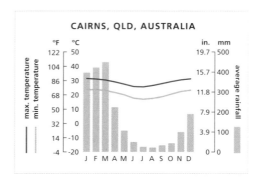

SCALE 1:8,000,000

BRIDGE AND BARRIER – NEW GUINEA AND CAPE YORK	
TERRESTRIAL MAMMALS FOUND IN:	NUMBER OF SPECIES
New Guinea only	250
New Guinea and Cape York	19
New Guinea, Cape York, and elsewhere in Australia	14
Cape York only	16
Cape York and elsewhere in Australia	35
Australia-wide	240

Homecoming
Marine turtles are among the world's longest-lived animals, with green turtle females breeding for the first time in their 60th year. Studies have shown they consistently return, as adults, to breed at the beach where they scrambled into the sea as tiny hatchlings.

CAIRNS, QLD, AUSTRALIA

Spectacled flying fox
Spectacled flying foxes are widely distributed in lowland New Guinea but in Cape York they roost in the rain forests and gallery forests at the tip of the cape and further to the south. Although they feed mainly on rain forest fruits, they have been persecuted by farmers for their habit of also raiding tropical fruit crops.

Striped possum
The striped possum of New Guinea and Cape York is Australasia's answer to the woodpecker. It uses its strong incisor teeth and elongated fourth finger to extract insect larvae from deep within tree branches, a characteristic it shares with the aye-aye, a Madagascan lemur.

Common brushtail possum
A highly variable species, the common brushtail possum occurs as a pale slender form inhabiting tropical savannas, and a dark form living in the rain forests of Cape York and the Atherton Tableland of far north Queensland.

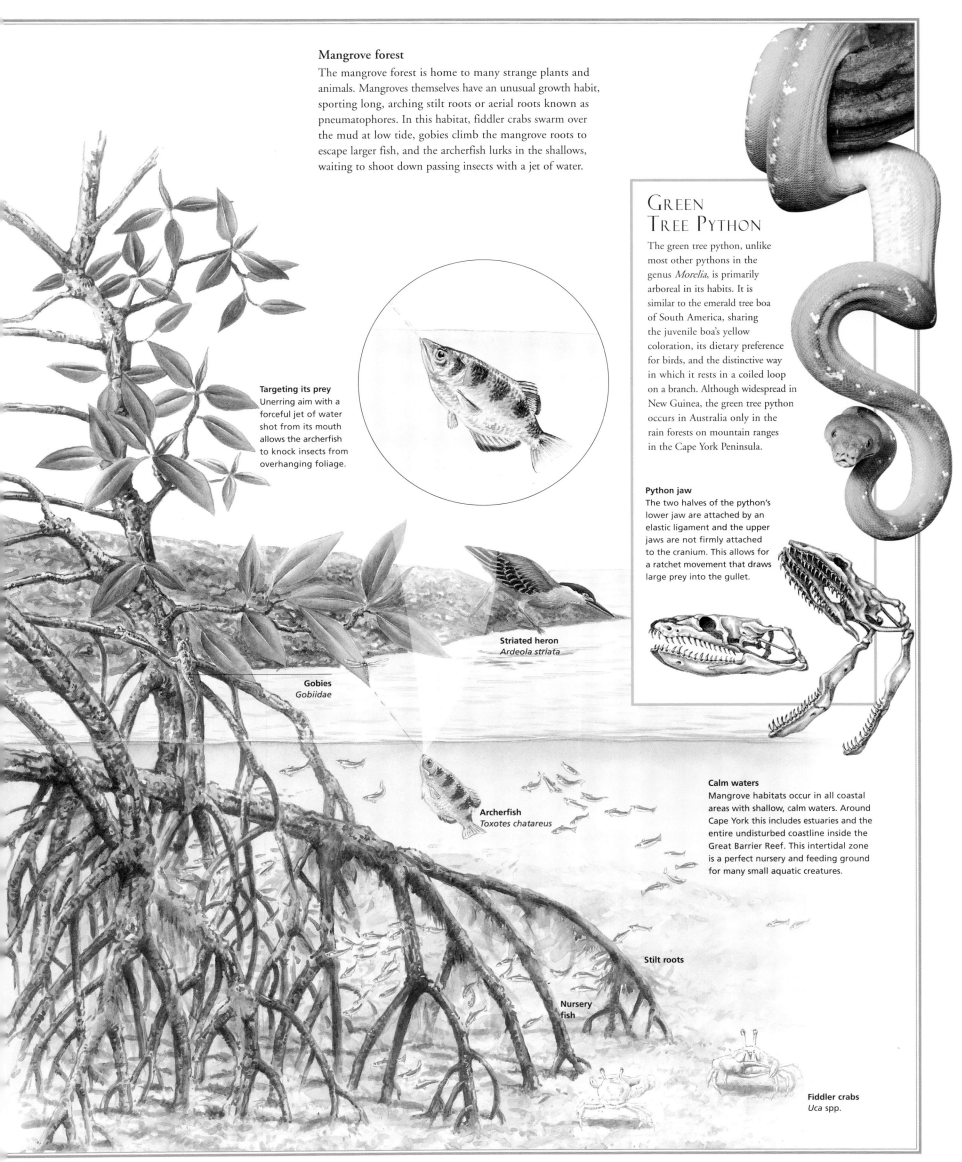

Mangrove forest

The mangrove forest is home to many strange plants and animals. Mangroves themselves have an unusual growth habit, sporting long, arching stilt roots or aerial roots known as pneumatophores. In this habitat, fiddler crabs swarm over the mud at low tide, gobies climb the mangrove roots to escape larger fish, and the archerfish lurks in the shallows, waiting to shoot down passing insects with a jet of water.

Targeting its prey
Unerring aim with a forceful jet of water shot from its mouth allows the archerfish to knock insects from overhanging foliage.

Striated heron
Ardeola striata

Gobies
Gobiidae

GREEN TREE PYTHON

The green tree python, unlike most other pythons in the genus *Morelia*, is primarily arboreal in its habits. It is similar to the emerald tree boa of South America, sharing the juvenile boa's yellow coloration, its dietary preference for birds, and the distinctive way in which it rests in a coiled loop on a branch. Although widespread in New Guinea, the green tree python occurs in Australia only in the rain forests on mountain ranges in the Cape York Peninsula.

Python jaw
The two halves of the python's lower jaw are attached by an elastic ligament and the upper jaws are not firmly attached to the cranium. This allows for a ratchet movement that draws large prey into the gullet.

Archerfish
Toxotes chatareus

Calm waters
Mangrove habitats occur in all coastal areas with shallow, calm waters. Around Cape York this includes estuaries and the entire undisturbed coastline inside the Great Barrier Reef. This intertidal zone is a perfect nursery and feeding ground for many small aquatic creatures.

Stilt roots

Nursery fish

Fiddler crabs
Uca spp.

WILDLIFE OF CAPE YORK
TROPICAL RAIN FORESTS

The Wet Tropics World Heritage Area (WTWHA) covers nearly 3,475 square miles (9,000 km²) of rich tropical rain forest that stretches from Townsville in the south to Cooktown in the north of northeastern Queensland. A verdant wonderland of rugged beauty, this region contains some of Australia's largest tracts of tropical rain forest. Most of the WTWHA, which was listed in 1988 on the basis that it met all four natural heritage criteria, is on public land and largely protected within a series of remote national parks. Where the rain forest extends to the coast it joins the Great Barrier Reef WHA. The rain forest ecosystems in the WTWHA contain more than 3,000 species of plants from more than 200 families, making this area one of the richest in botanical diversity in the world. The forests are home to several primitive forms of flowering plants and to many unique endemic species of animals, such as the musky rat-kangaroo.

Double-eyed fig parrot
The small but colorful double-eyed fig parrot is not often seen. It spends much of its time in the rain forest canopy where it enjoys a diet of native fig seeds. Its range also extends to New Guinea.

Musky rat-kangaroo
The musky rat-kangaroo is the smallest and most primitive member of the kangaroo group of families. It, alone, has retained the opposable first toe common to most other marsupial groups but absent in kangaroos. It forages during the day for fruits and fungi.

ENDEMIC SPECIES		
CLASS	**NO. OF SPECIES**	**EXAMPLE**
Mammals	8	Herbert River ringtail possum
Birds	13	Tooth-billed catbird
Reptiles	18	Chameleon gecko
Amphibians (frogs)	20	Torrent frog
Fish	78	Cairns rainbowfish
Invertebrates	Thousands	Cairns birdwing butterfly

Lilly pilly
Acmena smithii

Tropical rain forest floor

The floor of a tropical rain forest is a rich field for fruit and insect eaters, and an ideal habitat for a wide range of invertebrates, including centipedes, snails, and beetles. Frogs and lizards find both food and shelter in the leaf litter or in decaying branches. The canopy of dense vegetation overhead prevents much light from reaching the forest floor. Emerging seedlings grow slowly but fungi thrive.

Orange-thighed tree frog
Litoria xanthomera

Brush turkey
Alectura lathami

Rhinoceros beetle
Xylotrupes ulysses

Green ringtail possum
These rain forest possums are solitary creatures that do not build a nest or retreat to tree hollows but, instead, spend their daylight hours curled up asleep on a branch. The green tint to their thick, woolly fur is the result of the individual hairs diffracting light.

Northern bettong
A small nocturnal member of the rat-kangaroo family, the northern bettong is found only in north Queensland. It has a long tail, a forward-facing pouch, and moves by hopping. Fungi forms a major part of its diet, which also includes grass stems, insects, and leaves.

Cassowary
The cassowary's natural habitat is rain forest although it sometimes ranges into gardens and orchards in search of fruit. Like the emu and ostrich, the male incubates the eggs and rears the chicks, which remain in its care for about nine months.

Fruit dispersal
Cassowaries play an important role in forest life by helping disperse the seeds of forest trees, including the quandong. They swallow the fruits whole and their digestive tract activates the seed, which is returned to the earth conveniently encased in fertilizer.

Chameleon gecko
Carpodactylus laevis

Scrub python
Morelia amethistina

Giant forest cricket
Papuaistis sp.

Centipede
Scolopendridae

THE TROPICAL NORTH

The far northwest regions of Australia share a different climatic pattern from that of Australia's east-coast tropics. Annual rainfall is high, averaging more than 47 inches (1,200 mm) in Darwin, but it falls during a short monsoonal wet season between November and April. The rest of the year the weather is dominated by hot, dry winds. This results in a different suite of ecosystems dominated by grassy woodlands and savannas. Palm forests and vine thickets grow in moister gullies but large areas of rain forest are absent. The landscape and topography also differ, and include extensive plateaus and tablelands dissected by spectacular gorges that are fringed by an escarpment of rugged sandstone cliffs. The area is home to the second largest national park in the world, Kakadu, which contains many of the tropical north's unique plants and animals.

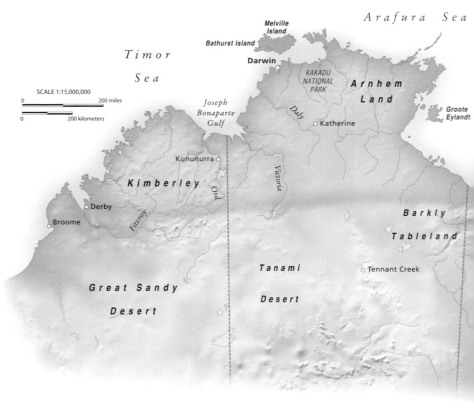

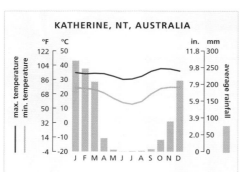

KATHERINE, NT, AUSTRALIA

Gouldian finch
Found only in Australia's far north, the beautifully colored Gouldian finch is a seasonal visitor to the coast but breeds inland, nesting in tree hollows.

KAKADU NATIONAL PARK	
Land area	7,646 sq mi (1,980,400 ha)
No. of visitors per year	200,000
World Heritage listing	1981, extensions 1987, 1992
Mammals	62 species
Birds	280 species
Reptiles	123+ species
Amphibians (frogs)	25 species
Fish	51 freshwater species
Invertebrates	More than 10,000

TAIPAN

The taipan is one of Australia's largest and most venomous snakes. It is a "strike and wait" predator, biting its unsuspecting victim once or twice before retreating and waiting for it to die. It is particularly dangerous to humans because of its habit of lurking in long grass, where it waits to strike prey, such as a passing bandicoot, rat, small marsupial, or bird.

Fang
The taipan's hollow fangs are fixed in the front of the upper jaw. A duct supplying venom leads from a gland in the back of the head.

Venom gland

Saltwater crocodile
Rightly feared as ferocious predators, saltwater crocodiles are found in northern Australian seas, estuaries, large rivers and, during the wet season, coastal flood plains. The female crocodile builds a mound nest of rotting vegetation, which she guards while her eggs incubate.

NORTHERN QUOLL

Cane toads, introduced to Australia in 1935, are one of the tropical north's greatest threats. Poison from the toad's parotoid glands is highly toxic to most native animals. Although some species seem to have found ways to avoid or even consume toads, the northern quoll has proven particularly vulnerable. The toad's relentless movement across Arnhem Land and Kakadu has coincided with the deaths of large numbers of quolls. A major effort is being made to save the northern quoll by establishing populations on toad-free islands north of Darwin.

Cane toads
Cane toads have been in the western Gulf of Carpentaria for many years but have recently expanded their range to the west, reaching Darwin in 2005.

Soldier
Soldiers are armed either with huge jaws or, in the case of the spinifex termite, a snout capable of squirting a sticky, toxic fluid.

King
The king's main role is to fertilize the queen but when the colony is first founded the king also cares for the young.

Termite fortresses

Most termite species build insignificant nests, either underground or inside a tree or log. But the magnetic termite mound is characteristic of the tropical north landscape, as is the giant, up to 25 feet (7.6 m) high, mound of the spinifex termite.

Brolga
The brolga, one of two Australian crane species, is well known for its elaborate ritual dancing, which involves bouncing or leaping, bowing, and outstretched wing display. Once widespread it is now common only in the tropical north. Breeding pairs share nest duties and care for their young for up to a year.

Queen
Queen termites lose their wings once they find a male. Together they establish a temporary shelter, where the first brood is born. The queen may live for 50 years and lay up to 2,000 eggs per day.

High-rise mounds
Impressively tall termite mounds dot the grasslands and woodlands of Australia's far north. Their shape, often narrow at the top, and their careful alignment in relation to the sun's rays, helps to keep them as cool as possible. This reduces moisture loss and regulates the temperature within the mound.

Many small cavities and channels in inner section of mound

Goannas often make their nest in the cool environment of a termite mound

Strong outer wall

Special chamber for queen

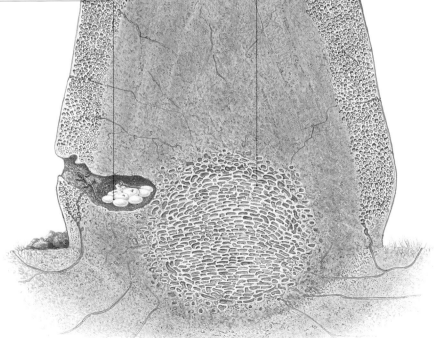

AUSTRALIAN OUTBACK

The term outback generally refers to the semiarid and arid lands of Australia's interior. The name also conjures up images of Uluru and the splendid gorges of the MacDonnell Ranges, but most of the outback is actually flat or rolling land sparsely covered with grasslands or low woodlands, featuring stunted trees such as the mulga and mallee. These apparently bleak ecosystems actually support a rich variety of wildlife. Ants abound in the desert, feeding on the seeds of grasses in competition with small parrots and hopping mice. Termites devour the dead grasses. Lizards, birds, and small mammals feed in turn on the ants and other insects. Water is a major limiting factor in the desert and, paradoxically, it appears in many strange places in the outback. Places such as Lake Eyre, rocky gorges, and the myriad of mound springs scattered around the rim of the Great Artesian Basin, a vast aquifer, defy notions of a barren continent.

LANDMASS

Outback 69%

Rest of Australia 31%

POPULATION

Rest of Australia 97%

Outback population 3%

ALICE SPRINGS, NT, AUSTRALIA

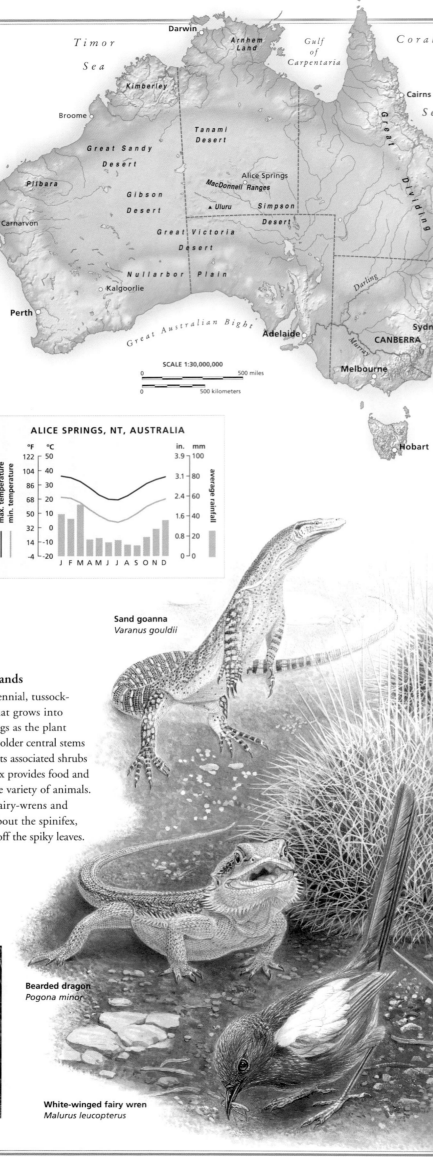

Sand goanna
Varanus gouldii

Spinifex grasslands

Spinifex is a perennial, tussock-forming grass that grows into characteristic rings as the plant expands and the older central stems die. Along with its associated shrubs and trees, spinifex provides food and shelter for a wide variety of animals. White-winged fairy-wrens and grasswrens flit about the spinifex, gleaning insects off the spiky leaves.

Thorny devil
The diminutive thorny devil's spiky skin provides protection from predators as it ranges the desert lapping up ants. Well-adapted to an arid climate, this lizard "drinks" moisture from dew on its scales.

Bearded dragon
Pogona minor

White-winged fairy wren
Malurus leucopterus

Bilby
Once widespread in the outback bilbies are now found in only a few refuges. These shy, nocturnal members of the bandicoot family, with ears and gait reminiscent of a rabbit, forage for fungi and insects. They spend the day in burrows to escape the inland heat.

risbane

Dingo
Members of the dog family, Canidae, dingoes occur widely in Australia from coastal to alpine regions, but they remain the quintessential symbol of the outback. They prey upon other mammals and birds, sometimes hunting in packs.

Spinifex tussock
Triodia sp.

Wedge-tailed eagle
The wedge-tailed eagle is Australia's largest bird of prey and is capable of taking a lamb or small kangaroo, but it feeds mainly on rabbits or carrion. Since the controlled decline of rabbits took effect, eagles have been forced to feed on roadkill and have fallen victim to vehicles themselves.

Emu
An "old man" emu leads its brood of chicks in search of food. Like kangaroos, the emu has benefited from pastoral development in remote areas, where dams and bores have assured these wide-ranging birds a reliable supply of water.

Mulgara
Dasycercus cristicauda

Sand-swimming skink
Lerista sp.

ROCKY GORGES

Flooding has carved outback gorges over millennia. During the wet season, rivers course through the gorges, filling waterholes in their deepest reaches. Plants such as figs and palms grow in the moist and sheltered sections, but most vegetation is adapted to the harsh dry season that follows, when wildlife relies on the gorges for survival. Prominent among these are the rock wallabies, which find shelter in the rocky gorge walls.

Black-flanked rock wallaby
At home in rocky gorges, rock wallabies are a familiar sight near water holes at many of Australia's most popular outback tourist sites, including Ormiston Gorge, in the West MacDonnell Ranges.

AUSTRALIAN OUTBACK
WATER IN THE DESERT

In many parts of the world, desert rivers such as Africa's Okavango or America's Colorado have their origins in adjacent high-rainfall regions. In Australia, the arid-zone rivers begin and end their journeys in the parched desert, where rainfall is a rare event. When it does rain, as a result of a massive frontal event or a cyclone penetrating far inland, the consequences are felt over vast areas and for many subsequent months. Rains falling on the inland plains of Australia's northeast, for example, make their slow way west into the Cooper and Diamantina systems. Rain further west swells the Finke River and all end up in the Lake Eyre Basin. These infrequent inundations provide the impetus for a massive, opportunistic breeding event, when all forms of life, from aquatic microorganisms to fish and birds, gather in vast numbers and multiply in the swelling lakes and billabongs.

Channel Country
The Diamantina River is a braided watercourse typical of the flat outback "Channel Country." The streambeds are often dry but, when rain does fall, can carry torrents of water to their ultimate destination, Lake Eyre. Vast areas of the surrounding flat country can be flooded for weeks after heavy rains.

Waiting for the rain
Long periods of drought in inland Australia make life impossible for frogs, which need to keep their skin moist. The water-holding frog has adapted to this harsh climate by burrowing into a chamber underground, shedding layers of skin to form a protective cocoon, and awaiting rain in a state of torpor. It then emerges to feed and mate.

The Lake Eyre drainage basin.

Area of the basin that is prone to flooding.

Digging in
The frog digs itself a small burrow and prepares to wait for rains to return.

Inactive underground
Enclosed in its cocoon, the frog enters a state of torpor, which may last many months.

Rain arrives
When rainfall softens the soil the frog digs its way out to the surface.

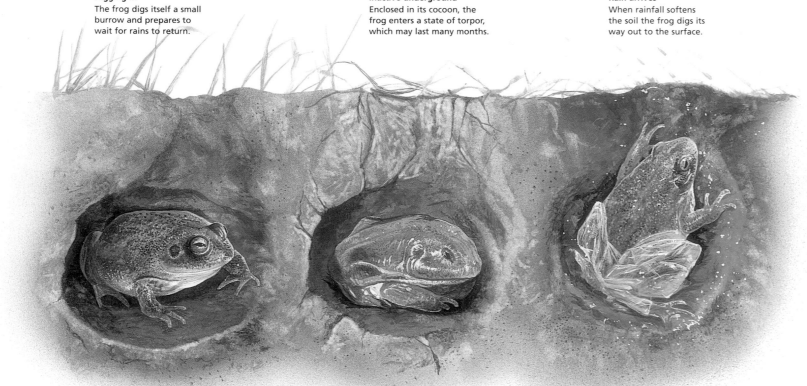

212

WATERBIRDS ON WETLANDS

The desert wetlands attract birds from all over Australia to the temporarily abundant feeding and breeding grounds. Ibis, egrets, spoonbills, and cormorants breed in trees fringing the rivers and billabongs. Pelicans, gulls, and terns nest on islands in the temporary lakes, and black swans, along with several duck species, nests in the reed beds fringing the wetlands.

Australian white ibis
Swamps are the favored feeding sites of the Australian white ibis, which dines on insects, crustaceans, fish, and frogs. While most birds breed in the Murray–Darling wetlands, some take advantage of ephemeral wetlands further inland on an opportunistic basis.

Royal spoonbill
The nomadic royal spoonbill, one of two species occurring in Australia, nests in small colonies scattered throughout northern and eastern Australia.

Pink-eared duck
The pink-eared duck is one of a group of nomadic species that takes advantage of the ephemeral waterways in the interior to breed when conditions are favorable. It retreats to coastal estuaries and lagoons when drought inevitably returns to the inland.

Australian pelican
Australian pelicans breed in several small breeding colonies around the continent's coastal fringe, but the major breeding site for vast numbers of pelicans is Lake Eyre. On the all-too-rare occasions when floodwaters reach the lake, it attracts many hundreds of birds.

Life in a billabong

Inland rivers may overflow their banks and flood surrounding plains after heavy rain, then shrink during drier times to form billabongs—isolated waterholes. The stagnant water in the billabong is an ideal habitat for smooth freshwater crayfish, or yabby, frogs, the long-necked tortoise, and myriad small fish and insects. Birds, including long-legged waders, are attracted to these rewarding feeding grounds.

Great egret
Ardea alba

Larvae of dragonfly

Yellowbelly
Macquaria ambigua

Snake-necked turtle
Chelodina longicollis

Yabby
Cherax sp.

Tadpoles

Temperate Forests and Heathlands

Australia's southern forests and heathlands are dominated by two large plant families—the Myrtaceae, containing the iconic eucalypts commonly known as gum trees, melaleucas, and bottlebrushes; and the Proteaceae, whose banksias and grevilleas regenerate quickly after the fires that periodically raze the landscape. All have massive flowering events that attract nectar-feeding mammals, such as possums and fruit bats, birds such as honeyeaters and lorikeets, and insects, all of which pollinate the plants as they gorge themselves on the abundant nectar. Vegetation types vary according to the rock and soil types, and prevailing climate. Large trees, such as the karris of the far southwest and the mountain ash of the continent's southeast, occur in areas with higher rainfall and richer soils. Drier areas with poorer soils support gnarled angophoras, ghostly scribbly gums, and heathlands of stunted trees and shrubs.

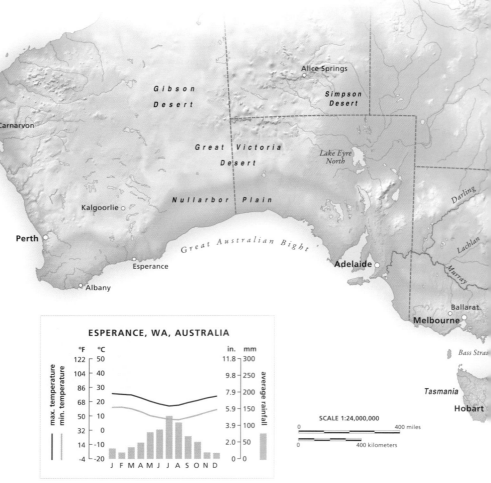

ESPERANCE, WA, AUSTRALIA

SCALE 1:24,000,000

New Holland honeyeater
This familiar resident of coastal woodlands and heath in the southeast and southwest of Australia is a frequent visitor to city parks and gardens. Often gathering in large flocks, it feeds on the nectar of shrubs and regards banksias and grevilleas among its favorites.

Other species in this habitat	
Common name	**Special feature**
Rock warbler	An endemic bird
Velvet worm	The link between worms and arthropods
Bristlebird	One of the oldest songbirds
Gilbert's potoroo	Endangered species, once considered extinct
Southern brown bandicoot	Numbers increasing in Sydney region
Brush turkey	Numbers increasing in Sydney region

Satin bowerbird
When the male satin bowerbird inherits or acquires a territory it changes into its deep blue–black plumage and builds a bower, which it lines with any blue objects it can find. The bird then hovers around the bower, burbling and calling to attract a mate.

Numbat
The numbat, a marsupial with a bushy tail and a pointed face, is exclusively a termite-eater. Its long tongue is a key player in its search for food as it explores feeding galleries of termites under the soil or in logs.

Forest fires
Many of the forests in the southern half of Australia are dependent on fire for their regeneration. Mature trees produce vast quantities of seed that cannot germinate until a massive fire burns off the old plants and simultaneously activates the seed.

Superb lyrebird
The superb lyrebird, named for the shape of its tail, is one of the oldest members of the songbird group that evolved in Australia before spreading to the rest of the world. The male lyrebird is an amazing mimic, capable of imitating almost any sound it hears.

⚡ CONSERVATION WATCH

The mountain pygmy possum is a true living fossil. It was first described from Pleistocene cave deposits, before living animals were discovered in 1966. Restricted to high alpine heathlands, it is highly endangered because of the threats of fire and global warming.

Winter warmth
During wintrer months the mountain pygmy possum survives in tunnels beneath the snow cover that forms an insulating barrier from the cold. Any reduction in the blanket of snow cover puts this tiny creature at risk.

Summer feast
During a time of plenty the mountain pygmy possum feasts on bogong moths, which come in their thousands to the possum's alpine habitat. Rich in fat, the moth is an ideal food for an animal that is about to enter a lean period.

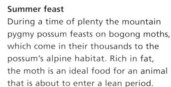

Kookaburra
The kookaburra is one of Australia's most familiar birds. A dry-land kingfisher, it preys on lizards, snakes, worms, and cicadas and is a highly efficient hunter. Its raucous laughing call, often heard pre-dawn, is a familiar sound in the Australian bush.

Red-necked wallaby
The red-necked wallaby, generally solitary, is one of the most common members of the kangaroo family and the only one to live in high alpine areas. Its thick winter fur was highly prized by Aboriginal people for making warm winter capes.

Brisbane

bo

Sydney

NBERRA

AUSTRALASIA & OCEANIA

COCKATOOS AND PARROTS

Parrots are characteristic of the three southern continents and southern Asia, with only a few species invading the northern tropics. Australia's parrot population is richly diverse and these colorful birds are a familiar sight in most parts of the country. Despite Australia having relatively few parrot species, 15 percent of the world's total, it has slightly more than its share of genera, 30 percent. Since the mid-19th century, when land clearing and urban development in Australia increased, many parrots have proven their adaptability. Several species of cockatoo are now more widespread than previously recorded and the distributions of other species have changed dramatically. Crimson rosellas are now resident year-round in lowland Sydney, where once they were only winter visitors. In many urban and suburban areas, the number of parrots has increased recently and, as forest areas decline, urban street trees have become popular roosting sites.

Turquoise parrot
A male turquoise parrot displays its beautiful wing and tail feathers as it prepares to land on a tree. The parrot occurs mostly in the eastern ranges, where it nests in tree hollows.

King parrot
The king parrot, distinguished by its brilliant red breast and head, is a large, forest-dwelling parrot. It feeds on the seeds of acacias and other understory shrubs and trees.

Black cockatoo
The handsome red-tailed black cockatoo feeds mostly on eucalypt seeds. In heavily timbered areas it feeds in the canopy but in more open country it is often seen on the ground.

Major Mitchell cockatoo
The pink or Major Mitchell cockatoo commonly travels in pairs or small groups. It inhabits ephemeral watercourses and remote billabongs, feeding in the nearby grasslands and dunes.

BILL TYPES

Parrots' bills, along with their bright plumage, are one of their most noticeable features. The upper bill is always downcurved but it varies in length from species to species. Some are long, ideal for digging into soft wood for insects or for cutting into ripe fruit. Others are short and strong, for breaking open cones or other tough seed cases.

Corella
The corella's long, narrow bill allows it to extract seeds from hard-coned plants and to dig up bulbs.

Double-eyed fig parrot
This parrot eats the seeds of soft-textured figs, slicing the fruit open neatly with the edge of its sharp bill.

Palm cockatoo
A huge bill and powerful jaw muscles allow the palm cockatoo to break open seed cases and unripe fruit.

Gang-gang cockatoo
The gang-gang cockatoo holds hard-cased fruit in one foot and cracks it open with its strong beak.

Rainbow lorikeet
Instead of using its bill, this lorikeet use its enlarged, hairy tongue to collect nectar and pollen from flowers.

Budgerigar
Sociable budgerigars create colorful spectacles in outback Australia. Frenetic flocks containing thousands of birds suddenly erupt from a waterhole and wheel around, only to alight briefly and take flight again.

Rainbow lorikeet
The rainbow lorikeet is found in the suburbs of most Australian cities with huge flocks roosting in gardens and dispersing during the day to feed on nectar-producing trees and shrubs.

Eastern rosella
Platycercus eximius

A VARIETY OF NESTS

The nests made by Australian parrots vary according to their range and the availability of safe sites. Hollows in tree trunks or branches are widely used as convenient nesting sites but parrots are found in a variety of habitats so nests may be on the ground, in grass, under rocks, or even in fence posts.

Ground nest
The ground parrot lives in grassy heathland and makes its nest on the ground, concealed by low-hanging foliage.

Tree nest
In common with many species of parrot, the Australian king parrot makes its nest in a deep hollow in a tree trunk.

Rock nest
Rock parrots, which live close to the coast, make their nest in a shallow depression protected by an overhanging rock.

Communal nest
Budgerigars nest in tree hollows but, unusually, they often nest communally, with several nests in one tree.

Termite nest
The golden-shouldered parrot makes its nest inside a termite mound at the end of a tunnel.

NEW ZEALAND

New Zealand's flora and fauna is a mixture of early Gondwanan elements, such as the Araucaria pines, tree ferns, moas, and kiwis, and species that have made the journey across the Tasman Sea or Pacific Ocean unaided. Most other native birds in New Zealand are close relatives of Australian species. However, the native bats are most closely related to a family of South American bats, and the four native frogs have even closer relatives living in Pacific coastal forests from British Columbia to California. New Zealand has 10 species of native mammals, three bats and seven pinnipeds, but it has 35 species of introduced mammals. Of these, the kiore and dog were introduced by the Maori and the rest, including a hedgehog, the rabbit, three rodents, and 16 ungulates, were brought by Europeans. Over the past 200 years these interlopers have had a devastating effect on native fauna and flora.

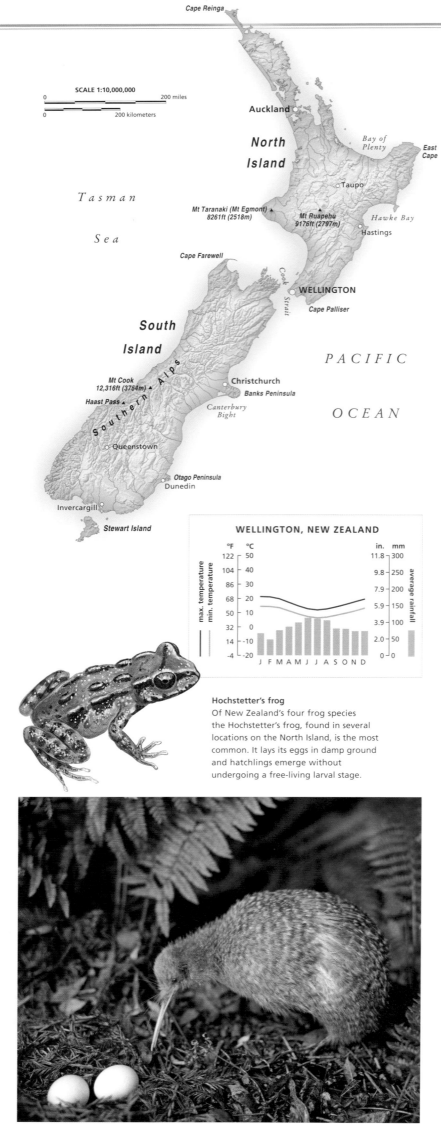

SCALE 1:10,000,000

Cape Reinga

Auckland

North Island

Tasman

Bay of Plenty

East Cape

Taupo

Sea

Mt Taranaki (Mt Egmont)
8261ft (2518m)

Mt Ruapehu
9176ft (2797m)

Hawke Bay

Hastings

Cape Farewell

Cook Strait

WELLINGTON

Cape Palliser

South Island

PACIFIC

Mt Cook
12,316ft (3754m)

Christchurch

Banks Peninsula

Haast Pass

Southern Alps

Canterbury Bight

OCEAN

Queenstown

Otago Peninsula
Dunedin

Invercargill

Stewart Island

WELLINGTON, NEW ZEALAND

Hochstetter's frog
Of New Zealand's four frog species the Hochstetter's frog, found in several locations on the North Island, is the most common. It lays its eggs in damp ground and hatchlings emerge without undergoing a free-living larval stage.

Kea
The kea is the alpine and subalpine parrot familiar to most visitors to New Zealand's Haast Pass, where it vandalizes the windscreen wipers of parked cars. It is also notorious for attacking sheep. Its numbers are declining.

Great spotted kiwi
The great spotted kiwi is the largest of the four kiwi species but, like the other three, its numbers are declining and it requires conservation. It is threatened by predation from domestic dogs and cats, as well as stoats.

Tuatara

Two species of tuatara survive on islands off New Zealand's coast. Despite their lizard-like appearance they are not lizards but belong to an ancient reptile order that predates the dinosaurs. They are now known only in New Zealand where half the population of the common species (*Sphenodon punctatus*) lives on Stephens Island in Cook Strait. They also occur on several other offshore islands.

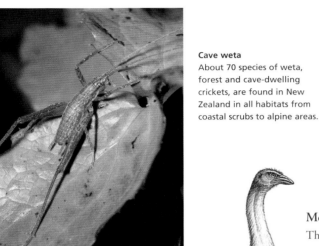

Cave weta
About 70 species of weta, forest and cave-dwelling crickets, are found in New Zealand in all habitats from coastal scrubs to alpine areas.

Moa

The moa was a medium to large bird, now considered more closely related to the emu and cassowaries of Australia and New Guinea than to surviving kiwis. The two largest species, the South Island giant moa and the North Island giant moa, grew to about 12 feet (3.6 m) in height and they weighed about 550 pounds (250 kg). These giant birds browsed on trees and shrubs and, before the arrival of the Maori in the 10th century AD, their only predator was the Haast's eagle. By 1400 AD the Maori had exterminated the two large moas.

⚡ CONSERVATION WATCH

The kakapo, considered the world's heaviest parrot, was once widespread throughout New Zealand. The clearing of forests and predation have forced it onto a handful of islands. Flightless and nocturnal, it lives on fruits and other plant parts, and breeds only every three to five years.

INTRODUCED BIRDS

Of 335 bird species recorded in New Zealand, 40 have been introduced in the past 200 years. Many have contributed to the decline of endemic species, mostly through competition for food and nesting sites, but threatened species are benefiting from captive breeding programs.

🔵 Black tomtit
This tomtit, a subspecies found only on Snares Island, and the black robin are the only black species of the three Australasian robins living in New Zealand and its neighboring islands.

Tomtit
The tomtit, a common bird in New Zealand, is found in forested areas where it pursues the insects that form its diet. It also occasionally eats fruit.

ISLANDS OF THE SOUTHWEST PACIFIC

The islands of the tropical southwest Pacific Ocean have two separate origins. New Caledonia is a remnant of the ancient supercontinent Gondwana, and the rest, from the Solomon Islands to Vanuatu, are volcanic uplifted blocks along the Pacific Rim of Fire. New Caledonia is home to many ancient plants that demonstrate its affinity with Australia, but there are many endemic plant families, indeed more than 75 percent of its plant species occur nowhere else. Vegetation on the volcanic islands shows greater affinity with New Guinea and the Bismarck Archipelago. The larger islands have a high percentage of endemic land birds, including the kagu of New Caledonia. The smaller, more isolated islands frequently host large breeding colonies of pelagic seabirds. Prominent among these are Norfolk and Lord Howe islands and their satellites, such as Balls Pyramid, to Lord Howe's southeast.

Coral Sea

Brisbane

PACIFIC

New Caledonia
NOUMEA

Norfolk Island

Port Macquarie

Lord Howe Island

OCEAN

Sydney

Tasman Sea

New Zeala

SCALE 1:43,000,000

0   400 miles

0   400 kilometers

NORFOLK ISLAND

°F	°C		in.	mm
122	50		11.8	300
104	40		9.8	250
86	30		7.9	200
68	20		5.9	150
50	10		3.9	100
32	0		2.0	50
14	-10		0.0	0
-4	-20			

max. temperature / min. temperature — average rainfall

J F M A M J J A S O N D

Land snail
A large ground-dwelling snail, endemic to Lord Howe Island, is known to reach more than three inches (8 cm) in length at maturity. It is at risk of predation by rats.

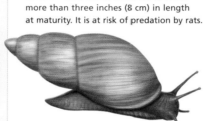

Purple swamphen
The purple swamphen, or pukako, is one of the most successful colonizers of islands throughout the South Pacific. As long as it has access to reed beds for nesting, it can live in any moist environment.

Sooty tern
The large breeding colony of sooty terns on Lord Howe Island's Mount Eliza is one of the island's major natural attractions. Bird breeding colonies are normally found on inaccessible islands, but here the birds gather in large numbers and are readily observed.

PROVIDENCE PETREL

The Providence petrel is a pelagic species with an unusually narrow distribution, occurring mainly in the warmer waters of the southwest Pacific Ocean. During the non-breeding season some individuals migrate to the North Pacific but during the breeding season dense colonies gather on Lord Howe Island. The birds nest in burrows, the parents taking turns to incubate the egg.

Hatching
The Providence petrel parents share the duty of incubating their egg in a small underground nesting chamber at the end of a burrow.

Nestling
The nestling, which is often alone while the parents fly far out to sea to seek feed, is in danger of predation by rats or other birds.

⚡ CONSERVATION WATCH

Species of rail tend to evolve into flightless forms after they invade remote islands, of which the Lord Howe Island woodhen is one example. It was widespread and common on the island until feral cats and pigs decimated its population. By 1973 only a few individuals survived on Mount Gower and Mount Lidgbird. A safe breeding colony was established and, by the mid-1980s, 85 captive-bred individuals were reintroduced into the wild. The current population is around 200 birds.

Stick insect
The Lord Howe Island phasmid, stick insect, population on the main island was wiped out by introduced rats but survivors were discovered in 2001 on an outlying island. A small captive colony was established and their progeny will be reintroduced following a planned rat eradication program.

Kagu
The kagu, a relative of the rails and cranes, is endemic to New Caledonia. Although its wings are a normal size for its body weight and shape it is flightless, so it is found only on the forest floor. It is highly susceptible to predation, particularly by dogs and cats.

Red-crowned parakeet
The red-crowned parakeet's range once extended across New Zealand's main islands but is now restricted to a few offshore islands. The bird has a distinctive red crown and red band across its cheek and eye. It feeds mainly on seeds, fruit, and berries.

Emperor penguins live in Antarctica and are one of the few animals to stay during winter. When penguin chicks are about six weeks old, they collect in a group, or crèche, and are looked after by a single adult. This allows other adult penguins to leave the colony and catch food—emperor penguins feed their own chicks for about nine months.

THE POLES

THE POLES

Polar regions at the ends of Earth are similar in their intense cold and seasonality, but different in their basic geography. The Arctic centers about a vast sea basin: a visitor to the north geographic pole stands on sea ice in the middle of a cold, deep ocean. The Antarctic centers on a high continent: a visitor to the south geographic pole stands on an icecap 9,301 feet (2,835 m) above sea level. Latitude for latitude the high continent makes the Antarctic region much colder than the Arctic. The geographical boundaries of these regions are the polar circles, located at 66° 33' N and S, each of 1,619 miles (2,606 km) radius and enclosing about 8 percent of Earth's surface. The Arctic region adjoins the temperate lands of the northern continents, and is constantly recruiting plants and animals overland from the south. Antarctica, an isolated continent, receives only the few plants and animals that can swim, fly, or be blown there. It also has fewer habitable areas to offer, hence its relative poverty of species. A small Arctic island may support as 90 species of flowering plant: the whole Antarctic continent supports only two.

The Arctic
The Arctic region is home to many land animals, although even the heavily furred polar bear must spend winter in a snow den.

SCALE 1:35,000,000

0   500 miles

0   500 kilometers

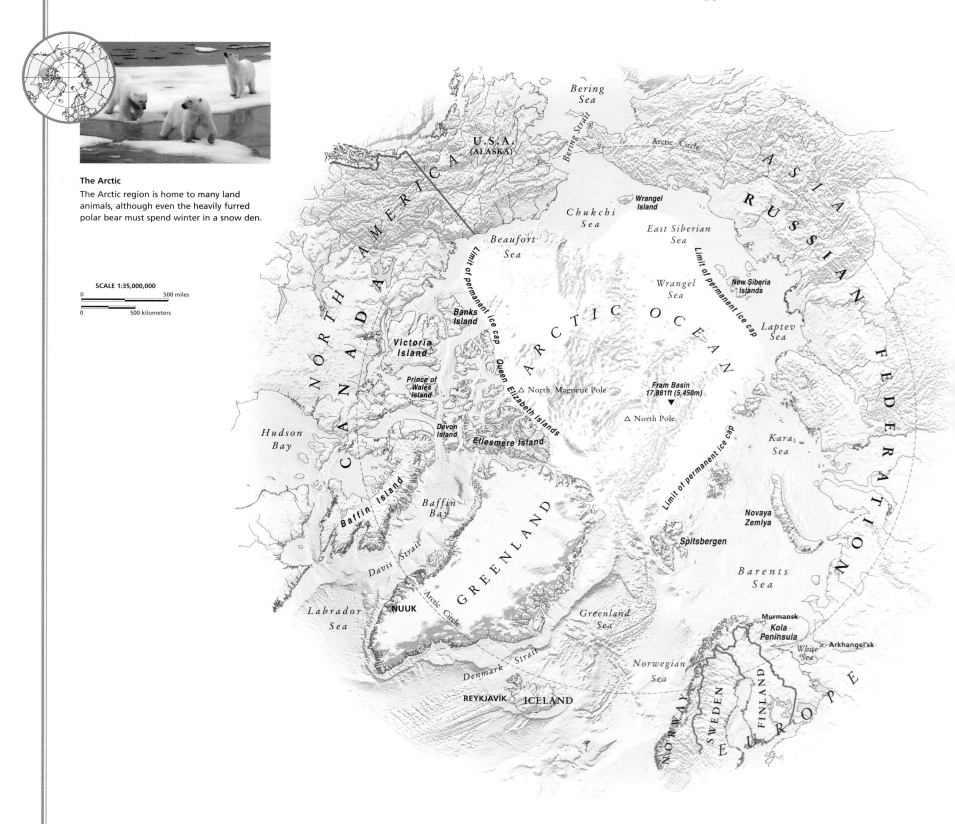

Bering Sea · Arctic Circle · ASIA · RUSSIAN FEDERATION · U.S.A. (ALASKA) · Bering Strait · Chukchi Sea · Wrangel Island · East Siberian Sea · Limit of permanent ice cap · New Siberia Islands · Laptev Sea · Beaufort Sea · Wrangel Sea · Limit of permanent ice cap · NORTH AMERICA · Banks Island · ARCTIC OCEAN · Victoria Island · Queen Elizabeth Islands · North Magnetic Pole · Fram Basin 17,881ft (5,450m) · Kara Sea · Prince of Wales Island · North Pole · CANADA · Devon Island · Ellesmere Island · Novaya Zemlya · Hudson Bay · Spitsbergen · Baffin Island · Baffin Bay · GREENLAND · Barents Sea · Davis Strait · Labrador Sea · NUUK · Arctic Circle · Greenland Sea · Murmansk · Kola Peninsula · White Sea · Arkhangel'sk · Denmark Strait · Norwegian Sea · NORWAY · SWEDEN · FINLAND · REYKJAVÍK · ICELAND · EUROPE

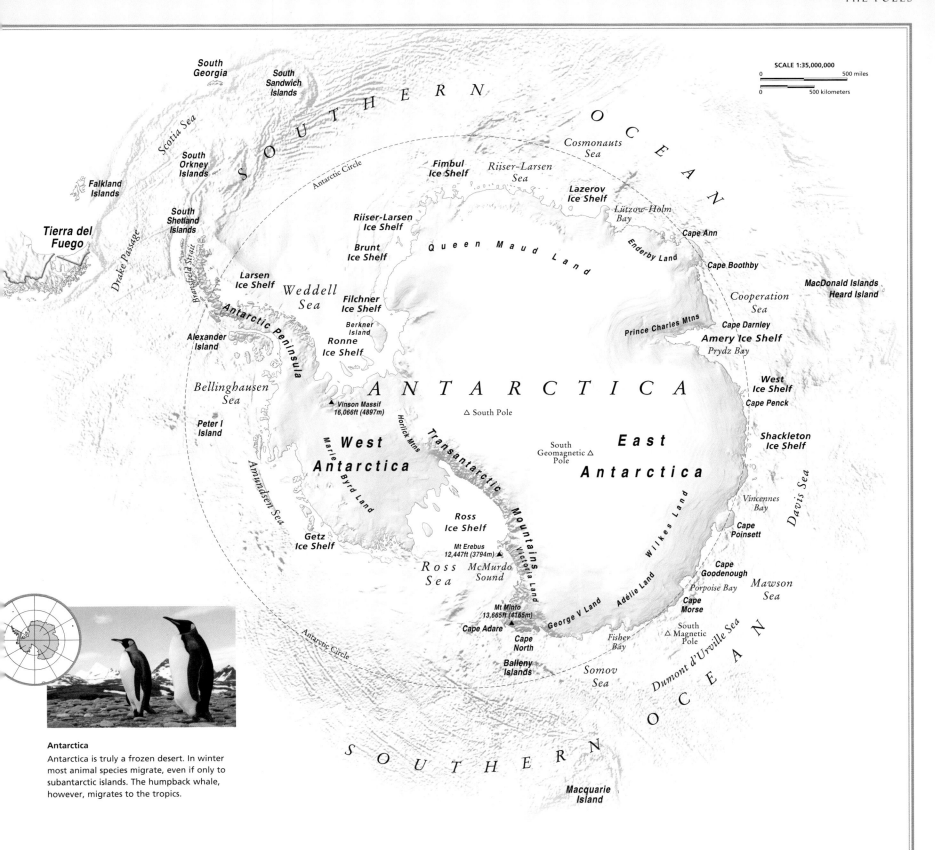

SCALE 1:35,000,000

South Georgia
South Sandwich Islands
SOUTHERN OCEAN
Scotia Sea
South Orkney Islands
Falkland Islands
Tierra del Fuego
South Shetland Islands
Drake Passage
Bransfield Strait
Antarctic Circle
Fimbul Ice Shelf
Riiser-Larsen Sea
Cosmonauts Sea
Lazerov Ice Shelf
Lützow-Holm Bay
Cape Ann
Enderby Land
Cape Boothby
Riiser-Larsen Ice Shelf
Queen Maud Land
Brunt Ice Shelf
Larsen Ice Shelf
Weddell Sea
Antarctic Peninsula
Alexander Island
Bellinghausen Sea
Peter I Island
Filchner Ice Shelf
Berkner Island
Ronne Ice Shelf
Vinson Massif 16,066ft (4897m)
West Antarctica
Marie Byrd Land
MacDonald Islands
Heard Island
Cooperation Sea
Prince Charles Mtns
Cape Darnley
Amery Ice Shelf
Prydz Bay
West Ice Shelf
Cape Penck
ANTARCTICA
△ South Pole
South Geomagnetic △ Pole
East Antarctica
Shackleton Ice Shelf
Horlick Mtns
Transantarctic Mountains
South Magnetic Pole
Wilkes Land
Vincennes Bay
Davis Sea
Cape Poinsett
Getz Ice Shelf
Ross Sea
Ross Ice Shelf
Mt Erebus 12,447ft (3794m)
McMurdo Sound
Victoria Land
Mt Minto 13,665ft (4165m)
Cape Adare
Cape North
Balleny Islands
George V Land
Adélie Land
Fisher Bay
Somov Sea
Dumont d'Urville Sea
Cape Goodenough
Porpoise Bay
Cape Morse
Mawson Sea
South △ Magnetic Pole
Antarctic Circle
SOUTHERN OCEAN
Macquarie Island

Antarctica
Antarctica is truly a frozen desert. In winter most animal species migrate, even if only to subantarctic islands. The humpback whale, however, migrates to the tropics.

THE ARCTIC

Climate

In the sunless winter, strong anticyclones form over the central core of pack ice, North America, Greenland, and Siberia, bringing mean temperatures of around -22°F (-30°C) to the central basin, -58°F (-50°C) over land. Through the rest of the year eastward-moving cyclones bring rain, snow, and winds. Mean monthly temperatures rise above freezing point from May to September.

Natural Resources

Marine life is limited in the Arctic Ocean but the more open oceans of the Barents, Greenland, and Bering seas support rich fisheries. Native peoples have long relied on sealing, whaling, and fur-trading. Seals are still hunted commercially on pack ice off Newfoundland and the White Sea: whaling is strictly limited for local communities. In northern Siberia and Alaska, huge reserves of oil, coal, and gas have been tapped.

THE ANTARCTIC

Climate

A persistent winter anticyclone over the continent makes the highest points of the plateau some of Earth's coldest places. The Russian station, Vostok, recorded a world record low temperature of -126.9°F (-88.3°C) in August 1960. Summer monthly mean temperatures rise to around -22°F (-30°C). Coastal stations and the Antarctic Peninsula are much warmer.

Natural Resources

Stocks of the Southern Ocean's whales and seals were hunted almost to extinction during the 19th and 20th centuries. They have recovered in recent years, especially since the International Whaling Commission declared most of the Southern Ocean a whale sanctuary in 1994. Of greater concern now is illegal fishing, which is steadily depleting stocks of Antarctic cod, finfish, and toothfish. Mining is banned under the Antarctic Treaty.

ARCTIC TUNDRA

Tundra is the rolling, treeless plains lying north of the boreal forests. Snow-covered in winter, it thaws in spring to reveal stony, wind-swept uplands and greener lowlands dotted with lakes, bogs, and marshes. Though underlain by permafrost, summer tundra supports mosses, grasses, rushes, and knee-high shrubs, brightened by patches of pink, white, blue, and yellow flowering plants. There is a brief fall of brown leaves, seeds, and bright red berries, before white winter sets in. Along its southern border tundra is fringed by a narrow zone of stunted trees and shrubs that merge with the forest itself. In the harsher north it thins gradually to near-sterile Arctic desert. Humans brought up in temperate conditions find tundra hostile, and wonder how plants and animals can survive there. Yet hundreds of kinds of living creatures, including humans, make their homes on tundra, either year-round or as summer migrants.

INSECTS

Insects disappear in winter, but emerge when the snow melts and the ground warms in spring. Moths, butterflies, hoverflies, and bumblebees search the flowers for nectar and pollen; blowflies breed on carcasses; damselflies, dragonflies, and caddisflies hover above the ponds; and swarms of midges, mosquitoes, and botflies plague the grazing caribou.

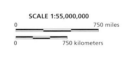

Bumblebee
Bumblebee queens spend winter deep in the soil, emerging in spring to warm up and find nesting holes near the surface. They collect pollen and nectar, and lay eggs to start their colonies.

Banded demoiselle
Damselflies spend years as larvae in ponds, feeding on other insects and growing slowly. When mature they climb out and fly for only a few days, long enough to mate and lay eggs.

SCALE 1:55,000,000

0 —————— 750 miles

0 —————— 750 kilometers

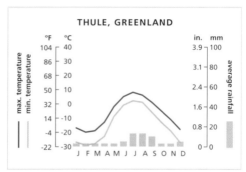

THULE, GREENLAND

Musk oxen
Musk oxen live in small wandering herds, feeding throughout the year on sedges, dwarf willows, and grasses. In fall they fatten and grow a dense, woolly coat. In winter they live only where the snow lies thin, so they can continue to find food.

Arctic fox
Gray or white in winter, brown or brown-and-white in summer, Arctic foxes live in well-drained hillside burrows, hunting constantly for ground squirrels, lemmings, and nesting birds. In winter many go out onto the sea ice, hunting for seal pups and scavenging after polar bears.

Life on the tundra

In winter much of the tundra lies blanketed in snow. Small animals, such as this ground squirrel, mice, and lemmings can continue living under cover—the ground is still warm and the blanket of snow protects them from the worst of the weather outside. Bigger animals cannot do this. Some, such as the caribou, migrate south to the shelter of forests. Others, such as musk oxen, fatten and grow massive coats to see them through winter.

Caribou

Thousands of caribou move north over the tundra in spring, giving birth to their fawns on the way. Shifting constantly, fattening on the new vegetation, they graze through the long summer days. In fall they mate, then turn south when the weather chills to spend winter in the forests.

KEEPING WARM

To stay active, warm-blooded animals such as mammals and birds must feed to maintain their body temperature around 99°F (37°C). Big animals like this grizzly bear carry thick fat and dense fur insulation, but cannot find enough food in winter to keep their temperature up. So they find a sheltered den and hibernate, chill down and sleep the winter away.

Snowy owl

Snowy owls live year-round on the tundra, generally favoring areas where snow is thin. They perch on rocks or low bushes from which they can watch for prey, then swoop silently and almost invisibly on hares, lemmings, mice, ducks, and other small mammals and birds.

Lemming

A snowy owl may take up to 1,600 lemmings in a year. In good years when the snow melts early and lemmings are easy to catch, snowy owls can raise ten or more chicks. In bad years they may lay only three or four eggs and lose them all.

227

THE ARCTIC
SUMMER BLOOM

Arctic land plants survive winter under tightly-packed snow, blanketed from harsh winds and extremely low temperatures. So do many insects, mice, lemmings, and other small animals. In spring, as the snow melts, the sun's rays penetrate to stimulate plant growth. Ponds and lakes thaw; algae, pondweeds, mosses, grasses, and flowering plants grow rapidly. As the air warms, insects by the million emerge, and birds and mammals that have wintered over begin to fatten. Now thousands of migrant birds fly north, some from as far as Africa, South America, and the southern USA, to feed and breed among the spring and summer abundance. Swans, divers, and ducks dabble in the streams and lakes. Geese browse the grasses and waders find insects among the grasses and shallow soils. Caribou and reindeer also move north, and porcupines, foxes, and brown and black bears emerge from the forests to hunt and scavenge.

Flowers that bloom in summer

For months this meadow in an Arctic corner of Newfoundland has been under snow. As winter ends the snow melts, lengthening days of sunshine warm the earth and vegetation, and the tundra springs to life. Arctic poppies and other quick-growing annuals appear first, providing a splash of color among the more sober perennial grasses.

Red fox
The common red fox of Eurasia and North America ranges up into the Arctic but not generally as far north as Arctic foxes. Unlike Arctic foxes, red foxes stay the same color throughout the year, though with a much denser coat in winter.

Willow ptarmigan
A hen willow ptarmigan in cryptic summer plumage. Known as willow ptarmigans because they feed almost entirely on leaves and buds of dwarf willows, these birds need year-round camouflage to protect them from predators. Mottled brown in summer and white in winter, they simply disappear into their background.

Willow ptarmigan
Winter plumage

Willow ptarmigan
Summer plumage

Poppies and bearberry
The tundra turns brilliant red in fall as the dwarf shrubs prepare to shed their leaves. Red berries appear, too, rich in nutrients for bears and other animals. Among them grow lacy reindeer moss— a lichen that is half fungus, half alga, which reindeer and caribou like to eat.

Caribou
Caribou are wild deer of Arctic North America; reindeer are the wild and domesticated herds of Europe and Asia. They migrate north in spring, south in fall across the tundra. Calves are born during the spring migration.

Daylight hours
As spring advances, hours of daylight increase rapidly; the further north the longer the days. After the fall equinox days grow shorter than nights. For every extra hour of summer daylight, there is an extra hour of darkness in winter.

	Jan	Feb	Mar	Apr	May	Jun	Jul	Aug	Sept	Oct	Nov	Dec
80°N	0	2.3	13.6	24	24	24	24	24	13.1	0.8	0	0
70°N	2.5	8.3	12.5	17.1	24	24	24	17.2	12.6	8.2	2.4	0
60°N	7.1	9.8	12.3	15.1	17.6	18.9	17.7	15.1	12.4	9.7	7.1	5.9

Grizzly Bear
Grizzlies are big bears, always hungry and ready to eat any kind of food they can find. In summer they snap up lemmings, ground squirrels, nesting birds, eggs, or sick or injured caribou. They also eat grasses, shoots, and berries. In winter they hibernate.

Barnacle geese
Branta leucopsis

GEESE MIGRATION

Millions of ducks, geese, and shorebirds that could not possibly survive Arctic winters spend winter instead in temperate regions. In early spring they fly north, reaching the tundra just as the snow is disappearing, the ponds are thawing, and the grass is beginning to grow. The summers here are short, so these seasonal migrants are always in a hurry to start nesting and laying their clutches of eggs.

Barnacle goose
Barnacle geese that nest in Svalbard winter in Britain: those that breed in the eastern Siberian Arctic spend their winters in the Netherlands. If spring comes late and the snow stays on the ground, they may not be able to breed at all.

Hunters and Hunted

The basic tundra foods are grasses, lichens, shrubs, roots, seeds, and berries. These are eaten year-round by lemmings, mice, ground squirrels, hares, musk oxen, ptarmigan, overwintering finches, and ground insects. In summer migrant reindeer, caribou, and geese arrive to feed on the fresh growth. These plant-eating mammals, birds, and insects are preyed on by foxes, wolves, weasels, owls, falcons, ravens, and skuas. Birds and small mammals fall prey to smaller hunters: wolves take the big musk oxen and caribou, leaving skin and bones to be picked over by foxes and scavenging birds. Summer-visiting shorebirds (waders) feed mainly on ground-living insects. In streams, ponds, and lakes, ducks dabble for weeds and aquatic insects or dive deeper for fish. Grizzly and polar bears feed on anything from berries to dead caribou, and polar bears and Arctic foxes go out onto the sea ice to feed on seals.

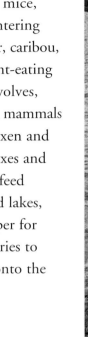

Ground squirrel
These little animals feed for only three to four months of the year—the summer months in which grasses and other new shoots are richest in nutrients and most plentiful. At the end of summer they accumulate fat, then sleep away the winter in nests underground.

TERRESTRIAL ANIMALS		MARINE ANIMALS
CARNIVORES & OMNIVORES	HERBIVORES & INSECTIVORES	CARNIVORES & OMNIVORES
Foxes	Lemmings	Orcas
Wolves	Mice	Seals
Weasels	Squirrels	Walrus
Falcons	Reindeer	Sharks
Owls	Caribou	Gulls
Bears	Birds	Ducks and other birds

Glaucous gull
These elegant gulls forage along the seashore for plankton washed up by the tide, and patrol the cliffs and beaches where other seabirds nest, watching for unattended eggs and chicks.

Feeding at Sea

The basic sea food is plankton—tiny plant cells and shrimplike crustaceans that proliferate when the sea ice melts in spring. Animals from small fish to big whales feed on plankton, and the fish in turn are eaten by most seals, dolphins, small whales, and seabirds. Bearded seals and walrus eat clams, which live on the seabed and feed on debris that falls from above.

Puffin
Puffins, sometimes called sea parrots, spend their summers in clifftop burrows, often in colonies numbering many thousands. They feed at sea, catching small fish that they carry home to their nestlings.

Orca
Also called killer whales, orcas are found all over the world including the Arctic. They hunt in packs for seals and other whales. An orca can eat seven seals in one meal.

Arctic fox

Like stoats, Arctic foxes hunt birds and small mammals, so need to change color from summer to winter. This one, in summer coat, is jumping on a mouse or lemming. In winter many move out onto the sea ice, scavenging on seals killed by polar bears.

Arctic wolf

Arctic wolves hunt in packs of a dozen or more, often following migrating caribou or musk oxen and killing the calves and older animals that cannot keep up with the herds. They feed also on birds and small mammals, but large mammals are their main prey.

Great gray owl

Great gray owls live in the northern forests and along the forest–tundra edge. Like snowy owls they hunt for voles, mice, and small lemmings, watching and listening for movement, then swooping and pouncing to carry off their catch. Males bring most of the food to the nests.

Stoat

In summer the stoat is brown; in winter it turns white, with a black tip to its tail, and is called an ermine. A fierce hunter of small mammals and birds, it stalks quietly and pounces without being seen. This one has found a deep-frozen Arctic hare to feed on.

Char

Some char live in lakes, others in streams and rivers, where they feed mainly on insects and smaller fish. Despite spending part of their lives in the sea, river char can also be found far up mountain streams where they feast on salmon eggs.

Harp seal

Harp seals live out on the sea ice, feeding on capelin, cod, and other shoaling fish. Pups are silky white for their first 12 days, then molt into harsher gray fur for swimming.

Greenland shark

The only sharks known in Arctic waters, these sluggish, bottom-living fish feed on seals and smaller fish. They are hunted for their oil and their sandpaper skin.

Walrus

Walruses look and swim like seals. They live on coastal sea ice and along Arctic shores, feeding by diving to the seabed, which they rake with their tusks for clams.

THE POLAR BEAR

Polar bears live around the Arctic Ocean and neighboring seas. Males weigh up to 1,322 pounds (600 kg), females are lighter, up to 550 pounds (250 kg): standing upright they are taller than a man. Unlike brown and grizzly bears, polar bears spend much of their lives on sea ice that, in winter, spreads along the coasts and covers the ocean. They live mainly on seals, which feed on fish and clams below the ice, but come up through cracks and holes to rest and produce their pups. As year-round residents in the Arctic, polar bears have to survive subzero temperatures. Their dense white fur, up to 12 inches (30 cm) thick, protects them from the worst polar weather. The fur is waterproof too, so bears can swim for hours in icy seas. In summer, when the ice softens and melts, they forage on land, eating grasses, berries, birds' eggs, and nestlings. In autumn they fatten on fish, particularly salmon and char, that they scoop from freshwater streams.

Defending their ground
Living where food is seldom plentiful, polar bears usually walk on their own. Two or three together are most likely to be a mother with cubs. When lone males meet they growl, roar, and even wrestle until one is driven away.

In search of food
Despite their weight and bulk, polar bears are agile. They leap from floe to floe and wander many miles every day in search of food. The ability to leave land and travel over sea ice gives them access to breeding seals—their main food in early spring.

Lone hunter
Polar bears are lone animals that live by their wits, always hungry and very strong—powerful enough to break into houses and food stores. Though still hunted in small numbers, they are protected by international agreement throughout the Arctic.

Family group
Cubs stay with their mother for up to two years, until almost fully grown. It is a hard life, especially in winter, and one or more in each family may die. Those cubs that survive wander off independently, then the mother is ready to find another mate.

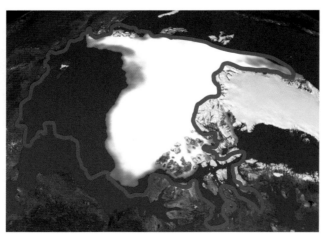

Sea ice changes

Areas of both permanent and annually-renewed Arctic sea ice grow smaller year by year and have lost 38 percent of their area over the past 30 years. Numbers of both seals and polar bears are likely to fall; they may disappear altogether from some areas. Climates are always changing: the Arctic has been both warmer and cooler in the past, and seals and bears have survived the changes before.

HUNTING TO SURVIVE

Polar bears spend part of their time on land, but more on sea ice in coastal channels and bays. Females give birth on land, but take their cubs onto the sea ice where food is easier to find. Food is never plentiful so, after mating, males and females go their separate ways. Mothers hunt and bring up the cubs on their own.

Seal meat
On the sea ice bears hunt for seals, which in spring are raising pups among the floes. The adult female knows how to find and kill the seals, providing a meal for herself and her cubs.

Whale carcass
Polar bears are always ready to eat whatever they can find. Here, a mother and her grown cubs have followed the scent to a dead whale, washed up on a Svalbard shore.

Ringed seal
Ringed seals live close inshore among the pack ice, where they produce their pups in spring, often in hidden dens among the floes. Polar bears hunt by scent for both adults and pups.

Protecting young cubs
Mother and cubs break out of their winter den in spring and move toward the sea ice. The cubs stay close to their mother because there are hungry predators about—foxes, wolves, even other polar bears— ready to kill and eat them. Females guard their cubs fiercely.

Winter in the den

Polar bears mate in summer. In autumn the pregnant females dig dens for themselves in snowbanks, where they sleep throughout winter. Around December each gives birth to one, two, or sometimes three rabbit-sized cubs, which feed on the mother's rich milk. Between feeds, mothers and cubs save energy by sleeping. By March or April the cubs are large enough to leave the den.

ANTARCTIC DESERT

Antarctica is truly a desert, the largest and driest on Earth, yet it contains 70 percent of the world's fresh water and 90 percent of its ice. Much of the Antarctic ice sheet is 2.5 miles (4 km) high and almost 3 miles (5 km) thick in places. It is also cold. A record low of –129.3° (–89.5°C) was recorded in 1983. Little rain falls but what does fall can remain frozen for up to one million years preserving an excellent record of climate changes. Deep within the ice there are vast lakes, kept above freezing temperature by Earth's heat. Life is rare on the ice sheet and restricted to the margins near the "warm" ocean. Water temperatures drop to a minimum of 28.7°F (–1.8°C) in winter beneath sea ice. At the margins of the continent, dark rocks absorb sunlight and heat, leading to the growth of algae and lichens on their warm surface.

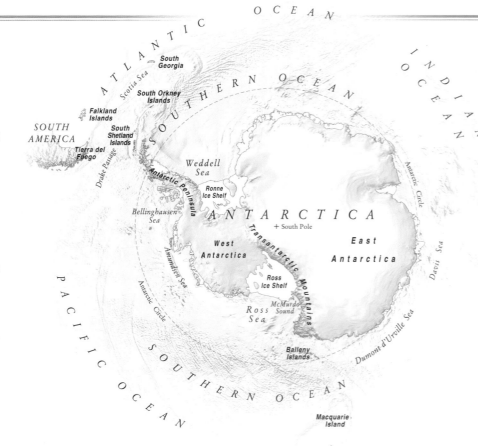

SCALE 1:70,000,000

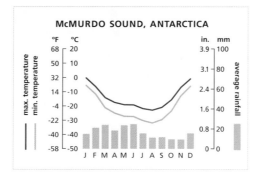

McMURDO SOUND, ANTARCTICA

CRABEATER SEAL DIET

Krill 94%
Fish 3%
Others (squid 2%, other invertebrates 1%)

LEOPARD SEAL DIET

Birds, seals, carrion 39%
Krill 37%
Fish 13%
Squid 3%
Other invertebrates 8%

Adélie penguins
Adélie penguins are a symbol of the Antarctic. They occur abundantly around the Antarctic margin, gathering in large rookeries to bear their young in summer. But much of their life is spent at sea where they hunt for fish and krill.

Blackfin icefish
The extreme cold of Antarctic waters is too severe an environment for most fish species. Some, however, have adapted to life here. The Antarctic icefish, such as the blackfin icefish, do not have hemoglobin in their blood, but have developed an "anti-freeze" capability.

Leopard seal
Leopard seals have a disproportionately large head and wide-opening, strong jaws. Their varied diet includes large catches such as penguins and young crabeater seals but they also filter seawater for krill. They are occasionally seen ashore on subantarctic islands.

Taylor Valley
This is one of the "Dry Valleys" in the McMurdo Sound region. These valleys, which receive almost no precipitation, are deserts of the most extreme type. They are largely ice-free, except for some permanently frozen lakes. Life here is limited to species such as mosses and algae.

234

Ross seal

The Ross seal's range encircles the Antarctic continent but it is most likely to be found in the Ross Sea. It feeds mainly on squid but also takes some fish and krill. Young are born on pack ice in early summer and are suckled by their mother for about four weeks. This is the rarest of the Antarctic seals.

Southern fur seal

These seals, which belong to the group known as eared seals, occur on islands close to the Antarctic continent but they do not breed on the ice. They spend most of the winter at sea, pursuing their diet of fish, krill, rock lobsters, and penguins.

Crabeater seal

The crabeater seal is the most abundant seal species on Earth. It inhabits Antarctic pack ice and its population is estimated at 11 to 12 million. This seal has characteristic tri-lobed teeth, allowing it to filter krill-rich water. Krill are its major food.

FEEDING GROUNDS

A crustacean central to the Antarctic food chain, krill lives near the margin of Antarctic sea ice and is the main food source of baleen whales, many seals, and penguins. The total mass of krill is more than 100 million tons making it the target of the world's largest single-species fishery. A krill's diet comprises microplankton such as diatoms.

Swarms

Krill are usually widely dispersed in the water, but periodically they come together in dense swarms, covering many square miles. These swarms, which color the sea red, provide a convenient food concentration for whales.

Food

A form of plankton, the krill uses its front legs to filter food and pass it forward to its mouth. Krill has high potential for human use as food and for biochemicals.

THE ANTARCTIC
LONG-DISTANCE MIGRANTS

Seasonal migration by wildlife is common in the natural world, allowing animals to move between distant environments to mate, bear young, and feed. Migration from the severe climatic conditions of polar regions is vital for many animals; food is plentiful in summer but in winter few animal species can survive. The emperor penguin is the only animal that is a year-round resident on the Antarctic ice. Others migrate, many of them long distances. Baleen whales, such as the humpback, migrate in both hemispheres along well-marked routes to the tropics during the polar winters. The northern and southern right whales, which have more restricted distributions and migration paths, also spend winter in warmer waters. The gray whale migrates from the northern Pacific Ocean to winter offshore from Mexico, a round trip of some 12,500 miles (20,000 km). Many bird and seal species also make long seasonal migrations from the high-latitude regions in winter.

Migration paths

Most aquatic migrating animals remain in their home hemisphere, even though they may travel long distances, but birds have no such limits and may migrate from one pole to the other. Whales migrate from polar regions, where they feed in summer, to the tropics where they mate and have their young. Seals migrate to bear their young on islands or other coasts in lower, subpolar latitudes.

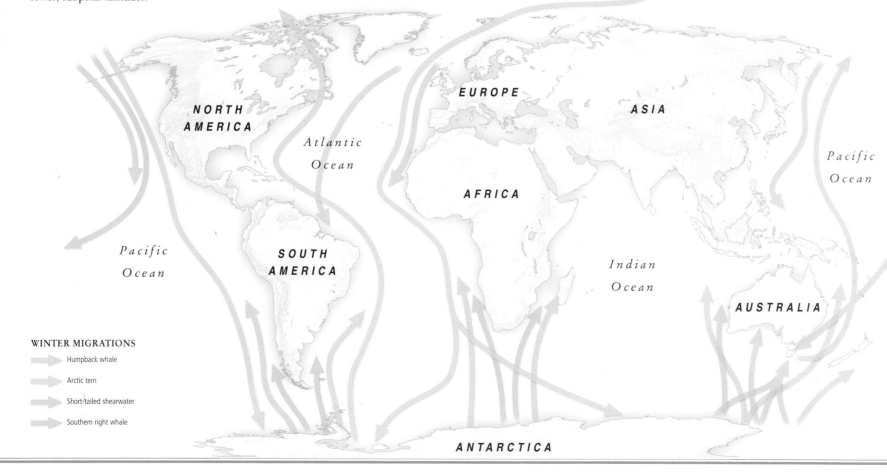

NORTH AMERICA

EUROPE

ASIA

Atlantic Ocean

Pacific Ocean

AFRICA

Pacific Ocean

SOUTH AMERICA

Indian Ocean

AUSTRALIA

WINTER MIGRATIONS

Humpback whale

Arctic tern

Short-tailed shearwater

Southern right whale

ANTARCTICA

Humpback whale

Humpback whales feed on swarms of krill in Antarctic waters (above). They gulp massive mouthfuls of krill and water, which are then filtered through their baleen "sieve" allowing them to retain and eat the krill. In the Arctic, humpback pods work cooperatively to form curtains of bubbles that concentrate krill in a restricted area. The humpback ends its migration in tropical waters, such as those off Tonga (left). Breaching may be a signal to others in the pod or elsewhere.

CONSERVATION WATCH

The Antarctic fin whale is second only to the blue whale in size. It is the fastest of the rorquals and cruises at 15 to 20 miles per hour (24–32 km/h). Its large size made it a desirable catch during the 20th-century whaling period and numbers have suffered.

Southern elephant seals

These juvenile elephant seals have migrated from the Antarctic winter and are resting in tussock grass on a subantarctic island. Elephant seals grow rapidly on their mother's rich milk and, weaned at about three weeks, can fend for themselves, feeding at sea.

Southern right whale

A southern right whale displays the unique callosities on its head and back. The species was named "the right whale" by whalers because it is slow, and therefore easier to catch, has a high oil content, and floats when dead.

MIGRATORY BIRDS

Birds that remain in the south polar regions year-round experience the maximum contrast between polar winters and summers. The Antarctic tern and several penguin species remain in the region; others, such as the albatross and the Arctic tern, travel vast distances.

Arctic tern

Arctic terns are renowned as great migrators—from their Arctic breeding grounds to the Antarctic. They can hover while observing small fish near the water's surface, then dive on their catch.

Arctic tern chick

Arctic tern chicks bred in the Arctic weigh only a few ounces. They migrate to the Antarctic for the southern summer.

Short-tailed shearwater

Short-tailed shearwaters breed in southeastern Australia and have two forms of migration—the traditional clockwise journey around the Pacific Ocean and a spring–summer round trip to Antarctic waters, gathering food for their young.

ANTARCTIC BIRDS

The Southern Ocean, circling Antarctica and covering almost 5 percent of the planet's surface, is home to a large and diverse seabird community including albatrosses, petrels, gulls, terns, and cormorants. It is also a destination for northern hemisphere migrants, such as Arctic terns during the southern summer. Early sailors dubbed the Southern Ocean winds the "Roaring '40s," the "Furious '50s," and the "Screaming '60s." These winds provide excellent flying conditions for albatrosses and petrels that use the energy from the wind for flight—their wingspans reach more than 12 feet (3.5 m). Small oceanic islands in the Southern Ocean serve as nesting sites for millions of seabirds, which seek prey in the surrounding seas. Their aerodynamically streamlined bodies reduce the energy required for flight, and enable them to forage far from land. Seabirds use a variety of methods to capture prey, including surface seizing and diving.

Snow petrel
Year-round residents of the Antarctic, snow petrels feed in open water among the ice. They are agile fliers and can survive winter storms. Snow petrels nest on the ground, laying one egg on bare rock in early summer.

South polar skua
South polar skuas are closely associated with breeding colonies of penguins. These predatory scavengers take eggs and small penguin chicks for food, but are aggressive in defense of their own breeding territories. The hook at the tip of their bill is used to rip flesh.

Subantarctic skua
These skuas are found on subantarctic islands and some temperate islands south of New Zealand. They nest on the ground using vegetation, if present, for their nest. Two eggs are laid, but typically only one chick survives.

SNOWY SHEATHBILL

Snowy sheathbills are found on the Antarctic Peninsula and on islands in the South Atlantic Ocean. Their breeding distribution is closely associated with penguins, other species of seabirds, and fur seal colonies. During the summer months they scavenge from these colonies, taking eggs, chicks, and carrion.

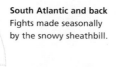

South Atlantic and back
Fights made seasonally by the snowy sheathbill.

Migratory flights
These birds are capable of flying from the Antarctic region to wintering sites in Patagonia, Tierra del Fuego, and the Falkland Islands. Flights may exceed 2000 miles (3200 km) in each direction.

Seasonal residents
Snowy, or pale-faced, sheathbills are named for the sheath, or shield, that is present around their bill. They lay up to four eggs in a nest constructed on the ground in a sheltered cavity.

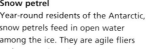

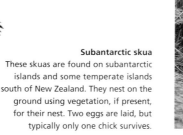

Wandering albatross on the wing

Albatrosses are perhaps the most efficient fliers on the planet. Their long wings generate enormous lift but prevent them from flapping the wings too rapidly. As a result, they are gliders, flying for long periods without flapping their wings. In light wind conditions they may rest on the water surface to conserve energy and await the next windy period. To take off from the water, they run into the wind with their wings outstretched.

Male display

Breeding males advertise themselves by bringing their wings to full stretch, raising their heads, and calling to prospective partners. Interested females approach and courtship rituals continue. The birds also use these behaviors to re-establish a bond between a pair that has bred before.

Air flow

Uplift

Aerodynamic design

A bird's wing is shaped so that air passes more quickly across the top, curved, surface than the bottom, providing essential lift.

Courtship rituals

Albatrosses use various courtship behaviors and vocalizations to establish the pair bond for the first time and, like many species of seabirds, they mate for life. A well-bonded pair has a greater chance of breeding successfully than first-time breeders.

Albatross chick

Perched on a nest made from vegetation and mud, this light-mantled sooty albatross chick waits for its next meal. Albatrosses lay just one egg and some species breed only every second year. Each season requires a coordinated effort by the parents to ensure their chick fledges.

Migratory path

Albatrosses make use of weather systems as they circumnavigate the globe. Strong and persistent westerlies are present over much of the southern hemisphere, and these winds provide the energy for the birds' long-distance flights. These flights are undertaken by non-breeding and juvenile birds, and by breeding adults that are restoring body reserves following a breeding season.

Pacific Ocean

SOUTH AMERICA

AFRICA

Indian Ocean

AUSTRALIA

ANTARCTICA

THE ANTARCTIC
PENGUIN PARADE

Of the 17 species of penguins, just four species are considered Antarctic: emperor, Adélie, chinstrap, and macaroni penguins. The remaining species are found on subantarctic and temperate islands as far north as the Galàpagos Islands at the equator, but all are confined to the southern hemisphere. Despite evolving from flighted ancestors, penguins are flightless but they "fly" through the water in order to feed. A variety of anatomical, physiological, and behavioral adaptations allow penguins to breed, feed, and survive. Their feathers are denser than those of any other bird, providing a streamlined and well-insulated body, and they have a thick layer of fat under the skin, providing further insulation and energy reserves for periods when they cannot feed. Up to 25 percent of a penguin's mass is in the breast muscles that power their flippers, which are used for swimming and for tobogganing over ice and snow.

Chinstrap penguin
Chinstrap penguins are so named because of the distinctive thin black line under their bills and on their cheeks. Their breeding colonies are found throughout the Antarctic Peninsula and on islands in the South Atlantic Ocean. A small breeding population is also found on the Balleny Islands, south of New Zealand.

Life on the ice
Penguins' feathers are highly adapted structures that form a dense layer to keep their body dry. They have strong feet with toes that provide a firm grip on ice and wet rocks.

Long toenails to grip onto ice

Feather layering

Nesting and feeding

Most penguin species nest close to the ocean. Diving underwater to feed, they seek prey concentrations such as krill swarms or schools of fish. All four species of Antarctic penguins breed around the Antarctic continent but the Adélie, chinstrap, and macaroni penguins choose only the coastal ice-free areas. Most colonies of emperor penguins, however, are found on the winter sea ice.

Distribution
Penguins are found along the coasts of all southern hemisphere continents, the Antarctic Peninsula, and on the small oceanic islands in the Southern Ocean.

Emperor penguins
Emperor penguins are the largest and heaviest penguins, with some individuals weighing more than 100 pounds (45 kg). They are capable of deep dives—the deepest recorded dive exceeded 1,600 feet (500 m) and took almost 20 minutes.

Penguin variety
Penguins are not just black and white, they are adorned with colorful crests, washes of rich oranges and yellows, and unique feather spots. Each species has a different shaped bill.

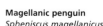

Emperor penguin
Aptenodytes forsteri

King penguin
Aptenodytes patagonicus

Chinstrap penguin
Pygoscelis antarctica

Adélie penguin
Pygoscelis adeliae

Yellow eyed penguin
Megadyptes antipodes

Magellanic penguin
Spheniscus magellanicus

Fiordland penguin
Eudyptes pachyrhynchus

Little penguin
Eudyptula minor

Adélie penguin
Adélie penguins are among the iconic species of penguin in the Antarctic and are the most widely distributed. Their diet is primarily crustaceans and fish, and they are capable of diving to 660 feet (200 m) to search for prey. Between dives, they rest on the surface or on ice floes to avoid predators such as leopard seals.

King penguin
King penguin colonies can number more than 100,000 pairs—so large the colonies are visible in satellite images. They are found on many of the subantarctic islands in the Southern Ocean where the maritime climate contrasts with the cold and dry climate of the Antarctic.

REARING OFFSPRING

Penguin chicks in the Antarctic face numerous threats from the moment they hatch. Temperatures can be extreme—as low as –40 degrees (–40°C) in midwinter when emperor penguins eggs hatch. Keeping the chicks warm is a full-time job for penguin parents as the newly hatched chicks are unable to keep themselves warm.

Protection
Until the chicks are quite large, almost half grown, they need their parents to protect them from the elements. Their own downy feathers do not protect them from low air temperatures.

Nest site
A rocky nest, built by the male, provides a home for the eggs and chicks. It is elevated above the surrounding terrain so that when the snow and ice melts during the summer it will not be flooded.

Bringing food
King penguins take more than a year to raise their chicks and, during winter months, a chick may wait weeks for its next meal. The parents forage over vast distances to provide their large chick with enough food.

Bottlenose dolphins live in the warm waters of the world. These social, active, and intelligent dolphins communicate with each other using a complex system of whistles, squeaks, and touch. They can travel at speeds of up to 18 miles an hour (30 km/h). All dolphins are cetaceans — a group that includes orcas and beluga whales.

THE OCEANS

THE OCEANS

Our Earth, the Blue Planet, is dominated by water. Some 70 percent of Earth's surface is covered by water, and life could not exist without it. About 200 million years ago, Earth was covered by one huge ocean with a single continent called Pangaea. Over the millennia, Pangaea broke up to form drifting continents, carried by great plates of Earth's crust. Today's five oceans—Pacific, Atlantic, Indian, Arctic, and Southern—were formed as continents drifted apart. The oceans comprise a vast three-dimensional space, where conditions at one spot on Earth can vary from bright, tropical warmth at the surface to perpetually dark, polar cold only a couple of miles below. Marine ecosystems can range from highly productive, brackish marshes, rocky coasts, and coral reefs to sterile mid-ocean regions bereft of nutrients. In this cornucopia of habitats, an extraordinary diversity of organisms has evolved with a wide array of adaptations to life in the sea.

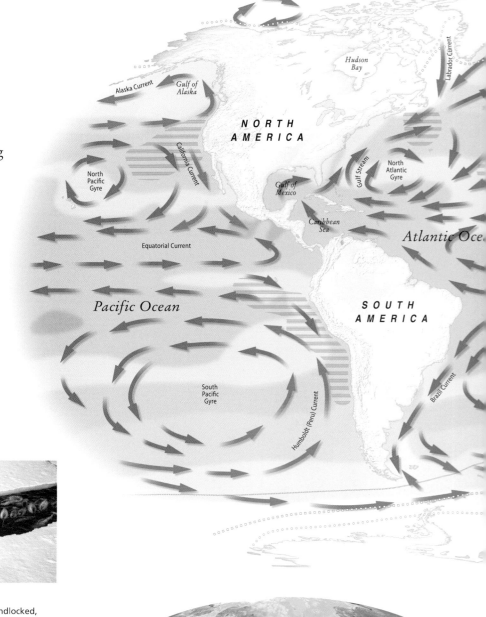

Pacific Ocean
The Pacific is the oldest and largest ocean. The coral reefs, stretching from Indonesia to the Great Barrier Reef off eastern Australia, harbor the most diverse marine fauna on Earth.

Arctic Ocean
The Arctic Ocean is essentially landlocked, and typified for aeons by permanent sea ice. Recent global warming is causing summer melting and threatens Arctic ecosystems.

Atlantic Ocean
The Atlantic formed 150 million years ago when the continents of Europe and North America broke apart, and Africa and South America separated along a submarine seam.

Southern Ocean
The nutrient-rich Southern Ocean, which flows around Antarctica, supports high plankton production. Great whales gather there in summer to gorge on shrimplike krill.

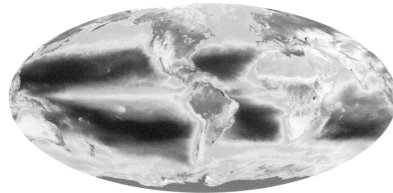

CHLOROPHYLL CONCENTRATION

Lowest | Very low | Low | Medium | High | Very high | Highest

Ocean productivity
Scientists use satellite measurements of chlorophyll concentration at the sea surface to estimate the production of phytoplankton around the world. The oceans' productivity is highest at higher latitudes, and in upwelling areas near the equator and along the western sides of continents. The most productive fisheries are found in these same high-nutrient areas.

Indian Ocean
The Indian Ocean shares much of its tropical marine fauna with the western Pacific, with which it is connected. Currents move freely around the Indonesian islands and Australia.

KNOWN SPECIES

Land species 84%

Marine species 16%

MARINE SPECIES

Benthic species 98%

Open-water species 2%

Marine species
Marine organisms make up only 16 percent of all known species. However, it is much easier to observe and collect plants and animals on land than in the oceans. A recent expedition to collect deepwater bottom animals off Antarctica discovered hundreds of new species.

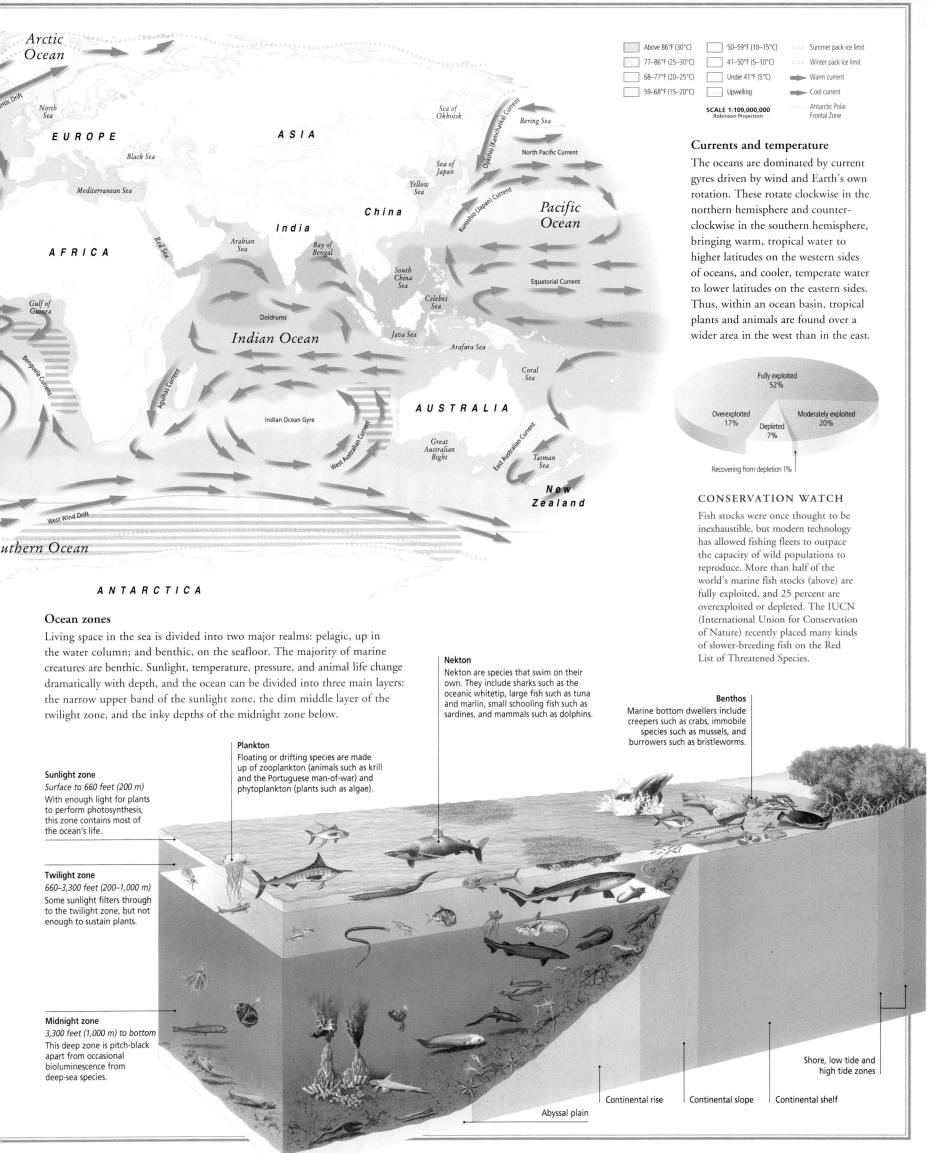

Legend:

- Above 86°F (30°C)
- 77–86°F (25–30°C)
- 68–77°F (20–25°C)
- 59–68°F (15–20°C)
- 50–59°F (10–15°C)
- 41–50°F (5–10°C)
- Under 41°F (5°C)
- Upwelling
- ⋯ Summer pack ice limit
- ⋯ Winter pack ice limit
- → Warm current
- → Cool current
- ⋯ Antarctic Polar Frontal Zone

SCALE 1:109,000,000
Robinson Projection

Currents and temperature

The oceans are dominated by current gyres driven by wind and Earth's own rotation. These rotate clockwise in the northern hemisphere and counter-clockwise in the southern hemisphere, bringing warm, tropical water to higher latitudes on the western sides of oceans, and cooler, temperate water to lower latitudes on the eastern sides. Thus, within an ocean basin, tropical plants and animals are found over a wider area in the west than in the east.

Pie chart:
- Fully exploited 52%
- Overexploited 17%
- Depleted 7%
- Moderately exploited 20%
- Recovering from depletion 1%

CONSERVATION WATCH

Fish stocks were once thought to be inexhaustible, but modern technology has allowed fishing fleets to outpace the capacity of wild populations to reproduce. More than half of the world's marine fish stocks (above) are fully exploited, and 25 percent are overexploited or depleted. The IUCN (International Union for Conservation of Nature) recently placed many kinds of slower-breeding fish on the Red List of Threatened Species.

Map labels:
Arctic Ocean, North Sea, Black Sea, Mediterranean Sea, EUROPE, AFRICA, Gulf of Guinea, Benguela Current, Red Sea, Arabian Sea, Agulhas Current, ASIA, India, Sea of Okhotsk, Bering Sea, Sea of Japan, Yellow Sea, China, Oyashio (Kamchatka) Current, North Pacific Current, Kuroshio (Japan) Current, Pacific Ocean, Bay of Bengal, South China Sea, Celebes Sea, Java Sea, Doldrums, Indian Ocean, Equatorial Current, Arafura Sea, Coral Sea, Indian Ocean Gyre, West Australian Current, AUSTRALIA, Great Australian Bight, East Australian Current, Tasman Sea, New Zealand, West Wind Drift, Southern Ocean, ANTARCTICA

Ocean zones

Living space in the sea is divided into two major realms: pelagic, up in the water column; and benthic, on the seafloor. The majority of marine creatures are benthic. Sunlight, temperature, pressure, and animal life change dramatically with depth, and the ocean can be divided into three main layers: the narrow upper band of the sunlight zone, the dim middle layer of the twilight zone, and the inky depths of the midnight zone below.

Nekton
Nekton are species that swim on their own. They include sharks such as the oceanic whitetip, large fish such as tuna and marlin, small schooling fish such as sardines, and mammals such as dolphins.

Benthos
Marine bottom dwellers include creepers such as crabs, immobile species such as mussels, and burrowers such as bristleworms.

Plankton
Floating or drifting species are made up of zooplankton (animals such as krill and the Portuguese man-of-war) and phytoplankton (plants such as algae).

Sunlight zone
Surface to 660 feet (200 m)
With enough light for plants to perform photosynthesis, this zone contains most of the ocean's life.

Twilight zone
660–3,300 feet (200–1,000 m)
Some sunlight filters through to the twilight zone, but not enough to sustain plants.

Midnight zone
3,300 feet (1,000 m) to bottom
This deep zone is pitch-black apart from occasional bioluminescence from deep-sea species.

Shore, low tide and high tide zones

Continental rise | Continental slope | Continental shelf

Abyssal plain

THE PACIFIC OCEAN

The sea's richest biodiversity and biological productivity occurs in the Pacific Ocean. This vast body of water acts as a great thermostat that cools passing air masses in summer and warms them in winter. Because the size of the Pacific has moderated its marine climate, many fewer species extinctions occurred there during glaciations and other periods of extreme global climate change. The relatively stable ocean environment has allowed complex ecosystems to evolve. Coral reef communities of the Indo-Australian archipelago have the greatest diversity of tropical marine species, while the rocky coasts and kelp forests of the eastern North Pacific are home to the greatest temperate biodiversity. The Pacific has some of the highest oceanic nutrient levels and heaviest marine plankton blooms. The Bering Sea, where plankton production soars during the long summer days, and the Humboldt Current off northern South America, support two of the most productive fisheries on Earth.

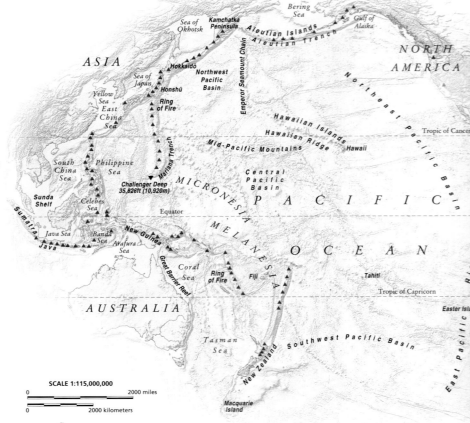

The dynamic Pacific

The central Pacific is marked by a long mountain ridge system from which Earth's crust arises and creeps west and east to collide with the continents. This violent tectonic activity—announced by earthquakes—causes mountain ranges and volcanoes to rise. Thus the perimeter of the Pacific is called The Ring of Fire.

OCEAN SHARE

Pacific Ocean
60.1 million sq miles
(155.6 million km²)
46%

All other oceans

Clown anemonefish
Amphiprion ocellaris

THE FACTS

Area	60.1 million square miles (155.6 million km²)
Average depth	13,127 feet (4,001 m)
Maximum depth	35,840 feet (10,924 m)
Maximum width	11,200 miles (18,000 km)
Maximum length	8,600 miles (13,900 km)
Coastline length	84,297 miles (135,663 km)

Boobies and anchovies

Boobies are the avian torpedoes of the sea, folding their wings and dropping like darts out of the sky to skewer their anchovy prey in a trail of bubbles. Boobies congregate in rich ocean areas, where plankton abounds to support productive ocean food webs and large shoals of forage fish, such as anchovies. During most years, upwelling off Peru brings cold, nutrient-rich water to the surface to boost a flourishing ecosystem including plankton, fish, and seabirds such as Peruvian boobies.

EL NINO

In Spanish El Niño means "The Christ Child," a name bestowed because this oceanographic phenomenon often begins around Christmas off Peru. Warm nutrient-poor water from the central Pacific spreads eastward, and upwelling that normally dominates the region stops. During La Niña, the opposite conditions prevail. Scientists call the event the El Niño/Southern Oscillation, or ENSO, and it has profound influences on global weather patterns.

El Niño
The warm water caused by El Niño can raise sea levels by up to 8 inches (20 cm). The white patch shows El Niño moving eastward along the equator across the Pacific in March 1997.

La Niña
Lower than average sea levels, caused by cooler water, are shown in purple, during a La Niña event in July 1998. El Niño and La Niña events occur in the Pacific Ocean in no fixed cycles.

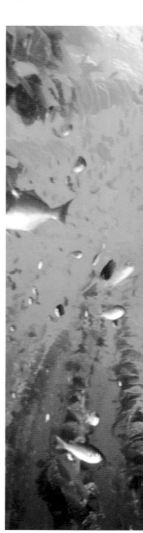

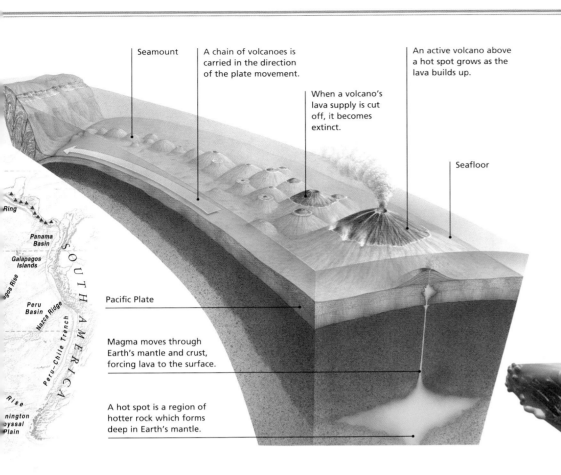

Seamount

A chain of volcanoes is carried in the direction of the plate movement.

When a volcano's lava supply is cut off, it becomes extinct.

An active volcano above a hot spot grows as the lava builds up.

Seafloor

Pacific Plate

Magma moves through Earth's mantle and crust, forcing lava to the surface.

A hot spot is a region of hotter rock which forms deep in Earth's mantle.

The Hawaiian hot spot

Most volcanic islands exist for only 10 million to 30 million years before eroding back beneath the sea. The Hawaiian archipelago, however, has been forming continuously over a volcanic hot spot in the Pacific Plate for at least 70 million years. The Big Island of Hawaii is still active and growing. Other islands formed over the same hot spot and were carried northwest on the plate.

Unique species

When a single hot spot gradually produces a series of new islands, shallow-water species can island-hop along the chain and unique species have time to evolve. Of the 600 or so species of shorefish in Hawaii, 25 percent are endemic (found nowhere else). They include the Hawaiian turkeyfish, a reef fish with venomous spines.

Kelp forest

Kelp are giant brown algae that may grow to 160 feet (50 m) or more in length. They require cool coastal temperatures and a rocky bottom upon which to attach. Kelp forests in the northeast Pacific provide a complex ecosystem that supports a wide variety of marine fish, such as these blacksmiths. Blacksmiths hover in the kelp and make forays into open water to feed on plankton.

Humpback whale
Large groups of black-and-white humpback whales gather to feed in summer in the plankton-rich waters off Alaska. In winter they swim halfway across the Pacific to warm subtropical haunts off Hawaii where their calves are born. Humpbacks are the most acrobatic of all the large whales, and often breach clear of the sea surface, falling with a giant splash.

⚡ CONSERVATION WATCH

The warm-blooded leatherback turtle can reach 1 ton (910 kg) in weight, and can dive more than 3,000 feet (914 m) to feast on jellyfish. Tens of thousands of leatherbacks once nested on the Pacific beaches of Central America, but no longer. Pacific leatherback populations have been decimated by capture in high-seas fisheries, and more frequent El Niño events are hampering their recovery.

THE ATLANTIC OCEAN

The North Atlantic Ocean appeared some 160 million years ago when North America began to pull away from Eurasia after the breakup of the supercontinent Pangaea. The South Atlantic formed later, after South America separated from Africa. Consequently, the Atlantic is a newer, smaller ocean than the Pacific. Climatic variations in the Atlantic Ocean have been more extreme, and species diversity is much lower because of periodic extinctions. Both the Mediterranean and the Caribbean seas were once tropical arms of the Atlantic. When glaciers covered much of Europe and North America 10,000 years ago, only the tropical species in the Caribbean survived. Even so, the Caribbean today has only about half as many species of reef fish as we see in the western Pacific. The Atlantic does include some of the world's richest fishing areas, and these were a major impetus to colonization of the New World.

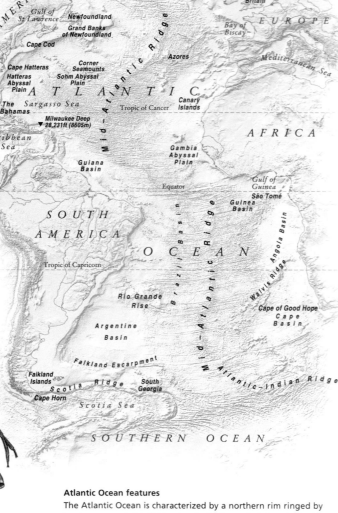

SCALE 1:125,000,000

OCEAN SHARE

All other oceans

Atlantic Ocean
29.7 million sq miles
(76.8 million km²)
23%

Caribbean spiny lobster
Panulirus argus

THE FACTS

Area	29.7 million square miles (76.8 million km²)
Average depth	11,827 feet (3,605 m)
Maximum depth	28,232 feet (8,605 m)
Maximum width	4,900 miles (7,900 km)
Maximum length	8,770 miles (14,120 km)
Coastline length	69,510 miles (111,866 km)

Atlantic Ocean features
The Atlantic Ocean is characterized by a northern rim ringed by landmasses and rich fishing banks, high tropical diversity in the west, cool temperate waters in the east, and a vast stretch of open ocean with productive converging water masses in the south.

Atlantic puffin
The Atlantic puffin is a streamlined diver with stubby wings and a colorful bill it uses to capture sand eels and other small fish. Puffins congregate to feed at productive North Atlantic fishing banks, and nest high on isolated island cliffs where they are safe from most predators.

Blue marlin
The blue marlin lives in tropical and subtropical seas around the world. Its long bill and streamlined shape make the marlin perfectly suited for the rapid acceleration needed to disable and capture mahimahi, tuna, and other fast-swimming prey.

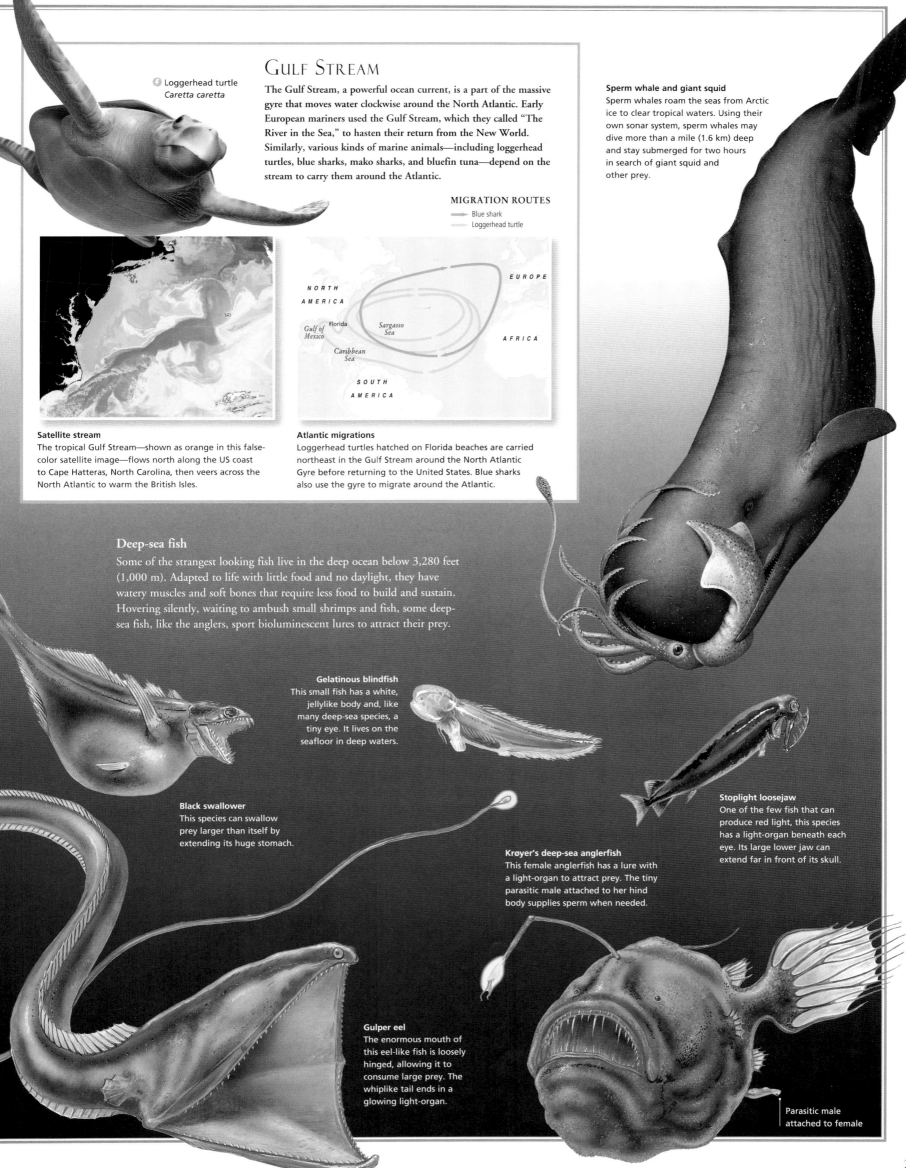

🄯 Loggerhead turtle
Caretta caretta

GULF STREAM

The Gulf Stream, a powerful ocean current, is a part of the massive gyre that moves water clockwise around the North Atlantic. Early European mariners used the Gulf Stream, which they called "The River in the Sea," to hasten their return from the New World. Similarly, various kinds of marine animals—including loggerhead turtles, blue sharks, mako sharks, and bluefin tuna—depend on the stream to carry them around the Atlantic.

Sperm whale and giant squid
Sperm whales roam the seas from Arctic ice to clear tropical waters. Using their own sonar system, sperm whales may dive more than a mile (1.6 km) deep and stay submerged for two hours in search of giant squid and other prey.

MIGRATION ROUTES
→ Blue shark
→ Loggerhead turtle

NORTH AMERICA
EUROPE
Gulf of Mexico
Florida
Sargasso Sea
Caribbean Sea
AFRICA
SOUTH AMERICA

Satellite stream
The tropical Gulf Stream—shown as orange in this false-color satellite image—flows north along the US coast to Cape Hatteras, North Carolina, then veers across the North Atlantic to warm the British Isles.

Atlantic migrations
Loggerhead turtles hatched on Florida beaches are carried northeast in the Gulf Stream around the North Atlantic Gyre before returning to the United States. Blue sharks also use the gyre to migrate around the Atlantic.

Deep-sea fish

Some of the strangest looking fish live in the deep ocean below 3,280 feet (1,000 m). Adapted to life with little food and no daylight, they have watery muscles and soft bones that require less food to build and sustain. Hovering silently, waiting to ambush small shrimps and fish, some deep-sea fish, like the anglers, sport bioluminescent lures to attract their prey.

Gelatinous blindfish
This small fish has a white, jellylike body and, like many deep-sea species, a tiny eye. It lives on the seafloor in deep waters.

Black swallower
This species can swallow prey larger than itself by extending its huge stomach.

Stoplight loosejaw
One of the few fish that can produce red light, this species has a light-organ beneath each eye. Its large lower jaw can extend far in front of its skull.

Krøyer's deep-sea anglerfish
This female anglerfish has a lure with a light-organ to attract prey. The tiny parasitic male attached to her hind body supplies sperm when needed.

Gulper eel
The enormous mouth of this eel-like fish is loosely hinged, allowing it to consume large prey. The whiplike tail ends in a glowing light-organ.

Parasitic male attached to female

The Indian Ocean

The Indian Ocean has a rich tropical shore fauna that stretches from South Africa, north to the Red Sea, east around the Indian subcontinent, and south through the Indo-Malayan archipelago to Western Australia. Coral reefs abound in the east and west, and sandy and muddy mangrove habitats dominate the Indian coast. Animal life of the Indian Ocean is closely related to that of the western Pacific, with many tropical shorefish species ranging from South Africa to the islands of the South Pacific. The Indian Ocean is home to a particularly wide variety of sharks, from small, bottom-grubbing catsharks to large, camouflaged wobbegongs and sleek requiem sharks. Olive ridley sea turtles gather to nest each year on Indian beaches. Productive upwelling across the central Indian Ocean supports tuna populations and the fisheries that pursue them.

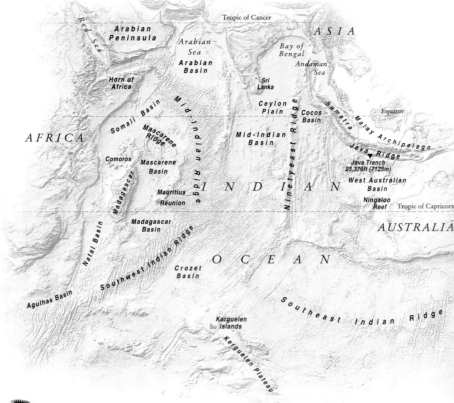

OCEAN SHARE

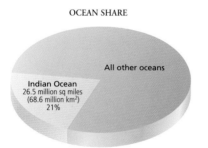

Indian Ocean
26.5 million sq miles
(68.6 million km²)
21%

All other oceans

The Facts	
Area	26.5 million square miles (68.6 million km²)
Average depth	12,644 feet (3,854 m)
Maximum depth	24,459 feet (7,455 m)
Maximum width	6,300 miles (10,200 km)
Maximum length	5,800 miles (9,400 km)
Coastline length	41,337 miles (66,526 km)

Yellow-lipped sea krait
Laticauda colubrina

SCALE 1:105,000,000

0 ————————— 2000 miles

0 ————————— 2000 kilometers

Indian Ocean formation
More than 100 million years ago, India, Australia, and Antarctica, together with Africa and South America, were joined in a southern supercontinent called Gondwana. India and Australia broke away and drifted slowly north and east to open the Indian Ocean basin.

Coelacanth

Coelacanths, primitive cousins of early fish that evolved into land vertebrates, were thought to have become extinct 65 million years ago. Then, in 1938, a trawler fishing off Mozambique dragged up a dark, bulky, rough-scaled monster of the deep. The creature was a coelacanth, in effect a living fossil. Today, remnant coelacanth populations have been found off East and South Africa, the Comoros Islands, Madagascar, and the Indonesian island of Sulawesi.

Living fossil
The discovery of a living coelacanth rocked the halls of science. Coelacanths frequent undersea volcanic slopes, hiding in caves by day and foraging at night as they drift with the currents.

Dolphins and baitball
Dolphins and several species of sharks follow migrating shoals of sardines, traveling south along the South African coast in summer and north in winter. Sardines and other schooling fish often form tight, spherical schools, called baitballs, when threatened by predators.

Coral communities

The Indian Ocean hosts a cornucopia of corals. Regions with little freshwater input and very clear water, such as the Red Sea (below), have particularly rich coral communities. Reef corals can occur deeper there because enough sunlight penetrates to allow photosynthesis by the algae that help nourish corals. Global warming and high sea temperatures cause potentially fatal coral bleaching.

GREAT WHITE SHARK MIGRATION

Great white sharks were thought to be coastal denizens until recent satellite tracking experiments showed that they can migrate thousands of miles across the open ocean. A mature female great white tagged off South Africa swam all the way across the Indian Ocean to Western Australia, then returned within the year. The reasons for such sojourns remain obscure, but breeding is a prime candidate.

Whale shark
Whale sharks (left and below) are the largest living fish, reaching 45 feet (13.5 m) in length, yet they are harmless plankton feeders. Large numbers gather each year to feast on billions of tiny eggs spawned by corals in places such as Ningaloo Reef off Western Australia.

Giant manta
Manta rays fly through tropical seas with flapping wings and mouths agape, filtering plankton as they go. The largest of all rays, they may reach 22 feet (6.5 m) in width. Mantas sometimes propel their huge bodies completely out of the water, landing with a thunderous splash.

THE ARCTIC OCEAN

Although the Arctic is the smallest ocean, its marine life is not well known because permanent sea ice and a harsh climate have made biological exploration difficult. Regardless, relatively few species inhabit the Arctic, a result of fluctuating climate during recent geological time. Sea ice has been a potent force in shaping the evolution of the creatures that do live there. The edges of the ice pack melt and shrink in spring and summer, providing a rich transition zone that supports lush phytoplankton growth. This primary production is the basis for most Arctic marine food webs. Several species of seals rest and pup on the ice surface while trying to avoid their polar bear predators. Beneath the ice, juvenile Arctic cod pursue tiny crustacean prey and hide from the seals and sleeper sharks that see them as potential meals. Great whales patrol the ice edge, engulfing tons of tiny zooplankton.

Arctic Ocean features
Surrounded by land, the Arctic Ocean has been subject to extreme climatic fluctuations and species extinctions over time. Today, most families of animals in the Arctic Ocean have evolved from North Pacific groups that entered through periodic openings of the Bering Strait.

OCEAN SHARE

All other oceans

Arctic Ocean
5.4 million sq miles
(14.1 million km²)
4%

SCALE 1:45,000,000

0 — 750 miles
0 — 750 kilometers

THE FACTS	
Area	5.4 million square miles (14.1 million km²)
Average depth	4,690 feet (1,430 m)
Maximum depth	18,455 feet (5,625 m)
Maximum width	2,000 miles (3,200 km)
Maximum length	3,100 miles (5,000 km)
Coastline length	28,203 miles (45,389 km)

Common feather star
Florometra serratissima

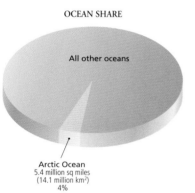

Arctic cod
Juvenile Arctic cod find shelter in crevices under the polar ice. Although members of the cod family are abundant and important in Arctic ecosystems, cods are the only fish family of Atlantic origin. All the other families, such as the sculpins, blennies, and flatfishes, came from the Pacific.

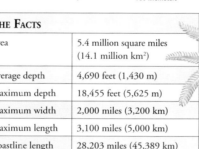

Sleeper shark
The huge Greenland shark and its close relative, the Pacific sleeper, are the apex predators in Arctic ecosystems—the marine equivalents of the polar bear. Curiously, the eyes of both species are commonly infected with a copepod parasite that may cause blindness but no other apparent health effects.

Whale species

There are two major types of whales: toothed species that feed on active fish and squid, and baleen whales that use long sheets of hairlike baleen to sieve out zooplankton and small fish from the water. Arctic residents include two toothed whales—the beluga and narwhal—and one baleen whale—the bowhead. Other baleen whales, such as the fin, minke, and North Atlantic right, arrive in summer to graze on zooplankton.

Minke whale
The minke whale is the smallest baleen whale in the Arctic.

Narwhal
The male narwhal has a single spiral tusk, like a unicorn's horn.

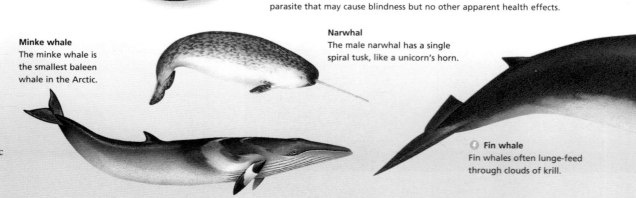

Fin whale
Fin whales often lunge-feed through clouds of krill.

Habitat zones

The Arctic summer brings birds to nest on the tundra and feed in the rich ocean waters. Explosive blooms of phytoplankton called diatoms support tiny grazing copepods and amphipods, both in the water and the pores of the ice. These in turn are consumed by small fish, such as capelin and herring, as well as by large whales. On the bottom, bristleworms, brittle stars, and clams abound.

ARCTIC JELLYFISH

Jelly animals are important predators in pelagic Arctic ecosystems. They include the 150 or so species of true jellyfish, or hydromedusae, and the eight species of colonial siphonophores. Both groups paralyze their prey with long, sticky, stinging tentacles, and eat fish, squid, shrimps, and even other jellyfish. A small number of harmless comb jellies have also been found in the Arctic Ocean.

Giant jelly
The Arctic lion's mane is the largest jellyfish in the world, with a bell-shaped body up to 7.5 feet (2.3 m) wide and tentacles 120 feet (36.5 m) long. Its venomous sting could kill a human.

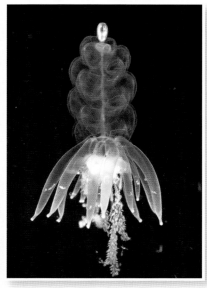

Hula skirt stinger
The hula skirt siphonophore grows to about 16 inches (41 cm) and, despite its small size, packs a powerful sting like its tropical cousin, the Portuguese man-of-war.

Beluga
Belugas are gray at birth but turn white by the time they are five years old.

Bowhead
The bowhead is hunted by Inuit people and is an important part of their culture.

North Atlantic right whale
With fewer than 350 individuals left, this species is near extinction.

THE SOUTHERN OCEAN

The Southern Ocean flows around the frigid continent of Antarctica. Thirty million years ago this cold circumpolar current did not exist because Antarctica was connected to the tip of South America, and the region was warmed by currents from the north. When the connection parted, the circumpolar current was born, sea temperatures dropped, warm-adapted animals became extinct, and the cold-adapted survivors evolved into a unique fauna. The Southern Ocean has provided a stable polar climate where cold-water animals have had time to evolve and diversify. Perhaps the greatest symbol of the Antarctic is the penguin, with its insulating feathers and torpedo-shaped body, efficient at conserving heat and swimming. The 90 species of notothenioid fish, which fill many ecological niches, are no less remarkable. They have special molecules in their blood called glycoproteins that act like antifreeze.

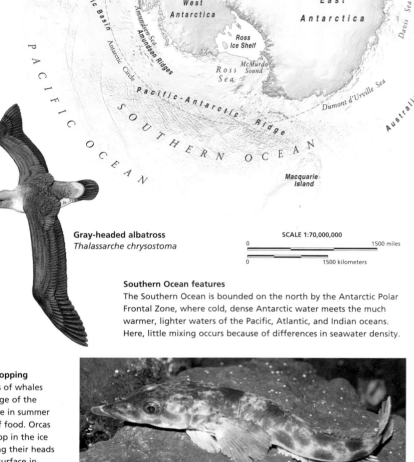

OCEAN SHARE

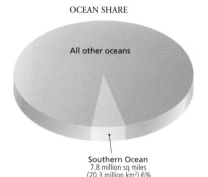

All other oceans

Southern Ocean
7.8 million sq miles
(20.3 million km²) 6%

THE FACTS	
Area	7.8 million square miles (20.3 million km²)
Average depth	14,750 feet (4,500 m)
Maximum depth	24,032 feet (7,235 m)
Maximum width	1,700 miles (2,700 km)
Maximum length	13,400 miles (21,500 km)
Coastline length	11,165 miles (17,968 km)

Gray-headed albatross
Thalassarche chrysostoma

SCALE 1:70,000,000

0 ————————— 1500 miles

0 ————————— 1500 kilometers

Southern Ocean features
The Southern Ocean is bounded on the north by the Antarctic Polar Frontal Zone, where cold, dense Antarctic water meets the much warmer, lighter waters of the Pacific, Atlantic, and Indian oceans. Here, little mixing occurs because of differences in seawater density.

Orcas spyhopping
Many kinds of whales visit the edge of the Antarctic ice in summer in search of food. Orcas often spyhop in the ice pack, poking their heads above the surface in search of resting seals or other prey that may be captured and consumed.

Naked dragonfish
The naked dragonfish, a common Antarctic bottom dweller, sits quietly waiting to ambush passing prey. This sit-and-wait strategy has reached its apex in closely related crocodile icefishes, which lack hemoglobin and take up all the oxygen they need from the frigid, oxygen-rich Antarctic water.

BOTTOM DWELLERS

Antarctic bottom communities are much more diverse than those of the Arctic. More than 90 percent of the invertebrates on the continental shelf originated in the Antarctic and occur nowhere else. Southern Ocean currents bring suspended zooplankton, phytoplankton, bacteria, and other microorganisms to bottom communities dominated by sponges, sea squirts, feather stars, and other filter feeders. In the deep Southern Ocean, hundreds of new species of worms and other tiny bottom creatures have recently been discovered.

Sea star
Sea stars are common members of Antarctic bottom communities. They prey on clams and other mollusks.

Anemone
Anemones are closely related to jellyfish. They prey on fish and other creatures that venture too close to their stinging tentacles.

Sea urchin
The Antarctic sea urchin grazes on algae, and camouflages itself with bits of shell and other debris to avoid predators.

KEYSTONE KRILL

Krill are small—1½ to 2½ inches (4–6 cm)—shrimplike creatures that swim in the Southern Ocean in swarms as dense as 13,000 per cubic yard (10,000 per m³). Living as long as five years, these small animals are the keystone food source upon which many species of fish, squid, penguins, seals, and whales depend for survival.

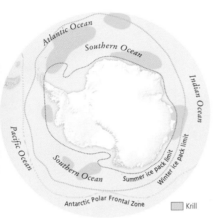

Commercial harvest
A ready source of protein, krill have attracted the interest of industrial fisheries. Large-scale harvest of krill has prompted concern that Antarctic food webs could be disrupted.

Southern distribution
Krill live in cold, productive seas at both ends of Earth, but reach their greatest concentrations in the Southern Ocean, where their phytoplankton food is at its most abundant.

⚡ CONSERVATION WATCH

The blue whale is the largest creature that ever lived on Earth, measuring up to 108 feet (33 m) in length, and weighing as much as 176 tons (160 t). Blue whales congregate in the Southern Ocean in summer to gorge on clouds of krill. In winter they head to more hospitable tropical climes to rest and have their calves.

King penguin
Unlike the five other species of Antarctic penguins that nest on the continent or the tip of the Antarctic Peninsula, king penguins prefer the more hospitable Southern Ocean islands, such as Macquarie Island. There they may be joined by a host of breeding seabirds, such as petrels, prions, and albatrosses.

Antarctic seals

The Antarctic is home to six species of seals, of which four—the Ross, Weddell, crabeater, and leopard seals—pup on the sea ice in spring. The Antarctic fur seal and the elephant seal breed in large colonies on beaches north of the pack ice. Most Antarctic seals include fish, squid, and krill in their diets, but the leopard seal also eats penguins and young seals.

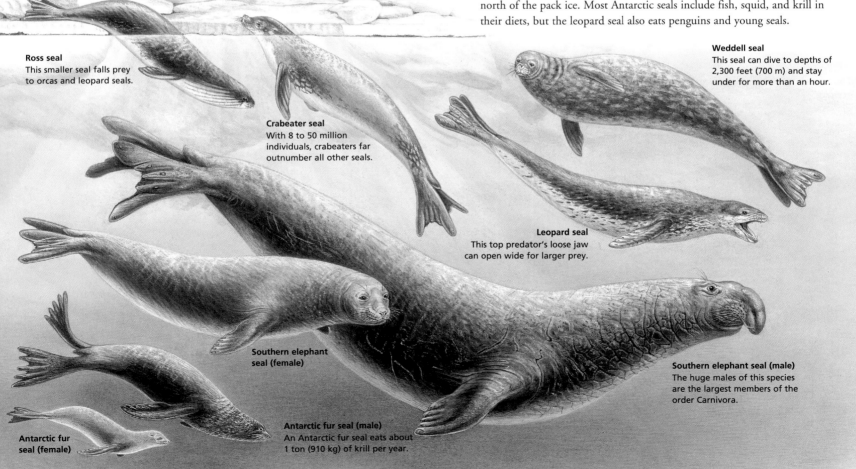

Ross seal
This smaller seal falls prey to orcas and leopard seals.

Crabeater seal
With 8 to 50 million individuals, crabeaters far outnumber all other seals.

Weddell seal
This seal can dive to depths of 2,300 feet (700 m) and stay under for more than an hour.

Leopard seal
This top predator's loose jaw can open wide for larger prey.

Southern elephant seal (female)

Southern elephant seal (male)
The huge males of this species are the largest members of the order Carnivora.

Antarctic fur seal (male)
An Antarctic fur seal eats about 1 ton (910 kg) of krill per year.

Antarctic fur seal (female)

This parrot snake is in Soberania National Park, Panama, Central America. It is eating a clutch of red-eyed tree frog tadpoles as they hatch from their eggs. All snakes are carnivorous and the parrot snake eats frogs, birds, lizards, and insects. Many snakes can lower their metabolic rate by 70 percent and eat only a few times a year.

FACTS ABOUT ANIMALS

Scientists have described and named at least 1.7 million species of plants, animals, and microorganisms, but new species are discovered almost every day and the total number of lifeforms is estimated at between 10 million and 30 million. The discipline of taxonomy provides a unique name for each organism and sorts organisms into hierarchies of increasingly exclusive groups, or taxa, based on their evolutionary relationships. The basic category is the species. Species are populations of organisms that share one or more similarities not found in related organisms, and can usually reproduce sexually only with each other. Each species is assigned a two-part scientific name. The first part, the generic name, gives the genus, the group of closely related organisms to which the species belongs. The second part, the specific name, is unique to that species within the genus. Animals are known by various common names around the world, so the scientific name is Latinized to avoid confusion. All taxa above the species level are meant to comprise an ancestral species and all it descendants. Recent genetic techniques have allowed comparison of organisms' DNA, forcing scientists to rethink the classification of many animals.

FACTFILE CONTENTS	
Mammals	p259
Birds	p268
Reptiles	p274
Amphibians	p275
Fish	p276
Invertebrates	p278

HOW TO USE THIS FACTFILE

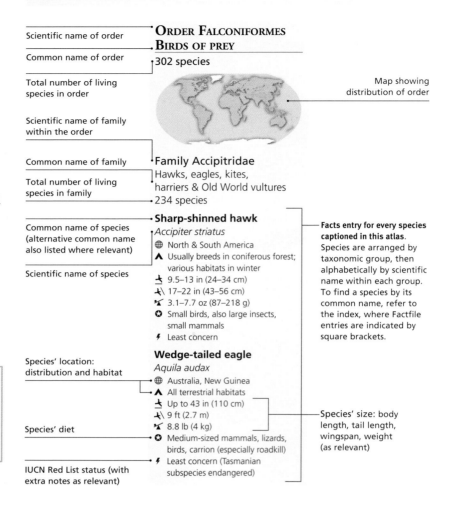

Scientific name of order — **ORDER FALCONIFORMES**
Common name of order — **BIRDS OF PREY**
Total number of living species in order — 302 species

Map showing distribution of order

Scientific name of family within the order

Common name of family — **Family Accipitridae**
Total number of living species in family — Hawks, eagles, kites, harriers & Old World vultures
234 species

Common name of species (alternative common name also listed where relevant) — **Sharp-shinned hawk**
Accipiter striatus
Scientific name of species
⊕ North & South America
⋀ Usually breeds in coniferous forest; various habitats in winter
⌁ 9.5–13 in (24–34 cm)
⌁ 17–22 in (43–56 cm)
⚖ 3.1–7.7 oz (87–218 g)
✿ Small birds, also large insects, small mammals
⚡ Least concern

Facts entry for every species captioned in this atlas. Species are arranged by taxonomic group, then alphabetically by scientific name within each group. To find a species by its common name, refer to the index, where Factfile entries are indicated by square brackets.

Species' location: distribution and habitat — **Wedge-tailed eagle**
Aquila audax
⊕ Australia, New Guinea
⋀ All terrestrial habitats
⌁ Up to 43 in (110 cm)
⌁ 9 ft (2.7 m)
Species' diet — ⚖ 8.8 lb (4 kg)
✿ Medium-sized mammals, lizards, birds, carrion (especially roadkill)
IUCN Red List status (with extra notes as relevant) — ⚡ Least concern (Tasmanian subspecies endangered)

Species' size: body length, tail length, wingspan, weight (as relevant)

KINGDOMS OF LIFE

All life on Earth can be classified into the six broad taxa known as kingdoms. These kingdoms are sometimes grouped into three higher domains: Bacteria (Eubacteria), Archaea (Archaebacteria), and Eukarya (Protista, Fungi, Plantae, and Animalia).

EUBACTERIA
Most known prokaryotes
10,000 species

These microorganisms were the only known prokaryotes, single-celled forms without a nucleus, until the discovery of archaebacteria in the 1970s. Eubacteria recycle nutrients in all Earth's habitats.

ARCHAEBACTERIA
Prokaryotes of extremes
18–23 phyla

Found in or around deep-sea vents, hot springs, and extremely salty water, these ancient lifeforms do not rely on oxygen. They are prokaryotes, but are very different genetically from other bacteria.

PROTISTA
Protists
250,000 species

Like fungi, plants, and animals, protists are eukaryotes, organisms with a cell nucleus. Protists are single-celled, or multicellular without specialized tissues. They include algae, cilia, and slime molds.

FUNGI
Fungi
100,000 species

Fungi include mushrooms, molds, and yeasts. They perform a vital ecological role in decomposing organic matter and recycling nutrients. Unlike plants, fungi cannot make their own food.

PLANTAE
Plants
350,000 species

The vast majority of plants create their own food through the process of photosynthesis and are the primary producers in ecosystems. They include flowering plants, mosses, and ferns.

ANIMALIA
Animals
1,350,000+ species

Animals make up the largest kingdom. It has about 30 phyla of invertebrates. A single phylum, Chordata, includes all the vertebrates—mammals, birds, reptiles, amphibians, and fish.

Animal classification
All lifeforms can be classified according to the Linnaean system. Each nested category contains organisms with progressively similar characteristics. This bobcat belongs to kingdom Animalia (all animals); phylum Chordata (animals with a centralized nerve cord); class Mammalia (all mammals); order Carnivora (with specialized teeth for eating meat); family Felidae (all cats); and genus *Lynx* (all lynxes). Finally, no other organism shares the scientific name of this species, *Lynx rufus*.

SPECIES
Lynx rufus
Bobcat

GENUS
Lynx
Bobcat, Eurasian lynx, Canadian lynx

FAMILY
Felidae
Bobcat, domestic cat, lion, leopard, jaguar

ORDER
Carnivora
Bobcat, seal, wolf, bear, skunk, meerkat

CLASS
Mammalia
Bobcat, kangaroo, human, dolphin, woolly mammoth

PHYLUM
Chordata
Bobcat, shark, salamander, dinosaur, albatross

KINGDOM
Animalia
Bobcat, stick insect, sea urchin, parrot, crocodile

MAMMALS

Mammals occupy all continents and almost all habitats. They nurse their young with milk from mammary glands, usually have body hair, and have a lower jaw bone that attaches directly to the skull. The 28 orders of the class Mammalia are divided into three major groups based on the structure of the reproductive tract. The most primitive are the egg-laying mammals, classified in a single order, the monotremes. Marsupials, which give birth to young in a very early stage of development, are now considered to consist of seven orders. The other 20 orders are made up of placental mammals. Recent DNA evidence indicates that there have been three major radiations of placentals in Africa, South America, and the northern hemisphere.

Icon key

⊕ Distribution	🐂 Tail length	✪ Diet
⋀ Habitat	✈ Wingspan	⚡ Status
🐂 Length	✕ Weight	♀♂ Female/male

PHYLUM CHORDATA
CHORDATES
53,000+ species

CLASS MAMMALIA
MAMMALS
4,791 species

EGG-LAYING MAMMALS
4 SPECIES IN 1 ORDER

ORDER MONOTREMATA
MONOTREMES
4 species

Platypus
Ornithorhynchus anatinus
- ⊕ Eastern Australia, Kangaroo Island, King Island
- ⋀ Freshwater streams, lakes, dams
- 🐂 Up to 16 in (40.5 cm)
- 🐂 6 in (15 cm)
- ✕ Up to 5 lb (2 kg)
- ✪ Aquatic invertebrates
- ⚡ Least concern

Short-beaked echidna
Tachyglossus aculeatus
- ⊕ Australia, New Guinea
- ⋀ All terrestrial habitats
- 🐂 Up to 14 in (35.5 cm)
- 🐂 3 in (7.5 cm)
- ✕ Up to 16 lb (7 kg)
- ✪ Ants, termites
- ⚡ Least concern

Long-beaked echidna
Zaglossus bruijni
- ⊕ New Guinea
- ⋀ Rain forest
- 🐂 Up to 25 in (63.5 cm)
- ✕ Up to 22 lb (10 kg)
- ✪ Worms
- ⚡ Endangered

MARSUPIALS
298 SPECIES IN 7 ORDERS

ORDER DIDELPHIMORPHIA
AMERICAN OPOSSUMS
70+ species

Brown-eared woolly opossum
Caluromys lanatus
- ⊕ South America
- ⋀ Tropical forest
- 🐂 31 in (78.5 cm)
- 🐂 16 in (40.5 cm)
- ✕ 1.1 lb (500 g)
- ✪ Fruit & nectar of flowering trees, seeds, leaves, soft vegetables, small invertebrates, carrion
- ⚡ Near threatened

Common opossum
Didelphis marsupialis
- ⊕ Mexico to Argentina
- ⋀ Forest, plantations
- 🐂 Up to 14 in (35.5 cm)
- 🐂 Up to 18 in (45.5 cm)
- ✕ ♂ 3.3 lb (1.5 kg)
- ✪ Fruits, small animals
- ⚡ Least concern

Virginia opossum
Didelphis virginiana
- ⊕ Eastern & central USA, Mexico, northern Costa Rica
- ⋀ Deciduous forest, urban areas
- 🐂 22.5–31.5 in (57–80 cm)
- 🐂 7–12 in (18–30.5 cm)
- ✕ 2.5–11.5 lb (1–5 kg)
- ✪ Fruits, nuts, grain, earthworms, insects, small vertebrates, carrion
- ⚡ Least concern

ORDER PAUCITUBERCULATA
SHREW OPOSSUMS
6 species

ORDER MICROBIOTHERIA
MONITO DEL MONTE
1 species

ORDER DASYUROMORPHIA
QUOLLS, DUNNARTS, NUMBAT & ALLIES
71 species

Brown antechinus
Antechinus stuartii
- ⊕ Eastern Australia
- ⋀ Forest, prefers wet sclerophyll forest
- 🐂 ♂ 6–10 in (15–25 cm), ♀ 5.5–8.5 in (14–22 cm)
- 🐂 Almost as long as body length
- ✕ ♂ 1–2.5 oz (29–71 g), ♀ 0.6–1.3 oz (17–36 g)
- ✪ Beetles, spiders, cockroaches, other invertebrates, mice, plants, pollen
- ⚡ Least concern

Northern quoll
Dasyurus hallucatus
- ⊕ Restricted areas in northern Australia
- ⋀ Rocky habitats, savanna, coastal eucalypt forest
- 🐂 9.4–13.8 in (24–35 cm)
- 🐂 8.3–12.2 in (21–31 cm)
- ✕ 10.5–31.5 oz (300–900 g)
- ✪ Small mammals, reptiles, beetles, ants, termites, grasshoppers, other invertebrates, figs, other soft fruits
- ⚡ Near threatened

Numbat
Myrmecobius fasciatus
- ⊕ Southwest Australia
- ⋀ Rain forest
- 🐂 Up to 11 in (28 cm)
- 🐂 4 in (10 cm)
- ✕ Up to 1.6 lb (725 g)
- ✪ Termites
- ⚡ Vulnerable

Tasmanian devil
Sarcophilus harrisii
- ⊕ Tasmania
- ⋀ Forest
- 🐂 Up to 25 in (63.5 cm)
- 🐂 10 in (25.5 cm)
- ✕ Up to 20 lb (9 kg)
- ✪ Carrion
- ⚡ Least concern (urgently needs updating; listed as Endangered in Australia)

ORDER PERAMELEMORPHIA
BANDICOOTS
24 species

Bilby
Macrotis lagotis
- ⊕ Central Australia
- ⋀ Acacia scrub, hummock grassland
- 🐂 Up to 18 in (45.5 cm)
- 🐂 11 in (28 cm)
- ✕ Up to 5 lb (2.3 kg)
- ✪ Arthropods, tubers, fungi
- ⚡ Vulnerable

ORDER NOTORYCTEMORPHIA
MARSUPIAL MOLES
2 species

ORDER DIPROTODONTIA
POSSUMS, KANGAROOS, KOALAS, WOMBATS & ALLIES
125 species

Suborder Vombatiformes
Koala & wombats
4 species

Koala
Phascolarctos cinereus
- ⊕ South & east Australia
- ⋀ Woodland, forest
- 🐂 Up to 32 in (81 cm)
- ✕ Up to 22 lb (10 kg)
- ✪ Leaves, shoots
- ⚡ Near threatened

Common wombat
Vombatus ursinus
- ⊕ Australia
- ⋀ Open forest, grassland
- 🐂 Up to 50 in (127 cm)
- 🐂 2 in (5 cm)
- ✕ Up to 80 lb (36 kg)
- ✪ Leaves, grass
- ⚡ Least concern

Suborder Phalangeriformes
Possums
64 species

Mountain pygmy possum
Burramys parvus
- ⊕ Australian Alps
- ⋀ Alpine rock scree above treeline
- 🐂 Up to 4.5 in (11.5 cm)
- 🐂 6 in (15 cm)
- ✕ Up to 3 oz (85 g)
- ✪ Insects, seeds, fruits
- ⚡ Endangered

Striped possum
Dactylopsila trivirgata
- ⊕ Australia, New Guinea, Pacific islands
- ⋀ Forest, savanna
- 🐂 Up to 11 in (28 cm)
- 🐂 14 in (35.5 cm)
- ✕ Up to 1.3 lb (600 g)
- ✪ Insects, fruits, honey
- ⚡ Least concern

Green ringtail possum
Pseudochirops archeri
- ⊕ Northeast Australia
- ⋀ Rain forest
- 🐂 14.5 in (37 cm)
- 🐂 14.5 in (37 cm)
- ✕ 2.2 lb (1 kg)
- ✪ Leaves of fig trees
- ⚡ Near threatened

Spotted cuscus
Spilocuscus maculatus
- ⊕ Northern Australia, New Guinea, Pacific islands
- ⋀ All forest types
- 🐂 Up to 22 in (56 cm)
- 🐂 22 in (56 cm)
- ✕ Up to 13 lb (5.9 kg)
- ✪ Leaves, shoots, fruit
- ⚡ Least concern

Honey possum
Tarsipes rostratus
- ⊕ Western Australia
- ⋀ Coastal heath
- 🐂 Up to 4 in (10 cm)
- 🐂 4 in (10 cm)
- ✕ Up to 0.4 oz (10 g)
- ✪ Nectar, pollen
- ⚡ Least concern

Bilby
Macrotis lagotis

Common brushtail possum
Trichosurus vulpecula
- ⊕ Southeast Australia
- ⋀ Forest, suburban gardens
- 🐂 Up to 20 in (51 cm)
- 🐂 16 in (40.5 cm)
- ✕ Up to 9 lb (4.1 kg)
- ✪ Leaves, flowers, fruits
- ⚡ Least concern

Suborder Macropodiformes
Kangaroos, wallabies & allies
57 species

Northern bettong
Bettongia tropica
- ⊕ Small range in tropical northeast Australia
- ⋀ Dry, open eucalypt woodland
- 🐂 12 in (30 cm)
- 🐂 11.5–14 in (29–36 cm)
- ✕ 2.2–3.3 lb (1–1.5 kg)
- ✪ Underground fungi, insects, leaves, stems
- ⚡ Endangered

Goodfellow's tree kangaroo
Dendrolagus goodfellowi
- ⊕ New Guinea
- ⋀ Rain forest
- 🐂 Up to 25 in (63.5 cm)
- 🐂 30 in (76 cm)
- ✕ Up to 15 lb (6.8 kg)
- ✪ Leaves, shoots
- ⚡ Endangered

Musky rat-kangaroo
Hypsiprymnodon moschatus
- ⊕ Far northwest Australia
- ⋀ Tropical rain forest
- 🐂 8 in (20 cm)
- 🐂 4.7–6.3 in (12–16 cm)
- ✕ 1.1 lb (500 g)
- ✪ Fruits, roots, stems, seeds, fungi
- ⚡ Least concern

Red-necked wallaby
Macropus rufogriseus
- ⊕ Eastern Australia
- ⋀ Forest, heathland, coastal scrub
- 🐂 Up to 36 in (91.5 cm)
- 🐂 35 in (89 cm)
- ✕ Up to 60 lb (27 kg)
- ✪ Leaves, shoots
- ⚡ Least concern

Red kangaroo
Macropus rufus
- ⊕ Australia
- ⋀ Grassland, desert
- 🐂 ♂ up to 4.6 ft (1.4 m); ♀ up to 3.6 ft (1.1 m)
- 🐂 3–3.3 ft (0.9–1 m)
- ✕ ♂ up to 187 lb (85 kg), ♀ up to 77 lb (35 kg)
- ✪ Grasses, herbs
- ⚡ Least concern

Black-flanked rock wallaby, Black-footed rock wallaby
Petrogale lateralis
- ⊕ South & west Australia
- ⋀ Rocky gorges & hills
- 🐂 Up to 23 in (58.5 cm)
- 🐂 20 in (51 cm)
- ✕ Up to 18 lb (8.2 kg)
- ✪ Grasses, herbs
- ⚡ Vulnerable

Red kangaroo
Macropus rufus

PLACENTAL MAMMALS
4,489 SPECIES IN **20** ORDERS

ORDER CINGULATA
ARMADILLOS
20 species

Nine-banded armadillo
Dasypus novemcinctus
- 🌐 Southern USA through to northern Argentina & Uruguay
- ▲ Grassland, forest
- 🔲 30 in (76 cm)
- 📏 13.5 in (34 cm)
- ⚖ 13 lb (5.9 kg)
- ✿ Mostly insects, also worms, snails, eggs, small amphibians, berries
- ⚡ Least concern

Three-banded armadillo
Tolypeutes tricinctus
- 🌐 Brazil
- ▲ Tropical forests on chalky grounds
- 🔲 8–10 in (20.5–25.5 cm)
- 📏 3 in (7.5 cm)
- ⚖ 4.4 lb (2 kg)
- ✿ Beetle larvae, ants, termites
- ⚡ Vulnerable

ORDER PILOSA
ANTEATERS & SLOTHS
9 species

Brown throated three-toed sloth
Bradypus variegatus
- 🌐 Central & South America
- ▲ Rain forest
- 🔲 23 in (58.5 cm)
- 📏 2.3 in (6 cm)
- ⚖ 11 lb (5 kg)
- ✿ Leaves, shoots, foliage
- ⚡ Least concern

Giant anteater
Myrmecophaga tridactyla
- 🌐 Central & South America
- ▲ Grassland, deciduous forest, rain forest
- 🔲 6.6 ft (2 m)
- 📏 35 in (89 cm)
- ⚖ 140 lb (63.5 kg)
- ✿ Ants, termites
- ⚡ Vulnerable

ORDER PHOLIDOTA
PANGOLINS
7 species

Ground pangolin
Manis temminckii
- 🌐 East & southern Africa
- ▲ Woodland, savanna, grassland
- 🔲 14–24 in (35.5–61 cm)
- 📏 12–20 in (30.5–51 cm)
- ⚖ 15–40 lb (6.8–18.1 kg)
- ✿ Ants
- ⚡ Near threatened

ORDER SORICOMORPHA
SHREWS, MOLES & SOLENODONS
370 species

Star-nosed mole
Condylura cristata
- 🌐 Southeast Canada, northeast USA to Georgia
- ▲ Moist fields, meadows, woods, marshes
- 🔲 5–9 in (12.5–23 cm)
- 📏 2–4 in (5–10 cm)
- ⚖ 1.4–3 oz (40–85 g)
- ✿ Worms, insects, insect larvae; also small crustaceans, mollusks, fish
- ⚡ Least concern

Water shrew
Neomys fodiens
- 🌐 Northern Eurasia
- ▲ Pond, marsh
- 🔲 Up to 4 in (10 cm)
- 📏 Up to 2.8 in (7 cm)
- ⚖ Up to 1.6 oz (45 g)
- ✿ Worms, crustaceans, fish
- ⚡ Least concern

Solenodon
Solenodon cubanus
- 🌐 East Cuba
- ▲ Wooded or brushy areas
- 🔲 11 in (28 cm)
- 📏 21 in (53.5 cm)
- ⚖ 2.2 lb (1 kg)
- ✿ Arthropods, worms, snails, small reptiles; also roots, fruits, foliage
- ⚡ Endangered

ORDER AFROSORICIDA
TENRECS & GOLDEN MOLES
47 species

ORDER ERINACEOMORPHA
HEDGEHOGS & GYMNURES
21 species

ORDER DERMOPTERA
FLYING LEMURS
2 species

ORDER SCANDENTIA
TREE SHREWS
17 species

ORDER CHIROPTERA
BATS
993 species

Golden-capped fruit bat
Acerodon jubatus
- 🌐 Philippines
- ▲ Primary & secondary forests from sea level to 3,600 ft (1,100 m)
- ⟷ 5–5.6 ft (1.5–1.7 m)
- ⚖ Up to 2.6 lb (1.2 kg)
- ✿ Figs
- ⚡ Endangered

Common fruit bat
Artibeus jamaicensis
- 🌐 Central & South America
- ▲ Rain forest, scrub forest
- 🔲 4 in (10 cm)
- ⟷ 16 in (40 cm)
- ⚖ 1.6 oz (45 g)
- ✿ Nectar, pollen, flower parts, insects
- ⚡ Least concern

Honduran white bat
Ectophylla alba
- 🌐 Central America, Caribbean
- ▲ Rain forest
- 🔲 1.5 in (4 cm)
- ⟷ 4 in (10 cm)
- ⚖ 0.18 oz (5 g)
- ✿ Fruits, seeds, flowers, pollen, insects
- ⚡ Near threatened

Southern long-nosed bat
Leptonycteris curasoae
- 🌐 Southern Arizona to Mexico & northern South America
- ▲ Arid scrub, arid grassland, oak forest, tropical dry forest
- 🔲 3–3.3 in (7.5–8.5 cm)
- ⟷ 14–16 in (36–40 cm)
- ⚖ 0.5–0.9 oz (15–25 g)
- ✿ Nectar & pollen of saguaro, other cacti, agaves, silk trees
- ⚡ Vulnerable

Spectacled flying fox
Pteropus conspicillatus
- 🌐 Northeast Australia, New Guinea, Pacific islands
- ▲ Rain forest, gallery forest, paperbark forest, mangroves
- 🔲 Up to 11 in (28 cm)
- ⟷ 5 ft (1.5 m)
- ⚖ Up to 2 lb (905 g)
- ✿ Fruits, nectar
- ⚡ Least concern

Mediterranean horseshoe bat
Rhinolophus euryale
- 🌐 Southern Europe, northern Africa
- ▲ Caves
- 🔲 Up to 3.5 in (9 cm)
- ⟷ Up to 12.5 in (32 cm)
- ⚖ Up to 0.6 oz (15 g)
- ✿ Moths, insects
- ⚡ Vulnerable

Mediterranean horseshoe bat
Rhinolophus euryale

ORDER PRIMATES
PRIMATES
291 species

Suborder Strepsirhini
Prosimians
63 species

Aye-aye
Daubentonia madagascariensis
- 🌐 East Madagascar
- ▲ Rain forest, deciduous forest
- 🔲 16 in (40.5 cm)
- 📏 16 in (40.5 cm)
- ⚖ 6 lb (2.7 kg)
- ✿ Invertebrates, seeds, fruit, nectar
- ⚡ Endangered

Indri
Indri indri
- 🌐 East Madagascar
- ▲ Montane forest
- 🔲 24 in (61 cm)
- 📏 20 in (51 cm)
- ⚖ 13–25 lb (6–11 kg)
- ✿ Leaves, fruits, seeds
- ⚡ Endangered

Ring-tailed lemur
Lemur catta
- 🌐 South Madagascar
- ▲ Deciduous forest, dry scrubland
- 🔲 17 in (43 cm)
- 📏 23 in (60 cm)
- ⚖ 5 lb (2.2 kg)
- ✿ Fruits, leaves
- ⚡ Vulnerable

Gray mouse lemur
Microcebus murinus
- 🌐 West Madagascar
- ▲ Secondary forest, spiny desert
- 🔲 5 in (12.5 cm)
- 📏 6 in (15 cm)
- ⚖ 3.9 oz (110 g)
- ✿ Fruits, invertebrates, flowers
- ⚡ Least concern

Slow loris
Nycticebus coucang
- 🌐 Southeast Asia
- ▲ Rain-forest canopy
- 🔲 12–15 in (30–38 cm)
- ⚖ Up to 4.4 lb (2 kg)
- ✿ Fruits, leaves, insects, bird eggs, young birds
- ⚡ Least concern

Greater bushbaby
Otolemur crassicaudatus
- 🌐 East & southern Africa
- ▲ Gallery forest, savanna woodland, montane forest
- 🔲 12 in (30.5 cm)
- 📏 16 in (40.5 cm)
- ⚖ 2.4 lb (1.1 kg)
- ✿ Gum, fruits, insects
- ⚡ Least concern

Coquerel's sifaka
Propithecus coquereli
- 🌐 Northwest Madagascar
- ▲ Dry deciduous forest
- 🔲 17 in (43 cm)
- 📏 23 in (58.5 cm)
- ⚖ 8–9 lb (3.6–4.1 kg)
- ✿ Leaves, flowers, fruits, bark
- ⚡ Endangered

Tarsier
Tarsius syrichta
- 🌐 Southeastern Philippines
- ▲ Primary & secondary forests
- 🔲 4–6 in (10–15 cm)
- 📏 About twice its body length
- ⚖ ♂ 5 oz (140 g), ♀ 4 oz (115 g)
- ✿ Insects, spiders, small lizards, birds
- ⚡ Data deficient

Red-ruffed lemur
Varecia rubra
- 🌐 East Madagascar
- ▲ Rain forest
- 🔲 20 in (51 cm)
- 📏 24 in (61 cm)
- ⚖ 8 lb (3.6 kg)
- ✿ Fruits, seeds, leaves
- ⚡ Endangered

Suborder Haplorhini
Monkeys & apes
228 species

Family Cebidae
Marmosets & allies
58 species

Pygmy marmoset
Callithrix pygmaea
- 🌐 West Amazon Basin in South America
- ▲ Rain forest
- 🔲 5 in (12.5 cm)
- 📏 6 in (15 cm)
- ⚖ 4.2 oz (120 g)
- ✿ Fruits, leaves, insects
- ⚡ Least concern

White-faced capuchin
Cebus capucinus
- 🌐 Central America, northwest South America
- ▲ Forest, mangroves
- 🔲 35 in (89 cm)
- 📏 18 in (45.5 cm)
- ⚖ 11 lb (5 kg)
- ✿ Fruits, insects
- ⚡ Least concern

Pied tamarin
Saguinus bicolor
- 🌐 Small region north of Amazon River in Brazil
- ▲ Rain forest
- 🔲 11 in (28 cm)
- 📏 16 in (40.5 cm)
- ⚖ 15 oz (425 g)
- ✿ Fruits, flowers, invertebrates
- ⚡ Critically endangered

Emperor tamarin
Saguinus imperator
- 🌐 Southwest Amazon Basin
- ▲ Tropical forest
- 🔲 10 in (25 cm)
- 📏 13 in (33 cm)
- ⚖ 14 oz (495 g)
- ✿ Fruits, nectar, plant sap, frogs, snails
- ⚡ Least concern

Family Aotidae
Night monkeys
8 species

Family Pitheciidae
Titis, sakis & uakaris
40 species

Family Atelidae
Howler, spider & woolly monkeys
24 species

Red howler monkey
Alouatta belzebul
- 🌐 Venezuela to upper Amazon Basin
- ▲ Forest canopy
- 🔲 28 in (71 cm)
- 📏 29 in (73.5 cm)
- ⚖ 15 lb (6.8 kg)
- ✿ Fruits, leaves, flowers, small birds, reptiles, mammals
- ⚡ Least concern

Mantled howler monkey
Alouatta palliate
- Central & South America
- Rain forest
- 6 ft (1.8 m)
- 35 in (89 cm)
- 19 lb (8.6 kg)
- Fruits, leaves and flowers
- Endangered

Family Cercopithecidae
Old World monkeys
81 species

Owl-faced monkey, Hamlyn's monkey
Cercopithecus hamlyni
- Albertine Rift in east Africa
- Bamboo, rain forest
- 16–26 in (40.5–66 cm)
- 20–26 in (51–66 cm)
- ♂ 10–22 lb (4.5–10 kg)
- Fruits, leaves
- Near threatened

Golden monkey
Cercopithecus kandti
- Albertine Rift in east Africa
- Montane, bamboo forest
- ♂ 19–26 in (48–67 cm), ♀ 18–21 in (46–53 cm)
- ♂ 10–25 lb (4.5–11.3 kg), ♀ 7.7–10 lb (3.5–4.5 kg)
- Leaves, bamboo, fruits
- Endangered

Blue monkey
Cercopithecus mitis
- East & central Africa
- Evergreen forest
- 17–27 in (43–68.5 cm)
- 21–43 in (53.5–109 cm)
- 11–15 lb (5–6.8 kg)
- Fruits, leaves
- Least concern

Black and white colobus
Colobus guereza
- East & central Africa
- Primary & secondary forest, riverine forest, wooded grassland
- 19–29 in (48–73.5 cm)
- 26–35 in (66–89 cm)
- 25–51 lb (11.5–23 kg)
- Leaves, fruits
- Least concern

Japanese macaque
Macaca fuscata
- Japan
- Subtropical to subalpine evergreen & deciduous forest
- Up to 31–37 in (79–95 cm)
- Up to 4 in (10 cm)
- ♂ 22–31 lb (10–14 kg), ♀ 12 lb (5.5 kg)
- Fruits; also seeds, young leaves & flowers, tree bark, insects
- Data deficient

Barbary macaque
Macaca sylvanus
- Northern Morocco, northern Algeria, introduced to Gibraltar
- Mixed oak, cedar forest
- Up to 30 in (76 cm)
- Up to 1 in (2.5 cm)
- Up to 29 lb (13.1 kg)
- Leaves, fruits, insects
- Vulnerable

Drill
Mandrillus leucophaeus
- West Cameroon, Nigeria, Equatorial Guinea
- Gallery & lowland rain forest, montane forest
- 24–29 in (61–73.5 cm)
- 2–3 in (5–7.5 cm)
- ♂ 55 lb (25 kg), ♀ 25 lb (11.5 kg)
- Fruits, seeds, invertebrates
- Endangered

Mandrill
Mandrillus sphinx
- Cameroon, Gabon, Congo
- Primary evergreen forest
- 22–32 in (56–81 cm)
- 3 in (7.5 cm)
- 24–59 lb (11–27 kg)
- Fruits, seeds
- Vulnerable

Proboscis monkey
Nasalis larvatus
- Lowland Borneo
- Mangrove swamps, riparian forest, rain forest
- 28 in (71 cm)
- 29.5 in (75 cm)
- ♂ 53 lb (24 kg), ♀ 26 lb (12 kg)
- Seeds, leaves, mangrove shoots, unripe fruit
- Endangered

Olive baboon
Papio anubis
- East Africa
- Woodland, savanna near rock outcrops
- ♂ 27.5 in (70 cm)
- 16 in (40 cm)
- ♂ up to 53 lb (24 kg), ♀ up to 31 lb (14 kg)
- Roots, fruits, flowers, leaves, insects, bird eggs, small mammals
- Least concern

Miss Waldron's red colobus
Piliocolobus badius waldronae
- West Africa (possibly Côte d'Ivoire)
- Rain-forest canopy
- 3 ft (1 m)
- Fruits, seeds, foliage
- Critically endangered (declared extinct in 2000)

Red-shanked douc monkey
Pygathrix nemaeus
- Cambodia, China, Vietnam, Laos
- Tropical forest
- 24–30 in (61–76 cm)
- 22–30 in (56–76 cm)
- ♂ up to 15 lb (7 kg), ♀ up to 11 lb (5 kg)
- Leaves high in fiber
- Endangered

Golden monkey
Rhinopithecus roxellana
- Central & southwest China
- Temperate montane forests
- ♂ 23–27 in (58–68 cm), ♀ 19–20.5 in (47.5–52 cm)
- Same as body length
- ♂ 44 lb (19.8 kg), ♀ 27 lb (12.4 kg)
- Lichens, trees, shrubs, vines, insects
- Vulnerable

Crested langur
Semnopithecus cristatus
- Myanmar, Indochina, Borneo
- Coastal, mangroves, riverine forest
- 18–20 in (46–51 cm)
- ♂ 26–30 in (67–75 cm), ♀ 20–23 in (50–58 cm)
- 12.5 lb (5.7 kg)
- Fruits, leaves, shoots
- Least concern

Common langur
Semnopithecus entellus
- India, Pakistan
- Subtropical or tropical dry forest, scrubland
- ♂ 20–31 in (51–78 cm), ♀ 16–27 in (40–68 cm)
- 27–40 in (69–101 cm)
- ♂ 40 lb (18 kg), ♀ 24.5 lb (11.2 kg)
- Fruits, buds, fruits, flowers, supplemented with insects
- Near threatened

Gelada baboon
Theropithecus gelada

Gelada baboon
Theropithecus gelada
- Ethiopia
- Montane grassland
- ♂ 27–29 in (68.5–74 cm), ♀ 19–25 in (48–63.5 cm)
- ♂ 18–21 in (45.5–53.5 cm), ♀ 12–20 in (30.5–51 cm)
- ♂ 44 lb (20 kg), ♀ 28 lb (12.7 kg)
- Leaves, grasses
- Near threatened

Family Hylobatidae
Gibbons (Lesser apes)
11 species

White-handed gibbon, Lar gibbon
Hylobates lar
- China, Indonesia, Malaysia, Myanmar, north Sumatra, Thailand
- Rain-forest canopy
- Up to 23 in (58.5 cm)
- 12.5–15.5 lb (5.7–7 kg), ♀ 11.5 lb (5.3 kg)
- Fruits, also tender leaves, flowers, shoots, insects, snails, bird eggs
- Near threatened

Capped gibbon
Hylobates pileatus
- Southeast Thailand, Cambodia
- Rain forest
- 16–26 in (40–65 cm)
- 9–18 lb (4–8 kg)
- Leaves, fruits, flowers, buds, insects, bird eggs, small birds
- Vulnerable

Family Hominidae
Great apes
6 species

Mountain gorilla
Gorilla beringei
- Uganda, Rwanda, Democratic Republic of Congo
- Montane & bamboo forest
- ♂ 4.6–6 ft (1.4–1.8 m), ♀ 4.3–5 ft (1.3–1.5 m)
- ♂ 350 lb (159 kg), ♀ 216 lb (98 kg)
- Leaves, shoots, stems
- Endangered

Western gorilla
Gorilla gorilla
- West & central Africa
- Primary & secondary forest, lowland swamp, montane forest
- ♂ 5.6 ft (1.7 m), ♀ 5 ft (1.5 m)
- ♂ 374 lb (170 kg), ♀ 158 lb (72 kg)
- Fruits, leaves, shoots, stems
- Critically endangered

Bonobo
Pan paniscus
- Democratic Republic of Congo
- Tropical rain forest
- ♂ 28–34 in (71–87 cm), ♀ 28–29 in (71–74 cm)
- ♂ 86 lb (39 kg), ♀ 68 lb (31 kg)
- Fruits, leaves, terrestrial herbs
- Endangered

Chimpanzee
Pan troglodytes
- West, central & east Africa
- Rain forest, dry woodland savanna, grassland
- 32 in (81 cm)
- ♂ 88–132 lb (40–60 kg), ♀ 70–103 lb (32–47 kg)
- Fruits, leaves, terrestrial herbs, flowers, insects, small vertebrates
- Endangered

Sumatran orangutan
Pongo abelii
- Sumatra
- Tropical rain forest
- ♂ up to 4.6 ft (1.4 m), ♀ 3 ft (0.9 m)
- ♂ up to 200 lb (90 kg), ♀ up to 100 lb (45 kg)
- Fruits, insects, bird eggs, small vertebrates
- Critically endangered

Bornean orangutan
Pongo pygmaeus
- Borneo
- Tropical rain forest
- ♂ up to 5 ft (1.5 m), ♀ up to 3.5 ft (1 m)
- ♂ up to 245 lb (110 kg), ♀ up to 135 lb (60 kg)
- Fruits, also young leaves, shoots, seeds, bark, insects, bird eggs
- Endangered

ORDER CARNIVORA CARNIVORES
275 species

Family Canidae
Dogs & foxes
34 species

Coyote
Canis latrans
- North America to Central America
- Desert, grassland, forest, farmland, suburbs, cities
- 30–39 in (75–100 cm)
- 10–16 in (25.5–40.5 cm)
- ♂ 17–44 lb (8–20 kg), ♀ 15–40 lb (7–18 kg)
- Mammals from mice to deer, birds, snakes, plant material, carrion
- Least concern

Gray wolf
Canis lupus
- Northern North America, parts of Eurasia
- Coniferous & deciduous forest, tundra, plains
- 34–51 in (87–130 cm)
- 14–20 in (35–51 cm)
- ♂ 66–176 lb (30–80 kg), ♀ 51–121 lb (23–55 kg)
- Deer, hares, other mammals
- Least concern

Dingo
Canis lupus dingo
- Mainland Australia
- Most Australian habitats, from desert to rain forest
- Up to 39.5 in (100 cm)
- Up to 14 in (36 cm)
- Up to 53 lb (24 kg)
- Kangaroos, wallabies, small mammals, birds, fruits
- Vulnerable

European wolf
Canis lupus lupus
- Europe, Asia
- Forest
- Up to 5.3 ft (1.6 m)
- Up to 22 in (56 cm)
- Up to 130 lb (59 kg)
- Carnivorous
- Least concern

Arctic fox
Vulpes lagopus

Ethiopian wolf
Canis simensis
- Ethiopia
- Montane grassland
- 35–39 in (90–100 cm)
- 10–14 in (25–35 cm)
- 26–39 lb (11.5–18 kg)
- Rodents & other small mammals
- Endangered

Maned wolf
Chrysocyon brachyurus
- South America
- Grassland, scrub forest
- 35 in (90 cm)
- 17.5 in (44.5 cm)
- 50 lb (22.5 kg)
- Rodents, hares, birds, fish, fruits, sugarcane, tubers
- Near threatened

Andean red fox, Culpeo
Lycalopex culpaeus
- South America
- Forest, prairie
- 44 in (112 cm)
- 13 in (33 cm)
- 13 lb (6 kg)
- Mammals, ungulates, vertebrates, poultry, livestock
- Least concern

African wild dog
Lycaon pictus
- Scattered in sub-Saharan Africa
- Woodland, savanna, grassland
- 29–44 in (74–112 cm)
- 12–16 in (30–41 cm)
- 39–79 lb (18–36 kg)
- Small to medium mammals such as antelopes
- Endangered

Raccoon dog
Nyctereutes procyonoides
- East Asia
- Deciduous woodland, mixed forest
- Up to 24 in (61 cm)
- Up to 7 in (18 cm)
- Up to 22 lb (10 kg)
- Invertebrates, frogs, lizards, rodents, birds, crabs, seeds, berries
- Least concern

Patagonian gray fox
Pseudalopex griseus
- Chile, Patagonia, Argentina
- Areas with lots of brush or woods
- 39 in (100 cm)
- 17 in (43 cm)
- 10 lb (4.5 kg)
- Hares, rodents, also berries, bird eggs, insects
- Least concern

Cape fox
Vulpes chama
- South Africa
- Grassland, steppe, semidesert scrub
- 24–24 in (54–61 cm)
- 11–16 in (28–40 cm)
- 5.5–7.7 lb (2.5–3.5 kg)
- Invertebrates, small vertebrates such as mice
- Least concern

Arctic fox
Vulpes lagopus
- Arctic tundra & forests
- Tundra, moorland
- Up to 27.5 in (70 cm)
- Up to 16 in (40 cm)
- Up to 18 lb (8 kg)
- Insects, small mammals, birds, carrion
- Least concern

Red fox
Vulpes vulpes
- 🌐 North America, Europe, northern & central Asia, northern Africa, Arabia, introduced in Australia
- ▲ Deciduous woodland, mixed forest
- ▭ Up to 32 in (81 cm)
- ▭ Up to 16 in (41 cm)
- ✖ Up to 15 lb (6.8 kg)
- ✿ Invertebrates such as insects & mollusks, small vertebrates such as rodents & birds, bird eggs, fruits
- ⚡ Least concern

Fennec fox
Vulpes zerda
- 🌐 Central Sahara
- ▲ Desert, steppe
- ▭ 15–16 in (38–41 cm)
- ▭ 7–8 in (18–21 cm)
- ✖ 1.8–3.3 lb (0.8–1.5 kg)
- ✿ Desert grasshoppers, other invertebrates, fruits
- ⚡ Data deficient

Family Ursidae
Bears & panda
9 species

Giant panda
Ailuropoda melanoleuca
- 🌐 Southwest China (Gansu, Shaanxi & Sichuan provinces)
- ▲ Bamboo & coniferous forests
- ▭ Up to 5 ft (1.5 m)
- ✖ 154–275 lb (70–125 kg)
- ✿ Bamboo leaves & shoots
- ⚡ Endangered

Sun bear
Helarctos malayanus
- 🌐 Southeast Asia
- ▲ Tropical rain forest
- ▭ 4 ft (1.2 m)
- ✖ 145 lb (65 kg)
- ✿ Fruits, insects
- ⚡ Vulnerable

Spectacled bear
Tremarctos ornatus
- 🌐 Tropical Andes
- ▲ Rain forest, cloud forest
- ▭ 6 ft (1.8 m)
- ▭ 3 in (7.5 cm)
- ✖ 180 lb (820 kg)
- ✿ Fruits, leaves, insects
- ⚡ Vulnerable

American black bear
Ursus americanus
- 🌐 Non-Arctic Canada & Alaska through USA to northern Mexico
- ▲ Diverse habitats from deciduous forest to desert, and subtropical forests to boreal forest & tundra
- ▭ 4–6.5 ft (1.2–2 m)
- ▭ 3–5.5 in (8–14 cm)
- ✖ ♂ 103–900 lb (47–409 kg), ♀ 86–520 lb (39–236 kg)
- ✿ Fruits, nuts, vegetation; also meat, insects
- ⚡ Least concern

Brown bear, Grizzly bear
Ursus arctos
- 🌐 Northwest North America, Europe south to Spain, north & central Asia
- ▲ Arctic tundra, boreal forest, open plains, edges of deserts
- ▭ 3–9 ft (0.9–2.7 m)
- ▭ 2.5–8 in (6.5–20 cm)
- ✖ 175–1,300 lb (80–590 kg) or more
- ✿ Plants, fungi, insects, birds, mammals, carrion
- ⚡ Least concern (though some subspecies are endangered)

European brown bear
Ursus arctos arctos
- 🌐 Pockets in northwest North America, Wyoming, western & northern Europe, Himalaya, Japan
- ▲ Mountain, forest
- ▭ Up to 9.2 ft (2.8 m)
- ▭ Up to 5 in (12.7 cm)
- ✖ Up to 460 lb (205 kg)
- ✿ Berries, fish, mammals
- ⚡ Least concern

Siberian brown bear
Ursus arctos collaris
- 🌐 Siberia, Mongolia, eastern Kazakhstan
- ▲ Taiga forest
- ▭ Up to 9 ft (2.8 m)
- ▭ Up to 5 in (12.7 cm)
- ✖ 220–1,500 lb (100–680 kg)
- ✿ Berries, roots, fungi, sprouts, insects, fish, small mammals
- ⚡ Least concern

Polar bear
Ursus maritimus
- 🌐 Arctic coastal areas
- ▲ Tundra, sea ice
- ▭ Up to 8 ft (2.5 m)
- ▭ 4 in (10 cm)
- ✖ ♂ up to 800 lb (360 kg), ♀ 200 lb (550 kg)
- ✿ Seals, fish, birds, eggs, carrion, berries
- ⚡ Vulnerable

Asiatic black bear
Ursus thibetanus
- 🌐 Afghanistan, Pakistan to China, Korea, Japan
- ▲ Forest (lowlands to hilly areas)
- ▭ 4.5–6.5 ft (1.4–2 m)
- ▭ Up to 4 in (10 cm)
- ✖ ♂ 220–480 lb (100–218 kg), ♀ 110–275 lb (50–125 kg)
- ✿ Plant matter such as acorns, nuts, bamboo & berries, insects, carrion, smaller vertebrates
- ⚡ Vulnerable

Family Mustelidae
Mustelids
56 species

Tayra
Eira barbara
- 🌐 Central America, South America, Trinidad
- ▲ Rain forest
- ▭ Up to 28 in (70 cm)
- ▭ 16 in (40 cm)
- ✖ Up to 13 lb (5.8 kg)
- ✿ Fruits, invertebrates, reptiles
- ⚡ Least concern

Wolverine
Gulo gulo
- 🌐 Northern North America, Europe, Asia
- ▲ Boreal forest, Arctic tundra
- ▭ 25.5–41 in (65–104 cm)
- ▭ 6.6–10.2 in (17–26 cm)
- ✖ ♂ 28–31 lb (12.7–14 kg), ♀ 18.3–21.8 lb (8.3–9.9 kg)
- ✿ Carrion of moose & caribou, ground squirrels, ptarmigan, snowshoe hares
- ⚡ Vulnerable

Northern river otter
Lontra canadensis
- 🌐 Canada & USA except southwest deserts & high Arctic
- ▲ Lakes, rivers, streams, swamps, marshes, estuaries
- ▭ 35–51 in (89–130 cm)
- ▭ 12–20 in (30–51 cm)
- ✖ 11–31 lb (5–14 kg)
- ✿ Fish, frogs, crayfish, turtles, birds, eggs, muskrats
- ⚡ Least concern

Eurasian otter
Lutra lutra
- 🌐 Europe, Asia, Africa
- ▲ River, wetlands
- ▭ Up to 43 in (110 cm)
- ▭ Up to 22 in (55 cm)
- ✖ Up to 26 lb (12 kg)
- ✿ Fish, crustaceans
- ⚡ Near threatened

Pine marten
Martes martes
- 🌐 Northern Europe
- ▲ Forest
- ▭ Up to 21 in (53 cm)
- ▭ Up to 10 in (25 cm)
- ✖ Up to 3.5 lb (1.6 kg)
- ✿ Small mammals, birds, frogs
- ⚡ Least concern

Sable
Martes zibellina
- 🌐 Siberia, northern Mongolia, China, Japan (Hokkaido)
- ▲ Forest
- ▭ 15–22 in (38–56 cm)
- ▭ 3.5–5 in (9–12 cm)
- ✖ 1.9–4 lb (0.9–1.8 kg)
- ✿ Small mammals, birds, fish
- ⚡ Least concern

European badger
Meles meles
- 🌐 Britain & western Europe to China, Korea & Japan
- ▲ Woodland, fields
- ▭ Up to 35.4 in (90 cm)
- ▭ Up to 8 in (20.5 cm)
- ✖ Up to 35 lb (16 kg)
- ✿ Earthworms, beetles, small mammals, reptiles, amphibians, eggs, fruits, roots, other plants
- ⚡ Least concern

Stoat
Mustela erminea
- 🌐 Arctic
- ▲ Tundra, moors, fields, marshes, boreal forest, woodland
- ▭ 10 in (25 cm)
- ▭ 4 in (10 cm)
- ✖ ♂ 7–16 oz (200–440 g), ♀ 5–10 oz (140–280 g)
- ✿ Insects, small amphibians, reptiles, birds, mammals, carrion
- ⚡ Least concern

Black-footed ferret
Mustela nigripes
- 🌐 Formerly, interior North America from southern Canada to northern Mexico
- ▲ Grassland, semidesert, desert
- ▭ 19–23.6 in (48–60 cm)
- ▭ 4.2–5.5 in (10.5–14 cm)
- ✖ ♂ 2–2.5 lb (905–1,125 g), ♀ 1.4–1.9 lb (635–860 g)
- ✿ Prairie dogs
- ⚡ Critically endangered (was extinct in the wild; zoo-bred animals have been reintroduced)

Least weasel
Mustela nivalis
- 🌐 North America, Europe, Asia
- ▲ Meadows, marshes, grassy fields
- ▭ Up to 10 in (26 m)
- ▭ Up to 3 in (7.5 cm)
- ✖ Up to 9 oz (250 g)
- ✿ Mice, voles, small rodents
- ⚡ Least concern

Polecat
Mustela putorius
- 🌐 Europe
- ▲ Wetlands, forest
- ▭ Up to 18 in (46 cm)
- ▭ Up to 9 in (23 cm)
- ✖ Up to 3.8 lb (1.7 kg)
- ✿ Rodents, birds, frogs
- ⚡ Least concern

Giant river otter
Pteronura brasiliensis
- 🌐 Southern Venezuela & Colombia to northern Argentina
- ▲ Amazon rain forest
- ▭ 6.5 ft (2 m)
- ▭ 3.3 ft (1 m)
- ✖ 75 lb (34 kg)
- ✿ Fish, crabs
- ⚡ Endangered

American badger
Taxidea taxus
- 🌐 Southwest Canada, USA, Mexico
- ▲ From alpine meadows to prairie, marshes & desert
- ▭ 23.5–31 in (60–79 cm)
- ▭ 4–5 in (10–13 cm)
- ✖ 9–26 lb (4–12 kg)
- ✿ Rodents (especially squirrels), birds, reptiles, insects
- ⚡ Least concern

Family Mephitidae
Skunks
13 species

Striped skunk
Mephitis mephitis
- 🌐 Southern Canada (except Pacific coast), USA, northern Mexico
- ▲ All habitat types except extremely arid ones
- ▭ 22.5–31.5 in (58–80 cm)
- ▭ 6.8–12 in (17–30 cm)
- ✖ 2.5–11.5 lb (1.1–5.2 kg)
- ✿ Insects, small rodents, rabbits, birds, eggs, carrion, fruits, vegetation
- ⚡ Least concern

Family Ailuridae
Red panda
1 species

Red panda
Ailurus fulgens
- 🌐 China, India, Bhutan, Laos, Nepal, Myanmar
- ▲ Mountain forest with coniferous & deciduous trees
- ▭ 16–24 in (40–60 cm)
- ▭ 12–24 in (30–60 cm)
- ✖ 6.5–13 lb (3–6 kg)
- ✿ Bamboo, berries, fruits, mushrooms, roots, acorns, lichen, grasses, also birds, fish, eggs, rodents, insects
- ⚡ Endangered

Family Phocidae
True seals
19 species

Leopard seal
Hydrurga leptonyx
- 🌐 Southern Ocean
- ▲ Antarctic pack ice, subantarctic islands
- ▭ 8–11 ft (2.4–3.3 m)
- ✖ ♂ 440–990 lb (200–449 kg), ♀ 485–1,250 lb (220–565 kg)
- ✿ Krill, penguins, fish, squid, young crabeater seals
- ⚡ Least concern

Weddell seal
Leptonychotes weddellii
- 🌐 Southern Ocean
- ▲ Fast ice & sea around Antarctica
- ▭ ♂ up to 9.5 ft (2.9 m), ♀ up to 11.5 ft (3.5 m)
- ✖ 880–1,320 lb (400–600 kg)
- ✿ Fish, squid, crustaceans
- ⚡ Least concern

Crabeater seal
Lobodon carcinophagus
- 🌐 Southern Ocean
- ▲ Pack ice, ice floes at pack-ice edge
- ▭ 8.5 ft (2.6 m)
- ✖ 750 lb (340 kg)
- ✿ Mainly krill, also squid, fish
- ⚡ Least concern

Southern elephant seal
Mirounga leonina
- 🌐 Argentina, New Zealand, subantarctic islands
- ▲ Subantarctic regions
- ▭ ♂ 16.3 ft (5 m), ♀ 9.8 ft (3 m)
- ▭ ♂ 19 in (48 cm), ♀ 11 in (28 cm)
- ✖ ♂ 4 tons (3.6 t), ♀ 0.8 tons (0.7 t)
- ✿ Cephalopods such as squid & cuttlefish, large fish such as sharks
- ⚡ Vulnerable

Monk seal
Monachus monachus
- 🌐 Coastal west Africa, Aegean Sea
- ▲ Coastal & island waters, sea caves for breeding
- ▭ Up to 7.8 ft (2.4 m)
- ✖ Up to 705 lb (320 kg)
- ✿ Fish, mollusks, octopus
- ⚡ Critically endangered

Ross seal
Ommatophoca rossii
- 🌐 Southern Ocean
- ▲ Pack ice
- ▭ 10 ft (3 m)
- ✖ 470 lb (214 kg)
- ✿ Squid, fish, krill
- ⚡ Vulnerable

Harp seal
Phoca groenlandica
- 🌐 Gulf of St Lawrence & Newfoundland, White Sea, Greenland Sea, ice-strewn seas further north in summer
- ▲ Arctic seas, pack ice
- ▭ 6–7 ft (1.8–2 m)
- ✖ 260–300 lb (118–135 kg)
- ✿ Capelin, Arctic cod
- ⚡ Least concern

European badger
Meles meles

Ringed seal
Phoca hispida
- ⊕ Arctic coasts & oceans, lakes in Russia & Finland
- ⋀ Inshore fast ice, pack ice
- ⬆ 4 ft (1.25 m)
- ⚖ 150 lb (65 kg)
- ✿ Planktonic crustaceans, fish, squid
- ⚡ Least concern

European harbor seal
Phoca vitulina vitulina
- ⊕ North Atlantic, North Pacific
- ⋀ Coastal, marine
- ⬆ Up to 6.2 ft (1.9 m)
- ⚖ Up to 375 lb (170 kg)
- ✿ Crustaceans, squid, fish
- ⚡ Least concern

Family Otariidae
Sea lions & fur seals
14 species

Southern fur seal, Antarctic fur seal
Arctocephalus gazella
- ⊕ Southern Ocean
- ⋀ Rocks, beaches & tussock grass thickets on subantarctic islands & particularly around Antarctic Peninsula
- ⬆ ♂ 5.5–6.5 ft (1.7–2 m), ♀ 3.3–4.3 ft (1–1.3 m)
- ⚖ ♂ 275–440 lb (125–200 kg), ♀ 55–88 lb (25–40 kg)
- ✿ Krill, fish, squid
- ⚡ Least concern

California sea lion
Zalophus californianus
- ⊕ West coast of North America
- ⋀ Coastal waters
- ⬆ 8 ft (2.4 m)
- ⚖ 660 lb (300 kg)
- ✿ Squid, fish
- ⚡ Least concern

Galápagos sea lion
Zalophus californianus wollebaecki
- ⊕ Galápagos Islands
- ⋀ Shallow coastal waters
- ⬆ 6.5 ft (2 m)
- ⬇ 11 in (28 cm)
- ⚖ 880 lb (400 kg)
- ✿ Sardines
- ⚡ Vulnerable

Family Odobenidae
Walrus
1 species

Walrus
Odobenus rosmarus
- ⊕ Circumarctic coasts (separate North Atlantic & North Pacific subspecies)
- ⋀ Shallow coastal seas
- ⬆ ♂ up to 16 ft (4.3 m), ♀ up to 8 ft (2.4 m)
- ⚖ Up to 1.8 tons (1.6 t)
- ✿ Bottom-dwelling bivalve mollusks
- ⚡ Least concern

Southern fur seal
Arctocephalus gazella

Family Procyonidae
Raccoons
19 species

Ringtail
Bassariscus astutus
- ⊕ Southwest USA, Mexico, Baja Peninsula
- ⋀ Rocky & mountainous terrain, arid shrubland, woodland
- ⬆ 24–32 in (62–81 cm)
- ⬇ 12–17 in (31–44 cm)
- ⚖ 2–3 lb (0.9–1.3 kg)
- ✿ Plants, small mammals, insects, fruits, acorns, lizards, birds, eggs
- ⚡ Least concern

Kinkajou
Potos flavus
- ⊕ Southern Mexico to Bolivia & Brazil
- ⋀ Rain forest
- ⬆ 22 in (56 cm)
- ⬇ 22 in (56 cm)
- ⚖ 7 lb (3.2 kg)
- ✿ Fruits, nectar from flowers
- ⚡ Least concern

Northern raccoon
Procyon lotor
- ⊕ North & Central America, introduced to Europe
- ⋀ All habitat types where there is water, including urban areas
- ⬆ 23.7–37.5 in (60–95 cm)
- ⬇ 7.5–16 in (19–40.5 cm)
- ⚖ 4–23 lb (1.8–10.4 kg)
- ✿ Insects, fish, crustaceans, mollusks, small rodents, birds, eggs, carrion, fruits, seeds
- ⚡ Least concern

Family Hyaenidae
Hyenas & aardwolf
4 species

Spotted hyena
Crocuta crocuta
- ⊕ Sub-Saharan Africa
- ⋀ Savanna, grassland
- ⬆ 3.3–6 ft (1–1.8 m)
- ⬇ 10–14 in (25–36 cm)
- ⚖ 88–198 lb (40–90 kg)
- ✿ Small to large mammals, carrion
- ⚡ Conservation dependent

Striped hyena
Hyaena hyaena
- ⊕ North & northeast Africa
- ⋀ Arid steppe, scrub, savanna
- ⬆ 39–47 in (100–120 cm)
- ⬇ 11–14 in (25–35 cm)
- ⚖ 55–121 lb (25–55 kg)
- ✿ Carrion, small mammals
- ⚡ Near threatened

Aardwolf
Proteles cristata
- ⊕ East & south Africa
- ⋀ Grassland, savanna
- ⬆ 21–31 in (55–80 cm)
- ⬇ 8–12 in (20–30 cm)
- ⚖ 17–26 lb (8–12 kg)
- ✿ Termites
- ⚡ Least concern

Family Viverridae
Civets, genets & linsangs
35 species

Fossa
Cryptoprocta ferox
- ⊕ Madagascar
- ⋀ Rain forest
- ⬆ 23–30 in (58–76 cm)
- ⬇ 22–28 in (55–70 cm)
- ⚖ 15–26 lb (7–12 kg)
- ✿ Small to medium vertebrates such as lemurs
- ⚡ Endangered

Malagasy civet
Fossa fossana
- ⊕ Madagascar
- ⋀ Primary forest
- ⬆ 16–18 in (40–45 cm)
- ⬇ 8–10 in (21–25 cm)
- ⚖ 3.3–4.4 lb (1.5–2 kg)
- ✿ Small mammals such as rodents
- ⚡ Vulnerable

Family Herpestidae
Mongooses
34 species

Indian gray mongoose
Herpestes edwardsii
- ⊕ Indian subcontinent, eastern Arabian peninsula, Sri Lanka, southeastern China
- ⋀ Open forest, scrubland, farmland
- ⬆ 14–17 in (35–43 cm)
- ⬇ 17 in (43 cm)
- ⚖ 2–4 lb (0.9–1.8 kg)
- ✿ Birds, reptiles, small mammals, insects
- ⚡ Least concern

Meerkat
Suricata suricata
- ⊕ Southern Africa
- ⋀ Bushland, scrub
- ⬆ 10–12 in (25–30 cm)
- ⬇ 7–9 in (18–24 cm)
- ⚖ 21–34 oz (590–955 g)
- ✿ Insects
- ⚡ Least concern

Family Felidae
Cats
36 species

Cheetah
Acinonyx jubatus heckii
- ⊕ Northern Africa
- ⋀ Woodland, savanna, grassland
- ⬆ 3–5 ft (1–1.5 m)
- ⬇ 26–35 in (65–90 cm)
- ⚖ 77–143 lb (35–65 kg)
- ✿ Small to medium mammals such as antelopes & gazelles
- ⚡ Endangered

Geoffroy's cat
Felis geoffroyi

Geoffroy's cat
Felis geoffroyi
- ⊕ Southern Bolivia & Paraguay to Argentina & Chile
- ⋀ Scrubby woodland
- ⬆ 36 in (90 cm)
- ⬇ 16 in (40 cm)
- ⚖ 7 lb (3 kg)
- ✿ Small lizards, insects, rodents, frogs, fish
- ⚡ Near threatened

Wildcat
Felis silvestris
- ⊕ Africa, Europe to western China & northwestern India
- ⋀ Mountain, forest
- ⬆ Up to 28 in (71 cm)
- ⬇ Up to 12 in (30 cm)
- ⚖ Up to 30 lb (13.6 kg)
- ✿ Rodents, birds
- ⚡ Least concern

Margay
Leopardus wiedii
- ⊕ Central & South America
- ⋀ Rain forest
- ⬆ 42 in (107 cm) including tail
- ⬇ 18 in (46 cm)
- ⚖ 20 lb (9 kg)
- ✿ Arboreal animals, birds, reptiles, insects
- ⚡ Vulnerable

Canada lynx
Lynx canadensis
- ⊕ Most of Canada & Alaska, south to northern Rocky Mountains
- ⋀ Boreal forest
- ⬆ 26–42 in (67–107 cm)
- ⬇ 2–5 in (5–13 cm)
- ⚖ 9–38 lb (4.5–17.3 kg)
- ✿ Snowshoe hares, other small mammals, deer, birds
- ⚡ Least concern

Eurasian lynx
Lynx lynx
- ⊕ France, Balkans, Iraq, Scandinavia to China
- ⋀ Mountain, forest
- ⬆ Up to 4.3 ft (1.3 m)
- ⬇ Up to 10 in (25 cm)
- ⚖ Up to 66 lb (30 kg)
- ✿ Deer, small mammals, rodents
- ⚡ Near threatened

Iberian lynx
Lynx pardinus
- ⊕ Formerly Spain & Portugal, now restricted to southern Spain
- ⋀ Grassland, woodland
- ⬆ 33–43 in (85–110 cm)
- ⬇ 5–12 in (12–30 cm)
- ⚖ ♂ 30–57 lb (13–26 kg), ♀ 20 lb (9 kg)
- ✿ Rabbits, small mammals, other vertebrates
- ⚡ Critically endangered

Bobcat
Lynx rufus
- ⊕ Most of USA, southern Canada, Mexico
- ⋀ Nearly all habitats from mountains to swamps & deserts
- ⬆ 2–4 ft (60–120 cm)
- ⬇ 3.5–8 in (9–20 cm)
- ⚖ ♂ 16–68 lb (7.2–31 kg), ♀ 8–53 lb (3.6–24 kg)
- ✿ Mammals from mice to deer fawns, especially rabbits; birds, reptiles, amphibians, insects
- ⚡ Least concern

Clouded leopard
Neofelis nebulosa
- ⊕ Southern China, Southeast Asia, eastern Himalaya, northeast India
- ⋀ Subtropical & tropical moist forests
- ⬆ 24–36 in (61–92 cm)
- ⬇ Up to 35.5 in (90 cm)
- ⚖ 33–51 lb (15–23 kg)
- ✿ Deer, pigs, primates, birds
- ⚡ Vulnerable

Lion
Panthera leo
- ⊕ Sub-Saharan Africa
- ⋀ Savanna, grassland
- ⬆ ♂ Up to 8 ft (2.4 m), ♀ 6 ft (1.8 m)
- ⬇ 23–39 in (60–100 cm)
- ⚖ ♂ 330–573 lb (150–260 kg), ♀ 269–401 lb (122–182 kg)
- ✿ Medium to large mammals
- ⚡ Vulnerable

Asiatic lion
Panthera leo persica
- ⊕ Gir Forest in state of Gujarat, India
- ⋀ Forest
- ⬆ ♂ 5.5–7 ft (1.7–2 m), ♀ 4.5–5.5 ft (1.3–1.7 m)
- ⬇ Up to 39.5 in (1 m)
- ⚖ ♂ 330–500 lb (150–225 kg), ♀ 220–330 lb (100–150 kg)
- ✿ Small mammals, deer, muntjac, sambar, wild boar, nilgai, cattle
- ⚡ Critically endangered

Jaguar
Panthera onca
- ⊕ Mexico to Argentina
- ⋀ Forest, grassland, pasture, ranches
- ⬆ 8.8 ft (2.7 m)
- ⬇ 30 in (76 cm)
- ⚖ 350 lb (159 kg)
- ✿ Meat, mammals, reptiles, fish
- ⚡ Near threatened

Leopard
Panthera pardus
- ⊕ Sub-Saharan Africa
- ⋀ Woodland, savanna, grassland
- ⬆ ♂ 4.9–6.3 ft (1.5–1.9 m), ♀ 3.3–4.6 ft (1–1.4 m)
- ⬇ 23–43 in (68–110 cm)
- ⚖ ♂ 77–198 lb (35–90 kg), ♀ 61–154 lb (28–70 kg)
- ✿ Small to medium mammals
- ⚡ Least concern

Sri Lankan leopard
Panthera pardus kotiya
- ⊕ Sri Lanka
- ⋀ Dry monsoon forest, tropical rain forest, montane forest
- ⬆ 3–7.8 ft (0.9–2.4 m)
- ⬇ 23–39 in (58–99 cm)
- ⚖ ♂ 125 lb (56 kg), ♀ 64 lb (30 kg)
- ✿ Small mammals, deer, muntjac, sambar, wild boar, monkeys, domestic dogs, cattle
- ⚡ Endangered

Tiger
Panthera tigris
- ⊕ India to Vietnam, Siberia to Indonesia
- ⋀ Forest
- ⬆ 9 ft (2.7 m)
- ⬇ 3 ft (1 m)
- ⚖ Up to 795 lb (360 kg)
- ✿ Deer, wild pigs, cattle
- ⚡ Endangered

Siberian tiger
Panthera tigris altaica
- ⊕ Far eastern Russia, northeastern China, North Korea
- ⋀ Taiga
- ⬆ 6.3–8 ft (1.9–2.5 m)
- ⬇ 3 ft (1 m)
- ⚖ ♂ up to 700 lb (320 kg), ♀ up to 400 lb (181 kg)
- ✿ Deer, goat antelopes, small mammals
- ⚡ Endangered

Bengal tiger
Panthera tigris tigris
- 🌐 India, Bhutan, Nepal, Bangladesh, Myanmar
- ⛰ Dry monsoon forest, mangrove swamp forest
- 📏 ♂ 8.8–10 ft (2.7–3 m), ♀ 7.8–8.5 ft (2.4–2.6 m)
- 📐 33–37 in (84–94 cm)
- ⚖ ♂ 400–570 lb (180–258 kg), ♀ 220–350 lb (100–160 kg)
- ✿ Deer, muntjac, sambar, wild boar, monkeys, wild cattle, livestock, serpents, birds
- ⚡ Endangered

Mountain lion, Puma, Cougar
Puma concolor
- 🌐 North & South America
- ⛰ Nearly all habitats except agricultural land & barren desert
- 📏 ♂ 3–6 ft (0.9–1.8 m), ♀ 3–5 ft (0.9–1.5 m)
- 📐 21–36 in (53–91 cm)
- ⚖ ♂ 1,000–2,000 lb (460–907 kg), ♀ 790–1,110 lb (358–504 kg)
- ✿ Mammals, including deer & other large hoofed species
- ⚡ Near threatened

Snow leopard
Unica unica
- 🌐 Mountains of central Asia (including the Himalaya), Afghanistan, northern Pakistan, eastern Tibet
- ⛰ Mountainous meadows, high rocky regions
- 📏 39–51 in (99–130 cm)
- 📐 32–39 in (81–99 cm)
- ⚖ 77–121 lb (35–55 kg)
- ✿ Wild goats, deer, small mammals, wild boar
- ⚡ Endangered

ORDER PROBOSCIDEA
ELEPHANTS
2 species (living)

Asian elephant
Elephas maximus
- 🌐 India, Nepal, Bangladesh, Bhutan, Sri Lanka, China, Thailand, Laos, Cambodia, Malaysia, Indonesia
- ⛰ Evergreen & dry deciduous forest, swamps, grassland
- 📏 Up to 24.5 ft (7.5 m)
- 📐 3.25–5 ft (1–1.5 m)
- ⚖ 3.3–5.5 tons (3–5 t)
- ✿ Grasses, leaves, bark, fruit
- ⚡ Endangered

African elephant
Loxodonta africana
- 🌐 Sub-Saharan Africa
- ⛰ Forest to semidesert
- 📏 29.6 ft (9 m)
- 📐 3 ft (1 m)
- ⚖ ♂ 4.4–6.9 tons (4–6.3 t), ♀ 2.4–3.9 tons (2.2–3.5 t)
- ✿ Grasses, woody plants
- ⚡ Vulnerable

Woolly mammoth
Mammuthus primigenius
- 🌐 North America, Eurasia, Siberia
- ⛰ Dry cold grassland & steppe
- 📏 11.5 ft (3.5 m); tusks to up to 16 ft (4.8 m) long
- ⚖ 5.6–13 tons (5–12 t)
- ✿ Grasses, sagebrush
- ⚡ Extinct c. 1,700 BC

Indian rhinoceros
Rhinoceros unicornis

ORDER SIRENIA
DUGONG & MANATEES
5 species

Family Trichechidae
Manatees
3 species

West Indian manatee
Trichechus manatus
- 🌐 Georgia & Florida to Brazil, Orinoco River
- ⛰ Shallow rivers, bays, estuaries, coastal waters
- 📏 12 ft (3.6 m)
- 📐 27 in (68.5 cm)
- ⚖ 1,600 lb (725 kg)
- ✿ Grasses, turtle grass, algae, mangrove leaves, water hyacinths
- ⚡ Vulnerable

Family Dugongidae
Dugong
2 species

Dugong
Dugong dugon
- 🌐 Red Sea to southwest Pacific islands
- ⛰ Shallow coastal waters
- 📏 Up to 4.5 ft (1.4 m)
- ⚖ Up to 900 lb (408 kg)
- ✿ Seagrasses
- ⚡ Vulnerable

Steller's sea cow
Hydrodamalis gigas
- 🌐 Bering Sea
- ⛰ Cold coastal waters
- 📏 Up to 29.5 ft (9 m)
- ⚖ More than 3.3 tons (3 t)
- ✿ Kelp
- ⚡ Extinct 1768

ORDER PERISSODACTYLA
ODD-TOED UNGULATES
18 species

Family Equidae
Horses, zebras & asses
9 species

Wild horse
Equus caballus
- 🌐 USA, some Atlantic coastal islands
- ⛰ Shrubby sagebrush plains & mountains, juniper woodland
- 📏 9.5 ft (2.9 m)
- 📐 35 in (90 cm)
- ⚖ 770–1,545 lb (350–700 kg)
- ✿ Grasses, forbs, shrubs
- ⚡ Feral domestic invasive in North America

Grevy's zebra
Equus grevyi
- 🌐 Ethiopia, Kenya
- ⛰ Grassland
- 📏 8.1–9.6 ft (2.5–3 m)
- 📐 16–29 in (40–74 cm)
- ⚖ ♂ 948 lb (430 kg), ♀ 849 lb (385 kg)
- ✿ Grasses
- ⚡ Endangered

Sumatran rhinoceros
Dicerorhinus sumatrensis

Indian wild ass, Khur, Onager
Equus hemionus
- 🌐 Gujarat Province (India)
- ⛰ Saline desert, grassland in arid zone, shrubland
- 📏 Up to 8.5 ft (2.6 m)
- ⚖ 550 lb (250 kg)
- ✿ Grasses, leaves, fruits
- ⚡ Data deficient

Przewalski's horse
Equus przewalskii
- 🌐 Mongolia
- ⛰ Semidesert steppe
- 📏 6.9 ft (2.1 m)
- 📐 2.9 ft (90 cm)
- ⚖ 660 lb (300 kg)
- ✿ Grasses
- ⚡ Critically endangered

Plains zebra
Equus quagga
- 🌐 East & southern Africa
- ⛰ Savanna, woodland
- 📏 7.2–8.2 ft (2.2–2.5 m)
- 📐 18–22 in (45–57 cm)
- ⚖ ♂ 485–710 lb (220–322 kg), ♀ 385–552 lb (175–250 kg)
- ✿ Grasses
- ⚡ Least concern

Family Tapiridae
Tapirs
4 species

Baird's tapir
Tapirus bairdii
- 🌐 Central America
- ⛰ Tropical forests
- 📏 6.5 ft (2 m)
- 📐 5 in (13 cm)
- ⚖ Up to 880 lb (400 kg)
- ✿ Plants, fallen fruits
- ⚡ Endangered

Brazilian tapir
Tapirus pinchaque
- 🌐 Tropical South America east of Andes
- ⛰ Tropical forest
- 📏 7 ft (2.1 m)
- 📐 3 in (8 cm)
- ⚖ 500 lb (227 kg)
- ✿ Ferns, horsetails, fruits, leaves
- ⚡ Endangered

Family Rhinocerotidae
Rhinoceroses
5 species

White rhinoceros
Ceratotherium simum
- 🌐 Central & southern Africa
- ⛰ Grassland
- 📏 11.8–13.7 ft (3.6–4.2 m)
- 📐 31–39 in (80–100 cm)
- ⚖ ♂ 2.2–4 tons (2–3.6 t), ♀ 1.5–2.2 tons (1.4–2 t)
- ✿ Grasses
- ⚡ Near threatened

Black rhinoceros
Diceros bicornis

White rhinoceros
Ceratotherium simum

Sumatran rhinoceros
Dicerorhinus sumatrensis
- 🌐 Malaysia, Sumatra, Sabah, Borneo
- ⛰ Rain forest, swamps, cloud forest
- 📏 8.3 ft (2.5 m)
- 📐 20 in (50 cm)
- ⚖ 1,100–1,700 lb (500–800 kg)
- ✿ Grasses, leaves, some fruit
- ⚡ Critically endangered

Black rhinoceros
Diceros bicornis
- 🌐 Southern Africa (also some central & eastern Africa)
- ⛰ Savanna, grassland, shrubland
- 📏 9.6–12.2 ft (2.9–3.7 m)
- 📐 23–27 in (68–68 cm)
- ⚖ 0.8–1.5 tons (0.7–1.4 t)
- ✿ Leaves, twigs, branches
- ⚡ Critically endangered

Indian rhinoceros
Rhinoceros unicornis
- 🌐 Nepal, Bhutan, Assam (India)
- ⛰ Tall grassland & forest in Himalayan foothills
- 📏 13.2 ft (4 m)
- 📐 2.3 ft (70 cm)
- ⚖ ♂ 2.4–3.3 tons (2.2–3 t), ♀ 1.8 tons (1.6 t)
- ✿ Grasses, leaves
- ⚡ Endangered

ORDER HYRACOIDEA
HYRAXES
Hyraxes
7 species

Rock hyrax
Procavia capensis
- 🌐 Throughout Africa
- ⛰ Mountain cliffs, rocky outcrops
- 📏 15–23 in (38–58 cm)
- ⚖ 4–12 lb (1.8–5.4 kg)
- ✿ Grasses, herbs
- ⚡ Least concern

ORDER TUBULIDENTATA
AARDVARK
1 species

Aardvark
Orycteropus afer
- 🌐 Sub-Saharan Africa
- ⛰ Savanna, grassland, woodland, scrub
- 📏 3.3–5.2 ft (1–1.6 m)
- 📐 17–25 in (43–63 cm)
- ⚖ 88–180 lb (40–82 kg)
- ✿ Termites, ants, larvae
- ⚡ Least concern

ORDER ARTIODACTYLA
EVEN-TOED UNGULATES
218 species
* DNA evidence shows that even-toed ungulates are more closely related to whales than to any other group.

Family Bovidae
Cattle, antelopes & sheep
136 species

Subfamily Bovinae
Cattle & spiral-horned antelopes
26 species

Bison, American bison
Bison bison
- 🌐 North-central Canada, throughout USA except coasts, northern Mexico
- ⛰ Midgrass & shortgrass prairies, forest meadows
- 📏 7–12.5 ft (2.1–3.8 m)
- 📐 17–35 in (43–90 cm)
- ⚖ ♂ 1,015–2,000 lb (460–907 kg), ♀ 790–1,110 lb (358–504 kg)
- ✿ Mixed grasses
- ⚡ Conservation dependent

Gaur
Bos frontalis
- 🌐 India, Bangladesh, Bhutan, Laos, Cambodia, peninsular Malaysia, Borneo, Nepal, Thailand, Vietnam, Myanmar
- ⛰ Tropical woodland, grassland
- 📏 8.2–12 ft (2.5–3.6 m)
- ⚖ ♂ 1.1–1.7 tons (1–1.5 t), ♀ 0.8–1.1 tons (0.7–1 t)
- ✿ Grasses, shoots, fruits
- ⚡ Vulnerable

Yak
Bos grunniens
- 🌐 Himalayan region of south-central Asia, Quinghai–Tibetan Plateau, Mongolia
- ⛰ Treeless uplands, mountains, plateaus
- 📏 10–11 ft (3–3.4 m)
- ⚖ Up to 1.3 tons (1.2 t)
- ✿ Grasses, lichens, other vegetation
- ⚡ Vulnerable

Nilgai
Boselaphus tragocamelus
- 🌐 Peninsular India
- ⛰ Grassland, scrubland, forest woodland
- 📏 6–6.5 ft (1.8–2 m)
- ⚖ 265–530 lb (120–240 kg)
- ✿ Grasses, leaves, buds, fruits
- ⚡ Least concern

Tamaraw
Bubalus mindorensis
- 🌐 Mindoro island in the Philippines
- ⛰ Tropical highland forest, prefers thick brush near open glade areas
- 📏 7.2 ft (2.2 m)
- 📐 24 in (60 cm)
- ⚖ ♀ 440–660 lb (200–300 kg)
- ✿ Grasses, young bamboo shoots
- ⚡ Critically endangered

African buffalo
Syncerus caffer
- 🌐 Sub-Saharan Africa
- ⛰ Grassland
- 📏 5.5–11 ft (1.7–3.4 m)
- 📐 20–31 in (50–80 cm)
- ⚖ 551–1,874 lb (250–850 kg)
- ✿ Grasses
- ⚡ Conservation dependent

Mountain nyala
Tragelaphus buxtoni
- 🌐 Ethiopia
- ⛰ Montane woodland, grassland
- 📏 6.2–8.2 ft (1.9–2.5 m)
- 📐 8–10 in (20–25 cm)
- ⚖ 440–660 lb (200–300 kg)
- ✿ Herbs, shrubs, grasses
- ⚡ Endangered

Bongo
Tragelaphus euryceros
- 🌐 West & central Africa
- ⛰ Rain forest with dense undergrowth
- 📏 5.5–8.2 ft (1.7–2.5 m)
- 📐 9–25 in (23–64 cm)
- ⚖ ♂ 529–893 lb (240–405 kg), ♀ 462–557 lb (210–253 kg)
- ✿ Leaves, shrubs, herbs
- ⚡ Near threatened

Greater kudu
Tragelaphus strepsiceros

Sitatunga, Marshbuck
Tragelaphus spekii
- 🌐 Central Africa
- ⛰ Swampland
- ⬛ ♂ 4.9–5.6 ft (1.5–1.7 m),
  ♀ 3.8–5.1 ft (1.1–1.6 m)
- 🦌 7–12 in (18–30 cm)
- ⚖ ♂ 176–286 lb (80–130 kg),
  ♀ 88–187 lb (40–85 kg)
- ❀ Shrubs, herbs, grasses
- ⚡ Least concern

Greater kudu
Tragelaphus strepsiceros
- 🌐 East & southern Africa
- ⛰ Woodland, evergreen forest
- ⬛ ♂ 6.3–8 ft (1.9–2.4 m),
  ♀ 6–7.7 ft (1.8–2.3 m)
- 🦌 12–22 in (30–55 cm)
- ⚖ ♂ 420–695 lb (190–315 kg),
  ♀ 265–475 lb (120–215 kg)
- ❀ Leaves, herbs, grasses
- ⚡ Conservation dependent

Subfamily Cephalophinae
Duikers
19 species

Blue duiker
Philantomba monticola
- 🌐 Central Africa
- ⛰ Lowland & montane rain forest
- ⬛ 22–35 in (55–90 cm)
- 🦌 3–5 in (7–13 cm)
- ⚖ 8–20 lb (3.5–9 kg)
- ❀ Fruits, leaves
- ⚡ Least concern

Subfamily Hippotraginae
Grazing antelopes
6 species

Addax, Screwhorn antelope
Addax nasomaculatus
- 🌐 Niger, possibly Chad; formerly
  northern Africa
- ⛰ Desert
- ⬛ 4–6 ft (1.2–1.8 m)
- 🦌 11–14 in (27–35 cm)
- ⚖ ♂ 220–298 lb (100–135 kg),
  ♀ 132–198 lb (60–90 kg)
- ❀ Desert grasses
- ⚡ Critically endangered

Sable antelope
Hippotragus niger
- 🌐 East & southern Africa
- ⛰ Miombo woodland
- ⬛ 6.2–8.3 ft (1.9–2.5 m)
- 🦌 16–30 in (40–75 cm)
- ⚖ ♂ 440–595 lb (200–270 kg),
  ♀ 418–507 lb (190–230 kg)
- ❀ Grasses
- ⚡ Conservation dependent

Scimitar-horned oryx
Oryx dammah
- 🌐 Formerly North Africa
- ⛰ Semidesert, grassland
- ⬛ 6.2–7.2 ft (1.9–2.2 m)
- 🦌 18–24 in (45–60 cm)
- ⚖ 298–308 lb (135–140 kg)
- ❀ Grasses, herbs, shrubs
- ⚡ Extinct in the wild

Gemsbok
Oryx gazella
- 🌐 Southwest Africa
- ⛰ Woodland, grassland
- ⬛ 6–6.4 ft (1.8–1.95 m)
- 🦌 16–19 in (40–48 cm)
- ⚖ ♂ 396–529 lb (180–240 kg),
  ♀ 396–496 lb (180–225 kg)
- ❀ Grasses, herbs
- ⚡ Conservation dependent

Arabian oryx
Oryx leucoryx
- 🌐 Arabian peninsula
- ⛰ Desert
- ⬛ 5–7.9 ft (1.5–2.4 m)
- ⚖ 154 lb (70 kg)
- ❀ Grasses, vegetation
- ⚡ Endangered (extinct in the wild
  1972, reintroduced after captive-
  breeding programs)

Subfamily Antilopinae
Gazelles, dwarf antelopes
& saiga
34 species

Springbok
Antidorcas marsupialis
- 🌐 Southwest Africa
- ⛰ Savanna, shrubland
- ⬛ 3.9–4.9 ft (1.2–1.5 m)
- 🦌 5–11 in (13–28 cm)
- ⚖ ♂ 66–130 lb (30–59 kg),
  ♀ 44–95 lb (20–43 kg)
- ❀ Grasses, shrubs
- ⚡ Conservation dependent

Thomson's gazelle
Eudorcas thomsoni
- 🌐 East Africa
- ⛰ Grassland, savanna
- ⬛ 23–35 in (58–90 cm)
- 🦌 9–14 in (23–36 cm)
- ⚖ 29–49 lb (13–22 kg)
- ❀ Grasses, herbs, shrubs
- ⚡ Least concern

Dorcas gazelle
Gazella dorcas
- 🌐 North Africa
- ⛰ Semidesert
- ⬛ 35–43 in (90–110 cm)
- 🦌 6–8 in (15–20 cm)
- ⚖ 33–44 lb (15–20 kg)
- ❀ Herbs, shrubs, grasses
- ⚡ Vulnerable

Gerenuk
Litocranius walleri
- 🌐 East Africa
- ⛰ Semiarid bushland
- ⬛ 4.6–5.2 ft (1.4–1.6 m)
- 🦌 9–14 in (23–36 cm)
- ⚖ 62–115 lb (28–52 kg)
- ❀ Tree leaves
- ⚡ Conservation dependent

Saiga antelope
Saiga tatarica
- 🌐 Kalmykia (Russia), eastern Mongolia,
  Kazakhstan
- ⛰ Semidesert steppe
- ⬛ 3.6–4.7 ft (1.1–1.46 m)
- 🦌 2.4–5.2 in (6–13 cm)
- ⚖ 80–139 lb (36–63 kg)
- ❀ Grasses
- ⚡ Critically endangered

Subfamily Caprinae
Sheep & goats
33 species

Takin
Budorcas taxicolor
- 🌐 Eastern Himalaya, including China
  & Bhutan
- ⛰ High bamboo forests
- ⬛ ♂ 7.2 ft (2.2 m), ♀ 5.6 ft (1.7 m)
- ⚖ Up to 770 lb (350 kg)
- ❀ Grasses, buds, leaves
- ⚡ Vulnerable

Markhor
Capra falconeri
- 🌐 Northern Pakistan, Turkmenistan,
  Afghanistan
- ⛰ Rugged, sparsely wooded hills &
  mountain slopes
- ⬛ 4.3–6 ft (1.3–1.8 m)
- 🦌 4–8 in (10–20 cm)
- ⚖ 90–240 lb (40–110 kg)
- ❀ Grasses, shrubs, trees
- ⚡ Endangered

Ibex, Alpine ibex
Capra ibex
- 🌐 Alps & other mountains in Europe
- ⛰ Protected mountainsides
- ⬛ Up to 5.6 ft (1.7 m)
- 🦌 Up to 12 in (30 cm)
- ⚖ Up to 264 lb (120 kg)
- ❀ Grasses, leaves, twigs
- ⚡ Least concern

Walia ibex
Capra walie
- 🌐 Ethiopia
- ⛰ Steep rocky areas at altitudes of
  8,200–14,800 ft (2,500–4,500 m)
- ⬛ Height: 27–43 in (68–109 cm)
- ⚖ 180–280 lb (80–125 kg)
- ❀ Bushes, herbs, lichens, shrubs,
  grasses
- ⚡ Critically endangered

Himalayan tahr
Hemitragus jemlahicus
- 🌐 Northern Himalayan region, Tibet
- ⛰ Rugged wooded hills, mountain
  slopes
- ⬛ 3.9–5.6 ft (1.2–1.7 m)
- ⚖ 286–397 lb (135–180 kg)
- ❀ Grasses, shrubs, trees
- ⚡ Vulnerable

Red goral
Naemorhedus baileyi
- 🌐 China, India, Myanmar
- ⛰ Tropical & subtropical dry forests &
  grasslands
- ⬛ 3 ft (1 m)
- ⚖ 44–66 lb (20–30 kg)
- ❀ Lichens, grasses, weeds, tender
  stems, leaves, twigs
- ⚡ Vulnerable

Mountain goat
Oreamnos americanus
- 🌐 Western North America
- ⛰ Cliffs & alpine meadows in high
  mountains, at or above treeline
- ⬛ 4.3–6 ft (1.3–1.8 m)
- 🦌 3.3–5.5 in (8–14 cm)
- ⚖ ♂ 100–300 lb (46–136 kg),
  ♀ 100–185 lb (46–84 kg)
- ❀ Grasses, herbs, ferns, lichens, twigs
- ⚡ Least concern

Musk ox
Ovibos moschatus
- 🌐 Arctic Canada, Greenland, Svalbard
- ⛰ Arctic tundra
- ⬛ 7 ft (2 m)
- 🦌 4 in (10 cm)
- ⚖ 660 lb (300 kg)
- ❀ Grasses, sedges, willow
- ⚡ Least concern

Bighorn sheep
Ovis canadensis
- 🌐 Rocky Mountains, desert southwest;
  once more widespread
- ⛰ Open, treeless mountain habitats
  with cliffs or steep terrain
- ⬛ 5–6.2 ft (1.5–1.9 m)
- 🦌 2.7–4.7 in (7–12 cm)
- ⚖ ♂ 165–298 lb (75–135 kg),
  ♀ 106–187 lb (48–85 kg)
- ❀ Grasses, forbs
- ⚡ Conservation dependent

Cyprus mouflon
Ovis orientalis ophion
- 🌐 Cyprus
- ⛰ Mountain
- ⬛ Up to 5 ft (1.5 m)
- 🦌 Up to 4 in (10 cm)
- ⚖ Up to 120 lb (54.4 kg)
- ❀ Short grasses, shrubs
- ⚡ Vulnerable

Chamois
Rupicapra rupicapra
- 🌐 Europe, introduced to New Zealand
- ⛰ Mountains
- ⬛ Up to 4.3 ft (1.3 m)
- 🦌 Up to 6 in (15 cm)
- ⚖ Up to 136 lb (62 kg)
- ❀ Grasses, leaves, fungi
- ⚡ Least concern

Subfamily Reduncinae
Reedbucks & lechwe
8 species

White-eared kob
Kobus kob
- 🌐 Sudan, Ethiopia
- ⛰ Grassland
- ⬛ 5.2–6 ft (1.6–1.8 m)
- 🦌 4–6 in (10–15 cm)
- ⚖ ♂ 187–267 lb (85–121 kg),
  ♀ 132–170 lb (60–77 kg)
- ❀ Grasses
- ⚡ Conservation dependent

Red lechwe
Kobus leche
- 🌐 Southern Africa
- ⛰ Swampland
- ⬛ ♂ 5.2–6 ft (1.6–1.8 m),
  ♀ 4.3–5.6 ft (1.3–1.7 m)
- 🦌 12–18 in (30–46 cm)
- ⚖ ♂ 187–287 lb (85–130 kg),
  ♀ 132–209 lb (60–95 kg)
- ❀ Grasses
- ⚡ Conservation dependent

Subfamily Aepycerotinae
Impala
1 species

Subfamily Peleinae
Rhebok
1 species

Subfamily Alcelaphinae
Wildebeest & topi
7 species

Wildebeest, Blue wildebeest
Connochaetes taurinus
- 🌐 Southern & east Africa
- ⛰ Grassland
- ⬛ 5.5–7.8 ft (1.7–2.4 m)
- 🦌 24–39 in (60–100 cm)
- ⚖ ♂ 364–639 lb (165–290 kg),
  ♀ 309–573 lb (140–260 kg)
- ❀ Grasses
- ⚡ Conservation dependent

Subfamily Pantholopinae
Chiru
1 species

Chiru antelope
Pantholops hodgsonii
- 🌐 Tibetan plateau
- ⛰ Semiarid grassland, alpine steppe
- ⬛ 3.9–4.3 ft (1.2–1.3 m)
- 🦌 7–12 in (18–30 cm)
- ⚖ 57–88 lb (26–40 kg)
- ❀ Grasses, forbs
- ⚡ Endangered

Family Cervidae
Deer
44 species

Moose, Elk
Alces alces
- 🌐 Northern North America, Eurasia
- ⛰ Boreal & deciduous forest near lakes
- ⬛ 7.9–10.5 ft (2.4–3.2 m)
- 🦌 3–5 in (8–13 cm)
- ⚖ 595–1,320 lb (270–600 kg)
- ❀ Leaves, twigs, aquatic plants
- ⚡ Least concern

Visayan spotted deer
Cervus alfredi
- 🌐 Panay island in central Philippines
- ⛰ Forests
- ⬛ Up to 4.3 ft (1.3 m)
- ⚖ 55–176 lb (25–80 kg)
- ❀ Grasses, leaves
- ⚡ Endangered

Red deer
Cervus elaphus
- 🌐 Europe, North America
- ⛰ Forest
- ⬛ Up to 8 ft (2.4 m)
- 🦌 Up to 8 in (20 cm)
- ⚖ Up to 650 lb (295 kg)
- ❀ Grasses
- ⚡ Least concern

Sardinian red deer
Cervus elaphus corsicanus
- 🌐 Sardinia
- ⛰ Mountain, forest
- ⬛ Up to 8.7 ft (2.7 m)
- 🦌 Up to 11 in (27 cm)
- ⚖ Up to 750 lb (340 kg)
- ❀ Short grasses, shrubs
- ⚡ Vulnerable

Eld's deer
Cervus eldii
- 🌐 India, Myanmar, Thailand,
  Cambodia, China, Vietnam, Laos
- ⛰ Open forest near rivers & marshland
- ⬛ 5–6 ft (1.5–1.8 m),
  ♂ antlers up to 6.6 ft (2 m)
- 🦌 8–12 in (20–30 cm)
- ⚖ Up to 330 lb (150 kg)
- ❀ Grasses, herbaceous plants, shoots
- ⚡ Vulnerable

Fallow deer
Dama dama
- 🌐 Mediterranean to southwest Asia
- ⛰ Deciduous woodland, meadow
- ⬛ Up to 5.3 ft (1.6 m)
- 🦌 Up to 9 in (23 cm)
- ⚖ Up to 187 lb (85 kg)
- ❀ Grasses, herbs, leaves
- ⚡ Least concern

Taruca, North Andean deer
Hippocamelus antisensis
- 🌐 Northern Andes (South America)
- ⛰ Rugged hills, mountain slopes,
  alpine grassland
- ⬛ 5.6 ft (1.7 m)
- 🦌 5 in (13 cm)
- ⚖ 143 lb (65 kg)
- ❀ Lichens, mosses, herbs, grasses
- ⚡ Data deficient

Indian muntjac
Muntiacus muntjak
- 🌐 Indian subcontinent, Sri Lanka,
  Southeast Asia
- ⛰ Dry monsoon forest, tropical rain
  forest, montane forest, scrubland
- ⬛ 35–53 in (90–135 cm)
- 🦌 5.2–9 in (13–23 cm)
- ⚖ 33–44 lb (15–20 kg)
- ❀ Grasses, leaves, fruits, tender
  shoots, seeds
- ⚡ Least concern

Mule deer
Odocoileus hemionus
- 🌐 Western North America into north
  & central Mexico
- ⛰ Mountains, forest, desert, brushland
- ⬛ 4.1–5.5 ft (1.25–1.7 m)
- 🦌 4.5–8.5 in (11–21 cm)
- ⚖ ♂ 88–265 lb (40–120 kg),
  ♀ 66–176 lb (30–80 kg)
- ❀ Plants including grasses, forbs, new
  twigs of trees & shrubs, acorns
- ⚡ Least concern

White-tailed deer
Odocoileus virginianus
- ⊕ Southern Canada, USA, northern South America
- ⋏ Diverse wooded habitats: northern temperate to semiarid to rain forest
- ▭ 2.8–7.8 ft (0.85–2.4 m)
- ▭ 7–12 in (17–30 cm)
- ⚖ 48–300 lb (22–137 kg)
- ✿ Green leaves, twigs, shoots, acorns, berries, seeds, grasses
- ⚡ Least concern

Northern pudu
Pudu puda
- ⊕ Southern Chile to southwest Argentina
- ⋏ Rain forest
- ▭ 23–33 in (58–84 cm)
- ▭ 3 in (8 cm)
- ⚖ 22 lb (10 kg)
- ✿ Twigs, bark, fruits, leaves, seeds
- ⚡ Vulnerable

Caribou, Reindeer
Rangifer tarandus
- ⊕ Northern North America, northern Eurasia
- ⋏ Boreal forest, Arctic tundra
- ▭ 4.6–6.9 ft (1.4–2.1 m)
- ▭ 4.3–7.9 in (11–20 cm)
- ⚖ ♂ 179–337 lb (81–153 kg), ♀ 139–207 lb (63–94 kg)
- ✿ Leaves of shrubs & plants in summer, lichen in winter
- ⚡ Least concern

Family Tragulidae
Chevrotains
4 species

Family Moschidae
Musk deer
4 species

Family Antilocapridae
Pronghorn
1 species

Pronghorn
Antilocapra americana
- ⊕ Mostly in lower 48 US states
- ⋏ Flat, rolling expanses from hot deserts to alpine plateaus without deep snow cover in winter
- ▭ 4.3–4.9 ft (1.3–1.5 m)
- ▭ 4–5.7 in (10–14.5 cm)
- ⚖ ♂ 93–130 lb (42–59 kg), ♀ 90–110 lb (41–50 kg)
- ✿ Variety of plants, especially forbs & shrubs
- ⚡ Least concern

Family Giraffidae
Giraffe & okapi
2 species

Giraffe
Giraffa camelopardalis
- ⊕ East & southern Africa; formerly throughout the northern, eastern & southern savannas
- ⋏ Acacia woodland, savanna
- ▭ 11.5–15.7 ft (3.5–4.8 m)
- ▭ 30–43 in (76–110 cm)
- ⚖ ♂ 2–2.1 tons (1.8–1.9 t), ♀ 0.5–1.3 tons (0.45–1.2 t)
- ✿ Tree leaves, shrubs
- ⚡ Conservation dependent

Okapi
Okapia johnstoni
- ⊕ Democratic Republic of Congo
- ⋏ Rain forest
- ▭ 6.2–6.9 ft (1.9–2.1 m)
- ▭ 12–16.5 in (30–42 cm)
- ⚖ 460–550 lb (210–250 kg)
- ✿ Leaves, fruits, ferns, fungus
- ⚡ Near threatened

Family Camelidae
Camels & llamas
6 species

Bactrian camel
Camelus bactrianus
- ⊕ Northwest China, Mongolia
- ⋏ Rocky desert, steppe grassland
- ▭ 10 ft (3 m)
- ⚖ 1,800 lb (815 kg)
- ✿ Grasses, leaves of shrubs
- ⚡ Critically endangered

Llama
Lama glama
- ⊕ From southern Peru to northwest Argentina
- ⋏ Puna, high Andes, paramo
- ▭ 6.5 ft (2 m)
- ▭ 9 in (23 cm)
- ⚖ 265 lb (120 kg)
- ✿ Grasses, halophytes
- ⚡ Domesticated

Guanaco
Lama guanicoe
- ⊕ Southern Peru to eastern Argentina & Tierra del Fuego
- ⋏ Puna, high Andes, paramo, Patagonian grassland
- ▭ 6.5 ft (2 m)
- ▭ 9 in (23 cm)
- ⚖ 330 lb (150 kg)
- ✿ Shrubs, lichens, fungi
- ⚡ Least concern

Alpaca
Vicugna pacos
- ⊕ Andes of Ecuador, southern Peru, northern Bolivia & northern Chile
- ⋏ Puna, high Andes, paramo
- ▭ 7.2 ft (2.2 m)
- ▭ 8 in (20 cm)
- ⚖ 99–174 lb (45–79 kg)
- ✿ Grasses, halophytes
- ⚡ Domesticated

Vicuña
Vicugna vicugna
- ⊕ Andes of southern Peru, western Bolivia, northwestern Argentina & northern Chile
- ⋏ Windswept, cold, semiarid plains or puna, high Andes
- ▭ 4.9 ft (1.5 m)
- ▭ 9 in (23 cm)
- ⚖ 110 lb (50 kg)
- ✿ Grasses, small forbs, lichens, water daily
- ⚡ Conservation dependent

Vicuña
Vicugna vicugna

Family Suidae
Pigs
14 species

Red river hog
Potamochoerus porcus
- ⊕ West & central Africa
- ⋏ Rain forest, swamp forest
- ▭ 3.3–5 ft (1–1.5 m)
- ▭ 12–18 in (30–45 cm)
- ⚖ 99–254 lb (45–115 kg)
- ✿ Roots, tubers, fruits
- ⚡ Least concern

Wild boar
Sus scrofa
- ⊕ Eurasia & northern Africa
- ⋏ River valley, forest
- ▭ Up to 6 ft (1.8 m)
- ▭ Up to 12 in (30 cm)
- ⚖ Up to 440 lb (200 kg)
- ✿ Grasses, nuts, berries, carrion, roots, tubers, insects, small reptiles
- ⚡ Least concern

Family Tayassuidae
Peccaries
3 species

Chacoan peccary
Catagonus wagneri
- ⊕ Paraguay, Bolivia, Brazil, Argentina
- ⋏ Dry briars or thorny bushes
- ▭ 38–46 in (96–117 cm)
- ▭ 1.2–4 in (3–10 cm)
- ⚖ 66–95 lb (30–43 kg)
- ✿ Cacti, roots, seedpods
- ⚡ Endangered

Family Hippopotamidae
Hippopotamuses
4 species

Pygmy hippopotamus
Hexaprotodon liberiensis
- ⊕ Guinean forests of West Africa, Liberia
- ⋏ Rivers
- ▭ 6.5 ft (2 m)
- ⚖ Up to 605 lb (275 kg)
- ✿ Riparian forest plants
- ⚡ Endangered

Hippopotamus
Hippopotamus amphibius
- ⊕ Sub-Saharan Africa
- ⋏ Grassland with permanent water
- ▭ 9–11.5 ft (2.8–3.5 m)
- ▭ 14–20 in (35–50 cm)
- ⚖ ♂ 0.7–3.5 tons (0.65–3.2 t), ♀ 0.6–2.8 tons (0.5–2.5 t)
- ✿ Grasses
- ⚡ Vulnerable

Hippopotamus
Hippopotamus amphibius

Order Cetacea
Cetaceans
81 species

Suborder Odontoceti
Toothed whales
68 species

Beluga
Delphinapterus leucas
- ⊕ Arctic & subarctic waters
- ⋏ Inlets, fjords, channels, bays, shallows, river mouths
- ▭ Up to 16.5 ft (5 m)
- ⚖ Up to 1.7 tons (1.5 t)
- ✿ Octopuses, squid, fish, crabs, snails
- ⚡ Vulnerable

Common dolphin
Delphinus delphis
- ⊕ Temperate to tropical oceans
- ⋏ Coastal waters
- ▭ Up to 6.5 ft (2 m)
- ⚖ Up to 440 lb (200 kg)
- ✿ Sardines, anchovies, squid
- ⚡ Least concern

Pink river dolphin, Amazon dolphin
Inia geoffrensis
- ⊕ Amazon River, Orinoco River
- ⋏ Main rivers, small channels, lakes
- ▭ 9.8 ft (3 m)
- ▭ 20 in (50 cm)
- ⚖ 198 lb (90 kg)
- ✿ Crustaceans, catfish, small freshwater fish
- ⚡ Vulnerable

Baiji, Yangtze river dolphin
Lipotes vexillifer
- ⊕ Yangtze valley (China)
- ⋏ Rivers, lakes
- ▭ Up to 8 ft (2.5 m)
- ⚖ 300–510 lb (135–230 kg)
- ✿ Fish
- ⚡ Critically endangered

Narwhal
Monodon monoceros
- ⊕ Arctic seas
- ⋏ Deep water near loose pack ice
- ▭ Up to 20 ft (6 m) without tusk
- ⚖ Up to 1.8 tons (1.6 t)
- ✿ Cod, squid, shrimps, some fish
- ⚡ Data deficient

Orca
Orcinus orca
- ⊕ Worldwide, especially polar seas
- ⋏ Coastal waters
- ▭ Up to 32 ft (9.8 m)
- ⚖ Up to 11 tons (10 t)
- ✿ Fish, squid, sea lions, seals, penguins
- ⚡ Conservation dependent

Sperm whale
Physeter catodon
- ⊕ Circumglobal, tropics to pack ice
- ⋏ Deep to surface waters
- ▭ Up to 61 ft (18.5 m)
- ⚖ Up to 77 tons (70 t)
- ✿ Giant squid, octopus, deepwater fish, sharks, skates
- ⚡ Vulnerable

Atlantic spotted dolphin
Stenella frontalis
- ⊕ Warm temperate to tropical Atlantic
- ⋏ Continental shelf, shallows
- ▭ 7.5 ft (2.3 m)
- ⚖ ♂ 310 lb (140 kg), ♀ 285 lb (130 kg)
- ✿ Fish, squid
- ⚡ Data deficient

Beluga
Delphinapterus leucas

Suborder Mysticeti
Baleen whales
13 species

Bowhead
Balaena mysticetus
- ⊕ Arctic & subarctic waters
- ⋏ Follow receding ice drifts; bays & estuaries in summer
- ▭ 49–59 ft (15–18 m)
- ⚖ Up to 110 tons (100 t)
- ✿ Plankton, krill, small fish
- ⚡ Conservation dependent

Minke whale
Balaenoptera acutorostrata
- ⊕ Northern hemisphere oceans from Arctic to tropics
- ⋏ Usually coastal waters
- ▭ Up to 36 ft (11 m)
- ⚖ Up to 11 tons (10 t)
- ✿ Plankton, krill, small fish
- ⚡ Near threatened

Blue whale
Balaenoptera musculus
- ⊕ All oceans except high Arctic
- ⋏ Open ocean
- ▭ Up to 110 ft (33.5 m)
- ⚖ Up to 209 tons (190 t)
- ✿ Plankton, krill, small fish
- ⚡ Endangered

Fin whale
Balaenoptera physalus
- ⊕ Circumglobal oceans, pack ice to subtropics
- ⋏ Open ocean, coastal waters
- ▭ Up to 82 ft (25 m)
- ⚖ Up to 88 tons (80 t)
- ✿ Plankton, krill, small fish
- ⚡ Endangered

Southern right whale
Eubalaena australis
- ⊕ Southern Ocean (summer), New Zealand, Australia, Argentina, Brazil, Chile, Mozambique, South Africa
- ⋏ Polar waters to feed; shallow continental shelves to bear young
- ▭ 50 ft (15 m)
- ⚖ 60 tons (65 t)
- ✿ Plankton, krill, small fish
- ⚡ Conservation dependent

North Atlantic right whale
Eubalaena glacialis
- ⊕ Subarctic to cold-temperate North Atlantic Ocean
- ⋏ Shallow coastal waters, deep basins
- ▭ Up to 59 ft (18 m)
- ⚖ Up to 99 tons (90 t)
- ✿ Plankton, krill, small fish
- ⚡ Endangered

Humpback whale
Megaptera novaeangliae
- ⊕ Circumglobal oceans, ice edge to tropics
- ⋏ Open ocean, coastal waters
- ▭ Up to 49 ft (15 m)
- ⚖ Up to 71.5 tons (65 t)
- ✿ Plankton, krill, small fish
- ⚡ Vulnerable

ORDER RODENTIA
RODENTS

2,015 species

Suborder Sciurognathi
Squirrel-like rodents, mouselike rodents & gundis

1,797 species

SQUIRREL-LIKE RODENTS
383 SPECIES IN 8 FAMILIES

American beaver
Castor canadensis
- 🌐 North America except desert & tundra regions
- ⛰ Lakes, ponds, streams
- 📏 39–47 in (100–120 cm)
- 📏 9–13 in (23–33 cm)
- ⚖ 35–66 lb (16–30 kg)
- ❂ Land & aquatic plants, tree leaves, inner bark, wood
- ⚡ Least concern

European beaver
Castor fiber
- 🌐 Western Europe to eastern Siberia
- ⛰ Rivers, marshes
- 📏 Up to 4.3 ft (1.3 m)
- 📏 Up to 12 in (30 cm)
- ⚖ Up to 75 lb (34 kg)
- ❂ Plants, bark, leaves
- ⚡ Near threatened

Black-tailed prairie dog
Cynomys ludovicianus
- 🌐 Great Plains of North America
- ⛰ Shortgrass & midgrass prairie
- 📏 13–17 in (34–42 cm)
- 📏 2.4–3.7 in (6–9.5 cm)
- ⚖ ♂ 20–53 oz (575–1,490 g), ♀ 27–36 oz (765–1,030 g)
- ❂ Grasses, herbs, seeds
- ⚡ Near threatened

Merriam's kangaroo rat
Dipodomys merriami
- 🌐 Southwest USA, northern Mexico, Baja Peninsula
- ⛰ Various dry habitats
- 📏 7.6–11 in (20–28 cm)
- 📏 4.7–7 in (12–18 cm)
- ⚖ 1.8–1.8 oz (33–53 g)
- ❂ Seeds, green vegetation, insects
- ⚡ Least concern

Northern flying squirrel
Glaucomys sabrinus
- 🌐 Northern North America, southern Appalachians
- ⛰ Conifer, mixed & deciduous forests
- 📏 11–13 in (28–34 cm)
- 📏 5–6 in (13–15 cm)
- ⚖ 2.6–5 oz (75–140 g)
- ❂ Mushrooms, other fungi, fruits, nuts, seeds, insects, bird eggs, flesh of small mammals & birds
- ⚡ Least concern (but Appalachian subspecies endangered)

Northern flying squirrel
Glaucomys sabrinus

Marmot
Marmota marmota

Gray squirrel
Sciurus carolinensis

Marmot
Marmota marmota
- 🌐 Mountainous areas in Europe, northern Canada, USA
- ⛰ Mountain
- 📏 Up to 21 in (54 cm)
- 📏 Up to 6 in (16 cm)
- ⚖ Up to 17.5 lb (8 kg)
- ❂ Grasses, herbs, insects
- ⚡ Least concern

Gray squirrel
Sciurus carolinensis
- 🌐 Eastern & central North America, introduced to Europe
- ⛰ Forest, now urban parks
- 📏 9–10 in (23–25 cm)
- 📏 6–10 in (15–25 cm)
- ⚖ 19 oz (540 g)
- ❂ Seeds, nuts, bark
- ⚡ Least concern

Red squirrel
Sciurus vulgaris
- 🌐 Western Europe to eastern Russia, Korea, northern Japan
- ⛰ Deciduous woodland, mixed forest
- 📏 Up to 9.5 in (24 cm)
- 📏 Up to 8 in (20 cm)
- ⚖ Up to 12 oz (350 g)
- ❂ Seeds, nuts, flowers
- ⚡ Near threatened

Arctic ground squirrel
Spermophilus parryii
- 🌐 Siberia, Alaska, Canada
- ⛰ Arctic tundra, open meadows
- 📏 14 in (35 cm)
- 📏 6 in (15 cm)
- ⚖ 32 oz (900 g)
- ❂ Grasses, herbs, berries, seeds, horsetails
- ⚡ Least concern

Eastern chipmunk
Tamias striatus
- 🌐 Eastern USA except southeast coast, southeastern Canada
- ⛰ Deciduous & boreal forest, suburban areas, cities
- 📏 8.5–11.5 in (22–29 cm)
- 📏 3–4.5 in (8–12 cm)
- ⚖ 2.8–5.2 oz (80–150 g)
- ❂ Nuts, small seeds, some vegetation, fungi, animal matter
- ⚡ Least concern

Red squirrel
Sciurus vulgaris

MOUSE-LIKE RODENTS
1,409 SPECIES IN 3 FAMILIES

Black-bellied hamster
Cricetus cricetus
- 🌐 Europe
- ⛰ Low-lying farmland
- 📏 ♂ 10.5–12.5 in (27–32 cm), ♀ 8.7–9.8 in (22–25 cm)
- ⚖ ♂ 16 oz (450 g), ♀ 12.5 oz (350 g)
- ❂ Grains, fruits, roots, plants
- ⚡ Least concern

Long-eared jerboa
Euchoreutes naso
- 🌐 China, Mongolia (Gobi desert)
- ⛰ Desert, semidesert
- 📏 Up to 0.35 in (9 mm)
- 📏 Up to 0.6 in (16 mm)
- ⚖ 0.8–1.3 oz (23–38 g)
- ❂ Insects
- ⚡ Endangered

Desert jerboa
Jaculus jaculus
- 🌐 North Africa
- ⛰ Desert
- 📏 7–13 in (17–32 cm)
- 📏 6–9 in (14–22 cm)
- ⚖ 1.8–2.5 oz (50–70 g)
- ❂ Seeds, stems, roots
- ⚡ Least concern

Steppe lemming
Lagurus lagurus
- 🌐 Russia, Ukraine
- ⛰ Steppe
- 📏 3–5.5 in (8–14 cm)
- 📏 0.3–0.8 in (0.7–2 cm)
- ⚖ 0.9–1.2 oz (25–35 g)
- ❂ Shoots, leaves, seeds
- ⚡ Least concern

Snow vole
Microtus nivalis
- 🌐 Europe
- ⛰ Mountain
- 📏 Up to 7 in (18 cm)
- 📏 Up to 4 in (10 cm)
- ⚖ Up to 1.5 oz (43 g)
- ❂ Grasses, plants
- ⚡ Least concern

Dormouse
Muscardinus avellanarius
- 🌐 Europe
- ⛰ Rocky areas, forest
- 📏 Up to 7.5 in (19 cm)
- 📏 Up to 6.5 in (16.5 cm)
- ⚖ Up to 7 oz (200 g)
- ❂ Plants, seeds, insects
- ⚡ Near threatened

Desert woodrat
Neotoma lepida
- 🌐 Southwest USA, Baja Peninsula
- ⛰ Desert scrubland, coastal sage scrub
- 📏 9–15 in (23–38 cm)
- 📏 3.7–7.5 in (9.5–19 cm)
- ⚖ 4.5–5.7 oz (128–162 g)
- ❂ Leafy vegetation, especially succulents
- ⚡ Least concern

Muskrat
Odontra zibethicus
- 🌐 North America from Alaska to southern USA
- ⛰ Brackish & freshwater lakes, ponds, streams, rivers, marshes
- 📏 16–24 in (41–62 cm)
- 📏 7–12 in (18–30 cm)
- ⚖ 1.5–4 lb (0.7–1.8 kg)
- ❂ Aquatic plants such as cattails, fish, crustaceans, snails
- ⚡ Least concern

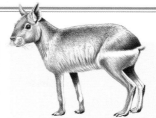

Patagonian mara
Dolichotis patagonum

Southern grasshopper mouse
Onychomys torridus
- 🌐 Mexico, southwest USA
- ⛰ Desert scrub
- 📏 Up to 5 in (13 cm)
- 📏 2.4 in (6 cm)
- ⚖ 0.8 oz (22 g)
- ❂ Mice, scorpions, beetles
- ⚡ Least concern

Cloud rat
Phloeomys pallidus
- 🌐 Philippines
- ⛰ Tropical forest, nests in hollow trees
- 📏 12–20 in (30–50 cm)
- 📏 Up to 5.5 lb (2.5 kg)
- ❂ Young leaves
- ⚡ Near threatened

Family Ctenodactylidae
Gundis

5 species

Suborder Hystricognathi
Cavy-like rodents

218 species

Patagonian mara
Dolichotis patagonum
- 🌐 Central & southern Argentina
- ⛰ Brushy areas with sandy soil, foothills, open grassland
- 📏 29 in (73.5 cm)
- 📏 2 in (5 cm)
- ⚖ 36 lb (16.3 kg)
- ❂ Leaves, grasses, herbs, fruits, cacti, seeds
- ⚡ Near threatened

North American porcupine
Erethizon dorsatum
- 🌐 Southern Canada, Alaska, western USA
- ⛰ Boreal forest, tundra, desert, chaparral, rangelands
- 📏 24–51 in (60–130 cm)
- 📏 7–10 in (18–25 cm)
- ⚖ 11–40 lb (5–18 kg)
- ❂ Bark, cambium, phloem tissue of coniferous trees
- ⚡ Least concern

Capybara
Hydrochaeris hydrochaeris
- 🌐 Panama to northeast Argentina
- ⛰ Ponds, rivers & lakes in habitats from savanna to rain forest
- 📏 24 in (61 cm)
- 📏 2 in (5 cm)
- ⚖ Up to 100 lb (45 kg)
- ❂ Grasses, aquatic vegetation
- ⚡ Least concern

Southern viscacha
Lagidium viscacia
- 🌐 Argentina, Bolivia, Chile, Peru
- ⛰ Rocky mountainous country
- 📏 Up to 16 in (40 cm)
- 📏 5 in (13 cm)
- ⚖ Up to 6.6 lb (3 kg)
- ❂ Grasses, mosses, lichens
- ⚡ Data deficient

Giant mole rat
Spalax giganteus
- 🌐 Ethiopia
- ⛰ Shrubland, grassland
- 📏 6–11 in (15–28 cm)
- 📏 0.4–3 in (1–8 cm)
- ⚖ 5.6–21 oz (160–600 g)
- ❂ Grasses, herbs
- ⚡ Vulnerable

ORDER LAGOMORPHA
HARES, RABBITS & PIKAS

82 species

Snowshoe hare
Lepus americanus
- 🌐 Canada, Alaska, western & northeast USA
- ⛰ Boreal forest
- 📏 14–20 in (36–51 cm)
- 📏 1–2.3 in (2.5–6 cm)
- ⚖ ♂ 2–3.7 lb (0.9–1.7 kg), ♀ 2–5 lb (0.9–2.3 kg)
- ❂ Snowshoe hares, other small mammals, birds, deer
- ⚡ Least concern

Black-tailed jackrabbit
Lepus californicus
- 🌐 Western USA, northern Mexico
- ⛰ Desert, prairie, chaparral, farmland
- 📏 18–25 in (46–64 cm)
- 📏 2–4 in (5–11 cm)
- ⚖ 2.8–7.3 lb (1.3–3.3 kg)
- ❂ Forbs, grasses, shrubs
- ⚡ Least concern

Alpine hare
Lepus timidus
- 🌐 Eurasia
- ⛰ Mountains
- 📏 Up to 24 in (60 cm)
- 📏 Up to 8 in (20 cm)
- ⚖ Up to 10.4 lb (4.7 kg)
- ❂ Leaves, twigs
- ⚡ Least concern

European rabbit
Oryctolagus cuniculus
- 🌐 Europe, introduced worldwide
- ⛰ Forest edges, fields
- 📏 Up to 18 in (46 cm)
- 📏 Up to 5 lb (2.2 kg)
- ❂ Grasses, other plants
- ⚡ Least concern

Amami rabbit
Pentalagus furnessi
- 🌐 Ryukyu Islands (Japan)
- ⛰ Dense old-growth forests, Japanese pampas grassland at forest edge
- 📏 17–20 in (43–51 cm)
- ⚖ 4.4–6.6 lb (2–3 kg)
- ❂ Bamboo shoots, berries, leaves & stems of sweet potato
- ⚡ Endangered

ORDER MACROSCELIDEA
ELEPHANT SHREWS

15 species

Snowshoe hare
Lepus americanus

BIRDS

Birds may be the most mobile of all the animals. They descended from reptiles that developed the ability to fly, and although some bird species have lost their flying ability, they all retain feathers. The American ornithologist Alexander Wetmore devised a classification of the orders and families of birds in the 1930s, basing it on structural similarities in limbs, skeletons, and feathers. Since then, DNA and other molecular studies have shown that many structural traits traditionally used for classifying birds are unreliable because of convergent evolution. The bird classification used here takes account of many of these changes.

Icon key

🌐 Distribution	🌙 Tail length	⭐ Diet
▲ Habitat	🌙 Wingspan	⚡ Status
🌙 Length	🌙 Weight	♀♂ Female/male

PHYLUM CHORDATA
CHORDATES
53,000+ species

CLASS AVES
BIRDS
9,743 species

ORDER TINAMIFORMES
TINAMOUS

74 species

ORDER STRUTHIONIFORMES
OSTRICH

1 species

Ostrich
Struthio camelus
- 🌐 East & southern Africa
- ▲ Savanna, desert
- 🌙 Height: 8.2 ft (2.5 m)
- 🌙 79 in (2 m)
- 🌙 ♂ 220–286 lb (100–130 kg), ♀ 198–242 lb (90–110 kg)
- ⭐ Grasses, seeds, leaves
- ⚡ Least concern

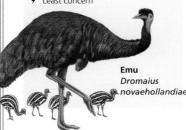

Emu
Dromaius novaehollandiae

ORDER RHEIFORMES
RHEAS

2 species

Rhea, Ñandú
Rhea americana
- 🌐 East, southeast & central-west South America
- ▲ Tall grassland, savanna, scrub forest, chaparral, desert
- 🌙 5 ft (1.5 m)
- 🌙 22 in (56 cm)
- 🌙 55 lb (25 kg)
- ⭐ Leaves, seeds, fruits, flowers, invertebrates, small vertebrates
- ⚡ Near threatened

ORDER CASUARIIFORMES
CASSOWARIES & EMUS

4 species

Southern cassowary
Casuarius casuarius
- 🌐 Seram (Indonesian island), southern New Guinea, northeast Australia
- ▲ Rain forest
- 🌙 Up to 6 ft (1.8 m)
- 🌙 Up to 140 lb (63 kg)
- ⭐ Fruits
- ⚡ Vulnerable

Emu
Dromaius novaehollandiae
- 🌐 Australia
- ▲ Open habitats including farmland
- 🌙 Up to 6.5 ft (2 m)
- 🌙 65–100 lb (30–45 kg)
- ⭐ Green leafy shoots, insects, fruits
- ⚡ Least concern

Indian peafowl
Pavo cristatus

ORDER APTERYGIFORMES
KIWIS

3 species

Great spotted kiwi
Apteryx haastii
- 🌐 South Island of New Zealand
- ▲ Forest, wetlands, tussock grassland
- 🌙 Up to 18 in (46 cm)
- 🌙 Up to 7 lb (3 kg)
- ⭐ Invertebrates, fallen fruits
- ⚡ Vulnerable

ORDER GALLIFORMES
GAMEBIRDS

290 species

Hazel grouse
Bonasa bonasia
- 🌐 Northern Eurasia, central & eastern Europe
- ▲ Dense mixed coniferous woodland
- 🌙 14–15 in (35–38 cm)
- 🌙 18–19 in (45–48 cm)
- ⭐ Plant matter, insects
- ⚡ Least concern

Greater sage grouse
Centrocercus urophasianus
- 🌐 Temperate North America
- ▲ Foothills, plains, mountain slopes with sagebrush
- 🌙 28–38 in (71–97 cm)
- 🌙 6–8 in (15–20 cm)
- 🌙 3–6.5 lb (1.4–3 kg)
- ⭐ Leaves, stems, flowers, fruits, insects
- ⚡ Near threatened

Willow ptarmigan, Willow grouse
Lagopus lagopus
- 🌐 Circumarctic Alaska, Canada, Eurasia, Greenland
- ▲ Tundra, boreal (birch) forest
- 🌙 15 in (38 cm)
- 🌙 24 in (61 cm)
- ⭐ Vegetation, insects
- ⚡ Least concern

Monal pheasant
Lophophorus impejanus
- 🌐 Himalaya, from eastern Afghanistan to western China
- ▲ Mountainous regions at 7,900–14,800 ft (2,400–4,500 m)
- 🌙 24 in (60 cm)
- 🌙 4–5.3 lb (1.8–2.4 kg)
- ⭐ Seeds, tubers, shoots, invertebrates
- ⚡ Least concern

Wild turkey
Meleagris gallopavo
- 🌐 Southern Canada to Mexico, Florida
- ▲ Hardwood forest, swamps, grassland, ponderosa pine, chaparral
- 🌙 3.5 ft (1.1 m)
- 🌙 3.9–5 ft (1.2–1.5 m)
- 🌙 5.5–24 lb (2.5–10.8 kg)
- ⭐ Nuts, seeds, fruits, insects, buds, salamanders
- ⚡ Least concern

Indian peafowl
Pavo cristatus
- 🌐 Indian subcontinent, Sri Lanka
- ▲ Monsoon forest, scrubland, deciduous forest
- 🌙 ♂ 7.3 ft (2.2 m) in full breeding plumage, ♀ 34 in (86 cm)
- 🌙 ♂ 11 lb (5 kg), ♀ 7.5 lb (3.4 kg)
- ⭐ Seeds, fruits, insects, reptiles, small mammals
- ⚡ Least concern

Black grouse
Tetrao tetrix
- 🌐 Northern Eurasia
- ▲ Forest, forest edge
- 🌙 Up to 19 in (48 cm)
- 🌙 Up to 28 in (72 cm)
- 🌙 Up to 2.6 lb (1.2 kg)
- ⭐ Buds, shoots, berries
- ⚡ Least concern

Western tragopan
Tragopan melanocephalus
- 🌐 Himalaya, from Pakistan to India
- ▲ Temperate forest, coniferous forest
- 🌙 19–24 in (48–60 cm)
- 🌙 ♂ up to 4.9 lb (2.2 kg), ♀ up to 3 lb (1.4 kg)
- ⭐ Leaves, shoots, seeds, invertebrates
- ⚡ Vulnerable

ORDER ANSERIFORMES
WATERFOWL

162 species

Mandarin duck
Aix galericulata
- 🌐 Eastern Russia, China, Japan
- ▲ Shallow lakes, marshes, ponds
- 🌙 16–19 in (41–49 cm)
- 🌙 26–30 in (65–75 cm)
- 🌙 15–24 oz (430–690 g)
- ⭐ Plants, seeds
- ⚡ Least concern

Wigeon, Eurasian wigeon
Anas penelope
- 🌐 Northern Eurasia
- ▲ Marshes, lakes
- 🌙 Up to 19 in (48 cm)
- 🌙 Up to 31.5 in (80 cm)
- 🌙 Up to 28 oz (800 g)
- ⭐ Leaves, shoots
- ⚡ Least concern

Barnacle goose
Branta leucopsis
- 🌐 Eastern Greenland & North Atlantic islands (summer); Scotland & Netherlands (winter)
- ▲ Tundra, cliffs, pasture
- 🌙 24 in (60 cm)
- 🌙 4.5 ft (1.4 m)
- 🌙 4 lb (1.8 kg)
- ⭐ Grasses, low herbs
- ⚡ Least concern

Abyssinian blue-winged goose
Cyanochen cyanoptera
- 🌐 Ethiopia
- ▲ Rivers, freshwater lakes, swamps
- 🌙 24–30 in (60–76 cm)
- 🌙 4.3–5.6 ft (1.3–1.7 m)
- 🌙 3.3 lb (1.5 kg)
- ⭐ Grasses, herbs
- ⚡ Near threatened

Abyssinian blue-winged goose
Cyanochen cyanoptera

Whooper swan
Cygnus cygnus
- 🌐 Northern Eurasia
- ▲ Wetlands, forest
- 🌙 Up to 5.3 ft (1.6 m)
- 🌙 Up to 7.8 ft (2.4 m)
- 🌙 Up to 33 lb (15 kg)
- ⭐ Aquatic plants, grasses
- ⚡ Least concern

Pink-eared duck
Malacorhynchus membranaceus
- 🌐 Australia
- ▲ All wetland types; highly nomadic
- 🌙 Up to 18 in (45 cm)
- 🌙 29 in (73 cm)
- 🌙 13 oz (370 g)
- ⭐ Aquatic invertebrates
- ⚡ Least concern

ORDER SPHENISCIFORMES
PENGUINS

17 species

Emperor penguin
Aptenodytes forsteri
- 🌐 Antarctica
- ▲ Ocean, ice sheet
- 🌙 Up to 5 ft (1.5 m)
- 🌙 48–82 lb (22–37 kg)
- ⭐ Fish, crustaceans
- ⚡ Least concern

King penguin
Aptenodytes patagonicus
- 🌐 Antarctica
- ▲ Islands, ocean
- 🌙 35–40 in (90–100 cm)
- 🌙 20–38 lb (9–17 kg)
- ⭐ Fish, cephalopods
- ⚡ Least concern

Adélie penguin
Pygoscelis adeliae
- 🌐 Antarctica
- ▲ Ocean, islands, ice
- 🌙 28 in (70 cm)
- 🌙 8–17.5 lb (3.8–8 kg)
- ⭐ Crustaceans, fish, squid
- ⚡ Least concern

Chinstrap penguin
Pygoscelis antarcticus
- 🌐 Antarctica
- ▲ Ocean, islands, ice
- 🌙 28–30 in (70–76 cm)
- 🌙 7.5–12 lb (3.5–5.5 kg)
- ⭐ Crustaceans, fish, squid
- ⚡ Least concern

Magellanic penguin
Spheniscus magellanicus
- 🌐 Antarctica
- ▲ Coastal areas, islands, remote continental regions
- 🌙 28 in (70 cm)
- 🌙 11 lb (5 kg)
- ⭐ Cuttlefish, sardines, squid, krill, other crustaceans
- ⚡ Near threatened

ORDER GAVIIFORMES
DIVERS

5 species

Bearded vulture
Gypaetus barbatus

ORDER PODICIPEDIFORMES
GREBES

19 species

Eared grebe

Podiceps nigricollis

- ⊕ Western USA & Canada, southern Mexico, Europe, Asia, Africa
- ▲ Freshwater lakes & ponds (breeding), salt water (winter)
- ⚊ 12–14 in (30–35 cm)
- ⚹ 20–22 in (51–55 cm)
- ⚖ 7–26 oz (200–735 g)
- ✿ Aquatic insects, spiders, brine shrimp
- ⚡ Least concern

ORDER PROCELLARIIFORMES
ALBATROSSES & PETRELS

112 species

Wandering albatross

Diomedea exulans

- ⊕ Southern Ocean, Australia
- ▲ Ocean, islands
- ⚊ 3–4.5 ft (1–1.4 m)
- ⚹ 8–11.5 ft (2.5–3.5 m)
- ⚖ 15–25 lb (6.5–11.5 kg)
- ✿ Cephalopods, fish
- ⚡ Vulnerable

Snow petrel

Pagodroma nivea

- ⊕ Antarctic continent & peninsula, South Georgia
- ▲ Islands, ice, ocean
- ⚊ 12–16 in (30–40 cm)
- ⚹ 30–38 in (75–96 cm)
- ⚖ 7–14 oz (200–400 g)
- ✿ Crustaceans, fish, cephalopods
- ⚡ Least concern

Providence petrel

Pterodroma solandri

- ⊕ Pacific Ocean, oceanic islands
- ▲ Salt water, nests on islands
- ⚊ Up to 16 in (40 cm)
- ⚹ 40 in (100 cm)
- ⚖ 17.5 oz (500 g)
- ✿ Fish, cephalopods, crustaceans
- ⚡ Vulnerable

Short-tailed shearwater

Puffinus tenuirostris

- ⊕ South & southeast coasts of Australia, North Pacific
- ▲ Islands around southeast Australia, New Zealand to breed
- ⚊ 16–17 in (41–43 cm)
- ⚹ 39 in (99 cm)
- ⚖ 7 oz (200 g)
- ✿ Fish, small krill
- ⚡ Least concern

Wandering albatross
Diomedea exulans

ORDER PHOENICOPTERIFORMES
FLAMINGOS

5 species

Lesser flamingo

Phoenicopterus minor

- ⊕ Eastern & southern Africa
- ▲ Saline lakes
- ⚊ 31–36 in (78–91 cm)
- ⚹ 38 in (96 cm)
- ⚖ 24–32 oz (680–905 g)
- ✿ Algae, crustaceans
- ⚡ Near threatened

Greater flamingo

Phoenicopterus ruber roseus

- ⊕ South America, southern Europe to Indian subcontinent
- ▲ Deltas, coastal lagoons
- ⚊ Up to 4.3 ft (1.3 m)
- ⚹ Up to 5.6 ft (1.7 m)
- ⚖ Up to 8 lb (3.6 kg)
- ✿ Crustaceans, algae
- ⚡ Least concern

ORDER CICONIIFORMES
HERONS & ALLIES

118 species

Roseate spoonbill

Ajaia ajaja

- ⊕ Southern USA to southern South America
- ▲ Coastal mangroves, swamps
- ⚊ 32 in (80 cm)
- ⚹ 48 in (122 cm)
- ⚖ 2.6–4 lb (1.2–1.8 kg)
- ✿ Fish, frogs, crustaceans
- ⚡ Least concern

Great blue heron

Ardea herodias

- ⊕ Alaska & Canada south to northern South America
- ▲ Calm seacoasts, freshwater lakes & rivers
- ⚊ 3.3–4.6 ft (1–1.4 m)
- ⚹ 5.6–6.6 ft (1.7–2 m)
- ⚖ 4.6–5.5 lb (2.1–2.5 kg)
- ✿ Mostly fish but also invertebrates & small vertebrates
- ⚡ Least concern

Black stork

Ciconia nigra

- ⊕ Europe (summer); tropical Africa, China (winter)
- ▲ Forest, wetlands
- ⚊ Up to 3.3 ft (1 m)
- ⚹ Up to 5 ft (1.5 m)
- ⚖ Up to 6.5 lb (3 kg)
- ✿ Fish, invertebrates
- ⚡ Least concern

Least bittern

Ixobrychus exilis

- ⊕ Southern Canada to northern Argentina
- ▲ Freshwater or brackish marshes with tall emergent vegetation
- ⚊ 11–14 in (28–36 cm)
- ⚹ 16–18 in (41–46 cm)
- ⚖ 1.8–3.6 oz (50–100 g)
- ✿ Small fish, insects
- ⚡ Least concern

Yellow-crowned night heron

Nyctanassa violacea

- ⊕ USA to northeast South America
- ▲ Swamps, marshes
- ⚊ 24 in (60 cm)
- ⚹ Up to 44 in (112 cm)
- ⚖ 22 oz (625 g)
- ✿ Crustaceans, mollusks, frogs, fish
- ⚡ Least concern

Common spoonbill

Platalea leucorodia

- ⊕ Breeds southern Eurasia, northern Africa; winters in tropics
- ▲ Wetlands, estuaries
- ⚊ Up to 3 ft (0.9 m)
- ⚹ Up to 4.6 ft (1.4 m)
- ⚖ Up to 3.3 lb (1.5 kg)
- ✿ Fish, crabs, frogs
- ⚡ Least concern

Royal spoonbill

Platalea regia

- ⊕ Australia, New Zealand, Indonesia, Papua New Guinea, Pacific islands
- ▲ Wetlands, estuaries
- ⚊ Up to 29.5 in (75 cm)
- ⚹ Up to 47 in (120 cm)
- ⚖ Up to 30 oz (850 g)
- ✿ Fish, crabs, frogs, aquatic invertebrates
- ⚡ Least concern

Glossy ibis

Plegadis falcinellus

- ⊕ North & South America, Eurasia, Africa, Australia
- ▲ Wetlands, estuaries
- ⚊ Up to 26 in (65 cm)
- ⚹ Up to 41 in (105 cm)
- ⚖ Up to 29 oz (820 g)
- ✿ Crabs, insects, small snakes
- ⚡ Least concern

Australian white ibis

Threskiornis molucca

- ⊕ Eastern & northern Australia
- ▲ Fresh & tidal wetlands
- ⚊ 25.5–29.5 in (65–75 cm)
- ⚹ 44–50 in (110–125 cm)
- ⚖ 3–5 lb (1.4–2.4 kg)
- ✿ Fish, aquatic invertebrates
- ⚡ Least concern

ORDER PELECANIFORMES
PELICANS & ALLIES

63 species

Australian pelican

Pelecanus conspicillatus

- ⊕ Australia, Papua New Guinea, western Indonesia
- ▲ Rivers, estuaries, lakes, water
- ⚊ Up to 6.2 ft (1.9 m)
- ⚹ 8.5 ft (2.6 m)
- ⚖ Up to 29 lb (13 kg)
- ✿ Fish
- ⚡ Least concern

Dalmatian pelican

Pelecanus crispus

- ⊕ Breeds in southern Eurasia, winters to India
- ▲ Swamps, shallow lakes
- ⚊ Up to 5.6 ft (1.7 m)
- ⚹ Up to 10 ft (3 m)
- ⚖ Up to 33 lb (15 kg)
- ✿ Fish
- ⚡ Vulnerable

Galápagos brown pelican
Pelecanus occidentalis urinator

Galápagos brown pelican

Pelecanus occidentalis urinator

- ⊕ Galápagos Islands
- ▲ Bays, ocean, beaches, lagoons
- ⚊ 3.6–4.6 ft (1.1–1.4 m)
- ⚹ 6.5 ft (2 m)
- ⚖ 10 lb (4.5 kg)
- ✿ Fish
- ⚡ Least concern

Blue-footed booby

Sula nebouxii

- ⊕ Northwest Mexico to northern Peru, Galápagos Islands
- ▲ Marine, tropical & subtropical islands
- ⚊ 32 in (81 cm)
- ⚹ 5 ft (1.5 m)
- ⚖ 3 lb (1.4 kg)
- ✿ Fish, squid, offal
- ⚡ Least concern

Peruvian booby

Sula variegata

- ⊕ Peru Current, Chile, Peru
- ▲ Marine
- ⚊ 30 in (76 cm)
- ⚖ Up to 2.9 lb (1.3 kg)
- ✿ Fish, squid, offal
- ⚡ Least concern

ORDER FALCONIFORMES
BIRDS OF PREY

302 species

Family Accipitridae

Hawks, eagles, kites, harriers & Old World vultures
234 species

Sharp-shinned hawk

Accipiter striatus

- ⊕ North & South America
- ▲ Usually breeds in coniferous forest; various habitats in winter
- ⚊ 9.5–13 in (24–34 cm)
- ⚹ 17–22 in (43–56 cm)
- ⚖ 3.1–7.7 oz (87–218 g)
- ✿ Small birds, also large insects, small mammals
- ⚡ Least concern

Wedge-tailed eagle

Aquila audax

- ⊕ Australia, Papua New Guinea
- ▲ All terrestrial habitats
- ⚊ Up to 43 in (110 cm)
- ⚹ 9 ft (2.7 m)
- ⚖ 8.8 lb (4 kg)
- ✿ Medium-sized mammals, lizards, birds, carrion (especially roadkill)
- ⚡ Least concern (Tasmanian subspecies endangered)

Golden eagle

Aquila chrysaetos

- ⊕ Northern Hemisphere
- ▲ Forest, mountains
- ⚊ Up to 32 in (82 cm)
- ⚹ Up to 7 ft (2 m)
- ⚖ Up to 11.7 lb (5.3 kg)
- ✿ Mammals, birds
- ⚡ Least concern (rare in Europe)

Galápagos hawk

Buteo galapagoensis

- ⊕ Galápagos Islands
- ▲ Tropical dry forest & shrubland
- ⚊ 21 in (54 cm)
- ⚹ 47 in (120 cm)
- ⚖ 24 oz (680 g)
- ✿ Lizards, snakes, rodents, birds, giant centipedes & other invertebrates, carrion
- ⚡ Vulnerable

Red-tailed hawk

Buteo jamaicensis

- ⊕ North & Central America
- ▲ Forest, desert, urban areas
- ⚊ 18–26 in (46–66 cm)
- ⚹ 3.6–5 ft (1.1–1.5 m)
- ⚖ ♂ up to 2.5 lb (1 kg), ♀ up to 3.5 lb (1.6 kg)
- ✿ Small mammals, birds, reptiles
- ⚡ Least concern

Northern harrier

Circus cyaneus

- ⊕ North & Central America, north & central Asia, north Africa
- ▲ Open grassland, woods along streams, wetlands
- ⚊ 18–20 in (46–51 cm)
- ⚹ 40–46 in (102–117 cm)
- ⚖ 10.6–26.5 oz (300–750 g)
- ✿ Mice, small mammals, small birds
- ⚡ Least concern

Bearded vulture

Gypaetus barbatus

- ⊕ Europe, Africa, India, Tibet
- ▲ Mountains, islands
- ⚊ Up to 9 ft (2.8 m)
- ⚹ Up to 9 ft (2.8 m)
- ⚖ Up to 15.5 lb (7 kg)
- ✿ Bones
- ⚡ Least concern

Bald eagle

Haliaeetus leucocephalus

- ⊕ North America
- ▲ Lakes, rivers, seacoasts
- ⚊ Up to 30 in (76 cm)
- ⚹ 6.5 ft (2 m)
- ⚖ 6.5–14 lb (3–6.3 kg)
- ✿ Fish, waterfowl, mammals, carrion
- ⚡ Least concern

Harpy eagle

Harpia harpyja

- ⊕ Southern Mexico to northern Argentina
- ▲ Tropical forest
- ⚊ 41 in (104 cm)
- ⚹ 7 ft (2.1 m)
- ⚖ 20 lb (9 kg)
- ✿ Sloths, monkeys, opossums, reptiles, birds
- ⚡ Near threatened

Red kite

Milvus milvus

- ⊕ Europe & northwest Africa
- ▲ Mountain, forest
- ⚊ Up to 25 in (63.5 cm)
- ⚹ Up to 6.6 ft (2 m)
- ⚖ Up to 3 lb (1.4 kg)
- ✿ Small mammals, birds, carrion
- ⚡ Near threatened

Philippine eagle

Pithecophaga jefferyi

- ⊕ Philippine islands (Luzon, Mindanao)
- ▲ Rain forest
- ⚊ ♀ 3 ft (1 m)
- ⚹ 6.5 ft (2 m)
- ⚖ ♂ 11 lb (5 kg), ♀ 15.5 lb (7 kg)
- ✿ Small arboreal mammals, reptiles
- ⚡ Critically endangered

Martial eagle

Polemaetus bellicosus

- ⊕ Sub-Saharan Africa
- ▲ Semidesert, savanna
- ⚊ 30–35.5 in (76–90 cm)
- ⚹ 6.2–8.5 ft (1.9–2.6 m)
- ⚖ 11.5 lb (5.2 kg)
- ✿ Birds, small mammals
- ⚡ Least concern

Lappet-faced vulture
Torgos tracheliotus
- ⊕ East & southern Africa
- ▲ Semiarid or desert areas
- ↥ 31–45 in (78–114 cm)
- ⤢ 8 ft (2.5 m)
- ⚖ 15 lb (6.7 kg)
- ✪ Carrion, live prey
- ⚡ Vulnerable

Family Pandionidae
Osprey
1 species

Osprey
Pandion haliaetus
- ⊕ North & South America, Eurasia, Africa, Australia
- ▲ River valley, coasts
- ↥ Up to 24 in (61 cm)
- ⤢ Up to 6 ft (1.8 m)
- ⚖ Up to 4.4 lb (2 kg)
- ✪ Fish
- ⚡ Least concern

Family Falconidae
Falcons & caracaras
60 species

Lanner falcon
Falco biarmicus
- ⊕ Africa, southeast Europe, northwest Asia
- ▲ Fields
- ↥ Up to 16.5 in (42 cm)
- ⤢ Up to 40 in (100 cm)
- ⚖ Up to 26.5 oz (750 g)
- ✪ Small birds, insects, mammals
- ⚡ Least concern

Eleonora's falcon
Falco eleonorae
- ⊕ Breeds on European islands, winters in Madagascar
- ▲ Scrub, cliffs
- ↥ Up to 15 in (38 cm)
- ⤢ Up to 47 in (120 cm)
- ⚖ Up to 12 oz (340 g)
- ✪ Insects
- ⚡ Least concern

Lesser kestrel
Falco naumanni
- ⊕ Sub-Saharan Africa
- ▲ Desert, grassland, steppe
- ↥ 11–13 in (28–33 cm)
- ⤢ 25–28 in (64–72 cm)
- ⚖ 4.5–6 oz (130–170 g)
- ✪ Insects, such as grasshoppers & termites
- ⚡ Vulnerable

Peregrine falcon
Falco peregrinus
- ⊕ Worldwide except extreme polar regions & New Zealand
- ▲ Mountain, river valley
- ↥ Up to 19 in (48 cm)
- ⤢ Up to 43 in (110 cm)
- ⚖ Up to 3.5 lb (1.5 kg)
- ✪ Birds, mammals
- ⚡ Least concern

Gyrfalcon
Falco rusticolus
- ⊕ Arctic coasts & islands of North America & Eurasia
- ▲ Tundra, mountains
- ↥ 19–26 in (48–66 cm)
- ⤢ 3.6–5.2 ft (1.1–1.6 m)
- ⚖ ♂ up to 3 lb (1.4 kg), ♀ up to 4.6 lb (2.1 kg)
- ✪ Other birds such as grouse; mammals such as marmots & hares
- ⚡ Least concern

American kestrel
Falco sparverius
- ⊕ Canada, USA
- ▲ Diverse open habitats from meadows & deserts to urban areas
- ↥ 9–12 in (23–30 cm)
- ⤢ 20–24 in (51–60 cm)
- ⚖ 2.8–5.8 oz (80–165 g)
- ✪ Small vertebrates, large insects
- ⚡ Least concern

Family Sagittariidae
Secretary bird
1 species

Secretary bird
Sagittarius serpentarius
- ⊕ Sub-Saharan Africa
- ▲ Grassland, savanna
- ↥ 4–5 ft (1.2–1.5 m)
- ⤢ 6.8 ft (2 m)
- ⚖ 7 lb (3.3 kg)
- ✪ Small mammals, lizards, snakes, large insects, young birds reptiles, insects
- ⚡ Least concern

Family Cathartidae
New World vultures
7 species
* Some schemes place this family into its own order, Cathartiformes.

Turkey vulture
Cathartes aura
- ⊕ North & South America
- ▲ Forest to grassland & desert
- ↥ 26 in (66 cm)
- ⤢ 5.6 ft (1.7 m)
- ⚖ 3 lb (1.4 kg)
- ✪ Scavenger, carrion
- ⚡ Least concern

American black vulture
Coragyps atratus
- ⊕ Southeastern USA to South America
- ▲ Open land with wooded or brushy areas; many other lowland habitats
- ↥ 24–27 in (61–69 cm)
- ⤢ 4.5–5 ft (1.3–1.5 m)
- ⚖ 3.5–5 lb (1.6–2.2 kg)
- ✪ Carrion
- ⚡ Least concern

Condor, Andean condor
Vultur gryphus
- ⊕ Andes (South America)
- ▲ Open grassland, mountains
- ↥ Up to 4.3 ft (1.3 m)
- ⤢ 10.8 ft (3.3 m)
- ⚖ Up to 33 lb (15 kg)
- ✪ Carrion from large & medium-sized mammals
- ⚡ Near threatened

ORDER GRUIFORMES
CRANES & ALLIES
212 species

Black-crowned crane
Balearica pavonina
- ⊕ Sub-Saharan Africa
- ▲ Marshes, swamps
- ↥ 40 in (100 cm)
- ⤢ 6.2 ft (1.9 m)
- ⚖ 8 lb (3.6 kg)
- ✪ Insects, reptiles, small mammals
- ⚡ Near threatened

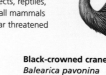

Black-crowned crane
Balearica pavonina

Lord Howe Island woodhen
Gallirallus sylvestris
- ⊕ Lord Howe Island (Australia)
- ▲ Rain forest
- ↥ Up to 18 in (46 cm)
- ⤢ Up to 20.5 in (52 cm)
- ⚖ Up to 18.7 oz (530 g)
- ✪ Insects, mollusks, invertebrates
- ⚡ Endangered

Whooping crane
Grus americana
- ⊕ Breeds in northwest Canada, winters in Texas; introduced central Florida & Wisconsin, USA
- ▲ Freshwater marshes, prairie, grain fields, shallow lakes, salt marshes
- ↥ 4.9 ft (1.5 m)
- ⤢ 7.5 ft (2.3 m)
- ⚖ 13–17 lb (6–7.8 kg)
- ✪ Plants, grain, fish, frogs, mollusks, crustaceans, insects
- ⚡ Endangered

Common crane
Grus grus
- ⊕ Breeds in northern Eurasia, winters in Africa & southern Eurasia
- ▲ Wetlands
- ↥ Up to 4.3 ft (1.3 m)
- ⤢ Up to 7.8 ft (2.4 m)
- ⚖ Up to 13.2 lb (6 kg)
- ✪ Leaves, berries, insects, small birds, mammals
- ⚡ Least concern

Red-crowned crane
Grus leucogeranus
- ⊕ Breeds in Siberia, Japan; winters in Korea, Taiwan, China
- ▲ Marshes, riverbanks, rice fields, other wet areas
- ↥ Height: 4.5 ft (1.4 m)
- ⤢ Up to 8 ft (2.5 m)
- ⚖ 17–22 lb (7.7–10 kg)
- ✪ Amphibians, fish, aquatic invertebrates, aquatic plants
- ⚡ Critically endangered

Brolga
Grus rubicunda
- ⊕ Tropical & eastern Australia
- ▲ Grassland, wetlands, farmland
- ↥ Up to 4.2 ft (1.3 m)
- ⤢ Up to 9 ft (2.7 m)
- ⚖ 13 lb (6 kg)
- ✪ Invertebrates, small vertebrates, tubers, shoots
- ⚡ Least concern

Hoatzin
Opisthocomus hoazin*
- ⊕ Orinoco delta & Amazon in South America
- ▲ Tropical rain forest
- ↥ 26 in (66 cm)
- ⤢ 40 in (100 cm)
- ⚖ 32 oz (900 g)
- ✪ Leaves, shoots of marsh plants
- ⚡ Least concern
* Some schemes place the hoatzin into its own order, Opisthocomiformes.

Great bustard
Otis tarda
- ⊕ Central Eurasia
- ▲ Open grassland
- ↥ 31.5–43 in (80–110 cm)
- ⤢ 5.9–8.2 ft (1.8–2.5 m)
- ⚖ ♂ 22–35 lb (10–16 kg), ♀ 8–11 lb (3.5–5 kg)
- ✪ Seeds, insects, worms, frogs
- ⚡ Vulnerable

Purple swamphen
Porphyrio porphyrio
- ⊕ Europe, Africa, tropical Asia, Australasia
- ▲ Wetlands, lakes, rivers, parks
- ↥ Up to 20 in (51 cm)
- ⤢ Up to 40 in (100 cm)
- ⚖ Up to 2.2 lb (1 kg)
- ✪ Aquatic vegetation, small invertebrates & vertebrates
- ⚡ Least concern

Kagu
Rhynochetos jubatus
- ⊕ New Caledonia
- ▲ Rain forest, montane forest
- ↥ Up to 22 in (56 cm)
- ⤢ Up to 32 in (81 cm)
- ⚖ Up to 2.4 lb (1.1 kg)
- ✪ Mollusks, worms, arthropods, lizards
- ⚡ Endangered

Rouget's rail
Rougetius rougetii
- ⊕ Eritrea, Ethiopia
- ▲ Marshy areas of montane grassland
- ↥ 5.5–20 in (14–51 cm)
- ✪ Seeds, aquatic insects, crustaceans
- ⚡ Near threatened

ORDER CHARADRIIFORMES
WADERS & SHOREBIRDS
351 species

Marbled murrelet
Brachyramphus marmoratus
- ⊕ Pacific coast of North America
- ▲ Breeds in coastal old-growth coniferous forest; winters offshore
- ↥ 9–10 in (23–25.5 cm)
- ⤢ 16 in (41 cm)
- ⚖ 9.1–12.6 oz (258–357 g)
- ✪ Small fish, shrimps, other crustaceans
- ⚡ Endangered

Subantarctic skua, Brown skua
Catharacta lonnbergi
- ⊕ Subantarctic, Antarctic
- ▲ Nests on islands; disperses over ocean in non-breeding season
- ↥ 20–25 in (51–64 cm)
- ⤢ 4–5 ft (1.25–1.6 m)
- ⚖ 3–5.5 lb (1.3–2.5 kg)
- ✪ Scavenges seabird eggs, chicks & adults, seal placentas & pups; predates burrowing petrels
- ⚡ Least concern

Piping plover
Charadrius melodus
- ⊕ Breeds in midwest Canada & USA, Great Lakes, Atlantic coast; winters along US Atlantic & Gulf coasts
- ▲ Open sandy beaches, alkali flats
- ↥ 7 in (18 cm)
- ⤢ 15 in (38 cm)
- ⚖ 1.5–2.2 oz (43–63 g)
- ✪ Insects, aquatic invertebrates
- ⚡ Near threatened

Dotterel
Charadrius morinellus
- ⊕ Northern Eurasia
- ▲ Mountain, tundra, mudflat
- ↥ Up to 8 in (20 cm)
- ⤢ Up to 23 in (59 cm)
- ⚖ Up to 3.8 oz (110 g)
- ✪ Insects, invertebrates
- ⚡ Least concern

Snowy sheathbill
Chionis albus
- ⊕ Breeds South Atlantic Ocean & Antarctic Peninsula; some winter in Falkland Islands
- ▲ Rocky islands & coast
- ↥ 14–16 in (35–40 cm)
- ⤢ 30–34 in (76–86 cm)
- ⚖ 16–28 oz (460–800 g)
- ✪ Scavenges carrion, eggs, placentas, feces, marine items
- ⚡ Least concern

Puffin, Atlantic puffin
Fratercula arctica
- ⊕ Breeds along North Atlantic coasts; winters in warmer seas
- ▲ Rocky coast & islands
- ↥ 14 in (36 cm)
- ⤢ 30 in (76 cm)
- ⚖ 18 oz (500 g)
- ✪ Small fish caught near surface
- ⚡ Least concern

Eurasian oystercatcher
Haematopus ostralegus
- ⊕ Western Europe, central Eurasia, eastern Asia
- ▲ Coastal
- ↥ Up to 16.5 in (42 cm)
- ⤢ Up to 33 in (83 cm)
- ⚖ Up to 19 oz (540 g)
- ✪ Mollusks, mussels, worms
- ⚡ Least concern

Little gull
Hydrocoloeus minutus
- ⊕ Breeds northern Eurasia, northern Canada; winters western Europe, northeast USA
- ▲ Estuaries, coastal marshes
- ↥ Up to 10 in (25 cm)
- ⤢ Up to 31 in (78 cm)
- ⚖ Up to 4.2 oz (120 g)
- ✪ Insects, fish, invertebrates
- ⚡ Least concern

Herring gull
Larus argentatus
- ⊕ North America, Eurasia
- ▲ Coastal
- ⬌ Up to 24 in (60 cm)
- ⤢ Up to 4.6 ft (1.4 m)
- ⚖ Up to 2.6 lb (1.2 kg)
- ✪ Omnivorous, scavenges food
- ⚡ Least concern

Laughing gull
Larus atricilla
- ⊕ US Atlantic & Gulf of Mexico coast
- ▲ Ocean coasts
- ↥ 15–18 in (38–46 cm)
- ⤢ 36–47 in (91–120 cm)
- ⚖ 7.8–13 oz (203–371 g)
- ✪ Aquatic & terrestrial invertebrates, fish, squid, garbage, berries
- ⚡ Least concern

Sooty tern
Onychoprion fuscatus
- ⊕ Tropical oceans
- ▲ Ocean, islands
- ↥ Up to 18 in (46 cm)
- ⤢ 36 in (91 cm)
- ⚖ Up to 10 oz (285 g)
- ✪ Fish
- ⚡ Least concern

Eurasian golden plover
Pluvialis apricaria
- ⊕ Breeds northern Eurasia; winters southern Europe, north Africa
- ▲ Fields, tidal flats, tundra
- ↥ Up to 11 in (28 cm)
- ⤢ Up to 28 in (72 cm)
- ⚖ Up to 7.7 oz (220 g)
- ✪ Insects, crustaceans, berries
- ⚡ Least concern

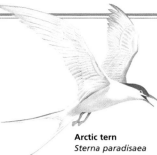

Arctic tern
Sterna paradisaea

Black skimmer
Rynchops niger
- 🌐 North & South America
- ⛰ Estuaries, coasts, ponds, lakes
- ↥ 16–20 in (41–51 cm)
- ⤢ 44 in (112 cm)
- ⚖ 7.5–15.8 oz (212–447 g)
- ✪ Small fish
- ⚡ Least concern (threatened or endangered in some US states)

South polar skua
Stercorarius maccormicki
- 🌐 Antarctica
- ⛰ Breeds on ice-free areas, typically in association with penguin colonies
- ↥ 20–22 in (51–56 cm)
- ⤢ 4.3–5.2 ft (1.3–1.6 m)
- ⚖ 1.3–3.5 lb (0.6–1.6 kg)
- ✪ Penguin eggs, chicks & adults, small fish
- ⚡ Least concern

Arctic tern
Sterna paradisaea
- 🌐 Circumpolar, breeds in the far north, winters in the far south
- ⛰ Hatches in the Arctic, migrates south to feed, returns north to breed
- ↥ 14 in (36 cm)
- ⤢ 30–34 in (76–85 cm)
- ⚖ 3.4–4.2 oz (95–120 g)
- ✪ Small fish, crustaceans
- ⚡ Least concern

Northern lapwing
Vanellus vanellus
- 🌐 Temperate Eurasia
- ⛰ Fields, mudflats
- ↥ Up to 12 in (31 cm)
- ⤢ Up to 28 in (72 cm)
- ⚖ Up to 7 oz (198 g)
- ✪ Insects, invertebrates
- ⚡ Least concern

ORDER PTEROCLIDIFORMES
SANDGROUSE
16 species

Burchell's sandgrouse
Pterocles burchelli
- 🌐 Southern Africa
- ⛰ Desert, scrubland
- ↥ 9–16 in (24–40 cm)
- ✪ Seeds
- ⚡ Least concern

Sandgrouse, Pallas's sandgrouse
Syrrhaptes paradoxus
- 🌐 Central Asia
- ⛰ Dry steppe
- ↥ 12–16 in (30–41 cm)
- ⤢ 27.5 in (70 cm)
- ⚖ 7–10.6 oz (200–300 g)
- ✪ Legume seeds, plant shoots
- ⚡ Least concern

ORDER COLUMBIFORMES
PIGEONS
313 species

Passenger pigeon
Ectopistes migratorius
- 🌐 Eastern North America
- ⛰ Forest, prairie edge
- ↥ 14 in (35 cm)
- ⤢ 8 in (20 cm)
- ✪ Seeds
- ⚡ Extinct

Dodo
Raphus cucullatus
- 🌐 Island of Mauritius
- ⛰ Forest
- ↥ 40 in (100 cm)
- ⚖ 44 lb (20 kg)
- ✪ Fruits, seeds
- ⚡ Extinct

ORDER PSITTACIFORMES
PARROTS
364 species

Australian king parrot
Alisterus scapularis
- 🌐 Eastern Australia
- ⛰ Rain forest, eucalypt forest, orchards, parks, gardens
- ↥ Up to 18 in (46 cm) including tail
- ⚖ Up to 9.7 oz (275 g)
- ✪ Seeds, fruits
- ⚡ Least concern

Blue-fronted parrot
Amazona aestiva
- 🌐 Bolivia, Brazil, Paraguay, northern Argentina; introduced Stuttgart, Germany
- ⛰ Tropical forest, palm groves
- ↥ 14 in (35 cm)
- ⤢ 8 in (20 cm)
- ⚖ 10 lb (4.5 kg)
- ✪ Avocado & other fruits, seeds
- ⚡ Least concern

Orange-winged parrot
Amazona amazonica
- 🌐 Tropical South America
- ⛰ Tropical forest
- ↥ 14 in (35 cm)
- ⤢ 35 in (90 cm)
- ⚖ 12 oz (340 g)
- ✪ Seeds, fruits, berries, flowers, nuts
- ⚡ Least concern

Scarlet macaw
Ara macao
- 🌐 Central America to Amazonian Peru & Brazil
- ⛰ Tall deciduous trees of forests & rivers
- ↥ Up to 36 in (91 cm) including tail
- ⤢ 45 in (114 cm)
- ⚖ Up to 2.5 lb (1 kg)
- ✪ Fruits, seeds, clay
- ⚡ Least concern

Major Mitchell cockatoo
Cacatua leadbeateri
- 🌐 Inland Australia
- ⛰ Mallee, mulga, timbered watercourses
- ↥ Up to 16 in (41 cm)
- ⚖ Up to 17 oz (480 g)
- ✪ Fruits, seeds
- ⚡ Least concern

Red-tailed black cockatoo
Calyptorhynchus banksii
- 🌐 Australia, especially northern half
- ⛰ Rain forest, woodland, shrubland, grassland
- ↥ Up to 4.6 ft (1.4 m)
- ⤢ 16 in (41 cm)
- ⚖ Up to 30.6 oz (870 g)
- ✪ Leaves, shoots
- ⚡ Least concern

Red-crowned parakeet
Cyanoramphus novaezelandiae
- 🌐 New Zealand offshore islands
- ↥ 10.5 in (27 cm)
- ⚖ 1.8–3.9 oz (50–110 g)
- ✪ Seeds, fruit, berries
- ⚡ Vulnerable

Double-eyed fig parrot
Cyclopsitta diophthalma
- 🌐 New Guinea, tropical coast of Australia
- ⛰ Rain forest
- ↥ Up to 6 in (16 cm)
- ✪ Fruits, fungi, lichens, insects
- ⚡ Least concern

Budgerigar
Melopsittacus undulatus
- 🌐 Drier parts of Australia
- ⛰ Scrubland, open woodland, grassland
- ↥ 7 in (18 cm)
- ⚖ 1–1.4 oz (30–40 g)
- ✪ Grass seeds
- ⚡ Least concern

Orange-bellied parrot
Neophema chrysogaster
- 🌐 Southwest Tasmania, coastal Victoria
- ⛰ Salt marsh, grassland
- ↥ 8 in (20 cm)
- ⚖ 1.6 oz (45 g)
- ✪ Seeds, berries, shrubs, grasses
- ⚡ Critically endangered

Turquoise parrot
Neophema pulchella
- 🌐 Eastern Australia
- ⛰ Grassland, open woodland
- ↥ 8 in (20 cm)
- ⤢ 16 in (40 cm)
- ⚖ Up to 1.4 oz (40 g)
- ✪ Seeds
- ⚡ Least concern

Kea
Nestor notabilis
- 🌐 South Island of New Zealand
- ⛰ Alpine areas, subalpine forest
- ↥ Up to 20 in (51 cm)
- ⤢ 40 in (100 cm)
- ⚖ Up to 2.2 lb (1 kg)
- ✪ Plants, beetle larvae, other birds, mammals including sheep
- ⚡ Vulnerable

African gray parrot
Psittacus erithacus
- 🌐 West & central Africa
- ⛰ Rain forest
- ↥ 13–16 in (33–41 cm)
- ⤢ 18–20 in (46–51 cm)
- ⚖ 16 oz (450 g)
- ✪ Seeds, fruits
- ⚡ Near threatened

Kakapo
Strigops habroptila
- 🌐 New Zealand offshore islands
- ⛰ Forest
- ↥ Up to 25 in (64 cm)
- ⤢ Up to 36 in (91 cm)
- ⚖ Up to 5 lb (2.5 kg)
- ✪ Fruits, leaves, stems, seeds
- ⚡ Critically endangered

Rainbow lorikeet
Trichoglossus haematodus
- 🌐 Australia, eastern Indonesia, Papua New Guinea, New Caledonia, Solomon Islands, Vanuatu
- ⛰ Rain forest, eucalypt forest, woodland, parks, gardens
- ↥ Up to 13 in (33 cm)
- ⤢ 7 in (17 cm)
- ⚖ 4.5 oz (130 g)
- ✪ Fruits, nectar
- ⚡ Least concern

ORDER CUCULIFORMES
CUCKOOS & TURACOS
162 species

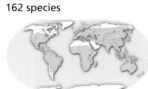

Greater roadrunner
Geococcyx californianus
- 🌐 Southwest USA, Mexico
- ⛰ Desert, scrubland
- ↥ 22 in (56 cm)
- ⤢ Up to 24 in (61 cm)
- ⚖ 10.5 oz (300 g)
- ✪ Insects, small reptiles, rodents
- ⚡ Least concern

Guira cuckoo
Guira guira
- 🌐 South America
- ⛰ Open scrubby areas
- ↥ 16 in (40 cm)
- ⤢ 3.6–5 ft (1.1–1.5 m)
- ⚖ 3.7 oz (105 g)
- ✪ Spiders, frogs, small mammals, smaller birds
- ⚡ Least concern

Lady Ross's turaco
Musophaga rossae
- 🌐 Central & southern Africa
- ⛰ Rain forest
- ↥ 15–18 in (38–46 cm)
- ⚖ 16 oz (450 g)
- ✪ Leaves, fruits
- ⚡ Least concern

ORDER STRIGIFORMES
OWLS
195 species

Tengmalm's owl, Boreal owl
Aegolius funereus
- 🌐 Northern North America & Eurasia
- ⛰ Mountain, boreal forest
- ↥ Up to 12 in (30 cm)
- ⤢ Up to 24 in (62 cm)
- ⚖ Up to 4 oz (114 g)
- ✪ Rodents
- ⚡ Least concern

Burrowing owl, Bolivian burrowing owl
Athene cunicularia
- 🌐 North & South America
- ⛰ Grassland, rangeland, desert
- ↥ 10 in (25 cm)
- ⤢ 22 in (56 cm)
- ⚖ 6 oz (170 g)
- ✪ Large insects, small rodents, reptiles
- ⚡ Least concern

Eagle owl, Eurasian eagle owl
Bubo bubo
- 🌐 Eurasia
- ⛰ Mountains, forest
- ↥ Up to 28 in (71 cm)
- ⤢ Up to 7 ft (2 m)
- ⚖ Up to 9 lb (4 kg)
- ✪ Small mammals
- ⚡ Least concern

Snowy owl
Nyctea scandiaca
- 🌐 Arctic Alaska, Canada, Greenland & Eurasia
- ⛰ Tundra, boreal forest
- ↥ Up to 28 in (70 cm)
- ⤢ 4.2–5 ft (1.3–1.5 m)
- ⚖ 4.4 lb (2 kg)
- ✪ Lemmings & other small mammals
- ⚡ Least concern

Spectacled owl
Pulsatrix perspicillata
- 🌐 Mexico, Central America, northern South America (not Andes)
- ⛰ Rain forest
- ↥ Up to 18 in (46 cm)
- ⤢ 36 in (91 cm)
- ⚖ Up to 32 oz (900 g)
- ✪ Mice, skunk, insects, spiders, caterpillars, bats, birds, frogs
- ⚡ Least concern

Great gray owl
Strix nebulosa
- 🌐 Northern hemisphere
- ⛰ Forest
- ↥ Up to 33 in (84 cm)
- ⤢ Up to 5 ft (1.5 m)
- ⚖ Up to 3.2 lb (1.5 kg)
- ✪ Rodents
- ⚡ Least concern

Ural owl
Strix uralensis
- 🌐 Scandinavia to Japan & Korea
- ⛰ Taiga forest
- ↥ 20–23 in (51–59 cm)
- ⤢ 45–49 in (115–125 cm)
- ⚖ ♂ up to 24.6 oz (700 g), ♀ up to 2.5 lb (1.2 kg)
- ✪ Rodents, smaller birds
- ⚡ Least concern

ORDER CAPRIMULGIFORMES
NIGHTJARS & ALLIES
118 species

White-winged nightjar
Eleothreptus candicans
- 🌐 Bolivia, Brazil, Paraguay
- ⛰ Dry lowland grassland
- ↥ 8 in (20 cm)
- ⤢ 11 in (28 cm)
- ⚖ 1.8 oz (50 g)
- ✪ Beetles, moths
- ⚡ Endangered

Orange-bellied parrot
Neophema chrysogaster

Scarlet macaws
Ara macao

ORDER APODIFORMES
HUMMINGBIRDS & SWIFTS
429 species

Costa's hummingbird
Calypte costae
- 🌐 Southwestern USA & Mexico
- ⛰ Desert, semidesert
- 📏 Up to 4 in (10 cm)
- ✈ Up to 4 in (10 cm)
- ⚖ 0.1 oz (3 g)
- ✿ Flower nectar, tree sap, small insects
- ⚡ Least concern

ORDER COLIIFORMES
MOUSEBIRDS
6 species

ORDER TROGONIFORMES
TROGONS
39 species

Resplendent quetzal
Pharomachrus mocinno
- 🌐 Central America
- ⛰ Montane cloud forest
- 📏 14 in (36 cm)
- 📏 ♂ 25 in (64 cm) tail streamer
- ✈ 16 in (40 cm)
- ⚖ 7.5 oz (210 g)
- ✿ Fruits, insects, frogs
- ⚡ Near threatened

ORDER CORACIIFORMES
KINGFISHERS & ALLIES
209 species

Red-knobbed hornbill
Aceros cassidix
- 🌐 Indonesia
- ⛰ Tropical rain forest
- 📏 27–32 in (70–80 cm)
- ⚖ ♂ 5.3–5.5 lb (2.4–2.5 kg)
- ✿ Mainly figs, also insects, other fruits
- ⚡ Least concern

European kingfisher
Alcedo atthis
- 🌐 Eurasia, northern Africa
- ⛰ Rivers, marshes
- 📏 Up to 6 in (16 cm)
- ✈ Up to 10 in (25 cm)
- ⚖ Up to 1.4 oz (40 g)
- ✿ Freshwater fish, also aquatic invertebrates
- ⚡ Least concern

Laughing kookaburra
Dacelo novaeguineae

Southern ground hornbill
Bucorvus cafer
- 🌐 Sub-Saharan Africa
- ⛰ Savanna, woodland, grassland
- 📏 3–4.3 ft (0.9–1.3 m)
- ✈ 3.9–5.9 ft (1.2–1.8 m)
- ⚖ 7–13.5 lb (3.2–6.2 kg)
- ✿ Small vertebrates, insects
- ⚡ Least concern

Laughing kookaburra
Dacelo novaeguineae
- 🌐 Eastern & southwestern Australia
- ⛰ Woods, open forest, gardens, parks
- 📏 Up to 18 in (47 cm)
- ✈ 25–26 in (64–66 cm)
- ⚖ 12 oz (340 g)
- ✿ Reptiles, frogs, invertebrates
- ⚡ Least concern

Northern carmine bee-eater
Merops nubicus
- 🌐 Sub-Saharan Africa
- ⛰ Savanna, woodland
- 📏 14 in (35 cm)
- 📏 12 in (30 cm)
- ✈ 11–12.5 in (28–32 cm)
- ⚖ 1.4–2.1 oz (40–60 g)
- ✿ Bees & other flying insects
- ⚡ Least concern

Southern yellow-billed hornbill
Tockus leucomelas
- 🌐 Southern Africa
- ⛰ Woodland, grassland
- 📏 19–24 in (48–61 cm)
- ✈ 5.9–7 ft (1.8–2 m)
- ⚖ 4–6 lb (1.8–2.7 kg)
- ✿ Seeds, insects
- ⚡ Least concern

Cuban tody
Todus multicolor
- 🌐 Cuba
- ⛰ Dry mountainous scrubland, tropical forest, mountainous evergreen forest, pine forest, seashore
- 📏 4 in (10 cm)
- ✈ 4.3 in (10.9 cm)
- ⚖ 0.2 oz (6 g)
- ✿ Small adult & larval insects, spiders, small lizards
- ⚡ Least concern

ORDER PICIFORMES
WOODPECKERS & ALLIES
398 species

Northern flicker
Colaptes auratus
- 🌐 North & Central America, West Indies
- ⛰ Open areas
- 📏 12 in (30 cm)
- ✈ 20 in (50 cm)
- ⚖ 4.5 oz (130 g)
- ✿ Insects, especially ants
- ⚡ Least concern

Versicolor barbet
Eubucco versicolor
- 🌐 Bolivia, Peru
- ⛰ Tropical forest
- 📏 9 in (23 cm)
- ✈ 27 in (68 cm)
- ⚖ 3.9 oz (110 g)
- ✿ Fruits, insects
- ⚡ Least concern

Northern flicker
Colaptes auratus

Gila woodpecker
Melanerpes uropygialis
- 🌐 Southwestern USA
- ⛰ Desert with saguaro & other large cacti for nesting; streamside woodland, dry forest
- 📏 9 in (23 cm)
- ✈ 16 in (41 cm)
- ⚖ 1.8–2.8 oz (51–79 g)
- ✿ Insects, fruits, seeds, bird eggs, lizards
- ⚡ Least concern

Keel-billed toucan
Ramphastos sulfuratus
- 🌐 Southern Mexico to Venezuela & Colombia
- ⛰ Rain forest
- 📏 25 in (63 cm)
- ✈ 16 in (41 cm)
- ⚖ 14 oz (400 g)
- ✿ Fruits, insects, bird eggs, tree frogs
- ⚡ Least concern

Toco toucan
Ramphastos toco
- 🌐 Central & eastern South America
- ⛰ Lowlands, swamps, savanna, canopy of tropical rain forest
- 📏 Up to 25 in (64 cm); bill length up to 8 in (20 cm)
- ✈ 24 in (61 cm)
- ⚖ 19 oz (540 g)
- ✿ Small fruits, berries
- ⚡ Least concern

Toucan barbet
Semnornis ramphastinus
- 🌐 South America
- ⛰ Tropical forest
- 📏 10 in (25 cm)
- ✈ 25 in (63 cm)
- ⚖ 3.5 oz (100 g)
- ✿ Fruits, insects
- ⚡ Near threatened

ORDER PASSERIFORMES
PASSERINES
5,754 species in 96 families, including the families listed below

Family Alaudidae
Larks
91 species

Horned lark, Shore lark
Eremophila alpestris
- 🌐 North America, northern Eurasia, mountains of southeast Europe
- ⛰ Shore, field, tundra
- 📏 Up to 8.3 in (21 cm)
- ✈ Up to 12.6 in (32 cm)
- ⚖ Up to 1.3 oz (37 g)
- ✿ Insects, seeds
- ⚡ Least concern

Family Cardinalidae
Cardinals
43 species

Rose-breasted grosbeak
Pheucticus ludovicianus
- 🌐 Breeds in Canada & eastern USA; winters from Mexico to northern South America & Caribbean
- ⛰ Woodland, orchards, parks, gardens
- 📏 7–8 in (18–20 cm)
- ✈ 11–13 in (28–33 cm)
- ⚖ 1.4–1.7 oz (39–49 g)
- ✿ Insects, seeds, fruits, buds
- ⚡ Least concern

Family Corvidae
Crows, magpies & jays
120+ species

Western scrub jay
Aphelocoma californica
- 🌐 Western USA, Mexico
- ⛰ Lowland scrub, woodland, gardens
- 📏 12 in (30 cm)
- ✈ 15 in (38 cm)
- ⚖ 2.8 oz (80 g)
- ✿ Arthropods, fruits, acorns, seeds
- ⚡ Least concern

Common raven
Corvus corax
- 🌐 Nearly worldwide
- ⛰ Open areas in diverse habitats including tundra, forest, prairie, desert, farmland, cities
- 📏 22–27 in (56–68 cm)
- ✈ 46 in (117 cm)
- ⚖ 1.5–3.5 lb (0.7–1.6 kg)
- ✿ Small mammals & birds, bird eggs, insects, grain, fruit, refuse, carrion
- ⚡ Least concern

Blue jay
Cyanocitta cristata
- 🌐 Southern Canada, eastern USA to central Texas
- ⛰ Edges of deciduous, conifer & mixed forests; gardens
- 📏 10–12 in (25–30 cm)
- ✈ 13–17 in (33–43 cm)
- ⚖ 2.5–3.5 oz (70–100 g)
- ✿ Insects, acorns, nuts, bird eggs, small mammals & birds
- ⚡ Least concern

Azure-winged magpie
Cyanopica cyana
- 🌐 China, Korea, Japan, Mongolia
- ⛰ Coniferous & broadleaf forests, gardens
- 📏 12–14 in (31–35 cm)
- 📏 6–8 in (16–20 cm)
- ✿ Acorns, pine nuts, insects, fruits, berries
- ⚡ Least concern

Spotted nutcracker
Nucifraga caryocatactes
- 🌐 Eurasia
- ⛰ Coniferous forest
- 📏 Up to 13.8 in (35 cm)
- ✈ Up to 21 in (53 cm)
- ⚖ Up to 6 oz (170 g)
- ✿ Nuts, seeds
- ⚡ Least concern

Siberian jay
Perisoreus infaustus
- 🌐 Northern Eurasia
- ⛰ Boreal forest
- 📏 12 in (30 cm)
- ✿ Insects, berries, bird eggs & nestlings, small mammals & birds
- ⚡ Least concern

Family Cotingidae
Cotingas
90 species

Andean cock-of-the-rock
Rupicola peruviana
- 🌐 Venezuela, Colombia, Ecuador, Peru, Bolivia
- ⛰ Rain forest
- 📏 13 in (33 cm)
- ✈ 14 in (35 cm)
- ⚖ 2.5 oz (70 g)
- ✿ Fruits
- ⚡ Least concern

Family Emberizidae
Buntings & American sparrows
400 species

Great pampas finch
Embernagra platensis
- 🌐 Argentina, Bolivia, Brazil, Paraguay, Uruguay
- ⛰ Tropical high-altitude shrubland, temperate grassland & swamps
- 📏 2.5 in (6.3 cm)
- ✈ 2 in (5 cm)
- ⚖ 1 oz (28 g)
- ✿ Seeds, insects
- ⚡ Least concern

Brewer's sparrow
Spizella breweri
- 🌐 Breeds southwestern Canada, western USA; winters southwestern USA, Mexico
- ⛰ Dense stands of sagebrush amid grassy areas
- 📏 5.5 in (14 cm)
- ✈ 8 in (20 cm)
- ⚖ 0.5 oz (14 g)
- ✿ Grasshoppers, beetles, other insects, seeds, some plant material
- ⚡ Near threatened

Family Estrildidae
Estrildid finches
130 species

Gouldian finch
Erythrura gouldiae
- 🌐 Northern Australia
- ⛰ Tropical woodland, spinifex grassland
- 📏 4.5–5.5 in (12–14 cm)
- ✿ Seeds, insects
- ⚡ Endangered

Family Icteridae
American blackbirds, New World orioles, grackles & cowbirds
88 species

Red-winged blackbird
Agelaius phoeniceus
- 🌐 North & Central America
- ⛰ Wetlands, grassy areas, open patches in woodland
- 📏 7–9 in (18–23 cm)
- ✈ 12–16 in (30–41 cm)
- ⚖ 1.1–2.7 oz (31–76 g)
- ✿ Insects, seeds, grain
- ⚡ Least concern

Rusty blackbird
Euphagus carolinus
- 🌐 Breeds Alaska, Canada, New England; winters throughout eastern & central USA
- ⛰ Swampy boreal forest in summer; swamps & wet woodland in winter
- 📏 8–10 in (21–25 cm)
- ✈ 15 in (37 cm)
- ⚖ 1.6–2.8 oz (45–79 g)
- ✿ Insects in summer; acorns, seeds, fruits in winter
- ⚡ Vulnerable

Brown-headed cowbird
Molothrus ater
- 🌐 Temperate to subtropical North America
- ⛰ Grassland, woodland edges, thickets, fields, prairie, pasture, orchards, suburban & urban areas
- 📏 7–9 in (18–23 cm)
- ✈ 11–14 in (28–35 cm)
- ⚖ 1.3–1.8 oz (37–51 g)
- ✿ Seeds, spiders, insects
- ⚡ Least concern

Gouldian finch
Erythrura gouldiae

Family Meliphagidae
Honeyeaters
182 species

New Holland honeyeater
Phylidonyris novaehollandiae
- Southern Australia
- Forest & woodland, heath
- 7 in (18 cm)
- 0.7 oz (20 g)
- Nectar, insects
- Least concern

Family Menuridae
Lyrebirds
2 species

Superb lyrebird
Menura novaehollandiae
- Southeastern Australia
- Rain forest, eucalypt forest, gullies
- Up to 40 in (100 cm)
- 2.2 lb (1 kg)
- Invertebrates, seeds
- Least concern

Family Mimidae
Mockingbirds & thrashers
30+ species

Chalk-browed mockingbird
Mimus saturninus
- Northeast Brazil, Bolivia, Paraguay, Uruguay, northern Argentina
- Savanna, shrubland, degraded forest
- 10 in (25 cm)
- 12 in (30 cm)
- 2.1 oz (59 g)
- Insects, worms
- Least concern

Curve-billed thrasher
Toxostoma curvirostre
- Southwestern USA, Mexico
- Desert, semidesert, thorn scrub, shrubby areas, open brushland
- 11 in (28 cm)
- 13 in (33 cm)
- 3 oz (85 g)
- Insects, seeds, berries
- Least concern

Family Paradisaeidae
Birds of paradise
40+ species

Huon astrapia
Astrapia rothschildi
- Huon Peninsula (Papua New Guinea)
- Rain forest
- Up to 27 in (68 cm)
- Fruits, insects
- Least concern

Superb bird-of-paradise
Lophorina superba
- New Guinea
- Rain forest
- Up to 10 in (23 cm)
- Up to 3 oz (85 g)
- Fruits, insects
- Least concern

Raggiana bird-of-paradise
Paradisaea raggiana
- New Guinea
- Tropical forest
- Up to 13 in (33 cm)
- ♂ 9.5 oz (270 g), ♀ 6.1 oz (173 g)
- Fruits, insects
- Least concern

Blue bird-of-paradise
Paradisaea rudolphi
- Southeastern New Guinea
- Rain forest, gardens
- Up to 12 in (30 cm)
- Up to 6.2 oz (176 g)
- Fruits, insects
- Vulnerable

King of Saxony bird-of-paradise
Pteridophora alberti
- New Guinea
- Rain forest
- Up to 9 in (22 cm)
- Up to 3 oz (87 g)
- Fruits, insects
- Least concern

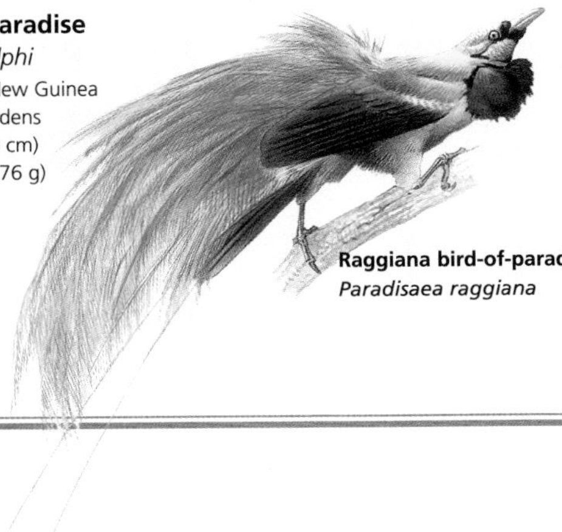
Raggiana bird-of-paradise
Paradisaea raggiana

Family Paridae
Tits, chickadees & titmice
64 species

Blue tit
Parus caeruleus
- Temperate & subarctic Europe & western Asia
- Deciduous or mixed woodland
- Up to 4.8 in (12 cm)
- Up to 7 in (18 cm)
- Up to 4 oz (113 g)
- Insects
- Least concern

Family Parulidae
New World warblers
119 species

Black-throated blue warbler
Dendroica caerulescens
- Breeds eastern North America; winters Caribbean & Central America
- Breeds in deciduous & mixed woodland; winters in tropical forest
- 4–5 in (10–13 cm)
- 7–8 in (18–20 cm)
- 0.3–0.4 oz (8–11 g)
- Insects, small fruits
- Least concern

Yellow warbler
Dendroica petechia
- Breeds in much of North America; winters in Caribbean, Central America & northern South America
- Willows & other moist thickets, shrubland, fields, mangroves
- 5 in (13 cm)
- 6–8 in (16–20 cm)
- 0.3–0.4 oz (9–11 g)
- Insects, spiders
- Least concern

Cape May warbler
Dendroica tigrina
- Breeds across Canadian boreal forest & south to northern USA; winters in Caribbean
- Breeds in coniferous forest; winters in various habitats
- 5 in (13 cm)
- 7–9 in (19–22 cm)
- 0.3–0.4 oz (9–12 g)
- Spruce budworms & other insects in summer; nectar & insects in winter
- Least concern

American redstart
Setophaga ruticilla
- Breeds southern Canada & eastern USA; winters Caribbean & from Mexico to northern South America
- Moist, shrubby second-growth deciduous forest
- 4–5 in (11–13 cm)
- 6–7 in (16–19 cm)
- 0.2–0.3 oz (6–9 g)
- Insects
- Least concern

Family Passeridae
True sparrows
40 species

Cape sparrow
Passer melanurus
- Southern Africa
- Savanna, grassland
- 6 in (16 cm)
- 10 in (25 cm)
- 1 oz (30 g)
- Seeds, insects
- Least concern

Family Petroicidae
Australian robins
45 species

Tom tit
Petroica macrocephala
- New Zealand
- Forest, scrub
- Up to 5 in (13 cm)
- Up to 0.4 oz (11 g)
- Insects
- Least concern

Black tomtit
Petroica macrocephala damnefaerdi
- New Zealand
- Forest, scrub
- Up to 5 in (13 cm)
- Up to 0.4 oz (11 g)
- Insects
- Not listed

Black robin
Petroica traversi
- Chatham Islands (New Zealand)
- Forested offshore islands
- Up to 6 in (15 cm)
- Up to 0.9 oz (25 g)
- Insects
- Endangered

Family Ploceidae
Weavers
155 species

Slender-billed weaver bird
Ploceus pelzelni
- Sub-Saharan Africa
- Savanna
- 0.6–0.7 in (14–19 mm)
- 2–2.5 in (5–6.5 cm)
- Insects & other small invertebrates
- Least concern

Family Ptilonorhynchidae
Bowerbirds
17 species

Satin bowerbird
Ptilonorhynchus violaceus
- Eastern Australia
- Rain forest, eucalypt forest, gardens
- Up to 12 in (32 cm)
- 7 oz (200 g)
- Leaves, fruits, insects
- Least concern

Family Sturnidae
Starlings
107 species

Red-billed oxpecker
Buphagus erythrorhynchus
- Sub-Saharan Africa
- Open savanna
- 8 in (20 cm)
- 1.8 oz (50 g)
- Insects, ticks, ungulate blood
- Least concern

Satin bowerbird
Ptilonorhynchus violaceus

European starling
Sturnus vulgaris
- Europe & southwest Asia; introduced North America, South Africa, Australia, New Zealand
- Gardens, fields
- 8 in (20 cm)
- 16 in (40 cm)
- 2–3 oz (60–90 g)
- Insects
- Least concern

Family Troglodytidae
Wrens
59 species

Cactus wren
Campylorhynchus brunneicapillus
- Southwestern USA to central Mexico
- Arid lowlands, mountain thorn scrub
- 7–9 in (18–22 cm)
- 5 in (12 cm)
- 1–1.7 oz (30–50 g)
- Insects, spiders
- Least concern

Family Turdidae
Thrushes & allies
305 species

American robin
Turdus migratorius
- Throughout North America to Mexico
- Forest, woodland, gardens
- 8–11 in (20–28 cm)
- 12–16 in (30–40 cm)
- 2.7 oz (77 g)
- Insects, earthworms, fruits
- Least concern

American robin
Turdus migratorius

BIRD SIZE COMPARISON

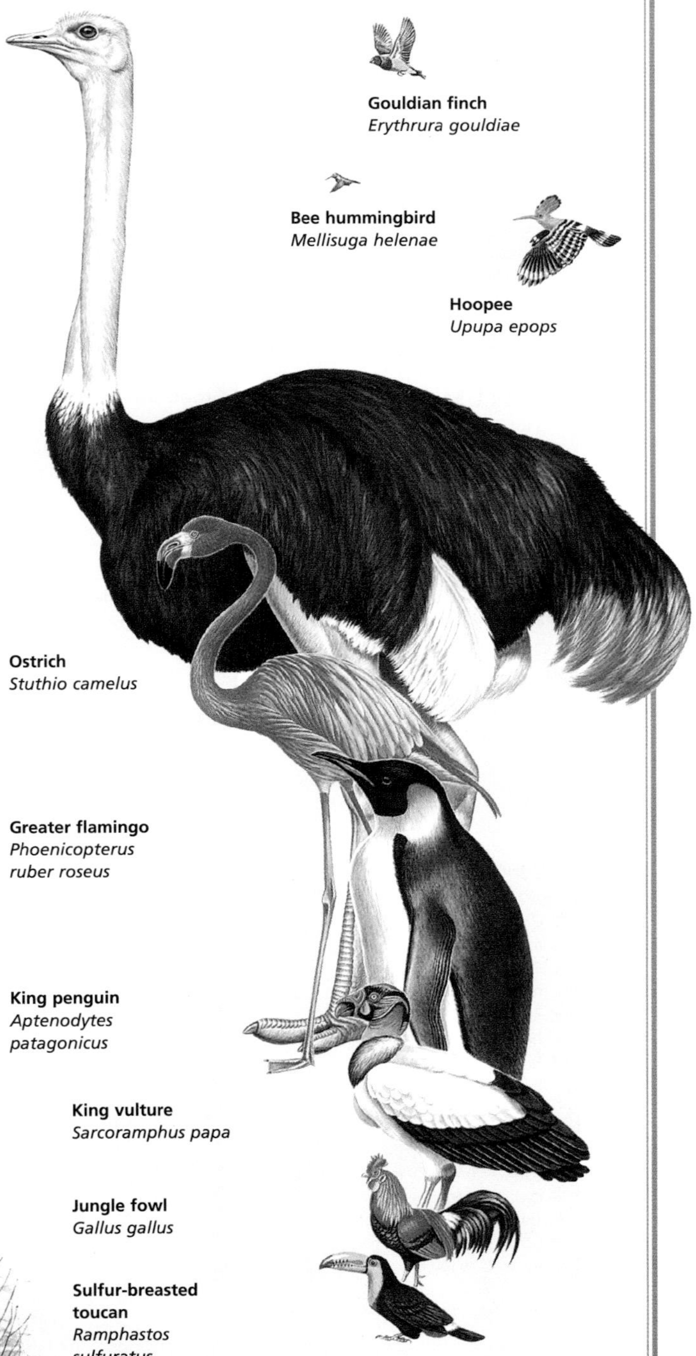
Gouldian finch *Erythrura gouldiae*
Bee hummingbird *Mellisuga helenae*
Hoopoe *Upupa epops*
Ostrich *Stuthio camelus*
Greater flamingo *Phoenicopterus ruber roseus*
King penguin *Aptenodytes patagonicus*
King vulture *Sarcoramphus papa*
Jungle fowl *Gallus gallus*
Sulfur-breasted toucan *Ramphastos sulfuratus*

REPTILES

Reptiles were the first animals to conquer land. With their impermeable scaly skin, internal fertilization, and closed eggs, they were able to live independently of water. The class Reptilia—living reptiles—traditionally includes the four orders of turtles, crocodilians, tuatara, and squamates (which contains suborders of lizards, snakes, and worm lizards). With DNA evidence, many relationships in this class have become controversial. The traditional reptile groupings have been used here, but most are currently under revision. Crocodilians are in fact most closely related to birds, and turtles may belong in a separate class altogether. The suborders within Squamata are artificial, as limbless lizards, snakes, and worm lizards all evolved from lizards that lost their limbs. Only the status of the tuatara as an ancient order by itself is agreed upon.

Icon key

⊕ Distribution
🗡 Tail length
✪ Diet
▲ Habitat
🗡 Weight
⚡ Status
⇌ Length
♀♂ Female/male

PHYLUM CHORDATA
CHORDATES
53,000+ species

CLASS REPTILIA
REPTILES
7,973 species

ORDER TESTUDINES
TORTOISES & TURTLES
293 species

Loggerhead turtle
Caretta caretta
⊕ Circumglobal, temperate to tropical oceans
▲ Oceanic & coastal waters, nests on beaches
⇌ 30–40 in (76–100 cm)
🗡 Up to 297 lb (135 kg)
✪ Mollusks, crustaceans, aquatic plants
⚡ Endangered

Pig-nosed turtle
Carettochelys insculpta
⊕ Australia, Indonesia, New Guinea
▲ Tropical freshwater streams
⇌ Up to 27 in (70 cm)
🗡 Up to 45 lb (20 kg)
✪ Omnivorous
⚡ Vulnerable

Green turtle
Chelonia mydas
⊕ Circumtropical
▲ Oceanic & coastal waters, nests on beaches
⇌ 5 ft (1.5 m)
🗡 Up to 452 lb (205 kg)
⚡ Endangered

Painted turtle
Chrysemys picta
⊕ North America
▲ Slow-moving shallow fresh water, ponds, lakes
⇌ Up to 10 in (25 cm)
🗡 2 oz (57 g)
✪ Mollusks, crayfish, small fish, aquatic plants
⚡ Not listed

Leatherback turtle
Dermochelys coriacea
⊕ Circumglobal, cool temperate to tropics
▲ Oceanic & coastal waters, nests on beaches
⇌ 6.5 ft (2 m)
🗡 550–1,984 lb (250–900 kg)
⚡ Critically endangered

Galápagos giant tortoise
Geochelone nigra (formerly *elephantopus*)
⊕ Galápagos Islands
▲ Tropical grassland, dry forest
⇌ 4 ft (1.2 m)
🗡 660 lb (300 kg)
✪ Cactus, grasses, leaves, sedges, vines, fruits
⚡ Vulnerable

Desert tortoise
Gopherus agassizii
⊕ Parts of Nevada, California, Utah, Arizona & Mexico
▲ Flat lands & rocky slopes in desert
⇌ Up to 14.5 in (37 cm)
🗡 8–15 lb (3.5–6.8 kg)
✪ Green & dried plants, spring wildflowers, cactus pads
⚡ Vulnerable

Big-headed turtle
Platysternon megacephalum
⊕ Southeast Asia
▲ Fast-moving streams & brooks
⇌ Up to 16 in (40 cm)
✪ Fish, mollusks, worms
⚡ Endangered

Spider tortoise
Pyxis arachnoides
⊕ South coast of Madagascar
▲ Woodland, bushland
⇌ 4 in (10 cm)
✪ Grasses, herbs
⚡ Vulnerable

ORDER CROCODILIA
CROCODILIANS
23 species

Philippine crocodile
Crocodylus mindorensis
⊕ Philippines
▲ Freshwater lakes, ponds, tributaries, marshes; nests & basks on land
⇌ Up to 10 ft (3 m)
🗡 Up to 220 lb (100 kg)
✪ Aquatic invertebrates, small vertebrates
⚡ Critically endangered

Nile crocodile
Crocodylus niloticus
⊕ Sub-Saharan Africa
▲ Freshwater marshes, mangrove swamps
⇌ Up to 20 ft (6 m)
🗡 Up to 1,609 lb (730 kg)
✪ Fish, mammals
⚡ Least concern

Saltwater crocodile
Crocodylus porosus
⊕ Southeast Asia, northern Australia
▲ Coastal waters, rivers, billabongs
⇌ Up to 24 ft (7 m)
🗡 Up to 1.1 tons (1 t)
✪ Fish, waterfowl, mammals
⚡ Least concern

Siamese crocodile
Crocodylus siamensis
⊕ Thailand, Laos, Cambodia, Vietnam, Indonesia
▲ Swamps, oxbow lakes, slow-moving sections of streams & rivers
⇌ Up to 4 ft (3 m)
✪ Critically endangered

Gharial
Gavialis gangeticus
⊕ Northern South Asia from Pakistan to Burma
▲ Larger rivers
⇌ 16 ft (5 m)
🗡 1,500 lb (680 kg)
✪ Fish
⚡ Critically endangered

Black caiman
Melanosuchus niger
⊕ Bolivia, Brazil, Colombia, Ecuador, French Guiana, Guyana, Peru
▲ Slow-moving rivers, wetlands, flooded savannas
⇌ 20 ft (6 m)
🗡 6.5 ft (2 m)
🗡 2,300 lb (1,043 kg)
✪ Fish, turtles, capybara, deer
⚡ Conservation dependent

ORDER RHYNCOCEPHALIA
TUATARA
2 species

Tuatara
Sphenodon punctatus
⊕ New Zealand
▲ Rodent-free offshore islands
⇌ Up to 24 in (61 cm)
🗡 2.2 lb (1 kg)
✪ Invertebrates
⚡ Least concern (needs updating, threatened by habitat loss & introduction of Polynesian rat)

ORDER SQUAMATA
LIZARDS & SNAKES
7,655 species

Suborder Amphisbaenia
Worm lizards
140 species

Suborder Lacertilia
Lizards
4,560 species

Spiny-footed lizard
Acanthodactylus erythrurus
⊕ Algeria, Morocco, Portugal, Spain
▲ Dry, sparsely vegetated habitats
⇌ Up to 8 in (20 cm)
🗡 Up to 8 in (20 cm)
✪ Insects
⚡ Least concern

Marine iguana
Amblyrhynchus cristatus
⊕ Galápagos Islands
▲ Shallow reefs, rocky coastlines
⇌ 18 in (46 cm)
🗡 9 in (23 cm)
🗡 4.4 lb (2 kg)
✪ Red & green marine algae
⚡ Vulnerable

Fiji banded iguana
Brachylophus fasciatus
⊕ Fiji, Tonga
▲ Arboreal
⇌ Up to 32 in (81 cm) including tail
🗡 Up to 24 in (61 cm)
🗡 10.6 oz (300 g)
✪ Trees, shrubs, hibiscus flowers
⚡ Endangered

Strange-horned chameleon
Bradypodion xenorhinus
⊕ Albertine Rift (east Africa)
▲ Montane forest
⇌ 11 in (28 cm)
✪ Insects
⚡ Not listed

Johnston's chameleon
Chamaeleo johnstoni
⊕ Albertine Rift (east Africa)
▲ Montane forest
⇌ 12 in (30 cm)
🗡 3 oz (85 g)
✪ Crickets, worms
⚡ Not listed

Land iguana
Conolophus pallidus
⊕ Galápagos Islands
▲ Arid lowlands
⇌ 39 in (100 cm)
🗡 21 in (53 cm)
🗡 28 lb (13 kg)
✪ Low-growing plants & shrubs, such as cactus, fallen fruits, cactus pads
⚡ Vulnerable

Greater earless lizard
Cophosaurus texanus
⊕ Southernmost Arizona & Mexico (summer only), dry parts of Mexico to northern South America
▲ Arid scrub & grassland, oak forest, tropical dry forest
⇌ 3.5 in (9 cm)
🗡 0.5–0.9 oz (15–25 g)
✪ Insects, spiders
⚡ Least concern

Panther chameleon
Furcifer pardalis
⊕ North Madagascar
▲ Forest, scrubland
⇌ ♂ 18 in (46 cm), ♀ 9 in (23 cm)
✪ Insects
⚡ Not listed

Gila monster
Heloderma suspectum
⊕ Southwest USA to northern Mexico
▲ Semiarid rocky regions of desert scrub & grassland
⇌ Up to 22 in (56 cm)
🗡 6 in (15 cm)
🗡 4 lb (1.8 kg)
✪ Small birds & mammals, eggs, lizards, frogs, insects, carrion
⚡ Near threatened

Sail-tailed water lizard
Hydrosaurus amboinensis
⊕ Southeast Asia, New Guinea
▲ Rain forest near rivers
⇌ Up to 40 in (100 cm)
✪ Plants, insects, rodents
⚡ Not listed

Thorny devil
Moloch horridus
⊕ Central Australia
▲ Sandy arid & semiarid habitats
⇌ Up to 4 in (10 cm)
🗡 4 in (10 cm)
🗡 1–3 oz (30–90 g)
✪ Ants
⚡ Not listed

Greater short-horned lizard
Phrynosoma hernandesi
⊕ Southern Canada through central and western USA to northern Mexico
▲ Shortgrass on the northern Great Plains, sagebrush in Great Basin
⇌ 2.5–6 in (6.4–15.2 cm)
✪ Invertebrates
⚡ Least concern

Italian wall lizard
Podarcis sicula
⊕ Western & central Europe; introduced USA
▲ Forest, shrubland, grassland, beaches, farmland & urban areas
⇌ Up to 8 in (20 cm)
🗡 Up to 5 in (13 cm)
🗡 Up to 0.5 oz (15 g)
✪ Plants
⚡ Least concern

Green turtle
Chelonia mydas

Central bearded dragon
Pogona vitticeps
- ⊕ Central Australia
- ▲ Rocky desert to dry woodland
- ↔ 24 in (61 cm) including tail
- ✖ 7 oz (200 g)
- ✪ Insects, mice, leaves, flowers
- ⚡ Not listed

Chuckwallah
Sauromalus obesus
- ⊕ Southwest USA to northern Mexico
- ▲ Rocky desert, lava flows, hillsides, rocky outcrops
- ↔ Up to 9 in (23 cm) without tail
- ↔ Up to 9 in (23 cm)
- ✖ 2 lb (900 g)
- ✪ Leaves, buds, flowers, fruits
- ⚡ Least concern

Desert spiny lizard
Sceloporus magister
- ⊕ Southwest USA
- ▲ Arid to semiarid regions with rock piles & crevices for shelter
- ↔ 10 in (25 cm)
- ✪ Insects, spiders, lizards, plant material
- ⚡ Least concern

Giant leaf–tailed gecko
Uroplatus fimbriatus
- ⊕ East Madagascar
- ▲ Primary rain forest
- ↔ 7 in (18 cm)
- ✪ Insects
- ⚡ Not listed

Gray monitor
Varanus griseus
- ⊕ North Africa, western Asia
- ▲ Desert & semidesert habitats
- ↔ 23 in (58 cm)
- ↔ Up to 34 in (87 cm)
- ✖ Up to 6.3 lb (2.8 kg)
- ✪ Insects, other lizards, snakes, frogs, small mammals, bird & reptile eggs
- ⚡ Not listed

Komodo dragon
Varanus komodoensis
- ⊕ Lesser Sunda islands, Komodo, Flores, Gili, Montang, Padar
- ▲ Arid forest & savanna on volcanic islands
- ↔ Up to 10 ft (3 m)
- ✖ 200 lb (91 kg)
- ✪ Carrion, deer, pigs, water buffalo
- ⚡ Vulnerable

Suborder Serpentes
Snakes
2,955 species

Puff adder
Bitis arietans
- ⊕ Sub-Saharan Africa
- ▲ Grassland, woodland, forest
- ↔ 27–35 in (68–90 cm)
- ✖ 13 lb (6 kg)
- ✪ Small mammals, birds, reptiles
- ⚡ Not listed

Sidewinding adder, Peringuey's desert adder
Bitis peringueyi
- ⊕ Southwest Africa
- ▲ Desert
- ↔ Up to 12 in (32 cm)
- ✪ Lizards
- ⚡ Not listed

Boa constrictor
Boa constrictor
- ⊕ Central America, South America, Caribbean
- ▲ Rain forest, savanna, semiarid areas
- ↔ Up to 13 ft (4 m)
- ✖ 60 lb (27 kg)
- ✪ Meat, birds, monkeys, peccaries, rodents, iguanas, young crocodilians, lizards
- ⚡ Not listed

Luzon mangrove snake
Boiga dendrophila divergens
- ⊕ Philippines
- ▲ Lowland rain forest, mangrove swamps
- ↔ 6–8 ft (1.8–2.4 m)
- ✪ Small mammals, lizards, frogs, snakes, fish
- ⚡ Not listed (but common)

Western rattlesnake
Crotalus viridis
- ⊕ Most of western USA, northern Mexico, southwestern Canada
- ▲ Open, dry habitats with rocky outcrops
- ↔ 3–4 ft (90–120 cm)
- ✪ Small mammals, birds, reptiles
- ⚡ Least concern

Spotted harlequin snake
Homoroselaps lacteus
- ⊕ Southern Africa
- ▲ Old termite mounds, grassland
- ↔ 12–24 in (30–60 cm)
- ✪ Legless lizards, snakes
- ⚡ Not listed

Carpet python
Morelia spilota
- ⊕ Australia, New Guinea, Indonesia
- ▲ Forest, woodland
- ↔ Up to 13 ft (4 m)
- ✖ Up to 11 lb (5 kg)
- ✪ Small mammals, birds
- ⚡ Not listed

King cobra
Ophiophagus hannah
- ⊕ South & Southeast Asia
- ▲ Dense forests
- ↔ Up to 18 ft (5.5 m)
- ✖ 20 lb (9 kg)
- ✪ Other snakes
- ⚡ Not listed

Taipan
Oxyuranus scutellatus
- ⊕ Australia
- ▲ Woodland, grassland
- ↔ Up to 10 ft (3 m)
- ✪ Small mammals, particularly rats & bandicoots
- ⚡ Not listed

Burmese python
Python molurus bivittatus
- ⊕ Myanmar, Thailand, Laos, Cambodia, Vietnam, Indonesia
- ▲ Rain forest, grassland, marshes, swamps, rocky foothills, woodland, river valleys
- ↔ Up to 23 ft (7 m)
- ✖ Up to 200 lb (91 kg)
- ⚡ Not listed (but uncommon)

Lataste's viper
Vipera latastei
- ⊕ Northern Morocco to northern Algeria, northwestern Tunisia
- ▲ Coastal dune, rocky crevice
- ↔ Up to 23 in (60 cm)
- ✪ Reptiles, small mammals
- ⚡ Near threatened

Lebetine viper
Vipera lebetina
- ⊕ Subspecies distributed in northern Africa & central Asia
- ▲ Desert & semidesert areas
- ↔ 7 ft (2 m)
- ✪ Small mammals, lizards
- ⚡ Not listed

Lebetine viper
Vipera lebetina

AMPHIBIANS

Amphibians have smooth skin without scales. They lay eggs in water and metamorphose from a water-breathing juvenile to an air-breathing adult. The living amphibians evolved from the same common ancestor and are grouped into three orders: the frogs and toads (Anura), the salamanders and newts (Caudata), and the caecilians (Gymnophiona).

Icon key
⊕ Distribution	↔ Length	✪ Diet
▲ Habitat	✖ Weight	⚡ Status

PHYLUM CHORDATA
CHORDATES
53,000+ species

CLASS AMPHIBIA
AMPHIBIANS
5,558 species

ORDER CAUDATA
SALAMANDERS & NEWTS
472 species

Mudpuppy
Necturus maculosus

Spotted salamander
Ambystoma maculatum
- ⊕ Eastern USA, southern Canada
- ▲ Deciduous forests with semi-permanent ponds
- ↔ 6–10 in (15–25 cm)
- ✪ Mollusks, earthworms, centipedes, millipedes, spiders, insects
- ⚡ Least concern

Japanese giant salamander
Andrias japonicus
- ⊕ China, Japan
- ▲ Brooks, ponds
- ↔ Up to 5 ft (1.5 m)
- ✖ Up to 55 lb (25 kg)
- ✪ Fish, insects, crustaceans, worms
- ⚡ Near threatened

Mudpuppy
Necturus maculosus
- ⊕ Eastern & central North America
- ▲ Ponds, streams, rivers
- ↔ Up to 19 in (48 cm)
- ✪ Crustaceans, fish, snails, insect larvae
- ⚡ Least concern

Red salamander
Pseudotriton ruber
- ⊕ Eastern USA
- ▲ Deciduous forests, under fallen bark, logs, rocks; leaf litter of streams & brooks
- ↔ 3–7 in (8–18 cm)
- ✪ Earthworms, insects, other salamanders
- ⚡ Least concern

European fire salamander
Salamandra salamandra
- ⊕ Western & southern Europe
- ▲ Deciduous forest close to streams
- ↔ Up to 10 in (25 cm)
- ✖ 0.7 oz (19 g)
- ✪ Insects, spiders, earthworms, slugs
- ⚡ Least concern

Alpine newt
Triturus alpestris
- ⊕ Europe from French Atlantic coastline east to the Ukrainian Carpathians, Romania, Bulgaria & the Balkans
- ▲ Forest, ponds
- ↔ Up to 5 in (12 cm)
- ✖ Up to 0.35 oz (10 g)
- ✪ Invertebrates
- ⚡ Least concern

ORDER GYMNOPHIONA
CAECILIANS
149 species

ORDER ANURA
FROGS & TOADS
4,937 species

Red-eyed tree frog
Agalychnis callidryas
- ⊕ Central America
- ▲ Forest near rivers & ponds
- ↔ 3 in (7.5 cm)
- ✪ Insects
- ⚡ Least concern

Oriental fire-bellied toad
Bombina orientalis
- ⊕ Korea, Japanese islands (Tsushima & Kyushu), northeast China, nearby parts of Russia
- ▲ In or near ponds, lakes, swamps, slow-moving streams
- ↔ 1.5–2 in (4–5 cm)
- ✪ Tadpoles eat algae, then insects; toadlets eat small invertebrates; adults eat beetles, ants, flies, other insects, worms, snails
- ⚡ Least concern

Cane toad
Bufo marinus
- ⊕ Rio Grande Valley of Texas south to central Amazon & southeastern Peru; widely introduced
- ▲ Forested areas with semi-permanent water
- ↔ Up to 10 in (25 cm)
- ✖ 4 oz (113 g)
- ✪ Insects, mollusks, lizards
- ⚡ Least concern

Golden toad
Bufo periglenes
- ⊕ Costa Rica
- ▲ Rain forest, cloud forest
- ↔ 2 in (5 cm)
- ✖ 0.6 oz (20 g)
- ✪ Small invertebrates
- ⚡ Extinct

Water-holding frog
Cyclorana platycephala
- ⊕ Australia
- ▲ Grassland, swamps, billabongs, claypans
- ↔ Up to 3 in (7.6 cm)
- ✪ Invertebrates
- ⚡ Least concern

Blue poison-dart frog
Dendrobates azureus
- ⊕ Suriname (South America)
- ▲ Ponds & streams
- ↔ Up to 2 in (5 cm)
- ✖ 0.11 oz (3 g)
- ✪ Insects
- ⚡ Vulnerable

Strawberry poison-dart frog
Dendrobates pumilio
- ⊕ Central America, especially Costa Rica
- ▲ Rain forest
- ↔ Up to 1 in (2.5 cm)
- ✪ Tadpoles eat unfertilized eggs from mother, then algae & detritus; adults eat small invertebrates
- ⚡ Least concern

Tomato frog
Dyscophus antongilii
- ⊕ Northeast Madagascar
- ▲ Primary rain forest, coastal forest, flooded areas
- ↔ 3 in (7 cm)
- ✪ Insects
- ⚡ Near threatened

Hochstetter's frog
Leiopelma hochstetteri
- ⊕ New Zealand
- ▲ Damp areas near streams
- ↔ Up to 1.8 in (4.5 cm)
- ✪ Insects
- ⚡ Vulnerable

Paradox frog
Pseudis paradoxa
- ⊕ South America
- ▲ Marshes, permanent ponds in savanna, open forest in tropical lowlands
- ↔ 2 in (5 cm)
- ✪ Larvae, small insects, tiny invertebrates
- ⚡ Least concern

Corroboree frog
Pseudophryne corroboree
- ⊕ Southeast Australia
- ▲ Alpine sphagnum bogs
- ↔ Up to 1.4 in (3.5 cm)
- ✪ Insects
- ⚡ Critically endangered

Corroboree frog
Pseudophryne corroboree

FISH

Fish are an immensely diverse array of animals, and most biologists regard the term "fish" as a convenient name, rather than a closely defined taxonomic entity, that describes aquatic vertebrates with gills and fins. There are various classification schemes for the fish but one of the most widely accepted recognizes five classes of living species grouped into two superclasses: the jawless fish of Agnatha, comprising hagfish and lampreys, and the jawed fish of Gnathostoma, comprising cartilaginous fish (sharks and rays), lobe-finned fish (lungfish and allies), and ray-finned fish (most bony fish).

Icon key

⊕ Distribution	⤝ Tail length	✪ Diet
⋀ Habitat	✕ Weight	⚡ Status
⬌ Length		

PHYLUM CHORDATA
CHORDATES
53,000+ species

SUPERCLASS AGNATHA
JAWLESS FISH
Lampreys & hagfish
105 species

SUPERCLASS GNATHOSTOMATA
JAWED FISH
c. 26,000 species

CARTILAGINOUS FISH

CLASS CHONDRICHTHYES
CARTILAGINOUS FISH
999 species

SUBCLASS ELASMOBRANCHII
SHARKS, RAYS & ALLIES
962 species

SUPERORDER SELACHIMORPHA SHARKS
415 species

Long-tailed thresher shark
Alopias vulpinus
- ⊕ Worldwide, cool to temperate oceans
- ⋀ Open ocean & coastal waters
- ⬌ Up to 25 ft (7.5 m)
- ✕ Up to 770 lb (348 kg)
- ✪ Schooling fish, crustaceans, squid
- ⚡ Data deficient

Great white shark
Carcharodon carcharias
- ⊕ Worldwide, temperate to subtropical oceans
- ⋀ Open ocean & coastal waters
- ⬌ Up to 20 ft (6 m)
- ✕ 2.1 tons (1.9 t)
- ✪ Fish, turtles, marine mammals
- ⚡ Vulnerable

Long-tailed thresher shark
Alopias vulpinus

Great white shark
Carcharodon carcharias

Whale shark
Rhincodon typus
- ⊕ Circumtropical and warm-temperate seas
- ⋀ Open ocean, coastal waters
- ⬌ Up to 46 ft (14 m)
- ✕ Up to 15 tons (13.6 t)
- ✪ Plankton
- ⚡ Vulnerable

Greenland shark
Somniosus microcephalus
- ⊕ Arctic Ocean to subtropical Atlantic Ocean
- ⋀ From beneath the ice in Arctic, to deep sea in subtropics
- ⬌ 24 ft (7.3 m)
- ✕ 1.2 tons (1.1 t)
- ✪ Bony fish, squid, cuttlefish
- ⚡ Near threatened

Scalloped hammerhead shark
Sphyrna lewini
- ⊕ Tropical & warm-temperate oceans
- ⋀ Open ocean & coastal waters
- ⬌ Up to 14 ft (4.3 m)
- ✕ Up to 330 lb (150 kg)
- ✪ Fish, cephalopods, crustaceans, other sharks
- ⚡ Near threatened

SUPERORDER BATOIDEA RAYS & ALLIES
547 species

Giant manta
Manta birostris
- ⊕ Circumtropical oceans
- ⋀ Open ocean
- ⬌ 30 ft (9.1 m)
- ✕ 3.3 tons (3 t)
- ✪ Tiny animals filtered from plankton
- ⬌ Near threatened

Giant devil ray
Mobula mobular
- ⊕ Eastern Atlantic: off Ireland, Mediterranean Sea, Portugal to Senegal, possibly northwest Atlantic
- ⋀ Marine waters over continental shelves & near oceanic islands
- ⬌ Up to 16.5 ft (5 m)
- ✕ Up to 77 lb (35 kg)
- ✪ Plankton, small fish
- ⚡ Endangered

Largetooth sawfish
Pristis microdon
- ⊕ Tropical Indian Ocean, Southeast Asia, New Guinea
- ⋀ Shallow coastal waters, river mouths, larger rivers
- ⬌ Up to 23 ft (7 m)
- ✕ 1,322 lb (600 kg)
- ✪ Benthic animals
- ⚡ Critically endangered

SUBCLASS HOLOCEPHALI
CHIMAERAS
37 species

BONY FISH

CLASS SARCOPTERYGII
LOBE-FINNED FISH
11 species

Coelacanth
Latimeria chalumnae
- ⊕ South Africa to Kenya, Comoros Islands, Madagascar
- ⋀ Underwater volcanic slopes 490–2,300 ft (150–700 m) below surface
- ⬌ 6.5 ft (2 m)
- ✕ 209 lb (95 kg)
- ✪ Cuttlefish, squid, octopus, fish
- ⚡ Critically endangered

Australian lungfish
Neoceratodus forsteri
- ⊕ Burnett & Mary rivers (Queensland, Australia)
- ⋀ Fresh water
- ⬌ Up to 5 ft (1.5 m)
- ✕ Up to 90 lb (40 kg)
- ✪ Frogs, fish, invertebrates, some plants
- ⚡ Vulnerable

CLASS ACTINOPTERYGII
RAY-FINNED FISH
c. 25,000 species

SUBCLASS CHONDROSTEI
BICHIRS & ALLIES
52 species

American paddlefish
Polyodon spathula
- ⊕ Mississippi River system, including Missouri River into Montana, Ohio River, major tributaries
- ⋀ Slow-flowing water of large rivers, usually deeper than 4 ft (1.2 m)
- ⬌ Up to 7 ft (2.2 m)
- ✕ Up to 220 lb (100 kg)
- ✪ Zooplankton
- ⚡ Vulnerable

SUBCLASS NEOPTERYGII
NEOPTERYGIANS
24,615 species

INFRACLASS HOLOSTEI BOWFINS & GARS
8 species

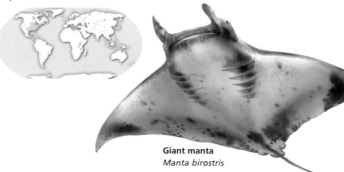

INFRACLASS TELEOSTEI TELEOSTS
24,607 species

SUPERORDER OSTEOGLOSSOMORPHA BONYTONGUES & ALLIES
221 species

Pirarucu
Arapaima gigas
- ⊕ Amazon River Basin, South America
- ⋀ Rain-forest rivers
- ⬌ Up to 15 ft (4.5 m)
- ✕ Up to 440 lb (200 kg)
- ✪ Catfish, small birds
- ⚡ Data deficient

SUPERORDER ELOPOMORPHA EELS & ALLIES
911 species

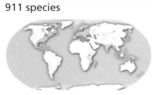

Gulper eel, Pelican eel
Eurypharynx pelecanoides
- ⊕ Worldwide, tropical to temperate oceans
- ⋀ Deep sea, at depths of 3,000–27,000 ft (900–8,000 m)
- ⬌ 24–40 in (60–100 cm), including long whiplike tail
- ✪ Other fish, shrimps, plankton
- ⚡ Not listed

SUPERORDER CLUPEOMORPHA SARDINES & ALLIES
378 species

SUPERORDER OSTARIOPHYSI CATFISH & ALLIES
7,023 species

Giant manta
Manta birostris

Sockeye salmon
Oncorhynchus nerka

SUPERORDER PROTACANTHOPTERYGII
SALMONS & ALLIES

502 species

Cutthroat trout
Oncorhynchus clarkii
- ⊕ Freshwater rivers & streams in western North America; Pacific Coast ocean; widely introduced
- ⋀ Relatively small streams, with gravel bottoms & gentle gradients; some live in ocean & spawn in streams
- ⬌ 6–40 in (15–100 cm)
- ✶ Up to 42 lb (19 kg)
- ✿ Small fish, crustaceans, insects
- ϟ Not listed

Sockeye salmon
Oncorhynchus nerka
- ⊕ Pacific coast of North America from Alaska to northern California; coastal northern Japan; Russian Far East north to Siberia
- ⋀ Winters in open ocean; enters rivers in summer; spawns in lake tributaries
- ⬌ Up to 33 in (84 cm)
- ✶ Average 5–8 lb (2.3–3.6 kg), but up to 15 lb (6.8 kg)
- ✿ Squid, small fish, plankton
- ϟ Not listed

SUPERORDER STENOPTERYGII
DRAGONFISH & ALLIES

415 species

Stoplight loosejaw
Malacosteus niger
- ⊕ Atlantic, Pacific & Indian oceans, South China Sea
- ⋀ Deep sea
- ⬌ 6–8 in (15–20 cm)
- ✿ Crustaceans
- ϟ Not listed

SUPERORDER CYCLOSQUAMATA
LIZARDFISH & ALLIES

229 species

SUPERORDER SCOPELOMORPHA
LANTERNFISH

251 species

SUPERORDER POLYMIXIOMORPHA
BEARDFISH

10 species

SUPERORDER LAMPRIDIOMORPHA
OPAHS & ALLIES

23 species

Oarfish
Regalecus glesne
- ⊕ Temperate to tropical Pacific & Atlantic oceans
- ⋀ Open ocean
- ⬌ Up to 26 ft (8 m), with unconfirmed reports of fish twice that length
- ✶ 600 lb (270 kg)
- ✿ Crustaceans, jellyfish, squid
- ϟ Not listed

SUPERORDER PARACANTHOPTERYGII
CODS, ANGLERFISH & ALLIES

1,382 species

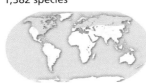

Gelatinous blindfish
Aphyonus gelatinosus
- ⊕ Eastern Atlantic, southwest Pacific, western Indian Ocean
- ⋀ Deep sea, benthic
- ⬌ 6 in (15 cm)
- ✿ Benthic organisms
- ϟ Not listed

Arctic cod
Boreogadus saida
- ⊕ Arctic Ocean
- ⋀ Under ice, water column
- ⬌ 16 in (40 cm)
- ✿ Zooplankton, benthic animals
- ϟ Not listed

Krøyer's deep-sea anglerfish
Ceratias holboelli
- ⊕ Circumglobal, tropical to temperate waters
- ⋀ Deep sea
- ⬌ 20–30 in (50–75 cm)
- ✿ Zooplankton, benthic animals
- ϟ Not listed

SUPERORDER ACANTHOPTERYGII
SPINY-RAYED FISH

13,262 species

Humphead wrasse
Cheilinus undulatus
- ⊕ Red Sea, Indian & Pacific oceans
- ⋀ Coral reefs, mangroves, seagrass beds
- ⬌ Up to 7.5 ft (2.3 m)
- ✶ Up to 421 lb (191 kg)
- ✿ Mollusks, fish, crustaceans
- ϟ Endangered

Black swallower
Chiasmodon niger
- ⊕ Atlantic, Indian & Pacific oceans
- ⋀ Tropical & subtropical waters
- ⬌ 10 in (25 cm)
- ✿ Bony fish
- ϟ Not listed

Blacksmith
Chromis punctipinnis
- ⊕ Temperate eastern Pacific
- ⋀ Shore waters
- ⬌ 10 in (25 cm)
- ✿ Planktonic invertebrates, benthic algae, weeds
- ϟ Not listed

Potato grouper
Epinephelus tukula
- ⊕ Indian & western Pacific oceans
- ⋀ Coral reefs
- ⬌ Up to 6.5 ft (2 m)
- ✶ Up to 242 lb (110 kg)
- ✿ Fish, crustaceans
- ϟ Not listed

Naked dragonfish, Ploughfish
Gymnodraco acuticeps
- ⊕ Southern Ocean
- ⋀ Near bottom at depths of 0–1,800 ft (0–550 m)
- ⬌ Up to 13.4 in (34 cm)
- ✿ Other fish, small crustaceans, bristleworms
- ϟ Not listed

Blue marlin
Makaira nigricans
- ⊕ Tropical to warm temperate Atlantic
- ⋀ Open ocean
- ⬌ 16.5 ft (5 m)
- ✶ Up to 1,800 lb (820 kg)
- ✿ Dolphinfish, tuna, squid
- ϟ Not listed

Black-spotted sweetlips
Plectorhinchus gaterinus
- ⊕ Indian Ocean
- ⋀ Coral reefs
- ⬌ Up to 18 in (46 cm)
- ✿ Crustaceans, mollusks
- ϟ Not listed

Hawaiian turkeyfish
Pterois sphex
- ⊕ Hawaiian waters
- ⋀ Coastal waters, benthic
- ⬌ 9 in (23 cm)
- ✿ Crabs, shrimps, fish
- ϟ Not listed

Hawaiian turkeyfish
Pterois sphex

Parrotfish, Stoplight parrotfish
Sparisoma viride
- ⊕ Tropical western Atlantic, including Caribbean Sea
- ⋀ Coral reefs
- ⬌ Up to 22 in (55 cm)
- ✶ Up to 3.5 lb (1.6 kg)
- ✿ Coral polyps, algae growing on rocks
- ϟ Not listed

Great barracuda
Sphyraena barracuda
- ⊕ Indian, Pacific & Atlantic oceans
- ⋀ Warm seas
- ⬌ 42 in (106 cm)
- ⤬ 4 in (10 cm)
- ✶ 88 lb (40 kg)
- ✿ Other fish
- ϟ Not listed

Yellowtail scad
Trachurus novaezelandiae
- ⊕ Australia, New Zealand
- ⋀ Cool to temperate coastal waters
- ⬌ Up to 20 in (50 cm)
- ✿ Crustaceans
- ϟ Not listed

FISH SIZE COMPARISON

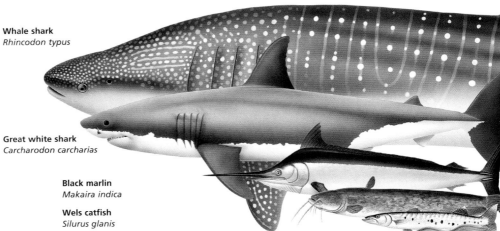

Whale shark
Rhincodon typus

Great white shark
Carcharodon carcharias

Black marlin
Makaira indica

Wels catfish
Silurus glanis

Great barracuda
Sphyraena barracuda

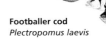

Green moray
Gymnothorax funebris

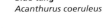

Footballer cod
Plectropomus laevis

Blackfin pacu
Colossoma macropomum

Red bigeye fish
Priacanthus macracanthus

Blue tang
Acanthurus coeruleus

Gelatinous blindfish
Aphyonus gelatinosus

Stoplight loosejaw
Malacosteus niger

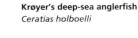

Krøyer's deep-sea anglerfish
Ceratias holboelli

INVERTEBRATES

More than 95 percent of animals are invertebrates. They are characterized by a structure that they all lack: a backbone or vertebral column. Invertebrates are divided into about 30 phyla, each displaying a distinct body form. Their evolutionary relationships can be inferred from their anatomy, their early development, and more recently from molecular analyses, particularly DNA. Features that define phyla include the organization of the body from a loose association of cells (Porifera), through tissue formation (Cnidaria), to the development of organs (Platyhelminthes). The acquisition of a fluid-filled body cavity was a defining point in evolution that allowed animals, such as Nematoda, Annelida, and many other phyla of worms, to move about by a hydraulic system driven by fluid pressure. While these phyla are soft-bodied, others are protected and supported by various types of skeletons, such as shells in Mollusca and a jointed exoskeleton in Arthropoda. The way in which embryos develop divide many advanced phyla into two lineages, one leading through the Echinodermata to the Chordata, the phylum to which vertebrates belong, the other containing the bulk of animal phyla. The continual identification of new invertebrate species indicates that the 1.3 million or so known invertebrates are nowhere near the full inventory.

Icon key

⊕	Distribution	✦	Wingspan	★	Diet
▲	Habitat	➶	Weight	⚡	Status
✳	Length				

PHYLUM CHORDATA
CHORDATES
53,000+ species

INVERTEBRATE CHORDATES
2,030+ SPECIES

SUBPHYLUM UROCHORDATA
SEA SQUIRTS
2,000+ species

SUBPHYLUM CEPHALOCHORDATA
LANCELETS
30 species

PHYLUM PORIFERA
SPONGES
9,000 species

PHYLUM CNIDARIA
CNIDARIANS
Sea anemones, corals, jellyfish & allies
9,000 species

Lion's mane jellyfish
Cyanea capillata
- ⊕ Arctic Ocean to northern Pacific & Atlantic oceans
- ▲ Open ocean
- ✳ Up to 120 ft (36.5 m) including tentacles; bell diameter 7.5 ft (2.3 m)
- ★ Zooplankton, small fish, comb jellies, moon jellies
- ⚡ Not listed

Hula skirt siphonophore
Physophora hydrostatica
- ⊕ East Pacific, West Atlantic
- ▲ Midwater
- ✳ Up to 16 in (41 cm) including tentacles
- ★ Phytoplankton, zooplankton
- ⚡ Not listed

PHYLUM PLATYHELMINTHES
FLATWORMS
13,000 species

PHYLUM NEMATODA
ROUNDWORMS
20,000+ species

PHYLUM MOLLUSCA
MOLLUSKS
Bivalves, snails, squid & allies
75,000 species

Giant squid
Architeuthis dux
- ⊕ All oceans but rare in tropical & polar regions
- ▲ Deep ocean, often near continental & island slopes
- ✳ ♂ up to 33 ft (10 m) including tentacles, ♀ up to 43 ft (13 m) including tentacles
- ➶ ♂ up to 330 lb (150 kg), ♀ up to 610 lb (275 kg)
- ★ Deep-sea fish, other squid
- ⚡ Not listed

Pacific banana slug
Ariolimax columbianus
- ⊕ Pacific coast of North America from Alaska to southern California
- ▲ Moist forest floor, under logs & other debris
- ✳ Up to 10 in (25 cm)
- ➶ 0.7–2.6 oz (21–75 g)
- ★ Fungus, leaves, dead plant materials, animal droppings
- ⚡ Not listed (but common)

Blue-ringed octopus
Hapalochlaena maculosa
- ⊕ Southern Australia
- ▲ Shallow coastal waters
- ✳ Body 2.5 in (5 cm), arms 4 in (10 cm)
- ➶ 1 oz (28 g)
- ★ Small crustaceans
- ⚡ Not listed

Caribbean reef octopus
Octopus briareus
- ⊕ Western Atlantic, Bahamas, Caribbean, coast of northern South America
- ▲ Coral reefs, rocks, seagrass beds
- ✳ 24 in (60 cm)
- ➶ 3.3 lb (1.5 kg)
- ★ Crabs, shrimps, lobster, fish
- ⚡ Not listed

PHYLUM ANNELIDA
SEGMENTED WORMS
12,000 species

Giant tube worm
Riftia pachyptila
- ⊕ Pacific Ocean
- ▲ Near deep-sea volcanic vents at depths of more than 1 mile (1.6 km)
- ✳ Up to 7.9 ft (2.4 m)
- ★ Relies on chemosynthetic symbiotic bacteria for nutrients
- ⚡ Not listed

PHYLUM ARTHROPODA
ARTHROPODS
1.1 million+ species

Caribbean reef octopus
Octopus briareus

Horseshoe crab
Limulus polyphemus

SUBPHYLUM CHELICERATA
CHELICERATES
81,000+ species

CLASS ARACHNIDA
ARACHNIDS
80,000 species

CLASS MEROSTOMATA
HORSESHOE CRABS
4 species

Horseshoe crab
Limulus polyphemus
- ⊕ East coast of North & Central America; spawns in Delaware & Chesapeake bays
- ▲ Sandy beaches for spawning; shallow bays for juveniles; ocean for adults
- ✳ Up to 2 ft (60 cm)
- ➶ Up to 10 lb (4.5 kg)
- ★ Sea worms, mollusks
- ⚡ Near threatened

CLASS PYCNOGONIDA
SEA SPIDERS
1,000 species

SUBPHYLUM MYRIAPODA
MYRIAPODS
Centipedes & allies
13,500 species

SUBPHYLUM CRUSTACEA
CRUSTACEANS
42,000 species

Krill, Antarctic krill
Euphausia superba
- ⊕ Southern Ocean
- ▲ Open ocean
- ✳ 1.5–2.5 in (4–6 cm)
- ➶ 0.4 oz (1 g)
- ★ Phytoplankton
- ⚡ Not listed (but abundant)

SUBPHYLUM HEXAPODA
HEXAPODS
1 million+ species

CLASS INSECTA
INSECTS
1 million+ species in 29 orders, including the 11 orders listed below

Azure damselfly
Coenagrion puella

ORDER ODONATA
DRAGONFLIES & DAMSELFLIES
5,500 species

ORDER MANTODEA
MANTIDS
2,000 species

ORDER BLATTODEA
COCKROACHES
4,000 species

ORDER ISOPTERA
TERMITES
2,750 species

ORDER ORTHOPTERA
CRICKETS & GRASSHOPPERS
20,000+ species

Cave weta, Wetapunga
Deinacrida heteracantha
- ⊕ New Zealand
- ▲ Rain forest
- ✳ Up to 4 in (10 cm)
- ➶ Up to 2.5 oz (70 g)
- ★ Leaves
- ⚡ Vulnerable

Migratory locust
Locusta migratoria
- ⊕ Africa, Asia, Australia
- ▲ Widespread
- ✳ 1.5–2.5 in (4–6 cm)
- ➶ 0.07 oz (2 g)
- ★ Vegetation
- ⚡ Not listed (but abundant)

ORDER HEMIPTERA
BUGS
80,000+ species

ORDER COLEOPTERA
BEETLES
370,000+ species

Seven-spotted ladybug/Seven-spot ladybird
Coccinella septempunctata
- ⊕ Europe, northern Asia, introduced North America & Oceania
- ▲ Orchards, gardens
- ✳ 0.2 in (5 mm)
- ★ Aphids
- ⚡ Not listed

Stag beetle
Lucanus cervus
- ⊕ UK, continental Europe, Turkey, Syria
- ▲ Oak forest, woodland, parks, gardens
- ✳ ♂ up to 3.5 in (9 cm) ♀ up to 2.5 in (6 cm)
- ★ Larvae feed on rotting wood; adults feed on sap
- ⚡ Not listed (but legally protected in several European countries)

Fog-basking beetle
Onymacris unguicularis
- ⊕ Namib Desert
- ▲ Sand dunes
- ✳ Up to 0.9 in (22 mm)
- ★ Detritus
- ⚡ Not listed

Monarch butterfly
Danaus plexippus

Camberwell beauty
Nymphalis antiopa

ORDER DIPTERA
FLIES

120,000 species

ORDER LEPIDOPTERA
BUTTERFLIES & MOTHS

165,000 species

Monarch butterfly
Danaus plexippus
- ⊕ North America (Canada to Mexico), Europe, Australia
- ▲ Forest, fields, roadsides, gardens
- ☀ 2 in (5 cm)
- ⛶ 4 in (10 cm)
- ✿ Larvae feed on milkweeds, adults feed on flower nectar
- ⚡ Not listed (abundant but wintering sites in Mexico in peril)

Julia butterfly
Dryas iulia
- ⊕ Southern Texas & Florida to Brazil
- ▲ Tropical forest
- ☀ 2 in (5 cm)
- ⛶ 3.5 in (9 cm)
- ✿ Flower nectar
- ⚡ Not listed

Common buckeye
Junonia coenia
- ⊕ USA, Mexico
- ▲ Open fields, beaches
- ☀ 1.1 in (2.8 cm)
- ⛶ 1.8–2.8 in (4.5–7 cm)
- ✿ Plants such as gerardias, toadflax & plantain
- ⚡ Not listed (but stable)

Red-spotted purple
Limenitis arthemis
- ⊕ Eastern USA, west to Mississippi River & south to Florida
- ▲ Moist woodland, suburban areas
- ☀ 1.6 in (4.1 cm)
- ⛶ 2.2–4 in (5.7–10.1 cm)
- ✿ Cherry trees, other trees
- ⚡ Not listed (but stable)

Blue morpho butterfly
Morpho menelaus
- ⊕ Central & South America
- ▲ Rain forest
- ☀ 6 in (15 cm)
- ⛶ 6 in (15 cm)
- ✿ Flowers, leaves, sap, juices
- ⚡ Not listed

Poseidon birdwing butterfly
Ornithoptera priamus poseidon
- ⊕ New Guinea
- ▲ Rain forest
- ⛶ Up to 5 in (12.5 cm)
- ✿ Vines
- ⚡ Not listed (but locally common)

Eastern tiger swallowtail
Papilio glaucus
- ⊕ Eastern North America
- ▲ Deciduous woodlands
- ☀ 2.2 in (5.5 cm)
- ⛶ 3.5 in (9 cm)
- ✿ Wild black cherry & tulip tree
- ⚡ Not listed (but stable)

Red Helen butterfly
Papilio helenus
- ⊕ Throughout South & Southeast Asia
- ▲ Evergreen forest
- ⛶ 4–4.7 in (10–12 cm)
- ✿ Larvae feed on plants in the family Rutaceae, including cultivated citrus species such as lime & orange
- ⚡ Not listed (but common)

Apollo butterfly
Parnassius apollo
- ⊕ Europe
- ▲ Mountain
- ⛶ 2.8–3.5 in (7–9 cm)
- ✿ Nectar
- ⚡ Vulnerable

Sphinx moth
(larvae = Tomato hornworm)
Protoparce quinquemaculata
- ⊕ North America
- ▲ Croplands
- ⛶ 3 in (7.6 cm)
- ✿ Larvae are pests of corn, cotton & tomato plants
- ⚡ Not listed

Painted lady
Vanessa cardui
- ⊕ Every continent except Antarctica
- ▲ Any open habitat
- ☀ 1.1 in (2.8 cm)
- ⛶ 2 in (5 cm)
- ✿ Larvae feed on thistles & other plants; adults feed on flower nectar
- ⚡ Not listed (but abundance varies from year to year)

ORDER HYMENOPTERA
BEES, WASPS, ANTS &
SAWFLIES

198,000 species

ORDER PHASMATODEA
STICK & LEAF INSECTS

3,000 species

Lord Howe Island phasmid, Land lobster
Dryococelus australis
- ⊕ Lord Howe Island Group (Australia)
- ▲ Shrubland, hollow trunks of living trees in forest
- ☀ Up to 5 in (12 cm)
- ✿ Leaves of *Melaleuca howea* & other trees
- ⚡ Critically endangered

Lesser purple emperor
Apatura ilia

Map butterfly
Araschnia levana

CLASS COLLEMBOLA
SPRINGTAILS
7,900 species

CLASS PROTURA
PROTURANS
500 species

CLASS DIPLURA
DIPLURANS
800 species

PHYLUM ECHINODERMATA
ECHINODERMS
Sea stars, sea urchins & allies
6,000 species

Antarctic sea urchin
Sterechinus neumayeri
- ⊕ Southern Ocean near Antarctica & subantarctic islands
- ▲ Benthic, most abundant in shallow waters
- ☀ 2.8 in (7 cm)
- ✿ Phytoplankton, zooplankton, sponges, bristleworms, seal feces
- ⚡ Not listed

PHYLUM NEMERTEA
RIBBON WORMS
900 species

PHYLUM ENTOPROCTA
GOBLET WORMS
150 species

PHYLUM TARDIGRADA
WATER BEARS
600 species

PHYLUM CTENOPHORA
COMB JELLIES
100 species

PHYLUM ROTIFERA
ROTIFERS
Wheel animals
1,800 species

PHYLUM HEMICHORDATA
HEMICHORDATES
Acorn worms
90 species

PHYLUM CHAETOGNATHA
ARROW WORMS
90 species

PHYLUM GASTROTRICHA
GASTROTRICHS
700 species

PHYLUM KINORHYNCHA
SPINY-CROWN WORMS
150 species

PHYLUM PHORONIDA
HORSESHOE WORMS
20 species

PHYLUM ONYCHOPHORA
VELVET WORMS
100+ species

PHYLUM BRACHIOPODA
BRACHIOPODS
Lamp shells
350 species

PHYLUM BRYOZOA
BRYOZOANS
Lace animals
5,000 species

PHYLUM SIPUNCULA
PEANUT WORMS
150 species

PHYLUM ECHIURA
SPOON WORMS
160 species

PHYLUM LORICIFERA
BRUSHHEADS
22 species

PHYLUM PRIAPULIDA
PHALLUS WORMS
17 species

PHYLUM NEMATOMORPHA
HORSEHAIR WORMS
240 species

PHYLUM ACANTHOCEPHALA
SPINY-HEADED WORMS
1,000 species

PHYLUM POGONOPHORA
BEARD WORMS
80 species

PHYLUM GNATHOSTOMULIDA
SAND WORMS
80 species

PHYLUM CYCLIOPHORA
CYCLIOPHORANS
3 species

PHYLUM PLACOZOA
PLACOZOANS
2 species

PHYLUM ORTHONECTIDA
ORTHONECTIDS
20 species

PHYLUM RHOMBOZOA
RHOMBOZOANS
150 species

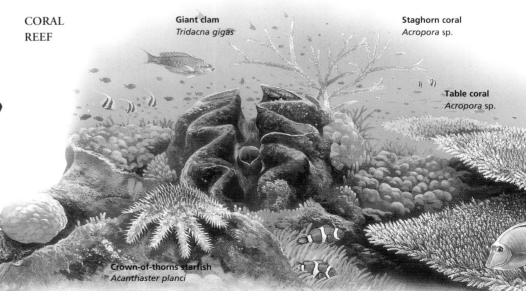

CORAL REEF

Giant clam
Tridacna gigas

Staghorn coral
Acropora sp.

Table coral
Acropora sp.

Crown-of-thorns starfish
Acanthaster planci

GLOSSARY

Adaptation

A change in an animal's behavior or body that allows it to survive and breed in new conditions.

Amphibian

A vertebrate animal, similar to a reptile, that lays its eggs in water and that spends its early life in water and its adult life on land.

Anal fin

An unpaired fin on the lower surface of a fish's abdomen. It plays an important role in swimming.

Antarctic Polar Frontal Zone

A zone, also known as the Antarctic Convergence, that surrounds Antarctica, where Antarctic waters mix with the warmer, more northerly, subantarctic waters.

Aquatic

Living all or most of the time in water; cf terrestrial.

Arboreal

Living all or most of the time in trees.

Arthropod

An animal with jointed legs and a hard exoskeleton; includes insects, spiders, crustaceans, centipedes, and millipedes.

Bacteria

Microscopic lifeforms that are usually just a single cell.

Baleen

The comblike, fibrous plates found in some whales; often referred to as whalebone.

Benthic

Relating to or occurring at the bottom of a body of water or the depths of the ocean.

Billabong

A waterhole in a branch of an Australian river that is dry during the dry season and that fills when the river is in flood.

Biodiversity

The total number of species of plants and animals in a particular location.

Biodiversity hotspot

An area where the diversity of plant and wildlife species is under threat.

Biogeography

The study of the way plants and animals are distributed.

Bioluminescence

Light produced by living organisms.

Biome

Large major habitat type that is generally identified with its dominant vegetation type. Biomes include grasslands, coniferous forests, deserts, and tundra.

Biosphere

The part of the world that can support life.

Bivalve

A mollusk, such as an oyster or a mussel, that has two shells that are joined at a hinge.

Braided watercourse

Part of a stream or river that has interlacing channels that combine and divide in irregular patterns.

Breach

The action of a whale as it springs upward from the water.

Browser

A plant-eating mammal that uses its hands or lips to pick leaves from trees and bushes.

Caecilian

A tropical, wormlike, burrowing amphibian.

Canopy

Of a forest, the upper layer composed entirely of trees.

Captive breeding

The breeding by humans of endangered animal species under controlled conditions.

Carapace

A hard outer covering, such as a turtle's shell; this provides protection for an animal's body.

Carnivore

An animal that eats mainly meat.

Carrion

The rotting flesh and other remains of dead animals.

Cartilaginous fish

A fish with a skeleton made of cartilage, such as a shark, ray, or chimaera.

Casque

A bony or horny protrusion on the head of some birds, such as cassowaries.

Cays

Small, sandy islands that form on coral reefs.

Cephalic fins

Hornlike extensions of the pectoral fins of manta rays and their relatives.

Cerebral cortex

The thin, outer layer of gray matter in the hemispheres in the brains of humans and upper mammals.

Colonial species

Species of birds and other animals that breed together in large groups.

Continental drift

The theory that the present distribution of continents is the result of the fragmentation of one or more pre-existing supercontinents that have drifted apart.

Copepod

One of a number of tiny freshwater and marine crustaceans.

Coral bleaching

The loss of color affecting coral reefs when the algae that live in them are killed or forced out.

Coteries

Groups of animals, within larger populations, that form communities and cooperate in providing food and shelter for their members.

Coverts

Small feathers that cover the base of a bird's wing and tail feathers.

Cranium

The skull of a vertebrate animal. The cranium encloses the brain.

Crepuscular

Becoming active around dusk or in the early evening.

Crop

A thin-walled, saclike pocket of the gullet, used by birds to store food before digestion or to feed chicks by regurgitation.

Cryptic

Hard to detect as a result of color, shape, or behavioral patterns.

Deciduous forest

An area dominated by woody perennial plants that shed their leaves at a particular time, season, or growth stage.

Decomposer

An organism, such as a bacterium or a fungus, that consumes dead organisms and returns them to ecological cycles.

Deep-sea hydrothermal vent

A spring of superheated, mineral-rich water found on some ridges deep in the ocean.

Deforestation

The cutting down of forest trees for timber, or to clear land for farming or building.

Dermal

To do with the skin, especially the dermis, the second layer of an animal's skin.

Diatom

One of many kinds of tiny algae in marine and freshwater environments.

Dimorphic

Having two distinct forms within a species. Sexual dimorphism is the situation in which the male and female of a species differ in size and/or appearance.

Display

Behavior used by an animal to communicate with its own species, or with other animals.

Diurnal

Active during the day. Most reptiles are diurnal because they rely on the Sun's heat to provide energy.

Diversity

The variety of plant and animal species in the natural world.

Dormant

To be in a sleeplike state, often because of environmental conditions; the body's activity slows for this period.

Echolocation

A system of navigation that relies on sound rather than sight or touch. Porpoises, dolphins, many bats, and some birds use echolocation.

Ecology

The interrelationship between organisms and the environment in which they exist, or the study of this interrelationship.

Ecosystem

A community of plants and animals and the environment to which they are adapted.

Egg tooth

A special scale on the tip of the upper lip of a hatchling lizard or snake. It is used to break a hole in the egg so that the newborn animal can escape.

Electroreceptors

Specialized organs found in some fish and mammals that detect electrical activity from the bodies of other animals.

El Niño

A warm current of equatorial water flowing southward down the northwest coast of South America. When pronounced and persistent, it results in rainfall and temperature anomalies.

Embryo

An unborn animal in the earliest stages of development. An embryo may grow inside its mother's body, or in an egg outside her body.

Emergent

A forest tree that is taller than those around it.

Emissions

Substances, such as gases and fluids, that are discharged into the environment.

Endemic

A species, or other taxon, found only in one habitat or region. For example, emus are endemic to Australia.

Ephemeral wetlands

Areas that become flooded in spring and early summer or after heavy rain.

Epiphyte

A plant that grows on a tree or other plant, but does not feed on or damage its host.

Estivate

To spend a period of time in a state of inactivity to avoid unfavorable conditions.

Evolution

Gradual change in plants and animals, over many generations, in response to their environment.

Exotic

A foreign or non-native species of animal or plant, often introduced into a habitat by humans.

Extinction

The death of a species.

Filter feeder

An animal that obtains food by straining small prey from seawater.

Fissure

A fracture in the ground. In volcanic areas, eruptions may occur as a line of vents along a fissure.

Flyway

A route regularly taken by birds when they migrate.

Food chain

A system in which one organism forms food for another, which in turn is eaten by another, and so on.

Forage

To search for and eat food.

Fossil

A remnant, impression, or trace of a plant or animal from a past geological age, usually found in rock.

Fry

Young or small fish.

Functionally extinct

Not completely extinct, but reduced to a point where extinction is inevitable.

Fungi

Lifeforms, such as mushrooms, molds, mildews, and yeasts, that contain no chlorophyll and that live parasitically on living and dead organisms.

Gastroliths

Stones swallowed by such animals as crocodilians, that stay in the stomach to help crush food.

Gelatinous

Viscous in texture, similar to the texture of jelly or gelatin.

Genera

The plural of "genus," which is the second lowest group in the scientific classification of living things.

Genetic material

The substance that stores the genetic information of a lifeform. The genetic material of almost all lifeforms is deoxyribonucleic acid (DNA).

Gestation period

The period of time during which a female animal is pregnant with her young.

Gills

Organs that collect oxygen from water and are used for breathing.

Gizzard

In birds, the equivalent of the stomach in mammals. Grit and stones inside the gizzard help to grind up food.

Glacial relics

Fossil remains of plants and animals that were originally preserved in glaciers or other bodies of ice.

Global warming

The increase in the temperature of Earth and its lower atmosphere due to human activity such as deforestation, land degradation, and the burning of fossil fuels. Global warming is also known as "the greenhouse effect."

Gullet

Found in birds, the gullet is the equivalent of the esophagus in mammals. This tube passes food from the bill to the gizzard.

Gyre

A circular motion in a body of water.

Habitat

The area in which an animal naturally lives. Many different kinds of animals live in the same environment, but each kind lives in a different habitat within that environment.

Harem

A group of female animals that mate and live with one male.

Herbivore

An animal that eats only plant material, such as leaves, bark, roots, and seeds; cf carnivore, omnivore.

Hibernate

To remain completely inactive during the cold winter months. Some animals eat as much as they can before winter, then find a sheltered spot and fall into a deep sleep.

Hierarchy

The different levels in the scientific classification of living things. "Phylum," "class," "order," "family," and "genus" are ranks in the zoological hierarchy.

Hybrid

The offspring of parents of two different species.

Hyoid bone

A single U-shaped bone or one of a number of bones at the base of an animal's tongue.

Incisors

The front teeth of an animal, located between the canines, used for cutting food.

Incubate

To keep eggs in an environment, outside the female's body, in which they can develop and hatch.

Insectivore

An animal that eats only or mainly insects or invertebrates. Some insectivores also eat small vertebrates, such as frogs, lizards, and mice.

Intertidal zone

The area of a seashore that is washed by tides. It is covered by water at high tide and exposed to the air at low tide.

Invasive species

Animal or plant species introduced by humans into areas where they do not occur naturally and which threaten species native to that area.

Invertebrate

An animal with no backbone. Many invertebrates are soft-bodied animals, such as worms, leeches, or octopuses, but most have an exoskeleton, or hard external skeleton.

Isthmus

A narrow strip of land, with water on both sides, that joins two larger landmasses.

Keratin

A protein found in horns, hair, scales, and feathers.

Keystone species

Animal or plant species that are so abundant in their environment that they make a strong impact on that environment.

La Niña

Periods of unusually cold ocean temperatures in the equatorial Pacific that occur between El Niño events.

Larva (pl. larvae)

A young animal that looks completely different from its parents. An insect larva, sometimes called a grub, maggot, or caterpillar, changes into an adult by either complete or incomplete metamorphosis.

Mammal

A warm-blooded vertebrate that suckles its young with milk and has a single bone in its lower jaw. Although most mammals have hair and give birth to live young, some, such as whales and dolphins, have little or no hair; others, the monotremes, lay eggs.

Mandible

Biting jaw of an insect.

Mangroves

Flowering shrubs and trees tolerant of saltwater, found on low-lying tropical coasts and estuaries.

Marsupial

A mammal that gives birth to young that are not fully developed. These young are usually protected in a pouch (where they feed on milk) before they can move around independently.

Mass extinction

The simultaneous extinction of an entire species or of a number of species, often as the result of a catastrophic event.

Microbial fermentation

The decomposition of foodstuffs, especially carbohydrates, by the action of microbes in an animal's large intestine.

Microhabitat

A very limited, isolated environment—such as a tree stump—in which an organism lives.

Microorganisms

Tiny lifeforms, such as bacteria, that can be seen only with a microscope.

Migration

A usually seasonal journey from one habitat to another. Many animals migrate vast distances to another location to find food, or to mate and lay eggs or give birth.

Mollusk

An animal, such as a snail or squid, with no backbone and a soft body that is often partly or fully enclosed by a shell.

Molt

To shed an outer layer of the body, such as hair, skin, scales, feathers, or the exoskeleton.

Monoculture

The use of agricultural or forest land for the cultivation of a single crop or organism.

Monotreme

A primitive mammal with many features in common with reptiles. Monotremes lay eggs and have a cloaca.

Montane forest

A forest that grows on the middle slopes of a mountain. Montane forests typically grow below higher coniferous forests.

Musth

In elephants, a time of high testosterone levels when the musth gland between the eye and ear secretes fluid.

Mutualism

An alliance between two species that is beneficial to both.

Mycorrhiza

A fungus that has a symbiotic association with the roots of a plant.

Natal burrow

The underground place where a burrowing animal gives birth to its young.

Natural selection

The process by which organisms adapt to their environment by reproducing in ways most favorable to their survival.

Nekton

Animals that swim freely in the sea and are not dependent on the action of waves or currents.

Niche

The ecological role played by a species within an animal community.

Nocturnal

Active at night. Nocturnal animals have special adaptations, such as large, sensitive eyes or ears, to help them find their way in the dark.

Omnivore

An animal that eats both plant and animal food. Omnivores have teeth and a digestive system designed to process almost any kind of food.

Opportunistic

Feeding on whatever food is available, rather than on a specific diet.

Opposable

Describing a thumb that can reach around and touch all of the other fingers on the same hand, or a toe that can similarly touch all of the other toes on the same foot.

Order

A major group used in taxonomic classification. An order forms part of a class, and is further divided into one or more families.

Organism

Any form of animal or plant life. An organism consists of separate parts that work together to support its existence.

Oviparous

Reproducing by laying eggs. Little or no development occurs within the mother's body; instead, the embryos develop inside the egg; cf ovoviviparous, viviparous.

Ovipositor

A tubelike organ through which female insects lay their eggs. The stinger of bees and wasps is a modified ovipositor.

Ovoviviparous

Reproducing by giving birth to live young that have developed from eggs within the mother's body. The eggs may hatch as they are laid or soon after; cf oviparous, viviparous.

Pair bond

A partnership maintained between a male and a female animal, particularly birds, through one or several breeding attempts. Some species maintain a pair bond for life.

Pampas

Extensive grassy plains in South America, east of the Andes.

Parallel evolution

The situation in which related groups living in isolation develop similar structures to cope with similar evolutionary pressures.

Parr

A young salmon that is able to feed independently in freshwater streams.

Passerine

Any species of bird belonging to the order Passeriformes. A passerine is often described as a songbird or a perching bird.

Patagium

A fold of skin between the forelimbs and hindlimbs of a gliding mammal or reptile, or a fold of skin on the front edge of a bird's wing.

Pelagic

Swimming freely in the open ocean; not associated with the bottom; cf benthic.

Pelvic fins

Paired fins, located on the lower part of a fish's body.

Permafrost

Ground that has remained frozen for at least two successive winters and the intervening summer.

Pheromone

A chemical released by an animal that sends a signal and affects the behavior of others of the same species.

Placental mammal

A mammal that nourishes its developing young inside its body with a blood-rich organ called a placenta.

Plankton

The plant (phytoplankton) or animal (zooplankton) organisms that float or drift in the open sea. Plankton forms an important link in the food chain.

Pleistocene

A geological epoch between about 1.8 million and 10,000 years ago, during which ice sheets advanced across northern Europe and North America. Modern humans appeared during the Pleistocene epoch.

Pneumatophores

Roots in certain marsh and swamp plants that act as respiratory organs.

Pollen

A dustlike substance produced by male flowers, or by the male organs in a flower, and used in the plant's reproduction.

Prairie

An extensive plain or undulating tract of land, covered mainly by grass, which in its natural state has deep, fertile soil.

Predator

An animal that lives mainly by killing and eating other animals.

Prehensile

Grasping or gripping. Some tree-dwelling mammals and reptiles have prehensile feet or a tail that can be used as an extra limb to help them stay safely in a tree. Elephants have a prehensile "finger" on the end of their trunk. Browsers, such as giraffes, have prehensile lips to help them grip leaves.

Prey

Animals that are hunted, killed, and eaten by other animals.

Pride

A group of lions.

Primate

A member of the mammalian order Primates. This order includes humans, apes, and lemurs.

Proboscis

In insects, a long, tubular mouthpart used for feeding. In some mammals, a proboscis is an elongated nose, snout, or trunk.

Progeny

The offspring or descendants of animals or plants.

Prokaryote

An organism, usually single-celled, in which the cell has no nucleus or membrane-bound organelles. Bacteria are prokaryotes.

Pupa (pl. pupae)

The stage during which an insect transforms from a larva to an adult.

Radiation

Energy radiated from a source as wavelengths or particles.

Rain forest

A tropical forest that receives at least 100 inches (250 cm) of rain each year. Rain forests are home to a vast number of plant and animal species.

Range

The entire geographic area across which a species is regularly found.

Raptor

A diurnal bird of prey, such as a hawk or falcon. The term is not used to describe owls.

Ratites

Flightless birds, such as emus, ostriches, cassowaries, and rheas, that lack a keel on their breastbone.

Receptors

Nerve endings through which animals receive sensory stimuli.

Red List of Threatened Species

A list of endangered animal and plant species compiled regularly by the International Union for the Conservation of Nature and Natural Resources (IUCN), which was established in 1963.

Reintroduction

The release into an area of a species that previously had lived there, but had disappeared from it.

Remnant population

A small number of surviving plants or animals in an area where they were previously abundant.

Reptile

One of about 6,000 species of animals that breathe air, are cold-blooded and have scaly bodies.

Rodent

A member of the order Rodentia. Rodents, which include mice, rats, squirrels, and beavers, are relatively small gnawing mammals.

Rudimentary

Describes a simple, undeveloped, or underdeveloped part of an animal, such as an organ or wing.

Ruminants

Hoofed animals—cattle, buffalo, bison, antelopes, gazelles, sheep, goats, and other members of the family Bovidae—with a four-chambered stomach.

Salt marsh

An area of soft, wet land periodically covered by saltwater, in temperate zones and generally treeless.

Scavenger

An animal that eats carrion—often the remains of animals killed by predators.

Seagrass

Long-leaved, grasslike marine plants that grow in coastal waters in temperate climates.

Sea ice

Ocean water that has frozen and formed ice. This occurs at temperatures of about 28.8°F (-1.8°C).

Seamount

An isolated submarine hill or mountain, usually of volcanic origin.

Siphonophore

One of various kinds of pelagic floating or free-swimming bell-like or disklike gelatinous invertebrates.

Smolt

A young salmon or sea trout that is ready to migrate from a freshwater stream to the sea.

Speciation

The formation of a new species by means of evolution.

Species

A group of animals with similar features that are able to breed together and produce fertile young.

Spermatophore

A container or package of sperm that is passed from male to female during mating.

Sphagnum bogs

Damp, spongy areas where decomposing mossy sphagnum plants combine with other plant materials to form deep layers of peat.

Stridulate

To make a sound by scraping objects together. Many insects communicate in this way, some by scraping their legs against their body.

Subtropical

The region that lies approximately between latitudes 35° and 40° in both hemispheres.

Symbiosis

An alliance between two species that is usually (but not always) beneficial to both.

Taxonomy

The system of classifying living things into various groups and subgroups according to similarities in features and adaptations.

Temperate

Describes an environment or region that has a warm (but not very hot) summer and a cool (but not very cold) winter. Most of the world's temperate regions are located between the tropics and the polar regions.

Terrestrial

Living all or most of the time on land; cf aquatic.

Territory

An area of land inhabited by an animal and defended against intruders. The area often contains all the living resources required by the animal, such as food and a nesting or roosting site.

Tertiary

A geological period that lasted from approximately 65.5 million years to 2.6 million years ago.

Thermal

A column of rising air, used by birds to gain height, and on which some birds soar to save energy.

Thermoregulation

The capacity of an organism to keep its temperature within a certain range.

Toothed whale

A whale that has slicing teeth and a throat that is able to swallow large pieces of prey.

Torpor

A sleeplike state in which bodily processes are greatly slowed.

Tropical forests

Forests growing in tropical regions that experience little difference in temperature throughout the year.

Tundra

A cold, barren area where much of the soil is frozen and the vegetation consists mainly of mosses, lichens, and other small plants adapted to withstand intense cold.

Turgid

Swollen or distended. The fluid content of a plant cell maintains the cell's level of turgor or turgidity.

Understory

The forest trees that form a canopy below the main canopy.

Vascular plant

A plant that has an internal system of cells that transport water, sugars, and other substances throughout the plant body.

Venom

Poison injected by animals into a predator or prey through fangs, stingers, spines, or similar structures.

Vertebrate

An animal with a backbone. All vertebrates have an internal skeleton of cartilage or bone.

Viviparous

Reproducing by means of young that develop inside the mother's body and are born live. Most mammals and some fish (such as sharks) are viviparous.

Vocalization

Vocal sounds, such as the howling of wolves, that animals use for communication.

Wadi

The Arabic name for a river channel in a desert. It is usually dry, but carries water occasionally.

Water column

The conceptual model of a body of water from the surface to the bottom.

Wetlands

Land that is covered for a part of the year with fresh or salt water. It has vegetation adapted to life in saturated soils.

INDEX

Page numbers in *italics* refer to illustrations and photographs. Numbers and letters in square brackets refer to page number and column location in the Animal Factfile.

In temperate and tropical seas tiger sharks *(Galeocerdo cuvier)* range over the
continental shelf and around islands. These active hunters feed on a variety
of other fishes as well as sea turtles and trash from vessels. They can grow to
about 16 feet (5 m), although such large specimens are increasingly rare.

THE ENCYCLOPEDIA OF
the Sea

Blue hole
Forming an almost perfect circle a quarter-mile
(0.4 km) in diameter, the Great Blue Hole of
Lighthouse Reef in Belize is one of the most
dramatic diving destinations in the world.
Several such sinkholes exist, all in coastal areas
where rising seas flooded a limestone cave
system and caused the roof to collapse.

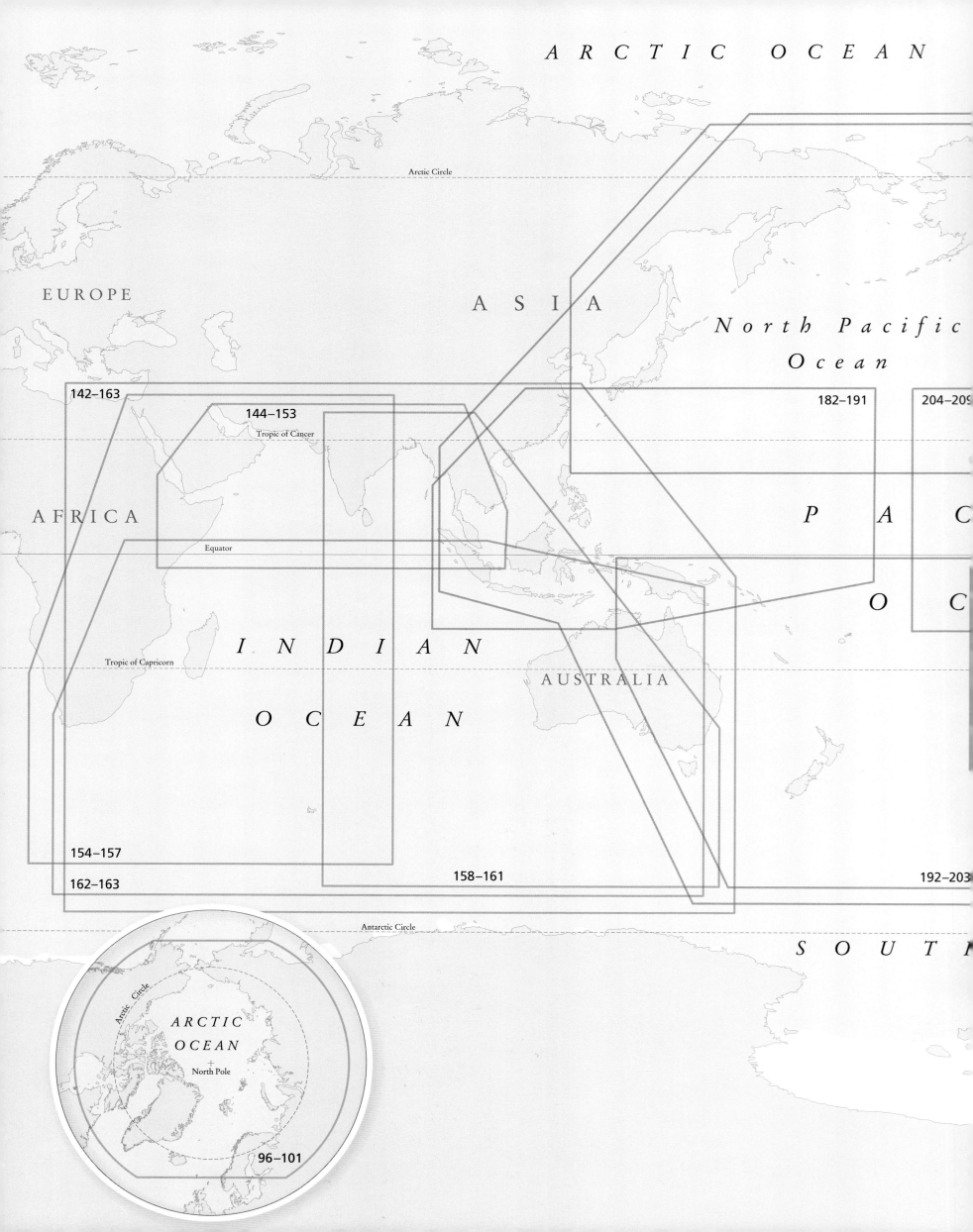

ARCTIC OCEAN

Arctic Circle

EUROPE

ASIA

North Pacific
Ocean

142–163

144–153

Tropic of Cancer

182–191

204–209

AFRICA

P A C

Equator

Tropic of Capricorn

O C

INDIAN

AUSTRALIA

OCEAN

154–157

162–163

158–161

192–203

Antarctic Circle

S O U T N

Arctic Circle

ARCTIC
OCEAN

+
North Pole

96–101

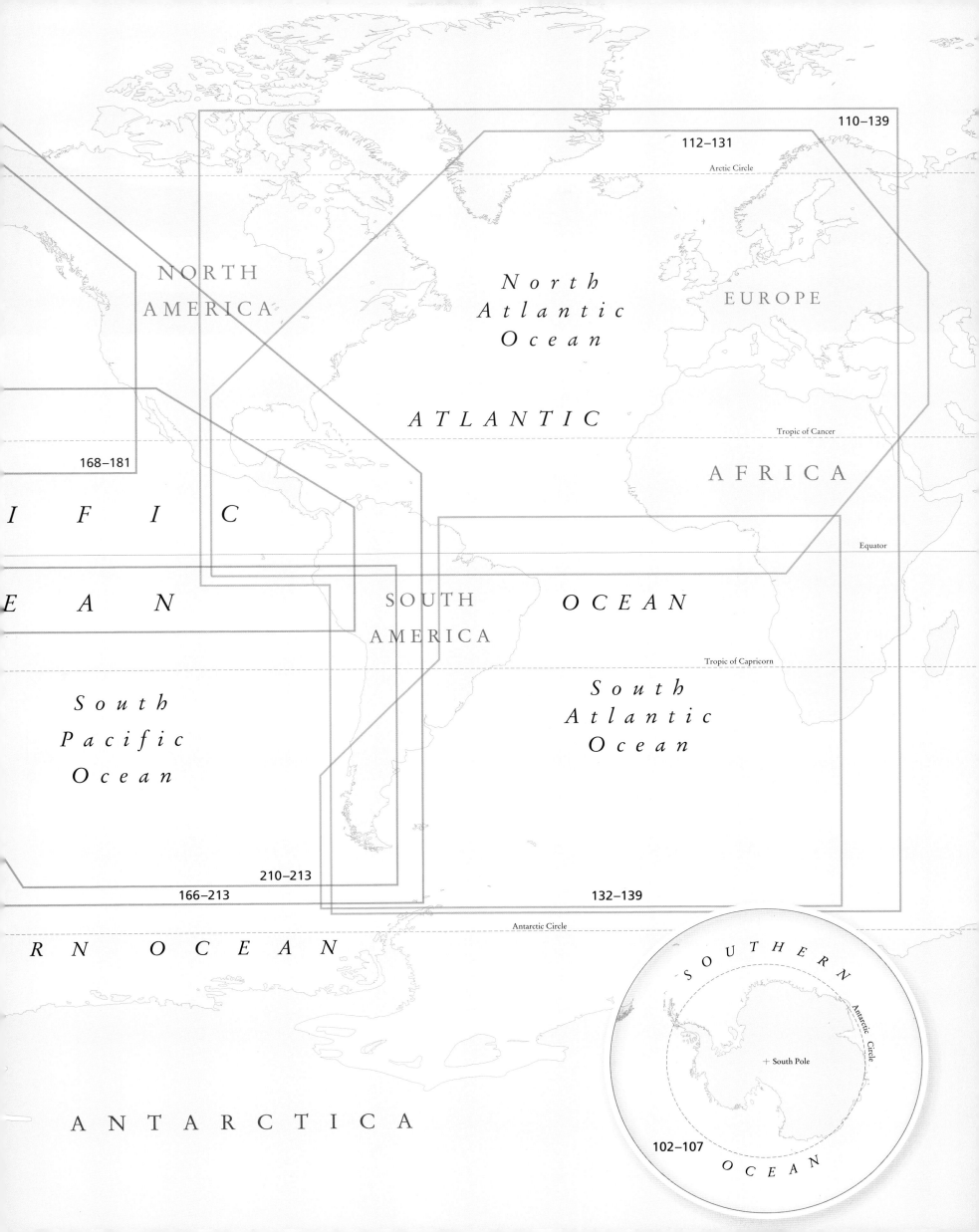

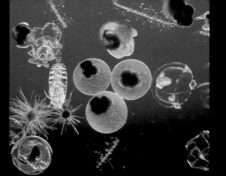
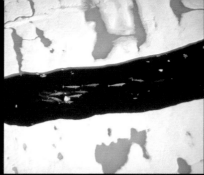

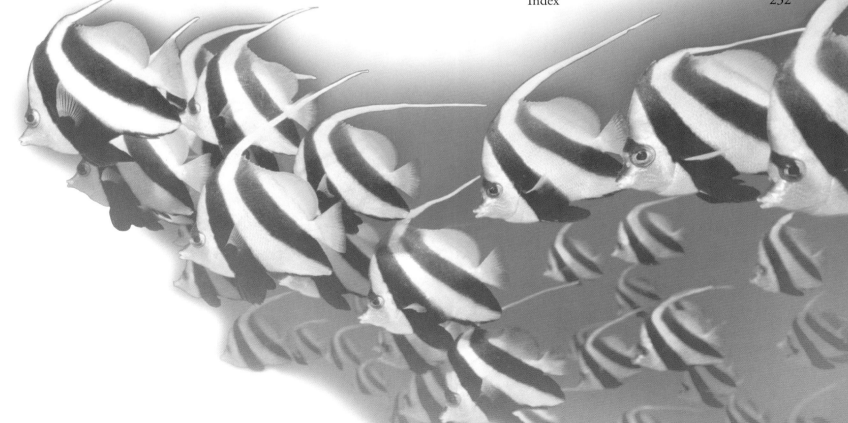

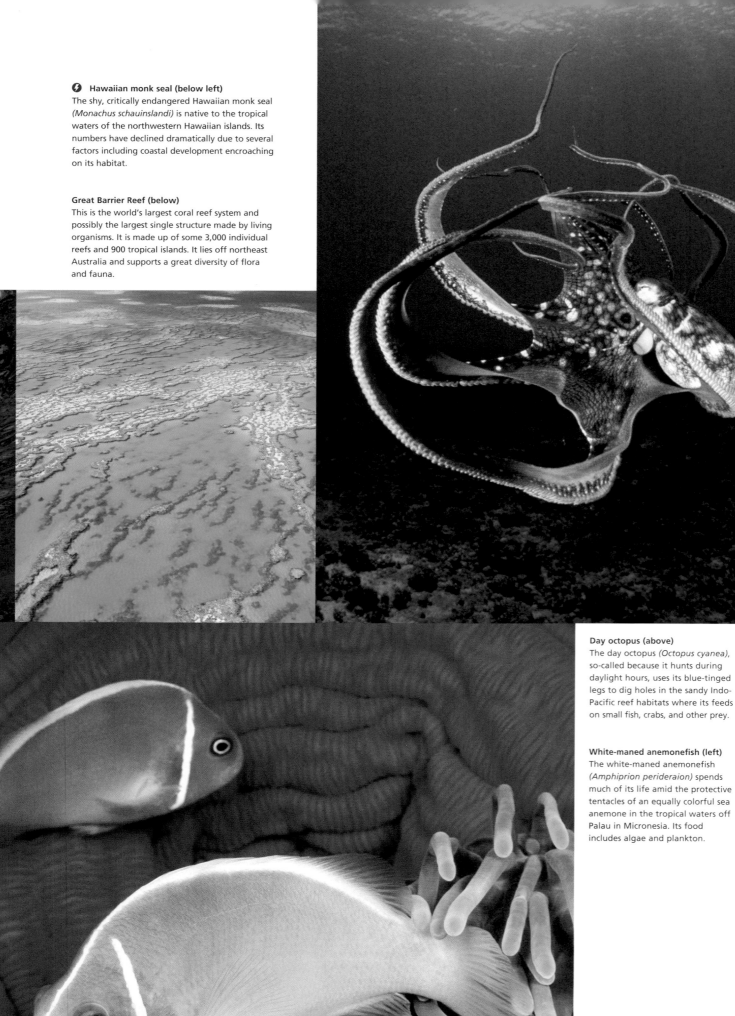

❷ Hawaiian monk seal (below left)
The shy, critically endangered Hawaiian monk seal (*Monachus schauinslandi*) is native to the tropical waters of the northwestern Hawaiian islands. Its numbers have declined dramatically due to several factors including coastal development encroaching on its habitat.

Great Barrier Reef (below)
This is the world's largest coral reef system and possibly the largest single structure made by living organisms. It is made up of some 3,000 individual reefs and 900 tropical islands. It lies off northeast Australia and supports a great diversity of flora and fauna.

Day octopus (above)
The day octopus (*Octopus cyanea*), so-called because it hunts during daylight hours, uses its blue-tinged legs to dig holes in the sandy Indo-Pacific reef habitats where its feeds on small fish, crabs, and other prey.

White-maned anemonefish (left)
The white-maned anemonefish (*Amphiprion perideraion*) spends much of its life amid the protective tentacles of an equally colorful sea anemone in the tropical waters off Palau in Micronesia. Its food includes algae and plankton.

FOREWORD

Producing an atlas is a daunting undertaking that requires an incredible breadth of knowledge, great attention to detail, creative skill in illustrative design and, of course, an ability to convey essential information with a well-written narrative. Indeed, producing an atlas of the oceans creates additional challenges in that the topography of the seafloor and of the ocean surface must be sensed remotely, and the marine life that inhabits the waters can be understood only from painstaking scientific research, much of which may not be widely available to the general public. Not only are the waters, the ocean floor, and the marine life complex and varied, but together they represent a coupled system with threads of connections that run throughout both time and space.

The *Illustrated Atlas of the Sea* is an amazing publication. It is more than an atlas in a traditional sense; it has nuggets of recent scientific research, ranging in scale from global to molecular that are embedded within the chapters. It contains stunning photographs to illustrate the diversity of marine environments and marine life and it offers much that is relevant in our lives through the inclusion of forays into climate change, pollution, natural resources, hurricanes, tsunamis, threatened sea life, and conservation. It is also more than a standard atlas in that it is comprehensive, easy-to-read, and offers an introduction to the casual scientist—yet contains much of interest to the more sophisticated scientific adventurer.

The *Illustrated Atlas of the Sea* is divided into nine chapters, the first four of which provide an overview of the water, its composition, circulation, and never-ending motion from waves and tides; its physical environments extending from the dynamic coastlines to the frigid dark plains of the deep sea; and its marine habitats, forms of life, and rich natural resources. The next four chapters, written by experts in their respective fields, are structured around the four ocean regions: Polar, Atlantic, Indian, and Pacific. It is here that the maps of the oceans can be found with color-coded bathymetric depths that are superimposed with hundreds of geographic names to depict the shoals, plateaus, ridges, basins, trenches, and other features that together make up 70 percent of Earth's surface. Each of these chapters is presented in a similar format that also includes, interspersed throughout the pages, dozens of helpful insets to convey ocean basin statistics, patterns of ocean currents, and the distribution of natural resources within the basins. A final reference chapter provides an encyclopedic fact file, glossary, and gazetteer. The large-format layout allows an ideal balance between maps, photographs, illustrations, and text.

Humans have always had a fascination for the oceans, and you will surely enjoy reading about them in this compelling reference atlas. It brings together in one volume all of the attributes that provide this fascination, ranging from the intensity of the ocean's physical processes, to the incredible diversity of marine life that lives in the waters, to the shape and structure of the basins that hold both the waters and the life. The *Illustrated Atlas of the Sea* will surely be a lasting contribution.

Dr John T. Wells
Dean and Director, Virginia Institute of Marine Science.

How to Use this Atlas

This atlas is arranged in two main sections. The first section provides a historical and physical overview of the global sea. Photographs, diagrams, and mapping illustrate information about different marine environments and species. The second section is a chapter-by-chapter cartographic survey of the world's major oceans and the sea divisions they encompass.

It includes details of seafloor topography, maps that show the key currents, and photographs and information about animal life and human activity in the region. A reference section completes the book and consists of a detailed fact file on the oceans and their subdivisions, a glossary, a gazetteer, and an index.

Thematic pages
The thematic pages include detailed world maps accompanied by illustrations, diagrams, charts, graphs, and photographs. They cover topics as diverse as the origins of water on Earth, exploration of the seas, ocean ecosystems, and conservation.

Introduction
This text gives a clear, concise overview of the most salient facts about the featured topic or sea.

Pie charts, tables, and graphs
Additional details about regions, or the animal life found there, is provided in the form of tables, charts, or graphs. This at-a-glance information adds to captions and photographs.

Diagrams and illustrations
These highlight relevant topics such as geological processes, ecosystems, wildlife, and oceanographic research equipment.

THEMATIC MAPPING

Marine life maps
Maps display marine life topics such as wildlife species range, migratory paths, and coral distribution.

Physical geography maps
Geographical features such as hot spots, ice extent, and continental margins are shown on thematic maps.

NASA and NOAA maps
Maps display data and information gathered using the latest satellite and sonar technology.

Thematic map key

Informative photography
Current photographs about the sea, marine life, and resources are included with captions.

Thematic maps
Thematic maps show a range of data from wildlife distribution, physical features, and sea depth.

Scale
The scale of the main map, plus a scale bar and projection information are included here.

Feature box
Special-interest subjects are shown in a feature box, with their own introduction and selected photographs or illustrations.

Locator map
This map indicates the location of the sea within its ocean.

The Facts
Charts detail the dimensions of the seas and oceans.

NASA imagery
Satellite photography provides up-to-date visual information.

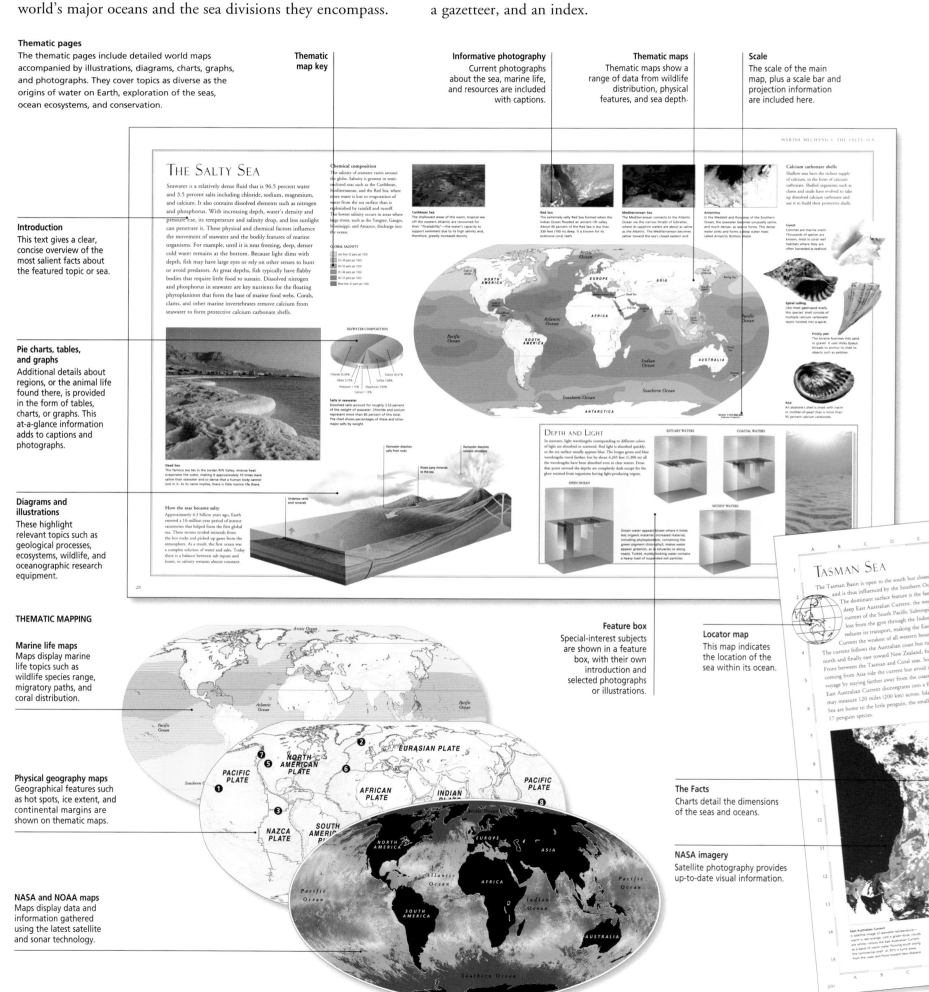

Cartographic pages
These pages show detailed maps of the world's oceans and seas, accompanied by illustrations, diagrams, charts, graphs, and photographs. The text describes the nature of each sea and its major currents and climatic influences.

Oceans
The introduction page for each chapter displays a large map of the entire ocean and provides an overview of natural resources, statistical information, and typical ecosystems.

Locator map
This map indicates the location of the ocean.

Pie chart
Facts about each ocean are presented in a pie-chart.

Cartographic map
Each map shows details of the seafloor including variations in depth, topography, and named features.

Natural resources
A small map carries icons to denote the natural resources to be found in each ocean area.

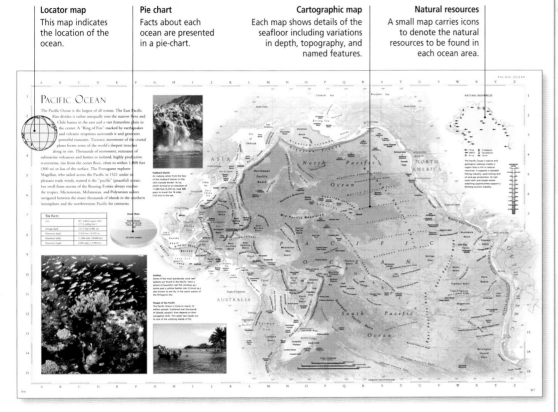

Seas
These pages take a close-focus look at a particular sea; a large-scale map shows the seafloor features in detail. Smaller supporting maps and images show key currents, natural resources, wildlife, and human activity.

Current map
A diagrammatic map shows the prevailing surface currents in the area.

Wildlife photography
Photographs from wildlife and undersea specialists show the animal life in the region.

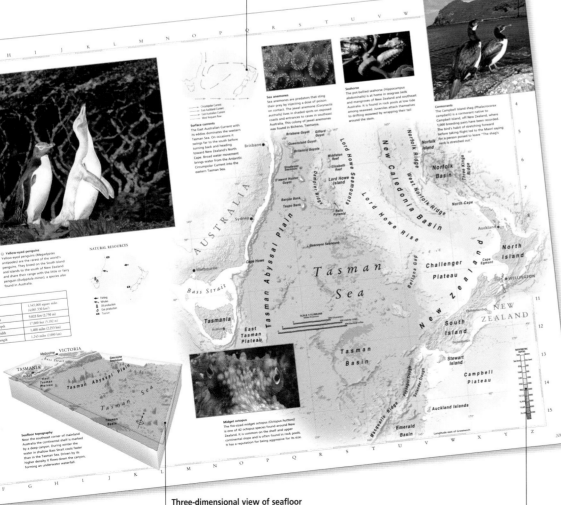

Three-dimensional view of seafloor
A computer-generated map reveals details of ridges, canyons, and other seafloor features.

Bathymetric depth scale

VISUAL KEYS

Conservation icons
The conservation status of endangered and critically endangered animals, as determined by the IUCN Red List of Threatened Species, is indicated by a red or yellow icon.

Critically endangered
Endangered

CARTOGRAPHIC MAPS

Map legend
The maps in this atlas contain a variety of labels, symbols, and other graphic devices to provide detailed information such as ocean floor depth and topography, and the location of undersea mountains, trenches, and volcanoes, rivers, cities, and country borders.

BATHYMETRIC DEPTHS

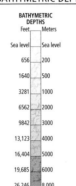

BATHYMETRIC DEPTHS	
Feet	Meters
Sea level	Sea level
656	200
1640	500
3281	1000
6562	2000
9842	3000
13,123	4000
16,404	5000
19,685	6000
26,246	8,000

SCALE AND PROJECTION

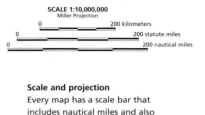

SCALE 1:10,000,000
Miller Projection

200 kilometers
200 statute miles
200 nautical miles

Scale and projection
Every map has a scale bar that includes nautical miles and also shows map projection details.

WATER FEATURES

Ocean	*PACIFIC OCEAN*
Sea	*Bering Sea*
Bay/gulf	*Gulf of Alaska*
Channel/strait	*Bering Strait*
Lakes	*Lake Nasser*
Rivers	*Nile*
Canal	*Suez Canal*
Seamount	▲ *Zheng He Seamount* 6,263ft (1,909m)
Bathymetric feature	*Madagascar Basin*

PHYSICAL FEATURES

Geographic feature	*Baja California*
Peninsula	*Cape York Peninsula*
Cape/point	*Beachy Head*
Island group	*Solomon Islands*
Island	*Isla Santa Maria*
Pole	North Pole

PLACE NAMES

Country names F R A N C E

City symbols

■ **Los Angeles**	Over 5 million	◼ **Bangkok**	National Capital
● **Houston**	1 million to 5 million	● **Hanoi**	National Capital
○ Miami	100,000 to 1 million	✹ Riga	National Capital

A sculpted and eroding rocky shore hints at the changeable physical
features of the undersea world beyond. Like ecosystems on land,
the marine environment is dynamic and varied. It encompasses an
array of geological forms as well as changing physical and chemical
conditions that establish the wide array of habitats where
communities of marine life may survive.

WATER ON EARTH

THE GLOBAL SEA

Liquid water covers more than 70 percent of the world's surface and is the defining feature of planet Earth. Salt water makes up 97 percent of this watery domain, forming a global sea that is subdivided into five named oceans. These interconnected marine regions are the vast Atlantic and Pacific oceans; the Indian Ocean, which stretches between eastern Africa and Australia; the Southern Ocean that encircles Antarctica; and the small, polar Arctic Ocean ringed by the northern fringes of North America and Eurasia. For much of recorded history this global sea has been a fascinating enigma. Its currents and weather patterns have challenged seafarers for centuries, while its undersea landscape and abundant marine life have largely been hidden beneath the waves. Only within the last two centuries have mariners and scientists begun to uncover the mysteries of Earth's oceans, providing an ever-deeper understanding of the global sea and the forces that have shaped it—and continue to do so today.

The marine map
A map of the global sea recognizes the five oceans and a wide array of subdivisions. Although the boundaries between these features may be rather arbitrary, geography and size are key factors in defining them. To geographers a "sea" is a large area of ocean that is partly enclosed by land. It may include a smaller arm called a gulf. Bays are smaller still.

Fresh water 3%

Salt water 97%

Salty and fresh water
Seawater makes up about 97 percent of Earth's water. The remainder is fresh water in lakes, rivers, groundwater, land ice, and water vapor.

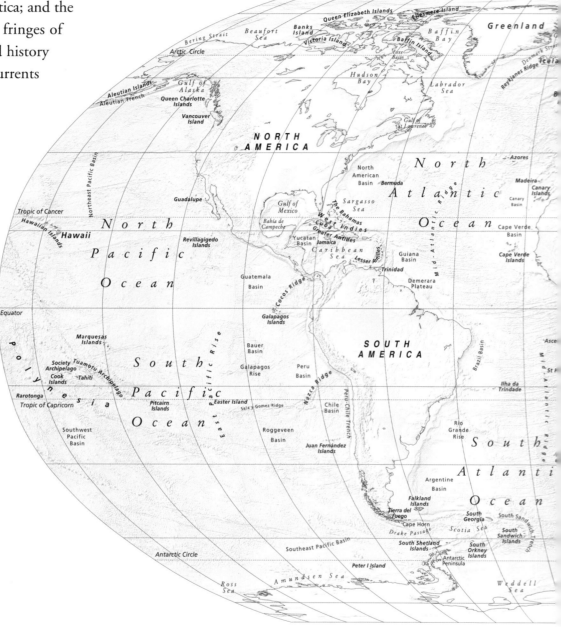

Earth from space
Orbiting astronauts called Earth "the big blue marble," noting the sapphire color of the global sea. Continents appear as patches of green and tan. Wisps of white are clouds formed when seawater evaporates.

GLOBAL SEA FACTS	
Total area	139 million square miles (361 million km²)
Total volume	310,000,000 cubic miles (1,347,000,000 km³)
Average depth	12,230 feet (3,730 m)
Greatest depth	35,840 feet (10,900 m)
Mean ocean crust thickness	4.04 miles (6.5 km)
Longest mountain range	10,000 miles (16,000 km)

OCEAN DEPTHS

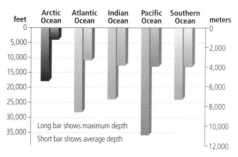

Ocean depths
For each ocean basin, the long colored bar shows maximum depth. The shorter bar indicates the basin's average depth.

OCEAN SIZES

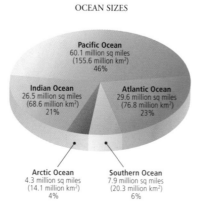

Pacific Ocean
60.1 million sq miles
(155.6 million km²)
46%

Indian Ocean
26.5 million sq miles
(68.6 million km²)
21%

Atlantic Ocean
29.6 million sq miles
(76.8 million km²)
23%

Arctic Ocean
4.3 million sq miles
(14.1 million km²)
4%

Southern Ocean
7.9 million sq miles
(20.3 million km²)
6%

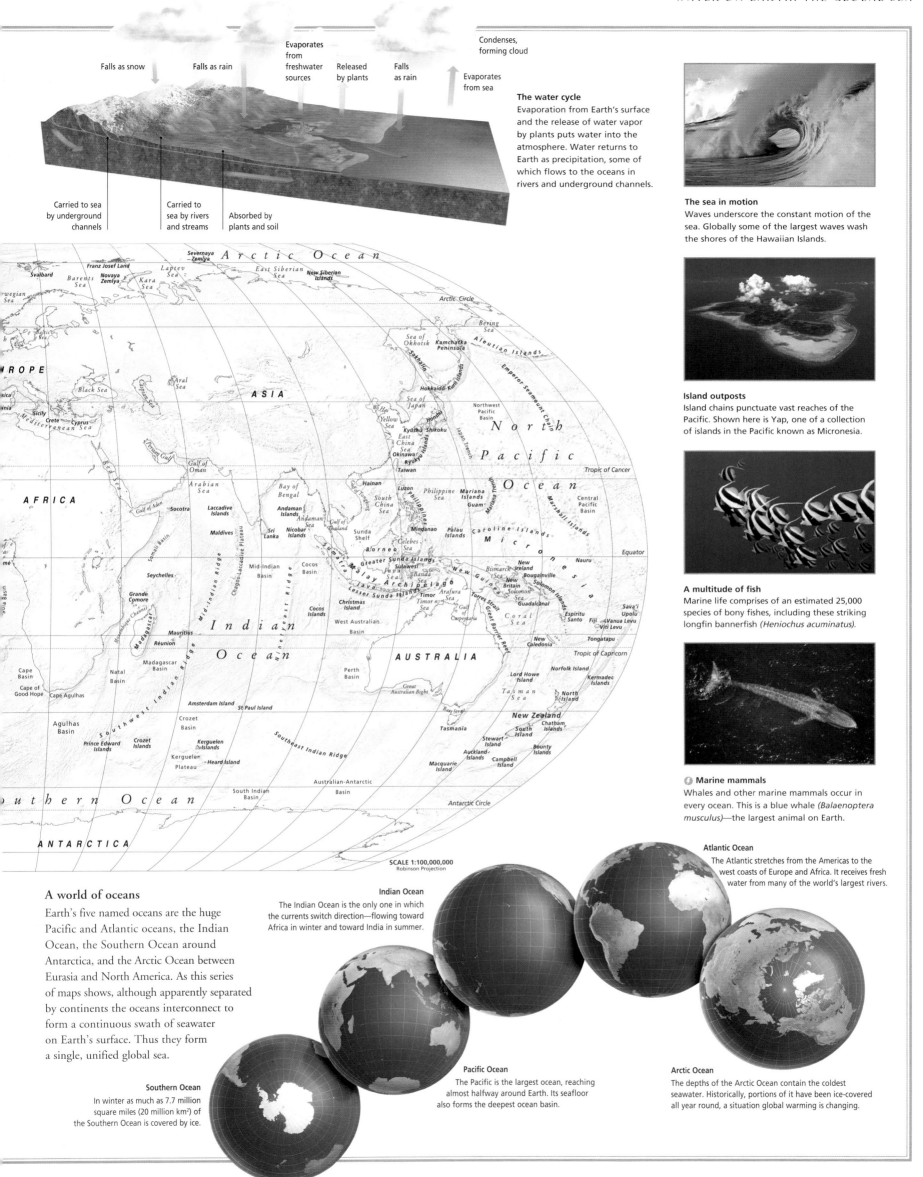

The water cycle
Evaporation from Earth's surface and the release of water vapor by plants puts water into the atmosphere. Water returns to Earth as precipitation, some of which flows to the oceans in rivers and underground channels.

Condenses, forming cloud

Falls as snow   Falls as rain   Evaporates from freshwater sources   Released by plants   Falls as rain   Evaporates from sea

Carried to sea by underground channels   Carried to sea by rivers and streams   Absorbed by plants and soil

The sea in motion
Waves underscore the constant motion of the sea. Globally some of the largest waves wash the shores of the Hawaiian Islands.

Island outposts
Island chains punctuate vast reaches of the Pacific. Shown here is Yap, one of a collection of islands in the Pacific known as Micronesia.

A multitude of fish
Marine life comprises of an estimated 25,000 species of bony fishes, including these striking longfin bannerfish (*Heniochus acuminatus*).

Marine mammals
Whales and other marine mammals occur in every ocean. This is a blue whale (*Balaenoptera musculus*)—the largest animal on Earth.

A world of oceans

Earth's five named oceans are the huge Pacific and Atlantic oceans, the Indian Ocean, the Southern Ocean around Antarctica, and the Arctic Ocean between Eurasia and North America. As this series of maps shows, although apparently separated by continents the oceans interconnect to form a continuous swath of seawater on Earth's surface. Thus they form a single, unified global sea.

Indian Ocean
The Indian Ocean is the only one in which the currents switch direction—flowing toward Africa in winter and toward India in summer.

Atlantic Ocean
The Atlantic stretches from the Americas to the west coasts of Europe and Africa. It receives fresh water from many of the world's largest rivers.

Southern Ocean
In winter as much as 7.7 million square miles (20 million km²) of the Southern Ocean is covered by ice.

Pacific Ocean
The Pacific is the largest ocean, reaching almost halfway around Earth. Its seafloor also forms the deepest ocean basin.

Arctic Ocean
The depths of the Arctic Ocean contain the coldest seawater. Historically, portions of it have been ice-covered all year round, a situation global warming is changing.

SCALE 1:100,000,000
Robinson Projection

Origin of a Watery World

The newly formed Earth was a turbulent, volcanic planet. No liquid water—and no life—could exist on its searing surface, but gases vented from volcanoes included water vapor that accumulated in dense, hot clouds. More steam rose from ice evaporating from comets that bombarded Earth's surface. As early Earth rapidly cooled, however, the clouds of steam began to condense into rain—the source of the first liquid water on the planet's surface. Water's chemical properties were crucial in the evolution of the seas and eventually of life itself. One is a high heat capacity, the ability to absorb a great deal of heat before water warms appreciably. As a result, temperatures in watery environments, including oceans and the bodies of organisms, remain remarkably stable. Water also dissolves many other substances, and it has surface tension—the cohesiveness that keeps individual molecules connected to one another in raindrops, rivers, and in the vast global sea.

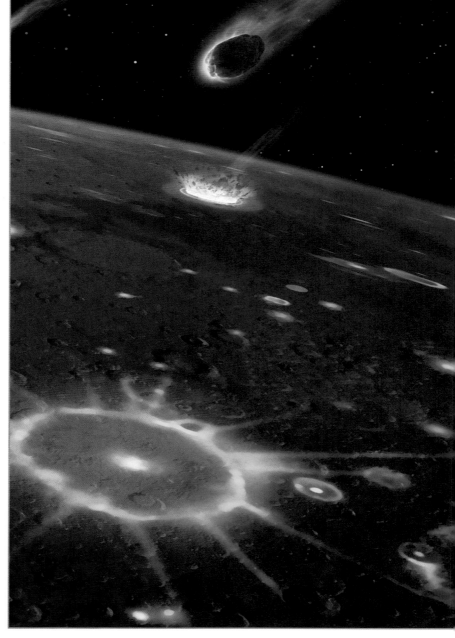

Evidence for Early Beginnings

Zircon crystals from ancient streambeds, such as Jack Hills in Western Australia shown below, form when water is present around melting granite. Dated to about 4.4 million years ago, zircons are remnants of Earth's first rocky crust, which was later destroyed by meteorite impacts. Their age strongly implies that conditions required for life—including liquid water—may have developed much earlier and faster than once thought.

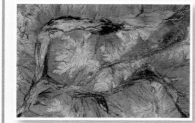

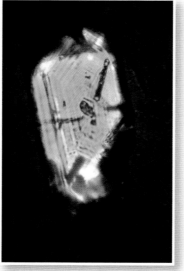

This enlarged image shows an ancient zircon crystal formed when searing heat, possibly from the impact of an ancient meteorite, melted granite in early Earth's crust.

Filling the oceans

Earth's first water supply probably was vaporizing ice from comets and asteroids that struck the hot planet over billions of years. As Earth cooled, water vapor condensed and fell. Erosion of volcanoes began and the ocean basins slowly filled with water and sediment.

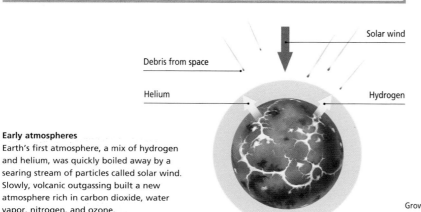

Early atmospheres
Earth's first atmosphere, a mix of hydrogen and helium, was quickly boiled away by a searing stream of particles called solar wind. Slowly, volcanic outgassing built a new atmosphere rich in carbon dioxide, water vapor, nitrogen, and ozone.

Solar wind

Debris from space

Helium

Hydrogen

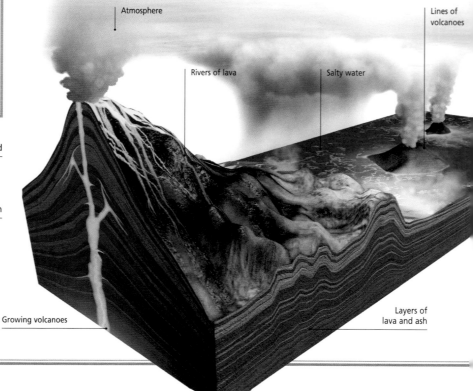

Atmosphere

Rivers of lava

Salty water

Lines of volcanoes

Growing volcanoes

Layers of lava and ash

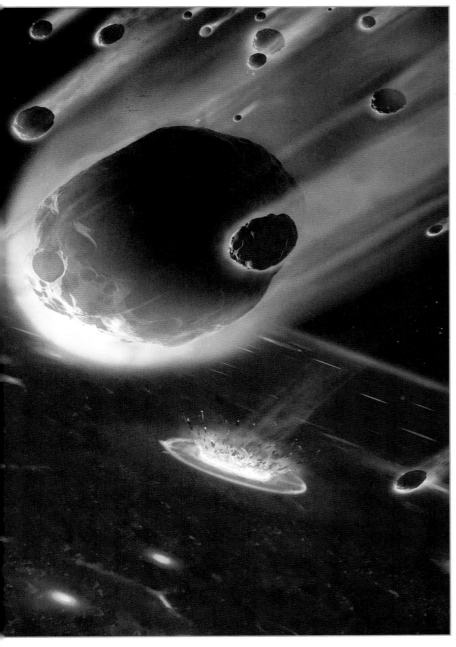

Properties of water

Water's properties make it one of the most extraordinary substances on Earth. Links between water molecules called hydrogen bonds cause water to lose or gain heat slowly, so temperatures in watery environments are quite stable. Water also is relatively dense, providing physical support for floating and swimming organisms. Yet water's solid form, ice, is less dense than liquid water, so ice floats—allowing aquatic life to survive beneath it.

Making a water molecule
A water molecule has an oxygen atom sandwiched between two hydrogen atoms, giving the molecule two arms with opposite electrical charges. This difference spurs the formation of hydrogen bonds that give water unique properties.

SOLID

Solid water
Below 32°F (0°C), bonds between water molecules form a rigid, open lattice, which makes ice less dense than liquid water.

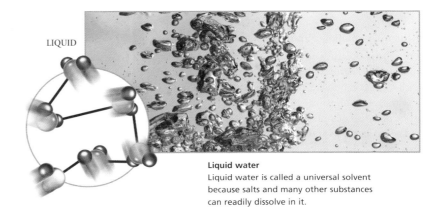

LIQUID

Liquid water
Liquid water is called a universal solvent because salts and many other substances can readily dissolve in it.

GAS

Gas
Water vapor is the gaseous phase of water. Water is the only substance on Earth that naturally exists as a solid, liquid, and gas.

Water from Earth or space?
At one time most scientists believed that Earth's first liquid water condensed from water vapor spewed by volcanoes along with other gases. Further study has supported the "heavy bombardment" theory that over billions of years ice-rich comets and asteroids brought water with them when they collided with Earth's atmosphere. Quite possibly, some combination of processes generated the planet's water supply.

Land and seas
Rain, formed by condensing water vapor, fed the oceans. The emerging waters lapped the volcanic granite that formed the first continents.

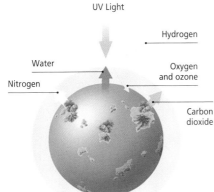

Earth's first ozone layer
Intense sunlight interacted with oxygen in the early atmosphere. This chemical reaction formed an ozone layer that protected Earth's surface from further harmful solar radiation. The ozone barrier paved the way for the evolution of more complex life.

THE WATER TABLE	
Boiling point	212°F (100°C)
Freezing point, pure water	32°F (0°C)
Freezing point, seawater	around 28.6°F (-1.9°C)
Weight of one gallon (2.2 L) at 68°F (20°C)	8.3 pounds (3.8 kg)
Seawater salt content	average 3.5%
Fresh water salt content	less than 0.1%
Pressure increase with depth	14.7 pounds (6.7 kg) per each 33 feet (10 m)
Average speed of sound in water at 46°F (8°C)	4,721 feet (1,439 m) per second
Greatest supply of fresh water	Antarctic ice (90%+)

THE EVOLVING SEA

As Earth cooled, a crust formed over its molten interior. This rocky skin's features included both highlands and basin-like depressions. As water vapor in the atmosphere condensed into droplets, torrential rains began to fill what would become ocean basins. Runoff from land areas contained eroded minerals, the beginnings of the salty global sea and a seafloor blanketed by layers of sediments. Geological evidence suggests that several times during Earth's early history the heat from massive asteroid impacts boiled away the oceans and any life they may have contained. By about 3.8 billion years ago, however, primitive cells became established, and over geologic time the evolution of animals and other major groups would be well underway. Meanwhile, climatic changes coincided with rising and falling sea levels, and shifts in Earth's crust were rearranging landmasses and ocean basins. By 200 million years ago, a vast global sea teeming with life washed the shores of a single huge continent, now called Pangea.

Millennia of change and loss

Over the ages Earth's ecosystems and the types of organisms in them have changed dramatically as climate shifts correlated with ice ages and fluctuating sea levels. Different factors have also triggered at least five mass extinction episodes, in which more than half of animal species were lost. Many ecologists today fear that a sixth mass extinction is underway due to unrestrained development and other human activities.

— Temperature
— Sea level (present at 0)
— Extinction rate
● Mass extinction event

A 444 mya
Ordovician extinction
Possible causes of this mass extinction include prolonged global glaciation and irradiation from an exploding star.

B 359 mya
Devonian extinction
A long series of smaller extinctions destroyed 70 percent of all species.

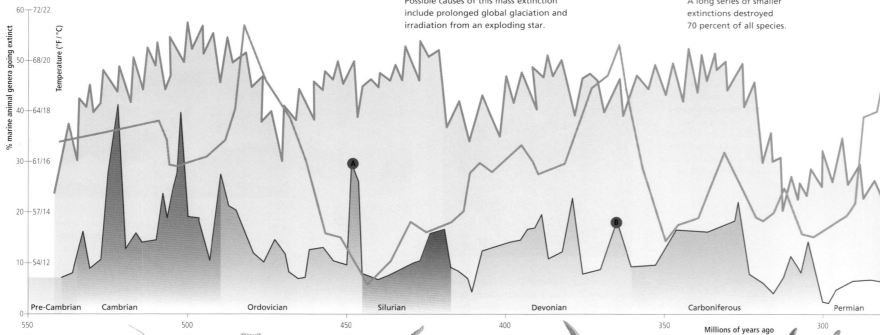

Cambrian period
542 mya Animals with shells and jawless fish (first vertebrates) evolve

Trilobites resembled bugs, but some grew more than 2 feet (60 cm) long.

Ordovician period
490 mya Jawless fish diversify and jawed sharks evolve

Sharks with jaws may have evolved from the jawless thelodonts.

Silurian period
435 mya Fish diversify; the first insects and amphibians appear

Life blossomed on land, as bony fish such as spiny *Nostolepis* swam with sharks.

Devonian period
408 mya First bony fish and first land plants and animals appear

Some modern sharks have spines in front of their dorsal fins, like *Ctenacanthus* did.

Carboniferous period
360 mya Golden Age of Sharks; the first reptiles appear

No one knows how the scissor-tooth shark used its weird whorls of teeth.

Evolving life

Bacteria were among the first lifeforms to evolve in early Earth's shallow seas. Some of these single-celled species, called cyanobacteria, carried out photosynthesis as plants do, using sunlight to manufacture their own food. Over time they formed domed mats—known today as stromatolites—that hardened into limestone as sediments and minerals accumulated in them. Fossil stromatolites have been dated radiometrically to about 3.5 billion years old. Shark Bay, shown left, in Western Australia is home to Earth's only living stromatolites. These specimens may be up to 1,000 years old.

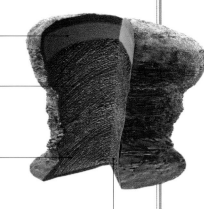

Stromatolite structure

Growth The mat of bacteria grows, mounding above the accumulating sediment.

Mineralization The bacteria secrete calcium carbonate, or limestone. The mineral secretions trap sediments that form darker layers.

Interior The interior of the stromatolite reveals concentric layers formed during previous growth.

Base The base of the stromatolite is firmly attached to the surface upon which the mound was originally established.

ICY TIMES

During an ice age, extensive ice sheets develop in certain regions, as in Antarctica and Greenland. By this measure, Earth is still in an ice age that began 2.6 million years ago. Sea level falls as large amounts of water become locked up in ice. The process continues during colder ice-age periods when glaciers advance. Sea level rises when glaciers retreat, a trend that accelerates as the overall ice age wanes.

Last Ice age

Ice now

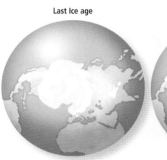

The supercontinent Pangea
About 260 million years ago a single supercontinent called Pangea was essentially a gigantic island surrounded by sea. The geologic changes that created Pangea would later break it apart, forming the modern position of continents and seas.

C 251 mya
Permian extinction
Loss of 96 percent of marine species followed global warming caused by volcanism and shifts in sea chemistry.

D 208 mya
Triassic extinction
About 20 percent of major marine groups and the last large amphibians vanished at this time.

E 65 mya
Cretaceous extinction
An asteroid impact and massive volcanism plunged Earth into years of "impact winter," killed off the non-avian dinosaurs and half of marine species.

Seal level (ft / m)

980/300

660/200

330/100

0

−330/−100

−660/−200

Last ice age

Quaternary

Pangea

Triassic   Jurassic   Cretaceous   Tertiary

250   200   150   100   50   0

☐ **Permian period**
286 mya Mass extinctions occurred both on land and in the seas

Permian rivers were home to eel-like sharks such as *Xenacanthus*.

☐ **Triassic period**
248 mya Early dinosaurs, mammals, and marine reptiles appear

Nothosaurus was a reptile with webbed toes and needle-like teeth.

☐ **Jurassic period**
208 mya First modern sharks and rays; mass extinctions in seas

Protospinax was an ancient relative of angel sharks and saw sharks.

☐ **Cretaceous period**
144 mya Sand tigers and some other modern shark lineages; first birds, dinosaurs

Top ocean predators included *Cretoxyrhina*—a relative of the great white.

☐ **Tertiary period**
65 mya to today Mammals, birds, and flowering plants diversify

Gigantic Megalodon ruled the oceans. On land, ancestors of modern humans evolved.

Into the future: Possible sixth mass extinction

A dramatic increase in species extinctions began in the Quaternary around 1.8 million years ago. These human-caused losses continue today.

Earth's Dynamic Crust

Earth's crust is divided into about a dozen sections or plates that move in different ways atop semi-fluid material underneath. Some contain all or part of the modern-day continents, while others, such as the Pacific Plate, lie entirely beneath the sea. By way of the process once called continental drift and now known as plate tectonics, plate movements slowly reposition continents, push up mountains, and recycle the crust of ocean basins. Such changes have been reshaping the seas for more than half a billion years. As ancient continents moved, the lifeforms on them were carried along, and researchers have been able to use fossil discoveries and the global distribution patterns of living species to help confirm hypotheses about continental movements. Today's continents have occupied the same general positions for about 10 million years. Even so, they are still on the move—on average, about 2 inches (5 cm) a year—as the age-old shifting of Earth's crustal plates continues.

Making ocean basins

Ocean basins form over millions of years as magma upwelling from Earth's interior gradually splits continental crust, creating an opening into which water can flood. About 150 million years ago, the Atlantic, Indian, and other modern ocean basins began to form as the supercontinent Pangea started to break apart. The same process is occurring today in parts of eastern Africa.

Moving Continents

Earth's crust is divided into movable rocky sections called tectonic plates that essentially float on the upper mantle. Over geologic time, moving plates have carried continental landmasses along with them in a process known as plate tectonics. When continents separate, the populations of species inhabiting them also may be separated, a phenomenon that helps explain the global distribution of certain plants and animals.

Today, the unusual plants called cycads occur on several continents. This ancient group first arose on Pangea and evidently cycads were carried around the globe as the supercontinent broke up.

200 million years ago

90 million years ago

Present day

60 million years from now

Birth of a rift valley
As a landmass begins to split apart, the land tilts and begins to subside, creating a wide valley.

Flooding the new ocean basin
When the valley floor subsides below sea level, seawater fills the depression. The formation of seafloor pushes the landmasses further apart.

Seafloor spreading
The ocean widens as spreading continues. As the seafloor moves outward it settles and sinks, leaving a ridge on either side of the rift.

Geological features

Earth's constantly moving tectonic plates are responsible for many of the planet's large-scale geological features, including those all or partly submerged under the sea.

Undersea collision
Arcs of volcanic islands occur where two ocean plates collide and one slides beneath the other.

Mid-ocean ridge
Where plates meet at mid-ocean ridges, new seafloor forms as crust material wells up from the mantle underneath.

Hot-spot volcanoes
Areas of unusually hot mantle beneath the interiors of crustal plates give rise to hot-spot volcanoes.

Coastal collision
Arcs of volcanic mountains occur where an oceanic plate collides with a continent and subducts beneath it.

Sliding plates
Transform faults occur where plates move past each other. Earthquakes occur where fault zones intermittently lock up, then release.

Continental rift
The tectonic splittin of a continent form deep valley. If the v floor continues to t seafloor spreading a new ocean basin.

Plate boundaries

Heat rising by convection from Earth's mantle drives the movement of crustal plates. The plates may slide past each other, spread apart, or collide, forming three general types of plate junctions—transform fault, divergent, and convergent boundaries. Volcanism and mountain building are common where plates collide. Examples are the volcano-dotted Andes, Cascades and other great mountain ranges along the coasts of continents.

Convergent boundary
When plates collide, the heavier one often is subducted into the mantle, slipping under the lighter one.

Divergent boundary
When plates move apart, new seafloor forms at oceanic spreading centers, or rifts, in continental crust.

Transform fault boundary
Where crustal plates mainly slide past each other, they form a transform fault boundary.

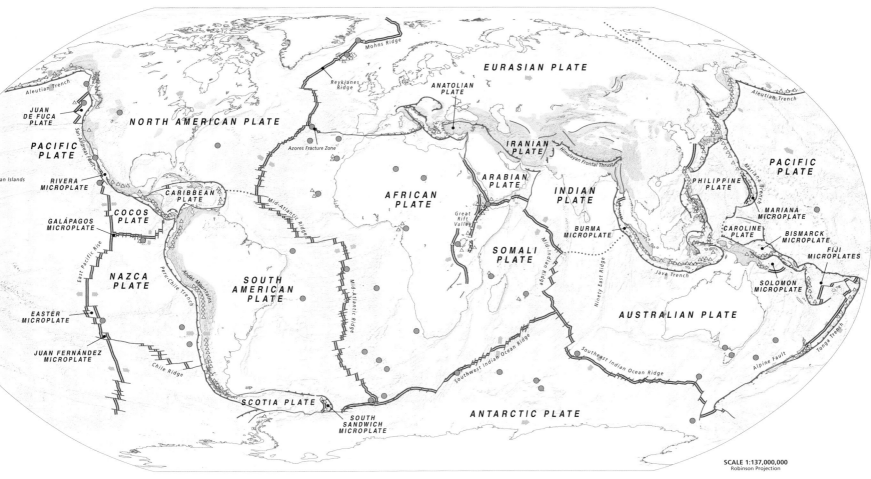

SCALE 1:137,000,000
Robinson Projection

Earth's tectonic plates

This map shows the present-day configuration of Earth's crustal plates. The red lines mark actively spreading ridges, features that occur in most ocean basins. Orange dots mark the major hot spots that have been active during the past 1 million years. Earthquake-prone areas correlate with subduction zones—for example, along the west coast of South America where the Nazca plate is sliding under and pushing up the South American plate.

TECTONIC FEATURES

- Earthquake zone
- △ Volcanic zone
- ● Prominent hotspot
- ⌃ Convergent margin
- ▬ Divergent margin
- — Transform fault
- ⋯ Diffuse or uncertain
- ▬ Direction of movement

Folding crust
Colliding continental plates cause the crust to thicken and crumple, which produces high mountains.

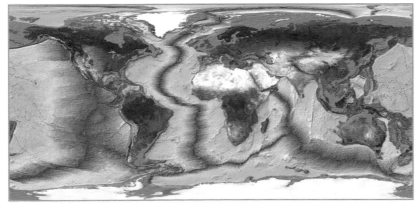

Age of the ocean floor
This computer-generated image shows the relative ages of seafloor areas, with the youngest (red) clearly aligned along mid-ocean spreading centers.

Million years
0 20 40 60 80 100 120 140 160 180 200 220 240 260 280

Pillow lava
As lava flows undersea, it quickly cools and forms a skin. As pressure builds within, new "pillows" burst through the skin.

SEA HIGHWAYS

Humans have taken to the waves for thousands of years, seeking food, commerce, new lands, treasure, and scientific understanding. The first intrepid mariners included Polynesians in dugout canoes and Egyptian traders in simple watercraft fashioned from bundles of reeds. Initially employing oars and sails, and later increasingly sophisticated engines, shipbuilding knowledge and technology advanced steadily over the centuries. Likewise, navigation tools evolved from devices such as the cross staff and astrolabe to the finely tuned chronometers developed by European watchmakers. By the 1400s, larger, sturdier vessels were expanding the range of ocean travel, transforming the seas into highways that could carry seafarers across whole oceans. Some coastal nations created navies that could extend their military might and support voyages of conquest. Eventually nearly every corner of the globe became accessible to those with the vision, vessels, and stamina to explore it.

Historic sea routes

Early records describe the intrepid journeys of an Egyptian explorer who sailed to Arabia in 2750 BC. Polynesians used outrigger canoes and celestial navigation to reach Tonga and Samoa in 1000 BC. Later, European, Chinese, and Muslim mariners all helped chart the oceans. By the 18th century, only the inhospitable seas of Antarctica remained unknown.

→ Polynesian expeditions
→ Viking expeditions
→ Chinese expeditions
→ Spanish expeditions
→ Portuguese expeditions
→ English expeditions
→ French expeditions
→ Dutch expeditions

SCALE 1:119,100,000
Robinson Projection

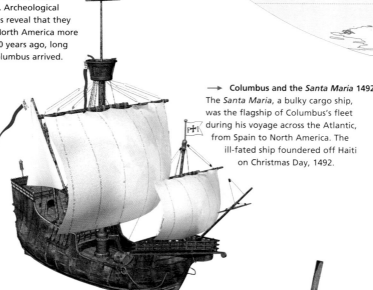

Cook's third voyage 1776-79
New
Hawaiian Islands (Sandwich Islands)
Acapulco
Ba
Cub
Hisp
Pa
Drake 1577-80
600
200-0 BC
Magellan-Del Cano 1519-22
Tahiti
Pitcairn Is. 700
Rapa Nui (Easter Island)
Cook's second voyage 1772-75
Cook's first voyage 1768-71
Cook's second voyage 1772-75

→ Viking mariners
Ancient Vikings braved the North Atlantic in sleek ships powered by oars and a sail. Archeological discoveries reveal that they reached North America more than 1,000 years ago, long before Columbus arrived.

→ Columbus and the *Santa Maria* 1492
The *Santa Maria*, a bulky cargo ship, was the flagship of Columbus's fleet during his voyage across the Atlantic, from Spain to North America. The ill-fated ship foundered off Haiti on Christmas Day, 1492.

FINDING THE NORTHWEST PASSAGE

The search for a Northwest Passage from the Atlantic to the Pacific beckoned a long line of explorers willing to challenge the harrowing conditions of the Arctic. Vitus Bering, James Cook, and Sir John Franklin all mounted unsuccessful expeditions, Franklin's ending in catastrophe. Eventually it was the savvy and meticulously prepared Norwegian explorer Roald Amundsen who discovered a route through the Arctic Ocean in 1906, after a four-year effort.

THE NORTHWEST PASSAGE, THE ARCTIC

▭ Franklin's route
Sir John Franklin and his crew were last seen in Lancaster Sound in July 1845. Expedition remains were found on Beechey Island five years later.

▭ Amundsen's route
Initially following Franklin's route, Amundsen had the good fortune to attempt the Passage when conditions in the Arctic were more favorable.

Vessels equipped to plow through ice and withstand its pressure have been essential to travel and exploration in polar seas. Early icebreakers were wooden sailing ships with an iron-sheathed hull. A modern icebreaker's hull is broad for added stability and its steel bow is reinforced. Rather than ramming through ice, the heavy bow slides up over and crushes it.

Finding the way

Mariners of old navigated by the sun and stars. Early celestial navigation tools such as the cross staff, astrolabe, and sextant measured latitude, a ship's location north or south of the equator. A later invention, the chronometer—essentially a seagoing clock—measured longitude, a ship's location east or west of a starting point. By combining latitude and longitude a seafarer could accurately plot a ship's position and progress.

Cross staff

Sextant

Astrolabe

Chronometer

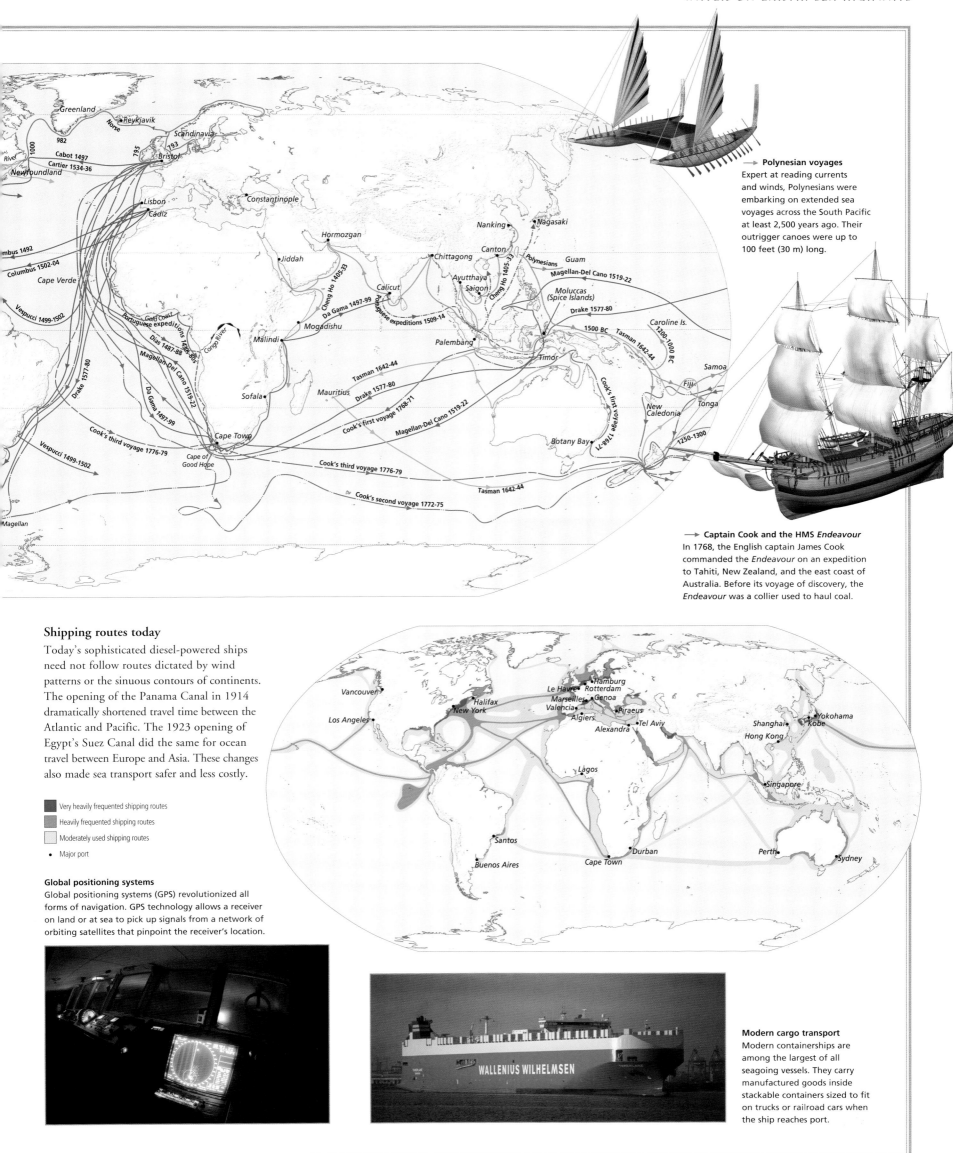

Polynesian voyages
Expert at reading currents and winds, Polynesians were embarking on extended sea voyages across the South Pacific at least 2,500 years ago. Their outrigger canoes were up to 100 feet (30 m) long.

Captain Cook and the HMS *Endeavour*
In 1768, the English captain James Cook commanded the *Endeavour* on an expedition to Tahiti, New Zealand, and the east coast of Australia. Before its voyage of discovery, the *Endeavour* was a collier used to haul coal.

Shipping routes today

Today's sophisticated diesel-powered ships need not follow routes dictated by wind patterns or the sinuous contours of continents. The opening of the Panama Canal in 1914 dramatically shortened travel time between the Atlantic and Pacific. The 1923 opening of Egypt's Suez Canal did the same for ocean travel between Europe and Asia. These changes also made sea transport safer and less costly.

■ Very heavily frequented shipping routes
■ Heavily frequented shipping routes
□ Moderately used shipping routes
• Major port

Global positioning systems
Global positioning systems (GPS) revolutionized all forms of navigation. GPS technology allows a receiver on land or at sea to pick up signals from a network of orbiting satellites that pinpoint the receiver's location.

Modern cargo transport
Modern containerships are among the largest of all seagoing vessels. They carry manufactured goods inside stackable containers sized to fit on trucks or railroad cars when the ship reaches port.

SURVEYING THE SEAS

People have long been drawn to explore remote mountains and jungles, study the heavens, and travel across the sea's surface, but for most of human history the ocean depths remained inaccessible. This changed in the 1800s with the advent of motorized winches and strong steel cables which enabled deep-sea sampling, and of diving gear that allowed humans to spend extended periods underwater. Today, underwater cameras and sophisticated sonar and sampling tools are transforming current scientific understanding of the dynamic marine landscape and its lifeforms. From space, satellites gather data about seasonal changes in ocean temperatures. Studies of Earth's shifting magnetic field and changes in ocean basins have helped confirm the effects of plate tectonics. Some of the most exciting discoveries have come from expeditions using remotely operated vehicles, which have revealed caches of vital mineral resources, bizarre communities at undersea vents, and details of the deep abyss.

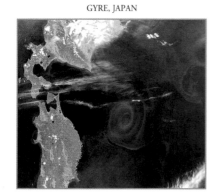

Mapping the sea surface

Satellites allow scientists to observe and compare ocean conditions on a global scale. Using advanced sensing technology, satellites relay data that is converted into computerized images. Among other benefits, the vivid map-like images provide previously unavailable information about shifts in ocean currents that affect climate. They also allow monitoring of ocean chemistry and phytoplankton—the foundation for sea food webs.

HISTORICAL STUDY

Long before oceanography was a recognized science, scholar-naturalists surveyed marine life and deepened understanding of currents and ocean basin features. The American Benjamin Franklin published a chart of the Gulf Stream in 1777. Later, Matthew Fontaine Maury did extensive research on currents and winds. Other 19th-century scientists probed the physical conditions and distribution of life in the oceans.

In 1873, scientists aboard the British vessel *Challenger* launched the first major voyage to study marine life and the seas. Traveling more than 79,000 miles (127,000 km) over three years, the expedition covered large areas of the Atlantic and Pacific oceans.

Sir John Murray was a driving force in interpreting the masses of data collected by the *Challenger* expedition.

SEAFLOOR OFF LOS ANGELES

Mapping the seafloor

Ship-based sonar devices allow scientists to map the seafloor. Pulses of sound waves directed at some part of the seafloor bounce off submerged objects and surfaces. Aboard ship, instruments convert these echoes into an image of the undersea landscape and objects, such as sunken ships, that might be there. In seismic surveying, sound waves directed into the seabed yield computer-generated images of the seafloor interior.

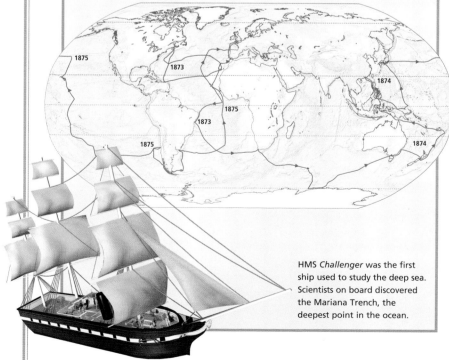

HMS *Challenger* was the first ship used to study the deep sea. Scientists on board discovered the Mariana Trench, the deepest point in the ocean.

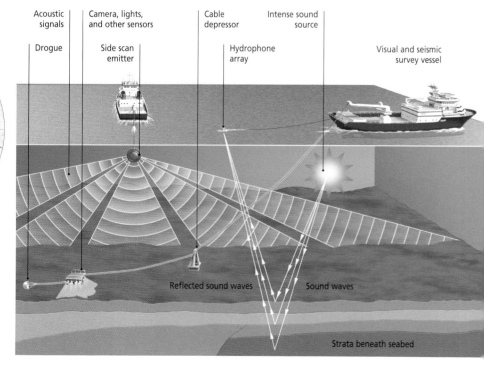

Acoustic signals

Camera, lights, and other sensors

Cable depressor

Intense sound source

Drogue

Side scan emitter

Hydrophone array

Visual and seismic survey vessel

Reflected sound waves

Sound waves

Strata beneath seabed

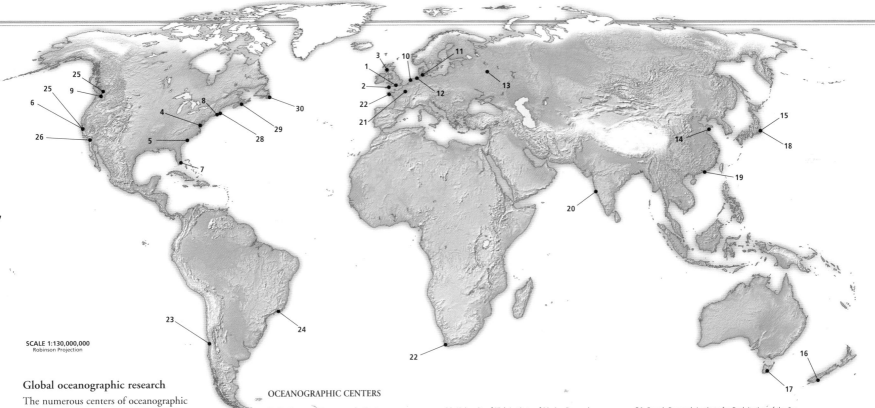

SCALE 1:130,000,000
Robinson Projection

Global oceanographic research

The numerous centers of oceanographic research and study throughout the world attest to the importance of the sea in human affairs. Governments continue to invest in new centers, equipped with the latest research facilities and vessels. Their discoveries have applications not only for improving basic understanding of the marine world, but also for naval operations and locating potential mineral resources such as oil and gas reserves.

OCEANOGRAPHIC CENTERS

1 Southampton Oceanography Centre
2 Plymouth Marine Laboratory
3 Dunstuffnage Marine Laboratory
4 Virginia Institute of Marine Science
5 Duke Marine Laboratory
6 Moss Landing Marine Laboratories
7 Rosenstiel School of Marine Science
8 University of Rhode Island School of Marine Science
9 University of Washington School of Marine Science
10 Netherlands Institute for Sea Research

11 University of Kiel, Institute of Marine Research
12 Alfred Wegener Institute for Polar and Marine Research
13 Shirshov Institute of Oceanology
14 Ocean University of Qingdao
15 Japan Agency for Marine-Earth Science and Technology
16 University of Otago, Department of Marine Science
17 CSIRO Marine Laboratories
18 University of Tokyo, Ocean Research Institute
19 University of Hong Kong, Swire Institute of Marine Science
20 University of Cape Town, Center for Marine Studies

21 French Research Institute for Exploitation of the Sea
22 Université de Bretagne Occidentale, Institut Universitaire Européen de la Mer
23 Universidad Catolica de Valparaiso, Escuela de Ciencias del Mar
24 University of São Paulo, Oceanographic Institute
25 Monterey Bay Aquarium Research Institute
26 University of California, Scripps Institution of Oceanography
27 University of Hawaii, School of Ocean and Earth Science and Technology
28 Woods Hole Oceanographic Institution
29 Bedford Institute of Oceanography, Ocean Sciences Division
30 Memorial University of Newfoundland, Ocean Sciences Center

Exploring polar ecosystems
Divers equipped for conditions under Antarctic ice gather information about the diets of sea life, including leopard seals, and penguins.

Investigating marine ecosystems
Research into marine ecosystems includes studies of lemon shark (*Negaprion brevirostris*) populations in the Bahamas.

Monitoring endangered species
Scientists at Monterey Bay Aquarium Research Institute monitor the endangered California southern sea otter (*Enhydra lutris nereis*).

Studying marine mammals
At Long Beach Marine Laboratory, California, scientists research the physiological mechanisms that allow mammals to dive for long periods.

EXPLORING THE DEEP

Submarines must be built to withstand the crushing pressure of the water around them —a pressure that grows steadily with depth. Research submersibles are smaller than military submarines and can go much deeper. In 1960, with a crew of two, the heavily reinforced bathyscaphe *Trieste*, a Swiss designed "deep boat," reached the bottom of the Mariana Trench, the deepest part of the global sea. No existing submersible can go as deep.

Undersea craft such as the bathyscaphe *Trieste* and research submersibles *Alvin* and *Shinkai* have allowed historic studies of the sea depths.

Safe operating depth

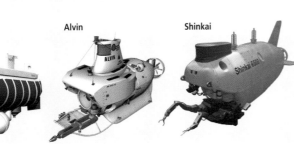

Trieste   Alvin   Shinkai

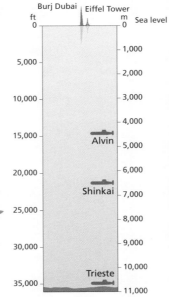

Burj Dubai | Eiffel Tower

ft		m	Sea level
0		0	
		1,000	
5,000		2,000	
		3,000	
10,000		4,000	
		5,000	Alvin
15,000		6,000	
20,000		7,000	Shinkai
		8,000	
25,000		9,000	
30,000		10,000	Trieste
35,000		11,000	

This one-person submarine, called *Deep Rover*, can descend to about 980 feet (300 m). Mechanical arms allow the operator to manipulate objects and collect samples.

From sunlit shallows to the greatest depths, the vast global sea is always in motion. The physical and chemical properties of seawater —salinity, the density or weight of water, its temperature, and the availability of light below the surface—all help determine where different marine species can survive. Seawater also continually interacts with the land it washes and the atmosphere above it.

MARINE MECHANICS

THE SALTY SEA

Seawater is a relatively dense fluid that is 96.5 percent water and 3.5 percent salts including chloride, sodium, magnesium, and calcium. It also contains dissolved elements such as nitrogen and phosphorus. With increasing depth, water's density and pressure rise, its temperature and salinity drop, and less sunlight can penetrate it. These physical and chemical factors influence the movement of seawater and the bodily features of marine organisms. For example, until it is near freezing, deep, denser cold water remains at the bottom. Because light dims with depth, fish may have large eyes or rely on other senses to hunt or avoid predators. At great depths, fish typically have flabby bodies that require little food to sustain. Dissolved nitrogen and phosphorus in seawater are key nutrients for the floating phytoplankton that form the base of marine food webs. Corals, clams, and other marine invertebrates remove calcium from seawater to form protective calcium carbonate shells.

Chemical composition

The salinity of seawater varies around the globe. Salinity is greatest in semi-enclosed seas such as the Caribbean, Mediterranean, and the Red Sea, where more water is lost to evaporation of water from the sea surface than is replenished by rainfall and runoff. The lowest salinity occurs in areas where large rivers, such as the Yangtze, Ganges, Mississippi, and Amazon, discharge into the ocean.

Caribbean Sea
The shallowest areas of this warm, tropical sea off the western Atlantic are renowned for their "floatability"—the water's capacity to support swimmers due to its high salinity and, therefore, greatly increased density.

GLOBAL SALINITY

	Less than 33 parts per 1000
	33–34 parts per 1000
	34–35 parts per 1000
	35–36 parts per 1000
	36–37 parts per 1000
	More than 37 parts per 1000

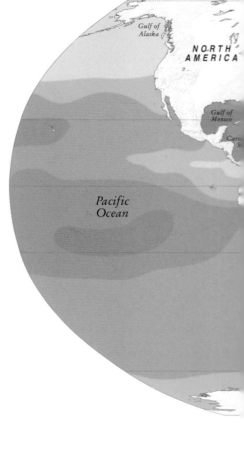

SEAWATER COMPOSITION

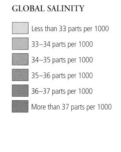

Chloride 55.04%
Others 0.72%
Potassium 1.10%
Calcium 1.16%
Magnesium 3.69%
Sulfate 7.68%
Sodium 30.61%

Salts in seawater
Dissolved salts account for roughly 3.53 percent of the weight of seawater. Chloride and sodium represent more than 85 percent of this total. The chart shows percentages of these and other major salts by weight.

Dead Sea
This famous sea lies in the Jordan Rift Valley. Intense heat evaporates the water, making it approximately 10 times more saline than seawater and so dense that a human body cannot sink in it. As its name implies, there is little marine life there.

How the seas became salty

Approximately 4.3 billion years ago, Earth entered a 10-million-year period of intense rainstorms that helped form the first global sea. These storms eroded minerals from the hot rocks and picked up gases from the atmosphere. As a result, the first ocean was a complex solution of water and salts. Today there is a balance between salt inputs and losses, so salinity remains almost constant.

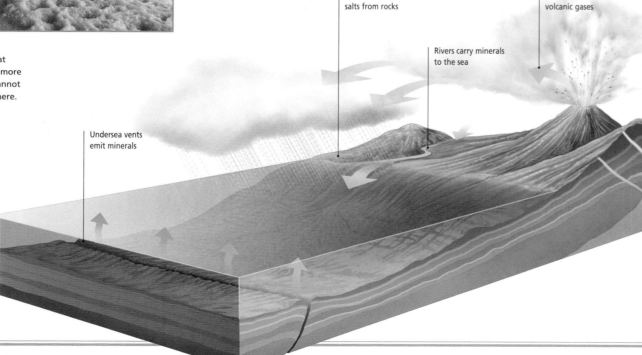

Rainwater dissolves salts from rocks

Rainwater dissolves volcanic gases

Rivers carry minerals to the sea

Undersea vents emit minerals

Red Sea
The extremely salty Red Sea formed when the Indian Ocean flooded an ancient rift valley. About 40 percent of the Red Sea is less than 330 feet (100 m) deep. It is known for its extensive coral reefs.

Mediterranean Sea
The Mediterranean connects to the Atlantic Ocean via the narrow Straits of Gibraltar, where its sapphire waters are about as saline as the Atlantic. The Mediterranean becomes saltier toward the sea's closed eastern end.

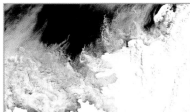

Antarctica
In the Weddell and Ross seas of the Southern Ocean, the seawater becomes unusually saline, and much denser, as sea ice forms. This dense water sinks and forms a deep water mass called Antarctic Bottom Water.

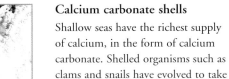

Calcium carbonate shells

Shallow seas have the richest supply of calcium, in the form of calcium carbonate. Shelled organisms such as clams and snails have evolved to take up dissolved calcium carbonate and use it to build their protective shells.

Conch
Conches are marine snails. Thousands of species are known, most in coral reef habitats where they are often harvested as seafood.

Spiral coiling
Like most gastropod snails, this species' shell consists of multiple calcium carbonate layers twisted into a spiral.

Prickly pen
This bivalve burrows into sand or gravel. It uses sticky byssus threads to anchor its shell to objects such as pebbles.

Abalone
An abalone's shell is lined with nacre or mother-of-pearl that is more than 95 percent calcium carbonate.

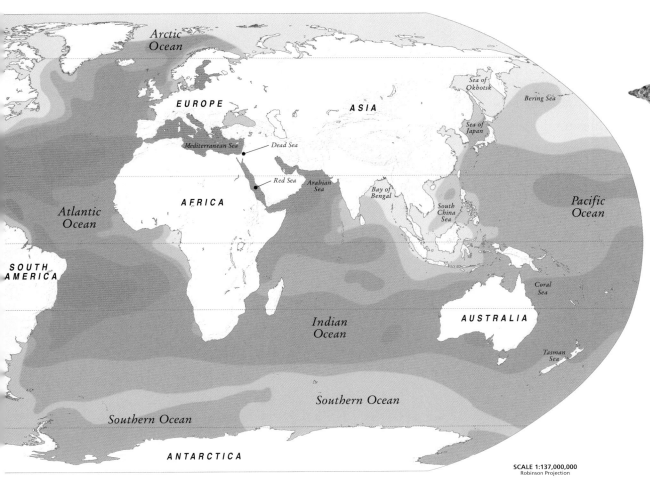

SCALE 1:137,000,000
Robinson Projection

DEPTH AND LIGHT

In seawater, light wavelengths corresponding to different colors of light are absorbed or scattered. Red light is absorbed quickly, so the sea surface usually appears blue. The longer green and blue wavelengths travel farther, but by about 4,265 feet (1,300 m) all the wavelengths have been absorbed even in clear waters. From that point onward the depths are completely dark except for the glow emitted from organisms having light-producing organs.

OPEN OCEAN

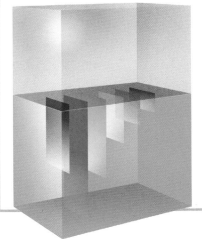

ESTUARY WATERS

COASTAL WATERS

MUDDY WATERS

Ocean water appears bluest where it holds less organic material. Increased material, including phytoplankton, containing the green pigment chlorophyll, makes water appear greenish, as in estuaries or along coasts. Turbid, muddy-looking water contains a heavy load of suspended soil particles.

In water, floating particles, density changes, and other factors change the trajectory of a light beam, a process called scattering that affects the water's color.

CURRENTS AND CIRCULATION

Currents are streams of moving water. Wind creates sea surface currents. Relatively warm water flows in some of these, including equatorial currents, while at higher latitudes water flows are much colder, such as the Labrador Current. The Gulf Stream and other boundary currents move along the edges of continents. Seawater also circulates in thermohaline currents, in which differences in temperature or salinity push water masses past one another, usually vertically. Thermohaline circulation distributes seawater into layers, with more salty, warmer water layered above colder, less saline water. Where surface currents drive water away from a coast, upwelling brings up deeper, nutrient-rich water to replace it. By contrast, downwelling occurs as surface water sinks when winds drive water toward a coast. In the largest oceans, surface currents include looping gyres in which water may be as much as 6.6 feet (2 m) higher in the center than at the edges. The combined effects of gravity and Coriolis forces drive the current in a horizontal spiral.

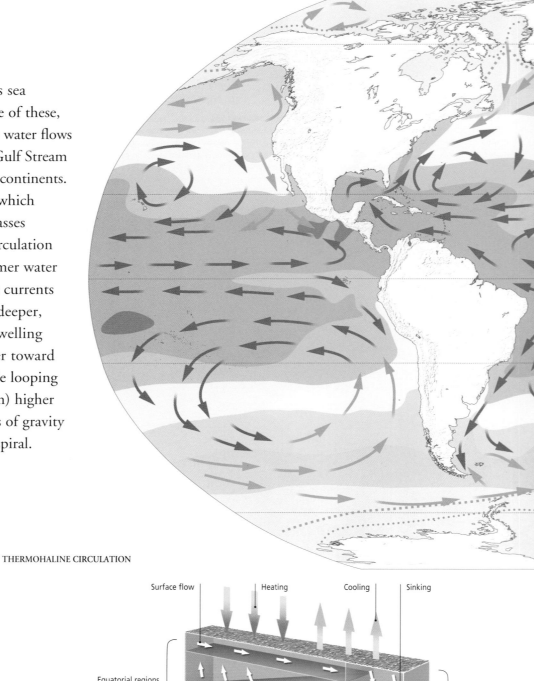

SURFACE AND DEEP OCEAN CIRCULATION

While dozens of small and large surface currents rapidly circulate upper ocean waters, deep-water masses simultaneously travel slowly around the global sea by thermohaline circulation. The North Atlantic Deep Water forms as water in the northern hemisphere sinks. Over an estimated 275 years it flows to the Antarctic, then onward to the deepest parts of the Indian and Pacific oceans before upwelling returns it to the surface.

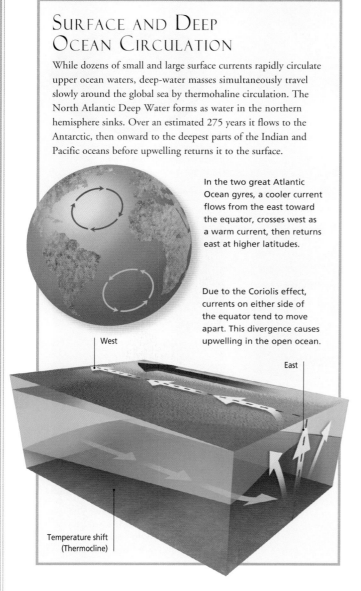

In the two great Atlantic Ocean gyres, a cooler current flows from the east toward the equator, crosses west as a warm current, then returns east at higher latitudes.

Due to the Coriolis effect, currents on either side of the equator tend to move apart. This divergence causes upwelling in the open ocean.

West

East

Temperature shift (Thermocline)

THERMOHALINE CIRCULATION

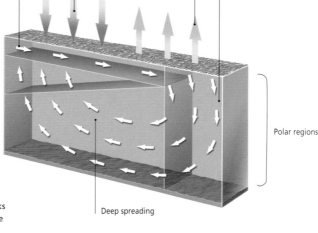

Surface flow   Heating   Cooling   Sinking

Equatorial regions

Polar regions

Deep spreading

Thermohaline circulation
Seawater becomes denser when it cools and less dense as it warms—changes that generate the force to move immense water masses. Dense cold water near the poles sinks and slowly travels toward the equator. These deep-water masses eventually rise again.

UPWELLING

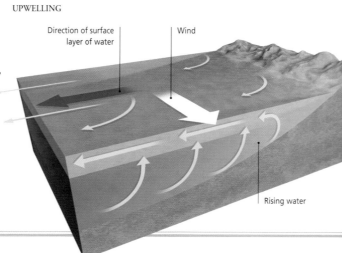

Direction of surface layer of water   Wind

Rising water

Upwelling and downwelling
Vertical thermohaline water movements, also called upwelling and downwelling, are vital for marine ecosystems. Sinking surface water replenishes oxygen in the deepest parts of all ocean basins, while rising deep-water masses return valuable sunken nutrients to the surface. Most of these vertical water movements occur along continental coasts.

Great global surface currents

Six huge currents, five of them gyres, move surface waters of the global ocean. The North Atlantic and North Pacific gyres circulate clockwise in the northern hemisphere. In the southern hemisphere the South Atlantic, South Pacific, and Indian Ocean gyres circulate counter-clockwise. Smaller, equatorial currents and countercurrents circulate immediately north and south of the equator. The sixth giant global current, called the Antarctic Circumpolar Current, transports more water than any other.

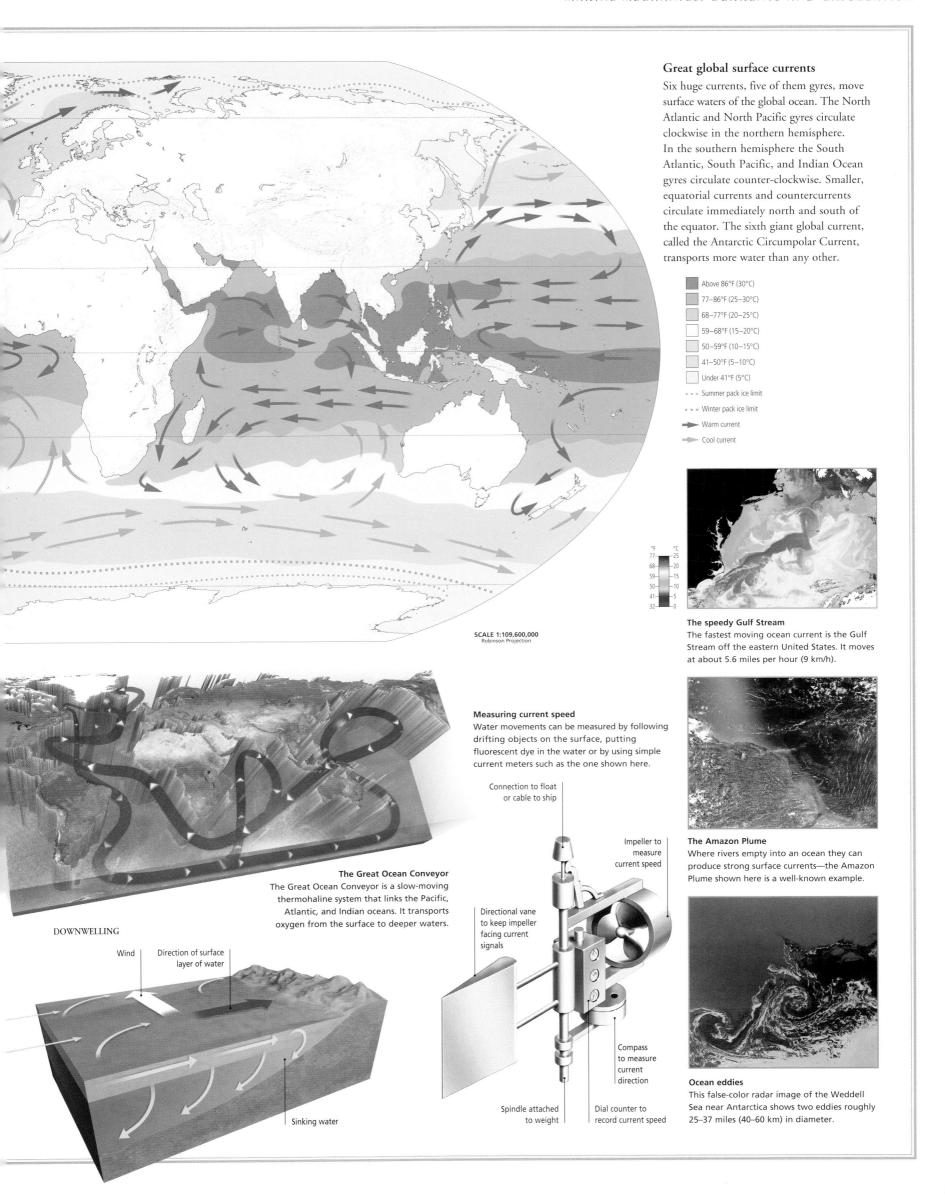

Above 86°F (30°C)
77–86°F (25–30°C)
68–77°F (20–25°C)
59–68°F (15–20°C)
50–59°F (10–15°C)
41–50°F (5–10°C)
Under 41°F (5°C)
• • • Summer pack ice limit
• • • Winter pack ice limit
→ Warm current
→ Cool current

SCALE 1:109,600,000
Robinson Projection

The speedy Gulf Stream
The fastest moving ocean current is the Gulf Stream off the eastern United States. It moves at about 5.6 miles per hour (9 km/h).

The Amazon Plume
Where rivers empty into an ocean they can produce strong surface currents—the Amazon Plume shown here is a well-known example.

Ocean eddies
This false-color radar image of the Weddell Sea near Antarctica shows two eddies roughly 25–37 miles (40–60 km) in diameter.

The Great Ocean Conveyor
The Great Ocean Conveyor is a slow-moving thermohaline system that links the Pacific, Atlantic, and Indian oceans. It transports oxygen from the surface to deeper waters.

DOWNWELLING

Wind
Direction of surface layer of water
Sinking water

Measuring current speed
Water movements can be measured by following drifting objects on the surface, putting fluorescent dye in the water or by using simple current meters such as the one shown here.

Connection to float or cable to ship
Impeller to measure current speed
Directional vane to keep impeller facing current signals
Compass to measure current direction
Spindle attached to weight
Dial counter to record current speed

31

CLIMATE AND THE SEA

A region's climate is the long-term pattern of weather conditions there. The sea strongly influences climate all over Earth through its interactions with the atmosphere, where sunlight first reaches Earth. About 49 percent of incoming sunlight is reflected back to space; the remaining 51 percent is absorbed. In response to the combined effects of solar heating and Earth's rotation on its axis, air in the atmosphere warms, rises, cools, and descends in masses known as cells. This general scheme of atmospheric circulation produces the global water cycle, and influences climatic patterns of seasonal temperatures and precipitation. It also translates into the wind patterns that drive surface ocean currents, and it affects long-term movements of water masses between the surface and the depths of ocean basins. Changes to the composition of the atmosphere, especially an increase in so-called greenhouse gases, are warming the atmosphere in ways that have begun to rapidly alter global climate.

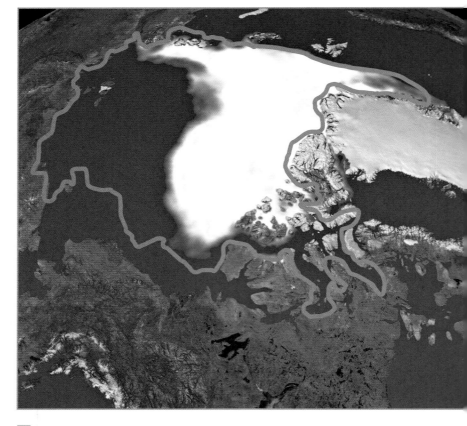

 Sea ice extent in the mid-1970s

The global energy equation

About 30 percent of the Sun's energy beamed toward Earth is immediately reflected back to space. Clouds and the lower atmosphere absorb another 19 percent. The remaining 51 percent of solar energy is absorbed by the sea and land, including a small amount that is temporarily captured by photosynthesizing plants. Over time, however, all solar energy that reaches Earth's surface is radiated back to space.

Sea ice changes

Both permanent and annually renewed Arctic sea ice have been decreasing in recent decades due to global warming. Both types of Arctic ice have declined by 38 percent since the mid-1970s. Ice provides crucial habitat for both Arctic seals and polar bears. Although such species have survived previous climate shifts, the numbers of both are likely to decrease and in some areas populations may disappear altogether.

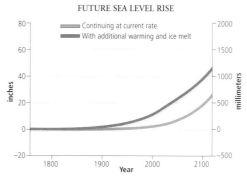

FUTURE SEA LEVEL RISE

Continuing at current rate
With additional warming and ice melt

Estimating sea level rise
At the current rate of sea level rise, sea level will gain 19 inches (480 mm) by 2100 (green line). Additional ice melting in Greenland or Antarctica could boost the increase to 39 inches (1,000 mm) or more (red line).

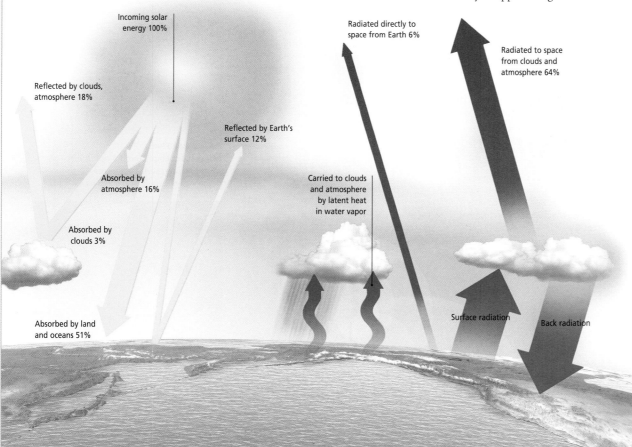

Incoming solar energy 100%

Radiated directly to space from Earth 6%

Radiated to space from clouds and atmosphere 64%

Reflected by clouds, atmosphere 18%

Reflected by Earth's surface 12%

Absorbed by atmosphere 16%

Carried to clouds and atmosphere by latent heat in water vapor

Absorbed by clouds 3%

Absorbed by land and oceans 51%

Surface radiation

Back radiation

GLOBAL WARMING, CORAL THREAT

One of the major impacts of global warming is a rise in ocean temperature. In tropical regions a temperature increase of only 2.7–3.6°F (1.5–2°C) above normal can lead to the loss of the symbiotic algae called zooxanthellae that nourish coral polyps. As the polyps become malnourished, they turn white, a phenomenon called coral bleaching. Affected corals can sometimes recover, but only if the bleaching is quickly reversed.

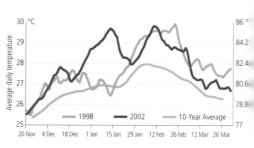

1998   2002   10-Year Average

During sustained periods of coral bleaching in 1998 and 2002 (yellow and orange lines), global sea temperatures were much higher than the 10-year average.

Monitoring sea surface temperature

Satellite-based instruments allow researchers to precisely measure the surface temperature of the world sea. The data used to generate this image was gathered over a period of 20 days in early spring. The coolest areas, around both the polar regions, show up as purple, while the warmest ocean regions show up as a red–orange band around the equator. A succession of such images allows scientists to monitor temperature shifts in different areas over time.

Atmospheric fireworks
As on land, a thunderstorm at sea can trigger the dramatic atmospheric discharge of electricity known as lightning. Bolts of lightning can travel an estimated 136,000 miles per hour (220,000 km/h).

1993
1947
1961
January 2002
March 2002

RETREATING LARSEN ICE SHELF

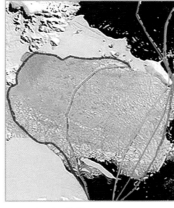

Retreating ice shelf
Over the years the extent of Antarctica's Larsen ice shelf has increased and decreased. In about 1960, however, the shelf began retreating due to prolonged global warming. Lines show ice shelf extent in 1947, 1961, 1993, and 2002.

Ice shelf collapse
In mid-March 2002, after shrinking steadily for 40 years, 1,255 square miles (3,250 km²) of the Larsen ice shelf collapsed, shattering into icebergs. The sudden event loosened 720 billion tons of ice into the sea.

Today, the predicted annual surface warming is 5.4°F (3°C) in the tropics and up to 14.4°F (8°C) in polar regions. Some species are shifting their habitat range to cooler areas, others are becoming extinct. Ice-dependent creatures such as penguins and polar bears are vulnerable.

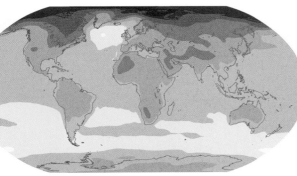

PROJECTED INCREASE IN SURFACE TEMPERATURE BY 2099

0–1.8°F (0–1°C)
1.8–3.6°F (1–2°C)
3.6–5.4°F (2–3°C)
5.4–7.2°F (3–4°C)
7.2–9°F (4–5°C)
9–10.8°F (5–6°C)
10.8–12.6°F (6–7°C)
12.6–14.4°F (7–8°C)

Corals stressed by warming seas may expel their resident zooxanthellae, or the algae may die. If conditions improve before the starving coral polyps die, they can take up new zooxanthellae and reestablish the life-sustaining symbiosis.

Coral polyps secrete a calcium carbonate skeleton that is covered by a layer of living tissue containing zooxanthellae. Warming seawater upsets the symbiosis in which the coral shelters its algal partner in return for sugars and oxygen, which leads to coral bleaching.

Healthy coral
1 Symbiotic zooxanthellae provide food and oxygen in exchange for protection.

Bleached coral
2 In bleached coral, polyp tissues no longer contain functioning zooxanthellae.

Dead coral
3 Surface algae blanket the bleached calcium carbonate skeletons.

EL NIÑO AND LA NIÑA

Interactions between the sea and Earth's atmosphere help shape both weather and climate. About 10 percent of seawater flows in wind-driven surface currents that have essential roles in climatic processes. In a roughly four-year cycle that unfolds along the coast of Peru, a tropical Pacific wind shift called the Southern Oscillation slows or reverses major currents. It also halts normal upwelling of cold, nutrient-rich water there. Spanish fishermen named this phenomenon El Niño (the Christ Child). It may last 18 months or longer. In the Americas and Southeast Asia, the abnormally warm, nutrient-poor El Niño current may mean disaster for fish and other wildlife that rely on seasonal upwelling for food. Increased evaporation of the warm surface water fuels an increase in severe storms that affect agriculture and other human activities. In an opposite phenomenon, La Niña, the sea surface remains uncharacteristically cool. It, too, produces abnormal weather patterns that extend around the globe.

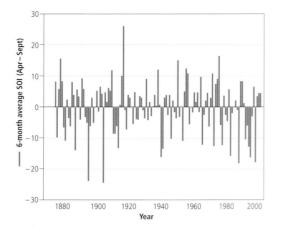

Southern Oscillation Index
The Southern Oscillation Index (SOI) tracks the air pressure difference between Tahiti and Darwin, Australia. When the SOI is strongly negative for several months, El Niño is underway. A strongly positive SOI marks La Niña.

Satellite monitoring of El Niño and La Niña
The TOPEX/Poseidon satellite monitors conditions in the oceans. Normal wind and current patterns were present in 2003. In 1997, however, satellite instruments tracked the development of El Niño. By October the mass of warm water (white area) had spread along the whole west coast of North and Central America. One year later, wind and current conditions had reversed and La Niña's cold water was upwelling.

Normal wind and current patterns
Normally in the tropical Pacific, surface winds blow westward, away from South America. Currents push warm water toward Indonesia, and upwelling replenishes nutrients and helps maintain normal weather patterns.

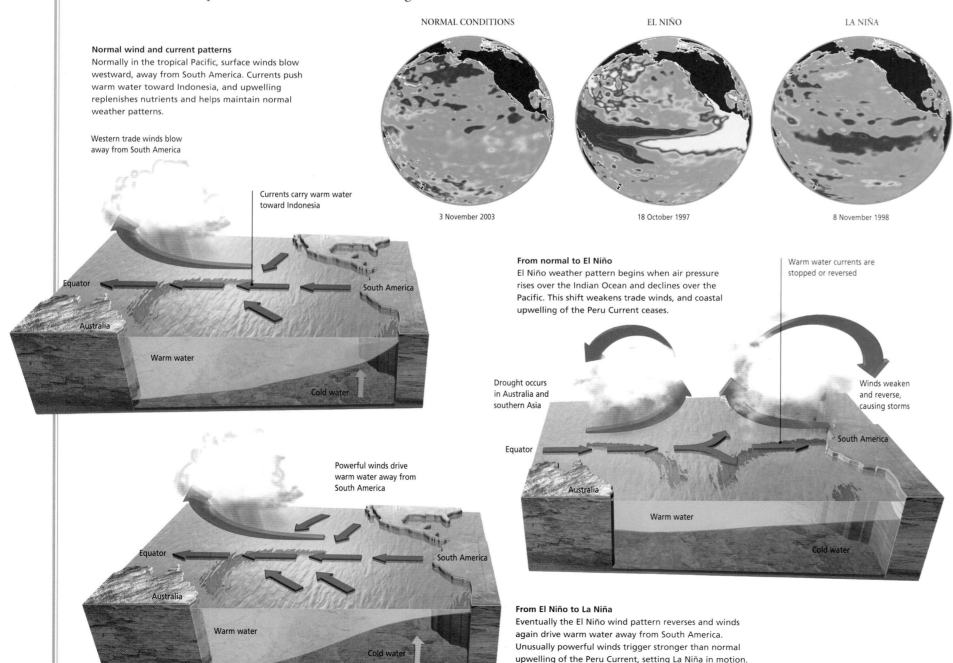

NORMAL CONDITIONS

EL NIÑO

LA NIÑA

3 November 2003

18 October 1997

8 November 1998

Western trade winds blow away from South America

Currents carry warm water toward Indonesia

Equator

South America

Australia

Warm water

Cold water

Powerful winds drive warm water away from South America

Equator

South America

Australia

Warm water

Cold water

From normal to El Niño
El Niño weather pattern begins when air pressure rises over the Indian Ocean and declines over the Pacific. This shift weakens trade winds, and coastal upwelling of the Peru Current ceases.

Warm water currents are stopped or reversed

Drought occurs in Australia and southern Asia

Winds weaken and reverse, causing storms

Equator

South America

Australia

Warm water

Cold water

From El Niño to La Niña
Eventually the El Niño wind pattern reverses and winds again drive warm water away from South America. Unusually powerful winds trigger stronger than normal upwelling of the Peru Current, setting La Niña in motion.

Shifting El Niño weather patterns

During El Niño, the arrival of an abnormal, large mass of warm water in the eastern Pacific may dramatically change precipitation patterns around the globe. Along the west coasts of North and South America, heavy downpours and tornadoes may wreak havoc in areas that are usually much drier, while extended drought develops in parts of Africa, Australia, and elsewhere.

- ▨ Dry and warm
- ▨ Warm
- ▨ Dry
- ▨ Wet and warm
- ▨ Wet
- ▨ Wet and cool

Starving seal
The 1997–98 El Niño had a serious impact on the marine food web along the west coast of the Americas. With its normal food supply of small fish greatly diminished, this sea lion pup (*Zalophus californianus*) is starving.

Coastal storm
Unusually frequent and severe storms and tornadoes are common during El Niño years. Coastal California has suffered huge losses in human life and property as storms triggered flooding, mud slides, and other damage.

Eye of the storm
Typhoon Fengshen slammed into coastal China, Macau, and the Philippines, causing over 1,400 deaths in 2008, La Niña year.

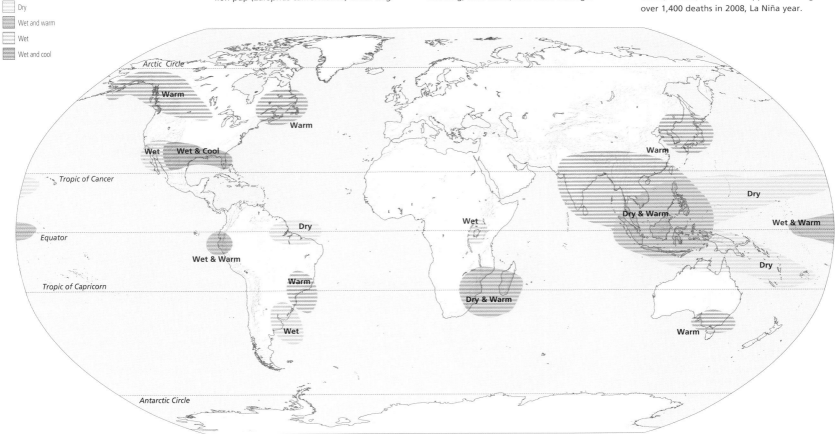

PERUVIAN ANCHOVY

The Peruvian anchovy *(Engraulis ringens)*, or anchoveta, is a small fish that is used to manufacture high quality fish meal. It is the target of the world's largest fishery. The anchovies feed heavily on zooplankton. Their populations appear to grow, then contract in cycles of about 30 years. During El Niño, however, the population plummets when normal upwelling stops and zooplankton become scarce.

This diagram shows the relative habitats of several important fish species in the eastern Pacific. Peruvian anchovies are vulnerable in El Niño periods because they depend on coastal upwelling close to shore.

Peruvian anchovy populations have probably always cycled between highs and lows related to spawning success and food availability. Heavy commercial fishing contributed to steep crashes that began in El Niño periods of the early 1970s and late 1990s.

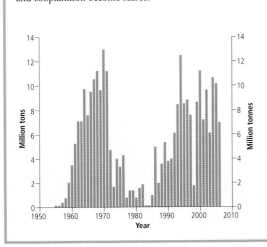

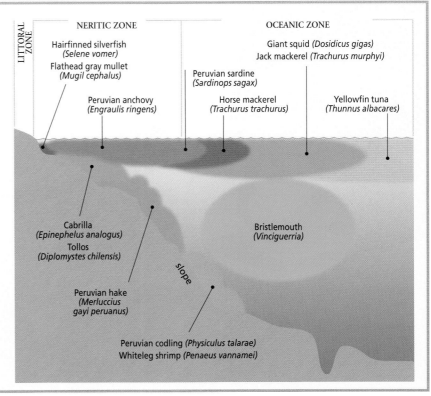

LITTORAL ZONE

NERITIC ZONE
Hairfinned silverfish (*Selene vomer*)
Flathead gray mullet (*Mugil cephalus*)
Peruvian anchovy (*Engraulis ringens*)

OCEANIC ZONE
Giant squid (*Dosidicus gigas*)
Jack mackerel (*Trachurus murphyi*)
Peruvian sardine (*Sardinops sagax*)
Horse mackerel (*Trachurus trachurus*)
Yellowfin tuna (*Thunnus albacares*)

Cabrilla (*Epinephelus analogus*)
Tollos (*Diplomystes chilensis*)

Bristlemouth (*Vinciguerria*)

slope

Peruvian hake (*Merluccius gayi peruanus*)

Peruvian codling (*Physiculus talarae*)
Whiteleg shrimp (*Penaeus vannamei*)

WIND

Wind is a force in driving ocean currents, including gyres that circulate around the fringes of the five largest ocean basins. Overall, air moves in patterns set by incoming solar energy. At lower latitudes, where sunlight is more intense, air warms, expands, and rises. At the poles air naturally cools, contracts, and falls. Earth's rotation shifts winds and currents to the right (clockwise) in the northern hemisphere and to the left (counter-clockwise) in the southern hemisphere. This shift is called the Coriolis effect. In addition, gravity pulls air from areas of high pressure, where the air mass is relatively cool, to areas of low pressure, where the air mass is warmer. Together these factors generate differing wind conditions over different ocean regions. In the ferocious rainstorms called cyclones or hurricanes, winds converge in an area of low pressure and spiral upward. An anticyclone develops over areas of high pressure and often correlates with fine weather.

WIND PATTERNS

Wind speed and direction
Data from NASA's satellite-based Scatterometer precisely measure wind direction and speed. Shown here are the Santa Ana winds that buffet Southern California, USA. The colored arrows represent various ranges of wind speed.

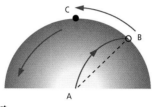

The Coriolis effect
The Coriolis effect can be understood by imagining that someone sitting at the center of a moving roundabout (point A) throws a ball to someone sitting at a point on the rim (point B). By the time the ball reaches B, the person on the rim will have moved to point C. To this person, the ball will appear to have curved away from them.

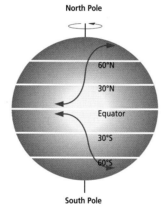

Spinning planet
On our spinning planet, freely moving objects including weather systems appear to follow a curved path. They turn to the right in the northern hemisphere and to the left in the southern hemisphere.

THE BERMUDA HIGH

A large, permanent region of high atmospheric pressure in the North Atlantic shifts with the seasons between the Azores and Bermuda. Air in this high picks up moisture from areas to the east. As the moist air circulates clockwise, it helps fuel the development of tropical storms and hurricanes that strike the Caribbean and the southeastern US during the summer and fall.

HURRICANE STRIKING NEW ENGLAND

HURRICANE MOVES INTO GULF OF MEXICO

Land and sea breezes
Coastal sea breezes develop early in the day when cooler air over the ocean rushes in to replace rising, warmer air over land. Overnight the process reverses, and land breezes develop.

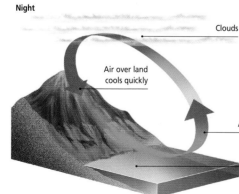

Night
Clouds
Air over land cools quickly
Air over sea cools slowly
Weak land breeze

Day
Thin clouds offshore
Warm air over land
Cool air over sea
Strong sea breeze

Seasonal monsoons
In summer, winds carry moist air across the Indian Ocean. The resulting monsoon rains begin in the south and spread northward. Monsoon season ends as winter cooling causes the wind direction to reverse.

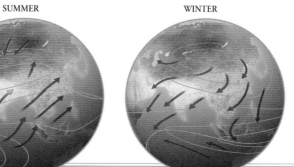
SUMMER   WINTER

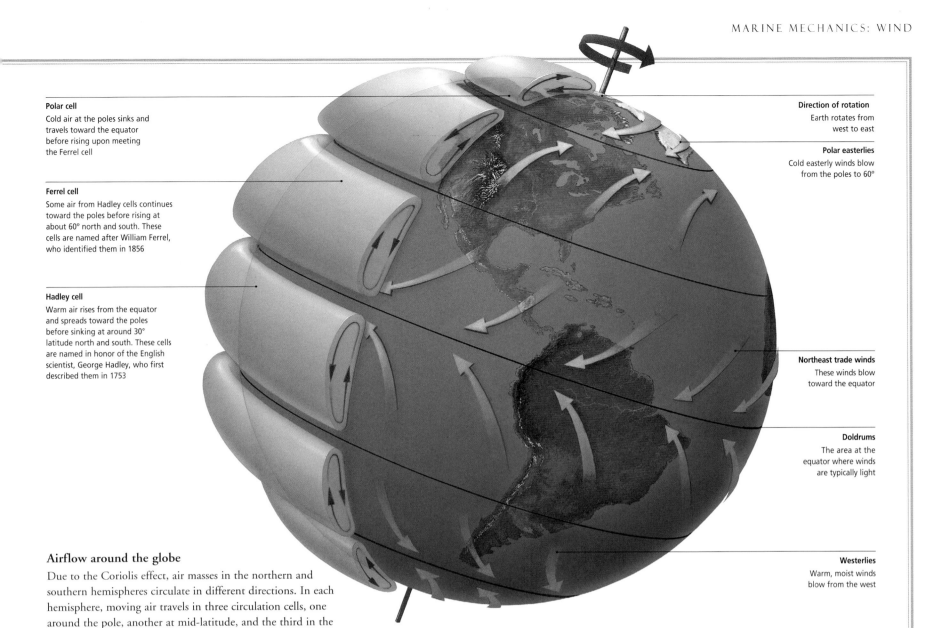

Polar cell
Cold air at the poles sinks and travels toward the equator before rising upon meeting the Ferrel cell

Ferrel cell
Some air from Hadley cells continues toward the poles before rising at about 60° north and south. These cells are named after William Ferrel, who identified them in 1856

Hadley cell
Warm air rises from the equator and spreads toward the poles before sinking at around 30° latitude north and south. These cells are named in honor of the English scientist, George Hadley, who first described them in 1753

Direction of rotation
Earth rotates from west to east

Polar easterlies
Cold easterly winds blow from the poles to 60°

Northeast trade winds
These winds blow toward the equator

Doldrums
The area at the equator where winds are typically light

Westerlies
Warm, moist winds blow from the west

Airflow around the globe

Due to the Coriolis effect, air masses in the northern and southern hemispheres circulate in different directions. In each hemisphere, moving air travels in three circulation cells, one around the pole, another at mid-latitude, and the third in the tropics bordering the equator. Among other effects, the circuits generate prevailing easterly winds in the tropics and high latitudes, and prevailing westerly winds in middle latitudes.

Stormy weather
Storms are atmospheric disturbances that develop when a region of high pressure envelops an area of low pressure. At sea, storm winds generate large, potentially dangerous waves.

Becoming becalmed
Mariners once dreaded becoming trapped in the doldrums, a belt of light winds in the tropics. A sail-powered ship might languish for days or weeks as supplies of food and drinkable water dwindle.

BEAUFORT WIND SCALE		
Force	Wind speed [mph (km/h)]	Description
0	below 1 (below 2)	calm
1	2–3 (3–5)	light air
2	4–7 (6–11)	light breeze
3	8–12 (12–19)	gentle breeze
4	13–18 (20–29)	moderate breeze
5	19–24 (30–38)	fresh breeze
6	25–31 (39–51)	strong breeze
7	32–38 (52–61)	near gale
8	39–46 (62–74)	gale
9	47–54 (75–86)	strong gale
10	55–63 (87–101)	whole gale
11	64–74 (102–120)	storm
12	above 74 (120)	hurricane

Beaufort Wind Scale

The Beaufort Wind scale ranks the force of wind at sea on a scale from zero (calm) to 12 (hurricane). The wind force determines how high wind-driven waves will be. It was devised to measure wind force on sailing ships.

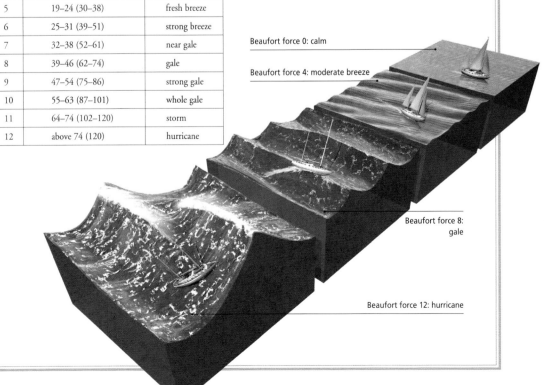

Beaufort force 0: calm

Beaufort force 4: moderate breeze

Beaufort force 8: gale

Beaufort force 12: hurricane

WAVES

From ripples to billowing swells and storm surges, waves are synonymous with the sea. All ocean waves are seawater set in motion by external energy. Most are wind waves that form as wind blows across the sea surface, its kinetic energy curling seawater up and forward. At a wave's crest, gravity pulls the water downward into a cuplike trough. Wind waves usually travel steadily across the surface, finally releasing energy when they reach the shore. Not surprisingly, the largest wind waves tend to occur in extremely windy ocean regions, such as the Southern Ocean encircling Antarctica. Along the southern coast of Australia, waves of nine–10 feet (2.7–3 m) are common. Storm winds often produce waves that reach 20 feet (6 m), although in areas such as the North Atlantic, wind and current conditions may produce so-called rogue waves that attain heights of 110 feet (33 m) or more.

A shore thing
A shoreline's structure helps determine the characteristics of the waves that wash it. Towering, curling breakers develop where waves arrive at a steep shore, as here, in Waimea Bay off the Hawaiian island of Oahu.

Making waves
Wind moving over the ocean generates corresponding movement in surface water. Steady wind over great distances tends to generate long, smooth undulations called swells. In the surf zone close to shore, water particles move in circles that become larger closer to the surface. When the orbiting water particles strike bottom in the shallows, they flatten out. The forward thrust near shore forms crests and breakers.

PARTS OF A WAVE

wavelength — crest

steepness

height

trough

Wave features
Wavelength is the distance between crests, while wave height is the vertical distance between a trough and a crest. Wave steepness is the angle from the bottom of a trough to the top of the neighboring crest.

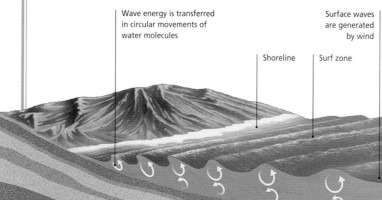

Wave energy is transferred in circular movements of water molecules

Surface waves are generated by wind

Shoreline | Surf zone

Movement of wind over the ocean generates corresponding movement in the water

Storm waves
As a storm builds, strengthening winds transfer a great deal of energy to the sea surface. Waves also interact with one another. This chaotic energy infusion may produce waves with a variety of wavelengths, heights, directions, and other physical characteristics, a phenomenon oceanographers term a wave sea. Rare rogue waves develop when many chaotic wind waves converge in a single spot.

1 Wind blowing across the sea surface produces small waves with rounded crests, narrow troughs, and a short wavelength.

2 As the waves continue to grow larger, the wave crests become more pointed and the troughs rounder.

3 Finally, the wave crests become less stable as gravity pulls them downward. Whitecaps form when the waves break.

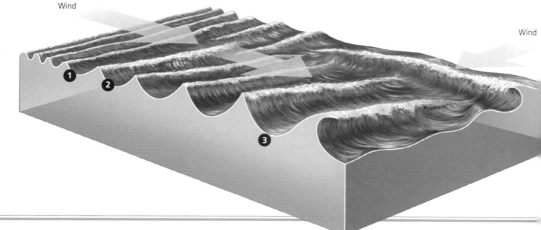

Wind

Wind

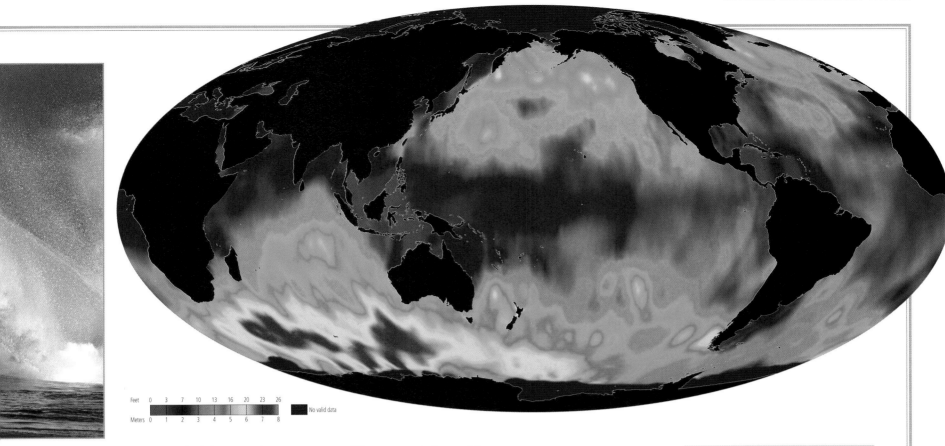

| Feet | 0 | 3 | 7 | 10 | 13 | 16 | 20 | 23 | 26 | | No valid data |
| Meters | 0 | 1 | 2 | 3 | 4 | 5 | 6 | 7 | 8 | | |

Wind waves on surface

Less dense water

Denser water

Internal wave
Waves can form below the sea surface, often at the bottom of a thermocline where a layer of warm water abuts a layer of colder, denser water. Generated by currents, tides, or winds, such internal waves can be more than 100 feet (30 m) high.

Waves around the world

This map shows the typical wave height in various regions of the global sea. Wave heights are color coded, from magenta for waves that are less than 3 feet (1 m) high, through blue, green, and yellow, to red for waves of 20–25 feet (7–8 m). The largest waves occur in the southern Indian Ocean and the Southern Ocean near Antarctica.

FIVE DIFFERENT WAVES	
Capillary wave	A tiny ripple-like wave that carries only a little amount of wind energy.
Plunging wave	A breaking wave whose crest curls into a tube as the wave advances toward a steeply sloping shore.
Deepwater wave	A wave traveling through water deeper than half the wave length.
Spilling wave	A breaking wave whose crest crumbles onto the wave base as the wave advances up a gently sloping shore.
Forced wave	A wave that persists because the energy that generated it continues.

Sea swell
The gently rising and falling ocean surface motion called "swell" consists of longer period waves that do not break. The arrival of swell in calm waters can indicate a storm is coming.

Storm-battered shores
Storm waves crashing on a Nova Scotia coast transfer their considerable energy to the shore. Many shorelines are regularly reshaped by the pounding force of storm waves.

WAVE POWER

Several coastal nations are exploiting ocean waves and winds as a renewable source of electrical energy that does not contribute to global warming. Technologies already in place include wave-powered generators, underwater turbines, and coastal wind farms that take advantage of steady sea breezes. The ceaseless motion of tides can also be used to produce electricity.

In a tidal power-generating system, a pump in a buoy drives seawater through a turbine, which in turn drives a generator connected to the shore.

Hydraulic pump encased in a buoy

Anchor and turbine

Generator in a canister

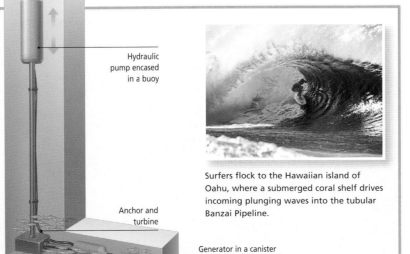

Surfers flock to the Hawaiian island of Oahu, where a submerged coral shelf drives incoming plunging waves into the tubular Banzai Pipeline.

Underwater
The slope of the bottom effects the way waves break over it. In this shallow Micronesian reef, the reef structure disperses the wave energy, so that the waves break gently on the shore.

TSUNAMIS

One of the most potentially dangerous ocean waves is a tsunami, a massive flood of water caused by a seismic shift such as a seafloor earthquake or an erupting undersea volcano. The term tsunami describes a speeding wall of water that can reach heights of 100 feet (30 m) or more and travel at a speed of 500 miles per hour (800 km/h). Typically, the triggering event launches a succession of huge waves as much as 45 minutes apart. Such waves may be imperceptible in the deep open ocean, but as a tsunami nears shore its height increases dramatically. In 1960, a tsunami generated by an earthquake off the coast of Chile raced 9,000 miles (14,500 km) to Japan where it caused massive damage and took 180 lives. Even more destructive was a 2004 tsunami that destroyed the Indonesian city of Banda Aceh and killed a total of more than 225,000 people.

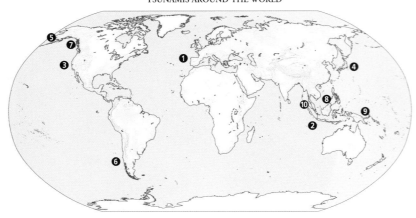
TSUNAMIS AROUND THE WORLD

Ten Worst Tsunamis		
1	1775	An earthquake in Lisbon generates a tsunami. More than 60,000 people die.
2	1883	Krakatau erupts and a tsunami sweeps over Indonesia; 36,000 people die.
3	1896	A tsunami hits Los Angeles on the Californian coast.
4	1896	The Sanriku tsunami strikes Japan and kills more than 26,000 people.
5	1946	Alaskan quake generates a tsunami. Hours later it kills 159 people in Hawaii.
6	1960	A tsunami kills 1,000 people in Chile, 61 people in Hawaii, and 180 people in Japan.
7	1964	Waves from an Alaskan quake sweep down the west coast, killing 122 people.
8	1976	A tsunami kills more than 5,000 people in the Philippines.
9	1998	A tsunami strikes the north coast of Papua New Guinea, killing 2,000 people.
10	2004	A powerful earthquake triggers waves that travel thousands of miles to crash onto the coastlines of at least 14 Asian and African countries. More than 225,000 people die.

Great wave in art
In the 1820s, Japanese artist Katsushika Hokusai captured the awesome power of huge ocean waves in his famous woodblock print *The Great Wave off Kanagawa*. The Japanese word tsunami roughly translates as "harbor wave."

Progress of a tsunami

After a shock launches a tsunami, it can travel across an ocean in less than a day. At sea the gathering tsunami may be less than 40 inches (1 m) high and vessels may hardly notice it. Nearing shore, the speed of tsunami waves slows and their height increases. The tsunami arrives as a series of wave crests and troughs 10 to 45 minutes apart.

Alaska 1964
In 1964, a tsunami struck southeastern Alaska with deadly force. Generated by a magnitude 9.2 earthquake beneath Prince William Sound, the gigantic wall of water wiped out several coastal villages and took 122 lives.

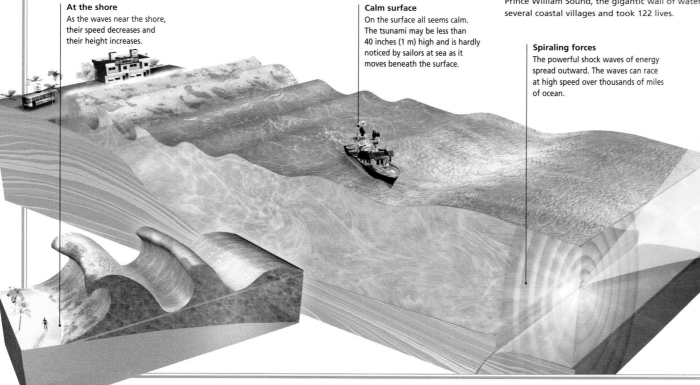

At the shore
As the waves near the shore, their speed decreases and their height increases.

Calm surface
On the surface all seems calm. The tsunami may be less than 40 inches (1 m) high and is hardly noticed by sailors at sea as it moves beneath the surface.

Spiraling forces
The powerful shock waves of energy spread outward. The waves can race at high speed over thousands of miles of ocean.

Submarine shock
Most tsunamis develop when an earthquake occurs deep in the ocean. Seafloor tectonic plates shift against one another, producing powerful shock waves. The energy of these waves then is transferred to the sea above.

Pre-tsunami
The Indonesian province of Aceh took the brunt of the December 2004 Indian Ocean tsunami. This aerial view shows the town of Lhokna in 2003.

Washed away
The tsunami washed away most buildings and vegetation in Lhokna, drowned nearby agricultural areas, and removed sand from the nearby beaches.

Monster tsunami

Throughout coastal Indonesia, the morning of December 26, 2004 held no sign of impending danger from the tsunami. Shortly before the first wave struck, however, the ocean off Aceh receded as water was pulled out toward the growing wave offshore. Then a series of waves up to 50 feet (15 m) high rushed toward the shore, crashed upon the beach, and pushed inland with massive force.

BEFORE THE TSUNAMI

WATER RETREATS

DISASTER STRIKES

AN ASIAN EARTHQUAKE AND TSUNAMI

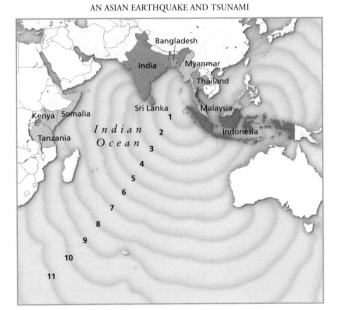

DEATH TOLL

■ >100 000	■ 10 000–100 000	■ 1 000–10 000
■ < 1 000	□ no data	**2** hours after event

Path to destruction
The Richter magnitude 9.2 or 9.3 earthquake that occurred on December 26, 2004 caused movement along a fault to the west of Sumatra. The sudden displacement in the sea floor sent a shock wave across the ocean. This map shows the hour-by-hour progress of the wave over 11 hours. When the wave reached shallow water it piled up into a devastating tsunami.

DETECTION AND WARNING

Tsunamis can hit coastlines both near to and far from the site of origin. In coastal nations around the world, early-warning systems help civil defense personnel predict when and where a tsunami will strike, and to inform the populace. The systems include sensors that monitor undersea earthquakes and other seismic shifts, and devices mounted on specialized buoys that track unusual shifts in the height of the sea surface.

This sign provides tsunami evacuation instructions at the beach on Koh Lipe, Thailand. Similar signs now appear in many beach areas vulnerable to tsunamis.

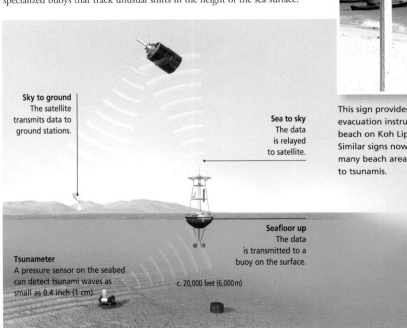

Sky to ground
The satellite transmits data to ground stations.

Sea to sky
The data is relayed to satellite.

Seafloor up
The data is transmitted to a buoy on the surface.

Tsunameter
A pressure sensor on the seabed can detect tsunami waves as small as 0.4 inch (1 cm).

c. 20,000 feet (6,000 m)

41

HURRICANES

Tropical cyclones are among the most powerful of all natural events. Called hurricanes in the Atlantic and eastern Pacific and typhoons in the western Pacific, these huge swirling storms generally develop over tropical seas where warm air soaks up evaporating surface water. Over several days, the air mass starts spinning counterclockwise in the northern hemisphere, attaining hurricane status when the wind speed reaches 74 miles per hour (118 km/h). Air in the calm center or "eye" of a hurricane is warmer and under lower pressure than in the spiraling rain bands farther out. The greater the pressure difference between the inner and outer regions, the greater a hurricane's intensity and the potential threat to life and property. The largest and most intense tropical cyclone on record is Super Typhoon Tip, which struck southern Japan in 1979 and caused major flooding and loss of life. Measuring 1,380 miles (2,220 km) in diameter, Tip generated maximum winds of 190 miles per hour (305 km/h).

Eye of a hurricane
In 2005, Hurricane Hernan developed into a huge storm off California and northwestern Mexico. Maximum winds measured 165 miles per hour (266 km/h). This satellite image clearly shows its eye, the calm area at a hurricane's center.

Pressure systems
In a low-pressure system, surface air converges counterclockwise toward the center, then rises and diverges in the opposite direction. The reverse happens in a high-pressure system. Air flows from high to low pressure, creating wind.

Convergence aloft

Divergence aloft

Subsidence

Uplift

Surface anticyclone

Surface cyclone

Southern hemisphere hurricane
A satellite tracks Hurricane Monica, building strength off northeastern Australia in April 2006, the southern hemisphere autumn. Its winds eventually peaked at 215 miles per hour (370 km/h). Colored areas correlate with rainfall, with red being the heaviest.

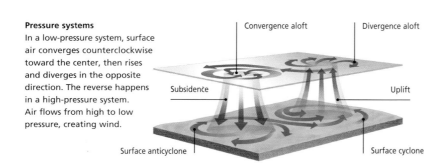

How a hurricane works

A hurricane forms when rising humid air begins rotating counterclockwise. As the air rises, it creates intense low pressure that essentially sucks in additional air over the sea surface. The circulating warm air typically holds a great deal of water vapor—a large hurricane can dump 20 billion tons (18 billion t) of rainwater in a day. Paired with high winds, the deluge can cause severe damage on land.

❶ Eyewall
The calm eye of a hurricane is surrounded by an eyewall—massive, dark storm clouds that produce the heaviest rain and strongest winds.

❷ Spiraling air
An upward spiral of warm, moist air is drawn into the central area of low pressure. Moisture sustains the formation of the storm clouds.

❸ Rain bands
As the storm builds, spiraling bands of rain clouds form. The outer bands may be more than 200 miles (320 km) from the eye.

❹ Approaching land
The eye forms and the hurricane is at its most dangerous approaching land.

❺ Over land
Without moisture from the sea, the hurricane starts to lose some of its energy.

❻ Hurricane dies
Farther inland the hurricane dissipates.

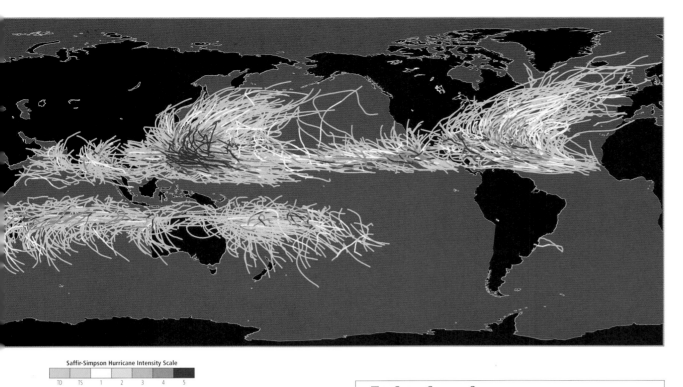

Distribution and paths
Hurricanes develop in the North Atlantic, North and South Pacific, and Indian oceans, in latitudes between 5° and 20°, where there is ample evaporation of water from warm currents and a strong Coriolis effect can start them rotating.

Hurricane Andrew's destruction, Florida, 1992

Shrimp boats blown ashore by Hurricane Katrina, 2005

Saffir-Simpson Hurricane Intensity Scale

| TD | TS | 1 | 2 | 3 | 4 | 5 |

Measuring hurricane intensity

Climatologists use the Saffir-Simpson Scale shown at right to categorize a hurricane's intensity. The most powerful hurricanes typically develop in the western Pacific, which historically has tallied more category 4 and 5 storms than anywhere else. By contrast, hurricanes are virtually unknown in the South Pacific and southern Atlantic oceans, where cold currents translate into cool air that gives off less water vapor to the atmosphere.

THE SAFFIR-SIMPSON SCALE

Category number	Wind speed [mph (km/h)]	Storm surge [ft (m)]	Damage
1	74–95 (118–152)	4–5 (1.2–1.6)	Minimal
2	96–110 (153–176)	6–8 (1.7–2.5)	Moderate
3	111–130 (177–208)	9–12 (2.6–3.7)	Extensive
4	131–155 (209–248)	13–18 (3.8–5.4)	Extensive
5	More than 155 (248)	More than 18 (5.4)	Catastrophic

TEN WORST HURRICANES
H = Hurricane, **T.S.** = Tropical Storm, **T** = Typhoon

	Year	Name and place	Deaths
1	1998	H. Mitch, Central America	11,000
2	1900	No name, Texas	6,000–12,000
3	1974	H. Fifi, Honduras	5,000
4	2004	T.S. Jeanne, Haiti	3,000
5	2005	H. Katrina, Louisiana & Mississippi	1,193
6	1979	H. David, Caribbean, Florida, Georgia, New York	1,000
7	1994	T. Fred, China	1,000
8	2004	T. Winnie, Philippines	(dead/missing) 1,000
9	1944	T. Cobra, Philippine Sea	790
10	2005	H. Stan , Central America	725

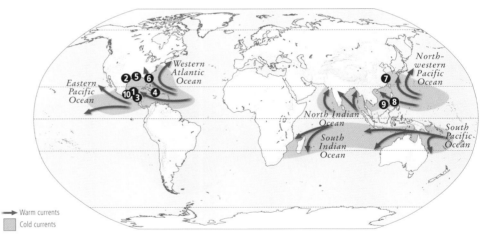

Warm currents
Cold currents

WATERSPOUTS

A tornado is a funnel of air rapidly spiraling upward into a cloud. It is the most violent of all climatic phenomena. Waterspouts are tornadoes that develop or pass over warm, shallow water, sucking up a whirling column of water that may rise as high as 300 feet (100 m). Waterspouts usually develop during tropical storms when masses of cold and warm air interact with the sea surface.

Not all waterspouts develop at sea. Some begin to form over land and then move to warm coastal waters offshore.

Mariners of old recounted frightening encounters with waterspouts. This 19th century painting clearly depicts multiple waterspouts threatening the sailing ship *Trombes*.

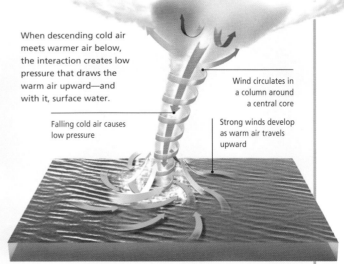

When descending cold air meets warmer air below, the interaction creates low pressure that draws the warm air upward—and with it, surface water.

Falling cold air causes low pressure

Wind circulates in a column around a central core

Strong winds develop as warm air travels upward

TIDES

Tides may be the sea's most predictable changes. In each tide cycle, the sea surface rises, then falls in conjunction with the shifting pull of gravity from the Moon and the Sun as Earth rotates on its axis. Lunar gravity exerts the strongest pull, so the sea bulges below the Moon's position above Earth. A corresponding bulge occurs on the planet's opposite side. As Earth rotates through the bulges, the result is a pattern of shallow, planet-sized waves that are visible as rising and falling water levels along the shore. The highest and lowest tides, called spring tides, occur year-round at two-week intervals corresponding to the full and new moon. "Neap tides"—the lowest high and highest low tides—occur during the Moon's first- and third-quarter phases. Regardless, because the Moon rises 51 minutes later each day, a tide cycle lasts 24 hours and 51 minutes and high tide occurs 51 minutes later each day.

Spring and neap tides

Spring tides result when Earth, the Moon, and the Sun all align. The combination of their gravitational effects increases both high tide height and low tide levels. Neap tides occur when Earth, the Moon, and the Sun form the points of a triangle. In this configuration, the Moon's gravitational pull is at right angles to that of the Sun and the Sun's gravity partly cancels it out.

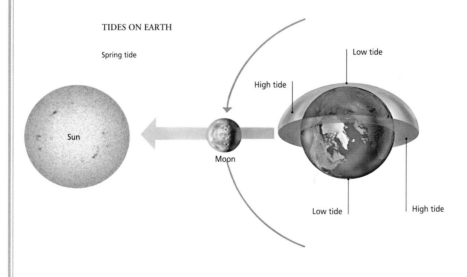
TIDES ON EARTH

Spring tide

Sun — Moon

Low tide / High tide / Low tide / High tide

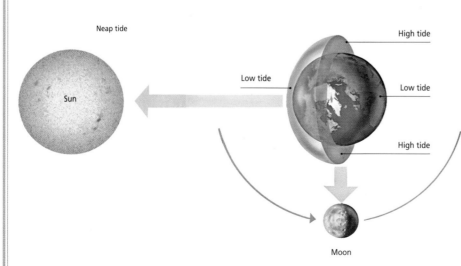

Neap tide

Sun

Low tide / High tide / Low tide / High tide

Moon

Tides around the globe

Three general tide patterns occur along Earth's coastlines. Most coastal areas experience semidiurnal, or twice daily, tides in which the levels of high or low tides are about equal. Also common are mixed tides—semidiurnal tides in which the levels of highs or lows are unequal. Along some coastlines tides follow a simpler diurnal pattern of one high and one low a day.

Highest high tide
The shape and depth of the Bay of Fundy, on Canada's east coast, give it perhaps the greatest tidal range in the world—56 feet (17 m). This photograph shows Hopewell Rocks at high tide, when the rock bases are submerged.

Lowest low tide
At low tide, Hopewell Rocks are completely above the water line and the shore is a broad mudflat. Tidal action has scoured out the rocks' pedestal-like bases and eventually will erode them away completely.

Pacific Ocean

NOR AMER

Gulf Mexi

Bea S

☐ Semidiurnal tides
☐ Diurnal tides
☐ Mixed tides

SCALE 1:146,000,000
Robinson Projection

Reef revealed
At Montgomery Reef in northwest Australia, the exposed reef visible at maximum low tide, when all the seawater drains into the ocean, extends over nearly 116 square miles (300 km²).

TIDE INFORMATION	
1 Nature of tide waves	Shallow water wave
2 Tide wave wavelength	About 12,400 miles (20,000 km)
3 Diurnal tide interval	24 hours, 50 minutes
4 Semidiurnal tide interval	6 hours, 12.5 minutes (high/low roughly equal)
5 Mixed tide interval	6 hours, 12.5 minutes (high/low unequal)
6 Speed of tide wave energy through ocean	About 435 miles per hour (700 km/h)

Hidden reef
At high tide at Montgomery Reef, the spectacular reef is submerged. The tidal range is about 33 feet (10 m), ranking second in the world after the Bay of Fundy in Nova Scotia.

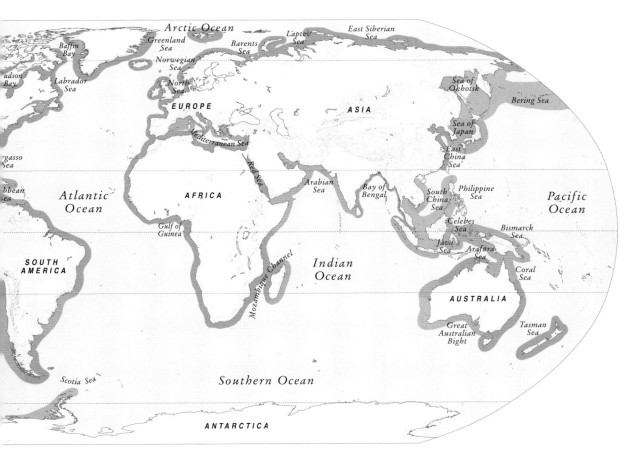

Bright red tide
A so-called "red tide" is a "bloom" of millions of rusty-hued phytoplankton called dinoflagellates. Toxic to fish or shellfish and other marine life, red-tide organisms can also cause poisoning and allergic reactions in humans.

TIDE CURVES FOR THE THREE COMMON TYPES OF TIDES

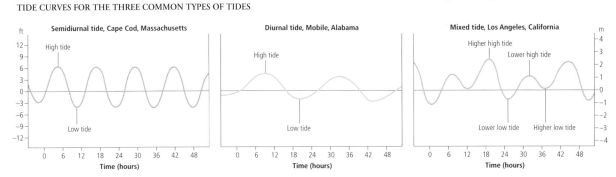

Tide curves
These graphs plot how water levels fluctuate during different types of tides over a 48-hour period. Although the water levels are unequal in mixed tides (pink), the shifting pattern repeats about every 12 hours 25 minutes.

THAMES BARRIER

In some harbor areas where extreme high tides or storm surge may threaten cities and towns, engineers have created barriers that can be moved into place to block the tidal flow. One of the largest protects areas of London, England from tidal flooding of the river Thames. Its water-filled, crescent-shaped steel gates can be rotated upward to block floodwater, then rotated back underwater when danger is past.

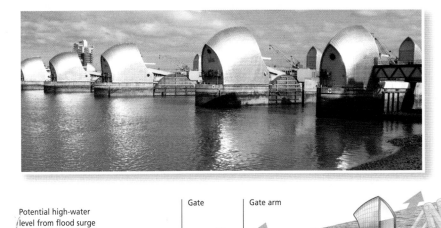

The Thames Barrier is just over 1,700 feet (520 m) long. Each of its 10 submerged gates spans 200 feet (61 m) and can rise 35 feet (10.7 m) above the Thames River's normal water level.

Barrier raised
The Thames Barrier is raised to protect against an impending flood and a remotely controlled gate arm pivots each gate upward. The gates can also be rotated 180 degrees for maintenance and are put through a test run every month.

Barrier lowered
The Thames Barrier is lowered when not in use and its curved gates nest in concave concrete foundations sunk into the riverbed. The depth of the channels above allows normal vessel traffic on the river.

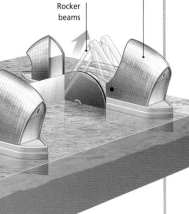

Steel-covered shells

Rocker beams

Potential high-water level from flood surge

Gate

Gate arm

Normal river flow

This photograph shows colonies of coral animals, each a polyp that
resembles a slender, white-tipped stalk. The polyps grow, they are
nourished, and they reproduce as they undulate with the current in
tropical shallows. The catalog of marine life encompasses a striking
array of animals, plants, and microorganisms, each with structures
and functions suited to survival in a particular undersea environment.

SEA ENVIRONMENT

Sea Depths

All forms of life on Earth are profoundly affected by their physical surroundings. In the sea, two of the most crucial physical factors are light and temperature conditions at different depths. Oceanographers divide the three-dimensional marine environment into the pelagic zone of open water and the bottom or benthic zone—each home to a striking diversity of marine life. The layers of the pelagic zone are defined by the amount of sunlight reaching them. The upper sunlight zone, where the most light penetrates, ranges from the surface to about 660 feet (200 m). Here marine life is most abundant, with the seas teeming with organisms ranging from bacteria to a wealth of fish and other species. Below, a dimmer, cooler, and less populated "twilight" zone extends down from 660–3,300 feet (200–1,000 m). The deep sea is a frigid, dark world where relatively few types of organisms survive.

Life at different depths

Similarly to land animals, sea creatures need a particular set of environmental conditions to survive. For example, like plants, phytoplankton and algae can only survive where there is enough sunlight for photosynthesis. Far more conspicuous are the thousands of species of marine fishes, some adapted for life near the surface of the sea, others that survive in mid-waters, and still others with features that suit them for great depths.

Surface for air
Sperm whales (*Physeter macrocephalus*) must surface to breathe, but they may dive as deep as 3,300 feet (1,000 m) in search of their giant squid prey.

Environments for life

Away from shore, the sea becomes a deepening universe of interacting physical and chemical factors. Although overall water depth varies greatly within different ocean basins, each of Earth's five oceans is subdivided into parts having different features. Horizontally an ocean includes nearshore and open waters. Vertically it has layered zones where depth-related shifts in temperature, salinity and other conditions set the ground rules for survival of marine species.

DEPTH	
Feet	Meters
Below sea level	
0	0
656	200
1,640	500
3,281	1,000
6,562	2,000
9,843	3,000
13,123	4,000
16,404	5,000
19,685	6,000
22,966	7,000
26,247	8,000

SCALE 1:143,100,000
Mercator Projection

Ocean zones
Ocean waters are subdivided broadly into a nearshore neritic realm and the oceanic realm. The pelagic realm encompasses the sunlit epipelagic and dimmer mesopelagic zones, the dark bathypelagic and abyssopelagic zones, and the hadal zone of seafloor trenches.

The Food-Rich Surface

The upper two percent of the global sea contains more living organisms than the rest of the ocean combined. Here sunlight fuels the growth of vast pastures of plant-like phytoplankton that sustain themselves by photosynthesis. They are the vital foundation for a global food web that includes zooplankton, tiny drifting animals preyed upon by species ranging from shrimps to whales. Food-rich surface waters also sustain a tremendous variety of fish species.

This species of krill (*Euphausia superba*) and the sea butterfly (*Clione limacina*) are types of zooplankton that drift or swim weakly with surface sea currents.

Krill

Sea butterfly

Diatoms are mostly single-celled phytoplankton with a hard, shell-like casing of silica that often forms an intricate pattern characteristic of each species.

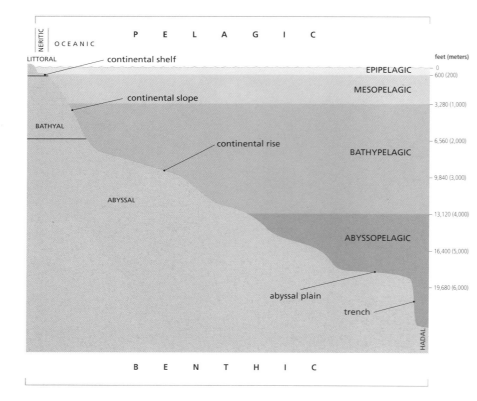

NERITIC OCEANIC
LITTORAL — continental shelf
PELAGIC
feet (meters)
EPIPELAGIC — 0
600 (200)
MESOPELAGIC
continental slope
3,280 (1,000)
BATHYAL
continental rise
6,560 (2,000)
BATHYPELAGIC
9,840 (3,000)
ABYSSAL
13,120 (4,000)
ABYSSOPELAGIC
16,400 (5,000)
abyssal plain
19,680 (6,000)
trench
HADAL
BENTHIC

Marine snow
Researchers deploy fine-mesh nets to collect "marine snow"—wastes and other decaying particles that drift toward the bottom. A crucial food source for many marine organisms, this material is the energy base for most deep-sea ecosystems.

Ribbon-like body
The longest bony fish in the ocean—the oarfish (*Regalecus glesne*)—grows to about 50 feet (15 m) and lives as deep as 3,000 feet (914 m). This specimen photographed in Kasari Bay, Japan, dwarfs the two divers swimming alongside.

Fast swimmer
The blue and silver mahi mahi (*Coryphaena hippurus*) closely match the hues of the upper ocean waters where these speedsters live and pursue darting flying fish.

Upward migrator
Lanternfish (*Diaphus* sp.) spend the day away from surface predators between 1,000 and 3,300 feet (303–1,000 m), but migrate upward at night to feed in the dark.

Deep-sea dweller
Humpback anglerfish (*Melanacetus johnsoni*) have a luminous fin spine on the head that attracts prey and potential mates. Several species live as deep as 6,600 feet (2,000 m).

Into the abyss
The abyssal cuskeel (*Abyssobrotula galatheae*) lives at extreme depths below 13,000 feet (4,000 m) in the abyssopelagic zone, where daylight never penetrates.

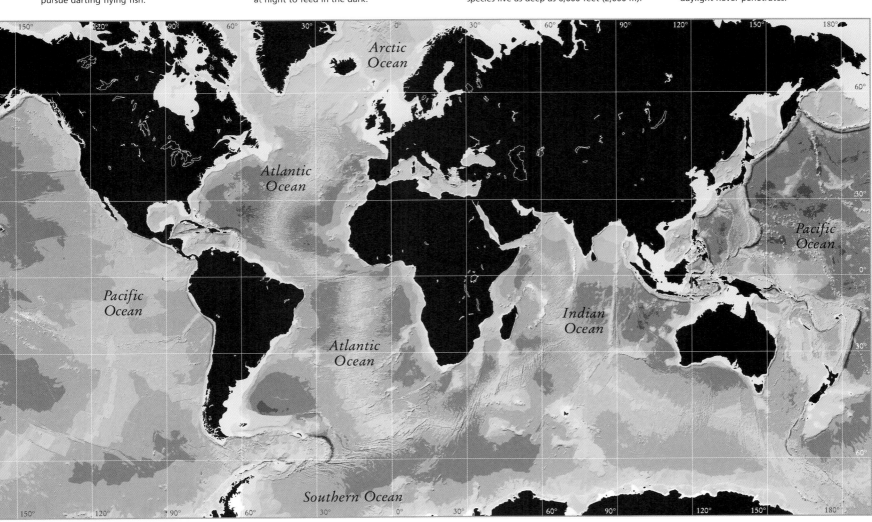

Arctic Ocean

Atlantic Ocean

Pacific Ocean

Pacific Ocean

Atlantic Ocean

Indian Ocean

Southern Ocean

DEEP-SEA VENTS

Hydrothermal vents may develop along crustal cracks where seafloor spreading is occurring. Dozens are known, all spewing a scalding blend of water and chemicals that may exceed 600°F (350°C). Some vents build into "smokers" that spout water chemically tinted gray or black. These towering structures have been known to rise 15 stories before collapsing. Vent communities include some of the strangest of all marine animals.

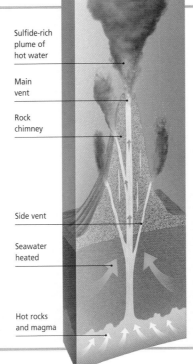

Sulfide-rich plume of hot water

Main vent

Rock chimney

Side vent

Seawater heated

Hot rocks and magma

Black smokers are the hottest vents. This one is releasing its chemical-laced plume at a hydrothermal spring in the mid-ocean ridge of the Atlantic.

Pale, oversized mussels (*Bathymodiolus* sp.) blanket an area near a hydrothermal spring in the Pacific. They share their real estate with crabs, shrimp, and limpets.

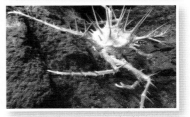

This aptly named, 2-inch (5-cm) spiny crab (species unknown) scuttles through a vent community hunting for live food, sometimes including other crabs.

Minerals in vent plumes harden into whitish rock chimneys that can be more than 63 feet (19 m) high. This relatively small example is about 3.3 feet (1 m) across.

UNDERWATER TOPOGRAPHY

It took centuries for marine scientists to begin to grasp the remarkable diversity of Earth's undersea landscapes. With the advent of increasingly sophisticated sonar, manned and remote-operated submersibles, advanced underwater cameras, and other methods, researchers today have a much fuller understanding of the sea's major topographic features. This physical portrait includes: the submerged, sloping margins of the continents; scores of submarine canyons; the vast plains of the deep abyss; plunging ocean trenches; approximately 20,000 inactive volcanoes that form structures known as seamounts and guyots; and about 40,400 miles (65,000 km) of sinuous undersea mountain ranges marking the submerged seams of crustal plates. Similar diversity marks the seafloor surface, which may be rocky, sandy, or a blend of sand and mud. Where tectonic events are actively producing new seafloor, surface sediments are usually thin. In contrast, at the "rise" where a continental shelf tapers to the deep ocean floor, deep blankets of soft sediments can develop.

The undersea landscape

Tools including satellite-based sensors and sonar are the stock-in-trade of bathymetry—literally measuring "the deep." Today, their computer-processed data provides a revealing and detailed portrait of the undersea landscape, with its varied array of continental shelves, huge undersea canyons, mid-ocean ridges, soaring peaks, vast trenches, and abyssal plains. These features include the deepest point on Earth and its tallest mountain—a peak that breaks the surface as the island of Hawaii.

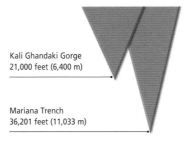

Kali Ghandaki Gorge
21,000 feet (6,400 m)

Mariana Trench
36,201 feet (11,033 m)

Mauna Kea
33,000 feet (10,000m)

Mount Everest
29,029 feet (8,848 m)

Deepest trenches
The Mariana Trench, the deepest part of the world seas, is more than 15,000 feet (4,572 m) deeper than the deepest land trench, Nepal's Kali Ghandaki Gorge.

Highest mountains
The marine volcano visible above the sea surface as Hawaii's Mauna Kea rises about 4,000 feet (1,219 m) higher than the tallest mountain on land, Mount Everest.

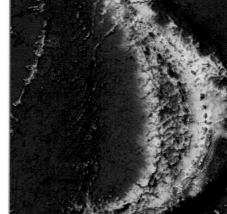

The Mariana Trench
The deepest point on Earth, the sickle-shaped Mariana Trench in the western Pacific, slices more than 36,100 feet (11,022 m) into Earth's crust. Due in part to the lack of food at that depth, life there is scarce.

SEDIMENTARY BASINS

Sediment blankets about 75 percent of the ocean basins and much of the continental shelves. Some of these sediments enter the marine environment as weathering rock and eroding soil washed or blown into the sea or carried there by rivers. Some form muddy deposits while others are converted to sticky clays. Still other sediments are soft "oozes" consisting of the decomposing remains of marine organisms.

Volcanic legacy
Researchers have ample evidence of past undersea volcanoes. These images compare the crater of an extinct land volcano, Crater Lake in the US state of Oregon, and the crater of an extinct marine volcano in the western Pacific.

SEDIMENTARY DEPOSITS

Onshore sedimentary deposits

Offshore sedimentary deposits

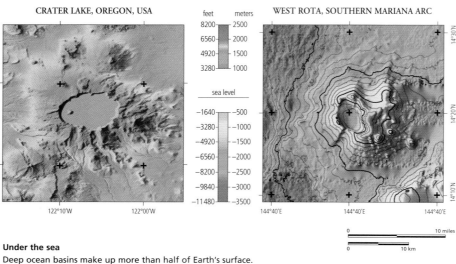

CRATER LAKE, OREGON, USA

WEST ROTA, SOUTHERN MARIANA ARC

feet	meters
8200	2500
6560	2000
4920	1500
3280	1000

sea level

-1640	-500
-3280	-1000
-4920	-1500
-6560	-2000
-8200	-2500
-9840	-3000
-11480	-3500

Under the sea
Deep ocean basins make up more than half of Earth's surface. Some of their most notable geologic features are canyons cleaving the continental slopes, mid-ocean mountain ridges, steep trenches, and broad, flat abyssal plains.

Continental shelf

Continental slope

Continental rise

Abyssal plain

Mid-ocean ridge

Trench

Sedimentary rock on land reveals the gradual layering of sediments over spans of time. This formation is in Death Valley National Park, California, USA.

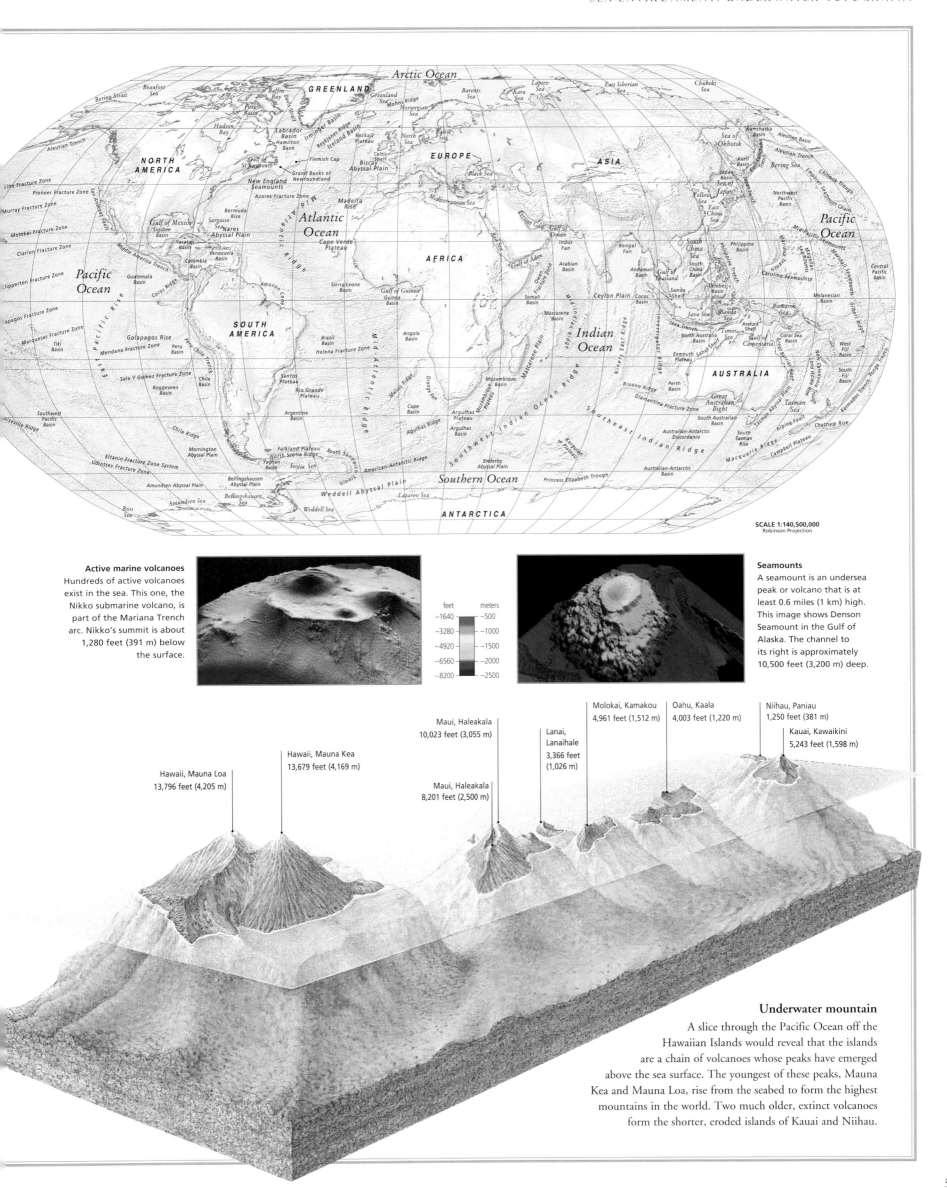

SCALE 1:140,500,000
Robinson Projection

Active marine volcanoes
Hundreds of active volcanoes exist in the sea. This one, the Nikko submarine volcano, is part of the Mariana Trench arc. Nikko's summit is about 1,280 feet (391 m) below the surface.

feet	meters
−1640	−500
−3280	−1000
−4920	−1500
−6560	−2000
−8200	−2500

Seamounts
A seamount is an undersea peak or volcano that is at least 0.6 miles (1 km) high. This image shows Denson Seamount in the Gulf of Alaska. The channel to its right is approximately 10,500 feet (3,200 m) deep.

Hawaii, Mauna Loa
13,796 feet (4,205 m)

Hawaii, Mauna Kea
13,679 feet (4,169 m)

Maui, Haleakala
10,023 feet (3,055 m)

Maui, Haleakala
8,201 feet (2,500 m)

Lanai, Lanaihale
3,366 feet (1,026 m)

Molokai, Kamakou
4,961 feet (1,512 m)

Oahu, Kaala
4,003 feet (1,220 m)

Niihau, Paniau
1,250 feet (381 m)

Kauai, Kawaikini
5,243 feet (1,598 m)

Underwater mountain
A slice through the Pacific Ocean off the Hawaiian Islands would reveal that the islands are a chain of volcanoes whose peaks have emerged above the sea surface. The youngest of these peaks, Mauna Kea and Mauna Loa, rise from the seabed to form the highest mountains in the world. Two much older, extinct volcanoes form the shorter, eroded islands of Kauai and Niihau.

51

HOT SPOTS

Volcanoes constantly reshape Earth's crust both on land and under the sea. The vast majority of volcanoes, including more than 450 in the famous Pacific Ring of Fire, result from collisions between crustal plates. Geologists estimate that there may be as many 10,000 hidden from view under the sea, most situated along mid-ocean ridges. Many are associated with some of the seafloor's most striking oddities, including hydrothermal vents, hot and cold seeps, and towering smokers, all home to an array of unusual species such as giant, rose-hued tube worms. Volcanoes also develop at so-called hot spots where heat from a site in the mantle erupts at the surface of the crust above it. The resulting volcano remains active until plate movements shift it away from the hot spot. Because the hot spot does not move, a new volcano then arises in crust that has moved into place above it. Iceland, the Galapagos Islands, and the Hawaiian Islands are examples of hot-spot activity.

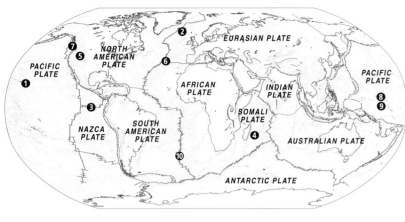

HOT SPOTS AROUND THE WORLD

10 Most Active Hot Spots	
1	Hawaii
2	Iceland
3	Galapagos Islands
4	Réunion Island (Indian Ocean)
5	Yellowstone National Park (continental)
6	Azores
7	Bowie (Queen Charlotte Islands, Canada)
8	Samoa
9	Marquesas
10	Tristan (Tristan da Cunha island, southern Atlantic)

Yellowstone geysers
Every 60 to 90 minutes, Old Faithful Geyser, a geothermal vent in Yellowstone National Park in the US state of Wyoming, spews a fountain of boiling water heated by hot-spot activity far below in Earth's mantle.

Iceland hot spot
Iceland's Strokkur Geyser erupts every five to 10 minutes, venting superheated water and steam as high as 70 feet (20 m). Iceland currently lies over one of the world's most active hot spots.

Réunion Island
Réunion Island in the Indian Ocean is one of the best known hot spots in the world. Its active volcano, Piton de la Fournaise, spews molten lava almost daily. The most recent major eruption occurred in 2007.

Galapagos Islands
Hot-spot volcanic activity that gave rise to the Galapagos Islands of Ecuador produced both the islet of Bartolomé and its landmark Pinnacle Rock. Eroding lava of various colors makes up much of Bartolomé's landscape.

The Ring of Fire

The Pacific Ocean basin contains numerous hot spots marked by features such as the Hawaiian and Samoan island chains. In addition, more than 50 percent of Earth's active continental volcanoes form the "Ring of Fire" that nearly encircles the basin. Unlike hot-spot volcanoes, these plate-boundary volcanoes rise where crustal plates are colliding. Volcanoes in Japan, Indonesia, and along the west coast of North and South America are prime examples.

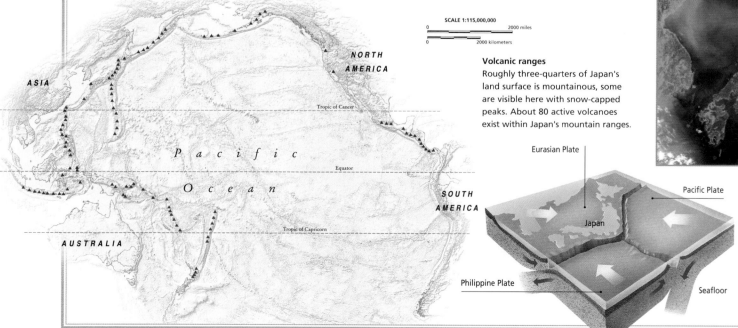

SCALE 1:115,000,000

0 — 2000 miles
0 — 2000 kilometers

Volcanic ranges
Roughly three-quarters of Japan's land surface is mountainous, some are visible here with snow-capped peaks. About 80 active volcanoes exist within Japan's mountain ranges.

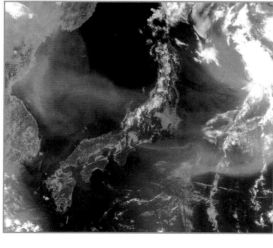

Eurasian Plate

Pacific Plate

Japan

Philippine Plate

Seafloor

The Japan split
There are three tectonic plates beneath Japan, but the Pacific Plate is moving about twice as fast as the Philippine Plate. This difference underlies the geologic activity that has formed many of Japan's volcanoes and that causes its frequent earthquakes.

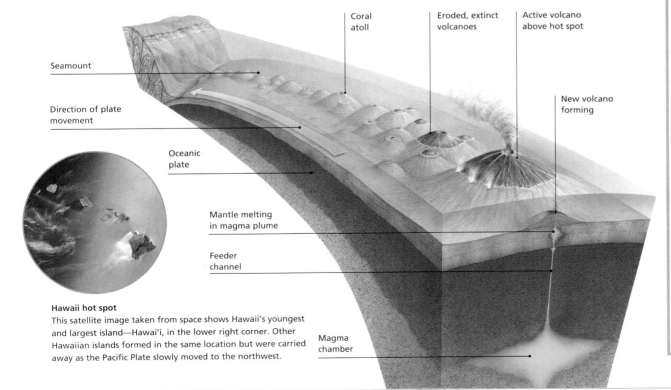

Formation of an island chain

Hawaii is a prime example of how hot spots may create marine island chains. The site of a hot spot's magma plume remains fixed while an oceanic plate slowly travels over it. Discharged magma gradually builds a volcano that breaks the surface as an island. As the plate moves over millions of years, a series of volcanic islands form, move away from the hot spot, become extinct, and erode.

Kilauea in action
Molten lava cascades regularly down the flanks of Hawaii's Mount Kilauea to the sea. Kilauea's current position atop the Hawaii hot spot makes it the most active volcano on Earth, erupting almost daily since January 1983.

Coral atoll

Eroded, extinct volcanoes

Active volcano above hot spot

Seamount

New volcano forming

Direction of plate movement

Oceanic plate

Mantle melting in magma plume

Feeder channel

Hawaii hot spot
This satellite image taken from space shows Hawaii's youngest and largest island—Hawai'i, in the lower right corner. Other Hawaiian islands formed in the same location but were carried away as the Pacific Plate slowly moved to the northwest.

Magma chamber

UNIQUE HAWAIIAN SPECIES

Hawaii's isolated location in the Pacific Ocean has triggered the evolution of a striking mix of endemic plants and animals—native species that occur nowhere else. Uniquely Hawaiian marine species include marine mammals, seabirds, fishes, and crustaceans. Endemic species may be unusually vulnerable to extinction if they face introduced predators or diseases against which they have few or no natural defenses.

⚡ The endemic Hawaiian monk seal (*Monachus schauinslandi*), Hawaii's state mammal, has become critically endangered due to hunting and other pressures. It is estimated only 1,200 individuals remain.

The Laysan albatross (*Phoebastria immutabilis*) is one of the most common of Hawaiian seabirds. Although they range widely over the North Pacific, the birds return to Hawaii to breed.

This banded spiny lobster (*Panulirus marginatus*) is a relatively common denizen of nearshore waters. Its distant cousins include spiny lobsters of the Caribbean and other tropical seas.

Divers may observe schools of these brightly colored Hawaiian squirrelfish (*Sargocentron xantherythom*) browsing among the coral heads of Hawaii's reefs.

COASTLINES

Coastlines, the boundaries where the sea meets land, are among the most dynamic places on Earth. Over geologic time, tectonic forces that move continents determine the location and overall shape of coastlines. A geologically young, emergent coast occurs where tectonic movements are pushing up the edge of a continent. Conversely, older coasts may gradually subside partly because of the weight of accumulating sediments. Sea level changes also submerge or expose coastal land as ice caps and glaciers form or melt, crustal plates shift, and the seafloor expands at mid-ocean ridges. Erosion by wave action, tides, and river flows mold the contours of the shore, forming beaches where the substrate is soft material such as sandstone. Along high-energy coastlines, where wave action is intense, erosion may sculpt dramatic features such as cliffs, caves, and arches. Seawalls and other human-made structures designed to forestall these natural processes attest to the sea's power to shape the land.

LONGEST COASTLINES

10 Countries with the Longest Coastlines	
1 Canada	151,485 miles (243,791 km)
2 Indonesia	33,999 miles (54,716 km)
3 Russia	23,396 miles (37,652 km)
4 Philippines	22,559 miles (36,305 km)
5 Japan	18,486 miles (29,750 km)
6 Australia	16,007 miles (25,761 km)
7 Norway	13,624 miles (21,926 km)
8 United States of America	12,380 miles (19,924 km)
9 New Zealand	9,404 miles (15,134 km)
10 China	9,010 miles (14,500 km)

Tectonically uplifted cliffs
The pale color of the famous cliffs along England's Dover coast comes from their main constituent calcium carbonate, remains of ancient marine zooplankton. The highest cliff rises 350 feet (106 m) above the sea.

Glacial coast
An ice-age glacier sculpted the rolling headlands typical of Orkney, an archipelago of more than 70 islands in northern Scotland. Erosion of underlying sandstone and volcanic granite produced the dark rock-strewn beach.

Lava flow coast
In geologic time, the Hawaiian island of Maui formed relatively recently as a hot-spot volcano and much of its coastline consists of lava rock. Over time, grinding wave action may produce beaches of coarse black lava bits.

Barrier island
Barrier islands form from sand deposited between two tidal inlets.

Coastal landforms

Vigorous waves and tides cut into rocky coasts, producing cliffs, terraces, blowholes and other landforms. The sea deposits the eroded material elsewhere, building sandbars and spits, and extending beaches. When sand accumulates and links an offshore rock or island with the mainland, the formation is called a tombolo, from an Italian word for mound.

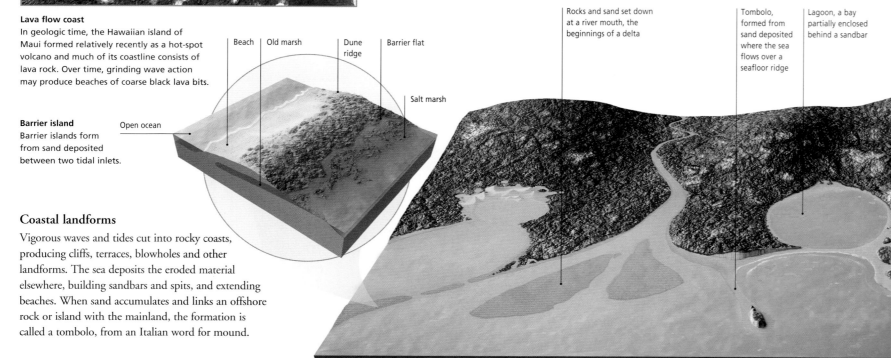

Beach   Old marsh   Dune ridge   Barrier flat

Open ocean

Salt marsh

Rocks and sand set down at a river mouth, the beginnings of a delta

Tombolo, formed from sand deposited where the sea flows over a seafloor ridge

Lagoon, a bay partially enclosed behind a sandbar

The Twelve Apostles
A set of 12 distinct sea stacks off the southern coast of Australia was named the Twelve Apostles in the 1950s. Since then, ongoing erosion has toppled four of the original stacks—a fate that will eventually claim them all.

Coast of barrier islands
Bald Head Island is one of a string of barrier islands along the coast of North Carolina, USA. Barrier islands typically are huge sandbars that develop where ocean currents and wave action promote the deposition of sand.

Cave
When coastal currents erode softer rocks from the face of a headland, a sea cave is hollowed out.

Arch
Wave action continues to widen the cave and eventually wears through the headland, producing an arch.

Stack
The top of the arch thins and collapses, leaving a sea stack separated from the shore.

Coastal formations

Coastal cliffs form when waves erode hills along the shore. As this process continues, the cliffs gradually retreat inland. Erosion due to wave action and weathering continues to play a major role in shaping subsequent coastal features, such as sea stacks, arches, and caves.

PROTECTING THE COAST

Coastal areas have always been vulnerable to damage from storm surges as well as day-to-day impacts of wave action and tidal fluxes. Seawalls and structures called groins are common solutions to these ongoing problems. A seawall protects developed coastal areas by deflecting wave energy back toward the ocean. Grouped groins help establish and maintain beaches by preventing the loss of sand or other sediments.

Modern seawalls are often reinforced concrete. This one in Zeeland, Holland was erected following major storm surge damage in 1953.

Sets of groins, typically constructed of rocks, wood or concrete, are a common sight in coastal areas where beach erosion is a recurring problem.

Spit, created by deposition of sand where the sea current slows down

Terrace in the cliff, cut by wave action

Blowhole, where the roof of a cave has collapsed

Stack, created by wave erosion at the end of a headland

Sand dunes built from accumulated windblown sand

Rocks at the foot of a cliff, where the cliff face is moving inland due to erosion

Beach, formed from sand set down by waves and tides

Caves hollowed out by wave action

Arch, where wave action has cut right through the headland

BEACHES AND DUNES

Along every coast a shoreline threads between the water's edge and the uppermost splash zone. Punctuating this seam between land and sea are beaches, some consisting mainly of sand or rocks, others of pebbles or mud. Beaches develop where coastal topography encourages the build-up of sediments. Depending on the location and other characteristics of a coast, beach material may be deposited by river or lava flows, nearshore currents and waves, by the wind or glacial action, or another source. Worldwide, sand beaches are the most common, often backed by dunes in places where strong onshore winds push beach sand landward. The largest coastal dunes may grow to more than 330 feet (100 m). Bangladesh claims the world's longest unbroken sand beach, which stretches some 80 miles (129 km) along the Bay of Bengal. Yet all beaches and dunes are in constant flux, shifting in size and shape in tune with shifts in the forces that mold them.

Beach makeup
Geologically a beach is a blanket of loose sediment particles deposited along the shore. Grinding wave action and erosion by wind and water produce these deposits from bedrock, coral, or lava, creating beaches of cobbles, pebbles, or sand. Many dazzling white tropical beaches consist of coral sand, while the dramatic black beaches of Iceland and some Hawaiian islands are the remains of lava flows.

Copacabana
The 2.5-mile (4 km) Copacabana Beach in Rio de Janeiro, Brazil, is one of the most famous beaches in the world.

SAND FILTER
Some of the water in waves advancing up a sand or shingle shore immediately returns to the sea, but some percolates down into the beach. This water is filtered of particulate matter as it trickles down through the beach sediments. Most of the filtered water eventually seeps back to sea, but some remains trapped in tiny spongelike spaces between the beach sediments.

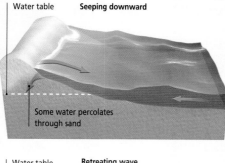

Advancing wave

Water table
Wave direction
Dry sand
Saturated sand

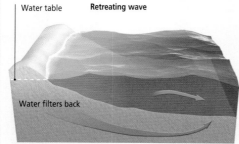

Water table
Seeping downward
Some water percolates through sand

Water table
Retreating wave
Water filters back

Dune systems
Coastal sand dune systems form where onshore winds pick up and redeposit sand from drier parts of a beach. A combination of factors determines dune size. The available supply of sand, grain size, and the strength of prevailing winds all contribute. Strong winds and abundant sand may sculpt dunes hundreds of feet high. Similarly, powerful storms may shift their location.

Towering dunes
The world's tallest dunes occur in the Namib Desert of western Africa. A narrow beach separates them from the Atlantic Ocean.

WIND-SHAPED DUNES

Transverse
Where sand is abundant, dune ridges develop at right angles, or transverse, to the wind.

Barchan dunes
Crescent-shaped dunes, with tips pointing downwind, form where the wind direction is constant but the sand supply is limited.

Star
Where winds come from three or more opposing directions, star dunes form as tall as 1,000 feet (300 m).

Longitudinal
Linear dunes form parallel to the average wind direction where sand is plentiful and wind direction is slightly variable.

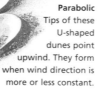

Parabolic
Tips of these U-shaped dunes point upwind. They form when wind direction is more or less constant.

Lava sand beach
This black beach at Vík í Mýrdal is one of numerous Icelandic beaches formed when basalt lava flowed into the sea.

Beach in transition
The sand beach at Cape Cod National Seashore, USA, is in transition. Rising sea level consumes as much as 3 feet (0.9 m) annually.

Coral sand beach
Bora Bora, part of the South Pacific nation of French Polynesia, is renowned for its sparkling white, often secluded coral sand beaches.

Brighton's shingle beach
Large pebbles mark a shingle beach at Brighton, England. Shingle beaches are composites of pebbles and sand.

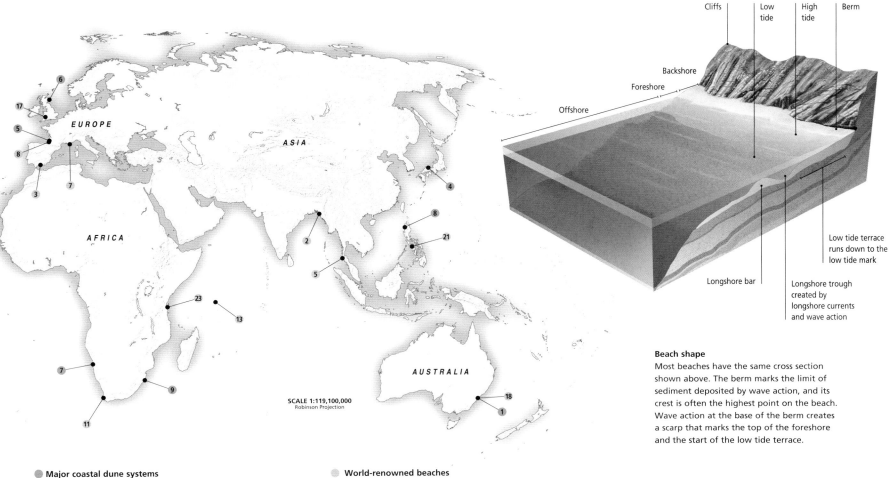

Beach shape
Most beaches have the same cross section shown above. The berm marks the limit of sediment deposited by wave action, and its crest is often the highest point on the beach. Wave action at the base of the berm creates a scarp that marks the top of the foreshore and the start of the low tide terrace.

Major coastal dune systems

1. Cronulla Sand Dunes/Kurnell Peninsula, Sydney, NSW, Australia
2. Nags Head, North Carolina, USA
3. Oregon Dunes National Recreation Area, Florence, Oregon, USA
4. Tottori Sand Dunes, Honshu, Japan
5. Great Dune of Pilat, Arcachon Bay, France
6. Sands of Forvie, Ythan Estuary, Scotland
7. Soussusvlai Dunes, Walvis Bay, Namibia
8. Paoay Dunes, Ilocos, Philippines
9. St. Lucia, South Africa

World-renowned beaches

1. Poipu Beach, Hawaii, USA
2. Cox's Bazar, Bangladesh
3. Costa del Sol, Spain
4. Ipanema Beach, Brazil
5. Khao Lak, Thailand
6. Matira Beach, Bora Bora
7. Saint Tropez, France
8. Biarritz, France
9. South Beach/Miami Beach, Florida, USA
10. Bandon Beach, Oregon, USA
11. Clifton Beach, South Africa
12. Pink Sand Beach, Bahamas (UK)
13. Anse Sourse Beach, Seychelles
14. Maroma Beach, Mexico
15. Cabo San Lucas, Mexico
16. Sarasota, Florida, USA
17. Swansea Bay, Wales, UK
18. Bondi Beach, Sydney, NSW, Australia
19. Big Sur, California, USA
20. Paracas Beach, Peru
21. Boracay Beach, Philippines
22. Palm Beach, Aruba
23. Spice Island, Zanzibar
24. Gold Coast, Barbados
25. Cape Cod National Seashore, Massachusetts, USA

RIP CURRENTS

A rip current, or a rip tide or undertow, is a small, strong current that flows out to sea. The current develops when a series of approaching waves causes water to accumulate in the surf zone faster than normal circulation patterns can disperse it. Some of this water then rushes back out to sea, possibly carrying a swimmer along with it.

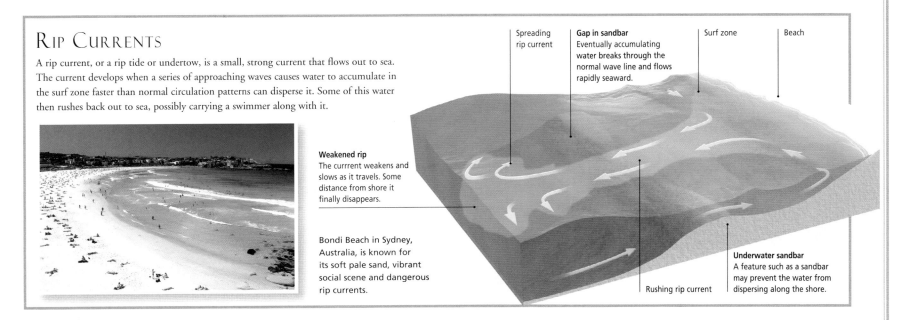

Bondi Beach in Sydney, Australia, is known for its soft pale sand, vibrant social scene and dangerous rip currents.

Weakened rip
The currrent weakens and slows as it travels. Some distance from shore it finally disappears.

Spreading rip current

Gap in sandbar
Eventually accumulating water breaks through the normal wave line and flows rapidly seaward.

Surf zone

Beach

Underwater sandbar
A feature such as a sandbar may prevent the water from dispersing along the shore.

Rushing rip current

CONTINENTAL MARGINS

A continent's dry land stops at the shore but the continent itself extends below the waves, its edge forming a gently sloping, submerged continental shelf that has "land" features such as hills and canyons blanketed with a thin layer of sediments. At plate boundaries, as off western South America, continental shelves are narrow but elsewhere they may be vast. In parts of the Arctic Ocean the shelf is more than 750 miles (1,200 km) wide. Shallow shelf waters are the most accessible areas of the sea where marine resources are most abundant. Continental shelves thus are the prime focus for fisheries and undersea mining. The outer edge of a shelf forms a feature called a continental slope. Beyond this steeply tilting area is the continental rise, where the continent ends. Where there is little or no tectonic activity, deep-sea sediments accumulate at continental rises. The sediment layer can be as thick as 6 miles (10 km) in some oceans.

From shore to sea

The continental shelf and slope make up the continental margin—the area of seafloor nearest the shore. The sloping transition from the edge of the sea to the ocean depths follows the same pattern around all continents. The continental slope and continental rise beyond give way to oceanic crust where the abyssal plain begins. Although these transitional areas vary greatly in their width and depth, by international agreement coastal nations claim jurisdiction over the first 200 nautical miles off their shores.

Continental shelf

Continental margin

200 nm (nautical miles)

NORTH AMERICA

Atlantic Ocean

Pacific Ocean

SOUTH AMERICA

Southern Ocean

Shallow shelf waters
Despite regional variations in the slope and the contours of continental shelves, the seas covering them are shallow. Shelf waters encompass only the epipelagic zone, the upper 660 feet (200 m) of the sea where light and life are abundant.

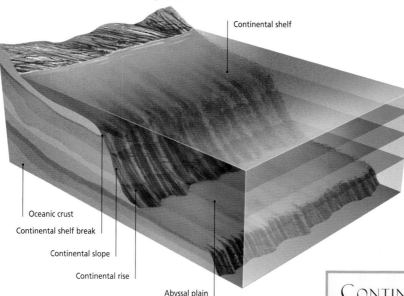

Continental shelf

Pelagic zone

Oceanic crust

Continental shelf break

Continental slope

Continental rise

Abyssal plain

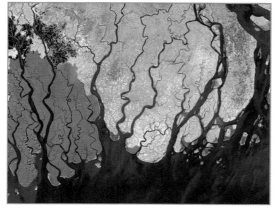

Meeting the shelf
The Ganges Delta, the world's largest river delta, is 220 miles (354 km) wide where it meets the coast of the Indian Ocean. Although very fertile, the delta is vulnerable to tidal flooding.

CONTINENTAL SHELF OFF EASTERN NORTH AMERICA

Off eastern North America the continental shelf overall is broad with a shallow incline. The northern portion of the shelf illustrated at the right also clearly shows the effects of the last ice age, when the sea level was much lower and the shelf was exposed to erosion. The shelf's submerged canyons, deep channels, and fanlike deltas were all carved by ancient river flows and similar events.

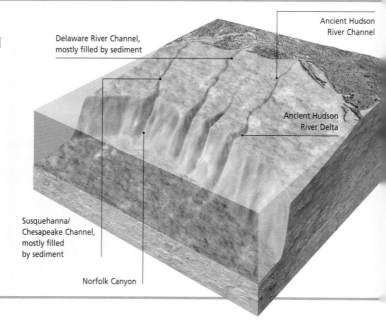

Delaware River Channel, mostly filled by sediment

Ancient Hudson River Channel

Ancient Hudson River Delta

Susquehanna/ Chesapeake Channel, mostly filled by sediment

Norfolk Canyon

Shelf variations

On mountainous coastlines, shelf zones are narrow, rough and steep. By contrast, they are smooth and gently sloping where plains meet the sea. Everywhere the shelf ends at a steep drop-off called the shelf break.

Broad and gentle
A broad gentle shelf with offshore ridges and sandbars often occurs at the boundary of the continent and an abutting oceanic plate with limited recent tectonic activity.

Barrier reefs
In shallow, tropical shelf areas the long-term activity of coral communities may produce a barrier reef landscape both below and above the sea surface.

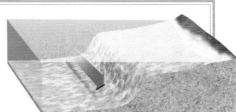

Cliff edge
Strong coastal currents, sometimes in combination with other factors, may scour out sediments and other material from the seaward edge of a continental shelf.

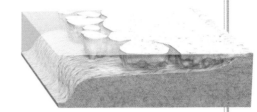

Ice age erosion
During the last ice age, so much seawater was locked in ice caps that previously submerged continental shelves were exposed. Ice streams and rivers carried exposed sediments seaward.

Geologic faulting
Where a continental plate and the adjoining oceanic plate are actively shifting, cracks or faults between plates may also alter the contours of the continental shelf.

Canyons and gorges
Erosion by moving water and sediment, often river flows or ancient flowing glaciers, creates steep-walled V-shaped submarine canyons and gorges cut deeply into the shelf and slope.

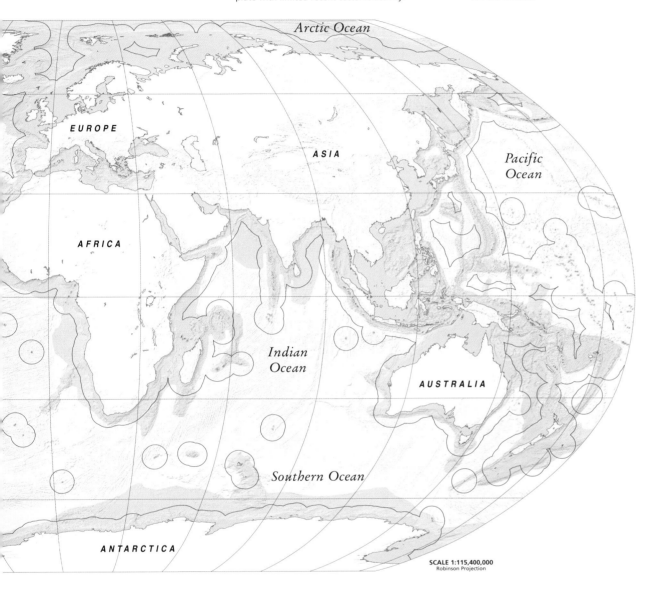

Arctic Ocean

EUROPE

ASIA

Pacific Ocean

AFRICA

Indian Ocean

AUSTRALIA

Southern Ocean

ANTARCTICA

SCALE 1:115,400,000
Robinson Projection

The dusky shark *(Carcharhinus obscurus)* frequents the shelf waters of temperate seas. Once abundant, the species is now threatened or endangered in many areas.

A banded butterflyfish *(Chaetodon striatus)* forages among yellow tube sponges *(Aplysina fistularis)*. Both are denizens of a coral reef in the Caribbean Sea.

This photograph shows eggs that have been deposited by a waved whelk *(Buccinum undatum)*, a North Atlantic snail. The species is a bottom dweller of the continental shelf.

Trailing a school of tropical fish, this large Pacific jellyfish *(Thysanostoma sp.)* navigates open shelf waters propelled by undulations of its bell.

CORAL REEFS AND ATOLLS

Coral reefs occur mostly in warm, shallow seas. Home to diverse communities of corals, fishes, sponges, and other species, coral reefs are the work of match head-sized coral polyps. Algae living within a polyp's tissues manufacture most of its food by the process of photosynthesis. Reef-building corals secrete a hard, protective limestone casing over their soft bodies, and over centuries, polyps of different species may produce vast reef systems such as Australia's Great Barrier Reef. At 1,250 miles (2,000 km) long and up to 95 miles (150 km) wide, it is the largest structure ever made by living organisms. A barrier reef is higher than the adjacent land, while fringing reefs form in the shallows around volcanic islands. A coral atoll develops when a volcanic island gradually erodes or sinks back into the sea, leaving sections of the reef behind. Recent coral bleaching —the untimely starvation of corals when their resident algae die—now threatens many coral reefs around the globe.

LARGEST KNOWN CORAL REEF AREAS		
Location	Area [square miles (km²)]	% of world total
1 Indonesia	31,700 (51,020)	17.95
2 Australia	30,400 (48,960)	17.22
3 Philippines	15,570 (25,060)	8.81
4 France (French Overseas Departments)	8,870 (14,280)	5.02
5 Papua New Guinea	8,600 (13,840)	4.87
6 Fiji	6,220 (10,020)	3.52
7 Maldives	5,540 (8,920)	3.14
8 Saudi Arabia	4,140 (6,660)	2.34
9 Marshall Islands	3,800 (6,110)	2.15
10 India	3,600 (5,790)	2.04

Coral life cycle
Most coral species have a multi-step life cycle. Eggs and sperm are released into the sea and unite. Fertilized eggs develop into young coral polyps. Colonies also expand as growing polyps reproduce asexually, by budding from the parent.

Sperm from different colonies fertilize eggs at random, preventing inbreeding.

Clusters rise to the sea surface, where they break up.

Reef colonies release eggs and sperm, which form floating clusters.

Fertilization produces embryos that may settle on a substrate.

Embryos that settle successfully undergo metamorphosis, forming polyps.

Colonies expand as calcification and budding continue over time.

Young polyps develop a mouth, tentacles, and a rudimentary calcified covering.

As algal partners are incorporated, calcification increases and budding begins.

ATOLLS

An atoll consists of a shallow lagoon surrounded by a coral reef. Hundreds exist in the global sea, although most occur in the central and southern Pacific. Atolls can be round, oval, or some other shape and usually occur in groups. Pacific atolls have generally developed as fringing reefs around a subsiding volcano. Elsewhere they may be atop subsided blocks of continental or oceanic crust.

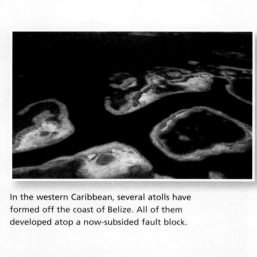

In the western Caribbean, several atolls have formed off the coast of Belize. All of them developed atop a now-subsided fault block.

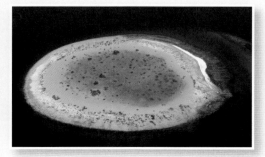

This atoll in the Maldives is still developing. As the coral heads grow together they will eventually encircle a shallow lagoon.

FORMATION OF AN ATOLL

1. Emerging volcano

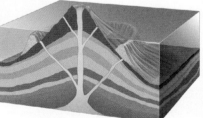

2. Fringing reef

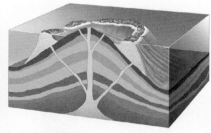

3. Volcano subsides

Where volcanoes emerge from the sea to form islands, fringing reefs may form around the sides. As the volcano subsides or erodes away, growing corals gradually encircle a central lagoon, forming an atoll.

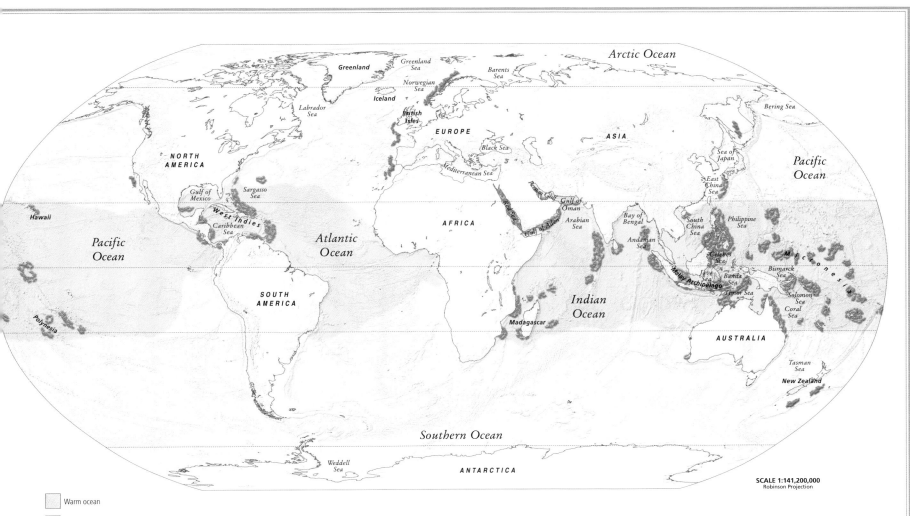

Warm ocean

Cold ocean

Warm-water coral reefs

Deep cold-water coral reefs

Cold-water coral communities
Anemones, warty sponges, and species of soft corals take hold on the rocky bottom in the cold waters of the Gulf of St Lawrence in eastern Canada.

Corals around the globe

Coral reefs occur in every ocean region except the Arctic and South Atlantic. Tropical reefs range in age from 6,000 to 9,000 years and have the most diverse array of species. Researchers are just beginning to identify aggregations of cold-water soft corals, some of which occur at great depths. To date they have been discovered in the territorial waters of more than 40 countries.

Brain coral
French grunts *(Haemulon flavolineatum)* forage around a giant brain coral *(Colpophyllia natans)* in the Florida Keys National Marine Sanctuary. Under ideal conditions, brain corals can live for an estimated 200 years, growing slowly to a maximum height of 7 feet (2 m).

Sea fan
The colonies of some coral species form branching fan-shaped structures that superficially seem plant-like. This bright crimson sea fan was photographed in its tropical habitat on a reef off the Fiji Islands.

HARLEQUIN SHRIMP

Reef animals often specialize in their diet, a natural mechanism for allotting resources in a highly competitive environment. The crimson spotted harlequin shrimp *(Hymenocera picta),* found in the Indo-Pacific, preys mainly on sea stars, often grazing on the echinoderm's tube feet. With a maximum size of only about 2 inches (5 cm), harlequin shrimps may devour their much larger but less mobile prey over a period of days.

SEA AND ICE

In polar seas, ice is a fact of life. Surface waters freeze into sea ice for much of the year in the Arctic. In the Antarctic, most sea ice melts during the southern hemisphere summer. Off Antarctica, Canada, and Greenland, ice shelves as thick as 3,300 feet (1,000 m) extend from the land and float on the sea surface. Antarctica's huge Ross Ice Shelf covers about 188,000 square miles (487,000 km²), nearly twice the area of New Zealand. Species in and around icy seas include fish with blood containing natural antifreeze, giant squids, whales, seals, Antarctic penguins, and Arctic polar bears. Antarctic ice shelves also produce the largest recorded icebergs. Propelled by ocean currents and winds, these bergs pose serious hazards to ocean-going vessels. As warming related to global climate change speeds the collapse of ice shelves, the risk of icebergs will rise, as will the threats to wildlife that depend on polar ice for their survival.

Arctic life

The Arctic Ocean boasts a wealth of species. Summer phytoplankton blooms support grazing copepods and amphipods, both in the water and in pores in the ice. These in turn are food for jellyfish, whales, and fish such as Arctic cod. Seabirds pluck prey from both water and ice. Skates and walruses feed on abundant clams and other invertebrates on the seafloor. Apex predators include huge sleeper sharks.

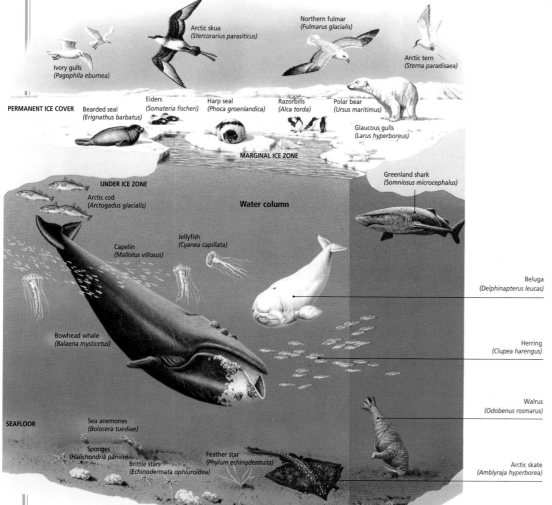

Ivory gulls (*Pagophila eburnea*)

Arctic skua (*Stercorarius parasiticus*)

Northern fulmar (*Fulmarus glacialis*)

Arctic tern (*Sterna paradisaea*)

PERMANENT ICE COVER — Bearded seal (*Erignathus barbatus*) — Eiders (*Somateria fischeri*) — Harp seal (*Phoca groenlandica*) — Razorbills (*Alca torda*) — Polar bear (*Ursus maritimus*) — Glaucous gulls (*Larus hyperboreus*)

MARGINAL ICE ZONE

UNDER ICE ZONE — Arctic cod (*Arctogadus glacialis*) — **Water column** — Greenland shark (*Somniosus microcephalus*)

Capelin (*Mallotus villosus*) — Jellyfish (*Cyanea capillata*) — Beluga (*Delphinapterus leucas*)

Bowhead whale (*Balaena mysticetus*) — Herring (*Clupea harengus*)

SEAFLOOR — Sea anemones (*Bolocera tuediae*) — Walrus (*Odobenus rosmarus*)

Sponges (*Halichondria panicea*) — Brittle stars (*Echinodermata ophiuroidea*) — Feather star (*Phylum echinodermata*) — Arctic skate (*Amblyraja hyperborea*)

Forms of sea ice

Sea ice comes in various types. So-called frazil ice is a thin, loose coating of ice crystals. In calm waters they may freeze into a thin layer called nilas ice. Other physical processes produce pancake ice and pack ice.

Frazil ice
Here a patchy glaze of frazil ice surrounds icebergs along the coast of Greenland. This type of sea ice is also called grease ice.

RUSSIAN FEDERATION

Arctic Circle

Laptev Sea — Kara Sea — White Sea — Barents Sea — FINLAND — SWEDEN — NORWAY

East Siberian Sea — Wrangel Sea — Arctic Ocean — Norwegian Sea

Bering Sea — Chukchi Sea — North Pole — Wandel Sea — Greenland Sea — Arctic Circle — ICELAND

Alaska (U.S.A.) — Beaufort Sea — GREENLAND

Labrador Sea

CANADA

Shrinking Arctic sea ice

More or less permanent ice once covered up to 5.6 million square miles (14.6 million km²) of the Arctic Ocean. Historically, only the outer portions of this frozen salt water melted in warmer months. Since the early 1950s, however, the maximum extent of Arctic sea ice has been steadily shrinking due to global warming.

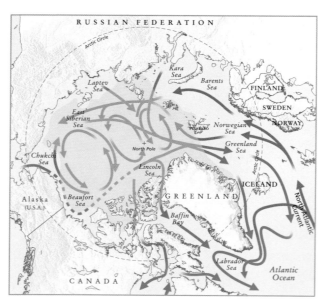

RUSSIAN FEDERATION

Arctic Circle

Laptev Sea — Kara Sea — Barents Sea — FINLAND — SWEDEN — NORWAY

East Siberian Sea — Norwegian Sea

Chukchi Sea — North Pole — Lincoln Sea — Greenland Sea — Arctic Circle — ICELAND

Alaska (U.S.A.) — Beaufort Sea — GREENLAND — North Atlantic Current

Baffin Bay — Labrador Sea — Atlantic Ocean

CANADA

Arctic seawater circulation

Currents flow in complex patterns in the Arctic. Warm surface water from the North Atlantic cools, sinks, and flows back southward, and influences Earth's climate.

Ice extent

Cool currents

Warm currents

Nilas ice
Recently formed nilas ice is thin enough to be transparent. As it thickens from the bottom up it eventually turns white.

Pancake ice
Flat plates of pancake ice form as swells and waves consolidate freezing slush that has formed on the sea surface.

Pack ice
Over time sea ice may be compressed into large, thick sheets called pack ice. Arctic pack ice is thickest, up to 9 feet (3 m).

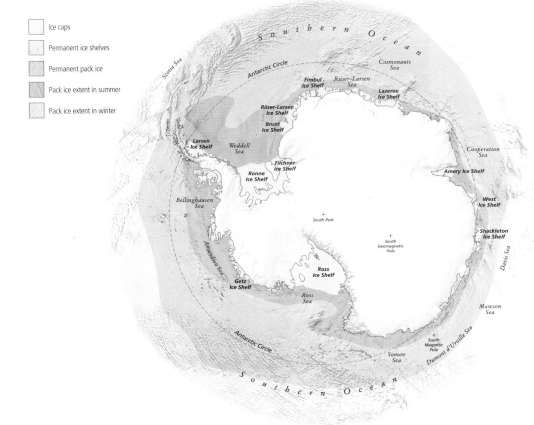

Ice caps
Permanent ice shelves
Permanent pack ice
Pack ice extent in summer
Pack ice extent in winter

Sea ice in the Antarctic
In the Antarctic, sea ice covers about 7.7 million square miles (20 million km²) in the depths of winter. It typically shrinks drastically, to about 1.5 million square miles (4 million km²), by summer's end. In contrast to the Arctic, the maximum extent of Antarctic sea ice has remained relatively stable. Even so, the Antarctic ice cap is melting more rapidly than scientific models predicted.

Icebergs
Icebergs are large, sometimes massive, chunks of ice that have broken off an ice sheet or glacier. This process, called calving, occurs when wave action, currents, or other forces produce enough physical stress to cut the berg away.

ICEBERG SHAPES

Icebergs come in a range of sizes and shapes. To qualify as a berg, the floating ice chunk must be at least 98 feet (30 m) wide at its visible base and rise a minimum of 16 feet (5 m) above the sea surface. Most of its bulk, however, lies unseen underwater. Huge icebergs that break off Antarctic ice sheets may exist for three years or longer before melting away.

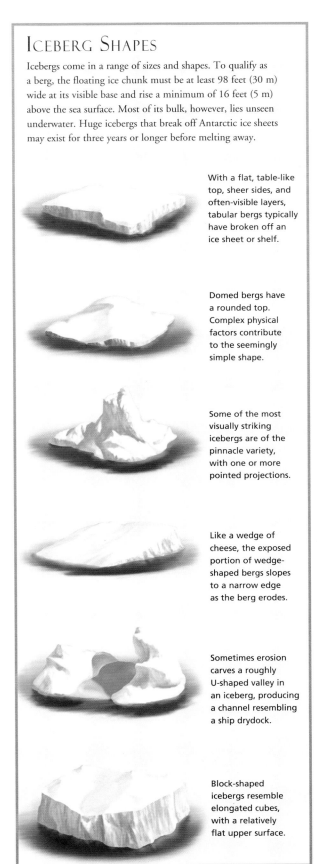

With a flat, table-like top, sheer sides, and often-visible layers, tabular bergs typically have broken off an ice sheet or shelf.

Domed bergs have a rounded top. Complex physical factors contribute to the seemingly simple shape.

Some of the most visually striking icebergs are of the pinnacle variety, with one or more pointed projections.

Like a wedge of cheese, the exposed portion of wedge-shaped bergs slopes to a narrow edge as the berg erodes.

Sometimes erosion carves a roughly U-shaped valley in an iceberg, producing a channel resembling a ship drydock.

Block-shaped icebergs resemble elongated cubes, with a relatively flat upper surface.

Between Land and Sea

An estuary is a partially enclosed body of water in which seawater mingles with fresh water from rivers and streams. Some estuaries are glacier-carved fjords, including Norway's Sognefjorden, the world's deepest estuary at just over 4,290 feet (1,300 m). Others are coastal lagoons protected by islands or sandbars and coastal plain estuaries such as Chesapeake Bay on the east coast of the United States. California's San Francisco Bay is a famed example of a tectonic estuary formed when seawater floods an area that is sinking due to movements of crustal plates. In tropical and some subtropical locales mangrove swamps line the fringes of estuaries, while elsewhere, brackish salt marsh skirts the water's edge. Conditions in estuaries constantly change. Salinity shifts with tidal fluxes and variations in rainfall and runoff from rivers and streams. Seasonal water temperature variations may also be extreme. Even so, estuaries are renowned for supporting abundant wildlife.

Estuary habitats

Estuaries are common features along the coastlines of every continent except Antarctica. Regardless of where an estuary occurs, however, it contains specialized communities of plants and animals adapted to cope with the ever-changing conditions. In temperate regions, grassy salt marshes fringe estuaries. In the tropics and subtropics, the shrubby tree species called mangroves are the dominant plant life. Each plant community supports a diverse assemblage of wildlife.

Roaming otter
In addition to living in totally freshwater habitats, southern river otters (*Lontra provocax*) may also thrive in estuaries and along rocky seacoasts.

Salt marshes

Mangrove forests

Salt marsh zones

A salt marsh has two zones that place differing demands on plant and animal life. Organisms in the low marsh must cope with daily flooding at high tide. Flooding is intermittent or rare in the drier upper marsh.

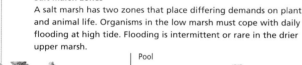

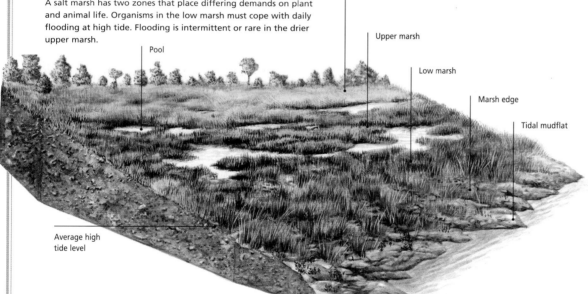

Upland area

Pool

Upper marsh

Low marsh

Marsh edge

Tidal mudflat

Average high tide level

Salt marshes

Salt marshes occur worldwide except in polar areas. This example is at the head of the Bay of Fundy, Nova Scotia, Canada, where North Atlantic high tides flood its lower zone with brackish water twice daily.

Osmoregulation

Estuarine fish and other aquatic wildlife have physiological means of osmoregulation—maintaining the slightly salty chemistry of their body fluids. In freshwater environments these mechanisms remove excess water that enters from outside. In the much saltier sea, osmoregulation removes excess salts. Barramundi (*Lates calcarifer*) are adapted to osmoregulate in both environments.

Australian barramundi live mostly in rivers. Once a year, however, adults move into brackish estuary waters to breed. After breeding, they and the juveniles swim back up into the river.

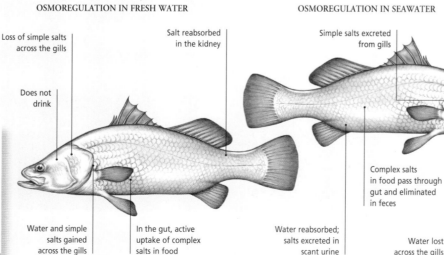

OSMOREGULATION IN FRESH WATER

Loss of simple salts across the gills

Salt reabsorbed in the kidney

Does not drink

Water and simple salts gained across the gills

In the gut, active uptake of complex salts in food

OSMOREGULATION IN SEAWATER

Simple salts excreted from gills

Simple salts gained across the gills

Complex salts in food pass through gut and eliminated in feces

Drinks seawater

Water reabsorbed; salts excreted in scant urine

Water lost across the gills

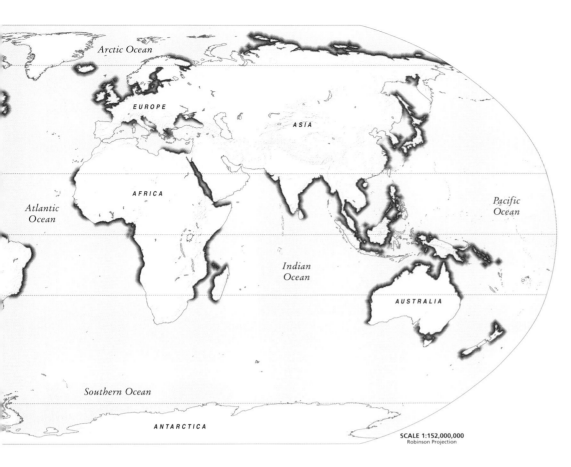

Submerged aquatic grasses

Submerged grasses and other aquatic vegetation flourish in the shallows of San Quintin Bay in Baja California, Mexico. Like mangrove habitats, such brackish coastal waters are vitally important nurseries for the young of many fish species. They also attract diverse wetlands birds, such as rails and herons. Clams and other small invertebrates live on or in the muddy bottom.

Estuaries
Various geological processes of formation, such as erosion and sedimentation, are used as part of a scheme to classify estuaries. The four main types are drowned river valleys, fjords, bar-built estuaries, and tectonic estuaries.

Floating through
The upside down jellyfish (*Cassiopeia xamachana*) inhabits a variety of tropical waters, such as mangroves. This specimen was photographed in a red mangrove swamp in the Bahamas.

Scarlet ibis
The scarlet ibis (*Eudocimus ruber*), native to northern South America, roams between coastal marshes and interior wetlands —a behavior common to many bird species that visit estuaries.

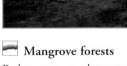

Mangrove forests

Red mangroves, photographed here in Florida, USA, are the dominant vegetation in saltier tropical estuaries. Black mangroves and white mangroves inhabit less saline estuarine environments.

Calm waters
Mangrove habitats occur in tropical coastal areas having shallow, calm waters. This intertidal zone is a perfect nursery and feeding ground for many small aquatic creatures.

Targeting its prey
Unerring aim with a forceful jet of water shot from its mouth allows the archerfish to knock insects from overhanging foliage.

Mangrove menagerie
Stilt-like mangrove roots support a diverse community of animal life. Gobies and other small fishes find food and shelter there, while fiddler crabs inhabit mud burrows below.

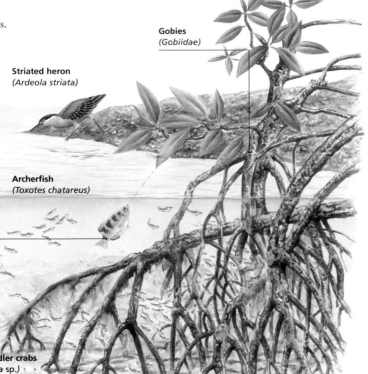

Gobies
(Gobiidae)

Striated heron
(*Ardeola striata*)

Archerfish
(*Toxotes chatareus*)

Fiddler crabs
(*Uca* sp.)

Stilt roots

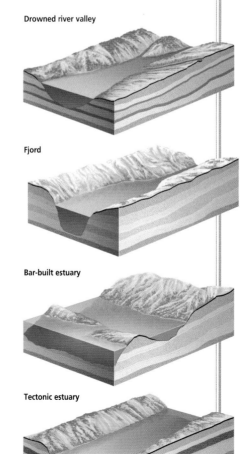

Drowned river valley

Fjord

Bar-built estuary

Tectonic estuary

SCALE 1:152,000,000
Robinson Projection

INLAND SEAS

Inland seas are branches of ancient oceans that are now enclosed by land. The Caspian Sea between southern Russia and northern Iran is the largest of these lakelike bodies of water, covering some 143,000 square miles (370,000 km²). Famous for its caviar-producing sturgeon, the Caspian is also home to abundant birdlife and other animals. The Caspian and the neighboring Black and Aral seas were cut off from the prehistoric Tethys Sea as plate movements raised the Himalaya and surrounding lands. The Aral Sea, in present-day Kazakstan and Uzbekistan, is rapidly disappearing because of diversions of feeder river water for human use such as irrigated farming. The world's saltiest inland sea is the Dead Sea, once a branch of the Mediterranean Sea. Like many other inland seas, the Dead Sea has no outlets. Evaporation and mineral build-up in the region's arid climate make the Dead Sea roughly nine times saltier than the ocean—far too saline for most life to survive.

Disappearing Dead Sea

The Dead Sea is actually a hypersaline lake in a basin created by the separation of crustal plates underlying the continents of Asia and Africa. Fed by rivers such as the Jordan, the Dead Sea has steadily been shrinking—and becoming saltier—as nearby countries divert river flows for agriculture and other uses.

Salty support
It is relatively easy to float in salt water because salt water is denser than the human body. The Dead Sea is roughly nine times saltier than any ocean. Floating in it is as simple as wading in and reclining.

Ancient inland sea
Some 300 million years ago an inland sea spread across the site of Arches National Park in Utah, USA. Slowly over time the sea evaporated and a thick layer of sandstone developed atop the salt bed left behind. Geologic upheavals and erosion produced the park's famous arches and other striking rock formations.

A nautical heritage
Tour boats and fishing vessels have long been a part of life along the shore of the Sea of Galilee. Today, the lake is mainly a tourist site, although small fishing operations still thrive.

Misnamed "Sea" of Galilee

Warm water and abundant life make the freshwater lake known as the Sea of Galilee a major aquatic resource in Israel. This "sea" is also the lowest freshwater lake on Earth, filling a shallow basin that is 686 feet (209 m) below sea level.

EVAPORITE DEPOSITS

Evaporite deposits are sediments laid down by the evaporation of salty water. During geologic time, multiple cycles of evaporation and replenishment of Dead Sea waters have created thick layers of evaporite salts, including halite—the rock salt from which table salt (sodium chloride) is refined. Chemical conditions near the bottom cause crystals of these salts to precipitate out on the lake floor. They also wash up along the shore.

Rock salt

Dead Sea salt deposits are the raw material of valuable commercial operations. Some consumers believe that salt-laden mud in the lake bottom also has health benefits.

As a salt lake dries out, minerals are deposited in predictable ring-like layers around what were once the margins of the original lake.

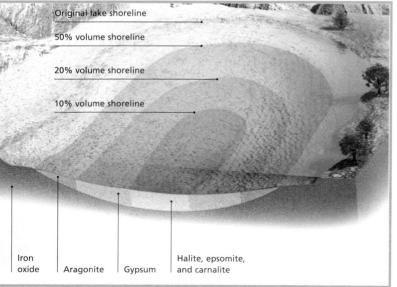

Original lake shoreline

50% volume shoreline

20% volume shoreline

10% volume shoreline

| Iron oxide | Aragonite | Gypsum | Halite, epsomite, and carnalite |

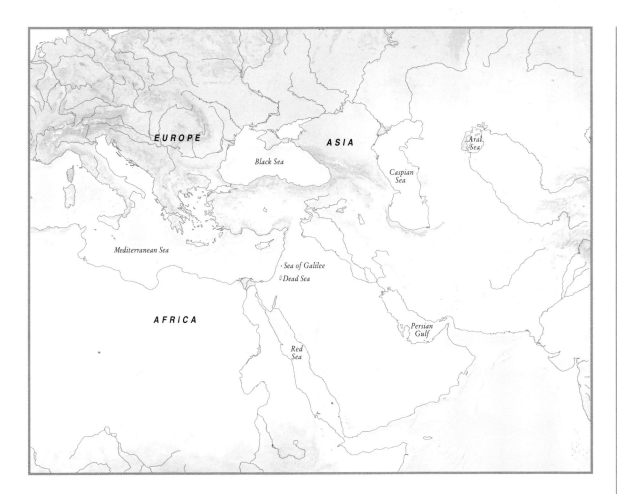

Cluster of inland seas

This map reveals the clustering of some major inland seas, including the Caspian and the Aral seas and the lakes known as the Dead Sea and the Sea of Galilee. These large bodies of water occur in rifts or basins created by tectonic shifts that slowly realigned crustal plates underlying the Arabian Peninsula and Eurasia. The plate movements correlate with the opening of the Indian Ocean about 300 million years ago.

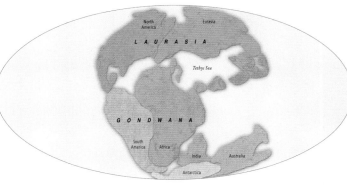

The prehistoric Tethys
A large, ancient Tethys Sea formed as Earth's supercontinent Pangea broke up into smaller landmasses. Drifting continents slowly produced the Indian Ocean and isolated remnants of the Tethys, including the Caspian and Aral seas.

Caspian Sea

The Caspian Sea is Earth's largest inland sea. Although some 130 rivers deliver fresh water to it, none flows out. Intensive fisheries, river-borne industrial pollution, and development along the shore have all taken a toll on the Caspian's ecological health. The discovery of significant oil and gas deposits under the Caspian is increasing pressure on the Caspian's natural systems and wildlife, including the sevruga sturgeon, seals, and birdlife.

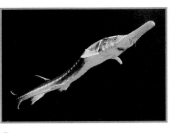

⊘ Endangered sturgeon
The sevruga sturgeon (*Acipenser stellatus*) has become endangered because of overharvesting of its eggs for sevruga caviar, pollution, and disruption of its natural spawning areas.

Caspian tern
The outsized Caspian tern (*Hydroprogne caspia*) has a maximum wingspan of about 4 feet (1.2 m). Caspian terns use freshwater and saltwater habitats around the globe.

A Dying Aral Sea

The Aral Sea was a vast lake that has been shrinking due to the loss of the river flows that once replenished it. Since the early 1960s, upstream damming and diversions for agriculture have dramatically reduced the lake's size, which can be seen in the photographs below. Today, only a few hypersaline ponds remain and the Aral Sea is rapidly becoming only a memory.

May 29, 1973
A NASA satellite photograph taken in the late spring of 1973 provided a baseline for monitoring changes in the Aral Sea coastline.

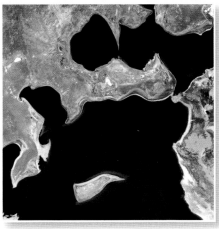

August 19, 1987
Fourteen years later, far more of the lake floor was exposed. Air-quality monitoring showed an increase in airborne dust and other pollutants in the region.

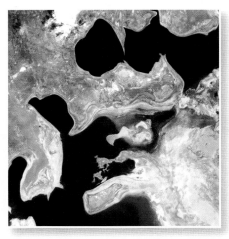

July 29, 2000
By 2000, the Aral Sea was seriously depleted and its wildlife all but wiped out. By 2008 less than 10 percent of the original lake remained.

Once considered a limitless trove of food fish and other commodities, the sea is a complex and fragile natural system. The modern challenge is finding ways to balance rising demand for marine resources with the need to sustain ecologically vulnerable marine habitats and species. Included in this category are green sea turtles (*Chelonia mydas*), an endangered species shown here amid colorful tropical fish.

Sea Life
& Resources

SEA HABITATS

At least several hundred thousand species of animals, plants, and other organisms inhabit the sea's varied environments. Roughly 98 percent of these marine organisms live in, on, or just over the seafloor that extends from the shore downward to the deepest abyss. The rest, from floating phytoplankton to sleek swimmers such as tunas, inhabit open waters—the pelagic realm. Water temperature establishes four overall marine regions: polar waters, the coldest; cold temperate seas; warm temperate seas; and the warmest, tropical seas. In all four regions, sunlight profoundly affects the abundance of marine life, with most species living within the sunlight zone that extends down to about 660 feet (200 m). Most marine animals, including familiar sharks, whales, and finfish, inhabit this top layer in temperate and tropical seas. Regardless of exactly where a species occurs, however, its biological design allows it to meet the constant challenges of living, finding food, reproducing, and evading predators in the undersea world.

Climate zones

Based on temperature, scientists divide Earth into four major climate zones. These zones correlate with the paths of warm and cold ocean currents, but they do not coincide exactly with geographic regions. For example, as the map at the right shows, cold currents extend the cold temperate zones up the west coasts of Africa and South America.

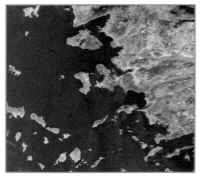

■ **Warm temperate zone**
Greek islands in the Aegean Sea are in the warm temperate climatic zone extending over the Mediterranean region and parts of western Asia. In this late-summer satellite view, much of the region's vegetation is brown.

- ☐ Tropical (over 69°F / 20°C)
- ☐ Warm temperate (50–69°F / 10–20°C)
- ☐ Cold temperate (40–50°F / 5–10°C)
- ☐ Polar (less than 40°F / 5°C)

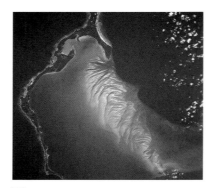

■ **Tropical zone**
The western Atlantic island of Eleuthera is a popular tropical destination. Warmed by equatorial currents and the Gulf Stream, the surrounding sea ranges in temperature from 70°F (21°C) in winter to 80°F (27°C) in summer.

Oceanic zones

Living space in the sea is divided into two major realms: pelagic, up in the water column; and benthic, on the seafloor. The majority of marine creatures are benthic. Sunlight, temperature, pressure, and animal life change dramatically with depth, and the ocean can be divided into three main vertical layers: the narrow upper band of the sunlight zone, the dim middle layer of the twilight zone, and the inky depths of the midnight zone below.

OCEANIC ZONES

ZONE	DESCRIPTION
1 Sunlight zone Surface to 660 feet (200 m)	With enough light for plants to perform photosynthesis, this zone contains most of the ocean's life.
2 Twilight zone 660–3,300 feet (200–1,000 m)	Some sunlight filters down into the twilight zone, but not enough to sustain plants.
3 Midnight zone 3,300 feet (1,000 m) to bottom	Apart from bioluminescence produced by deep-sea species, this deep zone is pitch-black.

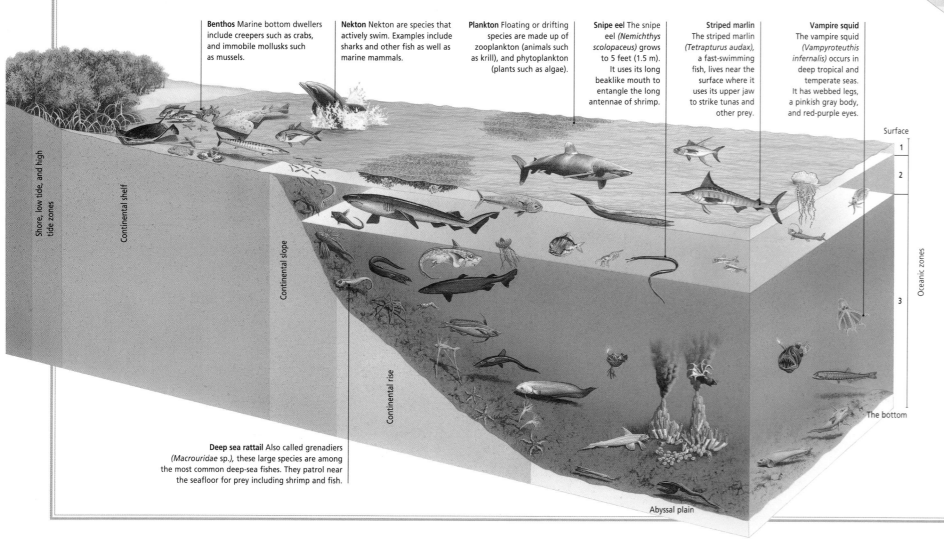

Benthos Marine bottom dwellers include creepers such as crabs, and immobile mollusks such as mussels.

Nekton Nekton are species that actively swim. Examples include sharks and other fish as well as marine mammals.

Plankton Floating or drifting species are made up of zooplankton (animals such as krill), and phytoplankton (plants such as algae).

Snipe eel The snipe eel (*Nemichthys scolopaceus*) grows to 5 feet (1.5 m). It uses its long beaklike mouth to entangle the long antennae of shrimp.

Striped marlin The striped marlin (*Tetrapturus audax*), a fast-swimming fish, lives near the surface where it uses its upper jaw to strike tunas and other prey.

Vampire squid The vampire squid (*Vampyroteuthis infernalis*) occurs in deep tropical and temperate seas. It has webbed legs, a pinkish gray body, and red-purple eyes.

Deep sea rattail Also called grenadiers (*Macrouridae sp.*), these large species are among the most common deep-sea fishes. They patrol near the seafloor for prey including shrimp and fish.

Shore, low tide, and high tide zones

Continental shelf

Continental slope

Continental rise

Abyssal plain

Surface
1
2
3
Oceanic zones
The bottom

Warm temperate

Tropic

Pac
Oc

Cold temperate zone
Influenced by the warm North Atlantic Current, a cold temperate climate prevails across the Scandinavian Peninsula, which includes Norway and Sweden. Glacier-carved fjords are common along the edges of the peninsula. Finland lies to the northeast.

Polar zone
Polar regions are colder than elsewhere because less solar heat reaches the poles. Around Antarctica the mixing of cold and warm ocean currents helps moderate climate. There is much less mixing in the nearly landlocked Arctic Sea.

Survival Strategies

All ocean species have body features and behaviors that help them survive in their habitats and produce young. These adaptations range from gills that enable fishes to acquire oxygen from seawater to the hydrodynamic body shape of fast swimmers such as mako sharks. Many adaptations are for defense. Camouflage, poisonous venom, and the ability to burrow into seafloor sediments all help protect the species from predation.

This common dab *(Limanda limanda)*, a flounder relative, burrows into bottom sediments as a means of avoiding the notice of both predators and prey.

Mats of sargassum, a brown alga, provide floating camouflage for small fish such as this sargassum frogfish *(Histrio histrio)* and other marine life.

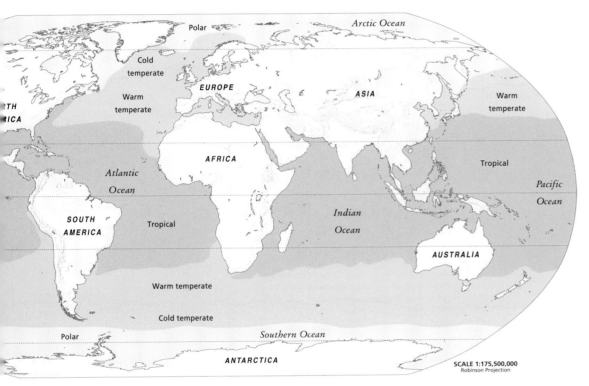

SCALE 1:175,500,000
Robinson Projection

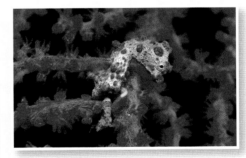

The coloration pattern of a pygmy seahorse *(Hippocampus bargibanti)* enables it to almost disappear against a gorgonian coral.

Phytoplankton soup
A gallery of phytoplankton from the tropical waters of the Great Barrier Reef, Australia, includes slender copepods, spiky radiolarians, larvae of marine mollusks, and photosynthesizing microorganisms known as cyanobacteria.

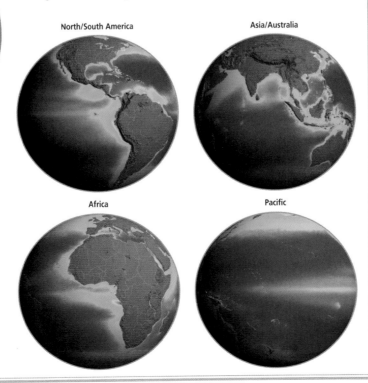

North/South America

Asia/Australia

Africa

Pacific

Monitoring the food base

The marine food web starts with phytoplankton, which survive by using photosynthesis to make their own food. Satellite instruments monitor light reflected from the sea surface to reveal how well or poorly this process occurs. The instruments measure chlorophyll, a pigment used in photosynthesis. Less photosynthesis occurs and food-web nutrients are scarcest in dark blue areas, but more plentiful in red and green areas.

Equipped with unusually long pectoral fins, an Atlantic flying fish *(Cypselurus melanurus)* glides through the air to escape predators.

LIFE ALONG THE SHORE

The sea begins where tides ebb and flow—the intertidal or littoral zone. Whether this narrow ribbon consists of rocks, sand, or mud, it is populated by communities of organisms equipped to survive its challenges. Buffeted by waves, high-energy rocky shores are home to organisms that attach to the hard substrate, such as barnacles, limpets, sea stars, and kelps and other seaweeds. Sandy shores are suited to burrowers such as clams, worms, and shrimplike amphipods. Mudflats may also have large populations of clams and worms. Shorebirds are a feature of every littoral community, and meadows of sea grass abound in areas of soft sediments, providing food and shelter for animals ranging from tiny shrimps to massive sea turtles. Intertidal habitats are increasingly threatened by coastal development, sewage, and accumulating trash. Globally, tens of millions of tons of garbage —an estimated 80 percent of it plastic—pile up along the shore, entangling or poisoning wildlife and degrading the seaside's natural beauty.

Mud communities

Muddy sediments conceal a thriving community of grazers, burrowers, and other life. In this illustrated community, mud snails graze along the surface, and moon snails and dog whelks hunt prey. Below the surface are buried worms, shrimps, and clams. These species extract food deposited on the surface or suspended in the water above it. Many more microscopic creatures inhabit the spaces between sediment particles.

Rocky and sandy coasts

Rock beaches, cliffs, and caves are prime features of erosional coasts, where wave action slowly wears away hard material forming the shore. Sandy beaches are a hallmark of depositional coasts, where rivers or wave action deposit sediment particles. Over a long time, erosional coasts retreat as the base material is worn away. Sandy coastlines tend to be more stable, but rising sea levels erode them.

Sea cucumber
Sea cucumbers occur in rocky or sandy shallows as well as on the deep seafloor. This specimen of sea cucumber (*Bohadschia argus*) is native to the Indian and southwestern Pacific oceans.

Venus clam
Venus clams (*Pitar* sp.) and other bivalves form colonies on sandy seafloors. Like other clams, they burrow into the soft substrate and filter bits of food from seawater.

Sediment life

Sand or mud beaches are extremely challenging environments. The Sun's heat, salt water, salt-laden winds, and constant wave action all are potential threats to survival. As a result, many species in the intertidal zone spend much or all of their time burrowed beneath the surface or in the shelter of driftwood and washed-up seaweeds and shells. Microscopic animals thrive in the spaces between sand grains.

Coastal cruiser
Purple sea urchins (*Strongylocentrotus purpuratus*) are common inhabitants of rocky coastal areas of western North America. They feed on kelps and other algae.

- Significant rocky coastlines
- Significant sandy coastlines

Isopod
Isopods (*Cyathura* sp.) are crustaceans with pairs of leg-like appendages and a flattened tail called a telson.

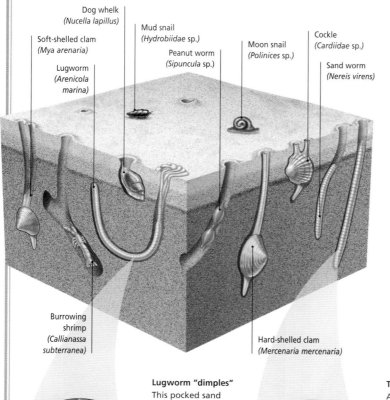

Dog whelk
(*Nucella lapillus*)

Mud snail
(*Hydrobiidae* sp.)

Soft-shelled clam
(*Mya arenaria*)

Peanut worm
(*Sipuncula* sp.)

Moon snail
(*Polinices* sp.)

Cockle
(*Cardiidae* sp.)

Lugworm
(*Arenicola marina*)

Sand worm
(*Nereis virens*)

Burrowing shrimp
(*Callianassa subterranea*)

Hard-shelled clam
(*Mercenaria mercenaria*)

Lugworm "dimples"
This pocked sand surface indicates a lugworm below. They can grow to 9 inches (23 cm) and anglers use them as bait.

Telltale cast
A lugworm takes in sand and digests microscopic organisms living between the grains. It expels the unwanted sand to the surface, leaving a cast.

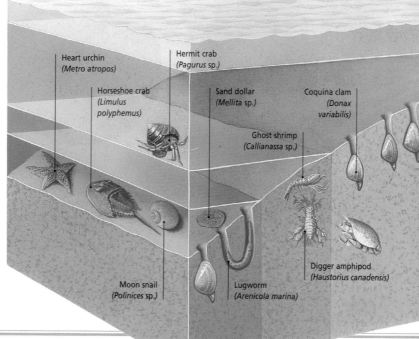

Highest high tide

High tide

Low tide

Lowest low tide

Heart urchin
(*Metro atropos*)

Hermit crab
(*Pagurus* sp.)

Horseshoe crab
(*Limulus polyphemus*)

Sand dollar
(*Mellita* sp.)

Coquina clam
(*Donax variabilis*)

Ghost shrimp
(*Callianassa* sp.)

Digger amphipod
(*Haustorius canadensis*)

Moon snail
(*Polinices* sp.)

Lugworm
(*Arenicola marina*)

NORTH AMERICA

SO AM

Southern sea otter
Southern sea otters *(Enhydra lutris nereis)* are marine mammals native to rocky coasts of the northeastern Pacific. They feed on urchins, shellfish, and small fish.

Blue-banded goby
The Galapagos blue-banded goby *(Lythrypnus gilberti)* darts through rocky nearshore reefs. It is 1.5 inches (4.5 cm) long and an aggressive predator.

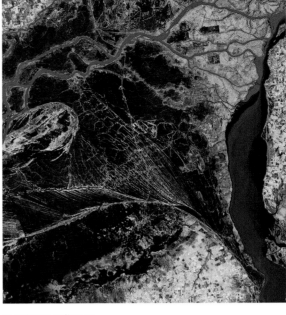

River-borne sediments
Rivers transport sediments to coastal areas, sometimes creating sprawling, fertile deltas. The forested and densely vegetated Parana River Delta shown here is northeast of Buenos Aires, Argentina.

Rocky shore life

Complex communities of marine organisms survive along rocky shores. Most of those living in the intertidal zone have shells or other adaptations that help protect them from wave action and the drying effects of air. Mussels, oysters, limpets, sea stars, chitons, and snails attach to the hard substrate. Small fish and creatures such as sea urchins are found only underwater, in the subtidal zone.

Gooseneck barnacle
Chunky gooseneck barnacles *(Pollicipes polymerus)* may attach to intertidal rocks or to floating debris such as driftwood.

Rock louse
(*Ligia occidentalis*)

Periwinkle
(*Littorina littorea*)

Limpet
(*Patellacea*)

White acorn barnacles
(*Balanus glandula*)

Chiton
(*Chitonidae*)

Highest high tide

Mussels
(*Mytilus californianus*)

High tide

Goose barnacle
(*Pollicipes polymerus*)

Blue mussels
(*Mytilus edulis*)

Low tide

Purple sea urchin
(*Strongylocentrotus purpuratus*)

Sea anemone
(*Urticina crassicornis*)

Hermit crab
(*Ceonobita* sp.)

Algae or seaweed
(*Enteromorpha* sp.)

Ochre sea star
(*Pisaster* sp.)

Beach flea
Beach fleas *(Orchestia* sp.) belong to the crustacean group called amphipods. Like fleas, they move by hopping.

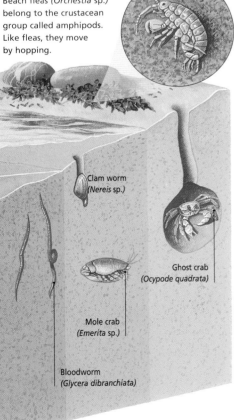

Clam worm
(*Nereis* sp.)

Ghost crab
(*Ocypode quadrata*)

Mole crab
(*Emerita* sp.)

Bloodworm
(*Glycera dibranchiata*)

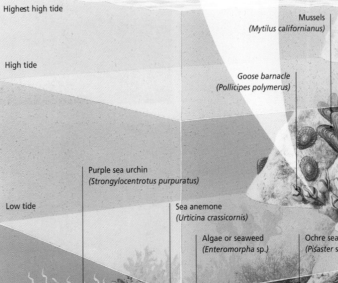

LIFE IN SHALLOW SEAS

Shallow, sunlit seas extend from the shore to the outer margins of continental shelves. This realm harbors the great bulk of sea life and also the greatest overall numbers of marine animals, plants, and other kinds of organisms. There are approximately 230,000 documented marine species, including thousands of bony fishes, sharks and their relatives, marine mammals and sea turtles, and invertebrates such as squids, shrimps, and the tiny floating animals collectively called zooplankton. Many more, yet undiscovered species of marine life are thought to exist, and some researchers estimate that the true tally may approach 1 million. Most fish and other pelagic marine animals spend their entire lives in shelf waters, while others pass through during seasonal migratory journeys. Sea grasses and an estimated 9,000 species of seaweeds live in coastal areas. In many parts of the world the cornucopia of life in shallow seas is under siege from overfishing, pollution, and the effects of global climate change.

Kelp forest
A California bat ray (*Myliobatis californica*) navigates a kelp forest in the Channel Island National Marine Sanctuary off southern California, USA. Kelps rise rapidly toward the sunlit surface. Some species grow as much as 20 inches (50 cm) a day.

SEA GRASS SPECIFICS

Type of sea grass	Ocean climatic zone	Interesting fact
Eelgrass	Temperate	Like other seagrasses, has tiny flowers at base of leaves
Widgeon grass	Temperate	Favorite food of wild ducks
Turtle grass	Subtropical Florida and Caribbean	Favored food of sea turtles and parrotfish
Shoal grass	Tropical, subtropical	Short, narrow blades only 0.08–0.1 inch wide (2–3 mm)
Posidonia	Temperate	May form colonies tens of thousands of years old
Johnson's seagrass	Subtropical Florida	Occurs only in Indian River Lagoon, Florida

Food from sunlight
Photosynthesis is the process by which green plants capture solar energy and use it to form sugars. These compounds fuel the plant's own growth and are also stored in plant tissues animals use as food. Specialized plant pigment molecules, mainly chlorophylls, initially trap sunlight. Its energy then drives chemical reactions that convert water and carbon dioxide into sugar. The reactions simultaneously release oxygen.

Sea grass meadows
Sea grasses undulate with the waves. Rooted in the soft bottom, sea grasses and algae growing on them provide food for grazing snails and small crustaceans. These densely vegetated beds also serve as cover for crabs and juvenile fish.

HUNTING ON THE WING

Keen-eyed seabirds have evolved a variety of methods for finding food. Some simply scavenge dead material floating at the sea surface. Others actively dive to snare fish or other prey near the surface. Still other seabirds excel at underwater hunting and are able to stay submerged for extended periods. Scientists have observed some penguins diving for eight minutes or longer without surfacing to breathe.

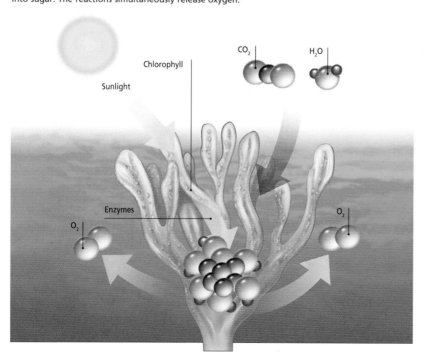

Chlorophyll

CO$_2$

H$_2$O

Sunlight

Enzymes

O$_2$

O$_2$

Shallow-water corals
Coral reefs in shallow, warm waters, like this strikingly colorful one in the Red Sea, are extraordinarily diverse marine habitats. Many species may coexist in a small area.

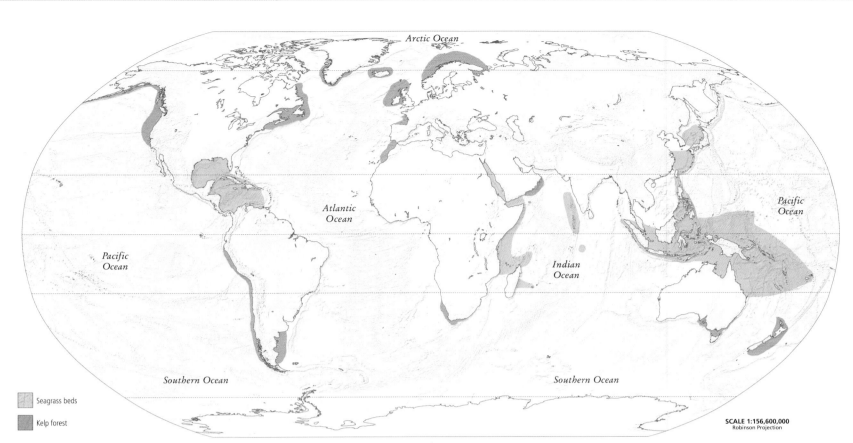

Seagrass beds

Kelp forest

SCALE 1:156,600,000
Robinson Projection

Coastal pastures

In tropical and temperate waters, sea grasses and the large seaweeds called kelp are crucial parts of many coastal marine communities. Growing in the nearshore shallows, this submerged vegetation provides small fish and other marine creatures with both food and shelter from predators. Sea grasses are common along sandy shores. Kelps form lush forests along some rocky coasts.

Giant clam
The tropical Pacific is home to giant clams (*Tridacna gigas*). This vulnerable species can grow, over many years, up to 4 feet (1.2 m) wide and can weigh 440 pounds (220 kg).

Versatile snake eel
The goldspotted snake eel (*Myrichthys ocellatus*) hunts after dark for crabs in sandy sea grass beds of tropical seas. It also burrows into the bottom with its hard, pointy tail.

Bottlenose dolphin
Bottlenose dolphins (*Tursiops truncatus*) occur in shallow waters of tropical and temperate regions of the global ocean. These sociable animals often travel in groups in search of fish.

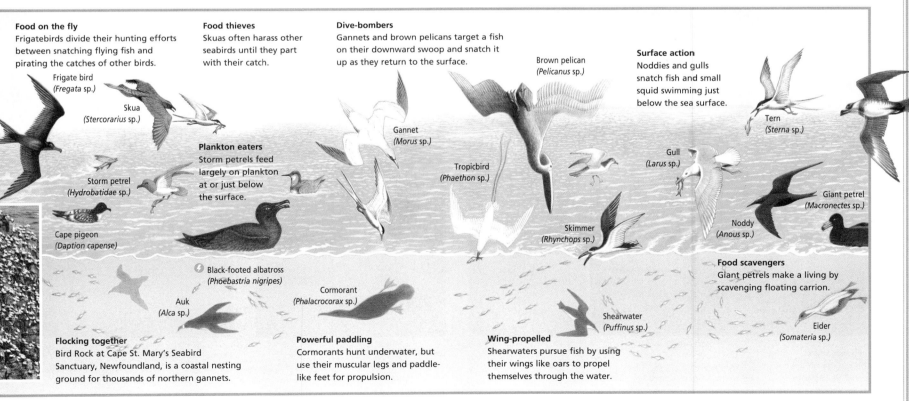

Food on the fly
Frigatebirds divide their hunting efforts between snatching flying fish and pirating the catches of other birds.

Frigate bird
(*Fregata* sp.)

Food thieves
Skuas often harass other seabirds until they part with their catch.

Skua
(*Stercorarius* sp.)

Dive-bombers
Gannets and brown pelicans target a fish on their downward swoop and snatch it up as they return to the surface.

Brown pelican
(*Pelicanus* sp.)

Surface action
Noddies and gulls snatch fish and small squid swimming just below the sea surface.

Tern
(*Sterna* sp.)

Gannet
(*Morus* sp.)

Plankton eaters
Storm petrels feed largely on plankton at or just below the surface.

Storm petrel
(*Hydrobatidae* sp.)

Tropicbird
(*Phaethon* sp.)

Gull
(*Larus* sp.)

Giant petrel
(*Macronectes* sp.)

Cape pigeon
(*Daption capense*)

Skimmer
(*Rhynchops* sp.)

Noddy
(*Anous* sp.)

Black-footed albatross
(*Phoebastria nigripes*)

Cormorant
(*Phalacrocorax* sp.)

Food scavengers
Giant petrels make a living by scavenging floating carrion.

Auk
(*Alca* sp.)

Shearwater
(*Puffinus* sp.)

Eider
(*Somateria* sp.)

Flocking together
Bird Rock at Cape St. Mary's Seabird Sanctuary, Newfoundland, is a coastal nesting ground for thousands of northern gannets.

Powerful paddling
Cormorants hunt underwater, but use their muscular legs and paddle-like feet for propulsion.

Wing-propelled
Shearwaters pursue fish by using their wings like oars to propel themselves through the water.

Beyond the Shelf

The open ocean begins where continental shelves end and ocean basins slope downward to the deepest seafloor. Sunlit and relatively warm near the surface, these waters become dimmer as the depth increases, and their temperature drops sharply as well. At about 3,300 feet (1,000 m), sunlight no longer penetrates and the temperature averages roughly 39°F (4°C). It stabilizes at a frigid 30°F (-1°C) in the deep abyss. Warmer surface waters teem with uncountable billions of floating phytoplankton, tiny plantlike organisms that are the foundation of the marine food web. Species with light-producing organs are common in the dimmer, cooler twilight zone below. Casting an eerie glow are many species of squids, red shrimps, and fishes whose eyes are 100 times more sensitive to light than those of humans. The sea becomes increasingly inhospitable to life with depth. Although the deep ocean contains more than 75 percent of the sea's total volume, relatively few species survive there.

Humpback whales
Humpback whales *(Megaptera novaeangliae)* are known for their acrobatic breaching—here, a rare double breach in the Pacific Ocean off Hawaii. Humpbacks occur around the globe, migrating seasonally between polar and temperate seas. They feed on fish and krill.

Built for speed
From its bullet-like body to its crescent-shaped tail, a bluefin tuna's *(Thunnus thynnus)* adaptations make it a powerful high seas predator. Its cruising speed is about 2 miles per hour (1.3 km/h), fast for a fish. When chasing prey, however, a tuna can accelerate in a burst of speed, reaching 12–18 miles per hour (20–30 km/h) in less than 10 seconds.

Crescent-shaped tail
The bluefin tuna has a narrow, stiff tail fin shaped like a crescent moon. This shape, and the "keels" on the sides of the tail, reduce turbulence or "drag" that can slow the tuna.

Dorsal fin | A predator's large eyes

Gills

Warm muscles
A network of blood vessels called a *rete mirabile*, or "wonderful net," keeps warm blood flowing to a tuna's muscles. This allows tunas to swim fast in cold waters.

Powerful swimming muscles
A tuna needs strong muscles for its lifetime of swimming. The bluefin tuna is globally endangered largely because its muscles are the "meat" that so many people prize as food.

Countershading
The back of a bluefin tuna is dark blue, while its underside and flanks are silvery. This countershading makes it harder for both predators and prey to see a bluefin in the water.

High seas shark
The oceanic white tip *(Carcharinus longimanus)* is one of the open ocean's large predators, growing up to 13 feet (4 m) long. Its sizable fins make this shark a target for fishers who slice off the fins and throw the doomed fish overboard.

Ocean sunfish
An adult sunfish *(Mola mola)* can weigh 2,200 pounds (1,000 kg) and feeds mainly on jellyfish. Sharks and killer whales prey on sunfish.

Chambered nautilus
The chambered nautilus *(Nautilus pompilius),* related to the octopus and squid, retracts its tentacled body into a multichambered shell.

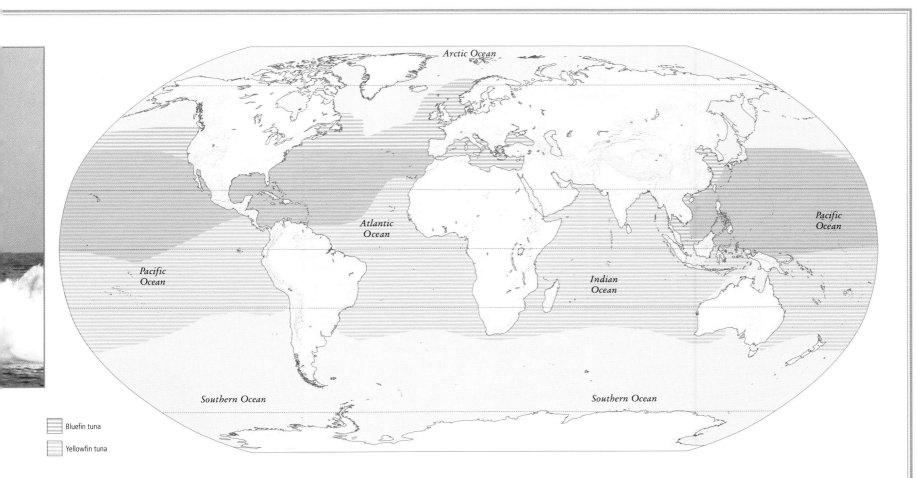

Bluefin tuna

Yellowfin tuna

Tuna geographic range

Two of the best-known tunas are the bluefin *(Thunnus thynnus)* and yellowfin *(Thunnus albacares)*. Both are somewhat "warm-blooded," with dense arrays of blood vessels that are warmed by the swimming muscles. This mechanism is most efficient in bluefin tunas, which spawn in tropical and subtropical regions but range in summer well up into cold temperate seas. Yellowfin tunas are restricted to tropical and subtropical waters year-round.

TUNA VITAL STATISTICS		
Common name	Bluefin tuna	Yellowfin tuna
Scientific name	*Thunnus thynnus*	*Thunnus albacares*
Average length	6.6 feet (2 m)	4.6 feet (1.4 m)
Maximum length	10 feet (3 m)	9 feet (2.8 m)
Maximum weight	1,500 pounds (680 kg)	880 pounds (400 kg)
Top speed	62 miles per hour (100 km/h)	50 miles per hour (80 km/h)
Maximum depth	3,000 feet (914 m)	820 feet (250 m)
Average life span	15 years	9 years

DEEP DWELLERS

In the eerie realm of the deep sea, many species including fishes, brittle stars, and squids are bioluminescent. Below about 3,300 feet (1,000 m) fishes and other creatures have soft bodies, and the fish species are small with large mouths. Some have large eyes; others are blind. Food is relatively scarce in this environment. Some predators have light organs that lure prey while others hunt using keen senses of smell and touch.

Normal fish eye
Eyes of upper and mid-water fish are rounded, with a moderate-sized lens and retina. This design works reasonably well for gathering ambient light.

Choroid layer

Iris

Tough outer layer

Suspensory ligament

Retina

Lens

Optic nerve

Optic nerve

Choroid layer

Retina

Lens

Tough outer layer

Auxiliary lens

Reflective layer

Tubular eye
Some deep-sea fishes have tubular eyes. The large lens and specialized, multi-layered retina help maximize the detection of available light in the depths.

Blackbelly dragonfish
This blackbelly dragonfish *(Stomias* sp.*)* is native to the central eastern Pacific, where it may be found as deep as 4,900 feet (1,500 m). Females sport long chin barbells equipped with light organs that may attract both prey and potential mates.

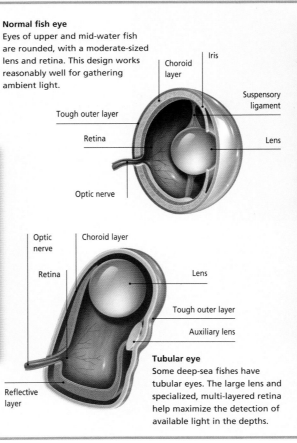

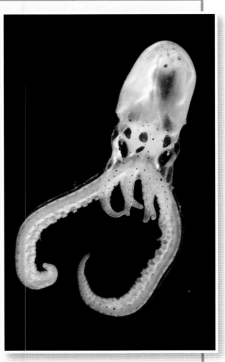

Atlantic longarm octopus
The delicate-looking Atlantic longarm octopus *(Octopus defilippi)* is named for elongated arms that stretch about five times the length of its body. It lives on or near the seafloor.

MIGRATIONS

Migration is a basic survival strategy for many marine creatures. Species ranging from fish and jellyfish to squids and plankton move vertically between the surface and deeper, darker waters in a daily rhythm that affords a balance between finding food and being less visible to predators. Sea turtles, whales, salmon, some sharks, and many seabirds migrate long distances to find mates, food, or to avoid harmful environmental shifts as seasons change. Cues from the sun, odors, sounds, or Earth's magnetic field are thought to guide these remarkable journeys. Female sea turtles are renowned for their long, magnetism-guided migrations to the nesting beach where they themselves were hatched. Humpback whales hold the record for a migrating marine mammal; they travel as much as 5,600 miles (9,000 km) between summer feeding grounds and winter breeding grounds. An Arctic tern traverses as much as 22,000 miles (35,400 km) in its annual migratory journey between the poles—the longest animal migration known.

Migration paths

Most migrating marine animals remain in their home hemisphere, even though they may travel long distances. Birds have no such limits, however, and may migrate from pole to pole. Whales migrate from polar regions where they feed in summer to the tropics where they mate and have their young. Seals migrate to bear their young on islands or other coasts in subpolar latitudes.

WINTER MIGRATIONS

➤ Humpback whale

➤ Arctic tern

➤ Short-tailed shearwater

➤ Southern right whale

Pacific Ocean

Phytoplankton

Phytoplankton species are known for their striking body architecture, which ranges from spiky or boxy to feathery, ball-like, and helical.

Daily vertical migration

Shifting light levels trigger the most massive marine migration, a vertical journey by numerous species moving up and down in the water column. For example, as day gives way to night copepods and jellyfish move upward, followed by their predators. The pattern reverses with the rising dawn. Some seabirds hunt at or near the surface regardless of the time of day.

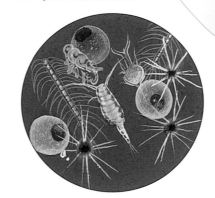

GULF STREAM TRAVELERS

🔵 Loggerhead sea turtles *(Caretta caretta)* are among a variety of marine migrators that take advantage of the powerful Gulf Stream traveling clockwise around the North Atlantic. Using different types of tracking devices, scientists have been able to monitor both the turtles' routes and the length of time they remain in the Gulf Stream. Loggerheads can detect and use Earth's magnetic field to navigate.

Satellite tags have revealed crucial information about loggerhead migration. The simpler "living tag" shown here is a pale plug from the turtle's plastron transplanted to its dark carapace. Living tags are used to mark wild turtles under study.

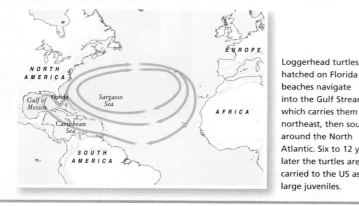

Loggerhead turtles hatched on Florida beaches navigate into the Gulf Stream, which carries them northeast, then south around the North Atlantic. Six to 12 years later the turtles are carried to the US as large juveniles.

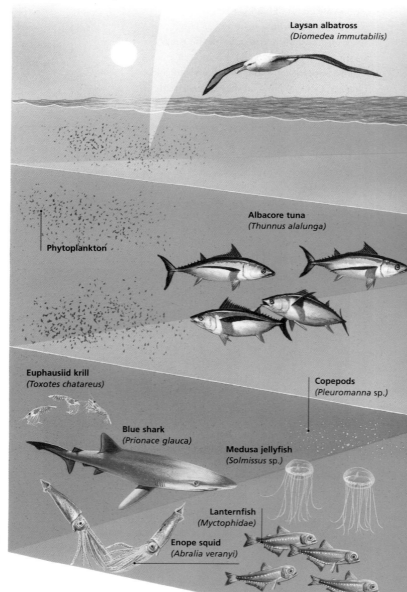

Day

Surface

100 feet (30 m)

660 feet (200 m)

3,300 feet (1,000 m)

Laysan albatross *(Diomedea immutabilis)*

Phytoplankton

Albacore tuna *(Thunnus alalunga)*

Euphausiid krill *(Toxotes chatareus)*

Copepods *(Pleuromanna sp.)*

Blue shark *(Prionace glauca)*

Medusa jellyfish *(Solmissus sp.)*

Lanternfish *(Myctophidae)*

Enope squid *(Abralia veranyi)*

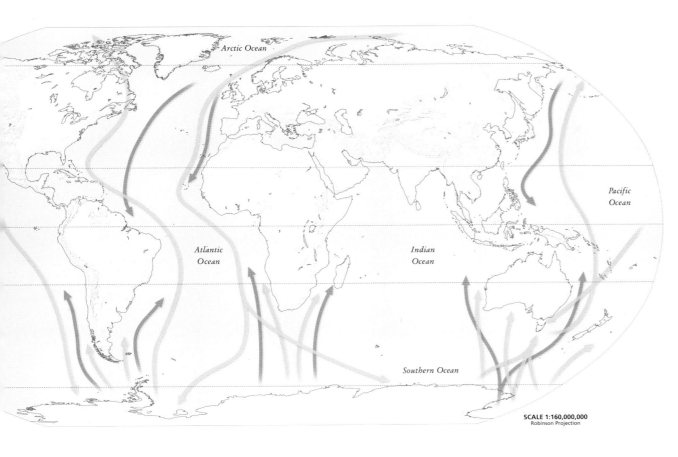

Short-tailed shearwater
Short-tailed shearwaters (*Puffinus tenuirostris*) migrate about 20,000 miles (32,000 km) around the Pacific. They return to Australia to breed.

Arctic tern
The Arctic tern (*Sterna paradisaea*) migrates between Antarctica and breeding grounds in the Arctic and subarctic regions.

Humpback whale
Humpback whales (*Megaptera novaeangliae*) feed in the Arctic in summer, but they do not eat while at their warmer winter breeding sites.

Southern right whale
The Southern right whale (*Eubalaena australis*) spends summer just off Antarctica and migrates northward to winter breeding grounds.

Night

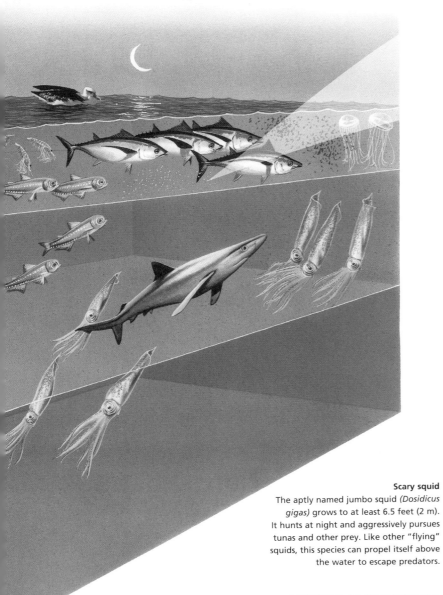

Copepods
Marine plankton includes countless billions of copepods, tiny crustaceans with long, bristly antennae, and nearly transparent bodies.

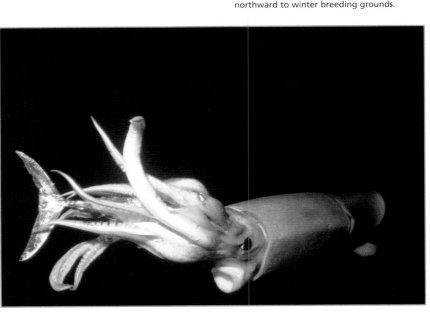

Scary squid
The aptly named jumbo squid (*Dosidicus gigas*) grows to at least 6.5 feet (2 m). It hunts at night and aggressively pursues tunas and other prey. Like other "flying" squids, this species can propel itself above the water to escape predators.

Gathering Together

Many marine species gather en masse to mate, migrate, or exploit a rich food supply. At the zenith of high spring and summer tides along Southern California beaches, hordes of wriggling grunions emerge from the surf to spawn in the sand, then return to the sea. In the Caribbean, Nassau groupers once formed huge local mating aggregations—gatherings that drew enough fishermen to drive several grouper populations extinct. Food can be a huge lure for many species. After pupping and mating elsewhere, hundreds of humpbacks and other whales arrive in the Gulf of Alaska to feed on a late summer explosion of krill. Approaching autumn may bring a million or more cownose rays to the mouth of Chesapeake Bay to prepare for a long southward migration. Some sea gatherings are scientific puzzles. Scalloped hammerhead sharks are normally solitary hunters, but for unknown reasons they converge during the winter at sites such as the Straits of Florida, only to disperse again over the continental shelf in summer.

Seal mating groups
Northern elephant seals *(Mirounga angustirostris)*—named for the dangling snout of the males—gather at mid-winter at several points along the central California coast; there pregnant females give birth. The cycle begins anew as adults mate before leaving the area.

Ray roundup
In early fall, a million or more Atlantic cownose rays *(Rhinoptera bonasus)* gather at the mouth of Chesapeake Bay, then migrate together to warmer Florida waters. Pregnant females carry unborn pups until the following spring, when they are born upon the rays' return.

Animals that Gather Together

Animal	Adaptive function	Typical season and location
Northern elephant seal *(Mirounga angustirostris)*	Mating/pupping	Winter, central California coast, USA
Horseshoe crab *(Limulus polyphemus)*	Mating/spawning	Spring, Delaware Bay, USA
Atlantic cownose ray *(Rhinoptera bonasus)*	Pre-migration	Early fall, mouth of Chesapeake Bay, USA
California grunion *(Leuresthes tenuis)*	Spawning	Spring/summer, Pacific coast, Mexico (Baja California) to central California, USA
Nassau grouper *(Epinephelus striatus)*	Spawning	Winter, Caribbean Sea
King penguins *(Aptenodytes patagonicus)*	Mating/nesting	Spring/summer, South Atlantic

Gathering Arthropods

Horseshoe crabs *(Limulus sp.)* occur in areas as distant as the Atlantic coast of North America and the Sea of Japan. At spawning season, males move close to shore. Females arrive some days later. Males attach to the egg-bearing females, which then drag the males along as they creep onto the shore. The males fertilize clusters of eggs the female deposits in a series of hollows scooped into the sand.

Female horseshoe crabs lure males in part by releasing a chemical trail of pheromones. Both sexes may also be able to visually identify potential mates.

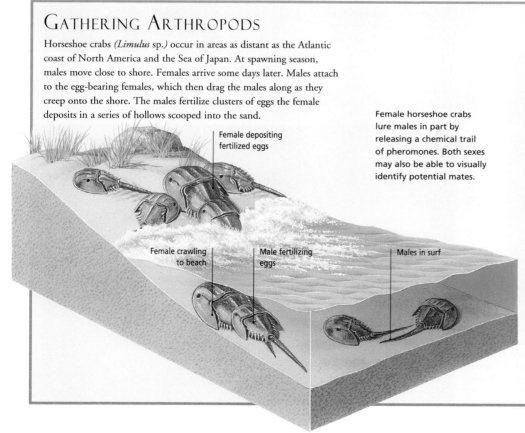

Female depositing fertilized eggs

Female crawling to beach

Male fertilizing eggs

Males in surf

The misnamed horseshoe "crab" is in fact a distant relative of spiders and scorpions. Late each spring masses of these large shelled arthropods creep up the beach in places such as Delaware Bay, USA, to spawn during a high tide.

Benefits of togetherness

When individuals of a marine species periodically gather in one location, the behavior is likely no accident. In particular, pre-migration gatherings, or those for mating, spawning, or protecting young, involve complex gene-based mechanisms for coordinating the activity of dozens, hundreds, or thousands of individuals. Such strategies improve chances that the members of a species, and the species as a whole, will survive.

King penguins
King penguins (*Aptenodytes patagonicus*) range far and wide in their usual foraging activities, but they gather into large breeding colonies.

California grunion
California grunions (*Leuresthes tenuis*) go ashore to spawn on spring and summer nights. After two weeks waves carry the young out to sea.

Naussau grouper
Mu ticolored male Nassau groupers (*Epinephelus striatus*) swim around a female. This triggers her egg release, which the males then try to fertilize.

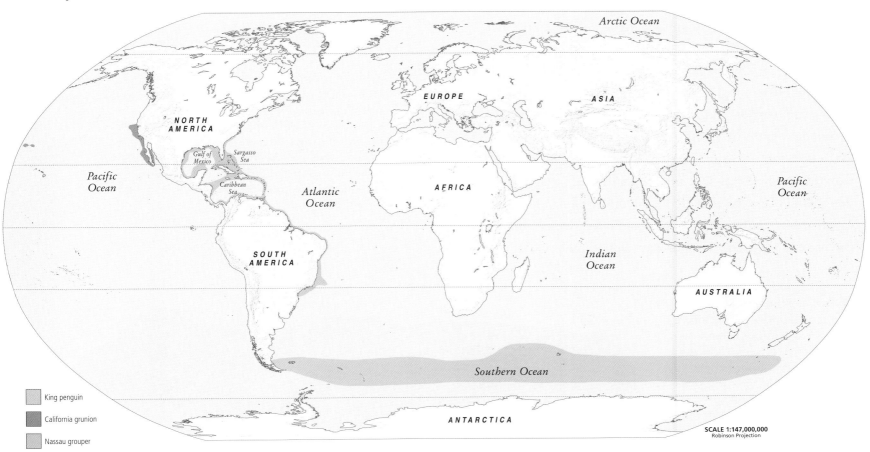

King penguin
California grunion
Nassau grouper

SCALE 1:147,000,000
Robinson Projection

RED KNOT RENDEZVOUS

Red knots (*Calidris canutus*) gather by the thousands to feed heavily before a long spring migration. A major stopover is Delaware Bay on the US Atlantic coast, where the birds' arrival tracks the spawning of horseshoe crabs. For countless generations of red knots, horseshoe crab eggs have been the key food resource fueling their migration. As human harvesting of horseshoe crabs has increased, red knot populations have been decreasing. Red knots migrate between subpolar regions of Eurasia and Canada and destinations in southern Europe, West Africa, South America, and Australia.

These red knots are but a few of the thousands that must build up their energy reserves before continuing their migratory journey.

RED KNOT MIGRATORY PATH

Staging/wintering areas
Staging areas
Wintering areas
Breeding areas
→ Migratory route
····> Hypothetical routes

Hungry sharks
Attracted by the presence of a rich food trove—a cluster of green jacks (*Caranx sexfasciatus*) off Cocos Island, Costa Rica—silky sharks (*Carcharhinus falciformis*) converge to feed.

Minerals

Minerals are among the sea's premier non-living resources. Commercial salt works, where impounded seawater slowly evaporates and leaves behind salt crystals, produce more than 30 percent of the world's table salt. Magnesium also is extracted from seawater for use in manufacturing precision metal parts. Huge deposits of methane hydrates—ice-locked methane, the main component of natural gas—occur in sediments of continental shelves. Highly promising as an alternative fuel source, methane hydrates also pose environmental challenges due to methane's status as a greenhouse gas that stokes global warming. Other sought-after industrial minerals include manganese, copper, and iron in seafloor fields of fist-sized nodules at depths of 13,000–20,000 feet (4,000–6,000 m). High extraction costs may stymie efforts to exploit this rich trove for the foreseeable future. By contrast, coastal beaches, dunes, and ocean bottom are heavily mined for sand used in construction, industrial processes, and beach replenishment. Intensive sand mining now threatens numerous coastal habitats.

METHANE HYDRATE DEPOSITS

SCALE 1:317,700,000
Robinson Projection

Methane hydrates

Methane is the main component of natural gas. Methane hydrates basically consist of methane trapped in slushy ice. Large deposits have been found under several continental shelves, and geologists estimate that the amount of methane they hold totals more than twice the world's reserves of other fossil fuels. Because the hydrates are located undersea, however, recovering them and safely extracting methane may prove both difficult and costly.

Mineral movements

Sand and many other minerals enter the sea when wind and rain erode them from land-based deposits. The eroded particles may fall into the sea or be transported there by rivers. If the seabed slope is steep, heavier particles will soon settle to the bottom. If the slope is shallow, currents and wave action may move sand or other sediments some distance along the shore, a process called longshore drift.

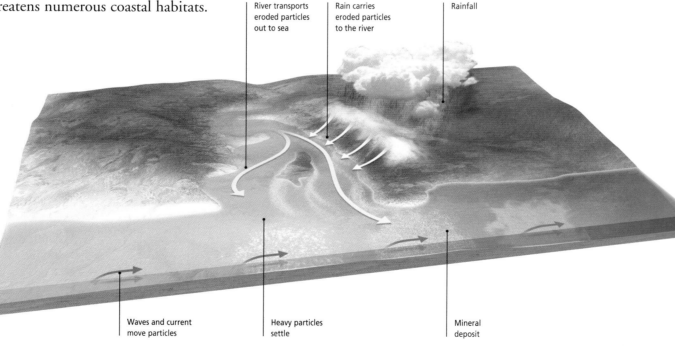

River transports eroded particles out to sea

Rain carries eroded particles to the river

Rainfall

Waves and current move particles

Heavy particles settle

Mineral deposit

Phosphate from the Sea

Earth's crust contains phosphates, which contain the mineral phosphorus used in fertilizers and other industrial chemicals. Phosphates are most accessible in land deposits. Despite this, one rich marine source is the accumulation of droppings of certain seabirds. This guano is collected and processed commercially, or used by local farmers who apply it directly to the soil—a centuries-old practice.

All plants require the mineral phosphorus to grow normally. Hence the use of phosphate-containing fertilizers on crops.

The Islas Ballestas off the coast of Peru are favored nesting sites for seabirds, making the rocky isles a major guano "mine." Scaffolding allows workers to collect the guano, which is then processed to extract phosphates.

Top Ten Phosphate Producers	
1 USA	6 South Africa
2 Russia	7 Egypt
3 China	8 Israel
4 Brazil	9 Morocco
5 Australia	10 Tunisia

Manganese-phosphorite rock

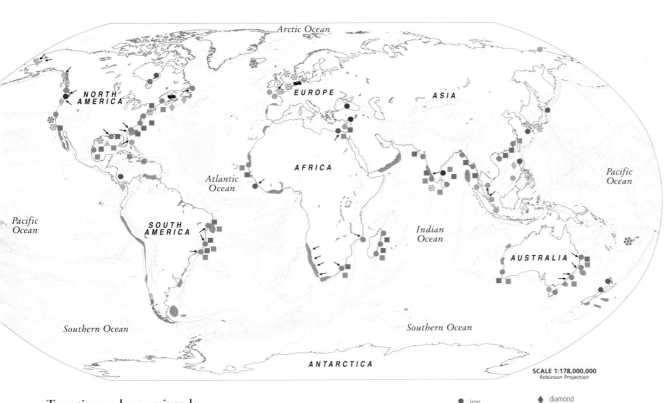

Arctic Ocean

NORTH AMERICA

EUROPE

ASIA

Atlantic Ocean

AFRICA

Pacific Ocean

Pacific Ocean

SOUTH AMERICA

Indian Ocean

AUSTRALIA

Southern Ocean

Southern Ocean

ANTARCTICA

SCALE 1:178,000,000
Robinson Projection

Targeting undersea minerals

A variety of potentially valuable mineral deposits exist in deeper offshore waters in various locations around the globe. Of these, oil and gas deposits in continental shelves in locales such as the North Sea and Gulf of Mexico currently have the most commercial appeal. As land-based sources diminish, it may become economically viable to pursue other deepwater mineral resources, including phosphates and manganese nodules.

- iron
- tin
- chrome
- copper
- titanium
- monazite
- zircon
- diamond
- gold
- sand and gravel
- shell sands
- coal
- sulfur
- phosphorite
→ derivation of placer

Desalination

Fresh water moves into salt water if a semi-permeable membrane separates the two. Applying pressure to the salt water stops this flow, called osmosis. Increasing the pressure causes reverse osmosis, in which pure water flows out of the salty solution.

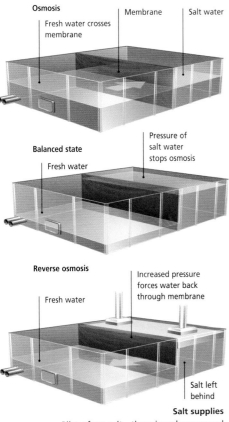

Osmosis
Fresh water crosses membrane | Membrane | Salt water

Balanced state
Fresh water | Pressure of salt water stops osmosis

Reverse osmosis
Fresh water | Increased pressure forces water back through membrane | Salt left behind

Salt supplies
Piles of sea salt—the mineral compound sodium chloride—are extracted in evaporation ponds, as shown here in Sicily. Windmills have been used to power the pumping of brackish water into the ponds since Medieval times.

MANGANESE NODULES

Lumpy nodules of manganese were first observed in the 1870s by the Challenger deep-sea expedition. The nodules lie scattered across the deep-sea floor of the world's oceans. Although not yet commercially viable because of the depths where they are located, manganese nodules are a potentially valuable source of nickel, copper, and manganese. Nodules enlarge as minerals accumulate, giving them an intricate interior structure.

Cross section

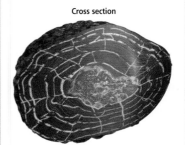

External view

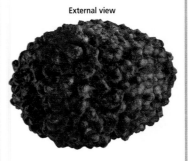

Researchers are developing methods to retrieve manganese nodules from as deep as 19,500 feet (6,000 m) below the sea. By current estimates the supply of key ores in the richest Pacific Ocean nodule fields could meet human needs for 20 centuries.

NODULE INGREDIENTS

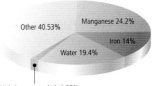

Other 40.53% | Manganese 24.2% | Iron 14% | Water 19.4% | Nickel, copper, cobalt 1.87%

On average a manganese nodule is about one-quarter manganese. Smaller amounts of other ores are valuable because the ores have such vital industrial uses.

OIL AND GAS

At dozens of sites around the globe, the seabed conceals major offshore fields of oil and natural gas. Both these fossil fuels formed over millions of years as buried, carbon-rich remains of animals and plants were compressed under accumulating rock layers. They gradually seep upward through porous rock strata until becoming trapped in pressurized pools under a hard, impermeable layer called caprock. Drilling at depths ranging from a few hundred feet to more than 34,000 feet (10,360 m) taps these pools and allows crude oil and natural gas to be piped to the surface. Extensive undersea oil and gas fields are known in the Middle East, in the North Sea, along the Gulf Coast of North America and off the east coast of South America, and the west coast of Africa. Due to the time span required for fossil fuels to form, they are finite resources that inevitably are being depleted as world demand for them grows.

Drilling support
Oil platforms are built on steel or concrete supports that must withstand the force of waves, currents, and in some areas ice. Some rigs float while others rest atop pillars sunk into the seafloor.

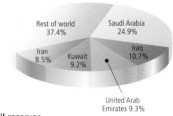

OIL

Rest of world 37.4%
Saudi Arabia 24.9%
Iran 8.5%
Kuwait 9.2%
Iraq 10.7%
United Arab Emirates 9.3%

Oil reserves
More than 60 percent of the world's oil reserves lie in the territory of five Middle Eastern countries. As global supplies dwindle, pressure is growing to tap other reserves.

GAS

Rest of world 37.3%
Russia 30.7%
Iran 14.8%
Qatar 9.3%
United Arab Emirates 3.9%
Saudi Arabia 4.0%

Gas options
Russia has the richest reserves of natural gas, but environmental concerns about this diminishing and highly valuable fossil fuel may limit its future use.

Remains accumulate
Dead organisms drop to the ocean floor and are quickly covered by mud and silt. Where little or no oxygen is present, remains only partially decay. Over time the remains are trapped within thickening sediment layers.

Controlled decay
As rock layers accumulate, organic remains trapped within them are subjected to moderate heat and increasing pressure. These conditions favor the formation of oil and gas from the buried remains.

Rise of fossil fuels
Once oil and gas have formed, they percolate upward through the overlying layers of rock. Both seep through porous sandstone, but eventually stop rising and pool when they reach higher, nonporous rock such as shale.

Settling remains

Sediment layers

Accumulating rock layers

Trapped organic material

Porous rock

Impermeable rock

Rising oil and gas

Access through rig

Oil and gas formation
Oil and natural gas form from the buried remains of marine life that have been compressed over millions of years between rock layers. These layers form as sediments are compacted in low-oxygen conditions, which preserve carbon compounds in decaying tissues. The modern-day inland location of many oil and gas deposits is due to tectonic movements and changing sea levels during Earth's geological past.

Formation of a reservoir
The oil and gas collect in reservoir rock that is porous. The nonporous caprock above prevents the pooled fossil fuels from leaking away. Drilling then allows access to these reservoirs.

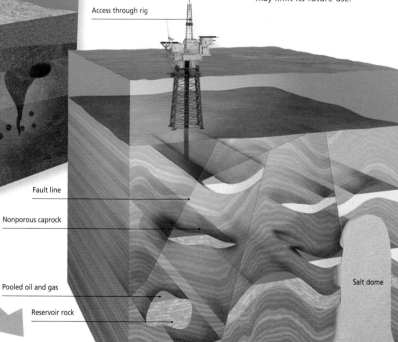

Fault line

Nonporous caprock

Pooled oil and gas

Reservoir rock

Salt dome

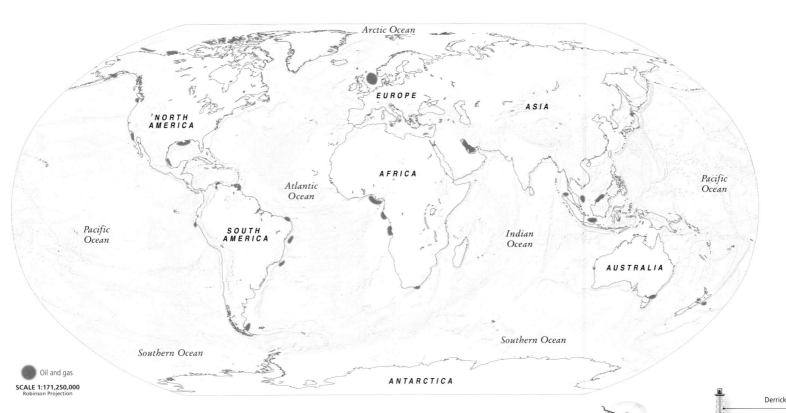

Oil and gas

SCALE 1:171,250,000
Robinson Projection

Oil and gas production

Offshore oil and gas production centers mainly in the Middle East, the North Sea, and Central and South America. Other important reserves have been found along the continental shelf off Nigeria, Egypt, and Indonesia. This map shows the most important areas of offshore oil and gas production at present. The multibillion-dollar oil and gas industry globally employs hundreds of thousands of workers.

Transporting oil
Fleets of supertankers move crude oil from its sources to refineries around the globe. Smaller vessels carry refined petroleum products to the market. The largest crude oil tankers transport 550,000 dead-weight tons (500,000 t) of oil, roughly 6 million barrels.

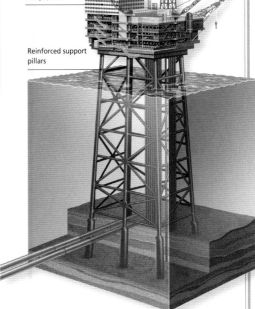

Derrick

Helipad

Office and living space

Reinforced support pillars

Oil platform
Oil platforms pump out millions of barrels of oil per day. Most stay operational for about 25 years. Large platforms may have living quarters for as many as 300 workers and derricks supporting multiple drills.

Top Ten Oil and Gas Consumers 2006

Country	Millions of barrels/day (combined oil and gas)	Country	Millions of barrels/day (combined oil and gas)
1 USA	20.59	6 India	2.53
2 China	7.27	7 Canada	2.22
3 Japan	5.22	8 Brazil	2.12
4 Russia	3.10	9 South Korea	2.12
5 Germany	2.63	10 Saudi Arabia	2.07

LIFE AROUND THE RIG

The submerged portions of oil platforms lure large numbers of marine organisms, especially where the seafloor lacks rocky surfaces that attract species requiring a hard substrate. In such places, hard platform supports may become home to thriving communities including corals and arrays of other invertebrates and fish. Platforms in warm and temperate seas have the most diverse marine life.

PLATFORM FIELDS WITH HIGH MARINE DIVERSITY

California coast

Gulf of Mexico

Coastal Venezuela

Persian Gulf

Indo-Australia

Rigs with significant wildlife

Hydroids (*Hydrozoa* sp.), marine invertebrates that superficially resemble plants, grow profusely on the support of an oil rig in warm waters of the Gulf of Mexico.

Orcas, or killer whales (*Orcinus orca*), pass by a New Zealand oil refinery where tankers offload crude oil to be processed.

This Green turtle (*Chelonia mydas*) was photographed in the Gulf of Mexico swimming around one of the many oil platforms.

SEA POLLUTION

Pollution is a serious threat to the seas, in part because roughly 40 percent of the world's population lives within 65 miles (104 km) of an ocean. Agricultural and urban runoff routinely contaminate coastal waters with trash, pesticides, and fertilizers that cause unnatural algal blooms. Industrial discharges to the air and waterways add toxins such as polychlorinated biphenyls (PCBs) and polycyclic aromatic hydrocarbons (PAHs) that accumulate in the tissues of marine organisms and eventually become magnified through the marine food web. Massive oil spills, such as the oil released after the 2002 sinking of the tanker *Prestige* off northwestern Spain, may damage coastal ecosystems and fisheries for as long as 15 years. Coastal cities routinely discharge minimally processed sewage. Although international regulations prohibit the once-common practices of ocean dumping of radioactive wastes, municipal garbage, sewage sludge, vessel trash, industrial wastes, and hazardous dredge spoils, enforcement is difficult and violations are common.

A sea of contamination

No part of the marine world is free from pollution. Areas where this contamination is worst include the Mediterranean Sea and many seacoasts. Much coastal pollution is due to the combined effects of coastal development and marine ship traffic to and from ports. Relatively speaking, the open ocean is the least contaminated. Fortunately, improvements to oil tanker design and operation have gradually reduced marine oil spills.

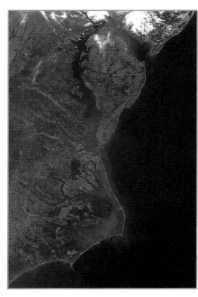

Coastal runoff
In Chesapeake Bay, the largest US estuary, runoff from farmland contains large quantities of fertilizers. This fuels the overgrowth of phytoplankton, which in turn leads to the depletion of oxygen in large "dead zones" in Bay waters.

- ⬛ Severely polluted sea areas
- ⬛ Less polluted sea areas
- ⬜ Areas of frequent oil pollution by shipping
- ● Sites of major oil tanker spills
- ▲ Major oil rig blow-outs
- ◼ Offshore dump sites for industrial and municipal waste

OCEAN POLLUTION SOURCES	
Type	Source
Land-based	• Runoff—nitrogen and phosphorus from farming fertilizers and pesticides • River-borne industrial chemicals • Dumping of waste at sea • Sewage, gray water, and waste water • Radioactive waste dumping • Improper garbage disposal
Airborne	• Pollutants such as wind-borne nitrogen and sulfur compounds deposited at sea • Acid rain
Maritime transportation	• Oil pollution from tanker spills • Waste and vessel sewage from tankers, naval ships, cruise liners, and recreational boats • Oil and gas platform waste

Agricultural inputs
Virginia is one of several US states bordering Chesapeake Bay. Many farmers there are experimenting with methods that can help reduce the use of agricultural chemicals.

OCEAN POLLUTANTS

Land-based sources 44%
Atmospheric inputs 33%
Other 11%
Maritime transportation sources 12%

ANIMALS IN TROUBLE

Floating garbage, noxious chemicals, and other pollution all harm marine wildlife. One of the worst offenders is plastic, in the form of discarded fishing lines and nets, trash bags, bottle holders, and other debris. Oil slicks that coat seabirds or other large wildlife also take a toll. Small organisms along oil-fouled coastlines may take a double hit, because they can be killed by some kinds of clean-up efforts.

Commercial fishermen often discard or lose nets at sea. These gray snappers *(Lutjanus griseus)* suffocated when they became entangled in a floating gill net.

A plastic garbage bag wrapped around this lemon shark *(Negaprion brevirostris)* may remain for years, assuming that the entangled shark can continue to function normally. The shark could be doomed if the plastic obstructs its gills.

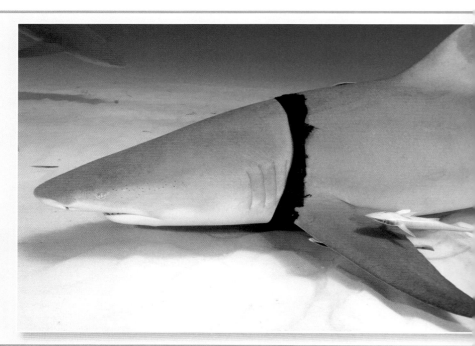

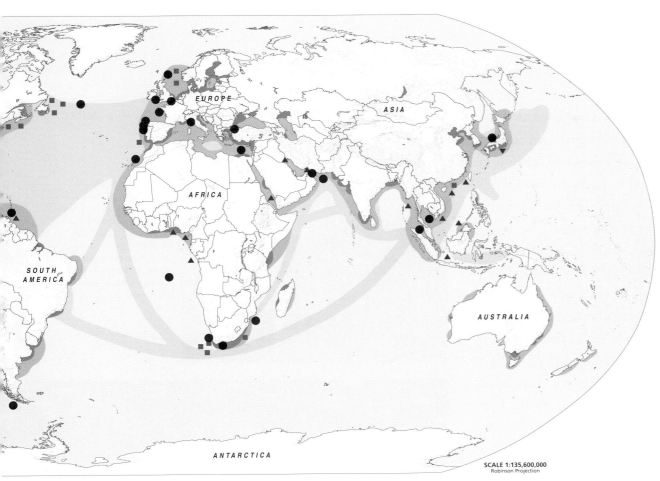

Blooming algae
Surplus nutrients in runoff fueled this algal bloom in Everglades National Park, Florida, USA. It depleted oxygen and killed life in the waters.

Most polluted Mediterranean
Industrial and agricultural wastes make up the majority of contaminants in the heavily polluted Mediterranean Sea.

Mumbai rubbish
Debris covering this beach in Mumbai, India, provides a mother pig and her piglets with food scraps, and they leave their droppings behind.

Oil-soaked coast
The Exxon Valdez oil spill had a severe impact on Alaska's Prince William Sound. About 11,000 tons (10,000 t) of the spilled oil came ashore, affecting wildlife and fisheries along more than 300 miles (480 km) of coastline.

SCALE 1:135,600,000
Robinson Projection

Pollution from Oil Tankers/Platforms		
Year	Tanker	Crude oil spilled [tons (t)]
1991	Iraqi tankers in Gulf War	up to 1.5 million (1.3 million)
1991	ABT Summer	260,000 (236,000)
1991	MT Haven	144,000 (131,000)
1988	Odyssey	132,000 (120,000)
1983	Castillo de Beliver	252,000 (229,000)
1980	Irenes Serenade	100,000 (91,000)
1979	Atlantic Empress & Aegean Captain	287,000 (260,000)
1979–80	Ixtoc I exploratory well	up to 480,000 (435,000)
1978	Amoco Cadiz	227,000 (206,000)
1972	Sea Star	115,000 (104,000)

Spill and aftermath
When the supertanker Exxon Valdez went aground in Prince William Sound, Alaska in 1989, only about one-fifth of the ship's cargo leaked from its damaged hull. Even so, clean up efforts took years, cost billions, and were only partially effective.

Shore effects
Oiled rocks and sand were blasted with hot, pressurized water. Later studies revealed the hot blasts killed many small animals.

When oil fouls the plumage of seabirds like this duck caught in the Exxon Valdez spill, they lose body heat and cannot fly. Hundreds of thousands of affected seabirds died, as did sea otters, whales, and millions of fish.

Aerial attack
Helicopters sprayed a strong detergent on the spreading slick. The spray only helped disperse about 5 percent of the oil.

Detergent spray

Oil slick
About 30 percent of the spilled oil formed a slick on the water's surface. Currents and wave action drove most of this oil ashore.

Containment
Containment booms enclose areas of oil above and below the surface. Much of the oil evaporates, some is burned off, and some is pumped out by skimmer ships.

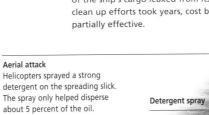

Commercial Fishing

The sea has supplied humans with food and other essentials for at least 40,000 years. From the Arctic to the Southern Ocean, early fishermen used nets, spears, ingenious traps, hook-and-line, and even their hands. Such low-impact practices helped sustain many generations of coastal peoples. Today millions of vessels using sophisticated electronic gear trawl, longline, or set massive nets along the continental shelves and on the high seas. This industrial fishery harvests billions of tons of sea creatures valued for food or fertilizer, including tunas, anchovies, shrimps, and squid, and earns annual revenues of more than US $400 billion dollars. Millions of tons of non-target "bycatch" species are simply discarded. By recent estimates, 52 percent of marine fish populations are being harvested to the maximum sustainable limit, while another 24 percent are being dangerously overharvested. Despite efforts at international controls, a few nations still conduct "scientific" whaling even though the populations of most whale species are a mere shadow of their former numbers.

Fishing Tradition

Peoples of the high Arctic traditionally traveled in skin-covered kayaks or larger craft called umiaks. They used woven nets and hook-and-line methods to catch fish, while seals, walrus, and the occasional whale were taken with spears or harpoons. Although some Inuit still use traditional methods, others employ motorized vessels and use a harpoon cannon or rifle to kill large prey, such as narwhals, beluga whales, and other species.

The term Inuit refers to Arctic peoples of Canada and Greenland. The shaded area on the map shows their traditional lands.

An Inuit fisherman may wait many hours at holes cut in the ice for Arctic char and other coveted fish species. This man is using a time-honored Inuit spear-fishing technique.

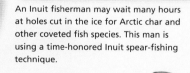

Knife used in preparing food

Detachable harpoon heads

Harpoon head

Fishing spear

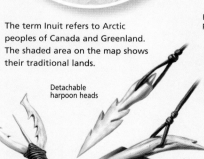

Traditional Inuit hunting tools are made from bone, animal hide, and walrus ivory. Spears are used to catch fish and harpoons to catch seals and whales.

Main fisheries

Fishing operations annually capture hundreds of millions of metric tons of fish used for human food, animal feed and fertilizers. Fisheries are spread around the global sea, but nearly 50 percent of this intensive harvesting occurs in different parts of the Pacific Ocean. Three nations—China, Peru, and the USA—account for nearly one-third of all catches. Nations neighboring the Indian Ocean and North Atlantic are other major producers.

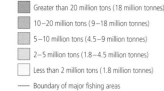

- Greater than 20 million tons (18 million tonnes)
- 10–20 million tons (9–18 million tonnes)
- 5–10 million tons (4.5–9 million tonnes)
- 2–5 million tons (1.8–4.5 million tonnes)
- Less than 2 million tons (1.8 million tonnes)
— Boundary of major fishing areas
10 (9) Production, tons (tonnes)

Open sea fishing
The deck of this commercial trawler is awash with Pacific cod caught off the coast of Alaska. Following an unsustainable 430 percent increase in the number of Pacific cod taken in recent years, the fishery today is more carefully regulated.

Fish to market
A Tokyo fish market features arrays of freshly caught tunas. Japan and other Asian nations operate roughly 70 percent of the world's motorized fishing vessels. These craft range from small powerboats to the high-tech vessels of industrial fishing fleets.

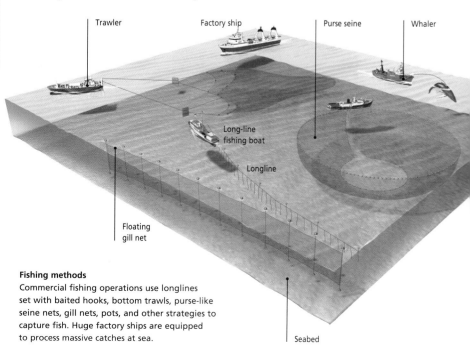

Trawler · Factory ship · Purse seine · Whaler

Long-line fishing boat

Longline

Floating gill net

Seabed

Fishing methods
Commercial fishing operations use longlines set with baited hooks, bottom trawls, purse-like seine nets, gill nets, pots, and other strategies to capture fish. Huge factory ships are equipped to process massive catches at sea.

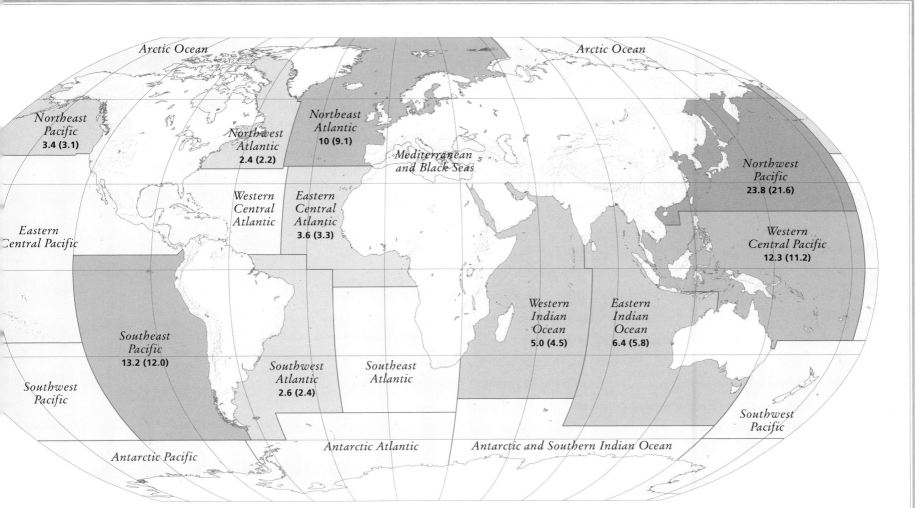

Arctic Ocean

Arctic Ocean

Northeast Pacific
3.4 (3.1)

Northwest Atlantic
2.4 (2.2)

Northeast Atlantic
10 (9.1)

Mediterranean and Black Seas

Northwest Pacific
23.8 (21.6)

Western Central Atlantic

Eastern Central Atlantic
3.6 (3.3)

Eastern Central Pacific

Western Central Pacific
12.3 (11.2)

Western Indian Ocean
5.0 (4.5)

Eastern Indian Ocean
6.4 (5.8)

Southeast Pacific
13.2 (12.0)

Southwest Atlantic
2.6 (2.4)

Southeast Atlantic

Southwest Pacific

Southwest Pacific

Antarctic Pacific

Antarctic Atlantic

Antarctic and Southern Indian Ocean

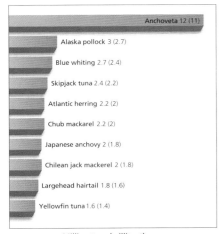

Anchoveta 12 (11)

Alaska pollock 3 (2.7)

Blue whiting 2.7 (2.4)

Skipjack tuna 2.4 (2.2)

Atlantic herring 2.2 (2)

Chub mackerel 2.2 (2)

Japanese anchovy 2 (1.8)

Chilean jack mackerel 2 (1.8)

Largehead hairtail 1.8 (1.6)

Yellowfin tuna 1.6 (1.4)

Million tons (million t)

Major commercial species, 2004
By weight the Peruvian anchovy (anchoveta) outstrips all other commercially caught wild fish. Other fish targeted by marine fisheries include tunas, and blue whiting, the latter a common ingredient in fish meal.

Target: lobsters
A lobster boat heads out into the western North Atlantic where baited pots will be set. In recent years catches of wild lobsters have begun to decline while consumer demand has risen.

Shrimping
Spot prawns are the catch in this small pot set in the cold waters of British Columbia, Canada. The majority of wild shrimp are caught with specialized trawl nets that rake in millions of tons annually.

WHALING

In the 20th century populations of many whale species fell as whaling fleets used spotter planes to locate animals and processed catches at sea on factory ships. The International Whaling Commission introduced protection for blue, gray and humpback whales in 1965. In 1985 an international moratorium banned nearly all whaling.

In Norway, Japan, and several other countries, whale meat is a prized delicacy. This photograph shows whale meat in a Norwegian market.

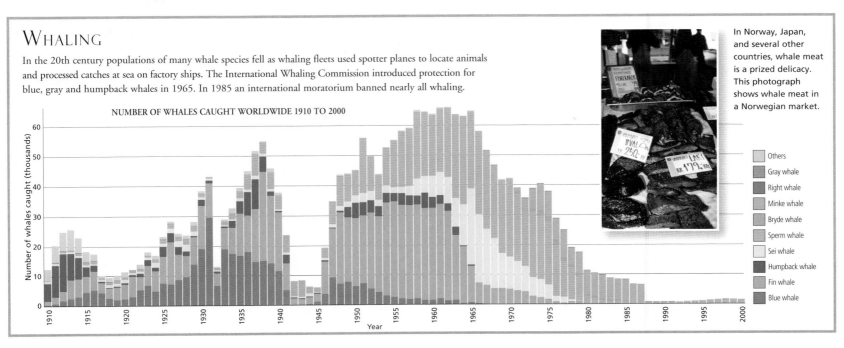

NUMBER OF WHALES CAUGHT WORLDWIDE 1910 TO 2000

Number of whales caught (thousands)

Year

Others
Gray whale
Right whale
Minke whale
Bryde whale
Sperm whale
Sei whale
Humpback whale
Fin whale
Blue whale

THREATENED SEA LIFE

Certain ocean areas and species have been hard-hit by aggressive fisheries, coastal development, pollution, and environmental changes due to global warming. Pollution, coral bleaching, and fishing with explosives have helped place coral reefs in the Caribbean and Indo-Pacific into the critically endangered category. Some scientists estimate that populations of vital reef predators such as sharks have declined as much as 50 to 90 percent. Development and oxygen-depleting nutrient pollution seriously threaten many estuaries that are major nursery grounds for many young fish and shrimp. The United Nations estimates that more than 20 percent of mangrove estuaries have been destroyed in recent years. Leatherbacks, hawksbills, and all other sea turtles are endangered, in part because humans consume their eggs and meat or use turtle shells for ornaments. Overfishing has decimated stocks of bluefin tunas, billfish, and shark species such as the sand tiger, and unrelenting whaling has nearly eradicated the blue whale, the largest animal ever to have existed on Earth.

On the brink

Scores of marine animals are listed as vulnerable, endangered, or critically endangered by the International Union for the Conservation of Nature (IUCN). Four of the five species pictured here are critically endangered, meaning that their numbers are so few that they may be on the brink of extinction. Human activities, including overharvesting and habitat destruction, have been the key factors placing these species in peril.

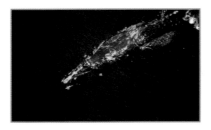

Northern right whale
Heavy whaling from the late 1840s to the mid-1880s decimated populations of the Northern right whale (*Eubalaena glacialis*).

Most Endangered Sharks
1 Ganges shark *(Glyphis gangeticus)*
2 Striped smoothhound *(Mustelis fasciatus)*
3 Pondicherry shark *(Carcharhinus hemiodon)*
4 Daggernose shark *(Isogomphodon oxyrhynchus)*
5 Angel shark *(Squatina squatina)*
6 Dumb gulper shark *(Centrophorus harrissoni)*
7 Borneo shark *(Carcharhinus borneensis)*
8 New Guinea river shark *(Glyphis* sp.*)*
9 Speartooth shark *(Glyphis glyphis)*
10 Narrownose smoothhound *(Mustelis schmitti)*
11 Smoothtooth blacktip *(Carcharhinus leiodon)*
12 Whitefin topeshark *(Hemitriakis leucopeript)*
13 Bizant river shark *(Glyphis* sp.*)*
14 Smoothback angel shark *(Squatina oculata)*
15 Sawback angel shark *(Squatina aculeata)*

THREATENED ANIMALS

North Atlantic right whale

Hawksbill turtle

Smalltooth sawfish

Mediterranean monk seal

Goliath grouper

SCALE 1:137,000,000
Robinson Projection

ACIDIFICATION

Increasing atmospheric carbon dioxide is a major phenomenon in global warming and climate change. As the level of carbon dioxide rises, related chemical reactions may be making the ocean more acidic. This change in turn can reduce the amount of calcium carbonate available to form the shells and skeletons of organisms such as corals, mollusks, and crustaceans. Concerned scientists are tracking shifts in acidification and monitoring their impacts.

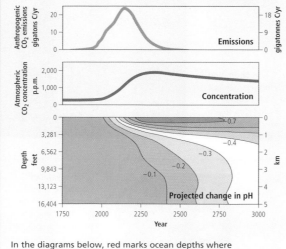

Starting in 1750, this model projects ocean acidification to the year 3000. The upper panels track carbon dioxide produced by human activity and in the atmosphere.

In the diagrams below, red marks ocean depths where too little calcium carbonate is (or will be) available for use by marine invertebrates.

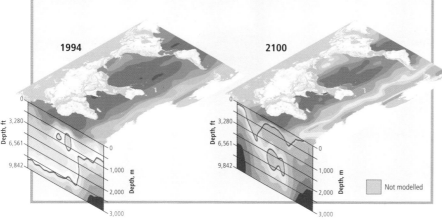

1994

2100

Not modelled

Shark mortality
South Africa, Australia, the USA, and Mediterranean nations all protect great white sharks (*Carcharodon carcharias*) in their waters. This 15-foot (4.6-m) specimen may have died when it tried to take fish hooked on a longline.

Death by finning
Fisheries for shark fins are destructive and wasteful. The fins are used in a luxury soup consumed in some Asian cultures. Typically, once fins are sliced off, the living shark is thrown back into the sea where it drowns.

⚡ Hawksbill turtle
Hawksbill (*Eretmochelys imbricata*) populations have been depleted by human consumption of its eggs and use of its shell for ornaments.

⚡ Smalltooth sawfish
Numbers of this tropical ray (*Pristis pectinata*) have perished in nets set for other species. Its habitat has been destroyed by development.

⚡ Mediterranean monk seal
Killing by fishermen, disturbed colony sites, and entanglement in fishing nets are some causes for this species (*Monachus monachus*) decline.

⚡ Goliath grouper
The grouper (*Epinephelus itajara*) is critically endangered due to intensive fishing pressure on its habitats and its slow rate of reproduction.

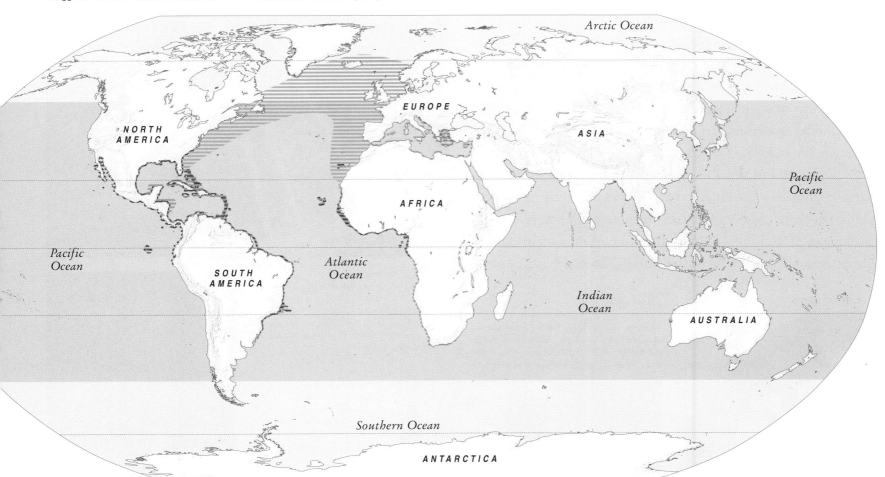

⚡ Ghost nets
Caught in an abandoned, drifting "ghost net," this endangered green sea turtle (*Chelonia mydas*) was unable to surface and breathe. Ghost nets probably also kill large numbers of sharks, which must swim unfettered in order to breathe.

Lethal bycatch
Lured by longline bait, sea turtles are sometimes taken as accidental bycatch on commercial longlines set for fish. Unless released in good condition the turtle will suffocate.

Death by dynamite
In some tropical regions fishermen use the highly destructive practice of dynamiting to "harvest" reef fish. This harmful practice is illegal, but unfortunately common.

EXTINCT MARINE ANIMALS

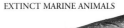

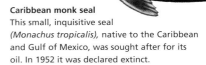

Caribbean monk seal
This small, inquisitive seal (*Monachus tropicalis*), native to the Caribbean and Gulf of Mexico, was sought after for its oil. In 1952 it was declared extinct.

Steller's sea cow
This immense 26-foot (7.9-m) long marine mammal, the steller sea cow (*Hydrodamalis gigas*) was hunted to extinction in less than three decades after it was discovered in 1741.

Great auk
The great auk (*Pinguinus impennis*) was flightless and therefore an easy target for hunters. It was last seen in Newfoundland, Canada, in 1852.

CONSERVATION OF THE SEAS

Until the mid-1800s the sea's bounty seemed inexhaustible, but by the early 1900s some northern waters were depleted of once vast stocks of cod, haddock, and oysters. Advances in fishing technology and storage allowed commercial fishers to pursue catches ever farther from shore, but by the 1970s overfishing and destruction of marine habitats began to be serious global concerns. In 1972 the United Nations Educational, Scientific and Cultural Organization (UNESCO) began its World Heritage program that now includes dozens of undersea sites around the globe. Today, governmental agencies and private organizations including the International Union for the Conservation of Nature (IUCN) and World Wildlife Fund work to help conserve marine habitats through scientific research, fisheries management, and public education. Major sanctuaries include marine reserves such as Palmyra Atoll, Kingman Reef, and Rose Atoll, a set of central Pacific islands that form the world's largest protected marine area.

Monitoring reef health
Using a digital camera, researchers photograph seaweed growing on a Hawaiian reef. These algae are an important part of the reef ecosystem. Long-term study of the sites allows scientists to monitor their health and track potential changes.

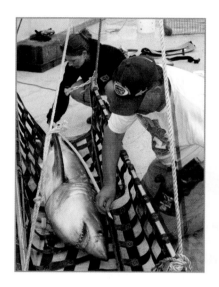

Shark tagging
This porbeagle shark (*Lamna nasus*) is being measured prior to being tagged and released back into the sea. Tagging studies allow marine scientists to gather data about shark migration and information on the ecology of populations.

Sustainable salmon
Sustainability is a major goal of the carefully managed Alaska salmon fishery, in which small vessels are the norm. This boat's purse seine encloses a load of chum (dog salmon), one of five species caught in Alaska waters.

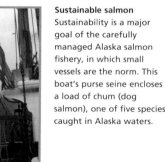

Turtle excluders
When shrimp trawl nets are equipped with turtle excluder devices (TEDs) like those shown here, sea turtles and large fish inadvertently caught in the nets are shunted back out through an opening in the device.

LEATHERBACKS

⚡ Leatherback sea turtles (*Dermochelys coriacea*) have a thick, leathery skin instead of hard scutes and grow to about 7 feet (2 m). They range through much of the global sea, with nesting beaches concentrated in the tropics and subtropics. The largest of living marine reptiles, leatherbacks are critically endangered due mainly to intensive human consumption of their eggs and meat. Conservation efforts focus on halting and possibly reversing the decline.

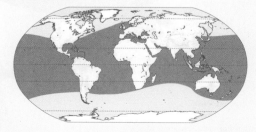

LEATHERBACK DISTRIBUTION

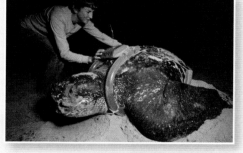

Satellite tracking allows researchers to monitor a leatherback's diving behavior and travel patterns through the ocean. The satellite tag, attached to a harness, feeds information to a satellite that transfers the data to a receiver on land.

Numbers painted onto a sea turtle's back allow scientists to identify it after it is released back into the wild.

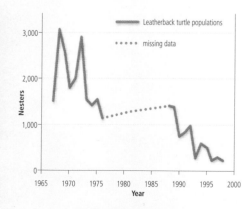

DECLINE OF LEATHERBACKS

— Leatherback turtle populations
···· missing data

DECLINE OF LEATHERBACKS

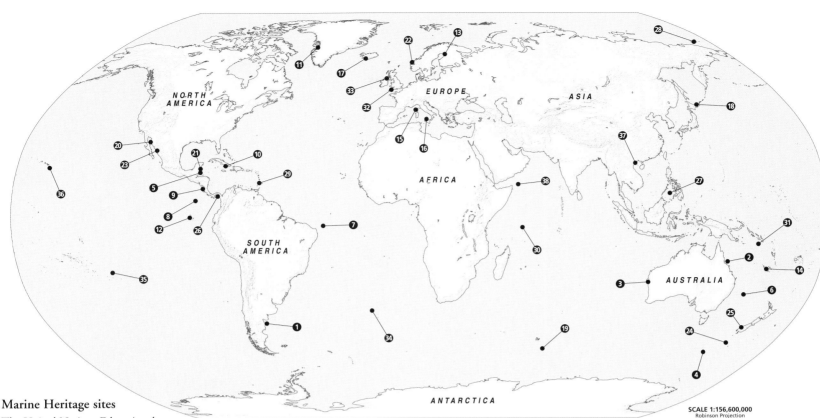

SCALE 1:156,600,000
Robinson Projection

Marine Heritage sites

The United Nations Educational, Scientific and Cultural Organization (UNESCO) designates protected Marine Heritage sites in coastal areas around the globe. The sites are selected for their outstanding natural and/or cultural significance. Site personnel receive training and support for state-of-the-science management methods to counter damage to the world's marine environments.

UNESCO MARINE HERITAGE SITES

1 Peninsula Valdés, Argentina
2 Great Barrier Reef, Australia
3 Shark Bay, Australia
4 Macquarie Island, Australia
5 Belize Barrier Reef Reserve System
6 Lord Howe Island Group, Australia
7 Brazilian Atlantic Islands
8 Cocos Island National Park, Costa Rica
9 Area de Conservacion, Guanacaste, Costa Rica
10 Desembarco de Granma National Park, Cuba

11 Ilulissat Ice Fjord, Denmark
12 Galapagos Islands, Ecuador
13 High Coast/Kvarken Archipelago, Finland & Sweden
14 The lagoons of New Caledonia
15 Gulf of Porto, Corsica
16 Isole Aolie (Aeolian Islands), Italy
17 Surtsey, Iceland
18 Shiretoko, Hokkaido, Japan
19 MacDonald and Heard Islands, Australia

20 Gulf of California, Mexico, Islands, and Protected Areas
21 Sian Ka'an, Mexico
22 West Norwegian Fjords, Norway
23 El Vizcaino Whale Sanctuary, Mexico
24 New Zealand Sub-Antarctic Islands
25 Tewahipounamu, Southwest New Zealand
26 Coiba National Park, Panama
27 Tubbataha Reef Marine Park, Philippines
28 Natural System of Wrangel Island Reserve, Russian Federation

29 Pitons Management Area, St. Lucia
30 Aldabra Atoll, Seychelles
31 East Rennell, Solomon Islands
32 Dorset & East Devon Coast, UK
33 Giants Causeway and Causeway Coast, UK
34 Gough and Inaccessible Islands, UK
35 Henderson Island, UK
36 Hawaii Volcanoes National Park, Hawaii, USA
37 Ha Long Bay, Vietnam
38 Socotra Archipelago, Yemen

Great Barrier Reef
The Great Barrier Reef of Australia is the world's largest coral reef system. It consists of hundreds of islands and nearly 3,000 separate reefs.

Giant's Causeway
The Giant's Causeway, located on the coast of Northern Ireland, consists of more than 4,000 basalt blocks formed by volcanic activity.

Ha Long Bay
The shimmering seawaters of Ha Long Bay in Vietnam encompass several thousand intriguingly shaped limestone islands.

Cocos Islands
The world-famous coral reef of Cocos Island, Costa Rica, is renowned for its sea life including whale sharks and hammerhead sharks.

MANATEES

Manatees *(Trichechus manatus latirostris)* are classified (with dugongs) as sirenians. Genetic studies suggest that elephants are the group's closest living relatives. Two of the three recognized species—the West Indian manatee and the West African manatee—spend time in salt water. All manatee populations are small and under threat. Manatees are known for lolling in tropical estuaries, rivers, and coastal waters where they feed on submerged grasses.

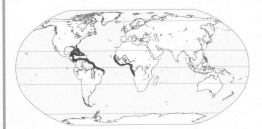

MANATEE DISTRIBUTION

Manatees have a blunt head and snout, short flippers used for slow swimming, and a flattened, rounded tail.

This researcher is attaching a satellite tracking device to a young Florida manatee before releasing it at a wildlife refuge.

Because manatees live mainly in the shallows, collisions with watercraft are common. In Florida boats cause up to 40 percent of manatee deaths.

BOAT SPEED KILLS

Penguins relax on a wave-sculptured iceberg of the Southern Ocean.
Ice covers both polar oceans in winter, melting and breaking up in
spring to release nutrients and surface food. On this annual bonanza
depend the fish, seals, whales, and seabirds abundant in polar oceans
both north and south. Icebergs provide sanctuary away from land for
penguins and other seabirds.

POLAR OCEANS

Arctic Ocean

During the 16th and 17th centuries, ship-borne explorers heading northward from Europe on early spring voyages soon found themselves among sea ice. Floes and towering, castle-like icebergs pressed dangerously around their ships, drifting steadily south from a seemingly endless reservoir located far to the north under Arctos, the pole star. Was there an Arctic Ocean, and could it be crossed to reach the wealth of China and the Indies? Penetrating the fringe seas east and west of Greenland, early Dutch and British explorers brought home tales of unimaginable cold and hardship. Those that headed northeast toward Russia, favored by warm currents from the north Atlantic Ocean, skirted the Siberian coast and became the first Europeans to enter the Arctic Ocean itself. The "Northeast Passage" to China evaded them, but traders who followed brought home cargoes of whale oil, baleen, walrus ivory, polar bear and reindeer skins, and later valuable furs from Siberia. The ocean was first crossed by Nansen's ship *Fram* in 1893–96.

Oil pipeline
Ice investing the northern shores of Alaska in winter makes year-round shipping impracticable. Oil drilled at Prudhoe Bay travels south instead by pipeline to Valdez, an ice-free port on the Pacific Ocean shore. The Trans-Alaska pipeline, which is 800 miles (1,280 km) long, was completed in 1977.

BATHYMETRIC DEPTHS

Feet	Meters
Sea level	Sea level
656	200
1640	500
3281	1000
6562	2000
9842	3000
13,123	4000
16,404	5000
19,685	6000
26,246	8,000

Ocean Share

All other oceans

Arctic Ocean
5.4 million sq miles
(14.1 million km²)
4%

The Facts

Area	5.4 million square miles (14.1 million km²)
Average depth	4,690 feet (1,430 m)
Maximum depth	18,455 feet (5,625 m)
Maximum width	2,000 miles (3,200 km)
Maximum length	3,100 miles (5,000 km)

NATURAL RESOURCES

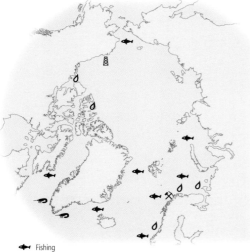

- 🐟 Fishing
- 🦐 Shellfish
- ⚒ Mining
- Oil production
- Gas production

There are rich fisheries in the Barents, Greenland, and Bering seas. Seals are still hunted commercially throughout the Arctic: whales are hunted off Norway, and Inuit communities take small numbers of whales and seals locally. Northern Siberia and Alaska have huge reserves of oil, coal, and gas.

Walrus herd
Walrus (*Odobenus rosmarus*) feed mainly on clams, which they seek in the mud of the nearshore seabed, using their whiskers as sensors and their tusks as rakes. Many thousands of walruses have been killed commercially for the solid ivory in their tusks, and for their tough leather hides.

Murmansk
Though north of the Arctic Circle, the port of Murmansk on Kola Peninsula remains ice-free throughout the year, warmed by waters of the North Atlantic Drift. Founded in 1916, it now has a population of more than 300,000. It is an important center for Arctic shipping.

(Map labels:) NORTH CANADA, Queen Maud Gulf, Corporation G., King William Island, Bo Pen, Hudson Bay, Southampton Island, Melville Peninsula, Coats Island, Mansel Island, Foxe Basin, Foxe Peninsula, Prince Charles Island, Hudson Strait, Baffin Isla, Ungava Bay, Cape Chidley, Dav, Labrador Sea, Labrador Basin, Nuuk

N

150° 160° 170° 180° 170° 160° 150°

V W X Y Z

1

2

3

Polar bear

White polar bears *(Ursus maritimus)* range along the Arctic shoreline, feeding mainly on seals that they catch from the pack ice, and salmon and other large fish that they scoop from rivers. Always hungry, in summer they scavenge the tundra for eggs, nestlings, deer, grass, shoots, and berries.

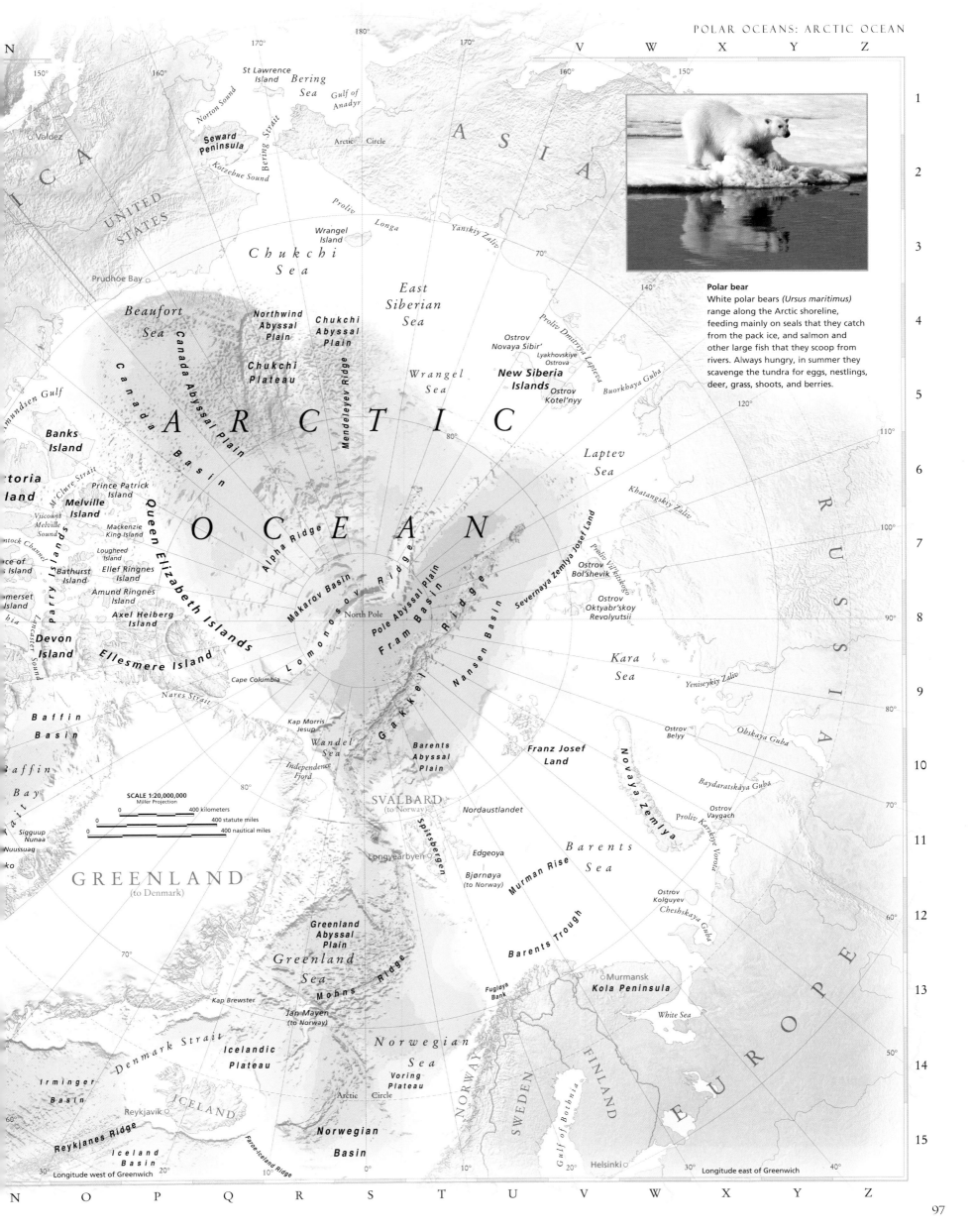

ICA

Valdez

St Lawrence Island

Bering Sea

Gulf of Anadyr

Seward Peninsula

Norton Sound

Bering Strait

Kotzebue Sound

Arctic Circle

UNITED STATES

Proliv Longa

A S I A

Wrangel Island

Yanskiy Zaliv

70°

Prudhoe Bay

Chukchi Sea

East Siberian Sea

Beaufort Sea

Northwind Abyssal Plain

Chukchi Abyssal Plain

Ostrov Novaya Sibir'

Proliv Dmitriya Lapteva

Amundsen Gulf

Canada Abyssal Plain

Chukchi Plateau

Mendeleyev Ridge

Wrangel Sea

New Siberia Islands

Lyakhovskiye Ostrova

Buorkhaya Guba

Banks Island

A R C T I C

Ostrov Kotel'nyy

Canada Basin

80°

120°

toria land

M'Clure Strait

Prince Patrick Island

O C E A N

Laptev Sea

110°

Viscount Melville Sound

Melville Island

Alpha Ridge

Queen Elizabeth Islands

Mackenzie King Island

Khatangskiy Zaliv

R U S S I A

ntock Channel

ce of s Island

Lougheed Island

Makarov Basin

Ellef Ringnes Island

Bathurst Island

Amund Ringnes Island

Pole Abyssal Plain

Lomonosov Ridge

Fram Basin

Nansen Basin

Severnaya Zemlya

Ostrov Bol'shevik

Proliv Vil'kitskogo

100°

Parry Islands

Axel Heiberg Island

North Pole

Gakkel Ridge

Ostrov Oktyabr'skoy Revolyutsii

90°

merset Island

hia

Devon Island

Ellesmere Island

Cape Columbia

Kara Sea

Nares Strait

Kap Morris Jesup

Yeniseykiy Zaliv

80°

Baffin Basin

Wandel Sea

Barents Abyssal Plain

Franz Josef Land

Ostrov Belyy

Obskaya Guba

affin

Independence Fjord

Novaya Zemlya

Baydaratskaya Guba

Bay

SVALBARD (to Norway)

Nordaustlandet

Ostrov Vaygach

70°

kait

SCALE 1:20,000,000
Miller Projection

0   400 kilometers
0   400 statute miles
0   400 nautical miles

Proliv Karskiye Vorota

Sigguup Nunaa

Nuussuaq

Spitsbergen

Edgeoya

Barents Sea

Ostrov Kolguyev

ko

GREENLAND
(to Denmark)

Longyearbyen

Bjørnøya (to Norway)

Murman Rise

Cheshskaya Guba

60°

Greenland Abyssal Plain

Barents Trough

Greenland Sea

Murmansk

Kola Peninsula

Mohns Ridge

Fugløya Bank

50°

Kap Brewster

Jan Mayen (to Norway)

Norwegian Sea

White Sea

Denmark Strait

Icelandic Plateau

Arctic Circle

E U R O P E

Irminger Basin

Voring Plateau

NORWAY

SWEDEN

FINLAND

Reykjavik

ICELAND

Gulf of Bothnia

Reykjanes Ridge

Norwegian Basin

Iceland Basin

Faroe-Iceland Ridge

Helsinki

30° 20° 10° 10° 20° 30° 40°

Longitude west of Greenwich   Longitude east of Greenwich

N O P Q R S T U V W X Y Z

4

5

6

7

8

9

10

11

12

13

14

15

EAST OF GREENLAND

Latitude for latitude this is by far the mildest sector of the Arctic. Except for the east coast of Greenland itself, the seas and coasts east of Greenland are warmed throughout the year by surface waters of the North Atlantic Drift—the northernmost branch of the Gulf Stream—which extends far into the Kara Sea. Without the North Atlantic Drift Britain, Iceland, and Norway would be as cold in winter as Labrador and Newfoundland; Archangel and Murmansk would be ice-bound for several months each year. The admixture of cold and warm currents brings fertility to the surface waters of these Arctic fringe seas. Generations of whalers, sealers, and fishermen have braved ice and foul weather to exploit their riches; deep-sea fishing for cod and prawns still brings prosperity to most of the neighboring countries. Seabed gas and oil have been exploited, and command continuing interest as reserves elsewhere are exhausted.

Hammerfest, Norway
Since the 16th century North Europeans have exploited the huge stocks of cod, herring, and other fish of cold North Atlantic and Arctic fringe waters. Today commercial fishing boats, like these in Hammerfest, Norway, continue to hunt for reduced stocks, working within scientifically-managed limits.

Kittiwakes
Crags and cliffs of hundreds of rocky islands provide breeding space, and the cold oceans provide rich feeding grounds, for these kittiwakes (*Rissa* sp.) and many other species of seabirds. This group has been foraging among the broken ice and open water in front of an active glacier.

Greenland shark
Up to 21 feet (7 m) long, Greenland sharks (*Somniosus microcephalus*) live in both shallow and deep water along the Greenland coast, usually close to the seabed, where they feed on other fish. Inuit hunters harpoon them for their meat, oil, and scaly sandpaper skin.

Surface currents
Strong surface currents leave the polar basin, carrying streams of old sea ice and icebergs southward between Greenland, Svalbard, and the Siberian islands, and blocking and chilling harbors along the coasts. Warm currents from the North Atlantic keep the shores of Iceland and Norway relatively ice-free.

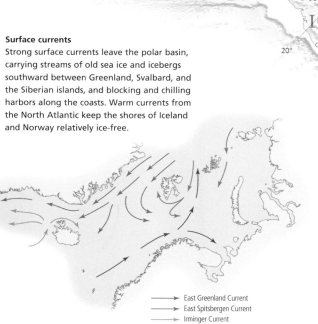

→ East Greenland Current
→ East Spitsbergen Current
→ Irminger Current
→ Norwegian Atlantic Current

GREENLAND

Narsarsuaq
60°
40°
Ammassalik
Kap Farvel
40°
Ittoqqortoormiit
Daneborg
Kap Brewster
Spar Fracture Zone
Jan Mayen Fracture Zone
Jan Mayen
Greenland–Iceland Rise
Denmark Strait
Kolbeinsey Ridge
Icelandic Plateau
Jan Mayen Ridge
60°
30°
Reykjanes Ridge
REYKJAVÍK
ICELAND
Arctic Circle
Irminger Basin
20°
Vik
Faroe–Iceland Ridge
Aegir Ridge
Norwegian Sea
10°
Faroe Islands
Faroe–Shetland Trough
60°
Shetland Islands
Ålesund
Bergen
0°
North Sea

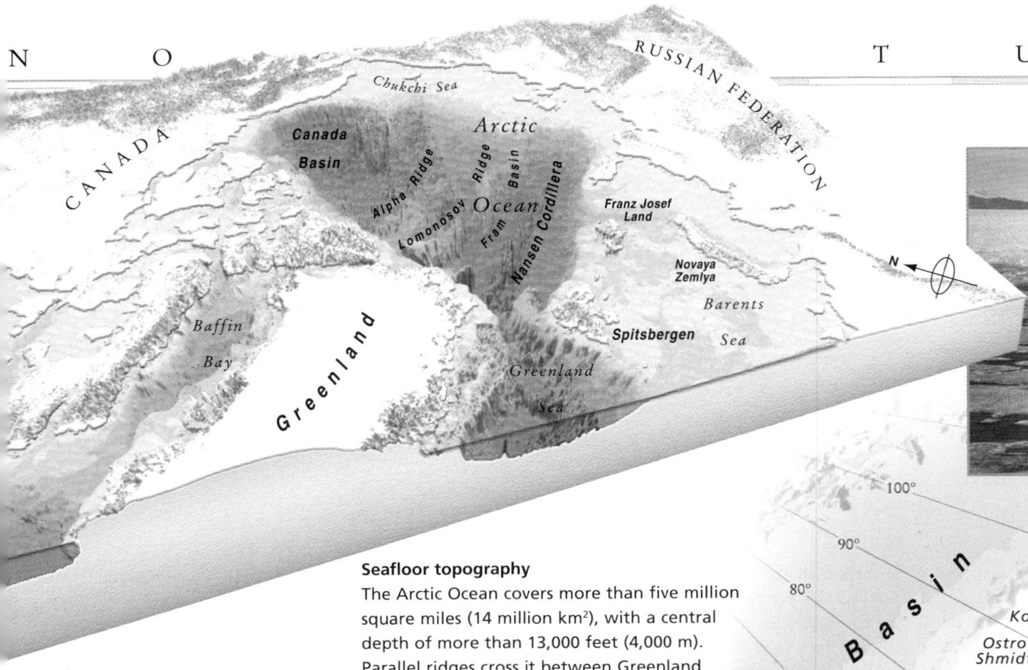

Inset locator map (top left):

CANADA

RUSSIAN FEDERATION

Chukchi Sea

Arctic Ocean

Canada Basin

Alpha Ridge

Lomonosov Ridge

Makarov Basin

Fram Basin

Nansen Cordillera

Franz Josef Land

Novaya Zemlya

Barents Sea

Spitsbergen

Baffin Bay

Greenland

Greenland Sea

N

Icebreaker

Owned by the Swedish Maritime Administration, *Oden* is one of a fleet of general-purpose icebreakers that open channels and act as tugs, escorts, and scientific research ships. Such ships are essential for keeping marine traffic moving through the sea ice of long Arctic winters.

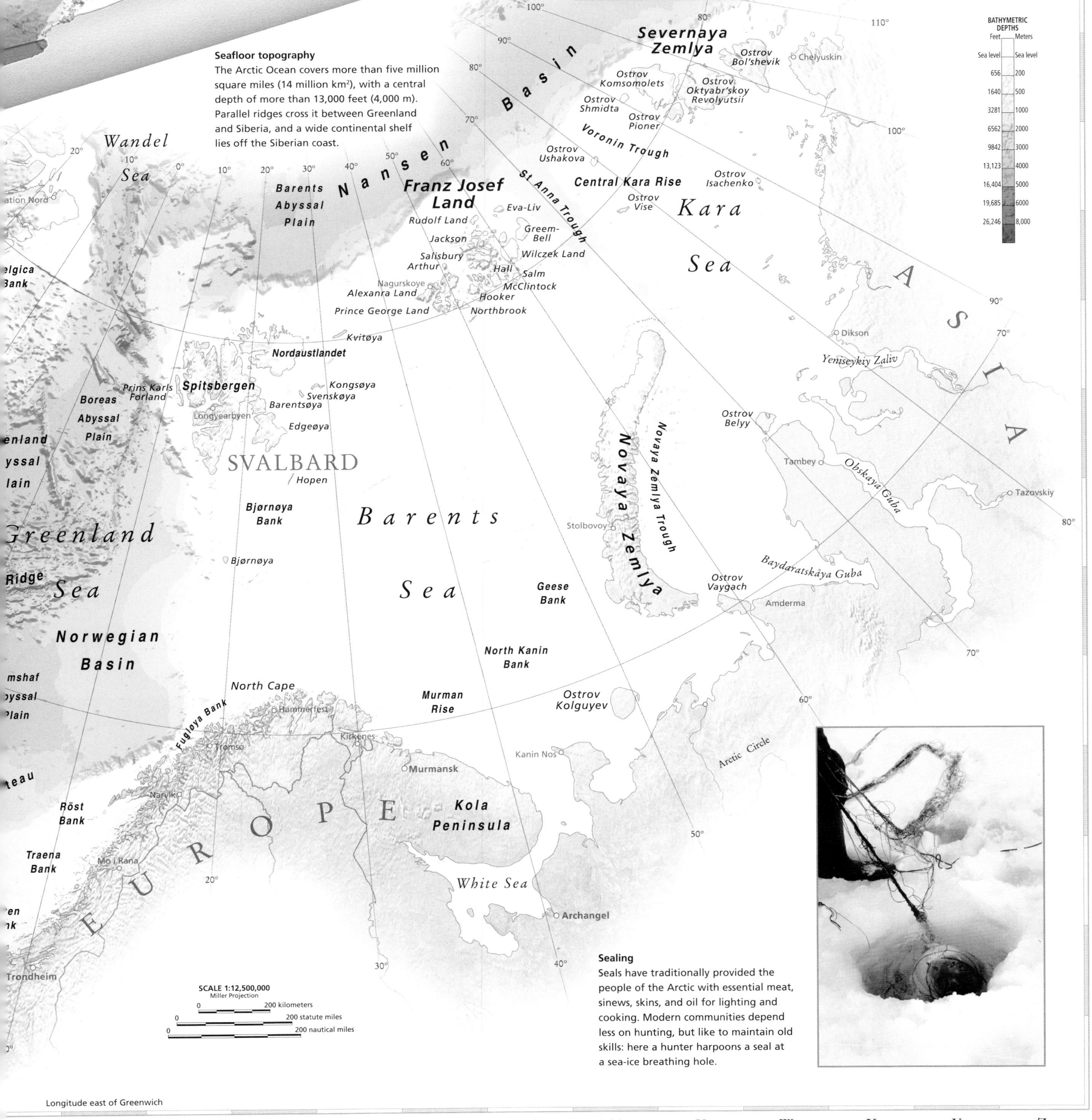

Seafloor topography

The Arctic Ocean covers more than five million square miles (14 million km²), with a central depth of more than 13,000 feet (4,000 m). Parallel ridges cross it between Greenland and Siberia, and a wide continental shelf lies off the Siberian coast.

Bathymetric depths scale:

BATHYMETRIC DEPTHS

Feet	Meters
Sea level	Sea level
656	200
1640	500
3281	1000
6562	2000
9842	3000
13,123	4000
16,404	5000
19,685	6000
26,246	8,000

Main map labels:

Severnaya Zemlya

Ostrov Bol'shevik

Ostrov Chelyuskin

Ostrov Komsomolets

Ostrov Oktyabr'skoy Revolyutsii

Ostrov Shmidta

Ostrov Pioner

Voronin Trough

Ostrov Ushakova

Central Kara Rise

Ostrov Isachenko

Ostrov Vise

Kara Sea

ASIA

Nansen Basin

St Anna Trough

Barents Abyssal Plain

Franz Josef Land

Eva-Liv

Rudolf Land

Greem-Bell

Jackson

Wilczek Land

Salisbury

Arthur

Hall

Salm

Nagurskoye

McClintock

Alexanra Land

Hooker

Prince George Land

Northbrook

Kvitøya

Nordaustlandet

Wandel Sea

Dikson

Yeniseykiy Zaliv

Spitsbergen

Kongsøya

Prins Karls Forland

Svenskøya

Boreas Abyssal Plain

Longyearbyen

Barentsøya

Edgeøya

Ostrov Belyy

SVALBARD

Hopen

Tambey

Obskaya Guba

Tazovskiy

Bjørnøya Bank

Barents Sea

Novaya Zemlya Trough

Novaya Zemlya

Bjørnøya

Stolbovoy

Baydaratskaya Guba

Greenland Sea

Geese Bank

Ostrov Vaygach

Amderma

Greenland Ridge

Norwegian Basin

North Kanin Bank

Ostrov Kolguyev

North Cape

Murman Rise

Fugløya Bank

Hammerfest

Kirkenes

Kanin Nos

Arctic Circle

Tromsø

Röst Bank

Murmansk

EUROPE

Narvik

Kola Peninsula

Traena Bank

Mo i Rana

White Sea

Trondheim

Archangel

Sealing

Seals have traditionally provided the people of the Arctic with essential meat, sinews, skins, and oil for lighting and cooking. Modern communities depend less on hunting, but like to maintain old skills: here a hunter harpoons a seal at a sea-ice breathing hole.

SCALE 1:12,500,000
Miller Projection

200 kilometers

200 statute miles

200 nautical miles

Longitude east of Greenwich

Northwest Passages

When geographers thought it likely that an ocean surrounded the North Pole, the search for the shortest sea route to China and the Indies began. Explorers sailing northward from Europe found concentrated ice off Svalbard. Sailing northeastward brought them little farther than northern Russia's Kola Peninsula. Exploration to the northwest was more promising: pioneering voyages by Davis, Baffin, and Hudson in the late 16th and early 17th centuries took them as far as Baffin Bay—to the gateway of this ice-bound archipelago forming the northeast corner of North America. The search was resumed in the late 18th and early 19th centuries, from Baffin Bay westward through the maze of islands and waterways. While Davis Strait and Baffin Bay became hunting grounds for British, Dutch, and German whalers, naval expeditions explored the archipelago right through to the Bering Sea. Not until the early 20th century was the passage completed in a single voyage, by the Norwegian explorer Roald Amundsen.

- → Baffin Island Current
- → Labrador Current
- → West Greenland Current

Surface currents
Cold surface currents carry icebergs and sea ice northward along the west Greenland coast toward Baffin Bay, to be joined by colder, ice-filled water from the polar basin. Baffin Bay and central Davis Strait contain year-round ice that drifts south with the Baffin Island and Labrador currents.

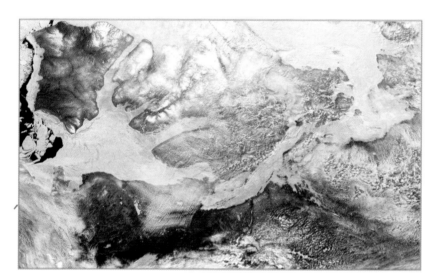

Arctic archipelago
Satellite imagery shows the complex of islands and ice-strewn channels of the Canadian Arctic archipelago. Here at the western end are Banks Island (left) and Victoria Island (center), separated from the Canadian mainland (bottom) by Amundsen Gulf, one of the western entrances to the Northwest Passages.

Drifting icebergs
Icebergs and pack ice drift south constantly from the Arctic. Remnants like these may reach shipping lanes, where they can become a danger to shipping. *Titanic* in 1912 was lost to an iceberg from Davis Strait. Satellite monitoring now reduces the risk considerably.

Whaling
North European ships, particularly German, Dutch, and British, hunted Arctic whales from the 17th to the 20th century, bringing home blubber for oil and baleen ("whalebone") for corset stays. Harpooning a 40-foot (12-m) whale from an open boat was a hazardous business.

N O P Q R S T U V W X Y Z

SCALE 1:10,000,000
Miller Projection

0   200 kilometers
0   200 statute miles
0   200 nautical miles

Lincoln Sea

Elizabeth Islands

Ellesmere Island

Nares Strait

Alert

60°
50°
40°
30°
70°
80°
90°
100°
110°

Sverdrup Channel

Nansen Sound

Peary Channel

80°

Kane Basin

Axel Heiberg Island

Ellef Ringnes Island

Amund Ringnes Island

Cornwall Island

Graham Island

Grise Fiord

Smith Sound

GREENLAND

Thule

Ummannaq

Bathurst Island

Cornwallis Island

Resolute Bay

Devon Island

Jones Sound

Parry Channel

Nuussuaq

Kangersuatsiaq

70°

Lancaster Sound

Prince of Wales Island

Somerset Island

Bylot Island

Borden Peninsula

Brodeur Peninsula

Prince Regent Inlet

Baffin Bay

Disko

Ilulissat
Qeqertarsuaq

Boothia Peninsula

Gulf of Boothia

King William Island

Haven

Baffin Island

Home Bay

Qikiqtarjuaq

Kangerlussuaq

70°

Rowley Island

Committee Bay

Parry Bay

Prince Charles Island

Air Force Island

Cumberland Peninsula

Davis Strait

A D A

Melville Peninsula

Repulse Bay

Foxe Basin

Cape Dorchester

Bowman Bay

Cumberland Sound

Cape Mercy

NUUK

Narsasuaq

Paamiut

60°

Vansittart Island

Southampton Island

Foxe Channel

Foxe Peninsula

Cape Dorset

Mill Island

Salisbury Island

Nottingham Island

Lemieux Islands

Hall Peninsula

Iqaluit

Meta Incognita Peninsula

Frobisher Bay

Loks Land

Big Island

Resolution Island

80°

Hudson Strait

60°

Cape Labrador

Killiniq

Labrador Sea

50°

60°
70°

1
2
3
4
5
6
7
8
9
10
12
13
14
15

INUIT CULTURE AND COMMUNITIES

Inuit, formerly called Eskimos, are the coastal people indigenous to the western Arctic. Traditionally they lived in small communities from Bering Strait to East Greenland, making seasonal nomadic movements. Today Inuit are more likely to be housed in settlements, with government-sponsored schools and medical facilities. Under their respective national governments they have increasing political self-determination.

In the vast, Arctic landscape there are few natural landmarks. This inukshuk, carefully constructed from local rocks, is a signpost or indicator of direction for travelers.

BATHYMETRIC DEPTHS

Feet	Meters
Sea level	Sea level
656	200
1640	500
3281	1000
6562	2000
9842	3000
13,123	4000
16,404	5000
19,685	6000
26,246	8,000

Harp seal
A seal of the Arctic and north Atlantic pack ice, the harp seal (Phoca groenlandica) is so-called from a characteristic harp-shaped dorsal patch of dark fur. This female, hunting for fish, has come up for air. Thousands of harp seal pups have been killed commercially each year for their white natal fur.

SOUTHERN OCEAN

Some call it the Antarctic Ocean, but Capt. James Cook, RN, the explorer who first defined it in the 1770s, called it the Southern Ocean. A ring-shaped ocean, its northern oceanographic limit is the Antarctic Convergence or Polar Front, where cold waters spreading north from Antarctica pass beneath warmer subtropical waters. Its southern limit is Antarctica itself. Persistent westerly winds drive surface waters eastward, except immediately around the continent where westward-flowing surface currents prevail. It is a deep ocean, dropping steeply from Antarctica to a mean depth of 14,750 feet (4,500 m). Of the total area, a high proportion is frozen over every winter, pack ice sometimes extending as far north as the Antarctic Convergence in the Pacific and Indian ocean sectors. In summer the ice edge retreats, but pack ice persists in many coastal areas. It is a permanent feature in the Weddell and Ross seas, the two great bights between East and West Antarctica.

Crabeater seals
Crabeater seals (*Lobodon carcinophagus*) breed on Antarctic pack ice. They feed on shoals of tiny shrimps that swarm in Antarctic waters in summer, filtering them through their trilobed teeth. Here a group surfaces to breathe off the west coast of the Antarctic Peninsula.

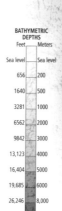

THE FACTS	
Area	7.8 million square miles 20.3 million km²)
Average depth	14,750 feet (4,500 m)
Maximum depth	24,032 feet (7,325 m)
Maximum width	1,700 miles (2,700 km)
Maximum length	13,400 miles (21,500 km)

Ocean Share

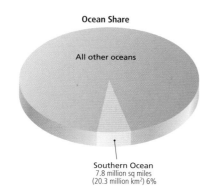

All other oceans

Southern Ocean
7.8 million sq miles
(20.3 million km²) 6%

POLYNYAS: ICE-FREE POCKETS

In both polar oceans, particular areas called polynas remain ice-free even in mid-winter. They may be formed either by strong winds blowing freshly-formed ice away, or by water at temperatures above freezing point upwelling from below. Either way they are important to wildlife, allowing whales and seals to breathe and birds to feed throughout the year.

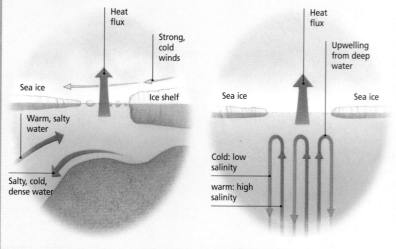

Wind-formed polynyas
These occur where strong downslope winds from land keep thin, newly-formed sea ice moving, sweeping it seaward and allowing relatively warm water to come up from below.

Upwelling polynyas
These occur on the open sea or channels at points where, for a variety of reasons, relatively warm vertical currents erode sea ice as fast as it forms. The result is persistent open water even in winter.

NATURAL RESOURCES

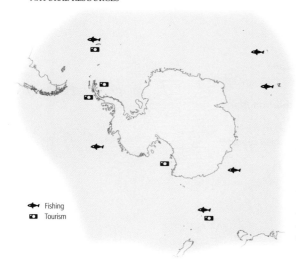

Fishing
Tourism

Natural resources
The Southern Ocean has no exploited seabed minerals, and mineral prospecting and development are prohibited within the area of the Antarctic Treaty (south of 60°S). Past industries have been based on a wealth of fur seals and whales: currently the region's resources support deep-sea fishing and tourism.

Russian Orthodox chapel
On a hilltop behind the Russian Bellingshausen Station, on King George Island, South Shetland Islands, stands this miniature Russian Orthodox church. Unusual but not unique: a neighboring Chilean station has a Catholic chapel, a bank, a hospital, and a supermarket.

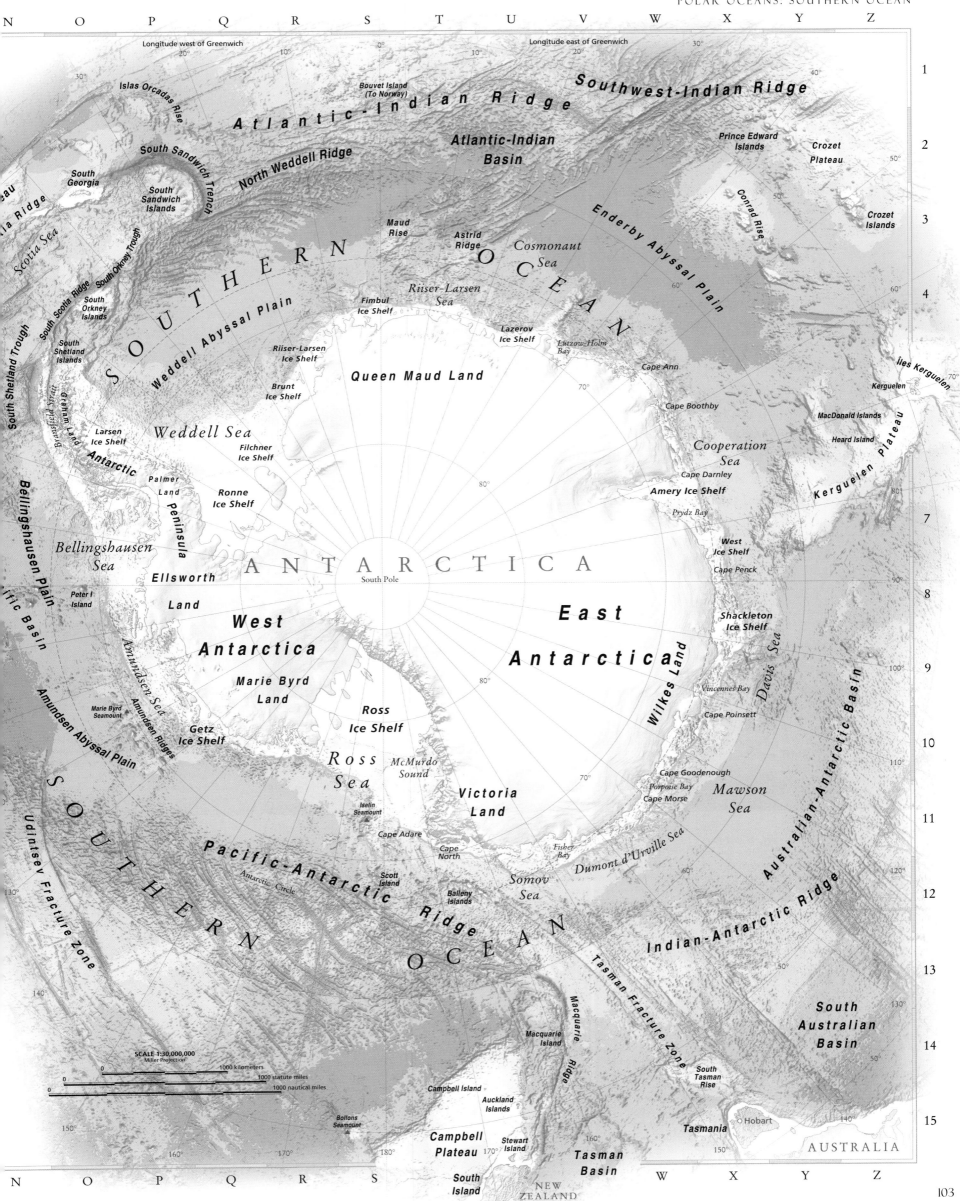

Longitude west of Greenwich
Longitude east of Greenwich

SOUTHERN OCEAN

Islas Orcadas Rise
Southwest-Indian Ridge
Atlantic-Indian Ridge
Bouvet Island (To Norway)
Atlantic-Indian Basin
Prince Edward Islands
Crozet Plateau
Crozet Islands

South Georgia
South Sandwich Islands
South Sandwich Trench
North Weddell Ridge
Conrad Rise

Scotia Sea
Maud Rise
Astrid Ridge
Cosmonaut Sea
Enderby Abyssal Plain

South Scotia Ridge
South Orkney Trough
Riiser-Larsen Sea
Fimbul Ice Shelf
Lazerov Ice Shelf
Lützow-Holm Bay
Iles Kerguelen

South Orkney Islands
Weddell Abyssal Plain
Queen Maud Land
Cape Ann
Kerguelen

South Shetland Islands
South Shetland Trough
Riiser-Larsen Ice Shelf
Cape Boothby
MacDonald Islands
Kerguelen Plateau

Graham Land
Bransfield Strait
Larsen Ice Shelf
Brunt Ice Shelf
Cooperation Sea
Heard Island

Weddell Sea
Filchner Ice Shelf
Cape Darnley
Amery Ice Shelf

Antarctic
Palmer Land
Ronne Ice Shelf
Prydz Bay

Bellingshausen Plain
Bellingshausen Sea
Peninsula
West Ice Shelf

Peter I Island
Ellsworth Land
ANTARCTICA
South Pole
Cape Penck

Pacific Basin
West Antarctica
East Antarctica
Shackleton Ice Shelf

Marie Byrd Land
Davis Sea
Wilkes Land
Australian-Antarctic Basin

Amundsen Abyssal Plain
Amundsen Ridges
Amundsen Sea
Marie Byrd Seamount
Getz Ice Shelf
Ross Ice Shelf
Vincennes Bay
Cape Poinsett

Ross Sea
McMurdo Sound
Victoria Land
Cape Goodenough
Porpoise Bay
Cape Morse
Mawson Sea

Iselin Seamount
Somov Sea
Fisher Bay
Dumont d'Urville Sea

Udintsev Fracture Zone
Pacific-Antarctic Ridge
Cape Adare
Cape North
Indian-Antarctic Ridge

SOUTHERN OCEAN
Antarctic Circle
Scott Island
Balleny Islands
Tasman Fracture Zone

Macquarie Ridge
Macquarie Island
South Australian Basin

SCALE 1:30,000,000
Miller Projection
1000 kilometers
1000 statute miles
1000 nautical miles

South Tasman Rise

Campbell Island
Auckland Islands
Tasmania
Hobart

Bollons Seamount
Campbell Plateau
Stewart Island
Tasman Basin
AUSTRALIA

South Island
NEW ZEALAND

103

ANTARCTIC PENINSULA

The Antarctic Peninsula and the islands of the Scotia Arc form stepping stones between South America and West Antarctica—a path first traced by early 19th-century sealers, and now followed each summer by thousands of cruise ship tourists. Geologically the peninsula is a southern extension of the Andes, heavily glaciated as the southern Andes formerly were, and invested with pack ice for several months each year. Climatically and biologically it forms a separate province, the Maritime Antarctic. It is much warmer year-round than continental Antarctica and has richer vegetation. The Weddell Sea, east of the peninsula, is renowned for its circulating pack ice that caught and destroyed Shackleton's expedition ship *Endurance*. Accessibility made the peninsula the most favored sector of Antarctica for early 20th-century exploration and the starting region for Antarctic whaling. Currently it is favored by more than 20 nations for research stations that give them access to membership of the Antarctic Treaty, and thus a political stake in Antarctica itself.

Cruise ships
Tens of thousands of tourists now visit Antarctica each summer, most of them on cruise ships that, like this one, land their passengers at penguin colonies and other points of interest. Bigger ships carrying more than 500 passengers cruise the scenic waterways but make no landings.

Peninsula scenery
While more than 95 percent of Antarctica's coastal scenery is ice cliffs, with no mountains visible, the west coast of the Antarctic Peninsula features spectacular mountains, islands, and channels, that in recent years have made it a major tourist attraction. Piedmont ice cliffs and glaciers line the shores.

Drifting icebergs
Icebergs breaking from Antarctic glaciers and ice shelves drift around the continent with the pack ice, taking several years to melt and crumble. Tourist visitors delight in their infinite variety. Scientists use satellite imagery to follow their progress, gaining information about sea currents and climatic variation.

Argentine station
The peninsula sector, which is more accessible than the rest of Antarctica through its longer summer period, supports the scientific research stations of many nations. The Argentine station, Esperanza, (above) is a small community with comfortable facilities for overwintering scientists and their families.

→ Antarctic Circumpolar Current
→ Antarctic Coastal Current
→ Weddell Sea Gyre

Farwell Island

Thurston Island

Abbot Ice Shelf

Eights Coast

Sherman Island

King Peninsula

Pine Island Bay

Walgreen Coast

Fur seals
From their discovery in the late 18th century, fur-seal (*Arctocephalus gazella*) colonies brought northern hemisphere sealers to the Antarctic Peninsula. Hundreds of thousands of seals were killed for their skins. Sealers explored the islands and channels, recording many geographical discoveries throughout the region.

Surface currents
The predominantly westward-flowing Antarctic Coastal Current, encountering the eastern shore of the peninsula, fills the Weddell Sea with a massive, persistent gyre of multi-year sea ice. This rotates southward along the Coats Land coast, and packs northward-moving masses of ice tightly against the peninsula flank.

N O P Q R S T U V W X Y Z

1

BATHYMETRIC
DEPTHS

Feet	Meters
Sea level	Sea level
656	200
1640	500
3281	1000
6562	2000
9842	3000
13,123	4000
16,404	5000
19,685	6000
26,246	8,000

SCALE 1:10,000,000
Miller Projection

0   200 kilometers
0   200 statute miles
0   200 nautical miles

Scotia

Sea

Ona
Basin

Shackleton Fracture Zone

South Scotia Ridge South Orkney Trough

Coronation
Island

Elephant
Island

Clarence
Island

South Shetland Trench

King George
Island

Loper Channel

South Orkney
Islands

Laurie
Island

South Shetland
Islands

Powell
Basin

Nelson Island
Greenwich Island

Livingston Island

Snow Island

Deception
Island

d'Urville Island

Joinville Island

Smith Island

Low Island

Bransfield Strait

Dundee Island

Vega Island

James Ross Island

Brabant Island

Snowhill Island

Cape Longing

Anvers Island

Robertson Island

Cape Disappointment

Aurora Canyon

Weddell

Renaud Island

Jason Peninsula

Yelcho Canyon

Antarctic Circle

Abyssal

Biscoe Islands

Lavoisier Island

Cape Alexander
Cole Peninsula

Graham Land

Larsen
Ice
Shelf

San Martin Canyon

Plain

Adelaide
Island

Hollick-Kenyon Peninsula

Endurance Canyon

Weddell *Sea*

Marguerite
Bay

Hearst Island

Antarctic Peninsula

Ewing Island

rcot
and

Rothschild
Island

Wilkins
Sound

Dolleman Island

Steele Island

Antarctic Canyon

ataday
land

Alexander Island

Palmer Land

George VI Sound

Black Coast

Odom Inlet

Uruguay Canyon

Beethoven
Peninsula

Kemp Peninsula

Cape Mackintosh

Deutschland Canyon

Ronne Entrance

Cape Deacon
Cape Brooks

General
Belgrano
Bank

Cape Norvegia

Smyley
Island

Spaatz
Island

English Coast

Lassiter Coast

Cape Fiske

Lyddan
Island

Riiser-Larsen Ice Shelf

berg
insula

Bowman Peninsula

Brunt Ice Shelf

Crown Princess Martha Coast

Gardner Inlet

nin Bay
st

Orville Coast

Caird Coast

Seafloor topography
This image shows the Antarctic Peninsula
emerging from the continent, with the off-
lying chain of South Shetland Islands to the
right. The Weddell Sea (left) is lined with ice
shelves ending in steep ice cliffs. Also visible
is the submarine ridge linking the peninsula
with southern South America.

Ronne
Ice Shelf

Evans Ice
Stream

Filchner Ice Shelf

Luitpold Coast

Coats Land

Korff
Ice Rise

Berkner
Island

Carlson Inlet

Henry
Ice Rise

Antarctica

Antarctic Peninsula

Weddell Sea

South
Shetland
Islands

Scotia
Sea

Shackelton Trench

A N T A R C T I C A

80° 100° 90° 80° 70° 60° 50° 40°

Longitude west of Greenwich

N O P Q R S T U

ROSS SEA

One of two great embayments in the flanks of Antarctica, the Ross Sea was discovered by Capt. James Clark Ross, RN, on a Royal Navy expedition of 1841. Despite its high latitude, circulation of pack ice within the Ross Sea allows ships of minimal icebreaking capacity to reach 78°S, making it a gateway for land expeditions to reach the South Pole. The southern limit of the sea is the Ross Ice Shelf, a huge floating sheet of glacier ice that descends from the high plateau of central Antarctica and terminates in a continuous ice cliff 500 miles (800 km) long. Land-based expeditions led by Scott, Shackleton, Amundsen, Borchgrevink, Byrd, and others made use of the gateway to explore inland, in particular to reach the south geographic and magnetic poles. McMurdo Sound is currently the site of McMurdo Station, Antarctica's largest township. Its population varies from about 250 in winter to 1,200 in summer.

Shackleton's team
Ernest Shackleton (centre left) and three companions in 1908-09 discovered a route from McMurdo Sound, in the southwestern Ross Sea, via Beardmore Glacier to the South Pole. The route is today used by US tractor trains to replenish Amundsen-Scott, the permanent US South Pole station.

Ice cliffs
On the southern flank of Ross Island, Windless Bight's heavily-glaciated cliffs face the Ross Ice Shelf. It was named by a party from Scott's Terra Nova expedition of 1910–13, who found it an oasis of calm on their otherwise storm-ridden journey to Cape Crozier.

Emperor penguins
Largest of all living penguins, emperor penguins (*Aptenodytes forsteri*) live in Antarctic coastal colonies as far south as Cape Crozier, Ross Island, incubating their single eggs on the sea ice in winter, and rearing their chicks through early spring. Fewer than 50 colonies are known around the continent.

McMurdo Station

McMurdo Station was established by the United States in 1955 as the logistical base from which Amundsen-Scott (South Pole) and other Antarctic stations and camps could be established and re-supplied. Currently involving some 90 buildings, it is a township with laboratories, workshops, garaging, fuel stores, airstrips, shops, and accommodation for more than 1,000 support staff and scientists.

Symbol of the past. Erected in 1902, this hut was an emergency depot for Scott's expedition ship *Discovery*, which lay frozen in close by. Solitary for half a century, it stands on the edge of McMurdo Station, Antarctica's largest and busiest community

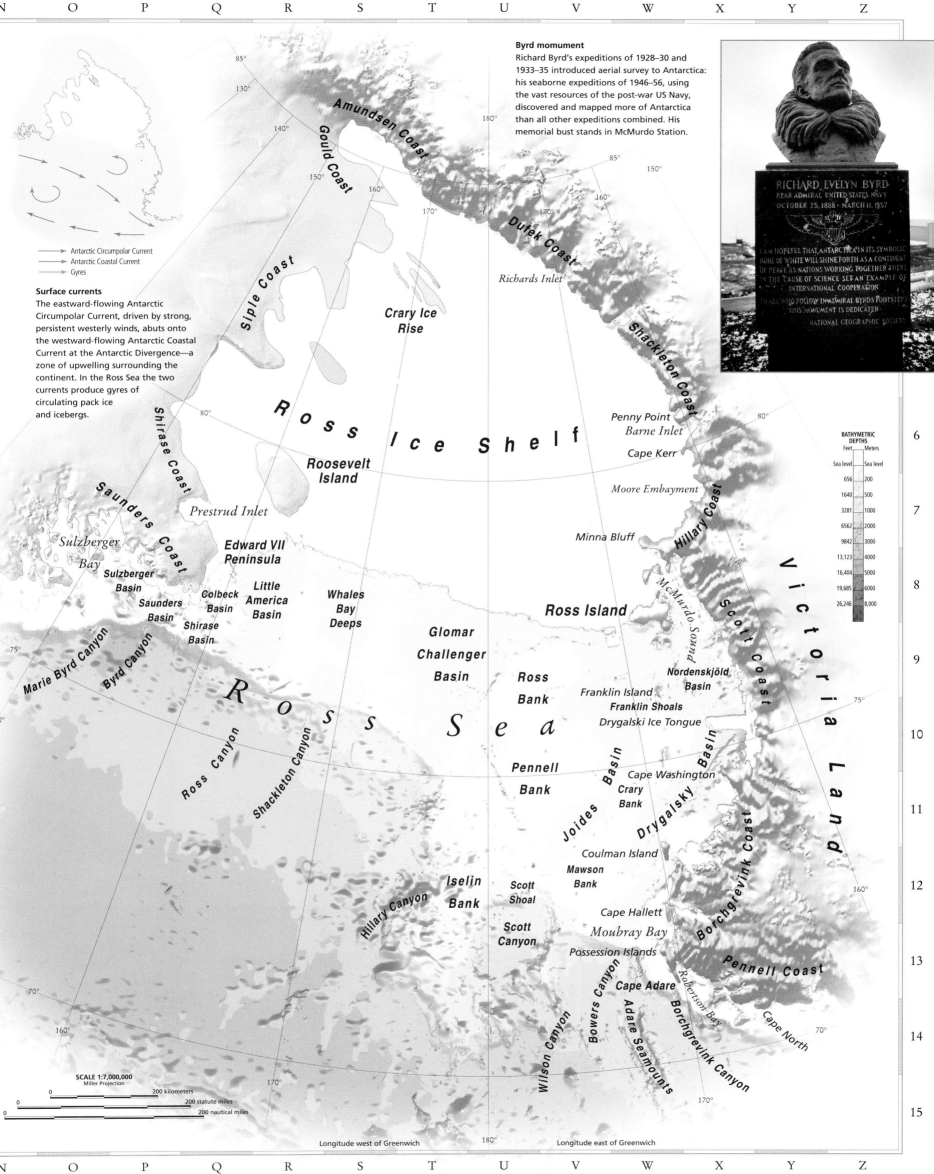

Byrd momument

Richard Byrd's expeditions of 1928–30 and 1933–35 introduced aerial survey to Antarctica: his seaborne expeditions of 1946–56, using the vast resources of the post-war US Navy, discovered and mapped more of Antarctica than all other expeditions combined. His memorial bust stands in McMurdo Station.

Surface currents

The eastward-flowing Antarctic Circumpolar Current, driven by strong, persistent westerly winds, abuts onto the westward-flowing Antarctic Coastal Current at the Antarctic Divergence—a zone of upwelling surrounding the continent. In the Ross Sea the two currents produce gyres of circulating pack ice and icebergs.

→ Antarctic Circumpolar Current
→ Antarctic Coastal Current
→ Gyres

BATHYMETRIC DEPTHS	
Feet	Meters
Sea level	Sea level
656	200
1640	500
3281	1000
6562	2000
9842	3000
13,123	4000
16,404	5000
19,685	6000
26,246	8,000

SCALE 1:7,000,000
Miller Projection

200 kilometers
200 statute miles
200 nautical miles

Longitude west of Greenwich   Longitude east of Greenwich

The rugged shoreline of southern Cape Breton Island, part of the
Canadian province of Nova Scotia, experiences frequent coastal fog.
The north Atlantic Ocean to the south and east, and the Gulf of
St Lawrence to the north and west, both have a considerable influence
on the weather here. Whale watching for pilot whales *(Globicephala
melas)* has become key to the island's economy.

ATLANTIC OCEAN

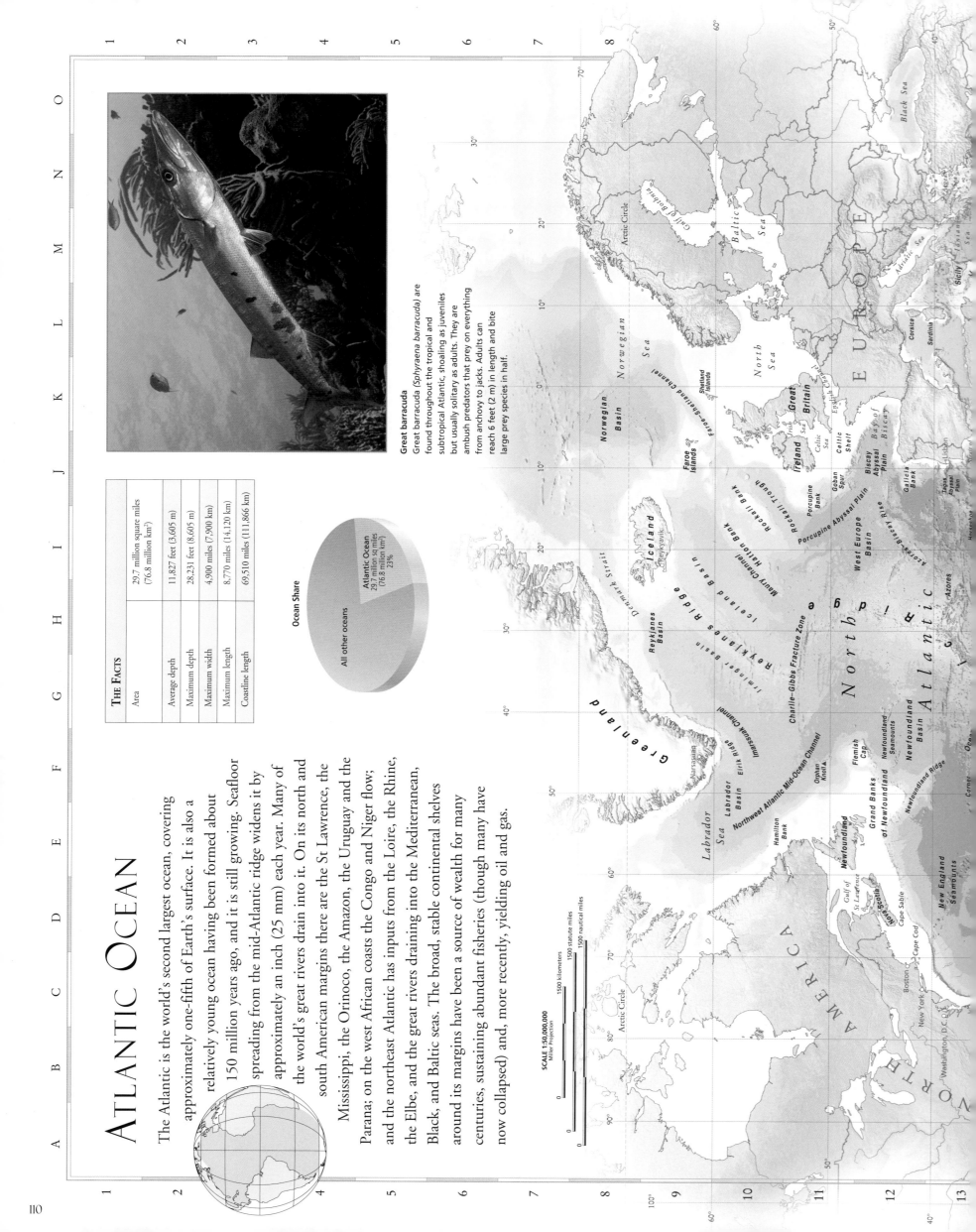

ATLANTIC OCEAN

The Atlantic is the world's second largest ocean, covering approximately one-fifth of Earth's surface. It is also a relatively young ocean having been formed about 150 million years ago, and it is still growing. Seafloor spreading from the mid-Atlantic ridge widens it by approximately an inch (25 mm) each year. Many of the world's great rivers drain into it. On its north and south American margins there are the St Lawrence, the Mississippi, the Orinoco, the Amazon, the Uruguay and the Parana; on the west African coasts the Congo and Niger flow; and the northeast Atlantic has inputs from the Loire, the Rhine, the Elbe, and the great rivers draining into the Mediterranean, Black, and Baltic seas. The broad, stable continental shelves around its margins have been a source of wealth for many centuries, sustaining abundant fisheries (though many have now collapsed) and, more recently, yielding oil and gas.

THE FACTS

Area	29.7 million square miles (76.8 million km²)
Average depth	11,827 feet (3,605 m)
Maximum depth	28,231 feet (8,605 m)
Maximum width	4,900 miles (7,900 km)
Maximum length	8,770 miles (14,120 km)
Coastline length	69,510 miles (111,866 km)

Ocean Share

All other oceans

Atlantic Ocean
29.7 million sq miles
(76.8 million km²)
23%

Great barracuda
Great barracuda (*Sphyraena barracuda*) are found throughout the tropical and subtropical Atlantic, shoaling as juveniles but usually solitary as adults. They are ambush predators that prey on everything from anchovy to jacks. Adults can reach 6 feet (2 m) in length and bite large prey species in half.

SCALE 1:50,000,000
Miller Projection

1500 kilometers
1500 statute miles
1500 nautical miles

EUROPE

Black Sea

Gulf of Bothnia

Baltic Sea

Arctic Circle

Norwegian Sea

North Sea

Adriatic Sea

Sicily

Corsica

Sardinia

Tyrrhenian Sea

Lisbon

Tagus Abyssal Plain

Azores

Azores–Biscay Rise

Bay of Biscay

Galicia Bank

Biscay Abyssal Plain

Goban Spur

English Channel

Celtic Sea

Celtic Shelf

Irish Sea

Ireland

Great Britain

Shetland Islands

Faroe Islands

Faroe–Shetland Channel

Norwegian Basin

Iceland
Reykjavik

Denmark Strait

Reykjanes Basin

Irminger Basin

Iceland Basin

Hatton Bank

Maury Channel

Rockall Bank

Rockall Trough

Porcupine Bank

Porcupine Abyssal Plain

West Europe Basin

Reykjanes Ridge

Charlie–Gibbs Fracture Zone

North Atlantic

Mid-Atlantic Ridge

Greenland

Narsassuaq

Eirik Ridge

Irminger Ridge

Northwest Atlantic Mid-Ocean Channel

Labrador Sea

Labrador Basin

Orphan Knoll

Flemish Cap

Newfoundland

Grand Banks of Newfoundland

Newfoundland Basin

Newfoundland Seamounts

Newfoundland Ridge

Hamilton Bank

Gulf of St Lawrence

Nova Scotia

Cape Sable

New England Seamounts

Cape Cod

Boston

New York

Washington, D.C.

NORTH AMERICA

Arctic Circle

110

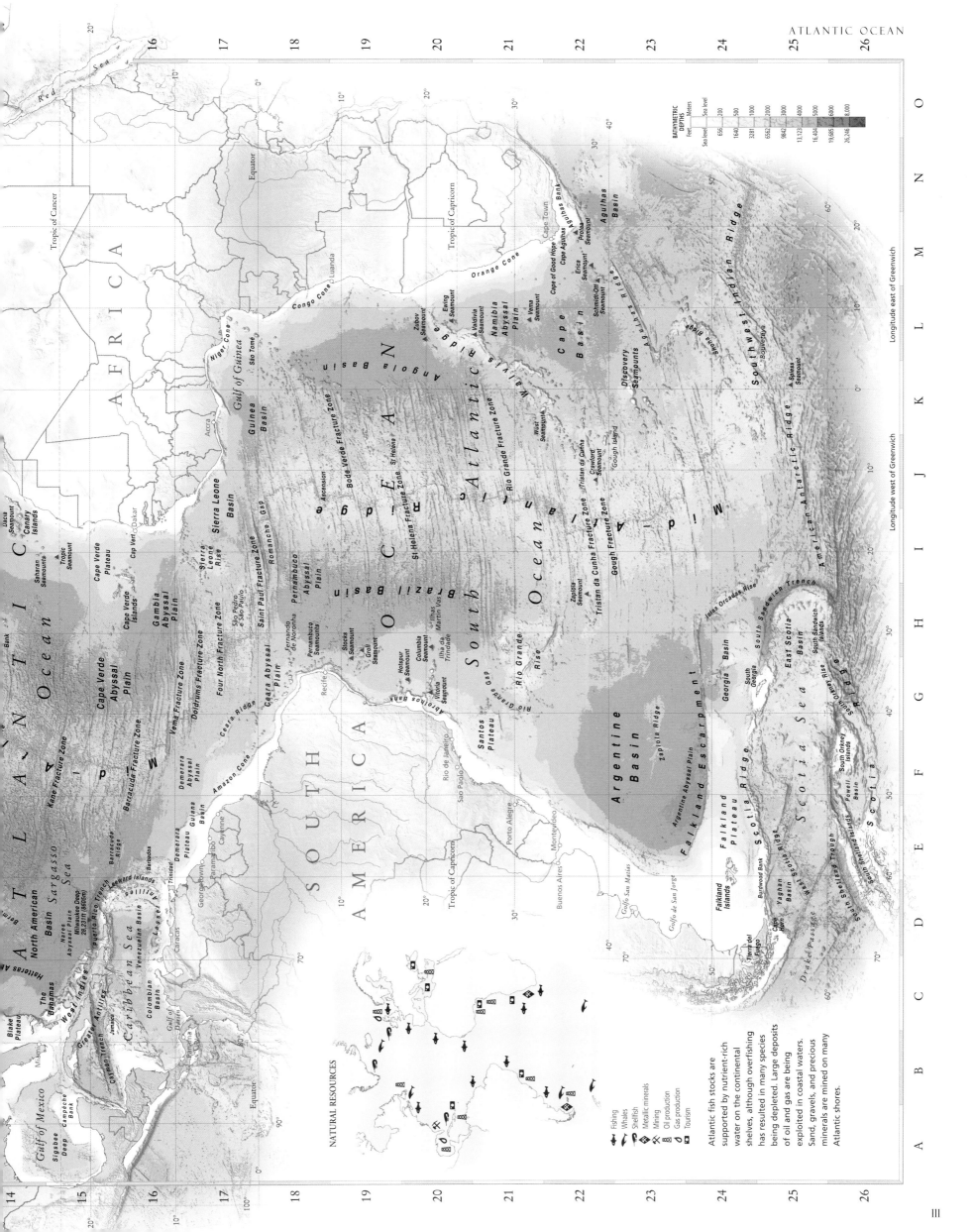

Northern Atlantic Ocean

The circulation of the water masses of the North Atlantic shapes the climate of adjacent landmasses. The Coriolis effect, produced by Earth's rotation, causes the water in the North Atlantic to circulate clockwise. This has the effect of causing warm water from the Gulf of Mexico and the Caribbean to be carried northward along the east coast of North America as the Gulf Stream. It meets the cold waters of the Labrador Current off Newfoundland, giving rise to the notorious fogs of the Grand Banks. Some of the warmer water continues eastward as the North Atlantic Drift that creates the relatively warm and wet climate of northwest Europe. The eventual cooling and sinking of the North Atlantic Drift water forms a deep water mass known as North Atlantic bottom water and helps to drive the "Ocean Conveyor" system of deep water currents that connect the world's oceans.

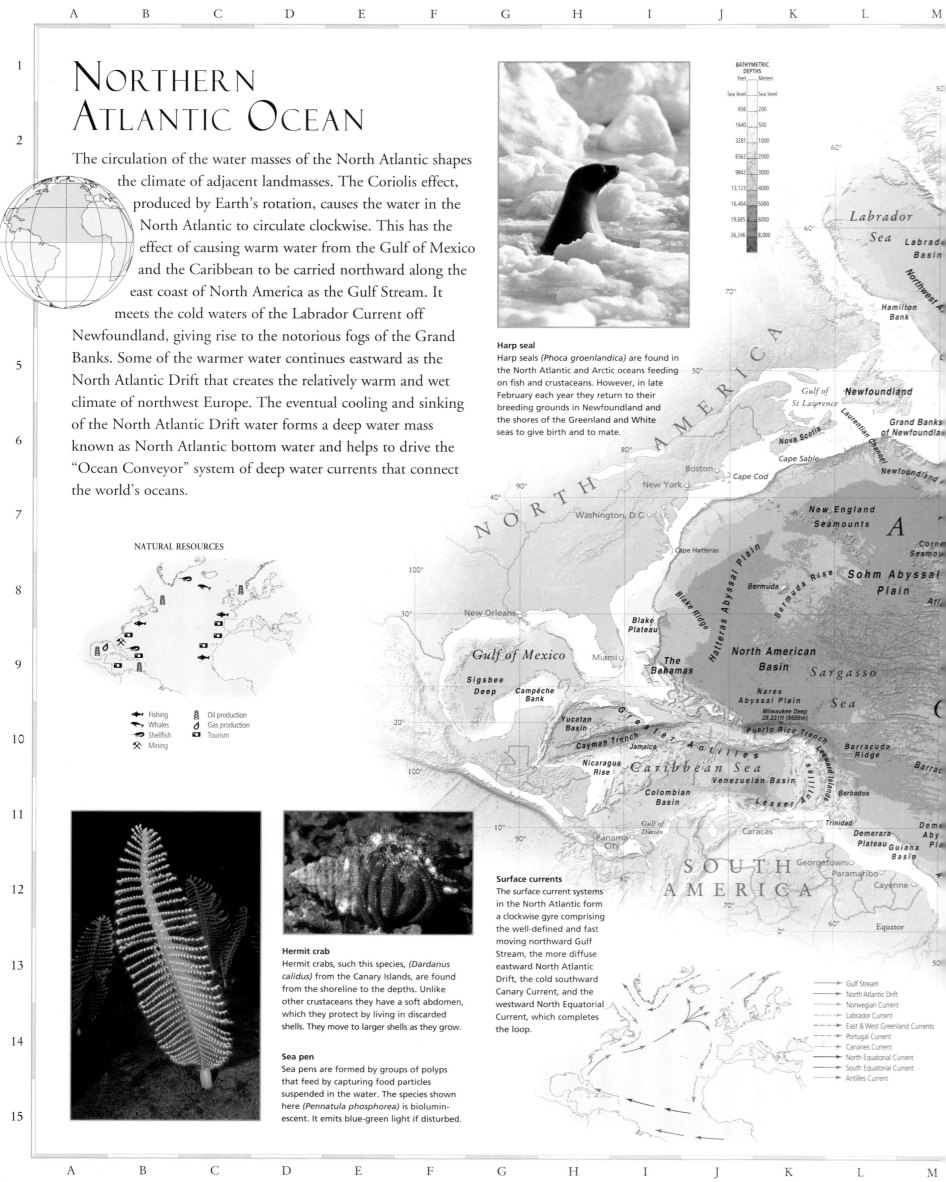

Harp seal
Harp seals (*Phoca groenlandica*) are found in the North Atlantic and Arctic oceans feeding on fish and crustaceans. However, in late February each year they return to their breeding grounds in Newfoundland and the shores of the Greenland and White seas to give birth and to mate.

NATURAL RESOURCES

Fishing
Whales
Shellfish
Mining
Oil production
Gas production
Tourism

Hermit crab
Hermit crabs, such this species, *(Dardanus calidus)* from the Canary Islands, are found from the shoreline to the depths. Unlike other crustaceans they have a soft abdomen, which they protect by living in discarded shells. They move to larger shells as they grow.

Sea pen
Sea pens are formed by groups of polyps that feed by capturing food particles suspended in the water. The species shown here (*Pennatula phosphorea*) is bioluminescent. It emits blue-green light if disturbed.

Surface currents
The surface current systems in the North Atlantic form a clockwise gyre comprising the well-defined and fast moving northward Gulf Stream, the more diffuse eastward North Atlantic Drift, the cold southward Canary Current, and the westward North Equatorial Current, which completes the loop.

Gulf Stream
North Atlantic Drift
Norwegian Current
Labrador Current
East & West Greenland Currents
Portugal Current
Canaries Current
North Equatorial Current
South Equatorial Current
Antilles Current

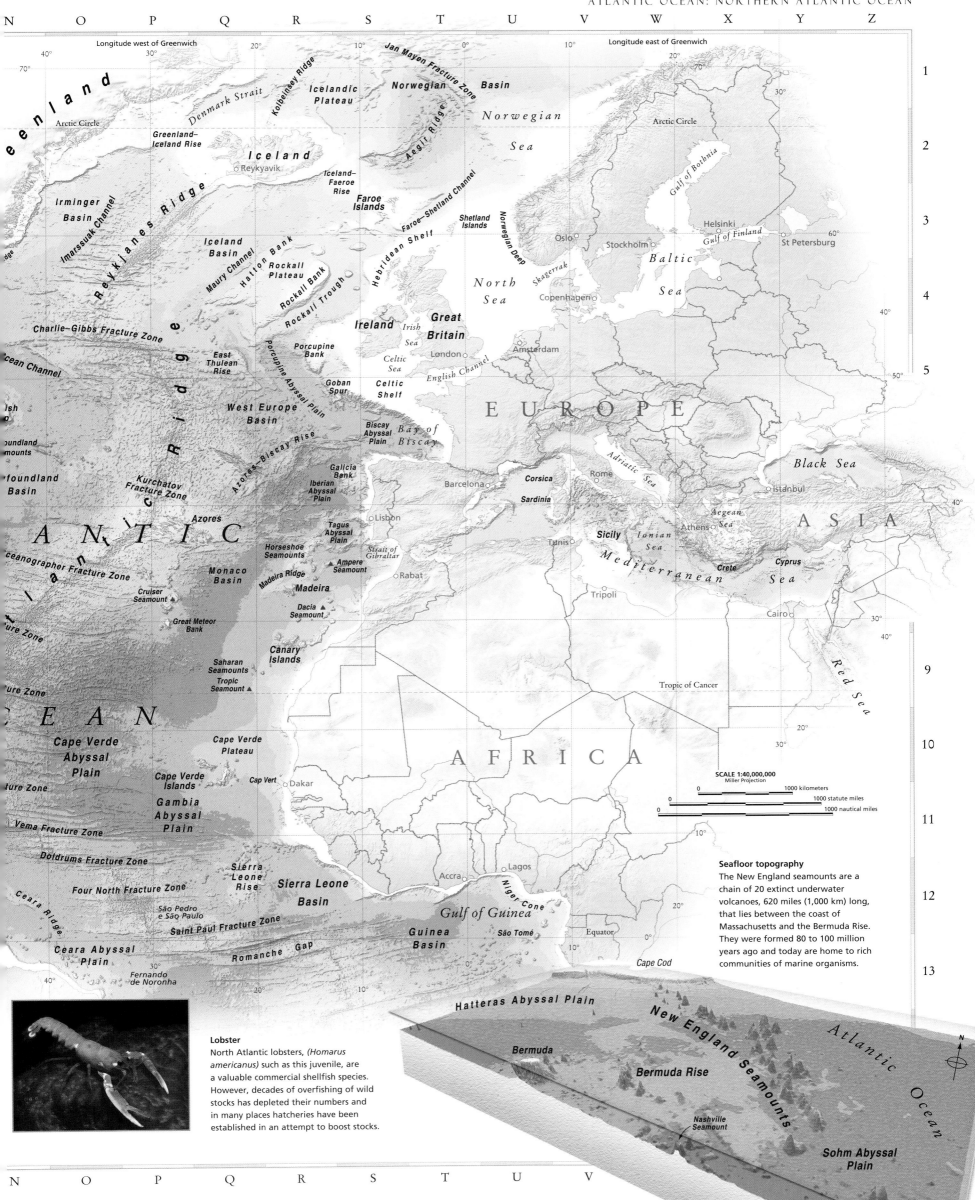

N O P Q R S T U V W X Y Z

Longitude west of Greenwich   Longitude east of Greenwich

eenland

Arctic Circle

Denmark Strait

Kolbeinsey Ridge

Icelandic Plateau

Jan Mayen Fracture Zone

Norwegian Basin

Norwegian Sea

Arctic Circle

Greenland–Iceland Rise

Iceland

Reykyavik

Gulf of Bothnia

Irminger Basin

Imarssuak Channel

Iceland–Faeroe Rise

Faroe Islands

Aegir Ridge

Helsinki

St Petersburg

Gulf of Finland

Iceland Basin

Maury Channel

Hatton Bank

Rockall Plateau

Rockall Bank

Iceland–Faeroe Shelf

Faroe–Shetland Channel

Shetland Islands

Norwegian Deep

Oslo

Stockholm

Baltic Sea

North Sea

Ridge

East Thulean Rise

Rockall Trough

Porcupine Bank

Skagerrak

Copenhagen

Charlie–Gibbs Fracture Zone

Ocean Channel

Porcupine Abyssal Plain

Ireland

Irish Sea

Great Britain

EUROPE

undland mounts

foundland Basin

West Europe Basin

Goban Spur

Celtic Sea

Celtic Shelf

London

Amsterdam

ish

Azores–Biscay Rise

Biscay Abyssal Plain

Bay of Biscay

English Channel

Black Sea

Kurchatov Fracture Zone

Galicia Bank

Iberian Abyssal Plain

Corsica

Rome

Adriatic Sea

Istanbul

L A N T I C

Azores

Barcelona

Sardinia

ASIA

Oceanographer Fracture Zone

Tagus Abyssal Plain

Lisbon

Sicily

Ionian Sea

Aegean Sea

Athens

Cyprus

ure Zone

Cruiser Seamount

Horseshoe Seamounts

Madeira Ridge

Ampere Seamount

Strait of Gibraltar

Rabat

Tunis

Mediterranean

Crete

Cyprus Sea

Monaco Basin

Dacia Seamount

Madeira

Tripoli

ure Zone

Great Meteor Bank

Canary Islands

Cairo

E A N

Saharan Seamounts

Tropic Seamount

Tropic of Cancer

Red Sea

Cape Verde Abyssal Plain

Cape Verde Plateau

AFRICA

ure Zone

Cape Verde Islands

Cap Vert

Dakar

SCALE 1:40,000,000
Miller Projection

0   1000 kilometers

0   1000 statute miles

0   1000 nautical miles

Gambia Abyssal Plain

Vema Fracture Zone

Seafloor topography
The New England seamounts are a chain of 20 extinct underwater volcanoes, 620 miles (1,000 km) long, that lies between the coast of Massachusetts and the Bermuda Rise. They were formed 80 to 100 million years ago and today are home to rich communities of marine organisms.

Doldrums Fracture Zone

Four North Fracture Zone

Sierra Leone Rise

Sierra Leone Basin

Accra

Lagos

Ceara Ridge

São Pedro e São Paulo

Saint Paul Fracture Zone

Guinea Basin

Niger Cone

Ceara Abyssal Plain

Romanche Gap

Gulf of Guinea

São Tomé

Equator

Cape Cod

Fernando de Noronha

Hatteras Abyssal Plain

New England Seamounts

Atlantic Ocean

N

Bermuda

Bermuda Rise

Lobster
North Atlantic lobsters, *(Homarus americanus)* such as this juvenile, are a valuable commercial shellfish species. However, decades of overfishing of wild stocks has depleted their numbers and in many places hatcheries have been established in an attempt to boost stocks.

Nashville Seamount

Sohm Abyssal Plain

N O P Q R S T U V

1 2 3 4 5 9 10 11 12 13

70° 40° 30° 20° 10° 0° 10° 20° 30° 60° 50° 40° 30° 20° 10° 40° 20° 30° 10° 30°

North Sea

The North Sea is a semi-enclosed arm of the North Atlantic, with most ocean water flowing in through the north-western opening between Scotland and Norway and smaller volumes through the English Channel and the Strait of Dover. There are also substantial freshwater inputs from major rivers such as the Rhine. The margins of the North Sea comprise one of the most diverse coastal regions in the world, with a great variety of habitats (fjords, estuaries, deltas, banks, beaches, sandbanks and mudflats, marshes, rocks, and islands). Its coastal margins are also heavily populated and vulnerable to catastrophic flooding caused by storm surges that cause water levels to rise dramatically as winter storms and tides force water southward into the narrowing southern North Sea. Its once-abundant fish stocks, particularly cod and herring, have been seriously over-fished and the oil and gas fields that were first exploited in the 1970s are becoming exhausted.

THE FACTS	
Area	222,100 square miles (570,200 km²)
Average depth	308 feet (94 m)
Maximum depth	2,165 feet (660 m)
Maximum width	373 miles (600 km)
Maximum length	621 miles (100 km)

Oil drilling

The broad continental shelf of the North Atlantic that includes the North Sea contains large reserves of oil and gas. The first offshore wells were drilled in 1964 and commercial extraction began in the 1970s, but intense storms in the region make it a difficult working environment. The peak of production has now passed and many rigs are being decommissioned.

The worldwide outcry against the proposed deep-water dumping of a decommissioned North Sea rig in the 1990s forced oil companies to scrap all old rigs on land.

Atlantic puffin
Atlantic puffins (*Fratercula arctica*) feed on small fish that they catch just below the water's surface. In the breeding season both parents bring fish in their beaks to feed their chick. Sixty percent of the world's Atlantic puffins breed in Iceland.

Cliff erosion
Soft sandstone, exposed to the force of North Atlantic waves on the west coast of the Orkney Islands, erodes rapidly, causing the formation of sea stacks and rugged cliff faces.

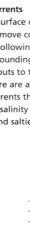

Coastal flooding
The low-lying coasts of the Netherlands and the east coast of England are vulnerable to flooding. In winter the funneling effect of the North Sea from north to south, high spring tides and strong northerly winds heap up the water in the southern North Sea.

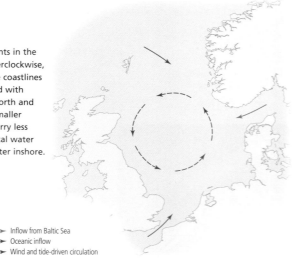

Hamburg Harbor
For centuries Hamburg has been the hub of sea-borne trade between central Europe and the rest of the world, firstly as one of the main Hanseatic league ports, in the 19th century as a major trans-Atlantic port, and now as a modern container port.

Surface currents
The main surface currents in the North Sea move counterclockwise, generally following the coastlines of the surrounding land with oceanic inputs to the north and south. There are also smaller surface currents that carry less dense low salinity coastal water offshore and saltier water inshore.

→ Inflow from Baltic Sea
→ Oceanic inflow
---→ Wind and tide-driven circulation

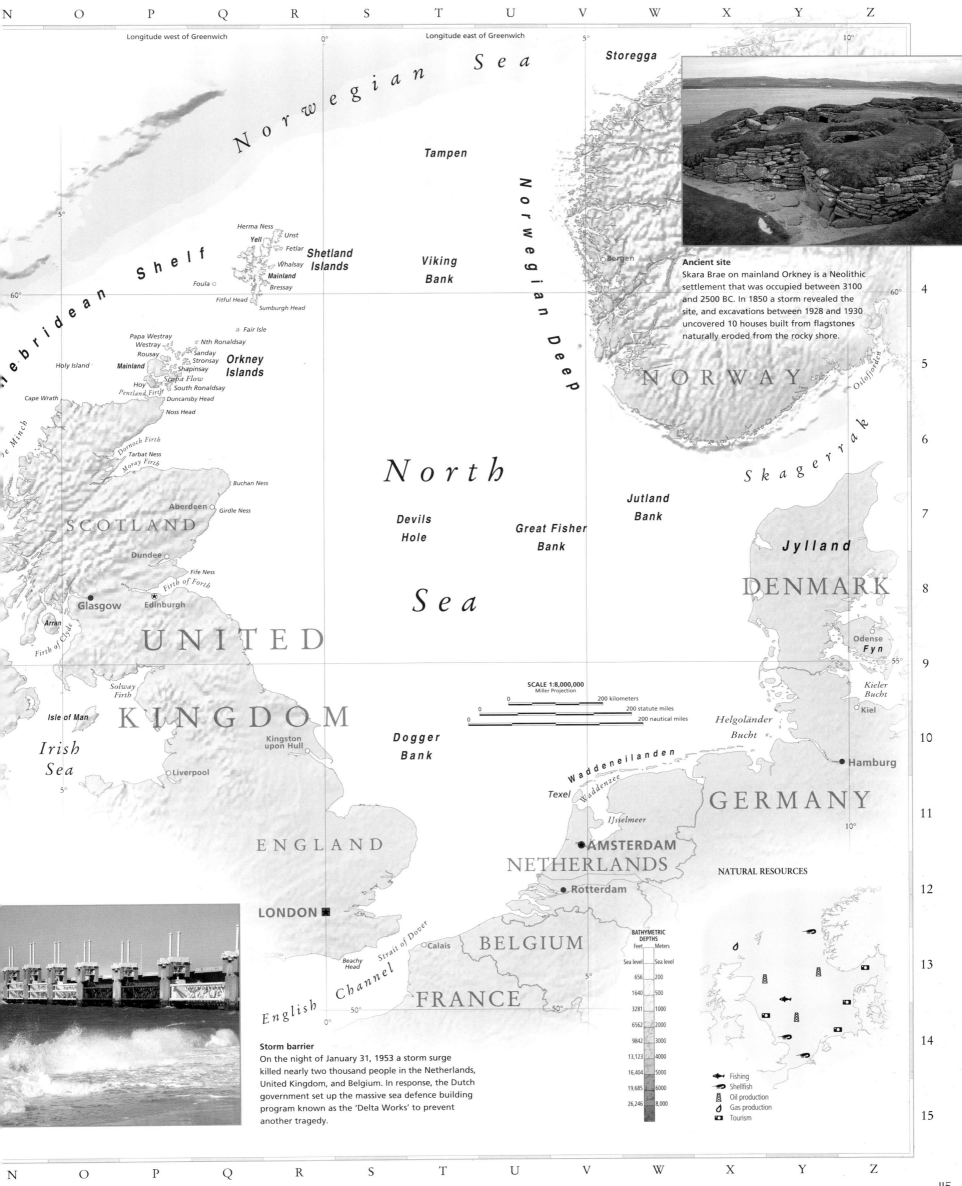

N O P Q R S T U V W X Y Z

Longitude west of Greenwich   0°   Longitude east of Greenwich   5°   10°

Norwegian Sea

Storegga

Tampen

Norwegian Deep

Herma Ness
Yell   Unst
Fetlar
Whalsay   **Shetland**
Mainland   **Islands**
Foula ◦   Bressay

Viking
Bank

Bergen

Fitful Head
Sumburgh Head

Fair Isle

Hebridean Shelf

Ancient site
Skara Brae on mainland Orkney is a Neolithic settlement that was occupied between 3100 and 2500 BC. In 1850 a storm revealed the site, and excavations between 1928 and 1930 uncovered 10 houses built from flagstones naturally eroded from the rocky shore.

60°   60°   4

Papa Westray
Westray
Rousay   Sanday
Mainland   Stronsay
Holy Island   Shapinsay
Hoy   Scapa Flow   South Ronaldsay
Pentland Firth   Duncansby Head
Cape Wrath   Noss Head

Nth Ronaldsay
Orkney
Islands

N O R W A Y

Oslofjorden

5

The Minch

Dornoch Firth
Tarbat Ness
Moray Firth

Buchan Ness

North

Skagerrak

6

SCOTLAND

Aberdeen   Girdle Ness

Dundee

Fife Ness
Firth of Forth

Devils
Hole

Great Fisher
Bank

Jutland
Bank

7

Sea

Jylland

Glasgow   **Edinburgh**

Arran
Firth of Clyde

U N I T E D

DENMARK

8

Solway
Firth

Odense
Fyn

55°   9

Isle of Man

K I N G D O M

Irish
Sea

Kieler
Bucht

SCALE 1:8,000,000
Miller Projection
0   200 kilometers
0   200 statute miles
0   200 nautical miles

Helgoländer
Bucht

Kiel

10

Dogger
Bank

Kingston
upon Hull

Hamburg

Liverpool

Waddeneilanden

Texel   *Waddenzee*

G E R M A N Y

11
10°

E N G L A N D

IJsselmeer

●AMSTERDAM

NETHERLANDS

NATURAL RESOURCES

12

● Rotterdam

LONDON ★

BELGIUM

Calais

Beachy
Head

Strait of Dover

BATHYMETRIC
DEPTHS

Feet   Meters

13

English

Channel

FRANCE

50°   50°

Sea level   Sea level
656   200
1640   500
3281   1000
6562   2000
9842   3000
13,123   4000
16,404   5000
19,685   6000
26,246   8,000

🐟 Fishing
🦐 Shellfish
Oil production
Gas production
Tourism

14

Storm barrier
On the night of January 31, 1953 a storm surge killed nearly two thousand people in the Netherlands, United Kingdom, and Belgium. In response, the Dutch government set up the massive sea defence building program known as the 'Delta Works' to prevent another tragedy.

15

N O P Q R S T U V W X Y Z

BALTIC SEA

The Baltic is the world's largest body of brackish water, with marine species found in the saltier waters at the western end, and species that are intolerant of any salt in the fresh water at the eastern end where there are significant river inputs. The circulation of water in the Baltic is complex, with irregular inflows of salt water from the North Sea entering approximately every 10 years. The salt water enters via the Danish straits and slowly mixes with the brackish waters of the central part of the Baltic. There is also a permanent surface current carrying brackish water out into the North Sea. Within the Baltic there is a general counterclockwise circulation of water. The Baltic occupies a basin that was created by glacial erosion and since the removal of the ice sheet the land around and beneath the Baltic has been rising because of post-glacial rebound, making the sea smaller and shallower. In the last cenury the whole area has risen by at least four inches (100 mm) and the inner part of the Gulf of Bothnia will rise above sea level within the next 250 years.

Helsinki archipelago
The Finnish capital, Helsinki, is approximately midway along an archipelago of more than 300 small islands that lies parallel to the Finnish mainland. The archipelago was created by a post-glacial rise in sea level that left the tops of coastal hills as islands.

Kiel Canal
The Kiel Canal was begun in 1887 and completed in 1895. Its construction was driven by the wish of the German navy and merchant shipping interests to have a direct link between the North Sea and the German Baltic ports, avoiding the need to sail around Denmark.

THE FACTS	
Area	163,000 square miles (422,200 km²)
Average depth	180 feet (55 m)
Maximum depth	1,380 feet (421 km)
Maximum width	324 miles (540 km)
Maximum length	795 miles (1,280 km)

Ice floes
Baltic sea ice usually starts to form in the northern end of the Gulf of Bothnia in mid-November and extends south and westwards so that the open waters of Bothnian Bay are frozen by February. The Gulf of Finland and the Gulf of Riga are frozen by early January.

Gulf of Finland
Fast ice, attached to the shoreline, develops first, and then thinner more mobile pack or rafter ice forms in open water. This satellite image shows the pack ice, driven by the wind into fast ice, piling up into ridges up to 50 feet (15 m) high.

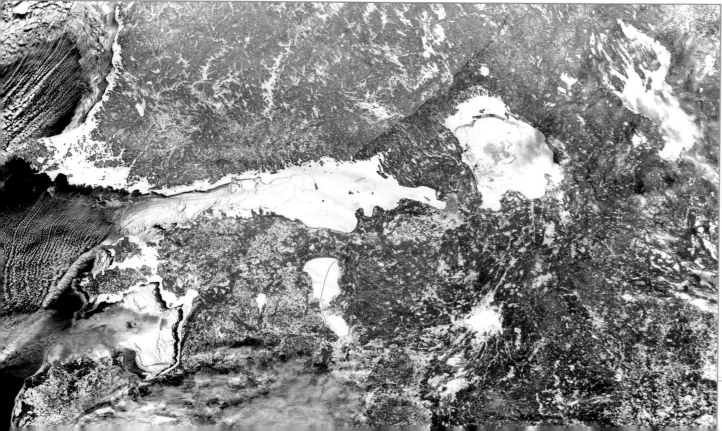

Surface currents
Apart from the well-defined outflow of brackish water through the Danish straits there is no clearly defined pattern of surface currents within the Baltic. Local surface currents are generated by prevailing winds and by the outflows of the larger rivers that discharge into the Baltic.

→ Outflow through Danish straits
→ Riverine inputs

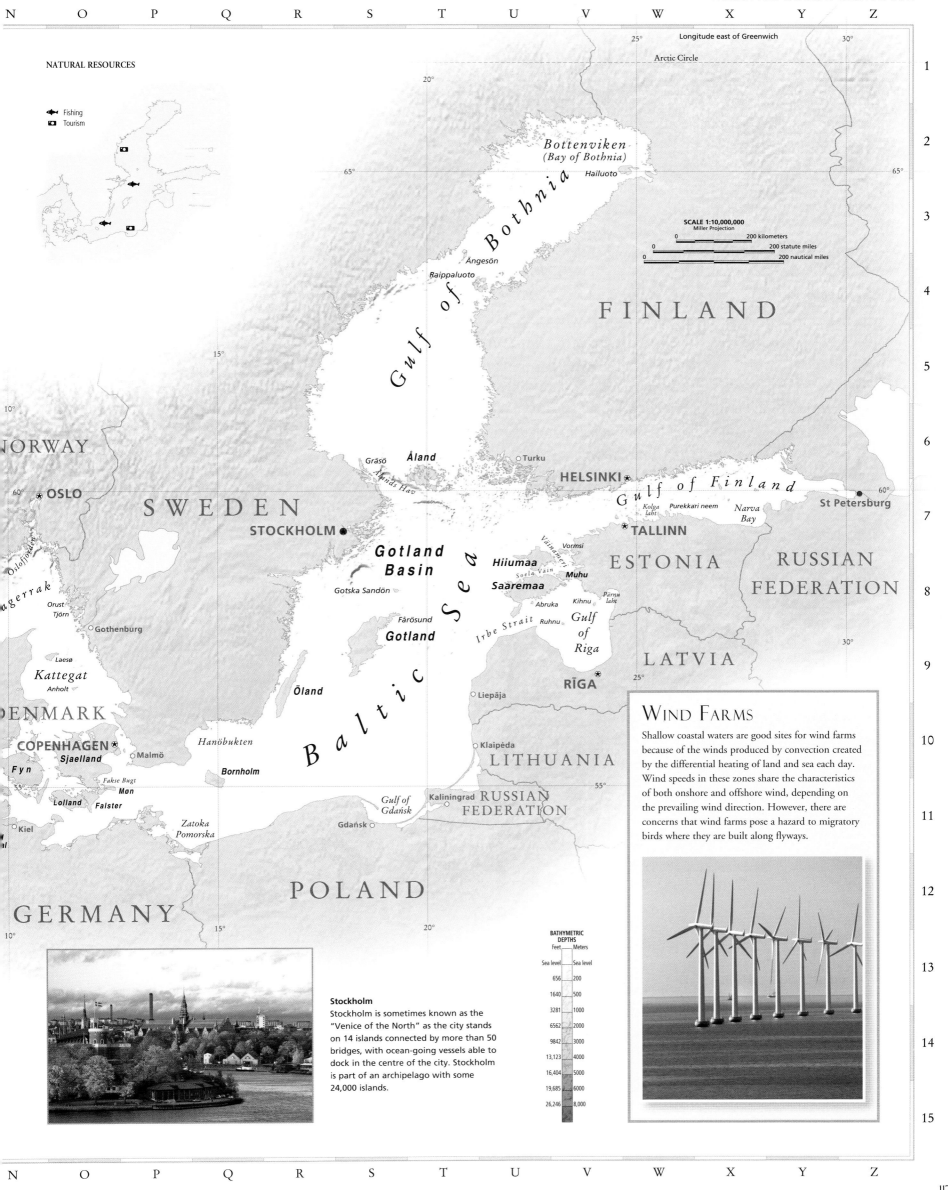

NATURAL RESOURCES

⚓ Fishing
📷 Tourism

Longitude east of Greenwich

Arctic Circle

Bottenviken
(Bay of Bothnia)

Hailuoto

SCALE 1:10,000,000
Miller Projection

0 — 200 kilometers
0 — 200 statute miles
0 — 200 nautical miles

Gulf of Bothnia

FINLAND

Ängesön

Raippaluoto

NORWAY

Gräsö
Ålands Hav
Åland

Turku

HELSINKI

Gulf of Finland

Kolga
laht
Purekkari neem
Narva
Bay

St Petersburg

SWEDEN

OSLO

STOCKHOLM

TALLINN

Oslofjorden

Gotland
Basin

Hiiumaa

Väinameri

Vormsi

ESTONIA

RUSSIAN
FEDERATION

Skagerrak

Orust
Tjörn

Gothenburg

Gotska Sandön

Soela Väin
Saaremaa

Muhu

Abruka
Kihnu

Pärnu
laht

Fårösund

Gotland

Irbe Strait
Ruhnu

Gulf
of
Riga

LATVIA

Laesø

Kattegat

Anholt

Öland

Liepāja

RĪGA

Baltic Sea

DENMARK

COPENHAGEN

Sjaelland

Hanöbukten

Klaipėda

LITHUANIA

Fyn

Malmö

Bornholm

Fakse Bugt

Møn

Lolland
Falster

Kiel

Zatoka
Pomorska

Gulf of
Gdańsk
Kaliningrad
RUSSIAN
FEDERATION
Gdańsk

WIND FARMS

Shallow coastal waters are good sites for wind farms
because of the winds produced by convection created
by the differential heating of land and sea each day.
Wind speeds in these zones share the characteristics
of both onshore and offshore wind, depending on
the prevailing wind direction. However, there are
concerns that wind farms pose a hazard to migratory
birds where they are built along flyways.

POLAND

GERMANY

BATHYMETRIC DEPTHS	
Feet	Meters
Sea level	Sea level
656	200
1640	500
3281	1000
6562	2000
9842	3000
13,123	4000
16,404	5000
19,685	6000
26,246	8,000

Stockholm

Stockholm is sometimes known as the
"Venice of the North" as the city stands
on 14 islands connected by more than 50
bridges, with ocean-going vessels able to
dock in the centre of the city. Stockholm
is part of an archipelago with some
24,000 islands.

GULF OF ST LAWRENCE

The Gulf of St Lawrence is considered to be the world's largest estuary, where the fresh water of the Great Lakes meets North Atlantic seawater. The size and shape of the gulf make it similar to an inland sea. It has a distinct ecosystem, characterized by partial isolation from the North Atlantic, a large freshwater runoff from the land, a deep trough running along its length, seasonal ice, the presence of a cold intermediate layer, shallow depths, and high biological productivity and diversity. The deep submarine trough, the Laurentian Channel, is a crucial component to the biology of the gulf as it brings in cold, nutrient-rich Atlantic water that slowly mixes and enriches the less dense overlying waters. The distinct qualities of the physical and biological components of the gulf combine to create its unique environment and its fishing grounds are an important regional economic asset. In the 1990s overfishing caused the collapse of cod and redfish stocks; the contribution of fishing to the regional economy is now maintained by the shellfish catch.

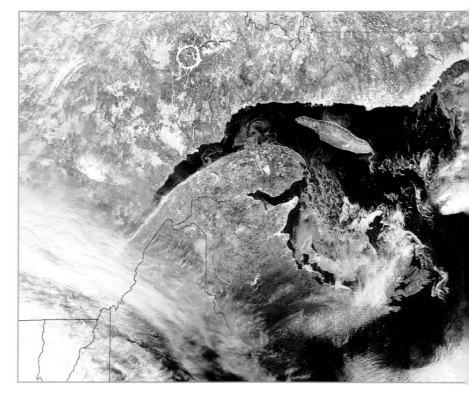

Gulf structure
The St Lawrence River flows northeastward, entering the gulf either side of Anticosti Island. The round shape in the upper middle of the image is Reservoir Manicouagan, which is a lake that now occupies a meteoric impact crater that was created 214 million years ago.

Navigation
Within the Gulf of St Lawrence the complex currents, numerous small islands, and the formation of winter ice are major hazards to navigation. The control of shipping movements and the provision of buoys, lighthouses, and other navigational aids are the responsibility of the Canadian Coast Guard.

Seafloor topography
Although the Newfoundland Ridge lies at the base of the North American continental shelf it was once part of the Iberian Peninsula. Geological studies show that as the early Atlantic widened, a small piece of continental crust was split off and subsided into the ocean.

Surface currents
Each spring, as the winter snows melt, the increased fresh water flows into the gulf from the St Lawrence River, the Saguenay River, and other rivers along the shores. This produces a low-salinity, higher-temperature surface layer of water that begins to flow toward the Atlantic Ocean.

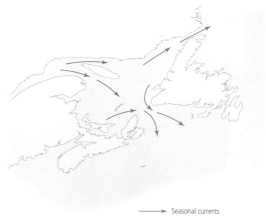

→ Seasonal currents

N O P Q R S T U V W X Y Z

Longitude east of Greenwich

55°

60°

Labrador

Belle Isle

65°

Strait of Belle Isle

Cape Bauld

Sea

C A N A D A
Q U É B E C

Grey Islands

White Bay

50°

Îles de Mingan

Détroit de Jacques-Cartier

Île d'Anticosti

Notre Dame Bay

Fogo Island

Pointe de l'Ouest

Détroit d'Honguedo

Pointe de l'Est

NEWFOUNDLAND AND LABRADOR

Bonavista Bay

Péninsule de Gaspé

Cap Gaspé

Gulf of

Cape St George

Newfoundland

Trinity Bay

Conception Bay

Chaleur Bay

Miscou Island

St Lawrence

St John's

Île Lamèque

Îles de la Madeleine

Île Brion

Cabot Strait

Île de l'Est

Avalon Peninsula

NEW BRUNSWICK

Miramichi Bay

Île du Harve Aubert

St Paul Island

Miquelon

Placentia Bay

St Mary's Bay

PRINCE EDWARD ISLAND

Cape North

Cape Breton Island

ST-PIERRE and MIQUELON (to France)

St-Pierre

ST-PIERRE

Fortune Bay

Prince Edward Island

Charlottetown

Northumberland Strait

St Georges Bay

Grand Banks of Newfoundland

Laurentian Channel

Chignecto Bay

Strait of Canso

Minas Channel

Minas Basin

Cape Canso

Grand Manan Island

NOVA SCOTIA

Halifax

Bay of Fundy

45°

Long Island

Ocean

55°

Gulf of Maine

Sable Island

Cape Sable Island

Atlantic

60°

65°

SCALE 1:8,000,000
Miller Projection

0   200 kilometers
0   200 statute miles
0   200 nautical miles

BATHYMETRIC DEPTHS

Feet	Meters
Sea level	Sea level
656	200
1640	500
3281	1000
6562	2000
9842	3000
13,123	4000
16,404	5000
19,685	6000
26,246	8,000

BARNACLES

Despite their appearance these goose or stalked barnacles are filter-feeding crustaceans. They begin life as larvae living in the water column but they will eventually settle on the surface of any floating object. Goose barnacles, unlike other encrusting barnacles, rely on external water movements, rather than the use of feathery limbs, known as cirri, to generate a feeding current.

NATURAL RESOURCES

Fishing
Whales
Tourism

Great cormorant
The great cormorant (*Phalacrocorax carbo*) is found throughout the world, with a sub-species that inhabits estuaries around the North Atlantic. In North America the only breeding colonies are found in the Canadian maritime provinces, with most found around the shores of the Gulf of St Lawrence.

N O P Q R S T U V W X Y Z

GULF OF MEXICO

The Gulf of Mexico is the ninth largest body of water on the planet and occupies a roughly circular basin whose formation continues to be the subject of geological debate. Seawater from the Caribbean Sea enters the gulf through the Yucatan Strait, circulates clockwise as the Loop Current, and exits through the Straits of Florida eventually forming the Gulf Stream. Portions of the Loop Current often break away forming eddies or gyres which affect regional current patterns. The gulf also receives huge volumes of fresh water from the river systems that drain into it, the largest being the Mississippi. However, excessive amounts of nutrients brought down by the rivers have caused algal blooms that create anoxic "dead zones" when they die. The wide continental margins of the gulf also contain large amounts of oil and gas that contribute a quarter of the United States' gas production and one-eighth of its oil production. In 2008 production was more than a million barrels of oil per day.

Mississippi Delta
This satellite image shows the algal blooms created by the upwelling of cold, nutrient-rich bottom water, caused by the plume of fresh water discharged from the Mississippi Delta. This river water does not fully mix with the surrounding seawater until it passes through the Straits of Florida.

Hurricane damage
Hurricane Katrina entered the Gulf of Mexico at the end of August 2005 and, although once it made its first landfall wind speeds dropped to 125 mph (205 km/h), it not only caused wind damage but also created a storm surge 20 feet (6 m) high, flooding nearly 80 percent of the city.

ⓘ Giant grouper
The giant grouper (*Epinephelus itajara*) is found in the Gulf of Mexico. However, this species is classified by the International Union for Conservation of Nature (IUCN) as critically endangered throughout its range. Its slow growth, low reproductive rate, and spawning behavior have made it especially susceptible to overfishing.

Algal blooms
Red tides, or "harmful algal blooms," in the Gulf of Mexico were first described by Spanish explorers in the 1530s and are mainly caused by *Gymnodinium breve*, a dinoflagellate. This organism produces powerful neurotoxins that cause fish-kills on a large scale and contaminate all forms of edible shellfish.

HURRICANES

Hurricanes, such as Katrina that devastated the Gulf Coast in 2005, form over warm tropical waters as rotating clusters of thunderstorms. The storm system spins faster as it moves away from the equator and the winds within increase in speed. Once the wind speed is above 74 miles per hour (120 km/h) it officially becomes a hurricane if it is in North America or the Caribbean.

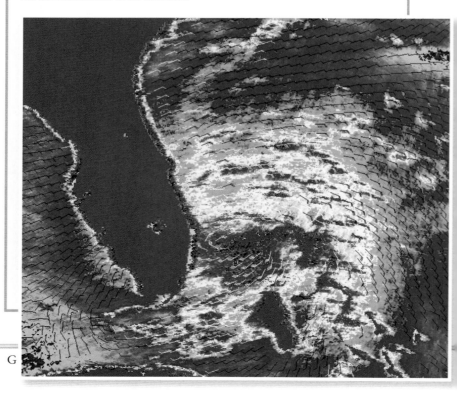

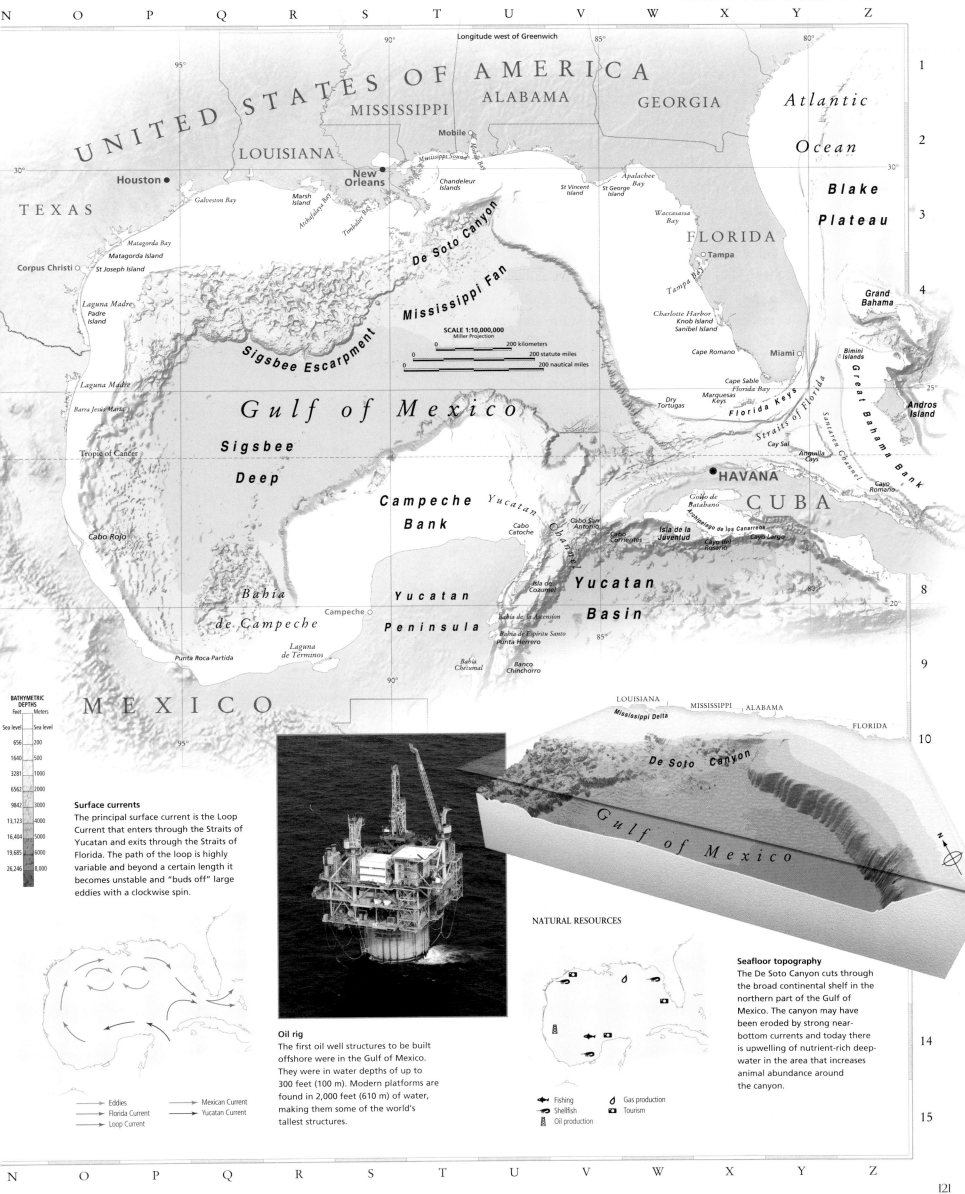

Map Labels

UNITED STATES OF AMERICA

MISSISSIPPI ALABAMA GEORGIA

Atlantic

Ocean

LOUISIANA

Mobile

Blake

TEXAS

New Orleans

Mississippi Sound *Mobile Bay*

Houston ●

Galveston Bay

Chandeleur Islands

St Vincent Island St George Island

Apalachee Bay

Plateau

Marsh Island

Atchafalaya Bay

Timbalier Bay

Waccasassa Bay

FLORIDA

Matagorda Bay

Matagorda Island

De Soto Canyon

○ Tampa

Corpus Christi ○ *St Joseph Island*

Mississippi Fan

Tampa Bay

Grand Bahama

Laguna Madre Padre Island

SCALE 1:10,000,000
Miller Projection

0   200 kilometers
0   200 statute miles
0   200 nautical miles

Charlotte Harbor
Knob Island
Sanibel Island

Bimini Islands

Laguna Madre

Sigsbee Escarpment

Cape Romano

Miami ○

Gulf of Mexico

Cape Sable *Florida Bay*

Great Bahama Bank

Andros Island

Barra Jesus Maria

Dry Tortugas *Marquesas Keys*

Florida Keys

Straits of Florida

Tropic of Cancer

Sigsbee

Deep

Cay Sal

Santaren Channel

Anguilla Cays

Cayo Romano

Cabo Rojo

Campeche

Bank

Yucatan Channel

Cabo San Antonio

HAVANA ●

Golfo de Batabanó

CUBA

Archipelago de los Canarreos

Cabo Catoche

Cabo Corrientes

Isla de la Juventud

Cayo del Rosario

Cayo Largo

Bahia de Campeche

Yucatan

Campeche ○

Isla de Cozumel

Yucatan

Basin

Peninsula

Bahía de la Ascensión

Bahía de Espíritu Santo
Punta Herrero

Punta Roca Partida

Laguna de Términos

Bahía Chetumal

Banco Chinchorro

MEXICO

BATHYMETRIC DEPTHS

Feet	Meters
Sea level	Sea level
656	200
1640	500
3281	1000
6562	2000
9842	3000
13,123	4000
16,404	5000
19,685	6000
26,246	8,000

Surface currents

The principal surface current is the Loop Current that enters through the Straits of Yucatan and exits through the Straits of Florida. The path of the loop is highly variable and beyond a certain length it becomes unstable and "buds off" large eddies with a clockwise spin.

→ Eddies

→ Florida Current

→ Loop Current

→ Mexican Current

→ Yucatan Current

Oil rig

The first oil well structures to be built offshore were in the Gulf of Mexico. They were in water depths of up to 300 feet (100 m). Modern platforms are found in 2,000 feet (610 m) of water, making them some of the world's tallest structures.

NATURAL RESOURCES

🐟 Fishing

🦐 Shellfish

⛏ Oil production

💧 Gas production

🏖 Tourism

Seafloor topography

The De Soto Canyon cuts through the broad continental shelf in the northern part of the Gulf of Mexico. The canyon may have been eroded by strong near-bottom currents and today there is upwelling of nutrient-rich deep-water in the area that increases animal abundance around the canyon.

LOUISIANA MISSISSIPPI ALABAMA

FLORIDA

Mississippi Delta

De Soto Canyon

Gulf of Mexico

CARIBBEAN SEA

The Caribbean Sea is a relatively shallow sea that occupies two main basins separated by a broad, submarine plateau. However, there are deep trenches such as the Cayman Trench that runs between Cuba and Jamaica and which contains the Caribbean's deepest point. The Caribbean Sea has a counterclockwise current that brings in Atlantic water between the Lesser Antilles.

Once in the Caribbean the water is warmed, and exits via the Yucatan Channel, where it eventually forms the Gulf Stream. The waters of the Caribbean are clear, warm and less salty than the Atlantic and the basin has a very low tidal range. These conditions are ideal for reef-building corals and the Caribbean has nine percent of the world's coral reefs that help attract tourists, who make a major contribution to the regional economy. Volcanic activity and earthquakes are common in the Caribbean, as are destructive hurricanes that gain energy from the warm water.

THE FACTS

Area	1.1 million square miles (2.7 million km²)
Average depth	8,685 feet (2,647 m)
Maximum depth	25,218 feet (7,686 m)
Maximum width	840 miles (1,400 km)
Maximum length	1,678 miles (2,700 km)

Schooling barracuda
Juvenile barracuda *(Sphyraena barracuda)* are frequently found in large schools. They are reputed to be good eating but there is an increasing problem with the toxin from the alga *Ciguatera* that causes severe food poisoning and which accumulates in the barracudas' muscles.

Yucatan coast
The "Temple of the Winds" at Tulum on the Yucatan Peninsula was built by the Mayans to act as a lookout and hurricane warning. As a hurricane approaches the strong winds blow across a hole in the top of the structure, producing a loud warning note.

Surface currents
Water from the equatorial Atlantic is carried by the North Equatorial, North Brazil, and Guiana currents between the Antilles to become the Caribbean Current. This carries large amounts of water northwestward, eventually entering the Gulf of Mexico and becoming part of the Yucatan Current.

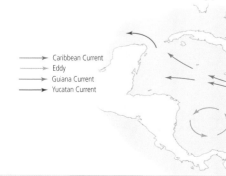

→ Caribbean Current
→ Eddy
→ Guiana Current
→ Yucatan Current

25° 75° Longitude west of Greenwich

R S T U V W X Y Z

Atlantic Ocean

THE BAHAMAS

Andros Island
Exuma Cays
Cat Island
Great Exuma Island
San Salvador
Rum Cay
Long Island
Crooked Island
Acklins Island
Mayaguana Island
North Caicos
Grand Caicos
East Caicos
TURKS AND CAICOS ISLANDS
COCKBURN TOWN
Grand Turk
Turks Islands
Caicos Islands
Little Inagua Island
Great Inagua Island

Great Bahaman Bank

CUBA

Cabo Lucrecia
Golfo de Guacanayabo
Archipiélago de Camagüey
Archipiélago de los Jardines de la Reina

Shipping hazard
The violent tropical storms and hurricanes of the Caribbean have always posed a serious threat to shipping in the region. The hurricane season lasts from June to December during which time there are usually nine or ten storms, about half of which reach hurricane strength.

Hispaniola Trough
Puerto Rico Trench

Punta de Quemado
Île de la Tortue
Cabo Isabela
Cabo Cabron
Bahía de Samaná

HAITI
DOMINICAN REPUBLIC
SANTO DOMINGO

Cabo Engano

Milwaukee Deep
28,231ft (8605m)

PUERTO RICO
SAN JUAN

Leeward Islands

VIRGIN ISLANDS
Anegada
St Thomas
ROAD TOWN
Tortola
THE VALLEY
Anguilla **ANGUILLA**
St John
CHARLOTTE AMALIE
VIRGIN ISLANDS (to USA)
St Martin St Barthélemy
St Croix
Saba St Eustatius St Kitts
BASSETERRE Nevis
ST KITTS AND NEVIS
ANTIGUA AND BARBUDA
ST JOHN'S
Antigua
Barbuda

20° 65° 4

PORT-AU-PRINCE
JAMAICA KINGSTON
Negril Point

Navassa Island
Île de la Gonâve
Golfe de la Gonâve

Greater Antilles

Jamaica Channel

Windward Passage

Isla Saona
Isla Beata
Cabo Falso
Cabo Beata
Isla Mona

Muertos Trough

PLYMOUTH
MONTSERRAT
GUADELOUPE
BASSE-TERRE
Marie-Galante
Dominica Passage

5

Pedro Bank

Beata Ridge

SCALE 1:10,000,000
Miller Projection
0 200 kilometers
0 200 statute miles
0 200 nautical miles

Caribbean Sea

ROSEAU
DOMINICA

Lesser Antilles

60° 15° 6

Colombia Basin

Venezuela Basin

FORT-DE-FRANCE
MARTINIQUE
St Lucia Channel
CASTRIES
ST LUCIA

Lesser Antilles

Grenada Basin
St Vincent Passage
Grenadines
St Vincent
KINGSTOWN
ST VINCENT AND THE GRENADINES
Bequia
Mustique
Carriacou
BARBADOS
BRIDGETOWN

7

ARUBA
ORANJESTAD

Curaçao
NETHERLANDS ANTILLES
Bonaire
WILLEMSTAD
Islas Las Aves
Islas Los Roques
Isla Orchila
Isla Blanquilla
Isla La Tortuga
Isla de Margarita

ST GEORGE'S
GRENADA
Grenada

Tobago Basin

Tobago

8

Gulf of Venezuela
Maracaibo
Barranquilla
Cartagena

CARACAS

Galera Point
PORT OF SPAIN
Gulf of Paria
Trinidad
Serpent's Mouth
Galeota Point
TRINIDAD AND TOBAGO

10° 9

COLOMBIA

Gulf of Darién
Golfo de Urabá

VENEZUELA

70° 65° 60°

Isthmus of Panama
PANAMA CITY
Gulf of Panama

Yucatan Peninsula

10

Havana

Cayman Trench

CUBA

PANAMA CANAL

The Panama Canal is a shortcut for shipping between the Atlantic and Pacific oceans. Construction began in 1880 under French control but disease and natural hazards caused its abandonment. The canal was eventually finished in 1914, after United States army engineers and doctors had eradicated the malaria and yellow fever that killed most of the 27,500 workers who died during the canal's construction.

11

JAMAICA
Kingston

Caribbean Sea

THE BAHAMAS

12

Port-au-Prince
HAITI

N

13

14

NATURAL RESOURCES

🐟 Fishing
🛢 Oil production
Tourism

Seafloor topography
The Cayman Trench between Jamaica and the Cayman Islands marks the boundary between the North American and Caribbean tectonic plates. Plans are underway for a team of scientists from the United Kingdom, to use a remotely-operated underwater vehicle to map the unexplored system of faults and underwater volcanic vents.

15

N O P Q R S T U Z

SARGASSO SEA

The Sargasso Sea is unusual in that it does not have limits defined by coasts or other geographic features. Instead, it is an area of the Atlantic Ocean characterized by large, floating, masses of brown sargassum seaweed that accumulate there. The sea is at the center of the North Atlantic Gyre, a group of clockwise north-Atlantic currents—the Gulf Stream, North Atlantic Current, Canary Current, and North Equatorial Current—which form a single, closed-circulation cell. This circulation causes everything that floats to become concentrated in the center of the gyre. Central gyres, such as the Sargasso Sea, have no local nutrient supply but studies have shown that Gulf Stream eddies can transport nutrient-rich waters into the Sargasso. A number of animals have co-evolved with the sargassum, taking on its brown-yellow coloration and living their entire lives in its camouflage. Also, the juveniles of some species make use of the weed as protection.

Sargassum crab
The ends of the fifth pair of legs of the sargassum crab *(Portunus* sp.*)* are modified into paddles so that it is able to swim between clumps of sargassum weed. The mottled shell is an effective camouflage when the crab is covered by strands of weed.

THE FACTS	
Area	1.4 million square miles (3.75 million km²)
Average depth	16,405 feet (5000 m)
Maximum depth	21,005 feet (6,402 m)
Maximum width	994 miles (1,600 km)
Maximum length	1,864 miles (3,000 km)

Gulf Stream
The Gulf Stream, shown in this satellite image in red, is known as "the river in the ocean." It is Earth's fastest moving ocean current, flowing at two to five miles per hour (3 to 8 km/h).

THE MYSTERIOUS LIVES OF EELS

The most famous inhabitants of the Sargasso Sea are not permanent residents. The European eel *(Anguilla anguilla)* and the American eel *(Anguilla rostrata),* delicacies in Europe and America, spawn here. The juvenile eels then migrate into the rivers of North America and Europe.

Parallel lives
The lifecycle of the European eel and its relative, the American eel, takes decades and up to 7,000 miles (11,250 km) to complete.

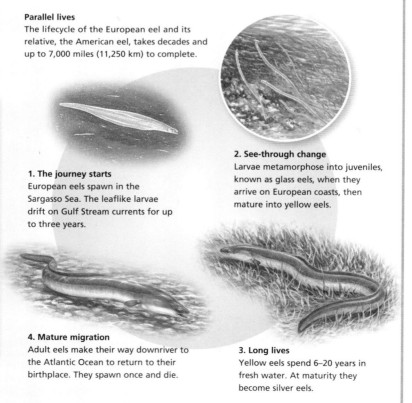

1. The journey starts
European eels spawn in the Sargasso Sea. The leaflike larvae drift on Gulf Stream currents for up to three years.

2. See-through change
Larvae metamorphose into juveniles, known as glass eels, when they arrive on European coasts, then mature into yellow eels.

3. Long lives
Yellow eels spend 6–20 years in fresh water. At maturity they become silver eels.

4. Mature migration
Adult eels make their way downriver to the Atlantic Ocean to return to their birthplace. They spawn once and die.

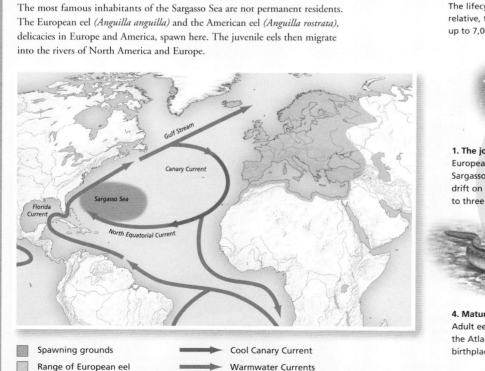

- Spawning grounds
- Range of European eel
- → Cool Canary Current
- → Warmwater Currents

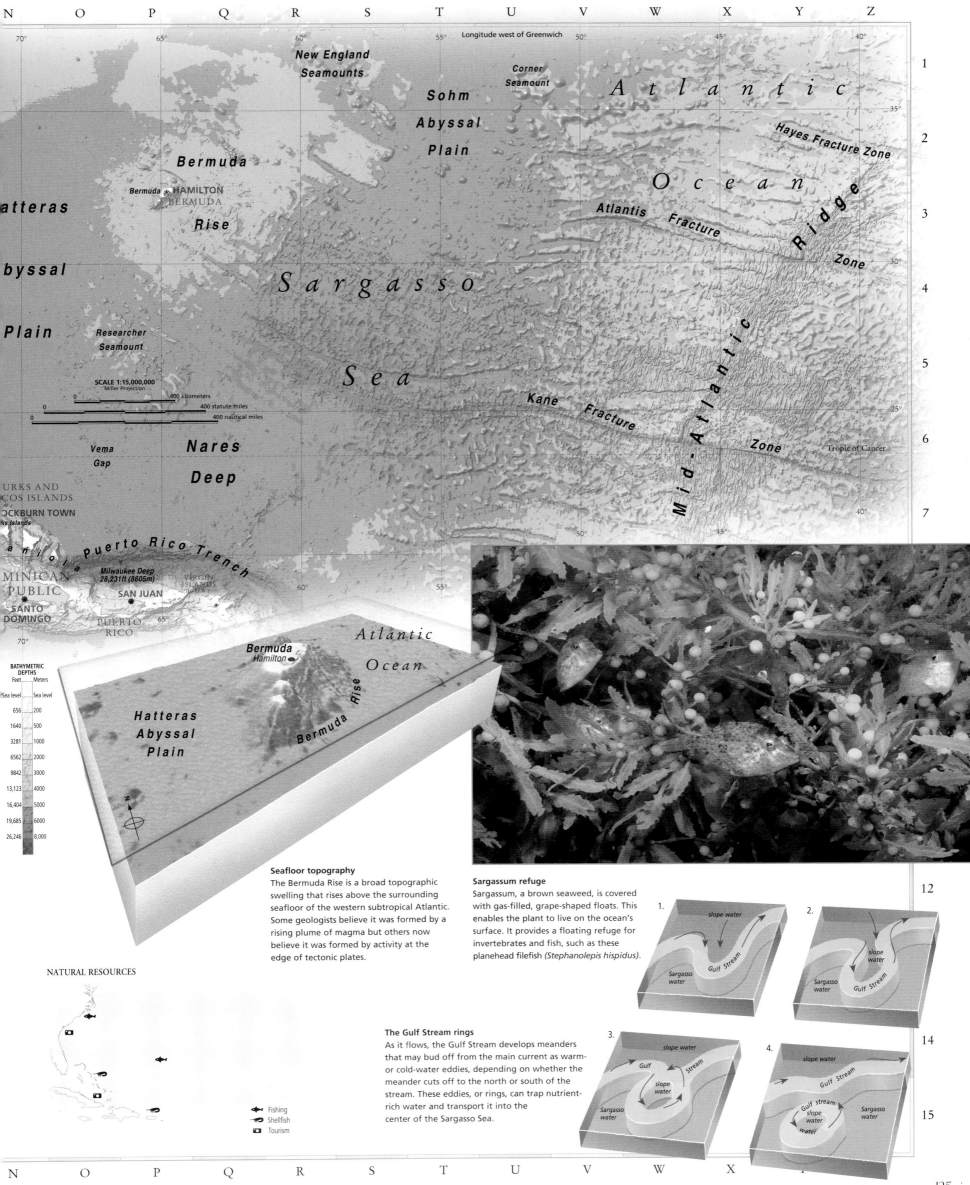

N O P Q R S T U V W X Y Z

70°   65°   60°   Longitude west of Greenwich   55°   50°   45°   40°

New England
Seamounts

Corner
Seamount

Atlantic

Sohm

Abyssal

Plain

Hayes Fracture Zone

Bermuda

Ocean

Bermuda ★ HAMILTON
BERMUDA

Rise

Atlantis   Fracture

Zone

atteras

Ridge

byssal

S a r g a s s o

Plain

Researcher
Seamount

SCALE 1:15,000,000
Miller Projection

Sea

Kane   Fracture

0   400 kilometers
0   400 statute miles
0   400 nautical miles

Zone

Tropic of Cancer

Mid-Atlantic

Vema
Gap

Nares

Deep

URKS AND
COS ISLANDS
OCKBURN TOWN
ks Islands

aniola   Puerto Rico Trench

MINICAN
PUBLIC
SANTO
DOMINGO

Milwaukee Deep
28,231ft (8605m)
SAN JUAN

VIRGIN
ISLANDS

PUERTO
RICO

70°   65°   60°   55°

Atlantic

Ocean

Bermuda
Hamilton ⊙

BATHYMETRIC
DEPTHS
Feet   Meters

Sea level   Sea level
656   200
1640   500
3281   1000
6562   2000
9842   3000
13,123   4000
16,404   5000
19,685   6000
26,246   8,000

Hatteras
Abyssal
Plain

Bermuda   Rise

N

Seafloor topography
The Bermuda Rise is a broad topographic
swelling that rises above the surrounding
seafloor of the western subtropical Atlantic.
Some geologists believe it was formed by a
rising plume of magma but others now
believe it was formed by activity at the
edge of tectonic plates.

Sargassum refuge
Sargassum, a brown seaweed, is covered
with gas-filled, grape-shaped floats. This
enables the plant to live on the ocean's
surface. It provides a floating refuge for
invertebrates and fish, such as these
planehead filefish (*Stephanolepis hispidus*).

1. slope water   Gulf Stream   Sargasso water

2. slope water   Sargasso water   Gulf Stream

NATURAL RESOURCES

The Gulf Stream rings
As it flows, the Gulf Stream develops meanders
that may bud off from the main current as warm-
or cold-water eddies, depending on whether the
meander cuts off to the north or south of the
stream. These eddies, or rings, can trap nutrient-
rich water and transport it into the
center of the Sargasso Sea.

3. slope water   Gulf   Stream   slope water   Sargasso water

4. slope water   Gulf Stream   Gulf stream slope water   Sargasso water

⊰ Fishing
🐟 Shellfish
📷 Tourism

1
2
3
4
5
6
7

12

14

15

BAY OF BISCAY

The Bay of Biscay is a semi-enclosed area of the northeast Atlantic that contains a wider than usual portion of continental shelf. This has made the bay relatively shallow and this, combined with the prevailing westerly winds that bring in waves that have traveled across most of the Atlantic, often makes its waters exceptionally stormy and rough. These waters have claimed countless vessels over the centuries. Circulation patterns within the bay are highly seasonal. From October to March, during winter season, a seasonal current flows along the slope of the continental shelf and this is known as the Navidad Current, so-called because it is present through the Christmas period. The Navidad Current flows eastward, along the north coast of Spain, and is an extension of the northward Portugal countercurrent. Where the current encounters irregularities on the continental slope, such as the Santander Canyon, it generates eddies, meanders, and warm-water lenses.

THE FACTS

Area	86,000 square miles (223,000 km²)
Average depth	7,874 feet (2,400 m)
Maximum depth	15,525 feet (4,735 m)
Maximum width	342 miles (550 km)
Maximum length	317 miles (510 km)

Shipwrecks
Despite modern navigation aids and accurate weather forecasting the Bay of Biscay still claims ships and lives. Storms develop quickly throughout the year, though these are fiercest and most frequent during the winter months when westerly winds whip up the waves into a cauldron of churning water.

Quiet inlet
Pont Goulphar is one of the numerous secluded inlets along the southwest coast of Brittany. The inlet and the surrounding rugged cliffs inspired the Impressionist painter Claude Monet to produce a series of famous seascapes. The area continues to attract large numbers of summer visitors.

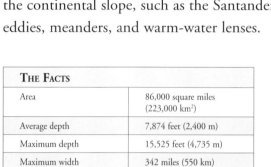

Porbeagle
Porbeagle sharks *(Lamna nasus)* are probably the most numerous of the large sharks in the Bay of Biscay, though overfishing in past decades has severely depleted their numbers in the North Atlantic and the species is listed as vulnerable by the International Union for Conservation of Nature (IUCN).

Gannet
The northern gannet *(Morus bassanus)* is the largest seabird in the North Atlantic, having a wingspan of up to six feet (2 m). Adults of the species are seen throughout the Bay of Biscay although they breed farther north.

La Rochelle Harbor
There has been a port at La Rochelle since the 10th century. Although always prosperous, as the most westerly Atlantic port in France the port also became strategically important in the 18th century when trade with French possessions in the New World expanded.

Surface currents
The surface currents of the Bay of Biscay have a clockwise circulation that is linked to the clockwise surface circulation pattern in the main part of the North Atlantic. In addition, there are strong coastal currents driven by the high tidal range within the bay.

→ Inshore tidal movement
→ North Atlantic Drift
→ Seasonal Navidad Current
→ Surface circulation

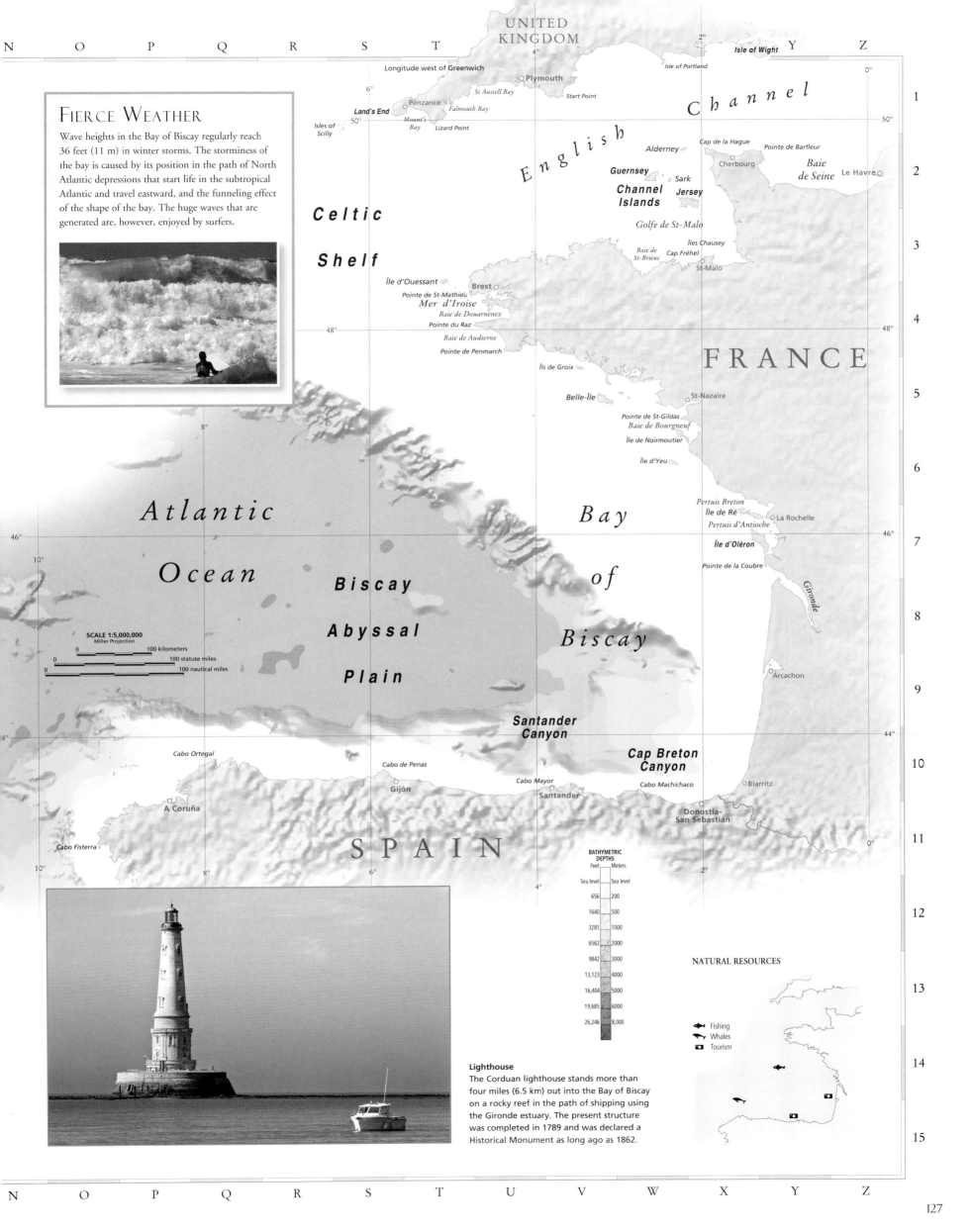

UNITED
KINGDOM

Longitude west of Greenwich

Plymouth

St Austell Bay
Penzance
Land's End
Mount's
Bay
Lizard Point
Falmouth Bay
Start Point

Isles of
Scilly

Channel

Isle of Portland

Isle of Wight

1

50°

Cap de la Hague
Alderney
Pointe de Barfleur
Cherbourg
Pointe de Barfleur
Guernsey
Sark
Channel
Islands
Jersey
Baie
de Seine
Le Havre

2

English

Golfe de St-Malo

Îles Chausey
Baie de
St-Brieuc
Cap Fréhel
St-Malo

3

Celtic

Shelf

Île d'Ouessant
Brest
Pointe de St-Mathieu
Mer d'Iroise
Baie de Douarnenez
Pointe du Raz
Baie de Audierne
Pointe de Penmarch

4

48°

48°

FRANCE

Îls de Groix

Belle-Île

St-Nazaire
Pointe de St-Gildas
Baie de Bourgneuf
Île de Noirmoutier

Île d'Yeu

5

6

Atlantic

Ocean

Pertuis Breton
Île de Ré
La Rochelle
Pertuis d'Antioche
Île d'Oléron
Pointe de la Coubre

7

46°

46°

Bay

of

Biscay

Biscay

Abyssal

Plain

Gironde

8

SCALE 1:5,000,000
Miller Projection
0   100 kilometers
0   100 statute miles
0   100 nautical miles

Arcachon

9

Santander
Canyon

44°

44°

Cabo Ortegal

Cabo de Penas

Cap Breton
Canyon

10

Cabo Mayor
Cabo Machichaco
Biarritz
Gijón
Santander

A Coruña

Donostia-
San Sebastián

11

Cabo Fisterra

S P A I N

0°

10°

8°

6°

4°

2°

BATHYMETRIC
DEPTHS
Feet   Meters

Sea level   Sea level

656 ____ 200
1640 ____ 500
3281 ____ 1000
6562 ____ 2000
9842 ____ 3000
13,123 ____ 4000
16,404 ____ 5000
19,685 ____ 6000
26,246 ____ 8,000

12

13

NATURAL RESOURCES

14

Fishing
Whales
Tourism

15

FIERCE WEATHER

Wave heights in the Bay of Biscay regularly reach 36 feet (11 m) in winter storms. The storminess of the bay is caused by its position in the path of North Atlantic depressions that start life in the subtropical Atlantic and travel eastward, and the funneling effect of the shape of the bay. The huge waves that are generated are, however, enjoyed by surfers.

Lighthouse
The Corduan lighthouse stands more than four miles (6.5 km) out into the Bay of Biscay on a rocky reef in the path of shipping using the Gironde estuary. The present structure was completed in 1789 and was declared a Historical Monument as long ago as 1862.

MEDITERRANEAN SEA

The Mediterranean Sea's only link with the Atlantic is through the Strait of Gibraltar, where dense salty Mediterranean water flows out beneath less dense Atlantic water. As a consequence, the tidal range in the Mediterranean is short and the circulation patterns are driven by evaporation and freshwater inputs. High evaporation in the eastern half causes the water level to decrease and salinity to increase eastward. This draws relatively low-salinity water from the Atlantic across the basin; it warms and becomes saltier as it travels east, then sinks in the region of the Levant and circulates westward, to exit at the Strait of Gibraltar. The Mediterranean Sea is largely populated by species that have entered via the Strait of Gibraltar and adapted to warmer more saline water than the Atlantic. However, since the opening of the Suez Canal in 1869 Red Sea species have begun to colonize the eastern Mediterranean.

City of Venice
Venice stands on 118 small islands within a saltwater lagoon bounded by the mouths of the River Piave to the north and the River Po to the south. During the Middle Ages and the Renaissance Venice was the dominant political and military power in the Mediterranean.

THE FACTS	
Area	959,210 square miles (2,484,342 km²)
Average depth	4,920 feet (1,500 m)
Maximum depth	16,897 feet (5,150 m)
Maximum width	497 miles (800 km)
Maximum length	1,250 miles (2,000 km)

Aegean Sea
The Aegean Sea is an embayment of the Mediterranean separating the Greek and Turkish mainlands. It was known to the Greeks as "Archipelago" referring to the large number of islands within it, though the term is now used to refer to island groups throughout the world.

SCALE 1:15,000,000
Miller Projection

0 400 kilometers
0 400 statute miles
0 400 nautical miles

Rhône Fan
Golfe du Lion
Cap de Creus
Barcelona
Valencia Trough
Balearic Islands
Majorca
Valencia
Valencia Basin
Balearic Channel
Ibiza
Minc
Kenc Plateau
Emile Baudot Escarpment
Algeri
Atlantic Ocean
Lisbon
Cabo de Palos
Mazarron Escarpment
Cabo de Gata
Habibas Escarpment
Algiers
Gibraltar Sill
Gibraltar
Strait of Gibraltar
Alborán Sea
West Alboran Basin
East Alboran Basin
Alboran Ridge
Cap des Trois Fourches
Rabat

Seafloor topography
The Strait of Gibraltar is the only natural connection between the Mediterranean Sea and the world ocean. It is 36 miles (58 km) long and narrows to 8 miles (13 km). Depths in the strait range between 980 and 3,000 feet (300 and 900 m).

Algerian Basin
Alboran Sea
SPAIN
PORTUGAL
Cadiz
Gulf of Cadiz
Gibraltar
Tangier
Strait of Gibraltar
Gibraltar Sill
MOROCCO
Rabat
Casablanca
Atlantic Ocean

Surface currents
Surface circulation of the Mediterranean consists of separate counterclockwise movements of the water in each of the two basins. The complexity of the northern coastline and of the numerous islands generates many small eddies and other local currents that contribute to the general surface circulation.

→ Atlantic surface inflow
→ Surface circulation

P Q R S T U V W X Y Z

Monk seal
The Mediterranean monk seal (*Monachus monachus*) is one of the world's most endangered animals; less than 500 individuals survive. Centuries of hunting, and pollution and disturbance in the sea in the past century, have brought them close to extinction. They are one of only three species of warm-water seals.

Fishing industry
The narrowness of the Mediterranean continental shelf means that most fishing is concentrated close to shore. Unfortunately, this is also where most young fish tend to congregate and are killed or removed so that fish stocks of hake, swordfish, sardines, and tuna are now in danger.

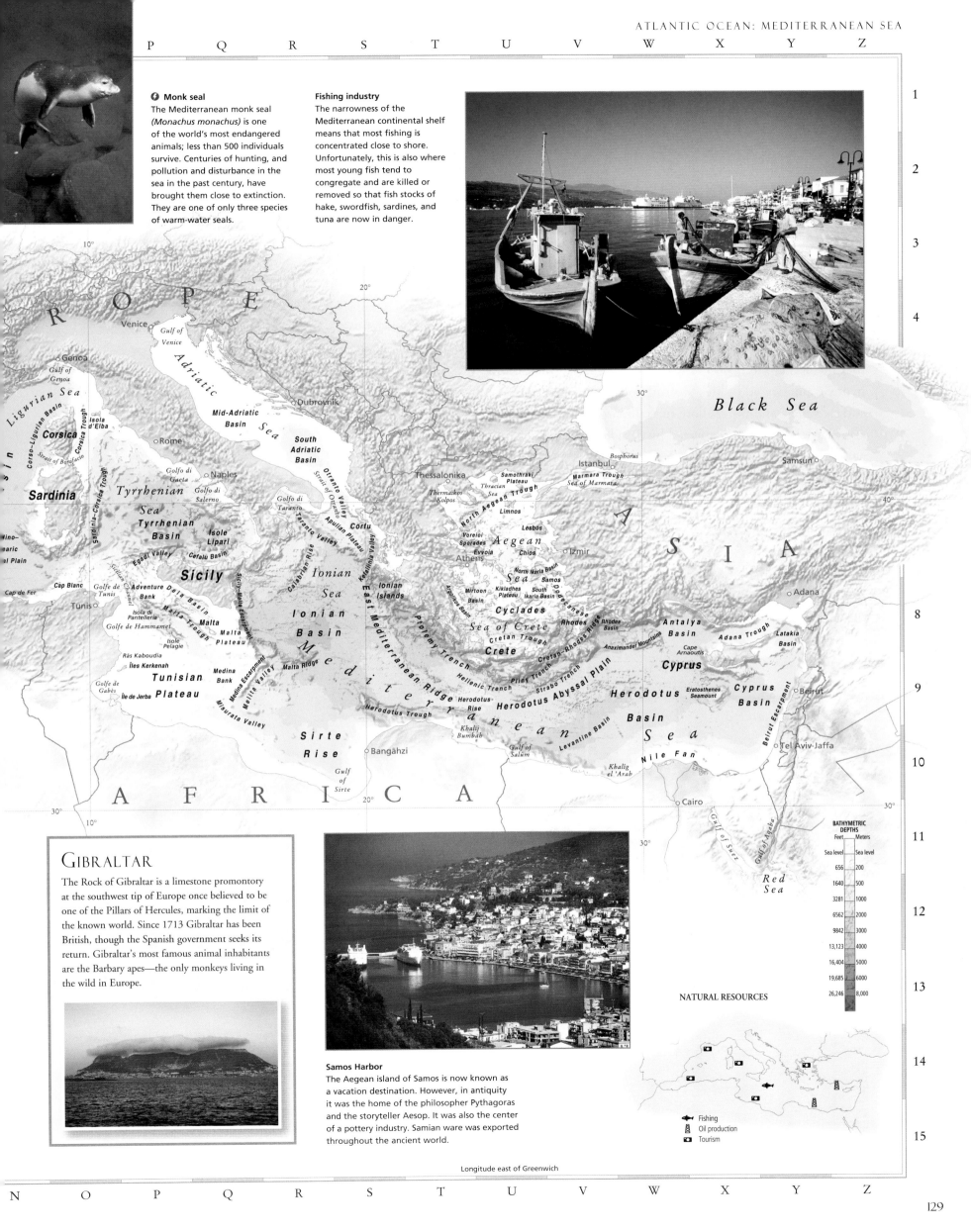

GIBRALTAR

The Rock of Gibraltar is a limestone promontory at the southwest tip of Europe once believed to be one of the Pillars of Hercules, marking the limit of the known world. Since 1713 Gibraltar has been British, though the Spanish government seeks its return. Gibraltar's most famous animal inhabitants are the Barbary apes—the only monkeys living in the wild in Europe.

Samos Harbor
The Aegean island of Samos is now known as a vacation destination. However, in antiquity it was the home of the philosopher Pythagoras and the storyteller Aesop. It was also the center of a pottery industry. Samian ware was exported throughout the ancient world.

BATHYMETRIC DEPTHS

Feet	Meters
Sea level	Sea level
656	200
1640	500
3281	1000
6562	2000
9842	3000
13,123	4000
16,404	5000
19,685	6000
26,246	8,000

NATURAL RESOURCES

Fishing
Oil production
Tourism

Longitude east of Greenwich

BLACK SEA

The Black Sea is believed by many geologists to have been a freshwater lake until about 8,000 years ago when the post-glacial rise in sea levels allowed seawater from the Aegean Sea to break through what is now the Turkish straits system (the Bosporus, Sea of Marmara and the Dardenelles). Even today the salinity of the Black Sea is only half that of full-strength seawater and the input of major rivers means that there is net positive outflow of water from the Black Sea into the Mediterranean. This fresh water causes much of the Black Sea to become stratified so that the deeper layers do not mix with the surface and become hypoxic and devoid of life. Most marine life is found in the surface waters and the shallow coastal margins, though these areas have been severely affected by decades of industrial and agricultural pollution brought down to the sea by rivers, principally the Danube.

THE FACTS	
Area	196,000 square miles (508,000 km²)
Average depth	4,062 feet (1,240 m)
Maximum depth	7,365 feet (2,245 m)
Maximum width	160 miles (260 km)
Maximum length	730 miles (1,175 km)

First Bosporus bridge
The Bosporus is less than half a mile (700 m) at its narrowest point. The first bridge, completed in 1973, stands beside the Oratokoy mosque. A second bridge was opened in 1988. A third bridge is planned and a railway tunnel is nearing completion.

Sea of Azov
The Sea of Azov is a body of brackish water that connects to the Black sea via the Kerch Strait and is the shallowest sea in the world. It has an average depth of 43 feet (13 m) and maximum depth of 50 feet (15.3 m).

BATHYMETRIC DEPTHS	
Feet	Meters
Sea level	Sea level
656	200
1640	500
3281	1000
6562	2000
9842	3000
13,123	4000
16,404	5000
19,685	6000
26,246	8,000

GREEC
Thessaloniki
Samot
Limnos
Aegea
Sea
Anatolian Trough

Moon jellyfish
In the 1970s there was a dramatic rise in the number of moon jellyfish (Aurelia aurita) in the Black Sea and it was suggested that this species, alone, was consuming 62 percent of all zooplankton produced in the surface waters. The zooplankton was food that previously supported important fisheries.

Stingray
The common stingray (Dasyatis pastinaca) lives on sandy or muddy bottoms in the Black Sea, often half-buried in the substrate, and near rocky reefs. It is usually found shallower than 197 feet (60 m). It is also tolerant of low salinity and may be found in estuaries.

Surface currents
There are two types of sea currents in the Black Sea: the surface currents that are driven by the counterclockwise pattern of the winds and the double currents in the Bosporus Strait and Kerch Strait, caused by the exchange of waters with adjacent seas.

→ Tidal exchange
→ Surface circulation

NATURAL RESOURCES

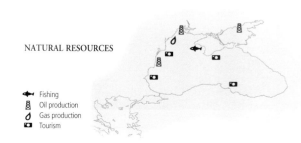

➤ Fishing
⚒ Oil production
◊ Gas production
▣ Tourism

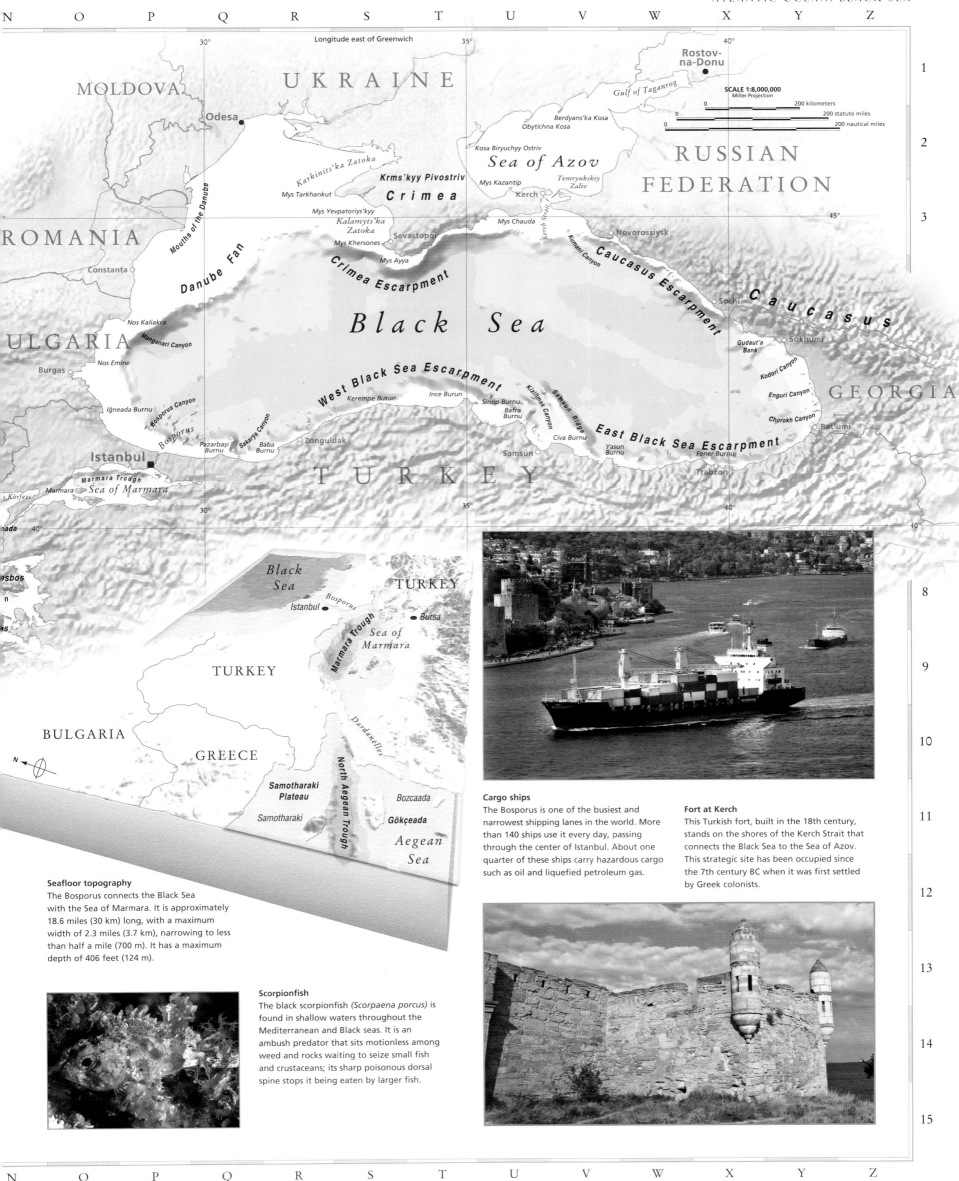

Seafloor topography
The Bosporus connects the Black Sea with the Sea of Marmara. It is approximately 18.6 miles (30 km) long, with a maximum width of 2.3 miles (3.7 km), narrowing to less than half a mile (700 m). It has a maximum depth of 406 feet (124 m).

Scorpionfish
The black scorpionfish (*Scorpaena porcus*) is found in shallow waters throughout the Mediterranean and Black seas. It is an ambush predator that sits motionless among weed and rocks waiting to seize small fish and crustaceans; its sharp poisonous dorsal spine stops it being eaten by larger fish.

Cargo ships
The Bosporus is one of the busiest and narrowest shipping lanes in the world. More than 140 ships use it every day, passing through the center of Istanbul. About one quarter of these ships carry hazardous cargo such as oil and liquefied petroleum gas.

Fort at Kerch
This Turkish fort, built in the 18th century, stands on the shores of the Kerch Strait that connects the Black Sea to the Sea of Azov. This strategic site has been occupied since the 7th century BC when it was first settled by Greek colonists.

SOUTHERN ATLANTIC OCEAN

Like the north Atlantic the south Atlantic has a central gyre of surface currents but these currents flow counterclockwise. The Brazil Current flows south from the equator, eventually turning eastward to become the South Atlantic Current which meets the Agulhas Current around the Cape of Good Hope. This creates an upwelling zone that brings cold, nutrient-rich waters to the surface and fuels intense biological activity in the area. However, the cold water that continues northward along the Namibian coast reduces the water vapor in the air over the coast, making it an arid desert sometimes known as the "Skeleton Coast." The loop is closed by the westward flowing South Equatorial Current. Exploitation of natural resources in the south Atlantic is much more recent than in the north Atlantic. There are established squid fisheries around the Falkland Islands and there is considerable interest in exploring the Falkland Plateau for oil and other minerals.

Reef squid
The reef squid (Sepioteuthis sepioidea) is found in warm, shallow waters around reefs in the Caribbean and tropical Atlantic. As the squid grow they move from very shallow water into deep water and adult squid are commonly found in waters up to 300 feet (100 m) deep.

NATURAL RESOURCES

- Fishing
- Whales
- Shellfish
- Metallic minerals
- Oil production
- Tourism

Great white shark
The great white shark (Carcharodon carcharias) is found in warm coastal waters. The best known Atlantic great white sharks are those that patrol the waters around Seal Island, South Africa during the seal breeding season, breaching spectacularly as they shoot up from the depths.

Surface currents
The counterclockwise gyre that covers the central south Atlantic is made up of four components: the South Equatorial Current, Brazil Current, Antarctic Circumpolar Current and Benguela Current. The waters that are isolated in the central portion of the gyre are nutrient-poor, forming a "blue desert."

- ‑‑‑‑> Equatorial Countercurrent
- ——> South Equatorial Current
- ——> Brazil Current
- ‑‑‑‑> South Atlantic Current
- ——> Falklands Current
- ——> Antarctic Circumpolar Current
- ‑‑‑‑> Agulhas Current
- ——> Benguela Current

BATHYMETRIC DEPTHS

Feet	Meters
Sea level	Sea level
656	200
1640	500
3281	1000
6562	2000
9842	3000
13,123	4000
16,404	5000
19,685	6000
26,246	8,000

Paramaribo
Cayenne
Amazon Cone
Equator
SOUTH
AMERICA
Tropic of Capricorn
Rio de Janeiro
Sao Paulo
Sant
Plate
Montevideo
Buenos Aires
Argentin
Basin
Zapi
Golfo San Matías
Argentine Abyssal Plain
Falkland Esca
Golfo de San Jorge
Falkland
Islands
Falkland
Plateau
Tierra del Fuego
Burdwood Bank
North Scotia Ridge
Cape Horn
Yaghan Basin
Shackleton Fracture Zone
West Scotia Ridge
Endurance Fracture Zone
Scoti
Drake Passage
Ona Basin
Protector Basin
Hero Fracture Zone
South Shetland Trough
South Shetland Islands
Powell Basin
South Orkn Islands
Scotia

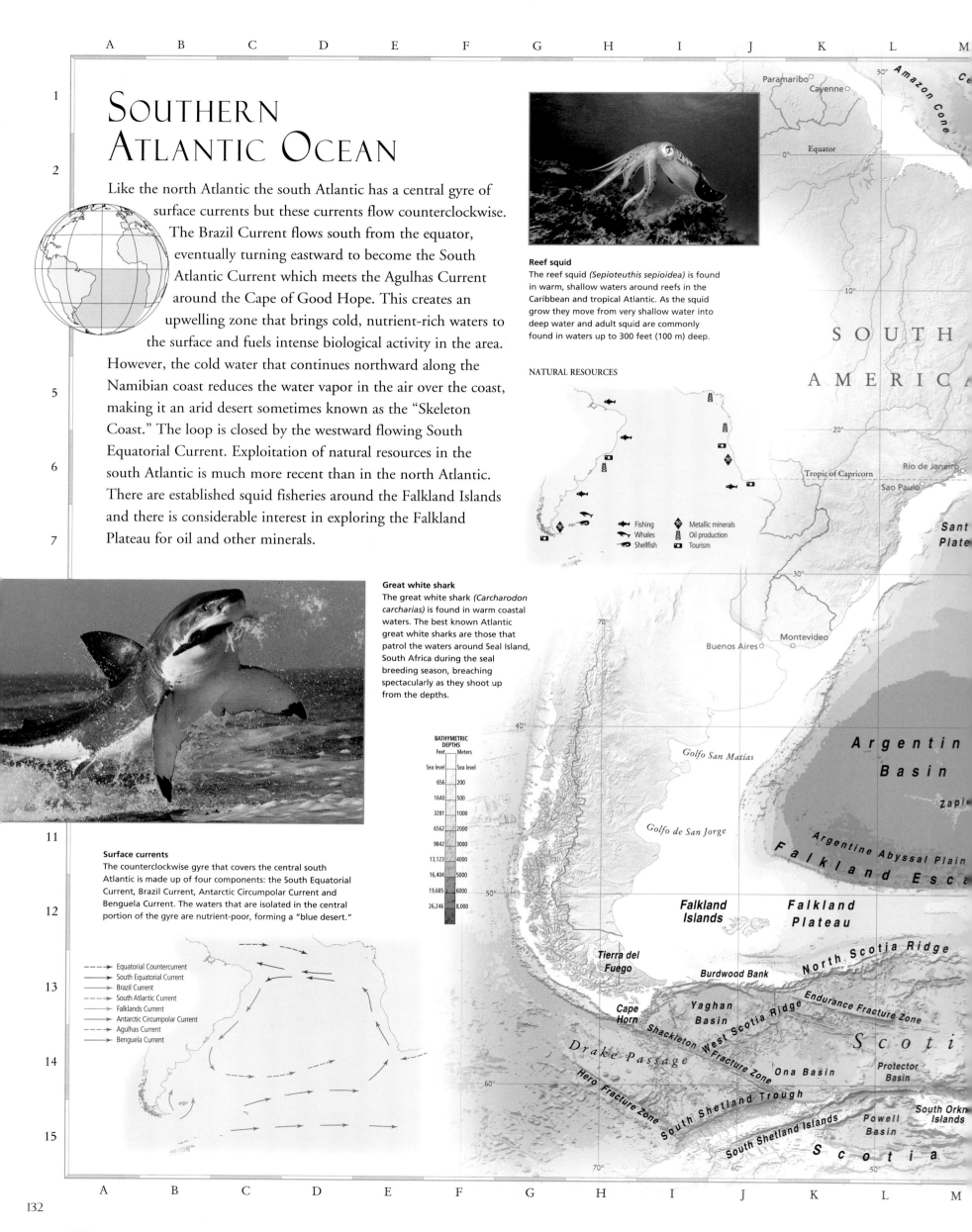

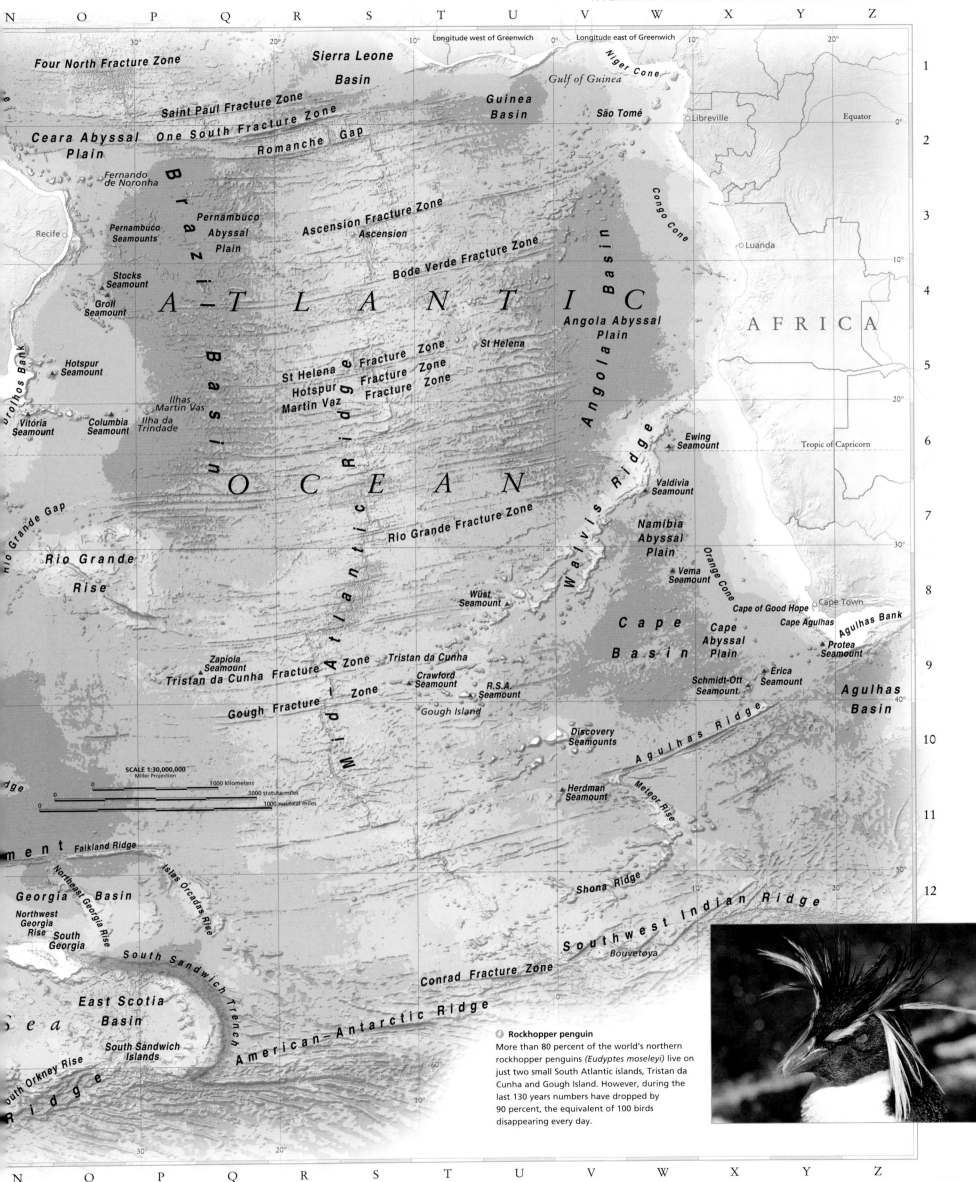

N O P Q R S T U V W X Y Z

30°   20°   10°   Longitude west of Greenwich   0°   Longitude east of Greenwich   10°   20°

Four North Fracture Zone

Sierra Leone Basin

Niger Cone

Gulf of Guinea

Saint Paul Fracture Zone

One South Fracture Zone

Guinea Basin

São Tomé

Libreville   Equator   0°

Ceara Abyssal Plain

Romanche Gap

Fernando de Noronha

B r a z i l   B a s i n

Congo Cone

Recife

Pernambuco Seamounts

Pernambuco Abyssal Plain

Ascension Fracture Zone

Ascension

Bode Verde Fracture Zone

Luanda   10°

A T L A N T I C

Angola Abyssal Plain

Angola Basin

AFRICA

Stocks Seamount

Groll Seamount

St Helena Fracture Zone

St Helena

Brolhos Bank

Hotspur Seamount

O C E A N

Hotspur Fracture Zone

Fracture Zone

Fracture Zone

Walvis Ridge

Ilhas Martin Vas

Martin Vaz

20°

Vitória Seamount

Columbia Seamount

Ilha da Trindade

Ewing Seamount   Tropic of Capricorn

Valdivia Seamount

Rio Grande Gap

Rio Grande Fracture Zone

Namibia Abyssal Plain

30°

Rio Grande Rise

Vema Seamount

Orange Cone

Wüst Seamount

Cape Town

M i d   A t l a n t i c   R i d g e

Cape of Good Hope

Cape Agulhas

Agulhas Bank

Zapiola Seamount

Tristan da Cunha Fracture Zone

Tristan da Cunha

Crawford Seamount

R.S.A. Seamount

Cape Abyssal Plain

Cape Basin

Schmidt-Ott Seamount

Erica Seamount

Protea Seamount

Agulhas Basin   40°

Gough Fracture Zone

Zone

Gough Island

Agulhas Ridge

Discovery Seamounts

SCALE 1:30,000,000
Miller Projection

0   1000 kilometers

0   1000 statute miles

0   1000 nautical miles

Herdman Seamount

Meteor Rise

Falkland Ridge

Shona Ridge   50°

Georgia Basin

Northeast Georgia Rise

Islas Orcadas Rise

Southwest Indian Ridge

Northwest Georgia Rise

South Georgia

South Sandwich Trench

Bouvetøya

East Scotia Basin

Conrad Fracture Zone

South Orkney Rise

South Sandwich Islands

American–Antarctic Ridge

Rockhopper penguin
More than 80 percent of the world's northern rockhopper penguins (Eudyptes moseleyi) live on just two small South Atlantic islands, Tristan da Cunha and Gough Island. However, during the last 130 years numbers have dropped by 90 percent, the equivalent of 100 birds disappearing every day.

N O P Q R S T U V W X Y Z

GULF OF GUINEA

The coastline of the Gulf of Guinea forms part of the western edge of the African tectonic plate and corresponds remarkably to the continental margin of South America running from Brazil to the Guianas. The coincidence between the geology and the geomorphology of these two coastlines constitutes one of the clearest confirmations of the theory of continental drift. The continental shelf within the gulf is narrower than that of most of the Atlantic margins but contains large and valuable oil and mineral resources, the best known are the oil and gas fields of the Niger Delta. The Benguela Current tends to trap warm water against the coast which is diluted by the inflow of large rivers such as the Niger and Congo. Where the cold Benguela Current water meets the warm waters of the Guinea Current there is upwelling and intense biological activity that sustains a wide variety of marine life. There are also areas of high biological activity, and fisheries, associated with fronts—the boundaries of the major water masses within the gulf.

Coast of Togo
The lagoon at Aneho, on the Togolese coast, is part of a 31-mile (50 km) system of dunes and lagoons. These have been built up from sediments carried westward by strong clockwise coastal currents and longshore drift along this part of the Gulf of Guinea.

ISLANDS OF THE GULF

The flora and fauna of the islands in the Gulf of Guinea have been studied for many decades by biologists seeking to understand the process and patterns of island colonization and biogeography. The gulf islands have each developed a unique community of plants and animals; many species are endemic to one island only.

The islet of Bom Bom to the north of the island of Príncipe has become a major tourist resort and the principal source of income for the local and regional economies.

⊘ Leatherback turtle
The leatherback turtle (*Dermochelys coriacea*) is one of four endangered sea turtle species in the Gulf of Guinea. The main nesting grounds are on Bioko, where it is threatened by the meat and egg trade. However, it nests in small numbers on the other islands.

NATURAL RESOURCES

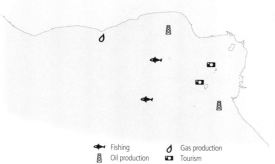

Fishing   Gas production
Oil production   Tourism

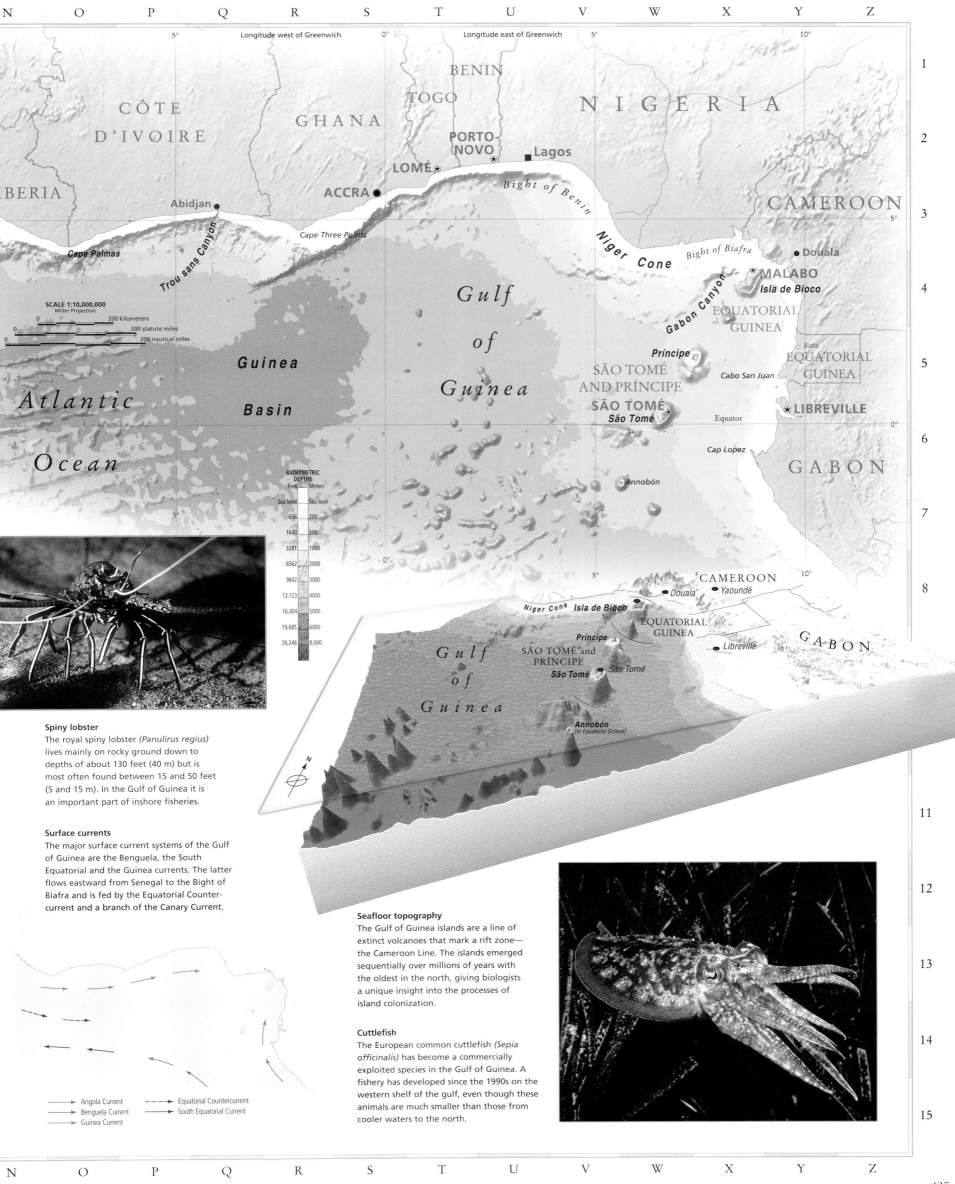

Spiny lobster

The royal spiny lobster (Panulirus regius) lives mainly on rocky ground down to depths of about 130 feet (40 m) but is most often found between 15 and 50 feet (5 and 15 m). In the Gulf of Guinea it is an important part of inshore fisheries.

Surface currents

The major surface current systems of the Gulf of Guinea are the Benguela, the South Equatorial and the Guinea currents. The latter flows eastward from Senegal to the Bight of Biafra and is fed by the Equatorial Countercurrent and a branch of the Canary Current.

→ Angola Current ⇢ Equatorial Countercurrent
→ Benguela Current → South Equatorial Current
→ Guinea Current

Seafloor topography

The Gulf of Guinea islands are a line of extinct volcanoes that mark a rift zone—the Cameroon Line. The islands emerged sequentially over millions of years with the oldest in the north, giving biologists a unique insight into the processes of island colonization.

Cuttlefish

The European common cuttlefish (Sepia officinalis) has become a commercially exploited species in the Gulf of Guinea. A fishery has developed since the 1990s on the western shelf of the gulf, even though these animals are much smaller than those from cooler waters to the north.

BATHYMETRIC DEPTHS

Feet	Meters
Sea level	Sea level
656	200
1640	500
3281	1000
6562	2000
9842	3000
13,123	4000
16,404	5000
19,685	6000
26,246	8,000

SCALE 1:10,000,000
Miller Projection

West African Coast

The surface waters of the southwest African coast are some of the most productive in the world, the abundant plankton sustains both fin fish and crustacean shellfish fisheries. This intense biological activity depends on cold, nutrient-rich water brought northward by the Benguela Current and brought to the surface by the upwelling produced by the prevailing south and south-easterly winds blowing over the sea surface. The cooling of the winds causes coastal fogs and the air that blows inland carries very little moisture, so that the adjacent land is some of the most arid in the world. Fishing is mainly centered around the seamounts in the region, which are also believed to have diamond deposits. However, suction dredging of these deposits causes major damage to the seabed wiping out local seabed communities and producing plumes of fine waste material that adversely affect a much wider area by smothering them. A decline in some commercial species such the rock lobster has been attributed to offshore mining activity.

Skeleton Coast
This part of the Namibian coast originally got its name from the bleached bones that once covered the shore, left by whaling and seal hunting. There are also more than a thousand rusting hulks from the numerous shipwrecks caused by the dense fogs and offshore rocks.

Black oystercatcher
The African black oystercatcher (*Haematopus moquini*) lives and breeds on the rocky coasts and islands of southern Africa. It uses its strong beak to open bivalves or to probe for worms. The species is now endangered and there are less than 5,000 adults left.

Ocean fog
On the west African coast the upwelling of the cold Benguela Current cools the air above it to the point where the water vapor in it starts to condense. This gives rise to dense ocean fogs, known locally as "cassimbo," that occur for most of the year.

Langstrand
In recent years tourists looking for isolation and privacy have sought places such as Langstrand on the Namibian coast. The town mainly consists of holiday homes and beach villas built close to water to catch sea breezes and escape the intense heat of the Namibian hinterland.

NATURAL RESOURCES

Fishing
Metallic minerals
Oil production
Tourism

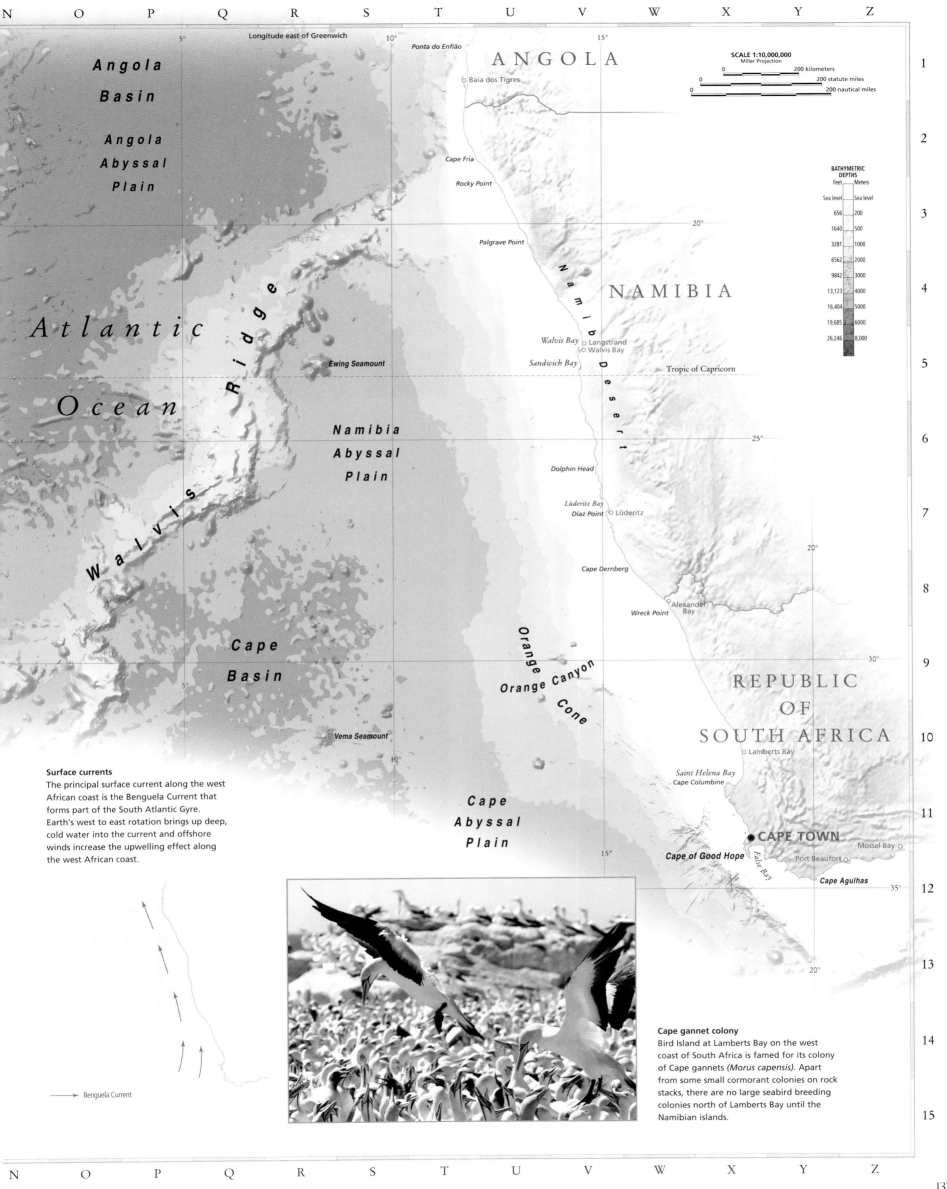

N O P Q R S T U V W X Y Z

Longitude east of Greenwich

Angola Basin

Angola Abyssal Plain

ANGOLA

Ponta do Enfião

○ Baia dos Tigres

Cape Fria

Rocky Point

Atlantic

Walvis Ridge

Palgrave Point

NAMIBIA

Ocean

Ewing Seamount

Namib Desert

Walvis Bay ○ Langstrand
○ Walvis Bay
Sandwich Bay

Tropic of Capricorn

Namibia Abyssal Plain

Dolphin Head

Lüderitz Bay
Diaz Point ○ Lüderitz

Walvis Ridge

Cape Dernberg

Cape Basin

Alexander Bay
Wreck Point ○

Orange Canyon
Cone

Vema Seamount

REPUBLIC OF SOUTH AFRICA

○ Lamberts Bay

Saint Helena Bay
Cape Columbine

Cape Abyssal Plain

● CAPE TOWN

Mossel Bay ○

Cape of Good Hope

False Bay
Port Beaufort

Cape Agulhas

SCALE 1:10,000,000
Miller Projection
0   200 kilometers
0   200 statute miles
0   200 nautical miles

BATHYMETRIC DEPTHS
Feet — Meters

Sea level — Sea level
656 — 200
1640 — 500
3281 — 1000
6562 — 2000
9842 — 3000
13,123 — 4000
16,404 — 5000
19,685 — 6000
26,246 — 8,000

Surface currents
The principal surface current along the west African coast is the Benguela Current that forms part of the South Atlantic Gyre. Earth's west to east rotation brings up deep, cold water into the current and offshore winds increase the upwelling effect along the west African coast.

→ Benguela Current

Cape gannet colony
Bird Island at Lamberts Bay on the west coast of South Africa is famed for its colony of Cape gannets *(Morus capensis)*. Apart from some small cormorant colonies on rock stacks, there are no large seabird breeding colonies north of Lamberts Bay until the Namibian islands.

CAPE HORN

It is a testament to the ferocity of the weather conditions in the area that for nearly a hundred years, until 1624, European sailors did not realize that Cape Horn was an island and not part of the mainland of Tierra del Fuego. Until the opening of the Panama Canal in 1914 the only route for ships traveling between the Pacific and Atlantic oceans was around Cape Horn, which meant sailors had to face the mountainous seas and year-round storms found there. At latitudes below 40°S, prevailing winds blow from west to east around the world, almost uninterrupted by land, giving rise to the "roaring forties" and the "furious fifties." The turbulence and speed of these winds intensify around Cape Horn as the funneling effect of the Andes and the Antarctic peninsula channel the winds into the relatively narrow Drake Passage. Wave heights here can reach enormous sizes. An area of shallow water around Cape Horn further increases wave heights and "rogue waves" can reach 100 feet (30 m).

Rounding Cape Horn
The Drake Passage is a body of water 600 miles (1,000 km) wide between Cape Horn and Antarctica that links the Pacific and Atlantic oceans. Its rough weather, ice, and mountainous seas make the passage a severe test of endurance for ships and their crews.

Whale migration
The southern right whale (Eubalaena australis) migrates northward to breed during the austral winter and is seen as far north as Brazil and Namibia. The population is estimated to be 12,000 animals and, since the hunting ban, stocks are estimated to have grown by seven percent a year.

Tierra del Fuego
Tierra del Fuego is an archipelago whose southern tip is Cape Horn. The islands have a cold, inhospitable subpolar climate. The archipelago gets its name from the smoke and fires lit by the indigenous people for warmth that were seen by the explorer Magellan in 1520.

Magellanic penguins
Magellanic penguins (Spheniscus magellanicus) have their main breeding grounds around Cape Horn, Tierra del Fuego and the Falkland Islands. During the austral winter the penguins from the Atlantic coast of South America and the Falkland Islands all migrate northward to the coast of Brazil.

Surface currents
The Antarctic Circumpolar Current is a wind-driven current that is able to circle the globe unimpeded by landmasses. However, the Drake Passage is a choke point so that some water is diverted northward into the Peru Current, the rest eventually linking with the South Atlantic gyre.

→ Antarctic Circumpolar Current
→ Cape Horn Current
→ Falklands Current

NATURAL RESOURCES

⌐ Whales
◆ Metallic minerals
▯ Oil production
▢ Tourism

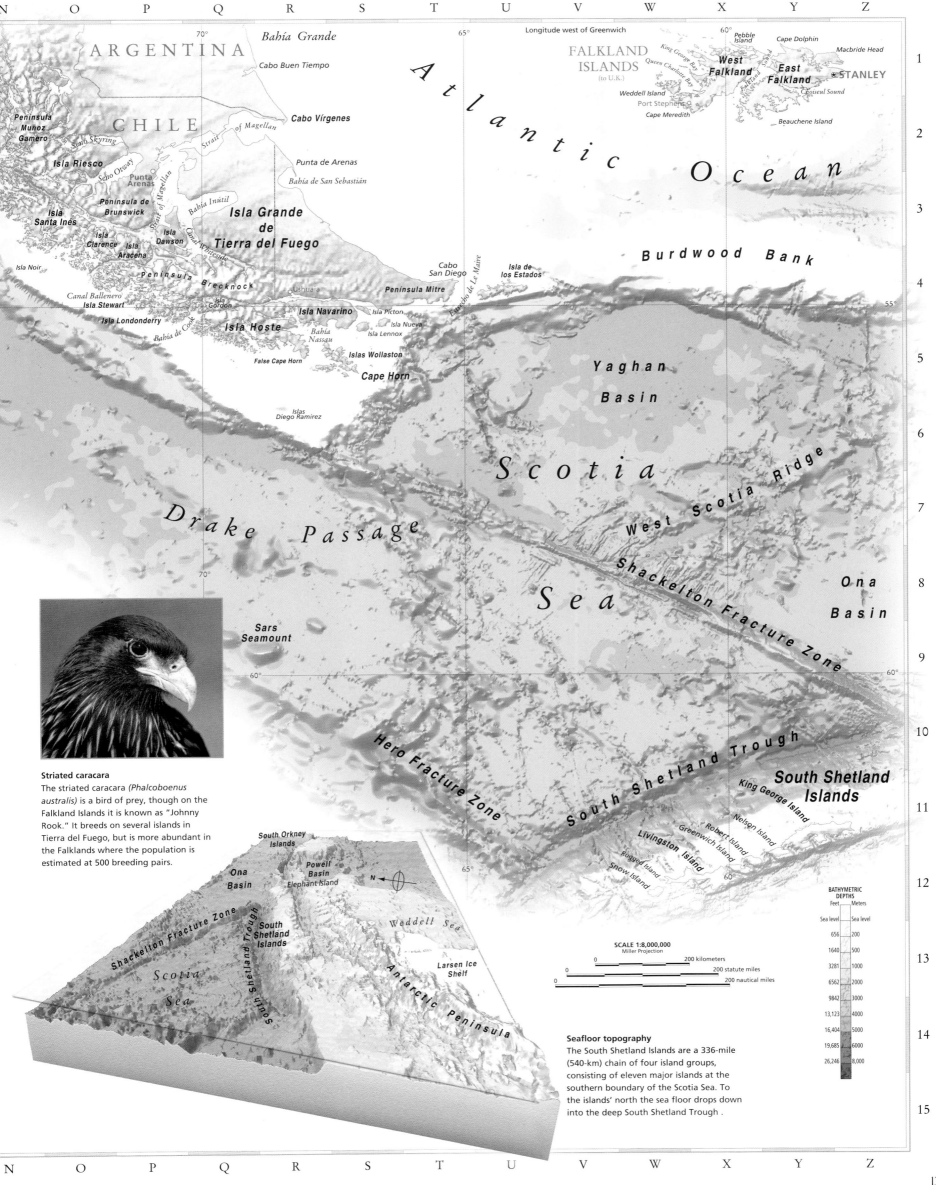

Striated caracara
The striated caracara (Phalcoboenus australis) is a bird of prey, though on the Falkland Islands it is known as "Johnny Rook." It breeds on several islands in Tierra del Fuego, but is more abundant in the Falklands where the population is estimated at 500 breeding pairs.

SCALE 1:8,000,000
Miller Projection

0	200 kilometers
0	200 statute miles
0	200 nautical miles

Seafloor topography
The South Shetland Islands are a 336-mile (540-km) chain of four island groups, consisting of eleven major islands at the southern boundary of the Scotia Sea. To the islands' north the sea floor drops down into the deep South Shetland Trough.

BATHYMETRIC DEPTHS	
Feet	Meters
Sea level	Sea level
656	200
1640	500
3281	1000
6562	2000
9842	3000
13,123	4000
16,404	5000
19,685	6000
26,246	8,000

The Andaman Islands, set in the tropical waters of the Indian Ocean's Andaman Sea, are fringed by coral reefs. The submarine scenery is spectacular and divers who make the trip to this site are richly rewarded. One of the group, Havelock Island, is home to some domesticated Indian elephants *(Elephas maximus)* that also relish a swim in the warm sea.

INDIAN OCEAN

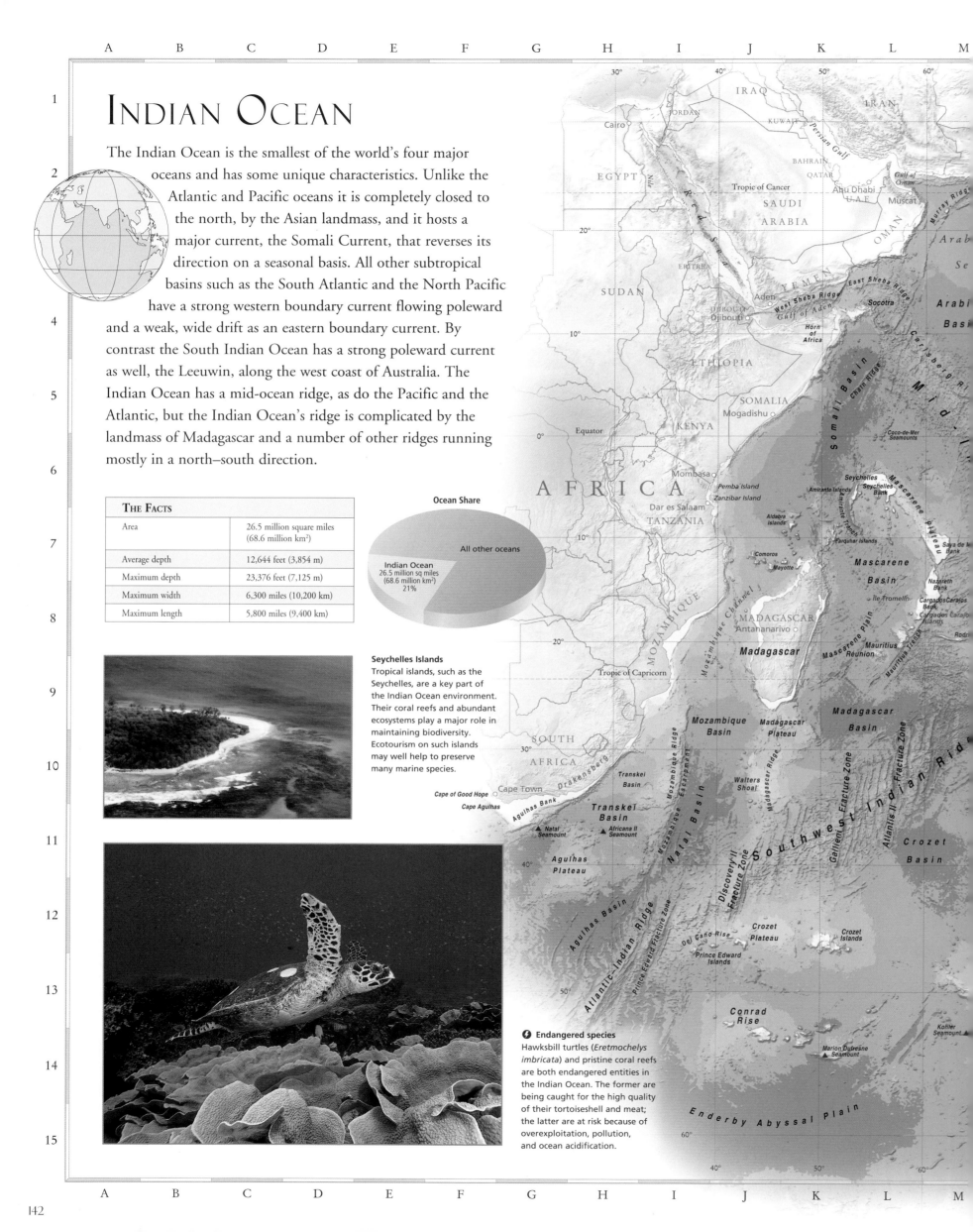

INDIAN OCEAN

The Indian Ocean is the smallest of the world's four major oceans and has some unique characteristics. Unlike the Atlantic and Pacific oceans it is completely closed to the north, by the Asian landmass, and it hosts a major current, the Somali Current, that reverses its direction on a seasonal basis. All other subtropical basins such as the South Atlantic and the North Pacific have a strong western boundary current flowing poleward and a weak, wide drift as an eastern boundary current. By contrast the South Indian Ocean has a strong poleward current as well, the Leeuwin, along the west coast of Australia. The Indian Ocean has a mid-ocean ridge, as do the Pacific and the Atlantic, but the Indian Ocean's ridge is complicated by the landmass of Madagascar and a number of other ridges running mostly in a north–south direction.

THE FACTS

Area	26.5 million square miles (68.6 million km²)
Average depth	12,644 feet (3,854 m)
Maximum depth	23,376 feet (7,125 m)
Maximum width	6,300 miles (10,200 km)
Maximum length	5,800 miles (9,400 km)

Ocean Share

All other oceans

Indian Ocean
26.5 million sq miles
(68.6 million km²)
21%

Seychelles Islands
Tropical islands, such as the Seychelles, are a key part of the Indian Ocean environment. Their coral reefs and abundant ecosystems play a major role in maintaining biodiversity. Ecotourism on such islands may well help to preserve many marine species.

Endangered species
Hawksbill turtles (*Eretmochelys imbricata*) and pristine coral reefs are both endangered entities in the Indian Ocean. The former are being caught for the high quality of their tortoiseshell and meat; the latter are at risk because of overexploitation, pollution, and ocean acidification.

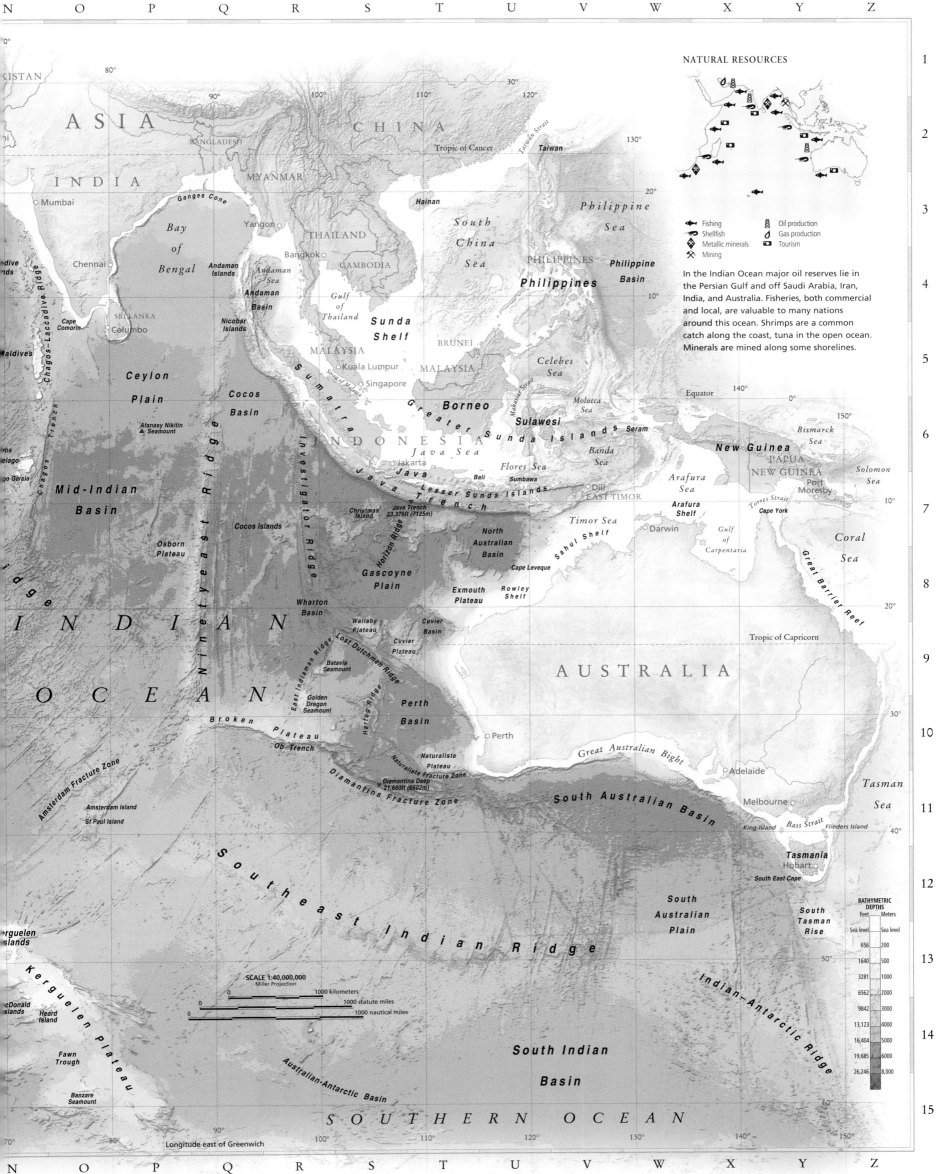

N O P Q R S T U V W X Y Z

80°
90°
100°
110°
30°
120°
130°

1

ASIA

CHINA

2

BANGLADESH

Tropic of Cancer

Taiwan

Tatvan Strait

INDIA

MYANMAR

Hainan

Yangon

*South
China
Sea*

20°

3

Mumbai

Ganges Cone

THAILAND

*Philippine
Sea*

*Bay
of
Bengal*

Bangkok

Andaman
Islands

*Andaman
Sea*

Chennai

GAMBODIA

PHILIPPINES

Philippine

*Philippine
Basin*

10°

4

Chagos–Laccadive Ridge

SRI LANKA

Andaman
Islands

Philippines

Cape
Comorin

Columbo

Nicobar
Islands

*Andaman
Basin*

*Gulf
of
Thailand*

*Sunda
Shelf*

BRUNEI

Maldives

*Ceylon
Plain*

MALAYSIA

Kuala Lumpur

MALAYSIA

*Celebes
Sea*

Equator

140°

0°

5

*Cocos
Basin*

Strait of Malacca

Singapore

*Molucca
Sea*

Seram

*Bismarck
Sea*

150°

6

Investigator Ridge

Borneo

Greater Sunda Islands

Sulawesi

*Banda
Sea*

*Arafura
Sea*

New Guinea

*Atanasy Nikitin
Seamount*

INDONESIA

Java Sea

PAPUA
NEW GUINEA

*Solomon
Sea*

*Mid-Indian
Basin*

Java

Bali

Flores Sea

Sumbawa

*Arafura
Sea*

Port
Moresby

Jakarta

Lesser Sunda Islands

Dili
EAST TIMOR

Timor Sea

*Arafura
Shelf*

10°

7

Chagos Trench

Java Trench

*Christmas
Island*

Java Trench
23,376ft (7125m)

*North
Australian
Basin*

Sahul Shelf

Darwin

*Gulf
of
Carpentaria*

Torres Strait

Cape York

*Coral
Sea*

go Garcia

Cocos Islands

Horizon Ridge

Cape Leveque

8

*Osborn
Plateau*

*Gascoyne
Plain*

*Exmouth
Plateau*

*Rowley
Shelf*

20°

INDIAN

*Wharton
Basin*

*Wallaby
Plateau*

*Cuvier
Basin*

Tropic of Capricorn

9

Lost Dutchmen Ridge

*Cuvier
Plateau*

AUSTRALIA

Ninetyeast Ridge

East Indiaman Ridge

*Batavia
Seamount*

OCEAN

*Golden
Dragon
Seamount*

Hartog Ridge

*Perth
Basin*

Broken Plateau

Perth

Great Australian Bight

30°

10

Ob Trench

*Naturaliste
Plateau*

Adelaide

*Tasman
Sea*

Amsterdam Fracture Zone

Naturaliste Fracture Zone

*Diamantina Deep
21,680ft (6602m)*

Diamantina Fracture Zone

South Australian Basin

Melbourne

11

Amsterdam Island

St Paul Island

King Island

Bass Strait

Flinders Island

40°

Tasmania

Hobart

South East Cape

12

Southeast Indian Ridge

*South
Australian
Plain*

*South
Tasman
Rise*

BATHYMETRIC
DEPTHS

rguelen
slands

Feet	Meters
Sea level	Sea level
656	200
1640	500
3281	1000
6562	2000
9842	3000
13,123	4000
16,404	5000
19,685	6000
26,246	8,000

50°

13

Indian–Antarctic Ridge

SCALE 1:40,000,000
Miller Projection

0   1000 kilometers

cDonald
slands

Kerguelen Plateau

Heard
Island

0   1000 statute miles

0   1000 nautical miles

14

*Fawn
Trough*

South Indian

*Banzare
Seamount*

Australian-Antarctic Basin

Basin

60°

15

SOUTHERN OCEAN

70°
80°
90°
Longitude east of Greenwich
100°
110°
120°
130°
140°
150°

N O P Q R S T U V W X Y Z

NORTHERN INDIAN OCEAN

The northern Indian Ocean, north of the equator, represents less than one-third of the total Indian Ocean. The waters here are generally warm, supporting coral reefs and extensive areas of mangroves. Sea turtles nest on the Indian coastline and many shark species thrive here. At the center of this expanse of ocean are the Indian subcontinent and its extension, the Chagos-Laccadive Ridge. Together these geographical features split this ocean into two roughly equal parts—the Arabian Sea and the Bay of Bengal. Adjacent seas, the Red Sea and the Persian Gulf, contribute their highly saline waters to those of the northern Indian Ocean. Currents here have a decided seasonality that is largely, but not entirely, driven by the monsoonal winds. During the northeast monsoon a westward North Equatorial Current is found at the equator and the circulation in both the Arabian Sea and the Bay of Bengal is clockwise. During the southwest monsoon the flow along the equator is eastward as the Southwest Monsoon Current; the flow in the Bay of Bengal is partially counterclockwise.

Seaside monument
The town of Kanniyakumari is situated at the southernmost tip of the Indian peninsula, where the Arabian Sea and the Bay of Bengal meet. Here, on a rocky islet, a monument has been erected to Swami Vivekananda, a Bengali religious leader, philosopher, and social reformer.

NATURAL RESOURCES

- 🐟 Fishing
- Shellfish
- ◆ Metallic minerals
- ⚒ Mining
- Oil production
- Tourism

Oman coastline
An abandoned fishing boat lies on the beach near Musandam, Oman. Subsistence and artisanal fisheries still play a major role in the economies of coastal communities around the northern Indian Ocean. They supply a significant part of the protein requirements of many people living near the coastline.

Surface currents
Northern Indian Ocean currents are influenced by monsoonal winds. The southwest monsoon blows from June to October, the northeast monsoon from December to April. The latter causes the reversal of the Somali Current and the formation of the Equatorial Countercurrent.

- ----- Equatorial Countercurrent
- → North Equatorial Current
- → Northeast monsoon

Lionfish
Lionfish (Pterois miles) are a venomous marine species; they have long poisonous dorsal spines. An Indo-Pacific fish, seen here in the Andaman Sea among soft gorgonian corals, they have been displaced to the Atlantic where they are now an invasive species.

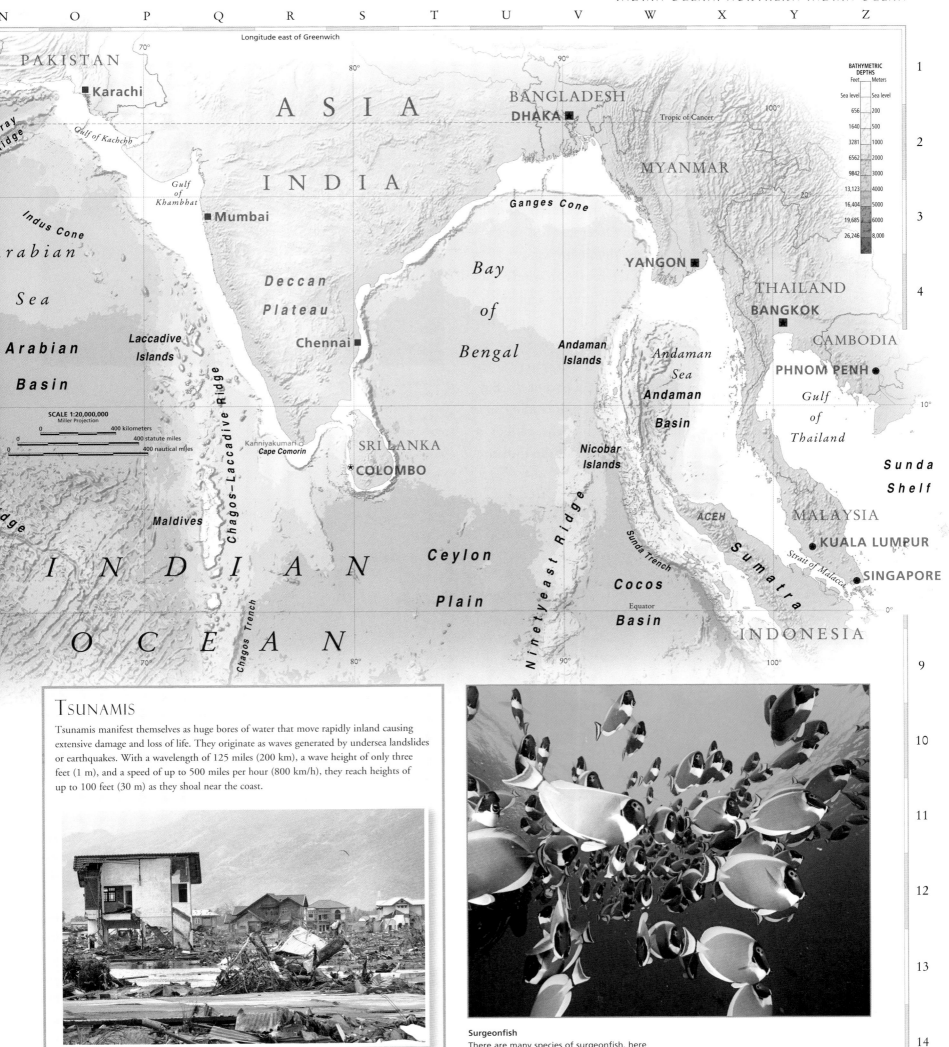

Map labels

Longitude east of Greenwich

PAKISTAN
Karachi
Gulf of Kachchh
ASIA
BANGLADESH
DHAKA
Tropic of Cancer
MYANMAR
INDIA
Gulf of Khambhat
Mumbai
Ganges Cone
YANGON
THAILAND
BANGKOK
Deccan Plateau
Bay of Bengal
Andaman Islands
Andaman Sea
CAMBODIA
PHNOM PENH
Arabian Sea
Chennai
Andaman Basin
Gulf of Thailand
Arabian Basin
Laccadive Islands
Sunda Shelf
SCALE 1:20,000,000
Miller Projection
0   400 kilometers
0   400 statute miles
0   400 nautical miles
Kanniyakumari
Cape Comorin
SRI LANKA
Nicobar Islands
MALAYSIA
ACEH
KUALA LUMPUR
Maldives
Chagos–Laccadive Ridge
COLOMBO
Ceylon Plain
Sumatra
Strait of Malacca
SINGAPORE
INDIAN
OCEAN
Chagos Trench
Cocos Basin
Ninetyeast Ridge
Sunda Trench
Equator
INDONESIA
ray idge
Indus Cone
Arabian Sea

BATHYMETRIC DEPTHS

Feet	Meters
Sea level	Sea level
656	200
1640	500
3281	1000
6562	2000
9842	3000
13,123	4000
16,404	5000
19,685	6000
26,246	8,000

Tsunamis

Tsunamis manifest themselves as huge bores of water that move rapidly inland causing extensive damage and loss of life. They originate as waves generated by undersea landslides or earthquakes. With a wavelength of 125 miles (200 km), a wave height of only three feet (1 m), and a speed of up to 500 miles per hour (800 km/h), they reach heights of up to 100 feet (30 m) as they shoal near the coast.

Devastation wrought by the 2004 tsunami on Aceh, the northern part of Indonesia. This was one of the most destructive tsunamis in modern history and cost the lives of thousands of people.

Surgeonfish
There are many species of surgeonfish, here the powder blue (Acanthurus leucosternon). Surgeonfish are invariably brightly colored, grow to 6–16 inches (15–40 cm), and are found among coral reefs in the tropics where they graze on algae. They have sharp spines at either side of the tail.

BAY OF BENGAL

This ocean region is not a bay in the usual coastal sense of the word, but constitutes the sea between India and Southeast Asia. The major currents here undergo seasonal reversal. From January to July the flow along the coast of India, the East Indian Current, is north-eastward; from September to December it is south-eastward, both contrary to the dominant wind directions. The main winds are the monsoon winds; the southwest or summer monsoon from about June to September and the northeast or winter monsoon from March to April. In winter the East Indian Current flows strongly with speeds exceeding 3.3 feet (1 m) per second and its fresher water is then fed into the adjacent Arabian Sea. A substantial part of the Bay of Bengal is less than 9,840 feet (3,000 m) deep, including all of the Andaman Sea along its eastern side. Much of the seafloor is flat, the result of sediment from the main rivers of the Indian subcontinent accumulating here over millenia.

Chlorophyll
In this satellite image of the Bay of Bengal the green coloration gives a good indication of the density of chlorophyll in the water, which in turn can be related to the presence of phytoplankton, marine algae. Regions colored red show where phytoplankton is abundant.

Subsistence fisheries
Fishermen in Orissa, India, remove a meager catch from their nets while others wait to take the fish to market. Subsistence or artisanal fisheries are found along the whole coastline of the Bay of Bengal, but in many places overfishing has caused fish stocks to collapse.

THE FACTS	
Area	838,613 square miles (2,172,000 km²)
Average depth	8,500 feet (2,600 m)
Maximum depth	15,400 feet (4,694 m)
Maximum width	1,000 miles (1,610 km)
Maximum length	1,300 miles (2,090 km)

NATURAL RESOURCES

➤ Fishing
◆ Metallic minerals

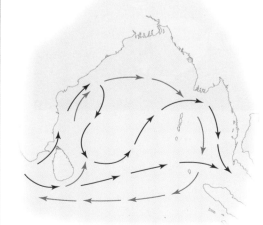

Surface currents
The surface currents here are affected by monsoonal winds. The currents off the northeastern coast of the Indian subcontinent reverse direction seasonally. However, the duration and intensity of monsoonal winds are not identical every year, so the currents also vary from year to year.

→ Summer
→ Winter

Colubrine sea krait
Banded sea snakes, such as this colubrine sea krait (Laticauda colubrina), are reptiles found in the ocean waters of the Indo-Pacific tropics. Females of this species may grow to 4.5 feet (1.4 m), nearly double the length of males. Sea kraits are venomous, but are not aggressive toward divers.

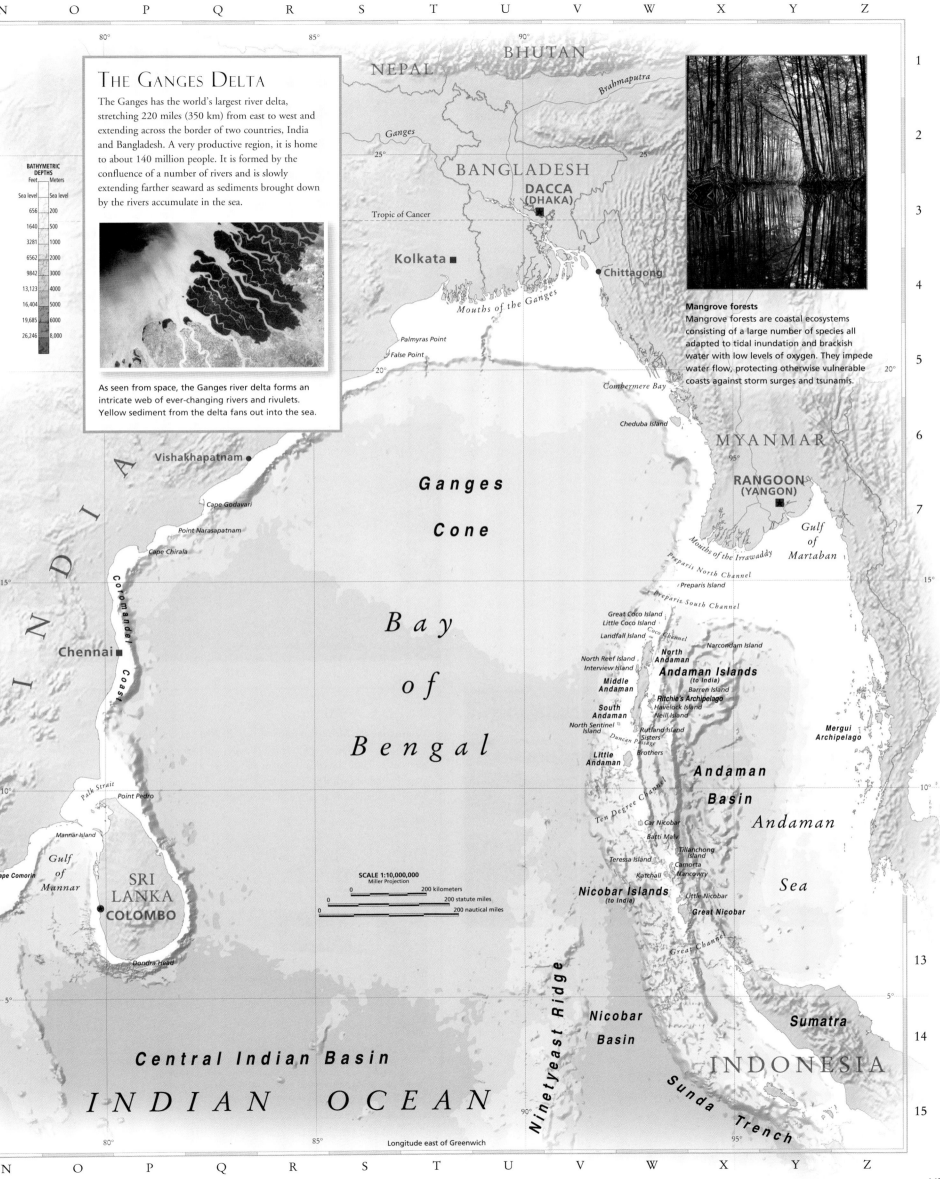

THE GANGES DELTA

The Ganges has the world's largest river delta, stretching 220 miles (350 km) from east to west and extending across the border of two countries, India and Bangladesh. A very productive region, it is home to about 140 million people. It is formed by the confluence of a number of rivers and is slowly extending farther seaward as sediments brought down by the rivers accumulate in the sea.

As seen from space, the Ganges river delta forms an intricate web of ever-changing rivers and rivulets. Yellow sediment from the delta fans out into the sea.

BATHYMETRIC DEPTHS

Feet	Meters
Sea level	Sea level
656	200
1640	500
3281	1000
6562	2000
9842	3000
13,123	4000
16,404	5000
19,685	6000
26,246	8,000

Mangrove forests
Mangrove forests are coastal ecosystems consisting of a large number of species all adapted to tidal inundation and brackish water with low levels of oxygen. They impede water flow, protecting otherwise vulnerable coasts against storm surges and tsunamis.

NEPAL
BHUTAN
BANGLADESH
DACCA (DHAKA)
Tropic of Cancer
Kolkata
Chittagong
Mouths of the Ganges
Palmyras Point
False Point
Combermere Bay
Cheduba Island
MYANMAR
RANGOON (YANGON)
Gulf of Martaban
Mouths of the Irrawaddy
Preparis North Channel
Preparis Island
Preparis South Channel
Great Coco Island
Little Coco Island
Landfall Island
Coco Channel
Narcondam Island
North Reef Island
Interview Island
North Andaman
Andaman Islands (to India)
Middle Andaman
Barren Island
South Andaman
Ritchie's Archipelago
Havelock Island
Neill Island
North Sentinel Island
Rutland Island
Sisters
Brothers
Duncan Passage
Little Andaman
Mergui Archipelago
Andaman Basin
Andaman Sea
Ten Degree Channel
Car Nicobar
Batti Malv
Tillanchong Island
Teressa Island
Camorta
Nancowry
Katchall
Nicobar Islands (to India)
Little Nicobar
Great Nicobar
Great Channel

INDIA
Vishakhapatnam
Cape Godavari
Point Narasapatnam
Cape Chirala
Coromandel Coast
Chennai
Ganges Cone
Bay of Bengal
Palk Strait
Point Pedro
Mannar Island
Gulf of Mannar
Cape Comorin
SRI LANKA
COLOMBO
Dondra Head

SCALE 1:10,000,000
Miller Projection
0   200 kilometers
0   200 statute miles
0   200 nautical miles

Ninetyeast Ridge
Nicobar Basin
Sumatra
INDONESIA
Sunda Trench
Central Indian Basin
INDIAN OCEAN
Longitude east of Greenwich

RED SEA

The Red Sea is part of a rift valley that formed when the African continent separated from Arabia. Lying between two desert regions, the Red Sea receives little runoff from land but experiences high levels of evaporation; some of the most saline waters in the world's seas are to be found here. The Red Sea is more than 6,560 feet (2,000 m) deep at its center but its access to the open sea is over a shallow sill at the Bab al Mandab strait that is only 360 feet (110 m) deep. As a result of this structure in the seafloor topography, fresher water moves in at the sea surface and dense, highly saline water with a low oxygen content escapes below the inflow. The extreme characteristics of Red Sea water allow it to be traced through most of the western Indian Ocean. It is even to be found in the Agulhas Current and the Agulhas Rings south of Africa.

THE FACTS	
Area	169,100 square miles (438,000 km²)
Average depth	1,608 feet (490 m)
Maximum depth	9,974 feet (3,040 m)
Maximum width	220 miles (355 km)
Maximum length	1,398 miles (2,250 km)

Bottlenose dolphin
The most common of ocean dolphins, bottlenose dolphins (*Tursiops truncatus),* inhabit warm seas worldwide. They live in pods of 15 or more and hunt small fish. They use echolocation to locate prey, and sound for communication. Many are killed as bycatch of tuna fisheries.

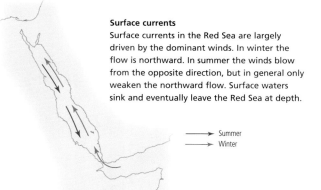

Surface currents
Surface currents in the Red Sea are largely driven by the dominant winds. In winter the flow is northward. In summer the winds blow from the opposite direction, but in general only weaken the northward flow. Surface waters sink and eventually leave the Red Sea at depth.

→ Summer
→ Winter

Hawksbill turtle
A hawksbill sea turtle (*Eretmochelys imbricata)* feeds on sea sponges over a coral reef, its preferred habitat. The hawksbill has a wide distribution but it is critically endangered; in some countries it is harvested for its meat. One of its major nesting sites is in the Red Sea.

Twobar anemonefish
At home among the tentacles of the sea anemone, the brilliantly colored twobar anemonefish (*Amphiprion bicinctus)* is safe from predators. Anemonefish are found in warm seas worldwide but particularly on coral or rocky reefs in the Indo-Pacific region.

SUEZ CANAL

Connecting the Mediterranean Sea with the Red Sea, the Suez Canal was opened to shipping in 1869. It is 120 miles (193 km) long and can handle ships of 150,000 tons displacement and 53 feet (16 m) draft. Up to 160 ships pass through it each day. There is a negligible difference in height between the waters of the oceans at each end, so no locks are needed in the canal.

A seagoing freighter sails through the Suez Canal on its way to the Red Sea. Ships pass through the canal at low speeds to avoid creating a bow wash that could erode the shoreline.

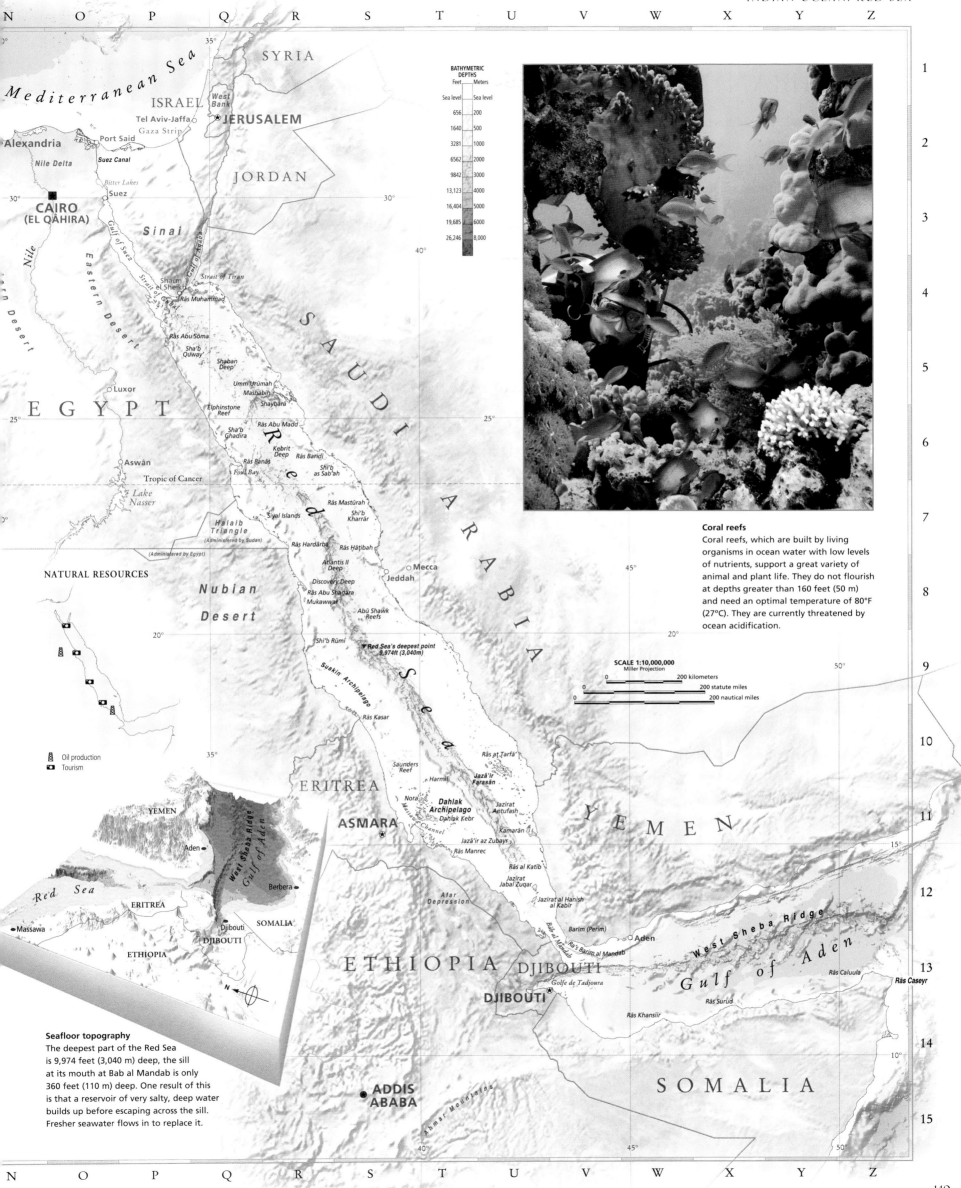

BATHYMETRIC DEPTHS

Feet	Meters
Sea level	Sea level
656	200
1640	500
3281	1000
6562	2000
9842	3000
13,123	4000
16,404	5000
19,685	6000
26,246	8,000

NATURAL RESOURCES

🛢 Oil production
🏝 Tourism

Coral reefs

Coral reefs, which are built by living organisms in ocean water with low levels of nutrients, support a great variety of animal and plant life. They do not flourish at depths greater than 160 feet (50 m) and need an optimal temperature of 80°F (27°C). They are currently threatened by ocean acidification.

SCALE 1:10,000,000
Miller Projection

0 — 200 kilometers
0 — 200 statute miles
0 — 200 nautical miles

Seafloor topography

The deepest part of the Red Sea is 9,974 feet (3,040 m) deep, the sill at its mouth at Bab al Mandab is only 360 feet (110 m) deep. One result of this is that a reservoir of very salty, deep water builds up before escaping across the sill. Fresher seawater flows in to replace it.

Mediterranean Sea

SYRIA
ISRAEL
West Bank
Tel Aviv-Jaffa
Gaza Strip
★ JERUSALEM
JORDAN
Alexandria
Port Said
Nile Delta
Suez Canal
Bitter Lakes
CAIRO (EL QÂHIRA)
Suez
Sinai
Gulf of Suez
Strait of Tiran
Gulf of Aqaba
Sharm el Sheikh
Râs Muhammad
Eastern Desert
Nile
EGYPT
Luxor
Aswân
Tropic of Cancer
Lake Nasser
Strait of Tiran
Râs Abu Sôma
Sha'b Quway
Shaban Deep
Umm Urumah
Mashâbih
Shaybarâ
Elphinstone Reef
Sha'b Ghadira
Râs Abu Madd
Kebrit Deep
Râs Baridi
Râs Banâs
Foul Bay
Shi'b as Sab'ah
Halaib Triangle
(Administered by Sudan)
(Administered by Egypt)
Siyal Islands
Râs Mastûrah
Shi'b Kharrâr
Nubian Desert
Râs Hardârba
Râs Hâtibah
Atlantis II Deep
Mecca
Jeddah
Discovery Deep
Râs Abu Shagara
Mukawwar
Abû Shawk Reefs
SAUDI ARABIA
Red Sea
Shi'b Rûmi
Red Sea's deepest point 9,974ft (3,040m)
Suakin Archipelago
Râs Kasar
Saunders Reef
Harmil
Râs at Tarfâ
Jazâ'ir Farasân
Jazirat Antufash
Nora
Dahlak Archipelago
Dahlak Kebir
Jazirat Antufash
Kamarân
ERITREA
ASMARA ★
Massawa Channel
Jazâ'ir az Zubayr
Jazâ'ir Manrec
Râs al Katib
YEMEN
Aden
Berbera
Jazirat Jabal Zuqar
Afar Depression
Jazirat al Hanish al Kabir
Barim (Perim)
Bâb al Mandab
Ra's Barim al Mandab
West Sheba Ridge
Aden
ERITREA
SOMALIA
Djibouti
DJIBOUTI
ETHIOPIA
Golfe de Tadjoura
DJIBOUTI
Gulf of Aden
Râs Surud
Râs Caluula
Râs Caseyr
Râs Khansiir
ADDIS ABABA
Ahmar Mountains
SOMALIA
West Sheba Ridge
Gulf of Aden
N

ARABIAN SEA

Maritime trade routes have crossed the Arabian Sea since ancient times and the modern-day vessels that use the Suez Canal continue to pass through here. Lying to the west of the Indian subcontinent and the Chagos-Laccadive Ridge, the Arabian Sea has two mediterranean seas that feed water into it, the Persian Gulf and the Red Sea. The flow in the Arabian Sea itself is seasonal with clockwise flow in summer, fed by the Somali Current, and a weak counterclockwise flow in winter. The winter flow along the west coast of India is about 250 miles (400 km) wide and 650 feet (200 m) deep before it is fed fresher water by a jet current from the Bay of Bengal. A notable feature of the region is strong, wind-driven upwelling on the east coast of Arabia. However, the strong East Arabian Current on the western boundary inhibits the build-up of a productive ecosystem by rapidly removing most of the phytoplankton that is produced. Upwelling is also found on the western Indian continental shelf during the southwest monsoon.

THE FACTS	
Area	1.5 million square miles (3.9 million km²)
Average depth	9,022 feet (2,750 m)
Maximum depth	15,262 feet (4,652 m)
Maximum width	1,490 miles (2,400 km)

NATURAL RESOURCES

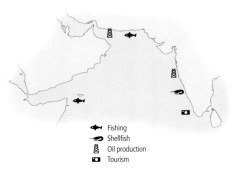

- Fishing
- Shellfish
- Oil production
- Tourism

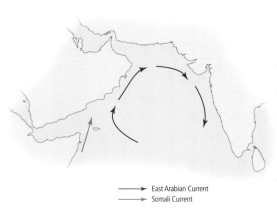

Surface currents
The Arabian Sea has surface currents largely influenced by the monsoonal winds and, as these winds may differ in duration from year to year, so do the currents. At depth the waters are influenced by the dense, salty water that emerges from the two adjacent seas, the Red Sea and the Persian Gulf.

East Arabian Current
Somali Current

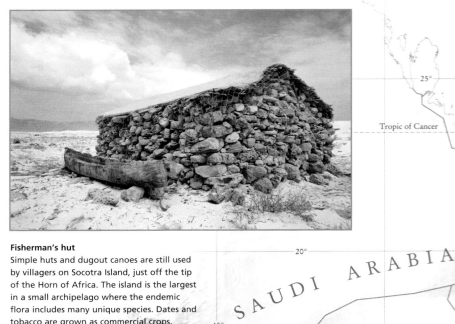

Fisherman's hut
Simple huts and dugout canoes are still used by villagers on Socotra Island, just off the tip of the Horn of Africa. The island is the largest in a small archipelago where the endemic flora includes many unique species. Dates and tobacco are grown as commercial crops.

BATHYMETRIC DEPTHS

Feet	Meters
Sea level	Sea level
656	200
1640	500
3281	1000
6562	2000
9842	3000
13,123	4000
16,404	5000
19,685	6000
26,246	8,000

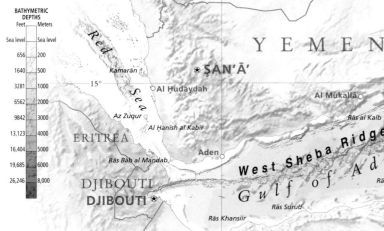

Oil slicks
A radar image of an offshore drilling field about 93 miles (150 km) west of Mumbai, India, shows the dark streaks of extensive oil slicks surrounding many of the drilling platforms, which appear as bright white spots. Radar images are useful for detecting oil pollution on the ocean's surface.

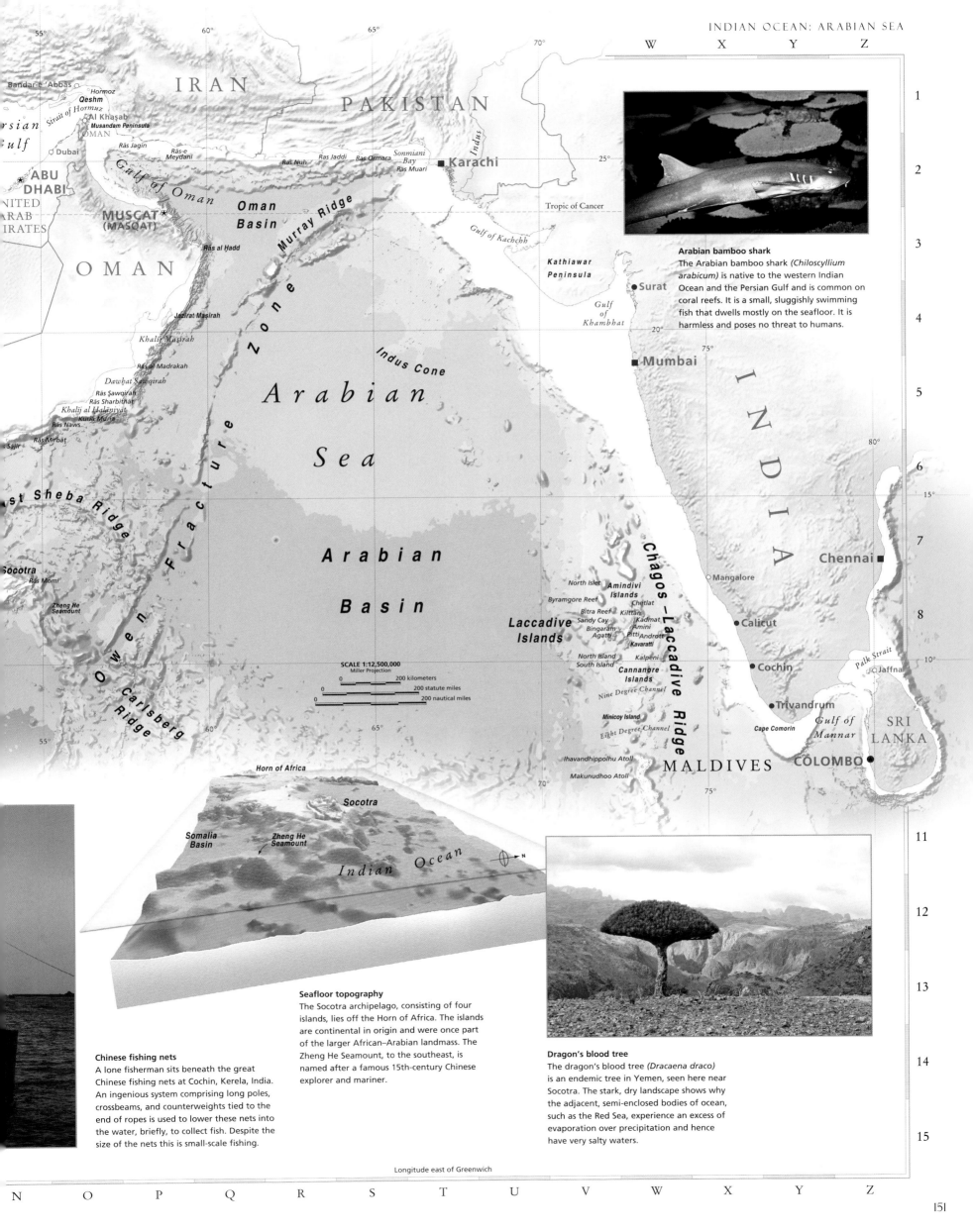

W X Y Z

Arabian bamboo shark
The Arabian bamboo shark (*Chiloscyllium arabicum*) is native to the western Indian Ocean and the Persian Gulf and is common on coral reefs. It is a small, sluggishly swimming fish that dwells mostly on the seafloor. It is harmless and poses no threat to humans.

55° 60° 65° 70°

IRAN
PAKISTAN

Bandar-e 'Abbas
Hormoz
Qeshm
Strait of Hormuz
Al Khaşab
Musandam Peninsula
OMAN
Dubai
Rās Jagin
Rās-e Meydani
Rās Nuh
Ras Jaddi
Ras Ormara
Sonmiani Bay
Ras Muari
Karachi
Indus

ABU DHABI
UNITED ARAB EMIRATES
MUSCAT (MASQAT)
Gulf of Oman
Oman Basin
Murray Ridge
Rās al Ḥadd

Tropic of Cancer

Gulf of Kachchh

Kathiawar Peninsula

Surat

OMAN
Jazīrat Maşīrah
Khalīj Maşīrah
Rās al Madrakah
Dawḥat Sawqirah
Rās Sawqirah
Khalīj al Ḥalānīyat
Kurīā Murīā
Rās Naws
Rās Mirbāţ
Sajir

Owen Fracture Zone

Indus Cone

Gulf of Khambhat

Mumbai

Arabian Sea

Arabian Basin

INDIA

East Sheba Ridge

Socotra
Rās Momi
Zheng He Seamount

Owen Carlsberg Ridge

Mangalore

North Islet
Amindivi Islands
Byramgore Reef
Bitra Reef
Chetlat
Sandy Cay
Kilttän
Kadmat
Bingaram
Amini
Agatti
Pitti
Andrott
Kavaratti
Laccadive Islands

Chagos-Laccadive Ridge

Chennai

Calicut

Cochin

Palk Strait
Jaffna

SCALE 1:12,500,000
Miller Projection
0   200 kilometers
0   200 statute miles
0   200 nautical miles

North Island
South Island
Kalpeni
Cannanore Islands
Nine Degree Channel

Trivandrum
Cape Comorin
Gulf of Mannar
SRI LANKA

Minicoy Island
Eight Degree Channel

Ihavandhippolhu Atoll
Makunudhoo Atoll

MALDIVES

COLOMBO

Horn of Africa
Socotra
Somalia Basin
Zheng He Seamount
Indian Ocean
N

Chinese fishing nets
A lone fisherman sits beneath the great Chinese fishing nets at Cochin, Kerela, India. An ingenious system comprising long poles, crossbeams, and counterweights tied to the end of ropes is used to lower these nets into the water, briefly, to collect fish. Despite the size of the nets this is small-scale fishing.

Seafloor topography
The Socotra archipelago, consisting of four islands, lies off the Horn of Africa. The islands are continental in origin and were once part of the larger African–Arabian landmass. The Zheng He Seamount, to the southeast, is named after a famous 15th-century Chinese explorer and mariner.

Dragon's blood tree
The dragon's blood tree (*Dracaena draco*) is an endemic tree in Yemen, seen here near Socotra. The stark, dry landscape shows why the adjacent, semi-enclosed bodies of ocean, such as the Red Sea, experience an excess of evaporation over precipitation and hence have very salty waters.

Longitude east of Greenwich

N O P Q R S T U V W X Y Z

1
2
3
4
5
6
7
8
11
12
13
14
15

PERSIAN GULF

The Persian Gulf region is the site of vast crude oil and gas reserves and the drilling operations that extract these valuable commodities put pressure on the natural environment. In both its geography and the salinity of its water the Persian Gulf is in many respects very similar to the Red Sea. It is long and narrow, with a narrow strait at its southern end, and is bordered by land that is predominantly arid. However, in contrast to the Red Sea it is very shallow. Its waters are also strongly saline because there is an excess of evaporation over rainfall. This salinity is formed despite the runoff into the Persian Gulf from the Tigris and the Euphrates rivers. The water that flows out of the gulf at the Strait of Hormuz is very salty, but with a much higher oxygen content than the outflow from the Red Sea. In some parts of the Indian Ocean this difference in dissolved oxygen values makes it possible to differentiate between waters coming from these two mediterranean seas.

THE FACTS	
Area	96,911 square miles (251,000 km²)
Average depth	164 feet (50 m)
Maximum depth	344 feet (119 m)
Maximum width	35 miles (56 km)
Maximum length	615 miles (989 km)

Sediment flow
A satellite image shows the true color of the sea at the head of the Persian Gulf. Here the combined waters of the Tigris and Euphrates rivers, laden with sediment, enter the sea. They appear light brown where they enter, and then dissipate into turquoise swirls as they drift southward.

Dugong
Dugongs (Dugong dugon) are large, placid marine mammals found in the Indo-Pacific. They eat seagrasses and are found largely in bays and mangrove channels, where they may be vulnerable to predators. Although capable of living for 70 years they are now extinct in many parts of their former range.

Oil rig
Oil platforms are enormous structures housing machinery for drilling wells into the seafloor in search of oil and gas, processing plants, and accommodation for workers. Platforms may be afloat or attached to the seafloor, depending on the depth of the water.

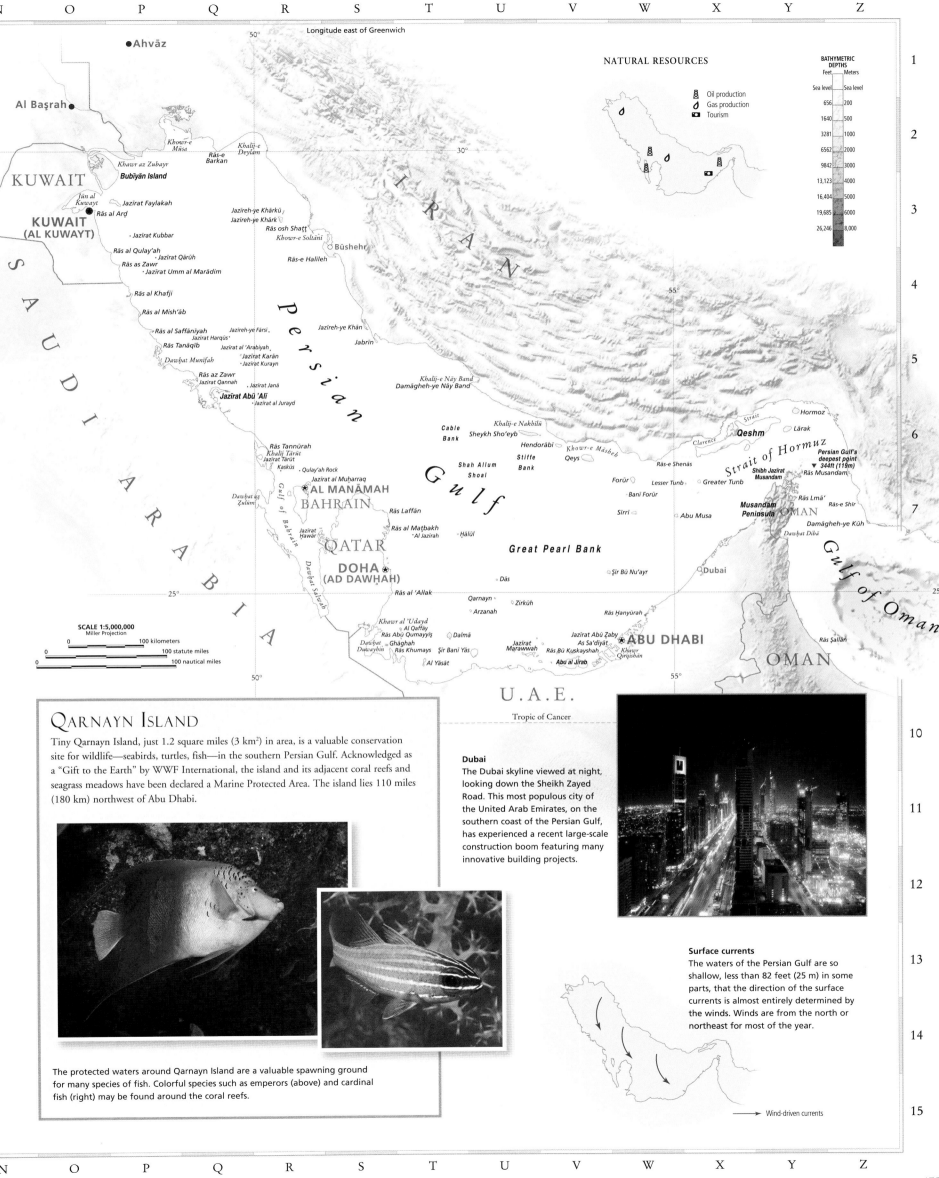

Longitude east of Greenwich

NATURAL RESOURCES

Oil production
Gas production
Tourism

BATHYMETRIC DEPTHS

Feet	Meters
Sea level	Sea level
656	200
1640	500
3281	1000
6562	2000
9842	3000
13,123	4000
16,404	5000
19,685	6000
26,246	8,000

●Ahvāz

Al Baṣrah ●

KUWAIT

Khowr-e Mūsā
Khalīj-e Deylam
Rās-e Barkan

Khawr az Zubayr
Bubīyān Island

Jūn al Kuwayt
KUWAIT (AL KUWAYT)
Rās al Arḍ
Jazīrat Faylakah

Jazīrat Kubbar
Rās al Qulayʿah
Jazīrat Qārūh
Rās as Zawr
Jazīrat Umm al Marādim
Rās al Khafji
Rās al Mishʿāb
Rās al Saffānīyah
Jazīrat Harqūs
Rās Tanāqib
Dawḥat Munīfah
Rās az Zawr
Jazīrat Qannah
Jazīrat Janā
Jazīrat Abū ʿAlī
Jazīrat al Jurayd

Jazīreh-ye Khārkū
Jazīreh-ye Khārk
Rās osh Shaṭṭ
Khowr-e Soltānī
○ Būshehr
Rās-e Halīleh

Jazīreh-ye Fārsī
Jazīrat al ʿArabiyah
Jazīrat Karān
Jazīrat Kurayn

Jazīreh-ye Khān
Jabrīn

I R A N

S A U D I   A R A B I A

P e r s i a n   G u l f

Khalīj-e Nāy Band
Damāgheh-ye Nāy Band

Cable Bank
Sheykh Shoʿeyb
Khalīj-e Nakhīlū
Hendorābī
Khowr-e Māsheh
Qeys

Shah Allum Shoal
Stiffe Bank

Rās Tannūrah
Khalīj Tārūt
Jazīrat Tārūt
Kaskūs
Qulayʿah Rock
Jazīrat al Muḥarraq
AL MANĀMAH
BAHRAIN

Forūr
Bani Forūr

Hormoz
Lārak
Qeshm
Strait
Clarence
Shibh Jazīrat Musandam
Rās-e Shenās
Rās-e Shir

Strait of Hormuz

Persian Gulf's deepest point
▼ 344ft (119m)
Rās Musandam

Lesser Tunb
Greater Tunb
Sirrī
Abu Musa

Musandam Peninsula   OMAN
Rās Lmāʿ
Damāgheh-ye Kūh
Dawḥat Dibā

Gulf of Oman

Gulf of Bahrain
Dawḥat az Ẓulim
Rās Laffān
Jazīrat Hawār
QATAR
Dawḥat Salwah
DOHA (AD DAWḤAH)
Rās al Maṭbakh
ʿAl Jazirah
Ḥālūl

Great Pearl Bank

Rās al ʿAllak
Qarnayn
Arzanah
Zirkūh
Das
Şīr Bū Nuʿayr
Rās Ḥanyūrah
Dubai

Khawr al ʿUdayd
Al Qaffay
Rās Abū Qumayyiş
Ghāghah
Dawḥat Duwayhin
Rās Khumays
Dalmā
Şīr Banī Yās
Jazīrat Marawwah
As Saʿdiyāt
Rās Bū Kuskayshah
Jazīrat Abū Ẓaby
ABU DHABI
Khawr Qirqīshān
Abu al Jirab
Al Yāsāt

U. A. E.

Tropic of Cancer

OMAN
Rās Ṣallan

25°   25°

SCALE 1:5,000,000
Miller Projection
100 kilometers
100 statute miles
100 nautical miles

QARNAYN ISLAND

Tiny Qarnayn Island, just 1.2 square miles (3 km²) in area, is a valuable conservation site for wildlife—seabirds, turtles, fish—in the southern Persian Gulf. Acknowledged as a "Gift to the Earth" by WWF International, the island and its adjacent coral reefs and seagrass meadows have been declared a Marine Protected Area. The island lies 110 miles (180 km) northwest of Abu Dhabi.

The protected waters around Qarnayn Island are a valuable spawning ground for many species of fish. Colorful species such as emperors (above) and cardinal fish (right) may be found around the coral reefs.

Dubai
The Dubai skyline viewed at night, looking down the Sheikh Zayed Road. This most populous city of the United Arab Emirates, on the southern coast of the Persian Gulf, has experienced a recent large-scale construction boom featuring many innovative building projects.

Surface currents
The waters of the Persian Gulf are so shallow, less than 82 feet (25 m) in some parts, that the direction of the surface currents is almost entirely determined by the winds. Winds are from the north or northeast for most of the year.

→ Wind-driven currents

153

WESTERN INDIAN OCEAN

From the head of the Arabian Sea to beyond the southern tip of the African continent, the western Indian Ocean covers a vast region. A number of complex currents are found here. Along the Horn of Africa the Somali Current flows northward during the southwest monsoon and southward during the northeast monsoon. Currents in the equatorial belt and in the Arabian Basin are also influenced by these changing monsoon winds. The powerful Agulhas Current carries water southward along southern Africa and part of the water from this current leaks into the South Atlantic as Agulhas Rings. Highly saline water from the Red Sea can be traced to the southern tip of Africa. Fresher water at intermediate depths comes from the Southern Ocean and moves northward. A number of north–south ridges such as the Mascarene Plateau and the Chagos-Laccadive Ridge influence the movement of deep and bottom waters. Localised coastal upwelling is found in the Somali, East Madagascar, and Agulhas systems, stimulating higher biological productivity.

Granite shores
Large boulders are common on the shoreline of granitic islands in the Seychelles, where endemic plants and large colonies of seabirds thrive. Human settlement displaced the giant tortoise *(Dipsochelys hololissa)* but it is found on many of the archipelago's coral islands.

Agulhas Current
The Agulhas Current is one of the world's major ocean currents. It extends to a depth of 9,845 feet (3,000 m) and flows swiftly. In this satellite image clouds are gray, warm Agulhas waters red, and colder water green.

NATURAL RESOURCES

- 🐟 Fishing
- Shellfish
- ⚒ Mining
- 🛢 Oil production
- Tourism

Surface currents
The surface flow along the east coast of Africa is dominated by three currents: the southward Agulhas Current, the northward East African Coastal Current, fed by the South Equatorial Current, and the seasonally reversing Somali Current. The Arabian Sea has clockwise flow in summer, counterclockwise flow in winter.

→ Agulhas Current
--→ Agulhas Return Current
→ Antarctic Circumpolar Current
→ East Madagascar Current
→ South Equatorial Current

Cargados Carajos Islands
Cargados Carajos Bank
Rodrigues Island
Mauritius
Mascarene Plain
Réunion
Mascarene Islands
Mauritius Trench
Indian Ocean
N

Seafloor topography
The islands of Réunion and Mauritius, which lie east of Madagascar, are both volcanic. The volcano on Réunion is quite active. North of Mauritius the shallow Mascarene Plateau forms a formidable barrier to east–west currents such as the South Equatorial Current.

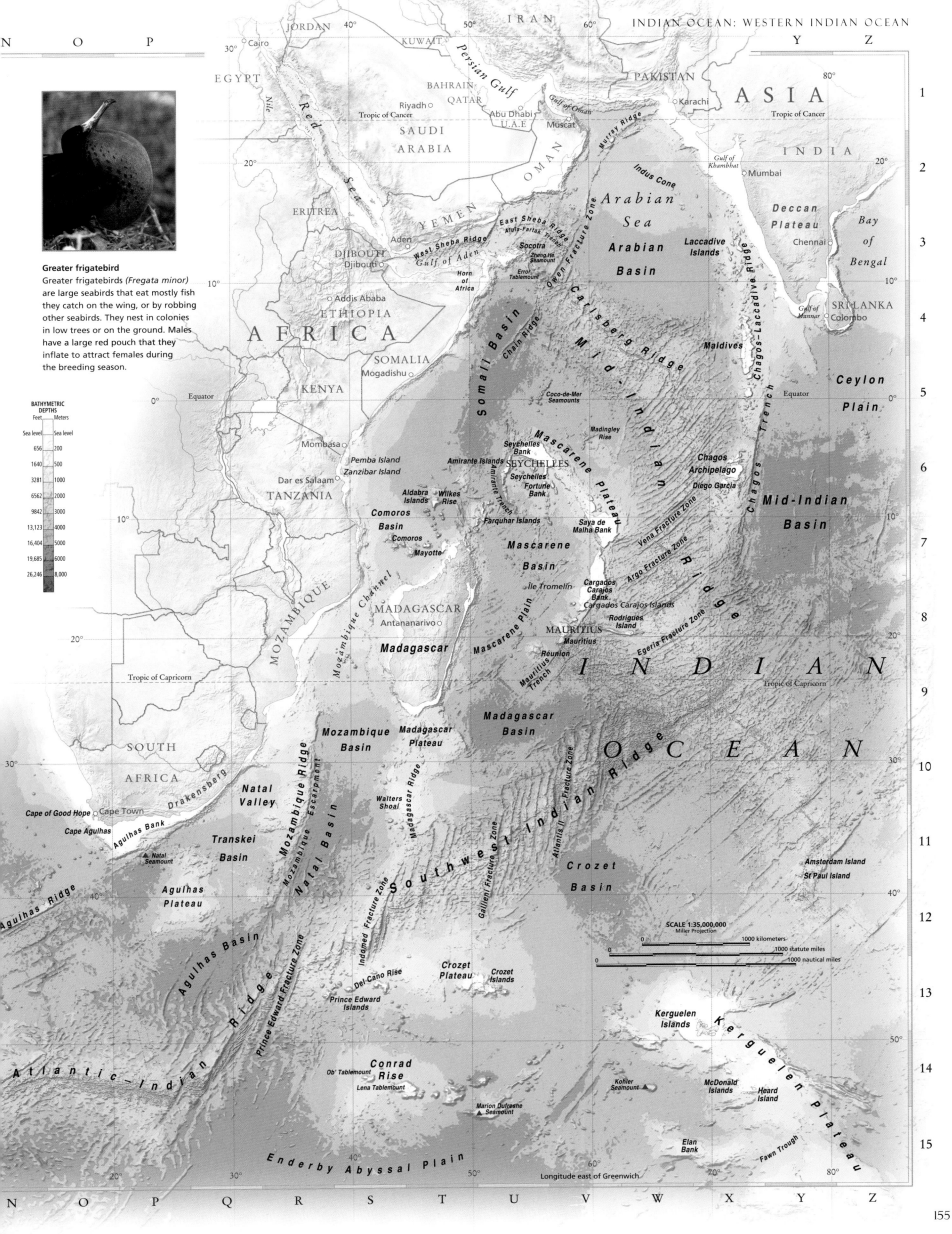

Greater frigatebird

Greater frigatebirds (*Fregata minor*) are large seabirds that eat mostly fish they catch on the wing, or by robbing other seabirds. They nest in colonies in low trees or on the ground. Males have a large red pouch that they inflate to attract females during the breeding season.

BATHYMETRIC DEPTHS

Feet	Meters
Sea level	Sea level
656	200
1640	500
3281	1000
6562	2000
9842	3000
13,123	4000
16,404	5000
19,685	6000
26,246	8,000

JORDAN   40°   50°   IRAN   60°

Cairo   KUWAIT   PAKISTAN   80°

EGYPT   30°   BAHRAIN   Persian Gulf   QATAR   Gulf of Oman   Karachi   ASIA

Riyadh   Tropic of Cancer   Abu Dhabi   U.A.E   Muscat   Murray Ridge   Tropic of Cancer

SAUDI ARABIA   OMAN   Gulf of Khambhat   INDIA   20°

Red Sea   20°   Indus Cone   Mumbai

Nile   YEMEN   Arabian Sea   Deccan Plateau   Bay of Bengal

ERITREA   Aden   East Sheba Ridge   Laccadive Islands   Chennai

DJIBOUTI   Atula-Fartak Trench   Socotra   Arabian Basin

Djibouti   West Sheba Ridge   Zheng He Seamount   10°

Horn of Africa   Gulf of Aden   Errol Tablemount   Owen Fracture Zone   SRI LANKA

Addis Ababa   Carlsberg Ridge   Gulf of Mannar   Colombo

ETHIOPIA   Maldives   Ceylon Plain

AFRICA   Mid-Indian   Chagos–Laccadive Ridge

SOMALIA   Somali Basin   Coco-de-Mer Seamounts   Equator   0°

Equator   Mogadishu   Chain Ridge   Madingley Rise

KENYA   Mascarene Plateau   Chagos Archipelago

Mombasa   Seychelles Bank   Chagos Trench

Pemba Island   Amirante Islands   SEYCHELLES   Diego Garcia   6°

Zanzibar Island   Seychelles   Mid-Indian Basin

Dar es Salaam   Aldabra Islands   Wilkes Rise   Fortune Bank

TANZANIA   Farquhar Islands   Vena Fracture Zone

Comoros Basin   Saya de Malha Bank   Argo Fracture Zone   10°

Comoros   Mascarene Basin   Ridge

Mayotte   Ile Tromelin   Cargados Carajos Bank

MADAGASCAR   Cargados Carajos Islands

Antananarivo   Mascarene Plain   Rodrigues Island   Egeria Fracture Zone

MOZAMBIQUE   MAURITIUS   20°

Madagascar   Mauritius   INDIAN

Mozambique Channel   Réunion   Tropic of Capricorn

Tropic of Capricorn   Mauritius Trench

Madagascar Basin   OCEAN

SOUTH AFRICA   Mozambique Ridge   Madagascar Plateau   30°

Drakensberg   Natal Valley   Southwest Indian Ridge

Cape of Good Hope   Cape Town   Walters Shoal   Amsterdam Island

Cape Agulhas   Agulhas Bank   Transkei Basin   Crozet Basin   St Paul Island   40°

Natal Seamount   Madagascar Ridge   Atlantis II Fracture Zone

Agulhas Ridge   Agulhas Plateau   Mozambique Escarpment   Natal Basin   Gallieni Fracture Zone

SCALE 1:35,000,000   Miller Projection

0   1000 kilometers

0   1000 statute miles

0   1000 nautical miles

Agulhas Basin   Prince Edward Fracture Zone   Indomed Fracture Zone   Crozet Plateau

Del Cano Rise   Crozet Islands

Prince Edward Islands   Kerguelen Islands   Kerguelen Plateau   50°

Atlantic-Indian Ridge   Conrad Rise   McDonald Islands   Heard Island

Ob' Tablemount   Kohler Seamount   Elan Bank

Lena Tablemount   Marion Dufresne Seamount   Fawn Trough

Enderby Abyssal Plain   40°   50°   60°   Longitude east of Greenwich   70°   80°

MOZAMBIQUE CHANNEL

Lying between the landmass of Africa and the island of Madagascar, the waters of the Mozambique Channel are influenced by both. The circulation in the channel and the local winds systems are both influenced by the adjacent land. Contrary to other parts of the east African coastline, the flow in the Mozambique Channel does not consist of an intense, continuous current. Instead it is characterized by a train of large eddies slowly drifting southward. These eddies are formed at the narrows of the channel and have an influence on the deep-sea ecosystems. Marine birds prefer to feed at their edges. The shallowest part of the channel is only about 6,560 feet (2,000 m) deep, thus preventing deeper water masses from flowing straight through it. Coral reefs are an important ecological component on the eastern side of the channel. On the western side major rivers, such as the Zambezi, influence the shelf waters, especially when they intermittently come down in flood, laden with silt.

Estuary flow
On the northwest coast of Madagascar, seawater penetrates inland to join the freshwater outflow of the Betsiboka River. Numerous islands and sandbars have formed from the sediment in this estuary and have been shaped by the push and pull of tides.

Coastal fishing
Villagers in Mozambique who rely on fishing have many challenges to contend with. Declining fish stocks, extreme weather events such as tropical cyclones, and regular flooding of low-lying villages by rivers bursting their banks make their trade a hazardous one.

Ghost crab
The ghost crab (Ocypode cordimana), which has one claw larger than the other, is common along Indo-Pacific shores. It is able to move rapidly and can disappear from sight with amazing speed. Ghost crabs may hibernate for up to six months through winter.

Seafloor topography
The seafloor structure of the Mozambique Channel and its surroundings is complex. The channel narrows toward the north and also becomes shallower, so water deeper than 6,560 feet (2,000 m) cannot pass through. The shallow Mozambique and Madagascar ridges extend southward at either side of the mouth of the channel.

Surface currents
The flow in the Mozambique Channel is not a continuous north to south current. It consists of a series of eddies, whirlpools of water that drift southward on the western side of the channel. They may draw coastal waters into the deep sea.

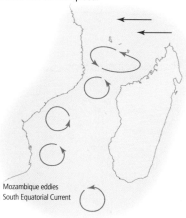

Mozambique eddies
South Equatorial Current

NATURAL RESOURCES

Fishing
Shellfish
Tourism

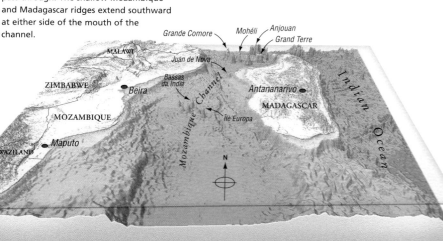

N O P Q R S T U V W X Y Z

Oceanic whitetip shark

The oceanic whitetip shark (*Carcharhinus longimanus*), seen here with pilot fish (*Naucrates ductor*) in the Mozambique Channel, is found mostly in warm waters. The population is under pressure because of the harvesting of fins for shark fin soup.

Wilkes Rise

Aldabra Islands
Assumption Island
Cosmoledo Island
Astove Island
Giraud Seamount

Cabo Delgado

COMOROS
Grande Comore *MORONI
Îles Glorieuses
St Lazarus Bank
Anjouan
Geyser Reef
Moheli
Mayotte
Tanjona Anorontany
Leven Bank
Nosy Mitsio
Baía de Pemba
Nosy Bé
Baía d'Ambaro
Baía do Lúrio
Lohatanjona Angadoka
Baía de Memba
Baía de Fernão Veloso
Nosy Lava
Baía de Narinda
Nacala

Baía de Mahajamba

Baía de Bombetoka
Mahajanga

Ilha Puga Puga
Tanjona Vilanandro
MADAGASCAR

Helodrano Antongila

COELACANTH

Coelacanths (*Latimeria chalumnae*) are highly unusual fish. Long considered to have been extinct for the past 70 million years, they were rediscovered in 1938 and have now been found along much of the east African coast. Weighing 180 pounds (80 kg) and with a length of 6 feet (2 m) individuals may live for 100 years.

Île Juan de Nova

Ponta Olinda

MOZAMBIQUE

Zambezi

Ponta Timbué

Îles Barren

A diver accompanies a slowly swimming coelacanth in the Mozambique Channel. These lethargic fish are found largely in caves in the continental shelf at depths up to 2,300 feet (700 m).

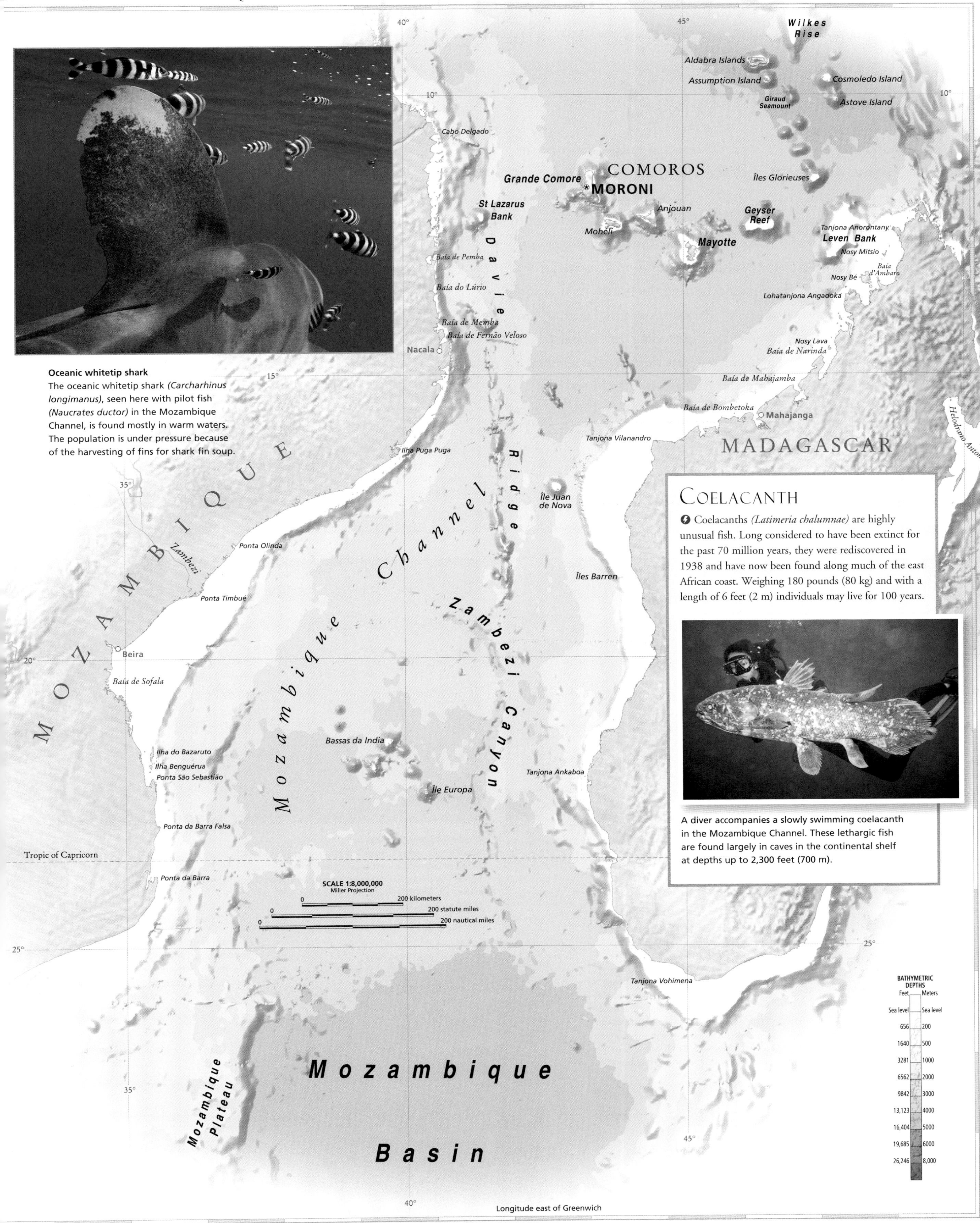

Beira

Baía de Sofala

Ilha do Bazaruto
Ilha Benguérua
Ponta São Sebastião

Bassas da India

Tanjona Ankaboa

Île Europa

Ponta da Barra Falsa

Tropic of Capricorn

Ponta da Barra

SCALE 1:8,000,000
Miller Projection

0   200 kilometers
0   200 statute miles
0   200 nautical miles

Tanjona Vohimena

Mozambique Plateau

M o z a m b i q u e

B a s i n

Longitude east of Greenwich

N O P Q R S T U V W X Y Z

BATHYMETRIC DEPTHS

Feet	Meters
Sea level	Sea level
656	200
1640	500
3281	1000
6562	2000
9842	3000
13,123	4000
16,404	5000
19,685	6000
26,246	8,000

Davie

Ridge

Mozambique Channel

Zambezi Canyon

1
2
3
4
7
8
9
10
11
12
13
14
15

40°
45°
10°
10°
15°
15°
35°
35°
20°
20°
25°
25°
40°

EASTERN INDIAN OCEAN

A large part of this ocean region is bisected north–south by the Ninetyeast Ridge, with the Mid-Indian Ocean Basin to its west and the Wharton Basin to the east. South of the equator the flow is dominated by the wide South Equatorial Current during the southwest monsoon. The flow of the Southwest Monsoon Current is eastward at the equator. During the northeast monsoon the westward currents, the North Equatorial current and the South Equatorial Current, are bisected by an eastward Equatorial Countercurrent. Throughout the year water flows into the Indian Ocean from the Pacific—the Indonesian Throughflow. In February, during the northeast monsoon, flow to the Indian Ocean is minimal but by August, during the southwest monsoon, currents flow strongly. The southward Leeuwin Current flows along the Australian coastline. The ocean's eastern boundary currents disrupt upwelling and biological productivity, which is therefore underdeveloped.

NINGALOO REEF

Ningaloo Reef, the longest fringing coral reef in the world, stretches for 125 miles (200 km) along the west coast of Australia, 745 miles (1,200 km) north of Perth. The reef is on the migratory route of dolphins, dugongs and humpback whales. It is now a declared marine park and its beaches are important breeding grounds for loggerhead, green and hawksbill turtles.

The whale shark (Rhincodon typus), a filter feeder, swims with its mouth open to capture plankton. Found at the Ningaloo Reef from March to June, these are the largest living fish species, growing to 40 feet (12 m) in length.

Ningaloo Reef's close proximity to the shore, less than 1,600 feet (500 m) in some places, adds to its attractions for those wanting to swim among the abundant marine life.

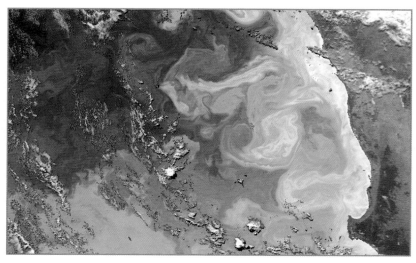

Leeuwin Current chlorophyll
A satellite image of chlorophyll shows a huge eddy or vortex in the Leeuwin Current off the west coast of Australia. The high concentrations of chlorophyll are yellow against an aquamarine background of lower concentrations, and come from coastal plankton, or marine algae, in the water.

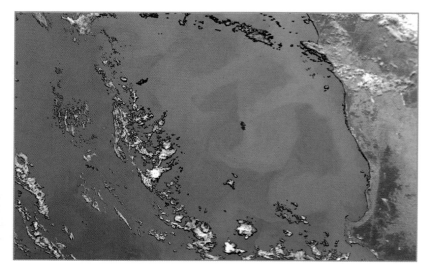

Leeuwin Current temperatures
A satellite image in thermal infrared shows sea-surface temperatures at the west coast of Australia. The huge eddies formed by the Leeuwin Current are visible. These eddies are about 125 miles (200 km) wide, 3,300 feet (1,000 m) deep, and spin at three miles per hour (5 km/h).

Surface currents
The eastern Indian Ocean is characterized by currents parallel to the equator, the Leeuwin Current flowing poleward along the west coast of Australia, and leakage of Pacific water through the Indonesian archipelago. Some water from the Great Australian Bight also enters the Indian Ocean.

→ Antarctic Circumpolar Current	⋯ South Equatorial Current
– – → Equatorial Countercurrent	→ Leeuwin Current
→ North Equatorial Current	→ Throughflow

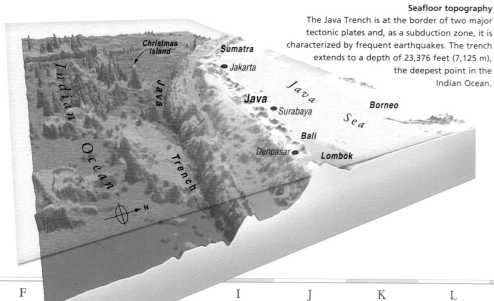

Seafloor topography
The Java Trench is at the border of two major tectonic plates and, as a subduction zone, it is characterized by frequent earthquakes. The trench extends to a depth of 23,376 feet (7,125 m), the deepest point in the Indian Ocean.

N O P Q R S T U V W X Y Z

80°
BANGLADESH
Dhaka
90°
Tropic of Cancer
100°

I N D I A
20°
Ganges Cone
MYANMAR
20°

Chennai
Yangon
THAILAND
Bangkok
Gulf of Thailand

Bay of Bengal
Andaman Islands
Andaman Sea

SRI LANKA
Gulf of Mannar
Colombo
Andaman Basin

Nicobar Islands
MALAYSIA
Kuala Lumpur
Strait of Malacca
Singapore

NATURAL RESOURCES

Leafy seadragon
Leafy seadragons (*Phycodurus eques*) are marine fish related to the seahorse. Found along the coast of western and southern Australia, their leafy body structures serve as camouflage. Moving slowly through the water they appear to be pieces of floating seaweed.

BATHYMETRIC DEPTHS	
Feet	Meters
Sea level	Sea level
656	200
1640	500
3281	1000
6562	2000
9842	3000
13,123	4000
16,404	5000
19,685	6000
26,246	8,000

Fishing   Mining
Shellfish   Oil production
Metallic minerals   Tourism

Ceylon Plain
Equator
Cocos Basin
BORNEO
130°
Equator
140°
1
2
3
4
5

Sunda Trench
Sumatra Ridge
INDONESIA
Java Sea
Jakarta
Sunda Sea
New Guinea
PAPUA NEW GUINEA
Port Moresby

Atanasy Nikitin Seamount
Investigator Ridge
Java
Bali
Lesser Sunda Islands
Dili
EAST TIMOR
Arafura Sea
10°

Mid-Indian Ocean Basin
Sunda Trough
Java Trench
Arafura Shelf
Torres Strait
Cape York
Coral Sea

Cocos Islands
Christmas Island
Java Trench 23,376ft (7125m)
North Australian Basin
Timor Sea
Sahul Shelf
Darwin
Gulf of Carpentaria

Horizon Ridge
Gascoyne Plain
Cape Leveque
Rowley Shelf

Osborn Plateau
Exmouth Plateau
7

Wharton Basin
Ningaloo Reef
20°

I N D I A N
Wallaby Plateau
Cuvier Basin
Lost Dutchmen Ridge
Cuvier Plateau

Tropic of Capricorn
East Indiaman Ridge
Batavia Seamount
Tropic of Capricorn

O C E A N
Golden Dragon Seamount
Hartog Ridge
Perth Basin
AUSTRALIA
30°

Broken Plateau
Ob Trench
Perth

Naturaliste Plateau
Great Australian Bight

Amsterdam Island
St Paul Island
Naturaliste Fracture Zone
Diamantina Deep 21,660ft (6602m)
Adelaide

Diamantina Fracture Zone
South Australian Basin
Melbourne
King Island
Bass Strait
40°

SCALE 1:35,000,000
Miller Projection
0   1000 kilometers
0   1000 statute miles
0   1000 nautical miles

Tasmania
Hobart
South East Cape

S o u t h e a s t   I n d i a n   R i d g e
South Australian Plain
South Tasman Rise
13

Kerguelen Plateau
Fawn Trough
Indian–Antarctic Ridge
50°

Banzare Seamounts
Australian-Antarctic Basin
South Indian Basin
14

80°
90°
100°
110°
120°
130°
140°
60°
15

Longitude east of Greenwich

N O P Q R S T U V W X Y Z

GREAT AUSTRALIAN BIGHT

The ocean area south of the Australian landmass is the easternmost extension of the Indian Ocean. In its extreme east it adds a cold-water connection to the Pacific Ocean. Warm water from the Leeuwin Current, which flows southward along the west coast of Australia, may round Cape Leeuwin on the southwest corner of the continent and penetrate into the bight. Bottom water formed at the coast of Antarctica moves north but, where its flow is obstructed by the Australian continental shelf, it moves in an easterly direction into the Indian Ocean. The flow at intermediate depths, around 3,280 feet (1,000 m), is also from the Great Australian Bight into the Indian Ocean, so the bight is inferred to have a greater influence on the Indian Ocean than on the Pacific. The dry atmosphere over parts of the bight causes excessive evaporation that forms highly saline, dense water, which descends to greater depths.

Great white shark
The great white shark (*Carcharodon carcharias*), the largest predatory fish in the world, can grow to 20 feet (6 m) and may weigh as much as 5,000 pounds (2,300 kg). It can dive to depths of 4,200 feet (1,300 m) and individuals have been tracked migrating from South African to Australian waters.

NULLARBOR COAST

The Nullarbor Plain is an extensive, flat, almost treeless region at the southern edge of the Australian continent, adjacent to the Great Australian Bight. This arid, semi-desert region receives only about seven inches (200 mm) of rainfall per year and is sparsely populated. Thought to have once been part of an ancient seabed, it is the largest limestone area on earth. Its daytime temperatures may reach 120°F (49°C).

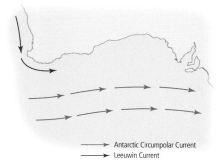

Surface currents
South of Australia, at the northern boundary of the Southern Ocean, the powerful Antarctic Circumpolar Current carries water west to east. On Australia's west coast, warm waters from the southward flowing Leeuwin Current occasionally flow east into the Great Australian Bight and penetrate the cold Antarctic waters.

→ Antarctic Circumpolar Current
→ Leeuwin Current

The spectacular 213-foot- (65 m) high Bunda Cliffs of the Nullarbor coast form part of the northern border of the Great Australian Bight. The cliffs are an excellent vantage point for whale-watching.

NATURAL RESOURCES

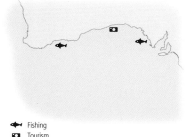

➤ Fishing
📷 Tourism

Kangaroo Island
Seal Bay Conservation Park, on the coast of Kangaroo Island, offers protected beaches where marine mammals, including the Australian sea lion (*Neophoca cinerea*), raise their young.

Australian sea lion
The Australian sea lion (*Neophoca cinerea*) is found only along the southern coast of Australia. It hunts for fish and squid at sea and comes ashore on rocky islands to breed. Members of the eared seal family, sea lions have small, furled ears. Males can weigh up to 660 pounds (300 kg) at maturity, females 176 pounds (80 kg).

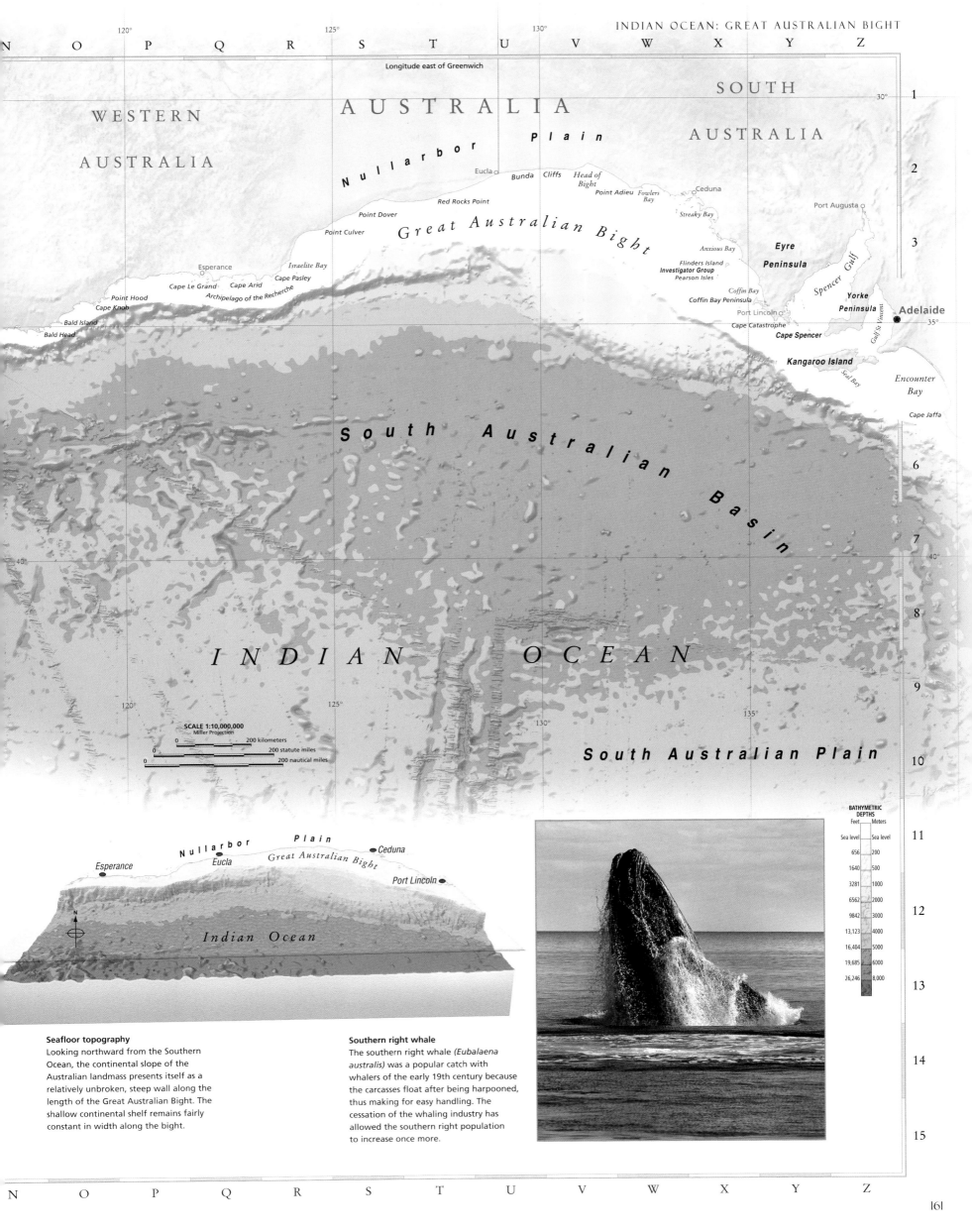

Longitude east of Greenwich

WESTERN AUSTRALIA

AUSTRALIA

SOUTH AUSTRALIA

Nullarbor Plain

Eucla
Bunda Cliffs
Head of Bight
Point Adieu
Fowlers Bay
Ceduna
Red Rocks Point
Streaky Bay
Point Dover
Point Culver

Great Australian Bight

Anxious Bay

Eyre Peninsula

Port Augusta

Esperance
Israelite Bay
Cape Le Grand
Cape Arid
Cape Pasley
Point Hood
Cape Knob
Archipelago of the Recherche
Bald Island
Bald Head

Flinders Island
Investigator Group
Pearson Isles

Coffin Bay
Coffin Bay Peninsula
Port Lincoln
Cape Catastrophe
Cape Spencer

Spencer Gulf

Yorke Peninsula

Adelaide

Gulf St Vincent

Kangaroo Island
Seal Bay

Encounter Bay

Cape Jaffa

South Australian Basin

INDIAN OCEAN

South Australian Plain

SCALE 1:10,000,000
Miller Projection

0   200 kilometers
0   200 statute miles
0   200 nautical miles

Seafloor topography
Looking northward from the Southern Ocean, the continental slope of the Australian landmass presents itself as a relatively unbroken, steep wall along the length of the Great Australian Bight. The shallow continental shelf remains fairly constant in width along the bight.

Nullarbor Plain
Esperance
Eucla
Ceduna
Great Australian Bight
Port Lincoln

Indian Ocean

Southern right whale
The southern right whale (*Eubalaena australis*) was a popular catch with whalers of the early 19th century because the carcasses float after being harpooned, thus making for easy handling. The cessation of the whaling industry has allowed the southern right population to increase once more.

BATHYMETRIC DEPTHS

Feet	Meters
Sea level	Sea level
656	200
1640	500
3281	1000
6562	2000
9842	3000
13,123	4000
16,404	5000
19,685	6000
26,246	8,000

SOUTHERN INDIAN OCEAN

The southern Indian Ocean extends from the African mainland to the west and south coasts of Australia, with the landmass of Madagascar as the only interruption. The general, wind-driven circulation is counterclockwise, except close to the equator, and it intensifies to the west where the strong Agulhas Current flows along the African coast, and the East Madagascar Current along the east coast of that island. The southern border of this ocean is the Subtropical Convergence, an oceanic front that separates South Indian Ocean waters from the colder, more nutrient-rich waters of the Southern Ocean farther to the south. The current that flows along this front is known as the Agulhas Return Current on the western side of the basin and as the South Indian Ocean Current to the east. On the west coast of Australia the warm Leeuwin Current flows southward; in the subtropics the South Indian Countercurrent carries water eastward against the general flow.

African penguins
African penguins *(Spheniscus demersus)*, formerly known as jackass penguins for their braying cry, live in colonies on islands off the southwest coast of Africa. The colony shown here is one of few on land. This 28-inch- (70 cm) tall penguin has black feet and a distinctive black stripe on the chest.

Phytoplankton
The southern tip of Africa as seen by satellite. The ocean color has been enhanced and shows the location of high levels of phytoplankton (green), particularly along the west coast where coastal upwelling brings nutrients to the sea surface.

NATURAL RESOURCES

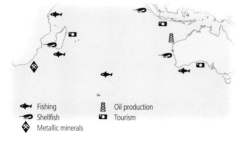

- Fishing
- Shellfish
- Metallic minerals
- Oil production
- Tourism

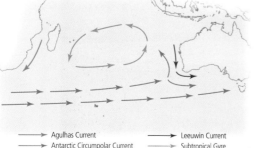

Surface currents
Surface flow is generally counter-clockwise in the gyres of all southern hemisphere basins. In the southern Indian Ocean it is highly concentrated in the western part and the strong Agulhas Current is the final recipient of much of this recirculating water.

→ Agulhas Current
→ Antarctic Circumpolar Current
→ Leeuwin Current
→ Subtropical Gyre

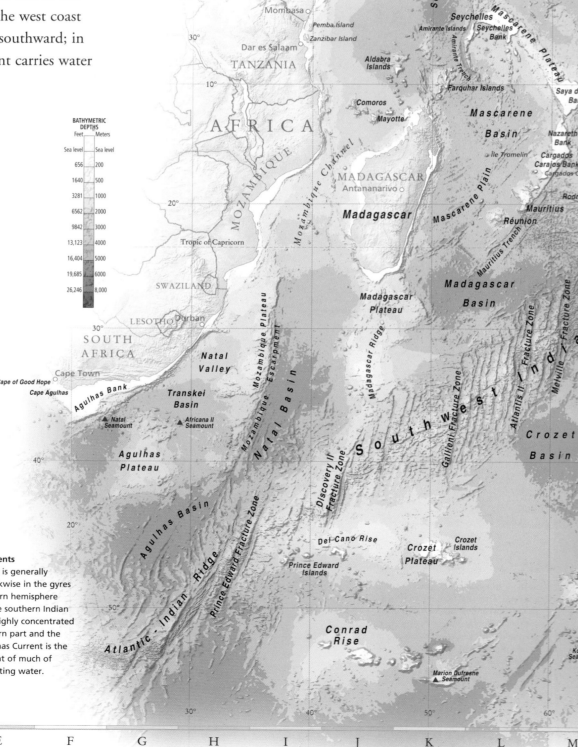

BATHYMETRIC DEPTHS

Feet	Meters
Sea level	Sea level
656	200
1640	500
3281	1000
6562	2000
9842	3000
13,123	4000
16,404	5000
19,685	6000
26,246	8,000

SOMALIA
KENYA
Equator
Mombasa
Pemba Island
Zanzibar Island
Dar es Salaam
TANZANIA
AFRICA
Comoros
Mayotte
Aldabra Islands
Somali Basin
Mascarene Plateau
Seychelles
Amirante Islands
Seychelles Bank
Amirante Trench
Farquhar Islands
Saya de Bar
Mascarene Basin
Nazareth Bank
Île Tromelin
Cargados Carajos Bank
Cargados C
Rodri
MADAGASCAR
Antananarivo
Madagascar
Mascarene Plain
Mauritius
Réunion
Mauritius Trench
MOZAMBIQUE
Mozambique Channel
Tropic of Capricorn
Madagascar Plateau
Madagascar Basin
Madagascar Ridge
SWAZILAND
LESOTHO
Durban
SOUTH AFRICA
Cape Town
Cape of Good Hope
Cape Agulhas
Agulhas Bank
Natal Valley
Mozambique Plateau
Mozambique Escarpment
Natal Basin
Southwest India
Atlantis II Fracture Zone
Melville Fracture Zone
Crozet Basin
Transkei Basin
Natal Seamount
Africana II Seamount
Gallieni Fracture Zone
Agulhas Plateau
Agulhas Basin
Del Caño Rise
Discovery II Fracture Zone
Crozet Islands
Crozet Plateau
Prince Edward Islands
Atlantic - Indian Ridge
Prince Edward Fracture Zone
Conrad Rise
Marion Dufresne Seamount
K Se

SARDINE RUN

The South African sardine run is one of the most spectacular natural migrations in the world. Between May and July of most years millions of sardines swim north along the east coast in schools more than four miles (7 km) long, one mile (1.5 km) wide, and nearly 100 feet (30 m) deep. They are followed by tens of thousands of predators such as dolphins, sharks, and gannets.

The sardine run is a bonanza for local fishermen and tourists. Sardines can be scooped from the sea by the bucketful from boats, and even by those wading in the shallows.

Predators such as dolphins drive sardines into tight groups known as bait balls, some 35–65 feet (10–20 m) in diameter, to facilitate feeding on them. Such balls are seldom maintained for more than 10 minutes.

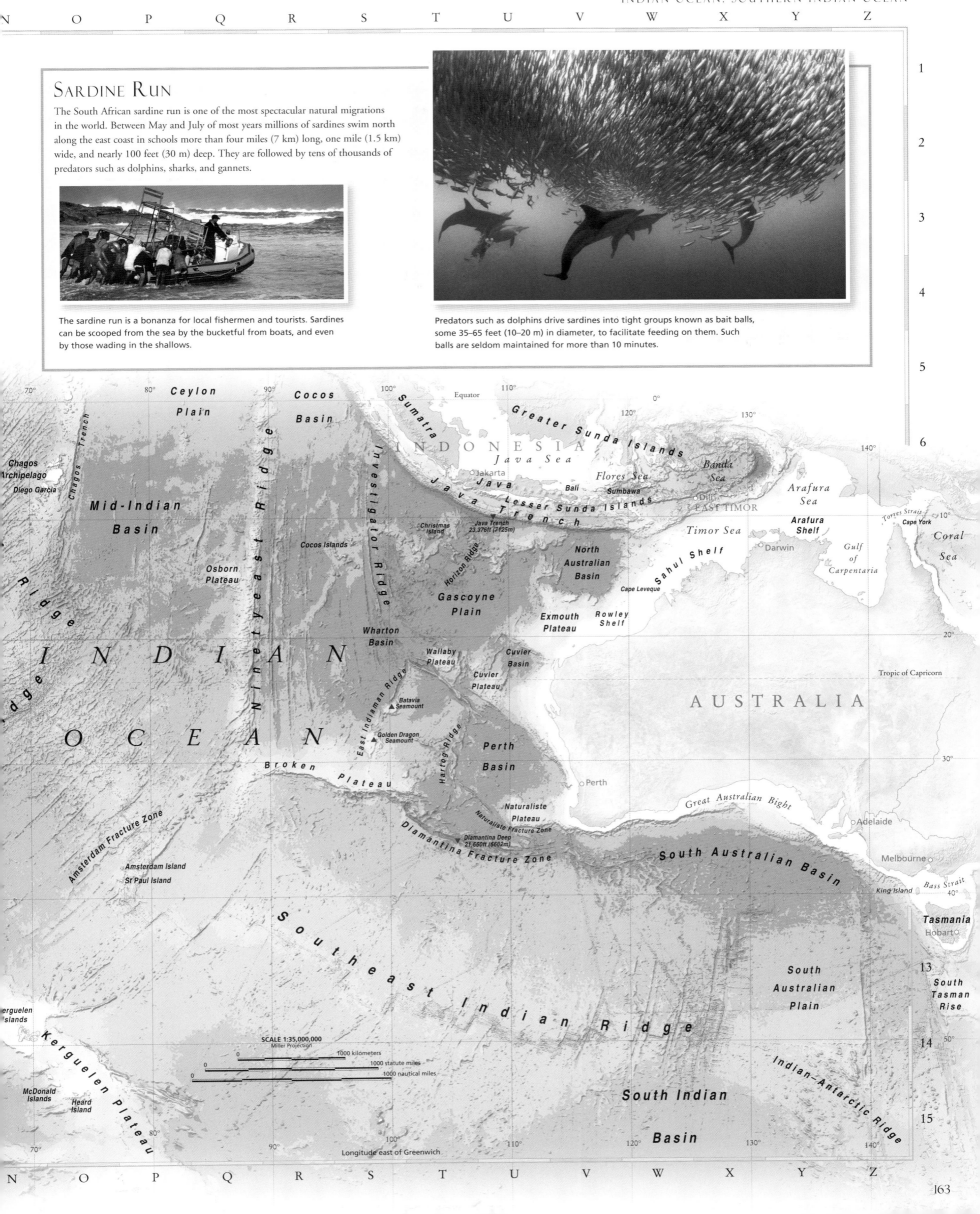

SCALE 1:35,000,000
Miller Projection

1000 kilometers
1000 statute miles
1000 nautical miles

Longitude east of Greenwich

A humpback whale (*Megaptera novaeangliae*) and her calf cruise the vast expanse of the Pacific Ocean, while the father, now a lone traveler far away, fills the ocean with his song for hours. Whale songs change over time, but at any one time all North Pacific humpbacks sing the same version. South Pacific humpbacks sing a different song.

PACIFIC OCEAN

PACIFIC OCEAN

The Pacific Ocean is the largest of all oceans. The East Pacific Rise divides it rather unequally into the narrow Peru and Chile basins in the east and a vast featureless plain in the center. A "Ring of Fire" marked by earthquakes and volcanic eruptions surrounds it and generates powerful tsunamis. Tectonic movement of the crustal plates forms some of the world's deepest trenches along its rim. Thousands of seamounts, remnants of submarine volcanoes and homes to isolated, highly productive ecosystems, rise from the ocean floor, often to within 1,000 feet (300 m) or less of the surface. The Portuguese explorer Magellan, who sailed across the Pacific in 1521 under its pleasant trade winds, named it the "pacific" (peaceful) ocean; but swell from storms of the Roaring Forties always reaches the tropics. Micronesian, Melanesian, and Polynesian sailors navigated between the many thousands of islands in the southern hemisphere and the northwestern Pacific for centuries.

THE FACTS	
Area	60.1 million square miles (155.6 million km²)
Average depth	13,127 feet (4,001 m)
Maximum depth	35,826 feet (10,920 m)
Maximum width	11,200 miles (18,000 km)
Maximum length	8,600 miles (13,900 km)

Ocean Share

Pacific Ocean
60.1 million sq miles
(155.6 million km²)
46%

All other oceans

Hubbard Glacier
An iceberg calves from the face of the Hubbard Glacier on the USA–Canada border. Its ice, which formed at an elevation of 11,000 feet (3,350 m), took 400 years to travel the 76 miles (122 km) to the sea.

Anthias
Some of the most spectacular coral reef systems are found in the Pacific. Here a school of beautiful reef fish (*Anthias* sp.) swims past a yellow feather star (*Crinoid* sp.), also known as sea lily, in the warm waters of the Philippine Sea.

People of the Pacific
The Pacific Ocean is home to nearly 10 million people. Scattered over thousands of islands, people's lives depend on their navigation skills. This water taxi heads out to one of the outlying islands of Fiji.

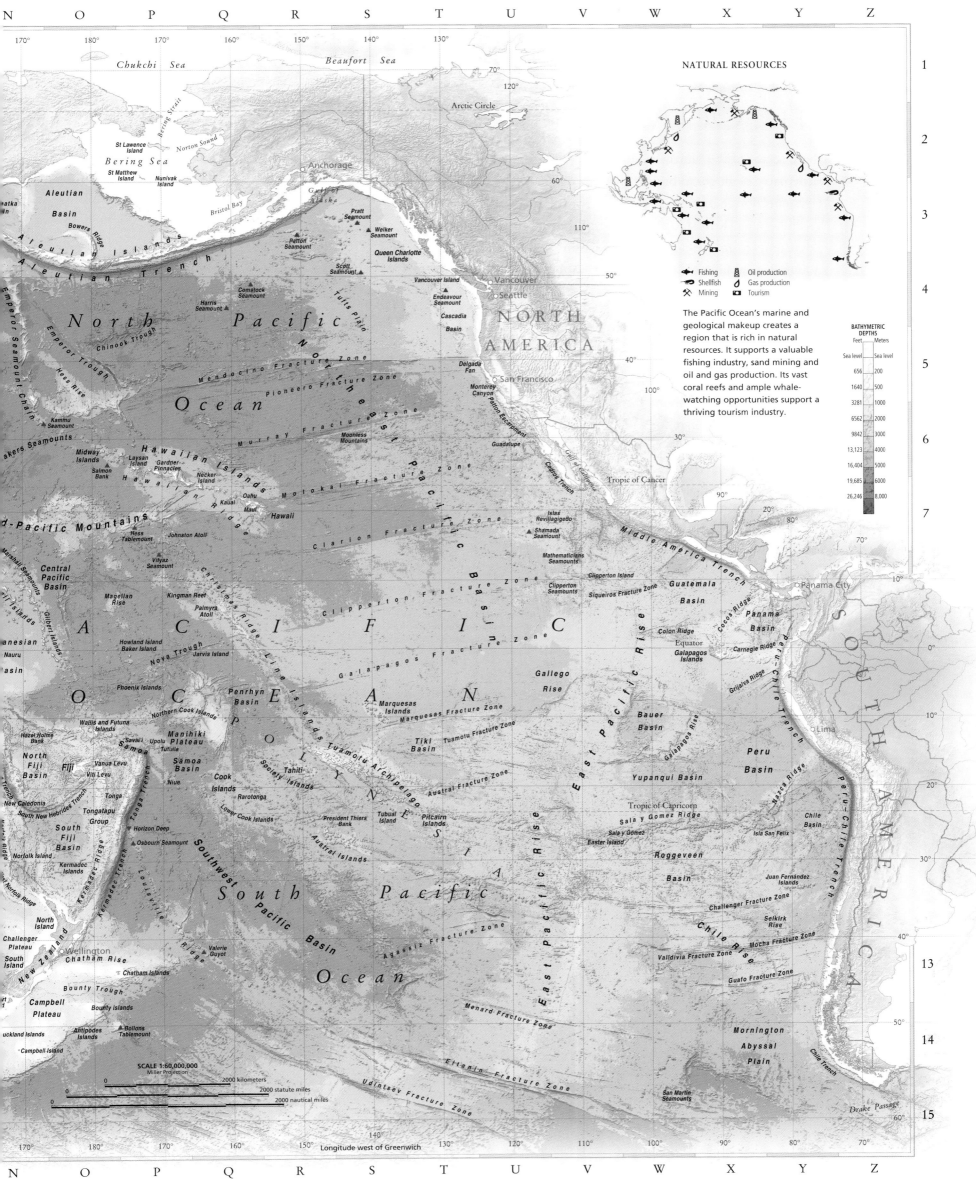

NORTHERN NORTH PACIFIC OCEAN

The northern sector of the North Pacific has the most uniform bathymetry of all ocean basins. Two big circulation systems dominate the region. The North Equatorial, Philippines, Kuroshio, North Pacific, and California currents form the clockwise circulation of the Subtropical Gyre. Water movement at its center is downward, depriving the upper ocean of nutrients, so its waters display the deep blue of the ocean's deserts. Plastic and other land-based or ship-derived garbage accumulates in the gyre, particularly between North America and the Hawaiian Islands. The Alaska Current, Alaskan Stream, Oyashio, and North Pacific currents form the counterclockwise circulation of the Subpolar Gyre, in which upward water movement brings nutrients to the surface, making it a region of high productivity and preferred fishing grounds. The Oyashio and Kuroshio currents meet along 35°N in the Kuroshio Extension, which forms a convoluted fast-flowing current across the Shatsky Rise and Emperor Seamounts, dominated by meanders and eddies.

Sea lion
The Steller sea lion *(Eumetopias jubatus)*, the largest of all sea lion species, is found from the Kuril Islands and the Sea of Okhotsk to the Gulf of Alaska and central California. Its numbers have been declining and it is on the endangered species list.

NATURAL RESOURCES

- ⤙ Fishing
- ▣ Tourism
- ⚒ Mining
- ⛟ Oil production

Aleutian Islands
Open sky between clouds in the south and in the north allows a clear view of the snow-covered peaks of the Alaskan Peninsula and the Aleutian Islands. More than 300 volcanic islands, in an arc 1,200 miles (1,900 km) long, form the southern boundary of the Bering Sea.

BATHYMETRIC DEPTHS

Feet	Meters
Sea level	Sea level
656	200
1640	500
3281	1000
6562	2000
9842	3000
13,123	4000
16,404	5000
19,685	6000
26,246	8,000

Surface currents
Two basin-wide gyres dominate the North Pacific. South of 40°N the American coastal waters experience upwelling from the California Current. Currents in the deep basin of the Bering Sea move counterclockwise while, over the shelf, northward movement feeds into the Arctic Ocean.

→ Bering Sea Gyre
→ California Current
→ Subpolar Gyre
→ Subtropical Gyre

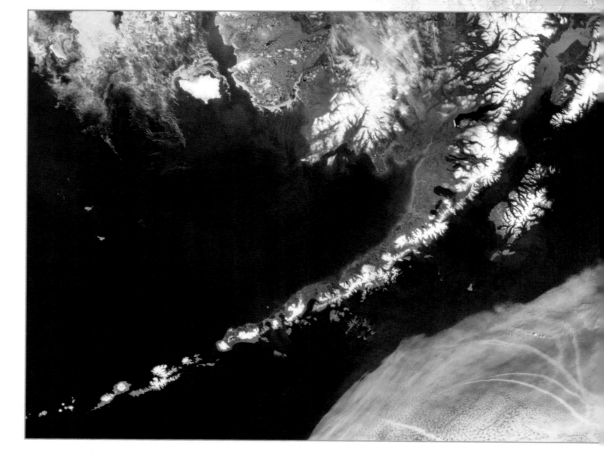

RUSSIA

Sea of Okhotsk

Tinro Basin

Deryugina Basin

Instituta Okeanologii Rise

Akademii Nauk Rise

Kuril Basin

Kuril Islands

Kuril–Kamchatka Trench

Zenkevich Rise

CHINA

Vladivostok

Japan Basin

Hokkaidō

NORTH KOREA

Sea of Japan

JAPAN

Northwest Pacific Basin

P'yŏngyang

Yamato Bank

Honshū

Tokyo

Japan Trench

Izu-Ogasawara Trench

Seoul

Yellow Sea

SOUTH KOREA

Yamato Basin

Isakov Seamount

Makarov Seamount

East China Sea

Kyūshū

Shikoku

Nankai Trough

Shikoku Basin

Shichito-Iōjima Ridge

Daitō Ridge

Kyushu-Palau Ridge

Oki-Daitō Ridge

Mid-Pacific

Tatarskiy Proliv

Sakhalin

N O P Q R S T U V W X Y Z

Longitude east of Greenwich   Longitude west of Greenwich
170°   180°   170°   160°   150°

Chukchi Sea

Bering Strait

Arctic Circle

ALASKA

E D E R A T I O N

Gulf of Anadyr

St Lawrence Island

Bering

Yukon

Anchorage

Sea

St Matthew Island   Nunivak Island

Albatross population
Before the 1930s millions of short-tailed albatrosses (*Phoebastria albatrus*) roamed the North Pacific. Hunted for its feathers, the bird was considered extinct by 1950. But some 50 juveniles survived at sea and began breeding again on Torishima Island in Japan. Today's population is estimated at 1,200.

Augustine Island   60°   140°   130°

Kamchatka Basin   *Aleutian Basin*   Pribilof Islands   *Bristol Bay*   Kodiak Island   *Gulf of Alaska*   **CANADA**   120°

Shirshov Ridge   Bowers Ridge   Pratt Seamount   Alexander Archipelago

Aleutian Basin   Bowers Bank   Patton Seamount   Welker Seamount   **Queen Charlotte Islands**

nsula   *Aleutian Rise*   *Aleutian Islands*   *Trench*   Tufts Abyssal Plain   Vancouver Island   50°

Aleutian Rise   Comstock Seamount   Endeavour Seamount   Vancouver

Emperor Seamount Chain   Harris Seamount   **Cascadia Basin**   Seattle

Chinook Trough   *Northeast*   **U.S.A.**   40°

Emperor Trough   **P A C I F I C**   *Pacific*   Mendocino Fracture Zone   Pioneer Fracture Zone   Delgada Fan   Monterey Canyon   San Francisco

Hess Rise   **O C E A N**   *Northwest Hawaiian Ridge*   Murray Fracture Zone   Moonless Seamounts   Los Angeles   30°

Kammu Seamount   Midway Islands   Murray Basin   Molokai Fracture Zone   Guadalupe   Tropic of Cancer

pmakers Seamounts   Salmon Bank   Laysan Island   *Hawaiian Islands*   120°   9

Gardner Pinnacles   Necker Island   Kauai   Oahu   Maui   20°

Mountains   *Hawaiian Ridge*   Hawaii   Clarion Fracture Zone   130°

170°   180°   170°   160°   150°   140°

SCALE 1:40,000,000
Miller Projection
0   1000 kilometers
0   1000 statute miles
0   1000 nautical miles

Siwash Rock
The moon sets over the approaches to the Port of Vancouver, Canada. Siwash Rock stands guard near the city's Stanley Park. A striking landmark during both calm and stormy days, the rock features in native American legends.

Mount Augustine
Augustine volcano on Augustine Island in Cook Inlet, Alaska, 174 miles (280 km) southwest of Anchorage, is one of several active volcanoes of the Ring of Fire. Steam plumes rich in sulfur dioxide disrupted air traffic in 1986, 1994, and 2006, and deposited ash on the city of Anchorage.

N O P Q R S T U V W X Y Z

BERING SEA

The Bering Sea is the world's third largest marginal sea (after the Arctic Ocean and the Mediterranean Sea). In the northeast it forms part of the highly productive Siberian–Alaskan shelf. In the south it consists of a deep basin that is subdivided by the Shirshov and Bowers ridges. The Aleutian Islands form part of the Ring of Fire and carry several active volcanoes. Bering Strait, its connection with the Arctic Ocean, is only 53 miles (85 km) wide and less than 160 feet (50 m) deep but is important for the global water budget by returning to the Atlantic the fresh water that came as rain across the Isthmus of Panama. Sea ice builds up in November and covers the shelf from January. Ice break-up begins in April; by July the entire region is ice-free. To protect spectacular cold-water "coral gardens," 60 percent of the Aleutian shallow water habitat is closed to bottom trawling.

Adak Island
Adak Island, in the Andreanof group of the Aleutian Islands, was abandoned by the native Aleut in the 1800s. During World War II its population grew to 6,000; today it has a population of about 300. In 1957 an earthquake in this region caused a tsunami that reached a height of 52 feet (16 m) in Hawaii.

THE FACTS

Area	884,900 square miles (2,291,880 km²)
Average depth	5,075 feet (1547 m)
Maximum depth	15,659 feet (4,773 m)
Maximum width	1,490 miles (2,398 km)
Maximum length	990 miles (1,593 km)

NATURAL RESOURCES

→ Fishing
→ Shellfish

Surface currents
Two systems make up the currents of the Bering Sea. Counterclockwise circulation in the deep basin supplies some water to the Oyashio through the Kamchatka Current, while water from the Alaskan Stream crosses the shallow eastern region to join the Anadyr Current toward Bering Strait.

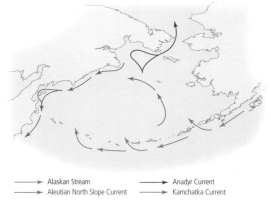

→ Alaskan Stream → Anadyr Current
→ Aleutian North Slope Current → Kamchatka Current

Humpback whale
Humpback whales (*Megaptera novaeangliae*) live in distinct populations in all polar waters during summer and migrate to give birth in subtropical or tropical waters in winter. Males communicate through songs that change from year to year.

Beluga
The beluga or white whale (*Delphinapterus leucas*), a whale species of the Arctic and subarctic oceans, grows to 15 feet (5 m) in length. It spends the summers in bays, estuaries, and shallow inlets and follows the progressing ice edge into open water in winter.

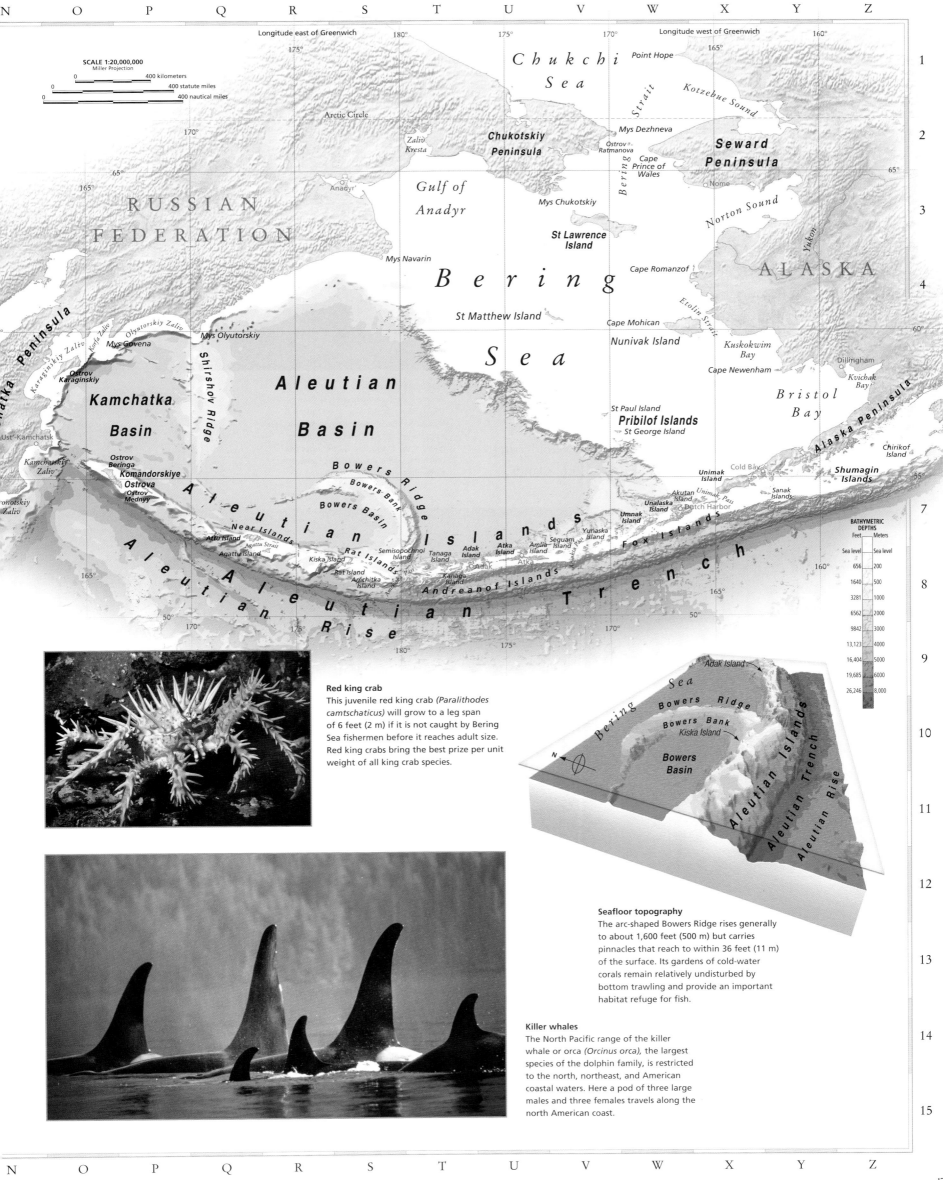

SCALE 1:20,000,000
Miller Projection

400 kilometers
400 statute miles
400 nautical miles

Longitude east of Greenwich
Longitude west of Greenwich

Chukchi Sea

Point Hope

Kotzebue Sound

Arctic Circle

Mys Dezhneva

Chukotskiy Peninsula

Ostrov Ratmanova
Cape Prince of Wales

Seward Peninsula

Zaliv Kresta

Bering Strait

Nome

RUSSIAN FEDERATION

Anadyr'

Gulf of Anadyr

Mys Chukotskiy

Norton Sound

Yukon

St Lawrence Island

Mys Navarin

B e r i n g

Cape Romanzof

ALASKA

S e a

St Matthew Island

Cape Mohican

Nunivak Island

Kuskokwim Bay

Dillingham

Kvichak Bay

Kamchatka Peninsula

Olyutorskiy Zaliv
Mys Govena

Mys Olyutorskiy

Karaginskiy Zaliv
Korfa Zaliv
Ostrov Karaginskiy

Kamchatka Basin

Shirshov Ridge

Aleutian Basin

Cape Newenham

Bristol Bay

Ust'-Kamchatsk

Kamchatskiy Zaliv

Ostrov Beringa
Komandorskiye Ostrova
Ostrov Mednyy

Onotskiy Zaliv

St Paul Island
Pribilof Islands
St George Island

Chirikof Island

Alaska Peninsula

Aleutian Rise

Bowers Ridge
Bowers Bank
Bowers Basin

Cold Bay

Unimak Island
Akutan Island
Unalaska Island
Dutch Harbor
Umnak Island

Sanak Islands

Shumagin Islands

Near Islands
Attu Island
Agattu Island
Agattu Strait

Kiska Island
Rat Island
Amchitka Island

A l e u t i a n I s l a n d s

Rat Islands
Semisopochnoi Island
Tanaga Island
Kanaga Island
Adak Island
Adak
Atka Island
Atka
Amlia Island
Seguam Island
Yunaska Island

Fox Islands

Andreanof Islands

A l e u t i a n T r e n c h

A l e u t i a n R i s e

BATHYMETRIC DEPTHS

Feet	Meters
Sea level	Sea level
656	200
1640	500
3281	1000
6562	2000
9842	3000
13,123	4000
16,404	5000
19,685	6000
26,246	8,000

Red king crab
This juvenile red king crab (*Paralithodes camtschaticus*) will grow to a leg span of 6 feet (2 m) if it is not caught by Bering Sea fishermen before it reaches adult size. Red king crabs bring the best prize per unit weight of all king crab species.

Bering Sea
Bowers Ridge
Bowers Bank
Kiska Island
Bowers Basin
N
Adak Island
Aleutian Islands
Aleutian Trench
Aleutian Rise

Seafloor topography
The arc-shaped Bowers Ridge rises generally to about 1,600 feet (500 m) but carries pinnacles that reach to within 36 feet (11 m) of the surface. Its gardens of cold-water corals remain relatively undisturbed by bottom trawling and provide an important habitat refuge for fish.

Killer whales
The North Pacific range of the killer whale or orca (*Orcinus orca*), the largest species of the dolphin family, is restricted to the north, northeast, and American coastal waters. Here a pod of three large males and three females travels along the north American coast.

GULF OF ALASKA

The circulation system in the Gulf of Alaska is determined by the eastern part of the Subpolar Gyre. Fed by the North Pacific Current, the Alaska Current and the Alaskan Stream follow the coast from the Alexander Archipelago to Unimak Island. Eddies measuring 120 miles (200 km) across are regularly found near Sitka and Queen Charlotte Islands. Fresh water from calving glaciers in Glacier Bay National Park and Preserve and other fjords lowers the salinity in the Alaska Current. The Inside Passage between the Alexander Archipelago and the mainland allows ships to avoid storms in the open gulf. The gulf is also exposed to tsunamis generated by earthquakes in the Queen Charlotte–Fairweather Fault System; the largest tsunami ever observed was triggered by a rockfall in Lituya Bay. A hot spot near Queen Charlotte Islands created the now-extinct volcanoes of the Kodiak-Bowie Seamount Chain. Cold-water corals are found near Kodiak and Queen Charlotte islands.

THE FACTS	
Area	592,000 square miles (1,533,273 km²)
Average depth	7,976 feet (2,431 m)
Maximum depth	16,500 feet (5,029 m)
Maximum width	240 miles (400 km)
Maximum length	1,200 miles (2,000 km)

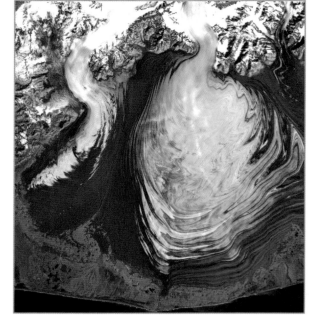
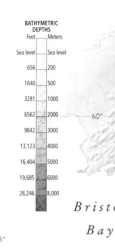

Malaspina Glacier
Where several valley glaciers spill onto the Alaskan coastal plain they form the Malaspina Glacier, seen here in a false-color satellite image. As a typical "piedmont glacier" the Malaspina Glacier does not reach the gulf but supplies its meltwater through streams from two lakes.

NATURAL RESOURCES

◄■ Fishing
▣ Tourism

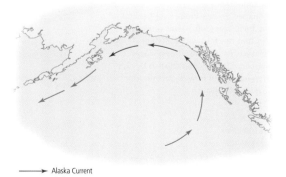

Surface currents
Water transport in the Alaska Current, also known as the Alaska Coastal Current, increases along its way due to freshwater input from meltwater and rivers. Its temperature, however, remains high, above 39°F (4°C), due to the supply of warm water from the North Pacific Current.

→ Alaska Current
→ Alaskan Stream
→ North Pacific Current

Prince William Sound
The "tidewater glaciers" that enter the many fjords of Prince William Sound are a favorite destination of tourist vessels. Tidewater glaciers supply meltwater through the calving of icebergs, which can create a huge wave. Cruise ships are well advised to keep their distance.

Breadcrumb sponge
A breadcrumb sponge (Halichondria panicea) is exposed at low tide on Kodiak Island. Breadcrumb sponges are common in the intertidal zone of all oceans. They occur in a wide range of forms and colors and have been described under more than 50 different names.

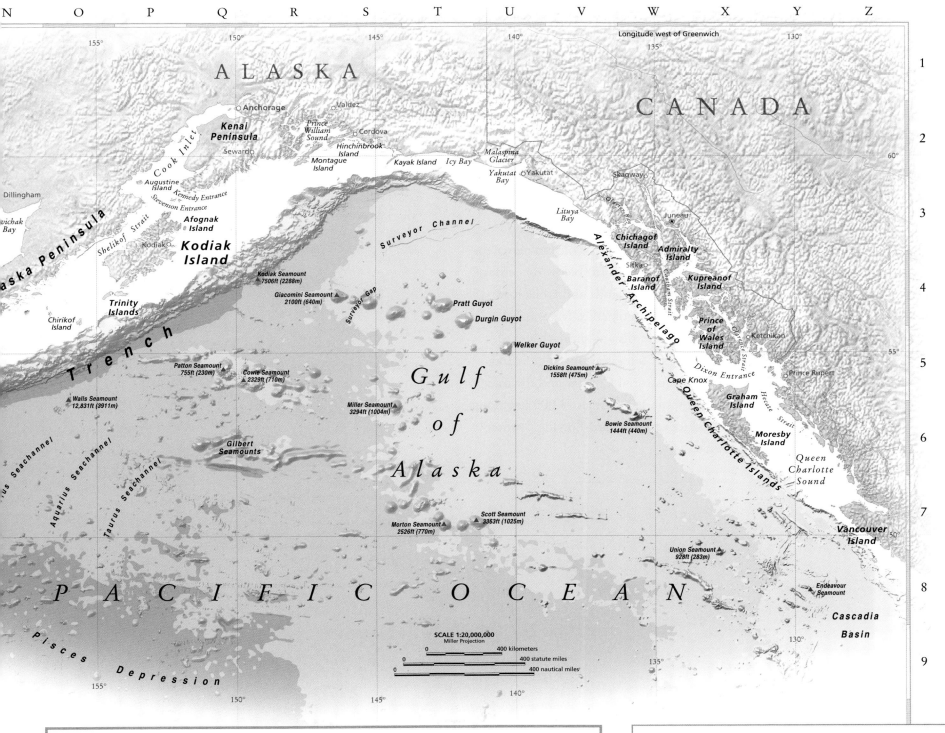

N O P Q R S T U V W X Y Z

ALASKA

CANADA

Anchorage
Valdez
Kenai
Peninsula
Prince
William
Sound
Cordova
Hinchinbrook
Island
Seward
Sewardo
Montague
Island
Kayak Island
Icy Bay
Malaspina
Glacier
Yakutat
Bay
Yakutat
Skagway
Dillingham
Cook Inlet
Augustine
Island
Kennedy Entrance
Stevenson Entrance
Shelikof Strait
Afognak
Island
Kodiak
Kodiak
Island
Lituya
Bay
Juneau
Chichagof
Island
Admiralty
Island
Sitka
Baranof
Island
Kupreanof
Island
Alaska Peninsula
wichak
Bay
Chirikof
Island
Trinity
Islands
Surveyor Channel
Kodiak Seamount
7506ft (2288m)
Giacomini Seamount
2100ft (640m)
Surveyor Gap
Pratt Guyot
Durgin Guyot
Welker Guyot
Alexander Archipelago
Prince
of
Wales
Island
Ketchikan
Dixon Entrance
Prince Rupert
Trench
Patton Seamount
755ft (230m)
Cowie Seamount
2329ft (710m)
Miller Seamount
3294ft (1004m)
Dickins Seamount
1558ft (475m)
Cape Knox
Graham
Island
Queen Charlotte Islands
Hecate Strait
Walls Seamount
12,831ft (3911m)
Gulf
of
Alaska
Bowie Seamount
1444ft (440m)
Moresby
Island
Gilbert
Seamounts
Queen
Charlotte
Sound
Aquarius Seachannel
Taurus Seachannel
Scott Seamount
3363ft (1025m)
Morton Seamount
2526ft (770m)
Vancouver
Island
Union Seamount
928ft (283m)
PACIFIC OCEAN
Endeavour
Seamount
Pisces
Depression
Cascadia
Basin

SCALE 1:20,000,000
Miller Projection

0   400 kilometers
0   400 statute miles
0   400 nautical miles

Longitude west of Greenwich

SOCKEYE SALMON

Sockeye salmon *(Oncorhynchus nerka)* are found in cold waters from northern Japan in the west to Canada in the east. They spawn in streams and lakes, where the young fish spend up to four years before they migrate to the ocean. After another one to four years they change from bluish–green to red, and return to the rivers to spawn.

Marine Highway
A ferry of the Alaska Marine Highway System, a ferry service that forms part of the National Highway System of the USA, makes its way through the Inside Passage. The ferries serve 32 destinations, some without road access, over a distance of 3,500 miles (5,600 km).

HAWAIIAN ISLANDS

Formed over a hot spot to their southeast, the Hawaiian Islands are a chain of 137 islands and atolls, numerous smaller islands, and seamounts that stretch northwestward to Midway and Kure atolls. Mauna Loa and Kilauea on Hawaii, the largest of the nine major islands and the closest to the hot spot, are the only active island volcanoes today. Loihi, a submerged volcano closer to the hot spot, is still 3,200 feet (975 m) below the surface but is growing and active. The smaller islands and atolls form a marine protected area, the Papahanaumokuakea Marine National Monument. Tsunamis from distant shores have reached the Hawaiian Islands on several occasions. The islands form an obstacle to the North Equatorial Current and the trade winds, and create a wake effect some 1,900 miles (3,000 km) long in the atmosphere. This produces an eastward-flowing counter-current on their western side.

Dynamic islands
Five volcanoes make up Hawaii's Big Island. Kohala is extinct, Mauna Kea and Hualalai are dormant. The two active volcanoes, Mauna Loa and Kilauea, add new layers of lava to the island, occasionally forcing the relocation of houses. Here lava from Kilauea reaches the ocean.

VOLCANOES

Hawaii's volcanoes are "shield volcanoes," built by the supply of low-viscosity lava that can flow over great distances. This false-color composite image of the Big Island (processed to simulate true color) shows the spreading range of Mauna Loa to the south, with Mauna Kea's crater to the north. Kilauea is in the east, Kohala in the northwest.

SCALE 1:10,000,000
Miller Projection

0   200 kilometers
0   200 statute miles
0   200 nautical miles

Surface currents
The Hawaiian Islands are located in
the center of the Subtropical Gyre, so
currents in their vicinity are relatively weak
and undefined. The prevailing flow follows
the North Equatorial Current but is
interrupted by several countercurrents
produced in the wake of the major islands.

→ North Equatorial Current
→ North Pacific Current
→ Subtropical Countercurrents

BATHYMETRIC
DEPTHS
Feet   Meters

Sea level   Sea level
656   200
1640   500
3281   1000
6562   2000
9842   3000
13,123   4000
16,404   5000
19,685   6000
26,246   8,000

Northwest Hawaiian Ridge

...naut Seamount
...018ft (310m)
...Seamount
(419m)

▲ Bousade Seamount
2016ft (614m)
▲ King George Seamount
329ft (100m)

Naifeh Seamount
717ft (219m) ▲
Volador Seamount
1299ft (396m) ▲
Volador Spur

...Seamount
(490m)
Laysan Island
Raita
Bank
Maro Reef
...pton
...unts

Gardner
Pinnacles

West St Rogatien Bank
St Rogatien Bank
Brooks Bank
Middle Brooks Bank

Baby Brooks Bank
**French Frigate
Shoals**

Necker Ridge

▲ Haydn Seamount
1792ft (546m)

Chopin Seamount
1819ft (554m) ▲

**Musicians
Seamounts**

Mendelssohn Seamount
2048ft (624m) ▲

Blackfin Ridge

H a w a i i a n I s l a n d s

Tropic of Cancer

Necker Island
Twin
Banks

West Bank   Middle Bank

Nihoa

Chauyauqua Seamount
1753ft (534m) ▲

Kauai

Niihau

Kaula Island

Molokai Fracture Zone

Honolulu
Oahu ★
Kauai Channel

Molokai

Lanai
Kahoolawe
Kailauea Channel

Maui

Mauna Kea
13,796ft (4205m) ▲
▲ Mauna Loa
13,678ft (4169m)

Hawaii

▲ Loihi Seamount

Hawaiian Trough

O C E A N

170°   165°   160°   155°

30°   25°   20°

Mauna Kea crater
The snow-capped crater of Mauna Kea,
which rises to 13,803 feet (4,207 m) above
the sea and 33,476 feet (10,203 m) above
its base on the ocean floor.

NATURAL RESOURCES

⚓ Fishing
▣ Tourism

🐢 **Green turtle**
The green turtle *(Chelonia mydas)* lives in
tropical and subtropical waters of all oceans.
Its Hawaiian subpopulation nests on French
Frigate Shoals 500 miles (800 km) northwest
of the islands. A tagging and research
program, begun in 1973, brought the
population back from near-extinction.

Lionfish
Lionfishes are found in the Indian and Pacific
oceans. Easily recognized by their long,
separated spines, they are among the most
venomous fish in the ocean. This Hawaiian
lionfish *(Pterois sphex)*, a species endemic to
Hawaii, rests in a slate pencil sea urchin
(Heterocentrotus mammillatus).

SEA OF OKHOTSK

The Sea of Okhotsk is set between the Siberian coast in the west and north, the Kamchatka Peninsula in the east, and the volcanically active Kuril Islands in the south. It falls off gradually from a wide shelf in the north to a deep basin in the south. Numerous deep passages between the Kuril Islands connect it with the main Pacific basins; straits east and west of Sakhalin Island provide connections to the Sea of Japan. During the winter monsoon (October–April) the sea is covered with drift ice, but storm winds from Siberia can still cause waves to rise up to 30 feet (10 m). Summer winds are light and calm conditions are encountered for 30 percent of the time. Currents circulate counterclockwise with moderate speed; in the south the Soya Warm Current, an extension of the Tsushima Current, passes rapidly from the Sea of Japan through the southern Kuril Islands.

THE FACTS	
Area	611,000 square miles (1,582,483 km²)
Average depth	2,818 feet (859 m)
Maximum depth	11,063 feet (3,742 m)
Maximum width	932 miles (1,500 km)
Maximum length	1,530 miles (2,463 km)

ICE FLOES

Salt lowers the freezing point of water, so the first ice to form is from fresh water in rivers. When the temperature drops to 28.8°F (-1.8°C) ice begins to form on the sea. Wind and waves break it up into pancake ice. Compacted pancake ice builds up to ice floes that drift with the current and can be piled up into pack ice.

A low winter sun shines on a thin sheet of new ice that forms in a river mouth. In the background the current carries parcels of older ice toward the sea.

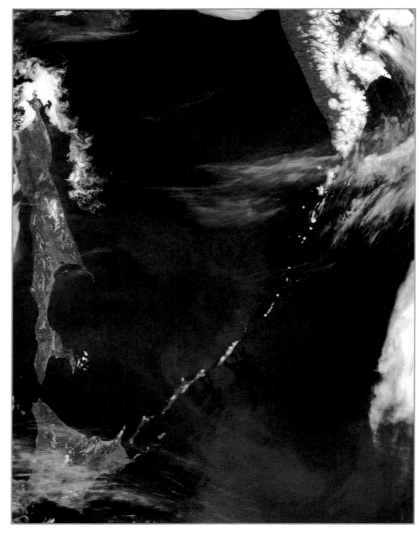

Kuril Islands
Snow covers the peaks of the 56 Kuril Islands that stretch for 700 miles (1,300 km) from Hokkaido, Japan, to Kamchatka, Russia. Different water coloration, visible under thin cloud cover, indicates patches of high productivity where the Soya Warm Current and the Kamchatka Current meet.

NATURAL RESOURCES

Fishing
Oil production

Oil rig
The shelf regions of the Sea of Okhotsk contain large oil and gas reserves that are difficult to access because of the extreme weather conditions in winter. This tanker-loading unit on the Sakhalin shelf is used to transfer oil from a pipeline to tankers.

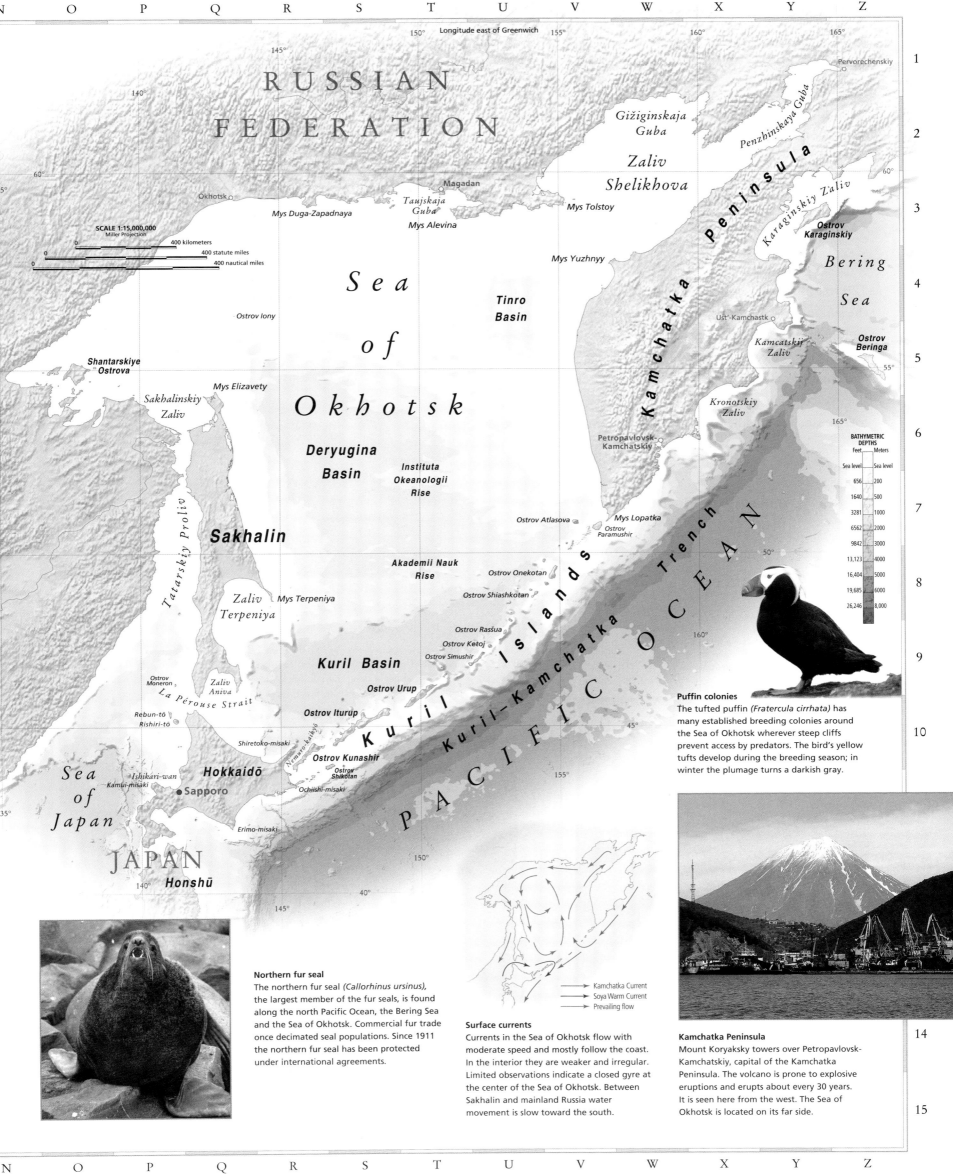

N O P Q R S T U V W X Y Z

150° Longitude east of Greenwich 155° 160° 165°

Pervorechenskiy 1

RUSSIAN

Gižiginskaja
Guba

Penzhinskaya Guba

2

FEDERATION

Zaliv
Shelikhova

Kamchatka Peninsula

Karaginskiy Zaliv

Magadan
Okhotsk· Mys Duga-Zapadnaya Mys Tolstoy Ostrov
Taujskaja Karaginskiy 3
Guba
Mys Alevina

SCALE 1:15,000,000
Miller Projection
400 kilometers
400 statute miles
400 nautical miles

Mys Yuzhnyy

Bering

Sea
of

Tinro
Basin

Ust'-Kamchastk

Sea 4

Ostrov Iony

Kamcatskij
Zaliv

Ostrov
Beringa 5

55°

Okhotsk

Shantarskiye
Ostrova

Mys Elizavety

Sakhalinskiy
Zaliv

Deryugina

Basin

Instituta
Okeanologii
Rise

Kronotskiy
Zaliv

Petropavlovsk-
Kamchatskiy

165° 6

BATHYMETRIC
DEPTHS
Feet Meters

Sea level Sea level

656 200
1640 500
3281 1000
6562 2000
9842 3000
13,123 4000
16,404 5000
19,685 6000
26,246 8,000

7

Tatarskiy Proliv

Sakhalin

Mys Lopatka
Ostrov Atlasova
Ostrov
Paramushir

Akademii Nauk
Rise

Ostrov Onekotan

Ostrov Shiashkotan

Kuril Islands

Kuril-Kamchatka Trench

PACIFIC OCEAN

8

Zaliv
Terpeniya

Mys Terpeniya

Ostrov Rasšua
Ostrov Ketoj
Ostrov Simushir

9

Ostrov
Moneron

Zaliv
Aniva

La Pérouse Strait

Kuril Basin

Ostrov Urup

Ostrov Iturup

160°

Puffin colonies
The tufted puffin (*Fratercula cirrhata*) has
many established breeding colonies around
the Sea of Okhotsk wherever steep cliffs
prevent access by predators. The bird's yellow
tufts develop during the breeding season; in
winter the plumage turns a darkish gray.

Rebun-tō
Rishiri-tō

Shiretoko-misaki

Nemuro-kaikyō

Ostrov Kunashir
Ostrov
Shikotan

Ochiishi-misaki

155° 45° 10

Sea
of
Japan

Iṣhikari-wan
Kamui-misaki

Hokkaidō

●**Sapporo**

Erimo-misaki

JAPAN
Honshū

140° 40°

145°

150°

Kamchatka Current
Soya Warm Current
Prevailing flow

14

135°

Northern fur seal
The northern fur seal (*Callorhinus ursinus*),
the largest member of the fur seals, is found
along the north Pacific Ocean, the Bering Sea
and the Sea of Okhotsk. Commercial fur trade
once decimated seal populations. Since 1911
the northern fur seal has been protected
under international agreements.

Surface currents
Currents in the Sea of Okhotsk flow with
moderate speed and mostly follow the coast.
In the interior they are weaker and irregular.
Limited observations indicate a closed gyre at
the center of the Sea of Okhotsk. Between
Sakhalin and mainland Russia water
movement is slow toward the south.

Kamchatka Peninsula
Mount Koryaksky towers over Petropavlovsk-
Kamchatskiy, capital of the Kamchatka
Peninsula. The volcano is prone to explosive
eruptions and erupts about every 30 years.
It is seen here from the west. The Sea of
Okhotsk is located on its far side.

15

N O P Q R S T U V W X Y Z

SEA OF JAPAN (EAST SEA)

The Sea of Japan, or East Sea, consists of isolated deep basins separated by a shallow ridge on which the Yamato Bank comes up to a depth of 177 feet (285 m). It connects with the Yellow Sea through Korea Strait, with the Sea of Okhotsk through La Perouse Strait and Tartar Strait, and with the main Pacific basins through Tsugaru Strait in the north and the narrow Kanmon Straits in the south. All of these straits are less than 120 feet (200 m) deep, so water in the basins is renewed through the sinking of cold surface water during winter. The North Korea Cold Current carries water from the Sea of Okhotsk to the sub-tropics. The warm Tsushima Current, a branch of the Kuroshio, flows swiftly northward. An unstable front between the two currents sheds eddies some 120 miles (200 km) wide every year. These eddies dominate most of the southern region.

THE FACTS	
Area	377,600 square miles (977,979 km²)
Average depth	5,748 feet (1,751 m)
Maximum depth	12,276 feet (3,742 m)

Moray eel
The tiger moray eel *(Enchelycore pardalis),* one of some 200 moray eel species, lives in coral reefs in shallow water of the tropical and subtropical Indo-Pacific. Morays are shy and reclusive. They rest in crevices during the day and are nocturnal predators.

Shark fins
Kesennuma in northeast Honshu is the center of a shark-fin industry. Shark-fin soup is a delicacy in China, where growing prosperity has led to increased demand. Many countries have banned the practice of cutting fins from living sharks and leaving the animals to die.

SPIDER CRAB

The Japanese spider crab *(Macrocheira kaempferi)* is the largest crab of the world's oceans. With a body of around 15 inches (40 cm) its legs reach a span of more than 10 feet (3 m). It lives around the islands of Japan at depths below 100 feet (300 m), where it feeds on dead animals and shellfish. At maturity it may weigh about 44 pounds (20 kg) and is believed to be very long-lived.

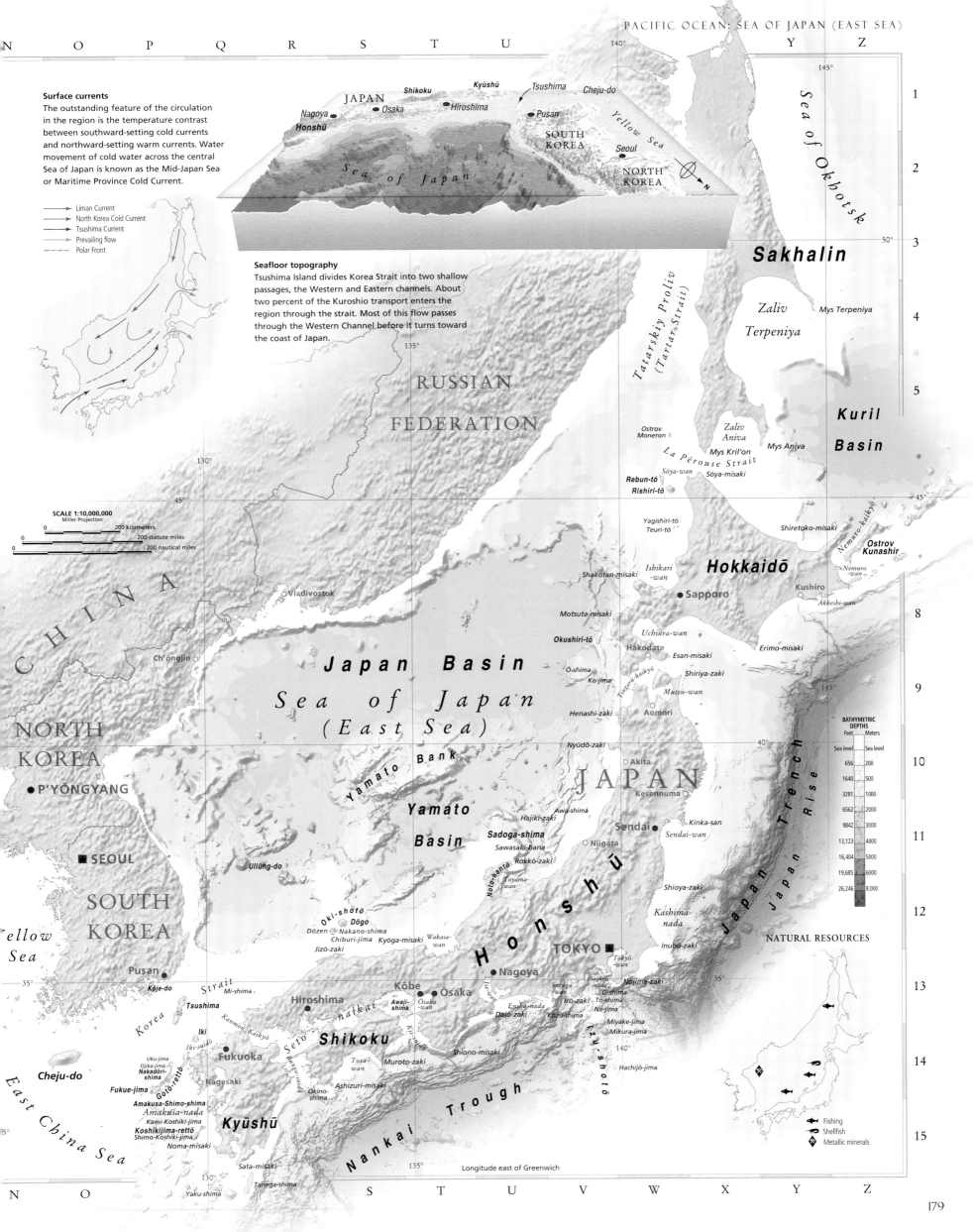

Surface currents

The outstanding feature of the circulation in the region is the temperature contrast between southward-setting cold currents and northward-setting warm currents. Water movement of cold water across the central Sea of Japan is known as the Mid-Japan Sea or Maritime Province Cold Current.

→ Liman Current
→ North Korea Cold Current
→ Tsushima Current
→ Prevailing flow
--- Polar Front

Seafloor topography

Tsushima Island divides Korea Strait into two shallow passages, the Western and Eastern channels. About two percent of the Kuroshio transport enters the region through the strait. Most of this flow passes through the Western Channel before it turns toward the coast of Japan.

JAPAN
Shikoku
Kyūshū
Tsushima
Nagoya
Honshū
Osaka
Hiroshima
Cheju-do
Pusan
SOUTH KOREA
Yellow Sea
Seoul
NORTH KOREA
Sea of Japan

Sea of Okhotsk

Sakhalin

Zaliv Terpeniya
Mys Terpeniya

Kuril Basin

Tatarskiy Proliv (Tartar Strait)

Ostrov Moneron
Zaliv Aniva
Mys Kril'on
Mys Aniva
La Pérouse Strait
Sōya-wan
Sōya-misaki

Rebun-tō
Rishiri-tō

RUSSIAN FEDERATION

Yagishiri-tō
Teuri-tō
Shiretoko-misaki
Ostrov Kunashir
Nemuro-kaikyō

Shakotan-misaki
Ishikari -wan
Hokkaidō
Kushiro
Akkeshi-wan
Nemuro-wan

Vladivostok

Ch'ŏngjin

Motsuta-misaki
Sapporo

Okushiri-tō
Uchiura-wan
Hakodate
Esan-misaki
Erimo-misaki

Japan Basin

Ō-shima
Ko-jima
Tsugaru-kaikyō
Mutsu-wan
Shiriya-zaki

Sea of Japan (East Sea)

Henashi-zaki
Aomori

Nyūdō-zaki

JAPAN

NORTH KOREA
Akita
Kesennuma

P'YŎNGYANG

Yamato Bank

Awa-shima

Yamato Basin

Hajiki-zaki
Sado ga-shima
Kinka-san
Sendai
Sawaski-bana
Sendai-wan
Niigata

SEOUL

Ullŭng-do

Noto-hantō
Rokkō-zaki
Toyama-wan

Shioya-zaki

SOUTH KOREA

Kashima-nada

Pusan

Oki-shotō
Dōgo
Dōzen
Nakano-shima
Chiburi-jima
Jizō-zaki
Kyōga-misaki
Wakasa-wan

Honshū

TOKYO
Tōkyō-wan
Inubō-zaki

Kōje-do
Korea Strait
Mi-shima

Nagoya

Kōbe
Ōsaka
Ōsaka-wan
Awaji-shima

Nojima-zaki

NATURAL RESOURCES

Tsushima
Iki
Kanmon Kaikyō
Iki-suidō

Hiroshima
Seto Naikai
Awaji-shima

Suruga-nada
Ō-shima
Irō-zaki
To-shima
Nii-jima

Miyake-jima
Mikura-jima

Cheju-do
Uku-jima
Ojika-jima
Nakadōri-shima

Fukuoka

Shikoku

Kii-suidō
Enshū-nada
Daiō-zaki
Kōzu-shima

Hachijō-jima

Fukue-jima
Gotō-rettō
Nagasaki

Tosa-wan
Muroto-zaki
Shiono-misaki

Izu-shotō

East China Sea

Amakusa-Shimo-shima
Amakusa-nada
Kami-Koshiki-jima
Koshikijima-rettō
Shimo-Koshiki-jima
Noma-misaki

Kyūshū

Ashizuri-misaki
Okino-shima

Nankai Trough

Sata-misaki

Yaku-shima
Tanega-shima

Longitude east of Greenwich

BATHYMETRIC DEPTHS

Feet	Meters
Sea level	Sea level
656	200
1640	500
3281	1000
6562	2000
9842	3000
13,123	4000
16,404	5000
19,685	6000
26,246	8,000

Japan Trench
Japan Rise

SCALE 1:10,000,000
Miller Projection
200 kilometers
200 statute miles
200 nautical miles

→ Fishing
→ Shellfish
◆ Metallic minerals

EAST CHINA SEA AND YELLOW SEA

The vast shelf region between Taiwan in the south and Korea in the north comprises two interconnected seas. The region south of a line between Kyushu and Shanghai is known as the East China Sea. It connects with the South China Sea through Taiwan Strait and with the main Pacific basins to the south of Kyushu and through passages between the Ryukyu Islands. The deep, fast-flowing, Kuroshio Current carries warm, saline water along its eastern perimeter. Dilution from the Yangtze River lowers salinity in the west. North of Shanghai the Yellow Sea connects to the Sea of Japan through Korea Strait. Sediment brought from China's loess plateau by the Yellow River (Hwang Ho), which enters the region through the Bo Hai Gulf, gives the Yellow Sea its name. Its wide intertidal mudflats are an important resting place for millions of wading birds during their migration from Siberia and Alaska to the southern hemisphere.

Sediment flow
A true-color satellite image reveals the effect of sediment carried by the Yellow River plume far out into the Bo Hai Sea. Some coastal waters are turbid from tidal current action. Farther south the coastal region is affected by the discharge of the Yangtze River.

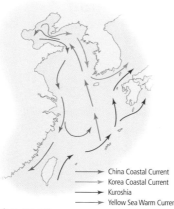

China Coastal Current
Korea Coastal Current
Kuroshia
Yellow Sea Warm Current

Surface currents
The circulation in the East China Sea and Yellow Sea is counterclockwise and follows the coast. A warm current branches off from the Kuroshio and flows into the center of the region. Another off-shoot from the Kuroshio enters the East China Sea from the south.

NATURAL RESOURCES

Fishing
Shellfish
Tourism

Yangtze River estuary
After flowing east for almost 4,000 miles (6,380 km), the waters of the Yangtze River finally reach the sea at Shanghai. The river's annual sediment load combined with that of the Yellow River makes up more than 10 percent of the total sediment flux to the world's oceans.

Gray whale
The endangered Asian population of gray whales (*Eschrichtius robustus*), which consists of less than 300 animals, migrates between the Sea of Okhotsk and Korea. Gray whales once also lived in the North Atlantic. Some 21,000 gray whales still migrate in the eastern Pacific between Alaska and California.

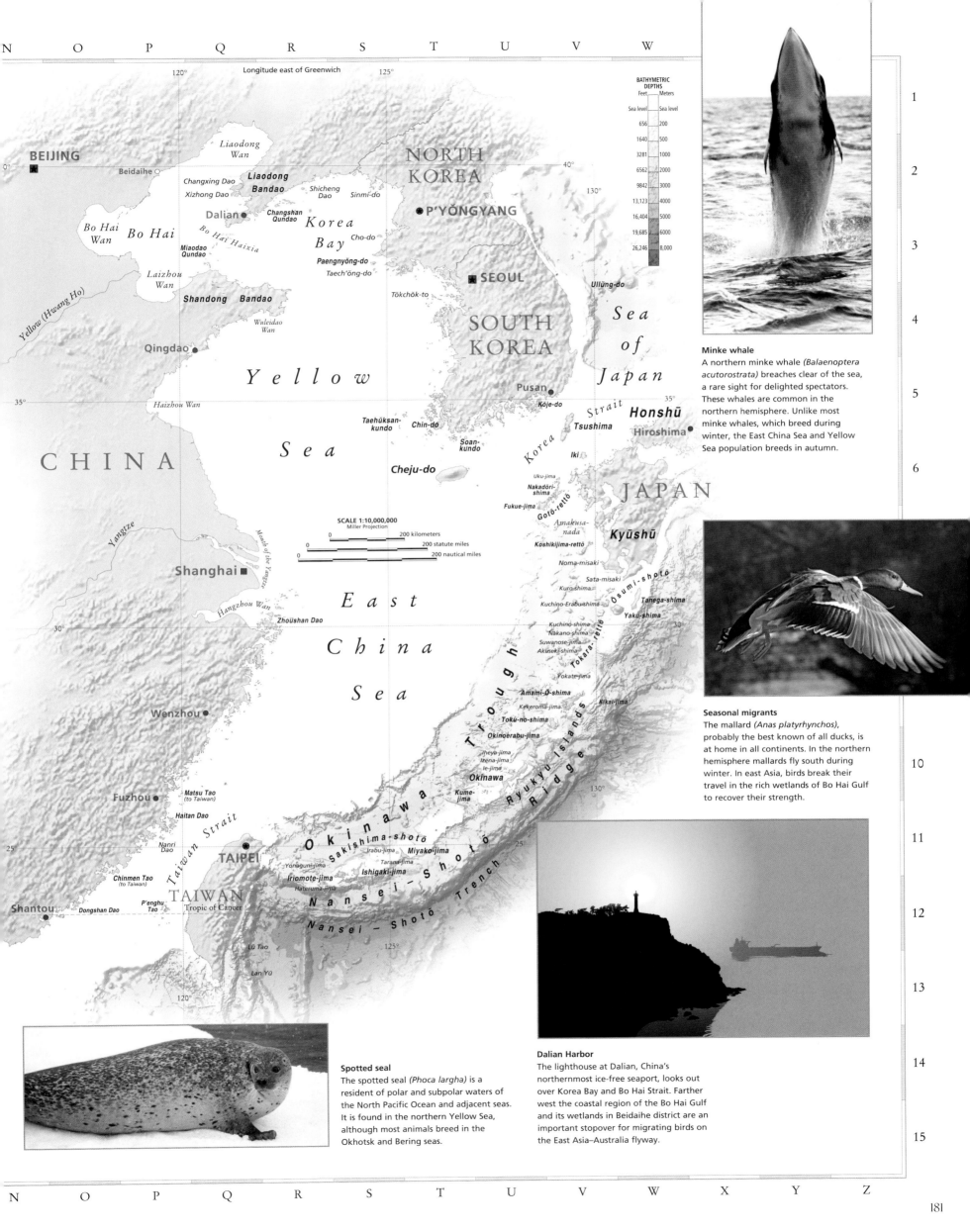

120°
Longitude east of Greenwich
125°

BATHYMETRIC
DEPTHS
Feet   Meters

Sea level Sea level
656   200
1640   500
3281   1000
6562   2000
9842   3000
13,123 4000
16,404 5000
19,685 6000
26,246 8,000

BEIJING

Beidaihe

Liaodong
Wan

NORTH
KOREA

40°

130°

Changxing Dao   **Liaodong**
Xizhong Dao   **Bandao**   Shicheng
                                     Dao   Sinmi-do
Bo Hai   Dalian   Changshan   **P'YŎNGYANG**
Wan   Qundao
        Bo Hai   Miaodao   Cho-do
Bo Hai Haixia Qundao   *Korea*
                                     Bay
Laizhou   **Paengnyŏng-do**
Wan   **Shandong Bandao**   Taech'ŏng-do
                                              ★ **SEOUL**
        Wuleidao   Tŏkchŏk-to
        Wan

Qingdao   **SOUTH**   Ullŭng-do
                                               KOREA   *Sea*
                                                                       of
35°   *Japan*
Haizhou Wan   *Yellow*   Pusan   35°
                                               Kŏje-do   *Strait*
                                    Taehŭksan- Chin-do   Tsushima **Honshū**
        CHINA   *Sea*   kundo   Iki   Hiroshima
                                    Soan-   *Korea*   Uku-jima
                                    kundo   **Nakadōri-**
Yellow (Hwang Ho)   **Cheju-do**   **shima**   **JAPAN**
                                               Fukue-jima Goto-rettō
                                               Koshikijima-rettō Amakusa-
Yangtze   SCALE 1:10,000,000   nada   **Kyūshū**
                                    Miller Projection   Noma-misaki
Shanghai   0   200 kilometers
                                    0   200 statute miles Sata-misaki Osumi-shotō
                                    0   200 nautical miles Kuro-shima Tanega-shima
                        East   Kuchino-Erabu-shima   Yaku-shima
Hangzhou Wan   Kuchino-shima
        Zhoushan Dao   *China*   Nakano-shima Tokara-rettō
30°   Suwanose-jima   30°
                                               Akuseki-shima
                        Sea   Yokate-jima
Wenzhou   Amami-O-shima
                                               Kekeroma-jima   Kikai-jima
                                               Tokū-no-shima
                                               Okinoerabu-jima
Fuzhou   Iheya-jima   Ryukyu Islands
        Matsu Tao   Izena-jima
        (to Taiwan)   Ie-jima
        Haitan Dao   **Okinawa**
        Nanri   Kume-   130°
        Dao   jima
25°   **TAIPEI**   Okinawa   Sakishima-shotō   25°
        Chinmen Tao   Sakishima-shotō Irabu-jima Miyako-jima
        (to Taiwan)   Yonaguni-jima Tarama-jima Ishigaki-jima
        TAIWAN   Iriomote-jima Hateruma-jima Nansei-Shotō Trench
Shantou Tropic of Cancer Nansei-Shotō
        Dongshan Dao   Nansei-Shotō Trench
                            Lū Tao
                            Lan Yü   125°

120°

Minke whale
A northern minke whale (*Balaenoptera acutorostrata*) breaches clear of the sea, a rare sight for delighted spectators. These whales are common in the northern hemisphere. Unlike most minke whales, which breed during winter, the East China Sea and Yellow Sea population breeds in autumn.

Seasonal migrants
The mallard (*Anas platyrhynchos*), probably the best known of all ducks, is at home in all continents. In the northern hemisphere mallards fly south during winter. In east Asia, birds break their travel in the rich wetlands of Bo Hai Gulf to recover their strength.

Spotted seal
The spotted seal (*Phoca largha*) is a resident of polar and subpolar waters of the North Pacific Ocean and adjacent seas. It is found in the northern Yellow Sea, although most animals breed in the Okhotsk and Bering seas.

Dalian Harbor
The lighthouse at Dalian, China's northernmost ice-free seaport, looks out over Korea Bay and Bo Hai Strait. Farther west the coastal region of the Bo Hai Gulf and its wetlands in Beidaihe district are an important stopover for migrating birds on the East Asia–Australia flyway.

1
2
3
4
5
6
10
11
12
13
14
15

WESTERN TROPICAL PACIFIC OCEAN

Deep trenches, isolated deep basins, myriad seamounts, and Micronesia's many hundred islands characterize the Western Tropical Pacific. The North Equatorial Countercurrent has its source here and the region is important for water exchange between ocean basins. North of New Guinea the South Equatorial Current and New Guinea Coastal Current combine to feed southern hemisphere water into the countercurrent, forming the Halmahera Eddy in the process. The North Equatorial Current adds northern hemisphere water through the Mindanao Eddy but also directs substantial amounts into the Indonesian seas toward the Indian Ocean. The heavily populated regions in its west, where fishing has been supplemented by aquaculture for centuries, contrast with the pristine conditions of the islands in the east and south. The high water temperatures of the "West Pacific Warm Pool" are the source of cyclones and play a key role in the El Niño–Southern Oscillation phenomenon.

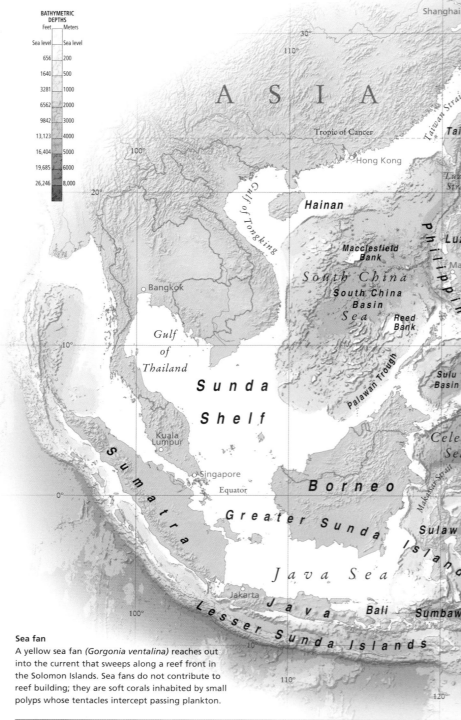

BATHYMETRIC DEPTHS

Feet	Meters
Sea level	Sea level
656	200
1640	500
3281	1000
6562	2000
9842	3000
13,123	4000
16,404	5000
19,685	6000
26,246	8,000

ASIA

Outrigger
Pacific islanders navigated their vast ocean space in outrigger canoes for centuries, using star constellations, swell patterns, and bird flight to guide them. This Melanesian is on a less challenging voyage; he heads for a nearby village to participate in a village festivity.

Surface currents
The western tropical Pacific plays a key role in the global oceanic circulation. It is the main region of the Pacific where currents transfer water between the two hemispheres, and it provides an opening into the Indonesian seas for water movement from the Pacific to the Indian Ocean.

Sea fan
A yellow sea fan (*Gorgonia ventalina*) reaches out into the current that sweeps along a reef front in the Solomon Islands. Sea fans do not contribute to reef building; they are soft corals inhabited by small polyps whose tentacles intercept passing plankton.

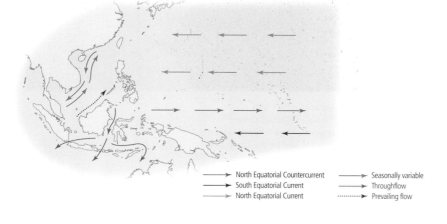

→ North Equatorial Countercurrent	→ Seasonally variable
→ South Equatorial Current	→ Throughflow
→ North Equatorial Current	⋯→ Prevailing flow

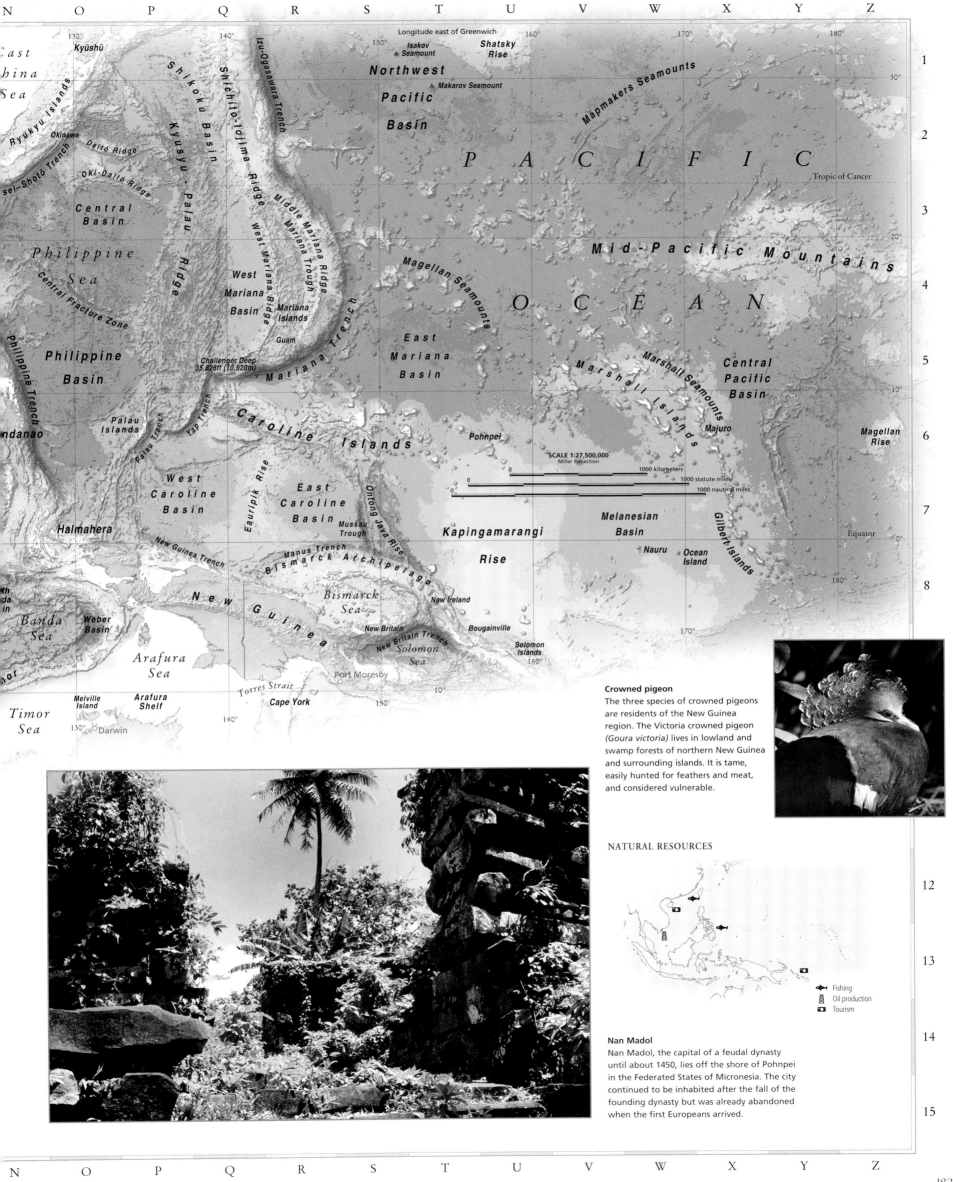

N O P Q R S T U V W X Y Z

Longitude east of Greenwich

Kyūshū

East China Sea

Ryukyu Islands

Okinawa

Daitō Ridge

sei-Shotō Trench

Oki-Daitō Ridge

Central Basin

Central Fracture Zone

Philippine Sea

Philippine Basin

Philippine Trench

ndanao

Palau Islands

West Caroline Basin

Halmahera

Banda Sea

Weber Basin

th da in

Timor Sea

Arafura Sea

Melville Island

Arafura Shelf

Darwin

Shikoku Basin

Kyusyu - Palau Ridge

Izu-Ogasawara Trench

Shichito-Iojima Ridge

Middle Mariana Ridge

West Mariana Ridge

Mariana Trough

West Mariana Basin

Mariana Islands

Guam

Challenger Deep 35,826ft (10,920m)

Mariana Trench

Yap Trench

Palau Trench

Eauripik Rise

Caroline Islands

East Caroline Basin

New Guinea Trench

Manus Trench

Bismarck Archipelago

Ontong Java Rise

Mussau Trough

New Guinea

Bismarck Sea

New Britain

New Britain Trench

New Ireland

Bougainville

Solomon Sea

Solomon Islands

Port Moresby

Torres Strait

Cape York

Isakov Seamount

Shatsky Rise

Northwest Pacific Basin

Makarov Seamount

Magellan Seamounts

East Mariana Basin

Mapmakers Seamounts

P A C I F I C

O C E A N

Tropic of Cancer

Mid-Pacific Mountains

Marshall Seamounts

Marshall Islands

Central Pacific Basin

Majuro

Magellan Rise

Pohnpei

Kapingamarangi Rise

Melanesian Basin

Nauru

Ocean Island

Gilbert Islands

Equator

SCALE 1:27,500,000
Miller Projection

0   1000 kilometers
0   1000 statute miles
0   1000 nautical miles

1
2
3
4
5
6
7
8

30°
20°
10°
0°

130°
140°
150°
160°
170°
180°

180°
170°
160°
150°
140°
130°

Crowned pigeon

The three species of crowned pigeons are residents of the New Guinea region. The Victoria crowned pigeon *(Goura victoria)* lives in lowland and swamp forests of northern New Guinea and surrounding islands. It is tame, easily hunted for feathers and meat, and considered vulnerable.

NATURAL RESOURCES

Fishing
Oil production
Tourism

12
13
14
15

Nan Madol

Nan Madol, the capital of a feudal dynasty until about 1450, lies off the shore of Pohnpei in the Federated States of Micronesia. The city continued to be inhabited after the fall of the founding dynasty but was already abandoned when the first Europeans arrived.

N O P Q R S T U V W X Y Z

SOUTH CHINA SEA

The South China Sea reaches from Taiwan in the north to Singapore in the south. It consists of an isolated deep basin, which is connected with the main Pacific basins through the 8,500 feet (2,600 m) deep Bashi Channel between Taiwan and Luzon, a wide shelf region in the east, and a vast shelf region between Indonesia and Malaysia in the south, where it connects with the Java Sea. Numerous tiny islands, most of them uninhabited and without much vegetation, along with hundreds of coral reefs, are the object of dispute between coastal states. The South China Sea connects with the Indian Ocean through the Strait of Malacca, one of the most important shipping lanes in the world. The strait has a minimum depth of 82 feet (25 m) and is dominated by large tidal currents that produce shifting sandbars 13–23 feet (4–7 m) high at its floor.

THE FACTS	
Area	895,400 square miles (2,319,075 km²)
Average depth	5,419 feet (1,652 m)
Maximum depth	16,456 feet (5,015 m)
Maximum width	840 miles (1,352 km)
Maximum length	1,182 miles (1,902 km)

NATURAL RESOURCES

- ⟨Fishing⟩ Fishing
- ⟨Shellfish⟩ Shellfish
- ⟨Tourism⟩ Tourism

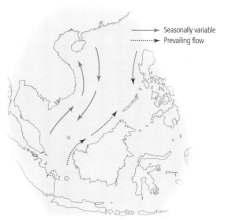

- → Seasonally variable
- ⋯→ Prevailing flow

Surface currents
Currents in the South China Sea are determined by the monsoon. During summer the southwest monsoon pushes water from the Sunda Shelf northward. During winter the northeast monsoon causes southward movement along the Vietnamese coast, but currents along Borneo continue to flow northward.

Halong Bay
The 1,969 limestone islands of Halong Bay in northern Vietnam are a UNESCO World Heritage site and a popular tourist destination. The islands' terrain is too steep for settlements, but the quiet waters between some islands support floating villages.

⊙ Turtle protection
The hawksbill turtle (Eretmochelys imbricata) lives in all tropical and subtropical oceans and is the main source of tortoiseshell. In Japan and Southeast Asia it is considered good eating. Hunting has severely reduced its numbers and many countries have banned trade in hawksbills and derived products.

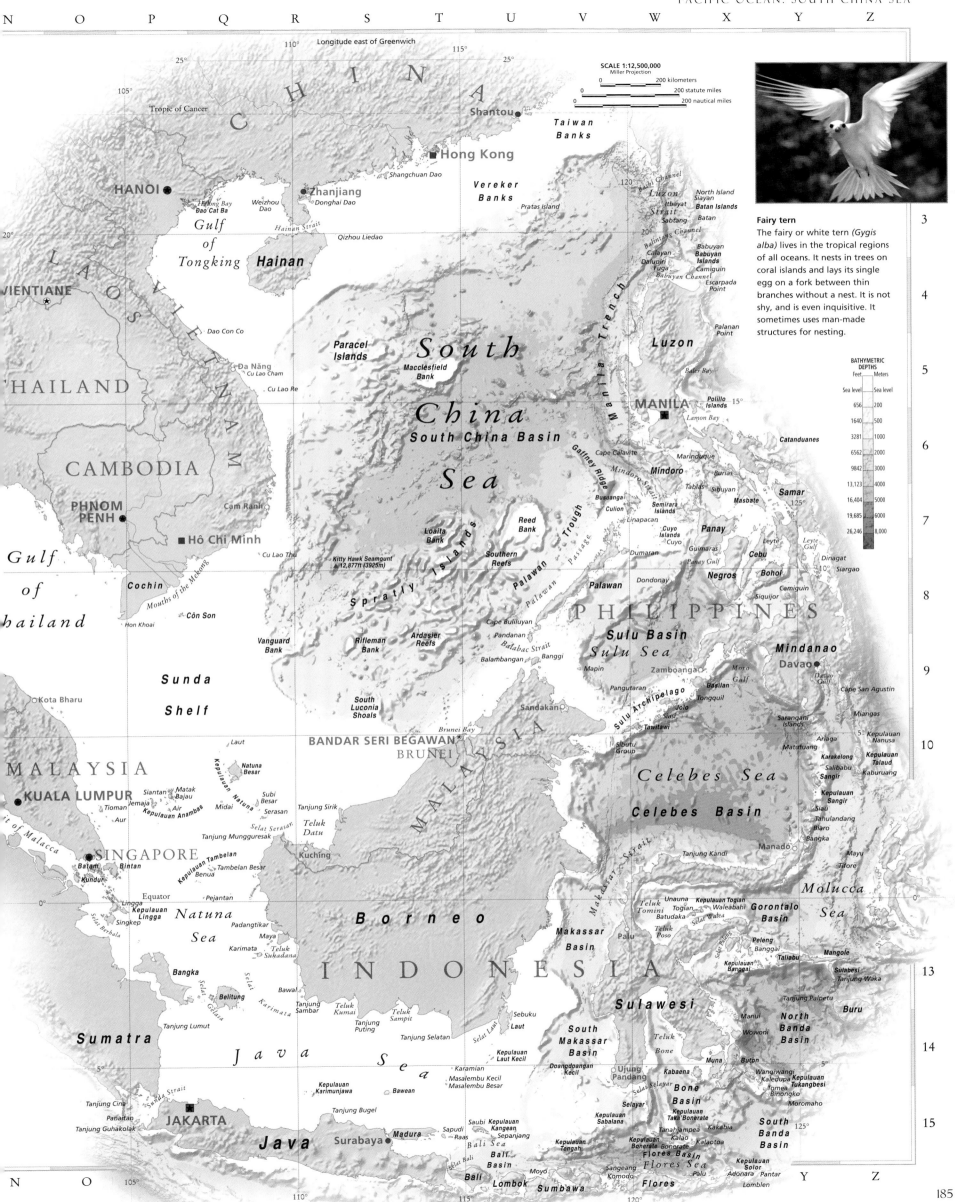

N O P Q R S T U V W X Y Z

SCALE 1:12,500,000
Miller Projection
0   200 kilometers
0   200 statute miles
0   200 nautical miles

Fairy tern
The fairy or white tern (*Gygis alba*) lives in the tropical regions of all oceans. It nests in trees on coral islands and lays its single egg on a fork between thin branches without a nest. It is not shy, and is even inquisitive. It sometimes uses man-made structures for nesting.

BATHYMETRIC DEPTHS
Feet   Meters

Sea level	Sea level
656	200
1640	500
3281	1000
6562	2000
9842	3000
13,123	4000
16,404	5000
19,685	6000
26,246	8,000

Longitude east of Greenwich
110°   115°
25°   25°
105°
Tropic of Cancer

C H I N A

Shantou

Taiwan Banks

Hong Kong

Shangchuan Dao   *Vereker Banks*

HANOI   Zhanjiang
Dao Cat Ba
Halong Bay   Weizhou Dao
Donghai Dao
Pratas Island
Gulf   Hainan Strait   Qizhou Liedao
of   20°
Tongking   **Hainan**

L A O S   VIENTIANE

Dao Con Co

V I E T N A M

Paracel Islands

Da Năng
Cu Lao Cham
Cu Lao Re

Macclesfield Bank

South China Sea

South China Basin

Hashi Channel
Luzon Strait   North Island
Siayan   Itbayat   Batan Islands
Sabtang
Calayan   *Balintang Channel*
Dalupiri   Babuyan Islands
Fuga   Camiguin
Babuyan Channel
Escarpada Point

Baler Bay

Luzon

Palanan Point

T H A I L A N D

CAMBODIA

PHNOM PENH
Cam Ranh

Hô Chi Minh
Côn Son
Cu Lao Thu

Gulf
of
Thailand

Hon Khoai

Mouths of the Mekong

Cochin

Gaffney Ridge

Palawan Trough

MANILA   15°
Lamon Bay
Polillo Islands

Cape Calavite   Marinduque
Mindoro   Burias
Mindoro Strait
Busuanga   Tablas   Sibuyan   Masbate
Culion   Semirara Islands
Linapacan   Panay
Cuyo Islands
Cuyo   Guimaras   Cebu
Dumaran   Panay Gulf
Negros   Bohol
Palawan   Dondonay   Siquijor

Reed Bank

Southern Reefs

Spratly Islands
Loaita Bank

Catanduanes

Samar
125°

Leyte
Leyte Gulf
Dinagat
10°   Siargao
Camiguin

Kitty Hawk Seamount
12,877ft (3925m)

P H I L I P P I N E S

Cape Buliluyan
Pandanan
Balabac Strait
Balambangan   Banggi

Vanguard Bank

Rifleman Bank   Ardasier Reefs

South Luconia Shoals

Sunda Shelf

Sulu Basin
Sulu Sea

Mindanao
Davao

Sandakan   Mapin   Zamboanga   *Moro Gulf*   Cape San Agustin

Pangutaran   Basilan   Miangas
Slasi   Tongquil   Sarangani Islands
Jolo   Ariaga   Kepulauan Nanusa
Sulu Archipelago   Tawitawi   Sibutu Group   Matutuang   Karakelong   Kepulauan Talaud
Kaburuang

Brunei Bay

BANDAR SERI BEGAWAN
BRUNEI

M A L A Y S I A

Celebes Sea

Celebes Basin

Salibabu   Kepulauan Sangir
Sangir
Siau
Tahulandang
Biaro
Bangka

MALAYSIA

KUALA LUMPUR

Laut   Natuna Besar
Siantan   Matak
Jemaja   Bajau   Subi Besar
Tioman   Air   Serasan
Aur   *Kepulauan Anambas*   Midai
Kepulauan Natuna   Serasan

Tanjung Sirik

Selat Serasan

Teluk Datu

Tanjung Mungguresak
Kepulauan Tambelan
Tambelan Besar
Benua

Kuching

Manado

Tanjung Kandi

Mayu
Titore

SINGAPORE
Batam   Bintan
Kundur

Lingga
Kepulauan Lingga
Singkep

Equator

Pejantan   Padangtikar   Maya   Karimata

Natuna Sea   Teluk Sukadana

B o r n e o

Makassar Strait

Teluk Tomini   Unauna   Kepulauan Togian
Togian   Waleabahi   Gorontalo Basin
Batudaka
Teluk Poso   *Selat Walea*

Makassar Basin

Palu

Peleng   Banggai
Kepulauan Banggai   Taliabu

Molucca Sea

Mangole

Sulabesi
Tanjung Waka

0°

I N D O N E S I A

Sumatra

Bangka

Belitung   *Selat Gelasa*   *Selat Karimata*

Tanjung Lumut

Palu
Makassar Basin

Tanjung Sambar   Teluk Kumai
Tanjung Puting   Teluk Sampit
Tanjung Selatan

Sebuku
Laut

Selat Laut

S u l a w e s i

Tanjung Palpetu

North Banda Basin   Buru

Java Sea
5°

Karamian
Masalembu Kecil
Masalembu Besar

Doangdoangan Laut Kecil

South Makassar Basin

Muna   Buton

Teluk Bone

Manui
Wowoni

Wangiwangi   Kaledupa   Kepulauan Tukangbesi
Tomea   Binongko

Kabaena

Kepulauan Karimunjawa   Bawean

Kepulauan Laut Kecil

Doangdoangan Besar
Kabia

Bone Basin

Tanjung Cina   Panaitan
Tanjung Guhakolak

Sunda Strait

JAKARTA

Saubi   Kepulauan Kangean
Sapudi   Sepanjang
Raas

Kepulauan Sabalana   Tanahjampea   Kakabia
Selayar   Kepulauan Taka Bonerate   Kalao   Kalaotoa
Kepulauan Taka Bonerate

South Banda Basin

J a v a   Surabaya   Madura

Bali Sea

Bali   Lombok   Sumbawa

Moyo

Kepulauan Tengah   Bonerate   Kalaotoa
Kepulauan Bonerate

Sangeang   Komodo

Flores Basin
Flores Sea

Kepulauan Solo   Kepulauan Adonara   Pantar
Flores   Lomblen

105°   110°   120°   125°

185

GULF OF THAILAND

The Gulf of Thailand is bowl-shaped and shallow. Rainfall exceeds evaporation here and creates a two-layered system, with low-salinity water leaving the gulf at the surface and water of oceanic salinity entering across the sill, 190 feet (58 m) deep, that separates the gulf from the South China Sea. The region is under the influence of the wet southwest monsoon from May to September and under the dry northeast monsoon from November to March. Forty-two islands near its eastern shore are scattered around a region where the gulf is less than 33 feet (10 m) deep; they form the Mu Ko Ang Thong National Park and are protected under international treaties. Turbid water and sediment from rivers support mangrove forests. The gulf also supports important artisanal and commercial fisheries. Oil and gas reserves are under dispute between Malaysia, Thailand, and Vietnam but developed jointly between the parties.

Lettuce coral
A school of anthias (Pseudanthias tuka) searches for food in a yellow scroll coral or lettuce coral (Turbinaria reniformis), a stony coral species popular for aquaria. Anthias are born female; if a dominant male dies, a female changes into a male to take its place.

Fishing fleet
Thai fishing boats anchor at Ko Samui, Thailand's third-largest island and the second most popular destination for tourists. Although tourism has shaped the face of the island, fishing vessels built from local teak still bring in a fresh catch in the morning.

THE FACTS	
Area	123,553 square miles (320,000 km²)
Average depth	148 feet (45 m)
Maximum depth	262 feet (80 m)
Maximum width	350 miles (563 km)
Maximum length	450 miles (724 km)

NATURAL RESOURCES

- Shellfish
- Tourism
- Oil production
- Gas production

Giant anemone
Anthias swarm around a giant anemone (Heteractis magnifica). In locations with good light and a strong, turbulent current, such as the wave zone on a reef front, giant anemones can grow to 3 feet (1 m) in diameter. They feed on vertebrates and invertebrates, including fish and crustaceans.

A B C

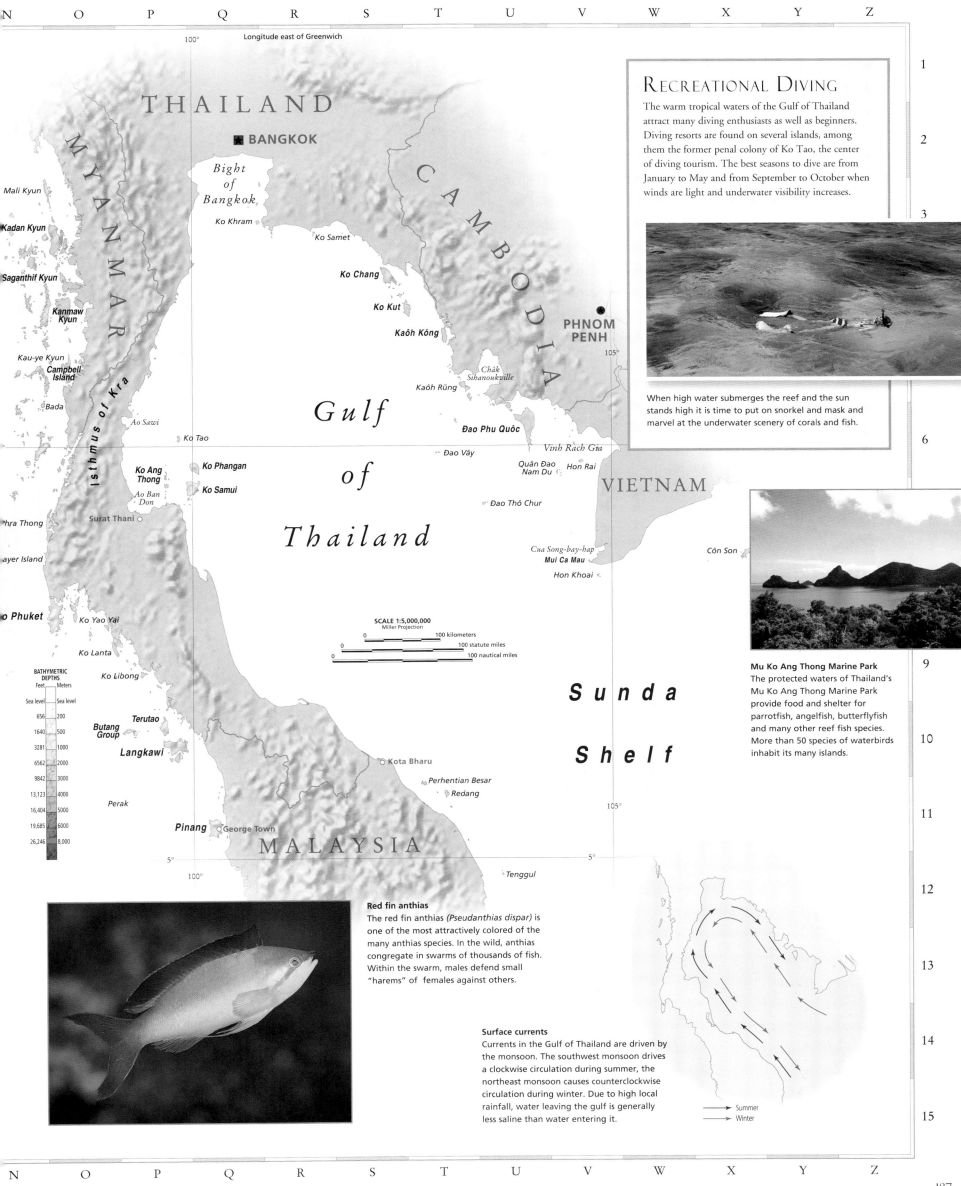

N O P Q R S T U V W X Y Z

1

Longitude east of Greenwich

100°

THAILAND

■ BANGKOK

2

Bight of Bangkok

Ko Khram

Ko Samet

CAMBODIA

MYANMAR

3

Mali Kyun

Kadan Kyun

Ko Chang

Saganthif Kyun

Ko Kut

Kanmaw Kyun

Kaôh Kŏng

PHNOM PENH

105°

Kau-ye Kyun

Campbell Island

Chắk Sihanoukville

Bada

Kaôh Rŭng

Isthmus of Kra

Ao Sawi

Gulf

Đao Phu Quốc

Ko Tao

Vinh Rach Gia

Đao Vây

of

Quân Đao Nam Du

Hon Rai

Ko Ang Thong

Ko Phangan

VIETNAM

Ao Ban Don

Ko Samui

Đao Thổ Chur

Thailand

hra Thong

Surat Thani

Đao Vây

ayer Island

Cua Song-bay-hap

Mui Ca Mau

Côn Son

Hon Khoai

o Phuket

Ko Yao Yai

SCALE 1:5,000,000
Miller Projection

0   100 kilometers

0   100 statute miles

0   100 nautical miles

Ko Lanta

BATHYMETRIC DEPTHS

Feet   Meters

Sea level   Sea level

Ko Libong

S u n d a

656   200

S h e l f

1640   500

Butang Group

Terutao

3281   1000

6562   2000

Langkawi

9842   3000

Kota Bharu

13,123 4000

Perhentian Besar

16,404 5000

105°

Redang

19,685 6000

Perak

26,246 8,000

Pinang

George Town

5°   5°

MALAYSIA

100°

Tenggul

Recreational Diving

The warm tropical waters of the Gulf of Thailand attract many diving enthusiasts as well as beginners. Diving resorts are found on several islands, among them the former penal colony of Ko Tao, the center of diving tourism. The best seasons to dive are from January to May and from September to October when winds are light and underwater visibility increases.

When high water submerges the reef and the sun stands high it is time to put on snorkel and mask and marvel at the underwater scenery of corals and fish.

Mu Ko Ang Thong Marine Park
The protected waters of Thailand's Mu Ko Ang Thong Marine Park provide food and shelter for parrotfish, angelfish, butterflyfish and many other reef fish species. More than 50 species of waterbirds inhabit its many islands.

Red fin anthias
The red fin anthias *(Pseudanthias dispar)* is one of the most attractively colored of the many anthias species. In the wild, anthias congregate in swarms of thousands of fish. Within the swarm, males defend small "harems" of females against others.

Surface currents
Currents in the Gulf of Thailand are driven by the monsoon. The southwest monsoon drives a clockwise circulation during summer, the northeast monsoon causes counterclockwise circulation during winter. Due to high local rainfall, water leaving the gulf is generally less saline than water entering it.

→ Summer
→ Winter

1
2
3
6
9
10
11
12
13
14
15

N O P Q R S T U V W X Y Z

BANDA SEA, CELEBES SEA, AND ADJACENT SEAS

The seas between Indonesia and the Philippines display the most complicated bathymetry of the world's oceans. Shallow sills divide the region into several deep basins. Water from the Pacific is transported through the various seas to the Indian Ocean, giving the region an important role in the global ocean conveyor belt. The "Indonesian Throughflow" enters south of Mindanao, passes through Makassar Strait, and leaves through the various passages between Bali and Timor. Annual rainfall exceeds evaporation by 6.5 feet (2 m), so Pacific water is strongly diluted during its passage and reaches the Indian Ocean with much-reduced salinity. Water renewal in the deep basins is slow, but faster than in the deep basins of the open Pacific due to strong mixing at ridges and sills. In the Weber Basin—at more than 23,000 feet (7,000 m) the deepest location of the region—the transit time is about 60 years.

Satellite view
Sun glint on the Molucca and Banda seas contrasts with the white of clouds that rise over the mountain ranges and highlight the convoluted coastlines of Indonesia's islands. The passage between Mindanao and Halmahera in the upper right is the entry point for the Throughflow.

Flores Island
Flores is one of the islands that form the border between the Pacific and Indian oceans. It carries several volcano craters and experienced a major earthquake and tsunami in 1992. The Throughflow passes through straits to the east and west of the island.

Seafloor topography
The Lesser Sunda Islands form part of the Pacific Ring of Fire and, in 1815, experienced the most violent volcanic eruptions in recent history. The narrow straits between the islands are an important passageway for the Indonesian Throughflow.

MAKASSAR STRAIT

Makassar Strait is a busy shipping route. Vessels that are too large to go through the Strait of Malacca, between mainland Malaysia and Sumatra, have to pass through this strait and continue through the Lesser Sunda Islands. The strait is shallow on the western side but deeper than 6,500 feet (2,000 m) in the east, where it is connected with the Celebes Sea.

Most of the Indonesian Throughflow passes from the Pacific to the Indian Ocean via Makassar Strait, thus giving this waterway between Borneo and Sulawesi an important role in global ocean circulation.

→ New Guinea Coastal Current
→ Prevailing flow
→ Throughflow

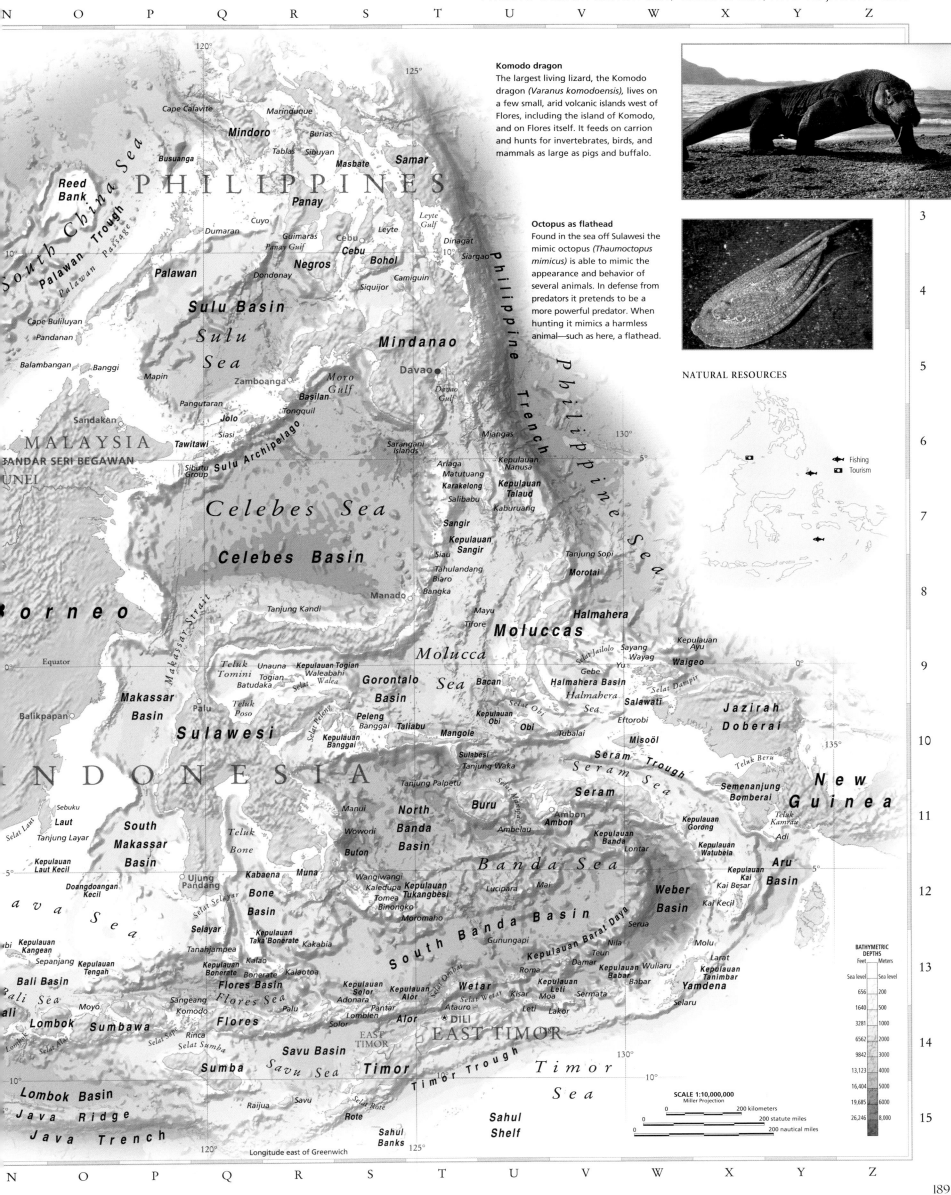

Komodo dragon
The largest living lizard, the Komodo dragon *(Varanus komodoensis)*, lives on a few small, arid volcanic islands west of Flores, including the island of Komodo, and on Flores itself. It feeds on carrion and hunts for invertebrates, birds, and mammals as large as pigs and buffalo.

Octopus as flathead
Found in the sea off Sulawesi the mimic octopus *(Thaumoctopus mimicus)* is able to mimic the appearance and behavior of several animals. In defense from predators it pretends to be a more powerful predator. When hunting it mimics a harmless animal—such as here, a flathead.

NATURAL RESOURCES

Fishing
Tourism

BATHYMETRIC
DEPTHS
Feet | Meters
Sea level | Sea level
656 | 200
1640 | 500
3281 | 1000
6562 | 2000
9842 | 3000
13,123 | 4000
16,404 | 5000
19,685 | 6000
26,246 | 8,000

SCALE 1:10,000,000
Miller Projection

0   200 kilometers
0   200 statute miles
0   200 nautical miles

PHILIPPINE SEA AND MARIANA TRENCH

The Philippine Sea is an isolated deep ocean region that contains some of the deepest trenches of the world's oceans. The Mariana Trench, the deepest depression in the ocean floor, lies east of the Mariana Islands—just outside the Philippine Sea—where the Pacific plate subducts under the Philippine plate. It was the place of the deepest ever ocean dive, when the bathyscaphe *Trieste* explored the Challenger Deep in 1960. In the west of the region is the Philippine Trench, the second deepest of ocean trenches, formed by subduction of the Philippine plate under the Eurasian plate. A sill depth of less than 9,000 feet (2,700 m) divides the region into the West Mariana Basin and the Philippine Basin. The North Equatorial Current enters the Philippine Sea from the east and continues as the Philippine Current and Kuroshio Current, the western boundary currents of the Subtropical Gyre.

NATURAL RESOURCES

➤ Fishing

Typhoon origins
The warm waters of the Philippine Sea present ideal conditions for the formation of tropical cyclones, known in the region as typhoons. A large pressure difference between the cyclone center and the surrounding ocean produces gale-force winds and torrential rain.

Surface currents
Most of the Philippine Sea experiences westward flow from the North Equatorial Current. The North Equatorial Countercurrent originates in the region and flows eastward near 5°N. Two eddies develop between these currents near Halmahera and Mindanao. The swift, deep-reaching Philippine Current flows northward along the Philippine coast.

→ North Equatorial Countercurrent	→ Philippine Current
→ South Equatorial Current	→ Mindanao Eddy
→ North Equatorial Current	····> Halmahera Eddy

SCALE 1:15,000,000
Miller Projection

0   250 kilometers
0   250 statute miles
0   250 nautical miles

BATHYMETRIC DEPTHS

Feet	Meters
Sea level	Sea level
656	200
1640	500
3281	1000
6562	2000
9842	3000
13,123	4000
16,404	5000
19,685	6000
26,246	8,000

Typhoon winds
A satellite image of winds and rain in Typhoon Nesat of June 2005. Color indicates wind speed, dark purple and light pink showing the strongest winds. White arrows near the center of the typhoon indicate heavy rain.

N O P Q R S T U V W X Y Z

Longitude east of Greenwich

130° 135° 140° 145° 150° 155° 160°

PACIFIC OCEAN

West Mariana Ridge

Farallon de Pajaros
Maug Islands
Asuncion

Agrihan
Pagan
Alamagan
Guguan

Mariana Islands

Mariana Trench

NORTHERN MARIANA ISLANDS

Middle Mariana Ridge

Sarigan
Anatahan
Farallon de Medinilla

Saipan
★ SAIPAN
Tinian

West Mariana Basin

Mariana Ridge

Mariana Trough

Rota

HAGÅTÑA
GUAM

Guam

Challenger Deep
35,826ft (10,920m)

Mariana Trench

East Mariana Basin

Magellan Seamounts

Central Fracture Zone

Philippine Basin

Palau Ridge

Caroline Islands

Ulithi

Yap

Gaferut

Sorol

Faraulep

Namonuito

Hall Islands

Murilo Atoll
Nomwin

Fayu

Ngulu

Yap Trench

West Fayu

Ulul

Chuuk Islands

Oroluk

Philippine Sea

Ngajangel
Palau Islands
KOROR ★
PALAU

Palau Trench

Caroline

Woleai

Halik

Elato

Pulap
Pulawat

Losap

PALIKIR
★ Pohnpei

Mwokil
Pingelap

Caroline

Eauripik

Pulusuk

Namoluk

Mortlock Islands

Ngetik Atoll

Seamounts

Sonsorol Islands

West Caroline Basin

Eauripik Rise

FEDERATED STATES OF MICRONESIA

Nukuoro

Pulo Anna
Merir

Solomon Rise

luccas
IA
ahera

Kepulauan Asia

Kepulauan Ayu
Equator

Kepulauan Mapia

East Caroline Basin

Mussau Trough

Sayang
Waigeo

Manim
Biak

Manus Trench

Ninigo Group

Hermit Islands

Mussau Island

St Matthias Group

Emirau Island

Yapen

Aua Island
Wuvulu Island

Admiralty Islands

Manus Island

Ysabel Channel

New Hanover

Tabar Islands
Lihir Group

Teluk Cenderawasih

New Guinea

Bismarck Archipelago

Manus Basin

New Ireland

New Guinea Basin

130° 135° 140° 145° 150° 155° 160°

20° 1
2
15° 3
4
10° 5
6
5° 7
8
0°

N O P Q R S T U V W X Z

14

15

MARIANA TRENCH

The highest point on Earth, the summit of Mount Everest, was first reached by climbers in May 1953. Seven years later, in 1960, the bathyscaphe *Trieste*, a specially built diving vessel capable of withstanding the tremendous pressure in the Mariana Trench, came close to the deepest point on Earth, reaching 35,797 feet (10,911 m). To the surprise of the occupants they saw shrimp and fish, even at such great depth.

Lieutenant Don Walsh of the United States Navy (left) and Jacques Piccard, oceanographer and designer of the bathyscaphe *Trieste* (center), in the diving cabin during the preparation for their dive.

Sea urchin
Sea urchins *(Echinoidea* sp.*)* are found in all oceans; more than 80 different species occur in the Philippine Sea. They are harvested for their roe, an important sushi ingredient in Japan, and rising demand has led to severe overfishing. Moves are now underway to control the fishery and to develop cultivation in sea-urchin farms.

Seafloor topography
The Mariana Trench is the deepest location on the surface of Earth. Its maximum depth of 35,826 feet (10,920 m) is in the Challenger Deep. It contains hydrothermal vents where acidic hot water of up to 570°F (330°C), laden with hydrogen sulfide, enters the ocean.

Mariana Islands
Guam
Mariana Trench

Challenger Deep
35,826ft (10,920m)

West Mariana Basin

Pacific Ocean

Yap Trench

Palau Trench

Palau

SOUTHWESTERN PACIFIC OCEAN

Coral islands, extensive plateaus and deep basins characterize the Southwestern Pacific. Where the Pacific plate subducts under the Australian plate the ocean floor is folded into island chains beside deep trenches. The region's hydrography is determined by the western part of the Subtropical Gyre of the southern hemisphere. The South Equatorial Current enters the Coral Sea from the east; its tropical waters are the source of the East Australian Current. Like all western boundary currents the East Australian Current is fast-flowing and extends to great depth. Loss of water from the Subtropical Gyre to the Indian Ocean through the Indonesian seas means that the East Australian Current transports less water than other western boundary currents, and it often disintegrates into eddies measuring up to 120 miles (200 km) across. The current turns east between the Coral and Tasman seas along the Tasman Front and continues along New Zealand's east coast as the East Auckland Current.

BATHYMETRIC DEPTHS

Feet	Meters
Sea level	Sea level
656	200
1640	500
3281	1000
6562	2000
9842	3000
13,123	4000
16,404	5000
19,685	6000
26,246	8,000

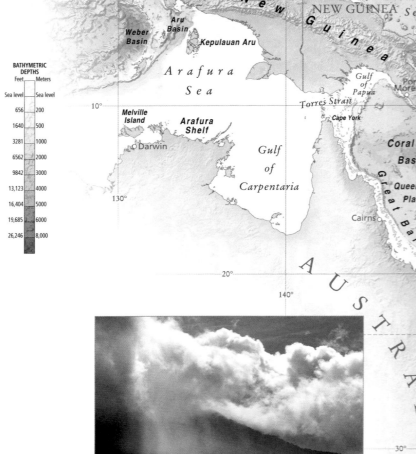

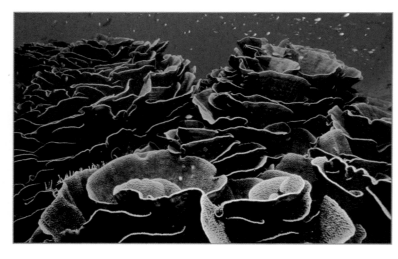

Tropical storm
The tropical southwestern Pacific receives some 10–13 feet (3–4 m) of rain every year. Rainfall is usually heavy and accompanied by strong wind but is localized and short-lived. Here a rainstorm passes over Kimbe Bay in West New Britain, Papua New Guinea.

Fiji
Fiji's 322 islands hold nearly 4,000 square miles (10,000 km²) of reef. In 2000, a crown-of-thorns starfish invasion posed a serious threat. Warm water temperatures in the following years led to extensive bleaching, and the reef area is declining.

Cabbage coral
Shallow reefs with good light conditions and strong current movement are the ideal habitat for the cabbage or lettuce coral (Turbinaria sp.), a favorite species for aquaria. The coral provides good shelter for many reef fishes that dart in and out in the search for food.

Surface currents
South of 45°S the Antarctic Circumpolar Current flows eastward. It has moderate speed but is deep-reaching and carries the largest transport of all currents. The western part of the Subtropical Gyre determines the circulation to the north. At its center currents are mostly weak and variable.

→ Antarctic Circumpolar Current → South Equatorial Current
→ East Auckland Current → South Pacific Current
→ East Australian Current

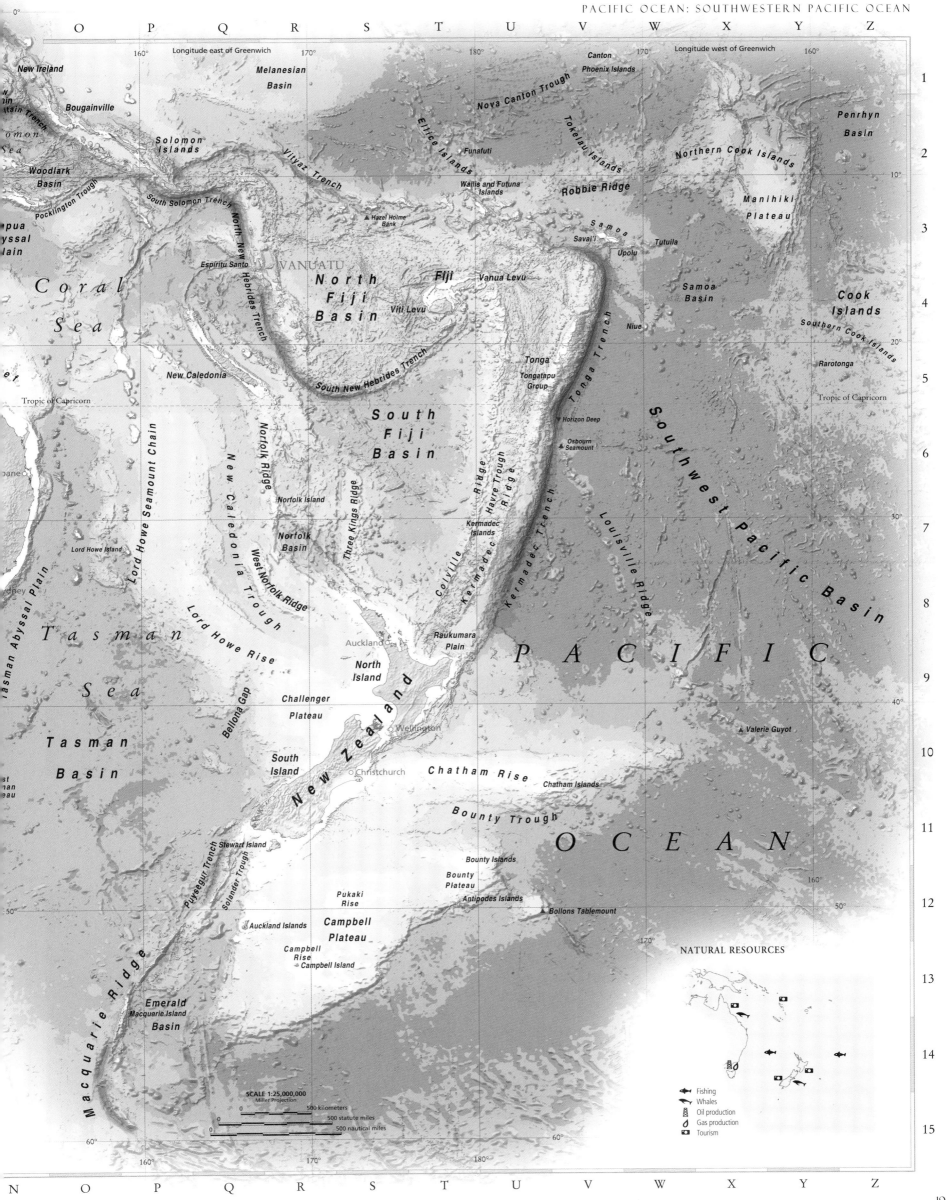

O P Q R S T U V W X Y Z

Longitude east of Greenwich 160° 170° 180° Longitude west of Greenwich 160°

1

New Ireland

Melanesian
Basin

Canton
Phoenix Islands

Bougainville

Nova Canton Trough

Penrhyn
Basin

2

omon
Sea

Solomon
Islands

Ellice Islands

Funafuti

Tokelau Islands

Northern Cook Islands

10°

Woodlark
Basin

Vityaz Trench

Wallis and Futuna
Islands

Robbie Ridge

Manihiki
Plateau

Pocklington Trough

South Solomon Trench

Hazel Holme
Bank

Samoa

3

pua
yssal
lain

Espiritu Santo

VANUATU

Savai'i

Samoa
Basin

Upolu

Tutuila

North
Fiji
Basin

Fiji

Vanua Levu

Coral

Viti Levu

Cook
Islands

4

Sea

New Caledonia

South New Hebrides Trench

Niue

Southern Cook Islands

20°

Tropic of Capricorn

South
Fiji
Basin

Tonga

Tongatapu
Group

Rarotonga

Tropic of Capricorn

5

Lord Howe Seamount Chain

Norfolk Ridge

Horizon Deep

Southwest Pacific Basin

Osbourn
Seamount

6

30°

New Caledonia Trough

Norfolk Island

West Norfolk Ridge

Three Kings Ridge

Ridge

Havre Trough

Louisville Ridge

7

Lord Howe Island

Norfolk
Basin

Colville

Kermadec
Islands

Kermadec Trench

PACIFIC

8

Tasman Abyssal Plain

Lord Howe Rise

Raukumara
Plain

Sydney

Auckland

North
Island

9

Tasman

Challenger
Plateau

Valerie Guyot

40°

Bellona Gap

Wellington

Sea

OCEAN

10

Tasman

South
Island

Christchurch

Chatham Rise

Chatham Islands

Basin

Bounty Trough

11

Puysegur Trench

Stewart Island

Bounty Islands

160°

Solander Trough

Bounty
Plateau

12

Pukaki
Rise

Antipodes Islands

Bollons Tablemount

50°

Auckland Islands

Campbell
Plateau

170°

13

Macquarie Ridge

Campbell
Rise

Campbell Island

NATURAL RESOURCES

14

Emerald
Macquarie Island
Basin

SCALE 1:25,000,000
Miller Projection

0   500 kilometers

0   500 statute miles

0   500 nautical miles

Fishing
Whales
Oil production
Gas production
Tourism

15

60°

160° 170° 180°

N O P Q R S T U V W X Y Z

ARAFURA SEA AND GULF OF CARPENTARIA

During the last ice age the Arafura Sea and the Gulf of Carpentaria formed a land bridge between Australia and New Guinea. Today they are shelf seas 150–250 feet (45–80 m) deep. The Arafura Sea adjoins the Indian Ocean where it meets the Timor Sea. In the east it connects with the Coral Sea through Torres Strait, which has a maximum depth of only 36 feet (11 m); large ships following the busy sea lane through the Arafura Sea have to wait for high tide before passing through the strait. Farther west the tidal range along the Australian coast exceeds 26 feet (8 m). The region is rich in marine life. Sea cucumbers are prized by Indonesian fishermen and shrimp fishing is a key industry in the Gulf of Carpentaria. The Morning Glory, a spectacular cloud band stretching from horizon to horizon, occurs along the gulf coast during September and October.

THE FACTS (ARAFURA SEA)	
Area	250,990 square miles (650,000 km²)
Average depth	230 feet (70 m)
Maximum depth	12,000 feet (3,660 m)
Maximum width	435 miles (700 km)
Maximum length	620 miles (1,000 km)

Sunset, Arafura Sea
The sun sets over the Arafura Sea at Mindil Beach in Darwin, Australia. Because the beach slopes gently toward the sea and the tidal range on Australia's north shore reaches up to 26 feet (8 m), the sea retreats a significant distance at low tide.

Starfish
Sea stars or starfish generally have five arms, which they can regenerate as long as at least one arm is still attached to the central disk. This starfish, found off Wessel Island east of Darwin, is regenerating two arms it had lost to predators.

Dugong
The dugong (Dugong dugon), a marine mammal and relative of Atlantic manatees, inhabits the Indo-Pacific region. Most of the population is found in northern Australian waters. This dugong and its calf graze the seagrasses of the Arafura Sea.

Cobourg Peninsula
Separated from Melville Island by Dundas Strait, the Cobourg Peninsula forms part of the northern boundary of Van Diemen Gulf in Australia's far northwest. It is nearly entirely Aboriginal land and has been declared a national park. It comprises coral reefs, wetlands, and rain forest and protects six species of sea turtles.

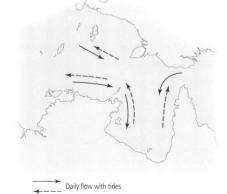

Daily flow with tides

Surface currents
The prevailing currents in the Arafura Sea and Gulf of Carpentaria are tidal, changing direction twice a day. The wind-driven currents are weak and usually of secondary importance. From November to April this pattern can be disturbed by cyclones and their associated strong currents.

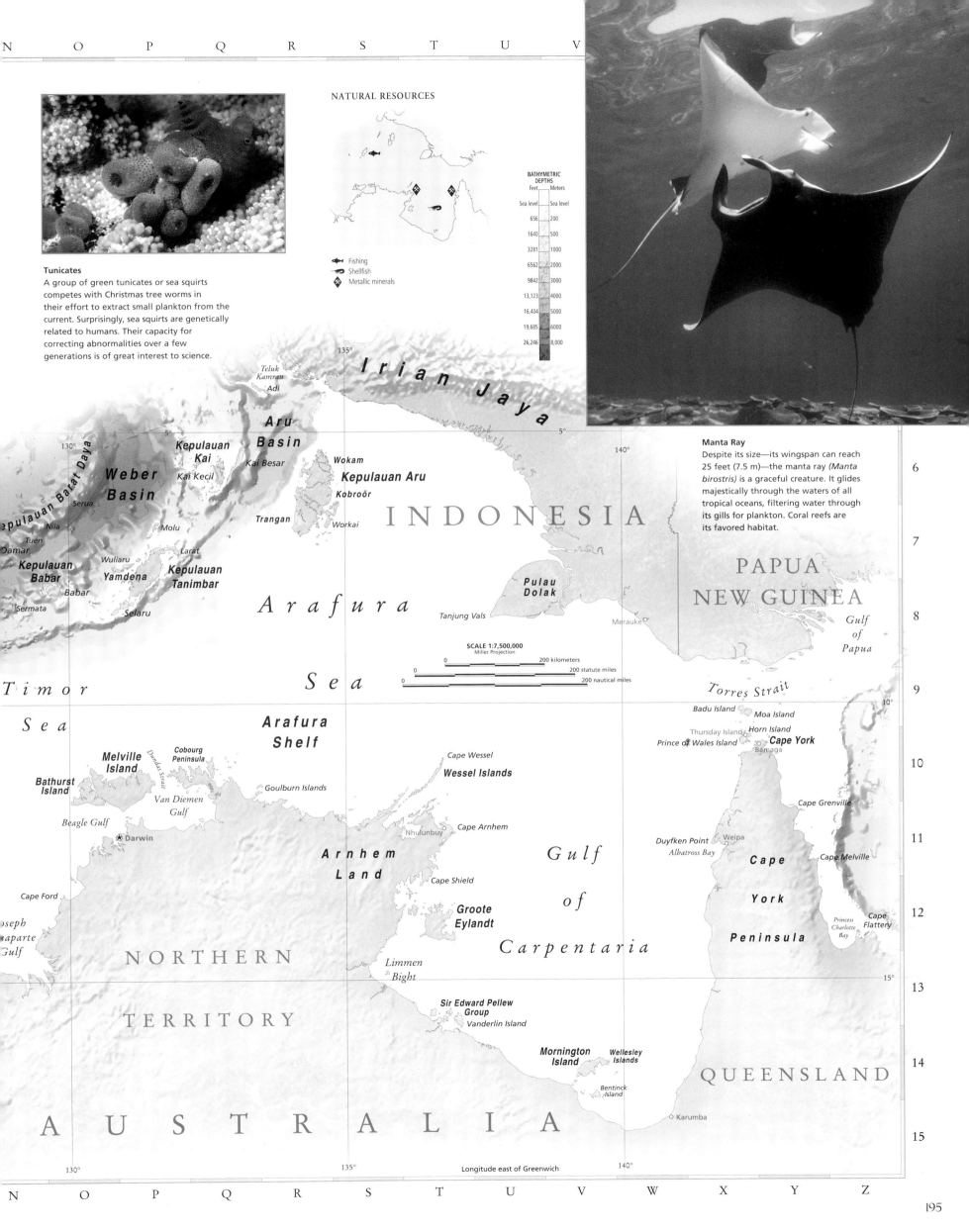

Tunicates

A group of green tunicates or sea squirts competes with Christmas tree worms in their effort to extract small plankton from the current. Surprisingly, sea squirts are genetically related to humans. Their capacity for correcting abnormalities over a few generations is of great interest to science.

NATURAL RESOURCES

BATHYMETRIC DEPTHS

Feet	Meters
Sea level	Sea level
656	200
1640	500
3281	1000
6562	2000
9842	3000
13,123	4000
16,404	5000
19,685	6000
26,246	8,000

→ Fishing
↪ Shellfish
◆ Metallic minerals

Manta Ray

Despite its size—its wingspan can reach 25 feet (7.5 m)—the manta ray (*Manta birostris*) is a graceful creature. It glides majestically through the waters of all tropical oceans, filtering water through its gills for plankton. Coral reefs are its favored habitat.

Teluk Kamrau
Adi

Irian Jaya

Aru Basin

Kepulauan Kai

Kai Besar

Kai Kecil

Wokam

Kepulauan Aru

Kobroör

Trangan

Workai

Weber Basin

Serua

Nila

Tuen

Damar

Wuliaru

Larat

Molu

Kepulauan Babar

Yamdena

Kepulauan Tanimbar

Babar

Sermata

Selaru

Kepulauan Barat Daya

INDONESIA

Pulau Dolak

Tanjung Vals

Merauke

PAPUA NEW GUINEA

Gulf of Papua

Arafura

Sea

Timor

Sea

Arafura Shelf

Torres Strait

Badu Island
Moa Island
Thursday Island
Horn Island
Prince of Wales Island
Cape York
Bamaga

Melville Island

Bathurst Island

Cobourg Peninsula

Dundas Strait

Goulburn Islands

Wessel Islands

Cape Wessel

Cape Grenville

Van Diemen Gulf

Beagle Gulf

Darwin

Nhulunbuy

Cape Arnhem

Arnhem Land

Cape Shield

Duyfken Point
Weipa
Albatross Bay

Cape York Peninsula

Cape Melville

Cape Ford

Gulf of Carpentaria

Groote Eylandt

Princess Charlotte Bay

Cape Flattery

Joseph Bonaparte Gulf

NORTHERN

Limmen Bight

Sir Edward Pellew Group

Vanderlin Island

TERRITORY

Mornington Island

Wellesley Islands

Bentinck Island

QUEENSLAND

Karumba

AUSTRALIA

SCALE 1:7,500,000
Miller Projection
200 kilometers
200 statute miles
200 nautical miles

Longitude east of Greenwich

CORAL SEA

Located between tropical Australia and the island arc formed by the Solomon Islands, Vanuatu, New Caledonia, and Norfolk Island in the south, the Coral Sea contains deep trenches in the east, deep basins in the north, part of the Lord Howe Rise in the south, and myriad coral reefs in the north and west. The South Equatorial Current enters it from the east, sending some of its water northward into the New Guinea Coastal Current, while the bulk of the current continues south to provide the source for the East Australian Current. January to April is the cyclone season, when palm trunks and other debris from devastation on land can be found drifting across the Coral Sea. Many marine life species that are endangered elsewhere are still found in healthy numbers in this sea, including reef and hammerhead sharks, manta rays, maori wrasse, and five of the seven species of turtles.

THE FACTS	
Area	1,849,000 square miles (4,788,888 km²)
Average depth	7,870 feet (2,398 m)
Maximum depth	25,134 feet (7,661 m)
Maximum width	1,500 miles (2,414 km)
Maximum length	1,400 miles (2,253 km)

Coral Sea diving
During summer the extremely venomous irukandji or box jellyfish keeps swimmers at bay; contact with its tentacles, which can be 3 feet (1 m) long, can be fatal. But in winter the Coral Sea is a diver's paradise. This diver is attracted by an alcyonarian, one of the soft coral species.

NATURAL RESOURCES

Reef shark
The non-aggressive whitetip reef shark (*Triaenodon obesus*) is a common shark found around coral reefs in the Indo-Pacific. It is nocturnal in habit; snorkelers often see it resting on the bottom during the day. Here a shark swims past a soft coral tree (*Dendronephtya* sp.).

Fishing
Whales
Tourism

Norfolk Island
The Norfolk Island Pine (*Araucaria heterophylla*) is adapted to life in an environment exposed to frequent sea spray. Its needles have a protective waxy coating. The tree dominates the scenery of Norfolk Island but has also been planted along the seafront of many cities.

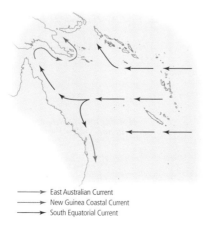

Surface currents
As the westward flowing South Equatorial Current approaches the Great Barrier Reef its flow is mainly directed northward and southward. Water exchange between the Coral Sea and the reef's lagoon is achieved by strong tidal currents that sweep through the narrow channels between individual reefs.

East Australian Current
New Guinea Coastal Current
South Equatorial Current

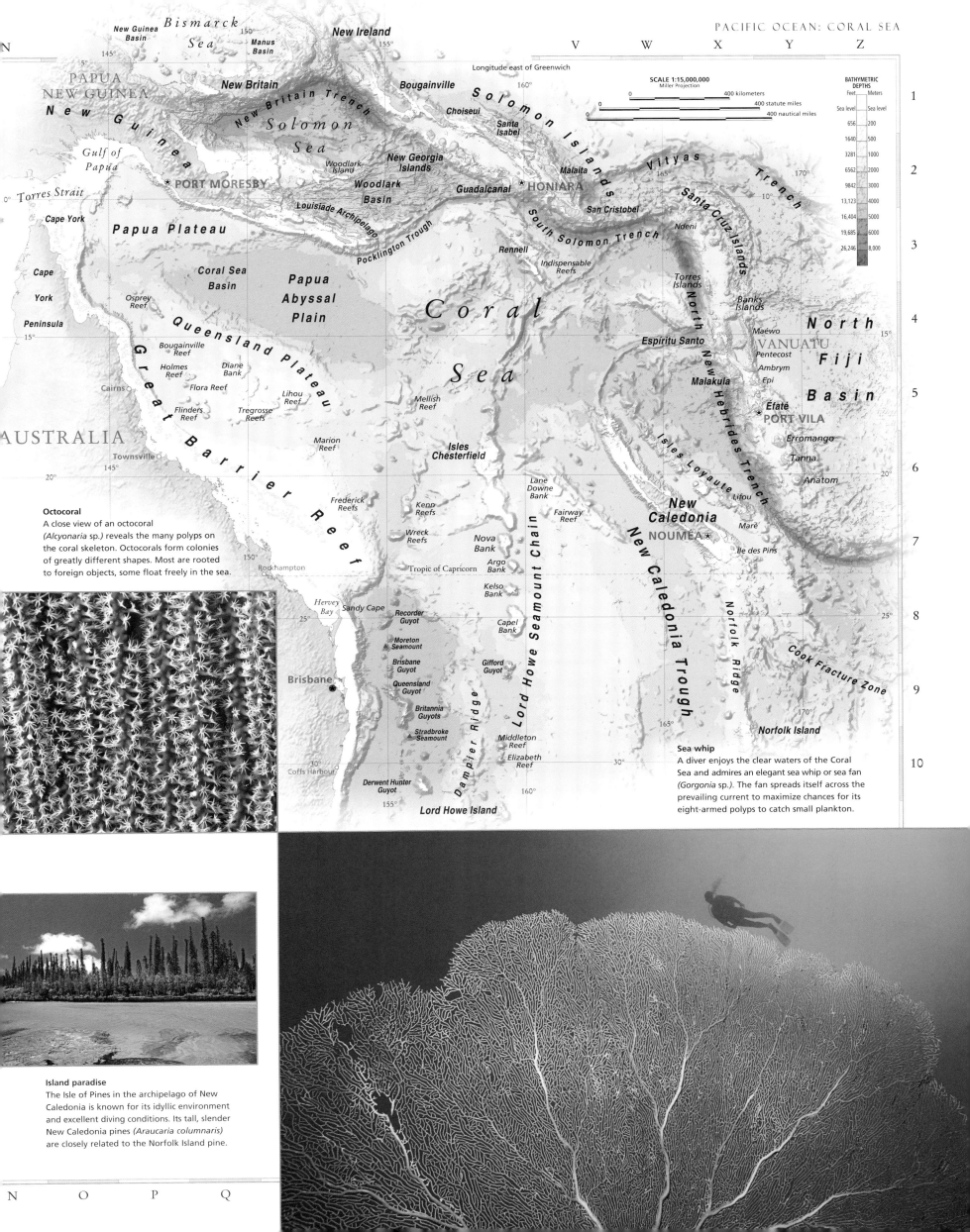

V   W   X   Y   Z

Longitude east of Greenwich

SCALE 1:15,000,000
Miller Projection

0 ———— 400 kilometers
0 ———— 400 statute miles
0 ———— 400 nautical miles

BATHYMETRIC
DEPTHS
Feet	Meters
Sea level	Sea level
656	200
1640	500
3281	1000
6562	2000
9842	3000
13,123	4000
16,404	5000
19,685	6000
26,246	8,000

Bismarck Sea
New Guinea Basin
Manus Basin
New Ireland
New Britain
Bougainville
Solomon Islands
Choiseul
Santa Isabel

PAPUA NEW GUINEA
New Britain Trench
Solomon Sea
Malaita
Vityas Trench

New Guinea
Gulf of Papua
Woodlark Island
New Georgia Islands
Woodlark Basin
Guadalcanal
*HONIARA
San Cristobel
Santa Cruz Islands

*PORT MORESBY
Louisiade Archipelago
Pocklington Trough
South Solomon Trench
Ndeni

Torres Strait
Cape York
Papua Plateau
Rennell
Indispensable Reefs
Torres Islands
Banks Islands

Cape York Peninsula
Coral Sea Basin
Papua Abyssal Plain
Coral Sea
Espíritu Santo
Maéwo
North Fiji Basin
VANUATU
Pentecost
Ambrym
Epi

Cape York
Osprey Reef
Queensland Plateau
New Hebrides Trench
Malakula

Cairns
Bougainville Reef
Holmes Reef
Diane Bank
Flora Reef
Lihou Reef
*Efaté
PORT VILA

Great Barrier Reef
Flinders Reef
Tregrosse Reefs
Mellish Reef
Isles Loyauté
Lifou
Erromango
Tanna

AUSTRALIA
Townsville
Marion Reef
Isles Chesterfield
New Caledonia
Maré
Anatom

Frederick Reefs
Kenn Reefs
Lane Downe Bank
Fairway Reef
NOUMÉA *
Île des Pins

Wreck Reefs
Nova Bank
Rockhampton
Tropic of Capricorn
Argo Bank
Kelso Bank

New Caledonia Seamount Chain
Hervey Bay
Sandy Cape
Recorder Guyot
Capel Bank

Lord Howe Seamount Chain
New Caledonia Trough
Norfolk Ridge
Cook Fracture Zone

Moreton Seamount
Brisbane Guyot
Gifford Guyot

Brisbane
Queensland Guyot
Dampier Ridge

Britannia Guyots
Stradbroke Seamount
Middleton Reef

Derwent Hunter Guyot
Elizabeth Reef
Norfolk Island

Coffs Harbour
Lord Howe Island

Octocoral
A close view of an octocoral (*Alcyonaria* sp.) reveals the many polyps on the coral skeleton. Octocorals form colonies of greatly different shapes. Most are rooted to foreign objects, some float freely in the sea.

Sea whip
A diver enjoys the clear waters of the Coral Sea and admires an elegant sea whip or sea fan (*Gorgonia* sp.). The fan spreads itself across the prevailing current to maximize chances for its eight-armed polyps to catch small plankton.

Island paradise
The Isle of Pines in the archipelago of New Caledonia is known for its idyllic environment and excellent diving conditions. Its tall, slender New Caledonia pines (*Araucaria columnaris*) are closely related to the Norfolk Island pine.

N   O   P   Q

GREAT BARRIER REEF

The Great Barrier Reef is the world's biggest single structure made by living organisms. Declared a Marine Park in 1975 and inscribed in the World Heritage list in 1981, it consists of more than 2,900 individual reefs and 900 islands and extends along Australia's east coast for 1,250 miles (2,000 km). The Great Barrier Reef Marine Park Authority manages its use in accordance with several international conventions. At least 400 species of hard and soft corals form the reef. The animal life found here includes more than 1,500 species of fish; 125 species of sharks, stingrays, and skates; 30 species of whales, porpoises, and dolphins; 6 species of turtles; and 17 species of sea snakes. Some 1.5 million birds breed on its islands. Saltwater crocodiles live in mangrove and salt marshes near the coast and most of the world's remaining dugong population is found on the reef where seagrasses are abundant.

THE FACTS	
Area	134,286 square miles (347,800 km²)
Length	1,250 miles (2,000 km)
Maximum width	95 miles (152 km)
Surface water temperature	75°–86°F (24°–30°C)
No. of hard coral species	More than 300
No. of fish species	More than 1,500
No. of sponge species	More than 400
No. of mollusk species	Approximately 4,000
No. of seaweed species	Approximately 500

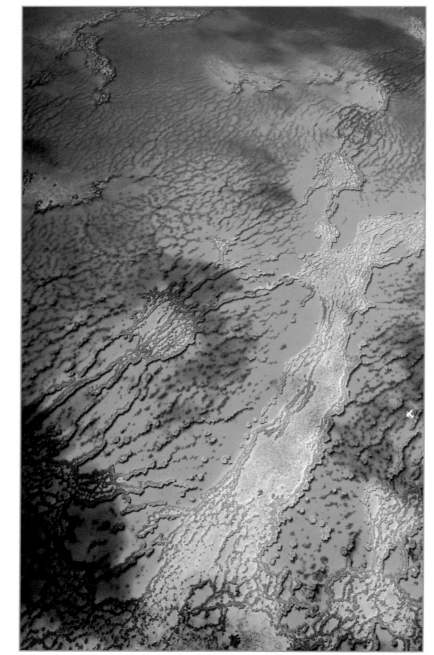

Above the reef
Australia's Great Barrier Reef is the only living structure on Earth that is visible from space. Here a small seaplane flies low over the reef, giving passengers a sweeping view.

Dwarf minke whale
In the northern Great Barrier Reef dwarf minke whales (*Balaenoptera acutorostrata* subsp.*),* known for being inquisitive, often meet boats and swimmers during "swim with whales" excursions.

CORAL BLEACHING

One of the main effects of global warming is an increase in ocean water temperatures. This can lead to coral bleaching, the loss of zooxanthellae—a symbiotic algae—from the polyps. A temperature increase of just 2.7–3.6°F (1.5–2°C) above normal can kill coral.

Mass bleaching
In 2002, the Great Barrier Reef suffered the worst coral bleaching event on record for the reef. Almost 55 percent of the reef suffered some degree of bleaching. On the map, pink indicates abnormally high temperatures.

2002 coral bleaching
- ● Extreme bleaching (>60% of corals affected)
- ● Very high bleaching (30–60%)
- ● High bleaching (10–30%)
- ● Moderate bleaching (1–10%)
- ○ No bleaching (<1% of corals affected)

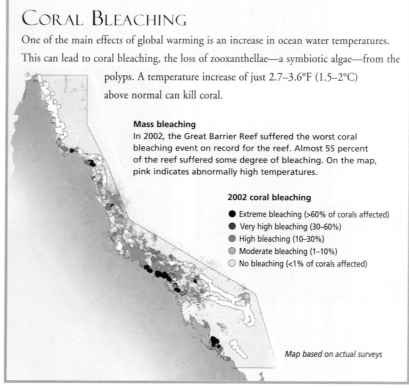

Map based on actual surveys

R S T U V W X Y Z

rres Strait

du Island | *Moa Island*
Thursday Island | *Horn Island*
of Wales Island
Cape York
Bamaga

10°
Eastern Fields

Ashmore Reef

Papua

Plateau

Pandora Entrance

Cape Grenville

Cape

York

Peninsula

Cape Direction

C o r a l

S e a

G r e a t

BATHYMETRIC DEPTHS

Feet	Meters
Sea level	Sea level
656	200
1640	500
3281	1000
6562	2000
9842	3000
13,123	4000
16,404	5000
19,685	6000
26,246	8,000

→ East Australian Current
→ Great Barrier Reef Undercurrent
→ South Equatorial Current

Mushroom coral
The solitary mushroom coral (*Actinodiscus sp.*) feeds at night. It does not form colonies and is not attached to the seabed, although it begins as a small disk attached to rock or dead coral.

Osprey Reef

Princess Charlotte Bay
Cape Melville

Lizard Island

Cape Flattery

15°

Cooktown

Bougainville Reef

Q U E E N S L A N D

Cape Tribulation

Trinity Bay
Arlington Reef

Cairns

145°

Surface currents
As the South Equatorial Current approaches the Great Barrier Reef it splits into southward and northward flow. Water exchange with the lagoon occurs through strong tidal mixing in the many passages between the individual reefs. Currents in the lagoon are determined by the wind and river runoff.

Holmes Reef

Diane Bank

150°

Flora Reef

Flinders Reef

Tregrosse Reefs

Anemonefish in sea anemone
Anemonefish (*Amphiprion sp.*) are protected by a mucous coating. This allows them to come into contact with the sea anemone's stinging tentacles without being affected.

NATURAL RESOURCES

Dunk Island

Hinchinbrook Island

Palm Islands
Halifax Bay
Magnetic Island

B a r r i e r

Townsville

🐋 Whales
Tourism

Marion Reef

Crown-of-thorns starfish
The crown-of-thorns starfish (*Acanthaster planci*) feeds on coral polyps, its venomous spines keeping predators at bay. On the Great Barrier Reef occasional population explosions have damaged entire reefs. Pollution and climate change have been suspected, but the reasons for these outbreaks are still unclear.

20°

A U S T R A L I A

R e e f

Whitsunday Group
Lindeman Island
Cape Conway
Brampton Island
Scawfell Island

Mackay

Frederick Reefs

Middle Island
Percy Isles

Swain Reefs

Saumarez Reefs

Long Island
Broad Sound
Townshend Island

Cape Clinton

Zooxanthellae

Sting cell

Tentacle cross section
Zooxanthellae give corals their color, while sting cells discharge to pierce the skin of prey.

Polyp tentacle

Formation of coral
In reef-building hard coral species, individual polyps secrete a limestone skeleton that partially encloses them. The polyps form communities in a variety of shapes, and their remains form reefs.

Polyp

Limestone skeleton

Great Keppel Island
Heron Island
Rockhampton
Curtis Island

Tropic of Capricorn

Round Hill Head

Sandy Cape
Hervey Bay

Fraser Island

Recorder Guyot

Double Island Point
Moreton ▲ Seamount

25°

SCALE 1:6,250,000
Miller Projection

0   200 kilometers
0   200 statute miles
0   200 nautical miles

150°
Longitude east of Greenwich

N O P Q R S T U V W X Y Z

1 2 3 4 5 6 7 8 9 10 11 12 13 14 15

TASMAN SEA

The Tasman Basin is open to the south but closed in the north and is thus influenced by the Southern Ocean at depth. The dominant surface feature is the fast-flowing and deep East Australian Current, the western boundary current of the South Pacific Subtropical Gyre. Water loss from the gyre through the Indonesian seas reduces its transport, making the East Australian Current the weakest of all western boundary currents. The current follows the Australian coast but turns offshore, north and finally east toward New Zealand, forming the Tasman Front between the Tasman and Coral seas. Southbound ships coming from Asia ride the current but avoid it on their return voyage by staying farther away from the coast. On occasions the East Australian Current disintegrates into a field of eddies that may measure 120 miles (200 km) across. Islands in the Tasman Sea are home to the little penguin, the smallest of the world's 17 penguin species.

Yellow-eyed penguins
Yellow-eyed penguins *(Megadyptes antipodes)* are the rarest of the world's penguins. They breed on the South Island and islands to the south of New Zealand and share their range with the little or fairy penguin *(Eudyptula minor)*, a species also found in Australia.

NATURAL RESOURCES

- Fishing
- Whales
- Oil production
- Gas production
- Tourism

THE FACTS	
Area	1,545,000 square miles (4,001,530 km²)
Average depth	9,023 feet (2,750 m)
Maximum depth	17,000 feet (5,182 m)
Maximum width	1,400 miles (2,253 km)
Maximum length	1,243 miles (2,000 km)

East Australian Current
A satellite image of seawater temperature—warm is red–orange, cold is green–blue, clouds are white—shows the East Australian Current as a band of warm water flowing south along the continental shelf. At 35°S it turns away from the coast and flows toward New Zealand.

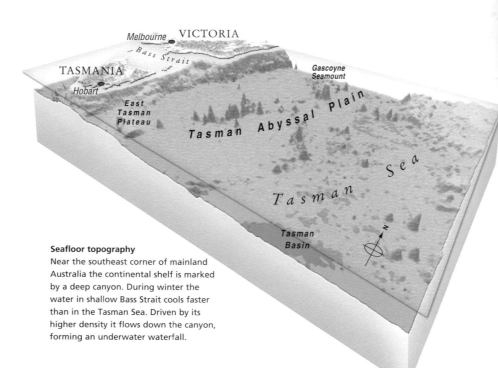

Seafloor topography
Near the southeast corner of mainland Australia the continental shelf is marked by a deep canyon. During winter the water in shallow Bass Strait cools faster than in the Tasman Sea. Driven by its higher density it flows down the canyon, forming an underwater waterfall.

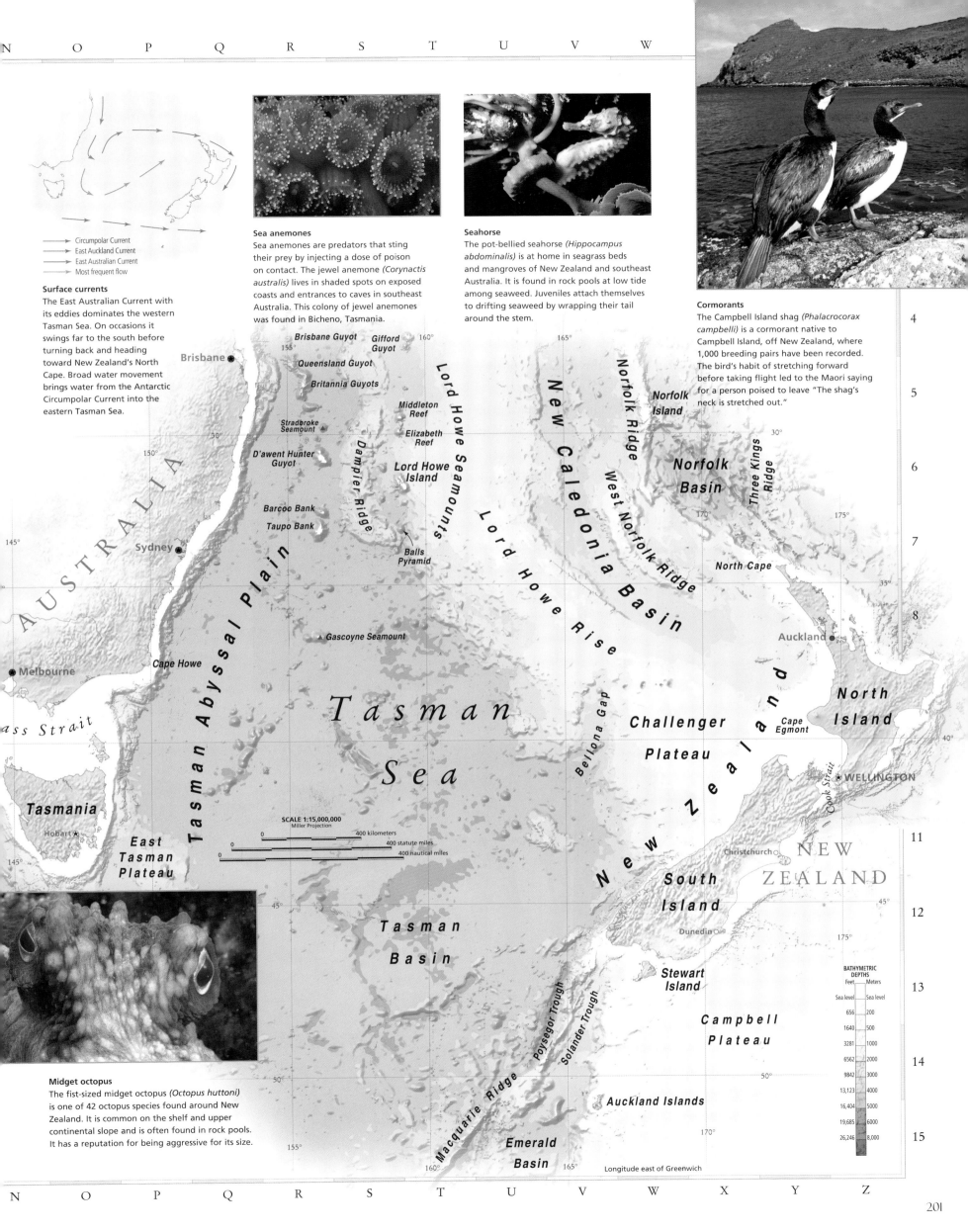

Surface currents

→ Circumpolar Current
→ East Auckland Current
→ East Australian Current
→ Most frequent flow

The East Australian Current with its eddies dominates the western Tasman Sea. On occasions it swings far to the south before turning back and heading toward New Zealand's North Cape. Broad water movement brings water from the Antarctic Circumpolar Current into the eastern Tasman Sea.

Sea anemones

Sea anemones are predators that sting their prey by injecting a dose of poison on contact. The jewel anemone (Corynactis australis) lives in shaded spots on exposed coasts and entrances to caves in southeast Australia. This colony of jewel anemones was found in Bicheno, Tasmania.

Seahorse

The pot-bellied seahorse (Hippocampus abdominalis) is at home in seagrass beds and mangroves of New Zealand and southeast Australia. It is found in rock pools at low tide among seaweed. Juveniles attach themselves to drifting seaweed by wrapping their tail around the stem.

Cormorants

The Campbell Island shag (Phalacrocorax campbelli) is a cormorant native to Campbell Island, off New Zealand, where 1,000 breeding pairs have been recorded. The bird's habit of stretching forward before taking flight led to the Maori saying for a person poised to leave "The shag's neck is stretched out."

Midget octopus

The fist-sized midget octopus (Octopus huttoni) is one of 42 octopus species found around New Zealand. It is common on the shelf and upper continental slope and is often found in rock pools. It has a reputation for being aggressive for its size.

Brisbane

Brisbane Guyot   Gifford Guyot

Queensland Guyot

Britannia Guyots

Middleton Reef

Stradbroke Seamount

Elizabeth Reef

D'awent Hunter Guyot

Lord Howe Island

Dampier Ridge

Barcoo Bank

Taupo Bank

Balls Pyramid

Lord Howe Seamounts

Lord Howe Rise

New Caledonia Basin

West Norfolk Ridge

Norfolk Ridge

Norfolk Island

Norfolk Basin

Three Kings Ridge

North Cape

Sydney

AUSTRALIA

Cape Howe

Gascoyne Seamount

Tasman Abyssal Plain

Melbourne

Bass Strait

Tasmania

Hobart

East Tasman Plateau

Tasman Sea

Challenger Plateau

Cape Egmont

North Island

New Zealand

Cook Strait

WELLINGTON

SCALE 1:15,000,000
Miller Projection

400 kilometers
400 statute miles
400 nautical miles

Tasman Basin

Bellona Gap

Christchurch

South Island

NEW ZEALAND

Dunedin

Stewart Island

Poysegor Trough

Solander Trough

Macquarie Ridge

Auckland Islands

Emerald Basin

Campbell Plateau

Auckland

Longitude east of Greenwich

BATHYMETRIC DEPTHS

Feet	Meters
Sea level	Sea level
656	200
1640	500
3281	1000
6562	2000
9842	3000
13,123	4000
16,404	5000
19,685	6000
26,246	8,000

CAMPBELL PLATEAU AND CHATHAM RISE

The Campbell Plateau, the Chatham Rise, and New Zealand once formed a microcontinent that separated from Antarctica. Today the major part of the Campbell Plateau is 1,200–3,000 feet (350–900 m) deep but breaks the surface in several places to form groups of islands and rises to 270 feet (82 m) in the Campbell Rise. The plateau steers the Antarctic Circumpolar Current along its flanks, isolating the region from cold polar waters. The smaller Chatham Rise is the shallower of the two, with depths of 600–1,800 feet (180–550 m), rising to 168 feet (51 m) at Mernoo Bank and breaking the surface at the Chatham Islands. The East Auckland Current brings warm subtropical water from the north and creates the Subtropical Front over the Chatham Rise. Mixing of subtropical and subantarctic water increases the productivity of the region; the Chatham Rise provides 60 percent of New Zealand's fish catch.

White Island
White Island, an active volcano in the Bay of Plenty off New Zealand's North Island, is known to Maori as Whakaari. It is 1.2 miles (2 km) wide and 1,053 feet (321 m) high. It was mined for sulfur until a landslide killed all 10 workers in 1914.

John Dory
The deep-sea predator John Dory (*Zeus faber*) is found at about 330 feet (100 m) along all coastal shelves except the Pacific east coast. A good table fish, it has been fished since the 1950s and supports a major commercial trawl fishery in New Zealand.

Sulfur
White Island has some of the most acidic lakes in the world. Runoff from lake water produces colorful sulfur deposits that create an eerie scenery on the mountain's flanks. An eruption in 2000 created a new crater and turned the earlier crater into a lake.

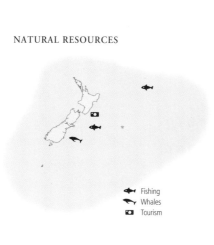

NATURAL RESOURCES

- Fishing
- Whales
- Tourism

Snares crested penguin
Snares crested penguin (*Eudyptes robustus*) breeds on The Snares, an island group off New Zealand's South Island. Its restricted distribution makes it a vulnerable species; the current population is estimated at around 30,000 breeding pairs. It feeds mainly on krill but occasionally takes squid and small fish.

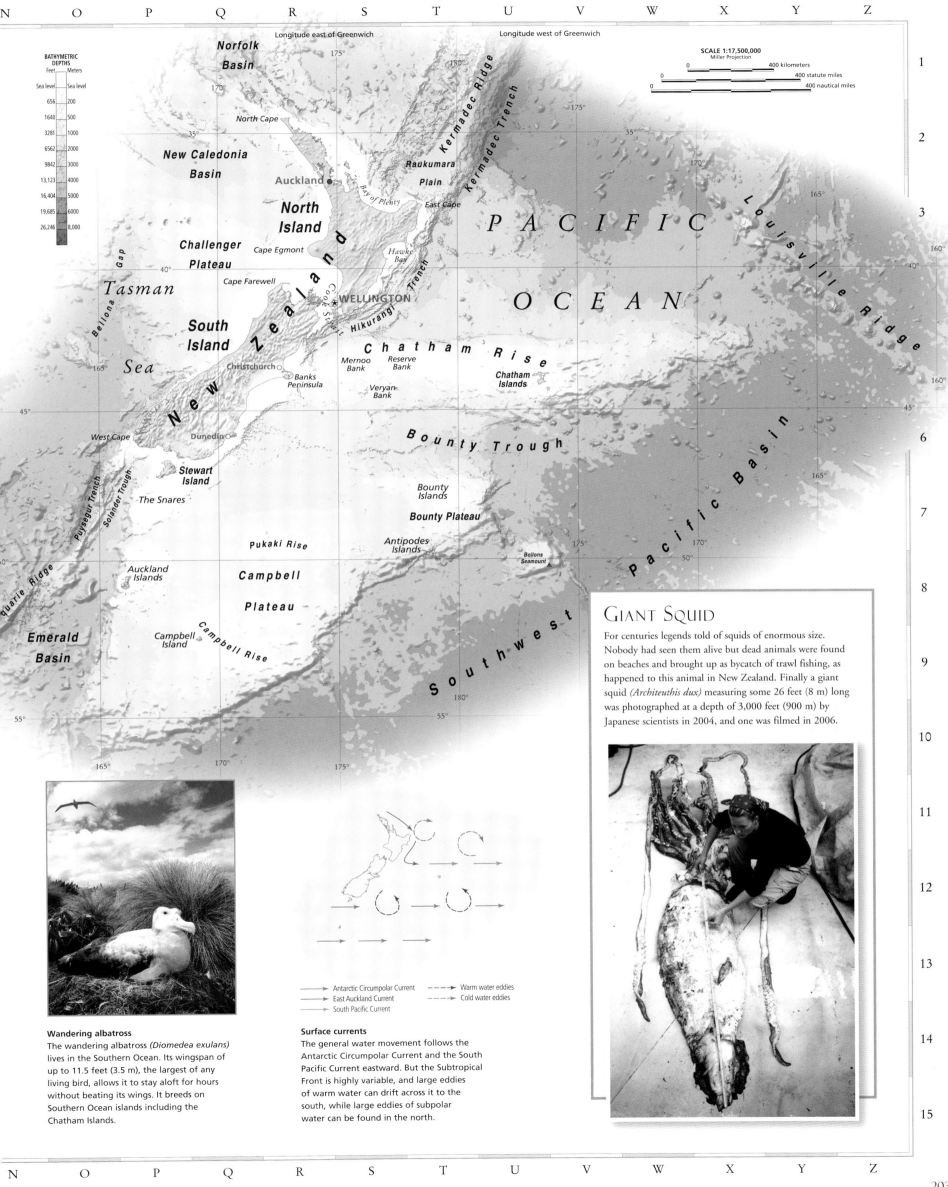

BATHYMETRIC DEPTHS

Feet	Meters
Sea level	Sea level
656	200
1640	500
3281	1000
6562	2000
9842	3000
13,123	4000
16,404	5000
19,685	6000
26,246	8,000

Longitude east of Greenwich

Longitude west of Greenwich

SCALE 1:17,500,000
Miller Projection

0   400 kilometers
0   400 statute miles
0   400 nautical miles

Norfolk Basin

North Cape

New Caledonia Basin

Auckland

North Island

Tasman Sea

Challenger Plateau

Cape Egmont

Cape Farewell

South Island

New Zealand

Christchurch

Banks Peninsula

Bay of Plenty

Raukumara Plain

East Cape

Hawke Bay

WELLINGTON

Cook Strait

Hikurangi Trench

Hikurangi Trench

Kermadec Ridge

Kermadec Trench

PACIFIC

OCEAN

Louisville Ridge

Gap

Bellona Gap

Mernoo Bank

Reserve Bank

Veryan Bank

Chatham Rise

Chatham Islands

West Cape

Dunedin

Stewart Island

The Snares

Puysegur Trench

Solander Trough

Pukaki Rise

Auckland Islands

Campbell Plateau

Campbell Island

Campbell Rise

Emerald Basin

quarie Ridge

Bounty Trough

Bounty Islands

Bounty Plateau

Antipodes Islands

Boilons Seamount

Pacific Basin

Southwest

Pacific Basin

GIANT SQUID

For centuries legends told of squids of enormous size. Nobody had seen them alive but dead animals were found on beaches and brought up as bycatch of trawl fishing, as happened to this animal in New Zealand. Finally a giant squid (*Architeuthis dux*) measuring some 26 feet (8 m) long was photographed at a depth of 3,000 feet (900 m) by Japanese scientists in 2004, and one was filmed in 2006.

Wandering albatross
The wandering albatross (*Diomedea exulans*) lives in the Southern Ocean. Its wingspan of up to 11.5 feet (3.5 m), the largest of any living bird, allows it to stay aloft for hours without beating its wings. It breeds on Southern Ocean islands including the Chatham Islands.

—→	Antarctic Circumpolar Current
—→	East Auckland Current
—→	South Pacific Current
--→	Warm water eddies
--→	Cold water eddies

Surface currents
The general water movement follows the Antarctic Circumpolar Current and the South Pacific Current eastward. But the Subtropical Front is highly variable, and large eddies of warm water can drift across it to the south, while large eddies of subpolar water can be found in the north.

EASTERN TROPICAL PACIFIC OCEAN

Most of the seafloor in the eastern tropical Pacific Ocean is a featureless plain, but deep trenches mark its eastern rim. Water in the Panama Basin is so stagnant that heating from Earth's interior raises its temperature by 0.5°F (0.3°C). The first chemosynthetic ecosystem around a hydrothermal vent was discovered in 1977 at the junction of the East Pacific Rise and the Galapagos Rift. Westward water movement dominates the region, interrupted by the eastward flowing North Equatorial Countercurrent. From August to February increased friction between the South Equatorial Current and the North Equatorial Countercurrent generates eddy-like disturbances in the flow field that are visible in satellite images. Upwelling along the equator supports an important tuna fishery. The region contains some of the smallest nation states in the world. Kiritimati (Christmas Island), the world's largest coral island, is home to several million seabirds, and the waters of the uninhabited Phoenix Islands form the world's largest marine protected area.

NATURAL RESOURCES

- 🐟 Fishing
- 🦐 Shellfish
- ⛏ Mining
- ⛴ Oil production
- Tourism

Sunfish

The sunfish *(Mola mola)*, a resident of tropical and temperate waters, has a stocky body that ends just behind the vertical fins but can grow to 10 feet (3 m). It feeds on jellyfish and likes to sunbathe, lying sideways, flat at the sea surface.

BATHYMETRIC DEPTHS

Feet	Meters
Sea level	Sea level
656	200
1640	500
3281	1000
6562	2000
9842	3000
13,123	4000
16,404	5000
19,685	6000
26,246	8,000

Fanning Island

Tabuaeran, also known as Fanning Island, is one of 32 atolls that belong to the island nation of Kiribati. The atolls, dispersed over 1.35 million square miles (3.5 million km²), are home to more than 100,000 people. If the sea level rises, most of these low-lying islands will disappear.

Guadalupe fur seal

The Guadalupe fur seal *(Arctocephalus townsendi)* was once common along the Californian and Mexican coast. It was hunted and disappeared from southern California by 1825. When hunting was banned in 1894 there were fewer than 100 animals left. Now 10,000 animals breed on Guadalupe again.

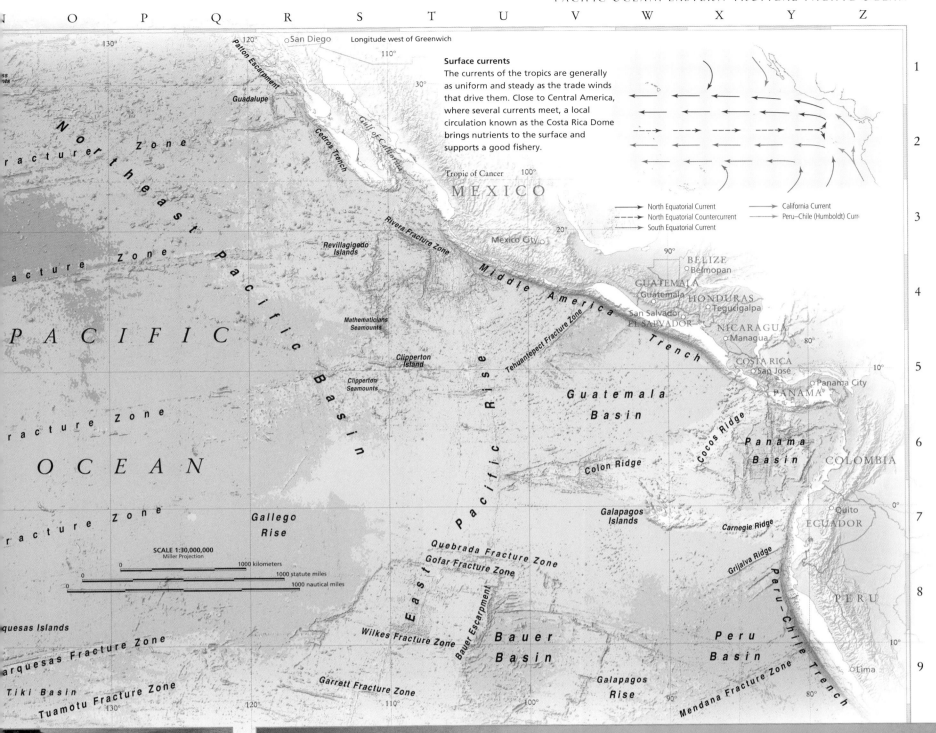

Surface currents
The currents of the tropics are generally as uniform and steady as the trade winds that drive them. Close to Central America, where several currents meet, a local circulation known as the Costa Rica Dome brings nutrients to the surface and supports a good fishery.

→ North Equatorial Current
--→ North Equatorial Countercurrent
→ South Equatorial Current
→ California Current
→ Peru–Chile (Humboldt) Curr

SCALE 1:30,000,000
Miller Projection

1000 kilometers
1000 statute miles
1000 nautical miles

Brown booby
Brown boobies *(Sula leucogaster)* live in the tropical Atlantic and Pacific, where they dive-hunt for fish and squid. Cocos Island, on the western Cocos Ridge, is one of their favorite nesting places. The island has been a World Heritage site since 1997.

Sailfish
Two sailfish *(Istiophorus platypteros)* cruise the tropical waters off the Mexican coast. Sailfish are among the fastest fish in the ocean. Their sail-like dorsal fin is usually folded but can be spread to make the fish look larger in case of danger, and during hunting.

GULF OF CALIFORNIA

Where the East Pacific Rise comes to the surface in Baja California Peninsula it creates a narrow sea with a rich and unique ecosystem, the Gulf of California, also known as the Sea of Cortez. Whales, rays, whale sharks, turtles, and many other migratory species are regular visitors to the region. There are resident populations of whales, sea lions, and elephant seals.

The more than 800 species of fishes support the major part of Mexico's fishery. There are more than 900 islands in the gulf and, of these, 244 are on UNESCO's World Heritage list and provide a sanctuary for hundreds of bird species. West of the peninsula and farther north, coastal upwelling creates one of the richest ecosystems in the world's oceans. Its once-vast schools of sardines disappeared through overfishing half a century ago, but sea otters still float among giant kelp, seaweed that grows 10 inches (27 cm) a day to reach 160 feet (50 m) at maturity.

THE FACTS	
Area	62,000 square miles (160,580 km²)
Average width	95 miles (153 km)
Maximum width (at mouth)	200 miles (320 km)
Maximum length	750 miles (1,200 km)

NATURAL RESOURCES

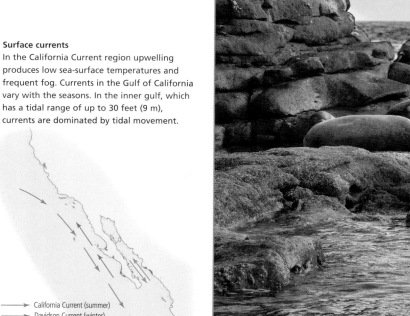

➤ Fishing
➤ Whales
▣ Tourism

Surface currents
In the California Current region upwelling produces low sea-surface temperatures and frequent fog. Currents in the Gulf of California vary with the seasons. In the inner gulf, which has a tidal range of up to 30 feet (9 m), currents are dominated by tidal movement.

→ California Current (summer)
→ Davidson Current (winter)
→ Tidal movement

KELP FORESTS

Kelp occurs worldwide where the water temperature does not exceed 68°F (20°C). It requires high nutrient supply, mixing from wave action, and light. In the Californian upwelling region giant kelp *(Macrocystis pyrifera)* grows into dense forests and provides habitat for many marine creatures. Supported by gas-filled bladders its fronds grow straight up to the surface, where they form a dense canopy.

Sea lions
The highly intelligent Californian sea lion *(Zalophus californianus)* is a common sight at Moss Landing in Monterey Bay. Sea lions feed on squid and fish and have learned to wait for prey near fish ladders. During the non-breeding season males and juveniles migrate north along the coast.

Blue whale

From December to March, blue whales (*Balaenoptera musculus*) in the Gulf of California are often accompanied by young calves. Many bear scars from encounters with killer whales. Along the northern Californian coast, blue whale populations have found new feeding grounds and are on the increase.

Monterey Bay

Once the center of an important sardine fishery, Monterey Bay is now part of the Monterey Bay National Marine Sanctuary. Famous for its kelp forests, it is home to many species of marine mammals. The old sardine cannery in Moss Landing now houses a world-renowned aquarium.

Californian sea otter

The endangered Californian sea otter (*Enhydra lutris*) forages for sea urchins, mollusks and crustaceans, which it dislodges and opens using small rocks as tools. It spends nearly its entire life in the ocean and wraps itself in kelp to avoid floating away while resting.

BATHYMETRIC DEPTHS	
Feet	Meters
Sea level	Sea level
656	200
1640	500
3281	1000
6562	2000
9842	3000
13,123	4000
16,404	5000
19,685	6000
26,246	8,000

SCALE 1:10,000,000
Miller Projection

0 — 200 kilometers
0 — 200 statute miles
0 — 200 nautical miles

Longitude west of Greenwich

207

GALAPAGOS ISLANDS

The Galapagos Archipelago was formed over a volcanic hot spot and contains some of the most active volcanoes in the world. Declared a World Heritage site in 1978, the islands are also home to 40,000 people. Their unique ecosystem gave Charles Darwin the observational material for his work *On the Origin of Species*.

Lacking mammal predators, island life is characterized by reptiles, among them giant tortoises, and land and sea iguanas. Among the many nesting birds are the blue-footed and red-footed boobies. The 13 main islands, 6 smaller islands, and 107 rocks and islets form an obstacle in the South Equatorial Current that produces a wake 600 miles (1,000 km) long. Upwelling in the wake brings cold water and nutrients to the surface, which leads to high productivity and provides ideal conditions for the Galapagos penguin, the world's northernmost penguin species and the only one to cross the equator.

Galapagos sea lions
The Galapagos sea lion *(Zalophus wollebaeki)* is at home on the Galapagos Islands and on the Isla de la Plata off the coast of Ecuador. It is a social animal that loves to play, sunbathe, and perform acrobatics in the surf. It is always popular with visitors.

Red rock crab
The red rock crab *(Grapsus grapsus)* is common along the Pacific coast of Central and South America and on the Galapagos Islands. It walks on tiptoe and can run in any direction. Its quick movement and fast reaction time have given it the name "Sally Lightfoot."

MARINE IGUANA

Among the many unique lifeforms encountered by Charles Darwin on his visit to the Galapagos, the marine iguana *(Amblyrhynchus cristatus)* is certainly the most specially adapted creature. It grazes on algae in cold water, yet being cold-blooded it can remain under water for only half an hour before it has to return to the shore. There it basks in the sun to raise its body temperature again.

Rocky shores
Red rock crabs live in swarms among rocks in the turbulent wave zone just above the limit of the sea spray, where they feed on algae and clean up carcasses.

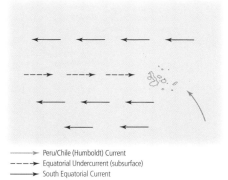

Surface currents
The waters around the Galapagos Islands are highly productive. Their position on the equator places the islands in the equatorial upwelling region. The wake of the South Equatorial Current in the west brings nutrients to the surface.

⟶ Peru/Chile (Humboldt) Current
--→ Equatorial Undercurrent (subsurface)
⟶ South Equatorial Current

Darwin called marine iguanas "disgusting clumsy lizards." They may be clumsy on land, but in the water they are graceful swimmers. This iguana soaks up the sun to prepare for its next dive.

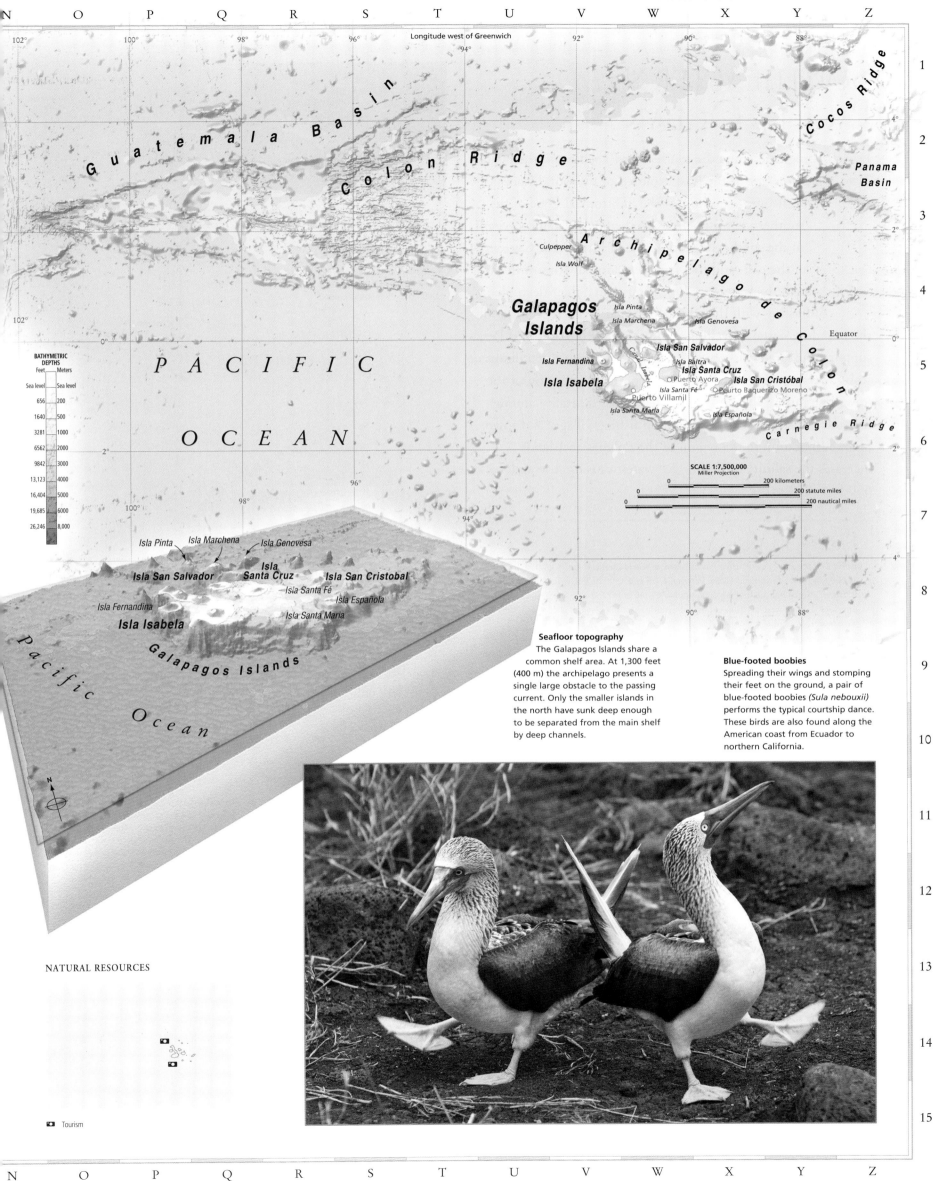

N O P Q R S T U V W X Y Z

102° 100° 98° 96° Longitude west of Greenwich 92° 90° 88°
94°

Guatemala Basin

Colon Ridge

Cocos Ridge

Panama Basin

Archipelago de Colon

Culpepper
Isla Wolf

Galapagos Islands

Isla Pinta
Isla Marchena   Isla Genovesa

Equator

Isla San Salvador
Isla Baltra
Isla Santa Cruz
Isla Fernandina
Isla San Cristóbal
Isla Isabela
○ Puerto Ayora
Isla Santa Fé   ○ Puerto Baquerizo Moreno
Puerto Villamil
Isla Santa Maria   Isla Española

Carnegie Ridge

PACIFIC

OCEAN

BATHYMETRIC DEPTHS

Feet	Meters
Sea level	Sea level
656	200
1640	500
3281	1000
6562	2000
9842	3000
13,123	4000
16,404	5000
19,685	6000
26,246	8,000

SCALE 1:7,500,000
Miller Projection

0   200 kilometers
0   200 statute miles
0   200 nautical miles

Isla Pinta   Isla Marchena   Isla Genovesa
Isla
Isla San Salvador   Santa Cruz   Isla San Cristobal
Isla Santa Fé
Isla Fernandina   Isla Española
Isla Santa Maria
Isla Isabela

Galapagos Islands

Pacific Ocean

N

Seafloor topography
The Galapagos Islands share a common shelf area. At 1,300 feet (400 m) the archipelago presents a single large obstacle to the passing current. Only the smaller islands in the north have sunk deep enough to be separated from the main shelf by deep channels.

Blue-footed boobies
Spreading their wings and stomping their feet on the ground, a pair of blue-footed boobies *(Sula nebouxii)* performs the typical courtship dance. These birds are also found along the American coast from Ecuador to northern California.

NATURAL RESOURCES

◻ Tourism

N O P Q R S T U V W X Y Z

SOUTHEASTERN PACIFIC OCEAN

Few shipping lanes cross the southeastern Pacific and the region remains one of the least explored of the world's oceans. It encompasses most of the Subtropical Gyre of the southern hemisphere, with the South Pacific Current in the south, the Peru–Chile or Humboldt Current in the east, and the South Equatorial Current in the north. Its waters are low in nutrients, their deep blue contrasting with the white sands and green vegetation of the islands. Coastal upwelling along the coast of Chile and Peru supports the largest fishery in the world and feeds the millions of seabirds responsible for rich guano deposits. Disruption of the upwelling during El Niño years causes mass mortality among fish and birds, and social upheaval in fishing villages and towns. High evaporation in the region of the Polynesian Islands increases the salinity of the surface water, causing it to sink to 650 feet (200 m).

Great barracuda
The great barracuda *(Sphyraena barracuda),* a voracious predator of all tropical oceans, grows to 6 feet (1.8 m) in length. It lies in wait in reefs and ambushes its prey, attacking with short bursts of speed up to 25 mph (40 km/h).

EASTER ISLAND

Isolated in the vast South Pacific, Easter Island, a World Heritage site, is located 2,237 miles (3,600 km) west of mainland Chile. Between 1250 and 1500 its Polynesian inhabitants, the Rapanui, created hundreds of large monolithic statues called moai. In the 18th and 19th centuries all moai were overthrown, probably during conflict between clans. Some 50 statues have been re-erected.

Atacama coast
Nowhere can the contrast between land and sea be greater than along the coasts of Peru and Chile. The Atacama desert, the driest on Earth, borders the coast and is nearly devoid of life. In the sea, upwelling provides nutrients for the oceans' richest fishing grounds.

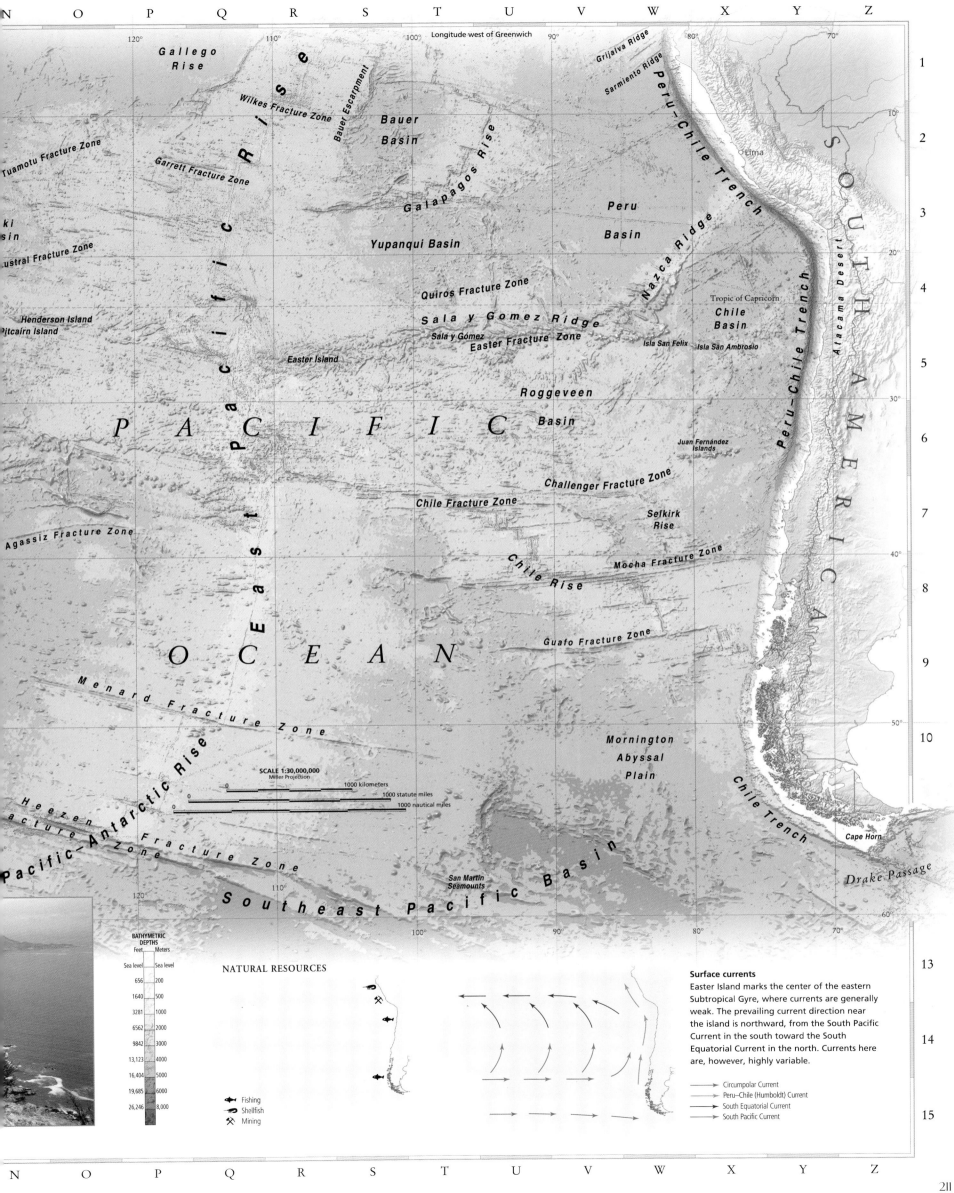

120°   110°   Longitude west of Greenwich   90°   80°   70°

Gallego Rise

Wilkes Fracture Zone

Tuamotu Fracture Zone

Garrett Fracture Zone

Bauer Escarpment

Bauer Basin

Grijalva Ridge

Sarmiento Ridge

Peru–Chile Trench

S O U T H

Lima

Austral Fracture Zone

Galapagos Rise

Peru Basin

Yupanqui Basin

Quiros Fracture Zone

Nazca Ridge

Tropic of Capricorn

Chile Basin

Atacama Desert

Sala y Gomez Ridge

Sala y Gómez   *Easter Fracture Zone*

Henderson Island

Pitcairn Island

Easter Island

Isla San Felix

Isla San Ambrosio

Peru–Chile Trench

A M E R I C A

Roggeveen Basin

P A C I F I C

Juan Fernández Islands

Challenger Fracture Zone

Chile Fracture Zone

Selkirk Rise

Agassiz Fracture Zone

Mocha Fracture Zone

Chile Rise

O C E A N

Guafo Fracture Zone

Menard Fracture Zone

Mornington Abyssal Plain

Pacific–Antarctic Rise

SCALE 1:30,000,000
Miller Projection

0   1000 kilometers

0   1000 statute miles

0   1000 nautical miles

Chile Trench

Heezen Fracture Zone

Cape Horn

Pacific–Antarctic Fracture Zone

San Martin Seamounts

Southeast Pacific Basin

Drake Passage

120°   110°   100°   90°   80°   70°

BATHYMETRIC DEPTHS

Feet	Meters
Sea level	Sea level
656	200
1640	500
3281	1000
6562	2000
9842	3000
13,123	4000
16,404	5000
19,685	6000
26,246	8,000

NATURAL RESOURCES

🐟 Fishing
🦐 Shellfish
⚒ Mining

Surface currents

Easter Island marks the center of the eastern Subtropical Gyre, where currents are generally weak. The prevailing current direction near the island is northward, from the South Pacific Current in the south toward the South Equatorial Current in the north. Currents here are, however, highly variable.

Circumpolar Current
Peru–Chile (Humboldt) Current
South Equatorial Current
South Pacific Current

POLYNESIAN ISLANDS

Several hot spots created the many island chains of the South Pacific. Young islands such as Tahiti have volcanic cones surrounded by fringing reefs. As the islands drift away from their place of formation they sink back into the ocean crust while their coral fringes grow into barrier reefs, as seen at Bora Bora. Eventually the islands disappear into the sea, leaving coral atolls such as the Tuamotus as their legacy. Located in the center of the South Pacific Subtropical Gyre the islands are surrounded by ocean of low productivity, which keeps the big fishing fleets away; but their reefs support a diverse ecosystem that provides for the island communities, whose diet depends on fish. Few shipping lines cross the region. Cyclones are a rare occurrence, and the fresh breezes that moderate the region's temperature make it a preferred tourist destination. Cruise vessels of various sizes operate a busy schedule around the islands.

School of bannerfish
A school of longfin bannerfish (*Heniochus acuminatus*) moves through the lagoon of Rangiroa Atoll in the Tuamotu Islands. Bannerfish, also known as butterflyfish, occur in several species on reefs of the Indian and Pacific oceans with water temperatures of 77–82°F (25–28°C).

THREE TYPES OF VOLCANIC ISLANDS

The Leeward Islands (south to north) demonstrate the development from volcano to atoll. Huahine, Raiatea, and Tahaa are tall volcanic islands with fringing reefs. Bora Bora's volcano has started to sink, a lagoon has opened around the island, and the reef has become a barrier reef. At Tupai the island has sunk below the surface, leaving an atoll with reef and an enclosed lagoon.

Coral trout
A coral trout (*Cephalopholis miniata*) hovers in a coral niche among cup corals, sponges, soft corals, feather stars, and sea fans. The abundance of sedentary plankton-feeders is an indication that the area is bathed in plankton-rich current. Coral trout are common in reefs of the tropical Pacific.

NATURAL RESOURCES

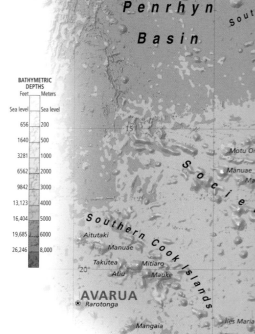

BATHYMETRIC DEPTHS	
Feet	Meters
Sea level	Sea level
656	200
1640	500
3281	1000
6562	2000
9842	3000
13,123	4000
16,404	5000
19,685	6000
26,246	8,000

Central Line Islands
155°
5°
Starbuck Island

Tongareva
10°

**Penrhyn
Basin**   South

15°

Motu One
Manuae
Maup

Society

Southern Cook Islands
Aitutaki
Manuae
Takutea   Mitiaro
20°   Atiu   Mauke

AVARUA
• Rarotonga

Mangaia   Iles Maria

COOK   Rimata
Tropic of Capricorn
ISLANDS

25°

**Southwest
Pacific
Basin**

30°
155°

↞ Fishing
▣ Tourism

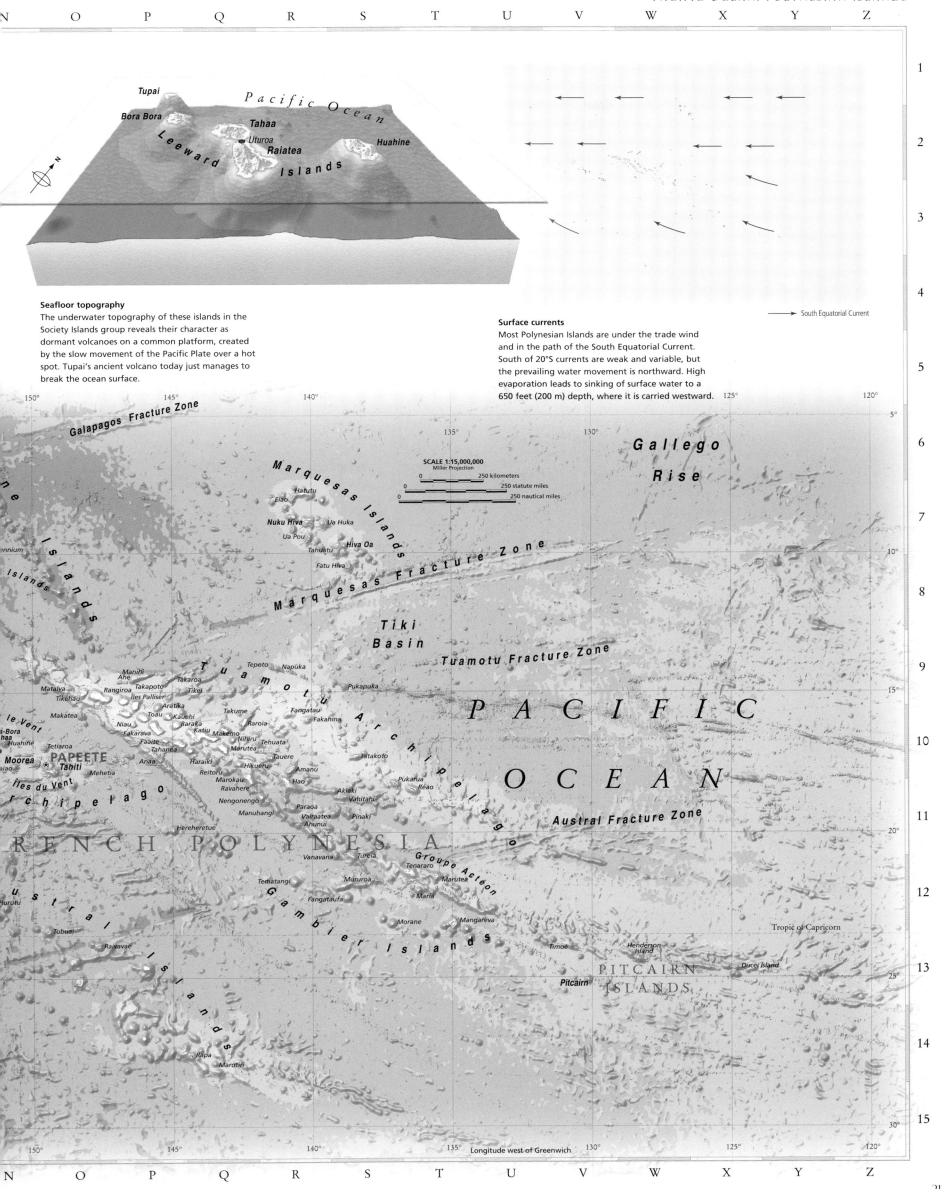

N O P Q R S T U V W X Y Z

1
2
3
4
5

Seafloor topography

The underwater topography of these islands in the Society Islands group reveals their character as dormant volcanoes on a common platform, created by the slow movement of the Pacific Plate over a hot spot. Tupai's ancient volcano today just manages to break the ocean surface.

Surface currents

Most Polynesian Islands are under the trade wind and in the path of the South Equatorial Current. South of 20°S currents are weak and variable, but the prevailing water movement is northward. High evaporation leads to sinking of surface water to a 650 feet (200 m) depth, where it is carried westward.

→ South Equatorial Current

Tupai
Bora Bora
Tahaa
Uturoa
Raiatea
Huahine
Leeward
Islands

Pacific Ocean

N

Galapagos Fracture Zone

Gallego Rise

Marquesas Islands
Hatutu
Eiao
Nuku Hiva
Ua Huka
Ua Pou
Tahuata
Hiva Oa
Fatu Hiva

Marquesas Fracture Zone

Tiki Basin

Tuamotu Fracture Zone

SCALE 1:15,000,000
Miller Projection
0   250 kilometers
0   250 statute miles
0   250 nautical miles

PACIFIC OCEAN

Manihi
Ahe
Takaroa
Matalva
Takapoto
Tepoto
Napuka
Rangiroa
Tikei
Tikehau
Iles du Palliser
Pukapuka
Aratika
Makatea
Takume
Niau
Toau
Kauehi
Fangatau
Fakahina
Fakarava
Raraka
Raroia
i-Bora
Faaite
Katiu
Makemo
-haa
Tetiaroa
Tahanea
Nihiru
Tehuata
Huahine
Anaa
Marutea
Tauere
Moorea
Haraiki
Hikueru
Tatakoto
PAPEETE
Reitoru
-iaio
Tahiti
Mehetia
Marokau
Hao
Akiaki
Pukarua
Réao
Ravahere
Vahitahi
Nengonengo
Paraoa
Manuhangi
Vairaatea
Pinaki
Hereheretue
Ahunui

FRENCH POLYNESIA

Vanavana
Turela
Groupe Actéon
Tenararo
Marutea
Tematangi
Mururoa
Maria
Fangataufa
Gambier Islands
Morane
Mangareva
Timoe
Henderson Island
Tropic of Capricorn
Ducei Island
PITCAIRN ISLANDS
Pitcairn

us-
urutu
Tubuai
Raivavae
-stral Islands
Rapa
Marotiri

150° 145° 140° 135° 130° 125° 120°
5° 6° 8° 10° 15° 20° 25° 30°

Longitude west of Greenwich

N O P Q R S T U V W X Y Z

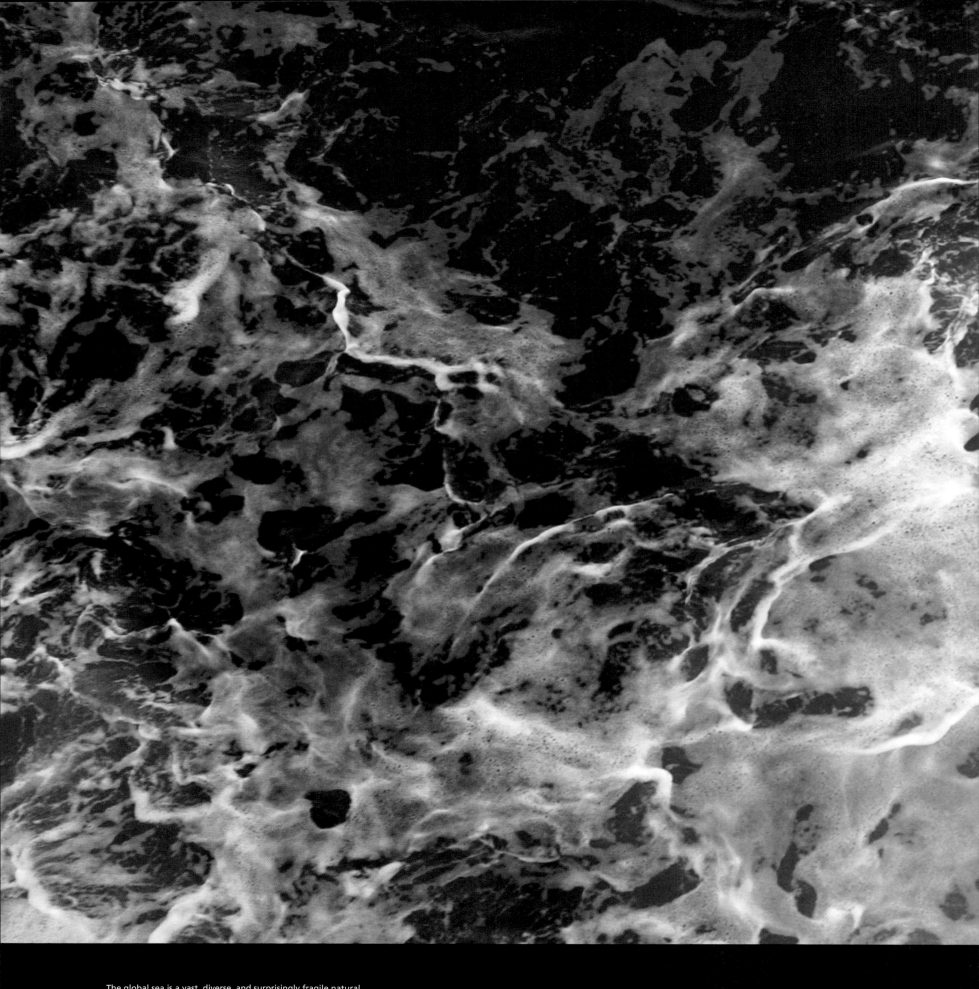

The global sea is a vast, diverse, and surprisingly fragile natural world. Despite centuries of marine exploration and avid human use of marine resources, the depths continue to reveal new wonders, pose new challenges, and spark the imagination and curiosity of each new generation.

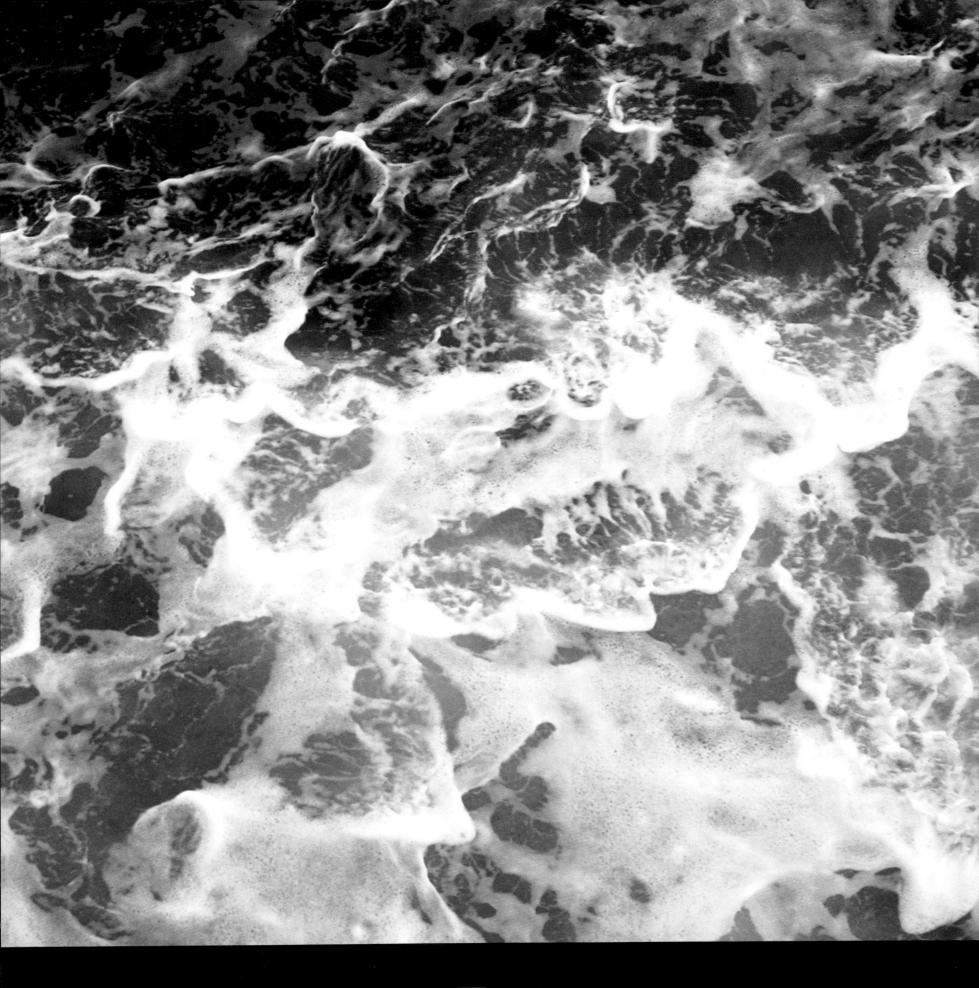

REFERENCE

OCEAN FACT FILE

Names of oceans and seas	Area square miles (km²)	Average depth feet (m)	Greatest known depth: feet (m)	Length miles (km)	Width miles (km)	Volume cubic miles (km³)
Planet Earth				(Equatorial circ.)*	(Polar circ.)*	
Planet Earth	196,930,000 (510,000,000)	–	–	24,902 (40,077)*	24,820 (39,942)*	–
The Continents (29.2% area of Earth)	57,510,000 (148,940,000)	–	–	–	–	–
The World Ocean (70.8% area of Earth)	139,420,000 (361,060,000)	12,430 (3,790)	36,201 (11,034)	–	–	329,070,000 (1,370,740,000)
The three main ocean basins						
Pacific Ocean including marginal seas and Pacific section of the Southern Ocean	69,380,000 (179,680,000)	13,220 (4,030)	36,201 (11,034)	10,106 (16,264)	to 11,185 (to 18,000)	173,770,000 (723,840,000)
Atlantic Ocean including marginal seas (Black, Mediterranean, Caribbean etc), the Arctic Ocean and the Atlantic section of the Southern Ocean	41,110,000 (106,460,000)	10,920 (3,330)	27,493 (8,380)	13,360 (21,500)	to 4,909 (7,900)	85,200,000 (354,900,000)
Indian Ocean including marginal seas and the Indian Ocean section of the Southern Ocean	28,930,000 (74,920,000)	12,790 (3,890)	24,460 (7,455)	6,351 (10,220)	to 6,338 (10,200)	70,100,000 (292,000,000)
The oceans						
Pacific Ocean, including marginal seas	65,590,000 (169,852,000)	13,127 (4,001)	36,201 (11,034)	8,637 (13,900)	to 11,185 (18,000)	163,100,000 (679,614,000)
Atlantic Ocean, including marginal seas	33,560,000 (86,915,000)	11,828 (3,605)	28,233 (8,605)	8,774 (14,120)	to 4,909 (7,900)	75,200,000 (313,352,500)
Indian Ocean, including marginal seas	26,980,000 (69,876,000)	12,645 (3,854)	24,460 (7,455)	5,841 (9,400)	to 6,338 (10,200)	64,720,000 (269,302,000)
Southern Ocean, including marginal seas	7,850,000 (20,327,000)	14,450 (4,500)	23,736 (7,235)	to 13,360 (21,500)	249–1,678 (400–2,700)	21,950,000 (91,471,500)
Arctic Ocean, including marginal seas	5,440,000 (14,090,000)	4,690 (1,430)	18,456 (5,625)	to 3,107 (5,000)	to 1,988 (3,200)	4,100,000 (17,000,000)

THE OCEANS AND SUBDIVISIONS IHO 23-4th: Limits of Oceans and Seas, Special Publication 23, 4th Edition June 2002, published by the International Hydrographic Bureau of the International Hydrographic Organization.

IHO	Names of oceans and seas	Area square miles (km²)	Average depth feet (m)	Greatest known depth: feet (m)	Length miles (km)	Width miles (km)	Volume cubic miles (km³)
	North Atlantic Ocean and subdivisions						
1	North Atlantic Ocean	–	–	28,233 (8,605)	4,636 (7,460)	to 4,909 (7,900)	–
1.1	Skaggerak	12,970 (33,600)	1,312 (400)	1,969 (600)	150 (240)	80–90 (130–145)	3,225 (13,440)
1.2	North Sea	222,100 (575,200)	308 (94)	2,165 (660)	621 (1,000)	93–373 (150–600)	12,974 (54,069)
1.3	Inner Seas (off West Coast Scotland)	4,630 (12,000)	82 (25)	266 (81)	174 (280)	43–62 (70–100)	72 (300)
1.4	Irish Sea	40,000 (100,000)	125 (38)	576 (175)	130 (210)	150 (240)	912 (3,800)
1.5	Bristol Channel	1,160 (3,000)	36 (11)	98 (30)	93 (150)	3–24 (5–40)	8 (33)
1.6	Celtic Sea	61,780 (160,000)	180 (55)	236 (72)	249 (400)	249 (400)	2,112 (8,800)
1.7	English Channel	34,700 (89,900)	272 (83)	394 (120)	249 (400)	21–112 (31–180)	1,726 (7,192)
1.7.1	Dover Strait	950 (2,450)	46 (14)	180 (55)	43 (70)	18–25 (30–40)	8 (34)
1.8	Bay of Biscay	86,000 (223,000)	7,874 (2,400)	15,525 (4,735)	317 (510)	342 (550)	128,419 (535,200)
1.9	Gulf of Guinea	324,360 (840,000)	12,796 (3,900)	16,405 (5,000)	435 (700)	746 (1,200)	786,064 (3,276,000)
1.10	Caribbean Sea	1,049,500 (2,718,200)	8,685 (2,647)	25,218 (7,686)	1,678 (2,700)	360–840 (600–1,400)	1,726,430 (7,195,075)
1.11	Gulf of Mexico	615,000 (1,592,800)	4,874 (1,486)	12,425 (3,787)	1,100 (1,770)	800 (1,287)	567,929 (2,366,901)
1.12	Straits of Florida	48,270 (125,000)	1,148 (350)	1,641 (500)	311 (500)	155 (250)	10,498 (43,750)
1.13	Bay of Fundy	3,600 (9,300)	328 (100)	656 (200)	94 (151)	32 (52)	223 (930)
1.14	Gulf of St Lawrence	62,530 (162,000)	197 (60)	656 (200)	280 (450)	261 (420)	2,332 (9,720)
1.15	Labrador Sea	222,030 (575,000)	6,562 (2,000)	12,468 (3,800)	to 870 (1,400)	to 492 (820)	275,938 (1,150,000)
	Other subdivisions of the North Atlantic Ocean						
–	Bay of Campeche	65,640 (170,000)	1,476 (450)	10,499 (3,200)	441 (710)	205 (330)	18,356 (76,500)
–	Block Island Sound	190 (500)	59 (18)	66 (20)	20 (32)	10 (16)	2 (9)
–	Cabot Strait	1,450 (3,750)	1,148 (350)	3,281 (1,000)	155 (250)	60–372 (100–320)	315 (1,313)
–	Canarias Sea	90,360 (234,000)	5,906 (1,800)	6,562 (2,000)	373 (600)	249 (400)	101,065 (421,200)
–	Cape Cod Bay	830 (2,150)	82 (25)	115 (35)	31 (50)	27 (43)	13 (54)
–	Chaleur Bay	1,680 (4,350)	82 (25)	164 (50)	90 (145)	15–25 (24–40)	26 (109)
–	Chesapeake Bay	5,800 (15,000)	23 (7)	80 (24)	193 (311)	3–25 (5–40)	25 (105)
–	Delaware Bay	970 (2,500)	23 (7)	70 (21)	52 (84)	6–25 (10–40)	4 (18)
–	Denmark Strait	54,060 (140,000)	3,281 (1,000)	8,203 (2,500)	300 (483)	180 (290)	33,592 (140,000)
–	Gulf of Cadiz	14,480 (37,500)	1,969 (600)	3,281 (1,000)	93 (150)	200 (320)	5,399 (22,500)
–	Gulf of Venezuela	10,190 (26,400)	8,203 (2,500)	9,843 (3,000)	75 (120)	150 (240)	15,836 (66,000)
–	Gulf of Honduras	30,890 (80,000)	2,953 (900)	8,203 (2,500)	249 (400)	9–240 (15–400)	17,276 (72,000)
–	Gulf of Maine	90,700 (235,000)	492 (150)	1,237 (377)	323 (520)	280 (450)	8,458 (35,250)
–	Long Bay	4,630 (12,000)	49 (15)	131 (40)	78 (125)	62 (100)	43 (180)
–	Long Island Sound	1,180 (3,056)	82 (25)	328 (100)	90 (145)	3–20 (5–32)	18 (76)
–	Massachusetts Bay	820 (2,123)	115 (35)	295 (90)	31 (50)	26 (42)	18 (74)
–	Mona Passage	8,500 (22,000)	656 (200)	3,281 (1,000)	112 (180)	68–87 (110–145)	1,056 (4,400)
–	Nantucket Sound	1,000 (2,600)	59 (18)	131 (40)	43 (70)	25 (40)	11 (47)
–	North Channel	2,320 (6,000)	328 (100)	656 (200)	124 (200)	11–36 (18–60)	144 (600)
–	Onslow Bay	5,790 (15,000)	66 (20)	164 (50)	103 (165)	62 (100)	72 (300)
–	Rhode Island Sound	580 (1,500)	23 (7)	33 (10)	25 (40)	24 (38)	3 (11)
–	Saint George's Channel	4,250 (11,000)	148 (45)	203 (62)	99 (160)	47 (76)	119 (495)

IHO	Names of oceans and seas	Area square miles (km²)	Average depth feet (m)	Greatest known depth: feet (m)	Length miles (km)	Width miles (km)	Volume cubic miles (km³)
Other subdivisions of the North Atlantic Ocean (continued)							
–	Sargasso Sea	1,448,020 (3,750,000)	16,405 (5,000)	21,005 (6,402)	1,864 (3,000)	994 (1,600)	4,498,990 (18,750,000)
–	Windward Passage	3,480 (9,000)	3,281 (1,000)	5,545 (1,690)	68 (110)	50 (80)	2,160 (9,000)
–	Yucatan Channel	16,600 (43,000)	3,281 (1,000)	6,693 (2,040)	135 (217)	124 (200)	10,318 (43,000)
Baltic Sea and subdivisions (North Atlantic Ocean)							
2	Baltic Sea	163,000 (422,200)	180 (55)	1,380 (421)	795 (1,280)	24–324 (40–540)	5,572 (23,221)
2.1	Central Baltic Sea	46,340 (120,000)	164 (50)	656 (200)	373 (600)	186 (300)	1,440 (6,000)
2.2	Gulf of Bothnia	45,200 (117,000)	200 (60)	965 (295)	450 (725)	48–150 (80–240)	1,684 (7,020)
2.2.1	Bothnian Sea	19,110 (49,500)	246 (75)	656 (200)	205 (330)	48–132 (80–220)	891 (3,713)
2.2.2	Bay of Bothnia	9,270 (24,000)	246 (75)	656 (200)	249 (400)	9–75 (15–125)	432 (1,800)
2.3	Gulf of Finland	11,600 (30,000)	85 (26)	377 (115)	249 (400)	12–80 (19–130)	187 (780)
2.4	Sound Sea	25,100 (65,000)	82 (25)	164 (50)	186 (300)	137 (220)	390 (1,625)
2.5	Gulf of Riga	7,000 (18,000)	131 (40)	144 (44)	109 (175)	24–72 (40–120)	173 (720)
2.6	The Sound	390 (1,000)	131 (40)	164 (50)	68 (110)	3–9 (5–14)	10 (40)
2.7	The Great Belt	460 (1,200)	85 (26)	164 (50)	47 (75)	9–12 (15–20)	7 (31)
2.8	The Little Belt	420 (1,100)	85 (26)	164 (50)	37 (60)	9–24 (15–40)	7 (29)
2.9	Kattegat	9,840 (25,485)	84 (26)	164 (50)	137 (220)	37–88 (60–142)	159 (663)
Other subdivisions of the Baltic Sea (North Atlantic Ocean)							
–	Gulf of Gdansk	1,660 (4,296)	180 (55)	197 (60)	62 (100)	43 (70)	57 (236)
–	Kiel Bay	970 (2,500)	131 (40)	131 (40)	50 (80)	22 (35)	24 (100)
–	Mecklenburger Bay	1,000 (2,600)	131 (40)	125 (38)	47 (75)	18–27 (30–45)	25 (104)
–	Pomeranian Bay	930 (2,400)	66 (20)	164 (50)	43 (70)	31 (50)	12 (48)
Mediterranean Sea and subdivisions (North Atlantic Ocean)							
3.1	Mediterranean Sea	969,000 (2,510,000)	4,920 (1,500)	16,897 (5,150)	2,500 (4,000)	497 (800)	860,636 (3,586,790)
3.1.1	Mediterranean Sea, Western Basin	328,220 (850,000)	-	12,000 (3,658)	1,250 (2,000)	497 (800)	-
3.1.1.1	Strait of Gibraltar	290 (750)	1,200 (365)	3,117 (950)	36 (58)	8 (13)	66 (274)
3.1.1.2	Alboran Sea	18,530 (48,000)	1,969 (600)	3,872 (1180)	249 (400)	48–120 (80–200)	6,910 (28,800)
3.1.1.3	Balearic Sea	123,560 (320,000)	2,461 (750)	4,987 (1,520)	497 (800)	120–420 (200–700)	57,587 (240,000)
3.1.1.4	Ligurian Sea	13,510 (35,000)	4,265 (1,300)	9,300 (2,850)	155 (250)	106 (170)	10,918 (45,500)
3.1.1.5	Tyrrhenian Sea	46,340 (120,000)	9,515 (2,900)	11,897 (3,626)	475 (760)	60–300 (97–483)	83,501 (348,000)
3.1.2	Mediterranean Sea, Eastern Basin	640,990 (1,660,000)	-	16,897 (5,150)	1,250 (2,000)	497 (800)	-
3.1.2.1	Adriatic Sea	52,220 (135,250)	1,457 (444)	4,035 (1,324)	497 (800)	99 (160)	14,409 (60,051)
3.1.2.2	Strait of Sicily	19,310 (50,000)	328 (100)	1,969 (600)	311 (500)	93 (150)	1,200 (5,000)
3.1.2.3	Ionian Sea	104,260 (270,000)	12,796 (3,900)	16,000 (4,900)	373 (600)	120–360 (200–600)	252,663 (1,053,000)
3.1.2.4	Aegean Sea	83,000 (214,000)	1,969 (600)	11,627 (3,543)	380 (611)	186 (399)	30,809 (128,400)
3.2	Sea of Marmara	4,430 (11,474)	1,620 (494)	4,446 (1,355)	175 (280)	50 (80)	1,360 (5,668)
3.3	Black Sea	196,000 (508,000)	4,062 (1,240)	7,365 (2,245)	730 (1,175)	160 (260)	151,147 (629,920)
3.4	Sea of Azov	14,500 (37,555)	23 (7)	45 (13)	210 (340)	85 (135)	63 (263)
Other subdivisions of the Mediterranean Sea (North Atlantic Ocean)							
–	Dardanelles	100 (250)	180 (55)	300 (92)	38 (61)	0.75–4 (1.2–6.5)	3.3 (13.8)
–	Gulf of Lion	11,580 (30,000)	246 (75)	276 (84)	93 (150)	60–138 (100–230)	540 (2,250)
–	Gulf of Venice	2,010 (5,200)	98 (30)	128 (39)	60 (95)	37 (60)	37 (156)
–	Bosporus	40 (105)	98 (30)	408 (124)	19 (30)	2.3 (3.7)	0.8 (3.2)
–	Sea of Crete	27,800 (72,000)	6,562 (2,000)	10,000 (3,294)	249 (400)	130 (210)	34,552 (144,000)
–	Thracian Sea	3,480 (9,000)	246 (75)	328 (100)	93 (150)	50 (80)	162 (675)
Southern Atlantic Ocean and subdivisions							
4	South Atlantic Ocean	–	–	27,651 (8,428)	4,139 (6,660)	to 4,680 (to 7,800)	–
4.1	River Plate	12,740 (33,000)	20 (6)	70 (21)	186 (300)	9 to 120 (15 to 200)	48 (198)
4.2	Scotia Sea	348,000 (900,000)	11,500 (4,500)	27,651 (8,428)	870 (1,400)	497 (800)	755,830 (3,150,000)
4.3	Drake Passage	308,910 (800,000)	11,000 (3,400)	15,600 (4,800)	497 (800)	621 (1,000)	652,653 (2,720,000)
Other subdivisions of the South Atlantic Ocean							
–	San Jorge Gulf	15,450 (40,000)	115 (35)	262 (80)	99 (160)	137 (220)	336 (1,400)
–	San Matias Gulf	6,950 (18,000)	98 (30)	230 (70)	99 (160)	24–90 (40–150)	130 (540)
–	Strait of Magellan	2,240 (5,800)	66 (20)	98 (30)	350 (560)	2–20 (3–32)	28 (116)
Indian Ocean and subdivisions							
5	Indian Ocean	26,500,000 (68,600,000)	12,644 (3,854)	23,376 (7,125)	5,800 (9,400)	6,300 (10,200)	64,720,000 (269,302,104)
5.1	Mozambique Channel	432,470 (1,120,000)	8,531 (2,600)	9,843 (3,000)	1,000 (1,600)	250–600 (400–950)	698,723 (2,912,000)
5.2	Gulf of Suez	4,050 (10,500)	82 (25)	295 (90)	180 (290)	15–35 (24–56)	63 (263)

OCEAN FACT FILE

IHO	Names of oceans and seas	Area square miles (km²)	Average depth feet (m)	Greatest known depth: feet (m)	Length miles (km)	Width miles (km)	Volume cubic miles (km³)
Indian Ocean and subdivisions (continued)							
5.3	Gulf of Aqaba	1,480 (3,840)	2,625 (800)	6,070 (1,850)	99 (160)	12–17 (19–27)	737 (3,072)
5.4	Red Sea	169,100 (438,000)	1,608 (490)	9,974 (3,040)	1,398 (2,250)	220 (355)	51,602 (215,058)
5.5	Gulf of Aden	205,000 (530,000)	4,922 (1,500)	17,586 (5,360)	920 (1,480)	300 (480)	190,757 (795,000)
5.6	Persian Gulf	96,911 (251,000)	164 (50)	344 (119)	615 (989)	35 (56)	1,957 (8,155)
5.7	Strait of Hormuz	4,630 (12,000)	213 (65)	2,953 (900)	99 (160)	35–60 (55–95)	187 (780)
5.8	Gulf of Oman	65,640 (170,000)	3,937 (1,200)	9,843 (3,000)	350 (560)	200 (320)	48,949 (204,000)
5.9	Arabian Sea	1,500,000 (3,900,000)	9,022 (2,750)	15,262 (4,652)	to 1,243 (2,000)	1,490 (2,400)	2,533,521 (10,558,708)
5.10	Lakshadweep Sea	289,600 (750,000)	7,874 (2,400)	14,765 (4,500)	to 932 (1,500)	to 620 (1,000)	431,903 (1,800,000)
5.11	Gulf of Mannar	11,740 (30,400)	3,281 (1,000)	5,906 (1,800)	99 (160)	80–170 (130–275)	7,294 (30,400)
5.12	Palk Strait and Palk Bay	5,780 (14,960)	98 (30)	295 (90)	85 (136)	40–85 (64–137)	108 (449)
5.13	Bay of Bengal	838,613 (2,172,000)	8,500 (2,600)	15,400 (4,694)	1,300 (2,090)	1,000 (1,610)	1,355,648 (5,649,800)
5.14	Andaman Sea	308,000 (797,700)	2,854 (870)	12,392 (3,777)	750 (1,200)	400 (645)	166,522 (693,999)
5.15	Timor Sea	235,000 (615,000)	459 (140)	10,800 (3,300)	609 (980)	435 (700)	20,659 (86,100)
5.15.1	Joseph Bonaparte Gulf	19,310 (50,000)	197 (60)	328 (100)	99 (160)	225 (360)	720 (3,000)
5.16	Arafura Sea	250,990 (650,000)	230 (70)	12,000 (3,660)	to 620 (1,000)	to 435 (700)	10,918 (45,500)
5.16.1	Gulf of Carpentaria	120,000 (310,000)	164 (50)	230 (70)	544 (875)	120–390 (200–650)	3,719 (15,500)
5.17	Great Australian Bight	366,830 (950,000)	7,218 (2,200)	14,765 (4,500)	1,740 (2,800)	to 620 (1,000)	501,487 (2,090,000)
Other subdivisions of the Indian Ocean							
–	Gulf of Bahrain	3,280 (8,500)	98 (30)	131 (40)	106 (170)	12–57 (20–95)	61 (255)
–	Strait of Tiran	440 (1,150)	262 (80)	400 (122)	31 (50)	16 (25)	22 (92)
South China and Eastern Archipelagic Seas (Pacific Ocean)							
6	South China & Eastern Archipelagic Seas	–	–	–	–	–	–
6.1	South China Sea	895,400 (2,319,000)	5,419 (1,652)	16,456 (5,016)	to 1,182 (1,970)	to 840 (1,400)	919,231 (3,830,988)
6.2	Gulf of Tonkin	46,340 (120,000)	246 (75)	230 (70)	311 (500)	150 (250)	2,160 (9,000)
6.3	Gulf of Thailand	123,553 (320,000)	148 (45)	262 (80)	450 (724)	350 (563)	3,455 (14,400)
6.4	Natuna Sea	135,150 (350,000)	148 (45)	328 (100)	559 (900)	60–390 (100–650)	3,779 (15,750)
6.5	Malacca Strait	25,000 (65,000)	90 (27)	656 (200)	497 (800)	40–155 (65–249)	421 (1,755)
6.6	Singapore Strait	1,000 (2,600)	131 (40)	164 (50)	65 (105)	10–18 (16–30)	25 (104)
6.7	Sunda Strait	4,440 (11,500)	131 (40)	164 (50)	103 (165)	16–70 (26–110)	110 (460)
6.8	Java Sea	167,000 (433,000)	151 (46)	689 (210)	900 (1,450)	261 (420)	4,779 (19,918)
6.9	Makassar Strait	81,090 (210,000)	2,625 (800)	6,562 (2,000)	497 (800)	80–230 (130–370)	40,311 (168,000)
6.10	Bali Sea	15,830 (41,000)	197 (60)	1,805 (550)	311 (500)	75 (120)	590 (2,460)
6.11	Flores Sea	93,000 (240,000)	6,890 (2,100)	16,860 (5,140)	435 (700)	108–360 (180–600)	120,933 (504,000)
6.12	Sumba Strait	6,490 (16,800)	328 (100)	2,461 (750)	130 (210)	36–60 (60–100)	403 (1,680)
6.13	Savu Sea	41,000 (105,000)	8,859 (2,700)	11,385 (3,470)	404 (650)	155 (250)	68,025 (283,500)
6.14	Aru Sea	30,890 (80,000)	6,562 (2,000)	11,484 (3,500)	311 (500)	78–102 (130–170)	38,391 (160,000)
6.15	Banda Sea	181,000 (470,000)	14,765 (4,500)	24,409 (7,440)	652 (1,050)	228–330 (380–550)	507,486 (2,115,000)
6.16	Gulf of Bone	12,740 (33,000)	6,562 (2,000)	9,843 (3,000)	186 (300)	36–102 (60–170)	15,836 (66,000)
6.17	Ceram Sea	31,280 (81,000)	7,218 (2,200)	11,484 (3,500)	360 (580)	68–120 (110–200)	42,758 (178,200)
6.18	Gulf of Berau	4,250 (11,000)	230 (70)	328 (100)	137 (220)	12–42 (20–70)	185 (770)
6.19	Halmahera Sea	28,570 (74,000)	2,461 (750)	3,281 (1,000)	186 (300)	186 (300)	13,317 (55,500)
6.20	Molucca Sea	77,000 (200,000)	9,187 (2,800)	15,780 (4,810)	373 (600)	150–258 (250–430)	134,370 (560,000)
6.21	Gulf of Tomini	23,170 (60,000)	3,937 (1,200)	4,922 (1,500)	261 (420)	60–123 (100–205)	17,276 (72,000)
6.22	Celebes Sea	110,000 (280,000)	13,780 (4,200)	20,406 (6,220)	420 (675)	520 (837)	282,177 (1,176,000)
6.23	Sulu Sea	100,000 (260,000)	11,484 (3,500)	18,400 (5,600)	490 (790)	375 (603)	218,351 (910,000)
Other subdivisions of the South China and Eastern Archipelagic Seas							
–	Luzon Sea	81,090 (210,000)	2,953 (900)	9,843 (3,000)	466 (750)	217 (350)	45,350 (189,000)
–	Luzon Strait	46,340 (120,000)	2,953 (900)	6,562 (2,000)	217 (350)	249 (400)	25,914 (108,000)
–	Karimata Strait	52,130 (135,000)	492 (150)	656 (200)	280 (450)	120–228 (200–380)	4,859 (20,250)
–	Yapen Strait	6,180 (16,000)	3,281 (1,000)	3,281 (1,000)	155 (250)	40 (65)	3,839 (16,000)
–	Cenderawasih Bay	18,150 (47,000)	2,297 (700)	3,281 (1,000)	174 (280)	54–252 (90–420)	7,894 (32,900)
North Pacific Ocean and subdivisions							
7	North Pacific Ocean	–	–	36,201 (11,034)	4,499 (7,240)	to 10,800 (18,000)	–
7.1	Philippine Sea	1,776,230 (4,600,000)	19,700 (6,000)	34,578 (10,539)	to 1,800 (3,000)	to 1,200 (2,000)	6,622,513 (27,600,000)
7.2	Taiwan Strait	21,240 (55,000)	197 (60)	230 (70)	286 (460)	100–174 (160–280)	792 (3,300)
7.3	East China Sea	284,000 (735,800)	574 (175)	8,913 (2,717)	684 (1,100)	435 (700)	30,897 (128,765)
7.4	Yellow Sea	180,000 (466,200)	131 (40)	338 (103)	600 (960)	435 (700)	4,475 (18,648)

IHO	Names of oceans and seas	Area square miles (km²)	Average depth feet (m)	Greatest known depth: feet (m)	Length miles (km)	Width miles (km)	Volume cubic miles (km³)
North Pacific Ocean and subdivisions (continued)							
7.4.1	Bo Hai	30,890 (80,000)	82 (25)	164 (50)	217 (350)	72–192 (120–320)	480 (2,000)
7.4.2	Liaodong Gulf	8,110 (21,000)	82 (25)	164 (50)	112 (180)	75 (120)	126 (525)
7.5	Inland Sea of Japan	8,500 (22,000)	121 (37)	197 (60)	233 (375)	6–105 (10–175)	195 (814)
7.6.1	Tatar Strait	23,940 (62,000)	246 (75)	3,281 (1,000)	311 (500)	78 (125)	1,116 (4,650)
7.7	Sea of Okhotsk	613,800 (1,589,700)	2,749 (838)	12,001 (3,658)	to 1,020 (1,700)	to 780 (1,300)	319,649 (1,332,169)
7.8	Bering Sea	884,900 (2,291,900)	5,075 (1,547)	15,659 (4,773)	1,490 (2,397)	990 (1,593)	850,746 (3,545,569)
7.8.1	Gulf of Anadyr	37,070 (96,000)	246 (75)	492 (150)	200 (320)	250 (400)	1,728 (7,200)
7.9	Bering Strait	29,350 (76,000)	133 (40)	164 (50)	236 (380)	60–180 (100–300)	729 (3,040)
7.10	Gulf of Alaska	592,000 (1,533,000)	8,203 (2,500)	16,405 (5,000)	to 1,200 (2,000)	to 240 (400)	919,594 (3,832,500)
7.11	Coastal Waters of Southeast Alaska and British Colombia	13,900 (36,000)	9,843 (3,000)	12,468 (3,800)	932 (1,500)	to 99 (160)	25,914 (108,000)
7.12	Gulf of California	62,000 (160,580)	3,937 (1,200)	10,000 (3,050)	750 (1,200)	200 (320)	44,054 (183,600)
7.13	Gulf of Panama	8,570 (22,200)	246 (75)	328 (100)	99 (160)	115 (185)	400 (1,665)
Other subdivisions of the North Pacific Ocean							
–	Amurskiy Liman	2,160 (5,600)	82 (25)	164 (50)	87 (140)	12–39 (20–65)	34 (140)
–	Bristol Bay	18,530 (48,000)	82 (25)	164 (50)	200 (320)	to 180 (300)	288 (1,200)
–	Cheju Strait	3,860 (10,000)	246 (75)	328 (100)	103 (165)	37 (60)	180 (750)
–	Gulf of Tehuantepec	12,160 (31,500)	984 (300)	3,281 (1,000)	326 (525)	75 (120)	2,267 (9,450)
–	Gulf of Santa Catalina	3,670 (9,500)	394 (120)	656 (200)	68 (110)	62 (100)	274 (1,140)
–	Hecate Strait	7,920 (20,500)	1,476 (450)	3,281 (1,000)	160 (257)	40–60 (64–129)	2,214 (9,225)
–	Strait of La Perouse	4,830 (12,500)	246 (75)	328 (100)	130 (210)	27–51 (45–85)	225 (938)
–	Korea Bay	13,900 (36,000)	98 (30)	164 (50)	165 (265)	121 (195)	259 (1080)
–	Korea Strait	2,510 (6,500)	295 (90)	328 (100)	62 (100)	30–48 (50–80)	140 (585)
–	Queen Charlotte Sound	7,410 (19,200)	1,575 (480)	3,281 (1,000)	124 (200)	75 (120)	2,211 (9,216)
–	Sakhalin Gulf	2,900 (7,500)	98 (30)	164 (50)	47 (75)	36–96 (60–160)	54 (225)
–	Santa Barbara Channel	2,320 (6,000)	1,312 (400)	1,641 (500)	75 (120)	31 (50)	576 (2,400)
–	San Pedro Channel	770 (2,000)	394 (120)	656 (200)	28 (45)	28 (45)	58 (240)
–	Sea of Japan	377,600 (978,000)	5,748 (1,752)	12,276 (3,742)	1,740 (2,800)	to 540 (900)	411,137 (1,713,456)
–	Strait of Georgia	1,450 (3,750)	328 (100)	1,200 (370)	138 (222)	17 (28)	90 (375)
–	Strait of Juan de Fuca	1,310 (3,400)	394 (120)	900 (275)	80–100 (130–160)	16 (25)	98 (408)
–	Gulf of Shelikhova	69,500 (180,000)	410 (125)	1,624 (495)	420 (670)	185 (300)	5,399 (22,500)
South Pacific Ocean and subdivisions							
8	South Pacific Ocean	–	–	35,704 (10,882)	4,139 (6,660)	to 10,800 (18,000)	–
8.1	Bismarck Sea	194,227 (503,000)	6,600 (2,000)	8,200 (2,500)	497 (800)	249 (400)	241,386 (1,006,000)
8.2	Solomon Sea	278,019 (720,000)	14,765 (4,500)	29,988 (9,140)	621 (1,000)	497 (800)	777,425 (3,240,000)
8.3	Coral Sea	1,849,000 (4,788,888)	7,870 (2,398)	25,134 (7,661)	1,400 (2,250)	1,500 (2,414)	2,758,421
8.3.1	Torres Strait	10,430 (27,000)	246 (75)	328 (100)	130 (210)	80 (130)	486 (2,025)
8.3.2	Great Barrier Reef	134,286 (347,800)	197 (60)	328 (100)	1,250 (2,000)	30–95 (50–152)	3,599 (15,000)
8.3.3	Gulf of Papua	14,670 (38,000)	213 (65)	328 (100)	95 (150)	225 (360)	593 (2,470)
8.4	Tasman Sea	1,545,000 (4,001,530)	9,023 (2,750)	17,000 (5,182)	1,243 (2,000)	1,400 (2,253)	2,639,407
8.4.1	Bass Strait	28,950 (75,000)	210 (60)	262 (80)	224 (360)	150 (240)	1,080 (4,500)
Other subdivisions of the South Pacific Ocean							
–	Bay of Plenty	3,090 (8,000)	328 (100)	820 (250)	99 (160)	37 (60)	192 (800)
–	Cook Strait	2,120 (5,500)	420 (128)	3,445 (1,050)	81 (130)	14 (23)	169 (704)
–	Foveaux Strait	970 (2,500)	98 (30)	164 (50)	43 (70)	22 (35)	18 (75)
–	Gulf of Guayaquil	5,410 (14,000)	82 (25)	197 (60)	124 (200)	87 (140)	84 (350)
Arctic Ocean and subdivisions							
9	Arctic Ocean	5,440,000 (14,090,000)	4,690 (1,430)	18,455 (5,625)	to 3,100 (5,000)	to 2,000 (3,200)	4,834,603 (20,148,700)
9.1	East Siberian Sea	361,000 (936,000)	328 (100)	510 (155)	777 (1,250)	497 (800)	22,459 (93,600)
9.2	Laptev Sea	250,900 (649,800)	1,896 (578)	9,774 (2,980)	528 (850)	497 (800)	90,120 (375,584)
9.3	Kara Sea	340,000 (880,000)	417 (127)	2,034 (620)	932 (1,500)	559 (900)	26,816 (111,760)
9.4	Barents Sea	542,000 (1,405,000)	750 (229)	1,969 (600)	808 (1,300)	650 (1,050)	77,201 (321,745)
9.5	White Sea	36,680 (95,000)	200 (60)	1,115 (340)	261 (420)	249 (400)	1,368 (5,700)
9.6	Greenland Sea	353,320 (915,000)	4,750 (1,450)	16,000 (4,800)	808 (1,300)	621 (1,000)	318,349 (1,326,750)
9.7	Norwegian Sea	328,220 (850,000)	5,254 (1,600)	13,020 (3,970)	870 (1,400)	684 (1,100)	326,327 (1,360,000)
9.8	Iceland Sea	111,980 (290,000)	3,701 (1,128)	9,843 (3,000)	404 (650)	280 (450)	78,491 (327,120)
9.9	Davis Strait	115,840 (300,000)	1,476 (450)	4,922 (1,500)	404 (650)	200–400 (322–644)	32,393 (135,000)

Ocean Fact File

IHO	Names of oceans and seas	Area square miles (km²)	Average depth feet (m)	Greatest known depth: feet (m)	Length miles (km)	Width miles (km)	Volume cubic miles (km³)
Arctic Ocean and subdivisions (continued)							
9.10	Hudson Strait	37,070 (96,000)	1,641 (500)	3,090 (942)	497 (800)	40–150 (65–240)	11,517 (48,000)
9.11	Hudson Bay	475,800 (1,232,300)	420 (128)	600 (183)	590 (950)	590 (950)	37,848 (157,734)
9.12	Baffin Bay	266,000 (689,000)	6,234 (1,900)	7,000 (2,100)	900 (1,450)	68–400 (110–650)	314,113 (1,309,100)
9.13	Lincoln Sea	57,920 (150,000)	2,461 (750)	9,394 (2,863)	249 (400)	236 (380)	26,994 (112,500)
9.14	Northwestern Passages	–	492 (150)	656 (200)	–	–	–
9.15	Beaufort Sea	184,000 (476,000)	3,239 (1,004)	15,360 (4,682)	684 (1100)	404 (650)	114,671 (477,904)
9.16	Chukchi Sea	225,000 (582,000)	253 (77)	7,218 (2,200)	559 (900)	435 (700)	10,753 (44,814)
Other subdivisions of the Arctic Ocean							
–	Fox Basin	55,600 (144,000)	492 (150)	656 (200)	280 (450)	249 (400)	5,183 (21,600)
–	James Bay	30,890 (80,000)	164 (50)	230 (70)	275 (443)	135 (217)	960 (4,000)
–	Kane Basin	7,720 (20,000)	492 (150)	656 (200)	124 (200)	62 (100)	720 (3,000)
–	Pechora Sea	34,750 (90,000)	20 (6)	689 (210)	249 (400)	162 (260)	130 (540)
–	Wandel Sea	28,960 (75,000)	1,148 (350)	1,955 (596)	186 (300)	155 (250)	6,299 (26,250)
Southern Ocean and subdivisions							
10	Southern Ocean	7,850,000 (20,327,000)	14,750 (4,500)	23,736 (7,235)	to 12,900 (21,500)	240–1,620 (400–2,700)	21,948,232 (91,471,500)
10.1	Weddell Sea	1,080,000 (2,800,000)	13,124 (4,000)	16,405 (5,000)	to 1,200 (to 2,000)	to 1,200 (2,000)	2,687,397 (11,200,000)
10.2	Lazarev Sea	185,350 (480,000)	11,484 (3,500)	13,124 (4,000)	497 (800)	373 (600)	403,109 (1,680,000)
10.3	Riiser-Larsen Sea	260,640 (675,000)	12,468 (3,800)	13,124 (4,000)	559 (900)	404 (650)	615,462 (2,565,000)
10.4	Cosmonauts Sea	386,140 (1,000,000)	14,108 (4,300)	16,405 (5,000)	621 (1,000)	621 (1,000)	1,031,768 (4,300,000)
10.5	Cooperation Sea	386,140 (1,000,000)	9,515 (2,900)	13,124 (4,000)	621 (1,000)	621 (1,000)	695,844 (2,900,000)
10.6	Davis Sea	347,520 (900,000)	6,562 (2,000)	9,843 (3,000)	621 (1,000)	559 (900)	431,903 (1,800,000)
10.6.1	Tryoshnikova Gulf	34,750 (90,000)	6,562 (2,000)	9,843 (3,000)	280 (450)	to 240 (400)	43,190 (180,000)
10.7	Mawson Sea	96,530 (250,000)	6,562 (2,000)	9,843 (3,000)	311 (500)	311 (500)	119,973 (500,000)
10.8	Dumont d'Urville Sea	185,350 (480,000)	5,906 (1,800)	13,124 (4,000)	497 (800)	373 (600)	207,313 (864,000)
10.9	Somov Sea	100,400 (260,000)	6,562 (2,000)	6,562 (2,000)	404 (650)	249 (400)	124,772 (520,000)
10.10	Ross Sea	370,000 (960,000)	656 (200)	2,625 (800)	684 (1,100)	621 (1,000)	46,070 (192,000)
10.10.1	McMurdo Sound	3,860 (10,000)	3,281 (1,000)	3,281 (1,000)	92 (148)	46 (74)	2,399 (10,000)
10.11	Amundsen Sea	297,330 (770,000)	6,562 (2,000)	9,843 (3,000)	684 (1,100)	435 (700)	369,517 (1,540,000)
10.12	Bellingshausen Sea	173,760 (450,000)	6,562 (2,000)	9,843 (3,000)	435 (700)	404 (650)	215,952 (900,000)
10.13	Drake Passage	308,910 (800,000)	11,000 (3,400)	15,600 (4,800)	497 (800)	621 (1,000)	652,653 (2,720,000)
10.14	Bransfield Strait	26,260 (68,000)	1,148 (350)	1,641 (500)	249 (400)	106 (170)	5,711 (23,800)
Inland Seas (salt lakes not seas)							
–	Caspian Sea	152,239 (394,299)	591 (180)	3,104 (946)	746 (1,200)	102–270 (170–450)	17,030 (70,974)
–	Aral Sea	13,000 (33,800)	52 (16)	223 (68)	266 (428)	176 (284)	130 (541)
–	Dead Sea	394 (1,020)	313 (96)	1,310 (399)	48 (78)	10 (15)	23 (97)
–	Salton Sea	344 (890)	30 (9)	51 (16)	30 (48)	10 (16)	2 (8)
–	Sea of Galilee	64 (166)	79 (24)	157 (48)	13 (21)	7 (11)	1 (4)
Largest subdivisions of the oceans by surface area							
8.3	Coral Sea	1,849,000 (4,790,000)	7,870 (2,400)	25,134 (7,661)	1,400 (2,250)	1,500 (2,414)	2,758,421 (11,496,000)
7.1	Philippine Sea	1,776,230 (4,600,000)	19,700 (6,000)	34,578 (10,539)	to 1,800 (3,000)	to 1,200 (2,000)	6,622,513 (27,600,000)
8.4	Tasman Sea	1,545,000 (4,000,000)	9,023 (2,750)	17,000 (5,200)	1,243 (2,000)	1,400 (2,250)	2,639,407 (11,000,000)
5.9	Arabian Sea	1,491,000 (3,862,000)	8,970 (2,734)	16,405 (5,000)	to 1,243 (2,000)	to 1,320 (2,200)	2,533,521 (10,558,708)
–	Sargasso Sea	1,448,020 (3,750,000)	16,405 (5,000)	21,005 (6,402)	1,864 (3,000)	994 (1,600)	4,498,990 (18,750,000)
10.1	Weddell Sea	1,080,000 (2,800,000)	13,124 (4,000)	16,405 (5,000)	to 1,200 (2,000)	to 1,200 (2,000)	2,687,397 (11,200,000)
1.10	Caribbean Sea	1,049,500 (2,718,200)	8,685 (2,647)	25,218 (7,686)	1,678 (2,700)	360–840 (600–1,400)	1,726,430 (7,195,075)
3.1	Mediterranean Sea	969,000 (2,510,000)	4,688 (1,429)	16,897 (5,150)	2,500 (4,000)	500 (800)	860,636 (3,586,790)
6.1	South China Sea	895,400 (2,319,075)	5,419 (1,652)	16,456 (5,015)	to 1,182 (1,902)	to 840 (1,352)	919,231 (3,830,988)
7.8	Bering Sea	884,900 (2,291,880)	5,075 (1,547)	15,659 (4,773)	990 (1,593)	1,490 (2,397)	850,746 (3,545,569)
5.13	Bay of Bengal	839,000 (2,173,000)	8,500 (2,600)	15,400 (4,694)	1,056 (1,700)	994 (1,600)	1,355,648 (5,649,800)
1.11	Gulf of Mexico	615,000 (1,592,800)	4,874 (1,486)	12,425 (3,787)	1,100 (1,770)	800 (1,287)	567,929 (2,366,901)
7.7	Sea of Okhotsk	611,000 (1,582,483)	2,818 (859)	11,063 (3,742)	1,530 (2,463)	932 (1,500)	319,649 (1,332,169)
7.10	Gulf of Alaska	592,000 (1,533,273)	7,976 (2,431)	16,500 (5,029)	1,200 (2,000)	240 (400)	919,594 (3,832,500)
9.4	Barents Sea	542,000 (1,405,000)	750 (229)	2,000 (600)	800 (1,300)	650 (1,050)	77,201 (321,745)
9.11	Hudson Bay	475,800 (1,232,300)	420 (128)	600 (183)	590 (950)	590 (950)	37,848 (157,734)
5.1	Mozambique Channel	432,470 (1,120,000)	8,531 (2,600)	10,000 (3,000)	1,000 (1,600)	250–600 (400–950)	698,723 (2,912,000)
10.4	Cosmonauts Sea	386,140 (1,000,000)	14,108 (4,300)	16,405 (5,000)	621 (1,000)	621 (1,000)	1,031,768 (4,300,000)
10.5	Cooperation Sea	386,140 (1,000,000)	9,515 (2,900)	13,124 (4,000)	621 (1,000)	621 (1,000)	695,844 (2,900,000)

IHO	Names of oceans and seas	Area square miles (km²)	Average depth feet (m)	Greatest known depth: feet (m)	Length miles (km)	Width miles (km)	Volume cubic miles (km³)
Largest subdivisions of the oceans by surface area (continued)							
–	Sea of Japan	377,600 (977,979)	5,748 (1,751)	12,276 (3,742)	1,740 (2,800)	to 540 (900)	411,137 (1,713,456)
10.10	Rose Sea	370,000 (960,000)	656 (200)	2,625 (800)	684 (1,100)	621 (1,000)	46,070 (192,000)
5.17	Great Australian Bight	366,830 (950,000)	7,218 (2,200)	14,765 (4,500)	1,740 (2,800)	to 620 (1,000)	501,487 (2,090,000)
9.1	East Siberian Sea	361,000 (936,000)	328 (100)	510 (155)	777 (1,250)	497 (800)	22,459 (93,600)
9.6	Greenland Sea	353,320 (915,000)	4,750 (1,450)	16,000 (4,800)	808 (1,300)	621 (1,000)	318,349 (1,326,750)
4.2	Scotia Sea	348,000 (900,000)	11,500 (3,500)	27,651 (8,428)	870 (1,400)	497 (800)	755,830 (3,150,000)
10.6	Davis Sea	347,520 (900,000)	6,562 (2,000)	9,843 (3,000)	621 (1,000)	559 (900)	431,903 (1,800,000)
9.3	Kara Sea	340,000 (880,000)	417 (127)	2,034 (620)	932 (1,500)	559 (900)	26,816 (111,760)
9.7	Norwegian Sea	328,220 (850,000)	5,254 (1,600)	13,020 (3,970)	870 (1,400)	684 (1,100)	326,327 (1,360,000)
1.9	Gulf of Guinea	324,360 (840,000)	12,796 (3,900)	16,405 (5,000)	435 (700)	746 (1,200)	786,064 (3,276,000)
10.13 + 4.3	Drake Passage	308,910 (800,000)	11,000 (3,400)	15,600 (4,800)	497 (800)	621 (1,000)	652,653 (2,720,000)
5.14	Andaman Sea	308,000 (797,700)	2,854 (870)	12,392 (3,777)	750 (1,200)	400 (645)	166,522 (693,999)
10.11	Amundsen Sea	297,330 (770,000)	6,562 (2,000)	9,843 (3,000)	684 (1,100)	435 (700)	369,517 (1,540,000)
5.10	Lakshadweep Sea	289,600 (750,000)	7,874 (2,400)	14,765 (4,500)	to 932 (1,500)	to 620 (1,000)	431,903 (1,800,000)
7.3	East China Sea	284,000 (735,800)	574 (175)	8,913 (2,717)	684 (1,100)	435 (700)	30,897 (128,765)
8.2	Solomon Sea	278,019 (720,000)	14,765 (4,500)	29,988 (9,140)	621 (1,000)	497 (800)	777,425 (3,240,000)
9.12	Baffin Bay	266,000 (689,000)	6,234 (1,900)	7,000 (2,100)	900 (1,450)	70–400 (110–650)	314,113 (1,309,100)
10.3	Riiser-Larsen Sea	260,640 (675,000)	12,468 (3,800)	13,124 (4,000)	559 (900)	404 (650)	615,462 (2,565,000)
5.16	Arafura Sea	250,990 (650,000)	230 (70)	12,000 (3,660)	to 620 (1,000)	to 435 (700)	10,918 (45,500)
9.2	Laptev Sea	250,900 (649,800)	1,896 (578)	9,774 (2,980)	528 (850)	497 (800)	90,120 (375,584)
5.15	Timor Sea	235,000 (615,000)	459 (140)	10,800 (3,300)	609 (980)	435 (700)	20,659 (86,100)
9.16	Chukchi Sea	225,000 (582,000)	253 (77)	7,218 (2,200)	559 (900)	435 (700)	10,753 (44,814)
1.2	North Sea	222,100 (575,200)	308 (94)	2,165 (660)	621 (1,000)	93–373 (150–600)	12,974 (54,069)
1.15	Labrador Sea	222,030 (575,000)	6,562 (2,000)	12,468 (3,800)	to 870 (1,400)	to 492 (820)	275,938 (1,150,000)
5.5	Gulf of Aden	205,000 (530,000)	4,922 (1,500)	17,586 (5,360)	920 (1,480)	300 (480)	190,757 (795,000)
8.1	Bismarck Sea	194,227 (503,000)	6,600 (2,000)	8,200 (2,500)	497 (800)	249 (400)	241,386 (1,006,000)
10.2	Lazarev Sea	185,350 (480,000)	11,484 (3,500)	13,124 (4,000)	497 (800)	373 (600)	403,109 (1,680,000)
10.8	Dumont d'Urville Sea	185,350 (480,000)	5,906 (1,800)	13,124 (4,000)	497 (800)	373 (600)	207,313 (864,000)
9.15	Beaufort Sea	184,000 (476,000)	3,239 (1,004)	15,360 (4,682)	684 (1,100)	404 (650)	114,671 (477,904)
6.15	Banda Sea	181,000 (470,000)	14,765 (4,500)	24,409 (7,440)	652 (1,050)	228–330 (380–550)	507,486 (2,115,000)
7.4	Yellow Sea	180,000 (466,200)	131 (40)	338 (103)	600 (960)	435 (700)	4,475 (18,648)
10.12	Bellingshausen Sea	173,760 (450,000)	6,562 (2,000)	9,843 (3,000)	435 (700)	404 (650)	215,952 (900,000)
5.4	Red Sea	169,100 (438,000)	1,611 (491)	9,974 (3,040)	1,200 (1,930)	190 (305)	51,602 (215,058
6.8	Java Sea	167,000 (433,000)	151 (46)	689 (210)	900 (1,450)	260 (420)	4,779 (19,918)
2	Baltic Sea	163,000 (422,200)	180 (55)	1,380 (421)	795 (1,280)	324 (540)	5,572 (23,221)

UNESCO Marine Heritage sites

UNESCO World Heritage sites are designated as part of the United Nations International World Heritage Programme. All have exceptional natural or cultural features. Like other natural areas recognized by UNESCO, marine sites must possess remarkable natural beauty or have extraordinary ecological importance; many meet both these criteria. To date nearly 900 sites in 145 nations have been designated including a growing number of marine coastal areas that are endangered by development, pollution, or other threats.

1	Península Valdés, Argentina
2	Great Barrier Reef, Australia
3	Shark Bay, Australia
4	Macquarie Island, Australia
5	Belize Barrier Reef Reserve System
6	Lord Howe Island Group, Australia
7	Brazilian Atlantic Islands
8	Cocos Island National Park, Costa Rica
9	Area de Conservacion, Guanacaste, Costa Rica
10	Desembarco de Granma National Park, Cuba
11	Ilulissat Ice Fjord, Denmark
12	Galapagos Islands, Ecuador
13	High Coast/Kvarken Archipelago, Finland & Sweden
14	The lagoons of New Caledonia
15	Gulf of Porto, Corsica
16	Isole Aolie (Aeolian Islands), Italy
17	Surtsey, Iceland
18	Shiretoko, Hokkaido, Japan
19	MacDonald and Heard Islands, Australia

20	Gulf of California, Mexico, Islands, and Protected Areas
21	Sian Ka'an, Mexico
22	West Norwegian Fjords, Norway
23	El Vizcaino Whale Sanctuary, Mexico
24	New Zealand Sub-Antarctic Islands
25	Tewahipounamu, Southwest New Zealand
26	Coiba National Park, Panama
27	Tubbataha Reef Marine Park, Philippines
28	Natural System of Wrangel Island Reserve, Russian Federation
29	Pitons Management Area, St Lucia
30	Aldabra Atoll, Seychelles
31	East Rennell, Solomon Islands
32	Dorset & East Devon Coast, UK
33	Giants Causeway and Causeway Coast, UK
34	Gough and Inaccessible Islands, UK
35	Henderson Island, UK
36	Hawaii Volcanoes National Park, Hawaii, USA
37	Ha Long Bay, Vietnam
38	Socotra Archipelago, Yemen

GLOSSARY

Abyssal plain

The flat area of an ocean basin between the continental slope and the mid-ocean ridge.

Abyssal zone

Ocean depths between 13,120 and 19,680 feet (4,000 and 6,000 m).

Adaptation

A change in an animal's behavior or body that allows it to survive and breed in new conditions.

Algae

Simple plants that are found as single cells or as seaweeds.

Antarctic circle

The line of latitude at 66°33'S marking the northern limit of the Antarctic region.

Aphotic zone

The part of the ocean where no surface light can penetrate.

Archipelago

A group of islands or an area that contains many small islands.

Arctic circle

The line of latitude at 66°33'N marking the southern limit of where the sun does not set in June or rise at December solstices.

Ascidian

The sea squirts—a group of invertebrates that produce a larvae with a primitive backbone.

Astrolabe

An early navigation instrument that was the forerunner of the sextant.

Atoll

A coral reef that has formed around a central lagoon.

Austral

Relating to the southern hemisphere.

AUV

Autonomous Underwater Vehicle—an unmanned, self-contained submersible.

Backwash

The water retreating down the shore after an incoming wave.

Baleen plates

Plates with frayed edges made out of keratin, the same material as hair and fingernails. Found in the mouths of certain whales instead of teeth, they are used for filter feeding.

Bar

A submerged or emerged mound of sand, gravel, or shell material built on the ocean floor in shallow water by waves and currents.

Barrier island

A ridge of sand, or gravel, that lies parallel to a coast.

Barrier reef

A coral reef around islands or along continental coasts, separated from the land by a deep lagoon.

Bathymetry

Study of the depth contours of all or part of an undersea area.

Bathypelagic zone

The ocean between 656 and 13,120 feet (200 and 4,000 m) deep.

Bathyscaphe

The earliest form of manned submersible.

Bay

A recess in the shore or an inlet of a sea between two capes or headlands, not as large as a gulf but larger than a cove.

Beach

The region of the shore where loose material, sand, mud, or pebbles, are deposited between high and low watermarks.

Benthic zone

The upper layers of the seabed and the water layer immediately above the seabed.

Berm

A horizontal ridge of sand or shingle running parallel to the shore, at the limit of wave action.

Biodiversity

The variety of plant and animal species found in a habitat on land or in the sea.

Bioluminescence

The generation of light by living organisms using the enzyme luciferin.

Bivalve

A mollusk, such as an oyster or a mussel, that has two shells that are joined at a hinge.

Bloom

The sudden increase in phytoplankton numbers, usually associated with seasonal changes.

Brash ice

Accumulations of floating ice made up of fragments not more than 6.6 feet (2 m) across; the wreckage of other forms of ice.

Cap rock

A hard, impervious rock that forms a layer above another rock and, as a result, seals it.

Carapace

The upper part of the shell of a turtle or tortoise.

Cephalopod

An advanced group of molluscs that includes the squids, octopuses, and cuttlefish.

Cetaceans

Whales and dolphins.

Channel

A body of water that connects two larger bodies of water (like the English Channel). A channel is also a part of a river or harbor that is deep enough to let ships sail through.

Chronometer

A watch or clock able to maintain its accuracy on long sea voyages.

Coelenterates

Gelatinous invertebrates with radial symmetry and sting cells.

Cold seep

Cold seawater, rich in methane, hydrogen sulphide, and hydrocarbons issuing from the seafloor.

Comet

A small astronomical body composed of ice and dust that orbits the Sun on an elongated path.

Continental drift

The theory that the present distribution of continents is the result of the fragmentation of one or more pre-existing supercontinents that have drifted apart.

Continental rise

The gently sloping base of the continental slope.

Continental shelf

The shallow, gently sloping edge of a continental landmass where it meets the sea.

Continental slope

The steeply inclined edge of continental plate below the continental shelf.

Copepod

One of a number of tiny freshwater and marine crustaceans.

Coral bleaching

The loss of color affecting coral reefs when the algae that live in them are killed or forced out.

Coriolis effect

The apparent tendency of a freely moving object to follow a curved path in relation to the rotating surface of Earth, similar to the apparent path of a ball thrown from a merry-go-round. Movement is to the right in the northern hemisphere and to the left in the southern hemisphere.

Crustaceans

Invertebrates with jointed limbs and hard chalky shells, such as lobsters, crabs, shrimps, and copepods.

Crustal plate

A segment of Earth's surface. Continental plates are about 25 miles (40 km) thick and oceanic plates 3.1 miles (5 km) thick.

Current

A flow of water in the sea, generated by wind, tidal movements, or thermohaline circulation.

Cyclone

An intense tropical wind system around a low pressure center with winds that move counterclockwise in the northern hemisphere, and clockwise in the southern hemisphere. Maximum sustained winds of 74 miles per hour (120 km/h) or greater. Also known as hurricanes or typhoons.

Deep-sea hydrothermal vent

A spring of superheated, mineral-rich water found on some ridges deep in the ocean.

Deep-sea trench

A long, narrow, steep-sided depression in the seafloor. Trenches occur at subduction zones, where one crustal plate sinks beneath another.

Density

The mass of a substance for a given volume.

Delta

A layer of sediment desposited at the mouth of a slow-moving river and protruding beyond the coastline.

Diatom

One of many kinds of tiny algae in marine and freshwater environments.

Dinoflagellate

One of many kinds of one-celled aquatic and mostly microscopic organisms bearing two dissimilar flagellae (long whip-like structures that let them turn, maneuver, and spin around), and having characteristics of both plants and animals.

Dune

An accumulation of windblown sand often found above the high tide mark on sand shores.

Ebb tide

The period of tide between high water and low water. A falling tide.

Echinoderms

Exclusively marine invertebrates with five-way symmetry and a water vascular system, including starfish, sea cucumbers and brittle stars.

Echiurans

A group of soft-bodied non-segmented worms found from the shore down to the bottom of ocean trenches.

Echolocation

The use of sound by whales and dolphins to sense objects.

Ecosystem

An interacting system of organisms and the environment to which they are adapted.

Eddy

A circular movement in the water produced by flows around obstructions or by interacting currents.

El Niño

The periodic warming of the surface waters in the east Pacific Ocean that stops upwelling of nutrients.

Endemic

A species, or other taxon, found only in one habitat or region.

Erosion

The wearing away of land by the action of natural forces. On a beach, the carrying away of beach material by wave action, tidal currents, littoral currents, or wind.

Estuary

A semi-enclosed area of water where the salinity departs strongly from ocean salinity, either from mixing with river water or from excessive evaporation.

Euphotic zone

The upper layers where there is sufficient light for photosynthesis.

Fast ice

Ice that is anchored to the shore or ocean bottom and does not move with the winds or currents.

Fetch

The distance over water in which waves are generated by a wind having a rather constant direction and speed.

Filter feeder

An animal that obtains food by straining small prey from seawater.

Flood tide

The period of tide between low water and high water. A rising tide.

Fossil fuels

Carbon-based materials, such as oil, coal, and natural gas, formed from the fossils of ancient plants and animals, and burned to produce energy and electricity.

Frazil ice

Frazil ice, a form of sea ice, refers to small ice crystals that form in the surface water when it reaches freezing temperature.

Fringing reef

A coral reef that forms around the shore of an island and gradually extends out to sea.

Gas bladder

The gas-filled buoyancy organ found in most bony fish.

Ghost net

A fishing net that has become detached from the vessel that set it and so floats freely in the sea where it may entangle marine life.

Gill

A structure used by aquatic animals to exchange dissolved gases and salts between their body fluids and the surrounding water.

Glacier

A mass of ice that moves over the underlying surface.

Global ocean conveyor belt

A circulation pattern that is driven by the sinking of cold water of high salinity in the North Atlantic and connects all oceans. Water moves into the Antarctic at depth and from there into the Indian and Pacific oceans, from where it returns to the North Atlantic at intermediate depth.

Gondwana

The southern supercontinent fragment comprising New Zealand, Antarctica, Australia, South America, Africa, and India. It existed as a separate landmass from 650 million years ago and began to break up only 130 million years ago.

Greenhouse effect

The warming of the lower layers of the atmosphere caused by the trapping of solar radiation by carbon dioxide and other gases.

Gulf

Part of the ocean or sea that is partly surrounded by land, usually on three sides; it is usually larger than a bay.

Gulf stream

The strong western boundary current flowing up the east coast of North America.

Guyot

A flat-topped seamount.

Gyre

A circular motion in a body of water.

Hadal zone

The ocean zone below 19,680 feet (6,000 m).

Headland

An area of high elevation more resistant to erosion than surrounding areas and less susceptible to flooding. Headlands can supply sand and gravel to beaches.

Hermatypic coral

Species living in tropical waters able to secrete sufficient calcium carbonate to form reefs.

High tide

The maximum elevation reached by each rising tide.

Holdfast

The multi-branched structure anchoring seaweeds to hard surfaces.

Holoplankton

Animals that live out their entire lifecycles floating in the water column.

Hot spot

In volcanology, local areas of high volcanic activity that do not occur at the edges of tectonic plates.

Hurricane

The name used for cyclones in the Atlantic and eastern Pacific oceans.

Hydrological cycle

The endless cycling of water between land, ocean, and atmosphere.

Hydrothermal vent

A spring of superheated, mineral rich water found on some ocean ridges.

Ice age

A cold phase in the climatic history of Earth during which large areas of land were covered by ice.

Ice sheet

The largest type of glacier.

Ice shelf

An area of floating ice, once part of a glacier, that is still attached to land.

Iceberg

A floated piece of ice broken off from glacier or ice sheet.

Intertidal zone

The area of a seashore that is washed by tides. It is covered by water at high tide and exposed to the air at low tide.

Invertebrate

A multicellular animal without a true backbone.

Kelps

A group of large fast-growing brown seaweeds.

Krill

A shrimp-like crustacean abundant in polar waters that is the principal food of baleen whales.

La Niña

Periods of unusually cold ocean temperatures in the equatorial Pacific that occur between El Niño events. An episode of La Niña brings these conditions for a minimum of five months.

Lagoon

A shallow body of water, as a pond or lake, usually connected to the sea.

Latitude
A measure of north-south location, relative to the equator at 0°.

Laurasia
One of the two continents that formed when the supercontinent Pangea separated. It includes Europe, North America, and Asia (not India). Similarity of plants and animals of these countries is explained by this former connection.

Littoral zone
The seashore between high and low tide marks.

Longitude
A measure of east-west location relative to the Prime Meridian (0°) that runs through the Greenwich Observatory, London, UK.

Longshore drift
The movement of beach material parallel to the coastline by combined wind and wave action.

Lophophore
The brush-like feeding organ of sea mats, horseshoe worms, and lamp shells.

Low tide
The minimum elevation reached by each falling tide.

Magma
Molten rock found below Earth's crust that is ejected by volcanoes and emerges at ocean ridges as lava.

Mangrove
Flowering shrubs and trees tolerant of salt water, found on low-lying tropical coasts and estuaries.

Mantle
The layer of Earth between the crust and the core.

Mariculture
The intensive cultivation of marine organisms in coastal areas in cages or on land in seawater ponds.

Medusa
The free-living bell or disc-like form of many coelenterates.

Meroplankton
The young stages of marine organisms that spend time in the plankton, before developing into non-planktonic adults.

Mid-ocean ridge
A region of the ocean floor where magma rises to the surface to create new ocean floor on either side of a central rift valley.

Migration
The movement of an animal from one place to another, often over long distances. Sea turtles, whales, seabirds, and many fish migrate through and above Earth's oceans.

Mollusks
A group of soft-bodied non-segmented invertebrates that includes sea snails, bivalves, and cephalopods.

Navigation
The science of position fixing and course plotting, using astronomical and other observations.

Neap tides
Tides with much smaller ranges than spring tides, that occur while the gravitational pulls of the Moon and the Sun on the oceans work against each other.

Neritic zone
The zone from high tide to the continental shelf break.

Nilas ice
A smooth thin sheet of sea ice formed of frazil sea ice crystals.

Ocean
One of the five great bodies of seawater defined by continental margins, the equator, and other arbitrary divisions.

Ocean desert
An ocean region devoid of nutrients and therefore of particularly high water clarity.

Oceanography
The scientific study of all aspects of the oceans.

Ore
A mineral or rock that contains a particular metal in a concentration that is high enough to make its extraction commercially viable. Hematite and iron ore are examples.

Osmoregulation
The regulation of the concentration of body fluids by aquatic animals.

Overfishing
The commercial fishing of natural populations so that breeding does not replenish what is removed.

Ozone
A gas that absorbs most of the harmful ultraviolet rays from the Sun and also prevents some heat loss from Earth; it occurs naturally in a thin layer in the stratosphere and is also an ingredient in photochemical smog.

Ozone layer
The thin layer of ozone gas, located roughly 15 miles (24 km) above Earth's surface, which shields us from ultraviolet rays generated by the Sun.

Pack ice
Sea ice that forms around the permanent ice sheets of polar regions in winter and which thins and retreats in summer.

Pancake ice
Uneven plate shapes of sea ice that occur when seawater movement disturbs newly melded ice crystals or nilas ice.

Pangea
The ancient supercontinent that once contained all of Earth's continents. It began to break up about 200 million years ago into Gondwana and Laurasia.

Pelagic zone
The water column above the benthic zone.

Photophores
Light-producing organs, especially common in deep-sea fish.

Photosynthesis
The biological conversion of carbon dioxide and water into sugars using solar energy.

Phytoplankton
Single-celled algae and other photosynthetic organisms floating in the surface layers of the oceans.

Piedmont glacier
A lobe of ice that forms when a valley glacier emerges from the mountain and spreads out on to the plain.

Pinnipeds
Seals, walruses, and sea lions.

Plastron
The bottom part of the shell of a turtle or tortoise.

Plate tectonics
The processes by which the plates that form Earth's surface are formed, moved, and destroyed.

Polar regions
The cold zones between the poles and either the Arctic or Antarctic circles.

Pollutant
A harmful substance or heat energy introduced into an ecosystem by human activities.

Polychaete
A group of marine segmented worms.

Polynesia
A large group of Pacific islands extending from The Hawaiian Islands south to New Zealand and east to Easter Island.

Polynyas
Areas of open water surrounded by sea ice, often of large extent that makes them navigable. Also spelled polynia.

Polyp
The sedentary body form of coelenterates, notably corals.

Predator
An animal that feeds by capturing and eating other animals.

Primary production
The biological conversion of inorganic carbon (carbon dioxide) into living material (organic carbon).

Projection
The system used to translate the three-dimensional form of Earth onto a two-dimensional map.

Radar
Radio Detection and Ranging, the use of pulsed radio waves to follow moving objects by analysing changes in reflected radio signals.

Remote sensing
The use of airborne or satellite sensors to map Earth's surface in space and time.

Reverse osmosis
The use of pressure to force water through semi-permeable membrane, leaving behind any dissolved salts. Used to obtain fresh water from seawater.

Roaring Forties
Areas of ocean either side of the equator between 40° and 50° N or S latitude, noted for high winds and rough seas.

Rogue wave
A single, unusually high wave created by the constructive interference of two or more smaller waves.

ROV
A Remotely Operated Vehicle, an unmanned submersible controlled and powered from the surface by an umbilical cord.

Salt marsh
An area of soft, wet land periodically covered by salt water, in temperate zones generally treeless with characteristic salt-tolerant plants such as reeds and samphire.

Sandbar
A low ridge of sand in shallow water close to a shore.

Scuba
Self-Contained Underwater Breathing Apparatus. The combination of a pressure compensated regulator or demand valve and high pressure compressed air cylinders for diving without an air supply from the surface.

Sea
A division of an ocean or a large body of salt water partially enclosed by land. The term is also used for large, usually saline, lakes that lack a natural outlet, such as the Caspian Sea and the Aral Sea. The term is used in a less geographically precise manner as synonymous with ocean.

Sea ice
Ice that forms when the surface of the ocean freezes.

Sea stack
A rocky tower or spire close to shore that has formed due to the erosion of a nearby headland by wave action, or by the collapse of a natural rock arch.

Seamount
A steep sided circular or elliptical projection from the seafloor that is more than 0.6 of a mile (1 km) in height.

Seasonality
The timing of major biological events cued by changes in light intensity and water temperature associated with the seasons in temperate latitudes.

Seawall
A vertical, wall-like coastal-engineering structure built parallel to the beach or duneline and usually located at the back of the beach or the seaward edge of the dune.

Sediment
Fine organic or mineral particles deposited on the seafloor, originating from the weathering of rocks and transported, suspended in, or deposited by air, water, or ice, or by other natural agents such as chemical precipitation.

Seismic survey
The use of high intensity sound waves to examine deep geological structures.

Sextant
A navigational instrument used to measure the angles between the Moon, the Sun, stars, and other objects such as the horizon.

Shear
The difference in speed of water movement in adjacent regions or layers creates friction and turbulence.

Shelf sea
The shallow but often highly productive seas over continental shelves.

Side-scan sonar
High resolution sound-imaging of the seabed.

Soft corals
Coral species that do not have a hard outer blanket of calcium carbonate. Soft corals do not form reefs.

Sonar
Sound Navigation and Ranging. The detection of objects in or on water using pulsed beams of sound waves and their reflected echoes.

Sponges
Invertebrates that consist of complex aggregations of cells, bound together by protein fibers and mineral spicules.

Spray zone
The area along a shore that is above the normal high-tide zone.

Spring tide
A tide that occurs at or near the time of a new or full moon with a large tidal rise and fall.

Strait
A narrow channel of water that connects two larger bodies of water, and thus lies between two landmasses.

Subduction zone
The area where one crustal plate is forced under another plate, giving rise to volcanic activity and earthquakes. These zones are usually marked by deep trench systems in the oceans.

Submersible
A small underwater vehicle designed for deep-sea research and other tasks.

Sunlight zone
The upper layer of the ocean where enough sunlight reaches to support the growth of phytoplankton.

Symbiosis
The close beneficial feeding relationship between two species.

Tethys Sea
The body of water partially enclosed by the C-shaped Pangean supercontinent. It was closed when Pangea split into Laurasia and Gondwana.

Thermohaline circulation
Water movement caused by differences in density produced by salinity and/or temperature changes.

Tide
The regular rising and falling of the sea that results from gravitational attraction of the Moon, the Sun, and other astronomical bodies acting upon rotating Earth.

Tide pool
A depression on a shore, usually rocky, that remains filled with seawater when exposed at low tide.

Tidewater glacier
A glacier that flows into the sea, producing icebergs as pieces break off.

Trade winds
The steady winds that blow from east to west, toward the equator to replace hot air rising from the equatorial region.

Transit time
The time it takes a water particle to travel through a described region. Also the time it takes to empty and replace all water in a described region.

Transport
The amount of water carried by a current in mass or volume per unit time.

Trench
A narrow deep depression in the ocean floor, often associated with the subduction of an oceanic plate at a continental margin.

Trophic web
The complex feeding relationships between plants and animals in a habitat.

Tropics
The zone between the Tropic of Cancer (23°27'N) and the Tropic of Capricorn (23°27'S) which approximates to the area of the ocean where water temperatures remain above 69°F (20°C).

Tsunami
A huge wave created by earthquake or volcanic explosion that can cause massive destruction in coastal areas. Mistakenly called a "tidal wave."

Typhoon
The name used for cyclones in the western Pacific Ocean, including the China Sea.

Upwelling
The rising of deep cold nutrient laden waters into the surface layers, close to continental coasts.

Water budget
The balance sheet of water entering and leaving a region; includes effect of currents, rainfall, evaporation, and rivers.

Water lens
A body of water wedged between two other layers of water and kept together in lentil-shaped form.

Wave
The disturbance in water caused by the movement of energy through the water.

Zooanthellae
Single-celled photosynthetic organisms that live in coral tissues in a symbiotic relationship.

Zooplankton
Small animals that spend all or part of their lifecycles floating in the surfaces layers of the ocean, either grazing on phytoplankton or preying on other zooplankton.

Abbot Ice Shelf–Brodeur Peninsula

GAZETTEER

Glossary of foreign terms

Archipièlag	archipelago
Bahía	bay
Baja, Bajo	shoal
Boca	channel, river
Bocche, Bogazi	strait
Cabo, Cap, Capo	cape
Cayo	key
Dao	island
Damagheh	cape
Dawhat	bay, cove, inlet
Denizi	sea
Ensenada	bay, cove
Golfe, Golfo	gulf
Île, Isla, Isola	island
Jazirat, Jazireh	islands
Kepulauan	archipelago islands
Ko, Koh	island
Khawr, Khowr	bay, channel, inlet
Kólpos, Körfezi	gulf
Laguna	lagoon
Mui	cape, point
Mys	cape, point
Peñón	point, rock
Punta	point
Ra's, Ras, Râs	cape
Selat, Stretto	strait
Tanjung	cape, point
Teluk	bay

A

Abbot Ice Shelf, *Sou.*	104	L-12
Abd al Kūrī, *Ind.*	150	M-8
Abrolhos Bank, *Atl.*	133	N-6
Abruka, *Atl.*	117	U-8
Abu al Jirab, *Ind.*	153	V-9
Abu Musa, *Ind.*	153	W-7
Abū Shawk Reefs, *Ind.*	149	S-8
Academician Berg Seamount, *Pac.*	174	H-2
Acklins Island, *Atl.*	123	Q-2
Adak Island, *Pac.*	171	T-8
Adana Trough, *Atl.*	129	X-8
Adare Seamounts, *Sou.*	107	W-13
Adelaide Island, *Sou.*	105	N-7
Adi, *Pac.*	189	Y-11
Admiralty Island, *Pac.*	173	W-4
Admiralty Islands, *Pac.*	191	T-9
Adonara, *Pac.*	189	S-13
Adriatic Sea, *Atl.*	129	P-4
Adventure Bank, *Atl.*	129	P-8
Aegean Sea, *Atl.*	129	U-7
Aegir Ridge, *Arc.*	98	K-11
Afanasy Nikitin Seamount, *Ind.*	159	O-5
Afognak Island, *Pac.*	173	P-3
Africana II Seamount, *Ind.*	162	H-11
Agassiz Fracture Zone, *Pac.*	211	N-7
Agatti, *Ind.*	151	V-8
Agattu Island, *Pac.*	171	Q-8
Agattu Strait, *Pac.*	171	Q-7
Agrihan, *Pac.*	191	T-2
Agulhas Bank, *Ind.*	155	O-11
Agulhas Basin, *Ind.*	155	P-13
Agulhas Plateau, *Ind.*	155	P-12
Agulhas Ridge, *Ind.*	155	N-12
Ahe, *Pac.*	213	P-9
Ahunui, *Pac.*	213	R-11
Air Force Island, *Arc.*	101	S-10
Aitutaki, *Pac.*	212	K-11
Akademii Nauk Rise, *Pac.*	177	S-8
Akiaki, *Pac.*	213	S-11
Akkeshi-wan, *Pac.*	179	Y-8
Akuseki-shima, *Pac.*	181	U-8
Akutan Island, *Pac.*	171	W-7
Al Ḩanīsh al Kabīr, *Ind.*	150	I-7
Al Jazirah, *Ind.*	153	T-7
Al Qaffāy, *Ind.*	153	T-9
Al Yāsāt, *Ind.*	153	T-9
Alamagan, *Pac.*	191	T-2
Åland, *Atl.*	117	T-6
Ålands Hav, *Atl.*	117	S-6
Alaska Peninsula, *Pac.*	173	N-4
Albatross Bay, *Pac.*	195	W-11
Alboran Ridge, *Atl.*	128	J-8
Alboran Sea, *Atl.*	128	I-8
Aldabra Islands, *Ind.*	157	W-1
Alderney, *Atl.*	127	W-2
Alenuihaha Channel, *Pac.*	175	W-7
Aleutian Basin, *Pac.*	171	R-5
Aleutian Islands, *Pac.*	171	P-7
Aleutian Rise, *Pac.*	171	P-7
Aleutian Trench, *Pac.*	171	Q-8
Alexander Archipelago, *Pac.*	173	V-3
Alexander Island, *Sou.*	105	O-8
Alexandra Land, *Arc.*	99	R-6
Algerian Basin, *Atl.*	128	L-8
Alijos Rocks, *Pac.*	207	S-11
Alor, *Pac.*	189	S-14
Alpha Ridge, *Arc.*	97	R-7
Alula-Fartak Trench, *Ind.*	155	U-3
Amakusa-nada, *Pac.*	179	P-15
Amakusa-Shimo-shima, *Pac.*	179	P-15
Amami-Ō-shima, *Pac.*	181	U-9
Amanu, *Pac.*	213	R-10
Amazon Cone, *Atl.*	132	L-1
Ambelau, *Pac.*	189	U-11
Ambon, *Pac.*	189	U-11
Ambrym, *Pac.*	197	Y-5
Amchitka Island, *Pac.*	171	S-8
Amchitka Pass, *Pac.*	171	S-8
American-Antarctic Ridge, *Atl.*	133	Q-14
Amery Ice Shelf, *Sou.*	103	W-7
Amindivi Islands, *Ind.*	151	V-8
Amini, *Ind.*	151	W-8
Amirante Islands, *Ind.*	155	T-6
Amirante Trench, *Ind.*	155	U-6
Amlia Island, *Pac.*	171	U-7
Ampere Seamount, *Atl.*	113	S-8
Amsterdam Fracture Zone, *Ind.*	163	O-12
Amsterdam Island, *Ind.*	163	P-12
Amukta Pass, *Pac.*	171	V-8
Amund Ringnes Island, *Arc.*	101	O-5
Amundsen Abyssal Plain, *Sou.*	103	N-9
Amundsen Coast, *Sou.*	107	S-2
Amundsen Gulf, *Arc.*	100	I-7
Amundsen Ridges, *Sou.*	103	P-9
Amundsen Sea, *Sou.*	103	P-8
Anaa, *Pac.*	213	P-10
Anatahan, *Pac.*	191	T-2
Anatolian Trough, *Atl.*	130	L-8
Anatom, *Pac.*	197	Y-6
Anaximander Mountains, *Atl.*	129	V-8
Andaman Basin, *Ind.*	147	W-11
Andaman Islands, *Ind.*	147	W-9
Andaman Sea, *Ind.*	147	X-11
Andreanof Islands, *Pac.*	171	T-8
Andros Island, *Atl.*	123	N-1
Andrott, *Ind.*	151	W-8
Anegada, *Atl.*	123	W-4
Ängesön, *Atl.*	117	T-4
Angola Abyssal Plain, *Atl.*	137	O-2
Angola Basin, *Atl.*	137	O-1
Anguilla, *Atl.*	123	W-4
Anguilla Cays, *Atl.*	121	Y-6
Anholt, *Atl.*	117	O-9
Anjouan, *Ind.*	157	V-3
Annobón, *Atl.*	135	W-7
Antalya Basin, *Atl.*	129	W-8
Antarctic Canyon, *Sou.*	105	U-9
Antarctic Peninsula, *Sou.*	105	P-6
Antigua, *Atl.*	123	X-5
Antipodes Islands, *Pac.*	203	S-7
Anvers Island, *Sou.*	105	O-5
Anxious Bay, *Ind.*	161	X-3
Ao Ban Don, *Pac.*	187	P-7
Ao Sawi, *Pac.*	187	P-6
Apalachee Bay, *Atl.*	121	W-2
Apulian Plateau, *Atl.*	129	R-7
Aquarius Seachannel, *Pac.*	173	O-7
Arabian Basin, *Ind.*	151	R-7
Arabian Sea, *Ind.*	151	R-5
Arafura Sea, *Pac.*	195	R-8
Arafura Shelf, *Pac.*	195	R-9
Aratika, *Pac.*	213	P-10
Archipelago de Colon, *Pac.*	209	V-3
Archipelago de los Canarreos, *Atl.*	122	L-2
Archipelago of the Recherche, *Ind.*	161	Q-4
Archipiélago de Camagüey, *Atl.*	123	N-2
Archipiélago de los Jardines de la Reina, *Atl.*	123	N-3
Archipiélago de Sabana, *Atl.*	122	M-1
Ardasier Reefs, *Pac.*	185	T-9
Argentine Abyssal Plain, *Atl.*	132	K-11
Argentine Basin, *Atl.*	132	K-10
Argo Bank, *Pac.*	197	U-7
Argo Fracture Zone, *Ind.*	155	W-8
Argolikos Basin, *Atl.*	129	T-8
Argonaut Seamount, *Pac.*	175	N-2
Ariaga, *Pac.*	189	T-6
Arlington Reef, *Pac.*	199	R-7
Arnhem Land, *Pac.*	195	R-11
Arthur, *Arc.*	99	S-6
Aru Basin, *Pac.*	189	Y-12
Arzanah, *Ind.*	153	U-8
As Sa'dīyāt, *Ind.*	153	V-9
Ascension, *Atl.*	133	S-3
Ascension Fracture Zone, *Atl.*	133	R-3
Ashizuri-misaki, *Pac.*	179	S-14
Ashmore Reef, *Pac.*	199	Q-1
Assumption Island, *Ind.*	157	W-1
Astove Island, *Ind.*	157	Y-2
Astrid Ridge, *Sou.*	103	T-3
Asuncion, *Pac.*	191	T-1
Atauro, *Pac.*	189	T-14
Atchafalaya Bay, *Atl.*	121	R-3
Atiu, *Pac.*	212	K-11
Atka Island, *Pac.*	171	U-7
Atlantic Ocean, *Atl.*	111	C-14
Atlantic-Indian Basin, *Sou.*	103	T-2
Atlantic-Indian Ridge, *Ind.*	155	N-14
Atlantis Fracture Zone, *Atl.*	112	M-8
Atlantis II Deep, *Ind.*	149	R-8
Atlantis II Fracture Zone, *Ind.*	155	V-11
Attu Island, *Pac.*	171	Q-7
Aua Island, *Pac.*	191	S-9
Auckland Islands, *Pac.*	203	P-8
Augustine Island, *Pac.*	169	T-3
Aur, *Pac.*	185	O-11
Aurora Canyon, *Sou.*	105	S-5
Austral Fracture Zone, *Pac.*	211	N-4
Austral Islands, *Pac.*	213	N-12
Australian-Antarctic Basin, *Ind.*	159	Q-14
Avalon Peninsula, *Atl.*	119	Y-5
Awaji-shima, *Pac.*	179	S-13
Awa-shima, *Pac.*	179	V-11
Axel Heiberg Island, *Arc.*	101	P-4
Az Zuqur, *Ind.*	150	H-7
Azores, *Atl.*	113	Q-7
Azores-Biscay Rise, *Atl.*	113	Q-6

B

Bāb al Mandab, *Ind.*	149	V-12
Baba Burnu, *Atl.*	131	R-6
Babar, *Pac.*	189	V-13
Babuyan, *Pac.*	185	X-3
Babuyan Channel, *Pac.*	185	W-4
Babuyan Islands, *Pac.*	185	X-3
Baby Brooks Bank, *Pac.*	175	P-5
Bacan, *Pac.*	189	U-9
Bada, *Pac.*	187	O-6
Badu Island, *Pac.*	195	X-9
Baffin Basin, *Arc.*	97	N-9
Baffin Bay, *Arc.*	101	S-7
Baffin Island, *Arc.*	101	Q-9
Bafra Burnu, *Atl.*	131	U-6
Bahía Chetumal, *Atl.*	121	T-9
Bahía Grande, *Atl.*	139	R-1
Bahía de Ballenas, *Pac.*	207	U-10
Bahía de Banderas, *Pac.*	207	Y-14
Bahía de Campeche, *Atl.*	121	Q-8
Bahía de Cook, *Atl.*	139	P-5
Bahía de Coronado, *Atl.*	122	K-9
Bahía de Espíritu Santo, *Atl.*	122	I-3
Bahía de la Ascensíon, *Atl.*	122	I-3
Bahía de La Paz, *Pac.*	207	V-11
Bahía de Samaná, *Atl.*	123	T-4
Bahía de San Juan del Norte, *Atl.*	122	K-8
Bahía de San Sebastián, *Atl.*	139	R-3
Bahía de Santa María, *Pac.*	207	W-11
Bahía Inútil, *Atl.*	139	Q-3
Bahía Magdalena, *Pac.*	207	V-11
Bahía Nassau, *Atl.*	139	R-5
Baía d'Ambaro, *Ind.*	157	Y-4
Baía de Bombetoka, *Ind.*	157	W-6
Baía de Fernão Veloso, *Ind.*	157	T-5
Baía de Mahajamba, *Ind.*	157	W-5
Baía de Memba, *Ind.*	157	T-4
Baía de Narinda, *Ind.*	157	X-5
Baía de Pemba, *Ind.*	157	T-4
Baía de Sofala, *Ind.*	157	O-9
Baía do Lúrio, *Ind.*	157	T-4
Baie de Audierne, *Atl.*	127	T-4
Baie de Bourgneuf, *Atl.*	127	W-5
Baie de Douarnenez, *Atl.*	127	T-4
Baie de Seine, *Atl.*	127	Y-2
Baie de St-Brieuc, *Atl.*	127	W-3
Baja California, *Pac.*	207	S-8
Bajau, *Pac.*	185	P-11
Baker Island, *Pac.*	167	P-9
Balabac Strait, *Pac.*	185	U-9
Balambangan, *Pac.*	189	N-5
Bald Head, *Ind.*	161	O-4
Bald Island, *Ind.*	161	O-4
Balearic Channel, *Atl.*	128	L-7
Balearic Islands, *Atl.*	128	L-7
Baler Bay, *Pac.*	185	W-5
Bali, *Pac.*	189	N-14
Bali Basin, *Pac.*	189	N-13
Bali Sea, *Pac.*	189	N-13
Balintang Channel, *Pac.*	185	W-3
Balleny Islands, *Sou.*	103	T-12
Ballons Seamont, *Pac.*	203	V-8
Balls Pyramid, *Pac.*	201	T-7
Baltic Sea, *Atl.*	117	R-10
Banco Chinchorro, *Atl.*	122	I-4
Banda Sea, *Pac.*	189	U-12
Banggai, *Pac.*	189	S-10
Banggi, *Pac.*	189	O-5
Bangka, *Pac.*	189	T-8
Banī Forūr, *Ind.*	153	W-7
Banks Island, *Arc.*	100	J-6
Banks Islands, *Pac.*	197	X-4
Banks Peninsula, *Pac.*	203	R-5
Banzare Seamounts, *Ind.*	159	N-15
Barīm (Perim), *Ind.*	149	V-13
Baranof Island, *Pac.*	173	W-4
Barbados, *Atl.*	112	L-11
Barbuda, *Atl.*	123	X-4
Barcoo Bank, *Pac.*	201	R-7
Barents Abyssal Plain, *Arc.*	99	Q-5
Barents Sea, *Arc.*	99	R-9
Barents Trough, *Arc.*	97	U-12
Barentsøya, *Arc.*	99	Q-8
Barne Inlet, *Sou.*	107	W-6
Barra Jesús María, *Atl.*	121	O-6
Barracuda Fracture Zone, *Atl.*	112	M-10
Barracuda Ridge, *Atl.*	112	L-10
Barren Island, *Ind.*	147	X-9
Bashi Channel, *Pac.*	185	W-3
Basilan, *Pac.*	189	R-5
Bass Strait, *Ind.*	159	Z-11
Bassas da India, *Ind.*	157	R-10
Batam, *Pac.*	185	O-12
Batan, *Pac.*	190	K-1
Batan Islands, *Pac.*	185	X-3
Batavia Seamount, *Ind.*	159	R-9
Bathurst Island, *Arc.*	101	N-6
Bathurst Island, *Pac.*	195	N-10
Batti Malv, *Ind.*	147	W-11
Batudaka, *Pac.*	189	Q-9
Bauer Basin, *Pac.*	211	S-2
Bauer Escarpment, *Pac.*	211	S-2
Bawal, *Pac.*	185	R-13
Bawean, *Pac.*	185	S-15
Bay of Bengal, *Ind.*	147	S-8
Bay of Biscay, *Atl.*	127	V-7
Bay of Fundy, *Atl.*	119	O-8
Bay of Plenty, *Pac.*	203	S-3
Baydaratskåya Guba, *Arc.*	99	W-9
Beachy Head, *Atl.*	115	S-13
Beagle Gulf, *Pac.*	195	O-11
Beata Ridge, *Atl.*	123	Q-6
Beauchene Island, *Atl.*	139	Y-2
Beaufort Sea, *Arc.*	97	P-4
Beethoven Peninsula, *Sou.*	105	N-9
Beirut Escarpment, *Atl.*	129	Y-10
Belgica Bank, *Arc.*	99	N-6
Belitung, *Pac.*	185	Q-13
Belle Isle, *Atl.*	119	X-1
Belle-Île, *Atl.*	127	V-5
Bellingshausen Plain, *Sou.*	103	N-7
Bellingshausen Sea, *Sou.*	103	O-7
Bellona Gap, *Pac.*	201	V-10
Benham Seamount, *Pac.*	166	J-7
Bentinck Island, *Pac.*	195	V-14
Benua, *Pac.*	185	Q-12
Bequia, *Atl.*	123	X-7
Berdyans'ka Kosa, *Atl.*	131	V-2
Bering Sea, *Pac.*	171	T-4
Bering Strait, *Pac.*	171	W-3
Berkner Island, *Sou.*	105	S-13
Bermuda Rise, *Atl.*	112	K-8
Bermuda, *Atl.*	112	K-8
Biak, *Pac.*	191	Q-9
Biaro, *Pac.*	189	T-8
Big Island, *Arc.*	101	T-13
Bight of Bangkok, *Pac.*	187	Q-2
Bight of Benin, *Atl.*	135	U-3
Bight of Biafra, *Atl.*	135	X-4
Bimini Islands, *Atl.*	121	Z-5
Bingaram, *Ind.*	151	V-8
Binongko, *Pac.*	189	S-12
Bintan, *Pac.*	185	P-12
Biscay Abyssal Plain, *Atl.*	127	S-8
Biscoe Islands, *Sou.*	105	N-6
Bismarck Archipelago, *Pac.*	183	Q-8
Bismarck Sea, *Pac.*	183	R-8
Bitra Reef, *Ind.*	151	V-8
Bjørnøya, *Arc.*	99	Q-9
Bjørnøya Bank, *Arc.*	99	Q-9
Black Coast, *Sou.*	105	Q-8
Black Sea, *Atl.*	131	S-5
Blackfin Ridge, *Pac.*	175	T-5
Blake Escarpment, *Atl.*	124	K-4
Blake Plateau, *Atl.*	121	Y-3
Blake Ridge, *Atl.*	124	M-3
Bo Hai, *Pac.*	181	P-3
Bo Hai Haixia, *Pac.*	181	Q-3
Bo Hai Wan, *Pac.*	181	O-3
Bode Verde Fracture Zone, *Atl.*	133	S-4
Bohol, *Pac.*	189	S-4
Bollons Seamount, *Sou.*	103	S-15
Bollons Tablemount, *Pac.*	193	U-12
Bonaire, *Atl.*	123	T-8
Bonavista Bay, *Atl.*	119	Y-4
Bone Basin, *Pac.*	189	Q-12
Bonerate, *Pac.*	189	Q-13
Boothia Peninsula, *Arc.*	101	N-9
Bora-Bora, *Pac.*	213	N-10
Borchgrevink Canyon, *Sou.*	107	W-14
Borchgrevink Coast, *Sou.*	107	X-13
Borden Island, *Arc.*	101	N-4
Borden Peninsula, *Arc.*	101	Q-8
Boreas Abyssal Plain, *Arc.*	99	O-8
Bornholm, *Atl.*	117	Q-10
Bosporus, *Atl.*	131	P-6
Bosporus Canyon, *Atl.*	131	P-6
Bottenviken (Bay of Bothnia), *Atl.*	117	U-2
Bougainville, *Pac.*	197	T-1
Bougainville Reef, *Pac.*	199	S-6
Bounty Islands, *Pac.*	203	T-7
Bounty Plateau, *Pac.*	203	T-7
Bounty Trough, *Pac.*	203	T-8
Bousade Seamount, *Pac.*	175	O-3
Bouvet Island, *Sou.*	103	S-1
Bouvetøya, *Atl.*	133	V-13
Bowers Bank, *Pac.*	171	S-7
Bowers Basin, *Pac.*	171	R-7
Bowers Canyon, *Sou.*	107	V-15
Bowers Ridge, *Pac.*	171	S-6
Bowie Seamount, *Pac.*	173	V-6
Bowman Bay, *Arc.*	101	R-12
Bowman Peninsula, *Sou.*	105	Q-10
Brabant Island, *Sou.*	105	O-5
Brampton Island, *Pac.*	199	U-10
Bransfield Strait, *Sou.*	105	P-4
Brazil Basin, *Atl.*	133	P-2
Bressay, *Atl.*	115	R-4
Brisbane Guyot, *Pac.*	197	T-9
Bristol Bay, *Pac.*	171	Y-6
Britannia Guyots, *Pac.*	197	T-9
Broad Sound, *Pac.*	199	U-12
Brodeur Peninsula, *Arc.*	101	P-8

Arc. Arctic Ocean *Atl.* Atlantic Ocean *Ind.* Indian Ocean *Pac.* Pacific Ocean *Sou.* Southern Ocean

Hokkaidō–Kotzebue Sound

Hokkaidō, *Pac.* 179 X-7
Hollick-Kenyon Peninsula, *Sou.* 105 P-7
Holmes Reef, *Pac.* 199 S-6
Holy Island, *Atl.* 115 O-5
Home Bay, *Arc.* 101 T-10
Hon Khoai, *Pac.* 187 V-8
Hon Rai, *Pac.* 187 V-6
Honshū, *Pac.* 166 K-5
Honshū, *Pac.* 179 U-13
Hooker, *Arc.* 99 S-6
Hopen, *Arc.* 99 Q-9
Horizon Deep, *Pac.* 193 V-6
Horizon Ridge, *Ind.* 159 S-7
Hormoz, *Ind.* 153 Y-6
Horn Island, *Pac.* 195 X-10
Horseshoe Seamounts, *Atl.* 113 R-7
Hotspur Fracture Zone, *Atl.* 133 R-5
Hotspur Seamount, *Atl.* 133 O-5
Howland Island, *Pac.* 167 P-9
Hoy, *Atl.* 115 P-5
Huahine, *Pac.* 213 N-10
Hudson Bay, *Arc.* 96 K-8
Hudson Strait, *Arc.* 101 U-13

I

Iğneada Burnu, *Atl.* 131 O-6
Iberian Abyssal Plain, *Atl.* 113 R-7
Ibiza, *Atl.* 128 L-7
Iceland, *Atl.* 113 Q-2
Iceland Basin, *Atl.* 113 Q-3
Iceland-Faeroe Rise, *Atl.* 113 R-2
Icelandic Plateau, *Arc.* 98 K-10
Icy Bay, *Pac.* 173 T-2
Ie-jima, *Pac.* 181 U-10
Ifalik, *Pac.* 191 T-6
Ihavandhippolhu Atoll, *Ind.* 151 V-10
Iheya-jima, *Pac.* 181 U-10
IJsselmeer, *Atl.* 115 V-11
Iki, *Pac.* 181 V-6
Iki-suidō, *Pac.* 179 P-14
Île Brion, *Atl.* 119 S-5
Île d'Anticosti, *Atl.* 119 S-3
Île d'Oléron, *Atl.* 127 X-7
Île d'Ouessant, *Atl.* 127 S-4
Île d'Yeu, *Atl.* 127 W-6
Île de l'Est, *Atl.* 119 S-5
Île de Jerba, *Atl.* 129 P-9
Île de la Gonâve, *Atl.* 123 Q-4
Île de la Tortue, *Atl.* 123 R-3
Île de Noirmoutier, *Atl.* 127 W-6
Île de Ré, *Atl.* 127 X-7
Île des Pins, *Pac.* 197 X-7
Île du Harve Aubert, *Atl.* 119 R-6
Île Europa, *Ind.* 157 S-10
Île Juan de Nova, *Ind.* 157 U-7
Île Lamèque, *Atl.* 119 Q-5
Île Tromelin, *Ind.* 155 U-8
Îles Barren, *Ind.* 157 V-8
Îles Chausey, *Atl.* 127 X-3
Îles de la Madeleine, *Atl.* 119 R-5
Îles de Mingan, *Atl.* 119 R-3
Îles du Vent, *Pac.* 213 N-10
Îles Glorieuses, *Ind.* 157 X-3
Îles Kerguelen, *Sou.* 103 Z-5
Îles Kerkenah, *Atl.* 129 P-9
Îles Maria, *Pac.* 212 M-12
Îles Palliser, *Pac.* 213 P-9
Îles Sous le Vent, *Pac.* 212 M-10
Ilha Benguérua, *Ind.* 157 P-10
Ilha da Trindade, *Atl.* 133 P-6
Ilha do Bazaruto, *Ind.* 157 P-10
Ilha Puga Puga, *Ind.* 157 S-6
Ilhas Martin Vas, *Atl.* 133 P-5
Îls de Groix, *Atl.* 127 U-5
Imarssuak Channel, *Atl.* 113 O-3
Ince Burun, *Atl.* 131 T-5
Independence Fjord, *Arc.* 97 R-10
Indian-Antarctic Ridge, *Ind.* 159 X-13
Indispensable Reefs, *Pac.* 197 V-3
Indomed Fracture Zone, *Ind.* 155 S-13
Indus Cone, *Ind.* 151 S-4
Instituta Okeanologii Rise, *Pac.* 177 T-6
Interview Island, *Ind.* 147 V-9
Inubō-zaki, *Pac.* 179 W-12
Investigator Group, *Ind.* 161 W-3
Investigator Ridge, *Ind.* 163 S-6
Ionian Basin, *Atl.* 129 R-8
Ionian Islands, *Atl.* 129 S-8
Ionian Sea, *Atl.* 129 R-7
Irō-zaki, *Pac.* 179 V-13
Irabu-jima, *Pac.* 181 S-11
Irbe Strait, *Atl.* 117 U-9
Ireland, *Atl.* 113 S-4
Irian Jaya, *Pac.* 195 S-5
Iriomote-jima, *Pac.* 181 R-12
Irish Sea, *Atl.* 113 T-4
Irminger Basin, *Atl.* 113 O-3
Isakov Seamount, *Pac.* 168 L-8
Iselin Bank, *Sou.* 107 T-12
Iselin Seamount, *Sou.* 103 S-11
Ise-wan, *Pac.* 179 U-13
Ishigaki-jima, *Pac.* 181 S-11
Ishikari-wan, *Pac.* 179 W-7
Isla Ángel de la Guarda, *Pac.* 207 U-8
Isla Aracena, *Atl.* 139 P-3
Isla Baltra, *Pac.* 209 W-5
Isla Beata, *Atl.* 123 R-5
Isla Blanquilla, *Atl.* 123 W-8
Isla Carmen, *Pac.* 207 V-11
Isla Cedros, *Pac.* 207 S-9
Isla Cerralvo, *Pac.* 207 W-11
Isla Clarence, *Atl.* 139 O-3
Isla Clarion, *Pac.* 207 T-15
Isla Coiba, *Atl.* 122 L-10
Isla Dawson, *Atl.* 139 P-3
Isla de Altamura, *Pac.* 207 W-11
Isla de Bioco, *Atl.* 135 X-4
Isla de Cozumel, *Atl.* 121 U-8
Isla de Guanaja, *Atl.* 122 J-5
Isla de la Juventud, *Atl.* 121 W-7
Isla de los Estados, *Atl.* 139 U-4
Isla de Margarita, *Atl.* 123 W-8
Isla de Providencia, *Atl.* 122 L-7
Isla de Roatán, *Atl.* 122 J-5
Isla de San Andrés, *Atl.* 122 M-7
Isla de Utila, *Atl.* 122 I-5
Isla Española, *Pac.* 209 X-6
Isla Espíritu Santo, *Pac.* 207 W-11
Isla Fernandina, *Pac.* 209 U-5
Isla Genovesa, *Pac.* 209 X-4
Isla Gordon, *Atl.* 139 Q-4
Isla Grande de Tierra del Fuego, *Atl.* 139 Q-3
Isla Guadalupe, *Pac.* 207 Q-9
Isla Hoste, *Atl.* 139 Q-5
Isla Isabela, *Pac.* 209 U-5
Isla La Tortuga, *Atl.* 123 V-8
Isla Lennox, *Atl.* 139 S-5
Isla Londonderry, *Atl.* 139 O-4
Isla Marchena, *Pac.* 209 V-4
Isla Maria Cleofas, *Pac.* 207 X-13
Isla María Madre, *Pac.* 207 X-13
Isla María Magdalena, *Pac.* 207 X-13
Isla Mona, *Atl.* 123 U-4
Isla Navarino, *Atl.* 139 R-4
Isla Noir, *Atl.* 139 N-4
Isla Nueva, *Atl.* 139 S-5
Isla Orchila, *Atl.* 123 V-8
Isla Picton, *Atl.* 139 S-4
Isla Pinta, *Pac.* 209 V-4
Isla Riesco, *Atl.* 139 O-2
Isla Roca Partida, *Pac.* 207 U-14
Isla San Ambrosio, *Pac.* 211 X-5
Isla San Benedicto, *Pac.* 207 V-14
Isla San Cristóbal, *Pac.* 209 X-5
Isla San Esteban, *Pac.* 207 U-9
Isla San Felix, *Pac.* 211 W-5
Isla San José, *Pac.* 207 V-11
Isla San Juanito, *Pac.* 207 X-13
Isla San Lorenzo, *Pac.* 207 U-9
Isla San Salvador, *Pac.* 209 W-5
Isla Santa Catalina, *Pac.* 207 V-11
Isla Santa Cruz, *Pac.* 209 W-5
Isla Santa Fé, *Pac.* 209 W-5
Isla Santa Inés, *Atl.* 139 O-3
Isla Santa Margarita, *Pac.* 207 U-11
Isla Santa Maria, *Pac.* 209 V-6
Isla Saona, *Atl.* 123 T-4
Isla Socorro, *Pac.* 207 V-15
Isla Stewart, *Atl.* 139 O-4
Isla Tiburón, *Pac.* 207 U-9
Isla Wolf, *Pac.* 209 V-4
Islas de la Bahía, *Atl.* 122 J-5
Islas del Maíz, *Atl.* 122 L-8
Islas Diego Ramirez, *Atl.* 139 R-6
Islas Las Aves, *Atl.* 123 U-8
Islas Los Roques, *Atl.* 123 U-8
Islas Marías, *Pac.* 207 Y-13
Islas Orcadas Rise, *Atl.* 133 P-12
Islas Revillagigedo, *Pac.* 207 t-15
Islas Wollaston, *Atl.* 139 S-5
Isle of Man, *Atl.* 115 N-10
Isle of Portland, *Atl.* 127 W-1
Isle of Wight, *Atl.* 127 X-1
Isles Chesterfield, *Pac.* 197 T-6
Isles Loyaute, *Pac.* 197 W-5
Isles of Scilly, *Atl.* 127 R-1
Isola d'Elba, *Atl.* 129 O-5
Isola di Pantelleria, *Atl.* 129 P-8
Isole Lipari, *Atl.* 129 Q-7
Isole Pelagie, *Atl.* 129 P-8
Israelite Bay, *Ind.* 161 R-3
Isthmus of Kra, *Pac.* 187 O-7
Isthmus of Panama, *Atl.* 123 N-9
Itbayat, *Pac.* 185 W-3
Izena-jima, *Pac.* 181 U-10
Izu-Ogasawara Trench, *Pac.* 168 K-7
Izu-shotō, *Pac.* 179 V-14

J

Jabrīn, *Ind.* 153 S-5
Jackson, *Arc.* 99 S-6
Jamaica, *Atl.* 112 I-10
Jamaica Channel, *Atl.* 123 P-4
James Ross Island, *Sou.* 105 Q-5
Jan Mayen, *Arc.* 98 L-10
Jan Mayen Fracture Zone, *Arc.* 98 L-10
Jan Mayen Ridge, *Arc.* 98 L-10
Japan Basin, *Pac.* 179 R-9
Japan Rise, *Pac.* 179 Y-12
Japan Trench, *Pac.* 179 X-12
Jarvis Island, *Pac.* 167 Q-9
Jason Peninsula, *Sou.* 105 Q-6
Java, *Pac.* 185 Q-15
Java Ridge, *Pac.* 189 N-15
Java Sea, *Ind.* 159 T-5
Java Trench, *Ind.* 159 S-6
Jazā'ir az Zubayr, *Ind.* 149 T-11
Jazā'ir Farasān, *Ind.* 149 T-10
Jazīrat Ḩawār, *Ind.* 153 R-7
Jazīrat Abū Ẓaby, *Ind.* 153 V-9
Jazīrat Abū 'Alī, *Ind.* 153 Q-5
Jazīrat al 'Arabiyah, *Ind.* 153 Q-5
Jazīrat al Hanish al Kabīr, *Ind.* 149 V-12
Jazīrat al Jurayd, *Ind.* 153 R-6
Jazīrat al Muḩarraq, *Ind.* 153 R-7
Jazīrat Antufash, *Ind.* 149 U-11
Jazīrat Faylakah, *Ind.* 153 P-3
Jazīrat Harqūs, *Ind.* 153 Q-5
Jazīrat Jabal Zuqar, *Ind.* 149 U-12
Jazīrat Janā, *Ind.* 153 Q-5
Jazīrat Karān, *Ind.* 153 Q-5
Jazīrat Kubbar, *Ind.* 153 P-3
Jazīrat Kurayn, *Ind.* 153 Q-5
Jazīrat Maşīrah, *Ind.* 151 P-4
Jazīrat Marawwah, *Ind.* 153 U-9
Jazīrat Qārūh, *Ind.* 153 P-4
Jazīrat Qannah, *Ind.* 153 Q-5
Jazīrat Tārūt, *Ind.* 153 R-6
Jazīrat Umm al Marādim, *Ind.* 153 P-4
Jazīreh-ye Fārsī, *Ind.* 153 Q-5
Jazīreh-ye Khān, *Ind.* 153 R-5
Jazīreh-ye Khārk, *Ind.* 153 Q-3
Jazirah Doberai, *Pac.* 189 X-10
Jemaja, *Pac.* 185 P-11
Jersey, *Atl.* 127 W-2
Jūn al Kuwayt, *Ind.* 153 O-3
Jizō-zaki, *Pac.* 179 R-12
Johnston Atoll, *Pac.* 167 P-7
Joides Basin, *Sou.* 107 V-11
Joinville Island, *Sou.* 105 R-4
Jolo, *Pac.* 185 W-10
Jones Sound, *Arc.* 101 P-6
Joseph Bonaparte Gulf, *Pac.* 195 N-12
Juan Fernández Islands, *Pac.* 211 W-6
Jutland Bank, *Atl.* 115 W-7
Jylland, *Atl.* 115 Y-7

K

Kabaena, *Pac.* 189 Q-12
Kaburuang, *Pac.* 189 U-7
Kadan Kyun, *Pac.* 187 N-3
Kadmat, *Ind.* 151 W-8
Kahoolawe, *Pac.* 175 V-7
Kai Besar, *Pac.* 189 X-12
Kai Kecil, *Pac.* 189 X-12
Kaiwi Channel, *Pac.* 175 V-7
Kakabia, *Pac.* 189 R-13
Kalamyts'ka Zatoka, *Atl.* 131 S-3
Kalao, *Pac.* 189 Q-13
Kalaotoa, *Pac.* 189 R-13
Kaledupa, *Pac.* 189 S-12
Kalpeni, *Ind.* 151 W-9
Kamarān, *Ind.* 149 U-11
Kamcatskij Zaliv, *Pac.* 177 X-5
Kamchatka, *Pac.* 166 M-3
Kamchatka Basin, *Pac.* 171 O-6
Kamchatka Peninsula, *Pac.* 171 N-6
Kamchatskiy Zaliv, *Pac.* 171 N-6
Kami-Koshiki-jima, *Pac.* 179 P-15
Kammu Seamount, *Pac.* 169 O-7
Kamui-misaki, *Pac.* 177 O-11
Kanaga Island, *Pac.* 171 T-8
Kane Basin, *Arc.* 101 R-4
Kane Fracture Zone, *Atl.* 125 V-5
Kangaroo Island, *Ind.* 161 Y-5
Kanmaw Kyun, *Pac.* 187 O-4
Kanmon Kaikyō, *Pac.* 179 Q-13
Kaôh Kōng, *Pac.* 187 S-5
Kaôh Rŭng, *Pac.* 187 T-5
Kap Brewster, *Arc.* 98 J-9
Kap Farvel, *Arc.* 98 D-8
Kap Morris Jesup, *Arc.* 97 R-9
Kapingamarangi Rise, *Pac.* 183 T-7
Kara Sea, *Arc.* 99 V-6
Karaginskiy Zaliv, *Pac.* 177 Y-3
Karakelong, *Pac.* 189 T-7
Karamian, *Pac.* 185 T-14
Karimata, *Pac.* 185 Q-13
Karkinits'ka Zatok, *Atl.* 131 R-3
Kashima-nada, *Pac.* 179 W-12
Kaskūs, *Ind.* 153 R-6
Katchall, *Ind.* 147 W-12
Katiu, *Pac.* 213 Q-10
Kattegat, *Atl.* 117 N-9
Kauai Channel, *Pac.* 175 U-7
Kauai, *Pac.* 175 U-6
Kauehi, *Pac.* 213 P-10
Kaula Island, *Pac.* 175 T-6
Kau-ye Kyun, *Pac.* 187 N-5
Kavaratti, *Ind.* 151 W-8
Kayak Island, *Pac.* 173 S-2
Kebrit Deep, *Ind.* 149 R-6
Kefallinia Valley, *Atl.* 129 S-8
Kekeroma-jima, *Pac.* 181 U-9
Kelso Bank, *Pac.* 197 U-8
Kemp Peninsula, *Sou.* 105 R-9
Kenai Peninsula, *Pac.* 173 Q-2
Kene Plateau, *Atl.* 128 M-7
Kenn Reefs, *Pac.* 197 T-7
Kennedy Entrance, *Pac.* 173 P-3
Kepulauan Alor, *Pac.* 189 S-13
Kepulauan Anambas, *Pac.* 185 P-11
Kepulauan Aru, *Pac.* 195 S-6
Kepulauan Asia, *Pac.* 191 O-8
Kepulauan Ayu, *Pac.* 189 W-9
Kepulauan Babar, *Pac.* 189 V-13
Kepulauan Banda, *Pac.* 189 V-11
Kepulauan Banggai, *Pac.* 189 R-10
Kepulauan Barat Daya, *Pac.* 189 U-13
Kepulauan Bonerate, *Pac.* 189 Q-13
Kepulauan Gorong, *Pac.* 189 W-11
Kepulauan Kai, *Pac.* 189 X-12
Kepulauan Kangean, *Pac.* 189 N-13
Kepulauan Karimunjawa, *Pac.* 185 R-14
Kepulauan Laut Kecil, *Pac.* 189 N-12
Kepulauan Leti, *Pac.* 189 U-13
Kepulauan Lingga, *Pac.* 185 P-12
Kepulauan Mapia, *Pac.* 191 P-8
Kepulauan Nanusa, *Pac.* 189 U-6
Kepulauan Natuna, *Pac.* 185 Q-10
Kepulauan Obi, *Pac.* 189 U-10
Kepulauan Sabalana, *Pac.* 185 V-15
Kepulauan Sangir, *Pac.* 189 T-7
Kepulauan Solor, *Pac.* 189 S-13
Kepulauan Taka'Bonerate, *Pac.* 189 Q-13
Kepulauan Talaud, *Pac.* 189 U-7
Kepulauan Tambelan, *Pac.* 185 P-12
Kepulauan Tanimbar, *Pac.* 189 X-13
Kepulauan Tengah, *Pac.* 189 O-13
Kepulauan Togian, *Pac.* 189 R-9
Kepulauan Tukangbesi, *Pac.* 189 S-12
Kepulauan Watubela, *Pac.* 189 X-11
Kepuluan Solor, *Pac.* 185 X-15
Kerch Strait, *Atl.* 131 V-3
Kerempe Burun, *Atl.* 131 S-5
Kerguelen, *Sou.* 103 Z-5
Kerguelen Islands, *Ind.* 163 N-13
Kerguelen Plateau, *Ind.* 159 N-13
Kermadec Islands, *Pac.* 193 T-7
Kermadec Ridge, *Pac.* 203 T-2
Kermadec Trench, *Pac.* 203 T-3
Khalīj al Ḩalānīyāt, *Ind.* 151 O-5
Khalīj Bumbah, *Atl.* 129 T-10
Khalīj Maşīrah, *Ind.* 151 P-4
Khalīj Tārūt, *Ind.* 153 R-6
Khalīj-e Deylam, *Ind.* 153 Q-2
Khalīj-e Nāy Band, *Ind.* 153 T-5
Khalīj-e Nakhīlū, *Ind.* 153 U-6
Khalīg el 'Arab, *Atl.* 129 V-10
Khatangskiy Zaliv, *Arc.* 97 W-6
Khawr al 'Udayd, *Ind.* 153 S-9
Khawr az Zubayr, *Ind.* 153 P-2
Khawr Qirqishān, *Ind.* 153 W-9
Khowr-e Māsheh, *Ind.* 153 V-6
Khowr-e Mūsa, *Ind.* 153 P-2
Khowr-e Soltānī, *Ind.* 153 R-3
Kiel Canal, *Atl.* 117 N-11
Kieler Bucht, *Atl.* 115 Z-9
Kihnu, *Atl.* 117 V-8
Kii-suidō, *Pac.* 179 T-14
Kikai-jima, *Pac.* 181 V-9
Kikladhes Plateau, *Atl.* 129 U-8
Kilttan, *Ind.* 151 W-8
King George Bay, *Atl.* 139 W-1
King George Island, *Sou.* 105 P-3
King George Seamount, *Pac.* 175 N-3
King Island, *Ind.* 159 Y-11
King Peninsula, *Sou.* 104 K-13
King William Island, *Arc.* 101 N-10
Kingman Reef, *Pac.* 167 P-8
Kinka-san, *Pac.* 179 X-11
Kisar, *Pac.* 189 U-13
Kiska Island, *Pac.* 171 R-8
Kittery Island, *Pac.* 174 K-3
Kitty Hawk Seamount, *Pac.* 185 S-8
Kizilimak Canyon, *Atl.* 131 U-5
Knob Island, *Atl.* 121 W-4
Ko Ang Thong, *Pac.* 187 P-6
Ko Chang, *Pac.* 187 S-4
Ko Khram, *Pac.* 187 Q-3
Ko Kut, *Pac.* 187 S-4
Ko Lanta, *Pac.* 187 O-9
Ko Libong, *Pac.* 187 O-9
Ko Phangan, *Pac.* 187 Q-6
Ko Phra Thong, *Pac.* 187 N-7
Ko Phuket, *Pac.* 187 N-8
Ko Samet, *Pac.* 187 R-3
Ko Samui, *Pac.* 187 Q-7
Ko Tao, *Pac.* 187 P-6
Ko Yao Yai, *Pac.* 187 O-8
Kobroör, *Pac.* 195 S-6
Kodiak Island, *Pac.* 173 P-3
Kodiak Seamount, *Pac.* 173 Q-4
Kodori Canyon, *Atl.* 131 Y-5
Kohler Seamount, *Ind.* 155 W-14
Kōje-do, *Pac.* 181 U-5
Ko-jima, *Pac.* 179 V-9
Kola Peninsula, *Arc.* 99 S-12
Kolbeinsey Ridge, *Arc.* 98 J-10
Kolga laht, *Atl.* 117 W-7
Komandorskiye Ostrova, *Pac.* 171 P-7
Komodo, *Pac.* 189 P-14
Kongsøya, *Arc.* 99 R-7
Korea Bay, *Pac.* 181 R-3
Korea Strait, *Pac.* 179 P-14
Korfa Zaliv, *Pac.* 171 O-5
Korff Ice Rise, *Sou.* 105 Q-13
Kosa Biryuchyy Ostriv, *Atl.* 131 U-2
Koshikijima-rettō, *Pac.* 181 U-7
Kotzebue Sound, *Arc.* 97 Q-2

Arc. Arctic Ocean *Atl.* Atlantic Ocean *Ind.* Indian Ocean *Pac.* Pacific Ocean *Sou.* Southern Ocean

Arc. Arctic Ocean   *Atl.* Atlantic Ocean   *Ind.* Indian Ocean   *Pac.* Pacific Ocean   *Sou.* Southern Ocean

Ndeni–Raroia

Ndeni, *Pac.*	197	W-3
Near Islands, *Pac.*	171	Q-7
Necker Island, *Pac.*	175	R-5
Necker Ridge, *Pac.*	175	O-7
Negros, *Pac.*	189	R-4
Neill Island, *Ind.*	147	W-10
Nelson Island, *Atl.*	139	X-11
Nelson Island, *Sou.*	105	P-4
Nemuro-kaikyō, *Pac.*	177	R-10
Nemuro-wan, *Pac.*	179	Z-7
Nengonengo, *Pac.*	213	Q-11
Nero Seamount, *Pac.*	174	J-3
Nevis, *Atl.*	123	X-5
New Zealand, *Pac.*	203	P-6
New Britain, *Pac.*	197	Q-1
New Britain Trench, *Pac.*	197	Q-2
New Caledonia, *Pac.*	197	X-7
New Caledonia Basin, *Pac.*	201	V-5
New Caledonia Trough, *Pac.*	197	W-7
New England Seamounts, *Atl.*	112	K-7
New Georgia Islands, *Pac.*	197	S-2
New Guinea, *Ind.*	159	Y-5
New Guinea Basin, *Pac.*	197	P-1
New Guinea Trench, *Pac.*	183	P-7
New Hanover, *Pac.*	191	V-9
New Ireland, *Pac.*	197	S-1
New Providence, *Atl.*	124	K-5
New Siberia Islands, *Arc.*	97	U-5
New Zealand, *Pac.*	201	V-12
Newfoundland, *Atl.*	112	L-5
Newfoundland Basin, *Atl.*	113	N-6
Newfoundland Ridge, *Atl.*	112	L-6
Newfoundland Seamounts, *Atl.*	113	N-6
Ngajangel, *Pac.*	191	P-5
Ngetik Atoll, *Pac.*	191	Y-6
Ngulu, *Pac.*	191	Q-5
Niau, *Pac.*	213	P-10
Nicaragua Rise, *Atl.*	122	L-5
Nicobar Basin, *Ind.*	147	V-14
Nicobar Islands, *Ind.*	147	V-12
Niger Cone, *Atl.*	135	V-3
Nihau, *Pac.*	175	T-6
Nihiru, *Pac.*	213	Q-10
Nihoa, *Pac.*	175	T-6
Nii-jima, *Pac.*	179	V-13
Nila, *Pac.*	189	V-13
Nile Fan, *Atl.*	129	W-10
Nine Degree Channel, *Ind.*	151	V-9
Ninetyeast Ridge, *Ind.*	163	R-10
Ningaloo Reef, *Ind.*	159	U-8
Ninigo Group, *Pac.*	191	T-9
Niue, *Pac.*	193	W-4
Nojima-zaki, *Pac.*	179	W-13
Noma-misaki, *Pac.*	181	V-7
Nomwin, *Pac.*	191	W-5
Nootka Seamount, *Pac.*	175	N-2
Nora, *Ind.*	149	T-11
Nordaustlandet, *Arc.*	99	Q-7
Nordenskjöld Basin, *Sou.*	107	W-9
Norfolk Basin, *Pac.*	201	X-6
Norfolk Island, *Pac.*	201	W-5
Norfolk Ridge, *Pac.*	201	W-5
North Aegean Trough, *Atl.*	129	T-7
North American Basin, *Atl.*	112	J-9
North Andaman, *Ind.*	147	W-9
North Atlantic Ocean, *Atl.*	110	G-11
North Australian Basin, *Ind.*	159	U-7
North Banda Basin, *Pac.*	189	S-11
North Caicos, *Atl.*	123	R-2
North Cape, *Arc.*	99	Q-11
North Cape, *Pac.*	201	X-7
North Fiji Basin, *Pac.*	197	Y-4
North Ikaria Basin, *Atl.*	129	U-7
North Island (NZ), *Pac.*	201	Y-9
North Island (Philippines), *Pac.*	185	X-3
North Island (USA), *Pac.*	174	L-3
North Island, *Ind.*	151	V-9
North Islet, *Ind.*	151	V-8
North Kanin Bank, *Arc.*	99	T-10
North New Hebrides Trench, *Pac.*	197	X-4
North Pole, *Arc.*	97	S-8
North Reef Island, *Ind.*	147	V-9
North Ronaldsay, *Atl.*	115	Q-5
North Scotia Ridge, *Atl.*	132	K-13
North Sea, *Atl.*	115	S-7
North Sentinel Island, *Ind.*	147	V-10

North Weddell Ridge, *Sou.*	103	Q-3
Northampton Seamounts, *Pac.*	175	N-4
Northbrook, *Arc.*	99	S-7
Northeast Georgia Rise, *Atl.*	133	N-12
Northeast Pacific Basin, *Pac.*	169	R-5
Northern Cook Islands, *Pac.*	193	W-2
Northumberland Strait, *Atl.*	119	Q-6
Northwest Atlantic Mid-Ocean Channel, *Atl.*	113	M-4
Northwest Georgia Rise, *Atl.*	133	N-12
Northwest Hawaiian Ridge, *Pac.*	175	N-2
Northwest Pacific Basin, *Pac.*	168	L-6
Northwind Abyssal Plain, *Arc.*	97	R-4
Norton Sound, *Pac.*	171	X-3
Norwegian Basin, *Arc.*	99	O-10
Norwegian Deep, *Atl.*	115	U-2
Norwegian Sea, *Arc.*	98	K-12
Nos Emine, *Atl.*	131	O-5
Nos Kaliakra, *Atl.*	131	P-4
Noss Head, *Atl.*	115	P-6
Nosy Bé, *Ind.*	157	Y-4
Nosy Lava, *Ind.*	157	X-5
Nosy Mitsio, *Ind.*	157	Y-4
Noto-hantō, *Pac.*	179	U-12
Notre Dame Bay, *Atl.*	119	X-3
Nottingham Island, *Arc.*	101	S-13
Nova Bank, *Pac.*	197	U-7
Nova Canton Trough, *Pac.*	193	U-1
Nova Scotia, *Atl.*	112	K-6
Nova Trough, *Pac.*	204	H-7
Novaya Zemlya Trough, *Arc.*	99	V-8
Novaya Zemlya, *Arc.*	99	U-8
Nuku Hiva, *Pac.*	213	R-7
Nukuoro, *Pac.*	191	X-7
Nunivak Island, *Pac.*	171	V-5
Nuussuaq, *Arc.*	97	N-11
Northwest Atlantic Mid- Ocean Channel, *Atl.*	110	E-10
Nyūdō-zaki, *Pac.*	179	V-10

O

Oahu, *Pac.*	175	U-7
Ob Trench, *Ind.*	159	R-10
Ob' Tablemount, *Ind.*	155	S-14
Obi, *Pac.*	189	U-10
Obskaya Guba, *Arc.*	99	X-8
Obytichna Kosa, *Atl.*	131	U-2
Ocean Island, *Pac.*	183	W-8
Oceanographer Fracture Zone, *Atl.*	113	N-7
Ochiishi-misaki, *Pac.*	177	R-11
Odom Inlet, *Sou.*	105	Q-9
Ojika-jima, *Pac.*	179	P-14
Oki-Daitō Ridge, *Pac.*	183	O-2
Okinawa, *Pac.*	181	T-10
Okinawa Trough, *Pac.*	181	R-11
Okinoerabu-jima, *Pac.*	181	U-10
Okino-shima, *Pac.*	179	R-14
Oki-shotō, *Pac.*	179	R-12
Okushiri-tō, *Pac.*	179	V-8
Öland, *Atl.*	117	R-9
Olyutorskiy Zaliv, *Pac.*	171	P-5
Oman Basin, *Ind.*	151	Q-2
Ona Basin, *Atl.*	139	Z-8
One South Fracture Zone, *Atl.*	133	P-2
Onslow Bay, *Atl.*	124	K-2
Ontong Java Rise, *Pac.*	183	S-7
Orange Canyon, *Atl.*	137	U-9
Orange Cone, *Atl.*	133	X-7
Orkney Islands, *Atl.*	115	Q-5
Oroluk, *Pac.*	191	X-6
Orphan Knoll, *Atl.*	112	M-5
Orust, *Atl.*	117	O-8
Orville Coast, *Sou.*	105	Q-11
Ōsaka-wan, *Pac.*	179	T-13
Osborn Plateau, *Ind.*	159	P-7
Osbourn Seamount, *Pac.*	193	V-6
Ō-shima, *Pac.*	179	V-9
Oslofjorden, *Atl.*	117	N-8
Osprey Reef, *Pac.*	199	S-4
Ostrov Atlasova, *Pac.*	177	U-7
Ostrov Belyy, *Arc.*	99	V-8
Ostrov Beringa, *Pac.*	171	O-6
Ostrov Bol'shevik, *Arc.*	99	W-4
Ostrov Iony, *Pac.*	177	Q-4
Ostrov Isachenko, *Arc.*	99	V-5

Ostrov Iturup, *Pac.*	177	R-10
Ostrov Karaginskiy, *Pac.*	171	O-5
Ostrov Ketoj, *Pac.*	177	T-9
Ostrov Kolguyev, *Arc.*	99	T-11
Ostrov Komsomolets, *Arc.*	99	U-4
Ostrov Kotel'nyy, *Arc.*	97	V-5
Ostrov Kunashir, *Pac.*	177	R-10
Ostrov Mednyy, *Pac.*	171	P-7
Ostrov Moneron, *Pac.*	179	W-6
Ostrov Novaya Sibir', *Arc.*	97	U-4
Ostrov Oktyabr'skoy Revolyutsii, *Arc.*	99	V-4
Ostrov Onekotan, *Pac.*	177	U-8
Ostrov Paramushir, *Pac.*	177	V-7
Ostrov Pioner, *Arc.*	99	U-4
Ostrov Rasšua, *Pac.*	177	T-9
Ostrov Ratmanova, *Pac.*	171	V-2
Ostrov Shiashkotan, *Pac.*	177	T-8
Ostrov Shikotan, *Pac.*	177	S-11
Ostrov Shmidta, *Arc.*	99	U-4
Ostrov Simushir, *Pac.*	177	T-9
Ostrov Urup, *Pac.*	177	S-9
Ostrov Ushakova, *Arc.*	99	T-5
Ostrov Vaygach, *Arc.*	99	V-10
Ostrov Vise, *Arc.*	99	U-5
Osumi-shotō, *Pac.*	181	V-8
Otranto Valley, *Atl.*	129	R-6
Owen Fracture Zone, *Ind.*	151	O-9

P

P'enghu Tao, *Pac.*	181	P-12
Pacific Ocean, *Pac.*	167	N-9
Pacific-Antarctic Ridge, *Sou.*	103	Q-12
Pacific-Antarctic Rise, *Pac.*	210	N-12
Padangtikar, *Pac.*	185	Q-12
Padre Island, *Atl.*	121	O-4
Paengnyŏng-do, *Pac.*	181	R-3
Pagan, *Pac.*	191	T-2
Palanan Point, *Pac.*	190	K-2
Palau Islands, *Pac.*	191	O-6
Palau Ridge, *Pac.*	191	P-6
Palau Trench, *Pac.*	191	P-6
Palawan, *Pac.*	189	P-4
Palawan Passage, *Pac.*	189	O-4
Palawan Trough, *Pac.*	189	N-4
Palgrave Point, *Atl.*	137	U-3
Palk Strait, *Ind.*	147	O-11
Palm Islands, *Pac.*	199	S-8
Palmer Land, *Sou.*	105	P-8
Palmyra Atoll, *Pac.*	167	Q-8
Palmyras Point, *Ind.*	147	T-5
Palu, *Pac.*	189	R-14
Panaitan, *Pac.*	185	O-15
Panama Basin, *Pac.*	205	X-6
Panama Canal, *Atl.*	123	N-Q
Panay, *Pac.*	189	R-3
Panay Gulf, *Pac.*	189	R-3
Pandanan, *Pac.*	189	N-5
Pandora Entrance, *Pac.*	199	Q-2
Pangutaran, *Pac.*	189	P-6
Pantar, *Pac.*	189	S-14
Papa Westray, *Atl.*	115	P-5
Papua Abyssal Plain, *Pac.*	197	R-3
Papua Plateau, *Pac.*	197	P-3
Paracel Islands, *Pac.*	185	S-5
Paraoa, *Pac.*	213	R-11
Pärnu laht, *Atl.*	117	V-8
Parry Bay, *Arc.*	101	Q-10
Parry Channel, *Arc.*	101	N-7
Parry Islands, *Arc.*	101	L-5
Passage Point, *Arc.*	100	L-6
Patton Escarpment, *Pac.*	207	P-6
Patton Seamount, *Pac.*	173	P-5
Pazarbaşi Burnu, *Atl.*	131	Q-6
Pearl and Hermes Atoll, *Pac.*	174	L-3
Pearson Isles, *Ind.*	161	W-3
Peary Channel, *Arc.*	101	N-4
Pebble Island, *Atl.*	139	X-1
Pedro Bank, *Atl.*	123	N-5
Pejantan, *Pac.*	185	Q-12
Peleng, *Pac.*	189	S-10
Pemba Island, *Ind.*	155	S-6
Península Brecknock, *Atl.*	139	P-4
Península de Azuero, *Atl.*	122	M-10
Península de Brunswick, *Atl.*	139	O-3
Península Mitre, *Atl.*	139	S-4
Península Muñoz Gamero, *Atl.*	139	N-2
Péninsule de Gaspé, *Atl.*	119	P-4

Pennell Bank, *Sou.*	107	U-11
Pennell Coast, *Sou.*	107	X-13
Penny Point, *Sou.*	107	W-6
Penrhyn Basin, *Pac.*	193	Z-2
Pentecost, *Pac.*	197	Y-5
Pentland Firth, *Atl.*	115	P-5
Penzhinskaya Guba, *Pac.*	177	X-2
Perak, *Pac.*	187	O-11
Percy Isles, *Pac.*	199	V-11
Perhentian Besar, *Pac.*	187	T-11
Pernambuco Abyssal Plain, *Atl.*	133	Q-3
Pernambuco Seamounts, *Atl.*	133	O-3
Persian Gulf, *Ind.*	153	R-5
Perth Basin, *Ind.*	159	T-9
Pertuis Breton, *Atl.*	127	X-6
Pertuis d'Antioche, *Atl.*	127	X-7
Peru Basin, *Pac.*	211	V-3
Peru-Chile Trench, *Pac.*	211	W-1
Pescadero Trough, *Pac.*	207	W-11
Peter I Island, *Sou.*	103	O-8
Philippine Basin, *Pac.*	191	N-3
Philippine Sea, *Pac.*	191	N-4
Philippine Trench, *Pac.*	190	L-3
Phoenix Islands, *Pac.*	193	V-1
Pinaki, *Pac.*	213	S-11
Pinang, *Pac.*	187	P-11
Pine Island Bay, *Sou.*	104	L-13
Pingelap, *Pac.*	191	Z-6
Pioneer Fracture Zone, *Pac.*	169	U-7
Pioneer Tablemount, *Pac.*	174	M-4
Pisces Depression, *Pac.*	173	N-9
Pitcairn Island, *Pac.*	211	N-5
Pitti, *Ind.*	151	W-8
Placentia Bay, *Atl.*	119	X-6
Pliny Trench, *Atl.*	129	U-9
Pocklington Trough, *Pac.*	197	S-3
Pohnpei, *Pac.*	183	T-6
Point Adieu, *Ind.*	161	V-2
Point Arena, *Pac.*	207	N-3
Point Arguello, *Pac.*	207	P-5
Point Conception, *Pac.*	207	P-5
Point Culver, *Ind.*	161	R-3
Point D'Entrecasteaux, *Ind.*	160	L-4
Point Dover, *Ind.*	161	S-3
Point Hood, *Ind.*	161	O-4
Point Hope, *Pac.*	171	W-1
Point Narasapatnam, *Ind.*	147	P-7
Point Pedro, *Ind.*	147	P-11
Point Reyes, *Pac.*	207	O-3
Point Sur, *Pac.*	207	O-4
Pointe de Barfleur, *Atl.*	127	Y-2
Pointe de l'Est, *Atl.*	119	S-4
Pointe de l'Ouest, *Atl.*	119	Q-3
Pointe de la Coubre, *Atl.*	127	Y-7
Pointe de Penmarch, *Atl.*	127	T-4
Pointe de St-Gildas, *Atl.*	127	W-5
Pointe de St-Mathieu, *Atl.*	127	T-4
Pointe du Raz, *Atl.*	127	T-4
Pole Abyssal Plain, *Arc.*	97	S-8
Polillo Islands, *Pac.*	185	X-5
Polynesia, *Pac.*	167	Q-10
Ponta da Barra Falsa, *Ind.*	157	P-11
Ponta da Barra, *Ind.*	157	P-11
Ponta do Enfião, *Atl.*	137	T-1
Ponta Olinda, *Ind.*	157	Q-7
Ponta São Sebastião, *Ind.*	157	P-10
Ponta Timbué, *Ind.*	157	P-8
Porcupine Abyssal Plain, *Atl.*	113	R-4
Porcupine Bank, *Atl.*	113	R-5
Porpoise Bay, *Sou.*	103	W-11
Port Royal Sound, *Atl.*	124	J-3
Possession Islands, *Sou.*	107	V-13
Powell Basin, *Sou.*	105	S-3
Poysegor Trough, *Pac.*	201	U-14
Pratas Island, *Pac.*	185	U-3
Pratt Guyot, *Pac.*	173	T-4
Pratt Seamount, *Pac.*	169	V-3
Preparis Island, *Ind.*	147	W-8
Preparis North Channel, *Ind.*	147	W-8
Preparis South Channel, *Ind.*	147	W-8
President Thiers Bank, *Pac.*	167	R-11
President Thiers Seamount, *Pac.*	210	K-4
Prestrud Inlet, *Sou.*	107	Q-7
Pribilof Islands, *Pac.*	171	W-6
Prince Albert Peninsula, *Arc.*	100	K-7
Prince Albert Sound, *Arc.*	100	J-8
Prince Charles Island, *Arc.*	101	R-11

Prince Edward Fracture Zone, *Ind.*	155	R-14
Prince Edward Island, *Atl.*	119	Q-6
Prince Edward Islands, *Ind.*	155	R-13
Prince George Land, *Arc.*	99	R-7
Prince of Wales Island (Aust.), *Pac.*	195	W-10
Prince of Wales Island (Can.), *Pac.*	173	X-4
Prince of Wales Island, *Arc.*	101	N-8
Prince of Wales Strait, *Arc.*	100	K-7
Prince Patrick Island, *Arc.*	100	K-5
Prince Regent Inlet, *Arc.*	101	O-8
Prince William Sound, *Pac.*	173	R-2
Princess Charlotte Bay, *Pac.*	199	P-4
Príncipe, *Atl.*	135	W-5
Prins Karls Forland, *Arc.*	99	O-7
Proliv Dmitriya Lapteva, *Arc.*	97	U-4
Proliv Karskiye Vorot, *Arc.*	97	W-11
Proliv Longa, *Arc.*	97	S-2
Proliv Vil'kitskogo, *Arc.*	97	V-7
Protea Seamount, *Atl.*	133	Y-9
Protector Basin, *Atl.*	132	L-14
Prydz Bay, *Sou.*	103	W-7
Ptolemy Trench, *Atl.*	129	T-8
Puerto Rico Trench, *Atl.*	123	U-3
Pukaki Rise, *Pac.*	203	Q-7
Pukapuka, *Pac.*	213	S-9
Pukarua, *Pac.*	213	S-11
Pulap, *Pac.*	191	V-6
Pulau Dolak, *Pac.*	195	U-8
Pulawat, *Pac.*	191	V-6
Pulo Anna, *Pac.*	191	O-7
Pulusuk, *Pac.*	191	V-6
Punta Abreojos, *Pac.*	207	T-10
Punta Arena, *Pac.*	207	W-12
Punta Baja, *Pac.*	207	S-8
Punta Burica, *Atl.*	122	K-10
Punta Cosigüina, *Atl.*	122	H-7
Punta de Arenas, *Atl.*	139	R-2
Punta de Mita, *Pac.*	207	Y-13
Punta de Perlas, *Atl.*	122	K-7
Punta de Quemado, *Atl.*	123	Q-3
Punta del Mono, *Atl.*	122	K-8
Punta Eugenia, *Pac.*	207	S-9
Punta Herrero, *Atl.*	121	U-9
Punta Mariato, *Atl.*	122	M-10
Punta Patuca, *Atl.*	122	K-6
Punta Roca Partida, *Atl.*	121	P-9
Punta Rosa, *Pac.*	207	V-10
Punta San Hipólito, *Pac.*	207	T-10
Punta San Pedro, *Atl.*	122	K-10
Purekkari neem, *Atl.*	117	W-7
Puysegur Trench, *Pac.*	203	O-7

Q

Qarnayn, *Ind.*	153	U-8
Qeshm, *Ind.*	153	X-6
Qeys, *Ind.*	153	V-6
Qizhou Liedao, *Pac.*	185	S-3
Quân Đao Nam Du, *Pac.*	187	U-6
Quebrada Fracture Zone, *Pac.*	205	T-7
Queen Charlotte Bay, *Atl.*	139	W-1
Queen Charlotte Islands, *Pac.*	169	W-4
Queen Charlotte Sound, *Pac.*	173	Y-6
Queen Elizabeth Islands, *Arc.*	100	M-4
Queen Maud Gulf, *Arc.*	100	M-10
Queen Maud Land, *Sou.*	103	S-5
Queensland Guyot, *Pac.*	197	T-9
Queensland Plateau, *Pac.*	197	P-4
Quiros Fracture Zone, *Pac.*	211	T-4
Qulay'ah Rock, *Ind.*	153	R-6

R

Raas, *Pac.*	185	T-15
Raiatea, *Pac.*	213	N-10
Raijua, *Pac.*	189	Q-5
Raippaluoto, *Atl.*	117	T-4
Raita Bank, *Pac.*	175	O-4
Raivavae, *Pac.*	213	O-13
Rangiroa, *Pac.*	213	O-9
Rapa, *Pac.*	213	Q-14
Raraka, *Pac.*	213	P-10
Raroia, *Pac.*	213	Q-10

Arc. Arctic Ocean *Atl.* Atlantic Ocean *Ind.* Indian Ocean *Pac.* Pacific Ocean *Sou.* Southern Ocean

Arc. Arctic Ocean   *Atl.* Atlantic Ocean   *Ind.* Indian Ocean   *Pac.* Pacific Ocean   *Sou.* Southern Ocean

INDEX

Page numbers in *italics* refer to illustrations and photographs.

ACKNOWLEDGMENTS

The Encyclopedia of Wildlife

Weldon Owen would like to thank the following people and organizations for their assistance in the production of this book: Robert Coupe, Dr. Theo Evans, Tony Gordon, Maria Harding, Ian Hutton, Hilda Mendham, Kathryn Morgan, Dr. Martyn Robinson, Noel Tait, Shan Wolody, DiZign, UNEP-WCMC (World Conservation Monitoring Centre of United Nations Environment Programme), Food and Agriculture Organization of the United Nations, World Resources Institute, Washington, United States Dept of Agriculture, Arctic Climate Impact Assessment, project of Arctic Council and International Arctic Science Committee, Australian Government Department of Environment, Water, Heritage and the Arts, Ramsar Convention on Wetlands, international treaty, National Center for Ecological Analysis and Synthesis, research center of University of California, Global Footprint Network, International Union for Conservation of Nature, 2007 Red List of Threatened Species, Intergovernmental Panel on Climate Change, Conservation International.

PHOTOGRAPHS

Key t=top; l=left; r=right; tl=top left; tcl=top center left; tc=top center; tcr=top center right; tr=top right; cl=center left; c=center; cr=center right; b=bottom; bl=bottom left; bcl=bottom center left; bc=bottom center; bcr=bottom center right; br=bottom right
AAP = Australian Associated Press; Aus = Auscape International; CBT = Corbis; GI = Getty Images; FL = Flickr; iS = istockphoto.com; MP = Minden Pictures; NHPA = Natural History Photographic Agency; PS = Photoshot; SH = Shutterstock; SP = Sea Pics; SPL = Science Photo Library; TPL = photolibrary.com.

Cover c CBT; tl, tl, cl, cl, cl iS; **Back Cover** c, tc, cr, cl, tr, tl iS; **1** SP; **2** CBT; **4** CBT; **6** tcl, tcr, tl, tr iS; **7** tcl, tcr, tl, tr iS; **8** bcr, bl iS; cl SH; l SP; tcr iS; **12** CBT; CBT; **14**tr iS; **14**tr iS; **15**c iS; r NHPA; t iS; tcl MP; tcr iS; tl NHPA; tr iS; **16** c, cl, cr, r iS; **18**tr NHPA; **19**b, bcr, br iS; cr NHPA; **20**c, tcr NHPA; **21**bcr, br,iS; **22**tr iS; **23**cr NASA; t,tcl, tcr, tl MP; **24**bcr NASA; **25**b iS; bcl MP; bcr iS; **26**bc NASA; br, t, MP; **27**b, bcr MP; cl iS; cr, l MP; r, tl, tr, iS; **28**bcr NASA; **29**bcr, br iS; cr, r MP; **30**tr MP; **31**bcr AAP; t iS; tcl, tcr, tl MP; **32**bcl NASA; **33**b MP; c iS; cl MP; **35**r NHPA; **36**c MP; br iS; cr NHPA; t, tcr, MP; **37**bl NHPA; br, cl, iS; tcl, tl iS; **38** CBT; **40**bcl SH; bl, l, cl, tl, c iS; b NHPA; **42**c NHPA; cr SH; **43**bc iS; br SH; cr iS; **44**cl iS; cr, l NHPA; tcl iS; tr MP; **45**cr MP; t NHPA; tcr, tl MP; **46**b MP; bcl SH; cl NHPA; **47**bc NHPA; tc MP; tr iS; **48**bl NHPA; br SH; cr NHPA; **49**bl SH; c SH; tl NHPA; **50**bl CBT; cl SH; **51**bc, bl, br MP; c, cr NHPA; tr NHPA; **52**c SH; tr NHPA; **53**b NHPA; c iS; cl TPL; tl NHPA; tr SH; **54**bcl iS; cl NHPA; **55**c iS; tr SH; **56**tc NHPA; tr SH; **57**br, cr NHPA; tcl SH; tr iS; **59**br NHPA; cr MP; tl NHPA; tr SH; **60**bl, bcr iS; c NHPA; **61**bcl NHPA; c SH; tcl iS; tr MP; **62**bc NHPA; bl MP; bcl iS; c NHPA; **63**bl MP; br, cl NHPA; cr MP; **65**bc, br MP; c SH; t NHPA; **66** CBT; **68**b iS; bcl MP; bl, c, cl, l, tl iS; **69**bcr MP; **70**br NHPA; cl MP; **71**b, bl, cr MP; tl NHPA; **72**b iS; bl, tr MP; **74**bcl, c SH; **75**br CBT; cr SH; t CBT; **76**bc, br, cl MP; **77**c NHPA; cr MP; t CBT; **78**cr NHPA; tr MP; **79**bc, bl, bcr, c, cr, tr, tcr iS; **80**bl NHPA; br MP; **81**tl NHPA; tr MP; **82**bl, bcr, tc MP; **83**bl, bcr CBT; cr MP; tc, tcr CBT; **84**b MP; c iS; **85**bl, br MP; c NHPA; t MP; **87**b MP; tc, tcl NHPA; tr iS; **88**bl PS; **89**br iS; c, tcl, tr MP; **90**b SH; cr SPL; tr CBT; **91**bl MP; bcl, cl iS; tc SH; tl iS; tcr NHPA; tr PS; **92**bc iS; bl, bcr MP; c SH; **93**bl, c, cl iS; tcr NHPA; **94**bl, tr MP; **95**bl MP; br, tl iS; **96**bl, bcl, c iS: c SH; **97**bcr, cr, tc, tcr, tr NHPA; **98**bl MP; br SH; cl NHPA; **99**cl SH; cr, tl MP; tr iS; **100**bc, bl, br iS; cl, tr MP; **101**bcr, br iS; cr iS; r SH; tr iS; **102** CBT; **104**cl SH; l, t iS; tc, tcl, tcr, tl SH **106**b NHPA; **107** bl, c, cl NHPA; tl MP; tr SH; **108** bl MP; bcl, cr iS; tr MP; **109**br, cl, cr, tl MP; **110**bl MP; bcr, tr NHPA; **111**bc NHPA; br, cl MP; **112**bcl, bcr, bl MP; br NHPA; **113**bl iS; c SH; cl iS; **114**bl MP/SH; br NHPA; cl MP; tr MP; **115**bl, br, c, tl MP; **116**bl MP; **117**bl MP; br iS; c, cl MP; tl iS; tr MP; **118**bl MP; cl iS; tc, tr MP; **119**bl MP; br, c CBT; **120**bl MP; **121**b, c MP; l SH; tl iS; **122**bl MP; br, NHPA; **123**cl, cr NHPA; tr MP; **124**bcr, bl NHPA; **125**b, tcr MP; **126**bl, br, cr NHPA; tr MP; **127**b MP; c, tl NHPA; **128**bcl iS; tr CBT; **129**tr NHPA; **130**b MP; c NHPA; **131** bl iS; cr CBT; tr MP; **132** NHPA; **134**b SH; bcl, bl iS; c MP; cl CBT; l, tl iS; **135**bcr, bl iS; br SH; **136**b, bl MP; cr NHPA; **137**bcl MP; cr iS; tcr NHPA; **138**bcr NHPA; bl CBT; c NHPA; r CBT; **139**bcr, l tcl MP; **140**cr NHPA; l, tcl MP; **141**cr NHPA; t CBT; tc, tcl NHPA; **142**b NHPA; c GI; **143**b, cr, tcr NHPA; **144**bcl, br, tcr NHPA; **145**bcr WWI; l, t CBT; **146**cl CBT; tcl MP; **147**t MP; tcr, tl NHPA; **148**bcr iS; l CBT; **149**bl MP; tcl, tcr CBT; **150**b, bl, cl iS; cr SH; **151**c, cr, l iS; t MP; tl NHPA; **152**bl, cl, cr MP; tr CBT; **153**cr NHPA; tc MP; tcl NHPA; tcr MP; tl NHPA; **154**bcr iS; bl MP; l NHPA; **155**c, cl, tcr iS; tl NHPA; **156**c MP; tcl NHPA; **157**t NHPA; tc TPL; tcr NHPA; **158**bcl SH; bcr NHPA; **159**b, bcl, cl NHPA; t SH; tcr NHPA; **160** CBT; **162**c, cl, l iS; t, tc SH; tcl iS; tl SH; **163**c SH; l SH r FL/Mark Harris; **165**bc MP; br NHPA; c NASA; cr MP/iS; tc MP; tl, tr NHPA; **166**br iS; cl NHPA; **167**bl MP; br CBT; tl NHPA; **168**cl MP; tr TPL; **169**cl, tr CBT; **170**bc, bcr NHPA; c MP; **171**bcl TPL; br MP; t NHPA; **172**bcl, bl NHPA; cr iS; tr MP; **173**bl CBT; br NHPA; c iS; cr MP; tl iS; **174**bcl, bl iS; c CBT; **175**b CBT; cl MP; cr CBT; tcl iS; tr CBT; **176**bl, br, c, tr MP; **177**c, cr, tl MP; **178**bl NHPA; cl MP; **179**br MP; bcr NHPA; cr MP; t NHPA; **180**bcr iS; **181**cl, tc NHPA; tcl iS; tr CBT; tcr MP; **182**bcl, bl iS; **183**br, t CBT; **184**bl, tr NHPA; **185**br, c MP; cl iS; cr MP; **186**bl iS; br NHPA; cr iS; **187**c iS; cr, tcr, tl NHPA; **188**bc, bcl, bcr MP; bl iS; c iS; **189**b iS; bcr MP; cl NHPA; cr iS; tl NHPA; **190**bcl FL/Mark Harris, bl FL/Silke Baron; c SP; bc FL/Mark Harris; **191**bcr SP; cr FL/Mark Harris; tc FL/Mark Harris, tr FL/ Christian Krause/www.flickr.com/alienx; **192** NHPA; **194**c, cl, l, t, tc iS; tcl IH; tcr iS; tl TPL; **196**b NHPA; **197**bcr NHPA; br SH; cr Aus; tcr NHPA; tl MP; **198**tr iS; **199**br, cr, tcr NHPA; **200**bcr MP; bl iS; **201**tc MP; **203**c iS; cr NHPA' tl MP; tr iS; **204**bl Aus; br NHPA; **205**tr Aus; **206**bl NHPA; tr Aus; **207**tc, tr NHPA; **208**bl NHPA; br MP; **209**bl Aus; tc iS; tl MP; **210**bc NHPA; cl MP; **211**bcr NHPA; bl, tl Aus; tr NHPA; **212**cl, tr Aus; **213**tc NHPA; tcl Aus; tr TPL; **214**bl NHPA; bcr SH; cl NHPA; **215**bc Aus; br, cl, tr NHPA; **216**c CBT; cr Aus; **217**tl Aus; tr CBT; **218**bl NHPA; br CBT; **219**bc, bcr, br Aus; tcl NHPA; **220**b NHPA; **221**bc, Aus; br MP; c, cr Aus; tl Aus; **222** CBT; **224**tl iS; **225**l iS; **226**cl, cr SH; l, tc, tcl iS; **227**cr NHPA; l, tcl, tl MP; **228**c iS; tcl MP; **229**cr NHPA; l, t MP; tcr iS; tr MP; **230**cl, cr, tcl, tcr, tr MP; **231**c TPL; cr SPL; l CBT; t MP; tcl, tcr NHPA; tl, tr MP; 232bl MP; tcr NHPA; tl SH; **233**cl NHPA; l iS; tc SH; tcl IS; tcr MP; tr iS; **234**bcr, bcl CBT; cl TPL; l NHPA; **235**bcl CBT; bcr, cr MP; l TPL; tcl CBT; **236**r, tr MP; **237**b CBT; bcr SH; bl, cl, tcr MP; tr SH; **238**br, c NHPA; cl, r MP; **239**cl iS; cr, tl NHPA; **240**cr MP; tcr iS; **241**b SH; bl, br iS; cr, tl MP; **242** MP; **244**bl, bcl, br, c, cl MP; **246**bc, bcl SPL; **247**bl, br SP, cr MP; **248**bcr NHPA; bl CBT; **249**tcl NASA; **250**bl NHPA; br MP; **251**c SP; cl SPL; tl SP; **252**bc SP; cl MP; cr SP; **253**cr, tcr MP; **254**bc, bcl SP; br, cr MP; **255**cl, cr MP; **256** MP; **258** cl, t, tc, tcl, tcr, tl iS; **288**c SP; **290**c SP.

ILLUSTRATIONS

Susanna Addario 93bc; **Mike Atkinson** 211cr; **Andrew Beckett** 18l; **Alistair Barnard** 189br; **The Art Agency** 240cl; **Richard Bonson/The Art Agency** 247tc; **Andre Boos** 147br; **Martin Camm** 169c, t, tc, tcl, tcr, tl, 249tr; **Robin Carter/The Art Agency** 34b, br, 35bc, 73bc, br, cr, tc, 99br, 129cl, cr, 247tr, 249bcr, bl, br, cl, cr, 251br, cr; **Dan Cole/The Art Agency** 49bcr, br, c, tcr, tr, 58bcr, br, c, cl, cr, t, tcr, tr, 59bc, c, cl, 70bl, bc, 74b, 100c, cr, r, 101c, cl, tc, 123bl, 167tr, 170r, 197b, c, 201b, c, cl, cr, bl, 205c, b, 213cr, 216 bc, bcl, bcr, bl, br, r, tr, 217bc, bcr, bcl, bl, br, 246br; **Fiammetta Dogi/The Art Agency** 20bcl, bcr, bl, br, 21bl, 93tc, tl, tr; **Mike Donnelly/The Art Agency** 20cr, l, r, 21c, cl, cr, tr, 113r; **Sandra Doyle/The Art Agency** 217cl, 56br, 86bl, 198c, 199l, 209br, c, cl, tc, 210br; **Jane Durston/The Art Agency** 85tr, 86tr, 91br, 93br, bcr, 109tc, tr, 116br, 131br, 153bl, 159br, cr, 164b, 178c; **Brin Edwards/The Art Agency** 88br, 96br, 98bc, bcr, 107cr, br, 119cl, cr, tc, 120cr, bcr, br, 127c, cr, tr, 131cr, 221tc, tr; **Simone End** 199bl; **Christer Eriksson** 15bcr, 25tr, 181br; **John Francis** 208br, 210bcl; **Jon Gittoes** 63t, 108br; **Ray Grinaway** 32t; **Tim Hayward** 45bl, 47br, cr, 56cl, 174br; **Steve Hobbs** 19br, **Bob Hynes** 155tc; **Ian Jackson/The Art Agency** 44cr, 64b, 77b, bcr, br, cr, 81br, tc, 95 c, cl, cr, tc, tcl, tr, 178br, 179bl; **Stuart Jackson-Carter/The Art Agency** 46cr, 52b, 82r, 115tc, tr, 157b, 182br, 202b, 206br, 212b, 213b; **David Kirshner** 14br, 15bl, 22bl, c, cl, l, 25r, 30br, 31bl, l, bcl, 35b, 42br, 54bl, 61cr, br, 75bl, 88l, 96tr, 108c, 115cr, 121tr, tcr, r, cr, b, br, bcr, bc, 122c, bc, 123br, 125tc, 144bc, 146c, 149br, 151tr, 154cr, 156bl, cr, 158l, cl, 166cr, 168br, bcl, 171cr, 177r, 180c, b, cl, 181bl, 189c, t, tr, 201tr, 204bc, 206c, 208c, 211tr, 217cr, 218c, 219cl, 220c, cr, 229cr, 250bl; **Frank Knight** 78br, 80bcl, 109bl, 111tr, 125tl, 157tl; **Iain McKellar** 42 bcl, bl, c, cl, l, 50cr, 207cr; **James McKinnon** 111bl, 151b, 219tr; **Magic Group** 76c, 168c, 189cr; **Rob Mancini** 14bcr; **Robert Morton** 239tr; **Yvan Meunier/Contact Jupiter** 96bc; **Peter Bull Art Studio** 63tl, 137tl, 140br,141br, 143bl, 147bl, 228br, 233br, 238b; **Sandra Pond/The Art Agency** 71bc, c, cl, cr, tc, 89cr, 94br; **Mick Posen/The Art Agency** 249tr; **Tony Pyrzakowski** 25t, 30bcr, 35bl, 56c; **Edwina Riddell** 149cr, 152br, 153tr, tc; **Trevor Ruth** 177b, 187b, 248c; **Peter Schouten** 18cl, 167tc, c; **Peter Scott/The Art Agency** 112cr; **Mario Sparaciari** 30bc; **Kevin Stead** 32cr, 196r; **Roger Swainston** 15bc; **Myke Taylor/The Art Agency** 54br, 55 bcl, bcr, bl, br, cr, tr, 63cr, 65cr, 111c, cr, tl; **Sharif Taraby** 14b; **Claude Thivierge/Contact Jupiter** 34tcr, 35c, cl, tr, 139b; **Guy Troughton** 17 c, cr, tcr, tr, 19cr, 34bl, 48cl, 49bl, 128bc, br, 129bl, 129bc, 168 bcr, br, 169br, bl, 184r, 187tr, 191bl, 198l, b, 200l, 203c, 209tr, 214br, 215c, cr; **Trevor Weekes** 32c; **Ann Winterbottom** 246cr.

MAPS & GRAPHS

Maps by Will Pringle and Laurie Whiddon/Map Illustrations, with additional graphic information by Andrew Davies/Creative Communication.
Infographics by Andrew Davies/Creative Communication.

The Encyclopedia of the Sea

Weldon Owen would like to thank the following people and organizations for their assistance in the production of this book: Malin Westman, Nina Paine, Tine Lund, International Union for Conservation of Nature, 2007 Red List of Threatened Species, Intergovernmental Panel on Climate Change, Conservation International.

PHOTOGRAPHS

Key t=top; l=left; r=right; tl=top left; tcl=top center left; tc=top center; tcr=top center right; tr=top right; cl=center left; c=center; cr=center right; b=bottom; bl=bottom left; bcl=bottom center left; bc=bottom center; bcr=bottom center right; br=bottom right
Aus = Auscape; CBT = Corbis Traditional Licensing; GI = Getty Images; iS = istockphoto.com; N = NASA; N_EO = NASA Earth Observatory; N_ES = NASA Earth from Space; N_G = Great Images in NASA; N_GS = NASA Goddard Space Flight Center; N_J = NASA Jet Propulsion Laboratory; N_L = NASA Landsat; NOAA = National Oceanic and Atmospheric Administration; N_V = Visible Earth; NRCS_VA = Natural Resources Conservation Service Virginia; SH = Shutterstock; SP = Sea Pics; USAP = U.S. Antarctic Program; Wiki = Wikimedia

1tl SH; tl, tr, tc SP; **2**bc, tr, t, tc, tl, t, c SP; **5**c SP; **8**cc iS; tr, bc, cl SP; **14**cl N; **15**tr SH; cr, tr, SP; **16**cc GI; cl N_V; **17**cr SH; cr, tr SP; **18**tr SP; **20**cr SH; **21**bc NOAA; br SP; **22**bl SP; **23**bc SP; **24**cr iS; cc NOAA; **25**br NOAA; cl, cc, cr SP; **28**cl SH; tr SP; **29**cr iS; tc, tl N_V; tl N; tr SH; cr SP; **31**cr, br N; **32**tr N_L; **33**cl iS; br SP; c, r N_L; **35**tr N_G; tl, tc SP; **36**cr, br N_J; **37**bl GI; cc iS; **38**t SP; **39** cr SH; cr, bc, br SP; **40**cr NOAA; **41**cr iS; tr N_V; **42**cr N_EO; tr N_V; N_GS; **43**bc iS; bl NOAA; cr SH; tr SP; **44**cc iS; cc SH; br, cc SP; **45**cc, tr iS; **48**tr, cl, bl SP; **49**br, bl NOAA; cr, br NOAA; tc, tl, tl, tr SP; **50**bl SP; **51**cr NOAA; **52**cr, cc, cc, cl iS; **53**bl N_V; tl, cr, br, tr, cr SP; **54**cl, cc, cr SH; **55**br iS; cr, cl, tl SH; **56**tr, cc iS; **57**bc, tr, tl, tc iS; tl SP; **58**bl N; **59**br, bc, bc, bl SP; **60**bl SH; cl, br SP; **61**bl, br, cr, cc SP; **62**tr SP; **63**tl Wiki/Mila Zinkova; bc, tr SH; tl SP; **64**cr, tc SP; **65**cl, cc, cc, tr SP; **66**bc, bl, tc iS; tr N_EO; cc, cl SH; **67**bc iS; bl N_V; bc SP; **70**tc N_ES; tr N_J; **71** tc, tl N_V; **72**bl iS; bc SH; **73**tr N_EO; tl SP; **74**bc iS; tr, cc, br SP; **75**cc SP; **76**tr, br, bl, bc SP; **77**bc, br SP; **78**cl SP; **79**cr, tr, br, cr SP; **80**cl, br, tr SP; **81**cc iS; br, tl, tr, tc SP; **82**bc iS; br NOAA; **83**bc SH; **84**t SH; **85**cc iS; bl, bc, br SP; **86**cc NRCS_VA; bl, br SP; **87**cr iS; cc NOAA; tr SH; tr SP; **88**tr, cr, cc SP; **89**br, cc, cr SP; **90**cr, tr, bc SP; **91**bc, tl, cr, tr, tc, cc, tl SP; **92**bc, cc, cl, tr, cr SP; **93**cc, cl iS; bc, cr, br SP; **96**cr iS; br, tc SH; **97**tr SP; **98**cl iS; tr SH; bl SP; **99**br iS; tc USAP; **100**br iS; cl N_V; bl NOAA; **101**tr SH; bl SP; **102**br SH; tr SP; **104**tr, cr, bl iS; cl SH; cc SP; **106**bl iS; br, cl NOAA; tr SP; **107**tr NOAA; **110**tl SP; **112**tc, bl, bc SP; **113**bl SP; **114**bc, bl iS; **115**tr iS; bl SH; **116**cr iS; bc N_EO; cc, tr SH; **117**br, bl iS; **118**tr N_V; bl SH; **119**br SH; bl SP; **120**bc, cr iS; br N_V; cl SP; **121**bc SH; **122**cr iS; bc SH; **123**br, tr SH; **124**cc NASA; tc SP; **125**cr CBT; **126**tr GI; cc, bc iS; cr SH; cl SP; **127**tl, bc iS; **128**tr iS; bl N_EO; **129**bl iS; tl, bc, tr SP; **130**tr, cr SH; cl, bl SP; **131**br SH; bl SP; **132**cl, tr SP; **133**br SP; **134**bl GI; tr iS; cr SP; **135**br, cl SP; **136**bl iS; cr, tr, cc SH; **137**bc iS; **138**tr CBT; bl N_EO; cc SH; cr SP; **139**cl SP; **142**bl SP; cl SH; c SP; **143**c SP; **144**bc SP; cl iS; cr SH; **145**br SP; bc SH; **146**tr N_V; cr SH; bc SP; **147**tl N_J; tr SP; **148**br SH; cl, cr, tr SP; **149**tr SH; **150**br iS; cc N_J; tr SH; **151**tr SP; br SH; **152**bl SP; br iS; **153**bc iS; cr SH; **154**cl N_GS; tr SH; **155**tl SP; **156**cr iS; tr N; cl SH; **157**cr, tl SP; **158**tr, tc SP; cl, cr N_EO; **159**tc SP; **160**tr, cl, br SP; cr SH; **161**br SP; **162**cl N_G; tr SH; **163**tl, tr SP; **166**bl SP; tc iS; br SH; **168**tc SP; br N_V; **169**tr SP; bl, br SH; **170**cr, br SP; tr iS; **171**bc, cl SP; **172**br SP; tr N_V; cr SH; **173**bc SP; br iS; **174**bc SP; br N_V; **175**br, bc SP; cc iS; **176**br iS; tr N_V; bl SH; **177**cr, bl SP; **178**br, tr, bl SP; **180**bc SP; cr iS; tr N_V; **181**bl, cr, tr SP; br iS; **182**br, cl iS; **183**bc NOAA; cr SH; **184**br SP; tr SH; **185**tr SP; **186**tr, br SP; cr SH; **187**bc SP; tr, cr SH; **188**tr N_V; cl SH; **189**tr, tr SP; **190**cc N_EO; br N_V; **191**cr SP; bc NOAA; **192**cr SP; br iS; cl SH; **194**cl, cr SP; tr iS; **195**tr, tl SP; **196**tr, br SP; cl iS; **197**br, cl SP; **198**bl SP; tr CBT; **199**cl SP; tr Aus; tr GI; **200**tr SP; bl N; **201**bl, tr, tl, tc SP; **202**br, cl SP; tr iS; **203**bl, br SP; **204**tc, br SP; bc iS; **205**br, cl SP; **206**br SH; tr SP; **207**bl, tr SP; **208**br SP; cl iS; tr SH; **209**br SP; **210**tc SP; cc, bc, br SH; **212**tr, cc SP; bl N_EO; **256**t iS

ILLUSTRATIONS

Richard Bonson/The Art Agency 19c, 20b, 51b, 53bc; **Peter Bull Art Studio** 14tr, 15b, 24br, 28b, 29b, 30cr, 36bl, 37br, 38c, cl, bl, 39c, bl, 41br, 42c, 43br, 45br, 57tcr, 58cl, 60c, bc, 63r, 64br, 65br, 72bl, tl, 74bl, tl, 76tl, 77bc, 83cl, l, bl, bcr, 85cr, 88bl, br, 199bl; **Leonello Calvetti** 22t, c, b, 23tr, 24bl, 48cl, bcl; **Robin Carter/The Art Agency** 18b, 19b; **Dan Cole/The Art Agency** 64cl, 65bc; **Tom Connell/The Art Agency** 19cl; **Barry Croucher/The Art Agency** 32bl, 58br, 59t, r; **Andrew Davies/Creative Communication** 14bcr, br, 17t, tc, c, bc, 18bl, 19br, 28c, 35b, 48cr, 50tr, 83br, 84cr; **Chris Forsey** 20tr, tcr, cr, bcr, 52bc, 56br; **Mark Garlick** 16tr, 17tl, 54, 55bl, 56cl, bcl, bl, 57br; **Jon Gittoes** [adapted from N.P. Ashmole and M.J. Ashmole, 1967, *Comparative Feeding Ecology of Seabirds on a Tropical Oceanic Island*, Yale Peabody Museum National History Bulletin 24] 75b; **Malcolm Godwin/Moonrunner Design** 25bl, 40b, 41cl, c, cr; **Gary Hanna/The Art Agency** 87br; **David Hardy/The Art Agency** 44bl; **Bob Hynes** 33br; **Ian Jackson/The Art Agency** 60cr, 62bl, 70b, 72bl, cr, 73br, 78r, 79l, c, 80bl; **Terry Pastor/The Art Agency** 16bcl, 17bl, 21t, 30bcl, 31bc; **Mick Posen/The Art Agency** 15tl, 16br, 19tr, 20c, 30bl, br, 31bl, 31cl, 34bl, 36bc, 49bc, 50br, 55cl, c, cr, 66br, 76cl, c, cr, 82c, 83cr, 84cl, c, bcr, br; **National Geographic Society** 42bl; **Oliver Rennert** 37t; **Claude Thivierge/Contact Jupiter** 91br.

MAPS & GRAPHS

Maps by Will Pringle and Laurie Whiddon/Map Illustrations, with additional graphic information by Andrew Davies/Creative Communication.
Infographics by Andrew Davies/Creative Communication.